AF756379

The History of Legal Education in the United States

Commentaries and Primary Sources

The History of Legal Education in the United States

Commentaries and Primary Sources

Volume II

Editor
Steve Sheppard

Salem Press, Inc.
Pasadena, California   Hackensack, New Jersey

Frontispiece: Portrait of a Law Lecturer at the University of Pennsylvania. Oil painting by Mary Franklin. In 1998, Cynthia Arkin, Associate Director for Special Collections of the Biddle Law Library of the University of Pennsylvania Law School, physically compared this portrait to portraits of Penn faculty members of the nineteenth century and identified the lecturer in the portrait as strongly resembling the official portrait of Edward Coppee Mitchell (1836-1887), dean of the law school from 1872 to 1887. The portrait is believed to have been painted in 1879. (*Reproduction rights courtesy of the Honorable Morris Arnold. Duplication courtesy of Hugh Lauter Levin Associates.*)

Copyright © 1999, by Salem Press, Inc.

All rights in this book are reserved. No part of this work may be used or reproduced in any manner whatsoever or transmitted in any form or by any means, electronic or mechanical, including photocopy, recording, or any information storage and retrieval system, without written permission from the copyright owner except in the case of brief quotations embodied in critical articles and reviews. For information address the publisher, Salem Press, Inc., P.O. Box 50062, Pasadena, California 91115.

∞ The paper used in these volumes conforms to the American National Standard for Permanence of Paper for Printed Library Materials, Z39.48-1992.

The history of legal education in the United States : commentaries and primary sources / edited by Steve Sheppard.
p. cm.
Includes index.
ISBN 0-89356-331-5 (set). — ISBN 0-89356-332-3 (vol. 1.). — ISBN 0-89356-333-1 (vol. 2)
1. Law—Study and teaching—United States—History. 2. Law schools—United States—History. I. Sheppard, Steve. 1963- .
KF273.H535 1999 98-41481
340'.071'173—dc21 CIP

FIRST PRINTING

PRINTED IN THE UNITED STATES OF AMERICA

The History of Legal Education in the United States: Commentaries and Primary Sources

Edited by Steve Sheppard

VOLUME I

E. Nineteenth-Century Legal Scientists

VOLUME II

F. Nineteenth-Century Legal Science

G. The Twentieth Century

II. Examinations and Evaluations

III. Skills Courses

IV. Students

VIII. Accreditation and Association

A. The American Bar Association

B. The Association of American Law Schools

IX. Technology and the Future

I. Teaching Books and Methods in the Lecture Hall

continued

F. Nineteenth-Century Legal Science

Chapter 44

Law and Geometry

Legal Science from Leibniz to Langdell

1986

M. H. Hoeflich

Michael Hoeflich is Dean of the University of Kansas School of Law and the editor of *The Gladsome Light of Jurisprudence* (New York: Greenwood Press, 1988). This article first appeared at 30 *American Journal of Legal History* 95 (1986). See also chapter 61.

Author's note: As always my debt to my friends and colleagues is great; thanks to Steve Presser, Alan Watson, John Nowak, Rick Marcus, Don Dripps, Harry Krause, John Orth, Peter Hay, Peter Stein, and Charlie Donahue. A version of this article was delivered on October 18, 1985 at the 1985 Annual Meeting of the American Society for Legal History. I want especially to thank Bob Gordon, Kent Newmyer, and Steve Conrad for their helpful comments at the meeting. All errors, of course, are mine alone.

I. Introduction

It should not be forgotten that law has an intellectual as well as a social history.[1]

There is a tendency when one speaks of the science of law to think in terms of experimental science with all its accoutrements. This is a perfectly understandable phenomenon, since, for most American lawyers, the notion of legal science is inevitably linked to Christopher Columbus Langdell, the introduction of the casebook method at the Harvard Law School in the 1870's, and Langdell's analogy of law to laboratory science.[2] The notion of legal science, however, greatly predates the Langdell era.

Without doubt, Christopher Columbus Langdell exercised a vast influence upon American legal education and scholarship. He is generally credited with the invention not only of the notion that law is a science, but also of the case-method of teaching law. In fact, Langdell invented neither of these things, although as Dean of Harvard Law School he did much to popularize both in the United States. In order to understand the Langdellian concept of legal science, however, it is necessary to understand its "prehistory" and the relationship of the Langdellian concept to the whole scientific movement in law from the seventeenth to the mid-nineteenth centuries.

It is the purpose of this brief essay to explore the nature and transmission of the dominant legal-scientific model of the pre-Langdellian era. That model was not experimental based upon the laboratory, but deductive based upon mathematical method. It is the idea that law can be reduced to a set of first principles, on the order of mathematical axioms, and that by the use of deductive method, these principles can yield all necessary consequences. In short, it is the notion that legal reasoning is syllogistic; that law is, like geometry, a deductive science.

Donald Elliott has suggested, in a memorable phrase, that law is a scavenger, feeding off the leftovers of other disciplines.[3] Such a characterization seems particularly apt these days in light of the succession of "law and . . ." subjects that have captured the imagination of legal academicians and jurists in the United States during the past few decades. One might argue that precisely because law does not possess one unique set of methodological assumptions dictated by its nature and process jurists must seek for methodological paradigms elsewhere.[4] Thus, the twentieth century has witnessed movements towards law and social science, law and psychology, and law and neo-Marxist critical theory. In each of these movements the major contribution of the ancillary subject has been the imposition of a special perspective and method upon law. In the Langdellian era experimental science also provided a special perspective and new method for legal scholarship. Professors at the newly invigorated university law schools could claim to take a place in their laboratories—law libraries—searching out the imperishable truths of legal science just as their colleagues in chemistry, biology, or physics were doing for their respective sciences.[5] Earlier in the century, however, jurists modeled their work on a different scientific paradigm, one which also provided both a perspective on law and a method of reasoning, which I have called, for convenience, the geometric paradigm.

II. Continental Learning and the Geometric Paradigm

One of the most interesting aspects of the development of the geometric paradigm in law is its relationship to the "new" Continental civilian learning of the seventeenth and eighteenth centuries and the rise of a new scientific paradigm during this same period.[6] From the twelfth through the fifteenth century there took place what has been called a "revival" of Roman law in the nation states of Western Europe.[7] Instigated by the rediscovery of complete manuscripts of the Byzantine *Corpus Iuris Civilis* and its compilation of classical Roman juristic argument, early modern jurists came to reject medieval national customs in favor of the more sophisticated learning of the Roman sources.[8] In point of fact, the texts contained in the *Corpus Iuris Civilis*, generally, tend to be neither systematic nor well-ordered.[9] The Corpus as a whole is plagued by *homonymiae*, tautologies, and *antinomiae*, inconsistencies. Nevertheless, what impressed a number of the early modern jurists was the method of argumentation adopted by the classical jurists and contained in those fragments preserved in the *Digest*. Roman juristic argument tends to be internally orderly and logical. More importantly, juristic discourse also often tends to proceed in a deductive fashion, and lends itself to an analysis starting from general analysis of facts leading to the derivation of first principles and moving thence again to a consideration of the application of those specific principles to another particular set of facts.[10] The ability to derive general principles, both explicit and implicit, from The *Digest* and the application of such principles in a syllogistic manner to a detailed factual pattern was viewed by jurists in the seventeenth and eighteenth centuries as contrary to and superior to the simple method of reasoning, closely fact-based, that had become traditional in national customary law texts.[11]

By and large, customary law tended to be what one might call "enumerative" rather than deductive. The collections of customs that one finds in the medieval and early modern European sources generally enumerate particular fact situations and then state a rule to govern such situations. There is little or no possibility of abstraction, no inherent method of legal reasoning.[12] Thus, for instance, a customal might well state that it is an offense to permit one's pig to do damage to a neighbor's vegetable patch. If such damage were done, then the pig's owner would be required to pay some set damages and little, if any, discussion would accompany this rule. Roman law, too, would have such a rule, but the juristic commentaries do not remain satisfied with a statement of the facts and a bare rule of resolution. On the contrary, it is characteristic of Roman juristic argument to make generalization possible and to utilize specific cases as a basis for extended argument. Indeed, Alan Watson has suggested that this often highly abstract and academic character of classical Roman juristic thought stems, in large part, from the closed nature of the Roman legal profession and the route to professional prestige therein.[13] In effect, jurists who could make the most clever and "elegant" arguments would gain the greatest prestige.[14] That this principled deductive aspect of *Digest* argument appealed greatly to university-trained jurists during the early modern period is notable, for it is in the work of one of the most remarkable of these university jurists that Roman law came to be the inspiration for the geometric paradigm in law.

During this same period in which jurists were moving away from the "chaotic" national customary laws towards the "elegance" of Roman legal method, scientists were moving away from medieval alchemy and primitive experimental science towards the development of a new, systematic scientific paradigm.[15] It was during the seventeenth and eighteenth centuries that the application of reason to the elucidation of scientific subjects came to the fore. As medieval law gave ground to a more systematic, more rational Romanist-influenced jurisprudence, medieval science gave way to early modern scientific method. Overwhelmingly during this period, leading scientists came to believe that not only was there a need for a reform of science and scientific method, an "*instauratio magna*" in Bacon's words,[16] but also a recognition of the unity of all the sciences, a unity deriving from a central scientific method, a characteristically "scientific" mode of reasoning.[17] The model for that new unifying method was mathematics and mathematical argument, including the syllogism and demonstrative proof.[18] Descartes who, with Francis Bacon and Gottfried Leibniz, was one of the leaders of this new scientific movement and formulator of the new methodological paradigm, commented:

> Those long chains of reasoning, simple and easy as they are, of which geometricians make use in order to arrive at the most difficult demonstrations, had caused me to imagine that all those things which fall under the cognizance of man might very likely be mutually related in the same fashion [19]

More importantly from the legal historian's perspective, it was also during this period that there was a major cross-fertilization between science and law on a personal level. Many of those individuals helping to create the "new science" were also active in formulating the "new jurisprudence."[20] For instance, Francis Bacon not only was instrumental in the new scientific *instauratio* in England, but also was a trained jurist, a practicing common lawyer, and a prolific legal author. For Bacon, law, like astronomy or chemistry, was a science, and thus was susceptible to the application of reason and the new scientific method.[21] Thus, by the end of the seventeenth century both science and law (especially under the influence of Roman law) were moving to new more systematic, syllogistic paradigms, based upon the belief that by reason and principled argument, legal truth could best be discovered.

It is not often that one can say with some confidence that a particular paradigm which becomes widely accepted in a special area of study originates primarily in the work of one individual. With regard to the development and popularization of the geometric paradigm in law, however, it is relatively clear that one jurist must be given principal responsibility. While Francis Bacon did much in England to develop the idea that law could be treated as a science and was thus susceptible to scientific method, it was Gottfried Wilhelm Leibniz who must be given fullest credit for the popularization and specific explication of the geometric paradigm in law.[22] Not at all surprising, Leibniz was also one of the founders of modern mathematics. He is probably best known as one of the independent codevelopers (with Isaac Newton) of the Calculus. Before he became active as a mathematician, however, Leibniz trained in the law and wrote several juristic treatises. Throughout his life his interest in the systematization and rationalization of law and juristic method continued. Furthermore, like all university trained Continental jurists during the seventeenth century, Leibniz concentrated his studies on Roman law (especially the *Digest*) and on the "new jurisprudence."

Both in his major Romanist treatise, the *Nova Methodus Discendae Docendaeque Iuris*,[23] and in his letters, Leibniz extensively developed the notion that law, indeed, must be understood as a principled deductive science on the model of classical geometry and that legal reasoning must follow the deductive, demonstrative model used in geometric proofs. For Leibniz, Roman law, as an illustration of such reason in practice, was no less principled and subject to deductive process than was geometry. In several of his letters and academic works Leibniz compared the work of the classical Roman jurists to that of the ancient mathematicians and geometers. In a letter to John Georg Graevius he commented: "I believe that neither Euclid nor Descartes, if they had applied themselves to this doctrine, would have been able to write more profoundly nor fully as Ulpian and Papinian."[24]

Based upon this statement, Fritz Sturm, in his study of Leibniz as a legal philosopher, has commented: "He saw in him an emanation of reason. He saw in him an intellectual accomplishment which was entirely able to compete with the accomplishment of the philosophers and mathematicians."[25]

Perhaps the clearest explication of this geometric paradigm comes in another Leibniz letter:

> There are enough substantial examples of proofs outside of mathematics and one may say that Aristotle had already given such in his Prior Analytics . . . Further, one may say that the jurists have numerous good proofs; above all, are the ancient Roman jurists, of whose work fragments have been saved for us in the Pandects. I am completely in agreement with Laurentius Valla, who could not admire these authors enough because they wrote in such a just and clear way and reasoned in a manner that approached [mathematical] proof and was often completely deductive . . . That precise manner of explanation to the point that all the jurists of the Pandects no matter how far in time from each other seem to speak in a single voice so that it would be virtually impossible to tell them one from the other were it not for the fact that their names are at the head of each [Digest] fragment; just as one is hard put to distinguish Euclid, Archimedes, and Appollonius in reading their proofs.[26]

Leibniz's development of the geometric paradigm to the fullest extent was significant on a number of grounds. First, because it illustrated clearly the methodological relationship between law and the natural sciences, it helped to establish the rightful place of legal scholarship and legal educaton in the early modern university. On the Continent this was no great revelation; Roman law had been a subject in the university curriculum since the twelfth century.[27] In England and in the United States during the next two centuries, however, the idea that law was a science susceptible to the application of "university" methodologies of reasoning and argument was innovative, and, as will be seen, quite significant.

The geometric paradigm in law as it developed in the seventeenth century was also of extreme importance to the development of ideas about law reform in this and subsequent periods. One of the most difficult problems facing lawyers and jurists in the early modern period was precisely that even the most advanced legal systems seemed to be chaotic. In England, the common law was still fully under the influence of the medieval writ system and the dark corners of feudal notions.[28] On the Continent, national legal systems were mired in the confusion of conflicting and often chaotic local and regional customs.[29] The geometric paradigm as a philosophical concept and a new method of legal reasoning, when allied with the newly discovered Roman law, which could provide not only an example of such a method in practice, but also a precise legal terminology to use in conjunction thereof,[30] provided a solution to this legal-philosophical Gordian knot. Once one accepted that law could be made logical and that legal argument could be shaped along deductive lines, legal results became more predictable, certain, and comprehensible. Once one combined commonly accepted principles of law with the deductive method of legal reasoning, law did, indeed, become a science. Law could now be seen as transcending the whim of an individual judge or confused case-law. Law, in theory and practice, became the application of logic and reason to first principles, and so long as the reasoning was sound, proper results would always follow. Instead of being a

set of irrational, positive rules to be learned by rote and applied by whim, law became a rational science. Leibniz himself worked throughout his life towards the production of a *Corpus Juris Reconcinnatum*, a reconstructed legal compilation modeled along deductive lines.[31]

Thus, in both pedagogy and in reform efforts, the geometric paradigm developed in Leibniz's work held out major promise for the future. The extent of the influence enjoyed by this paradigm in the works of subsequent jurists and legal scholars is, in fact, quite extraordinary.

III. The Continental Tradition After Leibniz

It is not at all surprising that the geometric paradigm in law continued to be strong after Leibniz. Earliest and undoubtedly first amongst jurists who adopted and popularized this paradigm must be Christian Freiherr von Wolff.

Wolff was born at Breslau in 1769 and studied philosophy and mathematics as a student of Leibniz at Jena. Lke his master, he embraced the idea of the "unity of sciences" and applied the geometric paradigm to legal materials. Indeed, Wolff's attempts at utilizing the geometric, deductive paradigm in law were even more extensive than those of Leibniz. In both his massive *Jus gentium Methoda Scientifica Petractatum*[32] and in his *Institutiones Juris Naturae et Gentium*[33] Wolff attempted to apply the geometric paradigm as Leibniz had suggested as a guiding principle for reordering existing law and rendering current legal arguments more exact and elegant. Ernst Landsberg has characterized Wolff's method as most illustrative of the "mathematical-demonstrative method":

> Wolff's philosophy distinguishes itself from all others primarily by its method—the mathematical demonstrative method—as he himself remarks occasionally. This method rests on an artful combination of carefully refined (exasciatae) definitions, principles taken from elsewhere, and more precise dogma; the latter must be provable by the two former.[34]

Indeed, in the introduction to the *Institutiones Juris Naturae et Gentium*, Wolff closely echoes Leibniz's comments on the relationship of law and geometry and lawyers and geometers:

> Therefore, these things may not be brought out into the light [of clarity], unless, setting oneself in the footsteps of Euclid, of the truer, stricter logic of the law; individual terms are defined by exact definitions, individual propositions are adequately demonstrated, and, no less, definitions are thus properly arranged, so that not only may consequences be entirely understood through their prior propositions, but also that the truth of these results be demonstrated through [the truth] of these preceding statements.[35]

Wolff not only adopted the Leibnizian analysis of law in terms of geometry, but he actually attempted to utilize it in his *Jus Naturae* as Leibniz had planned to do in his unwritten *Corpus Iuris Reconcinnatum*. This Wolffian synthesis of the Leibnizian geometric paradigm became quite important in Germany during the eighteenth century and gradually this geometric paradigm spread throughout Continental juristic circles. This is quite easily understood, since it was so closely consonant not only with the general "scientific" movement of the period, but also with the then popular natural law school and the idea that law must be an "emanation of reason." Natural law presupposed that there were preexisting "eternal" principles of law discoverable by men.[36] Many went a step further and believed that Roman law, especially the *Corpus Juris Civilis*, represented a distillation of such eternal principles of natural law. The geometric paradigm fit perfectly. Indeed, it may be suggested that natural law provided the principles and the geometric paradigm provided the method by which to reason from these principles. The geometric paradigm, as developed by Leibniz and popularized by Wolff, provided, also, an important philosophical basis for the development on the Continent and in Germany, especially, of the systematic or Pandectist movement in law, that movement whose practitioners attempted to reduce law virtually to a mathematical system consisting entirely of principles or axioms.[37]

The relationship between the geometric paradigm as a philosophical and methodological model and the eighteenth and nineteenth centuries' "systematic movement" in law can be best understood, perhaps, through a brief examination of the work of Anton Thibaut, the author of the *System des Pandekten Rechts*, published at Jena in 1803, in which this movement reached its high point.[38] The essence of Thibaut's work is abstraction, systematization, and rationalization of law. In the System, Thibaut explains the nature of law and legal systems:

> A legal system must present the substantive law in systematic unity. If the authors of the positive law had proceeded from a simple principle of law, and had they remained consistent in its implementation, there would be substantive unity, and each rule would be derived from the highest principle of law.[39]

Thibaut's *System* is, to a large extent, founded implicitly on the deductive, geometric paradigm developed by Leibniz and Wolff a century before. Law is to be understood as a set of axioms from which truths may be deduced. All is principle; all is abstraction. Legal consequences follow syllogistically from first principles. The method has, in fact, come to dominate the substance. Without the earlier work of Leibniz and Wolff, the systematizers like Thibaut would have lacked the philosophical and methodological foundation necessary for their work.

The geometric paradigm was not confined, however, only to the works of sophisticated jurists and legal scholars. It struck a chord in the larger, intellectual culture. For instance, the following passage is found in an odd work entitled *Jurisprudentia. Tresor des Anecdotes de Jurisprudence* published at Paris in 1858 by one M. Bréson,[40] identified only as an "ancien avocat":

> There is a thesis of Jean Botéon entitled: Geometriae cognitio Jureconsulto necessaria. I do not know the work itself but I believe it good and useful if it proves that the geometric spirit is essential to the practice of jurisprudence, just as in all the sciences where justice and certainty of reasoning are necessary, and if it shows well the application of geometric principles to the subjects of jurisprudence which are susceptible to them. If the work of Botéon does not do this, this is a book that ought to be written, and if it fulfills this task well, it will cause greater excitement in the "Republic of Letters" than that of Botéon.[41]

Perhaps the most interesting adoption of the geometric paradigm by a Continental jurist, however, is in the work of Freidrich Carl von Savigny. Savigny was the founder of the "historical school" of jurisprudence in Germany.[42] Throughout his career he was a staunch opponent both of codification and the Pandectist movement and its practitioners, including Thibaut. It was Savigny's theory that law was not merely *ratio scripta*, or an "emanation of reason." Rather, Savigny believed that law could only be understood as deriving from the society in which it developed.[43] Law, for Savigny, was, if anything, an "emanation" of a people and a nation and particular legal rules were intimately connected to national, historical circumstances. Nevertheless, even Savigny adopted the geometric paradigm as a model for legal reasoning in his earliest major work, the *Vom Beruf Unserer Zeit für Gesetzgebung und Rechtswissenschaft*.[44] After acknowledging that it is the nation in its historical development which is the source of law, he draws the analogy of geometry to legal science:

> In every triangle, namely, there are certain data from the relations of which all the rest are necessarily deducible: thus, given two sides and the included angle, the whole triangle is given. In like manner, every part of our law has points by which the rest may be given. These may be termed the leading axioms. To distinguish these, and deduce from them the internal connection, and the precise degree of affinity which subsist between all juridical notions and rules, is amongst the most difficult of the problems of jurisprudence. Indeed, it is peculiarly this which gives our labours the scientific character.[45]

Savigny, too, like Leibniz, saw Roman law as an especially excellent example of the congruence between legal method and geometric method:

> It has been shown . . . that, in our science, everything depends upon the possession of the leading principles, and it is this very possession which constitutes the greatness of the Roman jurists. The notions and axioms of their science do not appear to have been arbitrarily produced; these are actual beings, whose existence and genealogy have become known to them by long and intimate acquaintance. For this reason their whole mode of proceeding has a certainty which is found nowhere else, except in mathematics; and it may be said, without exaggeration that they calculate with their notions.[46]

It is in this latter passage that Savigny develops what is, perhaps, the most sophisticated version to date of the geometric paradigm. Savigny separates the sources of law from the proper method of legal analysis. As noted, for Savigny, law and legal notions derive from a nation's unique historical experience. Once so derived, however, they must be reduced to leading principles, the equivalent of mathematical axioms, so that jurists may "calculate with their notions." For Savigny, systematization does not require the derivation of law from reason, but only the application of reason to legal ideas once derived.

This distinction is extremely important. The development of the geometric paradigm on the Continent during the seventeenth and eighteenth centuries was, as noted above, to a large extent, connected to the natural law movement. The natural lawyers believed that positive law, law imposed upon society by its governors, derived from preexisting principles. These preexisting principles constituted natural law. Roman law itself was seen as a disembodied entity, reflecting "pure reason" and, thus, natural law. Indeed, the historical study of Roman law and the acknowledgement that Roman law was itself a "positive system of laws" and could be understood only in its own historical and social context came only in the nineteenth century with the work of Savigny and his followers.

The geometric paradigm fit easily within the natural law tradition. Since all positive law derived, in fact, from preexisting principles, once one could discover these preexisting principles one could deduce the proper rule of resolution for any dispute or question. Savigny, in adopting the geometric paradigm in the passage quoted above from the *Vom Beruf Unserer Zeit* went one step beyond the natural lawyers and integrated the geometric paradigm into an historical view of law in which there were no preexisting principles. Rather than begin with the idea of preexisting, natural principles of law, Savigny began with laws historically and socially derived. However, these laws, too, could be expressed as general rules. Once this was done, the geometric paradigm could still provide a legal methodology. Thus, for Savigny, Roman legal principles were seen not as written reason derived from nature, but rules of conduct derived from Roman history and society. Once so derived, however, they could function as mathematical axioms in the hands of the jurists.

IV. The Geometric Paradigm in Anglo-American Law

The spread of the notion that legal analysis must be modeled upon mathematical analysis was not limited to the Continent. The geometric paradigm also spread to England, Scotland, and the United States during the late eighteenth and early nineteenth centuries. One may speculate that it did so, generally, for several reasons. First, the mathematical-deductive method flourished where systematization of law was popular. Francis Bacon in his juristic writings in the seventeenth century laid the groundwork for such systematization of the common law.[47] This systematic tradition was carried on by Matthew Hale and, above all, William Blackstone, and continued into the nineteenth century.[48] This tradition, too, was intimately connected to Roman and civil law which was gaining ground in the common law countries at this time.[49] Roman and civil law tended to be used as an example of the deductive method and, as noted above, may have helped to inspire its spread. Thus, certainly the atmosphere of legal thought was conducive to the explicit adoption of the mathematical method, the geometric paradigm in England and the United States. Second, mathematics and geometry were basic elements of both English and American university education during this period, so that university educated jurists would have been familiar with the basic mathematical constructs and ideas.[50] Third, in Great Britain and in the United States, the early nineteenth century witnessed a renewed effort not only at some form of systematization and rationalization of the law, but also saw increased pressure to simplify and demystify the law so as to render it more predictable and certain. Finally, it was during this period that law began to be a university subject in England and, especially, in the United States, the geometric paradigm came to be viewed as legitimizing the place of law studies in the university curriculum and of law teachers on university faculties.

One of the earliest and most interesting appearances of the geometric paradigm is in the works of the Scottish moral philosopher, Dugald Stewart. In many respects, Stewart's professional career paralleled that of Leibniz.[51] He was born in Edinburgh in 1753. His father was a professor of mathematics at the University there. Stewart studied mathematics and moral philosophy at Edinburgh and attended Adam Ferguson's lectures there. He then moved to Glasgow where he continued to study moral philosophy under Thomas Reid. He was then called back to Edinburgh first to teach mathematics as a substitute for his father and then moral philosophy as a substitute for Ferguson. He succeeded to the chair of moral philosophy in 1785. He authored a number of books including the *Elements of the Philosophy of the Human Mind*,[52] the *Outlines of Moral Philosophy*,[53] and the *Philosophical Essays*.[54]

The *Elements of the Philosophy of the Human Mind* is a massive attempt to integrate all the knowledge then held about the process of human reasoning into a moral framework. In the first volume of the work Stewart included a chapter on "Reasoning and Deductive Evidence."[55] This chapter deals specifically with the process of reasoning, especially the contrast between the exercise of intuition and deduction. Stewart makes the point that mathematical reasoning, the art of deduction, is best utilized in sciences where terms are most precisely defined and delimited. He then goes on to discuss mathematical-geometric demonstration. This he defines as an exercise designed "to trace the logical filiation of consequences which follow from an assumed hypothesis."[56] At this point, Stewart moves to a significant conclusion, that "demonstrative reasoning might be employed in the moral sciences."[57] He points out that whether or not the consequences deduced will be true, will depend entirely upon whether or not the initial hypotheses are themselves true. Thus, the mathematical-geometric method described by Stewart is quintessentially a method of argumentation and reasoning, applicable to any subject for which one can state initial hypotheses. For Stewart, the best example of such a subject amongst the moral sciences, was jurisprudence:

> In those branches of study which are conversant about moral and political propositions, the nearest approach which I can imagine to a hypothetical science, analogous to mathematics, is to be found in a code of municipal jurisprudence; or rather, might be conceived to exist in such a code, if systematically carried into execution, agreeably to certain general or fundamental principles. Whether these principles should, or should not, be founded in justice and expediency, it is evidently possible, by reasoning from them consequentially, to create an artificial or conventional body of knowledge, more systematical, and, at the same time, more complete in all its parts, than, in the present state of our information, any science can be rendered, which ultimately appeals to the eternal and immutable standards of truth and falsehood, of right and wrong. This consideration seems to me to throw some light on the following very curious parallel which Leibnitz has drawn, with what justness I presume not to decide, between the works of the Roman civilians and those of the Greek geometers. Few writers certainly have been so fully qualified as he was, to pronounce on the characteristical merits of both.
>
> I have often said, that, after the writing of geometricians, there exists nothing which, in point of force and of subtlety, can be compared to the works of the Roman lawyers. And, as it would be scarcely possible, from mere intrinsic evidence, to distinguish a demonstration of Euclid's from one of Archimedes or of Apollonius, (the style of all of them appearing no less uniform than if reason herself was speaking through their organs,) so also the Roman lawyers all resemble each other like twin-brothers; insomuch that, from the style alone of any particular opinion or

argument, hardly any conjecture could be formed with respect to the author. Nor are the traces of a refined and deeply meditated system of natural jurisprudence anywhere to be found more visible, or in greater abundance. And, even in those cases where its principles are departed from, either in compliance with the language consecrated by technical forms, or in consequences of new statutes, or of ancient traditions, the conclusions which the assumed hypothesis renders it necessary to incorporate with the external dictates of right reason, are deduced with the soundest logic, and with an ingenuity which excites admiration. Nor are these deviations from the law of nature so frequent as is commonly imagined."[58]

John Austin, the first holder of the Chair of Jurisprudence at the University of London from 1827 to 1832, was the founder of the Anglo-American school of analytic positivism.[59] In his lectures at London published, in part, as *The Province of Jurisprudence Determined*, Austin utilized Bentham's notions of utilitarianism to develop a theory of law based upon a systematic development of first principles derived from the general principle of utility.[60] Austin's jurisprudence betrays, in many places, the influence of eighteenth and nineteenth century Continental and civilian learning.[61] Austin himself studied Roman law and Pandectist scholarship at Bonn from 1827 to 1828 as a necessary precursor to beginning his own lectures. Thus it is not at all surprising that Austin, too, adopted the geometric paradigm for legal reasoning.

In the third part of *The Province* Austin develops his notions of proper legal method. He begins with a discussion of the necessity to derive first principles of jurisprudence and the sciences of ethics and legislation by means of a Benthamite calculation of utilities. He chides the slowness with which those subjects had been developed and blames this upon the public's unwillingness to accept utilitarian ideas and, generally, to demand truth from writers on these subjects.[62] Then, he moves on to a discussion of method. Once first principles of law or ethics are derived from calculations of utility, what must follow? Here, Austin adopts the geometric paradigm as the proper method of reasoning:

> This general demand for truth (though it were clothed in homely guise), and this general contempt of falsehood and nonsense (though they were decked with rhetorical graces, would improve the method and the style of inquiries into ethics, and into the various sciences which are nearly related to ethics. The writers would attend to the suggestions of Hobbes and of Locke, and would imitate the method so successfully pursued by geometers: Though such is the variety of the premises which some of their inquiries involve, and such are the complexity and ambiguity of some of the terms, that they would often fall short of the perfect exactness and coherency, which the fewness of his premises, and the simplicity and definiteness of his expressions, enable the geometer to reach. But, though they would often fall short of geometrical exactness and coherency, they might always approach, and would often attain to them. They would acquire the art and the habit of defining their leading terms; of steadily adhering to the meanings announced by the definitions; of carefully examining and distinctly stating their premises; and of deducing the consequences of their premises with logical rigour. Without rejecting embellishments which might happen to fall in their way, the only excellencies of style for which they would seek, are precision, clearness, and conciseness: the first being absolutely requisite to the successful prosecution of inquiry; whilst the others enable the reader to seize the meaning with certainty, and spare him unnecessary fatigue.[63]

It is interesting to notice in this passage the parallels to Dugald Stewart's work. Austin, like Stewart, recognized that the truth or falsehood of conclusions reached by the deductive method of reasoning ultimately must depend upon the truth or falsehood of the principles upon which the deduction is based. Hence, Austin argued so strenuously for the importance of the proper derivation of these principles, that is, through application of the utilitarian calculus. Austin, like Stewart, also recognized that the difference between geometric deduction and legal deduction lay in the degree of precision with which terms are defined. The more precise the definitions, the more accurate the deduction. Indeed, it is reasonable to suggest that in this passage of *The Province*, Austin shows, perhaps, that he had both studied Stewart's *Elements* and been directly influenced by them.[64]

The geometric paradigm crossed the Atlantic as well. Here again the interplay between intellectual currents and personal networks comes into play. As will be seen, to a large extent, these "scientific" ideas parallel exactly English and Continental developments and, on occasion, are directly dependent thereupon.

The notion that law must be treated as a deductive science like geometry had several American supporters during the first half of the nineteenth century including Hugh Swinton Legaré, David Hoffman, and Daniel Mayes. The first, Hugh Swinton Legaré, was one of the leading American Roman law scholars of his era as well as a lawyer and statesman. Born and educated in South Carolina, he was a leading member of the Charleston Bar, American Chargé d'Affaires in Brussels, Belgium and, in 1842, Attorney General of the United States. His interest and expertise in civil law stemmed from a year's stay in Edinburgh in 1818-1819 where he matriculated as a law student and studied law under Professor Irving and moral philosophy under Dugald Stewart.[65]

At the peak of his career, Legaré was not only a successful lawyer and diplomat, but also one of the most acute and expert Civilians in the United States. He maintained friendships with other Americans interested in Roman and civil law, including Justice Joseph Story and Edward Livingston, as well as with noted European scholars including Savigny.[66] He was both a founder of the *Southern Review* and a frequent contributer thereto on law and classical literature. Legaré developed his theory of the geometric paradigm in two review articles which he published in the 1830's, the first on James Kent's *Commentaries on American Law* [67] and the second on a number of Civilian texts, entitled "The Origins, History, and Influence of Roman Legislation."[68] Throughout these two articles, the geometric paradigm furnishes the approved method of legal reasoning. Legaré begins the article on Kent's *Commentaries* with the proposition that law "is at once the most exact and the most complicated of the moral sciences."[69] Later he praises the systematic character of Roman and civil law and castigates the common law for its "irregularities" and incoherencies:

> Whatever may be the comparative merits of these two systems of jurisprudence, considered *per se*, it is certain that the Civil law has greatly the advantage of ours in the manner in which it has been expounded and illustrated . . . In comparing what the civilians have written upon any subjects that have been treated by the English text writers, or discussed in the English Courts, it is, we think, impossible not to be struck with the superiority of their truly elegant and philosophical style of analysis and exposition. *Their whole arrangement and method—the division of the matter into its natural parts, the classification of it under the proper predicaments, the discussion of principles, the deduction of corrolaries—everything, in short, is more unanimous and systematic—everything savors more of a regular and exact science.*[70]

And:

> It [the Common Law] seems to be a mass of irregularities and inconsistencies, which consists rather in particular usages and occasional decisions, than in immutable principles, or in consequences deduced immediately from the rules of natural justice.[71]

For Legaré, the scientific aspect of law was inextricably bound with utilization of the proper method of reasoning:

> It is evident . . . that the excellencies which have been alluded to as characteristic of the writings of the Civilians, do not arise out of anything in the nature of that law, but solely from the preparatory discipline and general intellectual habits of its professors.[72]

Thus, Legaré could argue, as had his teacher Stewart and his friend Savigny, that the deductive method of legal reasoning, the geometric paradigm, was not alien to the common law nor impossible of application to the common law, but, rather, could be applied to any substantive legal system so long as first principles could be established by some proper method. Indeed, Legaré aligned himself intellectually with Savigny and believed that such first principles must be derived from the positive laws of each nation, rather than simply from natural law.[73] In short, Legaré believed that Anglo-American common law could be made more precise and scientific by the application of principles of deductive reasoning.

There can be no doubt that these ideas about law as a deductive science, like geometry, derived from his work under Dugald Stewart. In the essay on Kent's *Commentaries*, Legaré specifically acknowledges Stewart's work in this area and the similarity of law to geometry. Indeed, Legaré quotes Stewart's quotation of Leibniz: "I have often said that, after the writings of the Geometricians, there exists nothing which, in point of force and subtlety, can be compared to the works of the Roman lawyers."[74] Legaré's work, therefore, acted as one conduit for these Continental ideas via Stewart into American jurisprudence. Legaré's essays were known to leading American jurists and thereby helped to introduce the geometric paradigm into the United States.

Another American example of the transmission of the geometric paradigm from the Continent is to be found in the work of David Hoffman. Hoffman was the first professor of law at the University of Maryland.[75] In 1817 he published *A Course of Legal Studies*[76] which he followed in 1836 with his *Legal Outlines* based upon his lectures at Maryland.[77] In 1832, the *American Jurist* published an excerpt from his lectures that encapsulated both the geometric paradigm, specifically attributed to Leibniz, and the relationship between the geometric paradigm and Roman and civil law:

> The praises of the Roman law, have been promulgated in the strongest language of eulogy; not by those only who admired its excellence, from ignorance of the merits of other codes; but by philosophers and publicists of the most enlarged views, and of the most extensive knowledge. The profoundly erudite Leibnitz, than whom no higher authority can be named on most subjects which engaged his inquisitive research, is of opinion, that nothing approximates so closely to the method of precision of Geometry, as the Imperial code; and this opinion has been echoed by many German, French, and Scottish civilians. The authority of the German jurists on all subjects relating to the civil law, stands justly preeminent, as none have cultivated it with equal ardor, or comparable success, with the exception of Pothier, and the Chancellor D'aguesseau, of France. The German lawyers regard Roman jurisprudence as an essential part of legal education, for the very reasons which strongly recommend it to our own careful attention. The common law of England, which lies at the foundation of American law, can no more be thoroughly and philosophically comprehended without frequent reference to the civil code, than can be the Jus Hodiernum of Germany, a system raised on the basis of that code.[78]

This excerpt is typical of Hoffman's jurisprudence. Throughout both *The Course* and *Legal Outlines* Hoffman argues for modeling Anglo-American common law upon Roman and civil law and for the adoption of the deductive method as the principal mode of legal reasoning.[79] Hoffman deplored the chaotic state of the common law and the unscientific nature of legal training. His adoption of the geometric paradigm was entirely consistent with his career oriented towards rationalization and systematization of American law.

Perhaps, the most interesting and significant American adoptions of the geometric paradigm in law are to be found in some of the pedagogical literature of the period. Of these, the most significant is clearly a lecture given by Daniel Mayes in 1832 entitled *An Introductory Lecture Delivered to the Law Class of Transylvania University on the 5th November, 1832* published at Lexington, Kentucky.[80] A long review of this lecture was published in the *American Jurist* in April, 1833 entitled "Whether Law is a Science."[81]

Mayes begins his lecture in the traditional way by stating that law is a moral science just as mathematics is an exact science and works a comparison of the two:

> The principles of mathematics are true, the instruments used by the mathematician, when he attempts to apply the principles of his science, to the purpose of art, are imperfect; and subjects

> to which he applies those true principles, are often such as not to admit of their exact application in practice . . . Give the mathematician the exact length and bearing of each line, and the principles of his science ascertain the contents with invariable accuracy.
>
> So of the law. Its principles are true in the abstract, and the difficulty lies in the imperfection of the instruments used, in making an application of those principles, in practice; and in the nature of those subjects to which those principles are to be applied. The abstract rule is to be applied to facts and intentions.[82]

For Mayes, the greatest problem facing American lawyers and law students was the absence of a proper method of analysis. The deductive method, as exemplified by geometry, provided a panacea for these ills:

> I have found that those who are new in the study of legal science, are often much perplexed when asked if advantage can be taken of certain errors [in procedure]. That they are prone to burden their memories with a number of detached instances, without classification, and have no process of reasoning by which they can come to the proper conclusion. *If a question is proposed of a case they have not seen, they are at a stand, for want of a rule, by which to test the case. This must ever be our condition, so long as we memorize cases, instead of studying principles. Cases are useful; but their greatest use is, that they serve to illustrate principles. If they are read and not resolved into elementary principles, the profit of the reading is not worth the time it occupies.*[83]

And:

> Most of the 'shadows, clouds, and darkness,' that rest upon the minds of some judges and lawyers . . . proceed from the fact that they wholly neglect analysis and classification.[84]

The reviewer in the *American Jurist* agreed whole-heartedly with Mayes:

> When we say that a branch of human knowledge is a science, we mean, in general, that it is founded on principles inherent in the subjects to which it relates. We mean also that those principles serve as a basis whereon we may classify the subjects of that particular branch of knowledge. We mean, further, that such branch of knowledge may be taught by commencing with generals and descending to particulars; and that in practice we do not grope in the dark, but each particular case, as soon as it arises, is illustrated, to the eye of the skillful observer, by the clear and steady light of general principles.[85]

The rationale for Mayes's support for the introduction of deductive, scientific analysis was twofold, and hearkened back to the ideas of his Continental predecessors. First, Mayes clearly believed that it was necessary to make law and law study more "scientific" if it was to be a university subject of instruction. Second, he believed that law and the legal process required more certainty and predictability if it was to retain its normative force in society. Indeed, he makes this point explicitly in the context of explaining how two judges might reach different results in the same case.[86] For Mayes, this variation could be attributable not to any inherent lack of certainty or to any defect in the method of decision, but rather to an imperfect application of the deductive method. According to Mayes such a difference could occur only because the judges involved either were "not masters of it [the science of law]" or because they had "fallen into some error."[87] Indeed, Mayes points out that two geometers might alao reach opposing conclusions because of their personal flaws.[88]Carrying this idea one step further, Mayes argues that judges' opinions are not laws *per se*, but rather only evidence of laws. In this particular sentiment, approved by the reviewer in the *American Jurist*, Mayes hearkened back to the natural lawyers, a point which may well reveal a Continental source for his use of the deductive, geometric paradigm.[89]

Mayes's two concerns, for certainty and predictability in the law, and for the "scientification" of law so that it could defend and maintain its place in the university curriculum, echo earlier seventeenth and eighteenth century sentiments in England and the Continent, and are also common themes throughout early nineteenth century American legal literature and may help to explain why the notion of law as a deductive science gained popularity in the United States during this period. As to the second point, the place of scientific law in the university, one can cite the remarks of Harvard President Josiah Quincy at the dedication of the Dane Law College at Harvard:

> The law, considered as a science, has so intimate a connection with the sciences in general, that, at first view, we are ready to wonder, why it was not made earlier a branch of education in Universities; or how it should have ever been deemed practicable to prosecute the study of it, successfully, elsewhere.[90]

Jurists and legal scholars were fighting a battle for legitimacy in the first part of the nineteenth century. Common law studies, both in England and in the United States, had traditionally been centered around an apprenticeship in the office of a practicing lawyer.[91] Now, suddenly, they were gaining a foothold in universities. In order to justify and legitimize their place in these institutions as well as to convince potential students to attend university law schools, it was necessary to develop some notion which would set university law studies apart from apprenticeship and would convince everyone that university law studies bestowed special expertise and status. The notion of legal science achieved these ends. First, by establishing law as a science, law *ipso facto* became a legitimate university subject. Indeed, the utilization of Roman and civil law as both an exemplar and a source for the developing legal science aided this legitimation process because the classical languages were the traditional treasures of the higher curriculum. The notion of law as a deductive science on the model of mathematics also served as a special selling point for attracting law students to the universities, for the apprenticeship system inculcated the traditional, writ-based, practice-oriented notions. It was only in the university law schools that students would be taught broad principles and the scientific mode of reasoning necessary to apply them.

The second rationale in the American context for the adoption of the geometric paradigm was the increasing dissatisfaction of the public with the seeming chaos and uncertainty of law and the legal process. While de Tocqueville may have been correct in his belief that lawyers were the true American aristocracy,[92] during this period popular distrust of lawyers and the legal system was growing. Many felt that the law was unpredictable, solely at the whim of lawyers and judges. For instance in a volume entitled *Sampson Against the Philistines or the Reformation of Lawsuits* written by one Jesse Higgins and published at Philadelphia in 1805, one finds the following indictment of the legal system:

> the whole body of common law, the whole body of pleadings, rules of evidence, etc. have no legislative acts to establish or even to define them. They depend wholly and entirely for their authority on notes taken by lawyers and clerks, about this very time, and hence the judges became the legislators. It is a fixed rule, maintained by every judge and lawyer, to follow the footsteps of those who have gone before them; so that whenever a lawyer can discover a case, bearing a resemblance to one now to be tried, that has been reported at some ancient time, by these very priestly lawyers, and adjudged by those sacred clerical judges, unless since altered by statute, he is sure of a judgment in his favor without paying any regard to the reason of the decision.[93]

The scientific theory of law eliminated this apparent incertitude, since it required first the discovery of general principles and then the application of these principles to facts by deductive logic. Indeed, this approach was perfectly consistent with even the most radical reformist idea, codification, since, by their very nature, codes invite application of deductive reasoning.[94]

V. Legal Science and Langdell

The scientific approach pioneered by Langdell in the 1870's had two components: empiricism and rationalism.[95] It was the empirical aspect of Langdell's concept that was most consonant with Harvard President Eliot's and other contemporaries' ideas about science. Science was something that one did. The term connoted investigation and experimentation. Thus, Langdell argued that jurists and legal scholars were also empirical investigators. They sought for legal principles rather than physical rules. The sources of their raw data were not chemical compounds or heavenly bodies, but rather legal facts, facts to be found in appellate cases. The rational aspect of the Langdellian notion of legal science dove-tailed with the empirical aspect. The rational aspect of the Langdellian model quite simply was the belief that legal reasoning must be deductive.

Langdell's notion of law as a rational science, therefore, was anything but unique or innovative. Indeed, to a very large extent, the Langdellian concept of legal science simply echoed Mayes, Legaré, Stewart, Leibniz, and other earlier jurists. Robert Stevens has commented, on this point, that "his [Langdell's] vision of legal science would have been acceptable to Bacon."[96] Langdell's "vision" is summed up in the preface to the first edition of his *Cases on Contracts*:

> Law, considered as a science, consists of certain principles or doctrines. To have such a mastery of these as to be able to apply them with constant facility and certainty to the ever-tangled skein of human affairs, is what constitutes a true lawyer.[97]

In fact, Langdell's major contribution to the notion of law as science was his emphasis on the empirical dimension by his insistence that the first principles to which deductive method must be applied could be attained not by reason or logic alone but through empirical research in the decided cases:

> We have also constantly inculcated the idea that the Library is the proper workshop of professors and students alike; that it is to us all that the laboratories of the university are to the chemists and physicists, the museum of natural history to the zoologists, the botanical garden to the botanists.[98]

In effect, Langdell's empirical case-method approach is but a means of deriving first principles. He noted that "the only way of mastering the doctrine effectually is by studying the cases in which it is embodied."[99] The empirical portion of Langdell's theory, that upon which he and his contemporaries placed most emphasis, is, therefore, totally consistent with the earlier developed deductive, geometric paradigm of legal reasoning. Indeed, the deductive method is crucial to the Langdellian model. The need for first principles was always a part of the deductive model of law, but the means of deriving these first principles was also always variable. Leibniz, Wolff, Thibaut, and the Pandectists looked to natural law and natural law in its best mundane manifestation, Roman law, for these principles. Savigny looked to the history and society of each nation, as did Legaré. Langdell looked to cases. Mayes, interestingly, also looked to cases. For him cases were only useful as sources for first principles. In this Mayes preshadowed—if not preempted—Langdell by nearly forty years.

The Langdellian notion of law as science, therefore, was hardly original. The various parts of his theory, even the empirical aspect, had been enunciated long before he took over the Harvard Law School and began to write. So, too, were the motivations behind the theory. The quest for certainty in law and the need to legitimize university legal studies both predated Langdell. Thus, to be fair to his predecessors, one should praise Langdell only for his popularization efforts, not for his innovativeness or originality.[100] Langdell was but a link in a chain of tradition stretching back two centuries and across the Atlantic.

Notes

1. Baker, *English Law and the Renaissance*, 44 Cambridge L.J. 46, 47 (1985).

2. See R. Stevens, Law School. Legal Education in America from the 1850's to the 1950's 35 (1983).
3. Elliott, *The Evolutionary Tradition in Jurisprudence*, 85 Colum. L. Rev. 38 (1985).
4. T.S. Kuhn, The Structure of Scientific Revolutions (2d ed. 1982); see also I.B. Cohen, Revolution in Science (1985).
5. On the influence of the science of geology and the development of evolutionary theory in biology and its impact on legal theory, see P. Stein, Legal Evolution. The Story of an Idea (1980) and Elliott, *supra* note 3. *Cf.* W.A.J. Watson, The Evolution of Law (1985).
6. See B. Shapiro, Probability and Certainty in Seventeenth Century England (1983) and Shapiro, *Law and Science in Seventeenth Century England*, 21 Stan. L. Rev. 727 (1969).
7. See Wieacker, *The Importance of Roman Law for Western Civilization and Western Legal Thought*, 4 B.C. Int'l & Comp. L. Rev. 257 (1981).
8. See W.A.J. Watson, The Making of the Civil Law (1982). On the medieval legal tradition, see F. Calasso, Medio Aevo Del Diritto (1954).
9. See Pringsheim, *The Inner Relationship Between English and Roman Law*, 5 Cambridge L.J. 347 (1935); F. Schulz, Prinzipien der Römischen Rechts 27 (1934) trans. as F. Schulz, Principles of Roman Law 40 (Wolff trans. 1936).
10. See Stein, *Elegance in Law*, 77 L.Q. Rev. 242 (1962); J. Bryce, *The Methods of Legal Science*, in Studies in History and Jurisprudence 629 (1901).
11. See comments of J. Bryce in *Inaugural Lecture*, in J. Bryce *supra* note 10, at 877.
12. Perhaps the greatest exception to this trend was the Iberian *Visigothic Code* of the seventh century A.D.; on this, see P.D. King, Law and Society in the Visigothic Kingdom (1972).
13. W.A.J. Watson, *supra* note 8, at 23.
14. See *supra* note 10.
15. See *supra* note 6, Kocher, *Francis Bacon on the Science of Jurisprudence*, 18 J. Hist. Ideas 3 (1957).
16. See *supra* notes 6 & 15.
17. See McCrae, *The Unity of the Sciences: Bacon, Descartes, and Leibniz*, 18 J. Hist. Ideas 27 (1957).
18. I. Bernard Cohen has suggested that Bacon's work on the "new science" of the seventeenth century was less important in its use of mathematical models than was that of Descartes; see Cohen, *supra* note 4, at 146-60.
19. *Quoted in* McCrae, *supra* note 17, at 36.
20. See *supra* note 6.
21. Shapiro, *supra* note 6, at 736-38; Kocher, *supra* note 15, at 4-6.
22. By far the best study of G.W.F. Leibniz's juristic work is F. Sturm, das Römische Recht in der Sicht von Gottfried Wilhelm Leibniz (1968).
23. G.W.F. Leibniz, Nova Methodus Discendae Docendaeque Iuris *printed in* G.W.F. Leibniz, Opera Omnia 214 (Dutens ed. 1768), and 1 G.W.F. Leibniz, Philosophische Schriften 261-364 (Dtsch. Akad. d. Wiss. ed. 1974).
24. ut credam nec Euclidem nec Cartesium, si se huic doctrinae applicuissent, potuisse scribere rotundius profundiisque, quam Ulpianum et Papinianum: ut quisquis his non lectis intellectisque magnum se juris naturae et gentium consultum fore sperat, procul a janua sit aberraturus. . . .
quoted in F. Sturm, *supra* note 22, at 19 n.34.
25. F. Sturm, *supra* note 22, at 19-20: "Er sieht in ihm eine Emanation der Ratio. Er erblickt in ihm eine geistige Leistung, die durchaus mit der von Philosophen und Mathematikern zu konkurrieren vermag."
26. Il y a des exemples assez considérables de démonstrations hors des Mathématiques, et on peut dire qu'Aristote on a donné déjà dans ses Premiers Analytiques . . . De plus, on peut dire que les Jurisconsultes ont plusieurs bonnes démonstrations; surtout les anciens Jurisconsultes romains, dont les fragmens nous on êté conservés dans les Pandectes. Je suis tout à fait de l'avis de Laurent Valle, qui ne peut assez admirer ces auteurs, entre autres parce qu'ils parlent tous d'une manière si juste et si nette et qu'ils raisonnent en effêt d'une facon qui approche fort de la démonstrative, et souvent est démonstrative tout à fait . . . Cette manière précise de s'expliquer, a fait, que tous ces Jurisconsultes des Pandectes, quoyque assez éloignés quelques fois les uns du tems des autres, semblent être tous un seul auteur, e tuk'on auroit bien de la peine à les discerner, si les noms des Escrivains n'êtoient pas à la tête des extraits; comme on auroit de la peine à distinguer Euclide Archimede et Apollonius en lisant leurs démonstrations sur des matières, que l'un aussi bien que l'autre a touchées
quoted in F. Sturm, *supra* note 22, at 22 n.43.
27. See 1 Rashdall, The Universities of Europe in the Middle Ages 87-175 (Powicke & Emden eds. 1936); see also K. H. Burmeister, das Studium der Rechte im Zeitalter des Humanismus (1974).
28. See the remarks of John Austin in J. Austin, Lectures on Jurisprudence 58 (Campbell ed. 1885), see also Hoeflich, *John Austin and Joseph Story: Two Nineteenth Century Perspectives on the Utility of the Civil Law for the Common Lawyer.* 29 Am. J. Legal Hist. 36, 43 (1985) and Stein, *Legal Theory and the Reform of Legal Education in Mid-Nineteenth Century England.* in 1 Educazione Juridica 185, 192 (1977).
29. See W.A.J. Watson, *supra* note 8.
30. On the importance of Roman legal terminology, see J. Bryce, *supra* note 10, at 878-79; see also Hoeflich, *supra* note 28, at 52-53. On the importance of precise language for deductive reasoning in law generally, see O. C. Jensen, The Nature of Legal Argument 21-28 (1957).
31. See F. Sturm, *supra* note 22, at 8-9, 16.
32. C. Wolff, Jus Gentium Methoda Scientifica Pertractatum (Halle 1774).

33. C. WOLFF, INSTITUTIONES JURIS NATURAE ET GENTIUM (Halle 1749).

34. Die Philosophie Wolff's unterscheidet sich von jeder andern am meisten durch ihre Methode, die mathematisch-demonstrative—so bemerkt er selbst gelegentlich. Diese Methode besteht in einer kunstvollen Verbindung von sorgfältig zugearbeiteten (exascitae) Definitionen, anderswoher genommenen Principien, scharfen Lehrsätzen; letztere müssen sich durch die beiden ersteren Gruppen beweisen lassen . . .

R. STINTZING & E. LANDSBERG, GESCHICHTE DER DEUTSCHEN RECHTSWISSENSCHAFT 198 (1898).

35. Ea igitur alio modo in lucem proferri non potuerunt, nisi, vestigius EUCLIDIS, legum verioris Legicae rigidi observatoris, insistendo, singuli termini exacta definitione explicarentur, propositiones singulae sufficienter determinarentur, & non minus definitiones ita ordinarentur, ut sequentes per antecedentes penitus intelligantur, sed propositiones quoque ita, ut sequentium veritas per antecedentes pateat,

C. WOLFF, *supra* note 33.

36. On natural law, see A.P. D'ENTREVES, NATURAL LAW (1965).

37. On the Pandectists, see 2 H. COING, HANDBUCH DER QUELLEN UND LITERATUR DER NEUEREN EUROPÄISCHEN PRIVATRECHTSGESCHICHTE (1976); F. Ebrard, *Über methoden, systeme, dogmen in der geschichte des Privatrechts,* 67 ZEITSCHRIFT FÜR SCHWEIZERISCHES RECHT 95 (1948).

38. A.F.J. THIBAUT, SYSTEM DES PANDEKTEN-RECHTS (1803). I have used the fifth edition published at Jena in 1818.

39. *Id.* at 7.

40. M. BRESON, JURISPRUDENTIA. TRESOR DES ANECDOTES DE JURISPRUDENCE (1858).

41. Il existe une dissertation de Jean Botéon, intitulé: *Geometriae cognitio Jureconsulto necessaria.* Je ne connais point l'ouvrage, mais je le croirais bon et utile, s'il prouvait du moins que l'esprit géometrique est essentiel dans la pratique de la jurisprudence commes dans toutes les sciences ou la justesse et la sûreté du raisonnement sont necessaires; et s'il montrait bien l'application des principles geométriques aux matieres de jurisprudence qui en sont susceptibles. Si l'ouvrage de Botéon n'est point fait ainsi, c'est un livre a faire; et s'il remplissait bien son objet, il ferait plus de bruit dans la republique des lettres que celui de Botéon.

42. On Savigny and the historical school, see J. REDDIE, HISTORICAL NOTICES OF THE ROMAN LAW AND OF THE PROGRESS OF ITS STUDY IN GERMANY (1826); G.P. GOOCH, HISTORY AND HISTORIANS IN THE NINETEENTH CENTURY 42-54 (1913); M. GUTZWILLER, DER EINFLUSS SAVIGNYS AUF DIE ENTWICKLUNG DES INTERNATIONAL PRIVATRECHTS (1923); see also the collection of articles printed in honor of Savigny's 200th birthday in 8 IUS COMMUNE (1980).

43. See J. REDDIE, *supra* note 42, at 111-14.

44. F. C. VON SAVIGNY, VOM BERUF UNSERER ZEIT FUR GESETZGEBUNG UND RECHTSWISSENSCHAFT (rev. ed. 1828); trans. as F. C. VON SAVIGNY, OF THE VOCATION OF OUR AGE FOR LEGISLATION AND JURISPRUDENCE (Hayward trans. 1831).

45. *Id.* at 38-39; the translation in the text is Hayward's.

46. *Id.* at 45; the translation in the text is Hayward's.

47. See Kocher, *supra* note 15.

48. See Hoeflich, *supra* note 28, at 43-47. See also the classic study of D. BOORSTIN, THE MYSTERIOUS SCIENCE OF LAW (1941).

49. Hoeflich, *supra* note 28.

50. See M. SANDERSON, THE UNIVERSITIES IN THE NINETEENTH CENTURY (1975).

51. Biographical details are drawn from 25 ENCYCLOPEDIA BRITTANICA 913 (11th ed. 1911); see also G. DAVIE, THE DEMOCRATIC INTELLECT, SCOTLAND AND HER UNIVERSITIES IN THE NINETEENTH CENTURY (1961); S. COLLINI, D. WINCH & J. BURROW, THAT NOBLE SCIENCE OF POLITICS 23-61 (1983).

52. D. STEWART, ELEMENTS OF THE PHILOSOPHY OF THE HUMAN MIND (1792-1827).

53. D. STEWART, OUTLINES OF MORAL PHILOSOPHY (1973).

54. D. STEWART, PHILOSOPHICAL ESSAYS (1810).

55. D. STEWART, *supra* note 52, at 405-90.

56. *Id.* at 424.

57. *Id.*

58. *Id.* at 424-25.

59. On John Austin, see W. L. MORISON, JOHN AUSTIN (1982); Rumble, *The Legal Positivism of John Austin and the Realist Movement in American Jurisprudence,* 66 CORNELL L. REV. 986 (1981); Hoeflich, *supra* note 28.

60. J. Austin, *supra* note 28.

61. Hoeflich, *supra* note 28, at 36-56; Schwarz, *John Austin and the German Jurisprudence of His Time,* 5 POLITICA 178 (1934).

62. 1 J. Austin, *supra* note 28, at 140.

63. *Id.*

64. Unfortunately, Austin's library was lost in the Second World War bombing of London. Schwarz, *supra* note 61 describes the library generally, but does not specifically mention Stewart's works as being a part of Austin's collection.

65. L. RHEA, HUGH SWINTON LEGARE (1934); see also Stein, *The Attraction of the Civil Law in Post-Revolutionary America,* 52 VA. L. REV. 403, 427-31 (1966); M. Hoeflich, Three Roman Lawyers of the Old South: Lieber, Legaré, and Walker (unpublished lecture given at the University of Chicago Legal History Workshop, Feb. 28, 1985); J. KRUMPELMANN, SOUTHERN SCHOLARS IN GOETHE'S GERMANY 6-22 (1965); 2 V. PARRINGTON, MAIN CURRENTS IN AMERICAN THOUGHT 114-24 (1927); see also the pioneering, albeit too brief, study of Perry Miller in P. MILLER, THE LIFE OF THE MIND IN AMERICA 156-64 (1965). Miller, I believe, understimates the influence of the European development of the deductive method in these remarks.

66. H. S. LEGARE, THE WRITINGS OF H. S. LEGARE (1934).
67. 2 H. S. LEGARE, *supra* note 66, at 102.
68. 1 H. S. LEGARE, *supra* note 66, at 517.
69. 2 H. S. LEGARE, *supra* note 66, at 104.
70. *Id.* at 110.
71. *Id.* at 112.
72. *Id.* at 112-13.
73. *Id.* at 135.
74. *Id.* at 113-14.
75. See Shaffer, *David Hoffman's Law School Lectures*, 1882-1833, 32 J. LEGAL EDUC. 127 (1981); Hoeflich, *Roman and Civil Law in American Legal Education and Research Prior to 1930,* [1984] U. ILL. L. REV. 719, 723-25. [See also chapters 18 and 19.]
76. D. HOFFMAN, A COURSE OF LEGAL STUDIES (1817).
77. D. HOFFMAN, LEGAL OUTLINES (1836).
78. Hoffman, *Ninth Lecture,* 8 AM. JURIST 203 (1832).
79. See Hoeflich, *supra* note 75.
80. D. MAYES, AN INTRODUCTORY LECTURE DELIVERED TO THE LAW CLASS OF TRANSYLVANIA UNIVERSITY ON THE 5TH NOVEMBER, 1832 (1833); see the remarks of A. W. B. Simpson on this lecture and its importance in Simpson, *The Rise and Fall of the Legal Treatise: Legal Principles and the Forms of Legal Literature,* 48 UNIV. CHI. L. REV. 632, 672 (1981).
81. Anon., *Whether Law Is a Science,* 9 AM. JURIST 349 (1843).
82. D. MAYES, *supra* note 80, at 3.
83. *Id.* at 17.
84. *Id.* at 7.
85. Anon., *supra* note 81, at 349.
86. D. MAYES, *supra* note 80, at 6.
87. *Id.*
88. *Id.*
89. *Id.*
90. J. Quincy, *Address on the Occasion of the Dedication of Dane Law College,* 9 AM. JURIST 48, 52 (1833); *cf.* the remarks of W. BLACKSTONE, A DISCOURSE ON THE STUDY OF THE LAW: BEING AN INTRODUCTORY LECTURE . . . (3d ed. 1759). "For sciences are of a sociable disposition, and flourish best in the neighborhood of each other: nor is there any branch of learning, but may be helped and improved by assistances drawn from other arts." *Cf.* the remarks of Simon Greenleaf in his lecture, *Law as a Liberal Science* contained in Huntington Library M.S. LI418, a version of which was published in the 1848 issue of the LAW REPORTER.
91. In England, in fact, legal education remained entirely unreformed in the Inns of Court until well into the nineteenth century; see Stein, *supra* note 28; see also REPORT FROM THE SELECT COMMITTEE ON LEGAL EDUCATION (1846).
92. A. DE TOCQUEVILLE, DEMOCRACY IN AMERICA (1835).
93. J. HIGGINS, SAMPSON AGAINST THE PHILISTINES OR THE REFORMATION OF LAWSUITS 16-17 (1805).
94. See J. VANDERLINDEN, LE CONCEPT DE CODE EN EUROPE OCCIDENTALE DU XIIE AU XIXE SIECLE. ESSAI DE DEFINITION (1967).
95. R. STEVENS, *supra* note 2, at 52-55; see also Grey, *Langdell's Orthodoxy,* 45 J. PITT. L. REV. 1, 16-20. Grey interestingly argues that in Langdell's period geometry was considered an inductive science as well as deductive.
96. *Id.* at 52.
97. C. LANGDELL, CASES ON CONTRACTS viii (1879).
98. *Quoted in* R. STEVENS, *supra* note 2, at 53. [Reprinted in whole in chapter 34 of this book.]
99. *Quoted in Id.* at 52.
100. It is useful to recall the remarks of the late Grant Gilmore about Langdell:
"Langdell seems to have been an essentially stupid man who, early in life, hit on one great idea to which, thereafter, he clung with all the tenacity of genius."
in G. GILMORE, THE AGES OF AMERICAN LAW 42 (1977).

Chapter 45

Before Langdell

The Roots of American Legal Science

1998

Howard Schweber

Howard Schweber is a historian, an attorney, and a doctoral candidate in government at Cornell University.

Author's note: I would like to thank Steve Sheppard, Greg Alexander, and Michael Dennis for their advice and assistance in the preparation of this paper. Paul Carrington, Michael Hoeflich, and Alfred Konefsky read earlier drafts and provided helpful comments that enabled me to avoid serious errors. This chapter is a revised and expanded version of an article that appeared previously in *Law & History Review*; the anonymous reviewers for that journal provided important and constructive guidance. A portion of this paper was also presented at the 1997 annual meeting of the American Society for Legal History in Minneapolis; R. Kent Newmyer, the panel's commentator, and listeners at the meeting provided valuable comments. Those errors that remain are, of course, entirely my own responsibility.

In the first half of the nineteenth century, a model of legal education called "legal science" became prominent in American universities. The idea of teaching law as a science was not new to American education. In 1823 Timothy Dwight wrote that Tapping Reeve, at Litchfield, taught law "as a science, and not merely nor principally as a mechanical business; nor as a collection of loose independent fragments, but as a regular well-compacted system."[1] Dwight, however, used "science" in its older sense of any organized body of knowledge. The new "legal science" of the nineteenth century, in contrast, represented an appropriation of the emergent sense of "science" as a method characteristic of the study of nature. In time, a version of this new model of legal science was to become the dominant approach to American legal education.

This paper attempts to situate the antebellum American idea of "legal science" in the historical context of nineteenth century natural science generally. The claim is not that direct links between natural and

23. George Sharswood (1810-1883) was chief justice of Pennsylvania and a professor at Penn. His view of science was very little changed from that of Blackstone, whom he annotated. (*Courtesy of the Biddle Library Department of Special Collections, University of Pennsylvania Law School.*)

legal scientists[2] are demonstrated here, although in some cases such links demonstrably existed (for example, by the prominent participation of lawyers in the early natural scientific associations of the 1820s and 30s). Instead, the primary focus is on the fact that writers about "legal science" grounded their claim that their methods were inspired by the natural sciences in a particular conception of the meaning and methods of "science."

The goal here is, in part, to remedy a tendency toward a kind of presentism in the history of ideas that confuses the *possibility* of a kind of thinking for evidence of its presence in an earlier period.[3] This is a particularly marked danger when dealing with a term that is as central to modernity's conception of itself as "science." The fact that nineteenth-century writers talked about "science" in a way that sounds like they could have meant what we mean by the same word is not sufficient to assure us that the meaning was the same in the two cases. I will argue, in fact, that the concept of natural science at work in antebellum American discourse was specific to its period, highly contested, and ideologically specific, and that a recognition of these facts requires us to reconsider some received truths about the meaning of legal science.

To demonstrate the meaning of "science" at work in American legal science, I will trace parallels in both the institutional and intellectual developments of legal and natural science. In many ways, the institutional developments in these fields demonstrated the patterns characteristic of nineteenth century professionalization generally: I have characterized these as a "movement upward" within society, toward elite status; followed by a "turning inward" away from the larger public sphere, as institutional gatekeeping mechanisms and an increasingly internalist discourse came to dominate the activities of scientific and legal educators.

This institutional account has significant consequences for the intellectual story. For one thing, when the natural sciences and legal education each "turned inward," the capacity for appropriation became sharply limited. Prior to that time, a governing conception of "science" was in free circulation in emphatically public associations and journals of general circulation. Where appropriation occurred after 1870 or so, it was from the much more open discourse of social science, itself prefigured in important ways by the ideas of the legal scientists. It was during the earlier period, however, that both the legitimating principles and method of natural and legal science were established in ways that were closely parallel.

The principles of legitimation for both natural science and legal science in their early "movement upward" phase were based on appeals to twin values of utility and improvement. Closely associated with liberal and republican norms, these two principles were invoked extensively and often simultaneously to define the mandates of the public enterprises of science. The idea of "utility"—captured in the coining of the word "technology" in 1829—emphasized the importance to society of rationalized, efficient, enterprises. Often expressed in exceptionalist terms, appeals to utility described a glowing American future of untold prosperity and millennial advancement. "Improvement," on the other hand, identifies claims that were made in both the natural and legal sciences that education would produce moral uplift. Applied to legal education, this also meant an immediate connection between legal training and republican jurisprudence. Legal science in its initial formulation was a fundamentally reformist movement, opposed both to the radicalism of codification and the legal conservativism of traditionalists such as James Kent.[4] An important part of this story is the gradual pulling apart of these two principles of justification into opposing ideological conceptions, a process that was under way by the 1820s and which reached fruition in the 1850s.

The particular method of the natural sciences that was adopted by legal science was characterized by a set of principles that I refer to under the rubric of "Protestant Baconianism." This was a set of values and assumptions quite unfamiliar to a modern reader. Closely connected to the religious roots of laissez-faire, grounded in the epistemology of Scottish Common Sense Realism, Protestant Baconianism had four outstanding characteristics: a commitment to natural theology, the doctrine that the study of nature proved religious truths; a commitment to a limited form of inductivism that defined science as the taxonomical classification of natural objects to demonstrate known first principles; a belief in a grand synthesis that bound all forms of knowledge together in a system of analogies; and the idea of improvement, a commitment to claims of moral and political consequences of scientific work closely connected to open discourse and public participation. These elements characterized both the tradition of legal science and the dominant tradition of natural sciences in the antebellum American universities.

In the natural sciences, the Protestant Baconian approach was exemplified and promulgated by a circle of friends centered around Alexander Dallas Bache.[5] In the 1840s, a circle of Bache's friends became the locus of development for the dominant public ideas about natural science. The "Bache circle," sometimes known as the "Lazzaroni," comprised, semi-officially, Bache, Joseph Henry,[6] Benjamin Peirce, Oliver Wolcott Gibbs, John F. Frazier, James D. Dana, Benjamin A. Gould, and Louis Agassiz, the most famous scientist of his age. The group was extremely influential in the development of national scientific associations, specialized journals, and university-based science education, particularly at Harvard and Yale.

Among antebellum American legal scientists, a handful of influential writers similarly stand out as exemplars of the approach that is the subject of this chapter, although unlike the natural scientists discussed here they did not form a unified group. They are: David Hoffman (University of Maryland),[7] Daniel Mayes (Transylvania University),[8] David Dudley Field,[9] Simon Greenleaf,[10] Nathan Beverley Tucker (College of William and Mary),[11] and George Sharswood (University of Pennsylvania).[12] These were the authors who promulgated the naturalistic turn in American legal science, a strand of intellectual development that existed separate from, and alongside, the idea of law as moral science developed by writers such as Joseph Story, Francis Hilliard,[13] and Silas Jones.[14]

It was by no means the case that legal science, however defined, immediately dominated legal education. For one thing, many lawyers continued to prepare by apprenticeship well into the twentieth century. Even in law schools, there was no universal acceptance of legal science.[15] As late as 1870, while Langdell struggled to attract a score of students, Thomas Cooley ran the largest and most successful law school in the nation based on the idea of providing practical training for future lawyers. Cooley's famous characterization of the law was "the common thoughts of men," an ideal far removed from the grandiose claims of either moralistic or naturalistic legal science.[16] In 1872 the provost of The Johns Hopkins University delivered an address to the law school in which he derided the idea of law as a science.[17]

Nonetheless, by the end of the century legal training had become both relentlessly professional *and* based on a particular model of legal science, that created at Harvard by Christopher Columbus Langdell.[18] Langdell was emphatic that his version of legal science was grounded in the natural, not the moral, sciences. The texts that are the primary focus of discussion in this section of this paper are chosen for their illumination of the roots of that naturalistic model of legal science, rather than based on a claim that they reflect the totality of university legal education.

Similarly, the claim here is not that the Bache circle's approach to the study of the natural sciences was the precursor to modern scientific practice. From early on there were scientists whose approach to their work was quite different, and in fact they would come to displace the Bache circle and the philosophy that they represented in the years following the Civil War.[19] The focus on Protestant Baconianism, however, captures the sense of the dominant public idea of science among educated elites in the antebellum period. It was that public idea, transmitted through what Alfred S. Konefsky has called "cultural nexes,"[20] that was received into the vocabulary of legal education by the specific agency of writers like Hoffman, Mayes, Field, Greenleaf, and Sharswood.

I. The Roots of American Legal Science

The idea of law as a science has been applied, retrospectively, as far back as Justinian's "Pandects," and in fact the form of the organization of the *Commentaries* of Blackstone, Kent and Story owed much to that model. In the Continental tradition references to law as a science continued from the medieval period, when law was declared one of the three great learned professions along with theology and medicine.

In its early sense, however, the term "science" implied no particular method, only the identification of the field as one appropriate for the efforts of men of learning. Throughout the medieval period, the project of determining a unified form of right reason equally applicable to theology, botany, and the law was the characteristic effort of the Scholastics.[21] The rediscovery of Arabic scientific texts in the thirteenth century forced the Church to acknowledge a separation between religious and natural knowledge; in the sixteenth century the reintroduction of Greek skepticism introduced a new vocabulary for the discussion of standards of verification and the nature of "knowledge" generally; the Reformation and Counter-Reformation connected positions about the knowledge of the natural world to religious and political ideologies.

Nonetheless, orthodox Calvinists no less than Jesuits held firmly to the position that a true understanding of the world was necessarily one which accorded with the dictates of Scripture despite the violence of their differences as to the content of those principles.[22] Thomist-inspired ideals of natural law continued to provide the connective tissue for the body of knowledge for both camps through the sixteenth century as they had in the fourteenth.[23] Legal doctrines were being created to deal with entirely new kinds of situations, such as early forms of insurance contracts that incorporated emerging concepts of probability and risk, but these were treated as exceptions or justified in terms of principles of religious morality.[24]

Faced with the decline in authority of traditional certainties, Rationalist writers exemplified by Leibniz and the Port Royal logicians began to attempt the creation of a mode of certain knowledge unconnected to religious presuppositions. Among many other projects, these authors turned their attentions to an attempt to describe legal science by deducing principles of law purely by the application of reason to known axioms. Others, such as Grotius and Locke, appealed to the historical legacy of an initial social contract and a secularized natural law derived from reason. In the eighteenth century, positive doctrines of law as a system of artificial arrangements made for the efficient accomplishment of social goods the basis for reordering the system of laws in new and allegedly more rational forms.

Applied to law, these three broad streams of historical development culminated in the nineteenth century in debates between the historical jurisprudence of Friedrich von Savigny and the German Pandectists, who sought a restored version of the Roman jus compendium; the Rationalist deductivism of Christian Wolff, who proposed to bring law into accordance with the new systems of geometry and mathematics; and Napoleonic proposals for codification championed by writers such as Anton Friedrich Justus Thibaut.[25] All of these different approaches asserted the claim that they were creating a "science" of law grounded in reason; none, however, drew a connection to the method of the natural sciences. The American version of legal science was something quite different, with its roots in England.

A. English Legal Science from Bacon to Blackstone

In the English common law tradition, the idea of legal science is related to the development of thinking about the study of nature from its outset. The idea that laws could be systematized, rationalized, and made understandable—and hence a proper subject for formal instruction—begins in the seventeenth century with the competing ideas of Coke and Bacon. Bacon was perhaps the greater jurist, although the extraordinary range of his endeavors has made him better remembered as the man who put his name on the modern idea of the natural sciences.[26] Bacon's great contribution to science was the inductive experimental method.[27] "The formation of ideas and axioms by true induction is no doubt the proper remedy to be applied for the keeping off and clearing away of idols."[28] Because Bacon's ideas about the study of the natural sciences figure prominently in this account, it is worth taking a moment to recall the basic elements of the experimental method of inductive reasoning.[29]

Bacon saw his task as overcoming the weight of traditional authority so as to make room for new methods of understanding.[30] Above all, this meant a rejection of the Aristotelian (or rather the Peripatetic gloss on Aristotelian) idea of deductivism and its replacement by a system of inductive reasoning.[31] In terms of earlier Christian teachings, Bacon's construction of the natural world meant that appeal to God as a moving first cause could never be an appropriate argument. God was taken to stand completely outside nature, which was itself a complete and closed system.[32] What was needed was immersion into the world without preconceptions about ordering first principles.[33] Mere observation, however, would not suffice, as human perceptions were "false mirrors" that yielded illusions of order generated by the mind of the observer[34]; the true order of things was hidden in false analogies and misleading correspondences.[35] As a result, not mere observation but rather an experimental method, one that studied Nature "vexed . . . forced out of her natural state, and squeezed and moulded,"[36] was the approach that alone could advance the sciences from their stagnant state, by revealing hidden as well as evident truths.[37]

Bacon's project was not restricted to the study of natural phenomena; rather it was part of a reform of knowledge *tout court.* All sciences had their roots in "one universal science," the *Philosophia Prima,* which he compared to the trunk of a great tree from which particular sciences emerge as branches.[38] The model for all the arts and science was to be natural philosophy, "the great mother of all the sciences," and their reform was to be accomplished by a return to the true methods of that study. "For all arts and sciences, if torn from their root, though they be polished and shaped and made fit for use, yet they will hardly grow."[39] The justification for attaining scientific knowledge combined values of utility and moral improvement. The perfection of knowledge of nature was desirable because it was the means to the Great Instauration, the restoration of man's domination over all aspects of the natural world, and the perfection of political and social institutions.

The systematization of legal knowledge, for Bacon, was similarly part of a project of reform and improvement. He complied three hundred legal maxims, of which twenty-five were published in 1630 as *Maxims of the Law.* His aim was "to sound into the true conceit of law by depth of reason.

> [I]n cases wherein the authorities do square and vary, to confirm the law, and to make it received one way; and in cases wherein the law is cleared by authority, yet nevertheless to see more profoundly into the reason of such judgments and ruled cases, and thereby to make more use of them for the decision of other cases more doubtful.[40]

Maxims "run through different matters of law"; hence governing principles for tort might be found in cases of contract, arrived at inductively by the examination of cases for negative instances to disprove affirmative propositions. This was the means of seeing through the illusions of rhetoric and the errors of reason to find the "hidden truths" of the common law. Like the truths of the natural world, those truths could be discovered only by those trained in its ways. "There is a great affinity and consent between the rules of nature, and the true rules of policy," he declared, "the one being nothing else but an order in the government in the world, and the other an order in the government of an estate. . . . I conclude there is . . . a congruity between the principles of Nature and Policy."[41]

To derive maxims, and the higher principles of justice that they embodied, Bacon looked to two kinds of sources. He proceeded first by induction from an examination of the norms of civilized society, which he supposed to be universally the same as expressions of a singular human reason. "There are in nature certain fountains of justice," he wrote, "whence all civil laws are derived but as streams."[42] Second, he found universal principles in Scripture; this distinguished legal science from the natural sciences, where Bacon had eschewed any claims of discovering natural truths through the examination of religious texts.[43] The organization of these maxims, moreover, was not hierarchical but aphoristic, "[f]or we see all the ancient wisdom and science was wont to be delivered in that form . . . but chiefly the precedent of the civil law. . . ."[44]

Thus crucial characterizing elements of Baconian natural science were the strict inductive experimentalism; the idea of a "grand synthesis" that unified all fields of knowledge under a single unifying method of reason; the emphasis on the direct connection between knowledge and improvement. All of these elements differentiated Baconian inductivism sharply from the older deductive systems and from the studies of mathematics or logic.[45] Each of these elements appeared in variously reconfigured forms in the American approaches to natural and legal science in the first half of the nineteenth century.

Bacon's approach to legal science drew a sharp contrast between himself and the earlier writings of Sir John Fortescue.[46] Fortescue had divided laws into those that were divine, those that were political (positively enacted) and those that were the product of custom (the common law.) Like Bacon, Fortescue had asserted that within each category, the logic of the law derived from maxims—"universal, self-evident, undemonstrable principles" acquired "by induction through the senses and the memory."[47] The different categories were incommensurable; in particular, the maxims of customary law could not be derived purely from reason but rather drew their authority from the fact of timeless custom.

> [T]hroughout the period of these nations and their kings, the realm has been continuously ruled by the same customs as it is now, customs which, if they had not been the best, some of those kings would have changed for the sake of justice or by the impulse to caprice . . . especially the Romans, who judged almost the whole of the rest of the world by their laws. . . . Hence there is no gainsaying nor legitimate doubt but that the customs of the English are not only good but the best.[48]

Bacon's striking departure from Fortescue's approach was his insistence that the application of reason, driven by a method learned from the study of nature, would produce a level of perfection in the laws unknown to past experience.

Bacon's contemporary and rival, Sir Edward Coke, drew on the idea of custom and combined it with Aristotelian deductivism to make the beginning of English legal science.[49] Coke's goal was different from Bacon's. Far from an attempt to radically reform the common law, Coke sought to enhance its authority by recording its rules in one place. His most important contribution was to turn Fortescue's general idea of validation by custom into an early version of the rule of precedent, i.e. the idea that a rule could be demonstrated to be in force by virtue of its having been articulated by a judge in a common law court. This was neither a positivistic argument, nor an appeal to natural law,[50] but rather the idea that judge's statements reflect rules whose source was the ordering logic implicit in established legal custom, what Coke called the "artificial perfection of reason" of the common law.[51] Coke's system, in other words, was designed around an hermeneutic principle of historical deductivism that treated the sum of English legal experience as the source for first principles.[52]

In the 1700s two great English legal writers, working from Coke's model, developed the idea of law as the science of historical jurisprudence further. The first was Matthew Hale. Hale's approach resurrected some of Bacon's prescriptions, particularly the emphasis on external sources drawing on philosophy, theology, and the natural sciences and the idea of arrangement in a "digest."[53] In other ways, however, Hale's approach continued the dominant tradition of Coke and Fortescue. In particular, Hale expanded on Coke's idea of the nature of precedent.

> Decisions of courts . . . do not make a Law properly so-called (for that only the King and Parliament can do); yet they have great Weight and Authority in Expounding, Declaring and Publishing what the Law of this Kingdom is, especially when such Decisions hold a Consonancy and Congruity with Resolutions and Decisions of former times, and though such Decisions are less than a Law, yet they are a greater evidence thereof than the Opinion of any private Persons, as such, whatsoever.[54]

What Hale added to Coke's formulation was an internalist conception of "custom." That is, the fact that a rule had been repeatedly accepted by judges—i.e. that it was the custom within the judicial system—indicated that the interpretation of the rule was correct. In fact, Hale posited nested layers of custom, since in his view judges themselves articulated the collective wisdom of the community.[55] This was not yet the rule of stare decisis, but it was the beginning of a connection between the idea of law as legitimated by its congruence with custom and the idea of the common law *as* custom.

This last equation would be made explicit by Blackstone.[56] In his 1759 address, "A Discourse on the Study of the Law," Blackstone expounded on his conception of his duties as the first ever professor of English common law. It was important, said Blackstone, for an Englishman to study English law, rather than the foreign principles of the civilian or classical traditions.

> [W]e must not carry our veneration [of the civil law] so far as to sacrifice our Alfred and Edward to the manes of Theodosius and Justinian: we must not prefer the edict of the praetor, or the rescript of the roman emperor, to our own immemorial customs, or the sanctions of an english parliament; unless we can also prefer the despotic monarchy of Rome and Byzantium, for whose meridians the former were calculated, to the free constitution of Britain, which the latter are adapted to perpetuate.[57]

The connection between "immemorial custom" and "the free constitutions of Britain" rings throughout Blackstone's work. A knowledge of the law was required for a gentleman, in particular, in order for him to display republican virtues and thus protect the freedom of England; for others, so much knowledge of the law was desirable as was required to allow them to carry out their business effectively.[58] Public duties such as sitting on juries, acting as lay magistrates, and above all service in Parliament, required formal advanced training in the law such as only a university could provide.[59] Throughout, Blackstone made the idea of university education an element of the dignity of the common law, comparing the grandeur of civilian legal education with the impoverished intellectual resources available to an aspiring member of the bar. This competitive theme was common in discussions of legal education, and following Coke's lead Blackstone and others intimated that the dignity of the common law was the dignity of Britain itself.[60]

Blackstone also made the idea of "law as a science" central to his effort in a way that had not been done previously in English legal writing. Hale's had been the first treatise that attempted to cover all of English common law under a single cover. He was inspired, in this effort, by German systematizers, from whom he developed the idea of dividing the common law into a series of topics and sub-topics. (In particular, Hale's approach had much in common with the historical jurisprudence of Savigny, who appealed to the idea that historical custom demonstrated *Volksrecht*, the particular genius of a people expressed as innate consciousness of legal principles.[61]) The relationships between the parts, however, were largely left out of the discussion, in part because Hale was writing as a jurist, not as a philosopher. Hale's treatise was thus not a system, merely an ordered collection and display. What set Blackstone's *Commentaries* apart was its emphasis on system.

Blackstone also focused his attention directly on legal education as a topic separate from the law itself, variously presenting ideas about the common law and about the most effective method for teaching that law to those who would become lawyers. Blackstone's claims on behalf of university legal education were not new, but due to his influence the idea of legal science became connected to the specific project of legal education, rather than simply a way of thinking and talking about law generally. Despite nearly universal acclaim for his *Commentaries*, Blackstone's educational proposals had little effect in England, due primarily to powerful resistance from the Inns of Court.[62] In America the idea of university-based education in law would take hold with considerable force. The form and meaning of that science, however, would be somewhat different from that envisioned by Coke, Hale and Blackstone.

B. The American Blackstone

As Edmund Burke famously remarked, Blackstone was as popular in America in the eighteenth century as he was in England. Following the Revolution, the ardor of Americans for the *Commentaries* began to cool.

For one thing, Blackstone was too ardent a Royalist, a logical consequence of his belief in the authority of "immemorial custom." In particular, Blackstone's substitution of natural law (in Coke) with the authority of timeless custom seemed to Jefferson and his fellows an inherently royalist manoeuver.[63] James Wilson, too, found Blackstone "inaccurate, simplistic and reactionary."[64] In response, American legal thinkers quickly began to move away from the model of historical jurisprudence.

The first response to Blackstone's unsuitedness was to turn to Montesqieu, whose *Spirit of the Laws* was by far the most-cited source of the late 1700s.[65] Montesqieu equated natural laws with civil regulations: "Laws, in their most extended significations, are the necessary relations which spring from the nature of things, and in this sense all beings have their laws; the Divinity has his laws; the material world has its laws; intelligences superior to man have their laws; the beasts have their laws; man has his laws."[66] Montesqieu therefore argued that laws must be understood from first principles, but that the first principles involved were the physical characteristics of each country and their influences on the climate, religion, laws, government, precedents, morals and customs of the inhabitants. *The Spirit of the Laws,* in other words, was constructed around an inductive principle that started from the observation of facts rather than from syllogistic principles internal to the system of law itself. The propriety of laws depended on the degree to which they accorded with the requirements of these physical characteristics, not the dictates of a people's history nor the conclusions of analytical reason.

Montesqieu's argument suited the American claim of exceptionalism. Based to a considerable degree on the physical fact of free land[67] and a belief in the efficacy of new technologies, the exceptionalist ideal held that the American experience was separated from historical European experience. This was an idea as old as the first Puritan settlements, but in the early 1800s it acquired new force in both liberal and republican thinking.[68] Among republicans, it was an article of faith that the new country would be free of the corruption of the old world, a view that combined a powerful element of nostalgia with a distinct reformist sense of mission.[69] For laissez-faire liberals exceptionalism was nearly eschatological. History simply began anew in 1776, as the *Democratic Review* stated in 1839: "Our national birth was the beginning of a new history . . . which separates us from the past and connects us with the future *only*."[70]

To Jefferson, in particular, the realization of a republican ideal required an emphasis on education, and especially legal education; universities, in his famous characterization, were to be "nurseries" for the generation of virtuous leaders.[71] Jefferson shared Montesquieu's (and Blackstone's) belief in the idea that legal education was both a necessary and a highly desirable form of moral training for the nation's political elites. He found the perfect man to bring his ideas into fruition at the College of William & Mary in George Wythe, appointed to a chair in "law and police" in 1779, established at Jefferson's insistence along with chairs in astronomy, medicine and chemistry.[72] Wythe, "the second professor of common law in the world," was a firm believer in natural law principles and the integral connection between law and civic virtue. He also incorporated important innovations in his approach to legal education, presiding over moot courts—to which he invited the public—and assigning clinical tasks as well as engaging in traditional lectures. He also invited the public in to hear moot court sessions. His reading list was a long list of classical texts, plus Blackstone's *Commentaries*; his lectures were based on Bacon's *New Abridgment of the Law.*[73] Wythe participated in revisions to Virginia's laws, and in 1788 became the state's Chancellor.[74]

In 1794 Alexander Hamilton arranged for the appointment of James Kent, a Federalist politician with ties to John Jay, to a professorship in law at Columbia University. Although Wythe and Kent stand as representatives of opposite sides of a crucial political division, from an intellectual perspective they stand together. No less than Wythe, Kent believed in the republican ideal of legal education, quoting Montesquieu in his opening address.[75] Furthermore, although both accepted Montesquieu's prescription for a new, uniquely American system, neither was willing to follow the philosopher's adoption of natural science—specifically Newtonian physics—as the direct model for the study of human society. Instead, Wythe and Kent stand together as the beginning of a strand of American legal thought that sought an Americanized version of the ancient ideal of law as an element of the moral sciences.

His espousal of natural scientific models was not the only reason that Montesquieu was not a perfect solution for republican-minded Americans, whether legal conservatives or reformists. Montesquieu was mistrustful of mass democratic rule, arguing that republican virtues could only be found in small,

Florentine-style city-states.[76] Furthermore, his comments were general, and of little immediate use in the construction of a curriculum for legal education. Blackstone remained the starting point for American legal education, but by the 1820s the need to Americanize his doctrines—the project that had been justified by the appeal to Montesquieu in the first instance—was clear.[77] The first writers did not strive to replace the old system, however, merely to clean it up a little.

In 1803 Wythe's successor, St. George Tucker, published the first American edition of Blackstone's *Commentaries*. Tucker denied outright the claim that English custom held binding force for Americans, giving credence only to those elements of English common law that had been recognized in pre-Revolutionary enactments. Tucker took pains to point out particular examples where Blackstone's version of the English common law did not fit the conditions of America, focusing especially on the all-important law of property.[78] He also excised what he viewed as anti-republican passages.[79]

Tucker's version of Blackstone was immediately adopted throughout the American university system.[80] Beginning in the early 1820s, however, a new strand in American legal science began to appear. This was an approach to thinking about law that resurrected Bacon's and Montesquieu's claims to directly connect thinking about the natural world to the study of law and politics. This turn to the natural sciences as the source for explanatory schema represented a uniquely American move, a departure not only from European precedents but also from the republican tradition of moral education. While the first important texts describing this approach came from David Hoffman, as noted earlier one of the best examples of the relationship between the two ways of thinking about American legal science was provided by Story and Greenleaf.

Greenleaf and Story, close friends as well as colleagues, were credited with building the Harvard Law School together. In the words of an article in the *Law Reporter*, "Story prepared the soil, and Greenleaf sowed the seed."[81] Story's republican idea of law as a moral science meant an emphasis on system, but not one that drew its models from the classification of natural objects.[82] Instead, Story's idea of legal science was essentially an anti-positivist conception of the meaning of law, exemplified in his famous opinion in *Swift v. Tyson*.[83] Greenleaf, discussed below, was one of the early important writers in the tradition of law as a form of natural science. The philosophical differences between the two were reflected in their teaching styles; Story was famous for his eloquence, while Greenleaf was revered for his meticulous, careful parsing of legal materials.[84]

Thus the growth of American legal science began with a double move in relation to Blackstone. First, republican moralists such as Story rejected the authority of custom in favor of the search for natural principles of morality and justice. Second, writers following the lead of Hoffman and Greenleaf turned the focus of law as a science away from the study of an innate national genius to a different kind of ahistorical abstraction, one based not on the inductive Baconian model of the natural sciences. To see how this latter move occurred, and the continuing influence that the appropriation of models from the natural sciences has had to this day, it is important to first recognize the parallels in the institutional developments of American legal and scientific education in the antebellum period. In the next section I will briefly outline those respective institutional stories, then turn to an examination of the parallels between the dominant ways of talking about "science" in these two contexts.

II. The Institutional Development of Legal and Natural Scientific Education

During the antebellum period, both American natural science and American law, like many other professions, demonstrated a two-stage process of institutional development that might be called separation upward and turning inward. "Separation upward" refers to attempts by practitioners of a craft to conceive of and present themselves as a meritorious elite, deserving of social status by virtue of their work. "Turning inward" identifies the institutional development of formal gatekeeping mechanisms, an internalistic discourse, and a focus on intracommunal concerns that characterized the development of nineteenth century professions. Each of these steps is evident in the historical development of nineteenth-century American scientific and legal institutions.

A. Lyceums, Surveys, and the American Association for the Advancement of Science

The development of institutions for the study of natural science in America begins very early indeed. American members of the social elite had demonstrated an interest in natural science from the time of settlement. In 1714, Cotton Mather became the first American-born member of the Royal Society, a pattern of overlap between clerical and scientific enterprises that was to continue through the 1840s.[85] In the eighteenth century, too, prominent Americans were drawn to science.[86] Lawyers and members of the clergy, prominent members of the social elite, played a prominent role in the public pursuit of science through participation in the early public institutions for the dissemination of scientific knowledge, the lyceums, and in early university appointments.[87] These were "gentlemen amateurs" (the gendered language is intentional and appropriate[88]) for whom an interest in science was both a sign of and a means toward elite status. Their fields of interest fell into two categories: natural history[89]—exemplified by geology and paleontology—and natural science, especially astronomy, botany and zoology. In other words, not only was it the case that in the public mind "science" identified a fundamentally taxonomical undertaking, but furthermore particular sciences were accorded prominence to the extent that they embodied a taxonomic ideal of scientific practice. These were the fields of endeavor that established the model from which legal science drew its inspiration; it is striking, for example, that there is no mention of Newtonian mechanics in any of the legal science texts.[90]

In the Jacksonian period, the number and scope of the lyceums increased dramatically, to a scale quite unknown in earlier eras. Gentlemen amateurs all over the country came together in associations to hear presentations on all manner of observations, presentations of matters published from elsewhere, and discussions about the methods of organization most suited to the project of creating an educated elite for the good of both themselves and of the society at large.[91] Nor was this a phenomenon solely among the well-established cultural elites of the East; between 1818 and 1860 thirteen institutes of scientific advancement were established in the Midwest, and in addition the Indiana town of New Harmony and the university museum at Ann Arbor acted as centers for the dissemination and display of scientific discoveries.[92]

Like the Eastern lyceums, the Western lyceum movement exemplified the Whig idea of science as a means of moral and social improvement, reflecting the aspirations of the elites in cities like Cincinatti and St. Louis to be considered the social equals of the best citizens of Philadelphia and Boston.[93] The capacity of scientific knowledge to uplift the populace was a popular justification for the investment of scarce resources. "The organization of a Lyceum in this place is at once an interesting and an important event. It is a strong illustration of the march of mind and civilization, and an evidence that this community have done with the insane rage of making fortunes in a day," declared the *Milwaukee Sentinel* on January 8, 1839.[94] The Rev. William G. Eliot, in 1836, urged his contemporaries to support the creation of the Western Academy of Natural Sciences in St. Louis, the largest and most successful of the Western lyceums, calling on those "who value literature and religion, and feel . . . the importance of education and morality . . . [to] come forward and establish institutions by which public opinion may be elevated, public feeling and taste purified."[95]

In addition, however, in the West these enterprises also exemplified a Democratic ethos of utility. In 1818 Daniel Drake had explained the need for the Western Museum Society of Cincinnati in an article in the *American Journal of Science*:

> Every citizen of the western country must feel the necessity of a speedy development of our mineral resources. To find beneath our soil an adequate supply of the various minerals which are now imported [from other parts of the United States] must be regarded by all as a matter of first and greatest importance. The Managers are anxious to be instrumental in the advancement of this useful work, and earnestly solicit the co-operation of the public.[96]

Two decades later the same themes still rang in the constitution and bylaws adopted by the Western Academy of Natural Sciences. "The geological peculiarities of the country are as yet but slightly known;

the immense mineral resources that it possesses also need development, for the little learned of them justifies the belief that when so developed they will create a new era in the arts and manufacturers of the West."[97]

These public institutions for the dissemination of scientific knowledge were not isolated local events. Newspapers and journals covered scientific disputes as important news of the day. In 1818, Benjamin Silliman, a lawyer and chemist, founded the *American Journal of Science*, the first journal devoted exclusively to discussions of natural phenomena.[98] This was a critical step in the move from purely local associations to the possibility for trans-communal organization on the basis of interest. In matters of theology this step had been taken long before, and it is a noteworthy indication of the closeness between clergy and lay researchers that authors published equally in both sorts of journal, a pattern that would persist into the 1840s. The *American Journal of Science* was initially significant more as a portent than as a direct step toward professionalization. There were no particular standards for determining the acceptability of articles, other than the preferences of Silliman himself, and Silliman was a broad-minded man. Not until the 1840s would the *AJS* be clearly identified as the journal of those who had a special interest in the advancement of scientific knowledge; when that happened, a rival journal—*Scientific American*—would emerge to take the place of the *AJS* as the primary organ of communication of lyceum research.[99]

In part, the Western lyceums' emphasis on the wealth-producing utility of science reflected their close association with the second institution of public science, the survey. The first state surveys were in North Carolina 1823 and South Carolina 1824, led by Denison Olmstead, a student of Silliman at Yale and a professor of chemistry at the University of North Carolina.[100] In 1830, the first real geological (as opposed to general) survey was initiated in Massachusetts, under the leadership of geologist Edward Hitchcock. Gov. Levi presented the survey to the legislature:

> Much knowledge of the natural history of the country would thus be gained, especially the presence of valuable ores, the extent of quarries, and of coal and limestone, objects of inquiry so essential to internal improvements, and the advancement of domestic prosperity would be discovered, and the possession and advantage of them given to the public.

In the 1830s and 40s surveys spread West; 20 other states sponsored surveys, based on similar justifications.[101] First Bache then Peirce served as consultants for the Nautical Almanac and U.S. Coast Survey.[102]

Throughout the antebellum period, the twin justifications of the lyceums and surveys—utility and improvement—were in tension with one another. Jacksonian Democrats, in particular, preached a public vocabulary that eschewed learning and research in favor of "the useful arts" of invention and engineering. Laissez-faire's grounding in Common Sense involved a conception that Nature existed to be catalogued and exploited, not to be made the subject of theoretical speculations and laboratory experiments. This conception was by no means unique to the West. "Sir," declared a Vermont congressman in 1846, "a laboratory is a charnel house, chemical decomposition begins with death, and experiments are but the dry bones of science."[103]

The derogation of cloistered study of knowledge was the flip side of a breathless public enthusiasm for invention. Technological advances had reached their zenith, a theme expressed in typically poetic fashion by the *Democratic Review* in 1845.

> Indeed it would almost seem as though [Man] were now but just entering on that dominion over the earth, which was assigned to him at the beginning. No longer, as once, does he stand trembling amid the forces of nature. . . . He has almost anhialated space and time.[104]

America's greatness would proceed out of this combination of the middle landscape and an American genius for "mechanism." In 1832 Charles Caldwell gave one of the great paeans to what might be called "technological exceptionalism."

> Objects of exalted power and grandeur elevate the mind that seriously dwells on them, and impart to it greater compass and strength. . . . The same will be true of our system of Rail-roads. Its vastness and magnificence will provide communicable, and add to the standard of the intellect of our country.[105]

Even the radical *Harbinger* joined in the chorus of approbation for the elevating social effects of new technology.

> The age that is to witness a rail road between the Atlantic and Pacific, as a grand material type of the unity of nations, will also behold a social organization, productive of moral and spiritual results, whose sublime and beneficent character will eclipse even the glory of those colossal achievements. . . .[106]

For conservatives and radicals alike, the advances of technology promised to transcend all previous history, demonstrating the greatness of the moment. "No age has illustrated so strongly as the present the empire of mind over matter . . . ," declared the editors of *Scientific American* in 1847. "It is a happy privilege we enjoy of living in an age, which for its inventions and discoveries, its improvement in intelligence and virtue, stands without a rival in the history of the world."[107] "Are not our inventors absolutely ushering in the very dawn of the millennium?," queried the same journal in 1860, agog over the development of a haymaker.[108]

The term "technology," in its modern usage, was coined in 1829 by Jacob Bigelow[109] in a book containing summaries of a course of lectures he had delivered at Harvard since 1815. Bigelow, a physician and botanist, was Rumford Professor "on the application of the sciences to the useful arts."[110] The term technology, according to Bigelow, captured the special place that useful applications of "arts . . . which involve applications of science, and which may be considered useful, by promoting the benefit of society together with the emolument of those who pursue them," a definition that he tied particularly to the greatness of the era, and America in particular, a nation of "ingenious mechanicians, skillful projectors, profound mathematicians, and men well versed in the useful learning of their time."[111] The ancients, he said, had excelled in the arts, "[b]ut in modern times there is a maturity, a cautiousness, a habit of induction, which is founded on the advanced state of philosophic knowledge."[112]

Bigelow's "technology" was not a synonym for science; the term referred to the application of "science" *to* the endeavor of creating useful artifacts.[113] The distinction was not a sharp one: "Our knowledge may be said to have been found out originally by discovery and invention. Discovery is the process of science; invention is the work of art. So common, however, is the connexion of the two with each other, that we find both a science and an art involved in the same branch of study."[114] In the 1820s, the twin justifications of the lyceums and surveys were mutually reinforcing; in time, they would begin to pull apart.[115] The Lawrence School of Science, proposed by Benjamin Peirce, was founded in 1849 as a separate and parallel program to the regular university designed to give engineering students skills "comparable with those enjoyed by students in the law and medical schools at Harvard." This marked Harvard's concession to growing public pressure for universities to offer education of a practical nature suitable for "young men not destined to enter the learned professions," which had already led to the creation of alternative curricula at Amherst, Brown, Union and Transylvania.[116] In that division, legal science would fall squarely on the side of improvement rather than utility . . . until Langdell.

Lyceums and surveys also benefitted from their claims to being public enterprises, an attitude that accorded equally well with Whig notions of improvement as with Democrat ideals of utility.

> Science has now left her retreats . . . her selected company of votaries, and with familiar tone begun the work of instructing the race . . . through the press, discoveries and theories, once the monopoly of philosophers, have become the property of the multitudes. . . . Science, once the greatest of distinctions, is becoming popular.[117]

One result of this attitude was that new theories—requiring new terminology and study—had been treated as threats to the Jacksonian ideal of public science.[118] The lyceum tradition was emphatically one of public education and outreach, fund-raising and politics.

Other scientific researchers expressed frustrations at the burden of the expectation that their work should be publicly intelligible. The chemist Robert Hare wrote to Benjamin Silliman, Sr.: "I was told . . . that many said they could not understand my memoir, who considered their standing such as to feel as if this were an imputation against me rather than themselves . . . there is our difficulty—we cannot write anything for the scientific few which will be agreeable to the ignorant many."[119] In 1841 William Whewell coined the term "scientist" to denote those whose professional calling was doing science, i.e. the improvement and expansion of knowledge about the natural world rather than the generation of wealth or material comfort.[120] Although the split was far from immediate,[212] Whewell's book marked the beginning of a counter-movement opposed to the lyceum ideals exemplified by the members of the Bache circle, one that would eventually lead the "turn inward" in which "scientists" would deliberately remove their efforts from the public sphere and move from lyceums to universities.[122] The most important institution for this transition was the American Association for the Advancement of Science.

Founded in 1840 by Edward Hitchcock as a society for survey geologists (as the American Geological Society), the AAAS quickly expanded its mandate to include all the natural sciences.[123] As its title indicated, the mission of the AAAS was the advancement, rather than the public dissemination, of scientific knowledge. This set the AAAS apart from the lyceum tradition in a crucial way. Stung by European disrespect for American science, and by the obvious inferiority of American scientific education to that of England and Germany, Bache and Henry had been discussing the idea of a national professional organization since 1838; when Hitchcock's organization appeared they quickly became its dominant members. From 1849 on, the presidents of the AAAS were, in order, Henry, Bache, Agassiz, Peirce, and Dana.

The members of the Bache circle used their position in the AAAS as well as their university appointments to promote the development of university education in science.[124] Their power over university science was sometimes exaggerated, as when an 1858 *New York Times* spoke of "a notorious society which boasts of its control over every scientific appointment of value in the country." Nonetheless, their influence was extraordinary. Peirce was responsible for reworking science curricula at Harvard, resulting in the founding of the Lawrence School of Science. Dana led the creation of the Sheffield Scientific School at Yale in 1846. At Yale's 1856 commencement Dana challenged the college: "Why not have here, the American university!" In 1861 Yale awarded the first American PhD's, including one in physics.[125] The Swiss-born Louis Agassiz may have been the greatest publicist and fund-raiser for science this nation has ever known: he gave regular public lectures to huge, adoring crowds, and between 1853 and 1860, including the sale by subscription of his *Contributions to the Natural History of the United States of America*, he raised an astounding $500,000 for a museum of comparative zoology at Harvard University—the Agassiz Museum, opened in 1860. The AAAS in general, and the Bache circle in particular, were instrumental in the creation of German-style graduate university science curricula; the creation of a national association of full-time scientists; the publication by its members of a range of journals devoted to specific scientific topics.[126] They were also close associates of some of the leading figures in the emerging social sciences, particularly Francis Lieber[127] and Daniel Coit Gilman.[128]

B. The Development of the American Law School

The institutional development of American legal education displayed the same two-step pattern of separation upward and turning inward, and the same separation between justifications based on utility and those based on claims of improvement. For a generation following the Revolution, conservative views held sway, despite Tucker's modifications to Blackstone's historicism. Conservatives such as Story and Kent resisted suggestions that the common law required significant revision, and viewed the task of legal education as the transmission of knowledge of the common law. From this perspective, the business of prescribing the ideal content of the law was not an element of legal education. Blackstone's valorization of legal knowledge in republican terms was a central element in the view that took the common law of England to be the great source of liberty, and hence viewed proposals for its alteration with suspicion.

There were a number of reasons why this outcome should not be surprising. First, anti-lawyer sentiment has almost certainly been exaggerated.[129] To be sure, radicals like Robert Rantoul and Orestes Bronson issued inflammatory statements—in 1839 the *United States Magazine and Democratic Review* proposed to do away with all existing laws in favor of a return to pure trial by jury, "the natural progenitor of democratic government"[130]—but their influence over the organization of the American bar was marginal, and their influence on legal education even less. Second, in point of fact lawyers *did* constitute a fairly closed, or at least inward-looking, elite class.[131] As a matter of ideology, finally, it is important to recognize, as writers of the day recognized, that the Revolution had been a politically radical but legally conservative effort. As a result, for a long time those who proposed significant changes in the doctrines of the common law were vulnerable to charges of disloyalty to the Glorious Cause, and familiar charges of corrupt foreign influences.

Thus to the limited extent that legal science was a topic of concern to early American legal educators, the conception that was at work in Kent's and Story's *Commentaries* would have been familiar to Blackstone and even Hale. Particular rules—particularly regarding real property and, to a lesser extent, evidentiary standards of proof at trial—underwent revisions, but the conception of the science of the common law as it was taught and discussed continued with only minor accommodations to the Montesqieu-inspired notion.

In the first half of the nineteenth century the setting of American legal education changed dramatically, as university and proprietary law schools went from an occasional specter to an industry.[132] The growth in institutions of legal education was closely connected to the growth in formal institutions of the bar generally, as judges exercised more control over juries and lawyers, and bar associations exercised more control over their members.[133] The legal profession, in general, developed an increasing degree of institutional self-awareness, exemplified in the proliferation of new independent legal journals (most of them short-lived) and law reviews.[134]

In part, no doubt, this was a defensive reaction to anti-lawyer sentiment and repeated legislative efforts to level a professional elite, marked in an 1847 *Pennsylvania Law Review* commentary:

> The tendency of the age is clearly marked. The voice of the multitude is against the legal community. Levelling begins with the mount of justice. . . . A cry is going out over the land. Radicalism is infectious as the pestilence. The tide of popular will must soon sweep away our prerogative, unless we stay its waters.[135]

This drew a strong connection between institutional and intellectual commitments, exemplified in the debate over the relative authority of statutory and common law. Codifiers, whether of a Benthamite or Napoleonic stripe, sought the outright replacement of the common law; early socialists called for an opening or an abolition of the profession; others called for a replacement of all positive laws by a pure jury system. Among those who argued, successfully, for a retention of the Common Law, there was a division between conservatives and reformers, a division that turned in part on the relationship between teaching law and making law.

Blackstone had compared the absence of university common law education unfavorably with the system of civilian teaching, in the 1820s and 30s promoters of university-based legal education in the United States compared their field with theology and the sciences. This meant, above all, that legal training should be an element of university education, as Mayes explained:

> Who can look upon the present state of the healing art, and believe for one moment that it could have arisen to the rank it now deservedly occupies, was medicine, like law, taught exclusively (almost), in the offices of private practitioners, and the halls of science abandoned by the sons of Aesculapius. To the honour of that learned body, and to the benefit of the human race, no young man who aspires to eminence in that profession, fails to avail himself of Academic instruction. With one unanimous rush they spring forward to drink in the streams of profes-

> sional learning, poured forth by our learned Faculty. When will the legal corps arouse itself from its lethargy and emulate so laudable an example?[136]

Greenleaf echoed his sentiments, noting that law stood with theology and medicine as the third of the traditional learned professions. "In the department of Theology the necessity of a learned ministry for the defence of our common faith against the common enemy has been urged with strength of argument and fervor of eloquence. . . . In Medicine too, the same necessity is felt and admitted. . . . And should less be done for the Law, in which our liberties have their being . . . ?"[137]

The idea, that the study of law was comparable to the study of other subjects, was the crucial move in the formulation of American legal science. This was not an appeal to a theory about law considered as a separate and discrete subject in itself, but a claim that law is experienced and understood in the same manner as other elements of the environment, as Nathan Beverley Tucker explained:

> [B]eing, in point of fact, born in the midst of law, habituated to it from our infancy, and accustomed to witness uniform obedience to its authority on the part of those whom we were taught to obey, we learn to regard it as a thing *in rerum natura*, rather than of human invention; a sort of moral atmosphere, which, like that we breathe, seems a very condition of our existence.[138]

In this Tucker departed from the modified Blackstonian jurisprudence of his father. His move was not entirely without precedent, however, as it built on the work of David Hoffman, the first and greatest of the American legal scientists.

In 1817 Hoffman published an *Outline of Courses* that initiated the process of transformation in the content of legal education. Recognizing that not every prospective lawyer would have the time or patience for the complete version, Hoffman identified the works that should be incorporated into a four-year and a two-year version. Moving from the shortest to the longest course identifies Hoffman's designation of core, secondary, and tertiary texts in the presentation of his philosophy of legal science. This is extremely helpful to a modern reader, since Hoffman's tendency to use glowing and (to our ears) overblown characterizations of the virtues of every assigned text could otherwise give the mistaken impression that each was as central to his enterprise as any other. In fact, Hoffman's core texts were the Bible, Cicero's *Offices*, Beattie's *Elements of Moral Science*, Paley's *Moral and Political Philosophy*, Reid's *Essays on the Powers of the Human Mind*, and his own *Legal Outlines*. His lists of secondary and tertiary texts were extensive.[139]

Even the shortest of Hoffman's courses was intended to be more than simply training for professional practice,[140] a theme echoed by Mayes, who spoke of those who viewed law solely as a profession as "standing in the same relation to law, that the cook does to chemistry" in 1834,[141] and Sharswood in 1870:

> There is no class of lawyers with us confined to the mere business of the profession, no mere attorneys, no special pleaders. . . . The American lawyer must be, to some extent at least, a jurist. He must extend his researches into all parts of the science, and is as frequently called upon to inquire what the law ought to be as what it is.[142]

The reformist emphasis of legal science was implicit in its use of naturalistic metaphors. The *American Jurist and Law Magazine*, the most important reformist journal of the early 1800s, characterized the common law in 1823 as: "[a] dark forest, where the most intrepid lawyer never thinks of exploring beyond the margin," a "territory" which must be "surveyed and laid out anew . . . to let in a little light."[143]

Legal educators who emphasized the practical benefits of their efforts for practitioners of the lawyer's craft drew a sharp distinction between lawyers and judges; legal scientists, devoted to the reformist ideal of marrying training and reform of the subject, insisted that "the Law" was a unified whole. "[I]t is to be remembered," wrote Sharswood, "that the bench and the bar are the same body—parts of the same administration. Not only is the bench exclusively taken from those who compose the bar, but they act and re-act on each other. A liberal, sound and thoroughly learned bar has a direct action and influence upon the bench, which none but those who are in the daily course of observation in the courts can fully appreciate."[144] Benjamin Butler and Thomas Cooley might treat laww school as merely useful; those who called their teaching "legal science" appealed to a loftier view that emphasized improvement.

Hoffman combined perfectly conservative legal doctrines (the book was dedicated to Story) with a new way of talking about law as a "science" that borrowed directly from ideas about the natural sciences generally. Hoffman's book extended the line initiated by the turn to Montesqieu, treating legal science as the study of a natural phenomenon whose history was to be studied not for its authority but as evidence of its character. To a significant extent this represented a rejection of the historicism of Coke, Hale and Blackstone in favor of a model drawn from the study of the natural sciences. The study of law, in this model, went beyond the study of the nation it served to the scientific study of the nature of humanity in general.[145]

Hoffman was followed in his universalism by the other legal scientists. Greenleaf encouraged comparative study, drawing on the model of "the comparative anatomy of a sister profession," but the results of that study were to be couched in timeless, universal truths of human nature expressed in principles of law[146]; Mayes said of law: "Man being its subject, and his happiness its object, its rules must necessarily be framed, in direct reference to his nature"; like Greenleaf, Mayes spoke of the need to study various nations, but always with the recognition that "[m]en also exist in a state of political society, their natures unchanged, their private social relations unaltered"[147]; Sharswood called for students to begin with "the principles of general jurisprudence, part from the peculiarities of any particular system."[148]

Furthermore, legal science sought to take its place not merely as one among others, but as the highest of all the sciences. The reason, said Field, was simple: the subject-matter of legal science was conceived of not as a special field of professional activity, but as the underlying significance of human civilization writ large:

> Compare this science with any of the other sciences; with those which are esteemed the greatest in extent, and the most exalted in subject. Take even astronomy, that noble science. . . . Sublime as this science is, it is but the science of inanimate matter, and a few natural laws; while the science which is the subject of our discourse governs the actions of human beings, intelligent and immortal, penetrates into the secrets of their souls, subdues their wills, and adapts itself to the endless variety of their wants, motives and conditions.[149]

Mayes declared that Man was to be "contemplated in every aspect in which he is found to exist, and in all the diversified relations which he bears to the persons and things, by which he is surrounded."[150]

The constant references to the study of history and the laws of other nations, in fact, spoke most strongly to the natural scientific tradition of the time. These references did not invoke the authority of timeless custom, but rather referred to pre-Darwinian evolutionary concepts that posited ascending stages of development along a divinely ordered scale.[151] Legal scientists, who viewed the scope of their study as the nature of human society itself, had arrived at the same working premise by their appropriation of natural scientific models of understanding. In this way American legal science presages American social science of the late nineteenth century. As a result of its immense scope and importance, the study of law demanded the highest of standards, and the most developed of methods.

> If, in the common concerns of life, and in our studies generally, method is of so great importance, there surely is no department of knowledge in which it is so imperiously requisite as in the science of jurisprudence. . . . He who aspires to a thorough acquaintance with legal science, should cultivate the most enlarged ideas of its transcendent dignity, its vital importance, its boundless extent, and infinite variety.[152]

That law was an exceptionally difficult science was a common theme among legal educators. "Law is a science simple in its elements . . . yet the stores of its learning, are so inexhaustible, that . . . much time and laborious study is indispensable to him, who would possess himself of all its treasures."[153] Sharswood complained of the unwillingness of students to devote the necessary efforts to learning.

> It is the characteristic of the youth of our country that they press too earnestly to enter early upon the arena of action. The time to train the athlete properly is not taken, and many a downfall succeeds in consequence. An apprenticeship of five or seven years is not deemed too long to learn a mechanical occupation, a period of two or three years is all that is allowed to make a lawyer.[154]

In large part, of course, this was an attempt by legal scientists to imbue their project with peculiar dignity and importance, but in part it may also have demonstrated the accurate recognition of the fact that the extension of the methods of the natural sciences to the study of law would be a difficult process.

III. Natural and Legal Science, 1820-1871: The Language of Protestant Baconianism

The vast increase in lyceums and surveys during the Jacksonian era had created an environment in which a new and peculiarly American approach to the study of both natural and legal science emerged.[155] An outgrowth of Common Sense, the approach to scientific investigation that characterized the lyceums and surveys can be characterized as "Protestant Baconianism." The approach was rooted in the teachings of Calvinism, whose most central tenet was the rejection of the idea of a priesthood whose intercession was required for understanding the divine edicts.[156] Evangelical Protestants in particular insisted that Scripture was "open," subject to the understanding of every man who approached the text with a proper attitude, which depended on having undergone a certain kind of adult conversion experience. Nature, "the second book of revelation," was equally held to be open to public understanding,[157] which made ministers obvious candidates for early natural science enthusiasm, as indeed they were.

The comfortable conjoining of scriptural interpretation with interest in the natural world that was a characteristic of early Calvinism was shattered in 1740 and the decades that followed by the Great Awakening. Protestant evangelicism, in the form of "enthusiastic" interpretations of Presbyterianism, Congregationalism, and other existing American polities, took over the countryside. The ideas of Calvinistic rationalism became the isolated provinces of urban elites, while otherworldly enthusiasm, faith in the presence of miracles, and rejection of formalistic doctrine became the dominating characteristics of huge portions of the rural, less wealthy, and less educated adherents. By the 1760s many denominations were in crisis, paralyzed by splits within their membership and their leadership.

The most important response to the challenge of enthusiastic evangelicism was initiated by the Presbyterians. In 1768 the Presbyterian Church, deadlocked in a split between enthusiastic, strict constructionist "New Lights" and the more traditionally liberal Old Lights, managed to arrive at a compromise when it invited Rev. John Witherspoon to take over the leadership of the College of New Jersey at Princeton. Witherspoon had been a leading figure in the Scottish Presbyterian Church, and a professor of divinity at Edinburgh.[158] He brought with him a set of ideas that were not only to define the positions of Protestant elites for the following decades, but also arguably to become the dominant intellectual tradition in American political thought right up to the Civil War. This was the tradition of Scottish Common Sense Realism, exemplified in the writings of its most prominent thinkers, Thomas Reid, professor of moral philosophy at Glasgow University, and his followers James Beattie and Dugald Stewart.[159]

The names Reid, Beattie and Stewart are familiar to any student of nineteenth century American history; these were the patron saints of laissez-faire, cited with (monotonous) regularity as the philosophers who had proved that nature dictated the ideal form of political economy. Common Sense, however, had not been initially developed either as a justification for political dogma nor as a form of Protestant compromise; instead, the ideas first developed by Thomas Reid were a direct response to the epistemological skepticism of Locke and, especially, Hume. Reid, in his book *An Inquiry into the Human Mind on the Principles of Common*

Sense, presented the argument that the experience of the perception of natural objects itself provided a certainty from which true knowledge could be ascertained. Since everyone shared in this experience of perception, Reid called it "common sense." This was little more than a revival of the Aristotelian nuos or the Cartesian cogito, but Reid's formulation involved two crucial additional points. First, Reid argued that the experience of perception contained within it the experience of faith in the veracity of that perception.[160] Second, by emphasizing the common—what might be called the "public"—character of perception, Reid restored the accessibility of true knowledge of the physical world. Common Sense philosophy thus laid the groundwork for the two characteristics of Protestant Baconianism: natural theology and an emphasis on taxonomical description.

Common Sense spread quickly in American academia. Witherspoon used Common Sense to transform his college, and his tradition was continued by his successor Samuel Stanhope Smith.[161] The influence of the movement spread, arriving at Congregationalist Yale with Timothy Dwight, and at Unitarian Harvard in 1790 with David Tappan and later through the teaching of Francis Bowen. When Congregational evangelicals split off from Harvard to form their own seminary at Andover, Scottish Common Sense Realism went with them, in the persons of Leonard Woods and Edwards Amasa Park. Bowen,[162] Woods and Dwight,[163] in particular, would later figure prominently in debates over legal education and science.

By the 1820s, evangelical Protestants had developed Protestant Baconianism into an art form. Natural theology—exemplified in William Paley's 1802 *Natural Theology*—was required reading in most American colleges.[164] Samuel Tyler, rejecting charges that the study of science must lead to atheism, declared the orthodox position: "the more Baconian philosophy has been cultivated, the more has natural theology advanced."[165] The result was to turn ministers into some of the most enthusiastic participants in the explosion of public knowledge about science.[166] Conversely, the lyceums themselves were intensely involved in questions of natural theology, at least partly by virtue of the number of clergymen among their most active members.

There were four major themes that characterized this approach. First and in many ways foremost, was natural theology, the doctrine that the study of nature confirmed scriptural truth. This was the "Protestant" element of Protestant Baconianism. With this addition, the other identifying features of the method were recognizably derived from versions of Bacon's own prescriptions. Inductivism was the methodological watchword, but as a result of its religious roots Protestant Baconianism preached a peculiarly constrained form of inductivism that operated within the constraints of known first principles; the ultimate goal was to see the grand synthesis, the idea that all areas of study contained lessons for every other area by means of analogic demonstration[167]; the language of justification for the project of science was suffused with the promise of public and personal improvement, the uplift that was the partner to the utility of technology.[168] Each of these themes was also strongly reflected in the "science" of American legal science in the period from the 1820s to the 1870s. To appreciate the parallels in both institutional and intellectual development between natural and legal science, it is worthwhile dealing with each of these four themes in turn.

A. Natural Theology

As noted above, the connection between science and natural theology was of great importance to nineteenth century Protestant theologians. It was equally was the grounding principle of much of American public science. For example the Lowell Institute, "America's most famous lyceum," was endowed by textiles manufacturer John Lowell in 1836, half of whose estate was left to create public lectures in Boston, "principally on evidence in support of Christianity and on various scientific subjects." The Lowell lectures were inaugurated with 12 lectures on geology by Benjamin Silliman, Sr. in 1839: "the rush for free tickets broke windows at the place of distribution, and thousands were turned away."[169] A typical later example of the Lowell Lectures was Francis Bowen's 1848 lecture on "Application of Metaphysical and Ethical Science to the Evidences of Religion."

The Lowell Lectures were the most famous, but far from an atypical, example of the religious mandate of respectable public science in the tradition of Protestant Baconianism.[170] When writers dared to suggest that science contradicted religion they were treated as vulgar and unlearned. This was most famously true in the case of Robert Chambers' popular and controversial 1844 book, *Vestiges of the Natural History of*

Creation, published in London and widely distributed in the United States. Chambers combined prevalent evolutionary notions[171] and Laplace's nebular hypothesis for planetary creation[172] and concluded that the development of life could be explained by a universal law of progressive development as fundamental as the law of gravity. While this concept was neither unusual nor incommensurable with Christian theology, Chambers took pains to push the point beyond the limits of acceptable religious principle. He described the creation of life as an electrochemical accident and the emergence of higher forms as the result of transmutation and spontaneous generation, events neither requiring nor confirming miraculous accounts. Although the book was published anonymously, the mere suspicion that he had written *Vestiges* was sufficient to cost Chambers considerable public embarrassment.[173]

The commitment to natural theology among the members of the Bache circle was strong. No one more completely embodied this continuing commitment than Agassiz, who by the late 1850s was the most famous member of the Lazzaroni. "A Thought of a Supreme Intelligence manifested in material reality; that is the view I take of the animal kingdom," was his famous statement of the matter in 1849.[174] "[R]elations and proportions which exist throughout the animal and vegetable world have an intellectual, and ideal connection in the mind of the Creator, matured in his thought, before it was manifested in tangible forms."[175] "We must acknowledge that the diversity among animals is a fact determined by the will of the Creator, and their geographical distribution part of the general plan which unites all organized beings into one great organic conception."[176] Others shared Agassiz' convictions. In an 1856 article in *The American Journal of Education*, Dana referred to science as "the handmaiden of theology."[177] Benjamin Peirce read Laplace's *Celestial Mechanics*, and far from finding encouragement for Chambers' materialism found the entire text a "vast teleological argument."[178] Agassiz protege and future Harvard president Thomas Hill, in his report on the 1849 session of the AAAS, wrote that "[t]he study of abstract law" leads "to a perception of the great thoughts of God."[179]

In legal scientific writings, natural theology was equally a grounding principle of justification and explanation in the study of law.[180] Hoffman, in particular, displayed close connections to the thinking of men like Edward Hitchcock, Benjamin Silliman, and Benjamin Peirce. The very first entry in the book is on the Bible, which is also the first element of his core curriculum. Hoffman's discussion of the importance of Scripture comprises a declaration of the connection between religion, law, and the study of nature.

> (Note 1.) THE BIBLE.—The Bible forms a very natural introduction to this Course, as recording a form of government and law originating in the great Legislator of the universe; whose pleasure it was to enjoin, by a direct communication of his will, those duties, and declare those obligations which, when by reasoning on the nature and relations of man, we have concluded to be such, we consider as the dictates of nature.[181]

Hoffman also relied on the Bible to define his position in relation to the scientific controversies of the day. "The Bible," he wrote, "affords *the only authentic history of the origin and multiplication of mankind.*[182] A nineteenth-century reader could not have missed this reference to the human origins question. Hoffman here forthrightly declared an allegiance between the study of law and natural theology against encroaching atheistic empiricism. The opposing principle to empiricism, in the jargon of nineteenth-century science, was inductivism in the service of religion, the grounding principle for natural theology and the hallmark of Protestant Baconianism. This connected closely with the Bible's most important role as the only source of the moral heart of the law. "[I]t is the foundation of the common law of every christian nation. The christian religion is a part of the law of the land, and, as such, should certainly receive no inconsiderable portion of the lawyer's attention."[183]

Simon Greenleaf adopted a less systematic tone, but his fervor for the cause of natural theology was no less than Hoffman's:

> We are therefore required by the strongest motives,—by personal interest, by the ties of kindred and friendship, by the claims of patriotism and philanthropy, to examine, and that not lightly,

> the evidences on which Christianity challenges our belief, and the degree of credit to which they are entitled. The Christian religion is part of our common law, with the very texture of which it is interwoven . . . while with swelling bosom he surveys the countless benefits rendered to his country by this his favorite science, let him [the lawyer] not withhold from the Fountain and Source of all Law the free service of undissembled homage.[184]

The word "evidences," again, would be unmistakable to a listener of the 1830s, a direct reference to the claim that the study of nature demonstrated the truths of Christian dogma. Greenleaf, in fact, not only authored an authoritative treatise on the law of evidence that went through eleven editions between 1842 and 1899 (not including a two-volume edition in 1866), but also a separate volume proving the truth of biblical accounts by application of legal standards of evidence.[185]

Nathan Beverly Tucker, too, made Christian education and the call to moral action a central tenet of his legal teaching, in sharp contrast to his father's conservative approach. Christian Roselius, in his 1854 "Introductory Lecture" at Tulane Law School described law as "a beautiful and harmonious system, devised by the profoundest wisdom and foresight . . . and founded, substantially, on the great and immutable principles of right and wrong, inscribed on the mind of man by the hand of his Creator."[186] Field appealed to Christian chivalry as an historical phenomenon, asserting that to it Americans owed "[t]he best part of our law of personal rights."[187] Sharswood not only appealed to the moral authority of the Bible, but also to the specific implications of nature for the proposition that "[t]rue conservatism is gradualism." "The world, neither physically, intellectually nor morally, was made to stand still. As in her daily revolutions on her own axis, as well as her annual orbit around the sun, she never returns precisely to the same point in space which she has ever before occupied, it would seem to be the lesson the Great Creator would most deeply impress upon mind, as He has written it upon matter: 'By ceaseless motion all that is, subsists.'"[188]

None of the other legal scientists discussed here were so overtly theistic in their beliefs. In part this may have been a reflection of the fact that the religious controversies of the time were scientific rather than legal; in the early 1800s religious journals were filled with articles about geology and the creation of mankind, not with debates over the religious basis for political authority as we can imagine they would have been in, say, the 1640s.[189] As we have seen, however, the natural sciences from which legal writers drew their inspiration were suffused with the language of biblicism; and as we shall see, even writers who did not acknowledge or understand the debt that their concept of "science" owed to Protestant theology clung to the methodological tenets that were characteristic of that theology with considerable force.

B. Inductivism

Above, a second identifying feature of the scientific thought of the gentlemen who ran lyceums and conducted surveys was an adherence to the highest values of "Baconianism." "[A]t the present day," wrote Edward Everett, editor of the influential Whig journal *North American Review* in 1823, "as is well known, the *Baconian* philosophy has become synonymous with the *true* philosophy."[190] As noted earlier, this was a particular version of Bacon's philosophy rooted in the requirements of Protestant theology, as John Brazier's 1835 Dudleian Lecture made clear:

> [T]hat a being, whom we call God, or Deity, exists, is a proposition to be proved, in the same way as the proposition that a certain law of relative forces reigns among the orbs of the planetary system;—namely, by that great organ or instrument of inquiry called the *inductive process* of reasoning; whose principles were first fully developed by Lord Bacon. . . . [191]

The relentless emphases on observation and the avoidance of hypotheses led many of these "Baconians" to reject the idea of formulating theoretical explanations for natural phenomena at all. This, scientific writers insisted, was the epitome of the inductive method of study in the natural sciences.[192]

The reason for this peculiarly constrained conception of inductivism was straightforward: inductive examinations of evidence always took place in the context of known, given first principles. To dabble in the development of explanatory theories—to speculate about the logic that connected the observations that one recorded—was the basic element of Bacon's inductive science, but it was anathema to the *Protestant* Baconianism, as William Stanhope Smith explained in 1815.

> [T]he extreme refinements of reason, which arise from the natural ambition of human pride, to extend its authority beyond its proper sphere, always tend to dogmatical error in bold and ardent minds, or to the cold indifference of skepticism, in minds of the opposite character.[193]

As Herbert Hovenkamp puts it, this was "scientific Antinomianism." "To extreme Baconians, terms like 'theory' and 'law' were part of metaphysics, not of true science."[194]

The commitment to limiting the "extremes of reason" is the sharpest mark of a distinction between this kind of constrained inductivism and deductive logic. The job of the good Protestant was to observe facts and record them, not to derive axiomatic principles from logical reasoning. As a good Protestant, moreover, there was no need to wait for these observations to yield laws of general applicability, since these had been prescribed *a priori* in Scripture. All that required explanation was the *how* of the obvious fact that scriptural laws dictated the pattern of observations. Translated into practice, this meant that the work of the natural scientist was taxonomy; the hallmark of Protestant Baconianism was the survey of forms and their compilation into catalogues.

This constrained form of inductivism-to-known-principles was a notable element of the legal science that dominated the writings of prominent legal educators. Simon Greenleaf called for a rejection of "bold empiricism" in favor of "reason."[195] The first lesson that Greenleaf drew from this imperative was the need to study history; not, however, to invoke Blackstone's (or Savigny's) authority of historically validated custom but, rather, to find universal and natural governing principles for human affairs.[196]

Other writers, following Bacon, looked to "the nature of man" as their starting point for evidence of first principles.[197] Hoffman based his recommendation of classical works on the basis that "we assume it as undeniable that pure Ethics and Natural Law lie at the very foundation of all laws. The original principles of law, as a science, are to be found in the moral nature of man. . . ."[198] Daniel Mayes, referring to Lord Bacon as "the prince of philosophers and light of the bar,"[199] argued that the study of history would yield an understanding of the nature of man, which would in turn yield principles that—in a complex system of combinations and recombinations—would demonstrate the proper form of every legal rule.[200] Sharswood, who cited Bacon's works more than those of any other writer, described the Law of Nature as "those rules of conduct for man which result from his nature and relations, whether discovered by the unassisted exercise of reason, or made known through the medium of a direct revelation." Examined the history and pre-history of the human condition and from that concluded that "government is an institution which necessarily grows out of the relations of men, and [is] therefore . . . an ordinance of God"; these elements, he wrote, defined the study of jurisprudence that underlay knowledge of the laws of any particular country[201]; only where the dual guides of reason and revelation provided no principle did law become a postivistic exercise in authority. Referring, for example, to differences in the form of governments he declared: "It follows from the mere silence of Scripture and nature on this subject, that it is left free to the determination of those to whom the general command is given."[202]

Beverly Tucker was an interesting case. Like his father, Tucker began with Blackstone, but whereas Blackstone had started with general topics (the origins of political and individual rights) and then worked his way down to the minutiae of legal practice, Beverly Tucker reversed the process, deriving principles from the examination of particular cases. Tucker's characterization of his approach is confusing to modern ears. He distinguished between philosophical analysis, "by which the different parts of a subject are so arranged, as to exhibit in distinct groups those things that depend on the same or like principles," and logical analysis, "by which different propositions are so arranged, as that no one of them shall ever be brought under consideration, until all others which may be necessary to the right understanding of that one, have been established and explained."[204]

The crucial point to recognize in these descriptions is that they are not deductive. That is, none of the systems described above propose moving from axioms internal to the study to construct or derive particular rules from the exercise of reason.[205] Hoffman used the idea of laws of nature precisely to draw the connection between induction and religious first principles. "[T]o the man of piety, it may be a matter of edification . . . to observe how nearly the rules discovered by reason and experience, as most conducive to the happiness of our present state, coincide with those precepts which are given in the Gospel, in order to fit us for a better [world.]"[206] As David Dudley Field put the matter in 1859, the range of historical evidences was too vast, and the set of principles too complex, to be treated as a mere deductive system.

> Will you compare it with one of the exact sciences; as, for example, with mathematics? . . . But the science of calculation is occupied with a single principle. This may go on to develop more and more, till the mind is almost lost in its immensity; yet the development of that one principle can never reach in extent, comprehensiveness and variety the development of all the principles by which the actions of men toward each other are governed in all their relations.[207]

Instead, legal science treated law as a species of natural object, a given element of the world whose historical development was to be examined in order to see *how* its ordering was consistent with timeless and universal first principles.[208] This was an exercise in taxonomy, not logic. The very openness of the system to non-legal sources of explanation (discussed below) emphasizes the cases occupied the position of objects to be examined for evidence of their origin—as though books of law had been found resting in the sediment of a streambed—rather than propositions whose validity were to be demonstrated by applications of the rules of the system in which they occurred.

C. Grand Synthesis, and Proof by Analogy

The third element of Protestant Baconianism was a belief in what I have called the "grand synthesis" idea, the thought that every field of study informed every other. An 1828 Yale report recommending the adoption of a single curriculum in matters of science had described the scope of its recommendations as covering "the various branches of mathematics, or of history and antiquities, or of rhetoric and oratory, or natural philosophy, or astronomy, or chemistry, or mineralogy, or geology, or political economy, or mental and moral philosophy."[209] This report, writes Mary Ann James, stood as a bulwark against rising demands for useful education with its clear preference for improvement over utility. "[T]he Yale Report made short shrift of visionaries. Mental discipline was the purpose of education. Vocational training had no place in a college."[210]

The particular method for drawing the connections among the elements of the grand synthesis that was favored by Protestant Baconians was one singularly suited to legal writers: reasoning by analogy.[211] Dana, for example, likened the stable categories of differentiation in biology to the unique weights of elements in the periodic table, describing Nature as a great "temple . . . of hewn and measured stones."[212] Benjamin Peirce, who designed Harvard's science curriculum under President Quincy, presented the attendees at the 1849 AAAS meeting with his discovery that the successive distances between nodes on plant stems were proportionate to the distances between orbits in the solar system. Agassiz protege and future Harvard president Thomas Hill was impressed by Peirce's arguments. "The study of abstract law" leads "to a perception of the great thoughts of God," he wrote in his report on the session.[213]

The grand synthesis idea, and its associated analogic mode of reasoning, was also prevalent in legal science, as Hoffman demonstrated with characteristic eloquence:

> How intimately are all the sciences connected, and how much mistaken is the idea entertained by many in this country, that the lawyer (whose province is reasoning,) can attain to eminence, though he restricts his inquiries within the visible boundaries of his peculiar science, chiefly as it is found in the treatises of municipal law.[214]

Greenleaf, as noted earlier, declared that to understand the law "[m]an is to be studies in every period of his social existence," and drew a connection between the study of law and "liberal learning."[215] Sharswood used the idea of natural law to connect moral and natural governing principles. "In a more general sense the term Law of Nature may comprise natural as well as moral relations, and in it there is evidently included all natural as well as moral science," extending to knowledge of the laws governing physical objects, rational creatures, "and as far as we can form ideas of them, in God himself."[216]

In legal science the ideal of the grand synthesis meant that analogies could be drawn from one area of law to another—from the duties of bailees to the rules governing liability to invited guests, or from contracts to torts—as well as from other areas of human history to the law generally. Hoffman, for example, had earlier quoted Sir William Jones, "than whom no authority is higher": "The great science of jurisprudence, like that of the universe, consists of many subordinate systems, all of which are connected by nice links, and beautiful dependencies; and each of them, as I have fully persuaded myself, is reducible to a few plain elements. . . . If law be a science and really deserve so sublime a name, it must be founded on principle, and claim an exalted rank in the empire of reason. . . ."[217] The same principle also enabled legal scientists to claim theistic authority for their enterprise: "International, constitutional and municipal law are but branches of this great original law, the fountain of all laws," said Sharswood, quoting Hooker and Cicero along with Montesqieu.[218]

D. Improvement

The last element of Protestant Baconianism was an externally oriented public character that supported the idea of "improvement." The social aspirations of the lyceums and the economic aims of the surveys appealed to a way of thinking about the study of science that emphasized its value both to the student and to the community at large. As noted earlier, this meant above all that natural science was public, a necessary condition for the claim that participation in scientific discussions was a source of improvement.

Legal science, too, was a form of discourse designed to mark an elite, to elevate the practitioner, and to improve the state of American civilization. "To be eminent in *our* profession," wrote Beverly Tucker, "is to hold a place among the great ones of the earth . . . to win *its* honors, and to wear them worthily, is to attain an elevation from which all other honors are accessible: but to turn aside disgusted with its labors, is to lose this vantage ground, and to sink again to the dead level of the common mass."[219] An anonymous Southern editorialist echoed Tucker's claims: "Can there be then aught better calculated to elevate the mind, to cause it to break off the shackles of prejudices, and attain to high moral beauty, than the full, faithful and conscientious studying of the law?"[220] In Greenleaf's classically republican formulation, law would rescue the heroic tradition of the Revolution from corruption. "[I]n later days, when the integrity of that charter has been invaded, its spirit violated, and its language perverted, whether to gratify the mad ambition of one partisan, or the cupidity of many; to whom have all eyes been imploringly directed for its preservation, but to the living and honored champions and expounders of constitutional law?"[221] As for the lawyer, his character "shines with mild but genial lustre."[222] Field echoed Blackstone when he declared that the study of law would elevate "both the head and the heart" of the diligent student.[223] "[I]f there be any science and any culture," said Field, "tending to invigorate and sharpen the intellect, they are legal science and discipline."[224] Sharswood called the law school "the nursery of sound literature and civil liberty."[225]

Like the natural sciences, legal science claimed for itself virtues of utility as well as improvement.

> [The law] is great, because it is essential. There is a necessity, not only for law, but for a system, with arrangement and a due relation of parts: for, without this system, the administration of government, both in its judicial and its administrative departments, would fall into irretrievable confusion. . . . Law, and the science of law, go therefore together, and both are as essential as industry, refinement, liberty, civilization.[226]

Utility and improvement combined in the nineteenth century legal scientists' emphasis on the connection between legal education and the larger project—closely linked to natural theology—of teaching moral conduct. Hoffman, for example, recommends the study of the works of Beattie and Paley because for a lawyer, "next to religion, nothing can be of more value than the science which teaches [Man] to see clearly the principles of his morals, and to define them with as much certainty as belongs to mathematical or physical truths. . . . The great object of moral philosophy is to demonstrate its truths, and by their systematic arrangement to present the whole as a connected scheme of moral action."[227]

Natural theology, bounded inductivism, grand synthesis, and public and personal improvement thus appear in antebellum American legal science in forms that closely parallel the contemporaneous dominant tradition in public science. By the 1870s, many of these parallels would break down (although, as noted at the outset, residual forms of both lyceum and legal science remained ubiquitous elements of the educational landscape.) A new form of legal science was invented; begun at Harvard and eventually destined to dictate the model of a modern law professor, the claim of this new model was that it had no relation to earlier forms and drew no inspiration from earlier, discredited forms of legal or natural science. The claim was false. Fundamental elements of Protestant Baconianism, incorporated into Langdell's legal science, continue to exert a profound influence on the teaching of American law to this day.

IV. Legal and Natural Science in the 1870s: Langdell and the New Legal Science

From the 1830s through the 1860s, a series of scientific controversies—over geologic time,[228] the causes for variations in animal and human forms,[229] and finally Darwinian evolution—rocked the intellectual foundations of Protestant Baconianism in the natural sciences. The members of the Bache circle found themselves committed to an entire tangled combination of ideas, none of which survived the Civil War with respectability:[230] biblicism, popular participation in science, anti-Darwinism, all coupled with support for the Southern cause.[231] Some members of the group, notably Gould and Dana, were able to revise their thinking.[232] Others, such as Agassiz, were gradually excluded from participation in discussions in the professional associations and journals.

By the end of the 1860s, the model of lyceum science had been driven out of the universities and scientific associations that it had helped to create. At Harvard, Asa Gray presided over an institutional "turning inward" that emphasized internalist discourse, disassociation from public affairs, a rejection of theological and political implications, an emphasis on the value of theoretical rather than practical scientific understanding and the development of explanatory theories rather than taxonomies. In 1864 Wyman wrote to a student, "The days of the *merely descriptive* naturalist have gone by . . . the *thinking* naturalist alone is the one who will command much respect."[233] In 1869 Gould, outgoing president of the AAAS and one of the original members of the Bache circle, would declare that one who supported science on the grounds of immediate practicality was "no true friend of science"; the incoming president, J. Lawrence Smith, could tellingly declare that there was "less connection between science and religion than there is between jurisprudence and astronomy, and the sooner this is understood the better it will be for both."[234]

Institutionally, Gray led a move toward an internalist discursive approach to scientific endeavors, both in terms of the language in which results were discussed and in terms of the audience for those discussions.[235] The nonscientific public was neither to be consulted nor informed in this conception; they were simply not part of the community of scientists, and hence not part of the process. By the 1860s the *American Journal of Science*, which had become the forum for "scientists," had a circulation of barely over a thousand; *Scientific American*, which had succeeded to the mantle of popular dissemination, had 40,000.[236] The "turn inwards" was most tellingly illustrated in the debate between Agassiz and Gray in 1859 over *The Origin of Species*. Apart from a short early piece in *The American Journal of Science*, Agassiz relied entirely on speeches before lay audiences and articles in theological and other nonscientific journals, drawing support from amateurs such as Francis Bowen and John A. Lowell who questioned the compatibility of Darwinism with Christianity.[237] By contrast, Gray published his arguments exclusively in the journals of science. This effectively represented Agassiz's abandonment of the field within the community of scientists.

The abandonment of the idea of a grand synthesis accompanied the abandonment of theology. As noted earlier, in the lyceums and surveys chemists had become the heads of geological surveys and doctors had presented papers on astronomy. By contrast, in 1842, Gray was appointed to a newly created endowed chair at Harvard (the Fisher chair) which unprecedentedly was not only confined to botany but also emphasized research as its primary duty.[238] In contrast, Agassiz's resistance to scientific specialization was finally one of the most enduring points in his beliefs. While other members of the Bache circle came to terms with the new ways of thinking about the natural sciences, Agassiz found an appropriate haven for his universalist approach as the first president of the American Social Scientific Association in 1865.

It would be going much too far to suggest that in the natural sciences, Protestant Baconianism in general or Agassiz personally had ceased to be important influences, particularly at Harvard. The Lawrence Scientific School, as Dupree points out, "never went very far in applied science but became instead the means of bringing Agassiz permanently to Cambridge."[239] It remained a stronghold of Agassiz's students; in 1863 Woolcott Gibbs took over the Rumford professorship after Charles Eliot was passed over for the position; Agassiz's students Frederick Ward Putnam (in anthropology) and Nathan Southgate Shaler (geology) continued the tradition of anti-Darwinism and natural theology and continued to play the role of scientist as public educator long after Agassiz's death in 1873.[240] Agassiz's continued influence on the Lawrence School, in fact, led to the development of a neo-Lamarckian version of evolution that became known as the American School of Biology.[241]

By the end of the 1860s, science at Harvard was divided institutionally and intellectually. The Lawrence School was dominated by students and followers of Agassiz whose thinking reflected what was left of Protestant Baconianism, and regard by the regular University, while the regular University, whose leading figure was Gray, represented the emergent culture of modern theoretical science. This was the environment of natural scientific research at Harvard when Christopher Columbus Langdell came to the Law School and began to create his own version of legal science. Before turning to that model, however, it is important to recognize the background and attitudes of the man who brought Langdell to Cambridge, Charles Eliot.

Eliot had been a chemist, becoming director of the Lawrence School in 1861. In 1863 Gibbs was made the third Rumford professor, a position that Eliot had wanted and expected to receive. Disappointed, Eliot resigned his position at the Lawrence School and spent two years in Europe—echoing the experiences thirty years earlier of Bache and Henry—examining models of scientific education. On his return in 1865, he became a professor of chemistry at William Barton Rogers' Massachusetts Institute of Technology, an experience that impressed him deeply. In 1869 Eliot published two articles in *Atlantic Monthly*, called "The New Education," in which he outlined his philosophy; it was largely on the basis of those articles that he was selected to become President of Harvard University later that same year.

Eliot, as his articles in *Atlantic Monthly* made clear, was concerned first and foremost with creating institutions of higher practical learning. His vision was exceptionalist; describing engineering as the ideal life for an American man, he stated that "[t]he average American does not eat, drink, sleep, work or amuse himself like an average European. He wants different tools, carriages, cars, steamboats, clothes, medicines, and houses." Eliot argued that what was needed was two distinct kinds of institution: classical colleges, at which subjects would be studied "for the love of them, without any ulterior objectives"; and institutions of technical education, in which students should have "a practical end constantly in view."[242] This idea, drawn directly from Eliot's experiences at MIT, embodied the strongest possible articulation of a division between science and technology. In Eliot's mind, at least, the separation between utility and improvement was not only real and important, it was the veritable starting-point for the construction of a university. The separation, however, was institutional rather than intellectual, and both were included in the overall scheme. The question of what philosophical and methodological baggage might accompany the definition of one or the other type of education does not appear to have greatly troubled Eliot's thinking. So long as Agassiz and Gray were both famous names in science, they stood together as assets to the university.[243]

Where did Langdell fit in this picture? One of the difficulties attendant on interpreting Langdellian legal science is that he himself did not leave an extensive written record, forcing historians to rely greatly on Eliot's characterizations. As we have seen, however, Eliot's vision of science was catholic as well as categorical, leaving open more than one possible interpretation of the place of Langdellian legal education in Harvard's heuristic scheme. In Eliot's mind, Langdell's revolutionary changes at the law school were part of a grand shift in the method of the university as a whole: "in all departments of the University," he wrote in his memoirs, "a careful observation of actual facts, an accurate recording of the facts determined, and a just and limited inference from the recorded facts have come to be the primary methods of study and research."[244] It was Eliot, not Langdell, who undertook the public defense of the case method through the 1870s and Eliot who famously analogized the study of cases to the experimental method.[245] In fact, Langdell's method *was* analogous to the experimental method applied to the taxonomical characterization of natural objects; it was not, however, analogous to the experimental method of Gray's theoretical science. This was not a matter of dissembling on Eliot's part, but may rather stand as an indication of the source for his reference. In this reading, the laboratories to which Eliot referred were those of the Lawrence School, not the Biology Department.

Langdell's approach to legal education is nearly uniformly treated by modern writers as an idea only arbitrarily attached to his conception of jurisprudence (and by some of his contemporaries who accepted one but not the other) despite their mutual inclusion by the man himself under the rubric of legal science.[246] It may well be true that Langdell's case method can be separated from its intellectual foundations in the sense that the influence of the case method has not depended upon a public acceptance of Langdell's and Eliot's depictions of legal science. Viewed as the culmination of a process of historical evolution, however, rather than as the beginning of a modern trend, Langdell's legal science demonstrates the precise contours of Eliot's practical scientific education generally, and with it the residual influences of Protestant Baconianism on legal science. The connection between Langdell's model and those of Hoffman, Mayes, and Greenleaf is drawn first and foremost from the mutual claims of each to make law a science on the order of the natural sciences. The crucial point of connection was in the characterization of cases as a species of natural objects to be discovered, examined and systematized, a point emphasized by Holmes when he compared Langdell's teaching to that of a biology teacher who "would give one of his pupils a sea urchin and tell him to find all about it he could."[247] What Holmes found objectionable was the implicit claim that observation could yield generally applicable principles; i.e. that law fit the model of inductive natural science.[248] This was an idea quite different from treating cases either as deductions from geometric axioms, expressions of timeless custom, or positivistic assertions of judicial or legislative power.[249]

Langdell's approach precisely echoed the search for ordering principles of taxonomy that survived in the Lawrence School. In his 1886 address to the Harvard Law School Association, Langdell made his famous analogy to laboratories. Quoted in full, the analogy is tellingly broad:

> We have also constantly inculcated the idea that the library is the proper workshop of professors and students alike; that it is to us all that the laboratories of the university are to the chemists and physicists, all that the museum of natural history is to the zoologists, all that the botanical garden is to the botanists.[250]

Botany and zoology were the prototypical taxonomical sciences, drawn from natural history, most prominently emphasized in the lyceums, and most closely associated with the ideals of Protestant Baconianism. The reference to "workshops" directly invoked the model of useful technology. Set between these two references, the conception of "chemists and physicists" to which Langdell referred appears clearly as the taxonomical study of Agassiz and his students in the Lawrence School. Lawbooks, famously associated with Langdell's teaching methods, were neither dialectical arrangements of rules nor histories of legislation, but collections of specimens.[251]

The emphasis on taxonomy as the goal of scientific inquiry was not the only connection to the pre-theoretical tradition of scientific practice. Langdell's legal science above all depended on retention of the strictly bounded inductivism of earlier natural scientific models. Deprived of the possibility of drawing first principles from the order of the universe or of the human soul, Langdell turned the focus of the discourse inward, a move that made the claim of "science" one purely of analogy rather than affinity. Extra-legal principles were entirely banished from consideration; the law was referential only to itself. Like the natural theologians of an earlier era, Langdell's students would reason by inference to already-determined principles, set out in summaries compiled first by Langdell and later by his student James Barr Ames.[252]

> Law, considered as a science, consists of certain principles or doctrines . . . much the shortest and best, if not the only way of mastering the doctrine effectually is by studying the cases in which it is embodied. But the cases which are useful and necessary for this purpose at the present day bear an exceedingly small proportion to all that have been reported. The vast majority are useless, and worse than useless, for any purpose of systematic study. Moreover the number of fundamental legal doctrines is much less than is commonly supposed. . . .[253]

Legal education was no surveying expedition: Langdell drew his students' attention only to those few cases that he knew to be accurate and clear demonstrations of principles known to him to be correct. To be sure, when beginning students in chemistry and physics recreated classic experiments the outcome was known in advance. The difference between that approach and Langdell's was that the science classes were intended to teach a method that could later be used to make *new* discoveries, while Langdell's students were introduced to a landscape with known and well-surveyed boundaries. The law case was fundamentally an object of contemplation, not analysis.

Langdell's inductivism, however, was different from that of the earlier legal sciences in its scope. The conclusions that he sought were secular, internalist propositions exclusive not only to law, but to a particular branch of the law.

> It seemed to me, therefore, to be possible to take such a branch of the law as Contracts, for example, and, without exceeding comparatively moderate limits, to select, classify, and arrange all those cases which had contributed in any important degree to the growth, development, or establishment of any of its essential doctrines; and that such a work could not fail to be of material service to all who desire to study *that branch of law* systematically and in it original source.[254]

This was the source of the famous "case method." The subject matter of legal study could only be legal cases, and at that only those cases involving the particular subject under study, and ideally only those few cases that fit the model of the ideal type. This was not merely an aspect of Langdell's method of instruction; it went to the heart of his conception of the nature of legal science. In his *Summary of the Law of Contracts*, Langdell eschewed any hierarchical ordering of subjects, instead presenting subjects in alphabetical order with the comment "every reader must exercise his own taste and judgment as to the order in which he will read them, or whether he will read them in any order."[255]

Earlier, I suggested that Langdell's approach might better be termed "legal technology" than "legal science" for its elevation of utility over improvement. With the decline of natural theology, legal science could no longer be described as a vehicle for moral uplift. This was probably one source of the affinity between Eliot and Langdell. As part of Eliot's liberal emphasis on practical education, he argued that law was to be promoted as "an apolitical, value-free, technocratic discipline" quite different from a republican enterprise to promote political virtues.[256] Instead, the point was to raise up a professional caste. "It should be the aim of the University's Law School," Eliot declared in 1875, "to train young men of good preliminary education and average ability, taken by the hundred, for the higher walks of the profession."[257] For Langdell, too, moral education was not an essential part of the project of law school. At the same time, however, Langdell's method remained grounded in the ideal of natural science in its treatment of law, especially common law, as a natural artifact to be discovered. This attitude aroused opposition to his method from eminent Harvard law professors such as constitutional law professor James Bradley Thayer and John Chipman Gray, who commented privately that Langdell's "intellectual arrogance and contempt is astonishing" and declared that "a school where the majority of the professors shuns and despises the contact with actual fact . . . will and ought to go to the devil."[258]

Made with reference to legal education, the assertion that Langdell's concept of legal science was grounded in claims of utility is non-controversial. Modern writers, however, have frequently accused Langdell of completely ignoring questions of practical consequence in his consideration of questions of legal doctrine. One of the most commonly cited examples arises in the context of his discussion of the mailbox rule.

> [Langdell] took note of the argument that the mailbox rule would best serve 'the purposes of substantial justice, and the interests of the contracting parties, as understood by themselves,' and responded that this was 'irrelevant'—a claim that has ever since been taken to express the wretched essence of his kind of legal thinking.[259]

In fact, this example of "wretchedness" relies on an incomplete quotation. The fuller quotation reads as follows:

> It has been claimed that the purposes of substantial justice, and the interests of contracting parties as understood by themselves, will be best served by holding that the contract is complete the moment the letter of acceptance is mailed. . . . The true answer to this argument is, that it is irrelevant; but, assuming it to be relevant, it may be turned against those who use it without losing any of its strength. The only cases of real hardship are where there is a miscarriage of the letter of acceptance, and in those cases a hardship to one of the parties is inevitable. . . . As to making provision for the contingency of the miscarriage of a letter, this is easy for the person who sends it, while it is practically impossible for the person to whom it is sent.[260]

This looks a great deal like the derivation of a rule from the observation of practical consequences recorded in cases, precisely the idea of an inductive legal science—however constrained the range of his induction—that Langdell had claimed to be exploring all along. If there is a general a priori principle at work, it is a singularly fact-based one: "The true protection for both parties is to have a binding contract made before performance begins . . . if they neglect this precaution, any hardship that they may suffer should be laid at their own door."[261]

On the other hand, Langdell's conception of legal education was decidedly not built around the experience of legal practice. As he famously remarked in an 1868 address, "[l]aw is a science; all the available materials of that science are contained in printed books."[262] This comment and the program that it reflected emphasized the connection between university-based education and the inward turn of legal science, as Langdell went on to point out.

> [I]f printed books are the ultimate sources of all legal knowledge; if every student who would obtain any mastery of law as a science must resort to these ultimate sources; and if the only assistance which it is possible for the learner to receive is such as can be afforded by teachers who have travelled the same road before him,—then a university, and a university alone, can furnish every possible facility for teaching and learning law.[263]

From a division between judges and lawyers perhaps more real than imagined, the teaching of law was now being directed toward a class of law professors with no claims to any connection to the activities of the profession. "What qualifies a person, therefore, to teach law is not experience in the work of a lawyer's office, not experience in dealing with men, not experience in the trial or argument of causes—not experience, in short, in using law, but experience in learning law."[264] From the 1870s forward critics of the case method argued that it did a poor job in teaching students the law as it was, but to no avail;[265] in 1873, Ames became the first full-time law instructor who had never practiced law.[266] As for the case method, in time it was adopted even by its critics at Harvard, and from there it soon spread across the country.[267]

Langdell's version of legal science was the intellectual counterpart to institutional developments in legal education and the profession.[268] In law as in the natural sciences, institutions turned inward in the 1850s and 60s, as lawyers became less and less identified as public intellectuals and more and more as professional specialists. "The young practitioner," commented Sharswood, "will find, in the long run, the good opinion of his professional brethren of more importance than that of what is called the public. . . . The good opinion and confidence of the members of the same profession, like the king's name on the field of battle, is a 'tower of strength'—it is the title of legitimacy."[269] As the antebellum period drew to a close lawyers began to withdraw from their roles as public intellectuals. The public improvement that had motivated earlier legal science was abandoned even as elements of its mode of analysis were incorporated into the new Langdellian regime.[270]

V. Afterword

In the natural sciences, both the respectable lyceum movement and the vulgar fascination with pseudoscience continued to flourish through the end of the nineteenth century, independent of the institutions and, for the most part, the community of professional scientists.[271] The Lowell Lectures continued with unabated popularity (as, indeed, they do to this day), and continued to marry scientific, social scientific, and legal topics. In 1881, arguably the single most famous Lowell Lecture ever given would be delivered by Oliver Wendell Holmes; the apotheosis of legal science, it was a study of evolutionary principles entitled "The Common Law."[272] It would be difficult to find a better illustration of the principles of natural theology and synthesis by analogy as the hallmarks of public legal science than a talk that was delivered in 1882. The speaker, a lawyer named John D. Thompson, delivered an address entitled "The Reign of Law" to the assembled members of the Vassar Literary Society, which was later published. Employing the same quotations from Montesqieu and Hooker that had inspired Sharswood, Thompson analogized mental derangement to crime,[273] described the laws of nature as divine principles of administration,[274] pointed out the logical unity of the workings of a steam engine,[275] and invoked the social scientific ideal of laws of social nature,[276] all based on his expertise as a lawyer.

In the study of law, too, residual forms of thinking persisted. Legal educators such as Christopher Tiedeman and Simeon Baldwin continued to express the ideals of legal science as an undertaking in moral improvement in the tradition of Story.[277] That version of legal science did not last long, however. Increasingly, the claim to the guardianship of republican virtue left legal study to become the province of the newly prominent social sciences. In 1834, Greenleaf had queried "to whom have all eyes been imploringly directed for its preservation, but to the living and honored champions and expounders of constitutional law?". In the 1870s, Andrew Dickson White proposed himself and his colleagues for that role. "The time is surely coming . . . when disheartened populations will hear brilliant preaching subversive of the whole system of social order . . . the only safeguard is in a thorough provision for the checking of popular unreason, and for the spreading of right reason."[278]

White's comments draw a connection that was alluded to earlier, between the treatment of law as a moral science in the 1830s and 40s and American social science fifty years later. White and, especially, Wayland inherited the program of law as an element of moral science at a time when it was decidedly on its way out from law schools. Francis Lieber's shift from legal science to political science followed (or perhaps led) the movement of moral science in the American academy. In later years, American social science took its own naturalistic turn, abandoning the humanistic universalism of Lieber's political science for a new version of the project of finding essential human truths in the order of nature. The difference was that the new breed of social scientist claimed no affiliation with other disciplines, whether in the science, theology, or the law. Social Darwinism, in particular, represented an extension of the "science of man" in just the areas in which natural scientists had withdrawn from the field of public debate. In their place a crude and debased version of evolutionary theory[279] was picked up by Herbert Spencer and William Graham Sumner and made the basis for the new science of sociology.[280] Social Darwinism fit well with laissez-faire, with its own ties to the Protestant Baconian ideal of law as natural science. Like the ideal of law as moral science, however, the claims of affinity between law school classrooms and laboratories fell into disfavor. In response to the claims of Social Darwinism, Progressive legal thinkers relied on new, reformist models of social science to formulate the "sociological jurisprudence" exemplified by Pound (a botanist by training) and Brandeis. In part this was due not only to the intellectual fashions of the time but also to the evident changes that industrialization had wrought on the social order.[281] Furthermore, the earlier debates had been built almost exclusively around consideration of the common law.[282] The increasing importance of public law at the end of the nineteenth century made the debates over whether the common law should be characterized as a natural, cultural, social artifact appear quaint.[283]

During the same period, however, the form of legal education became more and more homogeneously oriented around the case method. Legal educators long ago abandoned the attempts to derive theological truths, or to connect legal reasoning with every other aspect of the human condition, or to employ inductive reasoning to find a new path for the reformation of the system of the common law. At the same time, legal education still displays the inculcation of habits of constrained inductivism, the emphasis on taxonomy and analogic reasoning, the rejection of historical authority in favor of claims of evolutionary progress, and the characterization of cases as found natural objects. These are the skeletal remains of Protestant Baconianism, the amalgam of religious, political, and philosophical doctrines that defined America's public understanding of natural science one hundred and fifty years ago.

NOTES

1. Timothy Dwight, *Travels in New England and New York* (London: W. Baynes & Son, 1823), vol. IV, p. 295.

2. The reference to "scientists" raises the problem of anachronistic vocabulary, since the term was not coined until 1841. I have attempted for the most part to use historically appropriate terms, but where necessary I have also adopted Mario Biagioli's answer to this problem in his use of the term "science": "Here and elsewhere in the book I could have used more cumbersome terms such as 'natural philosophy' or 'mathematical natural philosophy.' . . . However, I have decided to adopt 'science' as a shorthand label for these activities—a label I am consciously using 'under erasure.'" Mario Biagioli, *Galileo Courtier: The Practice of Science in the Culture of Absolutism* (Chicago: University of Chicago Press 1993). Thus I will speak generally of the "natural sciences" when I am referring to the study of natural phenomena carried out in a way that was intended to conform to some governing model of "science." Those who participate in those activities are referred to as natural scientists, just as those who participated in the construction of legal science are here called "legal scientists." I do not intend "scientist," however, to indicate anything more than "a practitioner of a science." Where the particular sense of "scientist" as it was meant in 1841 is in use, I will attempt to make the parameters of that term clear in the context of the discussion in which it appears.

3. "In essence, [one] reasons that the concept X has components a, b, c; if we find a, b, c, then X has entered the realm of the thinkable. Alas for the clear-thinking historian, the contexts in which a, b, c occur may be so disparate from one another, or so alien to current sensibilities, that we can hardly glue these bits and pieces together to form any single notion at all, much less a familiar one." Lorraine Daston, *Classical Probability in the Enlightenment* (Princeton, NJ: Princeton University Press 1988), p. 12. Daston makes the intriguing argument that legal concepts of probability and evidence were powerfully influential on the construction of these same concepts in European science from the seventeenth through the nineteenth centuries. "[T]he works of the early probabilists turn out to be more about equity than about chances, and more about expectations than about probabilities. These ideas and the applications they stimulated—for example, to games of chance and annuities—came . . . largely from the law." *Ibid.*, p. 15.

4. By "conservative" here I mean only "opposed to radical changes in the system of common laws," not any particular set of policy preferences. Kent was quite progressive in the sense of being willing and even eager to countenance changes in legal rules in cases that would have the effect of promoting commerce; in this his sensibilities were eminently liberal. On the other hand, he was virulently opposed to codification, expanded reliance on statutes, and any other alteration in the traditional role of the common law. When the New York state legislature abolished, by statute, the Rule in Shelley's Case, Kent waxed poetic in his regret: "The juridical scholar, on whom his great master, Coke, has bestowed some portion of the 'gladsome light of jurisprudence,' will scarcely be able to withhold an involuntary sigh, as he casts a retrospective glance over the piles of learning, devoted to destruction by an edict. . . . He must bid adieu forever to . . . the multiplied specimens of profound logic, skillful criticism, and refined distinction, which pervade the varied cases in law and equity." *Commentaries*, iv, 226, n. a. Kent was also no democrat: nothing was more certain to him than that a levelling tendency would drag American society to its ruin. "My opinion is that the admission of universal suffrage . . . [is] incompatible with government and security to property and that the government and character of this country are going to ruin. This suffrage is too great an excitement for any political machine. It racks it to pieces and morals go with it." Letter to Moses Kent, Jr., April 3, 1835. In a letter to his friend Joseph Story, seven years later, Kent sounded even gloomier: "I have no hope that this corrupt and fanatical age can be reformed without harsh applications, and I think we are running down fast to the lowest depths of degradation." Letter to Joseph Story, October 5, 1842, both quoted at Gregory Alexander, *Commodity & Propriety: Competing Visions of Property in American Legal Thought, 1776-1970* (Chicago: University of Chicago Press, 1997), p. 41. Alexander's book provides an excellent discussion of Kent's thinking generally, with an emphasis on the tension between values of "liberalism" and traditionalism.

5. Bache was a remarkable figure: the great-grandson of Benjamin Franklin, he was related to three past secretaries of the Treasury and was the nephew of a vice president. First in his class at West Point, he taught there for three years, then became

a professor of natural history at the University of Pennsylvania at age 22. In 1836, at age 30, he became the first president of Girard College and was assigned to travel to Europe to examine schools there. On his return, Bache produced a 600-page report calling for the creation of universities on the German model to teach science in America. He later served as the head of the U.S. Coastal Survey. Robert V. Bruce, *The Launching of Modern American Science, 1846-1876* (Ithaca, NY: Cornell University Press 1987), p. 17; Thomas Haskell, *The Emergence of Professional Social Science* (Urbana: University of Illinois Press, 1977), pp. 70-71.

6. Bache and Henry met while travelling in Europe in 1836 while Henry was travelling on a grant from Princeton. In 1838 Henry wrote to Bache: "I am now more than ever of your opinion that the real working men in the way of science in this country should make common cause . . . to raise their own scientific character. To make science more respected at home to increase the facilities of scientific investigators and the inducements to scientific labours." Quoted at Bruce, *The Launching of Modern American*, p. 27. For a discussion of European travels by Americans interested in science, see Bruce Sinclair, "Americans Abroad: Science and Cultural Nationalism in the Early Nineteenth Century," in Nathan Reingold, ed., *The Sciences in the American Context: New Perspectives* (Washington, D.C.: Smithsonian Institute Press, 1979), pp. 35-54.

7. Hoffman, one of Maryland's most prominent attorneys, was an active supporter of the founding of the University of Maryland, where he began teaching in 1823. Sympathetic to Benthamite proposals for codification, Hoffman himself presented a much more broad-based approach to understanding the law in his *Course of Study*, discussed below. Twenty years after its initial publication, the editors of the *North American Review* said of the work: "If we were called upon to designate any single work, which had exercised a greater influence over the profession of the law in this country than all others . . . we should unhesitatingly select Hoffman's 'Course of Legal Study.'" 45 *North American Review* (October 1837), p. 482.

8. Mayes taught only briefly at Transylvania. For a discussion of the curriculum of Transylvania's school of law emphasizing its connections to the tradition of republican moralism, see Paul D. Carrington, "Teaching Law and Virtue at Transylvania University: the George Wythe Tradition in the Antebellum Years," 41 *Mercer Law Review* no. 2 (Winter 1990), p. 673.

9. David Dudley Field was a (distant) descendant of an English astronomer; his father had been a Congregational minister as well as a prominent member of Connecticut's Historical Society and the author of several books of local history. Field was a prominent New York attorney who appeared frequently before the Supreme Court. An anti-slavery Democratic politician, he was instrumental in the founding of New York University's Law School. Field was also one of the leading law reformers of his day, and the most prominent figure in the codification movement. He authored the Field codes for civil and criminal procedure that were adopted by New York State. The Field code eventually formed the model for the codes of civil procedure later adopted by most states and was influential in England as well. In 1857 Field headed a New York State commission that prepared penal, political, and civil codes as well. Although only the penal code was adopted by New York, all five Field codes were adopted in California, where David's brother Stephen Johnson Field was a member of the legislature (and later governor of the state and a justice of the U.S. Supreme Court). See, generally, James Grant Wilson and John Fiske, eds., *Appleton's Cyclopaedia of American Biography*, vol. II (New York: D. Appleton and Company, 1888), pp. 447-8; Allen Johnson and Dumas Malone, eds., *Dictionary of American Biography* (New York: Charles Scribners' Sons, 1932). For a specific discussion of the Field Code and Field's role in the codification movement, see Stephen N. Subrin, "David Dudley Field and the Field Code: A Historical Analysis of an Earlier Procedural Vision," 6 *Law & History Review* (November 1988), pp. 311-373. For a discussion of codification in America generally, see Charles M. Cook, *The American Codification Movement: A Study of Antebellum Legal Reform* (Westport, Conn.: Greenwood Press, 1981), p. 162.

10. Greenleaf was first Royall Professor of law at Harvard, and then later succeeded Story as Dane Professor. He was the author of an authoritative treatise on the law of evidence and real property, and an active Federalist politician, serving in the Maine legislature in 1820, where he was actively involved in drafting laws for the state. His brother, Moses Greenleaf, was a map maker and surveyor who had been an active promoter of Maine separatism. Moses was also a justice of the peace and in the court of common pleas.

11. The son of St. George Tucker, Beverly Tucker was a Southerner and an avid Romantic devotee of the Southern cause; he was one of the first prominent secessionists and boasted that none of his students left his care "without being, for the time, a Southern man in feeling and a States-rights man in conviction." This undoubtedly had something to do with the fact that his father had married the widow of John Randolph. See W. Hamilton Bryson, *Legal Education in Virginia, a Biographical Approach* (Charlottesville: University Press of Virginia, 1982). While both Northern and Southern sources are employed in this paper, one obvious point requiring further exploration is the influence of regional differences on the sense of "science," particularly in light of the role that questions of race and slavery played in natural scientific disputes (discussed below). On the issue of regional influences on legal development see, generally, James W. Ely, Jr., and David J. Bodenhamer, "Regionalism and American Legal History: The Southern Experience," 39 Vanderbilt Law Review 539 (April 1986); Paul Finkleman, "Exploring Southern Legal History," 64 North Carolina Law Review 77 (November 1985).

12. Sharswood is a somewhat odd fit with the rest of the writers discussed here. An avid believer in the idea of legal science, he also invoked the idea of law as a moral study and simultaneously sided with those such as Benjamin Butler who envisioned the university law school as an adjunct to, rather than a replacement for, apprenticeship. "Law belongs to the moral sciences, and cannot, like the medical art, which belongs to the natural sciences, and in most of its branches is demonstrative, be so advantageously taught by lectures. . . . I am firmly persuaded that nothing can nor ought to dispense with the necessity of a regular clerkship in the office of a practicing attorney." George Sharswood, *Lectures Introductory to the Study of Law* (Philadelphia: T & J.W. Johnson Co., 1870), p. 59. (Langdell, of course, would argue that law could not be taught by lectures because it *was* analogous to medicine and the natural sciences.) On the other hand, Sharswood defended the idea of stare decisis by drawing on the model of astronomy to argue that "true conservatism" was a principle of "gradual change" which implies the need for

"liberalism." Furthermore he was a reformer of the first order, who declared the duty of the lawyer "is as frequently called upon to inquire what the law ought to be as what it is." A utilitarian who rejected codification, he also railed against the evils of judicial rule-making, "invariably the precursor of uncertainty and confusion." (Sharswood, *Lectures*, pp. 81, 40, 39, 48.) His conception of legal science, ultimately, were squarely in line with those of Hoffman, Greenleaf, et. al. despite occasional contrary rhetoric.

13. Francis Hilliard was one of the most important reformers of the period. His 1835 treatise, *The Elements of Law*, begins by describing legal science in familiar terms: "in law, as in other sciences, there are certain broad and fixed principles, which embody the essence of the system, and remain unchanged amidst the fluctuations of successive ages." At the same time, however, Hilliard entirely eschewed the project of appropriating models from outside the field of legal practice, complaining that Blackstone's *Commentaries* "contain a large amount of matter, which is either in its nature not *legal*, but historical and political, or has no applicability, and even to the professional reader is of little use, in this country." Kent's books, too, spent significant time on matters having "more of a political than a strictly legal aspect" and are "speculative, historical, and discursive." In contrast, his own book is "designed to present American law, technically so called, *as it is* . . . it carefully abstains from all criticism, speculation, or history; and confines itself to a plain, brief statement of principles now in force, with occasional illustrations." Hilliard, *The Elements of Law: Being a Comprehensive Summary of American Civil Jurisprudence for the use of students, men of business, and general readers* (Boston: Hilliard, Gray, and Company, 1835), "Preface," pp. iii-iv (emphasis added). Hilliard's comments sound, in fact, remarkably like Langdell's "Preface" to his *Summary of the Law of Contracts* (discussed below).

14. Silas Jones was a prominent attorney who argued forcefully for reform of the common law. In many ways, his book contains a nearly perfect statement of the version of legal science that is presented in this paper. Jones, *An Introduction to Legal Science; Being a Concise and Familiar Treatise on Such Legal Topics as are Earliest Read by the Law Student should be Generally Taught in the Higher Seminaries of Learning; and Understood by Every Citizen, as a Part of a General and Business Education* (New York: John S. Voorhies, 1842). In his chapter on "Law Defined," Jones describes law as "that science which is instituted by the sovereign power of the state, to regulate civil conduct for the preservation and welfare of society. . . . Civil laws are neither divine nor natural, but are the institutions of society." On the other hand, there are a number of ways in which Jones appears to draw on prevalent ideas about the natural world. For example, despite his disavowal of civil laws as "natural," Jones relies on a theory of human nature that extends to analogies with animals to ground his political conception: "we find mankind every where united in societies, and eminently social beings. . . . In regard to the instinct of sociability, animals are divided into two classes, and man in this respect must rank, however undignified the position, with monkeys, sheep, geese, bees &c. . . . Society and government, taken together, make but one whole. They are each but parts of one complex machine. As is society, so is government, a natural institution." *Introduction to Legal Science*, pp. 7-8, 10. Jones also invoked a pre-Darwinian notion of evolutionary progress in his idea that societies develop to ever-higher states, and viewed legal science as both an element of a grand synthesis and itself possessed of internal overarching order. "Whenever any branch of knowledge rests on solid foundations, and has been so far cultivated and matured as to assume a systematic form, in learned treatises it is allowed to take its rank among the *sciences*. What branch of knowledge can be better entitled to this noble appellation, than that of law?" Finally, Jones' method of reasoning is difficult to specify. He is a devotee of the case method, organizing his discussions of substantive legal doctrines around illustrative cases, but he displays no interest in exploring the question of whether these cases define the common law rule or whether they are illustrative of rules already known and established, and at times he appears to invoke an almost Austinian positivism. His identification of law with state action, however, appears at times more an articulation of the pragmatic understanding of the practicing lawyer than a theoretical program. "Laws are made upon large and general considerations. . . . The law is made, and then the evil occurs, and lastly, the application of the law to the case follows." *Introduction to Legal Science*, pp. 18, 19.

15. Benjamin Butler's plan for a law school at New York University disavowed the idea of legal science and questioned the idea of university legal education in place of apprenticeship generally. Butler designed his program after serving as Jackson's Attorney-General; his approach reflected the ideals of a liberal Democrat. Butler's curriculum was relentlessly unphilosophical, oriented toward providing useful knowledge for working lawyers. "The organization of the school, and its whole system of instruction, should be specially adapted to students who design to pursue their professions within this State. . . . The great object of the School should be, to impart, within the given time, the largest amount of that kind of knowledge, which is best calculated to qualify the student for the practical duties of his profession; leaving it to him, in after years, and by diligent self-instruction, to fill up deficiencies." Butler, indeed, specifically identified himself as opposed to teaching law in the manner of a science. "Beginning with the primary department, I would propose an important departure from the ordinary scientific course pursued by the institutional writers. They more usually commence with the law of nature, as the foundation of all legal science, and go through a course of instruction in the law of nations, and in the Political or Constitutional Law of the country for which they write, before entering upon the peculiar system of Municipal Law when composes the great body of its civil and criminal jurisprudence. . . . The course adopted by the elementary writers, as just stated is undoubtedly the philosophical order in which the Law, as a general science, ought to be unfolded. And when the term of study is long enough to allow it, the same method may, with advantage, be pursued in a Law School; but then the student, until he reaches the practical branches of the Municipal Law, should not enter the office of the Attorney or Solicitor. . . ." Butler went on to suggest that all students ought to combine their university studies with office apprenticeships. Benjamin F. Butler, "A Plan for the Organization of a Law School in the University of the City of New York" (July 6, 1835 letter to Rev. J.M. Mathews, Chancellor of NYU), in Michael H. Hoeflich, ed., *The Gladsome Light of Jurisprudence: Learning the Law in England and the United States in the 18th and 19th Centuries* (New York: Greenwood Press, 1989), pp. 167-68, 171.

16. On the occasion of his receipt of an honorary degree from Harvard, Cooley delivered the comments that provided

Carrington's article with its title: "We fail to appreciate the dignity of our profession if we look for it either in profundity of learning or in forensic triumphs. . . . [T]he strength of the law lies in its commonplace character; and it becomes feeble and untrustworthy when it expresses something different from the common thoughts of men." Paul D. Carrington, "Law as 'The Common Thoughts of Men': The Law-Teaching and Judging of Thomas McIntyre Cooley," 49 Stanford Law Review 495 (February 1997). As Carrington points out, the story of Cooley and others like him is a unfairly neglected one. "The twentieth century has neglected, even scorned, Cooley, while elevating Langdell and Holmes: Langdell as the patron of a technocratic profession trained by Hessians, and Holmes as the patron of a disengaged academic subprofession. In the Jacksonian universe producing Cooley, there was little appreciation of the likes of either Langdell and his successors, or Holmes and his." *Ibid.*, p. 495. Cooley's—and Butler's—opposition to the pretensions of legal science reflected the approach characteristic of practicing lawyers. Even as judges-turned-law-professors were proclaiming the elite status of their subject matter, bar associations were trying hard to present themselves as open institutions composed of self-made men. "They come from the farm and the workshop," declared a law professor at Cumberland College in 1851, "from that condition of life to which the great majority belong. They are counted by the multitude as one of themselves, and they hail their elevation as a triumph of their own over all that looked like aristocracy." "Inaugural Address of Hon. A. Caruthers, Professor of Law in Cumberland University, Lebanon, Tennessee," 3 U.S. Monthly Law Magazine 542 (1851), quoted at Bloomfield, "Law vs. Politics," p. 313.

17. "It is the fashion among us to speak of the law as a science. . . . Jurisprudence is a science, certainly, and the noblest of all sciences, in so far as it applies to the regulation of human conduct that Eternal Law which 'is laid up in the bosom of God.' . . . Doubtless , the common law, in some of its titles and divisions, may justly be regarded as eminently scientific. But to call it, as a whole and with all its modifications, a science, or the exposition of a science, is really to trifle and delude. The rhetoricians who liken it to a great river, which has brought down upon its bosom all the treasures of the realms of time . . . seem to forget that great rivers bring down many things which are not treasures." S.T. Wallis, "Address Delivered Before the Law Class of the University of Maryland, June 15th, 1872," (Baltimore: John Murphy & Co, 1872), pp. 12-13. Wallis went so far as to cast doubt on the project of university legal training in general. "Professional opinion has been very much divided as to the advantage of university-instruction, by way of lectures, to students of law. My own experience and observation, I confess, have not inclined me towards that system, if pursued with any approach to exclusiveness. In England, the sentiment and custom of the profession have hitherto been strongly against it, and, even now, the effort to make it compulsory there is resisted by some of the ablest and broadest intellects of the Bar." *Ibid.*, p. 6. Unfortunately, we do not have a record of the reactions of Wallis' audience to his pronouncements.

18. In 1886 Cooley's Michigan Law School adopted the case method. Carrington, "Law as 'The Common Thoughts of Men,'" p. 520. As the quotations in the previous notes from Butler, Wallis, et. al., suggest, this was a victory for the idea of university-based legal education in general.

19. Among others who fit this mold were William Rogers, founder of the Massachusetts Institute of Technology, and Asa Gray. See A. Hunter Dupree, *Asa Gray* (Cambridge, MA: Belknap Press, 1959). Although Rogers and Gray were the most famous, they were far from the only scientific thinkers who rejected the tenets of Protestant Baconianism. One of the sharpest critics was Thomas Cooper of South Carolina, who accused Benjamin Silliman (see below) of "absolute unconditional surrender of his common sense to clerical orthodoxy." Ronald L. Numbers, "Science and Religion," 1 *Osiris* (second series, 1985), pp. 66-67. For other examples, see Charles Rosenberg's description of the development of agricultural experiment stations in the 1850s. Rosenberg, "Science and Social Values in Nineteenth-Century America: A Case Study in the Growth of Scientific Institutions," in *No Other Gods: On Science and American Social Thought* (Baltimore, MD: Johns Hopkins University Press, 1997,) Ch. 8.

20. Konefsky, "Law and Culture in Antebellum Boston," 40 *Stanford Law Review* 1119 (April 1988), p. 1121.

21. See, generally, Brian Vickers, ed., *Occult and Scientific Mentalities in the Renaissance* (Cambridge: Cambridge University Press, 1984).

22. For a discussion of the meaning of "right reason" for early Protestant writers, see Lotte Mulligan, "'Reason,' 'Right Reason,' and 'Revelation' in Mid-Seventeenth-Century England," in Vickers, ed., *Occult and Scientific Mentalities in the Renaissance*, pp. 375-402.

23. The classic work on the role of natural law in ideas about society across the early modern period is Otto Gierke, *Natural Law and the Theory of Society, 1500 to 1800*, Ernest Barker, trans. (Cambridge: Cambridge University Press, 1934). It should be noted that there is a difference between the idea of jus naturae—meaning laws the truth of which could be demonstrated by an appeal to nature—and the Christian ideal of natural law as a transcendent moral order imprinted in Creation by divine agency. In early Protestant writing, however, the distinction was often blurred; a classic and important example is the writings of Petrus Ramus, a dialectician who designed a system of analysis of phenomena designed to lead to a perception of the logic of the mind of God. Perry Miller famously assigned Ramus' thought great importance in American Puritanism. Miller, *The New England Mind* (New York: McMillan, 1939). While Miller's assessment has been challenged, it is noteworthy that Ramist logic and natural science was taught at Harvard until the end of the 17th century. Clark A. Elliott and Margaret W. Rossiter, eds., *Science at Harvard University* (Bethlehem, Pennsylvania: Lehigh University Press, 1992), p. 334. One of the most intriguing indications of the importance that American Puritans attached to Ramist ideas is the fact that John Eliot translated Ramist logic and principles of rhetoric into Algonquin, to be distributed with his Indian Bible. Stephen Foster, *The Long Argument* (University of North Carolina Press, Chapel Hill 1991), p. 333, n. 30. For a thorough presentation of Ramist thought, including an argument for its formative role in Puritan doctrine, see Walter J. Ong, *Ramus, Method, and the Decay of Dialogue* (Harvard University Press, Cambridge 1958). For a discussion of Ramist thought in the early humanist tradition see Margo Todd, *Christian Humanism and the Puritan Social Order* (Cambridge: Cambridge University Press 1987).

24. Grotius, for example, used an extended analysis of risk in investment to argue that Dutch bankers' charging high interest

on certain kinds of contracts did not constitute usury, and hence did not run afoul of church prohibitions. For a further development of this theme, see the discussion of aleatory contracts (contracts involving estimations of future risk) in the early seventeenth century in Lorraine Daston, *Classical Probability in the Enlightenment*, pp. 17-20.

25. Wolff argued that laws should be derived from the certain and imminent knowledge of human nature; Thibaut's call for a code was based on his devotion to an "historical-philosophical" approach that derived maxims from historical experience then developed codes embodying their essential principles; Savigny, a true historical jurisprude, rejected the claim that reason lay at the root of legal science at all. See Mathias Reimann, "Nineteenth Century German Legal Science," 31 *Boston College Law Review* 838 (July 1990). Reimann argues that German legal science had a great but diffuse influence on American legal science in the 1870s: great in that German inspirations were cited for numerous competing projects, diffuse in that there was no consensus on the question of what "German legal science" actually meant. There is a suggestion, then, that like Hoffman's invocations of Roman and Rationalist writers, late nineteenth century American legal writers opportunistically claimed the mantle of German legal science for its aura rather than on the basis of its content. For a discussion of Savigny's influence on English and Continental legal science, *see* Reinhard Zimmerman, "Savigny's Legacy: Legal History, Comparative Law, and the Emergence of a European Legal Science," 112 *The Law Quarterly Review* 576 (October 1996).

26. For descriptions of Bacon's thought generally, see Charles Webster, *The Great Instauration: Science, Medicine and Reform, 1626-60* (London: Duckworth Press, 1975) and Julian Martin, *Francis Bacon, the State, and the Reform of Natural Philosophy* (Cambridge: Cambridge University Press 1992). The relationship between Bacon's ideas of natural science, Aristotelean deductivism, and the traditions of legal science has been the subject of a number of accounts that take differing positions. For example, see Michael Hoeflich, "Law & Geometry: Legal Science from Leibitz to Langdell," 30 *The American Journal of Legal History* no. 2 (April 1986), pp. 95-121; Stephen A. Siegel, "The Aristotelean Basis of English Law, 1450-1800," 56 *New York University Law Review* (April 1981), pp. 18-59; Berman and Reid, "The Transformation of English Legal Science: From Hale to Blackstone," 45 *Emory Law Journal* no. 2 (Spring, 1996), pp. 438-522.

27. See generally, Brian Vickers, *English Science, Bacon to Newton* (Cambridge: Cambridge University Press, 1987).

28. Bacon, *New Organon*, Fulton H. Anderson, ed. (New York: Macmillan/Library of Liberal Arts, 1960), p. 48.

29. "Induction" derives from Aristotle's term "epagoge," referring to nondemonstrative arguments. "Epagoge," however, did not refer to induction as the opposite of deduction, it encompassed all forms of reasoning, as opposed to demonstration. Induction, by contrast, is ordinarily associated with the experimental method, while deduction is characteristic of syllogistic logic, mathematics, geometry, and other formal systems. There is a second distinction that needs to be drawn here. One of the characteristics of deductive systems is that they are "closed": that is, the axioms that provide the starting premises for the system, and the rules for moving from one proposition to the next in a "valid" way, are themselves elements of the system of propositions itself (subject to the exception of the Godel Theorem). Inductive systems of verification, on the other hand, are "open": that is to say, in theory at least the general propositions that are derived from observation of particulars are not required to occupy any particular relationship to the body of propositions that have been previously adduced in order to be "true" (as opposed to "valid.") Strikingly, Langdell's version of legal science was closed, whereas earlier models had been open.

30. "[N]ow of late by the regulation of some learned and (as things now are) excellent men . . . the sciences are confined to certain and prescribed authors, and thus restrained are imposed upon the old and instilled into the young; so that now . . . authority is taken for truth, not truth for authority. Which kind of institution and discipline . . . precludes all prospect of improvement." Bacon, *Natural and Experimental History for the Foundation of Philosophy* (London, 1622), p. xv.

31. In place of Aristotle's final and formal causes, Bacon returned to a pre-Platonic idea, exemplified by Democritus, of active matter, a single substance out of which all objects were composed and in accordance with whose universal dictates the behavior of all objects, conscious or unconscious, was determined. Observation of this matter would yield particulars, which could then be employed inductively to produce lesser axioms, then general rules ("middle axioms"), and finally unifying principles in accordance with which all philosophy was grounded in the study of nature. The central element of this approach was inductive reasoning. "Of induction, the logicians seem hardly to have taken any serious thought, but they pass it by with a slight notice and hasten on to the formulae of disputation. I, on the contrary, reject demonstration by syllogism. . . ." Bacon, "The Great Instauration," in *New Organon*, p. 19. For a discussion of the inductive nature of Bacon's legal philosophy and its relation to the "middle axioms" of his inductive experimental method, see Paul H. Kocher, "Francis Bacon and the Science of Jurisprudence," XVIII *Journal of the History of Ideas* no. 1 (January 1957). For a discussion of Bacon's theories of law and science and the influence of natural science on early English legal theories, see Barbara J. Shapiro, "Law and Science in Seventeenth-Century England," 21 *Stanford Law Review* 727 (1969). Shapiro argues that the dissemination of new scientific knowledge and the immense increase in the prestige of natural science influenced the vocabulary of legal reformers motivated by the desire to apply the highest forms of reason to questions of law.

32. See Robert McRae, "The Unity of the Sciences: Bacon, Descartes, and Leibitz," XVIII *The Journal of the History of Ideas* no. 1 (January 1957), p. 30. McRae points out that while both Bacon and Descartes preached the unity of all the sciences, "[f]or Bacon the basis of this unity is nature, for Descartes it is the mind." *Ibid.*, p. 34. The difference between an appeal to the evidence of nature and an appeal to the rational processes of the mind is precisely the difference between an inductive and a deductive approach to understanding.

33. "[W]e must entreat men again and again to discard . . . these volatile and preposterous philosophies, which have preferred theses to hypotheses, held experience captive, and triumphed over the works of God; and to approach with humility and veneration to unroll the volume of Creation, to linger and meditate therein, and with minds washed clean from opinions to study it in purity and integrity . . . becoming again as little children condescend to take the alphabet of it into their hands,

and spare no pains to search and unravel the interpretation thereof, but pursue it strenuously and persevere even unto death." Quoted at Bacon, *New Organon*, "Introduction," p. xv.

34. "[I]t is a false assertion that the sense of man is the measure of things. On the contrary, all perceptions as well of the sense as of the mind are according to the measure of the individual and not according to the measure of the universe. And the human understanding is like a false mirror, which, receiving rays irregularly, distorts and discolors the nature of things by mingling its own nature with it." Bacon, *New Organon*, p. 48.

35. "[T]he universe to the eye of the human understanding is framed like a labyrinth, presenting as it does on every side so many ambiguities of way, such deceitful resemblances of objects and signs, natures so irregular in their lines and so knotted and entangled." Bacon, *New Organon*, p. 12.

36. Francis Bacon, "The Great Instauration," in *New Organon*, pp. 25, 27. Robert Boyle was almost certainly following Bacon's example in "The Sceptical Chymist" when he has his character Carneades boast that his experimental results were achieved "when I took the pains impartially to examine the bodies themselves . . . and to torture them into a confession of their constituent principles." Boyle, "The Sceptical Chymist" (1661), reprinted at Vickers, *English Science, Bacon to Newton*, p. 71.

37. "[T]he discoveries which have been hitherto made in the arts and sciences are such as might be made by practice, meditation, observation, argumentation—for they lay near to the senses and immediately beneath common notions; but before we can reach the remoter and more hidden parts of nature, it is necessary that a more perfect use and application of the human mind and intellect be introduced." Bacon, *New Organon*, p. 13.

38. See McRae, "The Unity of the Sciences," p. 31.

39. Bacon, *New Organon*, p. 79.

40. Bacon, *Maxims of the Law*, quoted at Kocher, "Francis Bacon and the Science of Jurisprudence," p. 6. Kocher argues, persuasively, that for Bacon maxims in the law functioned as analogues to "middle axioms" in the natural sciences. "In natural science the utility of the middle axiom is to state a rule applicable to new physical situations. In jurisprudence the utility of the maxim is similarly to provide the premises by which new cases can be decided, contradictions in existing cases erased, and analogies more safely followed out." *Ibid.*

41. Quoted at Martin, *Francis Bacon, the State, and the Reform of Natural Philosophy*, p. 142.

42. Bacon, *The Advancement of Learning*, quoted at Martin, *Francis Bacon, the State, and the Reform of Natural Philosophy*, p. 10.

43. "For man is but the servant and interpreter of nature: what he does and what he knows is only what he has observed of nature's order in fact or in thought; beyond this he knows nothing and can do nothing." Bacon, "The Great Instauration," in *New Organon*, p. 29.

44. Bacon, Preface to *Maxims of the Law*, quoted at *New Organon*, p. 7.

45. "The art which I introduce . . . is a kind of logic, though the difference between it and the ordinary logic is great, indeed, immense. . . . [M]ine differs from it in three points especially—viz., in the end aimed at, in the order of demonstration, and in the starting point of the inquiry." Bacon, "The Great Instauration," in *New Organon*, p. 19.

46. Fortescue is credited with being the first author to argue that the British "ancient constitution" was directly connected to the authority of the common law, as well as with founding the study of comparative jurisprudence. Neal Wood, *Foundations of Political Economy: Some Early Tudor Views on State and Society* (Berkeley: University of California Press 1994). Fortescue was not the earliest writer on English law, of course, but Bracton's fourteenth century collections had little commentary and nothing in the way of explanatory theory.

47. J.G.A. Pocock, *The Machiavellian Moment: Florentine Political Thought and the Atlantic Republican Tradition* (Princeton: Princeton University Press, 1975), pp. 10-13.

48. Quoted at Pocock, *The Machiavellian Moment*, p. 13.

49. For a discussion of congruences between Aristotelean notions of practical knowledge and both Fortescue's and Coke's models of English law, see Siegel, "The Aristotelean Basis of English Law, 1450-1800," pp. 39-45. I have omitted a discussion of St. German in this article for reasons of length. St. German, who wrote in the early 1500s, adopted both the medieval ideas of revelation and divinely ordered laws of nature and the ideas of general and particular custom. For St. German, however, rules of custom were secondary to principles of equity and the dictates of religious revelation. Neither Coke nor Bacon followed down this particular path; St. German thus appears as the end of an earlier tradition rather than as an important figure in the beginning of the new. The important point of continuity between St. German and Coke is the reliance on first principles. Fortescue adopted a similar approach, but gave much greater weight to the authority of custom. *Ibid.*, pp. 23-28.

50. That Coke was not an adherent of Thomistic ideas of a law superior to and underlying human rules is demonstrated by his most important political conflict with Bacon. In 1613, Coke was made chief justice of the King's Bench, responsible for overseeing courts of law; Bacon, at the same time, was the King's Chancellor, with authority over the courts of equity. Over the next three years, Coke challenged the chancery courts' practice of overturning verdicts at law. In this, Coke was appealing to a tradition well-grounded in English custom. The originating idea of equity courts was precisely that they were courts of conscience rather than of law; in 1452, Fortescue countered a legal argument with the words "[w]e are to argue conscience here, not the law." Quoted at Baker, *An Introduction to English Legal History*, p. 124. Coke was politically outmaneuvered, and in 1616 James I issued a decree confirming the power of courts of equity to overturn verdicts at law. Later, that order was disregarded, and Bacon as Chancellor took pains to restore harmonious relations between the two systems. Nonetheless, in light of this history it is hardly surprising that Coke grounded his justification for the authority of the common law in something other than an appeal to transcendent moral principle, despite his reliance on deductivist principles. It is also significant that Coke is the person most identified with the tradition that treats common law as the fundamental law of England, rather than

as one among several competing systems. See Harold J. Berman, "The Origins of Historical Jurisprudence: Coke, Selden, Hale," 103 *Yale Law Journal* no. 7 (May 1994), 1651, 1680-81.

51. See Berman and Reid, "The Transformation of English Legal Science: From Hale to Blackstone," pp. 446-47.

52. See Berman, "The Origins of Historical Jurisprudence," pp. 1678-80. Berman notes that there is something misleading about the characterization of Coke's writings as a "theory," as though they comprised a clear and coherent methodology: "Coke's answer to the free monarchists' general theory of government and law was—no theory at all! . . . His answer to James was History, which he saw largely in terms of Tradition and Precedent." *Ibid.*, p. 1681. In searching for evidence of historically demonstrable principles Coke wandered far afield indeed. As Baker puts it: "[Coke] wrote like a helpful old wizard, anxious to pass on all his secrets before he died, but not quite sure where to begin or end. . . . [In a discussion of] a definition of fee simple . . . the commentary wanders through such disparate topics as etymology, alien status, misnomer in grants, interest rates and usury, the precedence of earth over the other elements, the correct Latin words for ponds, marshes, rushes, willows, elders, and boileries of salt, the Domesday Book, the eight parts of a deed, the styles and titles of the kings of England, the ownership of the Isle of Man, and the legal status of monsters and hermaphrodites." Baker, *Introduction to the History of English Law*, p. 218. As Baker notes, to make his system work Coke was required to distort, misstate, and even outright invent much of the precedent to which he appealed. Coke may therefore also stand, implicitly, as the earliest writer to acknowledge that the deductive model is poorly suited to the task of describing English common law.

53. Hale, *The Analysis of the Law: Being a Scheme or Abstract of the Several Titles and Partitions of the Law of England, Digested into Method* (New York: Garland Publishing, 1978); see Berman and Reid, "The Transformation of English Legal Science: From Hale to Blackstone."

54. Hale, *The History of the Common Law of England* (1713), quoted at Reid and Berman, "The Transformation of English Legal Science," p. 448.

55. See Gerald Postema, "Some Roots of the Notion of Precedent," in Laurence Goldstein, ed., *Precedent in Law* (New York: Oxford University Press, 1987).

56. Berman and Reid make the interesting point that a legal culture that employs the authority of custom as its legitimating vocabulary is particularly prone to employing "substantive legal fictions" to make changes in legal doctrine palatable. "The Transformation of English Legal Science," pp. 458-59.

57. William Blackstone, "A Discourse on the Study of the Law," (1759), reprinted in Michael Hoeflich, ed., *The Gladsome Light of Jurisprudence*, p. 54.

58. "I think it an undeniable position, that a competent knowledge of the laws of that society, in which we live, is the proper accomplishment of every gentleman and scholar; an highly useful, I had almost said essential, part of liberal and polite education. . . . [I]t is incumbent upon every man to be acquainted with those [laws] at least, with which he is immediately concerned; lest he incur the censure, as well as inconvenience, of living in society without knowing the obligations which it lays him under. And thus much may suffice for persons of inferior condition, who have neither time nor capacity to enlarge their views, beyond that contracted sphere in which they are appointed to move. But those, on whom nature and fortune have bestowed more abilities and greater leisure, cannot be so easily excused. These advantages are given them, not for the benefit of themselves only, but also of the public: and yet they cannot, in any scene of life, discharge properly their duty either to the public or themselves, without some degree of knowledge in the laws." *Ibid.*, pp. 54-55.

59. "[I]t is really amazing, that there should be no other state of life, no other occupation, art, or science, in which some method of instruction is not looked upon as requisite, except only the science of legislation, the noblest and most difficult of any. Apprenticeships are held necessary to almost every art . . . but every man of superior fortune thinks himself *born* a legislator. Yet Tully was of a different opinion: 'It is necessary,' says he, 'for a senator to be thoroughly acquainted with the constitution'; and this, he declares, is a knowledge of the most extensive nature. . . ." *Ibid.*, p. 57.

60. "The science thus committed to his charge, to be cultivated, methodized, and explained in a course of academic lectures, is that of the laws and constitution of our own country: a species of knowledge, in which the gentlemen of England have been more remarkably deficient than those of all Europe besides." *Ibid.*, pp. 53-54.

61. See Zimmerman, "Savigny's Legacy," *supra*.

62. See Michael H. Hoeflich, "Introduction," *The Gladsome Light of Jurisprudence*, p. 5. For later developments, emphasizing the influence of American educational reform on English legal education, see Hoeflich, "The Americanization of English Legal Education," 8 *Journal of Legal History* (December, 1987), pp. 244-59.

63. Jefferson wrote to Horatio G. Spafford: "I join in your reprobation of our . . . lawyers for their adherence to England and monarchy, in preference to their own country and its constitution. . . . I ascribe much of this to the substitution of Blackstone for my Lord Coke, as an elementary work." Quoted at Klafter, *Reason Over Precedents*, p. 37. Klafter notes that "staunch Federalists" such as Tapping Reeve and Peter Van Schaack had fewer reservations about the applicability of Blackstone's work. *Ibid.*, p. 36.

64. Paul D. Carrington, "The Revolutionary Idea of University Legal Education," 31 *William & Mary Law Review* 527 (Spring 1990), p. 540.

65. See Carrington, "The Revolutionary Idea of University Legal Education," pp. 527-29; see generally Donald S. Lutz, "The Relative Influence of European Writers on Late Eighteenth-Century American Political Thought," 78 *American Political Science Review* (1986), pp. 189-97. Lutz ranks various writers in terms of the number of times they were cited in American political writings published between 1760 and 1805; he finds that the most cited writers were, in descending order, Montesqieu, Blackstone and Locke. *Ibid.*, p. 93. Montesqieu continued to be universally included in lists of authors prescribed for students of American law; by contrast, English writers on legal science often did not share the Americans' enthusiasm. For example, in

1830 J.H. Dawson published "Suggestions as to the Course of Study to be Adopted, and the Selection of Books, by Parties Designed for Attorneys and Solicitors." Dawson included a long list of authors to whom students of the law might turn for Inspiration; Montesqieu was conspicuously absent from that list. Reprinted in Hoeflich, ed., *The Gladsome Light of Jurisprudence*, p. 92. Montesqieu is similarly not mentioned in Thomas J. Hogg, "An Introductory Lecture on the Study of the Civil Law" (1831), nor in Samuel Warren, "A Popular and Practical Introduction to Law Studies (How the Common Law Pupil Should Commence His Studies)" (1835), reprinted at Hoeflich, ed., *The Gladsome Light of Jurisprudence*, 183-200. On the subject of the scientific study of law, Warren did quote Fortescue's Aristotelean characterization: "Whoever desires to get a competent understanding in any faculty or science, must, by all means, be well instructed in the principles; for by reasoning from the principles which are universally acknowledged and uncontested, we arrive, at length, at the final causes of things: so that whoever is ignorant of these three—the principles, causes, and elements of any science—must needs be fatally ignorant of the science itself. On the other hand, when these are known, the science itself is known too. . . ." *Ibid.*, p. 196. Warren also quoted Dugald Stewart on the same subject: "It is evidently impossible to establish solid general principles, without the previous study of particulars: in other words, it is necessary to *begin with the examination of individual objects and individual events.* It is in this way that we can expect to arrive at general principles, which may be safely relied on, as guides to the knowledge of particular truths; and unless our principles admit of such a practical application, however beautiful they may appear to be in theory, they are of far less value than the limited acquisitions of the vulgar.'" *Ibid.*, p. 186. Warren's reading of Stewart, however, focuses on the need for *inductive* derivation of general principles.

66. Montesqieu, *The Spirit of the Laws*, Bk. I, ch. 3, quoted at Sharswood, *Lectures*, "On the Relation of Law to Moral Science," p. 72.

67. For a discussion of the role of free land in the formulation of American exceptionalist principles, see Eric Foner, *Free Soil, Free Labor, Free Men: The Ideology of the Republican Party Before the Civil War* (New York: Oxford University Press, 1995).

68. The relationship between republican and liberal political ideologies in the construction of American law and politics in the early years of the Republic has been the subject of a great deal of discussion. Famously, the description of an essentially republican order of public values has been challenged by Joyce Appleby's claim that liberal political ideology dominated American political discourse in the late eighteenth century. Joyce Appleby, *Capitalism and a New Social Order* (New York: New York University Press, 1984). On this same theme, see James T. Kloppenberg, "The Virtues of Liberalism: Christianity, Republicanism, and Ethics in Early American Political Discourse," *Journal of American History* 74 (June 1987) 9-33. In this essay the term "republican" is used broadly, to express the idea of a national character dependent on the existence of an ideal citizen type characterized by the possession of civic virtues exemplified by a sense of obligatory public participation in political—and hence legal—events.

69. Isaac Kramnick writes, "A persuasive case can be made for the Federalists as liberal modernists and the Antifederalists as nostalgic republican communitarians seeking desperately to hold on to a virtuous moral order threatened by commerce and market society." Kramnick, "The Great National Discussion," 45 *William & Mary Quarterly* no. 1 (Jan. 1988), p. 5.

70. Quoted at R.W.B. Lewis, *The American Adam: Innocence, Tragedy and Tradition in the Nineteenth Century* (Chicago: University of Chicago Press 1955). The theme was later extended to include historiography: "Inasmuch, however, as that the nature, the institutions, and the administration of the American nation are different from all others, so must its history be in an entirely different style." *Eighty Years' Progress of the United States, From the Revolutionary War to the Great Rebellion: 1781 to 1861* (Chicago: O.F. Gibbs, 1864), Preface, p. v.

71. Carrington, "The Revolutionary Idea of University Legal Education," p. 529.

72. Jefferson himself had studied law with Wythe; at various times, so did John Marshall, William Wirt, St. George Tucker, and Henry Clay. E. Lee Shepard, "George Wythe," in W. Hamilton Bryson, ed., *Legal Education in Virginia, 1779-1979: A Biographical Approach* (Charlottesville: University of Virginia Press, 1982,) p. 749. Regarding Jefferson's academic plan for the College of William & Mary, *see ibid.*, p. 660.

73. See Charles T. Cullen, "St. George Tucker," in Bryson, ed., *Legal Education in Virginia*, p. 657.

74. For a discussion of early American legal education methods generally, see Steve Sheppard, "Casebooks, Commentaries, and Curmudgeons: An Introductory History of Law in the Lecture Hall," 82 *Iowa Law Review* no. 2 (January 1997), pp. 550-644.

75. See Carrington, "The Revolutionary Idea of Legal Education," p. 542.

76. It was in response to this claim of the limited possible scale of republican rule that Jefferson appealed to a system of universities that would act as the "nursery" in which "statesmen, legislators, and judges" could be bred. Quoted at Carrington, "The Revolutionary Idea of Legal Education," p. 529.

77. Some writers also found Blackstone inadequately detailed and insufficiently rigorous for use as the basic curriculum for legal educations. "This is Blackstone's weakness," wrote Nathan Beverly Tucker in 1834, quoting his father St. George Tucker, "that in service of his philosophical project he fails to give the detail needed by a future lawyer. 'He treats most subjects in a manner too general and cursory to give the student an adequate knowledge of them. . . . After having learnt the advantage of the system, he is almost at the threshold of the science, turned back without a guide, to grope among the many volumes of our crowded libraries. This cannot be right.'" Nathaniel Beverly Tucker, "Lecture on the Study of the Law; Being an Introduction to a Course of Lectures on that Subject in the College of William and Mary," 1 *Southern Literary Messenger* 145-54 (1834-35) delivered October 27, 1834, reprinted at Hoeflich, *The Gladsome Light of Jurisprudence*, pp. 118-133.

78. "[A]s the common law is a collection of general customs, it may not be amiss to inquire whether particular customs have any, or what force, among us." Quoted at Klafter, *Reason Over Precedents*, p. 40.

79. See Klafter, *Reason Over Precedents*, pp. 40-46.

80. Carrington, "The Revolutionary Idea of University Legal Education," p. 540.

81. "Extracts from Prof. Parsons' Commemoration of Greenleaf," 6 *The Monthly Law Reporter* (new series), 413-17 (November 1853), p. 416. Greenleaf delivered the eulogy at Story's funeral. Story, in turn, was a great admirer not only of Greenleaf but also of Hoffman, calling his *Course of Study* "by far the most perfect system for the study of the law which has ever been offered to the publick." 6 *North American Review* 45-77 (November, 1817), p. 76.

82. "Scientific law assumed the mastery of rules and principles, but it was not legal taxidermy (the preservation of fixed rules) or a legal version of natural history (the hierarchical organization of fixed rules)." R. Kent Newmyer, *Supreme Court Justice Joseph Story: Statesman of the Old Republic* (New York: Oxford University Press, 1985), p. 44. Story came by his republican principles honestly; his father, a physician, had been a Son of Liberty and one of the "Indians" who dumped tea into Boston Harbor. Dumas Malone, ed., *Dictionary of American Biography* vol. IX (New York: Charles Scribners' Sons, 1931), 102-08.

83. "In the ordinary use of language it will hardly be contended that the decisions of courts constitute laws. They are themselves, at most, only evidence of what the laws are, and are not of themselves laws. . . . The law respecting negotiable instruments may be truly declared not the law of a single country only, but . . . principles established in the general commercial law." *Swift v. Tyson*, 41 U.S. 1, 18-19 (1842). Joel Seligman identifies Justice Story as occupying a "polar position in one of the great political debates of the Jacksonian period," referring to the contest between Federalists and Democrats on the question of the sources of the law. Story, by this account, was allying himself with Federalist appeals to natural law against Democrat preferences for legislation. Seligman, *The High Citadel* (Boston: Houghton Mifflin, 1978).

84. Rutherford B. Hayes described the respective styles of the two men in his diary: "Mr. G is very searching and logical in examination. It is impossible for one who has not studied the text to escape exposing his ignorance; he keeps the subject constantly in view, never stepping out of his way for the purpose of introducing his own experience. Judge Story, on the other hand, is very general in his questions, so that persons well skilled in nods affirmative and negative shakings of the head, need never more than glance at the text. . . . He is very fond of digressions to introduce amusing anecdotes." Quoted at Sheppard, "Casebooks, Commentaries, and Curmudgeons," p. 577.

85. Babbette M. Levy, *Cotton Mather* (Boston: Twayne Publishers, 1979), pp. 25-26. See, generally, Raymond P. Stearns, "Colonial Fellows of the Royal Society of London, 1661-1788," 3 *William & Mary Quarterly* (Third Series) (1946). pp. 208-68.

86. Among these were governors Francis Fauquier (of Virginia) and Robert Hunter Morris (of New York), who became members of Royal Society in the 1760s. Brook Hindle, *The Pursuit of Science in Revolutionary America: 1735-1789* (Chapel Hill: University of North Carolina Press, 1956).

87. Early lyceums included the Boston Philosophical Society (1683); the American Philosophical Society in Philadelphia (1769); the American Academy of Arts and Sciences in Boston; and the Society for Natural History in Cambridge, as well as Mechanics' Institutes established in various cities. For a good example of lawyers pursuing science in the universities, consider the case of Yale: the first two professors of "natural philosophy" were Josiah Meigs, appointed in 1794, and Benjamin Silliman, Sr., appointed in 1800 after Meigs left to found the University of Georgia. Both men were lawyers. Carrington, "The Revolutionary Idea of Legal Education," p. 543.

88. But see Bruce, *The Launching of Modern American Science, 1846-1876*, pp. 78-80 for a discussion of women who made significant contributions to American scientific institutions.

89. A typical example of popular statements on the subject appeared in the *Milwaukee Courier*, on November 2, 1842: "No one can reflect on the myriads of our species who have occupied this half of the globe—perhaps from times anterior to the flood—without longing to know something of their history; of their physical and intellectual condition; their language, manner and arts; of the revolutions through which they passed; and especially of those circumstances which caused them to disappear before the progenitors of the present red men." The *Courier* was a Whig publication, but Democrat and evangelical newspapers expressed similar sentiments. Quoted at Donald Zochert, 65 *Isis* 448-473, p. 450.

90. This omission is in sharp contrast to the eighteenth century French Philosophes, including Montesqieu, for whom Newton's causal explanations were the starting point for the enterprise of rationalizing and systematizing the messy world of human social and political life. This distinction points, again, to the divergence between American and Continental models of naturalistic legal science.

91. These institutions were clubbish and locally organized, often dominated by physicians and clergymen for whom natural history was a leisure-time activity. The Society for Natural History, for example was led in the 1830s by Charles T. Jackson, a physician who later became state chemist and geologist of Maine in 1837. One of the aspects of the development of American science that is regrettably overlooked in this paper is the role of the medical fraternity. Many of the key figures in the development of chemistry and botany—including Jacob Bigelow and Asa Gray as well as Jackson—were originally trained in medicine. Of the three learned professions of the premodern era—medicine, law, and the clergy—medicine was the one most involved in the development of experimental science. As a result, it is possible that many individuals with an interest in science pursued medical training as the best or only source of scientific education. See W.F. Bynum, *Science and the Practice of Medicine in the Nineteenth Century* (Cambridge: Cambridge University Press 1994). Moreover, many of the themes of Protestant Baconianism—the emphasis on taxonomy, reasoning by analogy, the search for unifying principles of Newtonian simplicity—also dominated the medical understanding of the late eighteenth and early nineteenth centuries. See also Hindle, *The Pursuit of Science in Revolutionary America: 1735-1789.* Interestingly, in this connection, Bynum points out that by the 1750s Scottish universities had replaced Dutch as the destination of choice for those seeking medical training overseas who lacked "the desire, money, religion, or connections to get into Oxford" (Bynum, p. 4).

92. See Walter B. Hendrickson, "Science and Culture in the American Middle West," 64 *Isis*, 326-40 (1973).

93. *Ibid.*

94. Quoted at Zochert, "Science and the Common Man in Ante-Bellum America," p. 450. Zochert notes, generally, that the sciences that held the greatest fascination for the general public were astronomy and geology.

95. Eliot had been a Congregational minister in New England. The founder of the Western Academy, Dr. George Engelmann, had also been involved in Eastern lyceums before moving West. The influence of the East, then, was transmitted West in just the way that the influence of Europe had reached across the Atlantic. Hendrickson, "Science and Culture in the American Middle West," *supra*.

96. Daniel Drake, promoter of the Western Museum Society of Cincinnati founded in 181, "An Address to the People of the Western Country," *American Journal of Science*, 203-04 (1818), quoted in Hendrickson, "Science and Culture in the American MIddle West," p. 335.

97. 5 *Act of Incorporation, Constitution and Bylaws of the Western Academy of Natural Sciences* (St. Louis, 1837), quoted in Hendrickson, "Science and Culture in the American Middle West," p. 14.

98. Of all the participants—certainly of all the lawyers—in the lyceum movement, none was more influential in its development than Silliman. He delivered the first Lowell lecture on natural theology (see below). More importantly, twenty years before Silliman had been responsible for taking the first step in the transformation of American lyceums into something more. Given a grant of money by a wealthy rock-collector, he founded a national journal of science in 1818. The *American Journal of Science and Arts*, known almost uniformly as "Silliman's Journal," was the first national journal devoted exclusively to the dissemination of scientific discoveries, debates over their significance, and descriptions of what was going on in various communities around the country.

99. See Nathan Reingold, "Science, Public Policy, and Popular Precepts: Alexander Dallas Bache and Alfred Beach as Symbolic Adversaries," in Reingold, ed., *The Sciences in the American Context: New Perspectives* (Washington, D.C.: Smithsonian Institution Press, 1979), 77-98.

100. North Carolina had established a Board of Internal Improvements, and Denison persuaded them that supporting scientific research would be profitable, a point emphasized by Silliman in the *American Journal of Science*: "From the intelligence, zeal and scientific attainments of Professor Olmstead, we cannot doubt, that (*if adequately encouraged by the local government, or by patriotic individuals*) the enterprise will produce important advantages to science, agriculture, and other useful arts, and will prove honorable to the very respectable state of North Carolina." Notice of a Geological Survey of North Carolina, *American Journal of Science* 5: 202 (1822), quoted at Walter B. Hendrickson, "Nineteenth-Century State Geological Surveys: Early Government Support of Science," 52 *Isis* 357-71 (1961).

101. The Maine Legislature's adoption in 1836 of a resolution authorizing a state survey described the enterprise as one that "may rightfully claim the encouragement of every class of industry, as involving more or less probable utility to each other and is intimately connected with the advancement of the arts and sciences, of agriculture, manufacturers, and commerce." In that same year, Charles T. Jackson, the leading geological surveyor of the period, wrote to Benjamin Silliman March 12, 1836: "The Geological Survey which have been made, or are now in progress . . . demonstrates that the communities are fully aware of the advantages, which must necessarily accrue to them, from a scientific examination of their mineral resources. It is certainly a source of congratulation that we find the American people so liberal and enlightened respecting the application of science to the arts, than the people of any European state. This is no doubt to be attributed to the generous diffusion of knowledge in our country." Quoted at Hendrickson, "Nineteenth-Century State Geological Surveys: Early Government Support of Science," 52 *Isis* 357-71, pp. 362-63 (1961).

102. Mary Ann James, "Engineering an Environment for Change: Bigelow, Peirce, and Early Nineteenth-Century Practical Education at Harvard" in Clark A. Elliott and Margaret W. Rossiter eds., *Science at Harvard University* (Bethlehem: Lehigh University Press, 1992), 55-75, p. 71.

103. Bruce, *The Launching of Modern American Science*, p. 64.

104. "Our Times," *Democratic Review* XVI (March 1845) 235-42.

105. Charles Caldwell, "Thoughts on the Moral and Other Indirect Influences of Rail-Roads," 2 *New England Magazine* (April 1832) 288-300.

106. "Rail Road to the Pacific," 4 *Harbinger* (Dec. 1846) 30-31, quoted at Leo Marx, *The Machine in the Garden: Technology and the Pastoral Ideal in America* (New York: Oxford Univ. Press), pp. 187-98.

107. "The Utility and Pleasures of Science," *Scientific American* (Aug. 1847), p. 381.

108. "Improved Hay-Maker," *Scientific American* (March 1860, new series) p. 216.

109. Bigelow did not claim to have invented the word. "To embody, as far as possible, the various topics which belong to such an undertaking, I have adopted the general name of Technology, a word sufficiently expressive, which is found in some of the older dictionaries, and is beginning to be revived in the literature of practical men at the present day." Jacob Bigelow, *Elements of Technology: Taken Chiefly from a Course of Lectures Delivered at Cambridge on the Application of the Sciences to the Useful Art, now published for the Use of Seminaries and Students* (Boston: Hilliard, Gray, Little, and Wilkins, 1829). The *Oxford English Dictionary* identifies the word "technology" (or "technologie") in use as early as the seventeenth century, at which time the word meant a book or treatise. Somewhat provincially, perhaps, the *Oxford English Dictionary* does not acknowledge Bigelow's contribution, but traces the modern usage of the term "technology" to an English author (P. Geddes) writing in the journal *Nature* in 1881, referring to a litany of fields of endeavor: "economics, physics, geology, botany, and zoology; of technology and the fine arts" (there is also a reference to an ambiguous use of the term by Jeremy Bentham in 1827, referring to "questions of technology in all its branches," by which term Bentham apparently meant any specialized knowledge). J.A. Simpson and E.S.C. Wiener, eds., *The Oxford English Dictionary* (Oxford: Clarendon Press, 1989) col. XVII, p. 705.

110. The terms of the original bequest that funded the position was a classic statement of the lyceums' justifications for

teaching science: Benjamin Thompson Count Rumford (born in Woburn, Massachusetts) instructed that the holder of the position was to "bear the character of a man of science, piety, and good morals," to teach "by regular courses of academical and public lectures, accompanied with proper experiments, the utility of the physical and mathematical sciences, for the improvement of the useful arts, and for the extension of the industry, prosperity, happiness, and wellbeing of society," to evaluate scientific discoveries and to present them to the public. James, "Engineering an Environment for Change: Bigelow, Peirce, and Early Nineteenth-Century Practical Education at Harvard."

111. Inaugural address, quoted at James, "Engineering an Environment for Change," p. 60. In *Elements of Technology* Bigelow wrote: "There has probably never been an age in which the practical applications of science have employed so large a portion of the talent and enterprise of the community, as in the present; nor one in which their cultivation has yielded such abundant rewards. And it is not the least of the distinctions of our own country, to have contributed to the advancement of this branch of improvement, by many splendid instances of inventive genius, and successful perseverance." Bigelow, *Elements of Technology*, p. v.

112. Bigelow, *Elements of Technology*, pp. 3-4.

113. "In common language we apply the name of *sciences*, to those departments of knowledge which are more speculative, or abstract, in their nature, and which are conversant with truths or with phenomena, that are in existence at the time we contemplate them. The *arts*, on the contrary, are considered as departments of knowledge, which have their origin in human ingenuity, which depend on the active, or formative processes of the human mind, and which without these would not have existed." *Ibid.*, p. 1. Bigelow's "technology" included a wide range of fields that a modern reader would recognize under the general rubric of "applied science": the study of materials from the mineral, plant and animal kingdoms; various "arts" including locomotion, illumination, and design; the study of forces, the combination of materials, timekeeping, and so on. Bigelow makes no mention of the learned professions (medicine, law, theology,) nor of moral philosophy nor the study of languages. Consistent with the definitions quoted above, Bigelow would have treated law as a non-scientific art. In order to be considered "scientists," then, legal scientists were required to push the idea of the grand synthesis further than some of their empirically-minded colleagues would have been willing to go.

114. *Ibid.*, p. 1. (citing the example of chemistry).

115. In 1830, at Bigelow's urging, President Quincy appointed Daniel Treadwell, president of the Boston Mechanics' Institute to take the post temporarily, and in 1834 Treadwell was named the second Rumford professor. An inventor who never graduated college, Treadwell was skeptical of the importance of theoretical science. "[I]nventions of great importance are often made without any scientific knowledge of the principles of laws on which their efficiency depends," he said, resulting from "the resources of genius, aided by industry and a careful observation of facts." James, "Engineering an Environment for Change," p. 63.

116. James, "Engineering an Environment for Change," pp. 61-69. Bruce Sinclair, however, asserts that the practical intent of Lawrence School "was almost immediately subverted" and "[t]he school . . . became instead a preserve of pure science ideology." Sinclair, "Harvard, MIT, and the Ideal Technical Education," in *Science at Harvard University*, 76-95, p. 77.

117. William Ellery Channing, Milwaukee *Sentinel*, Aug. 17, 1841, quoted Zochert "Science and the Common Man in Ante-Bellum America," p. 449.

118. As early as 1819, a physician and amateur chemist, reacting to the supplanting of Lavoisier's theories of chemical interaction, expressed outrage rather than embarrassment at his inability to appreciate the new discoveries in the field. "It is impossible for those of us, who have formed our ideas of the chemical operations of nature on the principles which he taught, to turn with complacency from a theory like his to a state of science so unsettled and so obscure, as modern chemistry now is . . . they have made it less captivating to the general scholar; they have lessened the interest with which it is viewed by those not immediately engaged in its pursuit, by rendering it more complicated and more difficult to be understood, and less applicable as a whole to the explication of those phenomena of the natural world with which we are most familiar." John Ware, "Gorham's Chemistry," 9 *North American Review* (June 1819), pp. 113-35, 134.

119. Letter, July 28, 1819, quoted at Daniels, "The Process of Professionalization in American Science: the Emergent Period, 1820-1860," (1976), p. 153. The frustration continued: William Rogers, at the time the state geologist of New Jersey and Pennsylvania, vented his frustration in a letter to his brother in 1838. "How can these gentlemen pretend to judge my reports? . . . the thought of a legislative body employing itself in venting spleen or exercising wit upon a paper of which but few of them have any adequate comprehension really fills me with indignation." Letter from William B. Rogers to Henry D. Rogers, letter of March 8, 1838, quoted at Hendrickson, "Nineteenth-Century State Geological Surveys: Early Government Support of Science," p. 143.

120. Whewell, *Philosophy of the Inductive Sciences, Founded upon Their History* (London: J.W. Parker, 1840).

121. While he is most famous for his development of the inductive scientific method, Whewell also was a natural theologian of the first order, whose other books included *Indications of the Creator: Extracts, Bearing upon Theology, from the History and the Philosophy of the Inductive Sciences* (London: J.W. Parker, 1842) and *The Elements of Morality, Including Polity* (New York: Harper, 1852); he also authored a translation of Grotius in 1853. Whewell's commitment to Baconianism is indicated by the title of the second part to the *Philosophy of the Inductive Sciences*: *Novum Organon Renovatum* (London: J.W. Parker, 1858). Thus Whewell covered natural theology, science, political science, and law, all from his vantage-point as an astronomer.

122. One may speculate, in fact, that the turn inward on the part of the scientific community encouraged legal writers to turn for their metaphors to the more readily available social sciences after the 1870s. For a discussion of the historiography of institutional development in American science, see Sally Gregory Kohlstedt, "Institutional History," 1 *Osiris* (second series, 1985), pp. 17-36.

123. The American Geological Society had its first meeting in 1840. There were seven members, all practicing geologists drawn from state geological surveys. At the second meeting in 1841, each member was allowed to invite six friends. Already the focus of the organization had moved beyond geology; the keynote speaker at the 1841 session was the ubiquitous and distinguished Benjamin Silliman, Sr. In 1842, in a session attended by Nathan Appleton (founder of the Lowell mills) as well as Charles Lyell, the association added "Naturalists" to its title and elected to permit membership to individuals belonging to any other scientific society. Sally Kohlstedt, "A Step Toward Scientific Self-Identity in the United States: The Failure of the National Institute, 1844," 62 *Isis*, 339-62 (September, 1971).

124. Quoted at Bruce, *The Launching of Modern American Science*, p. 224.

125. Bruce, *The Launching of Modern American Science*, p. 231.

126. In 1849, for example, the *Astronomical Journal* appeared. This journal was described by Gould as the first journal unequivocally dedicated to "not the diffusion, but the advancement" of scientific knowledge. Benjamin A. Gould, "On the Establishment and Progress of the Astronomical Journal," *AAAS Proceedings*, vol. III (1850), quoted at George H. Daniels, "The Process of Professionalization in American Science," p. 159.

127. Haskell, *The Emergence of Professional Social Science* (Urbana: University of Illinois Press, 1977), pp. 69-70. Addressing the opening session of Columbia College in 1858, Lieber declared that the scientific study of history depended on recognizing "three laws on which man's material well-being and . . . his civilization are founded": that "Man is no finding animal—he must produce"; that "[m]en are so constituted that they have far more wants . . . than other animals"; and that "the wants of men . . . infinitely increase and are by Providence decreed to increase with advancing civilization; so that his progress necessitates intenser production and quickened exchange." Lieber, "Address," in William Betts, *Addresses of the Newly Appointed Professors of Columbia College* (New York: Columbia University Press, 1858), pp. 80-81. Lieber is the most clearly social scientific of all the legal scientists, appealing to principles of "political economy" and "economics," "sociology" and German "scientific history," leading Paul Carrington to conclude that his work was a precursor to the sociobiological theories of E.O. Wilson. See Paul D. Carrington, "The Theme of Early American Law Teaching: the Political Ethics of Francis Lieber," 42 *Journal of Legal Education* no. 3 339-98 (September, 1992). Lieber also speaks of Christianity as "a co-efficient of the highest power of nearly all the elements of humanity and civilization," (*ibid.*, p. 111) in the course of an extended discussion of the opposing principles of "socialism and individualism." Lieber was a prolific and polymathic scholar; among other endeavors, he edited the early editions of *Encyclopaedia Americana* and a supplementary volume, *A Popular Dictionary of Arts, Sciences, Literature, History, Politics and Biography* (Philadelphia: Carey & Lea, 1831). The supplement contained a lengthy article on "Law, Legislation, Codes," which ended with the very social-scientific sounding proposition that "the part of true wisdom is, not so much to search out any abstract theory of universal jurisprudence, as to examine what, for each country in particular, may best promote its substantial interests, preserve its rights, protect its morals, and give permanence to its liberties." *Ibid.*, p. 592. Sharswood, interestingly, cited the *Encyclopaedia Americana* for a discussion of different methods of learning the law. Sharswood, *Lectures*, "On Legal Education," p. 57.

128. Perhaps the single most important product of the Sheffield School, in turn, was Daniel Coit Gilman, founding president of Johns Hopkins University and the "greatest academic professionalizer of the nineteenth century." Haskell, *The Emergence of Professional Social Science*, p. 75.

129. Historians who have focused on particular cases have invariably found that the legal profession emerged from the Revolutionary experience with much of its prestige intact. See, e.g., Dennis R. Nolan, "The Effect of the Revolution on the Bar: the Maryland Experience," 62 *Virginia Law Review* (1976); W. Hamilton Bryson, "The History of Legal Education in Virginia" 14 *University of Richmond Law Review* (1979). Tellingly, lawyers generally continued to play prominent roles in electoral politics throughout the first half of the nineteenth century. *See*, e.g., Maxwell Bloomfield, "Law vs. Politics: The Self-Image of the American Bar (1830-1860)," 12 *The American Journal of Legal History* 306-23 (1968).

130. Quoted at Charles M. Cook, *The American Codification Movement: A Study of Antebellum Legal Reform* (Westport, Conn.: Greenwood Press, 1981), p. 162.

131. See Gerard W. Gawalt, "Sources of Anti-Lawyer Sentiment in Massachusetts, 1740-1840." 14 *American Journal of Legal History* (1970), 223-232; Gary B. Nash, "The Philadelphia Bench and Bar," 7 *Comparative Studies in Society and History* no. 2 (1965) 203-220. Both Gawalt and Nash record high levels of social and economic insularity among lawyers, including patterns of intermarriage within the profession. For a general treatment of class in nineteenth century America, see E. Digby Baltzell, *Philadelphia Gentlemen: The Making of a National Upper Class* (Glencoe, Ill.: The Free Press, 1958).

132. See Robert Stevens, *Law School: Legal Education in America from the 1850s to the 80s* (Chapel Hill: University of North Carolina Press, 1983).

133. See William E. Nelson, *Americanization of the Common Law: The Impact of Legal Change on Massachusetts Society, 1760-1830* (Cambridge, Mass.: Harvard University Press, 1975).

134. Maxwell Bloomfield, "Law vs. Politics: The Self-Image of the American Bar" (1830-1860), 12 *The American Journal of Legal History* (1968), pp. 307-310. Bloomfield points out that the new independent journals were different from their forerunners. "Whereas earlier journals . . . tended to be speculative and treated many subjects of general interest to the educated community, the typical magazine of the post-1830 years conceived its function in rigorously utilitarian terms." The new journals were designed to serve "the workingmen of the profession, disdained theorizing and offered their readers a 'medium of communication concerning legal matters of fact' useful and interesting to gentlemen of the bar." Bloomfield's observations accord with the suggestion made earlier that the divergence between utility and improvement in ideas of legal education reflected a growing division between the ideas of working lawyers and legal educators.

135. Quoted at Bloomfield, "Law vs. Politics: The Self-Image of the American Bar," p. 307.

136. Daniel Mayes, "An Address to the Students of Law in Transylvania University," (1834), p. 160. Comparisons to medicine—while common—were almost always drawn as a call for greater prestige for the legal profession, recognizing law's status as one of the three traditional learned professions. Until Langdell's (and Eliot's) famous analogy of the library to the medical laboratory, however, legal scientists did *not* ordinarily call for an emulation of the methods of medical research. This is interesting, in part, in that medicine was much less affected by the tendencies of Protestant Baconianism than most of the natural sciences, in part because of its early separation from "natural philosophy" and natural history, its extensive early European (particularly Scottish) influences, and its early institutionalization in American universities. See, generally, Bynum, *Science and the Practice of Medicine in the Nineteenth Century.* For a discussion of the important role of physicians in American and European scientific associations in the early eighteenth century, see Hindle, *The Pursuit of Science in Revolutionary America*, pp. 36-37.

137. Greenleaf, "Inaugural Address," p. 139.

138. Tucker, "Lecture on the Study of Law," p. 121.

139. These included apparently anomalous entries such as works by Aristotle and Leibniz. Hoffman, however, credits Aristotle with being the true inventor of "the system of induction, so uniformly imputed alone to Lord Bacon"; he explains the inclusion of non-Christian and other authors as examples that provide good training for the mind, to produce "a manly intellectual vigour, an ingenuous modesty and dignity of habit, an energy of thought and diction, and a reach of comprehensive knowledge which distinguish the true English scholar," in contrast to "the feeble speculation which almost all modern systems of morality encourages." Hoffman, *Course of Legal Study*, pp. 95, 92.

140. "Should there be any (which we trust will never be the case) who will be content to glean a few works from the first and second Titles only of this volume, they may assume the name of DUPONDII, or students of small consideration, from the most common coin known in the Roman Empire, of the value of a penny sterling. Such Elementary attainments may sometimes pass them to the Bar; but as they have scarce attained 'ad limina legitimae scientiae,' they will never reap the honours of those 'qui juris nodos, legumque ainigmata solvunt.'" Hoffman, *Course of Study*, p. 53, note.

141. "There are to be found in our profession, as in every other, many, who either have not learned, or who having learned cease to remember, that there is a *science* of jurisprudence as well as an *art* of jurisprudence. Who standing in the same relation to law, that the cook does to chemistry, are actively engaged in practice during long lives, ignorant of the principles of the science upon which their art is founded. . . ." Mayes, "An Address to the Students of Law in Transylvania University," p. 145.

142. Sharswood, *Lectures Introductory to the Study of the Law*, pp. 38-39.

143. "Dane's Abridgment," 4 *American Jurist and Law Magazine* (1830) p. 66, quoted at Cook, *The American Codification Movement: A Study of Antebellum Legal Reform*, p. 81. The *American Jurist* was edited by George Hilliard, Charles Sumner and Luther Cushing. Hilliard was one of the most influential reformist writers; his son Francis authored the first national digest of torts in 1859. Francis Hilliard, *The Law of Torts or Private Wrongs* (2 vol.s) (Boston: Little, Brown & Co. 1859).

144. Sharswood, *Lectures*, "On Legal Education," p. 52.

145. Hoffman, *Course of Legal Study*, pp. 25-26. In Hoffman's view, in fact, the very idea of distinct "nations" was a thing of the past, soon to give way to the marvelous unity of the species wrought by technology. "Legislation, science, arts and literature, are no longer even national, but are fast becoming the common right and possession of the world. The remarkable melioration of the physical, moral and intellectual state of man . . . may be referred primarily to the numerous facilities which have overcome time and space . . . so that individual, local, and national habits and prejudices are fast disappearing, and the day approaching when the world may know but one homogeneous system of constitutions, laws, science, literature, and manners; and when morals, and even religion, shall so harmonize with the highest intellectual attainments, as to elevate our species far beyond the conceptions even of poets, or the imaginations of philosophers in their ideal republics." *Ibid.*, p. x.

146. "In this science, as in the comparative anatomy of a sister profession, we best understand our own system of laws by comparing it with those of other nations. Man is to be studied in every period of his social existence, from the savage to the civilized state, in order to perceive the great truth, that in every condition of freedom, of intelligence, of commerce, and of wealth, his habits, his virtues, his vices, the objects of his desires, and hence the laws necessary for his betterment, are essentially the same." Simon Greenleaf, "A Discourse Pronounced at the Inauguration of the Author as Royall Professor of Law in Harvard University" (1834), p. 139.

147. "Men also exist in a state of political society, their natures unchanged, their private social relations unaltered by this additional bond of union. They carry with them into the political community, of which they become members, all the duties that before rested on them as individuals, or as parties to a private social contract, and retain all the rights which belonged to them, when considered in either of the aspects before spoken of, except such as it is necessary to renounce, for the good of the community of which they form a part." Daniel Mayes, "An Address to the Students of Law in Transylvania University," (1834), p. 151.

148. Sharswood, *Lectures*, p. 41.

149. Field, *The Magnitude and Importance of Legal Science*, pp. 13-14.

150. Mayes, *Address*, p. 149.

151. See, generally, Peter J. Bowler, *Evolution: The History of an Idea* (Berkeley: University of California Press, 1989). For a discussion of the significance of pre-Darwinian evolutionary theories in nineteenth century American culture, see John Greene, *The Death of Adam: Evolution and Its Impact on Western Thought* (Ames, Iowa: Iowa University Press 1959). The issue of evolutionary models in the location of nineteenth century legal scientists on the natural scientific spectrum is a complex one. Cuvier, and his student Agassiz, were outright anti-evolutionists who argued that the forms of species were given and immutable. *Ibid.*, pp. 113-115. Cuvier thus rejected the earlier theories of Lamarck, who had suggested that forms change spontaneously in response

to their environments, resulting in an historical sequence of forms that accorded with an hierarchical order of complexity. Chambers, in *Vestiges*, adopted the idea promoted by German Idealists that existing forms of life transmutated into higher forms, while the British naturalist William Paley led a school of thought that saw God creating higher forms of life in successive stages as the condition of the planet "improved." *Ibid.*, Chapter III. The disagreements between these writers, however, were all encompassed within the general acceptance of some version of a "great chain of being," in which nature was seen as a carefully structured system, designed by God, with man at the top of a scale of natural forms. This idea appeared in the analyses of legal scientists as a theory of constant improvement in human society. Their more particular claims, moreover, were more firmly rooted in the scientific history of von Ranke and German Romantics than in any particular biological model. Later social scientists and legal writers, such as Sir Henry Maine and Holmes, would make the parallel between biological and social evolution explicit. Elliott points out, for example, that Savigny speaks of 'an organically progressive jurisprudence'; Sir Henry Maine, in 1861, spoke of stages of societal development; Oliver Wendell Holmes, in 1880, analogized the development of legal doctrine to the evolution of the feline clavicle. Elliott, "The Evolutionary Tradition in Jurisprudence," pp. 41, 44, 51.

152. Hoffman, *Course of Study*, p. 23.

153. Mayes, *Address*, pp. 151-52, 153.

154. Sharswood, *Lectures*, "On Legal Education," p. 54.155. I do not necessarily mean that each of these elements are unique to American natural and legal science. There are, however, two very sharp differences in the ways American ideas about "science" from the ways they developed elsewhere. In the natural sciences, while an emphasis on natural theology was common (witness Agassiz' success on his arrival from Switzerland in 1847), the connection to Common Sense as a justifying system was not. This distinction had limited consequences for natural science, beyond perhaps the fact that American universities were much later than their Continental counterparts in adopting laboratory-based experimental methods. The consequences of the connection to Common Sense had much more immediate significance, however, for the models of "science" that were available for appropriation by legal writers. The exceptional case among European nations was England, where writers shared the same access to and admiration for Common Sense that was prevalent in America. American writings were quite similar to those of some English writers at the same period. The difference in that case was that in England these remained essentially speculative criticisms; no significant changes were made to the model of legal education in England, due to institutional resistance from the Inns of court. In America, by contrast, the end of the story is that a Harvard-dominated version of legal science came to be the nearly universal model for legal education.

156. There is a rich literature devoted to exploring the relationship between Puritanism and scientific thought in England. Known as the "Puritans and science" debate, in its present state the general historical consensus denies the direct causal relation between Puritan values and the creation of the Royal Society of London. There were radical reformists who were involved in early scientific thought in seventeenth century England, but among the Wadham and Gresham College groups, and the founding membership of the Royal Society, moderate Puritans and liberal Anglicans predominated. Indeed, several of the Puritan figures who appear most prominently among the founders of the Royal Society later converted to Anglicanism and ended their lives as bishops. See I.B. Cohen, *Puritanism and the Rise of Modern Science* (New Brunswick, NJ: Rutgers University Press 1990), p. 221. The story is quite different in the American case, however. There, from the beginning, the methodological imperatives of Baconianism were interpreted through a strict Calvinist lens.

157. In 1643, for example, Thomas Browne referred to nature as "that universall and publick Manuscript that lies expans'd unto the eyes of all." Thomas Browne, *Religio Medici* (1643).

158. He would later be a revolutionary leader, a member of the Continental Congress and the New Jersey legislature, and a major figure in the campaign for New Jersey's ratification of the United States Constitution. See Carrington, "The Revolutionary Idea of University Legal Education," p. 527, 544.

159. The radical Republican writer William Leggett quoted Dugald Stewart on the virtues of laissez-faire in 1836: "Little else is required to carry a state to the highest degree of opulence, but peace, easy taxes, and a tolerable administration of justice; all the rest being brought about by the natural course of things. All governments which thwart this natural course, which force things into another channel, or which endeavor to arrest the progress of society at a particular point, are unnatural, and to support themselves are obliged to be oppressive and tyrannical. These sentiments, according to our view, comprise the essence of both democratick and economick theory." *Cleveland Plaindealer*, Dec. 17, 1836, reprinted in Lawrence H. White, ed., *Democratick Editorials: Essays in Jacksonian Political Economy by William Leggett* (Indianapolis: Liberty Press, 1984).

160. "[W]hen I perceive a tree before me, my faculty of seeing gives me not only a notion of simple apprehension of the tree, but a belief of its existence . . . and this judgment or belief is not got by comparing ideas, it is included in the very nature of the perception." Reid, *An Inquiry into the Human Mind on the Principles of Common Sense*, vol. 1, p. 209 (Edinburgh: Bell & Bradfute, 1801).

161. One of the key changes that this involved was the move away from training tutors in the classics, toward the development of textbooks that provided the authoritative right answers. This was largely an effort to consolidate control over unruly elements within the membership, but it had the effect of disassociating the Classical tradition from Protestant natural theology. The move to textbooks was, of course, also characteristic of legal science.

162. Bowen, who also introduced Kant to American colleges, is another fascinating figure in American intellectual history. He was a follower of Henry C. Carey, the leading theorist of the American school of political economy that provided the framework for the Whig's American System. In 1869, Charles Eliot transferred the teaching of political economy away from Bowen to a newly established professorship given to Charles F. Dunbar, a graduate of Harvard Law School. "Dunbar," writes Dorothy Ross, "quickly adopted the new scientific role and refrained from public advocacy." Ross, *The Origins of American Social Science*, p. 78.

163. See chapter 1 of this book.

164. William Paley, *Natural Theology: Or Evidences of the Existence and Attributes of the Deity, Collected from the Appearances of Nature* (London, 1802, reprinted at Cambridge, MA: Hilliard & Brown, 1830). Paley argued that adaptation of the structure of organisms to suit their functions was evidence of Providence, and hence proof of design; as Peter Bowler points out, Darwin's reliance on adaptation as the central process of evolution "turn[ed] the logic of Paley's argument on its head." Bowler, *Evolution: The History of an Idea*, p. 157.

165. As Tyler described it, Protestant Baconianism was a matter of humility in the face of the awesome splendor of Creation. "[T]he spirit of this philosophy is that in order to become philosophers truly so called, men must cast off that intellectual pride, which vainly strives to find out the secrets of nature by mere reasoning." Samuel Tyler, 12 "The Baconian Philosophy," *Biblical Repertory and Princeton Review* 362 (1840).

166. In time, in a pattern directly parallel to that of legal education, this would lead to the conclusion that the study of Scripture itself should be conducted by "that [method] which is pursued in the science of physics, by the maxims of Bacon and Newton." Leonard Woods, Jr., *Letters to Unitarians* (Andover, 1822), quoted at Hovenkamp, *Science and Religion in America*, p. 61.

167. The search for analogies as the source for a grand synthesis was eloquently described in 1852 by Harvard natural historian Thaddeus William Harris in his explication of the "Law of Unity": "[A]ll the observations of all the naturalists in all ages seem only to have elucidated this truth, that *creation is one*; different phenomena, different combinations, different planes, but the same identical law. . . . [The] work of science is to trace this clew through all modifications." Harris, "Man and Nature," 53 *Christian Examiner* 116-18 (1852). Harris was a follower of Agassiz, and rival of Gray for professorship in natural history (see below). In his article, Harris made the influence of German Idealism explicit, citing Fichte, Schelling, Goethe, and Hegel as his inspirations.

168. For a discussion of these same themes in a later period, see Samuel Haber, *Efficiency and Uplift; Scientific Management in the Progressive Era, 1890-1920* (Chicago: University of Chicago Press 1964).

169. Bruce, *The Launching of Modern American Science*, p. 42.

170. Edward Hitchcock, later the founder of the American Association of Geologists, was perhaps the exemplar case of the scientist as natural theologian. See Stanley M. Guralnick, "Geology and Religion Before Darwin: The Case of Edward Hitchcock, Theologian and Geologist," 63 *Isis* 529-43 (December 1972). Hitchcock, the most prominent surveyor of his day, held a chair in geology and natural theology at Amherst. Trained as a Congregationalist minister, as well as having studied chemistry with Silliman, Sr. at Yale, Hitchcock devoted a large part of his career to presenting "evidences" of God in nature. Hitchcock depended for his proof on both specific biblical citations and detailed analogies, such as one between the seasons of the year and the attributes of God, or another analogizing the metamorphosis of insects and the doctrine of resurrection, claiming of insect metamorphosis that "many able writers on natural theology have considered as direct proof of future resurrection." In the end Hitchcock's aim was to achieve the degree of certainty for the claims of religious philosophy that were promised for natural philosophy. "The manner in which I have endeavored to defend the Scripture doctrine of the resurrection of the body, by an appeal to certain principles of chemistry and physiology seems to me quite conclusive." Hitchcock, *Religious Lectures on Peculiar Phenomena in the Four Seasons*, quoted in Hovenkamp, *Religion and Science in America*, p. 42. Hitchcock's arguments by analogy, in fact, went farther than conservative theologians were willing to follow. Leonard Woods, who taught Scottish Realism at Andover Theological Seminary—which had split off from Harvard during the Unitarian Controversy—warned against "strict analogy" between God and the natural world, in "Dangers to be Avoided in Analogical Reasoning" Hitchcock's arguments, however, were squarely in line with the positions of the most radical evangelicals, figures such as Warren Burton, who used his review of William Whewell's *Astronomy and General Physics* as an opportunity to declare his ontological vision: "deity operated directly upon and through the material universe without the intervention of what philosophers call Laws . . . all the changes of nature proceed from the instantaneous impulses of his Almighty Will." Otherwise, God would be an "idle being" and the world "but a machine." Burton, "Divine Agency in the Material Universe," 18 *Christian Examiner* 315-21 (1835). As noted earlier, that a religious journal should carry Burton's review was far from unusual.

171. See discussion, below, under "Improvement."

172. The "nebular hypothesis" refers to the theory that planets formed out of clouds of dust that gathered in "nebulae" around stars. This theory replaced the older account that described the planets as having been produced when pieces of the Sun were knocked loose by massive collisions with stellar objects. The nebular hypothesis was the center of a huge controversy within and between the American communities of religious and scientific thinkers; Ronald Numbers, however, persuasively argues that the controversy demonstrates a successful strategy of accommodation between the two discourses rather than the beginning of an irrevocable split between the two. Numbers, *Creation by Natural Law: Laplace's Nebular Hypothesis in American Thought* (Seattle: University of Washington Press, 1977).

173. See Milton Millhauser, *Just Before Darwin: Robert Chambers and Vestiges* (Middletown, Connecticut: Wesleyan University Press, 1959). For a discussion of public attitudes toward evolutionary theory before Darwinism, see John C. Greene, *The Death of Adam; Evolution and Its Impact on Western Thought* (Ames, Iowa: Iowa State University Press, 1959).

174. Quoted at Bruce, *The Launching of Modern American Science*, p. 29.

175. Agassiz, "Essay on Classification" in *Contributions to the Natural History of the United States* (1857).

176. Agassiz, "Sketch of the Natural Provinces of the Animal World and their Relation to the Different Types of Man," in Nott and Gliddon *Types of Mankind* (Philadelphia, 1854), quoted at Lurie, "Louis Agassiz and the Races of Man."

177. "Science and Scientific Schools," 2 *American Journal of Education* 363 (1856), quoted at Daniels, "The Process of Professionalization in American Science: the Emergent Period, 1820-1860," p. 76.

178. Hovenkamp, *Science and Religion in America*, p. 104.
179. *Ibid.*, p. 105.
180. William LaPiana states the case nicely: "If one can identify a single problem in our modern understanding of American law in the first half of the 19th century, it is our inability to take seriously the proposition that Protestant Christianity was the strongest cultural force in the nation. Whatever ideas the legal profession had about the sources of public law and the nature of the Constitution, there was widespread agreement that the principles of private law were congruent with and dictated by the absolutely true requirements of Christian morality. Law was principles, and properly decided cases reflected those principles, which themselves, in the end, were God's plan for governing the nation." William LaPiana, "Honor Langdell," 20 *Law & Social Inquiry* no. 3 (Summer 1995), p. 762.
181. "Notes on the First Title" ("Moral and Political Philosophy").
182. *Ibid.* (emphasis added).
183. *Ibid.*, pp. 64-65, 67-71. Finally, Hoffman cited the Bible as a source for eloquence, an exemplar of "sublimity" in expression.
184. Greenleaf, "A Discourse Pronounced at the Inauguration of the Author as Royall Professor of Law in Harvard University," p. 144.
185. Simon Greenleaf, *A Treatise on the Law of Evidence* (Boston: C.C. Little & J. Brown, 1842) and *The Testimony of the Evangelists Examined by the Rules of Evidence Administered in Courts of Justice* (New York: James Cockroft, 1874).
186. Tucker, p. 224. An anonymous editorialist in the *Southern Literary Messenger*, writing three years after Tucker, called for an abandonment of the teaching of English law in favor of, inter alia, moral philosophy, "for by a contemplation of their duties as members of God's great family, the students would discover that the streams of the law descend from the great fountains of truth and justice. . . ." Anonymous, "Study of the Law," 3 *Southern Literary Messenger* 25-31 (1837) in Hoeflich, *The Gladsome Light of Jurisprudence*, p. 211.
187. David Dudley Field, "The Magnitude and Importance of Legal Science. An Address at the Opening of the Law School of the University of Chicago, September 31st 1859" (New York: William J. Read, 1859), p. 7.
188. Sharswood, *Lectures*, p. 40. Sharswood also quoted with approval "the advice given by one of the old lawyers of the interior of our State" to a newly appointed justice of the peace: "to read no lawbook but the Bible, and decide every case according to the dictates of his own conscience. He would find, in ninety-nine cases out of an hundred, that his decisions would be affirmed on an appeal."
189. It is noteworthy that where conflicts between religion and natural science were debated in the mid-1600s, they were in fact debated in political terms. For example, Hobbes' objection to Boyle's claim that he had produced a vacuum was that this was impossible, since where there was vacuum there was nothing over which the King could exercise sovereignty, and the King's sovereignty necessarily extended everywhere in England. See Steven Shapin and Simon Schaffer, *Leviathan and the Air-Pump: Hobbes, Boyle, and the Experimental Life* (Princeton, NJ: Princeton University Press 1985).
190. Edward Everett, "Character of Lord Bacon," *North American Review* 16 (1823), p. 300.
191. Brazer, "A Review of an Argument in Support of Natural Religion," 19 *Christian Examiner and Religious Miscellany* 140 (1835).
192. For extended discussions on the meaning of "Baconianism" in the early 1800s, see George H. Daniels, *American Science in the Age of Jackson* (New York: Columbia University Press, 1968); Theodore Dwight Bozeman, *Protestants in an Age of Science: The Baconian Ideal an Antebellum American Religious Thought* (Chapel Hill: University of North Carolina Press, 1977).
193. William Stanhope Smith, *A Comprehensive View of the Leading and Most Important Principles of Natural and Revealed Religion* (New Brunswick: Deare and Myer, 1815), p. 68.
194. Hovenkamp, *Science and Religion in America*, p. 33.
195. "In the department of Theology, the necessity of a learned ministry for the defence of our common faith against the common enemy has been urged with strength of argument and fervor or eloquence. . . . In Medicine too, the same necessity is felt and admitted. . . . And should less be done for the Law, in which our liberties have their being. . . . The age of mere fanaticism and cant, of bold empiricism and noisy declamation, of passionate appeals to prejudice, and forensic buffoonery, it is to be hoped, is passed away. Men are now to be addressed through their understandings. They are to be treated as rational beings, and convinced by argument and reason." Simon Greenleaf, "A Discourse Pronounced at the Inauguration of the Author as Royall Professor of Law in Harvard University" (1834), reprinted in Hoeflich, *The Gladsome Light of Jurisprudence*, p. 139.
196. "In this science, as in the comparative anatomy of a sister profession, we best understand our own system of laws by comparing it with those of other nations. Man is to be studied in every period of his social existence, from the savage to the civilized state, in order to perceive the great truth, that in every condition of freedom, of intelligence, of commerce, and of wealth, his habits, his virtues, his vices, the objects of his desires, and hence the laws necessary for his government, are essentially the same." Greenleaf, *Address*, p. 139. Greenleaf, like other writers discussed in this paper, treats "history" in the general model of natural history, i.e. the development of progressively superior forms. E. Donald Elliott identifies this idea as a pre-Darwinian form of evolutionary theory. Elliott, "The Evolutionary Tradition in Jurisprudence," 85 *Columbia Law Review* 38 (1985). For example, Savigny speaks of 'an organically progressive jurisprudence'; Sir Henry Maine, in 1861, spoke of stages of societal development; Oliver Wendell Holmes, in 1880, analogized the development of legal doctrine to the evolution of the feline clavicle. *Ibid.*, pp. 41, 44, 51.
197. An anonymous editorial entitled "The Legal Profession," 1 *The Law Reporter* (1839) quoted Bacon on "the science of Human Nature": "This knowledge [of human nature] is to man the end and term of knowledges." Reprinted in Hoeflich, *The Gladsome Light of Jurisprudence*, p. 218.

198. Hoffman, *Course of Study*, p. 82. One point that can cause confusion for modern reason was the tendency of nineteenth century writers to treat *all* prior great writings as elements of their own system. Thus Hoffman, for example, recommends the study of the works of Aristotle, despite his obvious lack of grounding in the Christian faith. Regarding Aristotle's *Ethics* Hoffman pronounces that it is "the most perfect specimen of scientific morality" the study of which will produce "a manly intellectual vigour, an ingenuous modesty and dignity of habit, an energy of thought and diction, and a reach of comprehensive knowledge which distinguish the true English scholar," in contrast to "the feeble speculation which almost all modern systems of morality encourages." *Ibid.*, p. 92. His version of reading Aristotle, however, again appeals to the Christian conscience. "Philosophy confines itself to the perishing interests of the present world; christianity, looking beyond those interests, takes a loftier aim. . . . Yet to the man of piety, it may be a matter of edification, to compare the virtue of philosophical firmness with the grace of christian patience; and to observe how nearly the rules discovered by reason and experience, as most conducive to the happiness of our present state, coincide with those precepts which are given in the Gospel, in order to fit us for a better [world.]" *Ibid.*, p. 94). Far from implying a fondness for geometric deductivism, however, Hoffman cites Aristotle as the true inventor of "the system of induction, so uniformly imputed alone to lord Bacon." *Ibid.*, p. 95.

199. Mayes, *Address*, p. 158.

200. "The subject, of all law, is man, its object, the promotion of his happiness. Man being its subject, and his happiness its object, its rules must necessarily be framed, in direct reference to his nature; and to this end, he is to be contemplated in every aspect in which he is found to exist, and in all the diversified relations which he bears to the persons and things, by which he is surrounded." Daniel Mayes, "An Address to the Students of Law in Transylvania University," p. 149.

201. Sharswood, *Lectures*, "Of Natural Law," pp. 112, 123, 116.

202. *Ibid.*, p. 123.

203. *Ibid.*, p. 121.

204. Tucker, "Lecture on the Study of the Law," pp. 124-25. "Of this last description are Euclid's elements, in which it is interesting to observe that no one proposition could with propriety be made to change its place. . . . Blackstone's Commentaries may be cited as an example of a *philosophical* analysis." Tucker proposed "to make occasional changes in [Blackstone's] arrangement, substituting one more logical, though perhaps less philosophical." *Ibid.*, p. 125, 126. Tucker's proposal to develop a legal science modelled after geometry was not so much an appeal to deductivism (as he, at least, would have understood it) as to a system characterized by what Thomas Gray has called "completeness," (Gray argues that "legal theories are defined by the relations they establish among five possible goals of legal systems: comprehensiveness, completeness, formality, conceptual order and acceptability." Gray, "Langdell's Orthodoxy," p. 6). This, however, may tell us more about Tucker's conception of geometry than about his ideas regarding the science of law. The point here is that to modern ears, deductivism is essentially the contradiction of the idea of natural science; in the early decades of the nineteenth century, Tucker thought of himself as appealing to the very latest in the inductive methods of Protestant Baconianism. Quoting his father, he points out the deficiencies in Blackstone's approach: "He treats most subjects in a manner too general and cursory to give the student an adequate knowledge of them. . . . After having learnt the advantage of the system, he is almost at the threshold of the science, turned back without a guide, to grope among the many volumes of our crowded libraries. This cannot be right." *Ibid.*, p. 125. The criticism of lack of specific detail is a characteristic nineteenth century natural scientist's challenge to deductivist philosophy.

205. The influence of Neoplatonism on the geometry-inspired deductivism of the Rationalists is a topic that has not received sufficient attention from writers who focus on the constant references to Aristotelean systems of classification.

206. Hoffman, *Course of Study*, p. 94.

207. Field, "The Magnitude and Importance of Legal Science," reprinted in this book as chapter 46.

208. "We can measure it best by tracing its progress. When men dwelt in tents and led a pastoral life, their laws might have been compressed in a few pages. . . ." Hoffman, *Course of Legal Study*,p. 7. "Its history is the history of the manners and opinions of a people advancing from barbarity, through many modes of thinking . . . to a high degree of civil and political liberty, of physical and intellectual improvement." *Ibid.*, p. 43.

209. Quoted at Stanley M. Guralnick, "Sources of Misconception on the Role of Science in the Nineteenth-Century American College," 65 *Isis* 352-66, p. 353.

210. James, "Engineering an Environment for Change: Bigelow, Peirce, and Early Nineteenth-Century Practical Education at Harvard," p. 61.

211. Proof by analogy was not the same thing as classification by analogy. For example, in 1831 Francis Wayland, 31 years old and already in his fifth year as the President of Brown University, presented an argument for reasoning by analogy as the way to get out from under the flood of new data that was overwhelming the capacity of scientific researchers to get beyond the stage of cataloguing—in other words, Wayland was preaching a reliance on analogies as a way out of the taxonomical limitations of Protestant Baconianism. In an 1831 lecture, entitled simply "Philosophy of Analogy," Wayland argued that natural phenomena are governed by laws, so that "By knowing the laws which govern any particular class of objects, we preclude the necessity of innumerable experiments and are enabled to predict, under given circumstances, what . . . will be the certain result." In turn, these specific laws expressed higher, more general laws in various manifestations. Thus magnetism and electricity, together, point to a higher law of attraction. These general laws were part of even more general laws, all the way up to some absolute single universal law of nature. The idea was to get away from the brute accumulation of facts. "Just as in proportion as the science of analogy is perfected, will the useless intellectual labor of the human race be diminished." Quoted at Hovenkamp, *Religion and Science in America*, pp. 101-02. The topic of classification—barely touched on in this article—is itself

a fascinating and potentially fruitful basis for comparison between legal and natural scientific modes of reasoning in various periods.

212. Analogic reasoning was one of the important factors that blurred the distinction between the inductive and deductive methods in the system of Protestant Baconianism, particularly regarding questions of classification. "Could we put in mathematical terms the precise law . . . which is the basis of the species . . . this mathematical expression would stand as a representative of the species; and we might use it in calculations, precisely as we can use any mathematical term." Dana, "Thought on Species," quoted at Hovenkamp, *Religion and Science in America*, pp. 114-15. The paper was published simultaneously in *The American Journal of Science* and *Bibliotheca Sacra*.

213. Hovenkamp, *Religion and Science in America*, p. 105.

214. Hoffman, *Course of Legal Study*, p. 104.

215. "[W]e see with what success the cultivation of liberal leaning may be combined with the study of law, as a constituent part of professional education. The law should be commended to good taste by classic purity of style, as well as to enlightened reason by the wisdom of its decisions; it is always more respected when administered with courtesy, than when it is morosely inflicted." Greenleaf, *Address*, p. 140.

216. Sharswood, *Lectures*, "Of Natural Law," pp. 112-113.

217. Hoffman, *Course of Legal Study*, pp. 25-26.

218. Sharswood, *Lectures*, "On the Relation of Law to Moral Science," p. 72.

219. Nathan Beverley Tucker, "Lecture on the Study of the Law," p. 119. To the republican conception of the elite that Jefferson had adopted (echoing Blackstone), however, Tucker added an updated, liberal gloss: "You this day put on the *toga virilis*, and enter on the *business of life*. This day you commence those studies on which independence, prosperity, respectability, and the comfort and happiness of those who will be dearest to you, must depend. . . ." *Ibid.*, pp. 118-19.

220. "Demosthenes, Pericles, Cicero, the elder Anthony and the elder Cato, were all lawyers in the strictest sense of the term; and minds more comprehensive than theirs seldom fall to the lot of man. The profession of Bacon, the man of universal lore, and who marked out the path for the progressive knowledge of succeeding centuries was the law. The names of More, of Mansfield, of Jones and of Broughan, need no comment, nor does that of Hamilton, the skillful warrior, legislator and statesman. . . . Law is a science and a lofty one. It is based on the rights of man by nature and society; its object is the elucidation of truth; its end the attainment of justice. . . . Can there be then aught better calculated to elevate the mind, to cause it to break off the shackles of prejudices, and attain to high moral beauty, than the full, faithful and conscientious studying of the law?" Anonymous, "Study of the Law" 3 *Southern Literary Messenger* 25-31 (1837), reprinted at Hoeflich, ed., *The Gladsome Light of Jurisprudence*, pp. 203-04.

221. "In the dark and lowering night, which succeeded that brilliant day, when the bonds of social order were loosened, and society was rapidly returning to its original elements when the only remedy was the infusion of new vigor into the social compact by the adoption of a more efficient constitution of government; the most distinguished disciples of the law were again among the framers of that instrument . . . and in later days, when the integrity of that charter has been invaded, its spirit violated, and its language perverted, whether to gratify the mad ambition of one partisan, or the cupidity of many; to whom have all eyes been imploringly directed for its preservation, but to the living and honored champions and expounders of constitutional law?" Greenleaf, "Address," p. 137.

222. *Ibid.*, p. 140.

223. William Blackstone, "A Discourse on the Study of the Law," (1759), reprinted in Hoeflich, *The Gladsome Light of Jurisprudence*, p. 71. Blackstone said that the study of law would inculcate "affectionate loyalty to the king, a zeal for liberty and the constitution, a sense of real honour, and well grounded principles of religion."

224. "Every science rewards those who study it, by enlarging their minds to a comprehension of its learning; and the greater the science, the greater the reward. But there is something in the conduct of litigation which makes the judgment severe and keen, beyond any other discipline to which it is subjected. While, therefore, the study of law has the effect of enlarging the vision of its practisers, it has also the effect of sharpening their intellect, leading to precision of thought and language, and acuteness in discovering the truth of facts." Field, *The Importance and Magnitude of Legal Science*, p. 17.

225. Sharswood, *Lectures*, "On the Profession of the Law," p. 4.

226. Field, *The Importance and Magnitude of Legal Science*, p. 16.

227. Hoffman, *Course of Study*, p. 101-02. Paley's utilitarianism is approached with a grain of salt. "On the subject of the utilitarian theory of moral philosophy . . . it is rather feebly supported by Paley; and somewhat quixotically advocated by Bentham and his disciples. The student will judge for himself on this point; we have some faith in it, but think it has not been clearly and dispassionately set forth." *Ibid.*, p. 105. The equation of mathematical and physical truths—again, a source of confusion for modern readers looking for a clear affiliation either with classical deductivism or modern, empirical inductivism—is characteristic of Protestant Baconianism's grounding of natural phenomena in the moral certainty of scriptural first principles, an approach sharply different from the deductivism of Cartesian geometry or Newtonian mathematics.

228. The leading theories of the 1820s (those of Cuvier and Buckland) emphasized uniformitarianism and catastrophism, holding that geological formations had been formed in discrete cataclysmic events and remained absolutely unchanged during the intervening eras. This was music to the ears of those who sought evidence to support natural theology. Creation, the Flood, the destruction of Sodom and Gomorrah, even Joshua making the sun stand still, all could be linked to evidence in the geologic record. In 1826 Lyell, extrapolating from local records, concluded that the age of the volcanic cones at Mt. Aetna far exceeded the posited age of the world; adding insult to injury, Lyell then observed that a layer of fossil-bearing limestone characterized by a preponderance of sea animals extended *under* the cones of Etna. Since the fossils in the limestone presumably dated from

the Flood, and since the layer of fossil-bearing stone extended beneath the volcanic cones, the date of the Flood must be even older than the date of the volcanoes, the age of which already exceeded that of the earth according to biblical creation . . . in short Lyell, in proper inductive fashion, had observed his way right into the concept of geologic time. The linchpins of Protestant Baconianism were beginning to buckle.

229. The challenge in this context began with the surveys' discovery of huge numbers of new animal forms, such as the sightless fish of Mammoth Cave, that seemed clearly adapted to highly specific environments. Even if catastrophism were preserved as a theory in geology, where was the biblical account to explain the adaptation of life forms to fit post-catastrophic conditions? The issue of explaining variation in forms led, inexorably, to the issue of explaining variations in the human form, a bedrock question for natural theology. To defend the connection between biological diversity and the Bible, Agassiz in a series of articles adopted the idea that there had been multiple Creations, occurring after each catastrophic event such as an Ice Age, and in each case populating the landscape with forms miraculously adapted to its current conditions. Agassiz, "Geographical Distribution of Animals," 48 *The Christian Examiner and Religious Miscellany* 181-204 (1850); "The Diversity of Origin of the Human Races," 49 *The Christian Examiner and Religious Miscellany* 110-145 (1850); "Contemplations of God in the Kosmos," 50 *The Christian Examiner and Religious Miscellany* 1-17 (1851).

230. Agassiz was an admirer of Southern writers such as Dr. Samuel George Morton, whose book *Crania Americana* (Philadelphia: J. Dobson, 1839) ranked races by order of abilities based on their cranial characteristics (employing a Linnaean morphological definition of species). Agassiz was also a staunch supporter of Josiah Clark Nott and George R. Gliddon, contributing an essay to their book *Indigenous Races of the Earth* (Philadelphia: J.B. Lippincott, 1854, subsequent republication in 1857), in which they argued that the scientific fact of multiple divine acts of Creation demonstrated the necessary inferiority of the Negro to the Caucasian race. Agassiz professed to be disinterested on the question of slavery: "It has been charged upon the views here advanced, that they tend to the support of slavery . . . we disclaim, however, all connection with any question involving political matters." Agassiz, "Diversity of Origins of the Human Races," p. 112. This disclaimer appears disingenuous, particularly in light of biographical details of which Gray was presumably unaware. See Lurie, "Louis Agassiz and the Races of Man," 45 *Isis* 227-42 (1954). Certainly the Southerners themselves had no doubt of the effect of Agassiz's support: in a letter to Morton, Nott wrote "[w]ith Agassiz in the war the battle is ours. . . . The parsons now are certainly in the way of being licked." Nott, letter to Morton, May 26, 1850, quoted at Lurie, "Louis Agassiz and the Races of Man," p. 156. Nott's reference to "the parsons" is suggestive of the extent to which Agassiz's position not only aided the pro-slavery cause but also inevitably alienated Northern religious abolitionists, driving a wedge between the constituencies of natural theology. Southerners frequently asserted a scientific basis for the institution of slavery. In another book, *Types of Mankind* (Philadelphia: J.B. Lippincott, 1871), Nott proudly claimed that Calhoun had consulted with Gliddon and Morton in formulating his positions. Alexander H. Stephens, Robert Toombs and Robert B. Rhett all also declared that their arguments were based on science, a position which Agassiz's theories strongly encouraged.

231. The members of the Bache circle, led by Agassiz (see preceeding note), tended to pro-Southern attitudes. Benjamin Peirce considered slavery beneficial; Joseph Henry called abolitionism the propaganda of "strong-minded women and weak-minded men from the North," and declared that "to liberate the Negro ever in this country [would be] certain death to the race"; James Hall blamed the War on "New England propagandists" and Negroes; Bache was a pro-Southern Democrat and an admirer of Jefferson Davis. (The exception was Woolcott Gibbs, who described James Hall's support for slavery as "moral insanity.") In contrast, their opponents tended to have Northern and/or abolitionist sentiments. Asa Gray turned down a position in Louisiana in 1837, declaring: "I do not like the Southern states." In 1857 William Chauvenet of the Naval Academy (along with Peirce one of the leading mathematicians of the day) turned down an offer of higher pay from South Carolina College; and in 1847 Benjamin Silliman, Jr., a chemist, turned down the offer of a chair at the University of Alabama, "such is my abomination of Negro slavery." Bruce, *The Launching of Modern American Science*, pp. 58-60, 271-74, 173.

232. Dana was able to remake himself as an evolutionist in the same mold as Gray, and thus to continue as a prominent and productive member of the scientific community. In the process, however, he suffered a nervous breakdown. See Hovenkamp, *Religion and Science in America*, p. 207.

233. Toby A. Appel, "A Scientific Career in the Age of Character: Jeffries Wyman and Natural History at Harvard" in *Science at Harvard University*, p. 105 (emphasis added).

234. Quoted at Daniels, "The Process of Professionalization in American Science," p. 77. In that same year, Andrew Dickson White, president of Cornell University, began the process of constructing an historiography that would present religion and science as timeless enemies in a lecture delivered to the Cooper Union in New York. "In all modern history, interference with Science in the supposed interest of religion . . . has resulted in the direst evils both to Religion and Science, and *invariably*. And on the other hand all untrammeled scientific investigation, no matter how dangerous to religion some of its stages may have seemed, temporarily to be, has invariably resulted in the highest good of Religion and Science." Quoted at Ronald L. Numbers, "Science and Religion," 1 *Osiris* (second series, 1985), pp. 59-80. Numbers' article presents an overview of the historiography of religion and science, emphasizing the use of battlefield metaphors to create a sense of historical opposition where, he argues, there was none.

235. Rogers, for example, took a much stricter line than Bache or Agassiz on the matter of keeping amateurs out of the AAAS. A survey geologist, he came from the government side of scientific enterprise, and had little patience for those of the old lyceum school who treated research as a leisure-time activity. During an 1855 session of the AAAS, Rogers interrupted the delivery of one paper in a section he chaired "on the grounds that the members of the Scientific Association did not meet as mere school boys to listen to elementary truths." In 1855, under Rogers' leadership, the AAAS adopted a resolution that "no

notice of articles not approved shall be taken in the published proceedings." Quoted at Bruce, *The Launching of Modern American Science*, p. 261.

236. See Reingold, "Science, Public Policy, and Popular Precepts: Alexander Dallas Bache and Alfred Beach as Symbolic Adversaries."

237. Gray insisted that indeed evolution and Christianity were compatible, a position that resulted in his exclusion from the inner circle of Darwin, Huxley et. al. despite the importance of his earlier support for *Origin*. Bruce, *The Launching of Modern American Science*, pp. 110-111.

238. Bruce, *The Launching of Modern American Science*, p. 40.

239. Dupree, *Asa Gray*, p. 154.

240. Shaler became a professor of Paleontology at the Lawrence School in 1869 at the age of twenty-eight; the title of his position was changed in 1888 to a professorship in Geology. He was an incredibly popular lecturer. In the 1880s his Geology 4 class, focusing on "the wonders of the natural world," had over 500 students; he was a regular contributor to *Atlantic Monthly*, *North American Review*, *Scribner's Magazine*, and the nativist *America*. "[H]e seemed," writes David Livingstone, "perfectly fitted to bring a 'scientific' perspective to the social problems unnerving genteel New Englanders." Shaler became Dean of the Lawrence School 1891; in the same year, he published *Nature and Man in America* in which he initiated the study of "cultural geography," a very direct descendant of the natural history of the lyceums. *See* David N. Livingstone, "A Geologist by Profession, a Geographer by Inclination: Nathaniel Southgate Shaler and Geography at Harvard" in *Science at Harvard*, quoted at pp. 150-51.

241. *Ibid.*

242. Sinclair, "Harvard, MIT, and the Ideal Technical Education," p. 81.

243. "To illustrate the failure of the system of the last 40 years to breed scholars," wrote Eliot, "let us take the most unpleasant fact which I know for those who have the future of this University to care for—Asa Gray, Benjamin Peirce, Jeffries Wyman and Louis Agassiz are all going off the stage and their places cannot be filled with Harvard men, or any other Americans that I am acquainted with. This generation cannot match them. These men have not trained their successors. This is a very grievous fact which had better not be talked about—it is altogether too significant." Quoted at Dupree, *Asa Gray*, p. 343.

244. Quoted at Anthony Chase, "The Birth of the Modern Law School," 23 *The American Journal of Legal History*, 329-348 (1979), p. 336.

245. "It is not simply that Eliot defended the case method more vigorously than did Langdell but rather that, with the exception of the introduction to his Contracts Casebook and a brief address in 1886, Langdell virtually did not defend his system at all." Chase, "The Birth of the Modern Law School," p. 338.

246. Sometimes the separation between teaching methods and legal philosophy is justified by the claim that Langdell himself was too dim to realize what he was about, as in Grant Gilmore's famous conclusion that Langdell was an "essentially stupid man." See, e.g., Thomas C. Grey, "Langdell's Orthodoxy," 45 *University of Pittsburgh Law Review* (Fall 1983), p. 2. It seems unlikely, however, that a man who was described by contemporaries as "the best read lawyer in New York" (*ibid.*, p. 706) can be so easily dismissed as an intellectual lightweight. Paul Carrington concludes that it was a matter essentially beyond Langdell's caring that his method "revealed a true picture of the political and atomized nature of American law, and . . . nurtured many of the civic virtues that American law teachers have sought to nurture since the time of George Wythe." Paul D. Carrington, "Hail! Langdell!," XX *Law and Social Inquiry* no. 3 (Summer 1995), pp. 693; 692; "Abstract," 691. Debates over the effects of that system as it has been put into practice are, of course, a different matter altogether; the 1995 issue of *Law & Social Inquiry* cited above contains short responses to Carrington's articles descriptively entitled "Honor Langdell" (William LaPiana), "Damn Langdell" (John Henry Schlegel), and "To Hell With Langdell" (Laura Kalman).

247. Carrington, "Law as 'The Common Thoughts of Men,'" p. 519.

248. "Law is not a science, but is essentially empirical. Hence, although the general arrangement should be philosophical, even at the expense of disturbing prejudices, compromises with practical convenience are highly proper." Holmes, "Codes, and the Arrangement of the Law," 5 *American Law Review* 1, quoted at Grey, "Langdell's Orthodoxy," p. 6. For a treatment of the idea of evolution in Holmes' thought, see Elliott, "The Evolutionary Tradition in Jurisprudence." See also note 274, below.

249. The nineteenth century also saw the beginnings of philosophical arguments to the effect that geometry itself was not purely deductive. Grey compares Millsian and Kantian descriptions of geometric axioms, and quotes Mill's 1889 use of the term "induction" to describe geometric axioms as generalizations derived from sense experience: "[t]he proposition, two straight lines cannot enclose a space . . . is an induction from the evidence of our senses." Rules derived inductively from observation could thereafter be employed as the premises for deductive arguments, an adaptation of Bacon's middle axioms. "When this structure—induction of axioms, deduction of theorems—is applied to law, it helps clarify the otherwise baffling talk of observation, experiment and the like that appeared in Langdellian literature, while the legal scientists so extensively devoted themselves to pure conceptual reasoning in their doctrinal work." Grey, "Langdell's Orthodoxy," pp. 18-19. What is at stake here, however, is the use of very specifically nineteenth-century meanings for both geometry and experiment. The phrase "pure conceptual reasoning" appeals to the Kantian idea of a priori apodeictic intuition, precisely what Mill was claiming geometry to be distinguishable from, and what Langdell—along with Holmes in the 1870s—denied was the ground for legal science. Kant, in fact, described geometry in much the same way as the rationalist philosophers against whom Bacon had initiated the program of natural science in the 1600s. See Immanuel Kant, *Critique of Pure Reason* (New York: St. Martin's Press, 1965), pp. 67-73. The Kantian version of induction, promoted by Whewell and Bowen, was the one that became dominant in natural science; Mill's formulations found greater acceptance among social scientists. In the first half of the nineteenth century, however, "science" was neither Kantian nor Millsian. Recognizing the historical construction of experimental science

demonstrates that Langdell's claims were not at all "baffling," but rather squarely within the established tradition of Protestant Baconianism.

250. Quoted in chapter 34.

251. Sutherland, *The Law at Harvard*, p. 167. Here again, interestingly, Langdell's approach is illuminated by a reference to Eliot's: regarding his own text on inorganic chemistry. Eliot wrote: "[y]ou will recognize the fact that a textbook is nothing but a compilation—our work has been simply one of selection and arrangement." Chase, "The Birth of the Modern Law School," p. 335. Carrington reads Langdell's reference to a chemistry laboratory to indicate that he "treated judicial decisions as experiments." "Cases not consistent with the principles that he detected by induction were simply wrong . . . experiments that had failed to apply correct logic; good law was good metaphysics." Carrington, "Hail, Langdell," pp. 707, 708-09. This a mixed metaphor: the experimental method is not a method that can be applied to either logic or metaphysics. The point is that the equation of "science" with the experimental method is a modern one. Langdell did not treat cases as experiments conducted by previous researchers but rather as found objects brought to the laboratory of the law school—*not* the courtroom—for contemplation and analysis, as Eliot pointed out in his Annual Report for 1873-74: "Medicine and surgery must be learned, partly, it is true, from books, but largely from the bodies of the sick and wounded; whereas law is to be learned almost exclusively from the books in which its principles and precedents are recorded, digested, and explained. . . . The law library, and not the court or law office, is the real analogue of the hospital." Quoted at Chase, "The Birth of the Modern Law School," pp. 341-42.

252. Ames extended Langdell's methods or organization from contracts to torts, producing the first torts casebook in 1874 after having offered the first separate classes in torts were offered at Harvard starting in 1870.

253. Langdell, *Summary of the Law of Contracts* (Boston: Little, Brown, and Company, 1880), p. ii.

254. Langdell, *Contracts*, p. ii.

255. Langdell, *Contracts*, p. v.

256. Carrington, "Hail, Langdell!," p. 707.

257. Chase, "The Birth of the Modern Law School," p. 337.

258. Carrington, "Law as 'The Common Thoughts of Men,'" p. 519. Gray was a kind of early Legal Realist who, working from a position of Austinian positivism, argued that law was what judges said it was. "[L]egislative acts, statutes, are to be dealt with as sources of Law, and not as part of the Law itself . . . in truth, all the Law is judge-made law." John Chipman Gray, *The Nature and Sources of the Law* (second edition, New York: MacMillan Publishing Co., 1921, reissued by Boston: Beacon Press, 1963), p. 125. Gray's objections to Langdell, then, were directed toward the lingering presence of elements of Protestant Baconianism. "[W]e do know enough to render it extremely doubtful whether there are any principles of Law which are so ingrained in human nature as to be immutable and necessary. The possibility of General Jurisprudence as a science of *necessary* principles rests on a theory of the universe which has, in these last days, been badly shaken, a theory which supposes a permanence in social relations the existence of which is very uncertain." *Ibid.*, p. 137. Ultimately Gray's objection was not to the claim that law should be scientific, but to his perception that Langdell's method was not. "In law the opinions of judges and lawyers as to what the law is, are the law, and it is in any true sense of the word as unscientific to turn from them, as Mr. Langdell does, with contempt because they are 'low and unscientific,' as for a scientific man to decline to take cognizance of oxygen or gravitation because it was low or unscientific." Letter from John Chipman Gray to President Eliot (January 8, 1883), quoted at Grey, "Langdell's Orthodoxy," p. 20. Thayer, in contrast, argued forcefully that judges should not interfere in the exercise of legislation. See, for example, Carrington, "Law as 'The Common Thoughts of Men,'" p. 525. Both Thayer and Gray are accurately characterized by Thomas Grey as "precursors of modernity." Grey, "Langdell's Orthodoxy," p. 38.

259. Grey, "Langdell's Orthodoxy," p. 4.

260. Langdell, *Contracts*, pp. 20-21.

261. *Ibid.*, p. 4. For a discussion of a similarly practical derivation of a solution to an unresolved legal issue, see the discussion of Langdell's treatment of the *Northern Securities Cases* in LaPiana, "Honor Langdell," p. 763.

262. Sutherland, *The Law at Harvard*, p. 175.

263. Sutherland, *The Law at Harvard*, p. 175.

264. Quoted at Carrington, "Law as 'The Common Thoughts of Men,'" p. 519.

265. Ephraim Gurney, the first Dean of Faculty, wrote to President Eliot in 1883 to complain about the increasingly Langdellian tone of the law school. "The whole tendency of the system, would be, to build a great school of law as an exact science, and divorce it more and more from its actual administration . . . it is . . . the attitude of mind, as following almost necessarily from a too academic treatment of a great practical profession which I do not wish to see control the School." Quoted at Sutherland, *The Law at Harvard*, 188.

266. Chase, "The Birth of the Modern Law School," p. 338.

267. Friedman, *A History of American Law*, pp. 615-17; Sheppard, "Casebooks, Commentaries and Curmudgeons," pp. 605-614. In 1915, the United States Bureau of Education reported that "the case method forms the principal, if not the exclusive, method of teaching in nearly all of the stronger law schools of the country." Quoted at *ibid.*, p 615.

268. This was a move characteristic of the increasing importance of liberal ideas in the language of the professions. As Carrington puts it, "[n]ew academic disciplines were devised around professional aspirations in education, librarianship, nursing, and social work, all of them claiming some basis in technology." Carrington, "Hail, Langdell," p. 703.

269. Sharswood, *Lectures*, "On Legal Education," p. 58.

270. For a discussion of the "divorce of law from politics," see Bloomfield, "Law vs. Politics." The tendency of lawyers to remove themselves from public life was of especial concern to writers who continued to harbor republican aspirations for their profession. Silliman, for example, reserved special outrage for lawyers who eschewed a role in political affairs. "We too often

hear men of standing and of culture proclaiming as a merit that they have nothing to do with politics. Such political nonentities would be fit subjects of a despotic power, but are worse than useless citizens of a Republic which depends for its life on the active opinions, and voices, and votes of its people. . . ." Silliman, "Address," p. 30. For a discussion of the decline of lawyers as public intellectuals generally, see Robert Ferguson, *Law and Letters in American Culture* (Cambridge: Harvard Press, 1984). E. Digby Baltzell has suggested that the shift in the conception of a respectable lawyer from a public leader to a closeted professional represents a shift in regional and cultural priorities from New England southward. Baltzell, *Puritan Boston and Quaker Philadelphia: Two Protestant Elites and the Spirit of Class Authority and Leadership* (New York: The Free Press, 1979). The pattern among physicians was quite different from that for other scientists; spurred by public health concerns, the public appetite for advice from physicians grew in the late 1800s, dramatically enhancing the authority of the profession. See Charles E. Rosenberg, *The Cholera Years: The United States in 1832, 1849, and 1866* (Chicago: University of Chicago Press, 1962).

271. An 1876 report on the Academy of Natural Sciences in Philadelphia commented on the character of its membership in familiar terms: "Though the register of its members contains the names of very many true scientists, a large majority of the members of the society always has been and is now composed of gentlemen who, to use an expression of the founders, are 'friendly to science' and its cultivation. Many of them pursue science only as a recreation during leisure hours, some are pleased to observe and know what others do, and others are content to encourage those who work." Bruce, *The Launching of Modern American Science*, p. 36.

272. This was the speech in which Holmes analogized the development of legal doctrine to the evolution of the feline clavicle. Quoted at Elliott, "The Evolutionary Tradition in Jurisprudence," p. 51. There is a debate among Holmes scholars that centers around the claim that there is a shift in his thinking between his earlier and later works. See G. Edward White, *Justice Oliver Wendell Holmes: Law and the Inner Self* (New York: Oxford University Press, 1993). By this account, in *The Theory of Torts* (1873) and *The Common Law* (1880), Holmes still identified himself with the ideal of legal science; it was only with *The Path of the Law* (1897) that Holmes eschews this search for general principles from which particular cases can be decided. "You can always imply a condition in a contract. But why do you imply it? It is because of some belief as to the practice of the community or of a class, or because of some opinion as to policy, or in short, because of some attitude of yours upon a matter *not capable of exact quantitative measurement*, and therefore not capable of founding exact logical conclusions." Quoted at Horwitz, *The Transformation of American Law: The Crisis of Legal Orthodoxy*, vol. II (New York: Oxford University Press, 1992), p. 38 (emphasis added). An alternative interpretation of Holmes' ideas is that they are consistent (albeit evolving) expressions of an approach to the law that has more to do with the late nineteenth-century idea of technology than of science, his occasional use of evolutionary metaphors notwithstanding. In this reading, Holmes' discomfort with Langdell had less to do with Landgell's system than with the claims that he made about it. My thanks to Eben Moglin for drawing this point to my attention.

273. "Mental derangement is none other than a breach of Law by the patient; oftener a Law of health than a Law of intellectual or moral integrity, possibly of both. The physician applies his cure to a restoration of the Law." John Thompson, Esq., "The Reign of Law; Read Before the Literary Section of Vassar Brothers' Institute March 7, 1882," (Poughkeepsie, N.Y.: A. V. Haight, 1882,) p. 12.

274. "God's Providential Government is doubtless *now* carried on through the agency of Law, and not by an interposition of the miraculous. The Laws of nature, therefore, are God's methods of administering the affairs of His empire according to a purpose and design, either apparent or concealed, and to come out afterwards." *Ibid.*, p. 17.

275. "[I]f one single law that governs the action of the slightest material of its composition is violated, it stands an inert mass of wheels, bolts, water, and iron,—the heart so to speak cut out of it—every mechanical Law must be observed or the machine is worthless." *Ibid.*, p. 8.

276. "What proportion of community *marry* and what fill the lists of bachelors and maids? What proportion are visionary and what thoughtful, what reformers and what conservative? And many other illustrations might be added, all proving by the results that society is belted by Law, that what seems the merest chance, is the movement of a beneficent Providence, the several steps putting at defiance all human calculation, but arranging and combining so as to educe harmony out of seeming confusion. . . . That while man has freedom of will, it is so curbed and restrained as to beget no rule of lawlessness." *Ibid.*, pp. 36-37.

277. Thomas Grey nicely describes Tiedeman and Baldwin as "Whig throwbacks." Gray, "Langdell's Orthodoxy," p. 38.

278. Quoted at Ross, *The Origins of American Social Science*, p. 61. White, writes Ross, had been persuaded in 1857 to accept a position in history at the University of Michigan by Francis Wayland's warning that "the country was shortly to arrive at a 'switching-off place' toward good or evil . . . [and] the West was to hold the balance of power, and to determine whether the country would prove a blessing or a curse in human history." Quoted at *ibid.*, p. 67.

279. Social Darwinism, it should be noted, had no basis in Darwin's own work, which included extended considerations of the possible evolutionary advantages of altruism.

280. When Sumner arrived at Yale 1872 to teach "social sciences," president Theodore Dwight Woolsey, a student of Lieber (who died in 1872) who had taught courses in history, politics and law before becoming President, forbade him to assign Spencer *The Study of Sociology*. In response to the ban Sumner publicly attacked "clerical domination" of the university, asserting that the history of learning was the freedom from "metaphysical speculation," a phrase that ironically echoes the claims of the theologians who brought Common Sense realism into American science in the early years of the nineteenth century. Ross, *The Origins of American Social Science*, p. 56.

281. Brandeis, in one telling example, reported a powerful change in his thinking in response to reading about the violent Homestead strike of 1892 while he was preparing a course in business law: "I saw at once that the common law, built up under simpler conditions of living, gave an inadequate basis for the adjustment of the complex relations of the modern factory system.

I threw away my notes and approached my theme from new angles." Interview July 27, 1914, quoted at Philippa Strum, *Brandeis: Beyond Progressivism* (Lawrence, Kansas: University of Kansas Press, 1993), p. 25.

282. Langdell's disciples James Barr Ames and Joseph Beale, for example, at one point threatened to withdraw their support from the University of Chicago Law School "because its organizers proposed to teach a substantial number of public law courses, thus violating the Harvard curricular dogma that students must be exposed only to scientific 'pure law' courses." Gray, "Langdell's Orthodoxy," p. 34.

283. Nonetheless, sociological jurisprudence recalled the initial impetus behind the legal science of Hoffman and his colleagues, as well as a healthy dash of moralism, both of which tendencies earned the movement the ire of Legal Realists. John Chipman Gray wrote that one approach to the study of the law "starts from the needs of society, and considers how far the Law is adequate or inadequate to those needs. As it deals with what the law ought to be, we may designate it as the deontological or ethical." In a footnote to the 1921 edition, Roland Gray added a dismissive comment: "Sociological Jurisprudence appears to be neither more nor less than Deontological Jurisprudence as thus defined." Gray, *The Nature and Sources of the Law*, p. 139, n. 1. The connection of sociological jurisprudence to the idea of law as science—or social science—was precisely the point of Legal Realism's attack on what Gerard Henderson called "the illusion of juristic necessity," beginning in the 1920s. Henderson, "Railway Valuation and the Courts," 33 *Harvard Law Review* 902, 913 (1920), quoted at Horwitz, *The Transformation of American Law*, p. 162.

Chapter 46

The Magnitude and Importance of Legal Science

1859

David Dudley Field

David Dudley Field (February 13, 1805-April 13, 1894) was a reformer of American civil procedure. This address was given at the opening of the law school of the University of Chicago on September 21, 1859, and was printed and distributed as a pamphlet.

Mr. President and Gentlemen: Twenty years ago there was depending in the Supreme Court of the United States a suit respecting the ownership of a tract of land on the southwestern shore of Lake Michigan. The parties in interest were, the Government of the United States on one side, and an Indian trader on the other. The controversy attracted much attention. It was debated with earnestness and ability, but the law was with the government, and the judgment of the Court confirmed its claim. Thereupon the lands came into market, and the City of Chicago now covers them with railroad stations, warehouses and dwellings. That tide which feels no ebb, that stream of people, which moves with the sun, westward, and which, first heard in murmurs on the eastern horizon, rises higher and louder, till it swells like the ocean, has passed over this shore, and is now breaking and dashing a thousand miles further west. Here and around this tract of prairie, for which the Indian trader contended with the government less than a quarter of a century ago, the stream has left a populous and opulent city, rivalling in mangnificence the oldest seats of government and commerce.

It seems but a graceful recognition of the benefits which Chicago received from that righteous judgment that she should now, in the fullness of her prosperity, found a school devoted to legal science. That, however, is the least of the reasons for the establishment of this Institution. The magnitude and importance of the science, the consequent necessity for its highest culture, the usefulness of a school above all other means of learning, the situation of Chicago, its commerce and influcence, and therefore its fitness as the place of such a school, are all but so many reasons for its establishment. Yours is the chief city of a great and flourishing State, and it has a position dominant over all the West.

In the Mississippi Valley, this marvelous region of abundance, there are few radiating points, and this is one of them. Whatever light is here kindled, shines through township and village, from the Alleghanies to the Rocky Mountains. This is not only a mart of commerce, but a workshop of the mind. You send your ships over these lakes even to the outer sea; you dispatch in different directions daily and nightly trains of heavily laden cars; but you can send abroad richer things than these; the products of your mind and the influence of your example.

This school, like the University of which it forms a department, owes its establishment chiefly to the liberality and foresight of citizens of Chicago. A right noble thing was it to found and endow them. Neither the possession of office, even the most exalted, nor the fame of statesmanship, however truly won, will give more certain satisfaction hereafter than the consciousness of having been their founder, or benefactor. For are not the cultivation and advancement of learning, the diffusion of it among men, and the promotion of a higher culture, more rational objects of ambition, than wealth or power? And however large may be a city, however beautiful its streets, and however great its traffic, there is no crown which it can wear, so truly light and graceful, as a seat of learning, with ample means of knowledge, with doors open to all who will receive it, where all the sciences are cultivated and all the arts can look for assistance.

This, is not however, the occasion to discourse of the value of the sciences or arts in general. We are to-day occupied with one of the sciences. And, even in discoursing of this, I must confine myself to a particular view of it, lest I should weary you. There are undoubtedly several topics, which might properly be considered, in connection with the establishment of this school; as for example, its relations to the public, to the university and to its own pupils, or the most advisable course of study; but I shall only ask you to consider with me now the magnitude and importance of legal science. And, although all knowledge has value, and all the arts their uses, yet, as there are differences in value as in use, I hope to show you that of all time sciences and all the arts, not one can be named greater in magnitude or importance than the science for which this school, as a permanent department of your university, is now founded; the Science of the Law.

Law is a rule of property and of conduct prescribed by the sovereign power of a State. The science of the law embraces therefore all the rules recognized and enforced by the State, of all the property and of all the conduct of men in all their relations, public and private. Wherever there appears material capable of appropriation, whether it be solid earth or flowing water; whether it be the product of the soil, or the workmanship of man's hand, there comes the law, and gives you the rule by which you may take it, use it, and transfer it. Wherever there is a community, wherever there is a family, wherever there is a man, the law prescribes the rights, the duties, the relations. No engagement can be entered into, no work undertaken, no journey made, but with the law in view. No man walks abroad in the morning, or lies down to sleep at night, or takes his bride to the altar, or lays his child in the cradle, but under the law's protection. This science therefore is equal in duration with history, in extent with all the affairs of men.

We can measure it best by tracing its progress. When men dwelt in tents and led a pastoral life, their laws might have been compressed in a few pages. They had, of course, some part of our law of personal rights, the law of succession, and of boundaries between the occupiers of adjoining pastures. This was the condition of the race in the primitive ages, and is even yet the condition of some parts of it. The Laplander in the North, the Bedouin in the South, the Nomadic tribes which roam over Central Asia, our American Indians, and the Southern Africans, are in this condition. The Bedouin encamps upon the edge of the sand, or along the declivities of the mountains, his tents, his flocks and herds, his scanty list of clothing and utensils being his only wealth. When he has exhausted one spot he removes to another, and if he is disturbed he flies to the desert. Nevertheless he is not without the pale of the law. He recognizes in many things more than the right of the strongest. His personal relations to his wife, his children, and his neighbors, are subjects of regulation, and when he dies his effects are parted according to rule among his kindred.

The next stage in the civilization of the race was the fixed habitation and the cultivation of the soil; and this brought with it the next stage in the development of the legal system—the law of land and of permanent structures—a department which, though it teaches of the most permanent of earthly things, has not partaken of their permanence, but has fluctuated with political condition. The distribution of the land has determined the policy and the fate of governments, and these in their turn have encouraged the aggregation or subdivison of estates, as they inclined to aristocratic or democratic institutions.

We cling, nevertheless, to the solid earth as we cling to no other possession. To possess land, to own an estate, to found a family, and to make for it an ancestral home, are objects of ambition almost universal. We seem to ourselves to be more firmly fixed when we are anchored in the soil. Where a man can stand beneath an ample roof and loof over broad meadows and cornfields, all his own, watch the reapers of his harvests, and the cattle in his pastures, he feels more stable in his fortunes, and fancies himself more abiding on the earth, than if his wealth were in ships or factories. Then, the pleasures of agriculture are the most favorable to a serene spirit and a happy life. The Fair, which has been so lately held in this city, and of which I hear so much, which so many thousands attended, and where the wealth of your soil was marvelously displayed, bears witness to the interest excited in this pursuit. And notwithstanding the enormous increase of personal property, in our modern society, the larger portion of man's wealth is still in the land. In the State of New York, the most commercial of our States, the assessed value of real property the last year was over a thousand millions of dollars, while that of personal property was but three hundred and sixty-seven millions; and even in its metropolitan city, where there is the largest aggregation of personal property, its assessed value was only one hundred and sixty-seven millions; and even in its metropolitan city, where there is the largest aggregation of personal property, its assessed value was only one hundred and sixty-two millions, while that of personal property was three hundred and sixty-eight millions.

For these reasons, the law, which regulates the possession, enjoyment and transfer of real property, has always been the subject of special attention. It has oscillated, as governments have swayed back and forth; at one time allodial, at another feudal; sometimes comparatively simple, then excessively complex; in one country natural, in another artificial. But in all countries, whether in the valley of the Nile, or in an English county, and under all systems, that of the Jews in Palestine, or of the Romans in Italy, or the Mohmammedans in India, or the French on the Seine, or the English in Australia, even under the simplest system that has ever been or can ever be devised, the law of real property has ever been and must be large and difficult. The acquistion and use of land, the different kinds of ownership, the exclusive and perpetual, or the joint and temporary title, the conflicting interests of adjoining owners, the relative rights of landlord and tenant, and a thousand other conditions and incidents, can only be regulated upon a careful and minute analysis, by a series of rules adjusted with nice discrimination and adapted to an almost infinite variety of circumstances.

In the next stage of civilization, the products of the soil were wrought into new forms, and manufactured fabrics added to the wealth and comfort of man. Manufactures required the purchase and collection of materials, the employment of workmen, and the sale of the fabric. Commerce led to navigation. Each of these operations added a new chapter to the law.

Of these three stages in civilization and in law, the ancient world was witness, but not in their highest development, though in forms of which the records will last forever. The accumulation of law-books became so burdensome, that, thirteen hundred years ago, it was found necessary to reduce them by substituting digests and codes. The historian of the "Decline and Fall of the Roman Empire," has given us, in a memorable chapter, an account of the men and the process by which this work was accomplished, in the reign, and under the orders of Justinian. Since then, however, materials have accumulated, greater by far than those, out of which the Roman Codes were constructed.

Of the vast fabric of our present law, it is not difficult to distinguish between what is ancient and what is modern, and we can see that not half of it is as old as Justinian. While our law of obligations or contracts came from Rome, our law of property and of personal rights came, most of it, from other quarters. The present law of real property in this country and in England was brought from the North, or Northeast, by those conquering tribes, whose scheme of civil polity was a gradation of ranks, bound together by feudal ties. This feudal system, after having flourished through several centuries, has been gradually softening and disintegrating under the double influence of commerce and peace. Our maritime law is also in great part of modern origin, for though the commerce of the ancients covered the Mediterranean and the Red Sea, and coasted along the adjacent shores of Europe and Asia, yet the rules by which modern commerce is governed began with the activity of the Middle Ages, and grew to maturity with the enterprise of our own times. The best part of our law of personal rights we owe to the spirit of Christianity and the influence of chivalry. A man's person is now sacred. You shall not confine it; you may not touch it. He may go or stay wheresoever he will; he may engage in any pursuit which pleases him; he may embrace any faith which appears right in his own eyes. Associations being more powerful than individuals, corporations scarcely known to the ancients, have become the most frequent and the most powerful agencies of modern society. During all the while the machinery of government has been increasing and expanding, till volumes are filled with the rules which relate to that alone. And last of all, there have just appeared the three most marvelous inventions of all time; the steamer, the railway, and the telegraph, which, while they have been making a revolution in the social life of man, have, at the same time, been adding three chapters to the books of his laws. And thus has it happened that the Body of the Law, the *Corpus Juris*, as we sometimes call it, has grown to its present colossal proportions; a structure so high and so vast that the mind is lost in the contemplation of its vastness as a whole, and the number and completeness of its parts.

The more perfect is the civilization, the more complete is the law. The latter is, in many respects, both the cause and the consequence of the former. They act and react upon each other. Ask the man who wonders that there are so many laws, to go with you to the neighboring prairie, and, standing in the door of the farm-house, with cornfields and pastures before you, explain to him the title by which the owner holds the land, how far his use is absolute, and how qualified by the rights of his neighbors, or the paramount rights of the State, the relative rights of the wife and husband, the persons who shall succeed when the owner dies, the rights of the adjoining proprietors in the stream which runs through the pasture, the rights of the tenant who tills the meadow, what right the owner has in the shore of the lake, how far he may build into it, and on what conditions, the relative rights of himself and the public in the highway before his house, the right which he has to the pew in the church, whose spire shines through the trees, and in the family vault where he expects in due time to be borne. Or take him with you to a point overlooking this city, and look down upon its network of streets, its long lines of private buildings, its public edifices, and its crowded port. The eye is weary with the infinite variety of objects on land and water; the ear stunned by the incessant roll of wheels and the tread of feet. The streets are thronged with men and women, intent on business or pleasure. Vessels are furling or unfurling their sails as they return to port or depart on their voyages. Steamers are plowing the lake; railway trains are arriving and departing. In all this scene of excitement and struggle, there is not a person, or an act, which the law does not sway, by an influence silent and unseen, perhaps, but none the less effective. Look into the banking-house, and see it at work dictating the form and use of commerical paper, by which the exchanges are effected; there is not a promissory note, or a bill of exchange, that is not in part the work of its hand. Look into the insurance office, and see the law guiding its operations; the insurance of dwellings, warehouses, vessels and cargoes, and the adjustment of losses from storm and fire. Look into the counting-room, the workshop, the market, and consider the rules which control the sale and delivery of all sorts of merchandise; those which regulate the building, freighting, manning and sailing of ships; the construction, repair and occupation of buildings. You see the offices of corporations and partnerships. These are the subjects of careful regulation, suited to all the purposes for which such associations are formed, from the smallest trade to the largest enterprise, whether the object be gain, or charity, or human culture. Dissolve this mass of busy men into its elements, and observe that there is a law for each, and peculiar to each; for the clergymen, the lawyer, the physician, the banker, the merchant, the artisan, the seaman. The scholar appeals to it for the protection of his patent. You see crowds hastening to the railway trains or the steamers. Every individual among them relies upon the law for the security of his person and the enforcement of his contract. You see a funeral procession. When the dead man is gathered to his fathers, and the procession has dispersed, his kindred will return to his tenant-less mansion to read his will, or to learn if he has left the disposition of his estate to the general laws of succession. Then comes into operation that long chapter of laws, regarding the distribution of the property of the dead, testate or intestate; the validity and interpretation of wills, the fact of marriage, the legitimacy of children, the death of the absent.

How are rights to be enforced? The State itself, of its own motion, undertakes the punishment of the graver violations of law. Hence the need of a penal code, with its definitions of crimes and its apportionment of punishments. These are great departments of the law, which have engaged and will ever engage the attention of the wisest men. The definition of every crime, for which a person may be punished, whether committed against the State or against individuals, and whether affecting property or person, and the just apportionment of punishment to each crime, according to its degree, are subjects of vast difficulty as of vast extent. Observe into what details it is necessary to descend. What acts it is expedient to visit with criminal punishment, who are to be deemed responsible, having regard to age, sex, mental capacity, and civil condition; who are to be treated as principals and who as accessories; what are the punishments, which it is proper for a Christian community to inflict upon offending members, and with what view, whether it should be vengeance, penalty, or reformation, there being different punishments adopted in different countries, some looking to degradation, some to forfeiture of property, some to bodily suffering or restraint, and some to deprivation of life; these are to be determined by considerations of private right and public policy, depending upon the condition of the offender, upon the degree of injury caused to society, and to individuals by particular acts, and upon the adoption of fit means to the end, which is the protection of society. In one stage of social existence an act may not even be punishable, which in another it may be necessary to meet with the severest penalties. Smuggling, for example, is an offense arising out of an artificial condition of society. In our present condition we include in the category of criminal acts not only such violations of the rights of persons and of property as are comprehended within the descriptions of murder, arson, mayhem, burglary, robbery, theft, forgery, and the like, but offenses against the elective franchise, against the Executive, the Legislative, or the Judicial power, against public justice, and against public order, the public health, and the public morals.

For the prosecution of criminals, as well as for judging between man and man, the State provides the machinery of tribunals and officers of justice, and a system of procedure, criminal and civil. The former prescribes the proceedings in criminal cases from the accusation through the subsequent stages, the warrant of arrest, preliminary examination, indictment, plea, trial, judgment and execution. The latter embraces all civil actions and proceedings, and all the steps in each, the various courts of justice, and the different grades of judicial officers, the parties who may sue or be sued, the times of bringing suits, the places of trial, the various provisional remedies of arrest, delivery, injunction, attachment and receivers, the written allegations of the parties, the elimination of the immaterial from the material allegations, the separation of the questions of fact from the questions of law, the different modes of trial, the formation of juries, the conduct of trials, the different kinds of evidence, and the means of its production, the verdict, the judgment, and the execution, the review of the questions of fact and of law, and the time and mode of appeal. There are besides in respect to special proceedings, a great number of particular provisions of immense importance, and relating among other things to the prerogative writs, including the great writ of *habeas corpus.*

The machinery of tribunals and officers of justice, though vast and intricate in details, is but a part of the machinery of government. Who that has studied the government of a country, though occupying but a single department in its laws, but wonders at the magnitude of the subject. A lifetime seems scarcely sufficient for its mastery. Political philosophy and history are its adjuncts. Take our political code, survey it generally, enter into its details, study its history, consider how many good and wise men have participated in its framing, how cautiously it has been contrived, amended, added to, debated, at every step in its progress, and then stand reverently before it as the grandest monument of human genius. Time would fail me if I were to attempt recounting even the principal epochs in its history; the long and hardy training of our forefathers beyond the sea, where their institutions were purified by blood and fire, the transplanting of those institutions hither, their curtailment of the monarchical portions, the amelioration which time and experience have wrought, the principle of federation, its origin and development, and the final completion of the vast structure of our government, federal and state, through all its parts. The magnificent dome which rises so high into the air and whose arches stretch across the continent, was built within infinite labor, out of an endless variety of materials; while the walls and columns upon which it rests were the slow work of centuries of suffering and patience. Large must be the book, which shall even describe adequately this double government of ours, larger still that which shall contain all the laws, by which it moves and all the functions which it performs; its various departments, legislative, executive and judicial, the powers and duties of all its public officers, its revenues, and the different branches of the public service.

These are general views, as when we look from an elevation upon a scene below. Its immensity is only half comprehended until we enter into details. It is as if upon a mountain top we look over and beyond hill and valley, lake and river, and great towns; we understand their distances; we have a general idea of vastness; but when we have descended and traveled over the scene, then and then only we know, how vast, how varied, how infinite in details it really was. The distant mountains which appeared to have sides as smooth and regular as a garment of fur, we find composed of giant ridges, deep valleys, torrents and waterfalls. The valley which seemed spread out like a map of level ground, is filled with winding streams, and roads, a succession of hill and vale, covered all over with villages and farm-houses, and vocal with the voices of men and animals.

So would it be with the law, if after the general view we have taken, you should enter into more minute details. Let us select for example a single department and follow out its subdivisions. Take if you will the contract of sale, and see into how many branches it divides itself. Whether the contract be written or unwritten, whether there be an actual transfer, or only an agreement to transfer, whether the thing agreed upon be already made or only to be made, whether it be sound or defective or deficient in quantity, whether there be fair dealing, concealment, or misrepresentation as to quality, existence or value, whether the thing has been delivered or paid for in whole or in part, whether the seller or the purchaser ever, and if so when and upon what terms, may rescind the contract and be reinstated; all these, and many more, are considerations affecting the transaction, which the law has carefully provided for, by an appropriate rule.

The law may be compared to a majestic tree that is ever growing. It has a trunk heavy with centuries, great branches equal themselves to other trees, with their roots in the parent trunk; lesser branches, and form those lesser branches still, till you arrive at the delicate bud, which in a few years will be itself a branch, with a multitude of leaves and buds. Or it is more fitly compared with the streams of your own Mississippi Valley, where there is the great parent stream, the father of rivers; into this pours the Arkansas, the Ohio, the Missouri; into these again pour lesser rivers; and still smaller into these last, and so on till you reach finally, the myriads of rivulets, all over the valley, and trace them to their springs. In like manner, the law appears infinite in its manifestations; the shelves of law libraries groan under the accumulation of their volumes. The curious in such matters have computed that the number of cases in the English Courts relating to practice alone equals twenty-five thousand, and that the common law has two million rules.

Compare this science with any of the other sciences; with those which are esteemed the greatest in extent, and the most exalted in subject. Take even astronomy, that noble science which numbers among its illustrious disciples Copernicus, Galileo, Kepler, Newton, La Place, which weighs the sun and the planets, measures their distances, traces their orbits, and penetrates the secrets of that great law which governs their motions. Sublime as this science is, it is but the science of inanimate matter, and a few natural laws; while the science which is the subject of our discourse governs the actions of human beings, intelligent and immortal, penetrates into the secrets of their souls, subdues their wills, and adapts itself to the endless variety of their wants, motives and conditions.

Will you compare it with one of the exact sciences; as, for example, with mathematics? Of this science I would always speak with profound respect. Clear, precise, simple in its elements, far-reaching and sublime in its results, it has disciplined and exalted some of the greatest minds of our race, and been the nursery of other sciences, and of the mechanic arts. Liebnitz, Euler and La Grange have been its teachers, and illustrious examples of the strength and elevation which it can give to the intellect. But the science of calculation is occupied with a single principle. This it may go on to develop more and more, till the mind is almost lost in its immensity; yet the development of that one principle can never reach in extent, comprehensiveness and variety the development of all the principles by which the actions of men toward each other are governed in all their relations. The law, it will be remembered, is the rule of all property and all conduct. Just so far as property is diversified (and it has scarcely a limit), so far is the law diversified; and as varied as are human actions, so varied are the rules applicable to them.

The differential and integral calculus is undoubtedly the most subtle instrument of calculation which was ever invented; yet it is but an instrument of calculation, after all.

As man is an object more interesting than any inanimate matter, or any abstract principle, or any instrument of calculation; as his actions are higher objects in the scale of the universe than the movement of any inanimate thing, so are the rules which are the guides of his conduct greater in extent, variety and interest than the rules of astronomy and mathematics.

This rapid survey may serve to give us some idea, imperfect, indeed, of the magnitude of legal science. Though it may be the most familiar of all things, it is also the most profound and immense. It surrounds us everywhere like the light of this autumnal day, or the breath of this all comprehending air. It sits with us, sleeps beside us, walks with us abroad, studies with the inventor, writes with the scholar, and marches by the side of every new branch of industry and every new mode of travel. The infant of an hour old, the old man of three-score and ten, the feeble woman, the strong and hardy youth, are all under its equal care, and by it alike protected and restrained.

It is hardly weakness for one, who loves it as I do, to seek to detect it in its invisible agencies; to see it govern where it is silent, and restrain where it is unheard; to fancy its invisible foot treading in all workshops and markets, and its invisible hand waving the crowds right and left; to follow its majestic governing and protecting presence into the lonely cabin on the prairie; into the little hamlet upon the side of the mountain; into the ship, struggling with the storm in the North Atlantic; into the room by the wayside, where a few disciples are worshiping God, according to their consciences, amidst a population of a different faith, but as undisturbed and as fearless as if they were surrounded by a battalion of armed men.

We have considered thus far the magnitude of legal science. Its importance is more than commensurate with its magnitude. Without it there could be no civilization, and no order. Where there is no law, there can be no order, since order is but another name for regularity, or conformity to rule. Without order, society would relapse into barbarism. The very magnitude of the law is a proof of its necessity. It is great, because it is essential. There is a necessity, not only for law, but for a system, with arrangement and a due relation of parts: for, without this system, the administration of government, both in its judicial and its administrative departments, would fall into irretrievable confusion. It is necessary, both for those who are to administer and those who are to obey. There is, besides, a natural tendency to assimilation where there is a great number of rules, just as there is a natural tendency in substances to crystallization. Law, and the science of law, go therefore together, and both are as essential as industry, refinement, liberty, civilization.

The science of the law is our great security against the maladministration of justice. If the decision of litigated questions were to depend upon the will of the judge or upon his notions of what was just, our property and our lives would be at the mercy of a fluctuating judgment, or of caprice. The existence of a system of rules and conformity to them are the essential conditions of all free government, and of republican government above all others. The law is our only sovereign. We have enthroned it. In other governments, loyalty to a personal sovereign is a bond for the State. Men cohere because they adhere to the throne. We have substituted loyalty to the State and the law, for what with others is loyalty to the person. In place of a government, of opposing interests, we have a double government of written constitutions. The just interpretation of these constitutions, and the working of the double machinery, so that there may be no break and no jar, are committed in a great degree, how great few ever reflect, to the legal profession, and are dependent upon their knowledge of the science of law in all its departments, political, civil, penal and remedial. Precisely, therefore, as free government and republican institutions are valuable, in the same proportion is the science of the law valuable as a means of preserving them.

My subject does not lead me to consider the dignity, value, or responsibilities of the legal profession. We are now concerned, rather with the science they cultivate, than with them. But if it were within the scope of this address, I might remind you that the law is lifeless without a sanction and a magistracy to enforce it. When the magistracy is established capable of judging, and independent in its judgment, the office of advocate begins and rises at once to dignity and power, as the means of communication between the magistrate and the suitor, and as assessor or aid to the magistrate.

I might also remind you that the law throws its own importance over the professor who teaches it and the advocate who practices it. Upon the learning, character, and fidelity of its practisers, its administration mainly depends as we know from their history, and as we might have inferred from their office. In all countries and at all times, the character of the lawyer, and the public consideration accorded to him, have been faithful witnesses of the freedom and civilization of the country and time. Where there is arbitrary power, there is no occasion to study the law; when the law begins to reign, its teachers and practisers come forth; the law and the lawyer go together, all the world over.

I might add, that if there be any science and any culture, tending to invigorate and sharpen the intellect, they are legal science and discipline. Every science rewards those who study it, by enlarging their minds to a comprehension of its learning; and the greater the science, the greater the reward. But there is something in the conduct of litigation which makes the judgment severe and keen, beyond any other discipline to which it is subjected. While, therefore, the study of the law has the effect of enlarging the vision of its practisers, it has also the effect of sharpening the intellect, leading to precision of thought and language, and acuteness in discovering the truth of facts. Who can unravel intrigues, lift the veil from hypocrisy, dissect evidence, and lay falsehood bare, like the practised lawyer? Better men have never existed, more exalted in intellect, or purer in motive, or more useful in action, than our profession can show. I should delight in placing some of them before you; and in asking my professional brethren to join with me, in saying: let us magnify our office; let us cherish it as full of great traditions, of illustrious examples; of beneficent results; let us fulfil it, as the best agent of political and social good; let us recommend it as requiring the highest talent, the purest intention, the most patient industry.

But I must return from this digression to the science which is the subject of this discourse. Am I not justified in saying of it, that while of the moral sciences it is the most exact, it is of all sciences the most comprehensive in its compass, the most varied and minute in its details, the most severe in its discipline, and the most important to the order, peace and civilization of mankind.

How shall this science best be learned? There are three methods: The private study of books; the advice and aid of practioners, amid the bustle and interruptions of practice, and the teaching of public schools. The inadequacy of the first is obvious; the disadvantages of the second are too painfully known to all of us who studied in that way; the third is beyond question the most efficient and complete. There is as much need of public schools for the law, as for any other science. There is more, for the greater the science, the greater the need. Above all others, this science, so vast, so comprehensive, so complicated and various in its details, needs to be studied with all the aids, which universities, professors, and libraries can furnish.

Where else so readily as here, will the student obtain a view of the law as a whole, and of all its parts in their several relations and dependencies; here, where are collected. the records of the science, where there are professors devoted to its teaching, where there are scholars emulous of distinction, and stimulating each other. If medical schools have an advantage over the former method of study and practice by the side of a practising physician, or if theological schools give better training than the private study of an ordained clergyman, busy with parochial duties, for similar reasons, a school of law, with its large library, its professors set apart to the duty, its lectures, its company of students, its discussious, oral and written, are helps above all that the private office of a busy advocate can offer to a complete legal education. Not that I would altogether dispense with or undervalue the observation of actual practice obtained by attendance in a lawyer's office, during the smaller portion of his legal course, preliminary to the student coming himself to the bar. After the general survey of the law, the comprehension of its parts, and the examination and study of all those parts in their different relations, which a thorough trinaing in a law school can best give, it would undoubtedly tend to the advantage of the youthful practitioner to pass a few months in the office of an elder brother, observe its methods, and participate in its active duties.

Forasmuch, therefore, Mr. President and gentlemen, as the science of the law is of proportions so vast, and of importance so urgent, the University of Chicago has established this Faculty of Law. It has appeared to you that the institution which your munificence has founded, would be incomplete without a department where should be taught the knowledge of American government and law. This department is now inaugurated. It has been studiously framed; it is anxiously watched. It is commended to the legal profession, to the magistracy, to the whole body of citizens.

So long as this University stands—and why should that not be centuries—so long may its Faculty teach sound law and its inseparable concomitants, pure morality and good citizenship. There are universities even in Europe, which were founded a thousand years ago, and which seem likely to last for a thousand years to come. Why may it not be said of the University of Chicago a thousand years hereafter, as of a still living and flourishing institution, that it was founded in the year 1859, and that this day its Faculty of Law was solemnly inaugurated, in the presence of Judges, lawyers and citizens. May it also in that day, as in all times hereafter, be said of it, that it has always been an instrument of good, that every generation has profited by its teachings, and that teachers and pupils without exception, have been true to the State and loyal to the law.

Chapter 47

Yale and the New Science of Jurisprudence

1915

Arthur L. Corbin

Arthur Corbin (October 17, 1874-May 4, 1967) was a contracts professor at Yale Law School from 1910 to 1957. This article first appeared at 21 *Case and Comment* 953 (1915).

From the day of Justinian to the present, much has been written of the science of jurisprudence and of methods of teaching. Yet the last word on the subject is still to be said, and when that last word is said we shall have ceased to have a living and developing law. In the administration of our law, whether statutory or customary in origin, the most influential part has been, and will continue to be, played by court decisions. These decisions, because of the great increase in population and the increasing complexity and volume of our social relations, have become as numerous as the leaves on the trees. The problems sought to be solved in these court decisions are in part the same as those of earlier days. We find the jurists of ancient Rome and the schoolmen of the Middle Ages considering and disputing about many of the questions with which our courts are actively concerned to-day. But, on the other hand, many of our problems are entirely new,—our ancestors did not find it necessary to determine the principles that should govern the application of electricity or the navigation of the air,—and to many of the old problems we must apply the additional knowledge gained in more recent experience.

The tremendous changes in our social and economic life have wrought a revolution in the methods of legal instruction as well as great changes in the content and administration of the law. They are placing upon our University law schools the responsibility of creating new types of legal scholars and investigators, of developing more intensively the study of jurisprudence as a science, and of raising the funds necessary for this development. In a recent address to the Dwight Alumni Association, Senator Elihu Root, while referring to the changes in the teaching of law since Professor Dwight's day, is reported to have said: "The young men in our great law schools to-day are being introduced, not merely to the bread-and-butter machinery of law, but are being started on the pathway of the science of jurisprudence. And this is fortunate, for there has been a great change in the conditions of the law and its relation to the world."

"In Professor Dwight's day it appeared simple and finished; but now that we have new relations between masses of organized capital and organized labor, and the vast extension of international commerce, we have passed beyond the ordinary slow growth of custom on which the old English and American law was based; and someone must be busy building up a new science of jurisprudence. The legislatures have been proceeding with great velocity, but without system; they have been hitting heads when they saw them; and there have been so many decisions that I don't know what is to become of the old principle of *stare decisis.* A new science of jurisprudence must be created."

In the earlier history of the common law, when recorded precedents were far less numerous then they are to-day, and when learned glosses and commentaries were few, it was more nearly possible for an industrious lawyer to know them all. Just as Dr. Samuel Johnson ventured to write a dictionary of the English language out of his own head, so did William Blackstone and James Kent attempt to state the entire common law. He would be a bold and an ill-advised man who would attempt to do either to-day. In their day it was possible to regard the opinion of a judge in a litigated case as the last word upon the subject of his decision. So, also, the opinions of the few learned commentators, like Coke and Blackstone and Kent, were regarded with much greater veneration than are the opinions of their modern successors. The modern judges and writers are often compared much to their disadvantage with these venerable masters of the past. But this is far from being wholly due to the superior learning and ability of the ancients; it is due in part to the greater simplicity of their problem, and in part to their lack of competitors on the top rounds of the ladder.

So long as the opinions of judges and commentators were regarded so highly by their more ignorant contemporaries and successors, the teaching of the law was bound to be a dogmatic process. The law was the word of the master, merely to be learned and understood by the student, seldom if ever to be criticized. The tremendous multiplication of decisions and treatises brought about a very different situation and new method of instruction. When two judges lay down different rules for the same set of facts, we cannot venerate them both in the same degree. Likewise, competition between commentators forbids us to swallow the dogmas of either without thorough mastication. We have been driven, to make a comparative study of decisions, thus leading directly to the case system; and in order to obtain a test of accuracy and a basis for selection, we have been compelled to study the sources, the purposes, and the practical working of the rules of law as laid down. This is creating what Senator Root described as "a new science of jurisprudence."

The Yale Law School, like the other law schools of this country, has been deeply affected by the influences above mentioned. The earlier dogmatic method of instruction has at Yale been replaced by the case system,—a comparative study of cases. This is the system of which Professor Josef Redlich, of Vienna, in his report to the Carnegie Foundation, says: "Law is conceived as the expression of social order in judicial form, which begins its separate existence all over again in every single case. Teacher and pupil approach it in the same way, the learner discovering it, under guidance of the teacher, as a new and original joint creation."

This system of instruction is far too well established to require any defense, and it is too well understood generally to require any explanation. It is not so generally understood or admitted, however, that there are other fields of legal development and investigation that must be entered by our law schools. We have long since ceased to limit our teaching by the covers of formal treatises; we must now become fully aware that there are other sources than the court decisions. We must indeed make a historical and critical study of our decisions to determine what are the principles upon which our courts have acted and are now acting; but in addition we must try to reduce those principles into a logical and harmonious system. To do this, we must, among other things, make a comparative study of other systems, and criticize our own in the light of this greater knowledge; we must determine the causes of dissatisfaction existing under our system, and discover means of eliminating them; we must determine the relative positions of our judiciary and our legislatures as lawmakers, and must improve the machinery of lawmaking.

To some of these problems the leaders of thought in the Yale Law School have for many years been alive. In no law school has the study of international law, general jurisprudence, Roman law, and modern continental law been encouraged to a greater degree than here. A graduate course, leading to higher degrees in law, has long been open to properly prepared students, and these degrees have been conferred upon graduates of many American and foreign law schools. The candidates for these degrees have been encouraged and required to take courses in the graduate school of the University, particularly in history, economics, and the social sciences. This work will be continued and improved, and new lines must be developed.

Professor Redlich, in his report to the Carnegie Foundation, states the problems before us here in America as follows: "Herewith, I believe, however, that the two great problems are revealed whose solution devolves upon American jurisprudence,—the creation of a scientific system of the common law, and a reform of the current law in the direction of that movement which is becoming more and more pronounced among the people of the United States in favor of a simplification, a greater efficiency and improvement, of substantive law as well as of civil and criminal procedure. Such a reform will, of course, not be produced by statutory decree alone. In my opinion this goal can be reached only through long and fruitful labor on the part of all elements of American legal life, the judges, the attorneys, the University law schools, and the legal scholars of the country."

In the solution of these problems the University law schools have a very large part to play. We cannot make a wise selection among those policies that may be proposed for the improvement of our law, unless we gain much greater knowledge than we have at present. This knowledge must be gained in part by experience, but in part also by study. The law schools now have practically all of our legal education in their hands. To them the people must look for a supply of trained lawyers and judges with the capacity to make intelligent use of their experience. It is largely to their faculties that we must look for men competent to draft and create a "scientific system of the common law." For this and for a reform of our current law, substantive and procedural, the mere personal experience of our bench and bar, indispensable though it may be, is not sufficient. We must have specialists, whose duty it is to devote their whole time to an acquisition and exposition of the experience and legal systems of other peoples and other periods. Final results will be attained only after long mutual collaboration and free universal criticism. The work of the scholar must be tested by the practical experience of the lawyer and the judge; and both must be brought into harmony with the prevailing folkways and customs and morals of the present, and with the desires and sentiments of the great majority, for whom law exists and without whose approval law is impossible.

The University law schools must supply the theoretical specialists, and must find the funds necessary to produce and maintain them. Such specialists are as necessary as are the bench and bar, the settlement workers, and the practical statesmen. Without them the results must be merely provincial and temporary, and will continue to be unsystematized, inconsistent, inharmonious, and piecemeal, just as they have been in the past. It is a condition, and not a theory, that now confronts us in legal administration, and it confronts us because in the past we have trusted too much to mere practical experience and have failed to develop a scientific theory.

Stare decisis was once a strong and well-constructed line of defense against the forces of disorder and inconsistency. Now, in the midst of the ever-increasing hosts of conflicting decisions, it often serves only as a shattered trench in which to bury the dead doctrine it was built to defend. The army of social unrest and dissatisfaction is in motion against our legal system. Capital, labor, politicians, social reformers, women, alike agree upon this, and join in the attack. Legal science, like Richard II. of old, must with wise discretion ride out to meet this rebellious host and disarm them all by saying, "I will be your leader." To develop such legal science and leadership will be expensive. Faculties must be increased, constructive thinkers must be recognized and gathered together for scientific team work. Surely it is the function of the Universities, where the plant and the atmosphere for such labor already exist, to undertake this service for society. The continental universities have long done it. Oxford and Cambridge are doing it. Will the American Universities, with faint heart and myopic vision, fail to grasp their opportunity? Haggling over the expense is penny wise and pound foolish. Justice is worth the price. Even the uninstructed public is becoming aware that in the absence of system harmony, unity, certainty, simplicity, and promptness of procedure, justice is difficult and expensive, or even at times wholly lacking. Our complex political system makes difficult of attainment these highly desirable qualities; but the expansion of our productive power that would follow such attainment would in a brief time create enough new wealth to finance a steel corporation.

It has been said, perhaps untruly, of the English that they trust in the ability of their government to muddle through somehow. We, too, are prone to drowse contentedly in a like belief. But there comes a time in national and social development when muddling fails to work, and when only a scientific organizer can save us from damage or destruction. The Universities must supply these scientific organizers, or fail miserably to serve the purpose of their creation.

G. The Twentieth Century

Chapter 48

The Law and the Law Schools

1915

Felix Frankfurter

Felix Frankfurter (November 15, 1882-February 22, 1965) was Associate Justice of the United States Supreme Court from 1939 to 1962, and a law professor at Harvard from 1914 to 1939. This article first appeared at 1 *American Bar Association Journal* 532 (1951).

Public opinion, the dominant factor in our national life, is also the most elusive. History is witness to the inherent difficulties and constant errors of contemporary judgments of the temper of a period. Occasionally, however, the intellectual tendency of the present is recalled as marking the culmination of a prior era. Apparently we are, for the moment at least, at the end of a period of agitation and wholesale criticism. The very term "muck-raking," is passing into disuse, and with it those energetic movements which produced its modern meaning. But this agitation has had a sound basis; it has not been fomented by irresponsible malcontents. Much of it has been crude, much has been indiscriminate. But the early expression toward any national betterment takes a rough-hewn form. However crude, however intemperate, however unjust in this or that detail, this great protest has had at its core a justifiable endeavor against remediable evils. Senator Root's speech before the New York Constitutional Convention the other day will help to give proper perspective toward an agitation which may at times have offended us. He said: "Let us bear in mind that there has been abundant cause for complaint. I have been in public life for 40 years and during that time the government of the State of New York has been about as representative and responsible as the government of Venezuela. Now the time has come when invisible government should give way to government that is accountable and responsive."

Senator Root thus soberly teaches us to analyze the aims back of this agitation, and not with passion or prejudice merely to denounce it. It is but natural that when social ills, and legal and political inadequacies, are surged against in a storm of protest, some of the protestants will offer hastily constructed and superficial remedies. But it is not sufficient for us merely to denounce as shallow or bungling or even evil such remedies as the recall of judicial decisions, the recall of judges, or what not. We must study causes. The times call for a searching diagnosis which may disclose deep-seated difficulties—difficulties needing correctives produced only by patient study and designed adjustment—difficulties responsive neither to quack remedies nor to quick remedies.

For something has happened; something is happening. We are in the midst of a changing set of ideas;

we are living through a change in direction; and a change in the thought and attitude of a people toward its national life must necessarily affect, as it always has affected, a large body of existing law.

We are not consciously the creators of these changes. Our changing opinions have been mostly effects, not causes. The fifty years since the Civil War have brought almost magical industrial growth. A vast nervous system of telephones and telegraphs has electrified our scattered country into one self-conscious unit. Radiating railroads have been the muscles which have pulled into a co-ordinate and articulate body the detached and sprawling members of our great domain. The concentration of life and activities in cities has scattered working ganglia throughout the nation. All these new physical forces, and the social changes which they produce, have brought increasing complexity in the problems of life. At the same time there has been a growing sense of obligation and increasing inventiveness to cope with these problems. Progress in education, growth of the scientific spirit, accumulation of scientific data affecting society, the advent of the specialist, national self-consciousness, social self-consciousness, have also come with these fifty years.

What does it all mean? Does it not mean that we are in the very midst of a definite shift of emphasis from individualistic ends to co-operative ends? Does it not mean that society is coming to the belief that the social purpose is to be attained not through individual self-assertion only, but through the conscious organization of society for social ends, guided by science and inspired by the democratic faith? Did the Marquis of Lansdowne, the Tory leader, have this in mind when he said before the Lords recently, "the old go-as-you-please system has broken down completely"?

And what of the law? These changes in the physical, economic and social aspects of life, all this new vast mass of facts, are necessarily so much raw material for the law. The finished product should be the legal means for accommodating the various interests of life. For law is not outside of life; it is part of it. The purpose of law, Justice Holmes has been one of the first to tell us, must be found in some help which law brings towards reaching a social end. These radical changes in the facts of life and in the attitude of our people present one of the greatest challenges ever thrown down before our common law system. A body of law adapted to a sparsely settled and primarily agricultural country, with a fairly homogeneous population, with comparatively few disparities of wealth, has suddenly and sharply been confronted with the task of adjusting itself to a vast democracy, drawn from many peoples, a nation containing thirty million wage-earners, with increasing pressure of conflicting interests. When our courts encountered these problems and applied, without elasticity or adjustment, old ideas to new facts, there was bound to follow dissatisfaction not only with specific decisions but with the legal system itself. This [l]ed the movement to tinker with the system, to attribute the causes for dissatisfaction largely to individuals, to throw the whole system overboard and start anew. Experience, however, has taught us to look deeper into causes. We now see more clearly that the difficulty is not primarily with the individuals who administer law, but with the accepted ideas consciously or unconsciously expressed by law.

Nor has the law been metallic. It has during the last decade clearly begun to respond to the temper and ideas and needs of the times. We are witnessing changes practically in the whole domain of the law—from procedural law to property, the branch of law which, one would suppose, age cannot wither. The reports during the last few years teem with illustrations. Take the United States Supreme Court. Compare the opinion of the court annulling the New York ten-hour law for bakers with its opinion, at the last term, upholding the California eight-hour law for women, and you will find not so much a reconcilable difference of decisions upon two statutes, as a radical difference in mental attitude—you will find a marked difference in point of view towards the need of governmental activity in meeting problems of the modern state. The difference spans a decade.

Take the Court of Appeals of New York. That state affords perhaps the most striking proof of a change in emphasis, of a modification, in those beliefs, mostly inarticulate, which largely determine judicial opinions. In 1907 that court animadverted upon the growing legislative activity of the time, emphasized the function of the courts to serve as barriers against such legislation, and declared unconstitutional a statute prohibiting nightwork for women. In 1915 the court expressly overrules that decision, recognizes the need of legislation for social ends, and refers to the economic and social facts justifying such legislative action.

Another example of a change in the point of view of courts is found in their present attitude towards the distribution of governmental functions. The law books continue to repeat as immutable doctrine that there can be no delegation of legislative power, but the Supreme Court sustains the tremendous power given by Congress to the Interstate Commerce Commission. Of course, the form of non-delegation may be preserved by dialectics, but the effect of the court's decisions is to recognize the pressure of economic facts and give the commission substantial control over interstate carriers. Within a decade throughout the country, in increasing variety of administrative commissions with what amounts to legislative power have been created. This means, in effect, the application of technical knowledge, developed by authoritative investigation and fair hearing, to modern complex industrial conditions. The creation of these commissions and the exercise of their power have, broadly speaking, been sustained by the courts as proper instruments for achieving appropriate ends.

24. Felix Frankfurter (1882-1965), here depicted in a photograph taken in 1917, was a professor at Harvard before becoming an associate justice of the U.S. Supreme Court. (*Courtesy of Art & Visual Materials, Special Collections Department, Harvard Law School Library.*)

So far as control over public utilities is concerned, it is only the machinery which is new. The principles of law supporting such control can be found in the Year Books. The machinery for exercising such control cannot be found in the Year Books. Means for making control effective have had to be devised. As result, problems of law enforcement, the relation of administrative action to legislature and courts, have brought to the fore a cloud of important questions calling for separate treatment as a substantially new branch of law in this country—administrative law.

The need for legislation has been amply responded to. Of making statutes there is no end. We have had a mass of legislation, some wise, some very foolish. Yet this mass of legislation, ill-considered and well-considered, apparently at times haphazard and piecemeal, constitutes on the whole, as Mr. Jethro Brown has shown, a body of law with common aims and a set of underlying principles.

But present conditions demand much more than new machinery, devised by legislation, for the effective application of old principles. And, to the extent that statutes effect changes in the substantive law, judicial decisions should not be uninfluenced by the reasons back of this legislation. For statute law and law developed through judicial opinions are, in reality, but two sides of the same activity. The two should harmonize. Both should express the same underlying premises, the same ends sought to be achieved by law. Particularly, in this country (passing for the moment the British self-governing dominions), in the last analysis, the whole field of law is for judicial development, because of the reviewing power of the courts.

These are conditions which demand new premises to fit the accumulation of new facts, from which to formulate new legal principles, just as the law, flexible common law, in Mansfield's day, absorbed the customs of merchants.

What have we done to work out new premises to fit present needs? To apply tried methods to new problems? To test new difficulties of adjustment by past experience? To remove what is obstructive or wasteful in old principles or old applications? Said Maitland a few years ago: "Are we facing modern times with modern ideas, modern machinery, modern weapons? I wish that I could think so. Some of our ideas seem to be inadequate, some of our machinery seems to me cumbrous and rusty, some of our weapons I would liken to blunderbusses, apt to go off at the wrong end."

What answer has this country for Maitland? Listen to one whose devotion to our legal system is best measured by the greatness of his contribution to it:

"Jurisprudence," writes Roscoe Pound, "is the last in the march of the sciences away from the method of deduction, from predetermined conceptions. The sociological movement in jurisprudence, the movement for pragmatism as a philosophy of law, the movement for the adjustment of principles and doctrine to the human conditions they are to govern rather than assumed first principles, the movement for putting the human factor in the central place and relegating logic to its true position as an instrument, has scarcely shown itself as yet in America."

Thus spoke Roscoe Pound in 1909. What has been accomplished? What further can be done? Can the law schools and law school teachers contribute anything?

As we have seen, the modern social conceptions have already begun to affect our courts. But this immense work of readjustment, the task of assimilating social and economic facts, of adapting old principles to present needs, of working out modern premises necessitated by new conditions, should not devolve upon the courts alone. They are already laboring under too heavy a pressure. Let figures tell their tale. The United States Supreme Court in the October term last year disposed of 472 cases. For the same period 100 years ago, the court passed on only 58 cases. In 1914 the Massachusetts Supreme Court wrote opinions in 470 cases, while during the same period 100 years ago a single volume of Massachusetts reports contains but 134 opinions. Johnson's reports for 1814, covering both law and chancery cases decided by two courts, disclose 228 eases, whereas the single New York Court of Appeals in 1914 disposed of 679 cases. These are the dry statistics of a fact known to all the Bar, that our supreme courts suffer from overburdening labor, putting cramping limits upon argument and deliberation and study. Their time and energy are exclusively devoted to deciding specific controversies submitted for their decision. To a very large degree they are practically compelled to choose from what is offered to them.

Nor is the need of working out the law as an entirety primarily a function of the Bar. By tradition and theory the American lawyer contributes to the development of law as the partisan in a controversy. An overworked and absorbed Bar can only assist in the problems now confronting the law so far as any concrete litigation demands consideration beyond the fringe of the field which it touches. Those few who do free themselves from the absorption of practice and turn their time into constructive contributions to the law are indeed of invaluable assistance to courts and practitioners.

No, the work is too exacting and too intimately connected with the welfare of the community not to be done consciously and systematically, and to be left to casual judicial contributions or the occasional incidence of a law suit. The work of assimilating the raw material, of restating the law in its entirety, must be done by those in position to give their entire time to the arduous task. Here the growing body of teachers of the law find a natural field. I do not mean to suggest the establishment of *ex cathedra* learning. Quite the contrary. The work involves humility, the trained humility of those who recognize that the ascertained is but a pitiably small fraction of the ascertainable. What we need are doctrinal writers—men who labor steadily upon law as an organic whole, who should produce tentative working hypotheses to be tested, revised and modified as the actualities of controversy require. For the work of the law schools must meet the tests and suffer the modifications of practical experience. Bench and Bar will apply such tests and make such modifications.

True enough, law is by no means a fixed science. In law, as Justice Holmes has pointed out again and again, we are dealing almost wholly with considerations of social advantage which very rarely permit of quantitative determination. This need not deter us from the scientific method; it all the more makes scientific treatment our soundest hope. While not to so large a degree as law, the whole history of medicine demonstrates that it is a science of probabilities and not of certainties. But for that very reason the medical schools have become organized experiment stations for working out theories which the practitioner applies, tests and corrects.

The same thing must be done for law by the law schools. The same thing was done at a previous stage in our legal history. In the formative days of our law, Story, as Professor Pound has so brilliantly told us, restated the English common law and thereby secured its acceptance as the basis of the American common law against the contending pressure of French law. In a similar way, if to a less degree, John Chipman Gray has furnished the basis for judicial decisions upon complicated questions of property law, and we are now witnessing the steady, wholesome influence of Dean Wigmore upon the law of evidence throughout the country. Story's and Gray's and Wigmore's works were essentially academic products.

Again, so long as the energies of courts necessarily are spent upon decisions of specific cases, the tendency is inevitably towards building up so-called local law. As a result there is an all too unfortunate emphasis upon local differences, and differences multiply into further separating anomalies. This tendency to particularism can only partly be arrested by the movement for uniform legislation. For the greatest field in the law is bound to remain development through decisions. Here likewise the law schools can help greatly. By the systematic treatment of the law, after thorough testing of all available jural matter, through the production of treatises of commanding authority and through a demonstration of identity of problems throughout the country, the law schools would further unity of decisions and thereby uniformity of law in the various jurisdictions.

Of course, great men—men like Ames and Holmes and Maitland and Thayer—will respond to the hunger of creation that is in them. But the scholarship that is now needed should not depend upon the accident of genius. Here, as elsewhere, opinion is in itself a creative force. If the Bar and Bench will require of law schools their needed share in the development of the law, the law schools will be compelled to meet the need. Therefore the profession should demand law schools fit for this work—the work not merely of training practitioners but of helping to develop the law, of participating in a great state service.

Not only by producing treatises to which they have devoted years of research, but in their class-room work, the law school teachers can assist the law in its needed response to present demands. It is not enough that young men should come from our schools equipped to become skillful practitioners, armed with precedent and ready in argument. We fail in our important office if they do not feel that society has breathed into law the breath of life and made it a living, serving soul. We must show them the law as an instrument and not an end of organized humanity. We make of them clever pleaders but not lawyers if they fail to catch the glorious vision of the law, not as a harsh Procrustean bed into which all persons and all societies must inexorably be fitted, but as a vital agency for human betterment.

Not so long ago sympathetic observers, like Lord Bryce, reported the loss of prestige of the profession. For the time being the lawyer was eclipsed because he went outside of his field; he became the subordinate to wealth, instead of the director of social forces. The lawyer is undoubtedly again coming into his own. Never were the demands upon him greater. Our society is becoming more and more complex, which means more law and not less law. The lawyer, by tradition and by training, is the expert in affairs. He must adapt old loyalties to new facts; he, above all, must find ways to reconcile order with progress. The problems ahead present to our profession opportunities for great leadership, but correspondingly they call for equipment adequate to the task; they call for fresh thinking, disinterested courage, and vision.

Chapter 49

The Work of the American Law School

1923

Roscoe Pound

Roscoe Pound (October 27, 1870-July 1, 1964) was dean of the University of Nebraska law school, from 1903 to 1907, professor at Northwestern from 1907 to 1909, the University of Chicago from 1909 to 1910, and Harvard from 1910 to 1947, serving from 1916 to 1936, and professor at UCLA from 1949 to 1953. This address was delivered at the dedication of the University of West Virginia College of Law building, November 17, 1923, and was first published at 30 *West Virginia Law Quarterly* 1-17 (1923).

Plato tells us that, of all kinds of knowledge, the knowledge of good laws may do most for the learner. A deep study of the science of law, he adds, may do more than all other writing to give soundness to our judgment and stability to the state. Indeed, he goes so far as to claim for it that it will confirm and advance the good in their goodness and reclaim the bad, except that incorrigible remnant for whom he conceives there is no help short of the gallows. It is true this high estimate of the study of law has two presuppositions that must give us pause. For one thing, the philosopher was thinking and writing of study of an ideal body of laws devised for an ideal social and political order, not of study of the code of legal precepts that happens to obtain at a given time in a given state. For another thing, he writes under the influence of the Socratic identification of wickedness with ignorance and the belief that when men are well informed as to the right they will not go wrong. Thus it might be questioned whether the study of law in a professional school is the same thing as that study of law which Plato commends so highly. Also it is not so clear to us today that we may combat evil with mere learning. With full allowance for this last consideration, however, we still have warrant for high claims for study of the science of law.

But, some one will say, is it a science of law that you study in the professional school of today? You study the Anglo-American common law. You study that common law in its practical application as set forth in the reported decisions of the courts. You investigate, not the principles of justice nor the ideal of the social and legal order, but the recorded experience of the administration of justice among English-speaking peoples. You study these materials in order to train lawyers for the practice of their profession. How are these things to achieve even a large measure of what Plato expected from the science of law?

Plato called for knowledge of good laws and for deep study of the science of law. We set up law schools to teach "law." But are these the same? Does "law" include "good laws"? Does the teaching of "law" involve deep study of the science of law? What is "law"?

To the lay mind the answer is simple: Law is an aggregate of laws, and laws are rules. Law is the whole body of legal precepts that obtain in the time and place. Indeed, some jurists have acceded to this lay view of the matter, and the analytical school, which was conspicuous in England and America in the last century, took this for its fundamental position. It held that lawyers were concerned only with the precepts which the state established, or which the state recognized and enforced through its tribunals. With the goodness or badness of these precepts lawyers had nothing to do. Nor was the science of law to go beyond an ordering and systematizing of these precepts. If this is the sound theory of law, and the true conception of the science of law, certainly it is not the good law and the science of law of which Plato wrote. Moreover, if such is to be our conception, we may well inquire whether there is much warrant for an academic school of law. We may well ask whether the aggregate of legal precepts applied for the time being in the particular place needs to be taught academically—whether it is not the best and the simplest course to learn them in the office of the practitioner, as was formerly the custom. We may well ask, even if it be thought that these precepts may be taught best in a school, whether it is worth while to devote large endowments and set up expensive university schools to teach a set of precepts that may be repealed by the next legislature.

In truth the matter is by no means as simple as the common sense of the laymen or the dogmatism of the analytical jurist make it appear. There is much more in law than a mere aggregate of legal precepts. Legal precepts are something much more complicated than the baseball rules or the football rules, or the constitutions and by-laws of clubs and fraternal orders, or the army regulations, or even than the municipal penal ordinances. Good laws in the sense of ideals are a large element in the apparatus by which causes are decided every day in the tribunals, and the science of law must take account of this element if it is to give us a true picture of the legal precepts that obtain for the moment. Likewise the science of law must do more than arrange and systematize those precepts. It must investigate the way they are given shape and are eked out and are developed with reference to ideals and by means of a juristic and judicial technique. It must investigate the means by which abstract formulas are made into living instru-

25. Roscoe Pound (1820-1964), a long-serving dean of Harvard and proponent of the use of social science in legal analysis, overtly relied on continental approaches to scholarship to promote a progressive view of the law. (*Courtesy of Art & Visual Materials, Special Collections Department, Harvard Law School Library.*)

ments of justice in their interpretation and application. Such a science of law may indeed give soundness to our judgment and stability to the state. It is no less a science that is taught in the American law school.

Three elements go to make up the law. The first element is legal precepts, the element to which Bentham referred when he said that law was an aggregate of laws. The second element is a traditional technique of deciding cases; a technique of finding the grounds of decision in legislation supplemented by traditional legal materials, or, in the absence of legislation, on the basis of the traditional materials alone; a technique of developing and applying legal precepts whereby those precepts are supplemented, extended, restricted, and thus adapted to the administration of justice. The third element is a body of ideas as to the end or purpose of law and as to what legal precepts ought to be in view thereof, an ideal picture of the social order with consequent pictures of the details of the legal ordering of society, with reference to which legal precepts and the traditional technique of decision are developed and applied and are continually given new shape or new content or new application in the changing circumstances of life.

No one questions that legal precepts are law. But if we mean by law that body of materials by means of which the courts decide the controversies that come before them, legal precepts are not all of the law. Indeed, it is impossible for them to be all of the law. Human wisdom does not suffice to provide a complete and perfect body of precepts for which no supplement and no gloss will be needed, and in which every human controversy can find its exact preappointed solution. No matter what the legal precepts may be for the time being, no matter what the last legislature may have prescribed or the justices of the highest appellate tribunal may have announced in the last lot of opinions handed down, interpretations and distinctions and analogical extensions and logical inferences and equitable applications will be called for by the infinite variety of human life to which the precepts must be applied. The precepts, the statutes, the judicial opinions will prove to be but materials from which tribunals must construct grounds of decision for states of fact which those who formulated the precepts, those who drew the statutes, those who wrote the opinions had never been called upon to consider. They are able to do this because of a certain judicial and juristic craftsmanship, because of a traditional technique, because of habits of mind which are the most enduring features of a legal system.

By way of example, consider four settled habits of mind of the common law lawyer—his attitude as to the force to be given to judicial decisions, his attitude toward specific redress and substituted redress, his attitude toward legislation, and his tendency to think in terms of relations. As a matter of course he attributes to judicial decision a controlling force in the decision of subsequent cases. As a matter of course he regards substituted redress as the normal type and specific redress as something exceptional, reserved for cases for which substituted redress is not adequate. As a matter of course he regards a statutory rule as something introduced arbitrarily into the general body of the common law, without any necessary or systematic relation thereto, in order to govern some special situation, and hence governing that situation only. As a matter of course he thinks in terms of relation—of husband and wife, landlord and tenant, master and servant, principal and agent, principal and surety, vendor and purchaser. So completely do these mental habits shape his legal thinking that he is at a loss to understand how the lawyers of half the world can think in radically different fashion upon each point. The civil-law lawyer finds his common law in texts and conceives of a judicial decision as determining nothing beyond the case in which it was rendered. He thinks of specific redress as normal and substituted redress as exceptional. He reasons by analogy from legislative texts and confines the force of a settled line of adjudication to the exact proposition it establishes. He thinks of will, where we think of relation, and speaks of the law of persons or family law, of usufruct, of the contract of letting services, of the contract of mandate, of the contract of suretyship, and of the contract of sale. We have a traditional technique of deciding with reference to the judicial decisions of the past, a traditional technique of developing the grounds of decision of particular cases on the basis of reported judicial experience. The civilian has a traditional technique of construing legal texts, and a traditional technique of developing the grounds of decision therefrom. In each case the art of working with legal precepts is more significant than the details of the legal precepts themselves.

But the administration of justice involves more than the interpreting and applying of given precepts by means of a traditional technique. It happens continually that courts must choose between competing principles, developing the one and distinguishing the other. They must choose to apply this precept by analogy and thus to extend its scope, and to restrict that precept that might well cover the case. They must choose to go in one path of legal analogy and not in another, where both lie open before them. The choice is not one of inexorable logic. Nor is it a matter of mere personal inclination or personal caprice. It is governed by settled ideals of the end of law and of what the legal order, and hence what legal precepts, should be in view thereof. These ideals give the background upon which judicial decision and juristic writing are projected. They determine the choice of starting points for judicial and juristic reasoning, the choice of analogies, and the selection of the concrete materials with which to fill out abstract formulas. Consider the test of applicability to American conditions that played a determining part in the formative period of American common law. How did courts ascertain what was applicable and what was not? There were no precepts defining applicability. The phrase had no historical content. They could only refer to an idealized picture of pioneer, rural, agricultural America of the fore part of the nineteenth century. That picture became part of the law. Other such pictures may be seen in connection with the criteria of conformity to "the nature of free government" or conformity to the "nature of American government" or to the "nature of American institutions," which have served as the basis of so many decisions on constitutional law; in connection with the hypothetical "old law of England," that idealization of parts of the medieval law to which so many things were referred a generation ago; and in connection with "the common law as it was at the time of colonization," an idealization of seventeenth-century law in terms and for purposes of the present, which still serves as the basis of decision in more than one of our commonwealths.

Nor are the legal precepts that make up the first and most obvious element of the law merely a body of simple commands and prohibitions. There are, indeed, many rules—many precepts in which a definite detailed legal consequence is attached to a definite detailed state of facts. But the lawyer knows well that he may seldom expect to find such a rule precisely applicable to his problem. Often he can hope only to find a principle—a generalization giving an authoritative premise for judicial and juristic reasoning. Often he must turn to some legal conception—to some critically defined type of situation to which he may refer or by which he may measure the facts of the case before him and thus find a basis for legal reasoning. Often there is no more than a standard—a general measure of conduct, to be applied with reference to the circumstances of each case, with wide margins of application, and an ultimate reference to what is fair and reasonable on the particular facts.

Thus rules are no more than a small fraction of the whole that we call law. Often they are the least stable part of the law. In a large view they are the least significant part. If one doubt this, let him compare the rules of 1800 with those of 1830, of 1860, of 1890, and of today. Where is the learning of real actions of 1800? Where are the nice rules of common law pleading of 1830? Where are the pedantic distinctions of bailments that obtained in 1860, or the minute precepts as to appellate procedure and error in trials at law that were at the height of their vogue in 1890? Yet how stable have principles and conceptions proved in comparison. If our law schools taught rules only, their teaching would be built upon the sand. It is because they must teach and do teach principles and conceptions and how to use them, standards and how to apply them, the traditional technique of the lawyers' and judges' craft, and the traditional ideals of what law is and what it is for—it is for these reasons that we may assert for the law school what Plato claimed for the study of law. When we train common-law lawyers, i. e., lawyers bred in the traditional art of decision that has grown up among English-speaking peoples, we give soundness to judgment and stability to the state. For our Anglo-American polity is a legal polity and our political institutions are legal institutions. But we seek to make common-law lawyers in whose hands the tradition shall further the progress of civilization. We seek to train common-law lawyers in whose hands the traditional Anglo-American technique of working out the grounds of decision from the judicial experience of the past shall continue to be an instrument of justice. In Plato's phrase, we seek to transmit a knowledge of good laws.

Although legal precepts in the narrowest sense, i. e., rules attaching a definite detailed legal consequence to a definite detailed state of facts, are the staple of ancient codes, it is not true, even in the beginnings of law, that the law is a mere body of legal precepts. In the beginning law is scarcely set off from other forms of social control. There is an undifferentiated social control by religion, ethical custom, and enacted rules. Hence knowledge of the traditional religious precepts and of the traditionally established ethical custom, as well as knowledge of the traditional interpretation of the written law, is even more important for the administration of justice than knowledge of the precepts promulgated in the code. Thus legal education is as old as law. For although the promulgated precepts are written out for all to read, the tradition must be transmitted through some sort of instruction. With the evolution of the legal order and development of the elaborate systems of the maturity of law, the relative significance of authoritatively established rules becomes even less and the demand for legal education continually increases.

In the modern world, legal education takes three forms: The Continental academic type, running back to legal education in ancient Rome; the English apprentice type, going back to the medieval conception of the profession as analogous to a craft, with its own government, its own traditional art or mystery, and its own instruction by the neophyte's serving as apprentice to a master; and the American academic professional type, growing out of the inapplicability of the English type to the conditions of the formative period of American law and the need of a rapid working over and adaptation of seventeenth-century English law in order to make of it a common law for America.

In the beginning of Roman law, the little-differentiated or undifferentiated body of religious precepts, ethical custom, and legal rules, by which the social order was maintained, was a tradition of the *pontifices*. Except as codified by the Twelve Tables, down to the fourth century B. C. this tradition was possessed exclusively by the patricians, who alone were eligible to the priesthood. The great man who knew the tradition sat in the court of his house and advised his dependents, drew legal documents for them, and, if need was, conducted causes for them. A turning point in legal history is the secularization of the law, which took place at Rome at the opening of the fourth century B. C. As a part of this process of secularization, the first plebeian *pontifex maximus* began to give consultations in public, so that students could listen and take notes. Also those who knew the law began to give advice to all comers, and had hearers, as they were called, who attended the consultations, learned the tradition and the traditional art, and in time, when they had become learned in the law, might themselves sit and give counsel. Thus in place of the priestly caste who have a class monopoly of the tradition, we get a profession with a sort of professional monopoly. When, in the reign of Augustus, the jurisconsults come to be licensed by the emperor, the transition is complete. At least as far back as the reign of Augustus we find that the jurisconsult is both counsellor and teacher, and this double function continues through the classical period. Not only do students attend consultations and take notes, but the jurisconsult lectures to them and even writes institutional treatises for them. Moreover, there is evidence that there were teachers of law in the classical period who were not practitioners.

Law schools as such developed in the period of maturity of law. The school of most importance was at Berytus, which in the fifth century was the chief seat of legal learning. The teachers of law in this school were men of culture, learned in the classical law, and possessed of an academic legal science only just short of the practical legal science of the classical jurists. From their time to the present, the academic law school has been the chiefest factor in the development of Roman law. Their notes upon the classical texts, editing them and bringing them down to date as statements of the actual law, as well as interpreting them and putting their details into a harmonious, logically constructed system, prepared the way for Justinian's Digest, which is the common law of at least half of the world today.

There is evidence of a continuity of law teaching in Italy from the law schools of Justinian's time to the rise of the great medieval teachers of law at Bologna in the twelfth century. Thus in a sense the methods of the school at Berytus set the standard for the teaching of Roman law for the modern world. But beyond this, the conditions of teaching at fifth-century Berytus and in twelfth-century Italy were the same. In the maturity of law in the ancient world, the writings of the chief jurisconsults of the classical era had been given statutory authority. Hence the task of the teacher was to interpret and expound these texts of the second and third centuries as a living body of law for the fifth and sixth centuries. In the same way in twelfth-century Italy the task was to interpret and expound the codification of Roman law by Justinian in the sixth century as a universal law of Christendom six centuries later. Thus from the beginning legal education in the modern Roman law was a training in the interpretation and application of written texts.

To understand the academic juristic method of the medieval Roman law, we must remember that medieval thought assumed the existence of a universal Christian society, which on its temporal side was a continuation of the ancient Roman empire. Postulating the continuity of the empire, the *Corpus Juris* was authoritative legislation binding upon the empire over which Justinian had ruled. It was an age of authority. Hence all that seemed permissible was analysis of the text and interpretation. Thinking of the Digest of Justinian as a statute and so of every text as written at one time, the academic teachers sought by means of analysis and formal logic to reconcile conflicting texts, to develop the implied content of each text, and to carry out the content to all its logical conclusions. As academic teaching of Roman law became the practical teaching of law for western Europe, a great part of the work of the teachers was application of the texts to hypothetical cases, leading to distinctions, analogical extensions, and generalizations in the form of maxims. Thus we get two characteristics of Roman-law teaching that persist to this day. First, it is primarily a teaching of the art of using authoritative texts as the basis for administering justice. Second, it is an academic teaching upon the basis of purely hypothetical cases and the opinions of the doctors as to the proper application of the texts to these cases. In consequence it has no immediate relation to actual cases. It ignores judicial experience. It discusses opinions on the texts and academic solutions of hypothetical cases, conceiving of the texts as laying down universal propositions, raising universal questions, and to be interpreted for all times, all places, and all men.

In the sixteenth century, the Humanists gave another direction to academic teaching of Roman law. The scholastic dialectical apparatus of the commentators, well adapted to organize any particular topic of the law, involved so diffuse and elaborate an exposition that only a small portion of the law could be treated in the reasonable limits of academic lectures. At most the professor could expound a few texts during a term, and for the rest the student must read by himself. The Humanists began to work out a system of Roman law as a whole. They engaged in a systematic exposition of the law derived from the texts instead of an exposition of the texts in their own order. Thus begins that search for a universal systematic arrangement, that quest for an analytical scheme whereby the whole law may be exhibited as a complete body of harmonious, logically interdependent precepts, flowing logically from a small number of established fundamental propositions, which has been characteristic of civilian exposition of law ever since and has exercised a profound influence upon systematic ideas in our own law.

After the Reformation and the consequent downfall of the canon law as an everyday agency of social control, Roman law was left in possession of the field as the one system of law with claims to universality. But by this time the idea of the continuity of the empire, and of the binding force of the Corpus Juris as authoritative legislation for all Christendom had broken down. It was apparent to jurists that they must find some test of the authority of a legal precept, or of a juristic principle, other than the text of the Corpus Juris. Accordingly lawyers began to study the actual course of decision in the courts in order to ascertain what parts of the Corpus Juris had been received as customary law and what had not. Thus they worked out the *usus modernus pandectarum* as a recognized system. Meanwhile the academic jurists sought to find a philosophical basis for the reception of Roman law upon which to rest the authority of its rules. This quest led them to adopt reason as the ultimate test of the validity of a legal precept. The result was a liberal, creative period, strikingly analogous to the classical period of Roman law in the ancient world. But in large part they assumed that the Roman law was embodied reason and reconciled authority with their rationalist philosophy in this way.

At the end of the 18th century and in the 19th century the law was codified in substantially the whole of the Roman-law world. But the modern codes assume a background of the modern Roman law, which is the common law in all the jurisdictions in which these codes obtain. Also the technique of development of code precepts, the technique of application of the codes, and the technique of judicial decision on the basis thereof, are the technique of the modern Roman law, derived from the classical Roman law and developed academically in the modern world. Hence in the Roman law world legal education is and must be a Roman-law education for the same reason that with us legal education is and must be a common-law education. Also it must be an academic education because the modern Roman law is a university-made law. Its spirit is the spirit of the university. Its organs are academic treatises. Its oracles are academic teachers. The great names in the civil law are not the names of great judges, or of great advocates. They are the names of great teachers.

If, then, the method of teaching law in the world of the modern Roman law is an academic method, by lectures and study of academic commentaries on authoritative texts, and of academic doctrinal treatises, it is because the modern Roman law demands such instruction. It is a university-made law. From its beginnings in ancient Rome, its technique has been a technique of developing and applying written texts, and its oracles have been teachers and academic commentators, not judges. Those who would introduce this method as a method of legal teaching in our law should reflect upon the intimate connection between the academic teaching of Roman law and the traditional technique which is taught thereby. They should consider how far such a method consists with the genius of our technique which has a wholly different history and has been developed by wholly different agencies.

For the common law, our story begins in the 13th century. In that century our law passes definitely into a stage of strict law, and it reaches its classical era in the 17th century. In the form which it took in the latter century it was received as the common law of America. Two points of contrast with the Roman law are decisive. In the first place, it had few or no authoritative texts. There are, it is true, Magna Charta, and the legislation of Edward I. But there is no complete authoritative statement. Bracton's treatise, "The Crown and flower of English medieval jurisprudence", was not official and did not receive legislative sanction, as did the classical Roman treatises, nor become the subject of commentary. The common law was the work of the King's justices, sitting in the King's courts and applying reason to judicial experience, rather than to juristic or legislative texts. For, in the next place, we must note that whereas in the classical Roman practice the judge was appointed for each case *pro hac vice*, and was not a learned lawyer, from the 13th century at least, the judges of the King's courts are permanent magistrates learned in the law. A Roman *iudex* could not follow his own decisions because he was not a permanent judge. He would not follow another *iudex* because the latter was not a learned lawyer and his opinion carried no weight. What counted was the opinion of the learned jurisconsult on which the *iudex* acted. The common-law judge, on the other hand, tended to follow his own decisions because he held a permanent office, and he tended to follow the decisions of other judges because they were learned lawyers and it was natural to imitate them. Thus from the outset the common-law technique becomes one of applying judicial experience—one of developing the grounds of decision out of the reported decisions of the past. What may fairly be called reports of decisions begin in the 13th century, and the doctrine of precedents may be found in the Year Books as early as the beginning of the 14th century.

Meanwhile, agencies of law-teaching had been growing up with the law. In another respect the common law as a system of law begins with the 13th century. For in that century there was in some sort a secularization of law. The non-clerical element came to predominate upon the bench, and a profession of non-clerical lawyers grew up to practice before the nonclerical judges. Apprentices of law were known already in the time of Edward I. How the societies of apprentices grew up we do not know precisely. Apparently certain masters of law took pupils, and the groups gradually expanded and became societies. After the manner of the Middle Ages, they came to be organized in colleges or corporations, self-perpetuating and self-governing. The path to the bar and to the bench was through these societies, not, as on the Continent, through the Universities. Since they were societies of professional lawyers, and practice before the courts of the common law was exclusively in their hands and in the hands of the sergeants, a guild or order selected from among them by the King, they controlled legal education by their control of admission to the profession. They were made up of benchers, the governing body, barristers and students. And the latter, after a probationary studentship, were called to the bar by their Inn.

A member of the bar, a "reader" or lecturer, was responsible during his term for teaching the students. The instruction was partly in the form of "readings" or lectures, taking the form of analysis and exposition of a statute, or of some section of a statute. Here we may see Roman influence, through imitation of the method of the universities. But statutes were too small a part of the law for these readings to suffice. And the bulk of the law, not formulated in written texts, but contained in the reported decisions, or in the tradition of what had been decided, did not lend itself to analytical and expository lectures in the scholastic manner. Hence the other form of instruction was by moots, in which students argued before a bencher and two barristers in the hall of the Inn. These moots were of such importance that the opinions of learned lawyers sitting in them as judges are sometimes reported, and some of them are cited as authority today.

The students learned by observing the lawyer in action in the courts, and by trying their hands in the moots. It was essentially an apprentice training.

We must remember that the common law was not taught in the universities. They taught the Roman law and the canon law, but had no professorships of English law until the 18th century. They had the training of advocates in the ecclesiastical courts and in Admirality, but after the 16th century, when for a time it seemed that there might be a reception of Roman law in England, the training of civilians became of relatively slight importance. Even today, when the English universities are beginning to take some part in the professional training of common-law lawyers, the basis of the instruction is Roman law, jurisprudence, and a historical and political introduction to law, followed by a rapid survey of what might be called the institutes of English law. There is a palpable gulf between professional instruction and academic instruction. Nor is this gulf to be wondered at. For the common law is not an academic system. From the beginning it has been a law of the courts as definitely as the modern Roman law, and indeed the Roman law since the 5th century, has been a law of the universities. The great names of English law are the names of judges, not of teachers. Indeed it used to be that a text book of the common law was of no persuasive authority and might not be cited unless written by a judge. Naturally legal education in England is as characteristically professional as legal education on the Continent is characteristically academic. In each case there is a decisive practical reason. For teaching of law is primarily a teaching of the traditional technique of developing the legal materials, and of developing grounds of decision of particular cases therefrom. In England the technique to be taught is a lawyer's technique of developing and applying the materials to be found in the law reports, not a teacher's technique of developing and applying written texts.

Although we received the political institutions of 17th century England, and in the latter part of the 18th and fore part of the 19th century, received the English common law, and although we set up our system of courts on an English model, there were compelling reasons why the English method of legal education could not be taken over for America. The systematic study which had been maintained in the Inns of Court almost to the 18th century had degenerated in that century to a few empty forms, and until the middle of the 19th century the real training was by study in the office of a practitioner, reading, observing, copying precedents and opinions, and drawing papers. In America we did not preserve the division of the profession into counsellors and attorneys. When we received English institutions and English law, the last remnants of the relationally organized society of the Middle Ages were thrown over. Craft organization had become obsolete, and only a few great companies preserved its memory. A purely individualist organization of society appealed both to Puritan and to pioneer. Moreover, the conditions of rural, agricultural, pioneer society demanded and produced a versatility, a distrust of specialization, and a proneness to allow everyone to demonstrate freely what he could do, that made organization of the profession in self-governing societies after the English model impossible. Immediately after the Revolution, law and lawyers were in much disfavor; the law because it could not escape the odium of its English origin in the period of bitter feelings after the war, lawyers because they alone seemed to thrive in the economic disorganization and disturbed conditions that followed peace. These circumstances and the radical Democratic notions of the Jeffersonian era determined our professional organization.

Another reason operated also to shape our organization of the bar, and to give character to our legal education. In England the courts were centralized at Westminster. Hence, the bar was centralized at the Inns of Court. But with us, in a country of long distances and expensive travel, central courts entailed an intolerable expense upon litigants. We decentralized the courts of general jurisdiction at law and in equity, almost from the start, and sought to set up a judicial organization that should bring justice to every man's back door. This decentralizing of the judicial system involved a decentralizing of the bar. As each of the old common-law courts had its roll of attorneys, so each local court of general jurisdiction had its own bar. There could be no such centralized system of admission to practice, and consequent centralized control of legal education, as the control of admission by the Inns of Court made possible in England.

While all these things were making for the system of reading in the office of a local practitioner, which obtained in this country until within a generation, and still obtains to some extent in certain localities, another force was acting to promote the academic professional training which is now characteristically American.

We received English law at the end of the 18th and in the fore part of the 19th century. But we could not receive it exactly as it stood in the English books. We had many things to be provided for which English legislation and English judges had never been called upon to consider. Much in English law was devised for social and political and economic conditions quite different from ours. Our courts were constrained to work out somewhat rapidly a system of legal precepts adapted to a new and growing country upon the basis of the somewhat stagnant English legal tradition at the end of the 18th century. For half a century at least our chief concern was to work out an American common law—to develop a system of certain and detailed legal precepts which should meet the requirements of American life. Apprentice trained lawyers, knowing only the traditional technique as the practitioners had learned it in the courts, could not rise to the exigencies of this demand. Indeed two things quite un-English, natural law and comparative law, played leading roles in the evolution of an American law, and for these, so far as they were made effective agencies of shaping our legal development and directing the growth of our law, we had to look to teachers.

Our first law schools, indeed, were but practitioners' offices. Certainly in the case of the first school of the common law in America, the one conducted at Litchfield, Connecticut, by Judge Reeve, there was a transition from law office to law school with no definite dividing line. As there were more students than in an office, the talks of the preceptor with the student turned into dictated lectures, but the spirit and method were those of an office apprenticeship.

On the other hand, the example of the Vinerian Professorship at Oxford and of Blackstone's lectures suggested a different method. That example was followed eagerly in the years when American law was formative. Wythe was professor at William and Mary in 1779-1780. James Wilson was professor at the College of Philadelphia in 1790-1791. Kent was professor at Columbia from 1793 to 1798. Isaac Parker became Royall professor at Harvard in 1815. But the general lectures which they delivered to academic audiences did no more than prepare the way. When the Harvard Law School was established in 1817 it was essentially a school of the Litchfield type; it afforded an improved method of study under a preceptor in a law office. It was not until the appointment of Joseph Story as Dane professor at Harvard that academic lectures and professional training under the direction of a common-law lawyer were brought into one system. Story was a common-law lawyer, and the traditions of English legal teaching insured that an Anglo-American academic law school under his guidance would be a professional school. But the philosophical ideas of the time in which Story had been trained insured that a school over which he presided would be a school of law, not a lawyer's office teaching rules of thumb. Also Story's zealous exposition of the doctrines of English law in the light of a natural-law philosophy and of comparative law, enabled the school in which he taught to remain a school devoted to the common law. From Story and Greenleaf to Parker and Parsons and Washburn, thence to Langdell and Ames, and thence to the American law schools of today, is a continuous evolution. It has given us a system of academic professional instruction that is as characteristically American as our American common law itself. It has given us a system of legal education that grows out of and expresses the spirit of our law as completely as the Continental system expresses the spirit of the modern Roman law, and as the English system expresses the spirit of the medieval common law. For if the modern Roman law is jurist-made, and English law is court-made, American law has been made by courts guided and inspired by jurists who worked scientifically upon a proved body of judicial experience in the administration of justice. Thus there are two elements in our technique as distinctly as there is but one element in the technique of the civilian and but one in the technique of the classical common law. Moreover, in the interpretation and application of constitutions we have had the same problem of developing a body of law from enduring texts, to which the academic legal science of the civilians has been addressed for centuries. Here also judges and teachers have each had a part. Along with the decisions of Marshall, the teaching of Story and of Cooley has given content to abstract formulas and determined the technique of constitutional interpretation which has become a distinctive feature of our law.

In the law school of a state university the American system of academic professional legal education cannot but be especially fruitful. A study of the local legal institutions and of the local law from a universal standpoint is made more effective through a close relation between the law school of the state and the organized bar of the state. There is no gulf between academic teaching of law and the law of the tribunals. Each reacts upon and corrects the other. Likewise where bench and bar are trained for the most part in the law school of the state university, the loyalty of the alumni which is the mainstay of American institutions of learning, must make of the law school a center of professional life such as we have never had in our decentralized judicial and professional organizations. Thus the sane measuring of what is by what ought to be, the intelligent testing of theories by the exigencies of concrete controversies, and the critique of judicial pronouncements with reference to rational principles, which have become the mark of our academic law schools, may come to be a part of the intellectual life of the whole profession.

There are many signs that our law is entering upon a new stage of development. Already there is call for juristic creative activity and for the same judicial resourcefulness and legislative inventive capacity that marked the formative period of our institutions. When we believed in the efficacy of effort, we were able to frame the Constitution of the United States, and we were able, almost at a stroke, to make the law of 17th-century England into a law for 19th-century America. Few creative periods in legal history can show greater achievements in so short a time. Today we need the same spirit, the same faith in our power to do things, the same determination to make of our traditional legal materials a machinery of justice under the conditions of time and place. If we are to do our duty by the common law in the 20th century, we must make it a living system of doing justice for the society of today and tomorrow, as the framers of our polity made of the traditional materials of their generation an instrument of justice for that time and for ours. And chiefly the responsibility for so doing will rest upon teachers and writers, as it did when Kent and Story published their academic lectures and assured that we should live under the common law; and as it did when Greenleaf gave form to the law of evidence, and when Parsons and Washburn guided the growth of our law of contracts and of our law of property.

May the creative juristic thought and creative juristic writing, which has been the life of American law from its beginnings, come forth in the fullest measure from the building you dedicate today.

Chapter 50

Some Phases of Legal Education in America

1924

Harlan Fiske Stone

Harlan Fiske Stone (October 11, 1872-April 22, 1946) was professor at Columbia Law School from 1898 to 1905 and dean from 1906 to 1924, Attorney General of the United States from 1924 to 1925, Associate Justice of the United States from 1925 to 1941, and Chief Justice of the United States from 1941 to 1946. This address was delivered by Attorney General Stone at Yale University, June 18, 1924, and was first published in 58 *American Law Review* 747 (1923).

The centennial anniversary, which we are here assembled to celebrate, gives emphasis to the fact that it was in America that the English Common Law first became the subject of university study, in a real sense and it is here that that study has reached its highest development. No chapter in the history of education so stirs the imagination; no educational achievement seems more worthy of commendation or more pregnant with consequences to the future welfare of our republic. To have made the common law the subject of university study in its highest and best sense, in a span of a little more than a generation was an accomplishment, but to have given to it a novel and successful method of exposition of legal science, which has won the enthusiastic approval of the educational world at home and abroad and to have assumed a position of leadership in our profession by virtue of their scholarship and their spirit of devotion to the highest interests of the profession are high achievements in which American schools of law and American universities may take a just pride.

It is a noteworthy fact that the beginnings of the teaching of the art of a profession have always originated in private initiative and enterprise. This was true of the exposition of principles of theology from both its Greek and mediaeval sources. Hypocrates, in the oath which he administered to his disciples, enjoined them to teach the principles of the art of medicine. To this rule Law has proved no exception. Both in England and America the first steps toward systematic training in the principles of common law were the private undertakings of lawyers especially skilled and especially interested in its exposition.

One has not far to seek for the explanation of the universality of this rule. The objective in the practice of a profession is always the ministration to the spiritual or physical needs of others. Its principles are, consequently, something more than mere intellectual abstractions. Nor is it ever completely subject to scientific laws, for it has its origin in the application of a practical art, not distinguishable in its early history from a trade or business. Knowledge of the art is at first acquired and transmitted through apprenticeship; later, its accumulated learning is expounded by those of its devotees especially fitted for the task by knowledge of its principles, and by skill in its exposition. Ultimately, when it rises to the full dignity of a learned profession, its learning must be subjected to analysis, and to classification. Its principles must be stated, and restated, and its underlying causes sought out, and appraised, by those processes of analysis and exposition which can be successfully carried on only in the university.

There is a theory of history that human progress, which is the real subject of history, moves in cycles, in which each cycle progresses from its beginnings, in the more primitive type of civilization, to its conclusion, in a more complex and higher type of social development, but that each successive cycle moves swiftly, and, consequently, in a shorter space of time, to its conclusion. However disputable this may be in the field of general history, the theory finds verification in the record of the development of legal science. From the primitive beginnings of Roman law—from its apprenticeship stage, to the time of its exposition as a learned art, in the mediaeval universities, spans nearly two thousand years, and it required some seven centuries more to develop, in the art of its exposition, a technique and resourcefulness comparable to that which today obtains in the teaching of the English common law in at least a half dozen American universities. The corresponding transition in methods of study of the English common law may be traced from its beginnings, in the twelfth century, to the first serious attempt to carry on instruction in law in public institutions of learning in both England and in America, in the last of the eighteenth century—a period of some six hundred years.

The still later period, which may be referred to as that of "the intensive development" of the methods and processes of the university study of the common law, corresponding to the period which reaches from the beginnings of the study of Roman law at Bologna to the intensive study and criticism of that system in France and Germany in the nineteenth century, has begun, and come to its present high estate, within the lifetime of many here present.

Until some fifty years or less ago, when there dawned what I like to think of as the golden age of legal education in America, its story was one of vague aspirations and crude beginnings.

To Ezra Stiles, president of Yale College, belongs the honor of first proposing the establishment of a professorship of law at an American seat of learning. In 1777, he drafted a plan for a university course of lectures in law and in medicine. His plan, so far as instruction in law was concerned, did not come to fruition until forty-seven years later, when Yale carried into practical operation a plan, not for the delivery of lectures on law in dilatante fashion, such as had characterized previous attempts, but for the establishment of a course of instruction intended to prepare prospective members of the bar for the practice of their profession. In the meantime, however, professorships in law somewhat evanescent in character, had been proposed at numerous institutions of learning, and had been actually established at William and Mary College, at Columbia College, when James Kent was called to a professorship, at Princeton, at the College of Philadelphia (later the University of Pennsylvania), at Middlebury, and at Transylvania.

The instruction given in these professorships bore little relation to the practical aims and needs of those seeking to enter the profession, and the time had not yet come for the penetrating analysis and reconstruction of legal doctrine which was to be the great work of the university schools of law of our own day, so that these early experiments failed for want of students and of popular support.

The first American institution which could be fairly described as a school for the training of lawyers was the private enterprise of Judge Tapping Reeve, who established his school at Litchfield, Connecticut, in 1784. This, and numerous other similar enterprises which thrived during the first years of the nineteenth century, marked the transition from the stage of apprenticeship to the beginings of university law study.

Harvard took the first step toward the founding of a school of law in 1817, a step, however, which was not effective in a real sense, until Judge Story was called to the Dane professorship of law in that institution in 1830. In the meantime, in 1824, Yale College took over, as a department of the college, the private law school conducted by Seth P. Staples in New Haven. Thus began the long and honorable career of the Yale

26. Harlan Fiske Stone (1872-1946) was Dean of Columbia before resuming an active practice and becoming U.S. Attorney General and Chief Justice of the United States. (*Photograph courtesy of Columbia University School of Law.*)

School of Law, the first century of whose existence and public service comes to a close during the present year.

That service has been marked by an elevated sense duty to the profession, by a steadfast maintenance and steady improvement of its standards and an active participation and capable leadership in the movement which, in our own day, is making our leading law schools in the United States, in the truest and best sense, university schools of law.

During the earlier and major part of the century just passed, American law schools treated somewhat lightly their university connections. They were the legitimate successors of the apprenticeship system of instruction in law. Their aspirations did not extend beyond the training of acceptable lawyers in the rudiments of their profession, so that they might pass their bar examinations and begin the practice of their profession. Rarely did their instructors take up legal research and investigation as a career. Often this work as teacher was a mere incident to the career of the practicing lawyer or the judge, or a reward bestowed upon the latter when he retired from judicial labors, to enjoy his ease with dignity.

To bring the study of law into its proper relation to the great enterprise of learning which it is the function of the university to promote and to make it worthy of the great task of systematic analysis and the reconstruction of the common law which awaited it, it was needful that there should come a new and larger conception of the function of legal education—a conception which embraced not merely a rule-of-thumb acquaintance with settled legal rules and doctrines for the use of the practitioner, but which aspired to bring to the service of mankind a more profound knowledge of legal principles and their more perfect adjustment to social and economic needs.

It was needful, too, if that conception was to be realized that there should be at least a generation of preliminary study of the vast accumulation of precedent which constitutes the repository in which the legal learning of the last seven centuries has been stored, to the end that the doctrines of the common law might be stated with exactness and precision; that their origin and history might be traced; that the anomalies of the law might be segregated, their boundaries accurately defined, and some indication given of those particulars in which the common law lacks harmony and system.

It is now a full half-century since it began to be evident that this new conception of law study was to be a dominant factor in guiding the progress of legal education in the United States. Whether its rise was due to the vision and faith of particular individuals, or whether the time had come when social and economic forces conspired to expand our views of law and its functions, and thus to impel us to renewed endeavors to solve its problems, just as the revival of commerce and industry led to the revival of study of the Roman law, need not now be inquired. That that conception was formed, and that it has been the impelling and inspiring motive in the leading law schools of the country, steadily increasing in power for a generation, are the significant facts.

During that fifty years, we have been engaged in what I have already referred to as a preliminary study of the common law. The common law is preeminently a system of case law, whose doctrines have been generated, in each instance, by the facts established in some particular litigation, and again moulded and expanded, step by step, by the creative force of the facts established in other litigations. It is a law, each rule and precept of which has been generated by the clash of actual controversy, and by reason of the very nature of its origin and the method of its creation, it is endowed with an extraordinary vitality, and it possesses, beyond all other systems, the advantages of flexibility and adaptability. But any system of law whose rules are always created *ad hoc*, must, at its best, lack form and symmetry. Its development is not systematic; its precedents, because of the very method of their creation, sometime lack the foundation of scientific and philosophical generalization on which all systems of law must ultimately rest, if they are to endure and do their appointed work. Its concepts, too often lack precision and definition, and consequently, they are not invariably used with certainty and precision, and the terminology with which they are expressed tends to become uncertain in its meaning and variable in its use.

This period of preliminary study had, therefore, necessarily had to be devoted to an analysis of our law as case law, and to an investigation of its historical origins. We have penetrated the jungle of judicial decisions, tracing the pathways of principle, defining and seeking the explanation of the anomalous, and endeavoring, perhaps without entire success, to classify so much of the law as conforms to principle. The process has been one mainly of defining and systematizing our knowledge of our law as it is, in clearing away non-essentials, so as to disclose its underlying philosophy, and of noting the methods and processes by which the law has been built up.

Having come now to the point in the development of legal education when we are apparently at the conclusion of what may be referred to as "The Period of Survey" of the materials of the Common Law, is it possible for us, looking to the future, to discern how the fruits of that investigation may be used, and then to suggest what the immediate problems of legal education may be?

It was, perhaps, inevitable, in view of the professional and educational experience through which we have passed, that the traditional attitude of our profession toward the law, should be that it is a body of technical doctrine, more or less detached from the social forces which have called it into being—to be studied and used in practice much as one studies and uses the rules of a game. In short, we have failed to recognize, as clearly as we might, that law, in the final analysis, is a method of social control intimately related to those social functions which are the subject matter of economics and social sciences generally.

The common law is technically more highly developed than any other system of law, and the law teacher of the last generation, as he engaged in the task of analyzing our case law, not unnaturally directed his energies principally towards the exposition of the law in its more technical aspects. It is not surprising, therefore, that teachers of law, as well as practicing lawyers, in their effort to master the intricacies of the common law, should have become absorbed in the study and exposition of its technique, as to have lost sight of its social function, and to regard it as a body of learning quite distinct from those social forces which created it, much as the scientist regards the body of natural law which he investigates, as something distinct and apart from social organization and development.

We have now come to that point in our legal thinking when we have a clearer understanding of this relationship, and the necessity is becoming apparent of embracing, within the field of law study, an investigation of those causal elements in legal science, which are fundamental to the development of its technical doctrine.

Our most distinguished and capable teachers of law now recognize that we can no longer deal with law as though it were a hermetically sealed compartment of social science, to be explored and its principles formulated without reference to those social and economic forces which call law into existence, and from which law must derive its form and substance, if it is to serve adequately its purpose. Our problem, then, is, building on this solid foundation of knowledge of the history and technical organization of the common law, which the last generation has given us, to come to a clearer, and more accurate understanding of the relation of law to these social functions, which it endeavors to regulate and control, and this must be accomplished by the study of the technical rules of law, as tools or devices placed in the hands of the lawyer, as the means of effecting that control.

This approach to the study of the common law involves, to some extent, the revision of the law curriculum in such a manner as to throw greater emphasis upon the coordination which the study of law from the aspect of social function brings about in the choice and use of technical legal doctrines—the tools of our profession, which, in the formulation of law school curricula, we have hitherto, too often, treated as being more or less unrelated.

Even more does it require, in the teaching of law, and in the formulation of its principles in legislation, in judicial decisions and in the restatement of the law, which is the great task now undertaken by our Bar and by the law-teaching professions, that we bring to bear on the actual exposition and judicial declaration of technical legal doctrine, a well-grounded knowledge of the social and economic phenomena of our times.

By far the greater proportion of our law relates to the institution of private property. Our dealings with property, which we accomplish through the aid of its legal incidents of ownership, alienability and control by contract, constitute the subject matter of the economics of modern business. The legal incidents of personality and family relationships again deep-rooted in social institutions, constitute, for all practical purposes, the balance of our law. We cannot, therefore, proceed far with the investigation of any legal rule, nor can we, in the development of law, relate logic and history to the requirements of social utility without dependence upon well organized knowledge of social institutions and of the methods of their functioning.

Whether the requisite acquaintance with the economics of the modern business world and with social institutions, is to come from an improved and more skillfully directed study of these subjects in American colleges, or whether law schools must take the initiative in bringing into closer relationship with their work, as at present defined, graduate studies in economics and social science, is one of the large problems in the field of legal education, to which no certain solution can yet be offered. But whatever that solution may be, if it is brought about by the scientific spirit and scholarly devotion which actuates this school, as well as other leading university schools of law, the ultimate effect will be to bring our law closer to the realization of its true ideals of justice and utility. Moreover, I venture to predict that in effecting that solution, in that spirit, it will be found necessary for a considerable period to subject the data of economics and of the social science to critical examination and analysis, comparable in extent and in method to the analytical and historical study of law which has been made in the last generation. Upon the basis of such a study of social phenomena which I believe is yet to be made, we may hope to correlate the technique of law with our social, economic and business institutions both in practice and in the law school in a manner which has not hitherto been possible.

The perfection of a system of substantive law does not bring with it, as a necessary incident, its wise or efficient administration. Substantive rules of law, however ideal in substance or in form, are not self-executing. Satisfactory law enforcement involves not alone the enactment of the law to be enforced. It involves the creation of an adequate machinery for enforcement and a procedure adapted to the translation of law at rest into law in action. It is idle for us to restate law, to create new laws by legislative action, if we do not set up adequate machinery for its enforcement; if we do not devise methods for securing the regular and constant functioning of that machinery and if the laws which we do enact, however ideal in the realm of morals and in legal theory, cannot be adapted or adjusted to the available machinery of enforcement. We have been so absorbed in the great work of investigating what may be called "static law," that we have neglected the problems of the law in action. We have not been sufficiently concerned with the relation of the rules of right and duty which constitute our substantive law, to the methods of making them effective in controlling human action, nor have we realized how fruitful a field of study it presents. We hear it said on every side that our system of enforcing law is breaking down; that through lax methods of administration of the law, there is a failure of law enforcement, and a growing lack of respect for law. That the execution of our laws depends in the first instance on the vigor and fidelity of public officials and upon the psychology and temper of the people, is undoubtedly true, but it is not the whole truth. It is likewise true that it depends, in a large measure, on the organization of law enforcement machinery; on the adaptability to it, on the one hand, of the law to be enforced, and, on the other hand, on its adaptability and that of the machinery of enforcement to the popular psychology. We cannot go on indefinitely with the creation of new laws leaving to chance or to the cumbersome machinery of an outgrown administrative system, the hazard of their enforcement. Here is a wide and untilled field for study and for investigation, testing to the fullest extent of our powers of observation and calling for the exercise of all the resources of scholarship.

The extension of the functions of government into new fields of activity, has developed enormously our administrative machinery, and has brought about the adoption of administrative devices in law enforcement, which have been steadily encroaching upon individual liberty in the supposed interest of celerity and efficiency of law enforcement. That, with the increasing complexity of government and its increasing contacts with the private citizen, the ancient methods of securing the legal rights of the Government by litigation in open court, cannot be adhered to in all cases, must be recognized, but it must be remembered also that one of the precious legal inheritances from eighteenth century England was the fundamental notions of personal right and liberty which then colored all our legal thinking and which found expression in our Bill of Rights and in the first ten amendments of the Constitution. That idea of personal liberty under law so nobly conceived and so dearly won must not be lightly surrendered, in our zeal to secure effective administration at the expense of private right and of the independence of the individual. To preserve the essential principles of individual liberty and to adjust to them a necessary and effective administrative system presents today problems of law and of government of the first importance, the proper solution of which should be of the deepest concern to the American people. Those problems cannot be solved in the field of politics and legislation alone. They must have brought to bear upon them by our University Schools of Law and Political Science, the same thoroughgoing research, the same analysis conceived and carried on in the spirit of science and scholarship as have hitherto been devoted to the problems of private law.

They will continue the work of analysis and research of legal doctrine so nobly begun. By the organization of their curriculums; by the emphasis of their teaching; by the coordination of their studies of technical legal doctrine with studies in Economics and Social Sciences, they will bring into closer and more appropriate relationship the technique of the law and the functions of organized society.

We look to them to extend the investigation of law from the study of its principles, as statements of rules of right and duty, to those processes by which those rules of law are translated into action and by which law is made effective in the control of human action, to the end that the administration of law may keep pace with our ever expanding faculty in the creation of it. We look to them, by the methods of science; by the force of scholarly and disinterested leadership, to point the way for the accommodation of our administrative system to the vital necessity of preserving in our legal system the fundamentals of personal liberty.

No nation can long endure, nor will it long deserve to endure, if it does not make its first concern the enactment of wise and just laws and strive for their honest and efficient administration. No nation can feel that concern whose people do not love justice and have faith in and respect for its institution for the administration of justice. It is for our profession and for our Schools of Law, which more and more voice the aspirations of our profession, to inspire that love and respect and to strengthen that faith.

It is for our schools of law to bring to the support and encouragement of popular sentiment for the observance of law and justice and of the due and orderly administration of law, the benefits of an enlightened scholarship; the aid and guidance of science and zeal for the truth.

Harlan F. Stone

Washington, D.C.

Chapter 51

On What Is Wrong with So-Called Legal Education

1935

Karl N. Llewellyn

Karl Nickerson Llewllyn (May 22, 1893-February 13, 1962) was the principal drafter of the Uniform Commercial Code and was Professor at Columbia Law School from 1925 to 1951 and at the University of Chicago from 1951 to 1962. His book, *The Bramble Bush,* is a classic of legal education. This article first appeared in 35 *Columbia Law Review* 651 (1935).

Author's note: This presents the substance of a talk delivered at Phillips Brooks House, Cambridge, on Jan. 22, 1935. It has, as of course in the circumstances, been duly submitted to the HARV. L. REV.; but as on other occasions their editor's canons of taste and policy did not jibe with mine.

Reactions from platform and floor were various: The ideals suggested were Utopian. . . . There had been practically nothing said that bore at all on legal education. . . . Would not segregated classes for slow men slow up the slow men further? . . . One professor, at last, had appreciated the point of view of a young man. . . . The speaker had no idea of where to stop. . . . Existing training was for a static world. We needed training for a world in flux. . . . The job of a law school was after all to train technicians. . . . There did seem to have been one point of interest. . . . Students were entitled to have what they came for. . . . This combination of lousy thinking and confessed incompetence. . . . The aim of the law was certainty, and such proposals would hinder the accomplishment of that aim. . . . What was meant, anyhow, by functional approach? . . . If a man went after roundedness in his first year, he lost out on the law review. . . . Could a curriculum, rather than the man himself, develop a rounded personality? . . . Why did the speaker sneer when he mentioned Wall Street practice? . . . Law students needed not only social fact, but the scientific theory of the social scientist.

The diapason throbbed to the belief that there is already too much Law to learn, whereas the suggestions here made call for further expenditure of needed time. No diapason could more adequately evidence the need for publishing the paper. Truly neither law students nor law professors, as masses, have begun to appreciate either their job, or what can be done with that job.

In the paper I am conscious of borrowing chiefly from Herman Oliphant, Young B. Smith, Robert M. Hutchins, Charles E. Clark, and Emma Corstvet. Details are hard to trace. There is included, somehow, a net impact of several hundred criticisms from students old and new, among them certainly and importantly Ralph Heymsfeld, Ambrose Doskow, Milton Handler, and Herbert Wechsler—these last, no less as colleagues. Handler, for instance, taught my sales book once—and I learned. The attempt has been to "revise and enlarge" my writings of five years back: *Über den Rechtsunterricht in den Vereinigten Staaten*, 79 IHERINGS JAHRB. (2. Folge Bd. 43) 233 (1929); the Introduction to CASES AND MATERIALS ON SALES (1930); *A Modern Law School*, 22 COLUMBIA UNIV. Q. 316 (1930); THE BRAMBLE BUSH (1930). Also to get some understanding of why performance tortoises so far behind desire.

If a person both can see and will do, he is, sociologically a freak. If he either cannot see, or seeing, will not do a thing non-traditional, he is normal; he is sane. The argument will base on the proposition that the health of any university, and more particularly of any law school, rests in departure from normality and deadly sanity. Freak persons and freak policies are needed; needed in very considerable measure. This is true always and everywhere. But it is peculiarly true in a discipline whose very essence is tradition; it is peculiarly true in a teaching profession at those epochs when their tradition of teaching has grown blind, and withers.

But, cries the Devil's Advocate, we cannot junk tradition, we need stability, we need continuity, tradition provides the skeleton, we must continue. Right, Sir. Precisely right, Sir. We *cannot* junk tradition. "Continuity with the past is not a duty; *it is only a necessity.*" There are a hundred odd men in American legal education who for some ten years have been striving to see new needed things, and do them. They stick in tradition as a body sticks in muck. They are tied hand, foot, and eyes. Five years of struggle gets one hand free, to wave for help. This is why freaks are not a danger: they are very few, they are so little freakish, they are so tradition-ridden in what freakishness they have.[1]

What, now, is the situation? If Adam, a Baby, or the Man from Mars, fresh-eyed and curious, should survey this scene of ours, what would he see?

(1) He could not talk or think of "American Legal Education in Law Schools"; variety overwhelms similarity. The training ranges from work which, year for year, cleanly surpasses any other system of university legal training in this world to work so wretched that I doubt the existence of a counterpart in other lands. Let us therefore talk only of what can be regarded as first-rate law school education. Let us, for science's sake and decency's, be concrete in our subject-matter. Let us choose a subject-matter we are acquainted with. I shall direct my comment at "legal education" as practiced at Columbia, Harvard, and Yale.[2] But I wish to make it clear that I am not attacking these three schools, as such, or any of them. *Shabby and silly as they are, I know of no schools less shabby or less silly.*

(2) For the second self-evidence is that American law school training at these, and all, institutions is, viewed in critical aloofness, blind, inept, factory-ridden, wasteful, defective, and empty. If you prefer verbs: it blinds, it stumbles, it conveyor-belts, it wastes, it mutilates, and it empties.

(3) The objectives of that education are a product of historical conditioning and chance. They miss most of what needs doing. They do not know what they miss, nor greatly care. Often they are plain wrong, plain vicious. Regularly, they are so confusedly perceived that they tangle one another's legs.

(4) The methods show, line for line, the lineaments of the objectives. A ghastly twinship.

(5) The trouble is as with the law itself. An outmoded tradition. A personnel which, in the large, clings inertly and incuriously to that tradition, as such, instead of viewing the tradition as one available tool, useful here, wasteful or futile there. A personnel which allows its aims to be dictated and limited by the existing tool, instead of seeking better or further aims, and then measuring the tool against the needed aims, and then setting itself to new invention when hammer and chisel are needed to supplement ax or adze. Or which Greenwich Villages into shrieking, miles beyond performance. In a word, an incompetent personnel: the conservatives blind, the radicals stickily quarter-baked.

All of this is understandable enough. It is pardonable. Law teachers are people. But the question is what is wrong with the job. The job is, too, not to explain merely, but to wrestle with my own conscience as a teacher. I find I come out worsted in the wrestling.

Objectives: What Do Lawyers Do?

By objectives I mean both the explicit objectives verbalized in that class of literature called Deans' Reports (as amazing a combination of reporting, propagandizing and suppression of the significant as man has yet devised) and those objectives implicit in the real workings of a school.

Both are alike in this: no faculty, and, I believe, not one per cent of instructors, knows what it or they are really trying to educate for.

Before the great case-book pioneers there seems to have swum a blurred composite photograph of the country-plus-city lawyer of about 1870. The shift even then occurring within the city-component received from the beginning less emphasis than was its due. The grosser evil lay in the over-simplification—as if there were a single kind of lawyer, with a single kind of practice, for which a single kind of training would suffice—and as if case-method were that single kind of training. That initial objective was and is false. But it is the initial objective which poses the problem, which frames the issue, for the future. No wonder subsequent work groans on a bias.

Anon, in the middle 20's, another composite photograph, no less blurred, began to swim before some innovators: the legal factory-hand, dedicated to the upper reaches of the corporation-factory. This was a needed correction. It involved, as most revolt-corrections do, a belated but vital perception of living, breathing, fact. But it involved, too, as most revolt-corrections do, too strong a swing toward the aspect newly perceived. Attempting to compass the new, we have whizzed by the old.

It is true that the 300-page corporate indenture is a part of today's life; it does need attention in the law school. But the old homestead is still being mortgaged. That needs attention too. And it is the effects of the new styles of mortgage-finance upon the old (and *vice versa*) which present the truly fascinating problem. Ancient rules and concepts of mortgage complicate and hamper the provision of corporate security. Ancient rules and concepts of trusteeship rise and walk, to defeat exemption clauses which should never have been drawn. While modern financing and modern statute draw farm and petty real estate mortgages into the orbit of a remodelled banking system. Such interactions cannot even be seen as long as either new phases or old are emphasized *alone*. So, through the other fields: I know for example no book on Corporations, and none on Business Units, that has *with due consistency* attempted to explore the differences between what one may call the investment and the family-corporation. We see beginnings. We do not see full performance. Because the Small and the Big are not sharply drawn as needing, *both*, attention. Nor as needing, *each*, its own regulation drawn to its own problems, its own needs.

Meantime, what pictures should we of today be making about the actual workings of "the" heterogeneous Bar?

Not rules, but doing, is what we seek to train men for. Rules our men need. Rules do in part control or shape, do in still greater part set limits to, their doing. But the thing remains the doing.

What *is* this doing of lawyers? Whither are we to head our students? We do not know. Haphazard personal observation, conditioned by fossil concepts: these are our eyes. It is, knowing this, a lovely and touching thing to watch our guildsmen in the classroom. They feel the needs, they grope for answer. Whenever experience suggests a concrete illustration, Property or Pleading lies neglected for five minutes, while "I had a case . . ." or "I once knew a lawyer . . ." (told with skill and care) makes the teller reawaken with his audience. The trouble is, that it happens by accident: haphazard, wasteful, only sometimes . . . because we do not know enough to choose or plan.

What do we *know* of the distribution of lawyers, by localities? What do we *know* of their work, quantitatively or qualitatively, or of the differences among them in their work? What do we *know*, as to how many law-trained men (or of our own graduates) are in law, and in what kind of law, or in what else? What do we *know* of their income; of their incomes by localities, or by specialties—*i.e.*, of what men can earn support, and how, from this long drawn-out "education"?

Nor does one find much interest in that other set of crucial problems: is the Bar's work too expensive to the people whom the Bar should serve, but whom it too often makes into milch-cattle? Can certain types of business be standardized and cheapened, and so made available to all who need counsel? Is the work as done, adequate? Where is it adequate, where is it not? Where, and for whom, are there gaps in the tasks actually performed? One suspects a piteous range of undone legal business; between the Legal Aid and the willing, paying client lies an unexplored, unexploited, *unattended* range of legal need. But how great is that need, and where does it lie, and what is it concerned with? We do not know. Do we care?

Yet if, as I premise, we claim to train men for a Profession, such things we need to know—and care about. *Know*, not guess at. Our graduates are to be placed. They are to be trained for their places. They are to make a living. They are to do the work a Bar is there to do. They are to do it decently, and for a decent price. As befits a government-protected monopoly, they are to do this for *all*. As befits a Profession, they are to do this—granted that they get a living—for those who cannot pay, or can pay little, quite as well as for those who pay the overhead or the installments on the Chrysler.

Neither may legal educators continue to overlook a further and major phase of law-work which we so thoroughly do overlook. Critique of law we not only too much neglect in class; when we do envisage it, then (bound in our technical Anglo-American tradition) we insist on viewing it from the angle only of the *judge*. But must law schools stay blind to the importance of the lawyer in political life? Can law schools not realize that political officeholders must reckon on displacement—that only the lawyer can hope to make immediate professional utilization, when displaced, of the publicity he gained while holding office? Can law schools overlook that even an unsuccessful campaign for public office affords that legitimate advertizing available otherwise only to counsel in a feature murder-trial? To politics, by the nature of our institutions, a good percentage of our graduates are predestined. For decent politics, what training do our law schools offer? A course in Constitutional Law, perhaps a sketchy course in Legislation. Trade Regulation may be added, or some new venture say on federal legislation. But what of *sustained* work, *throughout* the course, on the wherewithal for judging *and shaping* policy intelligently?

Let me repeat also what I have said elsewhere: I do not claim the absence in the orthodox curriculum of *occasional* intervention of policy-considerations when an instructor by personal accident *happens* to have acquired information, insight, and excitement. What "innovators" urge is the substitution of *sustained and consistent* labor with policy-facts and policy-choices for *occasional* flashes even of more-than-earthly beauty. Men see better by arc-light than by lightning.

To round out these considerations, one must include the recent trend of our law school graduates into government administration. That trend may be impermanent, Still, it demands reflection. To disregard the trend is to gamble on an hypothetical impermanency, while children in office are reaching decisions on which industries depend. Let me be plain: I do not often quarrel with their decisions. Far greater blindness and folly—where there is folly—lies, as I read it, in the opponents of these children. But, with more adequate training, there would be even happier results. Whereas we still stoutly train, not only for the blurred practice of 1870 alone, but for the technical phases of that practice only; even there, we spend most of our class-time playing checkers with pure "substantive rules."—No. I apologize. Checkers is much too solid. We play a cobweb chess. The pieces, clients, are fungible impersonalities: good old A, B and C. Michael Moriarty, The United States Steel Corporation; Al Capone, Secretary Mellon: "A," "B," or "C." Our graduate, if he is lucky, has learned enough theory to plead a bastard Ruy Lopez. The defendant answers. Our man brings out his "substantive" pawns and knights. He castles; he engages. He makes an oversight, for lack of *facts*. Mate! The poor client. . . .

Objectives: What Can Law Schools Do?

It does *per se* little good to show what is needed. The problem is, in view of what is needed, what can be done? Our immediate tools are a school and three years of time. Our excuses have been that we are merely a law school; that we have merely three years of time. I have heard Pound and Beale dig themselves in behind these flimsies, and Clark and Douglas, and Smith and Richard Powell. I, too, have found silly comfort in such digging in. For all of us, for each of us, I say now, such hiding makes out emotional and intellectual cowardice. Faced with a challenge, we slink to cover.

When business or government is confronted with a *Must*, business or government invents and improves. Or it goes under.

For law schools, the *Must* has today become inescapable. Either we produce, or our existing bankruptcy becomes an open shame. Demands on us rise by the hour. Either we make new payment in proportion to the rise, or we are exposed. As frauds. We have taken coin, we have usurped status, under the pretense of training for the law. While eyes and efforts have been fixed, and still are fixed, not on what *can* be done in a school in three years, but purblindly on what our predecessors, or ourselves, happen to *have been* doing.

Again, ground-clearing may require to be stump-pulling, if it is to give us an acre that yields more, and yet costs less to plough.

Consider the European schemes of legal education. In particular, consider the German in those days before party had become prerogative. There were seven semesters, spread over three and a half years, of academic training. Despite repeated reforms directed at making it more concrete, the university work remained over-theoretical. Compared with our best, it remained second-rate, or third. But complementing it was a further three years of *directed, rounded, apprenticeship.* Directed: no haphazardness of what office you might chance to find a place in; *a lawyer's legal duty was to take and train the man assigned to him.* The duty was abused. All duties are. But even exploitation trains. Rounded: the apprentice wandered from petty-court judge to appellate court, from courts to administrative agencies, from these to work with a practicing lawyer's office. He was to get an inkling of legal work at large. Three years of this, and then a *second* bar examination. Only after the second one was he let loose upon the public. *Meanwhile, throughout the apprenticeship, he received a modest stipend from the government.*[3] The State's interest was in raising judges and administrators. But it raised counsel, too.

Our schools face the absence of any apprenticeship at all. Why do they have to? What have we done to plug the gap? Where do you find signs that the problem has even been examined? We might, for example, look into the German system for its faults. I find nothing in it that really trains for the advocate's (as distinct from the judge's) job of legal argument; nor anything that trains for the lawyer's life-necessity of dealing with a client—or of getting one. I think of a certain old practitioner and his advice on how to avoid the conse-

27. Karl Llewellyn (1893-1962). A professor at Columbia and a formidable author of legal realist scholarship, Llewellyn was the principal drafter of the Uniform Commercial Code. (*Courtesy of Art & Visual Materials, Special Collections Department, Harvard Law School Library.*)

quences of a horseback opinion which had proved wrong. "Call your client back. Ask him to tell it all again, and with no prompting. He's sure to give you *some* new fact. Then hop on him: 'Why didn't you tell me *that* yesterday?'" This is not legal art, but legal artifice. Take, for contrast, the counsel of a veteran adviser of corporations: "Officers come to you to cover their own tracks. They want to do what they want; they want to have you to blame if it goes wrong. Your advice turns on the facts they give. Your reputation depends, therefore, on the record. So opinions do well to begin: 'You state that . . .' and to proceed: '*On the above facts*, my opinion is . . .'" This is not artifice; it is sense, it is decency, it is a solid, standard rule of thumb. Artifice or art: we purvey neither—save by accident. Though of course the curriculum is paved with good intentions.

Either of these stories brings home to a student the emptiness of rules without the facts, brings home the problem of turning legal or human knowledge into action. Their difference in tendency brings home to the observer the value of the full-time law-teacher who can hope to build perspective about which "practical" matters a Professional school can soundly inculcate. My own belief is: to fight wolves, you have to know wolves. And that wolf-study is a proper part of legal training. Ideals that cannot survive such study are stillborn.

Now are the virtues of sound case-training and full time instructors, obvious though they be, to obscure the need for complementing and supplementing the prevalent "best" training for the law?

A second line of semi-analogy lies in the care the medics exercise with regard to clinical service and to interneship. They have a longer theoretical training than ours. But they insist on *ordered* practical experience, before their graduates are certified to the helpless layman. Is medicine then more complicated than the law? I say, no. It is only that the standards for the law are lower. I have in mind a tentative questionnaire circulated recently among fifty lawyers. The question was, as to a long list of legal activities: From the angle of a client, but as knowing what *you* know, would you entrust to a person "of your experience" any one of the following matters? . . . The lawyers tried to answer honestly, despite certain ambiguities in the question (no mention of general skill, or of time available for research, *etc.*). The highest item found, out of the 50 questionees, 37 positive responses. The great bulk of lines of inquiry found no single lawyer-answerer who was ready to risk turning a case over to his equal.—No. Law is not simple. Well, then, is it no part of a law *school's* job to wrestle with the complexity? Or with the troublesomeness of turning rules into sensible *action?*

In a word: what have we tried to *do*, to make up for our inherent lacks, uncomplemented as they are by anything but chance—chance, which fails to make the dice turn up as we would want them?

Objectives: Deficient Preliminary Training

We know little, then, of the Whither of our graduates. Of the Whence of our entrants, we know a little more. But the more we see of that, the less we like it. They come unprepared. We know it. But about it, we do nothing. When we try, vaguely, to move, we find ourselves involved in hopeless controversy among ourselves.

I speak for no orthodox view, be it past or future, in regard to what pre-law-school work should be. As will appear, my belief is that *whatever pre-law-school work may be, it will never lighten the load on law instructors* for more than a moment at a time. Inadequate pre-law—school training forces law school men toward doubling the work they now do, in the accepted three years. More adequate pre-law training will ease the burden of doing what we are *now* doing. But it will not remove the yoke: it will indeed make heavier the labor of invention. For whatever we manage to be accomplishing, at any given time, and with any given human material, will always lag behind the demands bar and community are entitled to make upon us. Each upward shift of entrant-quality or training represents merely a new opportunity to take on an untouched piece of our own proper load. There will always be the obligation to strain toward doubling whatever, within the three years allotted us, we may happen to be turning out.

Yet at first glance it is disheartening that no agreement can yet be had, as to what pre-law-school work should be. Look at the records. The last report of the Committee of the Association reproduced three disparate opinions of non-members of the Committee. Then it abdicated. Again, a bankruptcy. The medics can agree. The lawmen cannot. They cannot even reach tentative compromise.

In part this rests on their inability to know whether they themselves would go. In part, on their ignorance of educational processes, a matter still to be discussed. Most of all, it rests on divergent views of what law school is for.

There is therefore only one immediate answer. Disruptive and unfortunate, it still is the only road of hope. School by school—if schools cannot agree—each faculty must lay down what *it* requires. And, as Oliphant and Handler have insisted, law schools must themselves take over a full share of the job of seeing that they get what they demand. Our own colleges, or those in our own cities, feed each of us in good part with our entrants. In good part enough to afford some test, as against students from other colleges, of whether our ideas on pre-law work, when tried out, will have the value we think they may have, toward *our* law study. The laboratory for experiment is clear, and open. Frame demands, enforce them as to our own colleges, and then, in our own schools, test the work of those who have fulfilled our demands against that of those from schools which have not. Five years will give light. . . . That is, it would give light if we did not scuttle past the laboratory door.

Of the matters to be developed before entrance into law school, each man, today, speaks purely for himself. I, for one, am for an entrance test that would go far beyond the "capacity-tests" in vogue at Columbia or Yale, and far beyond the college degree. *I want every law student to be able to read and write.* Half of my first-year students, more than a third of my second-year students, can do neither. I want any entrant to have a smattering of logic, American historical fact, descriptive economics, sociology of institutions, and psychology of human behavior; also some conception of organic evolution, and some conception of weighing statements of "fact" according to the "Authority" which has adduced the statement; finally some idea of quantitative, as opposed to purely qualitative thinking. Of none of these have 50% of my entrants, now, an inkling. Those that have one, lack another.

But larger than any such technique or knowledge looms the question of emotional and intellectual *interest*, or eagerness. In professional school we do profit by a certain stepping up of interest that depends on the entrant's perception that his living is at length at stake. Still, we miss out on half of them. They sit. Dough without yeast. If any law school teacher honestly doubts that, unhelped by circumstance (professional school) and ancient tradition (the case-book), he is a dub at teaching, let him tackle a college class (even of pre-law men), and try to bring out such eagerness as any capable teacher is able to produce. Experiment aids perception.

Meanwhile, I argue: pending reform of the college, we have to reform ourselves. Unless our men *go forth* equipped to read and write, and (leaving all else aside) with intellectual eagerness and with some grasp of policy-consideration, we fail in our duty to the community if *we* admit them to the LL.B. degree. We may shift the blame for not being able to graduate enough lawyers to serve the community (though on this I have yet to hear complaint from the community). *We can not shift blame for graduating incompetents. We can not shift blame for minting our incompetents as competent.* Are "best" schools to go on having graduates whom their professors will not recommend? Or, what is worse, whom their professors recommend with conscience qualms?

Law must have all the matters, all the skills, all the attitudes, in its lawmen, which we have been discussing. Else law's prestige will perish. Law *schools* must then provide these things—or get them provided. *Demands are rising.* The three creditors knock with the petition.

But we leave these things to chance. For comfort, we fix our telescope on graduates in high place, on the success of Law Review men, and the like. As gamblers chew over like a cud the one-time pleasure of four aces in a hand.

Objectives: Ideals, and the Full Life

This awful symbol Chance should neither drone nor whine in its reiterations. Rather should it be made Miltonian thunder down the pillared aisles, to blast our souls with organ-throbbing realization that we of the guild do but repeat the history of the race. Always Chance rules, until perception and invention come to serve and save. Always tradition smothers while she gives suck, fresh sacrifice eternal to a fresh spawn of Chance.

All of this is, I repeat, inevitably human. Almost the inevitability discourages. The sociological processes concerned are so clear. There is a tradition, at any given moment. Most of us, consequently, just fit in. Those that do not are freaks. But most freaks are crazy, and useless, even disruptive.[4] The tradition therefore goes on until it has been long outworn. Only a genius breaks through it, to living gain. Even such a genius as Langdell needed an Ames, a supplementary executing genius, and thirty years as well, to make his idea dent his guild. Even that great team dropped out much of the value or what they themselves had rebelled against, though they carried over (Ames, at least) into their own work the values of the earlier style of thinking. While the epigones, pygmies, lack both the balance and the tradition of the giants. Out of once succulent steak they make a hamburger that reeks its age.

It would, then, be discouraging if Students and Times did not squeeze upon that dog-wagon short-order man known as a law school teacher.

Students: they look around them, and rebel. They rebel no less (in the interest of the Grand Tradition) where they suspect themselves of being guinea-pigs, than in the centers of the Ancient Learning—where they suspect themselves of being sacrificed to idols. This is magnificent. One thing we overlook much too often is the value (in addition to the despair) that comes to us out of the stubborn resistance of our students. That resistance is not only magnificent, it is of course also often magnificently fallacious. Looking abroad, the student seizes on one or two Major Figures, and asks: "Why are not All of Ours as good as they?" While abroad, similar students are holding caucus on some similar question.—But, for all lacks in perspective, the students do stir. They stir not only in matters of the intellect. Students turn up, as well, persistently, insistently, consistently, with matters involving their souls, and their whole selves. And so awaken us.

Their souls: they have ideals. Surprising to one who has watched the Wall-Street-flocking over a decade and more is this number of youngsters who now show hunger to make law *do* something. The number who prefer a government job. The number who are pestered with the prospect of becoming prostitutes. The spontaneous gathering this year, at my school, for example, of boys who plan organized inquiry into what a lawyer *can* do, and still remain both a citizen and a person—and into how he can shape his work to be more of a person, and more of a citizen. (My guess is, their Report will jar their faculty.)

Now have we no obligation in the engendering, in the guiding, of such ideals? I do not refer to "teaching Legal Ethics," in a course. I refer to the setting up of every course to bear, *inter alia*, on what the job in society of that branch of law may really be, and on how well the job is being performed.

Again, let me avoid misconception. I hold that a lawyer's first job is to be a *lawyer*. I hold that we must teach him, first of all, to make a legal table or chair that will stand up without a wobble. Ideals without technique are a mess.

But technique without ideals is a menace. The boy must be hard-headed, with trained hands and brain. He must, as said above, be able to fight wolves. But is that all? I say, as well, that he must want to take wolves' pelts. The encouragement of that desire is a law school job. And if the man—as so many will—goes into legislation or administration, then it is the law school's job to give him, first, a decent fact-foundation from which to work; and second, understanding of the need of facts; and, third, a driving interest in their acquisition; and fourth, the first beginnings of the wherewithal to weigh them and their implications for a People. Techniques and interests, not merely as to "law," but as to "fact," and "policy." Peculiarly as to those *socially* vital facts which practice as such, in civil cases, so quietly and insidiously drops beneath the table.[5]

Neither does the job stop with this. Above I spoke of the student's whole self. That whole self needs attention. From the angle of a lawyer's dealings with clients, witnesses, jury, judge, and bench of five or seven. No less from the angle of a lawyer's living with self or children, after forty. Till forty—sometimes even till fifty—he can make out, after a fashion, on hard work, and (if he achieves it) on success.

But as in so many things, our law schools presuppose here some sort of ectogenic Culture, sprouted at home or in college, and somehow to be automatically reintroduced into the system in harmonious combination with whatever it is we teach. Now first, this Culture mostly has not sprouted. And second, our methods are such as to kill it if we can. "Make him think like a lawyer!" Park Culture at the door! This would be fine, if, *after* making the boy think like a lawyer, we really did reintroduce the Culture. Do we?

Indeed, the more "progressive" the school, the less time is left the student for anything but reading cases and chasing references—all with an eye as good as single to The Law. I think (and hope) that the Columbia level for a C+ man has now risen to over fifty hours a week of work. As a measure of a full time job, fine. But how of the work itself? Rules, always rules—or decisions—in the forefront of attention. (Yet a brief, in due course, will call also for composition, poetry and style.) Clear, legally artificial, dehumanized thinking—a touch of policy; but how much? (Yet trial or appeal in due course, will call also for "atmosphere," and some attention to what legislatures may have ordered.) The "issue" in legalistically procedural terms. (Yet life, in due course, will call no less for understanding human conflict, and the drama of human conflict.) Meanwhile some kid regrets that he has no time for piano practice; another yearns to compare Millay and MacLeish; the third knows none of these, and cannot understand the conversation.

The need is, in some fashion, for an integration of the human and the artistic with the legal. Not an addition merely; an integration. Attempt at such integration finds response. This is not yet the place allotted to discussion of means, yet discussion of means may here help clarify objective. I cite instances:

There were six photographs of Konenkov's bust of Holmes (the bust now at Columbia and Harvard). There were an equal number the anonymous Maria of Bamberg, and of the Uta of Naumburg, and of another modern head. The artist's chisel has reproduced the model for his Maria with tragic devotion. He loved her; he chose her as model for his Mary. He did not see or know, but he recorded, that she was venal, hard, treacherous, as well as lovely. So with the Uta. Though so idealized that the full face is ethereal, the profile shows up cat and shrew.—These photographs, then, spread before a group of law students, with comment on the differences that light and angle made—on walking around the whole, to see it whole—on how the subject had determined the job, despite all canons. Then suggestion on how the seemingly simple record of a case could change in the light of color and experience of the observer—how every time an instructor read his cases over he saw new facets and new form. Or on how a single opinion rounded out if one read it successively as a case in contracts, in waiver, in pleading, or in sales.—Or on how judges, like artists, can respond to facts their fingers notice, while their minds deny those facts.—One cannot easily catch faces or reactions into print. One simply knew that sculpture and cases had acquired, both, new meaning; *and new relation*. With similar pictures of the Winged Victory, what could be done!

There was that boy who had no time to practice music, and found his law antagonistic to piano. And who saw, then, how the Bach fugue was what an instructor might try his poor best to emulate in a case-book chapter, or a lawyer in a brief;—how the job of legal exposition might, and must, run upon the same lines as that of musical.

There was the attempt to study how to argue, with students turning back to all their college literature in search of style; and to their cases, in search of build-up and persuasiveness; and to novels (Sergeant Buzzfuzz' opening), and life, in search of keys to human nature.

So much for examples. But we need more than examples. The objective of a full life, though we starve it, is stubborn as a desert plant. We must not let law smother the man in his study of it, nor let it cut him off from what art has to offer for and in its practice. We must recapture, or find a substitute for, the old-time lawyer's Bible and his Shakespeare. But least of all must law cut its students off from living, from rich living, after they become lawyers. Professors who are sterile dissecting knives, *and are no more*, wreak tragedy. . . .

I said above, not only the students, but the Times, squeeze upon the comfort of our dog-wagon cook. But with a difference. The Students can in some measure be restrained by austerity, by authority, by their own ignorance, by their habit of submission. The Times cannot. Indeed, what we have by now in the way of semi-reform of the Ancient Routine, is directly a product of the Times. Those newer movements which strike toward reorganizing rules in terms of modern problems rest one and all on the discovery that some lawmen are no longer behaving along the lines presupposed by obsolescent legal formulae. *E.g.*, despite all talk of "no liability without fault," much liability simply has been happening in accordance with ideals about risk-distribution. So, despite all talk about "acceptance only in the terms dictated by the offer," some offerors are getting stuck before the terms dictated by the offer have been fulfilled. Thus run the cases, even in the courts. Much more does the pressure show, on counsel in the office. Most of all, outside either court or office.

Thus, in the mid-20 period of new courses, new case-books, curriculum revision, did the Times show their power upon the resistant shellfish of the schools. In these past few years, the power grows. When a Handler (who has been off New Dealing), reorganizes a course in Trade Regulation to build around the N.R.A., that is perhaps merely a pleasant sign of industry and of the effects of outside stimulus. But when a McLaughlin, though he regards the N.R.A. as "a joke, a tragedy, an abortion, and a fraud," devotes a semester to its study, and along original lines, we may see truly that the Times do press.

It seems, in short, as if Student and Times may yet jar even a Law School loose. If jarred, it must start fresh in some direction; and some of the directions we have canvassed. But are there *means*, to go?

Methods: Defenses and Excuses

Such a canvassing of objectives as the above may be relied on to meet with immediate evasion. The lines are familiar as Hamlet's soliloquies.

(1) Of course high ideals of education are lovely. Everybody likes them.

(2) But we are limited, we are hamstrung, by time and by student material and by personnel.

(3) We therefore render unto preliminary education the things that are preliminary education's.

(4) And unto practice the things that are practice's.

(5) Our own curriculum, meantime, is full. So are our hands.

(6) . . . We stay put. *Q.E.D.*

Now to this, and its ilk, several things need saying quickly. They will be dealt with more fully hereinafter.

(1) Necessity need not, of course, mother invention. Nobody can tell, until he courts necessity. But faint heart never won fair lady.

(2) Even on our present knowledge, waste of time in existing curricula is patent. The pure case-method—as fine a tool as teacher ever invented—completes its work with a quick student in a year; with even a slow student, it would do its work within two years, if the slow student, in the second year, were given sustained instruction sharply directed to *his* needs. Second year instruction, as practiced, falls between two stools: an attempt to keep the quicker man interested, and an attempt to bring the slower man along. The combination is wasteful. It is self-contradictory. The Law Review, as an expedient, helps a little, for some; but only a little, and only for some. Even for slow men, then, one year's time is available to try out something different, something that can uncork other techniques than pure analysis.

(3) Our teachers teach wastefully, and are content. They do not try to pool experience. Each knows that he is right. Despite this, the older men do not try to correct the mistakes or misguesses of those younger men who make up such a large proportion of our faculties. None cares to know any educational method but his own tradition. Moreover, in sublime conceit, we teachers attribute all failure to the student.—Here lies untapped possibility, thus far aborted, and inferred.—The range of that possibility we have been forced to see in one faculty that has labored with selective admission. *The students being reasonably certified, a flunkage of 20% must rest in good part on defective teaching.* Yet I know no better faculty.

(4) Some existing experiments in reorganization of material have definitely proved their worth, in getting more done in less time. Take Powell's condensation of Wills, Trusts, and Future Interests. Every such experiment makes room for further experiment.

(5) The practical certainty that many "C" men, given more individual attention, would get the knack of case-study more quickly by a year, has hardly been considered. Nor has the use of special sections in the second year, devoted to the special case-study problems of the slower men.

(6) The use, where the knack of analysis has been learned, of text and lecture and *reference* to a case-book to accomplish the *information* part of an upper class course, has hardly been tapped. This would free time for really working *with* the material, the student checking his reading of cases not by cross-examination in first year style on the well-known fifteen pages per hour, but by cross-examination on his *use* of the cases in drafting, argument, or advice.

All this merely by way of indicating that we have to reckon here not with counsels of perfection blowing lazily across the trees, but with a challenge. We *do* have room to move in. All signs indicate that we can make more room; much more room. So, instead of moving, we sit. This is a sleeping dog that needs a kick.

METHODS: WHAT LAWYERS DO

To train, we must know what we are training for. As will appear, there are many things we can turn to, even without more knowledge of this than we have already. But to provide either solid soundness or new vision, we must investigate the bar.

Can we, then, find out what lawyers are really doing? Already three lines of attack have been developed. The New York County Lawyers' Association has begun one opening canvass. Garrison has headed an illuminating and singularly canny survey of the Wisconsin Bar: a census of who is in practice, and where, and with what income, and with what type of academic record. Also an inquiry into how far, and where, true over-crowding seems to exist.[6] The next step in Wisconsin, already initiated for Illinois by the Illinois State Bar Association, is inquiry into the *what* of lawyers' doing: how much work, and how much specialization, and in what? How much competence for various lines of work among either general or highly specialized practitioners? Fees? All but the last are difficult to reach with any accuracy. But the mere presence of the movement is a heartening sign.

Beyond that, and as regards the jobs left undone by the bar, we have little definite information as yet save from the Legal Aid Societies and from such investigation as has given rise to Public or to Voluntary Defenders.

Nor have we clear information on what happens to our graduates. Yet an alumni law register could be made to yield some light on this last.

On cheapening and standardizing—and so developing—such types of business as lease-making or counselling on leases, or simple wills, we are in the realm of pure guesswork.

Taken as a whole: the field seems open for inquiry. The bar is interested as it has not been within our lifetimes; what lacks is imagination, initiative, interest. Methods are largely still to be developed, and the work is still to be done. But the need cries. Courses on The Legal Profession canvass chiefly the literature, which in turn is made up almost wholly of guess, or viewing with alarm, or prophecy. Whereas we need proved fact. We need proved information as to the typicality or non-typicality of what our haphazard experience suggests to us to be the fact. For instance, it has been objected: "Why worry in the schools about apprenticeship? The men get it." But how *many* get it? And with whom? And under what conditions favorable to learning? Do you *know?* Does anybody?

Personally, I suspect that when we do once discover what law-trained men are doing, we shall find that the objectives for which we are to train include much both from old-style and new-style teaching. But that they include much in addition to both. And therefore will require either expansion of the curriculum—which seems unfeasible—or new economy within it.

METHODS: BACKGROUND OF SOCIAL FACT

This matter of new economy comes to bear directly on the introduction of the background of social fact and policy. Unfortunate and often violent misconceptions fare abroad:

(1) There is the notion that introducing fact background means introducing it raw; *e.g.*, as extracts, reprints, or references that swallow social science studies whole. In rare cases, this may pay.

In very rare cases. For social scientists have not gathered their data to our use, but to their own; their data are focussed on the problem for which they have been gathered, and on the angle of that problem which interests the gatherer. However good, sound, thorough, illuminating, such a line of work, it intersects our lawyers' line at but a single point. Reading lines, to gather points, breaks the back. It is therefore normally the job of the instructor, and trebly the job of one who puts out a Materials book, to gather the strayed mass of materials together, and to extract from the intersections, in brief form, his *own* line of information. This costs editor's time; it means editor's education. *It overloads neither the student nor the curriculum.*

(2) There is the notion that adding social facts to The Law as law-course material makes the job harder, or longer, *for the student.*

This is sheer nonsense. The fact is that legal rules mean, of themselves, next to nothing. They are verbal formulae, partly conveying a wished-for direction and ideal. But they are, to law students, empty. A brilliant student told me recently of the pleasure of his course in Bills and Notes, in which he had been doing algebraic tricks. *This student had, however, never seen a bill.* (I had similar pleasure, once, in Bills and Notes.) It would not have been tactful to enquire into what he knew of foreign exchange, or the trade acceptance movement, or the use of acceptances in place of notes in England, or the differences in function and use between bills and checks. He could, however, and with real excitement, manipulate the Rules of Bills and Notes. I was reminded of how I used, in high school, to substitute {"$\frac{sin}{cos}\ \frac{a}{a}$"} for "tan a," successfully, to get the answer, but with no picture of a rectangled triangle, or of the relation of side to diagonal, or of a sine or tangent curve, or of the meaning of any of these things. It was fun; it was futile.

This type of manipulation, for all its values esthetic and sometimes practical, is vicious when left to itself. In a judge, it threatens us with the "strong decision" beloved of Parke, B. In an advocate, it leads to trusting gossamer to carry iron; it leads to disregarding the earthy sense of courts. But what is worse (for a brilliant man will in due course learn what else he needs to know) it leads to the slower student's groping in a three years' daze, with hold for neither right hand nor for left. The slower student, the concrete-minded student, does not even get to taste the fun.

Whereas to set rules into their social context, into the context of how men do things, and of what difference the rule makes to those men—this is to give body to a rule for any student. It has graphic value, it has movement value, it has memory value. Rules thus seen are not only more meaningful. *They are also easier to learn.* You *save* time, when you teach them thus. You also make *critique* of the rule take on its human content. You make critique inevitable, because the human content, once introduced, will never be denied.

Let me take an example; (1) No simple contract is valid without consideration. (2) Any bargained-for detriment, to the promisee, but only a bargained-for detriment to the promisee, is adequate consideration.—I suppose these are rules. Certainly they are current formulae.

Now put some cases from life. (a) A laborer is negligently injured, and worried over job, rent and food. The claim adjuster beats the ambulance chaser in. The laborer signs a release of claim in consideration of "one dollar and reemployment." He gets the dollar, and gets employment for a week. (b) One foreign exchange dealer gives another a "firm" offer for five minutes, and revokes after four of them. Both belong to the Foreign Exchange Club. (c) A brewer (or was it a pork-packer?) promises to pay a fixed sum per annum to his daughter after marriage to the Italian Count to whom she is engaged. They marry next day. Suit, years later, is, not by daughter or Count, but by a moneylender who has discounted the annuity. (d) Old Family Friend promises father to pay newborn son $10,000 if son is named after Old Family Friend. (e) An auto manufacturer of established reputation appoints an agent for Keokuk, the agent agreeing to seventeen things, the manufacturer to nothing; the agent has "bought out" his predecessor for $10,000. All five cases are bargains. What happens to "the" rules as they pass through the five cases, and what happens to "the" facts as the courts manhandle them to get decent results *despite the rules?* I claim these happenings not only give meaning to the rules, but make them stick in the head. Even a modicum of common sense embroidery has its justification. But, no less valuable, any real understanding of the social background typified in such cases *forces* policy-judgment.

The net result is: more effect, for less effort, for more men.

(3) The third notion abroad is that displacement of study-book space by "non-legal" material depletes the room for "necessary" "legal" material. I hold this idea fallacious; but I recognize its power. Judgments as to balance of convenience will differ.

Against the idea is to be argued, in addition to the *time-saving* just described,

(a) That our curriculum is already (and of necessity) so little representative of "legal" law at large that twenty or thirty per cent more or less makes little difference, provided more *and better* method be inculcated. (b) That much expansion of present courses has run in terms of merely adding, rather than of significant reselection. This development is a function of blindness (as to the whole), vision (as to the course), and vested interest (of the instructor), in triple combination.

(c) That digesting and shrinking of cases for use in course-books (always with an eye on *the whole case)* can save more space than technique has yet been evolved to prove. Shrinking is dangerous. But over the long haul, we all do it, one way or another. I hold it better, if conscientiously done, than mere excerpting. And I hold that case-books still too largely overlook the discussion-value of a shrunk case.[7]

(d) Finally, and as a lunge to the throat: that without the background material no case has any business to be used at all: *better less, with real understanding, than more of the ununderstood.*

The counter-arguments will occur to any reader. I shall not list them. The choice is a choice among values.

But room for one piece of personal testimony I must claim, making due advance allowance for bias and for idiosyncrasy. With a "standard" case-book, I spent *four* hours a week on Sales, and got poor results, on rules, on Act, on everything else. With a case-book and course built to set background for the rules, I get in *three* hours a reasonable understanding of the Act, the cases, and the business meaning of both. This may evidence personal incompetence in handling a standard case-book. But it certainly evidences that curriculum-time *need* not be sacrificed merely because the field of study is widened. Thus, Michael has added real logical training to his Evidence. He teaches the Law of Evidence as effectually as before. Little more time is called for; the excess heretofore called for is shrinking. The more light, the less time.

Method: Social Background: Conclusion

The upshot seems to be that, within our time-limitation, we either integrate the background of social and economic fact and policy, course by course, or fail of our job. The early urge, say about 1910, was to pile on such courses as Legal History, Legal Philosophy, Jurisprudence, Comparative Law, in a fourth year. I, for one, am glad the students refused to follow the suggestion. Merely added on behind, such matters are well-nigh as ectogenic as Economics from college, frozen into harmlessness in the law school refrigerator. The students' sabotage of the Fourth Year has had as its function to wake faculty-members up to the job of *integrating* background—social or philosophical—into *every* course. And I shall be greatly surprised if the new four-year curriculum projected by the Yale Law and harvard Business Schools does not, after a few years of experience, reconcentrate into a new and better Three Years.

The trouble lies of course with the instructor.[8] He knows his traditional technique. More than that, he values it as the center of his work. Other techniques are strange to him. Suppose, even, that he learns to deal with social science, or social science factual material: the job of building two things into a whole is, even for his *own* thinking, stiff to do. And after that, emerges a further job: extracting and shrinking the stuff *in its bearing on his course.* A gigantic task.

But, therefore, a task to be begun at once. Intensively. Again, and yet again, the argument is for *sustained* inquiry, along lines which every living law teacher indulges, which every living law teacher recognizes as needful, whenever fate happens to have thrown one golden apple into a passive lap.

Nor is it wholly apparent to the Man from Mars why all understanding must be had by way of Course or Class. Students, being Americans, do find the acquisition of knowledge or understanding apart from Courses somewhat hard to conceive. Students in large classes, being human, find it hard to labor when the chances of being called on are three to a hundred. Students, being practical, prefer courses that head directly for the bar exam.—But how much do *we* do, *for 100%* of the students, toward counteracting such herd-human drives?

Methods: Critique of Law

"My brother Gray," runs one garbled version of a story, "has taught you what the law Used to be; my brother Ames has taught you what the law Ought to be; I intend, with your indulgence, to give some attention to what the law Is." Such a goal, as *one* goal, no reformer will quarrel with. The first task of a law school is still to turn out as much a lawyer as it can. Historians who do not eat do not continue long to understand. Nor do reformers who do not eat, reform.

Yet critique is of the essence, not only of understanding and reform, but of practice. Critique, intelligent critique, derives only from knowledge of effect. And again, rules must be sized up in the light of *doing:* lawmen's doing, and the effect of such doing upon laymen. And yet again, isolated lightning-flashes do not do the work. *Day for day, week for week,* the background must be both provided and explored; and provided, and explored, not alongside, but as an inevitable part of, the rule-material studied. This, for understanding; this, for practical utilization; this, for criticism.

The social scientists make an interesting comment upon lawyers. "That rigid discipline," they say, "which lawyers take such pride in—that discipline shows sweetly in all purely *verbal* operations. [How an outsider can flatter!] In word-techniques, lawyers are admirable. Or on the facts of a particular case. [This compliment, now, is deserved—by any real lawyer.] But when it comes to broadly social facts, in their social bearings, lawyers are helpless—childish. They fall for the tripe that journalists talk to women's clubs, or politicians at a bankers' convention." The criticism is sound. Is there, for instance, anything sadder than the naîveté with which mere lawyers manhandle statistics? Say, on any aspect of crime, or on overcrowding of the bar?[9] Yet I think it demonstrated by work recently done in many schools on such topics as the N.R.A. that law students *can* learn to handle masses of social and economic fact, that they can learn this in law school, and that they can learn it with relatively small expenditure of curriculum hours. I do not refer in this connection to Law Review notes; those might show merely the ability of the chosen few. I rest my case on the work of the "C" man who, for a change, is given a chance.

It is patent, however, that personal investigation of social fact, or even personal canvass of the literature, is within a normal law curriculum a one-occasion business. It remains the faculty's job, course by course and case by case, to provide the material which will make it plain that judgment as to "the better rule" rests on more than ignorance and conceit. My experience is that "the better rule" is seldom either rule, but mostly an intelligent synthesis of the two, built in the light of the needs which each rule *partly* serves.

Methods: Techniques Other Than Analytical

As things stand, an LL. B. tends to indicate that its possessor has had some training in telling dictum from decision, has some information not yet wholly forgotten about a few rules of law, and can, under examination pressure, avoid wholly blowing up.

It does not indicate that the possessor can use a law library, or find a case in point. It does not indicate that he can draft language that will cover a point, much less that he can see a point to cover. It does not indicate that he has any ability to devise a rule of thumb to get around a rule of law, or any information as to what useful rules of thumb have already been devised. It does not indicate that he can argue, or try a case, or even draw a pleading.

Some of these things a school cannot teach. Let us grant that. None of them, however, can a school neglect.

Still, the use of a law library is one thing that can be taught. Law Review men learn it. Moot courts give first aid to many more. The term-essay has proved its worth in making the learning universal. All one has to do, to prove this, is to match the third year term-essay of a "C" student with the one he wrote his second year. Compulsory essays in both years should be introduced into every school.

Drafting is a harder job to handle. It is not easy to learn. Background is hard to give; and on background intelligent drafting must depend. Interest is hard to awaken—that interest which alone produces the seven reworkings out of which skill to draft develops. Yet some things *can* be done. In every course there crop up rules which the instructor abominates. His business is to provide facts enough to make his abomination plausible. Why does this not set a statutory or a contract-drafting problem? Why cannot an hour then be devoted to critique of what students have drafted? Let me be brutal: the first effort will be a mess. Seven out of a class, at most, will have attempted real thinking; the rest is hogwash. And, on discussion, ninety per cent of a class, instead of either thinking or criticizing, will dully note down the result. But the third, and the fourth, and the fifth efforts, if decent underpinning has been provided, will *not* be messes. The esthetic pleasure of tailoring words to a situation has an appeal that three-quarters of a law class can get; they set the tone, and the one-quarter comes along. I argue that drafting is a part of *every* law course.

So, too, of counselling, in all fields but procedure. Day by day, the question must recur: "In view of this decision, what will you advise a man in the loser's position to *do*, next time?" I have no patience with the archaic objection that the student does not know enough about the situation to respond. *If he does not, he cannot understand the decision. If he does not, he does not know the rule.* Competent teaching of decisions and rules requires the building of enough fact-background to provide some basis for a counselling-question. Indeed, from the instructor's angle, nothing reveals so searchingly his own inadequacies in getting background over as the first silly answers to his questioning on what to do. For this alone, counselling-questions should be made obligatory.

The neglect of opportunity along this line appears nowhere better than in the use of forms in "modern" materials books. Campbell as early as 1925 did include in his Mortgages a form of corporate mortgage. It stands at the end, unannotated, wholly unregarded. Even in 1930, I put my forms at the end of the book. Neither they nor their annotations are ever looked at. Hanna, Douglas and Berle inserted forms where they belong; square in the text. Yet not even they have has really milked the forms for their teaching value, for their value as review materials, for their value as problem-setters. Tradition still binds imagination. Yet, clearly, the outlook brightens.

When we come to court-work, the European model offers hope. Let us concede that practice-courts have thus far been successes only in the hands of notable teachers. Let us concede that the artificiality of the atmosphere is too great for most instructors to overcome. What of that? There remains the fact that law school is needlessly abstract, and needlessly removed from life. There remains the fact that seeing-it-done gives reading-it-in books new flavor, new perspective. If one afternoon a week, during one semester of one year, were free of other classes, and the students with an instructor should visit various courts; if written critiques of what had been observed were followed by the instructor's comment and criticism; if the lawyers concerned were invited to explain their own views on their strategy—

Or if law schools would deliberately set to work to plan an interstitial apprenticeship. Half of our students could afford to put in the first or second summer in a law office, for car fare and lunch money. There are enough lawyers who would cooperate, if anybody should go after them. Indeed, they could be induced to stretch a point; they could be induced to try to make the work rounded, for the student. But who tries to induce them? I do not believe, as Frank seems to, in the substitution of practice or clinic for theoretical instruction. But I believe with all my soul in the livening up, the making real, of theoretical work by practical complement.

Nor do I see reason why law schools should not deliberately set themselves to the job of planning and controlling a post-school apprenticeship. *And withhold the degree until that apprenticeship is served.*[10]

In 1919 Wigmore, stirred by Army method, built for law-students a "job-analysis." The aim was to take each of the operations a lawyer has to know, to devise a task which would test out or teach each of the necessary techniques, and then to put each student through each task. One of the most sweetly sparkling jewels yet cast before us.

Methods: Radical and Conservative

It has been argued above that the analytical technique in developing which the case-method is an incomparable tool can do its work for a quick student within a year, and, for any student who deserves to graduate, within two years. And it is ancient learning that as a purveyor of information the pure case-method is close to pure waste. To this one further observation should be added: with two exceptions, every superlative case-method class-room man I know of achieves his brilliance by so narrowing his base that only "law"-law is really under discussion. Once, or twice, or even three times, "law"-law, technically taught and consistently developed, is good training. Three times is enough. Four times is too many.

On the other hand, the innovators have proved little much worth proving. Man by man, almost all of them are quarter-baked. And where one of them does hit on something good, and useful, it remains his own. They build within so many schools, and in so many different directions, and with so little contact, that all they have in common is revolt. Yet the length and intensity of the fight to introduce the case-method itself evidences the inertia of the law-teacher. We need not only invention, but introduction. We need, then, not only creation, but transmission, and *machinery* for transmission. I look around in vain for any modem *transmissible* technique of teaching to supplement the one hydra-headed but limited tradition that we know.

METHOD: TOWARDS A THEORY OF TEACHING

We straddle, in a word, between regimentation and idiosyncrasy, both overdone. I think, because we have not taken thought. About the law, we have taken thought; and then about the judge. About the lawyer, we are beginning to. About our own procedures, no. Each man for himself. Teachers are born, not made. Selah!

Now as I marshal what I have seen, I find but one *born* teacher in my memories. The rest made themselves, and all but a few made themselves slowly. Most borrowed something from their own teachers. They went ahead then by trial and error. The students paid. (As, through years, clients pay for turning into lawyers the misbranded product with which we dare to flood the market.)

Admit that true artistry comes only to him who is born to become an artist. Still—can we not speed the work? We recognize that we can. We put out course-books, which make one man's experience in part available to many other men. But as to *method* of teaching—there we balk at communication, we balk at analysis. This is idiocy, plain and drooling. Until the would-be innovators pool knowledge and experience, until they approach one another's teaching technique with sympathetic criticism, they will bubble each his personal bubble, and burst—perhaps loudly, but without effect. It would help, if schools started swapping teachers for a year at a time. It would help more, if schools started faculty seminars on how to teach: "Who was the best teacher I ever had, and why?" "My original theory of teaching, and why I had to change it." A report from last year's class: from a "C" student, a "B" student, and an "A" student, on whom they liked, and whom they didn't like—and why. *Etc.* Then analysis and synthesis. For there *are* techniques, as well as vaudevillian mannerisms.

METHODS: INDIVIDUALIZATION

What with the case-book and the pseudo-Socratic monologue, we have grown sleepily comfortable among our conveyor-belts. And our Trustees have grown sleepily comfortable in the feeling that law schools are cheap. We can use an alarm-clock. It is time to challenge the regime of mass-production.

How do we teach? We rise and juggle balls before the class. Our more finished performers can juggle table, knife, and derby-hat. The class is supposed to learn by watching. It being mostly a simple type of juggling, the quicker men do learn it. The slower learn it partially, or not at all.

But these slower men are the crux of the problem. The slower men are the backbone of a graduate body. If they do not have eye and hand to get the juggling by mere watching, our job begins to be more than what we do. First, because we now squander their time and our own. Second, because without foundation there is no solid building. Experience shows that personal attention helps. Experience shows that three-quarters of those who need personal attention will not take the initiative in getting it. Experience shows that an awakened third-year class is more valuable than a corps of instructors, in giving personal attention to first-year men who still have not managed to get the knack.

Is all of this possibility to run off into the sewer, for mere lack of organization? Where is the best legal training in a law school? We all know: in the Law Review, *and under students*. Well?

IN SUM

Law School education, even in the best schools, is, then, so inadequate, wasteful, blind and foul that it will take twenty years of unremitting effort to make it half-way equal to its job.

That seems no reason for not beginning. What matters it where we begin? To right, to left, in front, are materials crying out for use. Enlistment of the student body is one. The professor's job lies in such enlistment, and in the organization, for use in his own courses, of the fact-background necessary to give to a policy-inquiry interest; to a rule, meaningfulness; to a counselling-question, body; to a critical evaluation, hands and feet. The bar, meanwhile, has teaching and apprenticeship powers not tapped these seventy years.

Law School faculties, as distinct from single professors, need to set about discovering what it is they are training for, that joint action may be sanely guided. Pending that, there is much to be done already: especially the widening of the techniques taught. That defectively trained student-material comes to us is no excuse for *our* stamping legal illiterates with an LL. B. Proper limitation of pure case-method, proper subdivision of our groups into quick and slow, and decent individualization of instruction, can give us ample room to move in. Introduction of adequate fact materials speeds, and does not slow up, the teaching process.

Altogether it makes one think of Pilgrim's Progress. But whether the stage be Slough of Despond or Vanity Fair is hard to tell.

NOTES

1. Take certain course-books I happen to know, all currently regarded as freakish, more or less: R. R. B. Powell's, both of Hanna's, and Jervey and Deak's, Havighurst's, Morgan and Maguire's, Chafee and Simpson's, and my own. The slaving to tradition, in any of these, accounts for 99 per cent of more of stuff, arrangement, treatment, and idea-content. The Man from Mars would find trouble finding significant differences between these books, or between any of them and a case-book of Langdell or Beale, or Costigan. It is not merely that all butterflies have wings, but that within one species of butterfly, color and spots are much alike; and all lay eggs that hatch out after their own kind. You need a micrometer to measure the freak-component. *Yet that is the component which gives the books such value as they have.*

2. It thus hardly needs to be made explicit that I am myself, with all my colleagues, on the receiving end of any bricks this paper heaves.

3. This varied by States, and by need, in recent years.

4. As indicated, this seems to me highly exceptional, so far as concerns their work and thought. But their personalities may sometimes work disruptively, within a faculty. In this they resemble saner folk. The problem is the same, with both.

5. So many folk have acquired the idea that realists are not interested in ideals or ethical problems that I want to guard against any misconstruction that this passage evidences a conversion, or coming round. The fact is that any would-be innovator, or changer of things-as-they-are-at-the-moment, is of necessity interested in ideals and in ethical evaluations. In my own case, I think that demonstrable in every paper or book published, at least since 1925.

6. Garrison tapped FERA funds. This had not occurred to other law school men. Garrison's methods and interpretation, moreover, would make most sociologists envious. The lawyer who becomes a social scientist seems to profit by his law. This does not contravene what is said below about the use of social science data by lawyers who remain *pure* lawyers.

7. There is one good by-product even of bad shrinking: students consult the original, and challenge.

8. The instructor has first of all to conquer inertia. It is hard to plough new ground, and one needs to plough around the field before he knows its nature and its possibilities. The instructor has, second, to keep his balance. I agree *in toto* with Goodrich's cautioning, *Our Black Ink Balance* (1932) 7 AM. L. SCHOOL REV. 385, at 394-5: The social sciences harbor both school-exaggeration and a lunatic fringe; nor can a man *master* (in one sense) many disciplines. Yet there is a chasm of difference between such "mastery" as means first-rate standing as a worker in neighboring ploughland, and such modest "mastery" as means only the ability to read critically, and to evaluate the findings read and the methods out of which they came. Only this last is called for. It is enough to rejog thinking, and to awaken appetite. True, shifting vocabulary solves no legal problems; but the concepts a new vocabulary adds, and the information which comes packaged in those concepts, may raise or clarify dozens of legal problems at a time.

Where I differ utterly from the net effect of Goodrich's paper at 395 is in my certainty that "collateral investigation" by the student "of all the fields of knowledge" is not of the essence of the problem; and in my belief that rightly prepared background simplifies and shortens the process of learning even legal analysis of decisions.

May I add two further observations?

(1) A black-ink *balance* is not produced by totting up assets. Sane accounting calls for a totting up, no less, of liabilities. Goodrich demonstrates his own point as to the dangers of playing with an unfamiliar vocabulary. But he demonstrates no less the value of emerging from the old, as an exclusive frame of thought. May there be more of him! May he go further!

(2) In no Continental country is there the hope our law education affords. *Our men specialize.* Whereas a Continental professor must be prepared, say, to teach all of Civil Law (Property, Estates, Obligation, Transactions, Representation, Family—and What Have You?), we have goodly numbers who teach Trusts and Torts, or Contracts and Sales, or such a combination plus but one or two other narrow courses. With such relative limitation of subject matter, the possibility of getting societal background becomes real.

9. Wickser and Garrison are notable exceptions. And a reasonable number of law school men have in recent years demonstrated their ability to do work more workmanlike. *Cf.* The Johns Hopkins studies, or the work of Warner, or Frankfurter and Greene.

10. I reserve here the possibility of some types of apprenticeship in business or finance, so far as demonstrable opening exists for specialization.

Chapter 52

Spartan Education

1943

Edward H. Warren

Edward H. Warren (January 11, 1873-July 24, 1943) was professor at Harvard from 1904 to 1943. He enjoyed a legendary reputation for generations of Harvard law students as the most fierce Socratic lecturer on the faculty. Known universally as "Bull Warren," he wrote these chapters for a book of prescriptions and reminiscences he privately published at the time of his retirement in 1942. In 1943, the Harvard Law School Association reprinted several chapters in shorter book, accommodating Warren's refusal to print no more than his initial 1,000 copies of the original. This reprint included the two chapters here reproduced. In the editor's foreword of the 1943 edition, editors Joseph Welsh and Reginald Heber Smith noted, "In the classroom he first terrified us then made us love him. It took a conscious effort on his part to terrify us, but his ability to make us love him was effortless. We suspect that 'The Bull' is only dimly aware of the affection in which he is held by the graduates of the School." Reprinted from *Spartan Education* (Cambridge, Mass.: Riverside Press, for The Harvard Law School Association, 1943).

Chapter Two: Effective Teaching Methods

This chapter is intended to be helpful to relatively young men (say, those who are still on the sunny side of forty), and particularly to those who offer a first-year course in a law school. The desirable methods of teaching a second-year or a third-year course differ from the desirable methods of teaching a first-year course, but much of what I say below is applicable to all teaching of law. I make the following points:

1. The giving of a substantial amount of reliable information and the training of the minds of the students are *both* important. But the instructor should lay about twice as much emphasis upon training as upon information.

2. If a choice had to be made between an exclusive use of the case method or an exclusive use of the lecture method, the case method should be used. But I see no reason why either method should be exclusively used. Do not make a fetish of the case method. So far as giving information is concerned, a considerable use of the lecture method is desirable.

3. The main thing is the training of students so that they may be enabled to become *accurate, clear,* and *terse* in their statement of facts and issues, and *sensible* in their exercise of judgment. It is wise not to try to do more for first-year students than to help them to be accurate, clear, terse, and sensible.

4. The first thing is to guide them in the making of abstracts. A student should first read a case rather rapidly so as to see what it is all about. Then he must determine with care *just what was the question which the court was called upon to decide.*

Most of the cases are cases in an appellate court, and the higher court will be considering the propriety of the actions of the trial judge. Did the trial judge err in receiving or rejecting certain testimony? Did he err in leaving the case to the jury or in directing a verdict? Did he err in his charge to the jury? This inventory of questions is not exhaustive, but it covers the ground in the bulk of cases.

Having reached his conclusion, the student should write that question or questions, accurately, clearly, tersely. This is the first part of the abstract.

Then he should write an accurate, clear, terse statement of so many of the facts and of so much of the pleadings as are pertinent to this question, *discarding all else.* Many students when they begin to write abstracts really do not do much more than to copy large portions of the report. This is all wrong. The pertinent facts and the pertinent pleadings can, with brains, usually be reduced to a few lines, and that reducing, eliminating process is very helpful in training the mind. This is the second part of an abstract.

Then the student should write what was the decision of the court. This can usually be done in a single word, or, at most, a single line. This is the third part of the abstract.

Then the student should write, accurately, clearly, tersely, what were the *reasons* given by the court for its result. Sometimes there is only a single reason given. But not infrequently the court will give alternative reasons. And not infrequently the court will drop a dictum or dicta (a dictum is something which a court sees fit to say as to the proper answer to a question which is *not* presented on the facts and pleadings in the case). Dicta are obviously of not so much weight as a reason or an alternative reason, but unquestionably they are given some weight and have played a substantial part in the development of the law.

Distinguish, therefore, between (*a*) a sole reason; (*b*) alternative reasons; (*c*) dicta. This is the fourth, and final, part of the abstract.

The ability to make a good abstract can come only after long practice. The dead-in-earnest student will usually find that in the first few months he will scrap his first draft, and write a second, and sometimes a third or fourth draft before he has achieved something which seems to him to be accurate, clear, and terse.

A student should make his abstracts in solitude, relying only upon himself. And even after he has made them, he should not compare them with those of any fellow student,—if he does look forward to a checking by comparing with others, it will weaken his sense of the necessity of doing the work *wholly* on his own.

There is one thing about abstracts which is so important that it will be made the subject of a separate point.

5. Encourage students to use the A, B, C technique. For example: In every pledge case let A stand for the pledgor; let B stand for the pledgee; let C stand for the assignee of the debt and security, if both are assigned to one person; and let C stand for the assignee of the debt and D for the assignee of the security, if the debt and security are assigned to different persons. This makes for terseness. It avoids discussion in class as to who was who. And—much more important—*it facilitates the comparison of one case with another.*

In *Margin Customers* (at pages 246-47), one of my seventeen adverse criticisms of Judge Cardozo's opinion in *Wood* v. *Fisk* is the fact that he cited the case of *Donald* v. *Suckling* as though it were pertinent to the case at bar. But in *Donald* v. *Suckling* the contest was between A and *C*, while in *Wood* v. *Fisk* it was between A and *B*. If Judge Cardozo had analyzed the two cases in the terms of the A, B, C technique, it is hardly thinkable that he would have cited a case as an authority for a proposition which was not before the court and upon which not one of the four judges even dropped a dictum.

Students do not see the value of the A, B, C technique at first. They are inclined to think that it is a fussy requirement,—much ado about nothing. Keep at them until they do see the value of it. If they are fit to be lawyers, they will eventually see it and will come to value it highly and to use it instinctively.

6. By far the most difficult part of teaching is to conduct, *in an effective manner,* the classroom discussions. Merely to lecture is pretty easy; the instructor gets the points in orderly arrangement in his mind, takes

the platform, and just tells the students what is what. *Some* straight lecturing is, I not only concede but urge, both permissible and desirable; *but* be on your guard against doing too much of it. You will be tempted to do a lot of it, not only because it is the easiest way, but also because the students lap it up. My experience leads me to believe that a large proportion of the students, on coming to a law school fresh from the *dolce far niente* college years, would rather walk two miles than think for three minutes. If the instructor will only give them something that they can write down and memorize, the students will rise up and call him blessed. But too much lecturing is bad for them,—very bad.

Put classroom discussions in the centre of the stage. The discussions cannot be cut-and-dried (as lectures may). To carry on discussions effectively, two things are requisite:

(1) The instructor must be a full man,—he must really have himself mastered the topic to be discussed so that he is quite clear as to what he thinks (at present), as to why he thinks it, and as to what the *present* state of the authorities is. In a word, he must know his business.

(2) The instructor must *also* be a ready man. He must be able to catch as catch can. He must be able to adjust himself, and quickly to adjust himself, to *any*thing that a student may say,—developing the good, demolishing the bad. Some instructors who are sound lawyers seem to be unable to acquire the suppleness and adroitness of mind which will enable them to carry on *stimulating* classroom discussions.

But if a young instructor has the ambition to be at the top of the teaching profession, he *must* be both a full man and a *ready* man. There is plenty of room at the top.

7. There are two points about classroom discussions which have given me much anxious thought, and about which I wish to write at some length, devoting a separate point to each.

When I joined the Harvard Law Faculty, my thought, often expressed, was that any student might ask any question at any time. I was (and am) strong for the ideal of freedom of thought and speech, and to give all students such unlimited opportunities seemed to me to be the right way to implement that ideal, as applied to classroom discussions.

But experience has convinced me that that just does not work. I deeply regret that, but 'tis so. The trouble is that an aggressive few speak again and again. There are many loquacious students who are really not much good. They thoroughly enjoy taking the floor, but the other students get bored,—the class goes dead. Nothing is so deadly to a class as a lot of cat-talk. Moreover, the very fact that some men do thus bore their mates by loose and excessive talking has a strong tendency to make talking unfashionable. The result is that many good men hesitate to speak lest they be classified as among the mouth-organs. The loquacious are usually (not always) weak; the strong are usually (not always) silent.

This is serious. After long pondering over the problem thus presented, I adopted, and in recent years have enforced, two regulations:

(1) No student shall speak unless he is called upon by name.

(2) No student shall raise his hand seeking opportunity to speak unless I call for volunteers (as I not infrequently do).

I go around the class so that in the course of the year each student shall have, approximately at least, as much chance to participate in the discussion as any other student, and I guard the talking student or students (for the oftener that two students with opposing views can be pitted against each other, the better) from any interruption whatever from other students.

There is reason in all things, and I believe that these two regulations make a reasonable limitation on freedom of speech. A few students kick against those regulations; they tell me that they never were subjected to anything like that in the good old college days (and it may well be that that is true); and they even object to such regulations as contrary both to the Declaration of Independence and to the Fourteenth Amendment to the Constitution of the United States. Sometimes the disregard by a particular student of such regulations is so persistent that it is necessary for me to write him a letter, setting forth why I think those regulations are desirable, and appealing to him to cooperate. But very few students give me any trouble; true it is that exasperators are a hardy annual, but during the year now drawing to a close I have had to write to only three. The great bulk of the students see the value in these regulations and cordially comply and cooperate.

I am clear that these regulations are for the good of a class, *considered as a whole.* If there are a few students who are troublesome, do not let that even dent your serenity; remember that no man can make an omelette without breaking a few eggshells.

8. The second point with regard to the classroom discussions is the use of the 'Yes' or 'No' technique. Answer the question put to you,—'Yes' or 'No.'

Is that fair? Well, it depends on the question put whether a 'Yes' or 'No' answer may fairly be expected. There are many, many questions to which such an answer cannot fairly be expected. Probably most of the readers have heard of the lawyer who on cross-examining a witness asked him: 'Have you stopped beating your wife?'

An *indispensable* condition to the use of the 'Yes' or 'No' technique is that the instructor should be able to frame, and should frame, his question so that a 'Yes' or 'No' answer may fairly be expected. But there are many, many such questions.

What I have the greatest difficulty in making the student realize is that the 'Yes' or 'No' answer does not *close* the discussion. It simply opens it. Further questions will surely follow. *In due time* he will be given opportunity to express all that is in his mind (if it is in coherent shape).

The 'Yes' or 'No' technique is a step-by-step technique. That's the point. Don't miss that. For example: There is a famous Pennsylvania case entitled *Rerick* v. *Kern* (14 S. & R. 267). A and B owned adjoining pieces of land; a stream flowed into A's land, then divided on A's land, and flowed onto B's land in two branches. B was minded to build a mill on his land, and he wanted to do acts on A's land which would prevent the division of the stream so that he might at his mill, when built, have the benefit of the waterpower of the whole stream. B asked A for permission to do such acts on A's land as would prevent the division of the stream. A said he had no objection. Thereupon B did those acts, and thereafter built his mill. Some time later A undid what B had done on A's land, so that thereafter the water flowed as it had been accustomed to flow before B had done these acts.

Now, what B obviously wanted was a right to have the water come to his land in one stream *indefinitely*. If he had such right, B would have an easement in A's land. The law is that an easement may be created only (1) by a writing under seal showing the intent to give such right, or (2) by adverse user. Even if an *oral* contract has been made for an easement, an obstacle to the specific enforcement of that contract is presented by the Statute of Frauds which provides that no interest in land may be created without a writing.

I consider that all of the questions listed below are questions to which a 'Yes' or 'No' answer may fairly be expected:

(1) Had there been any such lapse of time that there is any possibility that an easement had been acquired by adverse user?

(2) Was there any instrument in writing under seal creating such easement?

(3) Was there a contract for such an easement between A and B?

(4) Assuming that there was a contract, was there on the facts anything to take the case out of the Statute of Frauds?

(5) Had B tried to get something for nothing?

If a student will face these five questions and answer each of them 'Yes' or 'No,' he gradually clarifies the problem and narrows the issue. And at long last the question can be faced: Was there *anything* on these facts that should give B a right to complain of A? That is a very difficult question and courts have differed, and still differ, as to what the answer should be. But if a student assumes to answer that question without the preliminary, winnowing, 'Yes' or 'No' method, he will go round and round in ever-widening circles.

No lawyer can be an efficient cross-examiner unless he is master of the 'Yes' and 'No' technique. (Do not forget that one part of this is to be able to put questions to which such an answer may fairly be expected.) And I am convinced that no jurist on or off the bench can be an efficient jurist unless he is accustomed in his thinking to put 'Yes' or 'No' questions to himself, and to require himself to give an answer to himself in that form.

9. There is another problem, distinguishable from problems as to classroom discussions, but closely related to such problems.

The ideal lecture closes at a point where the students are in a turmoil of thoughts. Some of them, many of them, rush for the desk. They want the instructor right then and there to put them out of mental distress, to clear it all up, and put their minds at peace.

It is a mistake to do that for them. Let them go away, unsatisfied. Make them realize that they must do some mighty hard thinking themselves both by discussions with their fellow students out of class and ultimately by pondering in solitude.

But balance this by encouraging them, *after* they have discussed the matter with fellow students and have pondered over these things in their hearts, to reduce to writing (in accurate, clear, terse form) any question or questions which are still bothering them and hand those questions in. Collect the questions, arrange them in some order, and then hold, at rather frequent intervals, a question hour (which will often develop into a double-header) in which those questions are read, and the instructor gives his answers.

My experience is that that works, and works splendidly. The methods stated in points 6 to 9, both inclusive, have fourfold advantages: (1) they give to everyone his fair share of the instructor's time and attention; (2) they drive it home to the students that they *must* train their minds by helping themselves (the most important point of all); (3) there is something going on all the time which is of interest to the whole class; and (4) in due time the students receive the benefit of the instructor's own thoughts. Be clear, but do not be clear *too soon*.

10. *But* balance all that has been said above by insisting upon, and giving the fullest recognition to, the highly important fact that, after all has been done which can properly be done to clarify and narrow issues, there will frequently be questions, and perhaps many questions, on which intelligent men may well differ. Encourage the students to reach their own conclusions. Encourage them to disagree with you. Encourage them to think and let think. An instinct to think and let think, coupled with an intellectual conscience, is the supreme good.

11. Do not tell the students more than ten per cent of what you know about the subject matter of the course; and know so much that ten per cent of what you know will be as much as they can be expected to assimilate in their first year.

12. Keep a record of how the men have acquitted themselves in the classroom, and if an examination paper is on the doubtful line, re-read it with benevolent assumptions in favor of (but only in favor of) men with a pretty good classroom record.

13. Encourage them to regard discussions among themselves out of class as very important,—hardly less important than the discussions in class. A group of four is, usually, an ideal discussion group as to size.

14. Encourage them to give as high as a quarter of their time in the first year to participate in moot-cases (the Ames Competition at Harvard and similar competitions elsewhere).

15. Do not talk to the students as from the mount. Keep your eye on the receiving end. Aim at the low C men. Are you enabling others to see what you see? On the one hand never be cheap; never make a joke or coin an epigram for the sake of raising a laugh; let the jokes or the epigrams or the homely illustrations be spontaneous,—generated by something that a student has said. But, on the other hand, do not feel that it is *infra dig.* for you to use an apt, spontaneously generated, joke or epigram or homely illustration. That will often get the thought over when everything else has gone off the student's mind like water off a duck's back.

16. Do not get into a legal rut. Have some wholesome interests outside of the law. Law is only a small part of life, and it is impossible to achieve a proper philosophy of the law unless one has a proper philosophy of life.

17. Try to make the students realize that a satisfying lifetime at the bar usually requires four things: (1) a sound body; (2) a pleasing personality; (3) a good intellect; (4) a character that inspires confidence.

There are a good many young men who are unduly aggressive and are much more conscious of what is due to them from others than of what is due from them to others. Others avoid such men,—they just do not see them (if they see them first). Manners have a lot to do with attracting, and retaining, associates and clients.

Character has even more to do with attracting and retaining associates and clients. I know no asset that any man can have which will contribute so much to a legitimate and enduring success at the bar as the confidence of other people that he can be trusted always to do the decent thing.

Health, manners, brains, character,—it usually takes all four to have a permanent satisfying success at the bar. Don't let the students get brains too close to the camera. Brains are cheap in the marketplace. It takes brains to be a success at the bar, but brains alone will not get a man very far.

CHAPTER THREE: EFFECTIVE JURISTIC STYLE

The literary style, or lack of literary style, of many judges, professors of law, and editors of, and contributors to, law reviews is deplorable (or, at least, it so seems to me). What is the trouble? Three sources of trouble may be mentioned: (1) sloppy thinking; (2) a love for 'half-tones'; (3) a love for resounding words and expressions.

1. *Sloppy thinking.* There is a very close connection between sloppy thinking and sloppy writing. If the writer has not wrestled with the angel until his thoughts are clear in his own mind, how can he possibly write something which will be clear to the minds of others? An effective literary style is achieved only by an infinite capacity for taking pains.

The prevalent habit of dictating thoughts rather than writing them in longhand has done much, very much, to lower the general average of literary style. I am not in favor of the abolition of stenographers; no doubt dictation is an important time-saver with respect to routine matters, chatty letters, and the like. But woe to the jurist who dictates. Possibly some extraordinary men are safe in dictating on any subject; one marvels at the reputed (and probably actual) capacity of Julius Caesar in that respect. But there is at most only a tiny fraction of jurists who can safely dictate when they wish to express themselves on legal matters of any difficulty.

Sharpen the good old pencil. *Write* out your thoughts. The very fact that that is slower is all to the good,—your mind has a much better chance to keep up with your hand than with your tongue. The very fact that it is laborious is also all to the good,—it inclines you to brevity, and to the use of shorter words.

2. *A love for 'half-tones.'* 'Half-tones' are usually 'half-truths.' Distinguish sharply between (a) saying something which is half true and half false, and (b) an orderly marshalling of opposing considerations, each of which is entitled to *some* weight.

3. *A love for resounding words and expressions.* There are many persons who have that love. Once upon a time a clergyman was seeking to give comfort to a dying parishioner. 'You have found great comfort,' said he, 'in your Bible, have you not?' 'Yes, yes,' the dying old lady said. 'And what has been the word in the Bible that has been to you the source of the greatest comfort?' 'Mesopotamia,' answered the old lady. A word of six syllables. So far as I know, there is no word in the Bible of more than five syllables, except the names of persons or places, and there is only a small fraction of more than three. For example: In the fifty-first Psalm about seventy-four per cent of the words are words of one syllable, over ninety per cent are words of one or two syllables, and about ninety-eight per cent are words of one, two, or three syllables. Yet the old lady treasured most a word of six syllables, which was devoid of any spiritual light or leading.

Orators like Cicero and writers like Gibbon have rejoiced in resounding words and expressions. I am sorry to say that the list of other orators and writers who have relished the like is a very long list. And the use of such words and expressions no doubt does impress persons of a certain (or uncertain) grade of intelligence. The use of such words and expressions has done much to cause a revulsion against 'oratory.' I have always found that most jurymen like to have counsel express themselves in simple, homely words and expressions. That is wholesome.

Stop trying to impress people by the use of long words, or words with which the ordinary man is unfamiliar. I have read somewhere (although I cannot at the moment lay my hand on the quotation) a statement by an eminent jurist that it was not fitting that rules of law should be expressed in terms which those who are unlearned in the law could comprehend. Woe to such jurists.

There is nothing else that I have written that I so much desire should have a wide, enduring influence as the first two pages in the preface to the treatise on *Margin Customers,* which were as follows:

> *Style*: I note with deep and increasing regret that some jurists on the bench and many jurists off the bench evidence no instinct for simplicity and terseness of expression. They clothe their thoughts with a prodigality of drapery which ought to be as repulsive to the wholesome-minded as the rich plush which some decades ago was regarded as *le dernier cri* in the very best railroad, steamship, and hotel circles.

Some of these jurists must have been born with a long spoon in the mouth. They make four words grow where only one word grew before, and rejoice that it has been given to them to add to the national wealth. Some of them even invent new nomenclatures, juristic Mumbo Jumbo, words which are unintelligible, without explanation, to intelligent laymen. They build themselves stilts and thump about making loud noises, and are exceeding glad that they have grown to giant size, and ever and anon duck a low star.

How to correct this? If a student asks my advice, I say to him:

1. Never dictate anything which calls for careful thinking. Write out everything (except quotations) in longhand. If you dictate, you are likely to get into a habit of using words of many syllables like 'formulated' or 'constituted.' If you write in longhand you are likely to get into a habit of using words of one syllable like 'made' or 'was.'

2. Make it a habit of life to spend ten minutes a day in reading something in the Psalms or Proverbs or Gospels; and treasure the short, terse, depicting, dynamic, devastating words and expressions.

3. See to it that not less than sixty-six per cent of your words are words of one syllable, and that not less than eighty-three percent are words of one or two syllables.

4. Go over the drafts as they come back from the typist and rub and rub and rub again until you have massaged away every muddy word and every waste word.

5. If you are dealing with a tough juristic topic, lighten the strain from time to time. If one page has to contain a headache, balance it with another page that contains a smile. A joke may be the most effective of arguments, and the most dignified dignity is an unstilted dignity.

6. *But* avoid being 'cheap' as you would shun the plague. You are living in a picture age; picturesqueness is the order of the day. All right, adapt yourself, be picturesque; but never be cheap. And be keenly conscious of the fact that the line between the picturesque and the cheap is *not* a bright line.

7. Let learning be your servant, not your master; the deepest learning is the learning that conceals learning. The bread of an idea is worth more than a stone of information. Do not spread out in full your laboratory notes. Do not be *magis in operatione quam in opere*. Appraise your 'productivity,' not by quantity, but by quality. Read much, discuss much, ponder most, write a little.

Chapter 53

Law and the Law Schools

1948

Erwin N. Griswold

Erwin N. Griswold (July 14, 1904-November 19, 1994) was professor at Harvard from 1934 to 1967 and dean from 1946 to 1967. This speech is reprinted from a manuscript in the Harvard Law Library Department of Special Collections.

There are well over one hundred law schools in the United States. There are over 40,000 young men and women studying law. Not all of these students will eventually practice law, but many of them will—for many years. Obviously the law schools bear a very close relation to the legal profession and to the public. As one who is charged with the administration of a law school, I welcome the opportunity to talk with you about some current law school problems and some matters arising in the relations of the law schools to the bar.

There are many branches of the bar, but it has always seemed to me to be one great profession. There are the practicing lawyers, the backbone of the profession. Then there are lawyers in public office, and the judges. In recent years there have been a number of lawyers holding positions of responsibility in business. All of these are branches of the legal profession. But there are, too, the law students. I count them a real part of the profession, and I hope that the ties between the students and the other branches of the profession may be continuously strengthened and deepened. As I sit in my ivory tower it has seemed to me sometimes that the relation between the schools and the practitioners too remote. I would like to take advantage of this occasion, therefore, to discuss briefly a number of matters of common interest to these two branches of our common profession.

First, how about the numbers of law students. Can they all find opportunities in practice? Won't they overcrowd the bar? My own school has turned out over 900 graduates in this calendar year 1948. Haven't the schools, including my own, been lax and shortsighted in encouraging so many men to study law and in facilitating their entry into the profession?

There are a number of facts about this situation which should be understood. It is true that there are a large number of graduates this year, and that the schools have been operating in high gear, with an overdrive, for the past three years. But it should not be forgotten that there were nearly four years in which there were virtually no law school graduates. From 1942 to 1946 the law schools operated on a skeleton basis only, and there were many which were literally closed. It is true of our school, and I think of law schools generally, that we will not graduate more men in this decade than we would have graduated in a normal ten year period. In other words, we have not been more than making up the slack resulting from the war years. We have merely been making available a legal education to those men who lost their normal opportunity for law school training because of war service.

For the past two years we have admitted normal sized first year classes. Beginning with next June we shall have only one graduating class a year, and that of normal pre-war size. It is true that we have had many more applicants than in the pre-war years, and we have been forced to make difficult selections in forming our entering classes. This has been due in large part to the financial support made available for veterans by the Government. That will be running out before long. I expect the number of applicants for law schools will then diminish, but it is my best judgment that the number will nevertheless remain larger than it was before the war.

There are a number of questions which I would like to suggest. The great increase in applicants during this post-war period, thanks to the G.I. money available, shows very clearly that in normal times the cost, of legal education is a substantial deterrent to many well-qualified men. In other words we ordinarily have a heavy financial factor in the selection of law students. It may well be asked whether this is desirable. It is contrary to most of our professed notions. We have gone far to provide equal opportunity for educational advantages to those who are intellectually qualified, but this has not yet extended in full force to professional education. The G.I. benefits have in effect been a gigantic scholarship program. The question may well be asked whether we should not find some means to continue such a program on some scale so that well qualified young men may not be denied the opportunity of a legal education.

But how about numbers? Won't the bar be flooded with consequent difficulty for all? This is a real problem, but I do not believe that the answer is to be found in general shutting of the gates to law schools. That has never yet been the answer in this country as far as the law is concerned. Moreover it is nothing over which any individual law school has any real control. I often hear it said that "the law schools" ought to do something about the numbers of men that they turn out. The law school with which I am connected limits its numbers, as do many others. But there is no limit on the number of law schools. New ones are started every few months. There have been a number of new ones since the war. Many of these new ones are not really qualified. They do not have adequate library facilities or proper teaching standards. But it is difficult to believe that legal education should become some sort of a monopoly of the existing schools. Moreover it is quite beyond the power of the existing schools to prevent the establishment of a new school or to control the enrollment of such a school. The American Bar Association Section of Legal Education and Admission to the Bar does prescribe standards which are adopted by many state supreme courts, but not by all of them. The Association of American Law Schools prescribes standards for its members. But there are many schools which do not meet these standards, and which nevertheless turn out many graduates who are admitted to the bar examinations in a number of states. If the number of graduates of law schools taken as a whole is to be limited, it will have to be by action of the profession, and not by anything any individual school or group of schools can do. The simple fact is that there is no organization of schools which does or can control all of the schools, and as far as I can see there should not be.

Before the profession took any steps to limit the number of men who could qualify to take the bar examinations, I think some very serious thinking would have to be done. Time does move on, Young men do come to maturity. They are entitled to the same opportunity the rest of us have had. The legal profession has always been a competitive profession, in this country at least. It has always been our theory that we would set standards, but that the men who met that minimum would be entitled to make their way as best they could. I know that this method has raised a number of problems. I do not minimize these difficulties. They are serious. I only say that they seem to me to be less than the difficulties and injustices which would be inherent in any system of drastic limitations on the numbers of men who could go to law schools.

Now let me turn to another matter, the whole problem of instruction and teaching methods in the law schools. I think it fair to say that some of the best instruction to be found in any field of education is found today in American law schools, and also some of the worst. The law schools have a remarkable natural advantage in their students themselves. The other evening, I was reading the address which President Quincy of Harvard gave at the opening of Dane Hall of the Harvard Law School in 1832, at the very infancy of American legal education. Here is one of the passages which he used:

> "First, a great body of intelligent young men are here brought together, of about the same age and general range of attainments; all of them inspired with a love of study and ambitious of professional eminence. At least such is the fair conclusion from the fact, that they have voluntarily exchanged the absolute independence and irresponsibility of the private office, for the examination, the instruction, and responsibility established in this institution. From such minds, thus brought into contact, result honorable collision, concurrent inquiries, public discussions, comparison of themselves with each other;—all powerful stimulants of intellectual progress."

Late in the same address he quoted from the introductory lecture delivered at the University of London in 1829 by Professor Amos, who had said: "Young men, as far as their mutual information extends, are the best professors for each other."

Besides the teaching capacities of their own students, the law schools have also developed a remarkable educational tool, thanks to the pioneering of Dean Langdell and his colleagues, three quarters of a century ago. This is the case method. That is a generic term, which covers a multitude of educational devices. As long as forty years ago, it was said that there were as many forms of the case method as there were law teachers. As it is used today, it would be more accurate to call it the problem method. But whatever it is called it is a remarkable teaching tool, that deserves to be explored more thoroughly by educators in other fields. For one thing it has virtually eliminated the deadly lecture method from the law schools of the country. Originally it consisted of the study of lecture classes. Now it is often extended to other materials of almost unlimited form. But the essence of the case method is that the actual basic materials for discussion are put before the students, whether as a case, or a statute, or a legislative problem not yet solved, or an administrative issue. All of the students have an opportunity before coming to class to consider the same material. The class discussion is about something specific, and within the ken of all. The materials are discussed, analyzed, dissected, and built upon. One or more solutions are projected and debated. Simple problems, difficult problems, practical problems, and matters involving the most refined theory, can all be considered, not in the abstract, but on the basis of concrete materials. In the hands of a skilled teacher, there is no better class room method.

In recent years there have been two points of attack on traditional law school teaching. One of these has had a noticeable result. The other has not achieved much as yet beyond discussion. The first may be summarized with the phrase "non-legal materials," the other by the phrase "practical training."

More than a generation ago it was argued forcefully that law school training had become too narrow. The lawyer deals with complex social and economic problems, and not everything that should be known about these matters is found within the pages of the reports of decisions of courts of last resort. This is undeniably true. In many fields there was need for broadening the lawyer's outlook, and the place where this should be done was largely in the law school. There have been great discussions as to how this should be done. One method has been to bring on to the law school faculty a number of non-lawyers, who were specialists, in other fields, an economist, psychologist, sociologist, and so on. With certain conspicuous exceptions, this method has not worked too well. The difficulties of integrating the points of view are very great. Unless the expert in the other field has a genuine understanding of the legal problem, his effective contribution is not likely to be great, particularly when it is measured against the time he consumes, which necessarily must be taken from other studies.

The other method has been to try to develop law trained law teachers who had an adequate understanding of these other fields, and could bring it to bear on their law teaching. This method has not been completely successful either, as it is difficult to find men of the necessary breadth of training and interest. But it has had a measure of success. I think our current law school graduates are getting a broader outlook than was available to the graduates of thirty-five years ago. But there is still room for improvement here. On the whole, though, I think that the schools are ahead of the profession at large in this respect. And they should be.

Parenthetically, I would like to make brief mention of a problem which is peculiar to Ohio. The rules of the Ohio Supreme Court now prescribe some twelve or more subjects in which an applicant for the bar examinations must have taken a course in law school. No other state in the country has such a requirement, nor anything approaching it. The effect of course is virtually to prescribe the law school course, which from our point of view is unsound and unfortunate. The courses listed do not include many which are regarded as important in the schools today, such as administrative law, labor law, taxation. I am told that this requirement was adopted by the Court largely as a result of a misunderstanding as to the wishes of the League of Ohio Law Schools, and that there is a real likelihood that this rule, adopted in 1946, can be changed before much longer. I would like to state my hope that the rule will be changed. Its effect on Ohio students in our school is most unfortunate. No one questions the right of the Court to prescribe the subjects on which it will examine applicants for admission to the bar. But prescribing most of the courses which a student must take in School has the effect of largely freezing the curriculum and of preventing the student from studying several topics which are an active part of law practice today. I remember that when I took the Ohio bar examination twenty years ago, one of the subjects on which I was examination was Bailments.

The other matter of discussion in current legal education is that of practical training. Seventy-five to a hundred years ago, legal education was quite practical, and on the whole, rather bad. It was conducted either in law offices, or in law schools where most of the instruction was done by practicing lawyers who tore themselves away from their offices long enough to meet their classes and then went back to their offices again. Many of these practitioner-teachers were undoubtedly available and conscientious men, but law teaching was necessarily a secondary interest to them. Fifty years or so ago it began to be urged that law teaching should be done by full time teachers, and this has now become the standard in qualified law schools today. There is no doubt, I think, that a law teacher is a better teacher when teaching and the law school are his primary responsibility. He should be at the law school to meet students outside the class room and discuss problems with them. As it has been put, when he isn't thinking about something else he should be thinking about the law school and his teaching problems. Or to put it another way, his heart should be at the law school.

But the carrying into effect of this principle may have gone too far. It became a rather rigid rule that law teachers should spend full time at the law school. One consequence was that occasionally a man would go into law teaching because he couldn't make his way in the practicing part of the profession. Another consequence was to draw a rather sharp line between practitioners and teachers. Practitioners were inclined to think of law teachers as a rather visionary lot, who didn't know much about what was actually happening in the world—and not infrequently they were right.

In recent years there has been some tendency towards a middle ground, it never has been the rule at my school that teachers could not practice at all, Professor Gray of the Harvard faculty was an eminent practitioner, and Professor Williston always made himself available for consultation and other opportunities in practice, although he made a selection among the things which came to him. In the modern law there are many fields where the teacher must have a close acquaintance with the real world if he is to be an adequate teacher. These include Labor Law, Administrative Law, Taxation, Corporation Finance, some parts of Constitutional Law, not to mention Estate Planning, Trusts, Wills, Contracts, and so on. In recent years a modus vivendi has been worked out in many schools whereby the law teacher remains basically a law teacher, but he is free to maintain contacts in practice, within reasonable limits. I have often seen much of direct benefit to law teaching result from such active, though limited practice. One of the members of my faculty, working in the fields of estates and trusts, is a director of the Old Colony Trust Company. Others take part in labor arbitrations, in consultation with law offices, and in the actual handling of cases, particularly in appellate courts. There are difficulties and dangers here. The work in practice must be kept secondary. But it has been my experience that it can be kept secondary, and that the benefits to the teacher as a teacher are far greater than the risks involved. I think it can be said that in the very best sense, the law teacher of today is much more practical, that is, much more in contact with what actually goes on in law offices, than he was a generation ago.

But there is a further call for practical training. Judge Jerome Frank of the Court of Appeals for the Second Circuit, has long argued that law teaching should be much more tied to practice than it has been in the past. He draws the analogy of medical education, and argues that the law schools should provide

28. Erwin Griswold (1904-1994), dean at Harvard in the mid-twentieth century, promoted the case-method teaching of legal reasoning and lawyering, even as law schools increasingly emphasized instruction in specific rules and quiz-show classwork. (*Courtesy of Art & Visual Materials, Special Collections Department, Harvard Law School Library.*)

an internship in actual practice. He urges that the students should spend much time in court, seeing what actually happens there, and following cases from their beginning to their end. Though I have great respect for Judge Frank, and much appreciation for the stimulus which he has brought to legal education, I am not able to agree with him on this matter. It is too involved a question for full discussion here, but I will try to outline my thoughts. They may be summarized in two points: (1) The schools cannot do this sort of thing very well; and (2) There are other things that the schools can do better, and which the student cannot get nearly so well when he gets into actual practice. Moreover, Judge Frank seems to think that the only practical things a lawyer does are in court, and that students should get their practical training by spending their time on the sidelines in court rooms. This seems to me both to misconceive the nature of much of law practice today, and to overestimate the educational value of repeated court room visits as a spectator.

In this connection, we may consider another problem. The analogy of medical education has been referred to. Now there is one great characteristic of medical education; it is very expensive. The Harvard Medical School has an endowment of $20,000,000 and 400 students. The Harvard Law School has an endowment of $5,500,000 and at present 1700 students. Moreover, a medical education takes four years, and this is followed by a two year internship during which the young doctor gets virtually no financial return. The law schools do their work in three years, and the law student then goes out and gets a paying job. I am proud of the practicing members of the profession for their refusal to take economic advantage of the young lawyer, as has been done of the young doctor in the medical field. We know that law school graduates are not finished lawyers just as the law offices must know that fact, too. They have much to learn. Indeed, a lawyer always has much to learn. A competent lawyer's education is never finished. I think the first year or two in a law office, even the man's own law office if he hangs up his own shingle, should be looked on as an internship. That is the place where he should learn the ins and outs of practice. He can learn it much better there than it can ever taught to him in a law school. Moreover, to attempt to teach practice effectively in law school would involve the development of individual instruction methods which have made a medical education so costly. I think we have been wise to avoid such methods, even though we may well have gone too far into mass production, and there may be room to work out a more effective middle ground.

There is one more problem of instruction to which I should like to devote attention. That is the matter of imparting to the law student the standards and ideals of the profession, the responsibilities and opportunities for service of the lawyer. I do not speak of legal ethics. I am thinking of something broader, of something which includes the traditional canons of legal ethics and much more. The schools have long struggled with this problem, and without too much success. Courses in legal ethics are not effective. That much we know. It is almost inevitable that they should become courses in how far we can go without stepping over the line. Yet it is clear that there is much that can be taught to law students about the broad problems of the profession, and its responsibilities. It depends a great deal upon the teacher. It is said that Dean Ames of the Harvard Law School inspired his students in this respect in an almost unique manner. It is clear that the attitude and approach of the teacher can have a tremendous effect upon his students. If the teacher is cynical, if he suggests that it is smart for a lawyer or his client "to get away with something," if he indicates that the lawyer's craft consists largely in the development of "slick tricks," his students will be more deeply marked than by anything he can tell them about the rules of torts or contracts. If he has a love of the profession, an active appreciation of its standards and aspirations and responsibilities, he can make a great and lasting impress on them.

In this whole field I do not think that the law schools have yet measured up to their responsibilities. On the whole the general public does not like lawyers. They regard them as obstructionist, technical, narrow-minded, lacking in adequate appreciation of the public interest. On the whole it seems to me that lawyers as a class have been unduly conservative. There are many exceptions of course, and a wild-eyed lawyer can probably do more damage than a conservative one. Nevertheless it is my view that there is much room for improvement here, and that a large measure of responsibility rests upon the law schools.

About fifteen years ago, Mr. Justice Stone delivered an address at the University of Michigan Law School. It is entitled "The Public Influence of the Bar" and may be found printed in volume 48 of the Harvard Law Review. It deserves careful reading by practitioners and law students today. There are many significant passages in it, but there is one which I want to quote briefly merely in illustration of the point I have been making. Speaking in 1934, he said: "When the history of the financial era which has just drawn to a close comes to be written, most of its mistakes and its major faults will be ascribed to the failure to observe the fiduciary principle. . . . There is little to suggest that the Bar has yet recognized that it must bear some burden of responsibility for these evils." And responsibility here rests on the Schools as well. Students should be taught that their services are for sale, but that they need not sell their souls. The lawyer in advising a business man may sometimes have to be ahead of the business man, leading him, sometimes pushing him to standards higher than those of the market place. The Bar has a moral responsibility to the community, and the law schools have a responsibility to make law students aware of the moral influence they should wield.

There is one last topic on which I would like to say a few words that has to do with the relation of the organized bar with the law schools, particularly with the students in the schools. Perhaps that is the way to put it, as that relationship is almost nonexistent today. American Bar Association has no sort of student membership. It does no work in the law schools. It does nothing either to inculcate in the law student a feeling that he is becoming a member of a great profession or even to lead him so that he will become a regular member of the association on his admission to the bar. In this respect the National Lawyers Guild is much more active. It has a chapter on the Harvard Law School, and has performed real service for our students. It has provided speakers for them, advice about different types of law practice, and help in finding jobs. But there has been nothing of the sort from the American Bar Association. There is one exception to this statement. The American Bar Association Journal provides a special subscription rate for law students of $1.50 a year. But it does nothing to publicize this among the law schools.

I have several times called this to the attention of the officers of the Association, but as yet nothing has come of it. I know that the Association is large and cumbersome, and that it takes it a long time to get into action. I am neither impatient nor disappointed. I think there is a great opportunity here for the Association and the bar to provide ties between the practicing and the student members of the profession that such ties would be a great benefit to both groups. I suspect that many local associations do do a considerable amount of work with law students. In many ways it is easier to do it on that level. It may well be that your

Association maintains active relations with local law schools. That does not happen at my law school, and cannot happen very well, as our students come from every part of the country. Our contact with the organized profession must come largely through the American Bar Association, and as yet the connection is almost non-existent. I think that the schools would welcome the development of really active interest by the Association in law students, and that this would be of real and mutual benefit to all concerned.

I have tried to outline to you some of the problems that law teachers are thinking about today. I have tried to suggest the closeness of the tie that I think exists today between law schools, law students, law teachers and practitioners. In your eyes we may be an impractical lot. In our eyes, you are the backbone of the profession, whose cause we seek to serve. Without you, we would not be. If we can do our job better, we will better serve you, and through you the public whose servants we all should be.

Chapter 54

The Law Schools of the United States

1958

Lowell S. Nicholson

Lowell Starbuck Nicholson (1900-1992) was professor and dean of Northeastern University School of Law from 1946 to 1953. Reprinted from *The Law Schools of the United States: A Statistical and Analytical Report Based on 136 Completed Questionnaires and on Inspections of 160 Law Schools, Prepared for the Survey of the Legal Profession* (Baltimore: Lord Baltimore Press, Inc., 1958). This chapter presents a portion of this report, which was prepared for the survey of the legal profession.

---

§ 5. Curriculum

(A) In General

"Attention was paid to the breadth of the curriculum offerings, whether for the imparting of basic information, development of craft skills, or the cultivation of the mental faculties requisite to professional success. Measured by these standards, many curricula are superior. In such schools one finds virtually all of the initial experimentation and leadership in curricular changes during the past ten years—changes which have led to the inclusion of legal history, the legal profession, jurisprudence, legislation, comparative law, labor law, administrative law, taxation, trade regulation, legal accounting, and legal writing." (J.G.H.)

"The curricula are fairly well standardized. The vast majority of schools are either local or regional and the curricula have been fashioned largely around the subjects in which the graduates of the school must be examined for admission to practice. By and large, the law students have pressed for the 'bread and butter' courses and the subjects specified in the rules for admission to practice.[1] The law schools have tended, because of limited funds, inadequate facilities, and lethargy, to yield to the pressures. The result has been a failure to develop the whole professional man." (J.G.H.)

"There is need for further experimentation in course offerings and teaching techniques; the need for legal research was never greater; the call for distinctive programs was never louder; and the need for law school placement bureaus is great. And continuing education for lawyers, especially in the metropolitan areas, is in its infancy." (J.G.H.)

"There can be no such thing as a standard law school curriculum. This is particularly true today when the leading law schools of the United States are engaged in extensive programs of curriculum revision and reexamination of methods of instruction." (Calif. p. 52.)

"The number, character, and arrangement of courses in any law school must depend on a variety of factors peculiar to that school, including the number, experience, and scope of interest of the members of its faculty, the quality of its student body, and the school's library and physical facilities. The fundamental dilemma which perennially confronts American legal education: Whether to emphasize so-called practical subjects and thus run the danger of degenerating to mere trade school standards, or to emphasize legal history and theory, regarding the study of the law as simply one aspect of the study of the *universitas* of knowledge with which an institution of higher learning must be primarily concerned. The resolution of this dilemma can come only by continued, intelligent and free experimentation." (Calif. pp. 55-57.)

(B) Some Special Courses

"The first year also includes an 'Introduction to the Study of Law.' This program is given for three hours a day for the first two weeks of the entering semester. A book pertaining to 'Introduction to the Study of Law' has been prepared by members of the faculty and this book is sent to the students and is to be read by the students during the summer preceding their entrance into the law school. At the conclusion of these two weeks of introductory study, the regular courses begin."

"There was also added a course in Legal Accounting, for students without adequate previous training in the subject, and a course in Fundamentals of English Composition for those failing to pass the required entrance test in English. Both courses represent an interesting development in the infusion of new techniques in the traditional law school curriculum, and both are proving reasonably successful in achieving their desired objectives."

"There is a first year course in the Legislative Process which is designed to acquaint the student immediately with the importance of legislation and with methods of handling it. The course parallels one in the Judicial Process so that the student becomes acquainted with both fields at the same time and thus, presumably, does not learn to employ exclusively the common law approach to legal problems."

"It is unusual that Legislation and Jurisprudence are required courses. Perhaps the presence on the faculty of scholars who are especially notable in those fields explains the requirement."

(C) Practice Courses

"Unique in the curriculum is the program in Legal Research. Beginning in the first semester of the first year with a course in Legal Bibliography, one semester hour is required in each of the following three semesters in legal writing. The faculty is of the opinion that this program has not only resulted in improved writing skills but also in a better understanding of the substantive law as well."

"The school makes a vigorous attempt to make its instruction as practical as possible so that a student graduating and going into practice will already have had some experience with drafting pleadings, drawing wills and contracts, organizing corporations, writing briefs, and doing many of the things an office practice requires. This experience is largely gained in individual courses, but the legal research plan at the school has the same end."

"The school takes great pride in its practice courses and deservedly so. These courses begin with the general practice course in the first year and continue as required work throughout the entire law school program. Students gain experience in the actual preparation of legal documents, including pleadings, and in the actual preparation and conduct of cases for trial, and in perfecting appeals and arguing appellate cases. The work is closely supervised and approximates an apprentice system."

"Each graduate fellow takes a group of about sixteen students on field trips, the purpose of which is to see the procedure in various types of judicial and quasi-judicial proceedings. These supervised field trips visit trial courts, appellate courts and administrative hearings, etc. Before the trips the students are briefed upon the nature of the subject matter they will witness, and after the trip they are required to make a report."

(D) POST-ADMISSION COURSES

"Until comparatively recently, the thought of a practicing lawyer taking a graduate course in law school because it would help him in his practice would have been regarded by many as fanciful. This is rapidly ceasing to be so. The pioneer efforts of the New York University Law School have demonstrated that it is possible for a law school in a metropolitan area to contribute much to the post-admission education of members of the bar of that area in specialized technical fields. There can be no reasonable doubt that such systematic study in a law school is a more effective means of post-admission education than is merely listening to any series of lectures, no matter how well prepared." (Calif. pp. 134-135.)

"The significant suggestion out of this law school is the plan to attract students into continued legal education by specialized programs offering a Master of Laws degree in areas such as taxation, labor law, comparative law and international law. This experiment should be observed closely and its results made available to other law schools. This may be the solution through a graduate year of night school training to the problem of how to give the present day law students the additional training required by the increased emphasis on public law."

"The degrees planned are Master of Laws, Master of Laws in Oil and Gas Law, and Master of Laws in Taxation. As these titles indicate, the graduate study contemplated is to be primarily in special fields of particular interest to practicing lawyers and will be especially suited to lawyers practicing in the southwest. There is no plan to invade the usual function of graduate law study, which is the training of law teachers. As long as the graduate work is directed to the needs of practicing lawyers in the southwestern region, there is good reason to believe that it will serve a useful function of post-admission training in specialized fields where such training is needed."

[It is true that "the usual function of graduate law study" in the past has been "the training of law teachers." The training of law teachers is important; so important that the opportunities for practical training should be increased, and such opportunities should include some training in the *art of teaching* and in the meaning and use of the difficult but vital "case method of instruction." But the post-admission education of practicing lawyers is equally as important, possibly more so. The idea that the "usual function" of graduate law study is the "training of law teachers" should be abandoned. Law schools in metropolitan areas should emphasize the continuing education of practicing lawyers. No one now claims that a law student learns all the law he should know in law school. It is the two-fold responsibility of metropolitan law schools to offer opportunities for practical and effective post-admission courses and also to take measures to persuade practicing lawyers in the community to come back to school and continue their education in specialized fields of the law.]

"Although not a student activity, worthy of note is the Tax Law Club. Membership in the club leads to no advanced degree, it does not purport to serve as post law school education. A group of tax lawyers meets in the evening for the purpose of discussing recent tax cases—one member of the club is responsible for the presentation of a case or tax problem at each meeting. The purpose of the club is to keep the members abreast of current developments in tax law, both state and federal, and to afford the members an opportunity to discuss tax problems informally. The club has been unusually successful and the experiment might well be emulated elsewhere where graduate instruction is beyond the means of a school and yet there is a desire on the part of the school to maintain closer contact with members of the bar and to meet the needs of the bar for post law school education."

§ 6. SCHOLARSHIP STANDARDS

(A) RESPONSIBILITY TO THE PUBLIC

"It is important not only to young men and women seeking to enter the legal profession, but also to the public, that only those persons be admitted to practice who have the scholastic and legal training and the intellectual and personal qualities necessary to make an effective contribution to the discharge by the legal profession of its public responsibilities." (Calif. p. 35.)

"The danger of an inadequate legal education lies in the fact that it permits an unqualified person to become a lawyer if he can pass the bar examinations. And experience has shown that persistent candidates almost invariably succeed in gaining admission to the bar. In the final analysis it is the public interest which is the guide. Every reasonable step must be taken to protect the public against lawyers who do not measure up to reasonable standards of preparation and ability. One such precaution is to require adequate law school training."

"The unhappy conclusion one is forced to draw is that no law school in the area has the courage to shoulder its plain responsibility to the American community and to the legal profession of weeding out those students whose capacity-interest-effort characteristics call for such action. And the unavailability of authoritative bar examination statistics leaves blurred and confused the question of how the local bar examiners are handling this heavy and unwarranted burden thrust upon them by the failure of the law schools in the area to shoulder initially their responsibility in this respect. As matters apparently stand, the issuance of a District of Columbia license should carry with it no presumption of the attainment of any significant minima of knowledge or skill."

"The fact is that not every man or woman is fitted to be a lawyer. The sooner the incapable are discouraged from continuing law study the better it is for them, the better it is for the bar, the better it is for the scholastic standards of the law schools, and the better it is for the public." (Calif. p. 45.)

"If the standards of the American Bar Association are valid, the inference is plain that law schools not meeting them should not be allowed to qualify students for admission to the bar."

"This school is merely a demonstration of how poor facilities can be and still attract a few students who will put in the time in an effort to learn something. It is a tragedy that the organized bar does not take a firm position to eliminate such a school."

(B) Prelegal Requirements

[The subject of prelegal requirements has been covered extensively in books and articles during recent years. Accordingly, only a very few of the comments of the inspectors on this subject are included below. The first comment is general; the others contain ideas which are not frequently presented.]

"While the question of required specific prelegal subjects has been much discussed in the United States in recent years, not only has there been no agreement as to what those subjects should be, but there has been a general recognition of the fact that the value of a student's college work depends much more on his teachers than on the subject matter of his courses." (Calif. p. 43.)

"Although the law school does not prescribe required prelegal subjects, a counselling and guidance service to pre-law students is provided by a member of the law faculty assigned to that service."

"No particular prelegal subjects are specified. However, the school will give preference to applicants who have completed, with a distinguished record, college courses in English composition and public speaking, and in at least six of the following subject groups: social science: government, economics and sociology; philosophy and ethics; psychology and logic; English and American literature; English and American history; mathematics; accounting; laboratory science: biology, chemistry and physics; ancient or modern foreign languages."

"If a student appears to have a weak prelaw background he may be required to take a 'qualifying examination in expository writing.'"

"Each applicant for admission is required, upon enrollment, to stand an English Usage and Spelling Proficiency Examination, unless he holds a Bachelor's Degree."

"All entering students are required to pass a comprehensive English test, and those failing it must take a law school course on Fundamentals of English Composition."

(C) Easy Admission Policies

[The purpose of the inspectors was to obtain the "feel" of legal education in our law schools. A reading of the inspectors' reports gives one the "feeling" that there is almost a total absence of selectivity in the admission of beginning students to American law schools. The situation depicted in the following excerpts apparently exists in the vast majority of schools.]

"All qualified applicants have regularly been admitted to the law school in recent years."

"The school does not attempt to screen applicants over and above the determination that they have complied with the minimum qualitative and quantitative requirements."

"In almost all cases, admission of beginning students involves simply a computation of hours and grade averages."

"No personal interview with the dean or a faculty committee is required of applicants for admission. No opportunity, in advance of admission, is afforded to the law dean and the law faculty to evaluate the personality of the applicant, to judge the earnestness of his purpose, or to evaluate his probable aptitude for the study of law. Letters of recommendation are not required. No independent inquiry is made of the moral character of the applicant. All of this has resulted in the admission of students who are not qualified for the study of law. In the year 1948-49, 190 students entered upon the study of law in this school; only 91 remained in school at the beginning of the following year. Forty of the 190 were flunked out, and 59 others quit voluntarily, most of them persuaded so to do because of low grades. It would seem that a better system of selecting students might be devised."

(D) Interrelationship of Admissions and Exclusions

"In order to provide sound legal education, it is not only necessary to pursue a policy with regard to admission to law school which will exclude men and women incapable, by reason of lack of native endowments or lack of educational training, of profiting from law school instruction, but it is also essential to eliminate from the law school as soon as possible those students who are unable to demonstrate reasonable ability in the study of law. Failure to exclude demonstrably unfit persons from admission to a school or failure to eliminate them from the school when they have demonstrated their incapacity will result in lowering the standards of classroom instruction and will thus do harm to those of the student body who are capable of pursuing law school work to advantage." (Calif. p. 45.)

"The appropriate rigor of any particular school's policy with regard to elimination for scholastic deficiencies is necessarily related to the policy of that school with regard to entrance requirements." (Calif. p. 51.)

"This low standard for admission is reflected in a very high casualty rate. It might be more desirable to impose somewhat higher standards for admission and reduce the number of failures."

"The experience at some leading schools cause some to believe that a policy of selective admissions with a lower rate of exclusions is to be preferred over a policy of nonselective admissions and a high rate of exclusions. The former policy is thought to eliminate the waste and drag. There is no agreement on the point among legal educators." (J.G.H.)

(E) Voluntary Withdrawals

"In general, the inspections disclosed that approximately ten per cent of the entering students withdraw voluntarily and that another five per cent withdraw upon the advice of the dean and faculty during the course of the first year. By and large, these withdrawals are because of lack of capacity or time." (J.G.H.)

"There has been a tendency in the record-keeping of some of the schools to fail to differentiate between voluntary withdrawals during the year and exclusions for scholarship at the end of the year. The keeping of records showing separately withdrawals during or at the end of the academic year and exclusions for deficiency in scholarship at the end of the year is essential to the proper operation of a law school." (Calif. pp. 47-51.)

(F) Exclusion Policies and Practices

"Students with scholastic deficiencies generally are eliminated as soon as the deficiency appears. The usual practice is to make the exclusions at the end of the first year's study in the full-time division schools. While a few of the part-time division schools attempt to make such determinations at the end of the first year, the usual practice is to determine the exclusions in the second year." (J.G.H.)

"The scholarship standards have been strictly enforced. They have resulted in the dismissal of approximately 10.3% of all the students in the first-year class during 1948-1949. In view of the fact that this class was selected from a large group of applicants, this percentage of dismissals shows that the scholarship standards are quite satisfactory. The records show that it is very rare for a student to be dismissed after the end of his first year."

"The faculty promulgated in May, 1950, a very ingenious rule which should be watched with real interest by all other schools. A student who falls below a C average may (and if he falls far enough, he must) take a comprehensive examination over all work previously available to him. The examination is truly comprehensive without indication of courses or subject matter involved. If a student passes the examination successfully 'his slate is wiped clean' and he need only maintain a C average on work thereafter taken. If he fails the examination he may not re-enroll."

Liberal Exclusion Policies

"The rules governing probation and suspension are liberal. A student is dropped who, in any quarter, fails two thirds of his work."

"In the first-year courses although 62 people have received a grade of A, only 4 received failing grades and there were no conditions."

"Requirements for advancement are insufficient, grading seemed unusually lax and practically no students are excluded from the school, it being the policy to let the student continue until he becomes discouraged."

"The policy of the school to continue students with relatively low law school records appears to stem in part from the unwillingness on the part of the dean to face pressures which inevitably arise in state schools for the readmission of excluded students. That problem has been solved by not excluding students."

"Courses failed are not averaged in, in computing the student's general average. It follows that in numerous cases law students have deliberately failed courses rather than risk earning a low grade—the student may fail with impunity just so he does not in any semester fail one third of the semester hours for which he is registered."[2]

"The required average grade is readily attained by any student who selects his semester's schedule from the wide field of electives with an eye to getting good grades from easy professors that will sustain the required average for continuation in the school."

"The point simply is that the school as a whole is not working the students hard enough, is not holding them to high enough standards, and is not giving them as broad a legal education as they will need to compete with other young men in the legal world of today."

Exclusion Policies too Strict?

"While these strict standards of scholarship and severe policy of examination inevitably result in a good quality of work on the part of the students who pass, the result is disastrous for the individual student who fails. He must go down the scale and seek admission to a lower class law school, or he must give up the study of law. It would be much kinder, as far as he is concerned, to have more rigid qualitative standards for admission and to reject students with poor academic records before they enter the law school rather than after they have passed one or two years in it."

"The result of these policies is that scholastic mortality is high. Of 128 students who entered in the fall of 1948, 53 were eliminated in their first year. Only 43 returned to enter the second year in the fall of 1949, and of these there were 10 withdrawals during the first two terms, leaving 33 of the original entering class still enrolled in the spring term at the time of the survey visit. While such a rigorous policy undoubtedly produces a select group of graduates, it appears to have a repressive effect on student morale. It also tends to dissuade many of the better students from participating in law review work for fear of jeopardizing their grades in their regular courses."

(G) READMISSION

"Intimately related to the problem of exclusions for scholastic deficiency is the matter of readmission of students who have been excluded. A soft policy of readmission can defeat the strictest policy of exclusion." (Calif. p. 51.)

"The readmission of failed students was found in 46 of the approved schools. In some instances a failed student is required to remain away from school for one year and may then petition for readmission. This policy prevails most generally in the state university law schools. On the other hand, the inspections disclosed many glaring instances in which the number of exclusions was large but the number of readmissions was also large. In one instance a school had sent a mimeographed notice to all first-year students who had been excluded and invited them to file applications for readmission." (J.G.H.)

§ 7. Faculty

(A) Introductory

"In rating the faculty personnel account was taken of the diversity of training and experience, the classroom performance, and the contributions to legal literature. The most important consideration in each instance was the effectiveness of the classroom teaching. Particular attention was paid to whether the teacher could be heard by all students, whether he invited and answered questions, the use of correct English, clarity of explanation, logical analysis, synthesis, and his knowledge of the field of law being taught." (J.G.H.)

"The judgment of faculty quality is a complex matter involving a variety of factors, of which legal knowledge, adequate time for preparation, teaching experience, ability in classroom performance, competence in original investigation, contribution to legal scholarship, influence upon students, and influence upon the legal profession exerted through the organized bar are among the more important. Judgment cannot rest upon dry figures as to length of experience in teaching or in practice, number of advanced degrees, lists of published writings, or any other mechanical measures." (Calif. p. 57.)

"Classroom visits were directed primarily to securing impressions of the personalities, teaching methods and classroom effectiveness of the instructors visited, but with full realization that no single visit to any law class, whether for ten minutes or for an hour, would afford adequate data for a definitive judgment as to the ability of any particular faculty member. Such visits, however, are sufficient, when made by competent and experienced observers, to accomplish three purposes: (1) to identify teachers of extraordinary competence; (2) to identify teachers of extraordinary incompetence; and (3) when classes taught by all or substantially all the members of a law school faculty have been visited, to afford a basis for judgment as to the general level of ability of that faculty as a whole. Based on these classroom visits it is possible to say that the teaching performance of approximately 15% of the 186 teachers visited [of course, this number refers only to the California schools] was excellent to superior, that the teaching of 57% more was definitely above minimum standards, that the teaching of 19% was substandard without being incompetent, and that the teaching of 9% showed a degree of incompetence which could hardly be expected to be remedied by additional experience or any other means." (Calif. pp. 59-60.)

(B) Salaries

"By their salaries shall ye know them"

In General

"One of the most reliable, tangible, simplest-to-ascertain and most difficult to obscure or cloak or rationalize away, measuring sticks of a law school operation is its salary schedule. It directly reflects, for example, the judgment of a university on the value to the university and to the community of the operation and, except in highly unusual instances, affords a direct appraisal of the calibre of the faculty. By their salaries shall ye know them."

"Where the average or median salary was below $6,000 per academic year of nine months, it has been rated as 'inadequate.' Where the average or median salary was between $6,000 and $7,500 per academic year of nine months, it has been rated as 'adequate.'" (J.G.H.) [These figures relate to the academic year of 1949-50. See pages 164 and 170-172 for comments on salaries in the academic year 1953-54.1

"Difficulties have sometimes arisen in California, as elsewhere, in persuading university authorities of the need for adequately high faculty salaries in their law schools. The argument has been repeatedly made by other departments of the university that there is no reason why a law school professor should be paid any more than a professor of French or English or chemistry or agriculture. This argument is a wholly fallacious one, and one which the organized bar as well as the law schools must effectively combat in the public interest." (Calif. p. 63.)

"A senior professor in a law school is more than a teacher. He is an essential part of the machinery for the administration of justice. His function, as James Barr Ames pointed out almost half a century ago, is in many respects similar to that of an appellate court judge. (See Ames, *The Vocation of a Law Teacher*, 48 Am. L. Reg. 129 [1900].) The development of the law, the improvement of the administration of justice, and the reshaping of the substantive law to meet the demands of a changing age, are tasks which cannot be effectively carried out by an overburdened legislature and judiciary alone. If those tasks are to be effectively shouldered by law school teachers, it must be possible to recruit into law teaching men of the same calibre that should be chosen for the state and federal bench." (id. p. 63.)

"A man of outstanding ability and corresponding potential earning capacity at the bar may be willing to enter upon a permanent career in teaching, or to become a member of the judiciary, for a stipend, for example, of $15,000 a year. He will not do it if the maximum compensation he can hope to attain is $6,000 a year, as is the case in some of the California law schools today. [i.e., 1949.] When the problem is thus viewed—and it must be thus viewed if the public interest in its own good governance is to be served—consideration of comparative salaries in university departments outside the law school becomes obviously and properly irrelevant, and it becomes apparent that the proper measure for the salaries of senior law professors will be found in the salaries of the judiciary." (id. p. 63.)

"Without doubt the inadequate and low salary scales which obtain in 85 law schools have been harmful to the output of the schools. Nevertheless the national accrediting agencies have done little about it. Each dean has been left to his own resources in dealing with the problem. The accrediting agencies should tackle the problem." (J.G.H.)

Law Salaries Tied In with Other University Divisions

"Repeatedly the deans advised that a uniform salary scale prevails throughout all divisions of the institution and that their schools have been unable to pay salaries adequate to retain effective teachers and able scholars." (J.G.H.)

"To lock law faculty salaries into some general university schedule, or to key such salaries into some general hazy notion of prevailing salaries in this area, is to invite, if not guarantee, faculty mediocrity."

"The amount of money that a person qualified for law school teaching can make elsewhere must be considered, if properly qualified teachers are to be obtained. Possibly some able law school teachers teach for the love of teaching, but there are many able ones who also consider the matter of finances."

"The faculty salary problem seems, therefore, to be one of persuading the university administration to unlock law school salaries from the university salary schedule and to increase law school salaries to a point where they will be reasonably commensurate with those paid in other law schools in the community. A law school is not competing with other schools in the same university family but with other law schools in the immediate area."

Promotions More Rapid

"The maximum and minimum salaries for definite ranks are fixed by university regulations at the same figures for all divisions including the law school. Law school appointments, however, are usually at a higher rank and salary than corresponding appointments in most of the other divisions of the university for appointees of the same age and experience."

Salaries Not Tied In

"The law school has about a $1200 differential in its salaries as compared with the non-professional schools, but is about $1800 under the average salary in the School of Medicine. On the other hand, law school salaries are now (1949-50) some $600 better than the national law school average. Accordingly this school has not suffered any unusual faculty turn-over."

Great Turn-over

"The salary scale is considerably below the national average; as a result the school has had considerable turn-over in teachers."

"The faculty salaries are so low that if the young men prove to be exceptional they may be lured away by better offers."

"The salary level, however, has made it difficult to keep able men who become known in the law school world."

Young and Inexperienced Teachers

"The low-salary schools have been training schools for young and inexperienced teachers who have moved to higher-salary schools after having gained the necessary experience. This has been particularly true in the low-salary state university law schools and the secular institutions which have uniform salary scales throughout all divisions of the institution. While here and there in these schools one finds a devoted scholar and an effective teacher who remains content, for personal reasons, such is not the general practice." (J.G.H.)

"The school is following the wise course of paying its money to procure the best of the younger men rather than to keep older men of mediocre ability."

"The dean has followed the policy of getting young men who appear to be exceptionally well qualified rather than older men of inferior ability. He is forced to make this choice because of his inability to offer salaries which will attract and hold capable men."

"The faculty salary scale is too low to permit the school to replace the present staff with teachers of equal ability."

"The level of salaries at this law school is not adequate for the attraction and retention of well trained and experienced faculty members."

"The school now has a vacancy for a full-time teacher but is unable to fill it because the salary level is too low."

"The faculty of this school is only fair. The salary scale tends to retain those people who are ineffective and to encourage the better teachers to seek employment elsewhere. It is disgraceful that teachers should be asked to teach in a professional school at this salary level."

(c) Methods of Instruction

[One of the discouraging impressions gained from reading the inspectors' reports is that the true and effective "case method of instruction" is not in use in many schools. In most of the reports there is a surprisingly small amount of material on methods of instruction. A frequent statement is merely that "the school uses the case method." In most of the reports where this statement is amplified, the amplification creates a doubt as to the accuracy of the statement. Quite a few of the inspectors made reports somewhat similar to the following.]

"The case system of teaching is in use, in the sense that casebooks are the teaching materials, but the teachers have not become accustomed to efficient use of the true case method of teaching."

[Even more disturbing, many of the inspectors themselves seem to confuse the "case method" with something called the "casebook method."]

"The prevailing method of instruction is the case book method."

"The casebook is the basic method."

"The casebook method of instruction is used in all courses."

"Teaching is primarily under the casebook method."

"Classroom instruction, as observed in the classes visited, and student preparation and participation, measured up to standards of good legal education. The case-book method is predominantly used."

[This description of the method of instruction as the "casebook method" appears in a score or more of the inspectors' reports. An impression is gained from a reading of all of the reports that the "casebook" is used in nearly every American law school, but that the "case method of instruction" is used only in a very few schools.]

[An excellent explanation of the "case method," and almost the only one in all the inspection reports, is contained in Fuller's report on Legal Education in Pennsylvania. (Published in *Temple Law Quarterly*, Vol. XXV, No. 3, pages 249-300, January 1952.) Excerpts from this report follow.]

"Taking the Pennsylvania schools as a whole, good case method instruction is a rarity. In this I do not think they are different from other law schools, including our most famous, for I am convinced that there is a decline in the use of the case method over the country as a whole. To avoid misunderstanding, it should be added that by 'the case method' I mean generally a method which involves a joint exploration of problems by instructor and class as contrasted with a method designed primarily to convey information from the instructor to the class."

"Even in classes where instruction proceeded in the form of an exchange between professor and student often the object seemed not that of conducting a joint examination of issues but rather that of testing the student's knowledge by a kind of quiz. In these 'quiz' sessions the ratio of student talk to professor talk was high, but the student was there, not to analyse and think along with the instructor, but to demonstrate to his instructor and his classmates that he knew his way about the law. Where instruction thus proceeds by a kind of oral quiz, the significance of factual nuances tends to be lost. The effort is to stretch instruction over a complicated body of rules and exceptions, and the cases in the book serve about the same function as short hypothetical cases put orally by the teacher during the course of the quiz. There is no time to dig deeply into their facts. It is therefore small wonder that many students find the most convenient way of learning about the cases is through the canned brief since it yields all that is really essential in preparing for class."

"At the hands of a good teacher instruction by the quiz method can be a very lively and entertaining thing, but it lacks the vital spark of genuine student participation. The student is in no sense helping to bring a solution into existence. He is demonstrating that he knows and understands the solutions that have been produced by other people: judges, legislators and professorial restators of the law. When he reads the case in the casebook, he reads it, not as a problem, but as an illustration of one of these solutions."

"One cause for the tendency to resort to lecture lies in a feeling of insecurity on the part of the instructor. A truly free ranging discussion requires of the teacher either an extraordinarily nimble mind or a thorough advance preparation which includes not only studying the cases carefully but thinking through their implications and cross implications. Without this preparation a venture into the case method is a hazardous thing, and the man who sets out to emulate Socrates may find the roles reversed with himself an ineffective and self-contradicting Thrasymachus while the class plays the role of the triumphant Socrates. Such a reversal of roles may actually have the highest educational value for the student though neither he nor his instructor is likely to realize this at the time. At any rate it requires on the part of the instructor a tougher ego than is common even among case-hardened lawyers."

"In suggesting that the lecture method and what I have called the quiz method are deficient educationally, I do not rest simply on a philosophic conviction that in the long run better results will be achieved by a method of instruction that emphasizes problems rather than answers. For purposes of this report I am content to rest this conclusion entirely on direct observations in the classroom. There is an observable difference in the student interest commanded by lecture and quiz and by real cases and problems. The master of the case method, who takes the case itself as the point of departure, attains an intensity of student interest and participation that is beyond the powers of the most skillful lecturer or quiz master. This is not a matter of speculation but something that can be seen and experienced by any one who will visit a sufficient number of classes."

"During my visit to Pennsylvania I found that thoughtful and imaginative teachers in all schools were in substantial agreement about what obstructs good teaching, and about the steps that should be taken to improve legal education. In general they agreed that a determined effort must be made to shift student interest from answers to problems, or rather that a study of answers must be postponed until problems have been thoroughly understood. The student will not really understand a problem unless he has applied his own mind to its solution. He is not likely to do this unless he has worked for a while with his mind free from the inhibitive effect of the authoritative pronouncements contained in judicial decisions, statutes, treatises and restatements."

"It is my own opinion that legal education in Pennsylvania today is generally not giving the training it should in the analysis of problems, and that in particular the student does not learn the significance of inconspicuous factual nuances in the decision of cases. When this loss is taken into account, it becomes apparent that the student crammed full of second-hand knowledge about Pennsylvania law gained from lectures, texts, commercial outlines and cram courses may be a more dangerous man to turn loose on society than one who has a thoroughly good legal training but who knows little Pennsylvania law."

Good Examples

"Those teachers who were observed in action appeared to be well prepared, had the attention and interest of their classes and, by and large, did a good 'leading-out' job in their teaching. There appeared to be no particular indoctrination of any specific idea, but the students were made to think, analyze, and reach their own conclusions. If the conclusions were wrong in the teacher's opinion, he generally, without being dogmatic, led them around to what he considered a proper result. There was not a great deal of lecturing. Most of the teaching was done in the use of cases. Questions were asked and answered."

"In two of the classes visited the case method was used very successfully. In each of these classes the instructor showed excellent knowledge of his subject. Also, there was much student questioning and discussion; and the development of the discussion *appeared* to be by the students, but was carefully controlled and stimulated by the instructor. In most instances the solutions arrived at were reached through the participation of the students, and in many instances the solutions were 'discovered' by the students."

Bad Examples

"The case method is used but all teachers tend to lecture."

"The instructors were too ready to give answers without trying to make the students think for themselves."

"The casebook system as such is not employed because in the words of the dean 'It is too extravagant of students' time for use in an evening school.'"

"The only respect in which the casebook system is actually employed in the college is that casebooks are used instead of textbooks by the students."

"The teaching at the school, on the whole, is definitely unsatisfactory from the standpoint of modern law school practice. There is too much plain lecturing, too little student participation and discussion, and far too much of an attempt to inculcate into the student body dogmatic rules of law without sufficient endeavor to train the students in legal analysis and thinking. It is true that cases are used as the basis of legal teaching, but the teacher announces the rule of law illustrated by the cases, and the main cerebration required of the student consists of copying in his notebook the case citations and the rules they illustrate and then learning the rule."

"The basic objective of the school seems to be to teach rules of law rather than legal thinking and to furnish a key to the Massachusetts bar examination rather than to equip the student with the skills and training necessary for legal reasoning."

"The most dangerous thing in law practice is a blackletter mind. The public will not be well served by the lawyer whose whole course of legal study consisted in cramming his head full of information, however relevant to his practice that information might be if properly understood and applied."

"The lecture method flourished in its full glory with many professors merely dictating to students and then redictating to make certain that the students had written down completely and accurately their words of wisdom. No questions were asked in the classes attended."

"In order that the students may devote all of their time in listening to the lecturer the school passes out mimeographed notes and students are urged not to attempt to take notes in class."

"The teacher first named a student before posing a question, a habit which is not apt to arouse class interest in a problem."

"The visitor was apprised of an interesting variation on the case system of study. It seems that cases to be stated are assigned to particular students at the close of the preceding class period, so that each student knows what cases he will be called upon to state in advance of the class session. The visitor was told that this insured preparation by the students called upon and avoided the embarrassing and delaying effect of calling upon students who were unprepared. It also enabled other students to know that they would not be called upon and thus made unnecessary on their part the type of preparation which would be required if there was a possibility that they might be called upon to participate in class discussion."

(D) Teaching Load

"The members of the faculty are quite competent and are very sincere, and many are good teachers. However, they are laboring under much too heavy a load, and as a consequence general performance of the school suffers, and the members of the faculty do not find the adequate leisure and energy to engage in research, bar activities, and other things which would enrich their teaching."

"One may speculate how long a law teacher can continue to be effective while carrying nine courses a year, however interested, energetic, and healthy he may be."

"Teaching loads are too heavy—10 hours per week with no repeat courses, 12 hours per week with repeat courses."

"The teaching load is indefensible. Eight members of the faculty taught 9 or more hours (three taught 12 hours each) during one semester for the past year. In most instances there was no compensation for this load by a reduced schedule in the following semester."

(E) Research and Writing

"Research and writing by the faculty is not only strongly urged, but required for promotion. Activity in outside law organizations is also expected."

"University policy on promotions and salary increases is based largely on 'productive research' (writing for law reviews, textbooks, casebooks and the like). This does not mean that teachers who do not engage in such 'productive research' never receive salary increases and promotions, but it is true that they receive them much less frequently than their more 'productive' colleagues."

"Each faculty member seems interested in his work. There was every indication of careful and conscientious preparation for class. On the whole, however, the faculty does not seem to be sufficiently aware of the opportunities and obligations for legal research."

"There is one common need in these schools, and that is measures to promote the research work of the faculty. There is need for adequate funds to provide secretarial help, legal assistants, and mimeographing service. The provision of these aids would greatly improve the teaching effectiveness of the faculty. They would enable and encourage the faculty to keep their students abreast of developments by supplementing the casebooks with necessary local and other materials, to reorganize courses, and to try out their own teaching materials. The provision of the services would stimulate, too, the continued research and writing on legal problems which can form one of the major contributions of a law faculty. It is a sheer waste of university talents to fail to provide the relatively minor funds needed for the increased effectiveness of the teachers and scholars on the faculty."

(F) Inbreeding

"An unusually large proportion of both full-time and part-time teachers are recent graduates of the subject law school. The unfortunate effect of this 'inbreeding' is recognized, and the administration plans to alleviate the condition as future appointments are made."

"There appears to be a rather serious problem of inbreeding."

"None of the faculty has had legal educational experience outside the subject school."

"No information was obtained during the period of the visitation indicating that the dean or any of the full-time staff members had any interest in or were aware of any experiments in legal education being conducted at other schools. No information was obtained indicating that any member of the full-time staff had been in any kind of contact with any other law school during recent years."

(G) PART-TIME TEACHER

"In any field of endeavor, whether it be golf or law teaching, a reasonably competent professional is ordinarily superior to even a brilliant amateur or semi-professional. The full-time law teacher is a professional. He is not only in a position to devote adequate time to preparation for classroom instruction and to keeping up with developments in the law, but he is available for consultation with students to a degree that no part-time teacher can hope to be." (Calif. p. 58.)

"I view with a dim eye the practitioner law school which depends for its teaching on practicing lawyers whose main interest lies elsewhere. It is my view that this type of legal education belongs to the last century and we have now progressed beyond it. From the point of the law school administration, it is usually cheaper and much more flexible to have a part-time faculty, the members of which have no tenure and whose salaries can be cut to fit the school income if necessary. But if law school teaching is an art, which requires extensive preparation and continuous study and research, the full-time professional law teacher is better equipped for this than the practicing lawyer. The greater part of the instruction, but not necessarily all of it, should be given by the full-time faculty."

"Some of these men have a natural knack for stirring student interest, and the best of them were as good as any full-time teachers to be found in the state. On the other hand, some of the part-time instructors either lacked the native ability to teach, or were too preoccupied with their own affairs to have the time and energy necessary to read the cases carefully and to think through the problems of establishing contact with the student that must be solved before good teaching can take place."

"If practitioners could be found who would give a full measure of their powers to the law schools they could do much for legal education. Inevitably, practitioners who can afford to do this are rare. Yet the practicing lawyer does have much to contribute to law teaching. It is not in presenting systematically a body of law, in which he is at a great disadvantage with the full-time teacher. "It is in aiding the students to learn how to deal intensively and affirmatively with specific tough legal problems."

"Experience in law schools outside of California would indicate that part-time instruction may best be used in third-year courses of a practical nature, and particularly in specialist courses in fields with which the instructor is brought into particular contact by his daily practice." (Calif. pp. 60-61.)

§ 8. LIBRARIES

"The most essential equipment of a law school is its library. Adequate library facilities are not only necessary for the education of law students, but are equally important to make possible classroom preparation and individual research by members of the faculty and so to attract the right kind of faculty members." (Calif. p. 67.)

"The library is the laboratory of the law school. It is unfortunate that this laboratory is called 'library.' It is there that the students work with the tools of the profession which they expect to enter. Efficiency therefore dictates that there should be adequate materials and work space and an efficient, qualified staff to guide and assist the students in the use of the materials." (J.G.H.)

"The argument has been urged by some persons connected with California law schools having inadequate libraries, that a law school located somewhere near a bar association or other public law library does not require a library of its own, at least where the bar association or other library is itself an adequate one. That there is nothing in this argument is best evidenced by the fact that no first-rate law school anywhere in the United States proceeds, or ever has proceeded, on any such theory. The whole point of a law school library is to have it immediately available on the premises to teachers and students alike. A bar association library may well be extremely useful in providing access to rare material needed for research which it would be too expensive for a particular law school library to maintain. But with regard to the books in day-to-day use which are the tools of the trade of law student, law teacher and lawyer alike, these must be available at the law school where they can be readily found and used." (Calif. p. 68.)

"The library is operated under the theory that in order to justify itself it must be used. Therefore the students are given stack privileges and may freely enter the stacks and withdraw books. Likewise the library is made available to other departments of the university and operates a reference service. The students make great use of the library, and a major part of the available space is occupied by students most of the time."

"More important than physical equipment and space is the splendid library decorum that is maintained. Maintenance of proper standards of library conduct and restraint have become traditional and students take pride in carrying on that tradition. Many students seek its quiet and dignified reading rooms as a place where concentration is possible. A library smoking room is also provided."

"This law school has its librarian maintain a student check every hour of the day. It shows good usage and that in this school the law library is the center of the training program."

"Numerous special services are made available by the library staff to the faculty and other staff members of the law school. Thus, for example, a monthly mimeographed list of new book acquisitions is circulated, as is a weekly mimeographed summary of Texas Supreme Court decisions, a weekly mimeographed summary of the contents of legal periodicals currently received, and several mimeographed notifications of library service."

"One special feature of the library is a room designed for the use of attorneys who call at the library. In this special room are shelved practice sets dealing with such subjects as Federal procedure, automobiles, trial practice, etc., the United States Code Annotated, and other books thought to be of particular interest to practicing attorneys. It is the policy of the law library to extend every possible service to members of the bar. Pursuant to this policy, the library lends any book, except United States Supreme Court Briefs and the loose leaf services, to lawyers anywhere in the state."

"Principally, in addition to having the library serve the students and faculty, the librarian regards it as a source of reference material for the bar of the state. The dean shares this view and a good deal of progress has been made in performing reference service for the bar. A reference librarian who is a recent graduate of the school has recently been appointed. He answers inquiries for material sent in by lawyers throughout the state. The library does not furnish briefing service but does list applicable cases and statutes. It also has facilities for reproducing printed material and will make non-copyright material available at cost to persons requesting it."

"Only the inadequate use of the materials makes the library adequate."

"A probable explanation of the lack of use of the library lies in the fact that the teachers do not give the students citations to outside references nor indicate outside reading that should be done. Five classes were visited during the inspection, and during these visits not one citation or outside reference was given to any class nor was any suggestion for outside reading other than in the casebook offered. Very little written work is expected of the students."

"Student use of the law library has not developed to any appreciable extent. It is probable that if the teachers would give library assignments and recommendations for outside reading in connection with their regular teaching the use of the library would expand appreciably."

"The chief adverse criticism to be made of the library concerns the inaccessibility of many of the books. Except as previously stated, the books can be obtained only by filling out cards at the main desk and they are largely stored in an unheated loft which was inhabited by bats. Neither the temperature nor the fauna perturbed the librarian, however. Perhaps the point stated is unimportant since the books in regular use are either on open stacks or at the desk in the reading room. And since very little use is made of the library by the students in any case the location of the books may not be a matter of great significance."

"Because of the arrangement of the library only a few thousand volumes (particularly Wisconsin Reports and the three major law reviews) are readily accessible to the students. As a result the reading room becomes primarily a study hall and it is apparent that the student body does not make adequate use of the library facilities."

"Half of the books are inaccessible without the use of a ladder."

"Many books which are kept behind the desk, to be signed out by student assistants only on request, could well be in outside stacks accessible for greater student use were the physical facilities of the library better."

"Many of the books are in stacks that are not too accessible to students. The books may be had by asking for them, but such a situation does not conduce to browsing."

"The space provided for the law library is inadequate. The stacks in the library are less than 24 inches apart so that turning between shelves or bending over to read titles is practically impossible."

"The quarters occupied by the law library are unsatisfactory. The general reading room is a most unattractive room. The books are poorly arranged in the library, some books being placed horizontally on tops of other books shelved in the usual vertical fashion. The library is poorly lighted, gives the appearance of being very crowded, and some aisles in the library are obstructed at one end with small study tables."

"The University Library School has charge of the cataloguing of the law library. Disadvantages of this arrangement are offset by advantages."

"The expenditure for library materials has been such amount as necessary to retain accreditation."

"The judgment of the schools not accredited nationally, with few exceptions, seems to be that a library is not necessary. The deans of a few schools ventured the opinion that it is not even desirable in their schools." (J.G.H.)

"The law librarian is not a professional librarian. The dean stated that he 'would under no circumstances engage a person for this position who had "professional" library training.'"

"Without the services of a qualified and full-time law librarian, the students in the college do not have the benefit of the day-to-day guidance and assistance of a full-time librarian and the library does not have the benefit of the long term planning which can only be secured from a qualified full-time librarian."

§ 9. Students

(a) Extracurricular Activity

"An exceedingly effective form of student self-government exists in the life of the law school. Each member of the student body belongs to what is known as the 'Law Federation.' There are seven sections of this Federation and each student is a member of one and only one section. Each section has a distinct function to perform. These functions are indicated by the name of the section. The sections are as follows: Library Committee, Building Committee, Program Committee, Social Committee, Professional Integration Committee, Publication Committee, Publicity Committee. The chairmen of these various committees together with the officers of the Federation comprise the council of the Federation. This council serves as a liason between the student body and the faculty. The responsibility for the administration of the honor system rests with the Federation. The Federation has a specially elected honor board to handle all honor cases. The honor system functions admirably in the law school."

"There is a law review, a legal aid clinic, a moot court, the book mart, the student court, the Domesday Book, the embryo lawyer's club, and the coffee hour. All of these activities are well participated in and contribute not only to the professional education of the student but also to the student's orientation into the problems of law and society."

"One of the major problems of the law school lies in the fact that it is a part of a 'street-car' university. Most of its students live in their own homes or in rented apartments or rooms scattered over the city. Many have to travel considerable distances to attend classes. There is little opportunity for the kind of extracurricular education that takes place in a law school attached to a university that is itself a center of living and studying."

"The law review is one of the youngest of the many legal periodicals sponsored by law schools today, and is having as hard sledding as any of them. Few if any members of the law faculty have had previous experience with law reviews. Their hopes and purposes are good and what they are trying to do deserves encouragement. On the other hand it must be recognized that this law review is today not a very good law review. This does not by any means indicate that it should be abandoned, but rather that it needs to be improved and given more encouragement. Its difficulties are at present not financial. The budget is a small one, but is adequate, and the number of current subscriptions is reasonably good. The quality of student work in the law review, however, is not high, and ample encouragement is not given to students to do law review work. Physical facilities for student work are totally lacking. There is no law review work room nor any law review library. The law faculty recognizes this lack, and it has been called to the attention of the university administration. Probably it will be remedied when the new law school building is constructed. Other details of a plan to encourage more enthusiastic student work on the review will also have to be worked out if the review is to be a permanent success."

"Another publication is the Reading Guide. This publication was begun by the law librarian and has now received wide critical approval. It is published monthly, edited entirely by students. It consists of book reviews of current books of interest to law students. These are not technical law books, but books on related topics. The students do the book reviews and therefore another thirty students have an opportunity to work on a publication. The day the Reading Guide is published the library places on a separate book shelf copies of the books reviewed in that issue. This has stimulated other students to read the books and to discuss them. This appeals to the inspector as one of the most stimulating periodical developments in current legal education. The students are teaching themselves as well as being taught by their professors."

"One special project developed by the law school is the 'Series of Legal Handbooks,' originated in 1947-48, and published several times each year. It is primarily aimed at providing practicing attorneys with useful procedural materials, and is currently developing a complete set of jury instructions based upon, and selected from, local cases. Preparation of the Handbook is done by an editorial staff of top students, under faculty supervision. Sponsored in part by the law alumni association, the Handbook has a circulation of some 1800 copies, and apparently is well regarded by the bar and bench."

"The school maintains a briefing service under faculty supervision. Student membership on the briefing staff is based upon high scholarship. Lawyers without library facilities are invited to submit questions for briefing. The briefing staff prepares and returns to the attorney a complete brief on the question submitted. The service is of special value to lawyers in rural areas."

"The school operates a briefing service available only to lawyers in the nearby area. Some 172 briefs have been written during the past two years. Notice of the availability of the service goes forward each year to the lawyers in the area. A request for a brief is assigned to the professor whose subject category fits the problem. The professor in turn assigns the problem to his student group and supervises the brief."

(B) OUTSIDE EMPLOYMENT OF FULL-TIME STUDENTS

"The law schools too seldom take into account the outside employment of full-time law students. Full-time students should study law full time in an unhurried contemplative manner. Law school administrators should insist that they do so. The outside employment of full-time students should be held to the irreducible minimum. The standards of both national accrediting agencies are drafted in terms of full-time and part-time students. The inspections disclosed that students who carry a full-time schedule in law school often have outside employment. The accrediting agencies might well consider what effective steps might be taken to insure full-time study by full-time students in the accredited schools." (J.G.H.)

"The extent to which students do outside work while attending law school is not definitely known but is not believed to be great. The official policy of the school is to hold first-year students to a maximum of 15 hours of such employment per week but upper classmen in good standing may do more. Here, as in other schools, the problem of policing the regulation is extremely difficult."

"Practically all of the students are employed during the day, working an average of 24 hours per week. The school policy limits students to a total of 56 hours work a week, reckoned on a basis of 3 hours of preparation to 1 hour of recitation: if a student carries 7 recitation hours per week, he is not allowed to carry outside employment beyond 28 hours. Records of employment are carefully maintained, and the school's policy is in fact being carried out."

"A far more lengthy and probing visit might disclose in reference to most of the school that the day division students had part-time employment that precluded full utilization of the full-time faculty. It is obvious that the operation of a day division in a large metropolitan area is peculiarly subject to this risk. In respect to the subject school, the policy is that 'full-time students may not be employed for more than 20 hours a week.' The amount of such employment is not known."

"Possibly, scholarship standards would be improved if the school would insist that those students who have outside employment carry a lighter law school load. Between 55 and 60 percent of the students have outside employment. The average of outside-employment hours is 20.88 and of this group the average law-school hours is 14.36. In a sense the school is a part-time school. The law school load should be reduced in inverse proportion to outside workload."

"Students are not permitted to carry more than 8 hours a week outside work. Law review editors and graduate students are not allowed to engage in any outside activity."

"If a student needs to carry on outside work to an extent greater than 10 to 15 hours per week, he is expected to cut down his law school load and take a longer time to complete the course."

"The dean estimates that half of the day students are partially self-supporting. Outside work of day students is limited to fourteen hours per week."

"The dean regards twenty hours of work in any week as a maximum load which a student may carry if he is to maintain a full-time schedule in the school."

"Virtually all students are self-supporting. If a full-time student works in excess of 30 hours per week, he cannot take more than nine classroom hours of law work."

"The extent to which students do outside work while attending law school is not much of a problem. Day school students are expected to attend classes both morning and early afternoon."

"The dean reports that often the earning student may do better work, budget his time better, and become a better lawyer than the student who does no outside work."

(c) Placement

"The voluntary student committee on placement has done a very outstanding job in organizing a placement bureau. The 12 members of the committee have organized into two groups—one emphasizing counselling and the other operations. The counselling group seeks to procure information from the students and from the faculty as to the kind of job the graduating seniors are interested in and qualified for, and the operations group has sought to collect information concerning prospective employers in law firms, in legal departments or business organizations, and city, county and federal agencies. As part of the counselling operation lectures and seminars have been conducted for the purpose of acquainting the student body with the opportunities in the practice of law. Although the student committee in its report to the faculty emphasizes the necessity of a full-time placement director, the thoroughness with which the students have prepared their official forms, the insight they have shown in the problem of records and their use in placement, suggests that they may be as well qualified or better qualified to handle the job than a professional. Of course the danger continues to remain that the effectiveness of the program will depend on the capability and enthusiasm of each particular student group and will thus vary from year to year."

§ 10. Examinations

"The 'honor' system is used in supervising examinations. One wonders whether such a system can be used prudently in a law school other than one drawing most of its first-year students from colleges using the system."

"Proposed examination questions are exchanged and criticized by the faculty."

"Examinations are given only at the end of the course, except that examinations are given at the end of the first quarter for the student's information."

"One practice is worthy of serious consideration in other schools. At the end of the term the student appears for a series of four-hour examinations. At each of these examinations he is given eight questions relating to the work of the term. These questions bear no label to indicate the subject or subjects involved and it is up to the student to decide what issues are presented without the aid of such a label. In fact, each of the instructors in the full courses has prepared eight questions covering his own subject (with occasional cross-references to other courses studied during the year). These questions are then rearranged in the dean's office and presented to the student in a random series, so that the first question may involve Contracts, the second Agency, the third and fourth Torts, the fifth Contracts again, etc. The student writes his answer to each question in a separate book, and these books are then distributed by the dean's secretary among the various members of the faculty so that each grades the answers to the questions prepared by him."

"The comprehensive examination serves to unify a student's law course most effectively."

"Examinations and grades are not given in individual courses. The entire curriculum is completely prescribed. There are no electives. It is possible, therefore, to use one comprehensive examination at the close of each year. This is the practice followed. In order to prepare the freshman students for the ordeal of the comprehensive examination, they are given two sample examinations, one in November and another in January. The grades in these are posted, but they are not taken into consideration in the final grade. Questions on the comprehensive examinations must be approved by the entire faculty. Consequently, considerable faculty time is taken up in the meetings in discussing the questions submitted by the various professors in the courses which they teach. Not infrequently a question will be returned to a professor with suggestions for revisions, and until these are made the question will not be approved. Although time-consuming, this procedure results in certain side benefits since each faculty member gains a certain familiarity with the context of the curriculum as a whole; it also serves as a device to discover gaps and overlappings. The comprehensive examination at the end of the academic year lasts for three full days of seven hours each. The papers are graded anonymously, each instructor grading the questions which he submitted. The result is that a student fails or passes the entire year's work."

§ 11. Part-Time Schools

(A) Do Not Eliminate Part-Time Schools

"As an abstract proposition the superiority of full-time day instruction in law to part-time instruction is obvious. A student can get a better legal education if he devotes his entire time and energy to study in an educational institution whose faculty are themselves devoting their full time and energy to their job. In the abstract, there is no more reason why a lawyer should be permitted to take his professional training at night on a part-time basis than there is for letting a doctor work his way through a night medical school. However, if part-time legal study were not possible, a substantial number of able and ambitious young men and women would be barred from the legal profession because of their economic position. This has happened to a considerabre extent with the medical profession, with not too happy results. It would be far more serious if it happened with the legal profession. Under our form of government, law is so closely related to politics and to the operation of government that any barrier to the legal profession which would keep out the economically less fortunate would have serious political repercussions, and would ultimately impair the functioning of the democratic process. Even with the road to the legal profession open to all, it tends to become, as de Tocqueville pointed out so long ago as 1835, an essentially conservative group largely concerned with maintaining the social and economic status quo. (See de Tocqueville, *Democracy in America* [ed. Bradley, 1945] Vol. 1, 212, 280.) If the legal profession were to be recruited, as the medical profession now tends to be, mainly from the sons and daughters of the well-to-do, this tendency might well be accentuated to a degree seriously against the public interest. Hence, until some means is provided whereby young men and women not fortunately situated economically can be enabled to study law on a full-time basis, it is necessary to meet the demand for part-time professional instruction in law." (Calif. p. 82.)

"The proposal is made from time to time to eliminate the night school from American legal education. I would regard it as a real tragedy if this proposal were ever adopted. The basic need of our democratic society is that the gateways of opportunity be kept open, even at what may seem at times like disproportionate costs. One cannot attend classes like those at the two subject schools without acquiring a deep admiration for the courage and energy of the men and women who are able to prepare themselves for a difficult profession while holding down full-time jobs in other fields. If the time ever comes when night schools are abolished and ambitions of this order are blocked, we shall have lost not only an important source of effective lawyers but an inspiring example of sheer American grit."

"Among the students attending these two schools are accountants, engineers, civil-service employees and business men. Many of them are already in fields closely related to law, and will if they are successful in getting through law school and passing the bar bring to their law practices a valuable background of practical experience most lawyers lack. Some of the students do not intend to practice, but will utilize their legal training to widen their competence in other fields. This too represents a gain for the nation. It sets up a counter-current, however small it may be, against the general drift toward specialization. It tends in some measure to insure that when decisions are reached in industry or government there will be somebody there whose mind can embrace the problem as a whole—who knows what is really being decided. Without evening schools it is a safe assumption that the number of those with degrees in both engineering and law or in accounting and law would be very sharply reduced. I believe that we need not less but more of this kind of combined training."

"The evening division is being conducted at a substantial financial deficit. It is being conducted because the university believes that there ought to be some opportunity for employed persons to study law at night. It is the belief of the visitor that the evening division is making a very worthwhile contribution to legal education. At the present time there is not a substandard law school in the state, but if the school were too close its evening division, a substandard proprietary night school would probably be opened. The university is to be commended for its unselfish attitude in supporting this nonprofitable division of the law school. On the whole, this school is doing a creditable job of legal education even though its work cannot be classed as outstanding or distinguished."

"On the other hand, night law schools with proper standards can and do afford legal educational opportunities of as high quality as a daytime school can offer."

(B) Quality of the Part-Time Student

"An interesting observation—it was my feeling that the night school students were more aggressive, more interested and more alert even than the day school group. The explanation might well lie in the fact that this night law school attracts many students who could, because of their grades, choose their law school, but for the fact that they must work. It definitely indicates that there is a need for and a place for night school education carried on at the level found here. This school operates under the theory that the night school is every bit as good as the day school and it carries this theory into effect by using the same teachers in the night division as in the day division. In my opinion, the experiment is eminently successful."

"Many of the students in the first-year evening classes seemed tired, restless and inattentive. This had entirely disappeared in the two fourth-year classes visited, where the discussion was on a high level of interest and intellectual content. Particularly marked were the maturity of judgment and the sense of proportion displayed by the best of the students, who in these qualities certainly surpassed the younger and less experienced students one normally finds in our leading law schools."

"There is no doubt that the students are sincerely interested in getting a legal education and in many instances are making considerable sacrifices to do so. Their loyalty to the school is intense and they believe that they are getting sound training. They also believe that without a part-time night school many able and worthy people would be denied the opportunity of studying law and they feel that in spite of the handicaps under which they are working, they will measure up with the products of full-time schools."

"The great bulk of the school's alumni are graduates of its evening department. This is not, as one might suppose, a source of weakness, but probably one of strength. The alumni of the school are strongly attached to it, and they have served it in many ways, not only through gifts but through their services as teachers. The devotion of the alumni toward the school is readily understandable when it is recalled that if the school had not existed many of them could not possibly have become members of the legal profession. Their attachment to the school has deeper roots than a mere recollection of convivial gatherings or hours of pleasant discussion."

(c) Some Queries

"Not only can schools which only operate night classes not afford as a budgetary matter to pay full-time teachers, but they probably could not secure competent professional law instructors who would be willing to teach a full program entirely in night classes. It may well be preferable, therefore, for these schools, so long as they are operating, to follow the present policy in employing part-time teachers only. But this fact in itself is an almost conclusive argument against the existence of law schools giving instruction only at night. Proper night law teaching, making adequate use of professional personnel, can be conducted only in a school which also operates a day division." (Calif. p. 59.)

"The school operates both a day and evening division as do the other two schools in the city; and like the other two, the enrollment in the day division is approximately double that of the evening division. This uniform preference for day school instruction raises the question, not only whether *three* evening schools are justified in the area but also whether *any* evening schools are really necessary."

"This is a poor night school which has some ambition to be a good night school. It hopes ultimately to secure approval by the American Bar Association. In order to do so it should (1) become autonomous or at least independent of the Y.M.C.A., (2) improve its physical facilities, (3) acquire a faculty, (4) raise part-time salaries, (5) raise tuition, and (6) improve its grading and examinations. Even if it does all these things one may still raise the question as to whether it will serve a useful function as far as legal education is concerned. It will probably never do more than comply with minimum quantitative requirements and produce marginal lawyers. Whether this is enough must ultimately be decided by the profession."

"Both the president and the dean frankly state that they have no hope of meeting accrediting standards. However, they feel that at the state capital, there is a real need for a part-time school to serve ambitious young men and women who would otherwise find it impossible to obtain a legal education."

"Substandard night schools are worse than no schools at all; they mislead the student and the public into thinking that the fledging lawyer is being prepared to practice law when in fact he is not being so prepared."

(d) Same Standards in Both Divisions

"It is believed to be undesirable for a law school to establish lower admission standards for night students than for day students. Experience in other states indicates that a night division of a metropolitan law school is most successful when the day and night divisions of the school are placed on the same basis." (Calif. pp. 270-271.)

"The schools which operate both full-time and part-time divisions have encountered difficulty in holding the students in both divisions to the same standard of scholarship. In one instance the authorities were frank to admit that students were not held to the same level of performance, but other schools have attempted to exact the same level of performance by having a subject in both divisions taught by the same professor and subjecting the students to the same final examinations. Where a given course is not taught in both divisions by the same individual, the inspections disclosed a disparity in the grading standard." (J.G.H.)

"If part-time professional instruction in law is to be given, it is highly important that it be of the best possible quality. Studying law at night requires an unusual degree of perseverance, energy and concentration. The night law student needs help from his teachers more than does the day student. Particularly he needs the aid of experienced professional law teachers, especially in the first two years of his law school course. . . . It is important to have the maximum possible number of experienced teachers actually teaching in the night division of any school giving both day and night classes. This has been demonstrated by experience in mixed-type schools outside the state. The day students are better fitted to make up for the inevitable inadequacies of part-time instruction by outside study on their own responsibility than are night students." (Calif. pp. 82-83,58.)

"The full-time professors teach in both the day and evening divisions—usually the same professor handles the same subject in both divisions, using the same casebook and holding the students to the same standard of scholarship. A review of the grade sheets of the professors indicates that the scholarship standards are identical for the two groups. There has been no lowering of standards because of the establishment of the evening division."

"The combining of evening and day instruction produces special difficulties. One result of the combination of functions is that there is never a moment of repose for students or faculty from nine in the morning to nine at night. The seats in the classroom never get cold, and there is a constant coming and going that is not conducive to quiet study or reflection."

"In general, day classes are scheduled in the same manner as night classes; that is, a class scheduled for two hours a week meets for two hours in a row on one day. This, of course, merely follows a pattern already established in the evening division, and is probably found convenient by many faculty members, especially when their evening classes continue to be scheduled in this manner. At the same time, this method of scheduling classes may involve serious educational losses, particularly in the first year, as forfeiting the advantages of spaced study and demanding too lengthy an attention to one subject."

"There is another possible objection to having the same instructors teach both day and evening classes. This lies in the fact that it is impossible to expect of the evening classes the same degree of preparation that is expected of day classes. I refer here not to a mere reading of cases, but to a relaxed and leisurely exploration of their implications before coming to class. It would seem to me inevitable that a teacher who has to cut his demands down to the maximum that can reasonably be imposed on a group of evening students would tend inevitably to carry over the same standard in conducting his day classes."

(E) How Many Nights per Week? How Many Hours per Night?

[The inspection reports seem to indicate that evening schools most frequently operate for three nights a week, usually for three hours per night, occasionally for four hours. On the other hand, the inspectors are almost unanimous in recommending fewer hours per night, but more nights per week. For night students who live very near the law school, it may be that more nights is a better arrangement. But for students who live some distance away from the school the extra nights and the additional time of travel may create a time and physical handicap too great to be met.]

"For students who have worked during the day to concentrate for three hours at night in the classroom is a difficult task and it is believed to be preferable to spread evening classes over four or five nights a week so as to reduce the usual classroom load to two hours per night."

"In the evening division, classes meet only on Monday, Wednesday, and Friday from 6.45, and some classes go until 10.45. This seems too late for effective teaching and learning. Evening classes could meet five evenings per week or at least four. By this means some of the late classes could be eliminated. Hence, a readjustment of evening-division class schedules is advisable."

"To ask students, almost all of whom have worked during the day, to attend classes for four hours at night indicates either a complete lack of knowledge of legal pedagogy or a type of instruction which does not require much concentration on the part of the students."

"Extending classes over four periods in any evening would seem to be a questionable practice. Also, since a student is required to be at the law school for classes not oftener than three days a week, one may question whether the evening student acquires the library habit or is present often enough to obtain the desired acquaintance and opportunities for discussion with students and faculty. It might be suggested that classes could meet at least five days a week. This would give the students more contacts with the library, faculty and fellow students. Moreover, such a plan would make unnecessary classes over four periods in any one evening."

§ 12. Bar Examinations

(A) In General

"If the admissions are selective and the scholarship standards are high, the graduates of a school usually encounter little difficulty with bar examinations." (J.G.H.)

"These professional prerequisites (the high standards of the bar examinations, the requirements of the

A.B., or its equivalent, for admission to the bar, and the fact that admission is granted only to those who have attended schools approved by the Board of Law Examiners) have prevented the development of what might be called marginal educational enterprises and particularly those in which commercial considerations play a predominant role. The system of admissions to the bar can, therefore, be credited with the elimination of poor and marginal schools."

"The relationship between the Board of Law Examiners and the law school is not as close as it should be. Although upon invitation the law faculty has submitted questions for use on the bar examination, none of these questions has been used in recent years. Examination questions given by the law examiners are often based on literal provisions of the code and in quirks of the local common law decisions, the latter largely procedural. The need of improvement in this relationship is one of the principal problems of legal education in Georgia."

(B) Publication of Bar Examination Results

"The variations shown in bar examination success are extraordinary, and raise the question whether the acceptance by the State of California of law study in schools which have consistently been unable sufficiently to prepare their students that half of them at least can pass the bar examination is not just as much a trap to the unwary, and just as great an injustice to students who are led to waste time, energy and money, as is the toleration of correspondence instruction and law office and private study. No California law school approved by the American Bar Association has in any year since 1938 failed to have at least 50% of its students pass the bar examination the first time, and every such school shows a record of better than 55% bar examination success for the period 1932-49. On the other hand, no unapproved school shows 50% bar examination success for the period 1932-1949, as a whole, while certain schools show averages far below that figure. While there is substantial variation in bar examination success among the approved schools themselves, the difference between the approved and the unapproved schools in this respect seems to demonstrate a difference in kind rather than a difference merely in quality." (Calif. pp. 19-21.)

"There are factors in the California situation that need not be present in Pennsylvania, particularly a rivalry among several almost evenly matched schools to out-do one another in preparing their students for the bar examinations, comparative showings on these examinations being almost as much a matter of general interest and of school pride as comparative football scores. To prevent this kind of development, the Law Examiners should not follow the California example of publishing the results by schools."

[But most of the inspectors who commented on the matter were of the opinion that bar examination results should be published. One example follows.]

"In spite of this miserable showing by its students, the school has printed the following in its catalogue:

> 'The law school curriculum covers all subjects upon which are based the examinations for admission to the Bar, as well as several supplementary courses. The highly satisfactory bar examination record of its graduates affords convincing evidence of the thoroughness of instruction in the regular work of the Law School.'

The 'convincing evidence' of the 'thoroughness of instruction' at the school is that one person out of 8 from this school who took one of the seven bar examinations listed passed on the first attempt and only one out of every 15 subsequent attempts was successful. Publication of the examination results by the Board of Bar Examiners should put a stop to such flagrant misrepresentation."

(C) Stultifying Effects of Required Subjects

"So long as the present practice as to bar examination subjects and the present accreditation rule continue in effect, the inevitable result will be a freezing of the curriculum of every California law school, and something very close to a de facto prohibition on curricular experimentation and the introduction of new courses and new ideas. This will be true not because the faculties of the California schools necessarily prefer to follow old stereotypes, but because of student insistence on taking courses in all the subjects covered by the bar examination, leaving them no time for the exercise of intellectual curiosity in elective subjects." (Calif. pp. 53-55.)

"At one law school, for example, a student in order to take courses in all the bar examination subjects must devote 78 semester hours to those subjects out of a total of 84 semester hours required for graduation, in addition to five semester hours in courses required by the school, leaving only one semester hour of the regular course available for truly free election." (Calif. p. 53.)

"If the burden of preparing for a bar examination on local law were lifted from legal education in Pennsylvania, I think a substantial amount of classroom time would be freed for real thinking and analysis."

"No substantial attempt is made to extend the courses offered beyond those required by the prospects of the bar examination and those directed to the gainful practice of law."

"The Ohio bar examination requirements are notorious for this stultifying effect on curriculum committees."

"As long as the present detailed and extensive list of subjects given on the bar remains it will be difficult if not impossible to get students to elect any 'non-bar' courses.

"While New Jersey bar examination subjects are not the controlling influence in the curriculum, all such courses are of necessity covered. A reduction in the number of bar examination subjects would be of considerable value to this law school in its endeavor to broaden and strengthen its curriculum and to experiment in new fields of legal education."

"One may venture the guess that absent the whip of bar examination subjects, more evening schools would spend more time probing more deeply into fewer subjects."

NOTES

1. See § 12(c) of this chapter, page 55, on Bar Examinations, for comments on the stultifying effects of required bar examination subjects.

2. Analogous to the above practice of not using failure grades in computing the general average, is the policy of liberal permissions to take make-up examinations when a student has failed an examination or has omitted to take a regular examination when scheduled.

Chapter 55

Teaching Contracts with the Aid of Problems

1916

Henry Winthrop Ballantine

Henry Ballantine (1880-1951) was professor at Wisconsin from 1913 to 1916, dean at Illinois from 1916 to 1920, professor at Minnesota from 1920 to 1924, and professor at the University of California, Berkeley, to 1951. This article first appeared in 4 *The American Law School Review* 114 (1916). See also chapter 42.

The Socratic dialogue under the case method may be illustrated by the following discussion of a case in contracts:

Prof.: Mr. Greathead, will you state the case of Parker v. Russell (133 Mass. 74)?
Greathead (referring to his casebook or abstract): The defendant in this case, in consideration of the conveyance by the plaintiff to her of certain real estate, agreed to support the plaintiff, an old man, for the rest of his life. The defendant did support the old man for over five years, but unfortunately her house burned down, and for a period of two years she has neglected to furnish any support.

At the trial the defendant requested the judge to instruct the jury that damages could only be recovered for failure to furnish support prior to filing suit. The court, however, ruled that the plaintiff could recover compensation, not only for the past failure of the defendant to furnish support, but also full indemnity for the loss of future support.

The jury found that the value of the support from the date of the fire to the filing of suit was $377, but that the damages from the breach of the contract as a whole would amount to $972. The Supreme Court ordered judgment on the verdict for the larger sum, the entire value of the contract to the plaintiff.
Prof.: That is a very good statement of the case, Mr. Greathead. The plaintiff was allowed to recover prospective damages, including compensation for the future benefit he would probably have realized under the contract, based on the probable duration of his life and the value of

his support as measured by mortality and annuity tables. Do you agree with the decision?
Greathead: Why, yes, I suppose so.
Prof.: But how do you reconcile that holding with the doctrine in the case of Daniels v. Newton (114 Mass. 530), which we have just had?
Greathead: Let me see. I hadn't thought of doing that. That case held that an absolute refusal by the purchaser to perform a land contract before performance was due was not a breach of contract for which an action could be brought prior to the date of performance. The Massachusetts court refused to adopt the doctrine of anticipatory breach.
Prof.: Yes; now if we assume for the sake of argument that there can be no actionable breach of a contract before performance is due, how can a contract be entirely broken when the whole performance is not yet due? Is there any distinction on principle between this and the doctrine of anticipatory breach?
Greathead: Well, I had not thought of that. There may be one, but offhand I can't say.
Prof.: What would you say, Mr. Wiseman?
Wiseman: The Massachusetts court holds that it is not possible to break a contract before the date when its performance becomes due. But that is not inconsistent with allowing recovery for the entire value of a contract if it is entirely broken in the course of performance.
Prof.: Good; but does it necessarily follow that the recognition of any breach involves the recognition of a total breach? May there not be several partial breaches of the same contract; for example, in an installment contract for the sale of goods?
Wiseman: A contract would still continue after a minor breach, such as a slight delay; and I suppose there might be a right of election in the injured party to regard even a material breach as to one installment as being either a partial or a total breach of the contract.
Prof.: There is considerable doubt about any right of election, at least unless the other party assents to the waiver. See, for instance, the case of Pakas v. Hollingshead (184 N. Y. 211). Take the case of a contract of personal service. The plaintiff may usually bring suit before his term of service expires, and recover compensation for his whole loss, if he is wrongfully discharged. If he may do so, but sues only for his loss of wages to the date of the suit, a subsequent suit for the loss of wages accruing later would in most jurisdictions be entirely barred. Plaintiff must not split his cause of action, and his damages must include the loss of the entire contract, even though in one sense the damages have not yet been suffered.

Now, let me put you this case: Suppose a benefit insurance association wrongfully attempts to reduce the amount of benefit payable on a certificate or policy which it has issued from $5,000 to $2,000, and refuses to receive premiums or assessments on the $5,000 basis. May the holder of such a policy, which is payable to his wife, sue on the policy, upon which nothing will be due by its terms until his death?
Wiseman: I suppose not, except on the doctrine of anticipatory breach. I suppose that the Massachusetts court would say that the repudiation by the association of its contract amounts to no more than a notice of an intended breach of contract at a future time.
Prof.: The Massachusetts court so holds in the case of Porter v. American Legion of Honor, 183 Mass. 326. The New York court has made a similar holding (Kelly v. Security M. L. Ins. Co., 186 N.Y. 16), to the effect that the holder cannot recover the present value of the policy, because there is no breach of contract, but that the plaintiff might perhaps have a remedy by specific performance in equity, although an action at law will not lie. Yet it is hard to imagine any class of contracts where practical convenience demands an immediate right of action so much. The doctrine of anticipatory breach seems to be narrowly and illogically limited by some of those courts which recognize it, and these insurance cases would seem to furnish an instance of a breach occurring in the course of performance.

A repudiation or breach of contract does not "put an end" to the duty of performance, although it may excuse the other party from his duties. An action for damages for breach of contract is essentially an action to enforce the duty of performance by giving a substitute therefor, namely, the money equivalent of the performance which was bargained for, but which has not been rendered, or which evidently will not be rendered, and which the plaintiff is now excused from accepting or waiting for.

The professor then put the following problem to Mr. Mediokre:

B., who resides in Boston, promised to employ A. as housekeeper during his life, and to leave her a legacy of $500 at his death. He was also to furnish her board and lodging and pay her wages of $2 per week. After some years of service by A., B. said to her: "I am very glad, of course, to have you stay on here, and act as housekeeper for me, but I have concluded not to leave you that legacy of $500." (a) Can A. sue at once, and, if so, for what damages? (b) What different remedies are open to her? (c) When will the Statute of Limitations commence to run?

The professor then put the following problem to Mr. Woodhead:

A. employed B. to work for him on his farm at $50 a month, for one year, beginning January 1, 1911. Just before this day came, A. informed B. that he would not be wanted, and forbade B. to begin work. On February 10, 1911, B. sued A. for breach of contract. What is the measure of his damages? Can B. again sue A. on his contract?

An animated discussion ensued over these problems, which, however, cannot be reported herein.

The foregoing dialogue is no doubt an imperfect representation of a typical case method discussion, but it will serve to illustrate concretely certain undeniable characteristics thereof; particularly the extemporaneous nature of the colloquy, and the fact that only a few selected individuals are necessarily concerned in arguing out the solution of the questions.

If some of these problems which the professor put off-hand had been prescribed as part of the preparation for class in connection with the cases in the casebook, then all of the class would have had a fair opportunity to grapple with them. Then it would have been possible to hold the students responsible for a more definite formulation of their own ideas and opinions on the issues involved. Then some of the original thinking would have been done outside of the classroom, as well as in the cooperative effort of teacher and student.

What is the earnest law student supposed to do *before* entering the classroom? Is it sufficient that he carefully prepare an "abstract" summarizing the facts and holding in the cases he has read? It will be answered that he is supposed to do more than this; he is expected to reflect on the reasons given for the rulings, and to test their soundness in themselves and in comparison with other cases. The students are supposed to criticize and question what they read; they are to test the practical consequences of a proposition, trying its application to supposititious cases, like an opposing lawyer on the alert to take issue at any vital point.

But why should one suppose that the students actually do this? It is here that the students fall down, and it is at this critical point that the use of the problems comes in to fill the gap. It *forces* reflection and effort on the student's part at the stage where it is needed, before entering the classroom. It gives them the initiative, instead of leaving it all to the instructor.

The merit of the case method, it is believed, is mainly due to the fact that the cases present concrete problems in the application of legal principles to facts, and afford an opportunity for arguing how the rules of law should be formulated. But the student usually regards the cases, not as problems demanding solution, but as problems already solved by the judge, to be studied by him as authoritative statements of the law. His task is that of understanding the judicial opinion.

Even if the professor puts problems in the course of classroom discussion, that subject having been covered, the student does not take the problem home with him for individual original thought. In reading the cases it does not occur to him ordinarily to compare the various cases that he reads. The average student does not seem to have any adequate conception of what he is supposed to do with the cases assigned. He does not know what he is looking for, or what to put his effort upon. The study hours are confined largely to assimilative reading, and the abstracting and absorption of the doctrines laid down in the opinions.

Problems may then be advantageously employed for advance study, as well as for review. Instead of simply giving out problems in class after the cases have [been] covered, why not assign one or two [assignments] for each meeting of the course, [illegible] practical application of the [illegible] to be studied? Let oral or written solutions be prepared, using the casebook or text-book as the place for original research. In this way the student will seek for and grasp the principles of a case as something to be used, not merely to be studied and learned for its own sake. Under such stimulus the student should be able to read many more cases with much greater intensity of effort, concentration, and comprehension. If we are going to teach students to reason from fundamental principles, we have got to make them exercise that faculty as much as possible and do it outside of the classroom, as well as in it, instead of resting satisfied with the mere mechanical memorizing effort which now makes up the bulk of their preparation.

Law School and Bar Examinations are based on the idea that a mastery of the law is indicated by the power to apply it to concrete situations. It is curious that our present training does not lead up more directly by drill and exercises to the test we apply on examination. Examination papers are the best evidence that, in addition to the study of decided cases, the student needs to study and discuss problems.

The best results of case study are achieved when a number of cases are studied with reference to some central problem. If the student has a definite *objective*, and is looking eagerly for material, he will be apt to pursue a much more critical and creative method of reading his cases. His mind will not tend to wander so easily from what he is reading, and he will grasp and hold it better. With the stimulus of problems, many more cases can be read, and many more applications of law can be shown, in the given time.

Some teachers regard lack of time as a great obstacle to an extensive use of problems; but this objection is based on the erroneous assumption that the problems are just so much material super-added to the casebook, when in fact the problems will be closely connected with the cases, and what he should get out of them. The discussion of the cases should be expedited, rather than retarded, by the concurrent study of problems involving their application.

It is alleged by law teachers that the case system of instruction is used because that method not only enables men to learn the fundamental principles of the law, but gives the student practice in their application and enables him to acquire skill in legal analysis and argument and ability to deal with legal problems. It is submitted that there appears to be an inconsistency between the present-day justification of the case system, and the present-day method of the case system. It is justified on the ground that it trains the mind, but it is not worked in the way to train the mind most effectively. The addition of problems as a regular and formal part of the course will help secure the benefits which are now claimed for the case system without requiring any sacrifice of the books or methods now employed.

Chapter 56

How to Teach Law

An Outline and Bibliography

1949-1950

Committee on Teaching and Examination Methods, Association of American Law Schools

Introduction

Most literature on legal education in the United States deals with two questions: (1) WHAT should law students be taught, and (2) HOW should they be taught. The first relates to the aims and content of legal education; the second, to the methods of legal education.

This report deals with methods. It outlines most of the discussion that has been published on how American law students ought to be taught. We have searched Volumes 1-10 of the *American Law School Review*, Volumes 1 and 2 of the *Journal of Legal Education*, the handbooks of the Association of American Law Schools (1901-1949), and the *Index to Legal Periodicals* (1908-July 1950). The most obvious omissions are book reviews (cf. note 10, *infra*) and bar association publications. In addition, there are omissions caused by limitations on our research techniques. (To illustrate: We relied on titles to a great extent, but the title of an article does not always disclose its contents.)

Problems of method cannot, of course, be severed completely from problems of aims and content. The teacher of Adininistrative Law, for example, whose aim is training for private practice and whose materials are limited to court opinions and statutes, necessarily conducts his class differently from the teacher who hopes also to train for government service, and who adds agency documents to his materials. In working out a test stressing the HOW of law teaching, rather than the WHAT, we decided to exclude general comment on curricular reform. But we included materials dealing with courses now in the curriculum even when much of the discussion covered aims and content as well as method. We also included materials on the need for more public law, or more legal knowledge, or skills training, or policy science, or whatever else may have inspired a writer, when he proposed techniques that might aid other teachers in experimenting with his ideas. For example, under many of our headings we have cited excerpts from Dr. Esther Brown's study, *Lawyers, Law Schools, and The Public Service*, even though the study is primarily a critique of law school

29. John Chipman Gray (1839-1915), a Harvard professor is best known for his enormous treatise *Rule Against Perpetuities*, even though later in his career he lost interest in teaching property law. Despite his success as a lecturer and treatise man, Gray converted to the case method and became a leading exponent of case-method instruction and casebooks. Photograph taken in 1914. (*Courtesy of Art & Visual Materials, Special Collections Department, Harvard Law School Library.*)

objectives. We did this because her summary of experimental work in the law schools is probably the most comprehensive yet published.

For those who wish to investigate the problems of aims and content as well as method, we recommend Dr. Brown's book and also two committee reports of the Association of American Law Schools. The first report, surveying "the more or less typical law school curriculum of our time" appears in the 1947 Handbook of the Association, pp. 130-142.[1] The second, entitled "The Place of Skills in Legal Education," appears in the 1944 Handbook, pp. 159-201 (and also in 45 Columbia Law Review, pp. 345-391).[2] For all law teachers we recommend an article entitled "Lighthouse No Good" by Dean William L. Prosser, which states more vividly than any other document a few of the aches and aspirations characterizing our profession.[3]

We have had two purposes in preparing this report. The first was to rescue from obscurity a miscellany of writings that discuss law teachers and what they do, or could do, in the classroom. Some of this literature is stimulating; some dull. We think much of it could be helpful to new teachers, to teachers working on new courses, and to teachers who like to review or revise their established courses. Our second purpose was to create an outline that would help *identify* the problems of law teaching and, in addition, point up the profession's need for further research and writing. We think the outline and bibliography expose many inadequacies in past research and writing; and we hope that, once bared, some of these gaps will be filled.

Walter J. Blum, University of Chicago
Joe E. Covington, University of Arkansas
Archibald Cox, Harvard University (1949)
Delmar Karlen, University of Wisconsin (1950)
Jay W. Murphy, University of Alabama
James Snedeker, University of San Francisco (1949)
Samuel D. Thurman, Jr., Stanford University
Lehan K. Tunks, University of Iowa
Frank C. Newman, University of California, *Chairman*

December 28, 1950

The Methods of Legal Education
(An Introductory Outline)

I. Methods of teaching: Introduction
  A. Teacher training
  B. Teaching practices

II. The classroom
  A. The materials
    1. Casebook
    2. Syllabus
    3. Restatements
    4. Statutes
    5. Social science and other non-legal materials
  B. Classroom discussion
    1. In general
    2. The case method
    3. The problem method
  C. The teacher's other contributions
    1. Lectures (including introductions and summaries)
    2. Audio-visual aids
    3. Citations

III. Student work outside the classroom
  A. Preparation for class, and review
    1. Assigned readings, briefs, notes, summaries, etc.
    2. Supplementary readings
    3. Consultation
      a. With teachers
      b. With tutors
      c. With other students
  B. Research, writing, and oral expression
    1. In general
    2. For specific courses
    3. For law review
    4. For moot court, practice court, legal aid, etc.
  C. Observation
  D. Clinical training
  E. Inservice and apprentice training

IV. Specific courses
    1. Introductory courses
    2. Administrative law
    3. Agency
    4. Business associations
    5. Commercial law
    6. Comparative law
    6a. Conflicts
    7. Constitutional law
    8. Contracts
    9. Corporate finance
    10. Criminal law

11. Equity
12. Estate planning
13. Federal jurisdiction
14. International law
15. Judicial administration
16. Jurisprudence
17. Labor law
18. Legal accounting
19. Legal aid
20. Legal bibliography
21. Legal ethics
22. Legal history
23. Legislation
24. Military law
25. Natural resources
26. Practice and procedure
27. Property
28. Public utilities
29. Sales
30. Taxation
31. Torts
32. Trade regulation
33. Trusts, wills and estates

V. Appraisal (Examining and grading)
  A. Methods
    1. In general
    2. True-false
    3. Comprehensives
  B. Specific courses
    1. Constitutional law
    2. Contracts
    3. Legal bibliography
    4. Legal ethics

THE METHODS OF LEGAL EDUCATION

(A Selected Bibliography)

I. *Methods of Teaching: Introduction*

A. *Teacher Training*

Weihofen, "Education for Law Teachers"
43 Col. L. R. 423-448 (1943)

Cheatham, "A Seminar in Legal Education"
1 J. of Legal Ed. 439-442 (1949)

Leach, "Professorship of Legal Education Recommended"
2 J. of Legal Ed. 149-153 (1949)

Newman, "Lighthouses, Fog, and Law: A School for Teachers?"
1 J. of Legal Ed. 582-587 (1949)

Rodell, "Legal Realists, Legal Fundamentalists, Lawyer Schools, and Policy Science—Or How Not to Teach Law"
1 Vand. L. R. 5-7 (1947)

Frank, "A Plea for Lawyer-Schools"
56 Yale L. J. 1303, 1313-1315 (1947)

AALS Rep., "Educational Economizing"
1942 Handbook 94-101 (how to save time in law teaching; bibliography at p. 100); cf. AALS Rep. on the relative efficacy of massed and spaced instruction in the course in Contracts, 1944 Handbook 203-212

de Zulueta, "The Recruitment of Public Teachers of Law"
1933 J. Soc. Pub. Teach. Law 1-10

McCaskill, Smith, Kirkwood, "The Training of the Law Teacher"
7 Am. L. Sch. R. 420-428 (1932)

Lewis, "The Law Teaching Branch of the Profession"
5 Am. L. Sch. R. 447-455 (1925)

Stone, "The Importance of Actual Experience at the Bar as a Preparation for Teaching Law"
3 Am. L. Sch. R. 205-211 (1912)
37 A.B.A. Rep. 747-760 (1912)

Kales, "Should the Law Teacher Practice Law?"
25 Harv. L. R. 253-269 (1912)

Thayer, (Comment)
25 Harv. L. R. 269-273 (1912)

Ames, "The Vocation of the Law Professor"
48 Am. L. Reg. 129-146 (1900)

B. *Teaching Practices*

Pemberton, "Report of the National Law Student Conference on Legal Education (III. Teaching Methods Employed in the Law School)"
1 J. of Legal Ed. 232-240 (1948)

AALS Rep. (Skill training and treatment of policy considerations)
1948 Handbook 125-170

AALS Rep., "Methods of 'Covering Ground'" and "Skill Improvement"
1948 Handbook 194-227

AALS Rep. [F. R. Strong], "Investigational Possibilities in the Area of Techniques of Instruction"
1941 Handbook 134-139
9 Am. L. Sch. R. 1325-1329 (1942)

II. *The Classroom*

A. *The Materials*

1. *Casebook*[4]

Ehrenzweig, "The American Casebook: Cases and Materials"
32 Geo. L. J, 224-247 (1944)

Llewellyn, "On the Problem of Teaching 'Private' Law"
54 Harv. L. R. 775-810 (1941)

Kinnane, "Changing Materials in Teaching of Law"
19 A.B.A. J. 240-244 (1933)

Vance, "Of the Making of Casebooks"
6 Am. L. Sch. R. 4-10 (1926)

Parma, "The Origin, History and Compilation of the Case-book"
14 L. Lib. J. 14-19 (1921)
4 Am. L. Sch. R. 741-745 (1922)

Peterson, "A Defense of the Case System and A Criticism of Casebooks"
3 Am. L. Sch. R. 249-251 (1913)

Y.B. Smith, "The Study of Law by Cases. A Students Point of View"
3 Am. L. Sch. R. 253-256 (1913)

Chase, "A Comparison of the Use of Treatises and the Use of Case Books in the Study of Law"
3 Am. L. Sch. R. 81-83 (1912)

Cole, "A Case-Book Suggestion"
3 Am. L. Sch. R. 128-131 (1912)

Ashley, "The 'Failure' of Professor Langdell"
2 Am. L. Sch. R. 257-260 (1909)

Ballantine, "Adapting the Case-Book to the Needs of Professional Training"
2 Am. L. Sch. R. 135-141 (1908)

Kales, "The Next Step in the Evolution of the Case-Book"
21 Harv. L. R. 92-119 (1907)

Kales, "A Further Word on the Next Step in the Evolution of the Case-Book"
4 Ill. L. R. 11-26 (1909)

2. *Syllabus*

AALS Rep. ("Methods of 'Covering Ground'")
1948 Handbook 197-206

3. *Restatements*

Lewis, "The Value and Use of American Law Institute Restatements in the Teaching of Law"
7 Am. L. Sch, R. 735-739 (1933)
1932 Handbook 74-102

Goodrich, "The Law Institute and the Teacher of Law"
26 Mich. L.R. 351-360 (1928)
6 Am. L. Sch. R. 240-245 (1928)

Hadley, "Legal Education and the Restatement of the Law by the American Law Institute"
9 St. L. L. R. 118-129 (1924)

4. *Statutes*

AALS Rep., "The Implication of Modern Legislation to Law Teaching"
1934 Handbook 122-152
[and see "Legislation," "Corporate Finance," and "Equity," infra (IV, 23, 9, 11)]

5. *Social Science and Other Non-Legal Materials*[5]

Brown, *Lawyers, Law Schools, and The Public Service*
110-134 (1948); cf. pp. 142-145, 150-156

AALS Rep., Business and Social Science Materials
1949 Handbook 137-143
1948 Handbook 260-261
1947 Handbook 209-217

Johnston, "Sociological and Non-Legal Courses"
23 Rocky Mt. L. R. 71-74 (1950)

Ehrenzweig, "Teaching 'Integration'—A Comment on Law and Society"
2 J. of Legal Ed. 359-364 (1950)

Rostow, "The Study of Economics in Relation to Education in Law"
2 J. of Legal Ed. 335-343 (1950)

Hall, "Pedagogical Discovery Via the Seminar"
2 J. of Legal Ed. 209-212 (1949)

Llewellyn, "Law and the Social Sciences—Especially Sociology"
62 Harv. L. R. 1286-1305 (1949)

Sharp, "Biology and Law"
16 Chi. L. R. 403-413 (1949)

Katz, "Economics and the Study of Law—The Contribution of Henry C. Simons"
14 Chi. L. R. 1-4 (1946)

Katz, "What Changes Are Practical in Legal Education"
27 A.B.A.J. 759-762 (1941)

Llewellyn, "On the Problem of Teaching 'Private' Law"
54 Harv. L. R. 775, 800-810 (1941)

Harno, "Ideas and the Law"
26 A.B.A.J. 651-652 (1940)

Britt, "The Social Psychology of Law"
34 Ill. L. R. 802-811, 919-928 (1940)

Sharp, "Developments in the Law School Curriculum and in Teaching Methods"
8 Am. L. Sch. R. 1044-1049 (1938)

Frey, "Some Thoughts on Law Teachings and the Social Sciences"
82 U. Pa. L. R. 463-471 (1934)

Keyserling, "Social Objectives in Legal Education"
33 Col. L. R. 437-461 (1933)

Ebaugh and Jefferson, "Liaison Teaching of Psychiatry in Law Schools"
22 J. Crim. L. 724-733 (1932)

Spencer and Harno, "The Correlation of Law and College Subjects"
5 Am. L. Sch. R. 85-93, 130-132 (1923)

Lewis, "The Social Sciences as the Basis of Legal Education"
61 U. Pa. L. R. 531-539 (1913)

Runkle, "Application of Psychology to Law"
19 Case & Com. 835-836 (1913)

B. *Classroom Discussion*

1. *In General*

Hall, "A Pedagozical Discovery Via the Seminar"
2 J. of Legal Ed. 209-212 (1949)

Larson, "An 'Inductive' Approach to Legal Instruction"
1 J. of Legal Ed. 287-296 (1948)

Harno, "Disciplines in the Training of a Lawyer"
22 Boston U. L. R. 254-260 (1942)

2. *The Case Method*

[see "Casebook," *supra* (A. 1)]

AALS Rep. ("Values of 'the' Case-Method," "Current Difficulties in Case-Method," "Case-law Skills as an Explicit Focus of Case-Instruction")
1944 Handbook 165-178 (also 45 Col. L. R. 350-364)

AALS Rep. ("Methods of 'Covering Ground'")
1948 Handbook 198-199

Llewellyn, "The Current Crisis in Legal Education"
1 J. of Legal Ed. 211-220 (1948)

Nelson, "Do You Agree With This Case?"
36 Ky. L. J. 265-283 (1948)

Frank, "A Plea for Lawyer-Schools"
56 Yale L. J. 1303-1344 (1947)

Johnson, "A Lay View of Legal Education"
43 Col. L. R. 462-465 (1943)

Henderson, "Wherein Do the Law Schools Fail to Prepare a Law Student for Practice?"
9 Am. L. Sch. R. 1178-1184 (1941)

Hadaller, "On Teaching Law"
13 Calif. S. B. J. (No. 12) 1-6 (1938)

"The Case System in Legal Education"
4 Fort. L. J. 312-313 (1935)

Lichauco, "Studying Law Through Cases"
11 Phil. L. J. 48 (1931)

Rundell, "Problems of The Case Method"
6 Am. L. Sch. R. 698-701 (1930)

Landman, "Anent the Case Method of Studying Law"
4 N.Y.U.L. R. 139-160 (1927)

Brown, "An Experiment With a New Application of the Principles of the Case Method"
5 Am. L. Sch. R. 207-214 (1923)

Fessender, "The Rebirth of the Harvard Law School"
33 Harv. L. R. 493-517 (1920)

Kenny, "The Case Method of Teaching Law"
16 J. Comp. Leg. (N.S.) 184-194 (1916)

Redlich, "The Case Method of Instruction in American Law Schools"
1 S. W. L. R. 23-29 (1916)

Redlich, "Weaknesses of the 'Case Method' in American Law Schools: Suggestions Looking Toward Improved Instruction"
4 Am. L. Sch. R. 1-7 (1915)

Kocourek, "The Redlich Report and the Case Method"
10 Ill. L. R. 321-331 (1915)

Moore, "Legal Education in the U. S."
13 J. Comp. Leg. (N. S.) 207-212 (1913)
Cf. 25 Green Bag 467-470 (1913)

Y. B. Smith, "The Study of Law by Cases: A Student's Point of View"
3 Am. L. Sch. R. 253-256 (1913)

Carusi, "A Criticism of the Case System"
2 Am. L. Sch. R. 213-217 (1908)

O. J. Roberts, "Methods for Review and Quiz in 'Case System Law Schools"
1 Am. L. Sch. R. 222-224 (1904)

3. *The Problem Method*

AALS Rep., "The Problem Method"
1942 Handbook 86-94 (bibliography at pp. 89 and 93)

AALS Rep. ("Methods of 'Covering Ground'")
1948 Handbook 203-205

Brown, *Lawyers, Law Schools and The Public Service*
230-234 (1948)

Ruud, "A Commercial Counselling Seminar"
2 J. of Legal Ed. 505-509 (1950)

Taintor, "Required Summer Term and 'Problem' Course"
2 J. of Legal Ed. 347-350 (1950)

DeWitt and Volz, "Summer Course in Legal Problems"
1949 Wis. L. R. 336-340

Larson, "An 'Inductive' Approach to Legal Education"
1 J. of Legal Ed. 287-296 (1948)

Cavers, "In Advocacy of the Problem Method"
43 Col. L. R. 449-461 (1943)

Ballantine, "Teaching Contracts with the Aid of Problems"
4 Am. L. Sch. R. 115-119 (1916)

C. *The Teacher's Other Contributions*

1. *Lectures (including introductions and summaries)*[6]

AALS Rep. ("Methods of 'Covering Ground'")
1948 Handbook 205-206

2. *Audio-Visual Aids*

AALS Rep., "Educational Films"
1949 Handbook 55-58
1948 Handbook 171
1947 Handbook 148-149

Hunter, "Motion Pictures and Practice Court"
1 J. of Legal Ed. 426-429 (1949)

Joiner, "Motion Pictures and Practice Litigation"
35 A.B.A.J. 185-188, 274-275 (1949)

Joiner, "Motion Pictures As a Basis for Practice Litigation"
27 Mich. S.B.J. 26-29 (November 1948)

Jehring, "Audio-Visual Materials in Industrial and Labor Relations"
3 Indus. and Lab. Rel. R. 80-98 (1949)

Puente, "The Use of Maps in The Study of International Law"
6 Am. L. Sch. R. 507-514 (1929)

Weintraub, "Audio-Visual Media and Political Science Teaching"
43 Am. Pol. Sci. Rev. 766-776 (1949)

3. *Citations*[7]

AALS Rep., "Citation of Local Cases and Statutes in Law Classes"
1936 Handbook 179-189

Walz, "The State University Law School: III, Its Duty to Teach the Law of the Jurisdiction"
24 Green Bag 347-351 (1912)

III. *Student Work Outside the Classroom*

A. *Preparation for class, and review*

1. *Assigned Readings, Briefs, Notes, Summaries, etc.*

Larson, "An 'Inductive' Approach to Legal Instruction"
1 J. of Legal Ed. 287-296 (1948)

AALS Rep. ("Methods of 'Covering Ground'")
1948 Handbook 199-201, 205

Vold, "System of Study for Students Under the Case Method"
4 Am. L. Sch. R. 194-201 (1916)

2. *Supplementary Readings*

Roalfe, "The Relation of the Library to Legal Education"
31 Law Lib. J. 141-155 (1938)

AALS Rep., "Assignment of Topics to be Prepared or Problems to be Solved Without Classroom Discussion"
1936 Handbook 189-195
[and see "Legal Bibliography," *infra* (IV, 20)]

3. *Consultation* [cf. "Research, Writing, and Oral Expression," infra (B)]

a. With Teachers

b. With Tutors

Bathurst, "The Tutorial System: An Experiment in Legal Education"
9 Am. L. Sch. R. 695-697 (1940)

c. With Other Students

B. *Research, Writing, and Oral Expression*

1. *In General*

AALS Rep., "Legal Writing"
1948 Handbook 163-166; *cf.* 201-203

Cook, "Teaching Legal Writing Effectively in Separate Courses"
2 J. of Legal Ed. 87-91 (1949)

Roalfe, "Some Observations on Teaching Legal Bibliography and the Use of Law Books"
1 J. of Legal Ed. 361-377 (1949)

Kalven, "Law School Training in Research and Exposition: The University of Chicago Program"

I J.of Legal Ed. 107-123 (1948)

Volz and DeWitt, "Summer Work in Legal Problems"
1 J. of Legal Ed. 596-599 (1949)

Crampton, "A Plan for Law Student Participation in Real Cases"
30 J. Am. Jud. Soc. 173-174 (1947)

Westwood, "The Law Review Should Become the Law School"
31 Va. L. R. 913-919 (1945)

Henderson, "Wherein Do the Law Schools Fail to Prepare a Law Student for Practice?"
9 Am. L. Sch. R. 1178-1184 (1941)

McMurray, "The Place of Research in the American Law Schools"
5 Am. L. Sch. R. 631-639 (1926)
1925 Handbook 20-30

"Legal Research Work in Colleges"
30 Law Notes (N.Y.) 42-43, 161-162 (1926)

Oliphant and Bordwell, "Legal Research in Law Schools"
5 Am. L. Sch. R. 293-299 (1924)
1923 Handbook 99-111

Wigmore, "The Job Analysis Method of Teaching the Use of Law Sources"
16 Ill. L. R. 499-515 (1922)

Cooley, "'Manual Training' for Lawyers"
2 Am. L. Sch. R. 261-265 (1909)

2. *For Specific Courses*

AALS Rep., "Drafting Exercises in Connection with Regular Law School Courses"
1936 Handbook 195-204

Neff, "Laboratory Work in the Drafting of Pleadings as an Adjunct to the Study of Pleading"
4 Am. L. Sch. R. 150-153 (1916)

3. *For Law Review*

Hawkland, "Extracurricular Legal Teaching Methods"
20 Tenn. L. R. 728, 730-736 (1949)

Marsh, "The Law Review and The Law School"
42 Ill. L. R. 424-442 (1947)

Updegraff, "Management of Law School Reviews"
6 Am. L. Sch. R. 469-479 (1929)

4. *For Moot Court, Practice Court, Legal Aid, etc.*

[cf. "Clinical Training," *infra* (D); "Legal Bibliography," infra (IV, 20); "Practice and Procedure," *infra* (IV, 26) Hawkland, "Extracurricular Legal Teaching Methods"
20 Tenn. L. R. 728, 736-740 (1949)]

Frank, "A Plea for Lawyer-Schools"
56 Yale L. J. 1303-1344 (1947)

James, "An Arbitration Laboratory in Law School"
2 Arb. J. (N.S.) 79-83 (1947)

Green, "Realism in Practice Court"
1 J. of Legal Ed. 421-425 (1949)

Wilson, "More About Realism in Practice Court"
1 J. of Legal Ed. 569-572 (1949)

Hunter, "Motion Pictures and Practice Court"
1 J. of Legal Ed. 426-429 (1949)

Mertz, "A Law Student Looks at the Practice Court"
2 John Marshall L. Q. 542-559 (1937)

Blatt, "An Experiment in Moot Court Work"
8 Am. L. Sch. R. 417-420 (1936)

Folsom, "A Practical Practice Court"
8 Rocky Mt. L. R. 130-133 (1936)

Smith, "Law Club Work at Iowa"
6 Am. L. Sch. R. 499-507 (1929)

Hepburn, "Practice Court Work"
5 Am. L. Sch. R. 543-546 (1925)

Martin, "Practical Legal Education"
3 Am. L. Sch. R. 237-240 (1913)

Craig, "Moot Courts as a Part of a Law School Curriculum"
3 Am. L. Sch. R. 271-277 (1913)

Sunderland, "The Teaching of Practice and Procedure in Law School"
3 Am. L. Sch. R. 357-367 (1913)
1913 A.B.A. Rep. 908-923
[Discussion, 3 Am. L. Sch. R. 383-388
1913 A.B.A. Rep. 865-875]

Hastings, "Practice Courts"
3 Am. L. Sch. R. 182-189 (1912)

1912 A.B.A. Rep. 1010-1028
[Discussion, 3 Am. L. Sch. R. 189-196
1912 A.B.A. Rep. 937-954]

"The Ewing System of Conducting Trials in Moot Courts of Law Schools" (Ed. Note)
33 N. J. L. J. 260 (1910)
16 Va. L. Reg. 468-470 (1910)

C. *Observation*[8]

Roberts, "Performance Courses in the Study of Law"
36 A.B.A. J. 17-20, 84-87 (1950)

D. *Clinical Training*

[cf. "Practice and Procedure," *infra* (IV, 26)]

Bradway, *Basic Legal Aid Clinic Materials and Exercises on Taking Hold of a Case at Law* (1950)

Miller, "Clinical Training of Law Students"
2 J. of Legal Ed. 298-309 (1950)

Bradway et al., "Improving Legal Aid Clinic Technique"
18 Bar Examiner 46-56 (1949)

Hawkland, "Extracurricular Legal Teaching Methods"
20 Tenn. L. R. 728, 743-749 (1949)

Bradway, "'Case Presentation' and the Legal Aid Clinic"
1 J. of Legal Ed. 280-283 (1948)

Bradway, "Law Students Can Be Given Clinical Experience"
34 A.B.A.J. 103-106 (1948)

AALS Rep., "Legal Aid Clinics"
1948 Handbook 188-193
1946 Handbook 123-124
1943 Handbook 181-182
1941 Handbook 303-305
1940 Handbook 257-260

Vanderbilt, "Legal Aid and the Law Schools"
1 Record of N.Y. City Bar 296-300 (1946)

Patterson, "The Legal Aid Clinic—Benefits to Lawyers, to Law Students, and to Indigents"
21 Tex. L. R. 423-430 (1943)

Bradway, "Legal Aid Clinics Train Young Advocates"
26 J. Am. Jud. Soc. 14-16 (1942)

Bradway, "Classroom Aspects of Legal Aid Clinic Work"
8 Brooklyn L. R. 373-396 (1939)

Bradway, "The Objectives of Legal Aid Clinic Work"
24 Wash. U. L. Q. 173-192 (1939)

Fahey, "A Law School Briefing Service"
25 A.B.A.J. 502-504, 532 (1939)

Harris, "Educational Value of a Legal Aid Clinic"
3 Ohio St. L. J. 300-306 (1937)

Fuchs, "The Educational Value of a Legal Clinic—Some Doubts and Queries"
8 Am. L. Sch. R. 857-859 (1937)

Harris, "The Educational Value of A Legal Aid Clinic—A Reply"
8 Am. L. Sch. R. 860-864 (1937)

Shaw, "Legal Education and Legal Clinics"
[excerpts reprinted in 15 Can. B. R. 361-368 (1937)]

Bradway, "What We May Find Out About Law Students From Giving Them Clinical Training That We Do Not Find Out When We Give Them Casebook Training"
8 Am. L. Sch. R. 404-410 (1936)

Elliott, "Legal Aid Clinic Versus Legal Aid Society"
8 Am. L. Sch. R. 410-412 (1936)

Piel, "The Student Viewpoint Toward Clinic Work"
8 Am. L. Sch. R. 228-240 (1935)

Gardner, "Why Not A Clinical Lawyer-School?—Some Reflections"
82 U. of Pa. L. R. 785-804 (1934)

David, "The Clinical Lawyer-School: The Clinic"
83 U. Pa. L. R. 1-22 (1934)

Maguire, Legal Aid Clinics—A Definitional Comment"
7 Am. L. Sch. R. 1151-1153 (1934)

McClain, "Some Practical Problems to be Considered in Undertaking Clinical Work in Law Schools Located in Small Communities"
7 Am. L. Sch. R.1147-1151 (1934)

Bradway, "The Legal Aid Clinic as an Educational Device"
7 Am. L. Sch. R. 1153-1159 (1934)

Bradway, "Some Distinctive Features of a Legal Aid Clinic Course"
1 U. of Chi. L. R. 469-479 (1934)

Frank, "Why Not a Clinical Lawyer—School?"
81 U. of Pa. L. R. 907-923 (1933)

Bradway, "New Developments in the Legal Clinic Field"
13 St. L. L. R. 122-133 (1928)

Hepburn, "Law Schools and Legal Clinics"
6 Am. L. Sch. R. 245-249 (1928)

R. H. Smith, "Legal Clinics—The Student's Point of View"
24 Case & Com. 214-216 (1917)

Rowe, "Legal Clinics and Better Trained Lawyers—A Necessity"
11 Ill. L. R. 591-618 (1917)

"The Law Clinic [Univ. of Iowa]"
5 Am. L. Sch. R. 198-199 (1923)

Morgan, "The Legal Clinic"
4 Am. L. Sch. R. 255-258 (1917)

Hentig, "The Clinical Method in Teaching Criminal Law"
24 J. Crim. L. 1081-1087 (1933-1934)

MacNamara, "Teaching Legal Ethics by the Clinical Method"
8 Am. L. Sch. R. 241-245 (1935)

E. *In Service and Apprentice Training*

Brown, *Lawyers, Law Schools, and The Public Service*
33-40, 238-239 (1948)

AALS Rep., "Experiment in Training Students by Assignment to Government Agencies"
1943 Handbook 113-124

Report of Committee on Post Graduate Instruction
11 Cal. S. B. Proceedings 343-346 (1938)

Volz and DeWitt, "Summer Work in Legal Problems"
1 J. of Legal Ed. 596-599 (1949)

Silver, "'Experience-Employment' in Legal Education"
35 A.B.A.J. 991-994 (1949)

Souter, "Internship for Lawyers"
29 J. Am. Jud. Soc. 186-187 (1946)

Johnson, "A Lay View of Legal Education"
43 Col. L. R. 462-465 (1943)

Nathanson, "Internship for Lawyers"
38 Can. L. J. 667-(   )

Dawson, "The Sponsor System under Law School Auspices"
25 A.B.A.J. 849-851 (1939)

Morse and Fuller, "Law School Objectives and Methods; Training for Public Administration"
8 Am. L. Sch. R. 1049-1058 (1938)

Wheaton, "Law Teaching and Pragmatism"
25 Geo. L. J. 338-350 (1937)

Frank, "What Constitutes a Good Legal Education"
7 Am. L. Sch. R. 894-902 (1933)

Proceedings of Section on Legal Education of American Bar Association
7 Am. L. Sch. R. 944-951 (1933) [an exchange of ideas on apprenticeship training and deviation from traditional methods of instruction]

"Law School Graduate and Law Office Apprenticeship"
83 Cent. L. J. 102-103 (1916)

"Is Apprenticeship in a Law Office Desirable While Pursuing a Course of Study in a Law School?"
1 Am. L. Sch. R. 83-89 (1903)

IV. *Specific Courses*[9]

1. *Introductory Courses*

Jones, "Notes on the Teaching of Legal Method"
1 J. of Legal Ed. 13-27 (1948)

Peairs, "Method is For the Methodical"
10 Pitt. L. R. 511-523 (1949)

AALS Rep. (Skill training and treatment of policy considerations)
1948 Handbook 145-154

Brown, *Lawyers, Law Schools, and The Public Service*
135, n. 1 (1948)

Gavit, "A Course on the Introduction to Law"
8 Am. L. Sch. R. 413-417 (1936)

Cook, (Legal Method and Legal Analysis)
6 Am. L. Sch. R. 409-414 (1929)

Oliphant, "A Course in Brief Making and Legal Argument"
4 Am. L. Sch. R. 258-272 (1917)

2. *Administrative Law*

Brown, *Lawyers, Law Schools, and The Public Service*
174-204 (1948)

McGuire, "Reforms Needed in the Teaching of Administrative Law"
6 G.W.L.R. 171-180 (1938)

Hargreaves, "Administrative Law and the Teaching of Land Law"
1938 J. Soc. Pub. Teach. Law 15-23

Jennings, Robson, and Wade, "Administrative Law and the Teaching of Public Law"
1938 J. Soc. Pub. Teach. Law 10-15

Eastwood and Wortley, "Administrative Law and the Teaching of the Law of Contract"
1938 J. Soc. Pub. Teach. Law 23-35

3. *Agency*

Conard, "What's Wrong With Agency"
1 J. of Legal Ed. 540-562 (1949)

4. *Business Associations*

AALS Rep. ("Methods of Skill Improvement")
1948 Handbook 210-211

5. *Commercial Law*

Shestack, "Another Look At Commercial Law Instruction"
2 J. of Legal Ed. 466-471 (1950)

AALS Rep. ("Methods of Skill Improvement")
1948 Handbook 216-221

Llewellyn, "On the Problem of Teaching 'Private' Law"
54 Harv. L. R. 775-810 (1941)

Smith, "Changing Trends in the Field of Teaching Business Law"
9 Am. L. Sch. R. 1497-1503 (1942)

Chancellor, Lee, and Babb, "Methods of Teaching Business Law—Discussion"
8 Am. L. Sch. R. 1271-1286 (1938)

6. *Comparative Law*

Schlesinger, *Comparative Law: Cases and Materials*
468-469 [Bibliography on "Teaching of Comparative Law"] (1950)

Franklin, "On the Teaching of Advanced Foreign Civilians in American Law Schools"
2 J. of Legal Ed. 455-465 (1950)

Friedman, "The Teaching of Comparative Jurisprudence"
4 Res Judicatae 74-77 (1949)

Thayer, "The Teaching of International and Comparative Law"
1 J. of Legal Ed. 449-452 (1949)

Bishop, "Institute on the Teaching of International and Comparative Law"
42 Am. J. Int. L. 884-885 (1948)

Stone, "On the Teaching of Law Comparatively"
22 Tul. L. R. 158-172 (1947)

Ehrenzweig, "A Common Language of World Jurisprudence: Teaching Roman Law in Twenty Hours"
12 Chi. L. R. 285-294 (1945)

Murdock, "Teaching of Comparative and International Law"
19 Tul. L. R. 249-254 (1944)

Gutteridge, "The Teaching of International and Comparative Law"
23 J. Comp. Leg. 3d Ser. 60-64 (1941)

Kuhn, "The Function of the Comparative Method in Legal History and Philosophy"
13 Tul. L. R. 350-361 (1939)

Pound, "The Place of Comparative Law in the American Law School Curriculum"
8 Tul. L. R. 161-170 (1934)

Auld, "Roman Law in Canadian Law Schools"
11 Can. Bar. R. 530-538 (1933)

Hanbury, "The Place of Roman Law in the Teaching of Law Today"
J. Soc. Pub. Teach. Law 14-23 (1931)

Cassidy, "The Teaching and Study of Roman Law in the United States"
19 Geo. L. J. 297-305 (1931)

6a. *Conflicts*

Stimson, "The Preparation of Conflict of Laws Teaching Materials"
2 J. of Legal Ed. 351-358 (1950)

7. *Constitutional Law*

AALS Rep. (Skill training and treatment of policy considerations)
1948 Handbook 145-154

Brown, *Lawyers, Law Schools and The Public Service* ("Civil Liberties")
139-142 (1948)

8. *Contracts*

AALS Rep. (Skill training and treatment of policy considerations)
1948 Handbook 134-145

AALS Rep. (Relative efficacy of massed and spaced instruction in the course in Contracts)
1944 Handbook 203-212

AALS Rep. (Extent and content of courses on Contracts)
1941 Handbook 278-293

Eastwood and Wortley, "Administrative Law and the Teaching of the Law of Contract"
J. Soc. Pub. Teach. Law 23-35 (1938)

Havighurst, "A Classification of Contract Cases For Teaching Purposes"
7 Am. L. Sch. R. 844-847 (1933)

Ballantine, "Teaching Contracts with the Aid of Problems"
4 Am. L. Sch. R. 115-119 (1916)

9. *Corporate Finance*

AALS Proc. (Instruction in connection with Securities Act or Securities Exchange Act and similar legislation)
1937 Handbook 132-135

10. *Criminal Law*

Hertig, "The Clinical Method in Teaching Criminal Law"
24 J. Crim. L. 1081-1087 (1933-1934)

Ebaugh and Jefferson, "Liaison Teaching of Psychiatry in Law Schools"
22 J. Crim. L. 724-733 (1931-1932)

11. *Equity*

Simpson, "Use of Statutory Materials in the Teaching of Equity"
21 Geo. L. J. 457-470 (1933)

Hohfeld, "The Relations Between Equity and Law"
11 Mich. L. R. 537-571 (1913)

12. *Estate Planning*

Ritchie, "A Suggested Course in Estate Planning"
35 Va. L. R. 135-142 (1949)

Casner, "An Estate—Planning Course as a Substitute for Wills, Trusts and Future Interests"
1 J. of Legal Ed. 62-63 (1948)
[and see *Trusts, Wills, and Estates, infra* (33)]

13. *Federal Jurisdiction*

"A Course in Federal Jurisdiction" (editorial)
1 Iowa L. B. 77 (1915)

14. *International Law*

Thayer, "The Teaching of International and Comparative Law"
1 J. of Legal Ed. 449-452 (1949)

Bishop, "Institute on the Teaching of International and Comparative Law"
42 Am. J. Int. L. 884-885 (1948)

Carlston, "The Teaching of International Law in Law Schools"
48 Col. L. R. 516-533(1948)

Murdock, "Teaching of Comparative and International Law"
19 Tul. L. R. 249-254 (1944)

Gutteridge, "Teaching of International and Comparative Law"
23 J. Comp. Leg. 3d Ser. 60-64 (1941)

Akzin, "On the Teaching of International Law"
20 Iowa L. R. 774-784 (1935)

Hudson, "The Teaching of International Law in America"
15 A. B. A. 19-23 (1929)

Puente, "The Use of Maps in The Study of International Law"
6 Am. L. Sch. R. 507-514 (1929)

"International Law Teaching"
19 Am. J. Int. L. 362-363 (1925)

Gregory, "The Study of International Law in Law Schools"
2 Am. L. Sch. R. 41-48 (1906)

15. *Judicial Administration*

Brown, *Lawyers, Law Schools and The Public Service*
137-139 (1949)

Pirsig, "A Course in Judicial Administration"
30 Iowa L. R. 387-393 (1945)
30 J. Am. Jud. Soc. 37-41

16. *Jurisprudence*

Mermin, "The Study of Jurisprudence—A Letter to a Hostile Student"
49 Mich. L. R. 39-72 (1950)

Hall, Northrop, and Fuller, "The Place and Uses of Jurisprudence"
1 J. of Legal Ed. 475-507 (1949)

Friedmann, "The Teaching of Comparative Jurisprudence"
4 Res Judicatae 74-77 (1949)

Kalven, "Liberal Education, the Case-System and Jurisprudence"

14 Chi. L. R. 215-231 (1947)

Patterson, Llewellyn, and Kennedy, "A Required Course in Jurisprudence"
9 Am. L. Sch. R. 582-596 (1940)

Moore, "The Teaching of Jurisprudence"
J. Soc. Pub. Teach. Law 23-30 (1929)

Stewart, "Should Jurisprudence Be Taught at the Beginning or at the End of a Course in Law?"
40 Can. L. T. 647-653 (1920)

Corbin, "Yale and the New Science of Jurisprudence"
21 Case & Com. 953-956 (1915)

Patten, "The New Jurisprudence"
62 Pa. L. R. 1-16 (1913)

Brown, "Jurisprudence and Legal Education"
9 Col. L. R. 238-242 (1909)

17. *Labor Law*

Wirtz, "On Teaching Labor Law"
42 Ill. L. R. 1-28 (1947)

AALS Rep., "Round Table Council on Labor Law"
1947 Handbook 220-227

AALS Rep. ("Methods of Skill Improvement")
1948 Handbook 223-225

Jehring, "Audio-Visual Materials in Industrial and Labor Relations"
3 Indus. and Lab. Rel. R. 80-98 (1949)

18. *Legal Accounting*

Graham, "Accounting in the Law School Curriculum"
7 Am. L. Sch. R. 215-227 (1931)

19. *Legal Aid*

[see "Clinical Training," *supra* (III, D)]

20. *Legal Bibliography*

Moreland, "Legal Bibliography: A Factual Problem"
2 J. of Legal Ed. 489-491 (1950)

Peairs, "Legal Bibliography: A Dual Problem"
2 J. of Legal Ed. 61-70 (1949)

Roalfe, "Some Observations on Teaching Legal Bibliography and the Use of Law Books"
1 J. of Legal Ed. 361-377 (1949)

Hicks, "The Teaching of Legal Bibliography"
11 Law Lib. J. 1-8 (1918)

von Frech, "On Teaching the Use of Law Books"
30 Case & Com. No. 5 7-10 (1925)

Wigmore, "The Job Analysis Method of Teaching the Use of Law Sources"
16 Ill. L. R. 499-515 (1922)

Daly, "Finding the Law"
4 Am. L. Sch. R. 569-571, 750-751 (1920-21)

21. *Legal Ethics*

Hervey, "The Place of Professional Ethics in the Undergraduate Curriculum"
9 Am. L. Sch. R. 720-723 (1940)

MacNamara, "Teaching Legal Ethics by the Clinical Method"
8 Am. L. Sch. R. 241-245 (1935)

Turrentine, "Observations on the Teaching of Professional Ethics"
19 A.B.A.J. 305-308 (1933)

AALS Rep., (Teaching Professional Ethics in Law Schools)
1931 Handbook 157-162

Harris, "Teaching of Professional Ethics"
17 Va. L. R. 473-480 (1931)

Costigan, "The Teaching of Legal Ethics"
4 Am. L. Sch. R. 290-296 (1917)

Bond, "Present Instruction in Professional Ethics in Law Schools"
4 Am. L. Sch. Rev. 40-45 (1915)

22. *Legal History*

Bodenheimer, "An Experiment in the Teaching of Legal History"
2 J. of Legal Ed. 501-504 (1950)

Brown, *Lawyers, Law Schools and The Public Service*
146-150 (1948)

Kuhn, "The Function of the Comparative Method in Legal History and Philosophy"
13 Tul. L. R. 350-361 (1939)

Boorstin, "Tradition and Method in Legal History"
54 Harv. L. R. 424-436 (1941)

Froehlich, "Legal History and the American Law School"
7 Am. L. Sch. Rev. 739-760 (1933)

23. *Legislation*

Brown, *Lawyers, Law Schools and The Public Service*
135-136, 204-227 (1948)

AALS Rep. (Skill training and treatment of policy considerations)
1948 Handbook 145-154

AALS Rep. (Methods of Skill Improvement)
1948 Handbook 225-227

AALS Proc., "The Implication of Modern Legislation to Law Teaching"
1934 Handbook 122-152

Hawkland, "Extracurricular Legal Teaching Methods"
20 Tenn. L. R, 728, 740-743 (1949)

Jones, "Case Study in Neglected Opportunity: Law Schools and The Legislative Development of The Law"
2 J. of Legal Ed. 137-148 (1949)

Cohen, "On The Teaching of 'Legislation'"
47 Col. L. R. 1301-1312 (1947)

Hurst, "The Content of Courses in Legislation"
8 Chi. L. R. 280-295 (1941)

Elliott, "Requisites of Adequate Legal Training in the Legislative Process—From the Legislator's Viewpoint"
8 Am. L. Sch. R. 865-870 (1937)

Sly, "Requisites of Adequate Legal Training in the Legislative Process—From the Administrator's Viewpoint"
8 Am. L. Sch. R. 871-874 (1937)

Stone, "Law Students and Legislation"
7 Am. L. Sch. R. 1138-1147 (1934)

Van Hecke, "Ernst Freund as a Teacher of Legislation"
1 Chi. L. R. 92-94 (1933)

Dodd, "Statute Law and the Law School"
5 Am. L. Sch. R. 24-28 (1922)
1 N. C. L. R. 1-7 (1922)

Bigelow, "Training Young Lawyers in the Way Laws Are Made—Creighton University's 'Model House'"
84 Cent. L. J. 85-87 (1917)

24. *Military Law*

Ferrari, "Matter and Method in the Military Law Course"
7 Calif. L. Rev. 105-113 (1919)

25. *Natural Resources*

Martz, "The Study of Natural Resource Law"
1 J. of Legal Ed. 588-589 (1949)

Arnold, "Study of Public Land Law in the Western Law Schools"
4 Calif. L. R. 316-318 (1916)

26. *Practice and Procedure*

[see "Moot Court, Practice Court, Legal Aid, etc.," *supra*, (III, B, 4)]

Mueller and James, "Case Presentation"
1 J. of Legal Ed. 129-135 (1948)

Bradway, "'Case Presentation' and the Legal Aid Clinic"
1 J. of Legal Ed. 280-283 (1948)

AALS Rep., "Educational Films"
1949 Handbook 55-58
1948 Handbook 171
1947 Handbook 148-149
[see "Audio-Visual Aids," *supra* (II, C, 2)]

AALS Rep. ("Pleading" and "Evidence")
1948 Handbook 207-210

Wheaton, "The Teaching of Trial Practice"
15 A.B.A.J. 482-485 (1929)

Hale, "Why Blindfold Law School Students"
13 J. Am. Jud. Soc. 11-14 (1929)

Philbrick, "A Casebook for the First Year in Procedure"
6 Am. L. Sch. R. 123-127 (1927)

Magill, "An Introductory Course in Civil Procedure"
6 Am. L. Sch. R. 119-123 (1927)

Burke, "Law School Practice Courses and Moot Courts—Methods of Teaching Pleading and Practice"
5 Am. L. Sch. R. 539-542 (1925)

Wooten, "Classes in Court Practice and Procedure"
5 Am. L. Sch. R. 546-550 (1925)

McCaskill, "Teaching Pleading So As to Meet Future as Well as Present Needs"
5 Am. L. Sch. R. 286-292 (1924)

Sunderland, "An Inquiry Concerning the Functions of Procedure in Legal Education"
5 Am. L. Sch. R. 73-85 (1923)
29 W. Va. L. Q. 77-96 (1923)

Carlin, "Original Methods of Teaching Practice and Procedure"
26 W. Va. L. Q. 165-177 (1920)

Pound, "Teaching Civil Procedure"
4 Corn. L. Q. 143-147 (1919)

Gray, "Training Lawyers in Procedure"
1 J. Am. Jud. Soc. 86-89 (1917)

Branson, "The Science of Practice-The Young Practitioner's Need"
11 Ill. L. Rev. 489-494 (1917)

McCaskill, "Methods of Teaching Practice"
2 Corn. L. Q. 299-319 (1917)

Neff, "Laboratory Work in the Drafting of Pleadings as an Adjunct to the Study of Pleading"
4 Am.L. Sch. R. 150-153 (1916)

Amram, "Law School Instruction in Practice"
3 Am. L. Sch. R. 439-449 (1914)

Sunderland, "The Teaching of Practice and Procedure in Law Schools"
12 Mich. L. R. 185-197 (1914)

Sunderland, "Teaching Practice"
1913 A.B.A. Rep. 908-923
3 Am. L. Sch. R. 357-367 (1913)

Sunderland, "The Teaching of Practice and Procedure in Law Schools"
3 Am. L. Sch. R. 357-367(1913)

Sunderland, "The Art of Legal Practice"
7 Mich. L. R. 397-408 (1909)

Foster, "The Lawyer in His Office"
17 Law Students Helper 12, 44, 76, 172, 180, 213, 246, 279 (1909)

Van Zile, "Practice Work in the Law Colleges"
2 Am. L. Sch. R. 71-76 (1907)

Hall, "Practice Work and Elective Studies in Law Schools"
1 Am. L. Sch. R. 328-337 (1905)

Severson, "The Teaching of Procedure in the University of North Dakota School of Law"
12 Bar Briefs 56-60 (1935)

27. *Property*

Brown, *Lawyers, Law Schools and The Public Service* ("Real Property")
157-174 (1948)

Phipps, "Property, the Case Method, and McDougal"
2 J. of Legal Ed. 53-60 (1949)

Latty, "Sales and Personal Property Taught in One Package"
1 J. of Legal Ed. 430-437 (1949)

Leach, "Property Law Taught in Two Packages"
1 J. of Legal Ed. 28-62 (1948)

Effland, "Teaching, Real Property, and Law"
1948 Wis. L. R. 480-490

AALS Rep. (Methods of Skill Improvement: "Conveyancing")
1948 Handbook 215-216
[and see "Natural Resources" *supra* (25)]

28. *Public Utilities*

Brown, *Lawyers, Law Schools and The Public Service*
121-122 (1948)

29. *Sales*

Latty, "Sales and Personal Property Taught in One Package"
1 J. of Legal Ed. 430-437 (1949)
[and see Commercial Law, *supra* (5)]

30. *Taxation*

AALS Rep. ("Methods of Skill Improvement")
1948 Handbook 221-223; and see pp. 17-21 (Bittker)

Miller, "A Tax Program for the Undergraduate Law School"
1 J. of Legal Ed. 573-577 (1949)

31. *Torts*

AALS Rep. (Skill training and treatment of policy considerations)
1948 Handbook 126-134

Morris, "On the Teaching of Legal Cause"
39 Col. L. R. 1087-1109 (1939)

32. *Trade Regulation*

Edwards, "The Place of Economics in the Course on Trade Regulation"
1 J. of Legal Ed. 1-12 (1948); and see 1948 Handbook 261

AALS Rep. ("Methods of Skill Improvement")
1948 Handbook 225-227

33. *Trusts, Wills, and Estates*

AALS Rep. ("Methods of Skill Improvement")
1948 Handbook 212-215

Jacob, "Trusts, Future Interests and All That"
18 Corn. L. Q. 351-372 (1933)
[and see "Estate Planning," *supra* (12)]

V. *Appraisal (Examining and Grading)*

A. *Methods*

1. *In General*

AALS Rep., "Examination Frequency, and Marking"
1942 Handbook 101-107 (bibliography at p. 106)

AALS Proc., "Investigational Possibilities in the Area of Examination Techniques"
1941 Handbook 129-146
9 Am. L. Sch. R. 1329-1333

DeGraff, "Sources for Bar Examination Questions"
9 Am. L. Sch. R. 1197-1204 (1941)

"Legal education: The Examination Aspect"
1939 Scots Law Times (News) 81-83

Elliott, "Making and Marking a Bar Examination"
9 Am. L. Sch. R. 397-402 (1939)

Simmons, "Checking Bar Examinations"
9 Am. L. Sch. R. 426-431 (1939)

McDonald, "Preparation of Questions and Crediting of Papers in Missouri"
9 Am. L. Sch. R. 14-20 (1938)

Doubles, "Law School Examinations"
8 Am. L. Sch. Rev. 254-259 (1935)

Wood, "The Measurement of Law School Work"
24 Col. L. R. 224-265 (1924)
5 Am. L. Sch. R. 338-364 (1924)

Curtis, "Examinations in Law Schools"
1903 Handbook 41-50

Grant, "The Single Standard in Grading"
6 Am. L. Sch. R. 780-802 (1930)

Vold, "Impersonal Law Examinations"
5 Am. L. Sch. R. 214-219 (1923)

Lewis and Lile, "The Honor System of Conducting Examinations in Law Schools"
2 Am. L. Sch. R. 454-464 (1910)

"Final Examination Questions in Prominent Law Schools"
4 Am. L. Sch. R. 160-173 (1916)

2. *True-False*

AALS Rep. (Essay and objective-type examinations)
1945 Handbook 147-149, 152-167
(illustrative objective questions at pp. 153-167)

DeGraff. "Yes-No Questions"
16 Bar Exam. 7-11 (1947)

Clark, "Experiments with New Type Law Tests"
1928 J. Soc. Pub. Teach. Law 23-30

Atkinson, "The Use of True-False Examinations in Law Schools"
6 Am. L. Sch. R. 702-706 (1930)

Wigmore, "The 'New Type' Law Examination Defended"
19 Ill. L. R. 172-173 (1924)

Wood, "The 'New Type' Law Examination: A Reply to Professor Wigmore"
19 Ill. L. R. 442-444 (1925)

"Objective Law Examinations, A Correction"
19 Ill. L. R. 707 (1925)

Costigan, "Objective Law Examinations"
20 Mich. L. R. 514-526 (1922)

Kocourek, "Objective Law Examinations"
16 Ill. L. R. 304-317 (1921)

3. *Comprehensives*

AALS Rep., (The Comprehensive Examination)
1940 Handbook 162-179

Scott, "Comprehensive Examinations in the School of Law, Indiana University"
9 Am. L. Sch. R. 697-702 (1940)

Burdick, "The Comprehensive Examination at Cornell"
7 Am. L. Sch. R. 1124-1125 (1934)

Jacob, "Comprehensive Examinations in Law Schools"
7 Am. L. Sch. R. 1133-1138 (1934)

B. *Specific Courses*

1. *Constitutional Law*

Spayde, Strong, and Flesher, "The Validity of an Objective Examination in Constitutional Law"
1 J. of Legal Ed. 251-256 (1948)

(NOTE: Specimen Constitutional Law questions were distributed to all AALS schools in the spring of 1947.)

2. *Contracts*

Potthoff, "Examinations in Contract Law Courses," No. 2

U. of Ill. Studies in Higher Education (1942)

Oliphant, "A Sample of The New Type of Law Examinations"
6 Am. L. Sch. R. 490-498 (1929)

(NOTE: Specimen Contracts questions were distributed to all AALS schools in the spring of 1947.)

3. *Legal Bibliography*

Cooley, "Examination in legal bibliography"
2 Am. L. Sch. R. 509-511 (1911)

4. *Legal Ethics*

Robbins, "Examination in the Code of Ethics in Ohio"
76 Cent. L. J. 132-133 (1913)

NOTES

1. The chairman of this committee was Professor Edwin D. Dickinson, President of the Association in 1949.

2. The chairman of this committee was Professor Karl N. Llewellyn, President of the Association in 1950; and his speech on pp. 68-75 of the 1947 Handbook should be noted as a supplementary report. Also see Cavers, "'Skills' and Understanding," 1 J. of Legal Ed. 395-402 (1949).

3. 1 J. of Legal Ed. 257-267 (1949); cf. Harno, "Survey of the Legal Profession: The Legal Education Phase," 1 J. of Legal Ed. 508, 515 (1949).

4. See note 9, *infra.*

5. Law teachers do well to keep in mind that "The ghosts of defunct theories have a way of haunting the halls of other disciplines for at least a generation after they have been given decent burial in their original homes." Linton, "Psychology and Anthropology," 5 J. of Soc. Philos. 115, 116 (1940); cf. Wirtz, "Investigational Possibilities in the Area of Curriculum Construction," 9 Am. L. Sch. R. 1318, 1321 (1942).

6. "[N]ote-taking . . . is a student concern we think demands experimentation—whatever we finally conclude as to its role in the fifteen-hour classweek." Newman, "Lighthouses, Fog, and Law: A School for Teachers?," 1 J. of Legal Ed. 582, 585 (1949).

7. "I almost never cite authorities in class. I know that there are advantages in the contrary course; for one thing, it reminds the student that the cases in the book do not cover 'the law,' and that there are many distinctions not suggested by these cases. There are other ways of accomplishing this objective, however, and the discussion in class of authorities and precedents not reported in the book carries, in my opinion, a heavy price." Fuller, "Teacher's Notes to Fuller's *Basic Contract Law*" 4 (1948). This observation was of course made with respect to first-year instruction.

8. "Soundly conducted observational trips . . . would do more than months of reading to make the realities of the lawyer's task within the physical and cultural setting of America 'come alive.'" Brown, *Lawyers, Law Schools and The Public Service* 248 (1948).

9. Book reviews are not listed in this bibliography. Reviews of casebooks, however, contain some of the best discussion available on how to teach specific courses. (They can be found in the *Index to Legal Periodicals* by referring to the name of the author of the casebook.) On occasion book reviews contain very stimulating comment on how law should be taught, via the case method or otherwise. E.g., see Riesman, "Law and Social Science: A Report on Michael and Wechsler's Classbook on Criminal Law and Administration," 50 Yale L. J. 636-653 (1941).

Chapter 57

The State of the Art

A Survey of Teaching Practices in the American Law School Lecture Hall

1995

Steve Sheppard

The survey was distributed and the results collated with the kind assistance of Dana Aymond, Amy Headrick, and Kristin Keck. I am grateful to my colleagues and to Brian Gill and Mark Killenbeck for assistance in the developmental research and testing prior to this survey.

In 1995, a survey was distributed to the faculties of every accredited law school in the United States.[1] 422 law professors who teach in large lecture classes in 112 schools replied, answering 128 questions concerning themselves, their course materials, and their teaching methods in large lecture classes. This article presents an analysis of the responses, both considering answers of the group as a whole and comparing some answers among smaller groups, particularly teachers in code courses and common law courses, teachers who have published scholarly writings and those who have not, new and veteran teachers, teachers in first-year and upper-class courses, teachers in schools with selective admissions profiles and those in schools with democratic admissions profiles.[2]

The modern law school lecture consists of a mixture of tactics designed to accomplish a mixture of strategies. The tactics range from traditional methods, such as Socratic dialogues and professorial monologues, to recently popular methods such as role playing and computer simulation. The strategies seek to develop particular skills in the students, ranging from the analysis of judicial opinions to the construction of a basis for criticism of the idea of law. Despite such a variety of approaches, certain tactics and strategies remain widely accepted and overwhelmingly deployed, albeit with some variations in particular environments.

This article explores these tactics and strategies, by considering teachers' views of two distinct forms of tool used toward each end, teaching methods and teaching materials. The article presents a brief consideration of methods and teaching in sections one and two, followed by some comparisons among differing groups of teachers in section three, and a summary. An appendix describes the survey methodology and the survey questionnaire.

I. Teaching Methods

The average lecture is conducted with the professor employing a combination of monologue and dialogue to develop an understanding of the law by discussing case opinions and their contexts. Dialogue occupies the greater amount of time. Survey respondents were asked to rate the balance they employ between a monologue lecture and a dialogue with students.[3] No respondent used all monologue. 11% (46 respondents) marked "mainly monologue." 38% (160 respondents) recorded "roughly equal." 45% (190 respondents) employed "mainly dialogue." Only 3% (13 respondents) responded that their classes were "all dialogue."

The professor will typically begin a conversation with a student, who is selected from the whole class, usually without special warning of which student will have this opportunity.[4] By such means, the professor will elaborate the facts of the case and the reasoning of the opinion. The largest amounts of time devoted to a particular case are, however, spent in application of the case by analogy to hypothetical problems, and the next largest amount of time is spent in comparing it to other cases in the course. Among the facets of a case discussion surveyed, the next greater amounts of time were reportedly spent in elaborating social implications of opinions, discussing reasoning, and discussing facts. (See Table A.)

Table A - A Typical Case Discussion

Rank/ Survey Question		Most or All	More than Half	About Half	Roughly a Quarter	Little or None
1/90	Analogously applying the results of that case to hypothetical cases	%[a]10 N=42	%31 N=130	%49 N=206	%0 N=0	%0 N=2
2/89	Comparing the case to other cases discussed in the course	%2 N=7	%24 N=99	%23 N=96	%40 N=169	%6 N=25
3/91	Criticizing or elaborating on the social implications of the opinion	%2 N=10	%13 N=55	%78 N=329	%0 N=1	%0 N=0
4/88	Discussing a judge's reasoning or use of authority	%12 N=50	%1 N=5	%10 N=40	%69 N=290	%4 N=16
5/87	Discussing its facts	%0 N=0	%11 N=46	%38 N=160	%45 N=190	%3 N=13

[a] Percentages in this table are rounded to whole numbers and represent percentage of all respondents, not merely those respondents marking a given question. Thus, reported percentages for a single question may not total to 100%.

Just as there are common tactics in the consideration of a sample case, there are common strategies in using these tactics to expose students to particular considerations of the law. In a given week, respondents reported that class time is nearly equally divided among instruction in the black letter law of a course subject, instruction in its theoretical underpinnings, and in problem solving. This roughly tripartite allocation was apparently[5] seen by many of the respondents to signal a new emphasis, giving time not only to instruction in the case law and its theory but also to application of these principles to solve problems that are distinct from the cases of the casebook. This apparently recent increase in the use of problems is also suggested in responses by 61% (255 respondents) who believed they employ problems more than they were employed in their student days, and by 30% (126 respondents) who believed that they will use problems increasingly in the future. Respondents reported that they expect to see greater use of problems in the future than they reported expecting use of either discussion of the black letter law or theoretical foundations. (See Table B.)

TABLE B - A WEEKLY ALLOCATION OF TIME

Survey Question		None/ More	1-25%/ Less	25-50%/ The Same	50-75%	75-99%
92	In a week, how much time of a class is spent elaborating the "black letter law" in your field?	%6 N=27	%76 N=322	%10 N=42	%3 N=12	%0 N=0
93	Do you use this method more or less than it was used in this course when you were a student?	%35 N=148	%20 N=83	%35 N=147	%0 N=1	%0 N=0
94	Will you likely use this method more or less often in the future than you use it now?	%4 N=16	%8 N=35	%82 N=345	%0 N=1	%0 N=0
95	In a week, how much time of your class is spent solving problems illustrating the law in your field?	%7 N=28	%70 N=293	%15 N=63	%5 N=21	%1 N=5
96	Do you use this method more or less than it was used in this course when you were a student?	%61 N=255	%7 N=30	%25 N=104	%0 N=0	%0 N=0
97	Will you likely use this method more or less often in the future than you use it now?	%30 N=126	%1 N=3	%64 N=269	%0 N=0	%0 N=0
98	In a week, how much time of your class is spent considering theoretical underpinnings of your field?	%2 N=10	%80 N=337	%12 N=49	%2 N=7	%0 N=2
99	Do you use this method more or less than it was used in this course when you were a student?	%36 N=151	%16 N=67	%40 N=167	%0 N=0	%0 N=0
100	Will you likely use this method more or less often in the future than you use it now?	%16 N=67	%4 N=16	%74 N=311	%0 N=0	%0 N=0

Note: See the caution in note 5.

Of course, the most common forms of instruction are not the only forms of instruction. One distinct approach that was surveyed was the use of students as instructors for their peers, in the form of moot courts and role playing experiences in the lecture class. The bulk of respondents reported using some form of role play, including mock arguments.[6] 12% (50 respondents) reported doing so "frequently," 37% (156 respondents) "occasionally," and 24% (103 respondents) "rarely." Only 23% (94 respondents) did not use any role play or mock argument at all.

II. Teaching Materials

A. Assigning Readings in General

The overwhelming majority of lecture courses require the student to prepare for class from a casebook. Asked to describe the primary assigned text for their course, 98% selected "casebook" (412 respondents), and less than 1% selected "treatise" (2 respondents) or "problem book" (1 respondent).[7] Assignments from the casebook are, however, sometimes augmented with assignments from problem books, treatises, and materials selected by the teacher.[8]

The casebook was seen by the bulk of respondents as a reasonably effective tool for accomplishing several goals of legal pedagogy. Roughly three-quarters of the respondents who assigned a casebook considered it to be either effective or highly effective in extracting law from opinions, and nearly two-thirds believed it to be as effective in comprehending the reasoning of case opinions and in criticizing the law. However, this level of confidence in casebook effectiveness fell by half when the teacher was asked how well the casebook assists in preparing the student to represent clients, recognize law from non-judicial sources, or evaluate the role of lawyer in society. The responses to these questions from those who assigned a casebook are summarized in Table C.

Table C - Casebook Effectiveness

Rank/ Survey Question		Counter-productive	Ineffective	Neutral	Effective	Highly Effective
1/55	Extracting rules from opinions	%0 N=2	%5 N=19	%15 N=62	%61 N=256	%12 N=50
2/56	Comprehending reasoning	%0 N=1	%6 N=24	%24 N=100	%52 N=220	%9 N=39
3/63	Criticizing rules of law	%2 N=8	%10 N=40	%18 N=76	%46 N=192	%13 N=54
4/60	Reasoning by analogy	%1 N=3	%10 N=40	%26 N=108	%44 N=185	%10 N=44
5/59	Synthesizing conflicting cases	%0 N=1	%14 N=61	%32 N=135	%35 N=149	%8 N=34
6/58	Comprehensive synthesis of rules	%0 N=1	%12 N=52	%37 N=156	%35 N=149	%5 N=22
7/57	Understanding non-judicial law	%2 N=10	%24 N=100	%32 N=129	%28 N=119	%5 N=23
8/61	Preparing to represent clients	%4 N=18	%26 N=110	%30 N=127	%27 N=112	%4 N=15
9/62	Seeing the social role of lawyers	%3 N=14	%23 N=97	%31 N=131	%26 N=111	%6 N=26

The treatise, or hornbook, was the mainstay of the nineteenth-century lecture course, but it is now employed primarily as a secondary source for student preparation conducted primarily from casebooks.[9] In this guise, however, it is seen to perform a role that is complementary to certain areas of ineffectiveness in the casebook. Particularly, the treatise is believed to help students to synthesize rules of law and to coordinate a comprehensive view of the law that may be understood and criticized beyond the context of a particular case. The responses to these questions from those who assigned a casebook are summarized in Table D.

TABLE D - TREATISE EFFECTIVENESS

Rank/ Survey Question		Counter-productive	Ineffective	Neutral	Effective	Highly Effective
1/67	Comprehensive synthesis of rules	%1 N=3	%0 N=2	%4 N=18	%16 N=66	%4 N=15
2/68	Synthesizing conflicting cases	%0 N=2	%1 N=3	%6 N=26	%14 N=60	%3 N=11
3/72	Criticizing rules of law	%1 N=3	%2 N=7	%8 N=33	%12 N=49	%2 N=10
4/65	Comprehending reasoning	%1 N=4	%2 N=10	%7 N=31	%12 N=51	%3 N=11
5/64	Extracting rules from opinions	%1 N=4	%3 N=13	%6 N=25	%13 N=53	%3 N=13
6/66	Understanding non-judicial law	%1 N=3	%3 N=13	%9 N=39	%10 N=44	%2 N=8
7/71	Seeing the social role of lawyers	%1 N=6	%4 N=16	%11 N=46	%8 N=34	%1 N=5
8/69	Reasoning by analogy	%1 N=3	%4 N=16	%10 N=42	%9 N=39	%1 N=3
9/70	Preparing to represent clients	%2 N=7	%6 N=25	%10 N=43	%6 N=26	%1 N=3

Note: Percentages in this table are those of the respondents marking a particular answer as a portion of all respondents, even though a significant percentage of respondents did not mark any response to this question. Thus, the percentages do not total 100%.

It may be misleading to suggest that there is a difference between a modern casebook and a problem book, given both the idea that the cases of the casebook are meant in a significant way to serve as problems and the fact that many casebooks include a wide range of problems in them.[10] Even so, there are books designed more essentially as problem books, and these are used both as primary coursebooks and as supplemental readings.

The areas of greatest effectiveness for users of the problem book were also areas in which the casebook was seen to be effective, albeit with different emphasis. The problem book was reported to be most effective in developing skills of reasoning by analogy and client representation. (See Table E.)

TABLE E - PROBLEM BOOK EFFECTIVENESS

Rank/ Survey Question		Counter-productive	Ineffective	Neutral	Effective	Highly Effective
1/78	Reasoning by analogy	%0 N=0	%0 N=2	%1 N=6	%12 N=49	%7 N=28
2/79	Preparing to represent clients	%0 N=1	%1 N=4	%3 N=12	%13 N=54	%4 N=15
3/81	Criticizing rules of law	%0 N=0	%3 N=13	%5 N=21	%10 N=44	%3 N=12

continued on next page

TABLE E - *continued*

Rank/ Survey Question		Counter-productive	Ineffective	Neutral	Effective	Highly Effective
4/76	Comprehensive synthesis of rules	%0 N=1	%3 N=11	%5 N=20	%10 N=44	%2 N=9
5/77	Synthesizing conflicting cases	%0 N=0	%3 N=13	%7 N=29	%9 N=38	%1 N=6
6/75	Understanding non-judicial law	%0 N=1	%4 N=16	%5 N=22	%8 N=32	%3 N=14
7/80	Seeing the social role of lawyers	%1 N=3	%4 N=15	%6 N=27	%8 N=34	%2 N=9
8/73	Extracting rules from opinions	%0 N=2	%4 N=18	%6 N=26	%7 N=31	%2 N=9
9/74	Comprehending reasoning	%1 N=3	%4 N=18	%7 N=31	%7 N=30	%1 N=3

As well as the primary text, most respondents assigned some form of auxiliary reading, whether articles, anthologies, codes treatises, or histories.[11] Over three-quarters of the respondents assigned such readings, although the manner in which this material was used varied widely.[12] While half of the respondents reported discussing some of this assigned material in class,[13] less than a third reported examining students on such material.[14]

B. SPECIFIC QUALITIES DESIRED IN A PRIMARY COURSEBOOK.

The survey examined the desirability of various attributes of coursebooks, and the respondents measured the degree that forty-one attributes contributed to their decision to select one book over another.[15] A ranking[16] of these attributes according to the degree that preference would affect a decision to select a particular book is shown in Table F.

The significance of a few of these relative preferences deserves fuller mention. One of the most intriguing is the appearance of an ideal coursebook, derived from the most sought-after characteristics. The ideal casebook should logically relate the course topics together, using both classic and recent cases representative of the field, and not too many of either. The book should be short. It need not cover the entire field or dwell on minority state doctrines, but it should contain notes that both explain the major theories of the field and offer problems for student application. The book must be relatively neutral in ideological approach, but it must be sensitive to issues of gender and race. (See Table F.)

TABLE F - COURSEBOOK PREFERENCES

Rank/ Survey Question	Attribute	Prefer & Select	Prefer	Neutral	Reject	Reject & Select
1/35	Logical progression of topics covered	%66 N=277	%27 N=112	%5 N=23	%0 N=2	%0 N=0
2/1	Classic cases in the field	%57 N=240	%30 N=128	%9 N=37	%1 N=6	%1 N=6
3/2	Most recent cases in the field	%45 N=188	%34 N=142	%9 N=39	%0 N=2	%1 N=5

Table F - *continued*

Rank/ Survey Question	Attribute	Prefer & Select	Prefer	Neutral	Reject	Reject & Select
4/24	Teacher's manual or supplement with solutions to problems or questions in the student edition	%41 N=172	%34 N=143	%18 N=77	%3 N=11	%3 N=11
5/10	Notes concerning doctrine, policy, or theory with answers in the student edition	%41 N=171	%42 N=178	%10 N=41	%3 N=12	%3 N=11
6/13	More problems applying rules to hypotheses	%37 N=155	%35 N=146	%19 N=78	%5 N=21	%3 N=11
7/21	Teacher's manual or supplement availability	%35 N=149	%36 N=153	%21 N=90	%3 N=13	%2 N=9
8/25	Availability of an annual supplement with recent cases	%35 N=146	%32 N=136	%26 N=109	%3 N=13	%2 N=9
9/3	Reasoning in opinions (i.e., fewer cases but longer excerpts)	%35 N=148	%34 N=144	%14 N=60	%10 N=42	%4 N=15
10/30	Sensitivity to concerns of gender or racial diversity	%34 N=143	%35 N=149	%22 N=93	%3 N=12	%4 N=17
11/22	Teacher's manual or supplement with thorough discussion of cases	%29 N=122	%38 N=160	%26 N=109	%3 N=14	%2 N=8
12/7	Notes concerning rules of law with questions without answers in the student edition	%28 N=119	%40 N=167	%18 N=77	%8 N=33	%3 N=12
13/6	Notes explaining cases	%27 N=114	%33 N=137	%25 N=106	%9 N=39	%4 N=17
14/33	Absence of any apparent ideological direction in material selection or notes	%27 N=113	%34 N=142	%28 N=116	%4 N=16	%6 N=26
15/23	Teacher's manual or supplement with thorough discussion of doctrines of law	%22 N=91	%37 N=155	%33 N=139	%4 N=16	%3 N=12
16/37	Clear, light writing style of authors or editors employing mainly plain English	%50 N=209	%33 N=139	%13 N=55	%2 N=9	%0 N=0
17/9	Notes concerning doctrine, policy, or theory without answers in the student edition	%19 N=78	%32 N=134	%28 N=116	%16 N=66	%5 N=19
18/14	More sophisticated problems	%16 N=69	%38 N=160	%28 N=118	%10 N=44	%5 N=20
19/15	More elementary problems	%17 N=71	%27 N=115	%31 N=132	%14 N=61	%7 N=31

continued on next page

TABLE F - *continued*

Rank/ Survey Question	Attribute	Prefer & Select	Prefer	Neutral	Reject	Reject & Select
20/12	Notes describing scholarly approaches	%15 N=63	%47 N=196	%24 N=103	%8 N=32	%5 N=20
21/41	Large print and more pages	%13 N=56	%43 N=181	%32 N=135	%6 N=26	%3 N=14
22/17	Fewer pages of reading per class hour	%12 N=51	%27 N=115	%48 N=202	%7 N=28	%3 N=11
23/11	Notes describing state minority doctrines	%10 N=41	%30 N=125	%38 N=162	%15 N=63	%5 N=22
24/4	Rules of law in opinions (i.e., more cases but shorter excerpts)	%9 N=37	%30 N=124	%26 N=109	%19 N=82	%14 N=57
25/31	Apparent ideological direction in material selection or notes, favoring critical or progressive views	%6 N=24	%18 N=74	%29 N=120	%23 N=98	%23 N=98
26/34	Use of economic models and descriptions of rules or cases	%6 N=25	%30 N=126	%34 N=142	%18 N=75	%10 N=43
27/18	Fame or your respect for an author or editor	%5 N=21	%23 N=95	%60 N=252	%6 N=25	%5 N=21
28/5	Comprehensive coverage of law in the field	%5 N=22	%20 N=83	%31 N=132	%24 N=99	%18 N=76
29/8	Notes concerning rules of law with questions with answers in the student edition	%5 N=22	%20 N=83	%31 N=132	%24 N=99	%18 N=76
30/26	Pictures or graphics	%4 N=17	%22 N=94	%55 N=232	%10 N=41	%7 N=28
31/27	Amusement or entertainment value of selected cases or problems	%4 N=17	%22 N=94	%55 N=232	%10 N=41	%7 N=28
32/28	Similarity to materials you used as a student	%2 N=7	%9 N=39	%72 N=302	%8 N=34	%7 N=30
33/36	Similarity of progressions of topics covered to course you studied as a student	%2 N=10	%6 N=27	%77 N=323	%7 N=28	%6 N=25
34/19	Personal acquaintance with author or editor	%2 N=10	%16 N=69	%67 N=282	%6 N=26	%6 N=27
35/29	Lower price to students	%2 N=7	%9 N=39	%72 N=302	%8 N=34	%7 N=30
36/32	Apparent ideological direction in material selection or notes, favoring conservative or traditional views	%1 N=5	%7 N=30	%30 N=125	%32 N=133	%29 N=121

TABLE F - *continued*

Rank/ Survey Question	Attribute	Prefer & Select	Prefer	Neutral	Reject	Reject & Select
37/16	More pages of reading per class hour	%0 N=2	%6 N=24	%41 N=171	%31 N=132	%19 N=78
38/20	Fame of law school or institution that employs author or editor	%1 N=3	%0 N=2	%6 N=27	%1 N=4	%1 N=5
39/38	Traditional writing style of authors or editors employing numerous terms of art	%0 N=1	%14 N=57	%25 N=105	%38 N=162	%21 N=87
40/39	Use of double column text layouts	%1 N=3	%3 N=14	%39 N=164	%27 N=113	%28 N=118
41/40	Tiny print and fewer pages	%0 N=1	%1 N=3	%13 N=55	%34 N=144	%50 N=209

One of the more revealing aspects in this ideal book is that it omits lower cost. For the respondents, the cost of the book to the student appears to be no object. Whether this is because of approximate equivalence in price, a view that the price of the course's book is bound to be dwarfed by the costs of the course's tuition, or because professors do not buy books, the fact remains that price is much less a consideration in book selection than is the availability of a teacher's manual.

Beyond these general preferences, certain comparisons between particular attributes are more informative. Outstanding among these comparisons is the nearly uniform view that the book need not cover the field of law studied in the course.[17] The book is neither expected to present every detail of the field nor present minority jurisdiction doctrines.[18]

In general, respondents also sought an exposure of the students to hypothetical problems without disclosed answers, although these answers were sought in the teacher's manuals.[19] This preference was greater than for the students to be given problems with the answers supplied prior to class, except for problems based on legal theory.[20]

There was considerable agreement on material layout. Most respondents preferred fewer pages of reading per class hour,[21] although an increase in pages to allow for a larger typeface seemed acceptable.[22] Clear writing, excising unneeded terms of art, and an absence of double-column print were also desired.[23]

One factor strongly rejected as a basis for casebook selection was acquaintance with the author or editor of the casebook.[24] Even so, this rejection must be seen in the ironic light of many of the respondents' claims to know at least one editor or author of the materials they assign. When asked whether the respondent was personally acquainted with the author or editor of the book assigned,[25] 88% stated that they were.[26]

III. COMPARISONS AMONG GROUPS

It is possible to discern a variety of choices by distinct groups of teachers, whose preferences vary, at times, quite widely. The two most apparent divisions in views of course materials are between those who teach code courses as opposed to those who teach common law courses and between those who have published in their field and those who have not.

A. The Effect of Teaching Courses Based on Statutes or the Common Law

Comparing those responses from teachers of courses mainly from the common law, such as property and torts, to those mainly from statutes or cases, such as evidence and civil procedure, there is a slightly greater preference for casebooks in common law courses.[27] In common law courses, casebooks were selected by 93%of respondents, and in code courses 79%.[28]Respondents teaching code courses selected a treatise in 4% of responses and a problem book in 13%.

Respondents teaching common law courses are more likely than their code-teaching colleagues to select books that include classic cases,[29] longer excerpts that display more of the case's reasoning,[30] and fewer cases.[31] Teachers of code courses were more likely to select books based on comprehensive coverage of the law in their subject[32] and that included shorter excerpts of more cases,[33] more problems, pictures or graphics,[34] and a teacher's manual.[35] (See Table G.)

On the other hand, respondents teaching courses based on codes and the common law reported similarity regarding the role that policy arguments should play in the coursebook, with code course teachers only slightly more likely to select a book containing notes based on doctrine, policy, or theory. (See Table H.)

There is a slight, if unpronounced, difference between the perceptions of teachers in code and common law courses of the effectiveness of coursebooks. Common law teachers are somewhat more likely to see their coursebook as effective in encouraging students to apply law to new facts by analogy,[36] to develop skills to criticize the law,[37] and to synthesize law across conflicting cases.[38] Code teachers are more likely to see their coursebook to be effective in understanding law from non-judicial sources.[39] (See Table I.)

There are corresponding differences in the course methods employed by common law and code course teachers. Common law teachers report using more time in elaborating the black letter law and solving problems in class, while code teachers reported spending a slightly higher percentage of time each week considering theoretical underpinnings.[40] In considering a single case, there was a pattern of slightly greater emphasis by code teachers on particular components of case analysis than the more evenly weighted approach of common law teachers.[41] Common law teachers were less likely than code teachers to report that any component of case discussion—discussing facts, reasoning, case comparison or synthesis, and social criticism—occupied more than half of the discussion of a typical case. In contrast, code course teachers reported more specific emphases in considering a given case, with proportionally more respondents reporting that over half of the case discussion is spent in case comparison or synthesis. (See Table J.)

B. The Effect of Publication

Those who write in their fields are significantly more likely than teachers who do not[42] to believe that their coursebooks are effective in assisting students to accomplish course goals.[43] In measuring every one of the nine attributes of coursebook effectiveness, those who wrote articles were more likely than those who did not write to believe that the coursebooks were highly effective or effective. (See Table K.)

That scholars find the coursebooks to be more effective is not, however, based on significantly different tactics in employing them. Indeed, there is a striking similarity in the allocations of time in case discussion and emphasis on different components of course pedagogy between scholars and non-scholars. (See Table L.)

C. The Effect of Experience or Novelty in Law Teaching

Teachers who have taught longer are more likely than their less experienced colleagues[44] to see their coursebooks as effective in reaching pedagogical goals. This difference is not as pronounced, however, as is the difference between those who have written and those who have not. Particularly, veteran teachers reported a slightly higher view of coursebooks as effective or highly effective in student reasoning comprehension, case synthesis, professional preparation, and social and legal criticism. (See Table M.)

Veteran and new teachers reported a high degree of similarity in their approaches to strategic choices over a week of instruction,[45] but veteran teachers were somewhat likely to spend more time in discussing the facts of a single case than in considering the social implications of the case, when compared to more recently hired teachers.[46] (See Table N.)

D. The Effect of Teaching in the First Year or Upper Years

There is a considerable degree of agreement between teachers reporting views of coursebook effectiveness in first-year and upper-class courses.[47] The areas of difference suggest that first-year course teachers see the coursebook as more effective than their upper-class counterparts in encouraging students to extract rules from opinions but slightly less effective in understanding law from non-judicial sources and preparing students to represent clients.[48] Otherwise, there was, general agreement between the two groups regarding coursebook effectiveness or ineffectiveness. (See Table O.)

Unsurprisingly, there was a greater divergence in tactics and strategy between teachers in first-year and upper-class courses. Particularly, upper-class course teachers were more likely to emphasize particular attributes of a case discussion, while first year teachers reported spending time in a more balanced division of time in each component of a case discussion.[49] Teachers in the second and third years were, however, significantly more likely to spend greater amounts of time per case both in discussing a judge's reasoning and in comparison to other cases.[50] By contrast, first-year course teachers reported dedicating a somewhat larger portion of each week's lecture than their upper-year colleagues to teaching the black letter law and to problem solving.[51]

E. The Effect of Selective or Democratic Student Admissions

There is a very high degree of similarity between the views of respondents in law schools with competitive admissions from those with liberal admissions standards.[52] With the exception of a slightly higher report by selective school teachers of belief that the coursebooks assist the student to understand the role of the lawyer in society,[53] the responses of both groups showed considerable similarity of distribution to all other questions. (See Table Q.)

There is slightly less similarity in classroom technique between selective and democratic schools. The greatest differences are apparently only slight differences of emphasis. Particularly, teachers in selective schools report spending more time on each case in comparing it to other cases in the course, while teachers in democratic schools report spending more time on each case applying it to hypothetical problems.[54]

Interestingly, the question considering the allocation of time in a week to three aspects of the course in which respondents from select and democratic schools reported the highest similarity is in allocating class time to consider theoretical underpinnings of the field. There are nearly identical distributions by each group in answer to this question.[55]

F. Ideological Differences Among Teacher Groups

The survey incorporated several questions concerning the respondents' preference for ideological bias in the course materials. Specifically, respondents were asked if they would prefer or reject a book with progressive or conservative views, as well as with evident sensitivity to matters of gender or racial diversity.[56] A comparison of these responses among selected teacher groups isolated above—teachers of the code and common law, new and veteran teachers, teachers of first-year and upper-class courses, and teachers in schools with selective and democratic admissions profiles—demonstrates only a few groups within which there is significant ideological disparity.

There was a high degree of similarity in the comparisons of first-year and upper-class teachers, who demonstrated very nearly the same proportions of respondents who preferred and who rejected an apparent ideological biases.[57] Similarly, there was very little difference in the ideological bias reported by teachers in schools with selective admissions profiles from that reported by teachers in schools with democratic admissions policies.[58] Teachers of code courses sought a slightly more progressive ideological slant to the coursebook itself but were similar to common law teachers in the ratios by which they preferred or would select books with sensitivity to concerns of gender or racial diversity.[59]

The greatest degree of ideological difference among the groups studied is between recently hired and veteran teachers. While there was a similarity between newer and veteran teachers in the rejecting books favoring conservative or traditional ideological views, recently hired faculty members were significantly more likely to prefer a coursebook with a critical or progressive slant.[60]

A comparison of preferences for and against sensitivity to concerns for gender or racial diversity in the text follows a similar pattern. Most groups are consistent in expressing a preference for materials sensitive to issues of gender or racial diversity at a ratio of about two and a half times greater preference than neutrality or rejection. This pattern is roughly true for the preferences of first-year and upper-year course teachers,[61] teachers in selective and democratic schools,[62] and teachers of code and common law courses.[63] Recently hired teachers, on the other hand, expressed a preference for materials demonstrating sensitivity toward racial and gender diversity at a ratio over twice as high as that expressed by veteran teachers.[64]

G. The Use of Materials Employing Recent Technology

One area of course instruction that was heavily surveyed is the manner and degree the professor uses technology, particularly computers, as a tool for instruction. Computer use as a part of instruction was rare, although there are signs it may increase.[65] A quarter of the 1995 survey respondents use computer-assisted legal instruction, or "CALI," 4% (18) requiring, and 21% (88) recommending it. On the other hand, 64% (268) do not suggest its use, and an honest 7% (30) admitted to having no idea what CALI is. Very few respondents use interactive computer programs in class,[66] 6% (24) who do versus 88% (371) who do not. On the other hand, when asked if one might use them if the availability were known, 4% (17) replied "certainly"; and 30% (123) replied "yes, if the content is pedagogically sound." 26% (110) would use them "only as supplements to lectures." 20% (86) replied probably not, and 6% (27) replied flatly "no."

There is no reason to assume that the current scarcity of computer use is based upon a bias against all forms of technological delivery of instruction, particularly as a larger portion of teachers use audiovisual technology. Nearly a third of the respondents use films in conjunction with their lectures, most of them using them during the lecture.[67] 27% (113) use films during class. a small number provide films out of class, either as required viewing, 3% (13), or as an option, 5% (21). Even so, 60% (255) reported using no audiovisual materials.

III. Some Conclusions

The results of this survey are unlikely to surprise the modern law professor, or for that matter, the modern law student. The very nature of this form of survey is to reveal common patterns of activities, or at least common opinions regarding those patterns.

If there is a particular point that might be made from the data as a whole, it is the strong degree of homogeneity shown. By far, analysis of various groups' responses to some touchstone issues suggested agreement rather than division.[68] Even so, the factors that seem to suggest the greatest variation in a teacher's preferences or views of effectiveness are the number of years of teaching and degree of publication.

Appendix: The Survey

The survey was distributed through the deans of the ABA-accredited schools. Of 5,052 full-time law professors then reported as teaching in those schools, as of August 31, 1995, there were 513 responses, of which 422 related to traditional lecture hall courses.[69] Accounting for multiple responses by a single professor for multiple courses, the survey reflects an estimated response rate of 7% of the national professorate. The text of the appendix can be found at the end of this chapter's "Notes" section, following note 69.

TABLE G - A COMPARISON BETWEEN VIEWS OF COURSEBOOK ATTRIBUTES: CODE AND COMMON LAW

Survey Question		Code Prefer & Select	Code Prefer	Code Neutral	Code Reject	Code Reject & Select	C-L Prefer & Select	C-L Prefer	C-L Neutral	C-L Reject	C-L Reject & Select
1	Classic cases in the field	%41 N=31	%36 N=27	%18 N=14	%1 N=1	%4 N=3	%64 N=153	%29 N=70	%5 N=11	%1 N=3	%1 N=2
2	Most recent cases in the field	%37 N=49	%29 N=38	%5 N=7	%2 N=3	%2 N=3	%50 N=120	%40 N=95	%9 N=21	%0 N=0	%1 N=3
3	Reasoning in opinions (i.e., fewer cases but longer excerpts)	%17 N=13	%37 N=28	%26 N=20	%16 N=12	%3 N=2	%44 N=106	%35 N=84	%8 N=18	%8 N=20	%3 N=8
4	Rules of law in opinions (i.e., more cases but shorter excerpts)	%13 N=10	%30 N=23	%33 N=25	%13 N=10	%9 N=7	%8 N=19	%30 N=72	%22 N=52	%23 N=56	%15 N=37
5	Comprehensive coverage of law in the field	%51 N=39	%20 N=15	%13 N=10	%9 N=7	%7 N=5	%37 N=89	%38 N=92	%17 N=41	%5 N=13	%1 N=3
7	Notes concerning rules of law with questions without answers in the student edition	%3 N=21	%36 N=27	%41 N=31	%13 N=10	%7 N=5	%28 N=68	%44 N=104	%17 N=40	%8 N=20	%2 N=4
8	Notes concerning rules of law with questions with answers in the student edition	%11 N=8	%22 N=17	%32 N=24	%17 N=13	%17 N=13	%5 N=11	%19 N=45	%35 N=84	%24 N=57	%16 N=39
13	More problems applying rules to hypotheses	%55 N=42	%26 N=20	%12 N=9	%1 N=1	%3 N=2	%30 N=72	%40 N=96	%22 N=52	%6 N=15	%1 N=2
18	Fame or your respect for an author or editor	%0 N=0	%21 N=16	%66 N=50	%7 N=5	%5 N=4	%8 N=18	%26 N=61	%56 N=133	%6 N=14	%5 N=12
21	Teacher's manual or supplement availability	%53 N=40	%26 N=20	%16 N=12	%1 N=1	%3 N=2	%33 N=79	%36 N=87	%26 N=63	%2 N=5	%2 N=4
26	Pictures or graphics	%30 N=23	%51 N=39	%11 N=8	%7 N=5	%4 N=3	%3 N=7	%23 N=54	%56 N=135	%11 N=26	%6 N=14

Note: Percentages in this table reflect the percentage of respondents marking an answer as a portion of respondents marking that answer in the relevant pool, rounded to the nearest whole number.

TABLE H - A SELECTED COMPARISON BETWEEN VIEWS OF COURSEBOOK ATTRIBUTES: CODE AND COMMON LAW

Survey Question		Code Prefer & Select	Code Prefer	Code Neutral	Code Reject	Code Reject & Select	C-L Prefer & Select	C-L Prefer	C-L Neutral	C-L Reject	C-L Reject & Select
9	Notes concerning doctrine, policy, or theory without answers in the student edition	%25 N=19	%33 N=25	%20 N=15	%16 N=12	%5 N=4	%18 N=44	%32 N=77	%29 N=69	%17 N=40	%3 N=7
10	Notes concerning doctrine, policy, or theory with answers in the student edition	%46 N=35	%38 N=29	%8 N=6	%4 N=3	%3 N=2	%41 N=97	%45 N=108	%10 N=23	%3 N=6	%2 N=4

Note: Percentages in this table reflect the percentage of respondents marking an answer as a portion of respondents marking that answer in the relevent pool, rounded to the nearest whole number.

Table I - A Selected Comparison Between Views of Coursebook Effectiveness: Code and Common Law

Survey Question		Code Counter-productive	Code Ineffective	Code Neutral	Code Effective	Code Highly Effective	C-L Counter-productive	C-L Ineffective	C-L Neutral	C-L Effective	C-L Highly Effective
55	Extracting rules of law from opinions	%0 N=0	%7 N=5	%20 N=15	%54 N=41	%3 N=2	%0 N=1	%5 N=11	%13 N=31	%67 N=159	%13 N=32
56	Fully comprehend-ing the reasoning and statements written in opinions	%0 N=0	%4 N=3	%22 N=17	%53 N=40	%3 N=2	%0 N=1	%5 N=12	%23 N=54	%58 N=139	%11 N=26
57	Understanding law from non-judicial sources	%1 N=1	%21 N=16	%17 N=13	%33 N=25	%9 N=7	%3 N=7	%28 N=67	%36 N=85	%28 N=66	%3 N=8
58	Developing a comprehensive synthesis of the rules of law	%0 N=0	%18 N=14	%28 N=21	%32 N=24	%4 N=3	%0 N=0	%11 N=26	%43 N=102	%37 N=88	%7 N=16
59	Developing a synthesis of law across conflicting cases	%1 N=1	%20 N=15	%28 N=21	%29 N=22	%3 N=2	%0 N=0	%13 N=32	%35 N=83	%39 N=93	%10 N=25
60	Developing skills for the application by analogy of law to new problems	%1 N=1	%9 N=7	%28 N=21	%32 N=24	%12 N=9	%0 N=1	%10 N=24	%24 N=57	%51 N=121	%12 N=29
61	Generally preparing the student to represent clients	%7 N=5	%22 N=17	%26 N=20	%21 N=16	%5 N=4	%3 N=8	%31 N=73	%29 N=69	%31 N=74	%4 N=9
62	Understanding the role of the law, or of lawyers, in a social system	%3 N=2	%26 N=20	%26 N=20	%24 N=18	%3 N=2	%3 N=8	%25 N=59	%32 N=77	%29 N=70	%7 N=17
63	Developing skills to criticize law or the rules of law	%3 N=2	%9 N=7	%26 N=20	%32 N=24	%8 N=6	%2 N=5	%10 N=23	%17 N=40	%51 N=121	%16 N=39

Note: Percentages in this table reflect the percentage of respondents marking an answer as a portion of respondents marking that answer in the relevent pool, rounded to the nearest whole number.

TABLE J - A SELECTED COMPARISON BETWEEN TEACHING METHODS: CODE AND COMMON LAW

Survey Question	Time Spent per Case:	Code Most	Code Over 1/2	Code About 1/2	Code About 1/4	Code Little or None	C-L Most	C-L Over 1/2	C-L About 1/2	C-L About 1/4	C-L Little or None
87	Discussing its facts?	%0 N=0	%16 N=12	%49 N=37	%30 N=23	%1 N=1	%0 N=0	%9 N=22	%37 N=88	%50 N=120	%3 N=8
88	Discussing a judge's reasoning or use of authority?	%12 N=9	%3 N=2	%14 N=11	%62 N=47	%4 N=3	%11 N=27	%1 N=2	%8 N=19	%73 N=175	%4 N=10
89	Comparing the case to other cases discussed in the course?	%0 N=0	%64 N=49	%13 N=10	%17 N=13	%0 N=0	%0 N=1	%9 N=22	%26 N=62	%53 N=126	%8 N=18
90	Analogously applying the results of that case to hypothetical cases	%9 N=7	%55 N=42	%26 N=20	%0 N=0	%0 N=0	%10 N=25	%24 N=57	%59 N=140	%0 N=0	%0 N=1
91	Criticizing or elaborating on the social implications of the opinion?	%1 N=1	%20 N=15	%74 N=56	%0 N=0	%0 N=0	%2 N=5	%11 N=26	%82 N=196	%0 N=1	%0 N=0
92	In a week, how much time of a class is spent elaborating the "black letter law" in your field?	%1 N=1	%64 N=49	%22 N=17	%7 N=5	%0 N=0	%7 N=16	%82 N=195	%8 N=20	%2 N=4	%0 N=0
95	In a week, how much time of your class is spent solving problems illustrating the law in your field?	%3 N=2	%45 N=34	%34 N=26	%13 N=10	%1 N=1	%6 N=15	%80 N=191	%8 N=20	%3 N=7	%0 N=1
98	In a week, how much time of your class is spent considering theoretical underpinnings of your field?	%1 N=1	%89 N=68	%5 N=4	%0 N=0	%0 N=0	%3 N=6	%80 N=192	%14 N=33	%2 N=4	%0 N=0

[a] See the caution in note 5 concerning the reliability of these figures. They are included here solely for the potential for comparison between pools, in the assumption that respondents in each pool responded to the same questions similarly.

Table K - A Selected Comparison Between Views of Coursebook Effectiveness: Scholars and Teachers

Survey Question		S Counter-productive	S Ineffective	S Neutral	S Effective	S Highly Effective	Teacher Counter-productive	Teacher Ineffective	Teacher Neutral	Teacher Effective	Teacher Highly Effective
55	Extracting rules of law from opinions	%1 N=1	%3 N=5	%12 N=19	%62 N=99	%16 N=25	%0 N=0	%8 N=8	%12 N=12	%67 N=69	%8 N=8
56	Fully comprehending the reasoning and statements written in opinions	%1 N=1	%3 N=5	%12 N=19	%62 N=99	%16 N=25	%0 N=0	%8 N=8	%12 N=12	%67 N=69	%8 N=8
57	Understanding law from non-judicial sources	%3 N=5	%21 N=34	%31 N=50	%31 N=50	%7 N=11	%4 N=4	%36 N=37	%24 N=25	%26 N=27	%3 N=3
58	Developing a comprehensive synthesis of the rules of law	%0 N=0	%9 N=14	%43 N=68	%34 N=54	%8 N=12	%0 N=0	%17 N=18	%38 N=39	%36 N=37	%2 N=2
59	Developing a synthesis of law across conflicting cases	%0 N=0	%9 N=14	%35 N=56	%36 N=58	%13 N=20	%1 N=1	%17 N=17	%39 N=40	%32 N=33	%5 N=5
60	Developing skills for the application by analogy of law to new problems	%1 N=1	%8 N=12	%25 N=40	%46 N=73	%14 N=22	%1 N=1	%13 N=13	%34 N=35	%40 N=41	%6 N=6
61	Generally preparing the student to represent clients	%2 N=3	%23 N=37	%25 N=40	%38 N=61	%6 N=9	%8 N=8	%38 N=39	%26 N=27	%18 N=19	%3 N=3
62	Understanding the role of the law, or of lawyers, in a social system	%2 N=3	%19 N=30	%34 N=54	%27 N=43	%11 N=18	%6 N=6	%30 N=31	%33 N=34	%23 N=24	%1 N=1
63	Developing skills to criticize law or the rules of law	%2 N=3	%6 N=10	%17 N=27	%47 N=74	%20 N=31	%3 N=3	%17 N=18	%22 N=23	%38 N=39	%10 N=10

TABLE L - A SELECTED COMPARISON BETWEEN TEACHING METHODS: SCHOLARS AND TEACHERS

Survey Question		Scholar Most	Scholar Over 1/2	Scholar About 1/2	Scholar About 1/4	Scholar Little/ None	Teacher Most	Teacher Over 1/2	Teacher About 1/2	Teacher About 1/4	Teacher Little/ None
87	Discussing its facts?	%0 N=0	%17 N=27	%35 N=55	%44 N=70	%3 N=5	%0 N=0	%7 N=7	%38 N=39	%52 N=54	%2 N=2
88	Discussing a judge's reasoning or use of authority?	%16 N=25	%0 N=0	%8 N=13	%70 N=112	%3 N=4	%12 N=12	%4 N=4	%13 N=13	%66 N=68	%4 N=4
89	Comparing the case to other cases discussed in the course?	%1 N=1	%19 N=30	%27 N=43	%41 N=65	%9 N=14	%0 N=0	%23 N=24	%20 N=21	%47 N=48	%4 N=4
90	Analogously applying the results of that case to hypothetical cases	%11 N=17	%30 N=48	%51 N=81	%0 N=0	%1 N=1	%15 N=15	%29 N=30	%47 N=48	%0 N=0	%1 N=1
91	Criticizing or elaborating on the social implications of the opinion?	%1 N=2	%2 N=3	%8 N=12	%11 N=18	%5 N=8	%1 N=1	%21 N=22	%73 N=75	%1 N=1	%0 N=0
92	In a week, how much time of a class is spent elaborating the "black letter law" in your field?	%3 N=4	%80 N=127	%12 N=19	%3 N=5	%0 N=0	%6 N=6	%72 N=74	%18 N=19	%0 N=0	%0 N=0
95	In a week, how much time of your class is spent solving problems illustrating the law in your field?	%5 N=8	%72 N=115	%16 N=26	%4 N=7	%0 N=0	%7 N=7	%72 N=74	%12 N=12	%7 N=7	%2 N=2
98	In a week, how much time of your class is spent considering theoretical underpinnings of your field?	%3 N=5	%82 N=130	%14 N=22	%1 N=1	%0 N=0	%2 N=2	%84 N=86	%10 N=10	%1 N=1	%1 N=1

[a] See the caution in note 5 concerning the reliability of these figures. They are included here solely for the potential for comparison between pools, in the assumption that respondents in each pool responded to the same question similarly.

TABLE M - A SELECTED COMPARISON BETWEEN VIEWS OF COURSEBOOK EFFECTIVENESS: NEW AND VETERAN TEACHERS

Survey Question		New Counter-productive	New Ineffective	New Neutral	New Effective	New Highly Effective	Veteran Counter-productive	Veteran Ineffective	Veteran Neutral	Veteran Effective	Veteran Highly Effective
55	Extracting rules of law from opinions	%0 N=0	%5 N=9	%17 N=28	%62 N=102	%7 N=12	%0 N=1	%3 N=7	%12 N=25	%61 N=127	%15 N=32
56	Fully comprehending the reasoning and statements written in opinions	%0 N=0	%9 N=15	%24 N=40	%52 N=86	%5 N=8	%0 N=1	%3 N=6	%21 N=43	%55 N=114	%13 N=27
57	Understanding law from non-judicial sources	%2 N=4	%27 N=44	%29 N=48	%27 N=45	%4 N=7	%3 N=6	%23 N=48	%32 N=66	%30 N=63	%5 N=10
58	Developing a comprehensive synthesis of the rules of law	%1 N=1	%13 N=22	%36 N=59	%37 N=60	%4 N=6	%0 N=0	%13 N=26	%39 N=81	%33 N=69	%7 N=15
59	Developing a synthesis of law across conflicting cases	%1 N=1	%18 N=29	%33 N=54	%34 N=55	%5 N=9	%0 N=0	%13 N=26	%33 N=69	%35 N=73	%11 N=23
60	Developing skills for the application by analogy of law to new problems	%1 N=1	%11 N=18	%27 N=45	%43 N=70	%9 N=14	%0 N=1	%8 N=17	%23 N=48	%47 N=97	%13 N=28
61	Generally preparing the student to represent clients	%7 N=11	%31 N=51	%28 N=46	%22 N=36	%2 N=4	%2 N=5	%23 N=48	%30 N=62	%32 N=67	%5 N=11
62	Understanding the role of the law, or of lawyers, in a social system	%4 N=7	%27 N=44	%32 N=52	%24 N=40	%2 N=4	%2 N=5	%20 N=41	%32 N=66	%29 N=60	%9 N=19
63	Developing skills to criticize law or the rules of law	%3 N=5	%11 N=18	%24 N=39	%39 N=64	%11 N=18	%1 N=2	%8 N=17	%14 N=30	%50 N=105	%16 N=33

Note: Percentages in this table reflect the percentage of respondents marking an answer as a portion of respondents marking that answer in the relevent pool, rounded to the nearest whole number.

Table N - A Selected Comparison Between Teaching Methods: New and Veteran Teachers

Survey Question	Time Spent per Case	New Most	New Over 1/2	New About 1/2	New About 1/4	New Little or None	Veteran Most	Veteran Over 1/2	Veteran About 1/2	Veteran About 1/4	Veteran Little or None
87	Discussing its facts?	%0 N=0	%5 N=9	%40 N=66	%51 N=84	%2 N=3	%0 N=0	%15 N=31	%38 N=78	%40 N=84	%4 N=8
88	Discussing a judge's reasoning or use of authority?	%12 N=20	%2 N=4	%14 N=23	%64 N=105	%5 N=8	%12 N=24	%0 N=1	%7 N=14	%74 N=153	%3 N=6
89	Comparing the case to other cases discussed in the course?	%1 N=1	%26 N=43	%24 N=39	%40 N=66	%2 N=4	%1 N=3	%22 N=45	%22 N=45	%44 N=92	%8 N=16
90	Analogously applying the results of that case to hypothetical cases	%10 N=16	%29 N=48	%52 N=86	%0 N=0	%1 N=1	%12 N=24	%32 N=66	%48 N=99	%0 N=0	%0 N=1
91	Criticizing or elaborating on the social implications of the opinion?	%3 N=5	%20 N=33	%71 N=116	%1 N=1	%0 N=0	%2 N=4	%9 N=18	%84 N=175	%0 N=0	%0 N=0
92	In a week, how much time of a class is spent elaborating the "black letter law" in your field?	%4 N=6	%79 N=130	%11 N=18	%2 N=3	%0 N=0	%6 N=13	%75 N=156	%12 N=24	%3 N=7	%0 N=0
95	In a week, how much time of your class is spent solving problems illustrating the law in your field?	%6 N=10	%69 N=113	%15 N=25	%7 N=12	%0 N=0	%5 N=10	%73 N=151	%14 N=30	%3 N=7	%1 N=3
98	In a week, how much time of your class is spent considering theoretical underpinnings of your field?	%1 N=2	%83 N=136	%13 N=21	%0 N=0	%0 N=0	%3 N=7	%81 N=168	%11 N=23	%2 N=4	%0 N=1

[a] See the caution in note 8 concerning the reliability of these figures. They are included here solely for the potential for comparison between pools, in the assumption that respondents in each pool responded to the same questions similarly.

Table O - A Selected Comparison Between Views of Coursebook Effectiveness: First Year and Upper Years

Survey Question		1L Counter-productive	1L Ineffective	1L Neutral	1L Effective	1L Highly Effective	2&3 Counter-productive	2&3 Ineffective	2&3 Neutral	2&3 Effective	2&3 Highly Effective
55	Extracting rules of law from opinions	%0 N=0	%6 N=12	%11 N=21	%70 N=130	%11 N=20	%1 N=1	%2 N=4	%16 N=28	%57 N=101	%13 N=22
56	Fully comprehending the reasoning and statements written in opinions	%1 N=1	%8 N=15	%25 N=46	%57 N=106	%7 N=13	%0 N=0	%3 N=6	%20 N=35	%52 N=92	%12 N=21
57	Understanding law from non-judicial sources	%4 N=7	%34 N=64	%29 N=55	%26 N=49	%4 N=7	%2 N=3	%18 N=31	%31 N=55	%31 N=55	%6 N=11
58	Developing a comprehensive synthesis of the rules of law	%0 N=0	%13 N=25	%45 N=84	%34 N=64	%4 N=8	%0 N=0	%13 N=23	%33 N=58	%35 N=62	%6 N=11
59	Developing a synthesis of law across conflicting cases	%0 N=0	%17 N=31	%36 N=68	%36 N=67	%8 N=15	%1 N=1	%13 N=22	%33 N=58	%33 N=58	%9 N=15
60	Developing skills for the application by analogy of law to new problems	%1 N=2	%12 N=23	%25 N=47	%49 N=92	%9 N=16	%0 N=0	%9 N=15	%26 N=45	%41 N=73	%13 N=22
61	Generally preparing the student to represent clients	%5 N=9	%35 N=65	%28 N=53	%25 N=46	%5 N=9	%3 N=6	%22 N=38	%31 N=55	%29 N=51	%3 N=5
62	Understanding the role of the law, or of lawyers, in a social system	%4 N=7	%29 N=54	%28 N=52	%29 N=55	%6 N=11	%3 N=5	%20 N=35	%37 N=65	%23 N=41	%5 N=9
63	Developing skills to criticize law or the rules of law	%2 N=3	%13 N=24	%19 N=36	%46 N=86	%16 N=29	%2 N=4	%7 N=12	%20 N=36	%46 N=81	%10 N=17

TABLE P - A SELECTED COMPARISON BETWEEN TEACHING METHODS: FIRST YEAR AND UPPER YEARS

Survey Question	Time Spent per Case	1L Most	1L Over 1/2	1L About 1/2	1L About 1/4	1L Little or None	2&3 Most	2&3 Over 1/2	2&3 About 1/2	2&3 About 1/4	2&3 Little or None
87	Discussing its facts?	%0 N=0	%6 N=11	%33 N=61	%59 N=111	%2 N=3	%0 N=0	%12 N=15	%47 N=60	%30 N=39	%6 N=8
88	Discussing a judge's reasoning or use of authority?	%7 N=14	%1 N=2	%9 N=17	%76 N=143	%4 N=8	%18 N=31	%2 N=3	%10 N=18	%65 N=114	%2 N=4
89	Comparing the case to other cases in discussed in the course?	%1 N=1	%9 N=17	%21 N=40	%55 N=102	%8 N=15	%0 N=0	%40 N=70	%24 N=43	%28 N=50	%3 N=5
90	Analogously applying the results of that case to hypothetical cases	%10 N=19	%25 N=46	%58 N=108	%0 N=0	%1 N=2	%13 N=22	%38 N=66	%42 N=74	%0 N=0	%0 N=0
91	Criticizing or elaborating on the social implications of the opinion?	%2 N=4	%13 N=24	%81 N=152	%1 N=1	%0 N=0	%3 N=5	%15 N=26	%78 N=138	%0 N=0	%0 N=0
92	In a week, how much time of a class is spent elaborating the "black letter law" in your field?	%6 N=12	%82 N=154	%7 N=14	%2 N=3	%0 N=0	%4 N=7	%74 N=130	%16 N=28	%4 N=7	%0 N=0
95	In a week, how much time of your class is spent solving problems illustrating the law in your field?	%7 N=13	%79 N=148	%9 N=16	%3 N=6	%1 N=1	%4 N=7	%65 N=115	%21 N=37	%7 N=13	%1 N=2
98	In a week, how much time of your class is spent considering theoretical underpinnings of your field?	%2 N=3	%84 N=158	%12 N=22	%2 N=3	%0 N=0	%3 N=6	%81 N=143	%13 N=22	%1 N=1	%1 N=1

[a] See the caution in note 5 concerning the reliability of these figures. They are included here solely for the potential for comparison between pools, in the assumption that respondents in each pool responded to the same questions similarly.

Table Q - A Selected Comparison Between Views of Coursebook Effectiveness: Teachers in Schools with Selective and Democratic Admissions

Survey Question		Select Counter-productive	Select Ineffective	Select Neutral	Select Effective	Select Highly Effective	Demo Counter-productive	Demo Ineffective	Demo Neutral	Demo Effective	Demo Highly Effective
55	Extracting rules of law from opinions	%0 N=0	%6 N=7	%9 N=11	%65 N=76	%15 N=18	%1 N=1	%3 N=3	%11 N=10	%67 N=64	%9 N=9
56	Fully comprehending the reasoning and statements written in opinions	%0 N=0	%3 N=3	%21 N=25	%58 N=68	%12 N=14	%0 N=0	%8 N=6	%25 N=24	%47 N=45	%9 N=9
57	Understanding law from non-judicial sources	%2 N=2	%26 N=31	%34 N=40	%27 N=32	%6 N=7	%2 N=2	%25 N=24	%29 N=28	%29 N=28	%3 N=3
58	Developing a comprehensive synthesis of the rules of law	%0 N=0	%9 N=10	%49 N=57	%30 N=35	%8 N=9	%0 N=0	%12 N=12	%34 N=32	%37 N=35	%6 N=6
59	Developing a synthesis of law across conflicting cases	%0 N=0	%12 N=14	%35 N=41	%38 N=44	%10 N=12	%0 N=0	%16 N=16	%23 N=23	%25 N=24	%6 N=6
60	Developing skills for the application by analogy of law to new problems	%0 N=0	%6 N=10	%24 N=28	%48 N=56	%15 N=17	%0 N=0	%12 N=12	%23 N=22	%44 N=42	%8 N=8
61	Generally preparing the student to represent clients	%3 N=4	%26 N=30	%33 N=39	%29 N=34	%4 N=5	%6 N=6	%29 N=28	%23 N=22	%25 N=25	%4 N=4
62	Understanding the role of the law, or of lawyers, in a social system	%3 N=3	%28 N=33	%27 N=32	%26 N=31	%10 N=12	%3 N=3	%19 N=18	%33 N=31	%29 N=28	%4 N=4
63	Developing skills to criticize law or the rules of law	%2 N=2	%8 N=9	%15 N=18	%53 N=62	%16 N=19	%3 N=3	%6 N=6	%23 N=22	%42 N=40	%12 N=12

TABLE R - A SELECTED COMPARISON BETWEEN TEACHING METHODS: TEACHERS IN SCHOOLS WITH SELECTIVE AND DEMOCRATIC ADMISSIONS

Survey Question	Time Spent per Case	Select Most	Select Over 1/2	Select About 1/2	Select About 1/4	Select Little or None	Demo Most	Demo Over 1/2	Demo About 1/2	Demo About 1/4	Demo Little or None
87	Discussing its facts?	%0 N=0	%13 N=15	%38 N=45	%46 N=54	%1 N=1	%0 N=0	%9 N=9	%33 N=31	%52 N=49	%5 N=5
88	Discussing a judge's reasoning or use of authority?	%16 N=19	%0 N=0	%6 N=7	%73 N=85	%3 N=3	%9 N=9	%4 N=4	%9 N=9	%68 N=65	%5 N=5
89	Comparing the case to other cases discussed in the course?	%0 N=0	%20 N=23	%25 N=29	%43 N=50	%9 N=10	%0 N=0	%26 N=25	%16 N=16	%44 N=42	%6 N=6
90	Analogously applying the results of that case to hypothetical cases	%10 N=12	%31 N=36	%51 N=60	%0 N=0	%0 N=0	%8 N=8	%26 N=25	%57 N=54	%0 N=0	%2 N=2
91	Criticizing or elaborating on the social implications of the opinion?	%1 N=1	%11 N=13	%82 N=96	%1 N=1	%0 N=0	%3 N=3	%11 N=12	%80 N=76	%0 N=0	%0 N=0
92	In a week, how much time of a class is spent elaborating the "black letter law" in your field?	%3 N=3	%85 N=100	%8 N=9	%2 N=2	%0 N=0	%9 N=9	%73 N=690	%12 N=11	%4 N=4	%0 N=0
95	In a week, how much time of your class is spent solving problems illustrating the law in your field?	%3 N=3	%79 N=92	%15 N=17	%2 N=2	%1 N=1	%8 N=8	%62 N=59	%22 N=21	%5 N=5	%0 N=0
98	In a week, how much time of your class is spent considering theoretical underpinnings of your field?	%3 N=3	%81 N=95	%14 N=16	%1 N=1	%0 N=0	%2 N=2	%86 N=82	%8 N=8	%2 N=2	%1 N=1

[a] See the caution in note 5 concerning the reliability of these figures. They are included here solely for the potential for comparison between pools, in the assumption that respondents in each pool responded to the same questions similarly.

Table S - Ideological Preferences Compared Between Teacher Groups: First Year and Upper Class

Survey Question		1L Prefer & Select	1L Prefer	1L Neutral	1L Reject	1L Reject & Select	2&3 Prefer & Select	2&3 Prefer	2&3 Neutral	2&3 Reject	2&3 Reject & Select
30	Sensitivity to Concerns of Gender or Racial Diversity	%39 N=72	%35 N=65	%21 N=39	%2 N=3	%4 N=8	%32 N=57	%38 N=67	%23 N=40	%3 N=5	%3 N=5
31	Apparent ideological direction in material selection or notes, favoring critical or progressive views	%6 N=12	%22 N=41	%27 N=50	%18 N=33	%27 N=51	%4 N=7	%15 N=26	%35 N=61	%27 N=48	%18 N=32
32	Apparent ideological direction in material selection or notes, favoring critical or progressive views	%1 N=2	%7 N=14	%28 N=52	%27 N=50	%37 N=69	%2 N=3	%5 N=8	%35 N=62	%38 N=67	%19 N=34
33	Absence of any apparent ideological direction in material selection or notes	%28 N=53	%32 N=59	%27 N=50	%4 N=8	%9 N=17	%25 N=44	%39 N=68	%28 N=50	%3 N=5	%4 N=7

Table T - Ideological Preferences Compared Between Teacher Groups: Code and Common Law

Survey Question		Code Prefer & Select	Code Prefer	Code Neutral	Code Reject	Code Reject & Select	C-L Prefer & Select	C-L Prefer	C-L Neutral	C-L Reject	C-L Reject & Select
30	Sensitivity to Concerns of Gender or Racial Diversity	%36 N=27	%33 N=25	%26 N=20	%3 N=2	%1 N=1	%34 N=82	%36 N=86	%22 N=53	%3 N=6	%4 N=10
31	Apparent ideological direction in material selection or notes, favoring critical or progressive views	%3 N=2	%24 N=18	%25 N=19	%28 N=21	%20 N=15	%7 N=17	%16 N=38	%29 N=70	%20 N=48	%27 N=64
32	Apparent ideological direction in material selection or notes, favoring conservative or traditional views	%0 N=0	%5 N=4	%30 N=23	%38 N=29	%25 N=19	%2 N=5	%8 N=19	%29 N=69	%28 N=67	%32 N=77
33	Absence of any apparent ideological direction in material selection or notes	%21 N=16	%37 N=28	%29 N=22	%7 N=5	%5 N=4	%29 N=69	%33 N=80	%26 N=62	%4 N=9	%7 N=17

Note: Percentages in this table reflect the percentage of respondents marking an answer as a portion of respondents marking that answer in the relevent pool, rounded to the nearest whole number.

Table U - Ideological Preferences Compared Between Teacher Groups: New and Veteran Teachers

Survey Question		New Prefer & Select	New Prefer	New Neutral	New Reject	New Reject & Select	Veteran Prefer & Select	Veteran Prefer	Veteran Neutral	Veteran Reject	Veteran Reject & Select
30	Sensitivity to Concerns of Gender or Racial Diversity	%45 N=73	%36 N=59	%16 N=27	%1 N=1	%1 N=2	%25 N=53	%37 N=76	%26 N=54	%4 N=9	%5 N=11
31	Apparent ideological direction in material selection or notes, favoring critical or progressive views	%9 N=14	%25 N=41	%27 N=44	%21 N=35	%17 N=28	%3 N=7	%12 N=25	%32 N=66	%22 N=46	%28 N=59
32	Apparent ideological direction in material selection or notes, favoring conservative or traditional views	%0 N=0	%6 N=10	%29 N=48	%38 N=63	%25 N=41	%2 N=5	%7 N=15	%32 N=66	%25 N=52	%31 N=65
33	Absence of any apparent ideological direction in material selection or notes	%24 N=40	%35 N=58	%24 N=40	%5 N=9	%9 N=15	%28 N=59	%33 N=68	%29 N=61	%3 N=7	%4 N=8

TABLE V - IDEOLOGICAL PREFERENCES COMPARED BETWEEN TEACHER GROUPS: TEACHERS IN SCHOOLS WITH SELECTIVE AND DEMOCRATIC ADMISSIONS

Survey Question		Select Prefer & Select	Select Prefer	Select Neutral	Select Reject	Select Reject & Select	Demo Prefer & Select	Demo Prefer	Demo Neutral	Demo Reject	Demo Reject & Select
30	Sensitivity to Concerns of Gender or Racial Diversity	%26 N=31	%44 N=51	%24 N=28	%2 N=2	%3 N=4	%37 N=35	%30 N=28	%27 N=25	%2 N=2	%5 N=5
31	Apparent ideological direction in material selection or notes, favoring critical or progressive views	%4 N=5	%14 N=16	%32 N=38	%26 N=30	%23 N=27	%4 N=4	%22 N=21	%34 N=32	%19 N=18	%21 N=20
32	Apparent ideological direction in material selection or notes, favoring conservative or traditional views	%2 N=2	%7 N=8	%31 N=36	%28 N=33	%32 N=37	%0 N=0	%7 N=7	%35 N=33	%34 N=32	%24 N=23
33	Absence of any apparent ideological direction in material selection or notes	%25 N=29	%37 N=43	%29 N=34	%3 N=3	%6 N=7	%29 N=28	%29 N=28	%34 N=32	%3 N=3	%4 N=4

Notes

1. This survey was initially prepared to support an article surveying the history of teaching methods in American law schools from the 1760s to the present. See Steve Sheppard, Casebooks, Commentaries & Curmudgeons: An Introductory History of Law in the Lecture Hall, 82 Iowa L.Rev. 547 (1996).

2. This article is meant to disappoint the reader who enjoys arcane footnotes, as its notes hold little beyond cross-references or notes on the intentionally minimalist method. This note is the only bone for the dog of contextualism.

This survey is but one in a long tradition of surveys of American law school teaching methods. The earliest seems to be that of George-Auguste Matile, a one-time Swiss law professor at Neuf Châtel, who emigrated to the United States and became a state department lawyer in Washington, D.C. At the request of a former colleague, he contacted most of the American law schools, which then had "no coordination among universities or sharing of information about instructive methods, relying on accidental and personal contact." George-Auguste Matile, *A Letter Written by Him to M. Edouard LaBoulaye, Collège de France, Les écoles de droit aux États-Unis (Law Schools in the United States) extrait de la revue historique de droit français numéro de novembre-décembre 1863* (Published in Paris, A. Durand, 1864) (Harvard pamphlet S US 907 MAT).

The surveys that have had the greatest notoriety in this century are those of the Carnegie Foundation and the Survey of the Legal Profession. See Albert J. Harno, *Legal Education in the United States* (Westport, Conn., Greenwood Press, 1980); Alfred Z. Reed, *Training for the Public Profession of the Law: Historical Development and Principal Contemporary Problems of Legal Education in the United States with some account of Conditions in England and Canada* (New York, Carnegie Foundation for the Advancement of Learning, Bulletin Number 15, 1921); Lowell S. Nicholson, *The Law Schools of the United States: A Statistical and Analytical Report Based on 136 Completed Questionnaires and on Inspections of 160 Law Schools, Prepared by the Survey of the Legal Profession* (Baltimore, Lord Press, Inc., 1958). These surveys are discussed in Sheppard, "Casebooks, Commentaries, and Curmudgeons."

3. Question 87: "Is your average class primarily monologue lecture or dialogue with students?" The available responses were "(1) all monologue (2) mainly monologue (3) roughly equal (4) mainly dialogue (5) all dialogue."

4. Question 88: "If you use dialogue, do you give students whom you will call upon notice beforehand?" The available responses were "(1) yes, before class (2) yes, at the start of class (3) yes, occasionally (4) no." The responses were: (1)=12% (N=50) (2)=1% (N=5) (3)=10% (N=40) (4)=69% (N=290).

5. Note: A typographical error in the survey makes the answers to questions 92, 95, and 98 table unreliable. The error does not affect the answers to questions 93, 94, 96, 97, 99, and 100. The error is a classic in bad survey form editing, which was undetected until the compiled data was analyzed; there were two alternative meanings for the same entry. The answers available to respondents for these questions were "(1) none (2) 1-25% (2) 25-50% (3) 50%-75% (4) 75-99% (5) all." After discovering the error, I polled twelve respondents, and each declared to have read them in order, so that the second entry marked (2) was read to have been (3), and so on. As the original (5) was an unlikely choice, this could easily have been disregarded. Thus, I have estimated that the answers reflect a reading of the question as if it read "(1) none (2) 1-25% (3) 25-50% (4) 50%-75% (5) 75-99% (6) all" and choice (6) is not a choice. At the least, this is suggestive of high error and low validity. I do not believe, however, that this error affects the data collected in the comparative questions, asking whether these techniques are used by the professor now more or less than when the professor was a student, whether the professor will use these techniques more or less in the future.

6. Question 110: "Do you have students or others 'role play' in your classes, including mock arguments?" The available responses were "(1) frequently (2) occasionally (3) rarely (4) no."

7. Question 42: "Is your primary assigned text best described as a—" the available responses were "(1) Casebook (2) Treatise (3) Problem book." The descriptive value of these answers must be considered against the ratios of responses to questions 55 through 81, in which professors were asked to evaluate casebooks, treatises, and problem books "if you assign one." The average of responses for questions relating to casebooks is 397. The average of responses for treatises is 105. The average of responses for problem books is 85. The difference in these responses was expected, as question 42 surveys only the primary course book assigned, while questions 55-81 survey all books assigned, including supplemental materials.

8. See discussion in note 7 and the text accompanying notes 12 through 14.

9. See the comparative responses discussed in note 7.

10. This relationship is explored in Sheppard, "Casebooks, Commentaries & Curmudgeons."

11. Question 47: "Do you recommend auxiliary readings, such as articles, anthologies, codes, treatises, or histories?" Responses available were "(1) yes (2) no." Such assignments are also part of the presumed basis for overlapping opinions regarding problem books and treatises in courses that have a casebook assigned as primary readings. See note 7.

12. In common law courses, 78% (222 respondents) answered "(1) yes"; 21% (60) answered "(2) no." In code courses, 80% (164) answered "(1) yes," and 17% (35) answered "(2) no."

13. Question 48: "Do you discuss auxiliary readings in class?" Responses available were "(1) yes (2) no" Responses for (1) were 51% (N=215) and for (2) were 46% (N=193). These responses were consistent when the response pool was divided into common law and code courses: Common Law: (1): 52% (N=148) (2): 46% (N=130). Statute: (1): 50% (N=102) (2):48% (N=97).

14. Question 49: "Do you examine the students on auxiliary readings?" Responses available were "(1) yes (2) no." Responses for (1) were 32% (N=133) and for (2) were 64% (N=270). These responses were again consistent when the response pool was divided into common law and code courses: Common Law: (1):32% (N=91) (2):66% (N=186). Statute: (1):30% (N=61) (2): 66% (N=135).

15. The prefatory instruction to question one provided:

"In evaluating a coursebook for adoption, how have these attributes of books affected your decisions to adopt or reject?

Please darken (1), (2), (3), (4), or (5) on your answer grid for each question below, according to which statement most accurately reflects your view of these attributes of some books:
(1) = I would prefer a book to have this attribute and would base a decision on this preference in part."
(2) = I would prefer a book with this attribute, but I doubt that I would base a decision on this preference.
(3) = Honestly, I don't really think about this attribute in my selection process.
(4) = I would prefer a book not to have this attribute, but I doubt that I would base a decision on this preference.
(5) = I would prefer a book not to have this attribute and would base a decision on this preference in part."

16. Because the survey asked the likelihood that the teacher would select a book according to a particular attribute, the results are both qualitative regarding each attribute and capable of comparison among attributes.

17. See results in ranks 28, 24, and 9 in Table A.

18. See results in rank 23 in Table A.

19. See results in ranks 12, 17, and 29 in Table A.

20. See results in ranks 12 and 17 in Table A.

21. See results in ranks 22 and 37 in Table A.

22. See results in ranks 21 and 41 in Table A.

23. See results in ranks 16, 39, and 40 in Table A.

24. See results in rank 34 in Table A.

25. Question 45: "If you did not author or edit the primary text, is that person an acquaintance?" Responses available were "(1) yes (2) no."

26. Responses to question 45 were (1): 88.12% (N=371) (2): 4.99% (N=21)

27. Survey responses were divided into pools based on responses to question 111, which asked, "Do you consider the subject matter of the course to be primarily drawn from:" Responses available were "(1) Statutes/code (2) Federal court opinions (3) State court opinions (4) U.S. Sp. Ct. opinions (5) Administrative materials." Respondents who marked (1) or (5) were grouped into the code pool. Respondents who marked (2), (3), or (4) were grouped into the common law pool. The responses to the question were (1) 76 (18.05%); (2) 46 (10.93%); (3) 147 (34.92%); (4) 47(11.16%); and (5) 1 (0.24%). The pools thus created were 77 in the code pool, and 240 in the veteran pool. Survey responses were then sorted into a QuattroPro spreadsheet for the responses of each pool separately, from which the comparative tallies for the pools are drawn.

28. These responses are to question 42, described in note 7 and its accompanying text.

29. See question 1 in Table G.

30. See question 3 in Table G.

31. See question 3 in Table G.

32. See question 5 in Table G.

33. See question 4 in Table G.

34. See question 26 in Table G.

35. See question 21 in Table G.

36. See question 60 in Table I.

37. See question 63 in Table I.

38. See question 59 in Table I.

39. See question 57 in Table I.

40. See questions 92, 95, and 98 of Table J.

41. This comparative pattern is similar to that between teachers of first-year and upper-class courses. See the discussion accompanying Table P.

42. Survey responses were divided into pools based on responses to question 117, "How many scholarly articles have you published in the field of this course?" Responses available were "(1) 0 (2) 1-2 (3) 3-5 (4) 5-10 (5) More than 10." Respondents who marked (1) were grouped into the "teacher" pool. Respondents who marked (3), (4) or (5) were grouped into the "scholar" pool; responses of (2) were not placed here into either pool. The initial distribution among all respondents was (1) 103(24.47%); (2) 101(23.99%); (3) 78(18.53%); (4) 41(9.74%); and (5) 43(10.21%). The pools thus created of were 103 in the teacher pool, and 162 in the scholar pool. Survey responses were then sorted into a QuattroPro spreadsheet for the responses of each pool separately, from which the comparative tallies for the pools are drawn.

43. This essay makes no assessment of whether writers' greater belief in effectiveness is based on a stronger awareness of course materials results from the efforts of publication alone or from other factors, such as teaching the course over a longer period of time.

44. Survey responses were divided into pools based on responses to question 116, "How many years have you been teaching in a law school?" Responses available were "(1) 0-2 (2) 3-8 (3) 8-15 (4) 15-25 (5) More than 25." Respondents who marked (1) or (2) were grouped into the "new" pool. Respondents who marked (3), (4) of (5) were grouped into the "veteran" pool. The initial distribution among all respondents was (1) 34(8.55%); (2) 89(21.85%); (3) 88(20.90%); (4) 110(26.13%); and (5) 50(11.64%). The pools thus created were 123 in the new pool and 248 in the veteran pool. Survey responses were then sorted into a QuattroPro spreadsheet for the responses of each pool separately, from which the comparative tallies for the pools are drawn.

45. See responses to questions 92, 95, and 98 in Table N.

46. See responses to questions 87 and 91 in Table N.

47. Survey responses were divided into pools based on responses to question 126, "In what year do students usually take

your course?" Responses available were "(1) 1st year (2) 2d year (3) 3d year." Respondents who marked (1) were grouped into the "first year" pool. Respondents who marked (2) or (3) were grouped into the "upper-class" pool. The initial distribution among all respondents was (1) 187(44.18%); (2) 107(24.94%); and (3) 68(15.68%). The pools thus created were 187 in the first-year pool, and 175 in the upper-class pool. Survey responses were then sorted into a QuattroPro spreadsheet for the responses of each pool separately, from which the comparative tallies for the pools are drawn.

48. See responses to questions 55, 57, in 61 in Table O.

49. This comparative pattern is similar to that between teachers of code and common law courses. See the discussion accompanying Table J.

50. See responses to questions 88 and 89 in Table P.

51. See responses to questions 92 and 95 in Table P.

52. Survey responses were divided into pools based on responses to question 128, "From which level of competitiveness in the national pool of eligible law school candidates would you consider the students of your school to be admitted?" Responses available were "(1) Highest 10% (2) Highest 25% (3) Highest 50% (4) Lowest 50% (5) Lowest 25%." Respondents who marked (1) or (2) were grouped into the "selective" pool. Respondents who marked (4) or (5) were grouped into the "democratic" pool. The initial distribution among all respondents was (1) 29 (6.89); (2) 87 (20.43%); (3) 145 (34.44%) (4) 78 (18.53%); and (5) 20 4.75%. The pools thus created were 115 in the select pool, and 95 in the democratic pool. Survey responses were then sorted into a QuattroPro spreadsheet for the responses of each pool separately, from which the comparative tallies for the pools are drawn.

53. See responses to question 62, Table Q.

54. See responses to questions 89 and 90, Table R.

55. See responses to question 98, Table R.

56. Marking responses to the prefatory instructions in question 1, quoted above in note 15, respondents were asked to rate the attributes in

Question 30: Sensitivity to Concerns of Gender or Racial Diversity;

Question 31: Apparent ideological direction in material selection or notes, favoring critical or progressive views;

Question 32: Apparent ideological direction in material selection or notes, favoring critical or progressive views; and

Question 33: Absence of any apparent ideological direction in material selection or notes.

57. The ratio of first-year teachers who preferred a progressive to a conservative ideological bias was 53 to 16, or 3.3 to 1. The ratio of upper-class teachers who preferred a progressive to a conservative ideological bias was 33 to 11, or 3 to 1. The ratio of first-year teachers who rejected a progressive to a conservative ideological bias was 84 to 119 or .71 to 1. The ratio of upper-class teachers who rejected a progressive bias in favor of a conservative ideological bias was 109 to 128 or .85 to 1. For both groups, there was a slightly greater tendency for respondents to select material based on their ideological preference based on a progressive slant. See Table S.

58. The ratio of teachers in selective schools who preferred a progressive to a conservative ideological bias was 21 to 10 or 2.1 to 1. The ratio of teachers in democratic schools who preferred a progressive to a conservative ideological bias was 33 to 11, or 3 to 1. The ratio of teachers in selective schools who rejected a progressive bias in favor of a conservative ideological bias was 57 to 70 or .81 to 1. The ratio of teachers in democratic schools who rejected a progressive bias to a conservative ideological bias was 80 to 101 .8 or to 1. For both groups, there was a slightly greater tendency for respondents to select material based on their ideological preference based on progressive slant. See Table V.

59. The ratio of code course teachers who preferred a progressive to a conservative ideological bias was 20 to 4, or 5 to 1. The ratio of common law course teachers who preferred a progressive to a conservative ideological bias was 38 to 19, or 2 to 1. The ratio of code teachers who rejected a progressive bias in favor of a conservative ideological bias was 36 to 48 or .75 to 1. The ratio of common law course teachers who rejected a progressive to a conservative ideological bias was 112 to 134 or .84 to 1. For both groups, there was a roughly 3 to 1 tendency for respondents to select material based on their ideological preference based on progressive slant. See Table T.

60. The ratio of recently hired teachers who preferred a progressive to a conservative ideological bias was 55 to 10 or 5.5 to 1. The ratio of veteran teachers who preferred a progressive to a conservative ideological bias was 32 to 20, or 1.6 to 1. The ratio of recently hired teachers who rejected a progressive bias in favor of a conservative ideological bias was 63 to 104 or .6 to 1. The ratio of veteran teachers who rejected a progressive to a conservative ideological bias was 105 to 117, or .9 to 1. For both groups, there was a slightly greater tendency for respondents to select material based on their ideological preference based on progressive slant. See Table U.

61. The ratio of first-year teachers who preferred materials with sensitivity to concerns of gender or racial diversity was 137 to 50 or 2.74 to 1. The ratio of upper-class teachers who preferred materials with sensitivity to concerns of gender or racial diversity was 131 to 50 or 2.76 to 1. See question 30 in Table S.

62. The ratio of teachers in selective schools who preferred materials with sensitivity to concerns of gender or racial diversity was 82 to 34 or 2.41 to 1. The ratio of teachers in democratic schools who preferred materials with sensitivity to concerns of gender or racial diversity was 124 to 50 or 2.48 to 1. See question 30 in Table V.

63. The ratio of code course teachers who preferred materials with sensitivity to concerns of gender or racial diversity was 52 to 23 or 2.3 to 1. The ratio of common law course teachers who preferred materials with sensitivity to concerns of gender or racial diversity was 168 to 69 or 2.4 to 1. See question 30 in Table T.

64. The ratio of recently hired teachers who preferred materials with sensitivity to concerns of gender or racial diversity was

131 to 30 or 4.4 to 1. The ratio of veteran teachers who preferred materials with sensitivity to concerns of gender or racial diversity was 129 to 74 or 1.7 to 1. See question 30 in Table U.

65. "Do you suggest students perform supplemental computer assisted legal instruction (CALI)? (1) yes (2) no (3) I have no idea what this is."

66. "Do you use interactive computer programs in presenting any of your course material in class? (1) yes (2) no."

67. Question 109: "Do you use films or other audiovisual material with your course? (1) during class (2) required outside of class (3) optional outside of class (4) no"

68. This survey assumes that a difference in view concerning coursebook effectiveness, or a difference in approach toward pedagogy between converse groups of a population defined by a single characteristic would suggest some influence of that characteristic upon the view or approach. In other words, if a comparison between views of teachers in the first year and upper years that reveals a higher divergence of approach than the views of teachers in code courses differ from those of the common law, there is reason to believe that teaching in a particular law school year has a greater influence on views than teaching in courses based on codes or the common law. This assumption is highly inferential, and the cautious reader might not agree. Despite this caveat, a comparison of divisions of view regarding coursebook effectiveness and teaching methods reveal some interesting comparisons.

69. The inferential utility of the survey is limited by imprecision in distribution through third parties and the allowance of professors to submit multiple responses when one professor teaches different courses. As a practical matter, few professors did submit two forms and fewer still submitted more than two. Even so, the responses are considered by the author to be suggestive.

Course Book & Pedagogy Survey

Please complete as many forms as you wish. Please complete only one form for a divided course, such as Contracts I and Contracts II. If you complete one survey for a divided course, please answer part C for the course you teach most often.

AS ALWAYS, PLEASE USE A PENCIL.

In the segment "Your Last Name," please fill in the name of your course. (Abbreviate as necessary.)

In the segment "P I D," please fill in the number FIELD 3.

Please ignore all the remaining data fields, and begin answering from question 1.

Part A. About Your Course Materials—

Questions 1- 41: Please darken (1), (2), (3), (4), or (5) on your answer grid for each question below.

Which statement most accurately reflects your view of attributes below in selecting a casebook:

(1) = I would prefer a casebook with this attribute and would base a decision on this preference in part (or 1=Prefer & care).

(2) = I would prefer a casebook with this attribute, but I doubt that I would select for this reason (or 2 = Prefer but don't care).

(3) = Honestly, I don't really think about this attribute in my selection process (or 3=Don't care).

(4) = I would prefer a casebook without this attribute, but I doubt that I would select for this reason (or 4=Dislike but don't care).

(5) = I would prefer a casebook without this attribute and would select for this reason (or 5=Dislike & care).

1. Classic cases in the field.
2. Most recent cases in the field.
3. Reasoning in opinions (i.e., fewer cases but longer excerpts).
4. Rules of law in opinions (i.e., more cases but shorter excerpts).
5. Comprehensive coverage of law in the field.
6. Notes explaining cases.
7. Notes concerning elaborating general rules of law.
8. Questions with answers in the student edition.
9. Questions without answers in the student edition.
10. Notes concerning doctrine, policy, or theory.
11. Notes describing state minority doctrines.
12. Notes describing scholarly approaches.
13. More problems applying rules to hypotheses.
14. More sophisticated problems.
15. More elementary problems.
16. More pages of reading per class hour.
17. Fewer pages of reading per class hour.
18. Fame or your respect for an author or editor.
19. Personal acquaintance with author or editor.
20. Prestige of law school or institution that employs author or editor.
21. Teacher's manual or supplement availability in general.
22. Teacher's manual or supplement with thorough discussion of cases.
23. Teacher's manual or supplement with thorough discussion of doctrines of law.
24. Teacher's manual or supplement with solution to problems or questions in the student edition.
25. Availability of an annual supplement with recent cases.
26. Pictures or graphics.
27. Amusement or entertainment value of selected cases or problems.

Preferences with which to answer questions 1-41:
(1) = Prefer & care (2) = Prefer but don't care (3) = Don't care (4) = Dislike but don't care (5) = Dislike & care
28. Similarity to materials you used as a student.
29. Lower price to students.
30. Sensitivity to concerns of gender or racial diversity.
31. Apparent ideological direction in material selection or notes, favoring critical or progressive views.
32. Apparent ideological direction in material selection or notes, favoring conservative or traditional views.
33. Absence of any apparent ideological direction in material selection or notes.
34. Use of economic models and descriptions of rules or cases.
35. Logical progression of topics covered.
36. Similarity of progressions of topics covered to course you studied as a student.
37. Clear, light writing style of authors or editors employing mainly plain English.
38. Traditional writing style of authors or editors employing numerous terms of art.
39. Use of double column text layouts.
40. Tiny print and fewer pages.
41. Large print and more pages.

* * *

42. Do you have sole authority to select your coursebook?
(1) yes (2) no, it is chosen by a dean or chair (3) no, we choose them in a committee
43. Is your primary assigned text best described as a—(1) Casebook (2) Treatise (3) Problem book
44. How much of the assigned reading for your lecture as a whole is based on readings you have personally selected?
(1) none (2) 1-10% 20-(2) 40-60% (3) 60%-99% (4) all
45. Did you author or edit your primary assigned text? (1) no (2) author (3) editor (4) co-editor (5) co-author
46. How much of the material on your examination is discussed in class? (1) All (2) Nearly All (3) Most (4) Some (5) None
47. Do you recommend auxiliary readings, such as articles, anthologies, codes, treatises, or histories? (1) yes (2) no
48. Do you discuss auxiliary readings in class? (1) yes (2) no
49. Do you examine the students on auxiliary readings? (1) yes (2) no
50. Do you suggest students perform supplemental computer assisted legal instruction (CALI)?
(1) yes, I require it (2) yes, I recommend it (3) no, I do not suggest it (4) I have no idea what this is
51. How often have you changed the assigned primary text from one book to another (not counting revised editions)?
(1) each time the course is offered (2) after 2-3 times offered (3) after 4-5 years (4) never
52. If there is a comprehensive teacher's manual or supplement, how closely will your lecture follow the outline of that supplement in any particular class? (1) closely (2) closely for problems only (3) loosely (4) slightly (5) not at all
53. How do you react to student use of commercial briefs of cases? (1) Recommend (2) Discredit (3) Ignore
54. How do you react to student use of commercial outlines of your course? (1) Recommend (2) Discredit (3) Ignore

***Questions 56- 63**: If you assign a **casebook**, how effective do you find it in developing student skills in these areas:*
(1) = Counterproductive (2) = Ineffective (3) = Neutral (4) = Effective (5) = Highly effective.

55. Extracting rules of law from opinions.
56. Fully comprehending the reasoning and statements written in opinions.
Question 56 is the last question on side one of the answer grid.
Please turn the answer grid over to complete the remaining questions on side two.
57. Understanding law from non-judicial sources.
58. Developing a comprehensive synthesis of the rules of law.
59. Developing a synthesis of law across conflicting cases.
60. Developing skills for the application by analogy of law to new problems.
61. Generally preparing the student to represent clients.
62. Understanding the role of the law, or of lawyers, in a social system.
63. Developing skills to criticize law or the rules of law.

***Questions 64-72**: If you assign a **treatise**, how effective do you find it in developing student skills in these areas:*
(1) = Counterproductive (2) = Ineffective (3) = Neutral (4) = Effective (5) = Highly effective.

64. Extracting rules of law from opinions.
65. Fully comprehending the reasoning and statements written in opinions.
66. Understanding law from non-judicial sources.
67. Developing a comprehensive synthesis of the rules of law.
68. Developing a synthesis of law across conflicting cases.
69. Developing skills for the application by analogy of law to new problems.
70. Generally preparing the student to represent clients.

71. Understanding the role of the law, or of lawyers, in a social system.
72. Developing skills to criticize law or the rules of law.

Questions 73-81*: If you assign a* **problem book***, how effective do you find it in developing student skills in these areas:*
(1) = Counterproductive (2) = Ineffective (3) = Neutral (4) = Effective (5) = Highly effective.
73. Extracting rules of law from opinions.
74. Fully comprehending the reasoning and statements written in opinions.
75. Understanding law from non-judicial sources.
76. Developing a comprehensive synthesis of the rules of law.
77. Developing a synthesis of law across conflicting cases.
78. Developing skills for the application by analogy of law to new problems.
79. Generally preparing the student to represent clients.
80. Understanding the role of the law, or of lawyers, in a social system.
81. Developing skills to criticize law or the rules of law.

Part B. About Your Pedagogy, or Instructional Technique—

Questions 82-86*: Imagine a typical case, discussed half-way through your course. How much of the time devoted to that case will be spent in the following practices:*

82. Discussing its facts?
(1) most or all (2) more than half (3) about half (4) roughly a quarter (5) little or none
83. Discussing a judge's reasoning or use of authority?
(1) most or all (2) more than half (3) about half (4) roughly a quarter (5) little or none
84. Comparing the case to other cases discussed in the course?
(1) most or all (2) more than half (3) about half (4) roughly a quarter (5) little or none
85. Analogously applying the results of that case to hypothetical cases
(1) most or all (2) more than half (3) about half (4) roughly a quarter (5) little or none
86. Criticizing or elaborating on the social implications of the opinion?
(1) most or all (2) more than half (3) about half (4) roughly a quarter (5) little or none
* * *
87. Is your average class primarily monologue lecture or dialogue with students?
(1) all monologue (2) mainly monologue (3) roughly equal (4) mainly dialogue (5) all dialogue
88. If you use dialogue, do you give students whom you will call upon notice beforehand?
(1) yes, before class (2) yes, at the start of class (3) yes, occasionally (4) no
89. In a week, how much time of your class is spent **discussing cases** representative of your field?
(1) none (2) 1-25% (2) 25-50% (3) 50%-75% (4) 75-99% (5) all
90. Do you discuss cases more or less often than you remember was common in this course when you were a student?
(1) more (2) less (3) the same
91. Will you likely discuss cases more or less often in the future than you use it now?
(1) more (2) less (3) the same
92. In a week, how much time of a class is spent **elaborating the "black letter law"** in your field?
(1) none (2) 1-25% (2) 25-50% (3) 50%-75% (4) 75-99% (5) all
93. Do you elaborate on the "black letter law" more or less often than you remember was common in this course when you were a student?
(1) more (2) less (3) the same
94. Will you likely elaborate on the "black letter law" more or less often in the future than you use it now? (1) more (2) less (3) the same
95. In a week, how much time of your class is spent **solving problems** illustrating the law in your field?
(1) none (2) 1-25% (2) 25-50% (3) 50%-75% (4) 75-99% (5) all
96. Do you solve problems more or less often than you remember was common in this course when you were a student?
(1) more (2) less (3) the same
97. Will you likely solve problems more or less often in the future than you use it now? (1) more (2) less (3) the same
98. In a week, how much time of your class is spent **considering theoretical underpinnings** of your field?
(1) none (2) 1-25% (2) 25-50% (3) 50%-75% (4) 75-99% (5) all
99. Do you consider theoretical underpinnings of your field more or less often than you remember was common in this course when you were a student? (1) more (2) less (3) the same
100. Will you likely consider theoretical underpinnings of your field more or less often in the future than you use it now?
(1) more (2) less (3) the same
* * *

101. Do you use **interactive computer programs** in presenting any of your course material in class? (1) yes (2) no
102. Might you use **interactive computer programs** in your course, if you knew of their availability?
(1) certainly (2) yes, if the content is pedagogically sound (3) only as supplements to lectures (4) probably not (5) no
103. Do you use **computer-generated displays** of texts of classnotes in your course. (1) yes (2) no
104. Might you use **computer-generated displays** of text in your course.
(1) certainly (2) yes, if the content is pedagogically sound (3) only as supplements to lectures (4) probably not (5) no
105. Do you use **computer-generated displays** of graphics related to cases or rules in your course. (1) yes (2) no
106. Might you use **computer-generated displays** of graphics related to cases or rules in your course.
(1) certainly (2) yes, if the content is pedagogically sound (3) only as supplements to lectures (4) probably not (5) no
107. Do you communicate with students by computer?
(1) frequently (2) rarely (3) only in response to student posts (4) never (5) not possible here
108. If it is not now possible but becomes so in the future, would you probably communicate with students by computer?
(1) frequently (2) rarely (3) only in response to student posts (4) unlikely
* * *
109. Do you use films or other audiovisual material with your course?
(1) during class (2) required outside of class (3) optional outside of class (4) no
110. Do you have students or others "role play" in your classes, including mock arguments?
(1) frequently (2) occasionally (3) rarely (4) no

Part C. About you, your course, and your students—

Do you consider the subject matter of the course to be primarily drawn from:
This question is answered in answer boxes for both questions 111 AND 112.
111. 111(1) Statutes/code 111(2) Federal court opinions 111(3) State court opinions
111(4) U.S. Sp. Ct. opinions 111(5) Administrative materials
112. 112(1) Scholarly writings 112(2) Int'l materials 112(3) Foreign legal materials
112(4) Research or drafting problems 112 (5) Non-legal materials

113. How many hours' credit are assigned? (1) 1-2 hours (2) 3 hours (3) 4 or 5 (4) 6 or more hours (5) non-credit
114. Is your course required to graduate? (1) Yes (2) No
115. How many times have you taught this course? (1) 0-2 (2) 3-8 (3) 8-15 (4) 15-25 (5) More than 25
116. How many years have you been teaching in a law school? (1) 0-2 (2) 3-8 (3) 8-15 (4) 15-25 (5) More than 25
117. How many scholarly articles have you published in the field of this course?
(1) 0 (2) 1-2 (3) 3-5 (4) 5-10 (5) More than 10
118. How many scholarly articles have you published all together? (1) 0 (2) 1-2 (3) 3-5 (4) 5-10 (5) More than 10
119. How often do you read scholarly articles related to your field?
(1) never (2) when I have a specific question (3) when it is on my desk anyway (4) frequently (5) weekly or daily
120. How often do you read scholarly articles related to teaching (as in the Journal of Legal Education)?
(1) never (2) when I have a specific question (3) when it is on my desk anyway (4) frequently (5) weekly or daily
121. How often do you use electronic mail? (1) daily (2) 2-3 times a week (3) weekly (4) monthly (5) never
122. How much of your typical examination is computer-graded?
(1) none (2) 1-25% (2) 25-50% (3) 50%-75% (4) 75-99% (5) all
123. Do you use this method more or less than it was used in this course when you were a student?
(1) more (2) less (3) the same
124. Will you likely use this method more or less often in the future than you use it now? (1) more (2) less (3) the same
125. How much of your typical examination is an essay you evaluate personally?
(1) none (2) 1-25% (2) 25-50% (3) 50%-75% (4) 75-99% (5) all
126. In what year do students usually take your course? (1) 1st year (2) 2d year (3) 3d year
127. How many students are usually enrolled? (1) 30 or less (2) 31-50 (3) 51-90 (4) 91-150 (5) more than 150
128. From which level of competitiveness in the national pool of eligible law school candidates would you consider the students of your school to be admitted? (1) Highest 10% (2) Highest 25% (3) Highest 50% (4) Lowest 50% (5) Lowest 25%
129. Are students assigned to your course by the registrar or do they choose themselves? (1) Assign (2) Elect

Thank You For Your Time and Assistance !!

Please send completed answer forms to your Dean or to:

Steve Sheppard, Thomas M. Cooley Law School, 217 South Capitol Ave., P.O. Box 13038, Lansing, MI 48901

II. Examinations and Evaluations

Chapter 58

An Informal History of How Law Schools Evaluate Students, with a Predictable Emphasis on Law School Final Exams

1997

Steve Sheppard

Author's note: The discerning reader will discover references to an appendix included with the original publication of this essay. This appendix has not been reproduced here owing to its length but will be found at 65 *University of Missouri-Kansas City Law Review* 657, 696 (1997). I thank the editors of the *UMKC Law Review* for their invitation to write this article; without their exhibition of blind faith in agreeing to publish the unwritten, it would have remained so. I am also grateful to the Thomas Cooley librarians, particularly Sharon Bradley, Ardena Walsh, and Steve Boudette in locating some of the more obscure material for this odyssey, to Kristin Keck, Jill Pullum, and Cindy Hurst for their typing assistance. Frank Lorenz of Hamilton College, Kent McKeever and Whitney Bagnall of Columbia, and David Warrington and David DiLorenzo of Harvard were particularly helpful in locating some of the more critical bits of academic flotsam on which this paper is based.

Final exams play on a law student's world like some weirdly orbiting moon. They are always in sight; but while they're at a distance, they serve merely to create the tensions which swell daily like tides—to read, to keep pace, to understand. As exams draw close, however, . . . their gravitational force starts to shake the whole place to pieces.[1]

American law schools currently employ one essential, formal method of student evaluation—course-end examinations.[2] While informal evaluation, particularly observation of student oral class performances, does occur, the exams are usually the exclusive method by which a record of student performance is created. Examinations serve to measure the ability of the student to use the material assigned, whether they are fit or unfit for the practice of law, or for the recognition by the school that sufficient skill is had to award a law degree,[3] whether they should be recognized and identified for the employers as outstandingly fit,[4] and to signal the strengths and weaknesses of a student's work for the student's future development, as an incentive both to learn as much as possible during instruction and to review that instruction later.[5] The exams of the many American schools now follow a surprisingly few patterns based on a few hypothetical questions and, less often, on a group of many multiple-choice questions.

This pattern—of hypothetical essay examinations being the sole record of the students' performance—is a recent stage in the evolution of U.S. legal education. Once exams were only one form of evaluation to judge fitness, used in conjunction with class recitations, notebook inspections, and moot court performance. This complicated evaluation scheme was replaced by graduation exams, designed to measure the specific knowledge acquired over the whole course of study.

These in turn were followed by annual and course-end examinations. The questions of these exams evolved from brief didactic questions designed to measure rote memory to complicated hypotheticals designed to measure application. In this century, the objective question, the spiritual descendent of the then-obsolete didactic question emerged, allowing both faster evaluation of the student submission and broader coverage in the evaluation. This article describes this evolution, commencing with its English antecedents and influences.[6]

I. The English Experience to 1900: Trial and Error

A. Moots

Blackstone maintained that the English Inns of Court arose in response to the operation of Magna Carta and other acts fixing a permanent location of the law courts in London. "Here exercises were performed, lectures were read, and degrees were at length conferred in the common law, as at other universities in the canon and civil."[7] From the Fourteenth to the early Seventeenth Century, the Inns were power-houses of legal instruction,[8] and their primary form of education was the argument of moot cases,[9] which when done by the students, served as the student's oral examination.

The most spectacular of these moot arguments were performed semi-annually by senior barristers in the Readings, held in the Lent and Autumn vacations; student attendance was compulsory.[10] As reported by Nathaniel Bacon, the senior barristers would select a reader, who would choose a statute to describe and criticize, offering an argument for reform of the statute. This argument would then be challenged by other barristers in a debate that would last three or four days per week for two or three weeks.[11] Besides these showpiece arguments by the senior lawyers, the seniors observed student moots and arguments throughout terms and vacations, with varying degrees of participation by senior barristers.[12] The Readings set the standard and the style of the student moots. The problems assigned for student mooting, as for many of the Readings, tended to be hoary and well-tested, but this did not make the disputation easier. Professor Baker illustrates a typical moot problem from Lincoln's Inn:

> Two coparceners, seised of a manor by descent, have a tenant who holds the manor by homage and fealty and by the services of 20s. a year, repairing the mill and roofing the hall of the manor; the tenant grants part of the manor to a stranger, to hold of the chief lord of the fee by the services due; one of the parceners commits felony, for which she is attainted; the lord enters as in his escheat; and then they make partition between themselves, so that the mill is allotted to the lord and they hold the hall and the other services in common; and then they grant the hall to a man *pur terme d'autre vie*, during whose time the hall is unroofed; he for whose life the hall was leased dies; they enter as in their reversion; the lord makes a recognizance to a stranger to pay certain money at a certain day, at which day he does not pay, and so the other sues execution and has execution in respect of the mill; and during that time the mill falls down; the money is paid; the lord enters and distrains them; the tenants make replevin. Ceux?[13]

30. Austin Hall Library, 1902. Regardless of the class method, student preparation for an examination has, to date, been a practice of rereading the law while reviewing class notes and course summaries. (*Courtesy of Art & Visual Materials, Special Collections Department, Harvard Law School Library.*)

In observing students in the arguments lasting several hours, the senior lawyers both evaluated and coached their apprentices. The Inns' moots, however, were interrupted by the English civil war, an event from which they never fully recovered.[14]

B. Examinations

In the mid-sixteenth century, an oral examination was required of candidates to be called to the bar, examining, primarily, for satisfaction of residence, mooting, religious observance, and attendance requirements.[15] In 1596, the Readers of each Inn were given quotas of students who should be called, from the "fittest for then learning and honest conversation," although even such students should only be qualified to practice "very sparingly, in respect of the great multitude that there be already."[16] Thus, the exams were mere formality, and students were selected for professional qualification based on interview and on observation in such moots as were held, a state of affairs lasting from the Seventeenth to the Nineteenth century.[17] By the early Nineteenth century, however, even the moots had deteriorated to a series of desultory mechanical exercises held over lunch.[18]

Oxford, which had held lectures in Roman and, until Henry VII, canon law, since the twelfth century,[19] established examinations in its reforms under the Caroline Code of Archbishop Laud of 1636.[20] During the years of study,[21] a law student would be expected to attend lectures and to give disputations on set topics; thus, the education was said to be analytic and dialectic. The topics for argument in the disputations were usually posted on college walls, and the arguments were usually conducted in the afternoons before the officers of the university. Each student performed at least one disputation per term, and there were then four terms.[22]

The examinations to conclude the degree were oral, initially conducted with three examiners questioning a single student, although by the eighteenth century, students were examined in pairs.[23] Responding to the increasingly lax curriculum, the exams steadily eroded to a relatively ceremonial, formal exercise in which performance was often based on simple rote memory and in which failure was almost unknown.[24] By 1770, the examinations had become almost perfunctory, as witnessed by Lord Eldon's famous description of his examination for a double bachelor's degree:

> I was examined for a degree in Hebrew and in History.
> "What is the Hebrew for the place of a skull?"
> I replied, "Golgotha."
> "Who founded University College?"
> I stated (though by the way, the point is sometimes doubted), "that King Alfred founded it."
> "Very well sir," said the Examiner, "you are competent for your degree."[25]

Oxford's examination system was overhauled in 1800, with newly appointed examiners instructed to be more rigorous,[26] which had a rather interesting and unintended effect on instruction in common law. Law examinations were set solely for the bachelor's in civil law, and neither it nor any other degree required instruction in common law. Thus, even after Charles Viner established a professorship to teach the common law, held by William Blackstone and then Robert Chambers, there was little student demand for such instruction.[27] Still, common law instruction continued sporadically, even after civil law instruction had declined. By the mid-nineteenth century, the Professors of Civil Law in Oxford and in Cambridge had ceased to lecture, although the Vinerian lectures still attracted thirty-eight students who still were not examined in common law.[28]

Of course, Victorian Oxford was a time of reform, and the exams finally given in Oxford, which were printed and distributed in the United States, reflect a more thorough-going scrutiny of the preparation of the student than Lord Eldon suffered. The 1871 examination in Real Property lists a dozen questions, testing by rote the student's knowledge of the field.

1. What do you mean by tenure? What are the practical results of the fact that no one can have more than an estate in land?
2. Explain the following tenures—in frankalmoigne—by cornage—in gavelkind—ancient demesne.
3. The statute De Donis created estates tail. Show the exact meaning of this statement.
4. Trace successive means by which the holding of land in mortmain was restrained.
5. State the rule in Shelley's case, and show how it is related to the original interpretation of a gift to a man and his heirs.
6. What was the object of the Statute of Uses, and by what means was it evaded?
7. Explain the terms *general occupant, corruptio sanguinis, vivum vadium, reversion, defeazance.*
8. Enumerate the various forms of life estate, and specify the differences between them as regards the rights of the tenant over the land.
9. What changes were made in the rules of intestate succession by the statute 3 and 4 Wm.IV c.106? Show by examples the importance of the changes.
10. Explain the exact nature of Livery of Seisin, and show how the Statute of Uses was employed to evade it.
11. What is the origin of Dower? Trace the successive changes in the law on this subject.
12. Explain the effect of each of the following, and the reason for each:—
    (1) Feoffment to A and his heirs (before and after the Statute of Uses)
    (2) Grant to the use of A, to uses as B shall appoint.
    (3) Feoffment to A on condition that B dies before Christmas.
    (4) Verbal lease to A for five years.[29]

These exams were printed and then widely distributed, including distribution in the United States.[30]

Of course, the university exams were not alone in their reformation. The Law Society, which oversees the training of clerks who wish to become solicitors, introduced a compulsory written examination in 1835, a requirement enshrined in statute in 1843.[31] This examination was not an overwhelming burden, however, and a Parliamentary committee considered it no more than a "guarantee against absolute incompetency."[32] Indeed, the select committee, finding that legal education in England was nearly nonexistent, found that what little existed was overly concerned with the technicalities of law and insufficiently concerned with more general, doctrinal instruction.

It was about this time that England, or at least many of its public institutions, embraced the written examination. In 1853, the India Act made positions in the Indian Civil Service dependent upon performance of an examination, rather than upon patronage as had been the case; competitive exams for appointment were partially mandated for the Home Civil Service in 1855, becoming compulsory in 1870.[34] In 1850, secondary school admissions were first based on external examinations, and in 1857 and 1858, Oxford and Cambridge followed suit. By 1862, even government-supported elementary schools were required to give written examinations in reading, writing, and math. As a whole, examinations were seen as a method for the competitive and democratic movement from social preferment to merit as a means of access to education and position. The exams allowed classification of students, testing their skills for those believed to be needed in the professions, and providing opportunity in a slightly more egalitarian fashion.[35]

The Inns of Court first required trainee barristers to take a written exam in 1844, creating the Council of Legal Education in 1852 to create a standard exam, which was initially only required of students who had not attended lectures.[36] The exam became a universal requirement in 1872.[37] It was partly written and partly oral, and it was not demanding.[38]

The 1853 English Bar Exam questions are reproduced in full in part one of the Appendix to this article. It is clear that the exam questions performed several functions. The four preliminary questions echoed the ancient concerns of how long, what about, and with whom the student studied. Most of the questions in the five areas of subject matter—common law and practice; conveyancing; equity and procedure; bankruptcy and practice; and criminal law and procedure—require specific recitations of definitions or pleading elements. A significantly smaller number of questions are in the form of brief hypothetical requiring the student both to supply a particular doctrine and to give an opinion of its application to a few specific facts. There are some idiosyncratic questions, as well. Question eighteen requires the drafting a pleading and a judgement. Question twenty requires recitation of a history of conveyancing. (Many of these questions styles are also to be found in American bar exams in the following years, as in the New York exam also reprinted in part one of the Appendix.)

> The University of London commenced a course in English Law leading to the Bachelor's of Laws degree, graduating three students in 1836 and 135 by the century's end.[39] University-run legal education in nineteenth century England was not seen as a serious academic enterprise, remaining an unpopular professional option in the face of renewed instruction in the Inns and in local crash courses designed to prepare students for the Law Society exams.[40]

Despite these efforts at reform, the close of the nineteenth century found the professional examination still foundering. At the turn of the century, both English and American critics were alarmed at English instruction that represented about a third of the instruction of an American school and examinations that "do not afford any trustworthy test of adequate knowledge of the law."[41]

It is, perhaps, unfair not to describe the renaissance of English legal education and examination in this century, leaving the reader with an unwarranted impression that matters are as they were a century ago.[42] The parochial focus of this essay, however, is to consider English forms of educational evaluation and their contributions and their influence on American programs, which waned considerably in the twentieth century. That said, a useful summary of later styles of the English law exam is still had in the review of exam technique by University of London law professor L.C.B. Gower. Considering the English law exam in its collegiate and professional forms, he summarized its question formats in 1950 as falling roughly into three classes:

1. Pure tests of memory on points of detail. For example: "What is the order of succession in the case of deaths after 1925?" This type is common in the professional examinations.
2. Essay questions. For example: "Sketch the history of freehold tenures." This type is found principally in the university examinations.
3. Hypothetical problems. This type is now increasingly common in both university and professional examinations and there is no need to give examples.[43]

Of these forms, Gowers believed the hypothetical problem to be the most valuable, as it tests understanding of principles and practical proficiency more than mere knowledge.[44]

II. The American Examination Experience, Part I: Exams of the Commentators[45]

Examinations were part and parcel of early American legal pedagogy. While there were graduation examinations, the evaluation of the student through frequent written or oral questioning was integral to the lecture. Given the relationship of the lecture to the commentary style, the examination was really a measure of how well the student had recognized and could later remember and repeat the information in the commentary or, later, the treatise. This system was made longer and more thematically comprehensive in the graduation examination. As the commentary system came into competition with case method instruction, and as bar exams and foreign exams became more hypothetical, the questions evolved into the application of a doctrine or two to solve a simple fact pattern, requiring the student not only to recall the doctrine that applies in such facts, but to apply it to determine which hypothetical party's interests are favored under it. While these exams were often showpieces, many were given as graduation exercises that were held to high standards and that could be barriers to promotion into the second year or to graduation. Finally, as the exams became less frequent and more summary, used to conclude a course of study over a semester or a year, the exam began to test a smaller sample of the student's work.

A. Classroom Exercises and Annual Essays

The first professional law school in America, the Litchfield Law School of Tapping Reeve and James Gould, held examinations of its students every Saturday.[46] These quizzes, usually oral, were overseen by Judge Reeve during his ownership of the school, although Judge Gould hired two assistants, Jabez W. Huntington and Origen Storrs Seymour, to examine the students in his stead beginning in 1820.[47] The questions were meant to give "a thorough investigation of the principles of each rule, and not merely of such questions as can be answered from memory without any exercise of the judgement."[48] Given the structure of the Litchfield lectures,[49] it is a reasonable assumption that these questions were quite specific, created to measure the degree with which students could recall specific points of the week's lectures.

In the earliest days of Harvard's law school under Asahel Stearns, students were given oral or written examinations weekly as well as at the end of each text or topic.[50] Written examinations were not apparently required in every course, however. In 1826, Stearns' report to the school's overseers described the system of instruction included in regular exercises of the school: "1. *Recitations and Examinations* in several of the most important text books, such as *Blackstone's Commentaries, Cruise on Real Property, Saunders on Uses, Fearne on Remainders*, etc."[51]

A final examination, of a kind, was also required, covering the content of the entire course, in the form of set dissertations. The students were given topics set by the faculty, which they answered in descriptive essays. The 1820 dissertation questions were these:

1—The Rules of Descent and Distribution of Real and Personal Property by the Civil Law, the Law of England and the Law of Massachusetts.

2—The several injuries to which the Heir is liable in relation to his right of succession to Real Property, and the several remedies by Entry or Action which are furnished by the laws of England and of Massachusetts.[52]

After 1829 Judge Story and Professor Greenleaf gave quizzes and examinations in class, often several times a week, but these examinations were as voluntary as was class attendance.[53] This system persisted through Joel Parker's deanship.[54] So, from 1829 to 1871, Harvard seems to have had no formal examination of student performance that could bar a student from the degree. While this became a criticism of the program, the absence of exams was obviously not seen by Story, Greenleaf, Parsons, and the other lights of mid-nineteenth century Harvard as sufficiently problematic to cause them to institute any tests of greater rigor.[55]

B. The Graduation Examination and Annual Examinations

Of course, that Harvard abandoned the exam did not mean that it was not in flower elsewhere. The University of Virginia Law School, reorganized in 1829 under John Tayloe Lomax, required its graduates not only "to display a competent knowledge of the Common Law and the Law Merchant—embracing generally all of the branches of what is commonly considered 'municipal law,' [but also] to have passed an examination in English grammar and literature."[56] The Virginia exam was tough. Indeed, during the tenure of John B. Minor, who took up his post in 1845, a candidate was required to answer five-sixths of the questions on the graduation examination. In the first ten years of Minor's tenure, only fifty-nine of the 649 students who matriculated were awarded degrees.[57]

Examinations in law were necessary for those law schools whose students benefitted from the diploma privilege and could be admitted to the bar of the schools' states with no further exam. As schools were granted the right for their graduates to enter the profession without further examination by the local bar, the schools' examinations took on the role of both professional certification and justification of the privilege.[58] Thus, Theodore Dwight secured the diploma privilege for Hamilton College in 1855, under a legislative act allowing the court to appoint a committee of lawyers to examine Hamilton law students at the school.[59] In 1859, Albany Law School persuaded the New York legislature to designate its own faculty as bar examiners.[60] Dwight worked his magic again when he moved to Columbia, not only securing the diploma privilege for his own school's graduating class of 1860, but also representing both Columbia and New York University in suits to defend the privilege.[61] By 1870, nine schools held this privilege in their own states, although Oregon, which had no law school of its own, extended it to the graduates of everyone else's.[62]

In carrying out the new obligations of professional bar examiner, the faculties usually resorted to written exams, as well as daily or weekly quizzes. Thus, the Columbia course of instruction in 1864 included obligations for the student in two forms of examination. He must "prepare himself each day upon a subject selected by the Professor. He is then examined upon the subject studied. Having grappled with some of its difficulties, he is then prepared for the oral exposition which accompanies the examination."[63] Further, he was obliged to complete a "pass" or final examination at the close of the senior year, which were held before the Law Committee, a group of faculty and external examiners, and which lasted for three days.[64] These examinations were oral, and "adopted to secure greater familiarity with the subjects in which they had been instructed, every effort being made to avoid cramming."[65] Columbia also held prize exams administered to students prior to graduation, but which do not appear to have led to sanction for poor performance,[66] and daily quizzes held under third-year student tutors.[67] There are no apparent records of failures in these exams.

Whether through the influence of law-school examiners on the bar, or bar examiners on the schools, or both, a strong similarity in question form is evident between law school exams in the middle of the century with the bar exams. Bar exam questions in New York as late as 1888, reprinted in part one of the Appendix, mirror the patterns of the school exams.

That schools with the diploma privilege carried on examinations does not suggest that this is the only reason for them to do so. Virginia actively sought to avoid such a privilege, although it continued to require a rigorous exam,[68] and other schools, such as the St. Louis Law School, began to examine students without such a privilege.

The University of Iowa first required an examination for graduation of its class matriculating in 1865, a bar-like examination that included not only knowledge of the law but of character.[69] Four local attorneys were jointly appointed by the school and the Iowa Supreme Court as examiners, who held, apparently, oral examinations over three days. The earliest known written record of Iowa's exams is that of its Fall 1868 examinations. These were held on two days in its fall term, with two more supplementary days of exams of fall material given in January of the following year.[70] Each question was an elemental inquiry, requiring a recitation of a term, definition, or specification of a legal doctrine, and each exam drew questions from several topics of law. The first day's examination consisted of fifteen questions, which include intermingled questions of constitutional law, property, contracts, and commercial paper:

1. What are the sources of the Law of Nations?
2. When have the Federal Courts jurisdiction in common law cases?
3. What are the sources of municipal law in this country?
4. State the absolute rights of persons, and define each.
5. What constitutes a valid marriage at common law?
6. What interest had the husband at common law in each kind of his wife's property?
7. When is a father responsible for his child's contracts and torts?
8. State the distinction between real and personal property.
9. What are the essential elements of a valid contract?
10. What did the Statute of Frauds provide?
11. Define a bailment, and enumerate the various kinds.
12. What is the difference between a bill of exchange and a promissory note?
13. What is an easement?
14. State the difference between the present legal rights of [a] mortgagee, and those he had at common law.
15. What are the chief differences between our rules of descent and those of the common law?[71]

The second day's exam included questions, similarly constructed, touching on civil procedure and trial evidence, contracts, torts, and crimes. This exam's first question was a question of case reading, "What is an issue, and how is it to be reached?"[72] These questions followed instruction by Professors Hammond and Cole with student readings assigned in Kent's *Commentaries*, Stephen on Pleading, the Iowa Code of 1860, and Greenleaf on Evidence. Professor Hammond's Torts lectures appear not to have corresponded to a particular book.[73] Iowa's supplemental exams, given half on January 16 and half on January 30 of the next term, included more questions of a similar style, drawn from similar topics of law, but on a slightly more sophisticated plane. These are the questions of the first day:

1. State the difference between the Law of Nature and the Law of Nations.
2. Who are entitled to the rights of the native-born citizens of the U.S.?
3. Of what do the *written* and the *unwritten* law of this country severally consist?
4. What are the powers belonging to a corporation as such?
5. When & how far is a husband liable for his wife's debts?
6. When is the endorser of a note liable upon it?
7. How does a fee differ from a freehold, and what are the different kinds of fees?
8. How does a mortgage differ from a conditional sale?
9. Define each of these terms, reversion, vested remainder, contingent remainder.
10. What are the essential parts of a deed.
11. What do we mean by recording a deed, and what will be the effect of omitting to record it?
12. What is a noncupative will, & when is it valid?

13. How may a will be revoked?
14. What is the difference between the English rules of descent, and the American?
15. What is the right of eminent domain?[74]

Questions of the second day were based largely in pleading, evidence, tort, and crimes.[75]

The University of Chicago Law School, opening in 1859, required examinations of its students prior to graduation, and the exams were first given over three days in July of 1861.[76] Similarly, the St. Louis Law School, of Washington University in St. Louis, required an examination of the students of its first entering class, in 1867.[77] These students took not only termly exams that were written and graded by the professors but also graduation exams given at the end of the second year that were written and graded by an outside board of lawyers and judges.[78] Boston University Law School, opening its doors to the many who sought to avoid the Harvard case method in 1872, commenced its instruction with both annual and graduation examinations.[79]

The idea of the annual or termly examination as the sole method of evaluation did not, however, gain universal acceptance, and many schools continued to hold weekly or daily examinations. The University of Michigan established a general examination in 1860,[80] but it also hired recent graduates and young lawyers, called "quizmasters," who oversaw daily oral and written examinations of the material covered in earlier lectures, beginning in 1859.[81] These oral exams became increasingly rigorous over the years,[82] and, by 1883, students were barred by poor performance from promotion to the second year.[83]

This form of dual evaluation, of frequent quizzing with annual or graduation examinations, was not uncommon in many schools toward the last quarter of the century. Iowa's curriculum, designed by William Hammond, required quizzing, three termly final exams, and a graduation exam.[84] Cornell held daily examinations in all of its lecture classes, particularly in its elementary law class, as well as termly and graduation exams.[85] Penn held frequent examinations as well as a graduation exam.[86] Columbia's combination of daily quizzes, annual prize exams, and graduation exams, has been discussed.[87]

III. The American Examination, Part II: Examinations of the Case Scientists

Famously, the 1870's saw the advent of the case method of instruction, starting first at Harvard under the aegis of Dean Christopher Columbus Langdell. At the same time, Harvard reintroduced examinations.[88] The exams that accompanied case method instruction came, fairly quickly, to emulate the style of instruction, with examinations built around full-blooded essay questions of a complexity that increased over time. Over the century from 1870, these questions have placed a greater emphasis on developing the facts that might lead to a decision, on identifying the various doctrines that would govern those facts, on demonstrating the rationale of the doctrine and the manner in which it applies to the facts, and on an expectation that the student might criticize the rightness of the application of the doctrines that would seemingly govern the outcome.

These essay questions have required an increasing depth of analysis of fewer issues and subjects. The questions represent increasingly complicated choices by the examiners in the method of evaluation, sometimes requiring a greater portion of the anser to be occupied by policy analysis and criticism than by recitation or application of the applicable rules. For these reasons, and because of the influence of the bar exams, the essays have been augmented with the addition of batteries of short machine-scorable "objective" questions, which were initially true-false and then multiple choice.

Student performance on these end-of-term exams, whether or not they include shorter or machine-scorable questions, form the basis, almost universally in this century, of grades. The grades are, of course, averaged, allowing a student to be placed in rank order among other students, as well as given honors, allowed to graduate, or asked to leave.

A. From Quiz to Hypothetical Essay

Alfred Reed described Harvard's renewed use of annual exams as being made under the influence of the English examination movement and, perhaps, in recognition of disappointing bar exam performances by its graduates.[89] The Harvard Law School Circular of 1871 announced that the LL.B. would only be conferred upon

> students who shall pass satisfactory examinations in all the required subjects and in at least seven of the elective subjects,[90] after having been in the School for not less than one year. . . .
>
> The examinations for a degree will be of a thorough and searching character; but will be limited in scope to the ground covered by the instruction given in the School in the several subjects.[91]

This announcement "came upon the public as an innovation of a most startling character."[92] These exams were first administered between June 14 and 22, 1871.

> Printed questions were submitted in June to the candidates, covering all the principal topics of Law and Equity. These questions they were required to answer in writing; the answers being written in the presence of some member of the faculty, without consultation with other persons or with books.
>
> The examinations occupied six days, and judging by the questions and by such of the written answers as have been inspected, . . . it was an honest and thorough test of the acquirements of the student.[93]

A critical facet of the newly reconstituted Harvard exam was not only that it served as a guide to student progress, but also that it could be a bar to further attendance or receipt of the degree. With the 1872 exams, students who failed to pass the first-year exam were made ineligible for the degree, even though the degree would not have been conferred until the end of the second year.[94] In 1872, twenty-six students sat for the first-year exams, of whom nineteen passed but seven failed, disqualifying them for further study.[95] Passing a first-year exam required performance of at least seventy percent, and students could fail no more than two of the subject-specific exams.[96] In the 1871 second-year exams, which qualified for the degree, thirty-one had been examined; twenty-eight passed and three failed. This pattern continued in 1873, when forty-six of the fifty-six first-year examinees passed.[97]

Dean Langdell's exams followed the pattern of examinations in England, as well as in Litchfield, Columbia, and Iowa, in asking specific questions to measure specific knowledge of points of law. Thus, in 1871, typical questions from the exams were quite in keeping with the earlier models. Each question is designed to elicit a specific rule or law or definition. Agency questions included mere recognition of limits on capacity for agency of infants and married women,[98] and corporations, equity, and property questions all included demands for simple definitions.[99] This form of specific question was soon modified by the questions propounded by Langdell's faculty, if not by himself.

In his collection of examinations published in 1899, Northwestern Professor John Wigmore argued that the "most fair and practical test of the results of a law-student's work, and of his capacity to apply his knowledge and to give sound legal advice to future clients, is an examination consisting of practical problems in the form of concrete hypothetical cases."[100] Wigmore gave the credit for implementing these problems as the exclusive basis for an examination paper to James Barr Ames, in his 1873 examinations.[101]

In Harvard's 1878 exams, while Langdell's style remained as of old, and John Chipman Gray used hypotheticals on an earlier model, James Barr Ames was casting his questions in brief and more dramatic hypothetical. Langdell demanded a recitation of the use a particular pleading. Gray's exam was something between the extremes of Langdell and Ames, asking a more narrow question that would not have been out of place on the older English bar exams, designed to elicit an opinion on behalf of a sheep farmer.[102] Meanwhile, Ames has his students advise an employer about actions against a Lothario who seduced the employer's servant, making her leave his employ. Ames had set the stage for a the use of a number of specific facts for the application of a particular rule, which was not in itself novel. What made his stage important was to place the student in the role of acting in the drama. He made the student the lawyer, not merely the expositor of the law. In this way, the hypothetical essay question came, perhaps ironically, to resemble the moot court arguments of the early Inns. By giving the hypothetical characters a more human dimension, and by adding sufficient details to tailor the result to the problem assigned, the "practicality," which Wigmore cheered was achieved.

With Ames's hypothetical problems also came a greater range for student creativity became possible, including the pursuit of some ability to criticize the law or to discuss matters of policy. One sees questions of policy interjected into James Bradley Thayer's exams of 1887, which are profoundly evident in the significantly more fact-intensive questions he propounded in 1890.[103]

Thus, within the first decade of its re-employment at Harvard, the most essential ideas of the modern essay question had appeared and become the norm. Wigmore claimed that this exam style had, within ten years, become nearly universal in "a dozen schools."[104] One of the most important features of the new Harvard exam was that it not only determined whether students passed or failed but that it was graded.[105]

Under the leadership of Harvard poachee William Keener, Columbia's exams took on the character of the Harvard models, adapting them somewhat but employing both the short hypothetical and policy question, emphasizing the rationale for any conclusion. These questions were interspersed with questions in the older style demanding definition or explanation of specific points of law. The Spring 1894 exams illustrate this point nicely.[106]

First-year students were examined in separate exams on the elements of jurisprudence, contracts, and equity on May 24; common law pleading and practice on May 28; criminal law on May 29; torts on May 31; persons and domestic relations on June 4; real and personal property on June 5. Each examination begins with the italicized instruction, "Give your reasons for every answer." Second- and third-year students were examined on a similar schedule in their respective courses.

Some questions are clearly willing to represent unusual behavior for the purpose of eliciting an application of particular doctrines, such as the first question in equity. "1. A, who has already assaulted B, threatens to assault him daily and to enter upon his lands for that purpose if it is necessary. What are B's rights?"[107] The examination in first-year property is in a style typical of the other exams, and several of its questions are reproduced in the Appendix. It consists of three printed pages of nine questions. Two questions require specific doctrinal information to be related, mainly in the extent of current application of ancient doctrines. The other seven are hypotheticals presenting a set of facts among parties, from which the student is to ascertain the claims and defenses of various parties, including those rooted in minority doctrines, always giving "reasons for your answers." Each of these questions tends to require the application of several doctrines.

The new-fangled annual examination approach to the degree was not, however, readily and universally embraced. For instance Yale, during the 1880s, responded to what its dean saw as Harvard's over-reliance on an otherwise unchecked examination system.[108] Yale allowed office study to count toward time required for its law degree, and it gave a law degree to a student with one year's study, if that student had already passed a state bar exam.[109]

Other programs, unaffected by the squabbles of the East coast, continued to employ a graduation exam rather than an annual exam.[110] Hastings, under the rule of John Norton Pomeroy, required an examination at the close of the third year, covering topics from all three years, with an emphasis on recognition of doctrine rather than applications to facts.[111] Thus, an 1882 Hastings question in constitutional law asked

> Has the State of California, or any other State, power by statute to prevent Chinese or other foreigners from coming within the State to reside? Give the reasons for your answer. Where does the power of exclusion reside? Assuming that there are no treaties concerning the subject, has or has not the United States Government the power, under the International Law, to prevent the people of any foreign country from coming to and residing within the limits of the United States?[112]

The graduation examination continued in fitful popularity well into this century, popular because it could serve as a bar examination in itself and because it resembled the comprehensive examinations of graduate students in other academic departments of the university. In 1931, Cornell instituted a comprehensive examination at the end of its third year. The test was partly oral and partly written, and it was often drawn with elective questions that emphasized areas in which the student had performed poorly in the preceding five series of semester examinations.[113] This era seems to have one in which law comps. test were popular, judged at least by one attack against them.[114] As well as the graduation exam, some schools continued to rely on the effectively "comprehensive" bar examinations rather than internal examinations as their tests of fitness.[115]

By the turn of the century, the procedure of annual examination had spread among law schools, in part because of the influence of the American Association of Law Schools. At the Association's first meeting, Virginia Professor Raleigh C. Minor argued for the written examination as a requirement for law school graduation.[116] In the 1903 AALS meeting, St. Louis Law School Professor William Curtis described the parameters of the contemporary examination.[117] The exam for a given subject should last three or four hours and not much longer to avoid it becoming an endurance test for the students. He was also concerned that the exam receive neither a perfunctory nor a long-delayed review.

> Necessarily, then, the examination cannot extend beyond ten to twenty questions, supposing, of course, the questions to be carefully prepared in presenting concrete problems for the application of principles as well as calling for abstract rules and definitions. With fifteen questions the examiner, I contend, may test the student's knowledge of any one of the well-known topics in which the law finds itself divided. With a class of from fifty to seventy-five, the examiner cannot well report the results short of a week or ten days, employing his fragments of time, or of forty-eight hours in case he does nothing else. Long-delayed examinations are as great a nuisance as long-delayed decisions, and for much the same reason.[118]

Clearly, the questions Curtis had in mind were not dissimilar to the early Iowa questions or to Ames' Harvard questions, a group of fifteen or so specific questions of reasonable simplicity designed to identify, or to identify and apply, discrete knowledge of particular doctrines of law. One of the more important of Curtis's observations clearly applies no matter the form of the question, that the students should have feedback following the exam. He argued that individual students should be told the percentage of performance, with a mark on each question, not merely a pass or fail for the whole, because the student has a right to know both the nature of his error and the idiosyncrasies of the examiner. Further, he suggested that all of the papers written by the class should be accessible, so that students can compare answers and marks.[119]

One last component of the examination process was, perhaps, inevitable with the raised stakes the exam represented, the institution of standards against cheating. Law schools responded through the use of proctors to observe students in examination rooms and through the adoption of honor codes.[120]

As the mechanics of the exam began to reach a rough uniformity, the exams themselves did so, too. Through the first half of the twentieth century, an apparently uncoordinated but national transformation took place in the evolution of the essay questions. Slowly over the century, particularly in the years following the second world war, the forms of the essay exam evolved. Various customs grew up, as schools adopted local icons to replace, or at least supplement the venerable exam characters, the widow X, the son Y, and the devisee Z, or seller A, buyer B, and squatter C, who had so often had their rights to Blackacre and Whiteacre, located in the neverland of the common law assessed. In their place, Harvard examinees found themselves in the State of Ames, and Columbia's discovered their practice was in the State of Kent, as students of other schools moved in similarly mythic states and, as often, in real ones, to represent clients with ascribed names rather than letters.

Harvard exam questions collect in part two of the Appendix illustrate this transition. The questions of the 1870's move from stale statements of A sells to B in order to locate, gratuitously, the parties in Boston, New York, and Concord. By 1890, the parties to the hypotheticals include not just A, B, X, and "the owner" or "the carrier" but "The Corporation of Harvard College" and William Kemmler, the first convict to be executed in the electric chair. By 1935, the hypotheticals regularly include names or real and fictitious clients, decedents, beneficiaries, contractors, and so on, in a tremendously rich factual environment. By 1956, the exam questions include hypothetical statutes, and are . Rather well established in the pattern apparent in the survey of recent examinations in part five.

Similar patterns of evolution are apparent in the sample exam questions from Columbia, in Appendix part three, and Michigan in Appendix part four. Among the innovations in these examples, Karl Llewellyn's clear allowance for the student to alter or complete the hypothetical deserves special mention. His 1928 exam typically requires the student to "State any facts you find it desirable to assume." This instruction has become a commonplace, and a typical example of its current use is in Steven Shiffrin's exam in Appendix part five.

A modern question often demands the students to work with complex facts, which disguise multitudes of claims and defenses. The student must isolate the issues involved and perform a variety of forms of analysis in order to give reasoned support for conclusions about the interests of the hypothetical parties. Moreover, the questions themselves have grown more complicated and lengthy. Fact patterns began to include facts that were unnecessary to resolve the issues designed for student evaluation; they began to acquire red herrings.[121]

In response to this complexity, students both became more prolix and resorted to numerous artifices to give the appearance of scrutiny to the question and of recollection and reason in its reply.[122] In response, time, space, word, and page limits were devised, which both required the student to prioritize arguments and allowed the professor a shorter reading time in the evaluation. Harlan Fiske Stone threatened wordy students with a reduced grade, a penalty often asserted by his successors. Among the more entertaining solutions to student prolixity are admonitions to emphasize issue designation and legal reasoning over mere prose, such as Llewellyn's instruction to "*Think first, and don't write until you see where you are going.*" This instruction is compounded by his caveat that he would grade the questions on the structure of the analyses more than on their fullness, "It is not necessary to finish any question. State the law before you discuss or criticize it."

A signal degree of comparison in the form of exam instruction is that between the exams prior to the 1960's with many of those collected in part 5, offered over the last several years. Besides admonitory language such as Larry Tribe's "Concise answers will be rewarded in grading; unduly long answers will be penalized," he gives instructions on legible handwriting and clear typing. Similar instructions are given by Frank Michelman. These are brief compared to the instructions given by Ronald Rotunda at Illinois, which include similar concerns for clear thought and good organization, along with requests to be polite when leaving the examination room. It seems certain that the greater degree of specificity in these instructions is in response to occurrences within institutions, which in turn provoke clarifying instruction. If this is so, some unusual insight to student behavior in the examination room may be gleaned from such clarifications.

Beginning in the early years of the twentieth century, political, or at least theoretical, ideology began to be seen as a basis for examination. In Laura Kalman's study of legal realism at Yale, she noted that most of the realists' exams were conservative, or typical of the exams then used nationally. Even so, she noted that Morris Cohen's and Harold Laski's jurisprudence finals tended to be more daring. In 1930, Cohen required students to "state and criticize various views as to what law is and what it should be. When is a case wrongly decided? Indicate the relation of a science of law to the social sciences, to logic, to ethics, and to psychology."[123] In 1931, Laski asked his administrative law students to illustrate and discuss the gobbet, "[i]n a field where every case involves a multitude of pertinent elements which vary in importance from case to case it is impossible to find the criteria out of which legal rules emerge." Such concerns for policy in the Yale exams were not unusual, as in Fred Rodell's 1939 exam question, asking for criticism or defense of this: "It is practically useless to pass a pro-labor statute in these United States. The courts will emasculate it. . . . They already have."[124]

A later, and more common, approach combines require the student to deomonstrate both substantive evaluation and critical theory in providing a case for the student to analyze either as clerk or justice. A classic example of this genre is question one of Herbert Wechsler's 1976 Constitutional Law exam, reproduced in full in part three of the Appendix.

The desire to increase the effectiveness of the exam as a tool for evaluation, and the desire to do so more efficiently, and sometimes a wild-eyed desire to fiddle around have led professors into the design of numerous experimental questions. There have, of course, been experiments in question design that have failed. In the 1928-29 academic year, Leon Green reportedly set a Torts examination at Yale in which he posed eight complex hypotheticals and directed the students to list the questions posed by the problems but not to attempt to answer them. As Arthur Corbin related the story, "[h]ow happy that made the young pups! And how miserable they made Green. Not even the best ones, or Green himself, would know *all* the questions."[125] Green may have merely used Corbin's contracts grades for the same students instead of compiling his own grades from the botched torts exam.[126]

Despite such experimentation, which continues somewhat, there is a profound similarity in the construction of the essay questions offered by different professors in different faculties in American schools. The examinations collected in part five of the Appendix were chosen somewhat randomly, albeit from schools of national influence that distribute their exams. While there are differing emphases among them, there are dramatically more frequent similarities. Examinees are given a story, a narrative requiring the recognition of particularly appropriate legal doctrines, enunciation of the component requirements of the doctrines, application of those components to the myriad facts, which must be prioritized so that irrelevant facts are discarded, and, often criticism or extrapolation of the current rule.

The modern essay question was described by Tulane Professor Ferdinand Stone in his popular 1952 *Handbook of Law Study* as a test, not of knowledge of the law, but of its use. The essays are designed not to reward memorization but to reward application, which itself requires memory of the law being applied.[127] Such advice to students has been often echoed, not least in Stanley Kinyon's currently popular West Nutshell, *Introduction to Law Study and Law Examinations.*[128] The specific details of this "use" are, though, sometimes the subject of disagreement.

One of the more careful expositions of examination performance, by Philip Kissam, suggests that the blue book grade measures more than just use. Rather, he concluded that blue book performance measures more a series of work-performance capabilities.

> Successful performance on Blue Book exams appears to require some imprecise combination of four complex but general attributes. I call these attributes the internalization of doctrine; conventional legal imagination; the quality of legal productivity; and the capacity for self-study and self-learning in diffuse, complex, and uncertain situations.[129]

There have been occasional paeans to the modern hypothetical essay question as a measure of, or a mismeasure of, the student's ability to make a lawyerly application of the subject matter of the course to a particular problem.[130] The heart of this process of application is multi-faceted, although there is some continuity in the merit of each facet. In 1931, the Dean of Penn, Herbert Goodrich, quoted the New York board of bar examiners' instructions to candidates as a model of the component tasks of any essay examinee.

> The answer should show: A recognition of the problems; an analysis of the material facts; the doctrine of law applicable thereto; the solution, and the different steps of reasoning relied on by the applicant to support his solution. Clearness of expression and conciseness of statement will count. The applicant should confine himself to the particular problem presented and should not volunteer information that is not material to the solution. The value of an answer depends not upon its length, nor upon the mere correctness of conclusion, but upon the evidence it displays of the elements above mentioned. Unnecessary length and verbosity detract from the value of an answer.[131]

Throughout this century there has been an increasing pattern of professors writing their tests alone, although this practice is still not universal.[132] Even so, professors still very rarely provide feedback or evaluation of the final examination essay. Indeed, in many schools, return of the students' examination answers to the students is rare.[133] Exams have been given with greater concern for time between one exam and another.[134] Examinations have become anonymous.[135] One other development in examination administration in recent years is the growth of technology, primarily in allowing or requiring students to perform examinations on computers and in using multimedia components of the test construction.[136]

There are differing views as to the reliability of essay grading as an objective measure of student performance.[137] In Ben Wood's experiments at Columbia in the 1920s, there was greater variation among student performance on essay question performance than there was in the answer of true-false questions.[138] Even so, in an LSAC study twenty years later, seventeen contracts law professors in the study tended to agree on their evaluations of any typical essay. This result may not say so much about the particular exactitude of law professors; that same study showed that non-lawyers tended to also assign the same grades to the essays that the professors gave them.[139]

One other function that the essay question performs is to guide future student review to emphasize applications of the law to particular situations rather than rote memorization. This, along with encouraging professorial emulation, motivated Wigmore's decision to publish a comprehensive collection of exams in 1899.[140] Moreover, many law schools make institutional provision for universal access of their students to past exams, a practice that seems to have become relatively common at the beginning of the twentieth century.[141] Columbia published and distributed bound copies of its examinations every year from 1891 to 1945.[142] The University of Michigan continues to do so, a practice it began by at least in 1904.[143] Chicago and Indiana began to do so in 1906.[144] Cornell has done so at least since 1911.[145] Stanford published its finals in 1934.[146] Many law schools disseminate these examinations widely. Harvard published its examinations in the "red books," paper-bound copies of each year's questions, apparently first published in 1947 or 1948.[147] Each year, copies of the red books were placed in crates throughout the law school, which were taken away by students[148] as well as distributed to subscribers, usually to law libraries.[149] Harvard's last year for this practice was 1996, when examination questions were distributed through posting on the law school's web page.[150]

B. The Objective Test: True-False and Multiple Choice Questions

Of course, the essay question is not the only form of the modern law school exam. In the 1920's, in response to the new educational theory developed in schools of education and elsewhere, greater concern about the validity of measurement in the law school examination led to the development of short-answer questions. These questions could be answered by giving the student a statement regarding a doctrine or its application to a set of facts and then requiring the student to mark the statement as true or false.[151] The answers to such questions can then be quickly, and mechanically, tabulated and scored against a set of predesignated correct answers.

In 1921, Northwestern professor Albert Kocourek performed an experiment comparing student performance on "ratiocinative" or essay questions, compared to "dogmatic" questions that were answerable with a "yes" or a "no" or by the shortest possible answer if a yes or no were not possible.[152] In that experiment, the dogmatic or "objective" questions were asked aloud, and the student wrote the answers in a brief time following the reading of each of fifty questions, the first of which were:

1. Which is the broader term, "chattels" or "personal property."
2. Were chattels subject to feudal tenure?
3. Do chattels pass to the heir or to the executor?
4. May a gratuitous bailee maintain a possessory action?
5. Suppose that A is the owner of a chattel which he has leased to B for a year. If A retakes the chattel from B wrongfully before the end of the term, can B recover against A in trespass?[153]

From 1922 to 1925, Ben Wood at Columbia conducted similar research, administering true-false examinations, based in part on the construction of the federal civil service exams, to the contracts and property courses initially before expanding into twenty-two different courses.[154] One of his most significant conclusions was to find a strong correlation between objective question performance and essay question performance.[155] In 1928, Charles Clark reported that both Yale and Columbia had for several years been using true-false questions in combination with essays on their exams, and their use at Yale was no longer considered experimental but part of the regular program.[156] He acknowledged the difficulties in creating careful questions but dismissed concerns that the tests cannot examine lawyering skills, such as the recognition of causal effect, by stating that such limitations were only caused by the limits of the ingenuity of the author of the exam.

By the time of a 1929 survey, true-false examinations were given in forty-four of sixty law schools.[157] In those schools that used such tests, they were distributed across practically all courses, but two-thirds were used in first year subjects. Forty-nine professors of sixty-three surveyed believed the tests were successful, and the tests were generally more often employed in larger courses.[158] Eight professors relied solely on true-false questions, although most used the question for roughly half of the test.[159] Despite such wide acceptance, however, strong voices of doubt persisted, particularly that the chance to guess the right answers made these questions "an insult to the good student's abilities" but a "healthy gambling chance" for the poor student."[160] Despite such concerns, the AALS, during and soon after World War II examined the use of objective questions and recommended them in lieu of essay questions in examinations.[161]

> The objective question format did not long remain tied to the binary limitations of answers that are either true or false. There was considerable interest in the design of law exam questions to test a student's analytical skills with the precision being developed by the Educational Testing Service, the initial authors of the LSAT.[162] The Law School Admission Test was first developed in 1947, employing multiple-choice questions that are designed in a style similar to those of the true-false questions pioneered in the 1920's, in which there were objectively correct answers.[163]

By 1950, the true-false question was already fading from preference in favor of multiple-choice questions and, occasionally, questions that required sentences to be completed and questions that required matching of definitions to terms from a list.[164]

The first use of a multiple choice question at Harvard appears to have been in Robert Braucher's 1956 Legislation exam. A question from that exam required the student to mark one answer to the following:

> Check the best statement:
> A Lawyer who is retained to perform legal services in seeking the enactment of a private bill by Congress
> ____(a) is guilty of a federal crime if he contracts for a fee contingent on success.
> ____(b) is engaged in unethical practice if he charges a fee.
> ____(c) regularly finds that any bill enacted contains provisions limiting his fee.
> ____(d) may properly offer to pay fair compensation to a Congressman who sponsors and supports the bill, subject only to any limitation enacted as a part of the bill.[165]

Although interest in and use of multiple choice questions grew during the 1960's, the great interest in law school administration of such exams with such questions followed the advent of the multi-state bar examination. The Multi-State Bar Examination was first given in February 1972.[166]

The pedagogical advantages to the examiner of using multiple-choice questions were significant, beyond those of the earlier true-false format. The multiple-choice format reduces the benefit of students' guessing answers[167] and gives a correspondingly higher degree of validity.[168] It also allows for the construction of a greater variety of question formats by requiring students to judge among particular rationales or conclusions, rather than merely accepting or rejecting them. Furthermore, the examiner can test student ability to apply a specific doctrine with less distraction in ascertaining which doctrine is to be applied.[169] The objective question cannot easily be used to measure the student's process of analysis in reaching a conclusion, or style or correctness in writing the analysis or conclusion, and so many environments in which objective questions form a portion of the exam continue to incorporate essay questions.[170]

In a 1995 survey of law professors teaching traditional lecture class subjects, fully two-thirds did not report using computer-graded questions, although use was higher in classes in the first year and in statutory or code courses.[171] Of those professors who did use them, most used them for twenty-five percent of the examination or less.[172]

C. A Brief Word on Examinations and Grades[173]

An essential function of the modern law school examination is to serve as the method for generating grades. These grades in turn place the examinee into strata, including those unfit for graduation, those fit for graduation, those who are outstanding, and many gradations among them, including individual location in a class rank.[174]

There appears to be no record of grades in the modern sense being given in colonial and early federal law classes: the result of unsatisfactory quizzes was either to improve or to be dismissed, and the result of failure of the graduation exam was to be denied the degree.

Standards of performance required throughout the nineteenth century varied widely by time and school. Harvard, at mid-century, had no real standards at all, while Virginia failed a high percentage of its graduates. In 1901, Raleigh Minor reported that of nineteen of the "most prominent law schools," the standards to pass examinations were widely scattered. Two had no fixed percentage standards, one required fifty-five percent, three sixty percent, one sixty-five percent, five seventy per cent, three seventy-five percent, three eighty percent, and one eighty-three percent.[175]

Throughout this century, there have been numerous attempts to experiment and modify grading systems in order to achieve various ends. There has long been concern for grades that are not uniform among instructors in a single faculty. In 1920, Dean Wigmore at Northwestern calculated the percentages of good grades to all grades awarded by each member of his faculty. Among all courses, good grades accounted for anywhere between forty-one and one hundred per cent, although teachers in the large lecture courses varied only from fifty-six percent to seventy-four percent.[176]

In his 1921 report on legal education, Alfred Reed presented six concerns of the modern annual or semester-end exam, of which two were based on the integration of annual and semi-annual courses. He advocated intermittent recitations or quizzes by students, which would both provide an alternate method of testing proficiency and deter procrastination in student study. Perhaps more effectively, he also suggested that some differentiation among marks be made, allowing recognition of both unusual excellence in performance and greater significance of a course content. He argued for a more scientific method by which grades among instructors can be equalized.[177]

In line with such calls for reform, several schools re-evaluated their examination procedures. Columbia, under Dean Harlan Fiske Stone, adopted a new system of recording and averaging student grades in the annual examinations, based on Wood's research and requiring a minimum level of performance to remain enrolled. In its first year, the system led to the dismissal of seventy-eight students of an enrollment of 692.[178] This system replaced an older pass-fail system that had led to considerable attrition in its own rights,[179] but this system was itself replaced.[180] There is continuing concern, however, that these changes and reforms have yet to produce consistency in grades, and that, perhaps, such consistency is unattainable.[181]

Despite the general abandonment of pass-fail exams in favor of graded exams, pass-fail examinations have continued to find intermittent popularity, used both in particular courses and in particular years. Michigan even allowed students to opt for graded or pass-fail credit in any one course per semester in 1970, an option taken by thirty-one percent of the students, with mixed results.[182]

Further evolutions of the role of grades and the manner of grading have continued throughout this century, notably with the advent of targeted curves or distributions for a course grade list.[183] Students have sought and received greater procedural guarantees both within the law schools in the courts that grades are not overly arbitrary.[184] The most salient feature of these changes has occurred in the years following World War II, and particularly in the 1980's and 1990's. Law schools have markedly reduced the rigor of their grades and diminished the level of academic attrition; they have inflated their grades.[185] This change in standards may be attributable to increasing emphasis on careful admissions processes, competition among law schools for applicants, dissatisfaction by students, competition among schools for prestige, or, perhaps charitably, an increase in the quality of law school applicants.

IV. Evaluation Alternatives

A. Alternatives, Part I: Oral Performance: Moot Courts and Class Questions[186]

As the brief review of pre-revolutionary English legal education made clear, the moot argument was an essential tool not only of student instruction in the Inns and at Oxbridge but also of student evaluation. This was the state of affairs in the eighteenth and throughout the nineteenth century in American schools as well.

William and Mary held moot courts and mock legislatures under George Wythe.[187] James Wilson held "law exercises" every Saturday morning at the College of Philadelphia.[188] Litchfield held regular moot courts on weekday afternoons.[189] The predecessor of Yale Law School, the New Haven law school owned by Samuel J. Hitchcock, opened in 1824, and its first annual announcement specified that, "[a] moot court is held once a week, or oftener, which employs the students in drawing pleadings and investigating and arguing questions of law."[190] Moot courts, required in the curriculum, were long organized at Harvard under the auspices of student clubs, such as the Coke, Marshall, PowWow, Thayer, Ames, and Langdell clubs, which also held discussions, quizzes and other activities to enhance student understanding of the law.[191] Indeed, the Langdell club also begat the first staff of the *Harvard Law Review*.[192] Other schools' student associations were active in moot courts, perhaps most notably Michigan's Lawyer's Club.[193] Most schools opening in the nineteenth century included moot courts as part of their curriculum.[194]

Two changes in moot courts in the twentieth century are particularly of note. First is the advent of course credits and grades led eventually to participation and supervision of moot court programs receiving academic credit, albeit often on a pass/fail basis or writing credit only.[195]

The second major change is the development of interschool competitions. The Association of the Bar of the City of New York began sponsorship of a national competition following an interschool competition between Yale and Columbia in 1947, which was expanded by 1950 to a national competition.[196] In 1950, Georgetown beat Kansas,[197] arguing in the State of Jefferson the case of *Fayerweather v. Wetmore and Rain Control, Inc.*, over whether "a landowner can restrain an adjoining landowner from increasing the productivity of his soil by artificially withdrawing moisture from clouds above his land."[198] In the intervening years, several other competitions have developed, the most famous of which may be the Jessup competition in international law, which includes many foreign law schools and was begun in 1960.[199]

As well as moot courts held apart from the lecture hall, an important form of student evaluation based on oral performance occurs in student recitations in class.[200] Central to the case method, student response to questions is often the basis by which a student perceives success of failure in the classroom and by which teachers signal acceptable or poor performance,[201] but student participation is only occasionally a portion of the grading for a course.[202]

B. Alternatives, Part II: Writing Exercises, Legal Writing Programs, and Seminar Papers

The idea of a student writing requirement has been nearly a constant element of American legal education and has taken many forms. Students in England and early American schools maintained common-place books, in which definitions and applications of every doctrine they learned were recorded, subject to review by their teachers.[203] Students at Litchfield and other early schools not only copied their lectures in inspected notebooks but took written quizzes from oral questions.[204] As well as these programs, however, nineteenth century law schools frequently had graduation dissertation requirements and course thesis requirements.[205]

At the turn of the century, a new device for encouraging student writing arose, the student-edited law review. The first student-edited journal, the *Albany Law Journal*, was published in 1875, lasting only a year.[206] The first student journal of any influence appears to have been *The Columbia Jurist*, a publication started by six Columbia students in 1885, which, though also short-lived, influenced the founding of the *Harvard Law Review*, which published its first issue in 1886.[207] The Harvard journal served as a prototype for other schools, and in short order, law reviews had spread through the major law schools of the country.[208] Students selected for the staffs of law reviews are given considerable supervision in writing and editing, and the reviews are supported by their schools in many ways, both to enhance the prestige of the schools and to provide a writing and editing lab for their students. In most cases, however, only a small percentage of a law school class is needed for journal membership, and the remaining students are excluded from this experience.

The twentieth century law school, however, more often segregates instruction in legal writing into programs distinct from large-lecture courses.[209] The specialized writing programs are usually offered as classes in a first-year legal writing course, although there are upper-year seminar papers in which little writing instruction is given.

The legal research and writing course, in some regard, is an outgrowth of early courses in legal bibliography and programs in advocacy and rhetoric connected to moot courts.[210] One of the earliest legal writing programs, and still one of the best known, is that led by the Bigelow Teaching Fellows at Chicago, which was established in 1938.[211] In this year-long program, the first-year student was called on to write twelve assignments, including five legal memoranda, a précis, a radical condensation of a prior memorandum, two editorials, a preliminary question list, a preliminary definition of a field of research, and a book review. An early description of the program noted that the legal memorandum is the staple of the program and the other forms of assignment "are added for fun."[212] The students averaged roughly 300 hours of work time and wrote 25,000 words, receiving eight hours of credit from the year's forty-hour load.[213]

Other schools followed suit, some focusing on developing remedial skills, and others following Chicago's more developmental approach.[214] A typical course of this expansion is the second-year course in legal research and writing instituted at Michigan in 1957. It was staffed by instructors, recent graduates of Michigan and other law schools, under the supervision of a faculty member, initially Jack Pearce.[215] The Dean's Report of 1957-1958 described the program:

> The principal aim of the program was to train students to apply legal principles studied in their regular courses to legal problems presented in hypothetical fact situations. During the first semester, the students, in groups of 15 to 20, met weekly with the instructors for the purpose of discussing such problems as the drafting of wills, contracts, and forms of business transactions, statutory research and interpretation, and the elicitation and analysis of facts. Small groups made possible a large measure of individual participation together with criticism and evaluation of individual work. It was expected that the program would lend additional meaning to the regular classroom studies and this proved to be the case. Furthermore, it served to provide the students with more direct and personal familiarity with the law library and the research tools of the legal profession. . . .
>
> During the second semester, each student was required to engage in individual research in the preparation of a memorandum on some reasonably difficult legal proposition. Instructors met with the students individually during the progress of this work. In effect this phase of the program gave to all members of the second-year class the kind of opportunity that had hitherto been made available only to editors of the Law Review.[216]

Legal writing programs have proliferated,[217] increasingly run with tenured or tenure-track directors supervising contract instructors, who teach both research and writing in courses lasting two semesters of the first year, assigning grades based on the sufficiency of analysis and accuracy of writing.[218] These programs often include appellate brief writing exercises coupled with oral argument in a moot court, although moot court instruction in these programs has declined in recent years.[219] Legal writing classes usually include lectures,[220] although a critical feature of most legal writing programs is that of feedback. Students receive specific criticism of their work, which is usually the basis for subsequent redrafting of assignments, a trend increasing in recent years.[221]

V. Summary Observations

The exam as the sole method of grading has led to some obvious advantages, particularly in reducing faculty work-load. But its disadvantages are profound, particularly the difficulty of student improvement with so rare and sparsely evaluated feedback, the common limitation of oral performance and intermediate writing experiences from calculation in the grade, and the calculation of the grade from stressful and artificial circumstances. Part and parcel with these concerns is what Kissam has accurately described as the disengagement of professors from the learning of the student at the point of examination.[222] Not only do these disadvantages affect the utility of the evaluations for student improvement, they lead to a continuing skepticism among law students that the construction of their exam questions[223] or the review of their essays is thorough or fair.[224] Many variables may enter into the accuracy of the examination as an evaluation of student performance, not the least being stress.[225] Thus it is no surprise that many calls for reform in the curriculum, particularly in its evaluation methods, have been made of late.[226]

One of the most interesting of the recent efforts at reform has been the reinclusion of written work into the lecture course, alleviating many of the problems of absent feedback and improvement attendant with the course-end exam,[227] although, as in so many other "reforms" this movement not only echoes nineteenth century practices but also represents only the most recent incarnation of a cyclical reformation.[228] The use of written problems allows detailed feedback and guidance of individual student work concerning the course materials, as well as a broader base for formal evaluation of the student's performance.[229]

It is clear that, whatever changes there may be to evaluative methods, certain functions of the formal evaluation system will likely be retained. First, some method that faculties believe to be fair and valid will continue to be used to rank student performance within each group of students and graduates. This method will account both for changes in technology and in culture that attend not only other law school systems of evaluation but also examinations for law school admission and for bar admission. More than likely, this method will include components of measurement of both analytic skill in applying law to new situations and rote skill in recalling specific doctrines, thus measuring both depth and breadth of student ability to recall and apply the substance of each law course. Changes will likely also include a greater frequency of evaluation, coupled with methods of reducing professorial labor.

Student evaluation has almost universally been a part of the law school experience. With brief exceptions in the nineteenth century, the demands of the profession and of the faculty to evaluate the success of student learning have made some form of exam practically inescapable to the law student, even while the forms of the exams have evolved. That this will continue to be the case is practically certain. That it will remain in its current forms is doubtful.

NOTES

1. SCOTT TUROW, ONE L 157 (1986).

2. This near-uniformity of method is no accident. The American Bar Association demands it of schools that would remain accredited. Standard 304 requires the scholastic achievement of all students in lecture-hall courses to be tested with a "written examination of suitable length and complexity." ABA Standard 304(b) (1996).

3. These goals for examinations and their resultant grades are well established. See, e.g., Karl N. Llewellyn, *Lawyer's Ways and Means, and the Law Curriculum*, 30 IOWA L. REV. 333 (1945).

4. Again, these goals are old hat. See, e.g., John L. Grant, *The Single Standard in Grading*, 29 COLUM. L. REV. 920 (1929).

5. These goals are, unsurprisingly, less often noted in the literature of this century.

6. American legal education through the nineteenth century was strongly influenced by English traditions and practices. The moot court and the written examination had both been pursued in English institutions prior to independence, and this essay begins with a consideration of their methods of student evaluation. See, e.g., MARIAN C. MCKENNA, TAPPING REEVE AND THE LITCHFIELD LAW SCHOOL 1-7 (1986); 1 CHARLES WARREN, A HISTORY OF THE HARVARD LAW SCHOOL AND OF THE EARLIER LEGAL CONDITIONS IN AMERICA 31-45 (1970); LAWRENCE M. FRIEDMAN, A HISTORY OF AMERICAN LAW 84-88 (1973); Roscoe Pound, *Dedication Papers: The Law School and the Professional Tradition*, 24 MICH. L. REV. 156, 160 (1926). For the influence of Oxbridge graduates in early American colleges, see MARY LOVETT SMALLWOOD, AN HISTORICAL STUDY OF EXAMINATIONS AND GRADING SYSTEMS IN EARLY AMERICAN UNIVERSITIES: A CRITICAL STUDY OF THE ORIGINAL RECORDS OF HARVARD, WILLIAM AND MARY, YALE, MOUNT HOLYOKE, AND MICHIGAN FROM THEIR FOUNDING TO 1900, 3-5 (1935).

7. 1 WILLIAM BLACKSTONE, COMMENTARIES ON THE LAWS OF ENGLAND 23 (1765). For a more specific history of the origins of the Inns, see S.E. Thorne, *The Early History of the Inns of Court with Special Reference to Gray's Inn*, in S.E. THORNE, ESSAYS IN ENGLISH LEGAL HISTORY 137 (1985).

8. Not that the Inns were the sole professional law schools in Britain. For a discussion of the legal instruction in the Scottish Faculty of Advocates, see Steve Sheppard, *Casenotes, Commentaries, and Curmudgeons*, 82 IOWA L. REV. 547 (1997).

9. J.H. Baker identifies the term "moot" as a basis for both the description of the case and the forms of the disputation as

in use by 1428. J.H. Baker, *Learning Exercises in the Medieval Inns of Court and Chancery*, *in* J.H. BAKER, THE LEGAL PROFESSION AND THE COMMON LAW: HISTORICAL ESSAYS 15 (1986).

10. Richardson describes these readings in detail. W.C. RICHARDSON, A HISTORY OF THE INNS OF COURT, WITH SPECIAL REFERENCE TO THE PERIOD OF THE RENAISSANCE, 101-27 (1978). The proceedings from Readings and Moots are in S.E. Thorne's *Readings and Moots at the Inns of Court in the Fifteenth Century*, Vol.1 (Selden Society, vol. 71, 1954).

11. Nicholas Bacon et al., *An Analysis of the Structure, Government, and System of Education in the Inns of Court and Chancery* (1540), *reprinted* in EDWARD WATERHOUS, FORTESCUE ILLUSTRATUS (1663), *reprinted in* RICHARDSON, *supra* note 9, at 409. Holdsworth considered Bacon's report to be "the most authentic account" of the Inns' instruction. 2 W.S. HOLDSWORTH, HOLDSWORTH'S HISTORY OF ENGLISH LAW 503 (1923).

12. DAVID LEMMINGS, GENTLEMEN AND BARRISTERS: THE INNS OF COURT AND THE ENGLISH BAR, 1680-1730 77 (1990).

13. *Reprinted and translated in* J.H. Baker, *The Old Moot Book of Lincoln's Inn*, in J.H. BAKER, *supra* note 8, at 25, 28.

14. LEMMINGS, *supra* note 11, at 78-83. Lemmings collects citations of various scholars who disagree slightly over the dates of the beginning of the decline of the moots in the century prior to their interruption in 1642. *Id.* at 78 nn.7-9.

15. Inner Temple passed such a requirement in 1556. 1 Inner Temple Records 225-26 *cited in* RICHARDSON, *supra* note 9, at 171 n.15.

16. Rules of Government of the Inns of Court and the Inns of Chancery, Appendix 5, June 20, 1596, art 11. *reprinted in* RICHARDSON, *supra* note 9, at 175.

17. LEMMINGS, *supra* note 11, at 63, 261-63.

18. Bagehot recounted his moot from 1850:

> A slip of paper was delivered to you, written in legible law stationer's hand, which you were to take up to the upper table where the Benchers sat, and read before them. The contents were generally not intelligible: the slip often began in the middle of a sentence, and by long copying and no revision the text had become quite corrupt. The topic was, "Whether C. should have the widow's estate?" and it was said that if you pieced all the slips together you might make a connected argument for and against the widow. . . . [I]n 1850 the trial "case" had dwindled down to the everlasting question, "Whether C. should have the widow's estate?" The animated debate had become a mechanical reading of copied bits of paper, which it was difficult to read without laughing. Indeed, the Benchers felt the farce, and wanted to expedite it. If you kept a grave countenance after you had read some six words, the senior Bencher would say, "Sir that will do," and then the exercise was kept. But this favor was only given to those who showed due gravity. If you laughed you had to read the "slip" all through.

Walter Bagehot *in* 3 LITERARY STUDIES 252-53 (R.H. Hutton, ed., 1905), *quoted in* RICHARDSON, *supra* note 9, at 321-22.

19. The origins of Oxford legal education in the use of Vacarius's *Liber Pauperum* and the later vicissitudes of legal education there, are briefly described in Sheppard, *supra* note 7.

20. 1 OXFORD UNIVERSITY STATUTES, *Caroline Code or Laudian Statutes, Promulgated A.D. 1636* (G.R.M. Ward, trans., William Pickering 1845). For the apparent novelty of examinations as a degree requirement, see L.S. Sutherland, *The Curriculum*, in 5 L.S. SUTHERLAND & L.G. MITCHELL, THE HISTORY OF OXFORD UNIVERSITY: THE EIGHTEENTH CENTURY 469 (1986).

21. A student for the Bachelors of Laws would spend three years in residence, or five years if not a Master of Arts at his matriculation, the other two spent studying logic, moral philosophy, politics, and humane letters. 2 CHARLES E. MALLET, A HISTORY OF THE UNIVERSITY OF OXFORD 325 (1927), *citing Caroline Code*, VI, S, iv, c. I.

22. SUTHERLAND & MITCHELL, *supra* note 19, at 470-71.

23. *Id.* at 472.

24. Mallet, *supra* note 20, at 325. The experiences of Jeremy Bentham and others are reported in SUTHERLAND & MITCHELL, *supra* note 19, at 474.

25. *Oxford University Commission Report, 1852*, p. 59, *quoted in* MALLET, *supra* note 20, at 16. Note the skepticism as to Lord Eldon's veracity. *Id.* Lord Eldon was, of course, correct to suggest he answered one of his two questions inaccurately but to the happiness of the examiners; his answer conforms with what is now politely called the "Aluredian myth." Its origins as part of a fourteenth-century property fraud by the college fellows are illustrated in JAN MORRIS, THE OXFORD BOOK OF OXFORD 23-24 (1978).

26. OXFORD UNIVERSITY STATUTES, *supra* note 19, at 29, *University Statutes from 1767 to 1850.*

27. J.L. Barton, *Legal Studies*, *in* SUTHERLAND & MITCHELL *supra* note 19, at 604-05.

28. *Report of the Select Committee on Legal Education*, 10 BRITISH PARLIAMENTARY PAPERS 1, iv, xvi (25 August 1846), *described in* W.L. Twining, *Laws*, *in* THE UNIVERSITY OF LONDON AND THE WORLD OF LEARNING 1836-1986, 81-83 (F.M.L. Thompson, ed. 1990).

29. OXFORD EXAMINATION PAPERS, SECOND PUBLIC EXAMINATION, PASS, MICHAELMAS TERM, 1871. Only one component of the exam is reproduced above. The whole examination required fifteen sections, including several more on property, as well as several special sections on elective topics.

30. Harvard Law School has mid-nineteenth century examination papers from Oxford and from London that appear to have been received fairly contemporaneously to their publication. See UNIVERSITY OF OXFORD, OXFORD UNIVERSITY EXAMINATION PAPERS IN LAW AND MODERN HISTORY FOR THE ACADEMIC YEARS ENDING JULY, 1867 to 1872 (Oxford, J. Parker, 1872); THE EXAMINATION QUESTIONS, WITH FULL ANSWERS, FOR 1859 and 1860 (London: T.F.A. Day, 1860). Furthermore, the

general university collection held similar papers. See UNIVERSITY OF OXFORD, EXAMINATION PAPERS IN LAW AND MODERN HISTORY, FOR THE ACADEMICAL YEARS ENDING JULY, 1863 to 1868 (1868).

31. L.C.B. Gower, *English Legal Training*, 13 MOD. L. REV. 137, 140 (1950).

32. *Report of the Select Committee on Legal Education*, 10 BRIT. PARLIAMENTARY PAPERS 1, xvi (25 August 1846). Examples of early Law Society examinations, which were not all that difficult, may be found in *The Legal Observer*. See, e.g., *Questions at the Examination, Trinity Term, 1853*, 46 THE LEGAL OBSERVER, DIG. & J. OF JURISPRUDENCE 93 (1853).

33. A good description of this report and its effects is in Twining, *Laws*, *supra* note 27, at 81.

34. For a discussion of these statutes and a summary of the examination culture of the Nineteenth Century, see JOHN ROACH, PUBLIC EXAMINATIONS IN ENGLAND 1850-1900 (1971).

35. See Roach, *supra* note 33, at 8-34. That this rationale was somewhat of a driving force in the adoption of the exams may be seen in considering the arguments made by James Booth, vice-principal of the Liverpool Collegiate Institution in 1847. James Booth, *Examination the Province of the State: or the Outlines of a Practical System for the Extension of National Education* (1847), *discussed in* ROACH, *supra* note 33, at 56-60.

36. The idea of examination as requirement for entry to the bar was highly controversial. An effort to require examinations in classics in order to enter the Inns and to require an examination in law in order to be called to the bar was killed in the 1830's. See RAYMOND COCKS, FOUNDATIONS OF THE MODERN BAR 23 (1983).

37. Gower, *supra* note 30, at 141.

38. A popular student guide at the time noted that "The whole examination is an easy one—in fact, a great deal too easy, still it is impossible to pass it without some knowledge of the subject." WALTER R. BALL, THE STUDENTS' GUIDE TO THE BAR 22 (1879).

39. N. HARTE & JOHN NORTH, THE WORLD OF UNIVERSITY COLLEGE 1828-1978, 106 (1986).

40. Twining, *Laws*, *supra* note 27, at 96.

41. James Barr Ames, *The Vocation of the Law Professor*, *in* JAMES BARR AMES, LECTURES ON LEGAL HISTORY 354, 356 (1913), reprinted as chapter 72 of this book.

42. Although they have, indeed, improved markedly. See Twining, *Laws*, *supra* note 27, at 100-02 for a picture of the later years. An early description of the new reforms can be found in Dicey's rather unusual ad for B.C.L. students. See Albert V. Dicey, *The Extension of Law Teaching at Oxford*, 24 HARV. L. REV. 1 (1910). In part, these reforms were led by the departure from the study of civil law as the sole basis for the degrees in civil law. See, e.g., UNIVERSITY OF OXFORD, FACULTY OF LAW, EXAMINATION IN THE FACULTY OF LAW FOR THE DEGREE OF B.C.L. (1930); OXFORD UNIVERSITY, REQUIREMENTS FOR DEGREES, 1996 (1996). For a contemporaneous discussion of the 1922 requirement that Law Society examinees who would become solicitors complete a year of study in a law school prior to examination, see Frederick Pollock, *Learning the Law*, 159 LAW Q. REV. 287 (1924). For a reasonably current comparison of American and English programs, see Sandra R. Klein, *Legal Education in the United States and England: A Comparative Analysis*, 13 LOY. L. A. INT'L & COMP. L. J. 601 (1991).

43. Gower, *supra* note 30, at 137, 193.

44. *Id.* at 193.

45. This section and the next, concerned as they are with the evaluation of matriculated students, generally omit discussion of entrance examinations. The struggle to impose a uniform system of entrance examination was resolved with the advent of uniform use of the products of the Law School Admission Service, but that is a struggle beyond the scope of this essay.

46. Paul D. Carrington, *Training for the Public Professions of the Law: 1971*, *reprinted in* HERBERT L. PACKER ET AL., NEW DIRECTIONS IN LEGAL EDUCATION 95, 170 (1972). Judge Reeve oversaw the school from 1782 or 1784; he retired in 1820, and Judge Gould oversaw it until 1833. See James Gould, *The Litchfield Law School*, 1 U. S. L. J. 401-05 (1823). An overview of the school's history and a description of the teaching practices of Judges Reeve and Gould can be found in Sheppard, *supra* note 7.

47. MCKENNA, *supra* note 5, at 120, 171-72; ALFRED Z. REED, TRAINING FOR THE PUBLIC PROFESSION OF THE LAW 121, 356 (Carnegie Foundation for the Advancement of Teaching, Bulletin No. 15, 1921) (1976). While Seymour's contributions were late in the day and rather slight, Professor, later Justice, Brandeis seems to have been in error in declaring that Jabez Huntington, along with Reeve and Gould were "the only instructors whom the school ever had." Louis Brandeis, *The Harvard Law School*, 1 THE GREEN BAG 10, 12 (1889).

48. *Catalogue of the Litchfield Law School*, *quoted in* MCKENNA, *supra* note 5, at 85.

49. Few of the Litchfield notebooks have anything other than weekly lectures in them. None reviewed by the author to date had weekend questions, although it is likely that some of them do. For a discussion of the notebooks, see Sheppard, *supra* note 7. The time available in the drafting of this article did not allow review of the Litchfield notebook holdings in Yale. The publication of a transcribed Litchfield notebook in the Yale collection is forthcoming.

50. REED, *supra* note 48, at 357.

51. Asahel Stearns, *Report to the Overseers*, January 9, 1826, *quoted in* WARREN, *supra* note 5, at 334.

52. Report of John Lowell, Chairman of Examination Committee, August 29, 1820, 9 Harvard College Papers, *quoted in* WARREN, *supra* note 5, at 339.

53. ANNUAL REPORT ON HARVARD UNIVERSITY, 1829-30 XXVIII; ANNUAL REPORT OF THE UNIVERSITY OF CAMBRIDGE, 1847-48, 31, *cited in* REED, *supra* note 48, at 356 n.3; see also WARREN, *supra* note 5, at 434-36; Sheppard, *supra* note 7.

54. 2 CHARLES WARREN, A HISTORY OF THE HARVARD LAW SCHOOL AND OF THE EARLIER LEGAL CONDITIONS IN AMERICA 344-45.

55. Parker maintained that the professional examination was a task for the bar, not the schools, which provided an honorary

certification with the degree. JOEL PARKER, THE LAW SCHOOL OF HARVARD COLLEGE 32-32 (New York, Herd & Hoffman, 1871); WARREN, *supra* note 55, at 368-70 n.6.

56. University of Virginia, Faculty Minutes, April 5, 1828, *quoted in* JOHN RITCHIE, THE FIRST HUNDRED YEARS: A SHORT HISTORY OF THE UNIVERSITY OF VIRGINIA FOR THE PERIOD 1826-1926, 15 (1978).

57. *Id.* at 41. Virginia's exams remained tremendously exacting into this century. In 1901, UVA professor Raleigh Minor argued for strenuous standards for all law school graduation exams, even though "[o]bjection is frequently raised to a high and fixed examination standard" being unjust, particularly because of the examiner's potential, even if nonexistent, caprices. Raleigh C. Minor, *The Graduating Examination in the Law School*, 7 VA. L. REG. 468, 471 (1901).

58. For a history of the bar exams, see Robert M. Jarvis, *An Anecdotal History of the Bar Exam*, 9 GEO. J. LEGAL ETHICS 359 (1996), *reprinted in* CLOSSEN ET AL., HISTORY OF LEGAL EDUCATION (forthcoming). For a history of the diploma privilege, see James Peden, *A History of Law School Administration*, *in* CLOSSEN ET AL., HISTORY OF LEGAL EDUCATION (forthcoming).

59. N.Y. Laws 1855, c.310 (1855); see also REED, *supra* note 48, at 251.

60. N.Y. Laws 1859, c.267 (1859); see also REED, *supra* note 48, at 251.

61. N.Y. Laws 1860, c.202 (1860). Regarding the validity of the privilege for Columbia, see *Matter of Graduates*, 10 Abb. Pr. 348 (1860). Regarding New York University's privilege, see *In re Cooper*, 22 N.Y. 67 (1860).

62. REED, *supra* note 48, at 252-53 n.1.

63. Report of the Board of Trustees to the State Regents, 1863, *reprinted in* A HISTORY OF THE SCHOOL OF LAW, COLUMBIA UNIVERSITY 60 (Julius Goebel, ed., 1955) [hereinafter, HISTORY].

64. *Id.* at 62; Reed, *supra* note 48, at 356.

65. Theodore W. Dwight, *Columbia College Law School*, New York, 1 THE GREEN BAG 141, 152 (1889).

66. *Id.* at 154.

67. *Id.* at 157.

68. The diploma privilege statute passed in Virginia in 1842 allowed graduates of the College of William and Mary and of the University of Virginia to enter the bar based solely on their law school diplomas. This statute was repealed in 1849 at the request of Virginia's Professor John B. Minor, who argued that the law school and its graduates would be better off if the students' "fitness to practice law should be tested in the same way with students in private offices or in private law schools." COMMONWEALTH OF VIRGINIA, REPORT OF THE REVISORS 824 (1849), *quoted in* REED, *supra* note 48, at 350.

69. Helen S. Moylan, Note, *A Manuscript Record of the Early Days of the Iowa Law School*, 22 IOWA L. REV. 108, 109 (1936).

70. List of Questions Propounded at Examination, Fall Term, *in* Journal of William G. Hammond 58 (Special Collection, University of Iowa Law School Library). This journal is described more fully in Moylan, *supra* note 70, at 108.

71. Journal of William G. Hammond 58 (Special Collection, University of Iowa Law School Library).

72. *Id.*

73. Moylan, *supra* note 70, at 110-11.

74. *Id.* at 59.

75. *Id.*

76. *The Chicago Daily Tribune* of July 1, 1862, reported the content of the examination questions in detail. The property question entailed a fair portion of Washburn's property treatise, which was the assigned text:

> The intricate questions as to real estate were extremely well handled. In connection therewith, the various modes of holding property, from feudal days down to our own times, were closely examined and contrasted, and peculiar relations of lessors, lessees, tenants for life, tenants at will, and the various modes of conveyancing, fully considered. The multitudinous questions arising out of wills, divorces, and the rights of husbands in the property of wives were next entered into. The subjects of dower and jointure were treated.

quoted in James E. Babb, *Union College of Law, Chicago*, 1 THE GREEN BAG 330, 337 (1889).

77. REED, *supra* note 49, at 357. Charles Warren believed that this was the first law school examination in the country to be required for a degree. WARREN, *supra* note 5, at 364 n.1.

78. Charles C. Allen, *The St. Louis Law School*, 1 THE GREEN BAG 283, 285, 287-88 (1889). For examples of the questions of the examiners, which are not unlike those of the Iowa exam described above, see WASHINGTON UNIVERSITY SCHOOL OF LAW, CATALOGUE WITH MOOT COURT AND EXAMINATION PAPERS FOR THE SCHOOL YEAR 1882-83 (1882).

79. George W. Swasey, *Boston University Law School*, 1 THE GREEN BAG 54, 58 (1889).

80. ELIZABETH GASPAR BROWN, LEGAL EDUCATION AT MICHIGAN 1859-1959, 740 (University of Michigan Law School, 1959).

81. *Id.* at 192-94.

82. An example of the written questions of the quizzes appears to be found in the numerous quiz books that came from Michigan during this era. See, e.g., CHARLES CLINTON WALSH, THE STUDENT'S QUIZ BOOK, CONTAINING QUESTIONS, ANSWERS AND A HISTORY OF THE LEADING CASES IN ANSON ON CONTRACTS AND BLACKSTONE, AS TAUGHT BY THE PROFESSORS IN THE MICHIGAN LAW SCHOOL (1892).

83. University of Michigan Law School, Announcement 1885-1886, *quoted in* BROWN, *supra* note 81, at 197.

84. Emlin McClain, *Law Department of the State University of Iowa*, 1 THE GREEN BAG 374, 383-84 (1889).

85. Harry B. Hutchins, *The Cornell University School of Law*, 1 THE GREEN BAG 473, 484-85 (1889).

86. C. Stuart Patterson, *The Law School of the University of Pennsylvania*, 1 THE GREEN BAG 99, 107 (1889).

87. See *supra* notes 64-68 and accompanying text.

88. The case method is well-known to any survivor of the modern law school. Its dawn at Harvard and pre-dawn antecedents are described in Sheppard, *supra* note 7; see also WILLIAM P. LAPIANA, LOGIC & EXPERIENCE: THE ORIGIN OF MODERN AMERICAN LEGAL EDUCATION (1994).

89. REED, *supra* note 48, at 174, 357. For the institution of exams, see JOEL PARKER, *supra* note 55. For the timing of the exams with the institution of bar exams in Massachusetts, see ROBERT STEVENS, LEGAL EDUCATION IN AMERICA FROM THE 1850S TO THE 1980S, 94-95 (1983). The state of affairs prior to the reinstitution of exams is described by Louis Brandeis. "[P]rior to 1875, any person who had for three terms or eighteen months been enrolled as a member of the school was entitled to a degree without having necessarily attended a lecture or passed an examination." Brandeis, *supra* note 48, at 18.

90. Required courses were real property, personal property, contracts, torts, criminal law and procedure, civil procedure at common law, and evidence. Elective courses were (Commercial law) Sales of Personal Property, Real Property, Evidence, Domestic Relations, Marriage and Divorce, Wills and Administrations, Bailments, Agency, Partnership, Shipping and Admiralty, Insurance, Debtor and Creditor including Bankruptcy, Jurisdiction & Equity Procedure, Principal and Surety, Corporations, Conflicts of Law, and Constitutional Law. *Circular of the School of Law, 1870-1872* (Harvard University Law School Special Collections, Red Set).

91. *Id.*, *quoted in* WARREN, *supra* note 55, at 365.

92. *Id.* at 364.

93. *Report of the Visiting Committee, October 1871*, reprinted in WARREN, *supra* note 55, at 377-78.

94. A critical effect of the examination requirements was effectively to enhance the residence requirement of the law school. In 1878, Harvard extended its examination requirement to successful completion of each of the annual exams in all three years. By 1889, only seven men of the eighty-six who sat for the first year exams, and no one in the upper years, had not attended regular law school classes in Harvard. See REED, *supra* note 48, 174 n.1.

95. Christopher C. Langdell, *Report 1871-1872, reprinted in* WARREN, *supra* note 55, at 385 n.1.

96. These standards were set by faculty vote on June 24, 1872. WARREN, *supra* note 55, at 385 n.2.

97. *Id.* Such pass/fail ratios were not uncommon. Hastings College of Law examinees in the late 1880's fared similarly. In 1886, twenty-five seniors passed and five failed; in 1887, the ratio was twenty-one passed to three; in 1888 twenty-five passed to three, and in 1889 eleven passed but two were advised not to appear. Similar academic attrition occurred in lower-class annual exams. Charles W. Slack, *Hastings College of the Law*, 1 THE GREEN BAG 518 (1889).

98. See Appendix, part 2.

99. *Id.*

100. JOHN H. WIGMORE, EXAMINATIONS IN LAW: CONSISTING OF PRACTICAL PROBLEMS AND CASES COMPILED FROM PAPERS CONTRIBUTED BY VARIOUS LAW SCHOOLS iii (Chicago. Callahan & Co., 1899).

101. *Id.*

102. See Appendix, part 2.

103. *Id.*

104. WIGMORE, *supra* note 101. Wigmore noted that he drew his six-hundred-odd pages of exam examples from all of the schools known to him to employ the hypothetical question. *Id.* These included, in 1899, Cambridge, Colorado, Cornell, Harvard, Illinois, Iowa, NYU, Northwestern, Penn, and Oxford.

105. REED, *supra* note 48, at 357.

106. COLUMBIA COLLEGE, SCHOOL OF LAW EXAMINATION PAPERS FOR THE ACADEMIC YEAR 1893-94 (Woodbridge, Connecticut, Research Publications, 19th-century legal treatises, no. 52235). These exams are typical of the national trend at the time. See, e.g., EXAMINATIONS IN LAW, CONSISTING OF PRACTICAL PROBLEMS AND CASES COMPILED FROM PAPERS CONTRIBUTED BY VARIOUS LAW SCHOOLS (John Henry Wigmore, ed., 1899).

107. COLUMBIA COLLEGE, *supra* note 103, at 15.

108. Simeon E. Baldwin, *Graduate Courses at Law Schools*, 11 J. SOC. SCI. 123 (1880).

109. REED, *supra* note 48, at 174-75. Yale did, however, administer examinations in the course of its regular lectures, at least in 1889. See Leonard M. Daggett, *The Yale Law School*, 1 THE GREEN BAG 239, 250 (1889).

110. Tulane, for example, appears to have required its graduates to complete a "searching, accurate, and extended" exam after the "improved method of modern professional education." Lamar C. Quintero, *The Law School of the Tulane University of Louisiana*, 2 THE GREEN BAG 116, 118 (1890).

111. THOMAS G. BARNES, HASTINGS COLLEGE OF THE LAW: THE FIRST CENTURY 115 (1978).

112. EXAMINATION PAPERS FOR SENIOR CLASS 1882 ON CONSTITUTIONAL LAW, (Bancroft Library, Keith papers, shelf mark CB595 (carton 3)) *quoted in* BARNES, *supra* note 108, at 115.

113. Charles K. Burdick, *The Comprehensive Examination at Cornell*, 7 AM. L SCH. REV. 1124 (1934).

114. Francis W. Jacob, *Comprehensive Examinations in Law Schools*, 7 AM. L SCH. REV. 1133 (1934).

115. In 1889, the newly-opened Buffalo Law School required essays in certain courses, but it seems to have given no examinations; its graduates merely passed the state bar exam. See Charles P. Norton, *The Buffalo Law School*, 1 THE GREEN BAG 421, 435-36 (1889).

116. Raleigh C. Minor, *The Graduating Examination*, *in* AMERICAN ASSOCIATION OF LAW SCHOOLS, PROCEEDINGS OF THE FIRST ANNUAL MEETING 41 (1901).

117. William S. Curtis, *Examinations in Law Schools*, *in* AMERICAN ASSOCIATION OF LAW SCHOOLS, PROCEEDINGS OF THE THIRD ANNUAL MEETING 41 (1903).

118. *Id.* at 43-44.

119. *Id.*

120. See William Draper Lewis, *The Honor System of Conducting Examinations in Law Schools*, 5 AM. L. SCH. REV. 454 (1910). For an example of the preference for honor codes, see William Minor Lile, *The Honor System*, 5 AM. L. SCH. REV. 456 (1910), describing the adoption of Henry St. George Tucker's honor code at UVA in 1842, which required each candidate to certify on his examination answers, "I, A.B., do hereby certify on honor that I have derived no assistance during the time of this examination from any source whatever, whether oral or written or in print, in giving the above answers." *Id.* at 457. Lile's support for this system was unequivocal. When asked whether he believed in the honor system, he replied, "Yes, as I do in the Christian religion." *Id.* at 456.

121. Dean Goodrich defended the red herring in 1931.

> We cannot, in an examination, test the man's ability to dig out information and get together the factual material he needs. But we can test his ability to analyze his facts by giving him a more elaborate story than he needs, and watching his selection of the legally significant material out of it. That kind of test is worth making, although it cannot be done in every question for the practical reason that it takes too long a time.

Herbert F. Goodrich, *Law Schools and Bar Examiners* 18 A.B.A. J. 101, 103 (1932).

122. Some unfortunately accurate depictions of putative student responses to a modern question are presented in C. Steven Bradford, *The Gettysburg Address as Written by Law Students Taking an Exam*, 86 NW. U. L. REV. 1094 (1992).

123. LAURA KALMAN, LEGAL REALISM AT YALE, 1927-1960, 95 (1986).

124. *Id.* at 96.

125. Letter From Arthur L. Corbin to Karl Llewellyn, (Dec. 1, 1960) (Llewellyn Papers, University of Chicago Archives), *quoted in* KALMAN, *supra* note 117, at 261 n.113.

126. *Id.* Lewis Becker, at Villanova, describes a war-horse story of an experimental question failure. There is the probably apocryphal story of the professor whose examination question was: "Write an appropriate examination question for this course." The student response in the examination booklet was, "Write an appropriate examination question in this course." The student's answer is either an A or an F. Electronic Mail from Lewis Becker to Steve Sheppard, dated December 13, 1996. Notably, many stories of failed experiments in exams seem to be located in Yale, such as this one from John-Mark Stensvaag. Some Yale Professor apparently had an essay fact pattern in torts (or some such thing) concluding with the question "Can the Plaintiff recover?" Earlier, in the exam instructions, this teacher had said something like "the shorter the answer the better." One brash student turned in a bluebook with a single word: "Yes". This student got an "F." When the student complained to the teacher, sputtering about the instructions—"the shorter the answer the better"—the teacher brought the student up short: "There was nothing wrong with the brevity of your response. The problem was that a shorter, and accurate answer would have been: 'No'!" Electronic mail, John-Mark Stensvaag, of the University of Iowa College of Law, to Steve Sheppard, December 12, 1996.

127. FERDINAND F. STONE, HANDBOOK OF LAW STUDY 134-37(1952). For an argument to the contrary, recognizing the benefits of repetitious, ungrammatical misspelled, incomplete, and disorganized answers, see Jerry Phillips, *Thirteen Rules for Taking Law Exams*, 24 J. LEGAL EDUC. 76 (1971).

128. STANLEY KINYON, INTRODUCTION TO LAW STUDY AND LAW EXAMINATIONS (1971). This pamphlet is the successor to Lawrence Vold's *Suggestions on Studying Law and Writing Law Examinations*, which was also published by West. Vold presents models of sucessful and unsuccessful essay answers in *Types of Essay Law Examination Answers—Good and Bad*, 3 HASTINGS L.J. 85 (1951).

Of course, the desire of the student taking the test is restricted in many cases merely to passing the damned test rather than in commandingly demonstrating the knowledge sought by the examiner. See Louis B. Schwartz, *How To Pass Law School Examinations*, 11 J. LEGAL EDUC. 223 (1958) (noting that, while some students have passed without knowing anything about the subject, it would be a mistake to assume that ignorance is helpful).

129. Philip C. Kissam, *Law School Examinations*, 42 VAND. L. REV. 433, 458 (1989). This concern contrasts with earlier, more assured statements of what the examiner seeks in evaluating a blue book. See Frank J. Trelease, *Panel: What Examination Techniques Best Test Legal Capabilities? Criteria of Grading*, 23 ROCKY MTN. L. REV. 118 (1950)

130. See, e.g., Edwin W. Hadley, *Law Teaching and Problem Analysis*, 3 CASE AND COMMENT 2 (1932).

131. Goodrich, *supra* note 115, at 103. Dean Goodrich went on to characterize this task: "What we want to get at, then, is the examinee's ability to handle legal problems; to tear his set of facts apart, dissect out the problems and build up a solution, either in the form of a legal opinion, or a plan for action on the part of the client." *Id.*

132. See examples in the Appendix. There is an increasingly common practice of inter-school borrowing of exam questions, brought about by the exchange of questions through the Internet. It must be stressed that the mere fact, however, that two professors use the same exam question does not, depending on the question, lead to a conclusion that the professors would similarly or should similarly evaluate a particular answer to that question.

133. For a plaintive, if not lighthearted, explanation of the reasons for this national phenomenon, see James D. Gordon, III, *How Not to Succeed in Law School*, 100 YALE L. J. 1679, 1692 (1991).

134. A seemingly early example of this is the practice, established in North Carolina in the 1950's to space exams with at least one day between them. See Richard B. Amandes, *How We Examine*, 11 J. LEGAL EDUC. 566 (1959).

135. *Id.* at 568 ("One school" was exploring anonymous grading in 1959.).

136. Vincent R. Johnson, *The Video Essay Question: An Experiment in Teaching Professional Responsibility*, 50 MO. L. REV. 591 (1985).
137. In particular, see the analyzes in Kissam, *supra* note 128; Steve H. Nickles, *Examining and Grading in American Law Schools*, 30 ARK. L. REV. 411 (1977).
138. See Ben D. Wood, *The Measurement of Law School Work*, 24 COLUM. L. REV. 224 (1924); Ben D. Wood, *The Measurement of Law School Work: II*, 25 COLUM. L. REV. 316 (1925); Ben D. Wood, The Measurement of Law School Work: III, 27 COLUM. L. REV. 784 (1927). These articles are discussed in Hadley, *supra* note 123, at 23.
139. Stephen P. Klein & Frederick M. Hart, *Chance and Systematic Factors Affecting Essay Grades*, 1 REPORTS OF LSAC SPONSORED RESEARCH, 1949-1969, 511 (LSAC Report 68-4). This study is reprinted as chapter 60 in this book.
140. WIGMORE, *supra* note 106, at iii-iv.
141. St. Louis Law School Professor William Curtis argued that exams should be printed in sufficient number for the students who take them to keep them and to freely distribute to subsequent classes. William S. Curtis, *Examinations in Law Schools*, *in* AMERICAN ASSOCIATION OF LAW SCHOOLS, PROCEEDINGS OF THE THIRD ANNUAL MEETING 41, 43 (1903).
142. COLUMBIA UNIVERSITY SCHOOL OF LAW, EXAMINATION PAPERS (Columbia Law School Treasure Room shelf mark CU C735 Ex15).
143. See, e.g., LAW SCHOOL EXAMINATIONS— 1904 (University of Michigan Library).
144. UNIVERSITY OF CHICAGO LAW SCHOOL, EXAMINATION QUESTIONS (Columbia Law School shelf mark T C43e); INDIANA UNIVERSITY SCHOOL OF LAW, EXAMINATION QUESTIONS, THE INDIANA UNIVERSITY SCHOOL OF LAW (Columbia Law School shelf mark T In27e).
145. The Columbia law school catalog lists publication beginning in 1911. Cornell Law Examinations (Columbia shelf mark T C8141).
146. STANFORD UNIVERSITY SCHOOL OF LAW, FINAL EXAMINATIONS (Columbia Law School shelf mark T 15368f).
147. In 1996, access to the Red Set at Harvard Law Library was curtailed owing to renovation and construction. Based on a review of the catalogs, David Warrington, director of special collections of the library, assessed the belief that the first entries for red books of exams was either 1947 or 1948. Telephone Interview with David Warrington, Director of Special Collections (Dec. 9, 1996).
148. TUROW, *supra* note 1, at 157.
149. Telephone Interview with Mark Slassen, Assistant Registrar, Harvard Law School (Nov. 18, 1996). In recent years prior to 1996, approximately 85 copies were annually distributed in this way.
150. *Id.* Harvard Law School Web Page (visited December 15, 1996) <http://www.law.harvard.edu/academics/registrar/95-96_exam.html>.
151. Albert Kocourek, *Objective Law Examinations*, 16 ILL. (Nw. U.) L. REV. 304 (1921).
152. *Id.* Kocourek's views were, to say the least, controversial. For an assault on both Kocourek's methods and his conclusions by a professor at Northwestern, see George P. Costigan, Jr., *Objective Law Examinations*, 20 MICH. L. REV. 514 (1922).
153. Kocourek, *supra* note 143, at 309.
154. See Wood, *supra* note 131.
155. *Id.*
156. Charles E. Clark, *Experiments with the New Type Law Tests*, 1928 J. PUB. TEACHERS OF L. 23, 29.
157. Thomas E. Atkinson, *The Use of True-False Examinations in Law Schools*, 6 AM. L. SCH. REV. 702 (1930).
158. *Id.* at 703.
159. *Id.* at 704.
160. M. Ray Doubles, *Law School Examinations*, 8 AM. L SCH. REV. 254, 255 (1935).
161. ASSOCIATION OF AMERICAN LAW SCHOOLS, 1945 REPORT OF THE COMMITTEE ON TEACHING AND EXAMINATION METHODS 147-48 (1945).
162. See Munroe H. Freeman, *Testing For Analytic Ability in the Law School Admission Test*, 24 J. LEGAL EDUC. (1958).
163. LSAS/LSAC, *The Law School Admission Test: Sources, Contents, Uses* 1-2 (September 1991). The questions were initially designed after the structure of tests given by the U.S. Navy and by the Pepsi-Cola Scholarship Test, which later became the NMSQT. Thomas O. White, *A Retrospective Examination of Law School Admission, the Law School Admission Council, and Law School Admission Services*, *in* WALTER RAUSHENBUSH, LAW SCHOOL ADMISSIONS, 1984-2001: SELECTING LAWYERS FOR THE TWENTY-FIRST CENTURY 25 (Walter B. Raushenbush, ed., Law School Admissions Service, 1986).
164. Henry Weihofen, *Panel: What Examination Techniques Best Test Legal Capabilities? Types of Questions*, 23 ROCKY MTN. L. REV. 110, 112 (1950). Weihofen also described short answer and "master list" questions in which a student identified gobbets from opinions according to the author, as well as a matching and comparison questions that require a logical sorting of statements that support or oppose other statements. This form of matching and comparison question was then used in federal civil service exams for lawyers. See Henry Weihofen, *The Written Federal Attorney Examination*, 11 U. OF CHI. L. REV. 154, 167 (1944). Weihofen's example of a multiple choice question has a complicated fact pattern from which the student is to identify the principal issue in dispute.
165. *Examinations*, *supra* note 99, at 16.
166. Jarvis, *supra* note 59, at 380-81.
167. For a careful discussion of the manner in which questions are constructed in order that this might be the case, see Howard J. Gensler, *Valid Objective Test Construction*, 60 ST. JOHN'S L. REV. 288 (1986). See also Wood, *The Measurement of Law School Work III*, *supra* note 131, at 803-26. For an illuminating argument that "multiple guess" questions do not achieve this

goal, see Eileen N. Wagner, *Multiple Choice Exams are Ineffective for Teaching the Nuances of Law. True or False?*, 20 STUDENT LAW. 42 (Dec. 1991).

168. See Lawrence W. Ross, Jr., *The Construction and Selection of Objective Business law Examination Questions*, 17 AM. BUS. L. J. 547 (1980); Howard J. Gensler, *Valid Objective Test Construction*, 60 ST. JOHN'S L. REV. 288 (1986).

169. John A. Winterbottom, *The Use of Essay and Objective Techniques in Bar Examinations*, 38 THE BAR EXAMINER 5 (1968). Interestingly, Dr. Winterbottom took pains to discredit the use of true/false questions, recommending only the use of multiple-choice questions in lieu of the essay.

170. Of course, there is still controversy regarding the effectiveness of both essay questions and objective questions and which is the superior in these tasks. See Vaughn C. Ball, *Objective Questions in Law Examinations*, 12 J. LEGAL ED. 567 (1960). A fine sample of the recent debate is in Norma Redlich & Steve Friedland, *Challenging Tradition: Using Objective Questions in Law School Examinations*, 41 DEPAUL L. REV. 143 (1991); Norma Redlich & Steve Friedland, *A Reply to Professor Jacobs: Right Answer, Wrong Question*, 41 DEPAUL L. REV. 183 (1991); Michael S. Jacobs, *Law School Examinations and Churchillian Democracy: A Reply to Professors Redlich and Friedland*, 41 DEPAUL L. REV. 159 (1991).

171. Question 122 of the survey asked, "How much of your typical examination is computer-graded? (1) none (2) 1-25% (2) 25-50% (3) 50%-75% (4) 75-99% (5) all."

Of all respondents teaching lecture courses, the responses were (1) N=278 or 66%; (2) N= 69 or 16%; (3) N=15 or 4%; (4) N=1 or 0%; (5) N=5 or 1%.

When answers were sorted according to the year in which the course was taught, the responses for first-year classes were (1) N= 160 or 70%; (2) N=50 or 22%; (3) N=10 or 4%; (4) N=0 or 0%; (5) N=3 or 1%. In contrast, responses for second-and third-year courses were (1) N=103 or 80%; (2) N=15 or 12%; (3) N=4 or 3%; (4) N=1 or 1%; (5) N=2 or 2%.

When answers were sorted according to the subject matter of the course, the responses for statutory or code courses were (1) N= 37 or 49%; (2) N=9 or 12%; (3) N=3 or 4%; (4) N=4 or 5%; (5) N=10 or 25%. In contrast, responses for common law courses were (1) N=177 or 74%; (2) N=47 or 20%; (3) N=9 or 4%; (4) N=1 or 0%; (5) N=3 or 1%.

The results of question 122 roughly correspond to the results of question 125, which asked "How much of your typical examination is an essay you evaluate personally? (1) none (2) 1-25% (2) 25-50% (3) 50%-75% (4) 75-99% (5) all." Of all respondents teaching lecture courses, the responses were (1) N=7 or 2%; (2) N= 25 or 6%; (3) N=80 or 20%; (4) N=47 or 12%; (5) N=205 or 49%. When answers were sorted according to the year in which the course was taught, the responses for first-year classes were (1) N= 4 or 2%; (2) N=14 or 6%; (3) N=57 or 25%; (4) N=30 or 13%; (5) N=117 or 51%. In contrast, responses for second- and third-year courses were (1) N=3 or 2%; (2) N=11 or 9%; (3) N=17 or 13%; (4) N=15 or 12%; (5) N=77 or 60%.

When answers were sorted according to the subject matter of the course, the responses for statutory or code courses were (1) N= 9 or 12%; (2) N=4 or 5%; (3) N=52 or 68%; (4) N=0 or 0%; (5) N=0 or 0%. In contrast, responses for common law courses were (1) N=3 or 1%; (2) N=13 or 5%; (3) N=47 or 20%; (4) N=32 or 13%; (5) N=141 or 59%.

The methodology and distribution of this survey are described in Steve Sheppard, *The State of the Art: A Survey of Teaching Practices in the American Law School Lecture Hall* (chapter 57 in the current volume).

172. *Id.*

173. While inexorably linked in a modern discussion of exams, the subjects of grades, grading systems, and the history of their use in law schools is too large a subject to be reasonably treated here except in the most cursory fashion. Still, some few points seem necessary in order to place the evolution of the method of evaluation through law school exams in some context.

174. For a general description of grades and their relationship to examinations, see Jay L. Feinman, *Grades*, 65 UMKC L. REV.—(1997); Nancy H. Kaufman, *A Survey of Law School Grading Practices*, 44 J. LEGAL EDUC. 415 (1994); Nickles, *supra* note 136; W.B. Schrader, *Law School Grading Practices, 1970 Survey* (LSAC Report 71-6), *in* LAW SCHOOL ADMISSION COUNCIL, 2 LAW SCHOOL ADMISSION RESEARCH 165 (Law School Admission Council, 1976). For the origins of grading systems in America, see SMALLWOOD, *supra* note 5, at 40-45. For the idea that the examinations are designed to separate the fit student from the unfit, see STONE, *supra* note 121, at 134. For the idea that such a division is necessary as part of the case method see sources collected in WILLIAM R. JOHNSON, SCHOOLED LAWYERS: A STUDY IN THE CLASH OF PROFESSIONAL CULTURES 126-27 (1978). For the effect of the stratification of students upon self-image, see WAGNER THIELENS, JR., THE SOCIALIZATION OF LAW STUDENTS 331 (1980). For the idea that grades and examinations affect the development of a student's character, see Duncan Kennedy, *Legal Education as Training for Hierarchy*, *in* DAVID KAIRYS, THE POLITICS OF LAW: A PROGRESSIVE CRITIQUE 40 (1982); Duncan Kennedy, *Legal Education and the Reproduction of Hierarchy*, 32 J. LEGAL EDUC. 591 (1982). For the idea that the methods by which this is done are generally invalid, see, e.g., Douglas A. Henderson, *Uncivil Procedure: Ranking Law Students Among their Peers*, 27 U. MICH. J. L. REFORM 399 (1994).

175. Minor, *supra* note 58, at 474-75.

176. Kocourek, *supra* note 143, at 305 n.2.

177. Lastly, he argued for a reduction in the labor necessary to grade, to avoid "this deadening intimacy with ignorance and mental fog," which saps a professor's strength from classrooms and ambition from scholarship. REED, *supra* note 48, at 359-60.

178. COLUMBIA REPORTS, 1922, 70, *cited in* HISTORY, *supra* note 64, at 233. See also the Wood studies, *supra* note 131 and accompanying text. The last study related to this change is John Grant's survey of grading practices at Columbia through 1928. John L. Grant, *The Single Standard in Grading*, 29 COLUM. L. REV. 918 (1930).

179. In 1900, Columbia lost one-third of its class between matriculation and graduation, a currently unknown percentage of which apparently left for failing exams. HISTORY, *supra* note 64, at 188.

180. John L. Grant, *Justice in Grading*, 9 J. LEGAL EDUC. 186, 187 (1956).

181. See, e.g., John L. Grant, *Justice in Grading*, 9 J. LEGAL ED. 186 (1956). For an argument that the pursuit of such uniformity in grading is chimerical at best, see Janet Motley, *A Foolish Consistency: The Law School Exam*, 10 NOVA L. J. 722 (1986).

182. Richard Lempert, *Law School Grading: An Experiment with Pass-Fail*, 24 J. LEGAL EDUC. 251 (1972).

183. An illustration of this common practice is in Richard A. Epstein, *Grade Normalization*, 44 S. CAL. L. REV. 707 (1971) (USC's grade curves).

184. See Penn Lerblance, *Legal and Educational Aspects of Student Dismissals: A View from the Law School*, 33 SOUTHWESTERN L. J. 605 (1979); Thomas Doniger, *Grades: Review of Academic Evaluations in Law Schools*, 11 PAC. L. J. 733 (1980). An interesting related question now moving through the legal community is the degree of accommodation a student with disabilities, including learning disabilities, must be given in law school. See James Peden, *The ADA in the Law School* (forthcoming).

185. Carl T. Bogus, *The Death of an Honorable Profession*, 71 IND. L. J. 911, 929 (1996); J. Harvie Wilkinson III, *Legal Education and the Ideal of Analytic Excellence*, 45 STAN. L. REV. 1659, 1662 (1993).

186. This section presents but a cursory glance through the history of moot arguments. For a fuller description, see Ralph Brill, *Legal Research and Writing Programs*, *in* CLOSSEN ET AL., A HISTORY OF LEGAL EDUCATION (forthcoming). See also William Adams, *Trial Practice, Clinical and Moot Court Programs. Id.*

187. LYON G. TYLER, EARLY COURSES AND PROFESSORS AT WILLIAM AND MARY COLLEGE (1904), *cited in* REED, *supra* note 46, at 117 n.1.

188. REED, *supra* note 48, at 122.

189. The account of Augustus Hand's unfortunate moot argument one Friday afternoon in 1828 is reprinted in McKenna, *supra* note 5, at 170.

190. Yale College Catalog, November 1826, *reprinted in* Frederick C. Hicks, *Yale Law School: The Founders and the Founders' Collection* 24-25 (Pamphlet 39, Tercentenary Commission of the State of Connecticut) (1935).

191. WARREN, *supra* note 55, at 319-31.

192. Samuel Williston, *Joseph Henry Beale, A Biographical Sketch*, 56 HARV. L. REV. 685, 686 (1943).

193. BROWN, *supra* note 81.

194. For example, Iowa established an organized moot court in its first program in 1868. Moylan, *supra* note 70, at 110-11. Despite the relative universality of moot court programs until World War II, see ROBERT STEVENS, LAW SCHOOL: LEGAL EDUCATION IN AMERICA FROM THE 1850S TO THE 1980S, 229 n.88 (1983), they were not uniformly applauded. See *Law Apprenticeships*, 5 ALBANY L. J. 97 (1872).

195. See, e.g., COLUMBIA UNIVERSITY SCHOOL OF LAW, CATALOG 1985-1986, 104 (moot court participation satisfies writing credits requirements).

196. ASSOCIATION OF THE BAR OF THE CITY OF NEW YORK YOUNG LAWYER'S COMMITTEE, 1 NATIONAL MOOT COURT COMPETITION: 1950 (William S. Hein Co., ed., 1983).

197. *Id.*

198. *Id.*

199. ASSOCIATION OF STUDENT INTERNATIONAL LAW SOCIETIES AND THE AMERICAN SOCIETY OF INTERNATIONAL LAW, PHILIP C. JESSUP INTERNATIONAL MOOT COURT COMPETITION, 1960-1968 (William S. Hein Co., ed., 1981). The first competition, then named the International Law Moot Court Competition, was argued over Cuban agrarian reform, among Harvard, Yale, and Columbia. Harvard won. An illustration of the use, not only of Jessup arguments but of moot arguments in general as a basic learning device is in Craig Brown, *The Jessup Mooting Competition as a Vehicle for Teaching Public International Law* 16 CAN. YRBK. INT'L L. 332 (1978).

200. A discussion of class recitations both before and after the adoption of the case method is in Sheppard, *supra* note 7. For the purposes of this essay, the importance of oral student questioning prior to the case method may be seen in Butler's plan for the first-attempted New York University Law School, in 1835, which required the use of occasional interrogatories, such that the Professor should put at least one question to each member of the class every lecture. See Benjamin F. Butler, *A Plan for the Organization of a Law School in the University of the City of New York*, *reprinted in* THE GLADSOME LIGHT OF JURISPRUDENCE: LEARNING THE LAW IN ENGLAND AND THE UNITED STATES IN THE 18TH AND 19TH CENTURIES 164, 178-79 (Michael J. Hoeflich, ed., 1988).

201. For the idea that students must not be discouraged by rejecting class answers as "wrong" see Paul T. Hayden, *On Wrong Answers in the Law School Classroom*, 40 J. LEGAL EDUC. 251 (1990). For opposing views see Joseph R. Paul, *Yes, Virginia, There Are Wrong Answers: A Reply to Professor Hayden*, 40 J. LEGAL EDUC. 473 (1990). See also David P. Leonard, *On "Right" and "Wrong" Answers: A Reply to Professor Hayden*, 40 J. LEGAL EDUC. 477 (1990).

202. There have been occasional attempts to restore the oral exam as a basis for the grade. See, e.g., Steven I. Friedland, *Towards the Legitimacy of Oral Examinations in American Legal Education*, 39 SYRACUSE L. REV. 627 (1988).

203. For a description of commonplace books, including John Marshall's student book, see Sheppard, *supra* note 7.

204. For copybook examples, see Sheppard, *supra* note 7. For a discussion of the oral quiz, see *supra* notes 171-186 and accompanying text.

205. Buffalo required theses on set topics concerning the constitution in its first constitutional law class, in the 1890's. Norton, *supra* note 110, at 433. Boston University required a graduation thesis of all of its students in the 1880's. Swasey, *supra* note 80, at 60.

206. Michael I. Swygert & Jon W. Bruce, *The Historical Origins, Founding, and Early Development of Student-Edited Law Reviews*, 36 HASTINGS L. J. 739, 764 (1985).

207. *Id.* at 766-69.

208. The history of this movement is amply described in Swygert & Bruce, *supra* note 190, and in Michael Clossen, *The History and Influence of the Law Review Institution*, 30 AKRON L. REV. 15 (1996), *reprinted in* CLOSSEN ET AL., HISTORY OF LEGAL EDUCATION (forthcoming). Representative views of the modern and future law review are to be found in Peter Stein, *Essay: Law Reviews and Legal Culture*, 70 TUL. L. REV. 2675 (1996); Bernard J. Hibbitts, *Last Writes? Reassessing the Law Review in the Age of Cyberspace*, 71 N.Y.U. L. REV. 615 (1996).

209. There are, of course, other methods of evaluating students through their writing of current vintage; one of these being the student journal. James R. Elkins, *Writing Our Lives: Making Introspective Writing a Part of Legal Education*, 29 WILLAMETTE L. REV. 45 (1993) (journals used in lieu of exams in West Virginia's Introduction to Law course).

210. For antecedent legal bibliography courses and their influence on early writing programs, see Marjorie Dick Rombauer, *First-Year Legal Research and Writing: Then and Now*, 25 J. LEGAL EDUC. 538 (1973). For antecedent advocacy courses, see *infra* notes 198-99 and accompanying text.

211. Harry Claven, *Law School Training in Research and Exposition: The University of Chicago Program*, 1 J. LEGAL EDUC. 107 (1948). The fellows are named for the former Dean, Melville M. Bigelow.

212. *Id.* at 110.

213. *Id.* at 109.

214. See Rombauer, *supra* note 194, at 542. A typical developmental program, built deliberately on the Chicago model, but with some remedial modifications, is that of Wisconsin. See Stewart Macauley & Henry G. Manne, *A Low-Cost Writing Program—The Wisconsin Experience*, 11 J. LEGAL EDUC. 387 (1959). For a later view of the Wisconsin programs, see Barbara J. Cox & Mary Barnard Ray, *Getting Dorothy Out of Kansas: The Importance of an Advanced Component to the Legal Writing Programs*, 40 J. LEGAL EDUC. 351 (1990).

215. Dean Stason's Report to the President, 1957-1958, *reprinted in* BROWN, *supra* note 81, at 223.

216. *Id.*

217. Descriptions of specific legal writing programs may be found in Maureen Arrigo-Ward, *How to Please Most of the People Most of the Time: Directing (Or Teaching) in a First-Year Legal Writing Program*, 29 VAL. U. L. REV. 557 (1995), and in Jan Levine, *Response: "You Can't Please Everyone, So You'd Better Please Yourself": Directing (Or Teaching in) A First-Year Legal Writing Program*, 29 VAL. U.L. REV. 611 (1995); John Sonsteng et al., *Learning by Doing: Preparing Law Students for the Practice of Law*, 21 WM. MITCHELL L. REV. 111 (1995) (Legal practicum course, a hybrid between a clinical and lecture hall environment); Franklin M. Schultz, *Teaching "Lawyering" to First-Year Students: An Experiment in Constructing Legal Competence*, 52 WASH. & LEE L. REV. 1643 (1995) (small section late first-year course in law office problems, moot court, drafting). A description of Columbia's Legal Research and Writing Program is in Lorne Sossin, *Discourse Politics: Legal Research and Writing's Search for a Pedagogy of Its Own*, 29 NEW ENG. L. REV. 883 (1995).

218. Regarding supervision, see Jan M. Levine, *Voices in the Wilderness: Tenured and Tenure-Track Directors and Teachers in Legal Research and Writing Programs*, 45 J. LEGAL EDUC. 530 (1995). While this staffing is the norm, it is not universal. Thomas M. Cooley Law School, for example, has five tenured or tenure-track professors teaching legal writing courses full time. Regarding semester requirements, see Jill Ramsfield, *Legal Writing in the Twenty-First Century: A Sharper Image* (forthcoming publication on behalf of the Legal Writing Institute).

219. *Id.* See also *supra* notes 29-43 and accompanying text.

220. For a criticism of the standard lecture pedagogy of the legal writing classes, see Mary Kate Kearney & Mary Beth Beazley, *Teaching Students to "Think Like Lawyers": Integrating Socratic Method with the Writing Process*, 64 TEMP. L. REV. 885 (1991) (encouraging the use of a Socratic inquiry method in legal writing classes).

221. *Id.* at nn.46-55. For a view that the content of these writing exercises should be expanded to include documents and instruments more akin to the first Chicago program, see Lucia Ann Silecchia, *Legal Skills Training in the First Year of Law School: Research? Writing? Analysis? Or More?*, 100 DICK. L. REV. 245 (1996).

222. Kissam, *supra* note 129, at 436, 489-90.

223. Cooley Howarth at Dayton reports a complaint of unfairness based on insensitivity to student ideology. The exam question revolved around the proper interpretation of the word "creed" in an antidiscrimination statute. The statute prohibits discrimination on the basis of "race, color, creed, religion, ancestry, national origin, etc.

> The fact pattern has a luncheon delivery business refusing to deliver to an abortion clinic on religious grounds. The clinic owner sues claiming that her "non-religious philosophical moral and political beliefs" in support of abortion fall within the statute's prohibition on discrimination on the basis of "creed."
>
> . . .
>
> The student objected to having to answer this question because of her "strongly held pro-life" beliefs and her reluctance (I guess that's the right word, perhaps distaste might fit as well) to having to make arguments on behalf of the clinic's interpretive position. She added that such a topic was particularly inappropriate in the context of an examination given under a time limit and its inherent "pressures." She felt that I should have been more sensitive to such issues in the design of the examination.
>
> . . .
>
> My response to her was that while I regretted her discomfort, this exam question was based upon a legitimate issue of statutory interpretation taken from a real case and not an issue of constitutional law, and, from a practical point of view, there seemed little I could possibly do for her at ten minutes into the exam. She did not feel that I was really "sorry" and left quite abruptly.

Electronic mail, Cooley R. Howarth, Jr, to Steve Sheppard, Friday, December 13, 1996.

224. Alex Tanford relates this story from his 1975 second-year exam in Trusts and Estates at Duke under Bertel Sparks, then known as "a cranky and feared old codger."

> We were all convinced, based on the randomness of our 1st year grades, that the professors did not read our exams. One student wrote on the next-to-last page, "I am certain you will not actually read this. The class will be at the student union at [a certain date and time] to buy you a milkshake. If you don't show up, our belief that professors never read the exams will be confirmed." At the appointed hour, there must have been fifty law students waiting to see if he would show up—he did.

Electronic Mail, Alex Tanford to Steve Sheppard, December 13, 1996.

225. Joshua Dressler, at McGeorge School of Law, examined an English-speaking law student who wrote her entire 3-hour exam in French, her undergraduate major, and did not realize that until it was brought to her attention when he tried to grade it. Electronic mail, Joshua Dressler to Steve Sheppard, Friday, December 13, 1996.

226. See, e.g., Section on Legal Education & Admission to the Bar, American Bar Association, *Legal Education and Professional Development—An Education Continuum* (The Report of The Task Force on Law School and the Profession: Narrowing the Gap) (American Bar Association 1992) (The "McCrate Report"); Edward J. Imwinkelried, *On Achieving Synergy in the Law School Curriculum*, 66 NOTRE DAME L. REV. 739 (1991); Kristine Strachen, *Curricular Reform in the Second and Third Years: Structure, Progression, and Integration*, 39 J. LEGAL EDUC. 523 (1989). For the specific complaint that the grade is insufficient feedback and a call for other forms, see Michael E. Elvine, *Toward Descriptive Grading*, 44 S. CAL. L.REV. 696 (1971).

227. The scholarship in this field is imposing. Jay N. Feinman & Marc Feldman, *Achieving Excellence: Mastery Learning in Legal Education*, 35 J. LEGAL EDUC. 528 (1985); Jay N. Feinman & Marc Feldman, *Pedagogy and Politics*, 73 GEO. L.J. 875 (1985) (Rutgers-Camden program integrating writing into classroom work in contracts and torts); Kathleen Bean, *Writing Assignments in Law School Classes*, 37 J. LEGAL EDUC. 276 (1987); Gordon D. James III, *An Integrated First-Year Legal Writing Program*, 39 J. LEGAL EDUC. 609 (1989) (BYU's program of legal writing requirements in substantive law courses); John M. Burman, *Out-of-Class Assignments as a Method of Teaching and Evaluating Law Students*, 42 J. LEGAL EDUC. 446 (1992) (including examples of assignments); Nancy M. Maurer & Linda Fitts Mischler, *Introduction to Lawyering: Teaching First-Year Students to Think Like Professionals*, 44 J. LEGAL EDUC. 96 (1994) (Albany's first-year program combining clinical experiences with legal writing coursework).

228. At the turn of the century, Penn professor Owen J. Roberts, joining in and responding to criticism of the case method, instituted the distribution of exam-like hypothetical questions for his students to solve during the semester. Owen J. Roberts, *Methods for Review and Quiz in "Case System" Law Schools*, 1 AM. L. SCHOOL. REV. 222 (1904).

229. The author of this article employs frequent written assignments for courses in property and constitutional law and finds this to be the case; in his school institutional policy even bars scores from these assignment being factored into a final grade. For a experiments in a similar, but graded, exercise regime see John M. Burman, *Out-of-Class Assignments as a Method of Teaching and Evaluating Law Students*, 42 J. LEGAL ED. 447 (1992). For a similar experiment based more strictly on exam question answering, see Louisa D. Del Duca & Donald B. King, *Student Examination Answers: Education Tool or Incinerator Fuel?*, 13 J. LEGAL ED. 499 (1961).

Chapter 59

The Graduating Examination in the Law School

1901

Raleigh C. Minor

Raleigh Colston Minor (1849-1923) was professor at the University of Virginia from 1893 to 1923. This paper was read before the American Bar Association's Section on Legal Education in August, 1901, and was first printed in the *Proceedings* for that meeting and then was reprinted at 7 *Virginia Law Register* 468 (1901). This paper is discussed in chapter 58.

Let me express at the very outset my profound sense of the honor done me in inviting me to address this illustrious body of men, banded together, not for their own advantage, but for the cause of legal education and for the benefit of the youths of our land, who yearly congregate at our institutions of learning, to drink deeply there of that great well-spring of justice and morals—the Common Law.

In the expansion of that great system of jurisprudence to meet the needs of every business, every country and every clime, the judge, the practitioner and the teacher of the law, each takes a part, and neither plays an inferior role. It were an invidious task to institute a comparison between the service rendered by each of these in perfecting that system which now commands the enlightened admiration of the world. Rather let us turn our thoughts to a consideration of the ways and means whereby the teacher may increase his usefulness to his profession and to his country.

This honorable body has already in many directions rendered incalculable aid to the cause of legal education. In every law school the effect of your efforts is seen in the lengthening and expansion of courses, in higher standards of attainment, and in all the various ways suggested by an intelligent comparison of methods and results.

Everywhere the law school is now alive to the dignity and importance of its functions. It is exacting of the student good honest work in the class-room. It is requiring him in his preparation for the bar to take the time to ponder, reflect and digest, as well as to acquire. In some instances it is requiring, as a preliminary to legal studies, a thorough academic training. It is demanding of the student more original legal investigation, the better to prepare him for the professional duties that lie before him. The value of these things is now too well appreciated to need further discussion.

But there is one matter connected with legal education, the value of which, as an educational force, it has seemed to me, we have not appreciated perhaps as we should. I refer to the Graduating Examination.

I have concluded, therefore, to consider briefly the nature, character and purposes of the examination, not with the expectation of advancing new ideas, but simply with the hope that it may provoke a helpful discussion.

The Examination, I apprehend, should fulfill a two-fold function. In the first place, it operates as a test of the student's knowledge of principles, his ability to apply them, and his fitness to enter upon the practice of his profession. In this aspect it is not to be regarded as a teaching force, but merely as a means of ascertaining how successful has been the teaching. It is simply a measure, a standard by which the student's acquirements are to be weighed.

But in its second aspect the Examination is much more than a mere test of knowledge. It is susceptible of use as a great educational factor in itself, because the student is thereby compelled to review the work he has done for the class-room with a thoroughness not otherwise attainable.

To obtain a proper acquaintance with any branch of learning, it is essential that it should be studied not only in detail, but as a whole. The student must familiarize himself with the relations of the parts to the whole, and to each other, as well as with the *minutiae* of each part. The class-room work furnishes the minute knowledge of detail, but permits only imperfect glimpses of the whole and of the correlated parts. The latter can only be attained by a systematic and rapid review.

Should one of us desire in a limited time to obtain a thorough familiarity with this beautiful city, he could select no way of achieving this result so quickly and thoroughly as by examining first the details of every street and park, and then, mounting to some glittering tower, obtain a view of the whole city, thus fixing permanently in his mind the relations and directions of all the various parts, which before he had studied in sections. So, one who desires an accurate and philosophic knowledge of any subject may best acquire it by the careful study of detail under competent teachers, supplemented by his own thorough review of the whole.

In the study of the law, perhaps more than in that of any other science, "damnable iteration," the most thorough and constant review of past work, is essential to the student's successful mastery of the subject. Review! Review! Review! Too much emphasis cannot be laid upon this advice to the student of law, nor can it be repeated too often, nor enforced too stringently. For alas! human beings are so constituted as always to be anxious to attain a desired goal with the least possible effort, and ever to be allured by names rather than things, by shadows rather than substance. When applied to a candidate for a law degree in one of our schools, these characteristics of human nature work out in many cases the peculiar result that the student worships and labors for the degree, rather than the knowledge which the degree represents, and will attain the coveted diploma with the least possible effort, consistent with certainty of success.

In such cases—and they constitute the rule rather than the exception—it is bootless to explain the advantage and necessity of review in order to the acquisition of a thorough knowledge of the subject. In the abstract, the student recognizes that he is seeking knowledge, but in the concrete he is seeking the degree—pursuing the shadow, not the substance. Unless therefore, by means of searching examinations, a review is made essential to the degree, the student will rarely commit the (to him) unpardonable folly of doing more work than is called for.

It is for the most part practically impossible, nor indeed is it desirable, that the review should be personally conducted by the teacher or his assistants. In this matter the student must usually work out his own salvation. Nothing short of the requirement that he must pass searching examinations for his degree will induce him to enter voluntarily upon this arduous task.

It is this office of the graduating examination that differentiates it from the examination for admission to the bar. The latter has no other purpose than to test the candidate's knowledge and his fitness to practice his profession, while the graduating examination, as a review-compelling medium, fills an important place in the teaching of the law, in addition to its function as a mere measure of attainment. It may therefore well bear a closer scrutiny of the principles which should regulate it in order to its most successful application in both its aspects.

I. Written or Oral?

The first practical question that arises is: Should the examination be written or oral? In the absence of some insurmountable practical obstacle, there can be little doubt in the mind of one who has used both forms that the written examination is greatly preferable, not only because it avoids the danger of personal embarrassment on the part of the student (sometimes a very patent source of failure), but also and chiefly because it is much more fair and just both to the student and to the school.

II. Long or Short?

In the next place, should the examination be long or short? As a test of the student's knowledge, the ideal examination would be that which would require for the attainment of the perfect mark the correct and accurate rendition by the student of every principle comprised in the particular course upon which the examination is being held. The accurate grading of such a paper would show with precision the exact percentage of knowledge possessed by the student. In other words, the ideal examination is that which asks an indefinite or infinite number of questions upon the subject.

But to give such an examination is, of course, as utterly impracticable as it is impossible that two parallel lines should meet. All we can hope for is a remote approximation to this ideal. That the approximation should be other than very remote is rendered impossible by many practical considerations, the chief of which are the impracticability in general of devoting more than one day to a single examination and the physical limitations of the student.

Practically therefore the extreme limit of time to be allotted to an examination should not exceed eight hours—that is, it should be arranged to occupy the average student for no longer period. Perhaps six hours would be a more reasonable limit.

Subject to these practical limitations, and others dictated by convenience in particular cases, the principle seems plain: The more the student is required to tell, the fairer is the test of his knowledge.

III. Theoretical or Practical?

Another point arises with respect to the character of the questions to be asked. These may be either theoretical or practical.

The *theoretical* question is one which may be answered in the very words of the text-book or teacher. The student is called upon to *remember* the statements of definitions and principles, but not to *apply* them.

Upon the *practical* examination, on the other hand, the questions are stated more or less in the form in which they would be apt to arise in practice, and the student is forced to rely for his answers, not only upon his knowledge and memory of principles stated, but also upon his ability to apply the principles he has learned.

In another form of the practical examination, which, for want of a better term, we may call the ultra-practical examination, the student is compelled not only to apply to a concrete case the principles he has learned, but to reason in a legal way from those principles to new and more advanced conceptions which he has never seen formulated.

Each of these forms of question has its peculiar advantages. Probably the least valuable is the theoretical, for it in the main tests the memory rather than the understanding. The sort of examination that constitutes the fairest test for one type of mind may not be so fair in the case of a different type. It is to be noted also that each of these forms of examination represents a different sort of knowledge, each sort being occasionally needed by the practitioner. It would seem reasonably to follow that the fairest general test would be an examination wherein all these varieties of question are judiciously mingled.

IV. The Honor System

I would be recreant to my duty should I fail, in this noble presence, to lift my voice in favor of one feature of the Examination, which, unfortunately, I cannot but believe, does not prevail in all our institutions. I refer to the examination conducted upon the Honor System.

Originated in 1842 at Jefferson's noble creation, the University of Virginia, which I am proud to serve, its intrinsic merit has led to its adoption in many of the schools and colleges of the country.

With the theory of the Honor System you are doubtless all more or less familiar. It relies upon the principle of student self-government, and can only be successfully supported by the favorable sentiment of the student-body. It may be extended to other matters beside examinations, but in its application to the latter, the student makes it a point of honor to give and receive no assistance upon any examination, and at the University of Virginia the student-body itself punishes any offender against its code of honor by summary expulsion, the faculty's kind offices towards that end being unnecessary. Such a punishment is terrible in its consequences to the individual, for it marks him for life with the brand of dishonor.

I hope I shall live to see the Honor System adopted by the free voice of the students themselves in every great institution of our country.

V. The Grading of Examination Papers

Objection is frequently raised to a high and fixed examination standard that it is unfair and unjust, since the student's percentage will depend in large measure upon the whim or caprice of the person grading his paper; or at least that it is fluctuating and uncertain, since a certain grade with one teacher or at one institution may mean a very different thing from the same grade as used by another teacher or at another institution.

And it must be admitted that the grading of papers cannot, in the nature of things, be quite mathematically exact. Neither for that matter can the grading of a student's answers in the class-room. But I contend earnestly that, given a conscientious examiner, disposed to do full justice both to his school and his student, there can be made a very near approach to mathematical certainty.

My own personal observation and experience, if you will pardon a reference to it, has clearly demonstrated to my mind that a student's percentage in an examination under one professor will furnish a very close index to his percentage upon an examination held under a different professor about the same time. There may be a variation of two or three points in the hundred, but rarely more. Numerous instances of this fact each year in my own experience surprise me by their strong testimony to the accuracy with which papers may be graded.

I assert therefore with the profoundest conviction of the truth of the statement that, given examiners who desire to administer *exact justice* between the student and the institution they serve, there is no danger that an examination standard fixed at a certain point will be materially varied from. The important condition is that the examiner should be imbued with the desire to administer *exact justice*.

Indeed, a sufficiently high numerical value being attached to each question, the grading can be made very accurate. Something of course must be left to the examiner's judgment in ascertaining the value of an answer—more and more as the examination becomes more practical in its character. But in any event the examiner's discretion can properly be invoked only within very small limits. There is room only for small errors of judgment, and these are apt to cancel one another.

VI. The Examination Standard

Thus far, in discussing the various attributes of the Examination, we have regarded it merely in its aspect as a measure or test of the student's knowledge. The next and last point upon which I wish to touch—the

Examination Standard—introduces also into the discussion that other most important view-point of the examination—its aspect as a review-compelling medium.

While the percentage required for graduation must depend in some measure upon the form of examination, the modes of instruction and the customs and traditions of each school, there are some general principles which we may look to as proper to regulate this very important matter.

One thing is certain, the higher the examination standard, the more thoroughly will the student be compelled to do his work both for the class-room and by way of review, and the more law must he know when he comes into the examination room.

It has been objected that a high examination standard leads the student to cram his head full of propositions for examination purposes, which he will forget immediately afterwards. There are some great law schools in this country which require of the applicant for honors a much higher percentage upon examination than is demanded of the ordinary candidate for the degree. Ask these institutions whether their honor-men are regarded as below par—ranking below the average candidate for the degree because of the increased standard?

But the objection scarcely needs this refutation. One who has once learned principles so thoroughly that he can turn and twist and apply them to any concrete case likely to arise is not liable to forget them afterwards, even though the primary purpose in learning them is to pass a searching examination. Exactly the same objection may be applied to a high standard in the class-room work.

The truth is that the student does forget a good deal of what he learns either for recitation or examination, but he also remembers a great deal. He finds little difficulty in recalling what he has once learned and he has had the benefit of the mental discipline and training undergone in once learning it. A higher examination standard merely compels him to review and grasp more firmly the principles learned in the class-room.

In the preparation of this paper, I have written to nineteen of the most prominent law schools in this country, with the intention of ascertaining their examination standards. They very courteously replied giving me the information desired, which may be summarized as follows: Two schools had no fixed standard, requiring only that each professor be satisfied with his students' attainments; one required *fifty-five* per cent. as the standard for general graduation; three required a standard of *sixty* per cent.; one required *sixty-five* per cent.; five required *seventy* per cent.; three, *seventy-five* per cent.; three, *eighty* per cent; and one, *eighty-three* per cent.

As a practical illustration of the advantages of a high examination standard, let us suppose a standard of eighty per cent. as opposed to sixty-five per cent. Is it not apparent that the higher standard would compel the average student to do much more thorough work in class and by way of review? And would it not follow that the degree would stand for much higher attainments on the part of the average graduate?

Let me not be misunderstood. I do not mean to imply that the student would thus be given greater opportunities to learn. Indeed at some of our law schools those opportunities could hardly be improved. Along those lines our standards have been greatly elevated during the last few years, largely through your efforts.

Nor would it imply any particular advance on the part of the best students, who would probably reach the higher mark in any event.

It would simply mean that the *average* student would be forced to take more advantage of the opportunities afforded, do more thorough work and prepare himself better for graduation and finally for his profession.

Would not this body do well to look into this matter, and inquire whether advantage would not result to the cause of legal education by a hearty effort to bring about a greater uniformity and an elevation of the examination standards in our law schools? The reforms you have already advocated have done much to raise the standard of attainment of our best graduates. The adoption of higher examination standards would go far towards elevating the rank and file.

Chapter 60

Chance and Systematic Factors Affecting Essay Grades

1976

Stephen P. Klein and Frederick M. Hart

This study first appeared in 1 *Reports of LSAC Sponsored Research: Volume I, 1949-1969* 511 LSAC Report 68-4. It is discussed in chapter 58.

The authors wish to express their appreciation to the Law School Admissions Test Council for their support of this research; to the professors who participated in it; and to Susan Beidler, Frank Evans, and Susan Pierson for their invaluable assistance.

The research dealing with the prediction of grades in law school, like the prediction of other graduate and undergraduate grades, has focused mainly on the predictors. Comparatively little attention has been paid to the criterion against which these selection instruments are usually validated, i.e., grades on essay examinations. Investigations into the nature of this kind of criterion are important, however, since they may reveal certain *systematic* factors which bias essay grades in a manner that could lead to the adoption of a selection instrument that was not truly relevant to the goals of the curriculum. This situation might occur if a student's grade was a function of such things as how fast he could write or whether he was pedantic. In other words, measures of writing speed or the tendency to use long sentences would appear as useful predictors even though a professor did not wish to have these characteristics influencing the grades he assigned.

A second reason for examining the criterion is to find out whether there are *chance* factors affecting grades in a way that would lower the potential validity of any predictor of them.[1] For example, a student's score might be biased if his paper was graded immediately after an exceptionally good or poor paper and/or read near the beginning or end of the grading session (Godshalk, Swineford, & Coffman, 1966).

There are, of course, several kinds of chance factors that could influence the predictability of essay grades. These have been discussed at length elsewhere (e.g., Coffman, 1968; Ebel, 1965), but whether or not any of them are operating can be assessed by studying the reliability of the grades themselves. This is usually accomplished by examining one or more of the following three types of data: (1) whether a student gets the same grade on different essay questions, (2) whether a grader assigns the same score to the same paper on different occasions, and (3) whether a paper receives the same score from different graders.

Although Coffman (1968) and others have reviewed the findings with these three kinds of data along with the conditions under which various systematic and chance factors operate, their conclusions are based almost entirely on studies with English themes and/or essays produced in conjunction with nationwide testing programs (e.g., Swineford, 1964). Thus, relatively little is known about the degree to which extraneous factors influence the grades given by teachers to their own students in content-oriented courses. And to the writers' knowledge, there has not been a single published report of whether these factors affect the scoring of the essay examinations that actually are used in graduate or professional schools for assigning course grades.

The purpose of the present study was to examine this latter issue. To achieve this end, it was decided to investigate the nature of essay grades at 16 different law schools when they were based on answers to a typical question that was asked as part of a regular final examination.

PROCEDURE

PROFESSORS

The 17 professors (*Ps*) who participated in this research taught Contracts in law school. One of them, however, was not teaching this course when the study was being conducted. A survey of the backgrounds and characteristics of these *Ps* indicated that they were quite heterogeneous on a number of salient variables. For example, almost all the *Ps* received their LLBs at different schools; they ranged in age from 32 to 69; they used a variety of casebooks; and they taught at a diverse group of private, state, and religious schools. The 16 schools represented by these *Ps* also varied in geographical location and in student selection standards.

COMMON QUESTION

The *Ps* met and discussed the relevancy of four tentative essay questions to their own courses. The question that was preferred almost unanimously was then selected (hereafter referred to as the CQ), and all 16 *Ps* who were currently teaching Contracts included it in their regular final examinations.[2]

The *Ps* judged that a student could write an adequate answer to the CQ in about one of the three hours usually allotted for finals; however, the CQ was not timed separately or otherwise identified as being special. It also was decided that a 30-minute "warm-up" question of a *P's* own choosing should precede the CQ, but no controls were placed on the student to insure that he answered the CQ second.

GRADING CLASS PAPERS

Each *P* graded the papers for his own class. The instructions to the *Ps* regarding such grading read in part as follows: "Use your own normal procedures for grading all student papers. Please provide a separate grade for the common question as well as the student's overall grade." The only exception to normal grading practices was that the *Ps* were not to make any marks or comments on the student's answer to the CQ. To insure realism, a student's score on the CQ was included in his grade on the final examination.

SELECTING THE COMMON SET

Student papers. After a *P* graded the papers for his own class, he sent to ETS five student answers to the CQ that represented the full range of the grades he assigned to it, i.e., one of his best papers, one of his worst, and three that fell at various points in the middle. This procedure resulted in a pool of 80 papers.

Layman's answer to CQ. One of the 80 papers was illegible and was replaced by one written by an intelligent layman who received her bachelor's degree in English. Although she was given unlimited time for this task, she wrote her answer without any outside assistance.

Grading the Common Set

A Xerox copy of the final set of 80 answers to the CQ was sent to each *P* and he was asked to grade them according to the following instructions:

> Please read the papers in the order in which you receive them . . . [each *P* had a different order so that possible sequence effects were counterbalanced]. It is suggested, however, that you glance through a few of them to get an idea as to their range of quality before you begin assigning grades. Assign grades along a five point scale, i.e., 1 through 5. The *higher the number, the better the paper.* Try to spread your grades across the five categories as much as possible . . . [and] . . . each of the five grades should be used at least twice.

The *Ps* did not know that a layman's paper was included in the set of 80.

Student Characteristics

Scores on the following three tests were obtained for 74 of the 79 students (*Ss*) whose papers were included in the common set: Law School Admissions Test (LSAT), Writing Ability (WA), and General Background (GB).[3] The LSAT *Bulletin of Information for Candidates* (ETS, 1967) contains a description of these measures and sample items.

Scores for all 79 students were computed for undergraduate grade-point average (UGPA) and first-year grade-point average in law school (Law-GPA). This was done by obtaining a student's rank on these variables relative to the other five students in his class whose papers were included in the common set (e.g., if he had the highest UGPA and the lowest Law-GPA, his scores on these measures would be 5 and 1, respectively).[4]

Paper Characteristics

Each of the 80 papers in the common set was scored for the following four characteristics: (1) Length (as measured by the total number of words written), (2) Handwriting quality (as evaluated by eight independent raters), (3) English composition, and (4) a layman's impression of its "correctness." The latter two scores were the average grades assigned by two college graduates who majored in English and who had never taken a law course. No instructions were given to these graders regarding what was a good or poor answer.

Analyses and Results

Criterion Reliability

The three issues dealing with criterion reliability that were studied and the results of these examinations were as follows:

(1) Did a student get the same grade on different essay questions? The results presented in Table 1 indicate that he did since the average part-whole correlation between a student's grade on the CQ and his grade in Contracts was .71 and the mean grade on the CQ (i.e., across the 17 *Ps*) had an average correlation of .80 with Law-GPA. It may be argued, however, that this latter $\bar{r}$ may have been inflated indirectly by the technique used in selecting the papers at each school. A partial answer to this criticism is that the *Ps* mean grade correlated .62 with Law-GPA across the 79 students (see Table 3). In other words, the correlation between the *Ps*' mean grade and Law-GPA was still highly significant even when there were no corrections for the inadequacies in the scaling of Law-GPA or adjustments for school differences.[5] It may be concluded, therefore, that a student's performance on the CQ was highly related to his performance on other essay questions used in law school.

(2) Did a professor assign the same grade to the same paper on different occasions? Two kinds of data were used to answer this question. The first was the correlation between the scores a *P* assigned to his five papers when he graded them in his own class and the scores he assigned about eight weeks later when he

graded them in the common set. An inspection of Table 1 indicates that all the *Ps* except #5 graded their own five papers almost identically on the two occasions ($\bar{r}$=.93).

TABLE 1: EVIDENCE OF PROFESSOR AND STUDENT CONSISTENCY[a]

P#	Number of *Ss* in *P's* class	r between CQ and course grade for al *Ss* in *P's* class[b]	r between *Ss*' mean grades on CQ in common set and Law-GPA (n-5)[c]	r between grade on CQ in class and in common set (n-5)[c]	r between *P's* grades on the common set and the mean grades of the other *Ps* (n=80)
1	57	.54	.78	.96	.81
2	102	.53	.55	.86	.73
3	87	.86	.85	.99	.81
4	56	.66	.83	.86	.60
5	68	.65	.86	.14	.68
6	117	.69	.71	.88	.72
7	123	.75	.61	.93	.72
8	39	.73	.70	.98	.78
9	58	.75	.62	.99	.81
10	63	.87	.91	.98	.77
11	114	.58	.93	.91	.78
12	90	.63	.93	.97	.74
13	75	.71	.83	.97	.85
14	83	.83	.78	.92	.81
15	192	.69	.76	.79	.71
16	99	.64	.71	.90	.80
17	—	—	—	—	.77
		r=.71	r=.80	r=.93	r=.76

[a] Fisher's z′ transformation was used in obtaining the average ($\bar{r}$) correlation.
[b] This r was based on all the *Ss* in a *P's* class, i.e., not just the ones whose papers he selected for the common set.
[c] n=4 for *P* #5 since one of the papers he submitted was replaced by the layman's paper.

The second analysis involved computing the student's z score in his own class on the CQ and the z score he received when his paper was graded in the common set by his own *P*. The correlation between these two z scores across the 79 students was .70. This indicated that a *P* tended to give a paper the same relative grade in the common set as he did when he graded it with all the papers in his class. For example, if one of his papers was in the top 10% of his own class, he also tended to put it in the top 10% of the grades he assigned in the common set. Thus, it may be concluded that a *P* used essentially the same grading criteria in the common set as he did in his own class. In other words, these two analyses indicated that a *P* not only ranked his own papers the same way twice, he even appeared to grade the common set of 80 as if they were a random sample of papers from his own class.

(3) Did a paper receive the same grade from different *Ps*? This is a complex question since a *P's* grades could differ from those assigned by other *Ps* in the following three ways: (1) variability (i.e., how much a *P* spread his grades across the five-point score range), (2) leniency (i.e., mean grade), and (3) relative order (i.e., whether there was agreement as to which papers were best, average, and worst). It also is possible

that some *Ps* grade one way and another cluster grade in a different manner, i.e., there may be separate schools of thought (or points of view) as to what makes one paper better or worse than another, and only within each viewpoint would *Ps* agree on what constitutes a "good" answer. For example, *Ps* holding one viewpoint might give more credit to *Ss* who cited relevant cases, whereas *Ps* holding a different point of view might stress the appropriate application of legal principles.

The results obtained in investigations of each of these considerations with the grades assigned to the 80 papers may be summarized as follows: (1) Cochran's C test for homogeneity of variance (Winer, 1962) indicated that the *Ps* did not differ significantly in variability (C=.082), (2) an analysis of variance (see Table 2) indicated that some *Ps* were significantly more lenient than others (F=2.14), and (3) there was a high degree of agreement on how the papers should be ordered (the intraclass correlation was .58 and the reliability of the mean ratings was .96). A second indicant of the consistency among the *Ps* in how they ordered the 80 papers was that the average correlation between a *P's* grades and the mean grades assigned by the other 16 *Ps* was .76 (see Table 1). Further evidence of their agreement came from factor analyses of the inter-*P* cross-products, covariance, and correlation matrices in that only one viewpoint was obtained regarding which papers were considered good, average, or poor.[6]

Position Effects

A 4 x 17 analysis of variance was computed to determine whether a *P* tended to give higher or lower grades near the beginning or end of his set of 80 papers. Since each *P* read the papers in a different order, it was decided to break each set into four groups, i.e., the first 20 read, the second 20, etc. The results of this analysis appear in Table 2 and indicate that although the *Ps* differed in leniency, there was no evidence that one or more of them were influenced by whether they read a paper near the beginning, middle, or end of the set of 80.

Table 2: Analysis of Position and Professor Ethics

Source	df	MS	F
Positions	3	1.72	1.20
Professors	16	3.06	2.14**
Positions x Professors	48	1.85	1.29
Within Cell (Error)	1292	1.43	
Total	1359		

**p < .01

Correlations Between Student and Paper Characteristics

Table 3 contains the correlations of paper and student characteristics with the average grades the 17 *Ps* assigned to the 80 answers. An inspection of this table indicates that this average grade is predicted moderately well by LSAT and WA scores, and even better by Length and the laymen's impression of "correctness." There also was a low but statistically significant correlation between Handwriting and Mean Grade

When various student and paper characteristics were combined, it was found that the team of Length plus the laymen's impression of "correctness" yielded the best prediction of the *Ps'* average grade (R=.70). Since the reliability of the latter measure was only .54, it seems reasonable to assume that this correlation would be increased were the laymen's "correctness score" based on the judgments of several rather than just two laymen. An essentially equally high level of prediction was achieved by the combination of Length and LSAT (R=.68). In other words, the students who received the better grades were both intelligent (as measured by LSAT) and verbose.

TABLE 3: CORRELATIONS AMONG STUDENT AND PAPER CHARACTERISTICS

	P's Mean Grade	LSAT	WA	GB	UGPA	Law-GPA	Length	Handwriting	English Comp.	Laymen's "Correctness" Score
P's Mean Grade		.45**	.47**	.11	.02	.62**	.56**	.25*	.44**	.63**
LSAT			.60**	.37**	-.09	.40**	.15	.27**	.27**	.44**
Writing Ability (WA)				.55**	.11	.35**	.20*	.18	.41**	.44**
General Background (GB)					-.02	.13	.06	.11	.27**	.25*
Undergraduate GPA						-.10	.14	.12	.08	1.04
Law-GPA							.32**	.19*	.21*	.25*
Length								.20*	.34*	.47**
Handwriting									.41**	.29**
English Composition										.78**
Mean Score	2.84	574.70	57.26	53.53	3.01	3.00	813.11	2.95	2.94	2.88
Standard Deviation	.94	70.62	8.27	8.55	1.38	1.45	306.92	1.33	.84	.94
Reliability	.96	.90	.83	.80	[a]	[a]	[a]	.97[b]	.45[c]	.54[c]

[a] The reliability of this measure was not available.
[b] The reliability of the mean Handwriting score was obtained by analysis of variance.
[c] This is the reliability for the mean scores across the two laymen. It was computed by "stepping up" the correlation between them to account for the papers being graded by two laymen.
*p .05
**p .01

Discussion

A comparison of the foregoing results with those obtained in other studies of essays (e.g., Diederich, French, & Carlton, 1961; Myers, McConville, & Coffman, 1966) suggests that the grades assigned by a *P* were quite reliable.[7] The "average" (intraclass) correlation of .58 was particularly impressive since no attempt was made to achieve agreement among the *Ps* in how they assigned grades, i.e., there were no scoring guides or similar aids. This finding was somewhat surprising in light of the fact that when the *Ps* discussed the nature of the CQ, there did not appear to be any consensus on what they considered to be a "good" answer. Thus, despite the heterogeneity in the law schools, in the types of *Ps* who participated, and in the opinions as to what an adequate answer to the CQ should involve, all the *Ps* agreed on what a "good" essay was when they read one.

Since it can be demonstrated that reliability is increased substantially as more essays by the same student are graded (Coffman, 1966) and since a student generally answers a few questions on each of several examinations during his first year in law school, the preceding results suggest that first-year Law-GPA probably has a very high reliability. It appears, therefore, that the potential validity of a measure in predicting Law-GPA is not limited greatly by *chance* factors influencing grades.

On the other hand, certain *systematic* factors, such as handwriting, were associated with the *Ps*' grades. The most striking of these was Length, but it is not known just what facets of Length were producing this high relationship. Since Length is essentially unrelated to LSAT (r=.15), one cannot dismiss its impact by saying that the intelligent student knows more and thus writes more. It just is not so! The combination of LSAT and Length, however, does yield a very good prediction of the *Ps*' grades (R=68). This finding is quite consistent with Bracht and Hopkins' (1968) study of essay grades in educational psychology since they found that essay grades correlated .44 and .46 with SAT scores and Length, respectively, and that the latter two measures were essentially unrelated. Similar results also have been obtained with college freshmen and high school students (e.g., Diederich et al., 1961; Page, 1967).

One hypothesis to explain this latter phenomenon is that essay examinations may place a high premium on both writing speed and intelligence rather than on knowledge per se. Three pieces of evidence supporting this hypothesis are as follows: (1) the layman's answer to the CQ was written under untimed conditions and received a slightly higher than average grade (3.15), (2) the laymen's evaluation of the 80 papers was significantly correlated with the *Ps*' grades (r=.63), and (3) the grades assigned by a typical *P* correlated with the grades assigned by the other *Ps* only slightly higher than the scores based on the combination of Length and LSAT (.76 versus .68, respectively). Thus, it appears that the *Ps* gave high grades to persuasive "common sense" answers to the CQ without much regard to whether the students used technical principles and/or jargon appropriately. If this was indeed the case, and if such an answer involved dealing with several salient characteristics of the question, then students who could write both quickly and intelligently would get the better grades. There are, of course, other hypotheses that might account for the success of the Length and LSAT combination, but an examination of which hypotheses are most tenable will require further research.

Conclusions

The foregoing results have led to the following conclusions:

(1) Students tend to be consistent in their performance on different essay questions used in law school.

(2) The level of agreement among the *Ps* in how they graded a single typical essay was high enough to expect that law school grades are potentially quite predictable.

(3) Although the basis for the *Ps*' agreement was not clear, they did have a marked preference for longer answers and for those written by brighter students. Since measures of length and intellectual ability were unrelated, a combination of them yielded a very high correlation with the *Ps*' grades.

(4) Individuals who had no law training generally assigned the same grades to the papers as did the

Ps. It appeared, therefore, that the *Ps* were at least in part giving good grades to those papers that presented a persuasive "common sense" answer to the question.

References

Bracht, G.H. & Hopkins, K.D. Objective and essay tests: Do they measure different abilities? Paper presented at Annual Meeting of the American Educational Research Association, Chicago, February 2, 1968.

Coffman, W.E. On the validity of essay tests of achievement. *Journal of Educational Measurement*, 1966, *3*, 151-156.

Coffman, W.E. Personal communication, 1968. (Draft of chapter on Essay Tests for *Educational Measurement* to be published by the American Council on Education.)

Cronbach, L.J. *Essentials of psychological testing*. (2nd ed.) New York: Harper, 1960.

Diederich, P.B., French, J.W., & Carlton, S.T. *Factors in judgments of writing ability*. Research Bulletin 61-15, Princeton, N.J.: Educational Testing Service, 1961.

Ebel, R.L. *Measuring educational achievement*. New York: Prentice-Hall, 1965.

Educational Testing Service. *Bulletin of information for candidates*. Princeton, N.J.: Educational Testing Service, 1967.

Godshalk, F.I., Swineford, Frances, & Coffman, W.E. The measurement of writing ability. College Entrance Examination Board, *Research Monograph No. 6*, 1966.

Jøreskog, K.G. Umlfa, A computer program for unrestricted maximum likelihood factor analysis. Research Memorandum 66-20. Princeton, N.J.: Educational Testing Service, 1966.

Klein, S. & EvanS, F.R. An examination of the validity of the nine experimental tests for predicting success in law school. *Educational* and *Psychological Measurement* (in press), 1968.

Myers, A., McConville, Carolyn, & Coffman, W.E. Simplex structure in the grading of essay tests. *Educational and Psychological Measurement*, 1966, *26*, 41-54.

Page, E. Grading essays by computer. In *Proceedings* of the *1966 Invitational Conference* on *Testing Problems*. Princeton, N.J.: Educational Testing Service, 1967. Pp. 87-100.

Swineford, Frances. Test analysis, Advanced Placement Examination in American History, Form MBP. Statistical Report 64-53. Princeton, N.J.: Educational Testing Service, 1964.

Winer, B.J. *Statistical principles in experimental design*. New York: McGraw-Hill, 1962. Pp. 92, 124-129.

Notes

1. It can be shown that the validity of a perfectly reliable test can never be greater than the square root of the criterion's reliability (Cronbach, 1960, p. 132).

2. Appendix A containing a copy of the CQ has been deposited with the American Documentation Institute. Appendices to this article may be obtained from the ADI Auxiliary Publications Project, Photoduplication Service, Library of Congress, Washington, D.C. 20540. Cite Document number 10062 and remit $1.25 for photoprints, or $1.25 for 35mm microfilm. Advance payment is required. Make checks or money orders payable to: Chief, Photoduplication Service, Library of Congress.

3. One of the *Ps* taught at a school that did not participate in the LSAT program, and thus, scores on the LSAT, WA, and GB were not available for the five students whose papers he submitted.

4. This appeared to be the most practical system for scaling these scores; however, it was very crude and tended to make distinctions between students where there were no differences. This was especially true of UGPA. The relatively low correlations with UGPA presented in Table 3 were, therefore, probably a function of this poor scaling rather than any lack of relationship between it and other variables.

5. The *Ss* in the present study had a mean of 575 and standard deviation of 71 on the LSAT. These results are quite comparable to those found in validity studies of the LSAT with first-year law students. For example, Klein and Evans (1968) have reported that the LSAT mean and standard deviation across seven law schools were 575 and 72 respectively. Thus, the *Ss* in the present study did not appear to be unduly heterogeneous on ability relative to the population of law students.

6. This conclusion was based on inspections of the latent roots and vectors and on the fact that the first principal axis in the three analyses accounted for 94%, 63%, and 64% of the variance, respectively. Jøreskog's (1966) method for obtaining communalities was used in the factor analysis of the inter-P correlation matrix, and the results of this analysis indicated that

the probability of there being more than one factor was less than 5 in 100. The latent roots obtained in these analyses are presented in Appendix B, deposited with the American Documentation Institute.

7. Coffman (1966) and others have noted, however, that the reliability of students' grades on an objective test is likely to be considerably higher than that on an essay test scored by only one grader. There are several reasons for this, among which are that essay tests are relatively limited in their sampling of course content and that scores on them are a function of both grader and student factors rather than just the latter. It should be noted also that a grader's reliability can be increased by the use of scoring guides and similar aids.

III. Skills Courses

Chapter 61

Plus Ça Change, Plus C'est la Même Chose

The Integration of Theory and Practice in Legal Education

1993

M. H. Hoeflich

Michael Hoeflich is Dean of the University of Kansas School of Law and the editor of *The Gladsome Light of Jurisprudence* (New York: Greenwood Press, 1988). This article first appeared in 66 *Temple Law Review* 123 (1993). See also chapter 44.

Author's note: I wish to thank my colleagues Dean Braveman and Arlene Kanter for their conversation about this article. I also wish to acknowledge the help in acquiring the materials used in this article of scholarly and resourceful booksellers, Bob Rubin of Brookline, Mass. and Steve Resnick of Cazenovia, N.Y.

In recent years one of the "hot" topics in legal education has been the debate over the extent to which it is desirable and possible to integrate a more practical approach into the predominantly theoretical classroom model of legal education used in most American law schools. The reasons for this debate occurring now are complex and several. First, there has been a growing discontent among many law teachers over the last decade with the classic Langdellian doctrinal approach to teaching law.[1] The gap between the doctrinal/rules-oriented Socratic method and the realities of the legal profession has grown in recent years. Tied to this has been the growing dissatisfaction of many practicing lawyers with the products of traditional legal education.[2] Unfortunately, when most law students graduate they are not ready to *practice* law but instead are only ready to *begin to learn* to practice law through the apprenticeship they will experience as associates.[3] Also, and in the past decade especially, clinical legal education, broadly defined to include actual clinics, externships, and simulations, has gained many proponents throughout the United States. More and more often today, clinicians are taking their places as full members of law faculties who are able to enter into serious discourse with their more traditional colleagues on issues of pedagogical methodology.[4]

As a dean and as a law teacher I find myself delighted with this debate and hope that it will result in a far more pragmatic and less doctrinal approach to legal education. At the same time, as a legal historian I find myself bemused at the claims of many of the most vocal proponents of this integration of practice into theory that this is a new and "revolutionary" idea. Like so much else that appears to be new to those without a historical sense, the debate about the integration of theory and practice in legal education is far from new. Indeed, it is a debate that took place and had extensive practical impact during the first phase of American university-affiliated legal education, in the period between the founding of the first professorships in law in American universities in the late eighteenth century and the development of the modern law school beginning in 1870 with the accession of C.C. Langdell to the deanship of the Harvard Law School. It would, perhaps, be worthwhile for today's law teachers engaged in this important debate to become a bit more familiar with the shape of this debate and its results as they occurred over a century ago.

I. The First Era of American Law Schools

Prior to the American Revolution the principal model of legal education in the United States was apprenticeship.[5] Beginning in the last quarter of the eighteenth century, under the influence of Thomas Jefferson's appointment of George Wythe to the first chair in law at William and Mary, a number of universities appointed law professors to lecture to undergraduates.[6] It was not until 1817, however, the year which marked both the inauguration of the Dane College of Law at Harvard and the publication of the first edition of David Hoffman's *A Course of Legal Study*, that the antebellum university affiliated law school became a reality.[7] During the period between 1817 and 1860, law schools were initiated at a number of major universities, including Harvard, Transylvania,[8] New York University, and Columbia.

Not surprisingly, the founding faculties of these new university affiliated law schools found themselves in direct competition with the well-established apprenticeship system.[9] A university law degree was by no means a necessary requirement for law practice. Indeed, in many parts of the country such a degree might be viewed as a liability.[10] The law school experience was time-consuming and expensive. It was a delay in "getting down to business." Thus, the faculty members at those universities that had established law schools found that they needed to develop a mission for their schools which would differentiate them from the apprenticeship system and would convince potential law students that the time and expense of obtaining a university related legal education was justifiable.

Interestingly, the debate that arose from this need centered upon the relationship between theoretical and practical training and the integration of the two in university related law schools. Equally interesting is that this nineteenth century debate took as its starting point the wholly practical, nontheoretical model of apprenticeship as the norm and therefore required justification for introducting a theoretical element into legal education. Conversely, the starting point for this early debate is precisely the opposite of that of today's debate. Today the debate about the integration of theoretical and practical components in legal education is motivated by a growing repudiation of the doctrinal and theoretical Langdellian approach now predominant in American legal education.

There is a rich literature from the antebellum period on the integration of theoretical and practical learning in law schools. Some of the greatest law teachers of the period, including Joseph Story, James Kent, Simon Greenleaf, Benjamin Butler, Daniel Mayes, and David Dudley Field, made contributions.[11] Unfortunately, most of this literature has been forgotten by modern law teachers and even by legal historians. In part, it has been overshadowed by the outpouring of literature on legal education that occurred after 1870 as part of the Langdellian revolution in pedagogy and, in part, it has been forgotten because of the form in which it was published. To a very large degree, these contributions came in the form of discourses pronounced at the inauguration of these early law schools, at the beginning and end of law school terms, and at the annual meetings of honorary societies such as Phi Beta Kappa.[12] These discourses were occasionally printed in the periodicals of the time such as the *North American Review* or the *Southern Literary Messenger*,[13] but most often appeared only as pamphlets in limited print runs. Today these pamphlets are often extremely rare and found only in a few libraries, if that. I have spent the better part of ten years collecting these pamphlets precisely because they provide a rich source for the history of legal pedagogy and can shed light on such issues as the integration of theoretical and practical learning in law schools.

II. The Antebellum Debate

The central problem for the university related law schools was one of differentiation. They had to develop a model which was both different from and more appealing than the traditional apprenticeship model. The apprenticeship model had several factors in its favor. First, it had been the predominant model for well over a century.[14] The greatest American lawyers of the late eighteenth and early nineteenth century, including Jefferson, Hamilton, Webster, and Clay, were all products of this system.[15] Second, it provided the apprentices with an established professional network, since they would apprentice themselves to well-known and successful judges or lawyers.[16] Third, it was relatively inexpensive since the apprenticeship experience for most young would-be lawyers took place in their home communities.

The apprenticeship model also had several disadvantages. First, it was wholly practical. The young legal tyro would learn only what he encountered in his master's practice or from his master's tutelage, if he were lucky enough to be affiliated with a lawyer or judge who provided some formal instruction to his clerks. Second, learning by the apprenticeship model tended to be conservative. The young apprentices would learn how law was practiced but would not learn how law might be changed from the existing models. Finally, the apprenticeship model depended to a great extent upon the availability of successful lawyers and judges willing to train younger lawyers. In locales where such persons were not available, the model was unsuccessful.

Not surprisingly, the pedagogical theoreticians of the new university affiliated law schools played upon these weaknesses in appealing to would-be students. They explained that law was more than a simple craft, that it was, in fact, a liberal science.[17] Legal training, in their arguments, prepared law students not only for the technical necessities of law practice but also for the burdens of citizenship in the new republic, as law reformers and, indeed, intellectuals. They contrasted the product of the apprenticeship system, the narrowly educated "pettifogger,"[18] with the broadly trained legal scientist who understood not only the technicalities of pleading and conveyancing but also the history and philosophy of the law. Perhaps the clearest exposition of this argument is to be found in the anonymous article entitled "Study of the Law" published in the 1837 volume of the *Southern Literary Messenger*.[19] The author of this article contrasts office study with study in a university affiliated law school:

> But supposing the student to have made choice of his office, and that he has opportunity for study, and uses it; he cannot have those advantages which he should have. The system itself is wrong, fundamentally wrong. For those young gentlemen of independent fortune, who take up the profession of the law, merely because, in this country, a young man without any pursuit or profession would be an anomaly; or for those who adopt it because it is eminently honorable, or because it is considered the high road to place and power, without any determination of trusting to it as a profession, the present course of study is fully sufficient. But for him who desires, if entrusted with power, to use it rightly, or who intends to make the law his business and his study—who is anxious to become master of the law and its spirit—who expects to devote his whole life to its ardent pursuit,—to such a one, how utterly inappropriate and inadequate is the present method of study! It allows barely sufficient time to obtain a general knowledge of the local laws, but is altogether incompetent to imbue the mind with a deep and solid

> acquaintance with its broad and general principles. He cannot go up to the source of the stream and drink from its fountains, but he must receive it polluted and adulterated as it has floated down to him. His time is divided between the business of the office and his studies; and in the regulation of the latter he has to trust to his own judgement, or at best, to the casual advice of one more competent. Why should such a plan be pursued in regard to students of the law, when one so different is deemed necessary for those of other liberal professions.[20]

The proponents of university affiliated legal education could not reject outright the importance of providing instruction in the practical techniques of the law, however. To have done so would have been to render these new law schools irrelevant to would-be practitioners who demanded practical training. They were forced, by the nature of their definition of university affiliated legal education, to design educational programs that would combine the practicality of instruction in the apprenticeship system with the theoretical richness contained in their ideas of law as a liberal science. In an 1817 review of *A Course of Legal Study* by David Hoffman, Joseph Story captured the spirit of these pioneers of university affiliated law schools and the way in which they both had to differentiate their schools from the apprenticeship system and at the same time appeal to the practical instincts of would-be lawyers:

> We have another motive, besides the intrinsic value of the work, for commending it [Hoffman's book] earnestly to the perusal of our readers. It will demonstrate to the understanding of every discerning man the importance, nay, the necessity, of the law-school, which the Government of Harvard College have, so honorably to themselves, established at Cambridge. No work can sooner dissipate the common delusion, that the law may be thoroughly acquired in the immethodical, interrupted, and desultory studies of the office of a practicing counsellor. Such a situation is indispensable after the student shall have laid the foundation in elementary principles, under the guidance of a learned and discreet lecturer. He will then be prepared to reap the full benefits of the practice of an attorney's office.[21]

Baltimore lawyer David Hoffman was one of the least appreciated and most significant innovators in American legal education. His *A Course of Legal Study* was an ambitious plan to provide a thorough university affiliated legal education to American students.[22] For a short time Hoffman was able to put his educational ideas into practice through a series of lectures on law which he delivered at the University of Maryland, though their ultimate lack of success prevented him from instituting the "legal seminary" which he had envisioned.[23] Nonetheless, Hoffman's writings on legal education were widely known and he corresponded with men such as Associate Supreme Court Justice and Harvard law professor Joseph Story on the topic.[24]

In his *Introductory Lecture*, published at Baltimore in 1823, Hoffman explained his theory of legal pedagogy.[25] He rejected the apprenticeship model for two principal reasons. First, most of the apprentice lawyer's theoretical knowledge came from reading a few books, e.g. *Blackstone's Commentaries*.[26] Hoffman believed that it was impossible for a young would-be lawyer to acquire a knowledge of the voluminous literature of the law simply through solitary reading without guidance from a more experienced and knowledgeable master.[27] This guidance, he believed, was best provided by lectures, a practice not found in law offices. Second, Hoffman opposed the notion of solitary study for another reason. He believed that learning should be a "social" activity, something best accomplished with a large group of fellow students engaged in the same learning process.[28] Hoffman believed that a group of students learning the law *together* would each help to reinforce the others' learning processes and facilitate discussion of new ideas. Again, this was best accomplished at a university rather than in a law office.

Hoffman's emphasis on lectures on the general principles of law shows clearly the importance he placed upon theoretical and doctrinal education in his syllabus. This is not suprising, since it was one of the two primary ways in which he differentiated his university based system from the competing apprenticeship model. Nevertheless, Hoffman was also quite aware of the need to provide practical training to his students as an accompaniment to his lectures. He proposed to do this by three methods, the inspiration for which he drew upon the history of legal education in England at the Inns of Court.[29] Hoffman proposed that law students at his university engage in trial practice, stating:

> . . . the organization of a tribunal for the argument of supposed cases, brought before it with a strict regard to all the forms of good Pleading, and the rules of Evidence, and prosecuted with a rigid attention to all the decorums of forensic disputation. This tribunal will have the name of Moot Court. . . .[30]

Second, he proposed to establish a "distinct association, denominated the Rota," which would provide a forum for discussion and debate of those legal issues that did not lend themselves to the moot court context.[31] Finally, he proposed to establish four prize essay competitions for law students that would provide a forum for them to write extensively upon topics of legal significance.[32] Thus, in Hoffman's scheme, the theoretical education of the lecture hall would be supplemented by the practical exercises of the moot court, the debating hall, and the writing competitions.

Hoffman's ideas on legal education and the integration of theoretical and practical instruction were followed at a number of the contemporary law schools, including Harvard.[33] One of the most innovative of these law schools, from the perspective of blending theoretical and practical instruction, was that begun in the City of New York by Benjamin Butler.[34] Butler had a distinguished career at the Bar. He served as Attorney-General of the United States during the Jackson administration and subsequently as United States Attorney for the Southern District of New York.[35] In addition to his practicing career he was also profoundly concerned with legal education. Butler's attempt to start a successful law school in New York City, like Hoffman's attempt in Maryland, also failed. However, he did publish, in 1835, a pamphlet on his educational ideas. Butler's *Plan for the Organization of a Law Faculty and for a System of Instruction in Legal Science in the University of the City of New York* shares many features in common with Hoffman's *A Course of Legal Study*.[36] Butler starts at the same point as Hoffman and the other legal reformers of the period, rejecting the apprenticeship system:

> Instruction in Law Offices is necessarily quite imperfect. A course of reading is usually marked out for the student; and if he be industrious and attentive, he will have opportunities to acquire considerable knowledge of the Practice. But as gentlemen engaged in extensive business can seldom find time to pay much attention to the improvement of their clerks, the progress of the latter in the Principles of Legal Science, is usually tardy and laborious. In many cases they are left to grope their way in the dark, with little or no assistance from their principals.[37]

Butler, however, shied away from the "legal seminary" approach of Hoffman and others in designing his law school plan. Butler recognized that most contemporary law schools were located in small towns and thus were situated differently from a law school in New York City.[38] Butler proposed to incorporate theory and practice in his new law school far more directly than his contemporaries, for he proposed to integrate actual law practice into the law school curriculum. His idea was that law students should serve as law clerks in practitioners' offices and attend law school simultaneously.[39] He envisioned that the students would work as clerks during the morning and early afternoon and then attend law school classes in the late afternoon and evening hours. In this manner, during part of each day they would have the practical experience of actual lawyering and be exposed to the principles of legal science through attendance at lectures as well.[40] Interestingly, however, Butler did not abandon the idea of moot court exercises, but instead saw these as part of the law school curriculum and as a substantial addition to the law office experience.[41]

Butler's ideas on the integration of theory and practice, combining clerkship experience simultaneously with classroom experience, were unusual for his time. Undoubtedly, the richness of the New York City Bar helped to shape his views which were remarkably ahead of his time, foreshadowing by half a century the YMCA law school models which similarly attempted to integrate theoretical classroom instruction with actual law office experience.[42] Of especial interest is the way in which Butler planned to weave together the theoretical instruction students would gain in the classroom with the practical instruction they would acquire in the law office. In order to fully integrate the student's experience, Butler proposed that the subject matter and schedule of courses be designed to complement the types of experience the student would encounter as a law office clerk. Thus, Butler proposed that in the first year students learn pleading, jurisdiction, admiralty, equity, and criminal law since these would be the subjects to which they would be exposed in their practice as clerks.[43] In so doing, Butler hoped to make both the practical and the theoretical experiences more valuable:

> The ordinary labors of the law office, properly explained to the intelligent student, will immediately become to him subjects of interest, and sources of improvement. What might otherwise be regarded as intolerable drudgery, will now be valued as instructive occupations and he will therefore apply himself to his duties as a clerk with alacrity and diligence.[44]

At the same time, the students also would attend lectures on legal history, constitutional law, and the law of nature and nations.[45] In the second year the students had courses in family law, personal property, criminal law, and evidence, again designed to parallel the experiences a more experienced clerk might have.[46] Finally, in the third year the student attended lectures on real property and conveyancing, as well as Roman law and professional ethics. These complex subjects would round out both their theoretical and practical education.[47]

31. Penn Students at Play. Law students of the University of Pennsylvania, not studying, in 1910 on the courts behind the law school. (*Courtesy of the Biddle Library Department of Special Collections, University of Pennsylvania Law School.*)

Butler's *Plan* shared some of the same philosophical premises outlined by Joseph Story in Story's 1817 *North American Review* article, which first popularized the notion of a university affiliated law school and set forth the theoretical justifications for students to attend such a school rather then enter an apprenticeship. Both Story and Butler, unlike Hoffman, recognized that a university affiliated law program ought to be tied to the law office clerkship experience.[48] But where Story proposed the theoretical law school experience as a one year precursor of the clerkship experience, Butler proposed a full, simultaneous integration of the two.

Closer to the Hoffman model than either the Story or Butler model was the organization of the law school at Transylvania University in Lexington, Kentucky.[49] Transylvania was one of the earliest and most successful university affiliated law schools of the antebellum period.[50] Its faculty was drawn almost exclusively from the ranks of the South's most distinguished jurists, including Judges George Robertson and Daniel Mayes.[51] Both have left, in pamphlet form, introductory lectures outlining their theories of legal education and providing other views on the subject of the integration of theoretical and practical elements in the training of young lawyers. Robertson's lecture on the importance of the Constitution to the maintenance of a free society and of the importance of the law and lawyers in its preservation is of little interest for our present purposes.[52] Mayes' lecture, however, is another matter.

Daniel Mayes' *Introductory Lecture*, presented at Transylvania in 1833, is one of the most comprehensive statements of legal educational philosophy to survive from the antebellum period.[53] Mayes begins his analysis by drawing an important distinction between the notion of the law as an *art* and as a *science*:

> There are to be found in our profession, as in every other, many, who either have not learned, or having learned cease to remember, that there is a *science* of jurisprudence as well as an *art* of jurisprudence. Who standing in the same relation to law, that the cook does to chemistry, are actively engaged in practice during long lives, ignorant of the principles upon which there science is founded . . . Just so it sometimes is in our profession . . . He dreams not that there is any thing of science to be taught from what he has done, and laughs at the idea, that a sensible reason ought to be sought for in everything connected with the profession . . . His students are engaged in reading, without comprehending, and impressing on the memory, without being instructed by adjudged cases, and forms of proceeding.[54]

Indeed, as his final telling blow against the value of the apprenticeship system, Mayes cites Blackstone for the proposition that "if practice be the whole he [a lawyer] is taught, practice must also be the whole he will ever know."[55]

Having established his basic premises, Mayes goes on to describe his vision of how law should be taught, a vision implemented at Transylvania. In each branch of the law the professor chose "the best elementary treatises" as texts.[56] These were the subject of class assignments. Classes were structured as recitations; each student was expected to interpret the text and thereby show not only that they had memorized the principles, but also had learned legal analysis, the ability to work with the principles so learned.[57] As part of these classes, the professor would tell the students of relevant cases and statutes.[58] This was the theoretical portion of the educational program that took place during the week. On Saturdays, however, the lectures ceased and each student was required to participate in a moot court.[59] This practical portion of the program functioned as follows:

> Here the students sufficiently advanced to engage in its exercises, apply their theory to practice. They are exercised in all the forms of professional duty, such as drafting pleas, declarations, bills, answers, etc.; and in debating such legal questions as arise in the course of their exercises; and they are instructed in the practice in courts of law and equity as fully as the nature of a moot court will admit of. [60]

Mayes also introduced an important new element into the debate. Mayes argued that the best law teachers would not necessarily come from the ranks of the best practitioners.[61] On the contrary, he foreshadowed the introduction of the professional law teacher, which occurred at Harvard in the late nineteenth century.[62] In his 1834 lecture he advocated that university affiliated law schools seek to create a class of professional law teachers:

> It is by no means true that he who is most learned is generally best qualified for the business of instruction. All other things being equal he would be so. He is best suited to the business of instruction in a given subject, who has a thorough understanding of the subject so far as it is proposed to teach it, whose ambition it is to teach successfully, and who has no views or ambition beyond this; who is gifted with that peculiar tact which enables the instructor at once to ascertain the character of mind, and the state of improvement, of him who is to be instructed; who can speedily know exactly the wants of the students and most simply and immediately supply those demands upon him which grew out of such wants: who can and will let himself down to the exact level of the beginner's ignorance, and patiently and perseveringly enlighten that ignorance, and raise up the pupil step by step, in regular method, to the desired point of knowledge . . .[63]

Again, it is important to recognize that Mayes did not expect his law school to entirely supplant the apprenticeship system. On the contrary, he saw attendance at Transylvania as a necessary precursor to entrance into a law office and an apprenticeship. Thus, his attempt to blend the theoretical element during the daily lectures with the practical element of the Saturday moot court was understood in the context that further practical training would follow once the pupil had entered into a law office. Indeed, Mayes was not willing to abandon practical training entirely: he retained one day each week for moot court and its practical exercises.

Clearly, it was the widespread belief of the founders of university affiliated law schools that a proper course of legal education would blend the theoretical with the practical. Such is to be found in the writings of Simon Greenleaf, for instance, in regard to his own duties as Royall Professor at Harvard and in his plan for the establishment of a new law school at Bowdoin College.[64] What is important is to understand the premises upon which this belief depended and the circumstances within which this belief developed and flourished. University affiliated legal education was a novelty in the antebellum period in the United States. The notion that legal education ought to integrate both the theoretical and the practical served to differentiate the university affiliated law schools from the existing, dominant apprenticeship system, and thereby helped create a market for these programs. It would be a mistake, however, to understand this new theory of an integrated course of legal study as arising solely as a marketing device. To do so would be to vastly underrate these early pioneers of legal education.

To understand the origins of this new integrated model of legal education and its explicit rejection of the exclusively practical training offered by the apprenticeship system one must understand the growth of the reform movement in law during this period. It is in this movement that the new university affiliated law schools and their integrated model of education were born.

During the antebellum period there existed in the United States a strong anti-common law movement. The movement spanned the new society and attracted adherents both among the broad masses and among the educated elite. It was rooted in a form of proto-populism that rejected what was perceived to be a highly complex legal system that was expensive, arbitrary, and which denied access to justice to a large portion of the population. As such, this system was held to be antidemocratic and violative of those principles upon which the new republic was built.[65] Throughout the antebellum period, this anti-common law movement found a number of vocal proponents.

One of the most vociferous attacks on the legal system and the legal profession was published by Jesse Higgins in Philadelphia in 1805. His work, *Sampson Against the Philistines or the Reformation of Lawsuits*, presented the case against the common law and the common lawyers.[66] Obviously the work of an individual familiar with the law and with legal history, it begins with an exposition of the right to trial by jury, moves on to an analysis of the extant system of pleading, and from there engages in a wholesale attack against lawyers and the legal profession.[67] Lawyers are seen as obscurantist, profiting from the complexity of a system which, in the words of a later commentator, had become a "mysterious science" open only to those who had been trained in the intricacies of special pleading, jurisdictional rules, and complex forms of action.[68] According to Higgins, the legal system was so complex and so closed that the only hope for justice to triumph was its radical reformation and simplification and its opening up to all and sundry, thereby requiring the virtual abolition of the legal profession.[69] Without such a reformation, in Higgins' view, the law would remain the preserve of profiteering lawyers and arbitrary judges, closed to the vast majority of citizens.

Higgins' views were echoed, in a more moderate manner, by Robert Rantoul, himself a Harvard trained lawyer, in his famous oration at Scituate in 1836.[70] Rantoul also recognized the closed nature of the legal system and what, in his view, was the arbitrary nature of judge-made law. His solution was to reduce radically both the complexity of law and the status of the legal profession through the codification of all law. Such a codification, he believed, when combined with a concomitant ban against interpretation would eliminate ambiguity and place the layman on an equal footing with the lawyer.[71] In this way, lawyers would lose their monopoly on knowledge of the law and the ability to manipulate law and judicial decisions.

Inherent in the theories of both Higgins and Rantoul, as well as the other opponents of the antebellum legal system and legal profession, was a fundamental objection to the notion that law was a closed system, and a belief that the monopoly of lawyers and judges derived from the complexity of procedural rules that had grown up over centuries. Certainly, the early nineteenth century rules of pleading and jurisdiction, as well as the forms of action, appear remarkably complex to a modern lawyer. To these nineteenth century critics, this complexity and the professional monopoly to which it had given rise were socially and morally unacceptable. Their calls for radical reform and the abolition of the existing legal profession were taken seriously by many and posed a very real threat to that profession. Many lawyers and judges who believed in the system understood that these critics must be answered if their attacks were not to ultimately succeed. What was required was reform, not radical reform, but reform by lawyers and judges that would eliminate the system's worst excesses and thereby help to preserve its continued existence.

What was necessary was the development of university legal education and a cadre of broadly educated lawyers who both understood and could explain the legal system. Lawyers trained solely in law offices were ill-read and unfamiliar with the underlying principles of the law. These mere "pettifoggers" could not be reformers nor could they satisfactorily defend the legal system against its detractors; they represented precisely the type of lawyer that had fueled the opposition. Men such as Story, Butler, Greenleaf, and Mayes were determined to produce lawyers who could both convincingly defend the existing system by recourse to principled argument and analysis and, at the same time, were knowledgeable in both theory and current practice and could reform the system where reform was necessary. In effect, the new model of university affiliated education, with its underlying pedagogical notion of integrating theory and practice, was part of a movement by the defenders of the American legal system both to preserve the system and to reform it by building up a body of lawyers with the requisite theoretical and practical training that would enable them to undertake this daunting task.

In point of fact, these pioneers of university affiliated legal education were successful in their endeavors. During the antebellum period they were able to produce such lawyers, and through their actions and their writings these men did preserve the system against its opponents. At the same time, they also laid the groundwork for the vast number of reforms that transformed the system from its near feudal state into the modern system we have today.

As university affiliated legal education became a fixture on the antebellum scene, the notion of the integration of theory and practice continued to exercise substantial influence among reformers such as David Dudley Field.[72] One of the greatest of the nineteenth century legal reformers, lawyer, congressman, antislavery statesman, Field was the greatest proponent of codification in the nineteenth century.[73] He brought together his views on law reform and legal education in a speech he delivered at the inauguration of the law school at the University of Chicago in 1859 entitled, *The Magnitude and Importance of Legal Science.*[74] In this speech, Field recited the development of law throughout history and of its role as the preserver of social order and the protector of individual rights. In his words, "Where there is no law, there can be no order, since order is but another name for regularity, or conformity to rule. Without order, society would relapse into barbarism."[75]

In fact, Field turned the arguments of the earlier attacks on the legal system to his own purpose. For Field, "the science of the law is our great security against the maladministration of justice."[76] Unlike earlier proponents of codification, Field did not support the abolition of the legal profession's monopoly, since he wrote at a time when university affiliated law schools were producing lawyers who took a philosophical view of the law and were reforming its worst aspects. He supported such education fully and supported as well the integration of theoretical and practical learning that had become its hallmark:

> Where else so readily as here, will the student obtain a view of the law as a whole, and of all its parts in their several relations and dependencies; here where are collected the records of the science, where there are professors devoted to its teaching, where there are scholars emulous of distinction, and stimulating each other. If medical schools have an advantage over the former method of study and practice by the side of a practicing physician, or if theological schools give better training than the private study of an ordained clergyman, busy with parochial duties, for similar reasons, a school of law, with its large library, its professors set apart to the duty, its lectures, its company of students, its discussions, oral and written, are helps above all that the private office of a busy advocate can offer to a complete legal education. Not that I would altogether dispense with or undervalue the observation of actual practice obtained by attendance in a lawyer's office, during the smaller portion of his legal course, preliminary to the student coming himself to the bar.[77]

In 1858, Theodore W. Dwight, the founder of the modern Columbia Law School, delivered his inaugural.[78] His subject was "Our Municipal Law and the Best Mode of Acquiring It."[79] He echoed those who had gone before him in favoring university affiliated legal education and the integration of theory and practice therein. Dwight believed that law students must study law both historically and systematically. He recognized that the common law is complex, but argued that it was through an understanding of its guiding principles that the complexities could be resolved:

> The complexity and intricacy of legal principles . . . is the price we pay for our free, advancing and refined state of society—an intricacy only to grow more intricate, and a complexity to grow more complicated. Yet it is safe to say that he, who is thoroughly familiar with the fundamental principles of law, has the thread in his hand by which he can be guided through the labyrinth.[80]

Dwight also understood that law was both a science of principles as well as an *art*, and, therefore, law schools must train their students in both the art and the science of law:

> It is at this point [the integration of theory and practice, art and science] that law schools find their justification and found their claim to support. In my judgement, they ought, in this country, when fully organized, to combine both the gymnasium and the university. They should train the student and teach him how to study, and after the work is done, or while it is being done, communicate information on special topics by full courses of lectures. The period of study should be long enough to accomplish both results. The instruction should be mainly scientific; so far as it can at the same time be practical, it must be. While, on the one hand, a law school should not be a mere school of practice, on the other hand it should not prepare its students to be mere lovers of the science of law. They should be lawyers, or, at least, their studies so shaped as not to give them a distaste for the practical side of the profession.[81]

III. The Langdellian Revolution and the Current Debate

There is currently a tendency by those who believe that the current structure of legal education does not sufficiently integrate theory and practice to blame this upon the innovations wrought by C.C. Langdell at Harvard during his deanship. These critics of Langdell tend to characterize the Langdellian method as too theoretical and doctrinal, and opposed to integrating practical elements into the law school curriculum. This is a serious misapprehension. Langdell did, indeed, revolutionize legal education through the substitution of the study of cases for the study of treatises.[82] But Langdell's doctrinalism is not philosophically much different from that of his precedessors discussed above. Indeed, it was the earlier pioneers of legal education like Story, Mayes, and others who championed doctrinalism. However they, like Langdell who was their heir, did not attempt to eliminate the practical from legal education. Langdell, like his predecessors, accepted that legal education had to integrate both theory and practice, to include both the lecture room and the moot court exercise.[83] Langdell and his contemporaries, like Butler and Hoffman and their contemporaries, also assumed that a lawyer's education would take place both in the law school and in the law office. The notion that legal education would be confined solely to the period in which an individual was enrolled in a law school was alien to them. All of the nineteenth century legal educators understood legal education to be a seamless web covering both a student's time in law school as well as his period of clerkship in a law office.[84] We should not blame Langdell for what we perceive as the increasing isolation of law school curriculum and pedagogical theory from practice. Instead we must look to more modern developments.

As I have shown above, throughout the antebellum period legal educators propounded an integrative theory of law study. This theory continued to be influential in the Langdellian decades. What has happened today to cause concern is the result of several recent trends. First, law schools have become increasingly alienated from the practicing Bar.[85] Law faculty have become, in the eyes of practitioners, too much university professors, adopting many of the attitudes and beliefs of the liberal arts faculties while rejecting the professional side of their existence as anti-intellectual. This, in itself, would not present enormous problems so long as the division of educational labor continued in effect as it did in the nineteenth century. Increasingly, however, the practicing Bar has rejected any serious educational role for itself while at the same time increasing its complaints regarding the quality of newly graduated lawyers.[86] For economic reasons, the Bar now generally expects law school graduates to spring from law school as fully grown lawyers. What has happened, in short, is that many law professors during the past few decades have abandoned the traditional law school notion of integrating theory and practice, both in law school and beyond, and redefined their roles to be more like humanities or social science faculty. At the same time the Bar has redefined its role as mentors and teachers of practical skills. In the past several years, a backlash has begun to grow against these movements. Increasingly, law faculties are coming to believe that they must reintroduce practical training into the law school curriculum, while the practicing Bar is coming to realize that it must also accept some burden in the training of young lawyers after they graduate from law school. There is even beginning to be the gleanings of a realization by both law professors and practicing lawyers that learning the law is a process that joins law schools and the Bar and that law teaching must straddle the two worlds of academia and practice. As these discussions continue it will be useful to be aware of their history and that, perhaps, we yet have things to learn from our antebellum predecessors.

Indeed, it is interesting to speculate whether again, as in the antebellum period, the integration of theory and practice will become the focal point for law reform and reform of the legal profession. Increasingly, non-lawyers are coming to view the legal system as too complex and too easily manipulated by lawyers. As their negative perceptions grow and are reflected in anti-lawyer legislation and other activities, the Bar may once again begin to feel seriously threatened. Perhaps, as this process continues, we will again come to realize that the solution lies in a better educated and better informed Bar consisting of lawyers who both understand the theory of law and its actual workings and can use this integrated knowledge to accomplish the needed reforms. Here, perhaps, lies the greatest value in understanding the history of this important debate.

NOTES

1. C. C. Langdell, appointed dean of the Harvard Law School in 1870, helped to create the modern paradigm for legal education. He was instrumental in establishing the use of casebooks and the Socratic method at Harvard. On the Langdellian approach, see generally Thomas C. Grey, *Langdell's Orthodoxy*, 45 U. PITT. L. REV. 1 (1983); Michael Hoeflich, *Law & Geometry: Legal Science from Liebnitz to Langdell*, 30 AM. J. LEGAL HIST. 95 (1986).

2. In 1989, the American Bar Association ("ABA") appointed a Task Force on Law Schools and the Profession to review the issues surrounding the adequacy of skills training at law schools. This Task Force issued its final report on August 9, 1992 at the ABA convention in San Francisco, California. See *Legal Education and Professional Development—An Educational Continuum*, 1992 ABA Sec. Leg. Educ. 233-325 [hereinafter "ABA Report"] (task force concluded that law schools must do more to provide law students with practical skills and that legal profession must recognize that education does not stop with law school graduation).

3. I recognize that such a statement is troubling coming from a law school dean. Yet, I have come to believe over the years that law school is only the beginning of legal education, not the end. Even if we are able to integrate a strong practical element into the three year law school curriculum, I do not believe that we can ever fully replace the apprenticeship learning experience of young lawyers in a law firm setting. Indeed, I have been fortunate enough to be able to experiment with continuing legal education in the law firm context at the firm of Bond, Schoeneck, & King in Syracuse, an experience I intend to document in a later article.

4. At my own school, Syracuse, we have initiated faculty-wide discussions on the further integration of practice training into the traditional curriculum. This has led to the creation of several new clinical programs.

5. On the apprenticeship model, see generally Paul M. Hamlin, Legal Education in Colonial New York 35-38 (DaCapo Press 1970) (1939) (development of three to five year apprenticeship for attorneys discussed); see also Catherine Fennelly, The County Lawyer in New England *1790-1840* (1968).

6. See Robert Stevens, Law School: Legal Education in America from the 1850's to the 1980's, 4 (1983) (history of law schools reflects clash between elitism and democracy); Paul D. Carrington, *The Revolutionary Idea of University Legal Education*, 31 Wm. & Mary L. Rev. 527, 533-73 (1990) (appointment of law professors at colleges throughout United States following William and Mary's trend-setting example detailed); Paul D. Carrington, *Teaching Law and Virtue at Transylvania University: The George Wythe Tradition in the Antebellum Years*, 41 Mercer L. Rev. 673 (1990) (success of Transylvania's legal education explored).

7. See Stevens, *supra* note 6, at 4 (first real success of university level law school at Harvard); see also Charles Warren, A History of the Harvard Law School and of Early Legal Conditions in America (DaCapo Press 1970) (1908) (detailed account of events surrounding founding of Harvard Law School in 1817).

8. See *infra* note 49 and accompanying text for a discussion of Transylvania University, which operated one of the first and best university-affiliated law schools in 19th century America.

9. See Hamlin, *supra* note 5, at 125 26 (New York's experience of apprenticeship competing with formal legal education discussed). In addition, a number of "law schools" developed out of the apprenticeship model, building upon the reputation of noted practitioners or lawyers who were not affiliated with a university. The best known of these was the Litchfield Law School founded by Trapping Reeve in Litchfield, Connecticut. See Marian C. McKenna, Tapping Reeve and the Litchfield Law School (1986) (Reeve's contributions to legal education described).

10. See Hamlin, *supra* note 5, at 95 (apprenticeship provided local connections through which practitioner could acquire clients and valuable experience). One must remember that law practice during this period was very much *local* practice and the best way to acquire clients was through local connections. Apprenticeship to a prominent attorney provided such connections.

11. Joseph Story taught at Harvard for much of his career. James Kent was a professor of law at Columbia. Simon Greenleaf was a colleague of Story's at Harvard. Benjamin Butler founded the Law school at N.Y.U. Daniel Mays was a professor in the Law Department of Transylvania, and David Dudley Field was both judge and a major figure in U.S. law reform in the mid-19th century. See *infra* notes 34-37 and accompanying text for a discussion of Butler's contribution to the literature on legal education. See *infra* notes 53-63 and accompanying text for a discussion of Mayes' writings. See *infra* note 48 and accompanying text for a discussion of Story's ideas concerning legal education. See *infra* notes 72-77 for a discussion of Field's ideas on legal education.

12. Phi Beta Kappa, the earliest of the American academic honor societies, was founded in 1776. It has been a tradition since its founding that each chapter have an annual lecture, usually at the time of the annual meeting and election of new members. In the antebellum period, the texts of these speeches were often published and many reflect the thinking of the period's most prominent lawyers. They have been virtually unused as a source by modern legal historians. See Richard H. Current, Phi Beta Kappa in American Life 66 (1990) (Phi Beta Kappa noted for its addresses by famous graduates).

13. See generally Robert Ferguson, Law & Letters in American Culture (1984), for background on the literary activities of antebellum lawyers in the U.S.

14. See Hamlin, *supra* note 5, at 1-6 (overview of legal education from 1664-1765); see also Stevens, *supra* note 6, at 3 (apprenticeship regarded standard for legal training); The Earliest Diary of John Adams 64-68, 77 (L. H. Butterfield, ed. 1966) (apprenticeship model discussed). On Adams, see generally Daniel R. Coquillette, *Justinian in Braintree: John Adams, Civilian Learning, and Legal Elitism*, 1758-1775, *in* 62 Law in Colonial Massachusetts, 1630-1800, 359-69 (1984).

15. See generally Stevens, *supra* note 6, at 3.

16. See Hamlin, *supra* note 5, at 95 (apprentices provided to serve "consequential personages").

17. See Hoeflich, *supra* note 1, at 95-99 (European roots of scientific paradigm in law outlined); Michael H. Hoeflich, *The Americanization of British Legal Education*, 8 J. Legal Hist. 244, 245 (1987) ("scientific" aspect of legal education most significant feature during period between 1790 and 1850); see also Michael H. Hoeflich, The Gladsome Light of Jurisprudence 7-9 (1988) [hereinafter "Gladsome Light"] (evolution of law as liberal science described). See *infra* note 54 and accompanying text for a discussion of law as a science.

18. The term "pettifogger" was common throughout England in the 16th, 17th, and 18th centuries and was imported to the United States. It referred to those lawyers who specialized in the narrow, technical aspects of the law, such as special pleading, and was generally a term of derision. See generally C.W. BROOKS, PETTYFOGGERS AND VIPERS OF THE COMMONWEALTH (1986).

19. Anonymous, *Study of the Law*, SOUTHERN LITERARY MESSENGER (1837), *reprinted in* GLADSOME LIGHT, *supra* note 17, at 201.

20. *Id.* at 207.

21. Joseph Story, *Course of Legal Study*, *in* THE N. AM. REV. (1817), *reprinted in* W.W. STORY, THE MISCELLANEOUS WRITINGS OF JOSEPH STORY 66, 91-92 (William W. Story ed., 1972) (1852).

22. DAVID HOFFMAN, A COURSE OF LEGAL STUDY (1817) (comprehensive legal education outlined). On Hoffman, see Michael H. Hoeflich, *Roman and Civil Law in American Legal Education Prior to 1930*, 1984 U. ILL. L. REV. 719, 723-28 (Hoffman's commitment to Roman and civil law models and his influence on American legal education explored); Thomas L. Shaffer, *David Hoffman's Law School Lectures, 1822-1833*, 32 J. LEGAL EDUC. 127, 127 (1981) (Hoffman's *A Course of Legal Study* described as "most perfect system for study of law"); see also Story, *supra* note 21, at 91 (importance of formal law school training in attorney's education highlighted).

23. See Shaffer, *supra* note 22, at 138 (Hoffman continued trying to espouse his methods despite surrender of his school and university positions). By using the term "legal seminary," Hoffman was attempting to describe a law academy based upon clerical training, i.e. an educational institution devoted solely to the study of law which would, in effect, "cloister" its students away from the distractions of everyday life. See DAVID HOFFMAN, A LECTURE INTRODUCTURY TO A COURSE OF LECTURES NOW DELIVERING IN THE UNIVERSITY OF MARYLAND 36 n.25 (1823).

24. There is in my personal collection a letter from David Hoffman to Joseph Story dated May 1836. In this letter Hoffman relates his then current pecuniary problems as a result of his lack success as a law teacher and his thought of publishing a new book which would help to popularize his pedagogical theories. Letter from David Hoffman to Joseph Story (May 1936) (on file with author).

25. DAVID HOFFMAN, A LECTURE INTRODUCTORY TO A COURSE OF LECTURES NOW DELIVERING IN THE UNIVERSITY OF MARYLAND (1823).

26. *Id.* at 16 (". . . I cannot but express, on this occasion my disapprobation of the mode recently recommended by an able lawyer of a neighboring state, who insists, (strange as it may appear) on students actually getting by rote the whole of Blackstone's Commentaries, and some other elementary works. I would urge you, on the contrary, to study the general and pervading principles of the science.").

27. *Id.* at 33-34 (". . . [the] true province of a lecturer [is]—to collate and select with diligence and discernment—to trace his doctrines from their first germ to their final growth, through all the variations of judicial opinions—to mark the accordance of decided cases with general principles, or the exceptions and deviations—to declare what has been said, not *merely* and *indiscriminately*, but with a view to general results, and with an examination of its consistency with legal analogy and reason . . .").

28. *Id.* at 39.

29. *Id.* at 66-68. There has been a strong tradition of cross-fertilization between Britain and the United States in law and legal education, particularly during the nineteenth century. See generally RICHARD A. COSGROVE, OUR LADY THE COMMON LAW: AN ANGLO-AMERICAN LEGAL COMMUNITY 1870-1930 (1987); Michael H. Hoeflich, *The Americanization of British Legal Education*, 8 J. LEGAL HIST. 244 (1987).

30. HOFFMAN, *supra* note 25, at 50.

31. *Id.* at 50.

32. *Id.* at 50-51.

33. See generally STEVENS, *supra* note 6, at 4-10.

34. See David S. Muzzey, *Benjamin F. Butler*, *in* II DICTIONARY OF AMERICAN BIOGRAPHY 356-57 (1929) (biographic information about Butler).

35. *Id.* at 356.

36. BENJAMIN F. BUTLER, PLAN FOR THE ORGANIZATION OF A LAW FACULTY AND FOR A SYSTEM OF INSTRUCTION IN LEGAL SCIENCE IN THE UNIVERSITY OF THE CITY OF NEW YORK (New York, N.Y., 1835), *reprinted in* THE LAW SCHOOL PAPERS OF BENJAMIN F. BUTLER: NEW YORK UNIVERSITY SCHOOL OF LAW IN THE 1830'S (Ronald L. Brown ed., 1987).

37. *Id.* at 115.

38. *Id.* at 120. Indeed, Butler took inspiration for his plan from the great Prussian law schools, through knowledge gained from discussions with Baron de Roenne and through reading an article by F.C. Von Savigny, the great Prussian legal scholar, see *id.* at 8 n.9. See generally Michael H. Hoeflich, *Savigny and his Anglo-American Disciples*, 37 AM. J. COMP. L. 17 (1989) (Savigny's influence on American law described).

39. BUTLER, *supra* note 36, at 122-26.

40. *Id.* at 120.

The great number of Law offices in this city, in which a varied and instructive business is carried on, will afford facilities for the acquisition of practical knowledge which may be turned to great account. Instead of withdrawing the Law Clerks from the labors of the office, the University should endeavor so to regulate its Law Department, as to give new value to those labors, and to render them auxiliary to a systematic course instruction in the principles of Legal Science.

Id.

41. *Id.* at 132.

As a further means of promoting emulation, and with the higher view of preparing the students for speaking and writing on legal subjects, it will be useful to exercise their minds by forensic debates in moot courts, and by requiring from them written opinions on questions of law, and readings and dissertations on statutes and other themes, as circumstances may admit.

Id.

Another who viewed moot court exercises as a necessary adjunct to theoretical lectures was William Merrick, a professor at the Columbian College Law School in Washington, D.C. In his *Introductory Address* of 1865 he told his students: "The moot court, which will be an accessory for your instruction, gentlemen, as it is in all well appointed law schools, will, for you, furnish sufficient opportunity for reading and examining particular cases and giving the semblance of real life to your otherwise tranquil investigations of truth." WILLIAM MERRICK, INTRODUCTORY ADDRESS TO THE STUDENTS OF THE COLUMBIAN COLLEGE LAW SCHOOL (Wash., D.C., 1865).

42. See STEVENS, *supra* note 6, at 80-81 (YMCA model was cooperative, workstudy model, with first semester spent in classroom; next in internship).

43. BUTLER, *supra* note 36, at 122-26.

44. *Id.* at 124.

45. *Id.* at 126. This would be in what Butler referred to as the "general or parallel course." *Id.*

46. *Id.* at 126-27.

47. *Id.*

48. See *id.* ("appropriate" elements of law school curriculum discussed).

49. See Charles Kerr, *Transylvania University's Law Department*, 31 AMERICANA 3 (1937); see also Carrington, *supra* note 6, at 557-59 (Transylvania's organization and approach detailed).

50. The Transylvania Board of Trustees resolved to establish a law professorship on January 8, 1799, having already established a law library on October 10, 1798. On October 10, 1805, Henry Clay was elected to fill the Chair in Law, replacing its first holder, George Nicholas. The first commencement of the "Law Department" was held on March 3, 1823. This information is drawn from transcripts of extracts from the Board's member books kindly supplied to me by Carolyn D. Palmgreen, Curator, Special Collections at Transylvania University.

51. On Mayes and Robertson, see *infra* notes 52 & 53. Mayes and Robertson are best known for their lectures.

52. GEORGE ROBERTSON, INTRODUCTORY LECTURE DELIVERED BEFORE THE LAW CLASS OF TRANSYLVANIA UNIVERSITY, November 12th, 1836 (Lexington, Ky., 1836).

53. DANIEL MAYES, AN ADDRESS TO THE STUDENTS OF LAW IN TRANSYLVANIA UNIVERSITY (Lexington, Ky. 1834), *reprinted in* GLADSOME LIGHT, *supra* note 17, at 145-64.

54. *Id.* at 145-47.

55. *Id.* at 147 (quoting Blackstone's *Introductory Lecture*).

56. *Id.* at 153.

57. One of the themes constantly sounded in the literature emanating from antebellum, university affiliated law schools is the importance placed in these schools on understanding the principles of the law, rather then simply learning the forms by rote. Thus, in this, Mayes was echoing the sentiments of many of his contemporaries, including Simon Greenleaf at Harvard. In his writings, in regard to his duties as Royall Professor at Harvard and in his plan for the establishment of a new law school at Bowdoin College, Greenleaf blended the theoretical elements of legal education with the practical. See generally Simon Greenleaf, Law as a Liberal Science (unpublished manuscript, on file with the Harvard Law School Library) and SIMON GREENLEAF, A DISCOURSE PRONOUNCED AT THE INAUGURATION OF THE AUTHOR AS ROYALL PROFESSOR OF LAW IN HARVARD UNIVERSITY (Cambridge, Mass. 1834), *reprinted in* GLADSOME LIGHT, *supra* note 17, at 134-44 (legal profession's influences on society discussed); see also J.R. TYSON, DISCOURSE ON THE INTEGRITY OF THE LEGAL CHARACTER 15 (Philadelphia, Pa., 1839) ("The law is not only a learned but a liberal profession; and the lawyer, of all men, should elevate and fortify his principles by various and enlarged studies . . .").

58. It is important to remember that during this period there were very few printed American case reports. See ERWIN SURRENCY, A HISTORY OF AMERICAN LAW PUBLISHING 37 (1990) (development of regular publishing system for legal decisions in the United States detailed); see also Benjamin Silliman, Address Before the Graduating Class of the Law School of Columbia College (New York, N.Y., 1867), at 10-11.

59. MAYES, *supra* note 53, at 154.

60. *Id.*

61. *Id.* at 158-59. In this call for professional law teachers, Mayes foreshadowed the Harvard Law School of Langdell and Ames.

62. STEVENS, *supra* note 6, at 51.

63. MAYES, *supra* note 53, at 159.

64. See *supra* note 57. Professor Fred Konefsky of the University of Buffalo is presently engaged in writing a biography of Greenleaf. The plan for a law school at Bowdoin College prepared by Greenleaf is contained in a manuscript now in the Greenleaf Papers at the Harvard Law School Library.

65. For a view of American law in the antebellum period and its sociological and literary context, the best account remains the classic work of Perry Miller. See generally PERRY MILLER, THE LIFE OF THE MIND IN AMERICA (1962).

66. JESSE HIGGINS, SAMPSON AGAINST THE PHILISTINES OR THE REFORMATION OF LAWSUITS (Philadelphia, Pa., B. Graves 1805).

67. See *id.* at iv (book's coverage prefaced).

68. See *id.* at 22-44 (only lawyers benefit from complex common law system). On the tradition of law as a "mysterious science," see DANIEL BOORSTIN, THE MYSTERIOUS SCIENCE OF LAW 68, 102 (1941) (complexities that had evolved in common law system discussed).

69. In this, of course, Higgins was an early proponent of the Jacksonian movement against the organized Bar and the "everyman his own lawyer" movement that generated a flood of books and pamphlets throughout the antebellum period.

70. Robert Rantoul, *Oration at Scituate, reprinted in* LUTHER HAMILTON, MEMOIRS, SPEECHES AND WRITINGS OF ROBERT RANTOUL, JR. (Boston, Ma., 1854).

71. *Id.*; see generally CHARLES COOK, THE AMERICAN CODIFICATION MOVEMENT, A STUDY OF ANTEBELLUM LEGAL REFORM (1981) and MILLER, *supra* note 65, at 220, for a useful discussion of the nineteenth century codification movement.

72. On Field, see COOK, *supra* note 71, at 189-97 (David Dudley Field's contributions to law discussed); see generally Philip J. Bergan, *David Dudley Field: A Lawyer's Life, in* THE FIELDS AND THE LAW 21-51 (1986).

73. See Cook, *supra* note 71, at 189-97.

74. DAVID D. FIELD, THE MAGNITUDE AND IMPORTANCE OF LEGAL SCIENCE, ADDRESS OF DAVID DUDLEY FIELD AT THE OPENING OF THE LAW SCHOOL OF THE UNIVERSITY OF CHICAGO (Chicago, Ill., 1859), reprinted as chapter 46 of this book.

75. *Id.* at 15-16. Interestingly, this passage derives directly from the writings of James Lorimer, a Scottish legal philosopher of the period. I acknowledge with thanks Prof. Alan Watson for this reference.

76. *Id.* at 16.

77. *Id.* at 18-19.

78. Theodore W. Dwight, *An Introductory Lecture, Delivered Before the Law Class of Columbia College New York on Monday, November 1, 1858, in* INAUGURAL LECTURES OF THEODORE W. DWIGHT AND OF GEORGE P. MARSH IN COLUMBIA COLLEGE (1859).

79. Reprinted as chapter 23 of this book. It is important to understand the meaning of "municipal" in this nineteenth century context. Dwight used the phrase as a synonym for domestic or national. *Cf.* JOHN NORTON POMEROY, MUNICIPAL LAW 10 (New York, D. Appleton and Co. 1864) (municipal law defined as law of particular state).

80. Dwight, *supra* note 78,at 38.

81. *Id.* at 52.

82. See *supra* note 1 and accompanying text for a discussion of Langdell's method. Some of Langdell's contemporaries at Harvard believed that his accomplishments were *less* than advertised. See generally JOEL PARKER, THE LAW SCHOOL OF HARVARD COLLEGE (New York, N.Y., 1871).

83. See STEVENS, *supra* note 6, at 35.

84. This realization is again coming to the attention of modern legal educators through the recently released report by the ABA Task Force. See *supra* note 2 and accompanying text for a discussion of the task force's findings.

85. Of course, some degree of alienation has been present for at least a century. See generally Jerold S. Auerbach, *Enmity and Amity, Law Teachers and Practitioners, 1900-1922, in* LAW IN AMERICAN HISTORY 551 (Donald Fleming & Bernard Bailyn eds., 1971).

86. But see ABA Report, *supra* note 2, at 233-36, 260-68 (practicing Bar's role in teaching lawyering skills and values discussed).

Chapter 62

The Legal Clinic

1917

John H. Wigmore

John Henry Wigmore (1863-1943) was a founder of the *Harvard Law Review* (see chapter 71) and was an influential evidence professor and dean of Northwestern from 1901 to 1929. This article first appeared in 23 *Case and Comment* 973 (1917).

And why not a legal clinic as well as a medical and surgical clinic? What does a clinic do? It combines two things, education and charity; and it combines them effectively, without loss to either. And it doubles the possibilities for both; *i.e.*, it does for education and for charity also an indispensable service that could not otherwise have been performed.

Medical education is now far ahead of legal education. Formerly the young medical student got his clinical experience by driving the doctor about to his patients, and joining him in his bedside inspection,—sometimes by holding his horse outside at the curbstone while the doctor went alone into the patient's house. Nowadays the medical student gets his clinical experience by attending a real case, brought into the amphitheater where a skilled specialist demonstrates to the student group the lessons of the case.

Formerly the law student got his clinical experience in the same way as the antique doctor. He sat at a table in the outer office; and when the client came in, the embryo lawyer said, "Mr. Counselor is engaged; please wait." Then, half an hour later, when the client emerged from the consulting room, the counselor handed a paper to the young law graduate with the order, "Take this over to the probate court and file it." Once in a while the eminent counselor, by way of varying the monotony, gave the young law graduate a small piece of silver, with the order, "Go over to Joe's place, and get me a packet of Cairo cigarettes, usual brand." Gradually, the young law graduate thus gathered a few useful clinical hints.

Nowadays,—but what are we saying? Nowadays things are still as they were formerly. The "formerly" of medical practice continues to be the way of law practice. The great achievement of medical education—the hospital clinic—is still practically unknown in legal education.

It is on the verge of arriving, however, and it is as sure to arrive soon, and on a large scale, as every great and inherently true thing is sure to come to pass.

It will come to pass as it did in medical education. The medical schools affiliated with the hospitals, and the professors became the demonstrators in the hospital clinics. So, too, the law schools will affiliate with the legal aid societies, and will turn them into legal clinics. The legal aid societies are here. It remains only to provide the method of affiliation.

Two methods thus far obtain, but both are imperfect. One is the method of allowing lawschool students to volunteer for a small part of their time in the legal aid work, while still undergraduates. The fault of this method is that the student in his first or second or third year is not mature enough to profit by what he does and sees.

The other method is to appoint a law graduate to a position on the legal aid staff, upon his graduation. The faults of this method are two. In the first place, there is no systematic supervision by a professor of practice; hence the educational benefit is relatively small and casual; and there is the same waste of duplicated and unguided effort as in a law office. In the second place, there is no stipend to enable the legal aid hospital to secure the services of all of the best graduates, for the salaries of the prosperous law offices compete for the graduates, and naturally most of the young men must accept these salaried places.

There is only one sound method, the method of the future, and it is this,—for each legal aid clinic there will be from ten to fifty positions (according to the size of the community), each having a stipend of the amount usually paid in local law offices. These positions will be filled by competitive appointments. The funds will be supplied either by private endowment of the society, or by university endowment, or by bar association contributions.

A professor of practice will be in charge of these young attorneys; and at his call will be a staff of specialists for special classes of litigation. The professor of practice will so conduct the work as to give it the maximum educational value.

Moreover, as the four-year law course comes gradually into vogue (Northwestern University has already prescribed it; California, Yale, and others, are due to follow; Manila prescribed it two years ago), this clinical service will be required as a part of the fourth year's work for a degree. The young man thus equipped will be ready for setting up his own law office on graduation, just as the young medical graduate now does. For in the six months of supervised clinical experience he will have received all of the benefit that now comes from a year or two in the ordinary office. And he will have received much more, too; for he will have come into direct daily contact with the client,—a vital benefit which he seldom or never gets in the usual law office.

A dream, do you say? Not at all. It is precisely the plan which has already been devised and approved by the Chicago Bar Association, nearly two years ago, and now awaits only the raising of the necessary funds. It is precisely the plan approved by the New York Bar Association's Committee on Legal Education. The chairman of that committee, W. V. Rowe. Esq., has eloquently set forth the plan in the "Illinois Law Review" for April, 1917; and will urge it zealously throughout the country. It is feasible in every large city, and it is feasible in every university town where there is a law school. If the town is too small to supply either a medical or a legal hospital with sufficient variety of cases, then (as in the case of medical schools) this part of the law-school work can be carried on in the nearest metropolis.

The objection, by the way, that the range of cases in legal aid work is not sufficiently varied, has sometimes been raised by members of the bar, even in large cities. But a full acquaintance with the work of an active legal aid society would dispel the objection. The variety of cases is certainly far greater than in any single law office. Do you know that the largest law office in the United States is the Legal Aid Society of New York with nearly 40,000 new cases annually? Do you know that the next largest law office is the Legal Aid Society of Chicago, with 12,000 new cases annually? The number used to reach 16,000, but lack of funds obliged us to close the doors at noon so as to reduce mechanically the number of cases to be handled. Here is a list of the kinds of cases arising in one year's work: Wage claims; miscellaneous claims for collection; support matters; claims for collection of alimony; chattel mortgages; wage assignments; complaints growing out of domestic relations; cases in which clients were advised as to their legal rights; matters between attorney and client; matters between landlord and tenant; cases of advice and help on claims; cases of recovery of personal property; real estate matters; contract matters; sundry matters; insurance matters; probate, wills, estate, etc.; complaints against employment agencies; cases of insanity; cases involving custody of children; complaints against pawn shops; foreign matters; cases of crime against women and children; bastardy and rape; miscellaneous criminal matters; miscellaneous matters.

The litigation arising out of these cases ran into every court in the county, and involved the use of practically every variety of legal document. In more than one case, the society's attorneys helped to make law both in the supreme court and in the legislature's sessions.

The following selection of cases, made at random from recent annals of the society's work, will illustrate for the skeptical the value of the legal clinic as a finishing feature in the training of a responsible lawyer:

File No. 2424.12. Mr. H. was sued by the X Business College for "family expenses and necessaries" to the sum of $23.75, being a balance alleged to be due for schooling furnished Mr. H.'s daughter, Ida, a minor. The facts were that a solicitor of the business college had called on Ida and had represented that a course in shorthand would cost $50; that most students finished in six months; and that as much time could be taken by the student as was necessary to finish, without extra charge. Ida's brother signed an enrolment slip for a "six months' shorthand course," promising to pay therefor $50. Mr H. was not present during the conversation, and did not know about the arrangement until two weeks after Ida had started the course. Mr. H. was a poor man, making about $15 per week. He could not afford to send Ida to business college, but permitted her to attend because her brother was paying for it. Ida failed in some of her tests, so the business college informed her, and she was obliged to go two months more, for which the charge was $20 extra, plus $3.75 for stationery. During the seventh and eighth months Ida worked in the business college office, writing letters and mailing bills. Many of these bills were for extra tuition in cases similar to hers. Many complaints were registered by parents who refused to pay these bills. It appeared to us that the college was working a scheme to extort money from parents, and we opposed it. The court held that the schooling was furnished under an express contract with Ida's brother for a fixed amount, which had been paid; that the father could in no event be held for necessaries for her, had had nothing to do with the matter, and, furthermore, his income and station in life negative the theory that a business college education was, as to his daughter, a necessity. The business college then paid Mr. H. $10 for witness fees and mileage taxed as costs, and gave to Ida her diploma, which had been withheld.

File No. 2406.14. Harold C. had borrowed in various sums from a loan company a total amount of $90. In that same year he had repaid on the claim $82.50. The loan company from which he had borrowed then went out of business and sold out to another company. This latter company in turn sold out to a third company, who this year took up the claim against Harold C., doubtless thinking that he had destroyed his receipts for the money paid. The loan company claimed that $105 was still due, and upon refusal of Harold C. to pay they sued him for this amount. He then came to us. We found that with the balance due on the original loan and the interest thereon, the sum due was $18.65. When the attorney for the loan company learned that we would contest the suit, he agreed to have the case dismissed, and, upon payment of $21.65 by our client, the matter was settled and we recovered his papers for him.

File No. A9764.1. Fred C. came to the office with a vague statement about some money—the amount not known—that was due him from a Eastern railroad for which he had worked as a switchman in the year 1905. He claimed to have quit his work with the railroad before the regular pay day, and gone to Kentucky. From there he had written for the amount due him, but had been informed that he would have to present himself personally to the paymaster in New York before the money would be paid. As he was unable to go to New York, Fred C. let the matter drop for the time being. Three years later he again wrote for his money, and again received a letter stating that he must apply for it personally. At the time he came to us he had this letter, which bore the date of March 2, 1908. He had been in the Army from the time he received that leter up to a short time before he came to us, and had never gone back to New York. We took the matter up with the railroad, an investigation was made, and the sum of $23.60 was found to be due our client. This amount was forwarded to us immediately, and almost nine years from the date he had earned the money the same was turned over by us to Fred C.

File No. 190.34. Man, having wife and two children, aged six and eight years, was indicted for embezzlement. He was suffering from tuberculosis, and when he was arrested, his wife, also suffering with tuberculosis, was sent to a sanitarium, and the two children were sent to the Home for the Friendless. Upon close inquiry we found that the wife had been very ill, that the man had become discouraged and had begun to drink, which he had done twice before in his life, and, being in a position where he handled funds, he could easily take same without detection. The temptation under the circumstances was too great, and when he was arrested he had no idea how much money he had taken. It appeared that he had taken considerable, but the circumstances under which he had committed the offense and his family's condition were such that we could see no good to be gained if he were sent to the penitentiary. It was the first time that he had been arrested, and he fully realized what he had done. Arrangements were made with the man who had secured the position for him and gone on his bond to give him work and to have the loss repaid, and we therefore appealed to the court, who gave him a very light sentence. He is now repaying the debt, and has his family with him again.

File No. 92.25. She was a little dark-eyed German lady, and so excited when she came into the office that all she could say was, "My boy Erick, you must get him for me." Her tale was a most pathetic one. Her husband had deserted her and left her penniless and almost starving in Battle Creek, Michigan. In this hour of her extremity she had placed the little boy with people whom she had supposed to be friends, and had come on to Chicago, where she could get work. Every few months she had visited her boy and each time had been treated more and more coldly. Finally, having made a place for herself here and feeling that she could now obtain the object of all her struggles, she sent for her boy. She was answered with a legal notice, telling her that her son had become a ward of the state of Michigan and had been given out for adoption to the people with whom she had left him.

It was at this time that she turned to the office of the Legal Aid Society. After a long and bitter struggle, lasting about two years, a habeas corpus proceeding was finally terminated successfully and the boy was restored to his mother.

File No. 8284.1. Our client in this case was employed by a building contractor, who was utterly irresponsible financially, and did carpenter work upon two new flat buildings, the owners of which were unacquainted with the mechanic's lien law and took no precautions to protect themselves against liens. We instituted suit against both owners in accordance with the statute and obtained a judgment for $28 against one and $12.50 against the other, both of which were paid in full, with costs. By this means we not only obtained the wages that our client was justly entitled to, but also taught the owners a valuable though costly lesson.

File No. 218.29. The defendant in this case was arrested on a warrant charging him with being the father of the illegitimate child of our client, and, upon his being found guilty, was committed to the Bridewell for six months in default of furnishing satisfactory security for the payment of money for the support of the child, as required by the statute relating to bastardy. Upon the expiration of his sentence we instituted suit upon the order for the payment of money, which was entered in the quasi criminal proceedings, and after judgment, followed by garnishment proceedings, we succeeded at last in demonstrating to the man that he could legally be compelled to support the child, and he has for the last twenty months been paying to our client through this office regularly the sum of $1 per week.

Chapter 63

Is Apprenticeship in a Law Office Desirable While Pursuing a Course of Study in a Law School?

1909

This collection of commentaries first appeared in 1 *American Law School Review* 83 (1909) Henry Rogers (Oct. 10, 1853-Aug. 16, 1926) taught at Michigan and Yale, and was President of Northwestern from 1890 to 1900. He was professor and dean at Yale, leaving to join the Second Circuit by 1913. W. S. Pattee (Sept. 19, 1846-1911) taught equity and contracts at Minnesota, where he was dean. William Borland (Oct. 14, 1867-Feb. 21, 1919) taught probate and wills and was dean at Kansas City. Chester Cicero Cole (June 4, 1828-Oct. 4, 1913) was dean of Iowa, where he taught for forty-seven years. H. H. Ingersoll (Jan. 20, 1844-Mar. 17, 1915) taught corporations and procedure and was dean at Tennessee. Bernard Steiner (Aug. 13, 1867-Jan. 12, 1926) taught constitutional law and was dean at Baltimore. Clarence Ashley (July 4, 1851-Jan. 26, 1931) taught contracts and was dean at New York University. William P. Rogers (Mar. 3, 1857-Oct. 4, 1921) was a contracts professor and dean at both Indiana and Cincinnati. W. O. Harris (Feb. 5, 1847-1911) was dean at Louisville. George E. Gardner was a professor at Boston University Law School, R. M. Bashford taught at the University of Wisconsin College of Law, and Edward R. Taylor was dean of the Hastings College of Law, University of California.

All students entering upon a course of legal instruction, with the intention of practicing law, are confronted by many perplexing problems. Prominent among the questions which first arise for consideration is the one pertaining to study and work in a law office. The editor of the American Law School Review, therefore, with a view to publication, submitted the question, "Is apprenticeship in a law office desirable while pursuing a course of study in a law school?" to a number of well-known legal educators, whose many years' experience in law school work has afforded them an excellent opportunity for observation along this line. We take pleasure in publishing the answers received, as we are sure they will prove of especial interest and value to our readers.

From Henry Wade Rogers, Professor Yale University Law School

"Is apprenticeship in a law office desirable while pursuing a course of study in a law school?" My answer to that question is decidedly, No. In a law school of the first class the work is planned to occupy the student's full time, and it ought to be so planned. If the student in such a school does his work as he should, he has no time to give to the work of the office. And it may be added that if he does the work of the office properly he has no time to do the law school work. It is certainly important that every law student should spend some time in a good law office. That is the best place for him to learn matters of practice, as the law school is decidedly the best place for him to learn the substantive law. My advice to the student is to spend three years in the best law school he can afford to attend, and then go after graduation for six months or a year into the best office into which he can be admitted in the state in which he proposes to practice. A poor office, like a poor law school, is a place to be avoided. The student will form bad habits in either, and be apt to start in his professional career with very limited acquirements and very poor ideals, if he be fortunate enough to have ideals at all.

From W. S. Pattee, Dean of the University of Minnesota College of Law

In ancient days an "apprenticeship" in a law office, like an "apprenticeship" in a carpenter's shop or elsewhere, signified the gaining of knowledge in the particular trade or profession under the instruction of a master. Should a student in a law school supplement his daily school work by an additional amount of instruction in a law office, it would of course be beneficial to him. Should he be under the instruction of a lawyer sufficiently interested to properly instruct him in pleading, conveyancing, and in the art of practice generally, I should say that the student might profitably spend his time in such an office while pursuing his studies in a law school. But, on the other hand, if a student simply spends his time in an office, gaining only such instruction as he may pick up, unaided by any competent and interested instructor, serving papers occasionally, and occupying the office when the proprietor is away, I should say that he better devote all of his time exclusively to his daily work in the school. Apprenticeship does not signify now what it once did. The practicing lawyer does not now devote much of his time to the instruction of his pupil. The student in an office picks up such instruction as he can, unaided, as a general rule, by the attorney in whose office he happens to be. This fact has led the law schools to provide extensive courses in practice by means of moot courts. It is possible to give students instruction in practice and this is now being done successfully during the senior year in our leading schools.

From Wm. P. Borland, Dean of the Kansas City Law School

I have always regarded apprenticeship in a law office not only desirable, while pursuing a course of study in a law school, but I regard it as the ideal way for a student to study that profession. It is just as important to the law student to be connected with a law office, and to be thrown into contact with the actual practice of the law and the machinery of the courts, as it is for a medical student to have hospital work while pursuing his medical course, or for an engineering student to attend surveying camps. The average person learns faster by example than by precept. Office experience alone is incomplete because the student has not the necessary theoretical knowledge or breadth of view to understand what he is doing and why he is doing it that way. It tends to make narrow and technical lawyers. On the other hand, I believe that all a law school can do for a student is to give him the foundation principles which he must otherwise learn to apply, either in somebody else's law office, where he sees experienced men at work with the same tools, or in his own law office, where he must experiment with much loss of time and labor.

From Chester C. Cole, Dean of the Iowa College of Law

From a somewhat extended observation from each end of the line, as proprietor of a law office and as dean of a law school, I am of the opinion that such an apprenticeship is not desirable at all during the first year, is barely tolerable during the second year, and more or less desirable for the third year of the law course of study. An apprenticeship in the office of a practicing lawyer, full of business, involves necessarily frequent interruptions in the reading or study by the student. These interruptions prevent the full appreciation of the text he may be reading, as he would appreciate it if permitted to give a continuous reading until the close of the particular subject or branch of it. These interruptions necessarily interfere with the development of mental discipline and dwarf the grasping of the subject before him. These objections are not at all compensated for by the more or less semi-occasional suggestions coming from his principal, whose time and thought are occupied in his business ordinarily quite too much to afford an opportunity or leisure requisite for any considerate instruction. The almost universal experience of students in a busy lawyer's office is that he must absorb from the duties and incidents occurring therein any knowledge which is to be acquired by him therefrom. He gets none, practically or generally, from his principal. The student's capacity for absorption is by no means comprehensive and grasping until he has acquired some knowledge of the law, fully as much as could be acquired in the first year's study, and probably quite as much as could be acquired in the two years. At all events, his extended opportunity for gaining some knowledge of the law would better fit and prepare him for absorption of knowledge from the current observations and experiences in a law office. After this measure of the knowledge of substantive law shall have been acquired, then an apprenticeship in an office which would afford him more or less of opportunity for the application of such knowledge would be of advantage. Further than this, the course of study in the law school will have afforded him such mental discipline as that the interruptions, coming from the current duties ordinarily devolving upon an attorney's clerk, would not interfere, but would, in fact, add to it, by its demands for the application of the knowledge acquired to the current items of practice and pleading involved in his regular duties as such clerk.

From H. H. Ingersoll, Dean of the Law Department of the University of Tennessee

Waiving the real meaning of "apprenticeship," and discussing generally the topic of experience in a law office, I think it very desirable for a student of law. The progress from the known to the unknown is greatly facilitated by familiarity with the atmosphere and surroundings of the journey: and the most formidable obstacles to progress by the student of law is his want of understanding and appreciation of the exact meaning and application of legal terms. From my office experience with young stenographers, as well as my class room experience with students of law, I am persuaded that more mistakes are made, more worry caused, and more time lost from want of familiarity with our technical vocabulary than from any other cause. This want can best be supplied in the lawyer's office, and occasionally in the court room, by listening to the legal vernacular, reading law papers and periodicals, copying process, pleadings, and documents, and thus obtaining some familiarity with the lawyers' ways. He will thus be enabled to better understand and comprehend, not only what he reads in the text-books, but also what he hears in the class room, and his progress in learning the law will be much more rapid. This part of legal training is usually deferred until the close of the course of study, and then the alumnus picks up this experience as best he can. This is putting syntax before spelling. A year in a lawyer's office before beginning the course, or three hours daily during the course, would give the legal alumnus better preparation by fully one-third for the active duties of his calling.

From Bernard C. Steiner, Dean of the Baltimore Law School

When the law school curriculum has advanced to the point now reached by the courses of study in medical schools, men will no more apprentice themselves in law offices than they do in the offices of physicians. The medical education of the country has passed through three stages. At first a man entered a physician's office, then he took lectures from a medical school and had a physician as a preceptor, and lastly he received all instruction, chemical and laboratory work, as well as lectures, from the medical school. When law schools have properly developed that side of their work, which corresponds to laboratory work and clinics, it will be so much more systematic and comprehensive than work in a lawyer's office that it will entirely supersede it.

From Clarence D. Ashley, Dean of the New York University School of Law

Upon beginning his law studies the first question which confronts the student is whether to study in a law school, a law office, or to combine both. In his perplexity he naturally turns to some lawyer in practice, and generally follows the advice received, although the chances are that the adviser may not have given attention to questions of legal education for years. While most lawyers to-day advise a course in the law school, many at the same time recommend attendance at the office. In my opinion, no worse advice could be given. Why is it that the profession is so wedded to this idea, when it must be apparent to any thoughtful observer that the modern law office is no place for a student until he has completed his course of study? During his first year he learns practically nothing there, and, while later he may pick up some points of practice, it is at the expense of priceless time, which should be devoted to laying the foundations of his legal career. Just in proportion to his acquisition of points of practice he becomes valuable to the office, begins to come late to his lectures, and then to absent himself. His interest inevitably becomes engrossed in the office work to the neglect of his studies. This often leads to failure and disappointment in examinations, and always to poor equipment for his life work. Can it be said that this pays? If he does not do his systematic study while in the law school, is there much chance that he will do it afterwards? With the hard work of actual practice, is one likely to do much general study? Every year lawyers of standing and ability seek opportunity to teach some subject in a law school, and I am often told that the applicant desires to devote careful study to that topic, and needs the spur of necessity to compel him to do so. The conservatism of our profession probably explains the position taken by so many lawyers, and the belief in the efficiency of office work is probably due to the fact that law schools are of comparatively recent date, and that for years the law office was the sole place to obtain a legal education. In those days, however, the modern rush and push had not begun. The would-be student of law entered the office of some able leader of the bar. The lawyer considered that he owed a duty to the student, personally supervised his studies, examined him upon his work, and drew upon his own rich experience to aid and instruct. Such young men received for years the benefit of private tuition from great teachers—from men so imbued with a love of their profession, its worth and dignity, that the fortunate student found a liberal legal education in such intercourse. With the progress of events all this is changed. Vast accumulations of wealth have thrown heavy burdens upon the lawyer, every moment is precious, and, instead of the old-fashioned supervision of law students, he hardly knows they are in his office, and they become little better than errand boys. When the school work is well finished the student can take his plunge into the active life of the profession with some comprehension of what it all means, and the least service which he performs will serve to educate him, because he understands what it portends. It seems to me that the profession at large, and the law schools themselves, should discourage in every possible way office work in advance of or during the course of legal study.

From W. P. Rogers, Dean of the Law Department of the University of Cincinnati

I should say that the most desirable thing for the student pursuing a course of study in a law school is to give his whole time to the law school work. He should by no means consider his daily task completed when he has read the lesson assigned, but should follow out to the utmost limit of his time the various topics which each day's work brings before him. These will lead him into unlimited fields of research, and if he has access to a good library he will soon learn that, instead of having time for work outside of the law school, he has not sufficient time to follow up, and settle to his own satisfaction, the numerous questions of interest which arise. There is no other period in the lawyer's life when he can give so much time to such work in general as when a student in the law school, and he should be encouraged, at this period, to give himself wholly to it. Later, in his practice, he will delve deeper into special subjects in which he finds the particular case he has in hand, but the opportunity for thus getting a glimpse at the whole field of the law as a system comes only to the diligent student, willing for the time to keep all things else out of view. The apprenticeship in the law office should come later, after he has secured from the law school all it can give him. There will be for him, between the end of his law school course and the period when the rush of clients comes, plenty time for his term of service in a lawyer's office.

From W. O. Harris, Dean of the Law Department of the University of Louisville

I think apprenticeship in a law office is not desirable while pursuing a course of study in a law school. To my best judgment, my experience as a teacher leads me to this conclusion. In addition to this, my opinion as a priori proposition is the same. The practice of any science is more attractive and interesting than the elementary principles, and the pupil who commences with the practice is attracted by it, and never adequately learns the elements. To start a law student in the law office is to recur in part, at least, to the mode of instruction in use before there were any law schools. A pupil in music is not allowed to sing or play tunes until he has learned the scales. The tune is more attractive, and is reserved as a reward for him after he has gone through the drudgery of the scales. I think the same principle applies to learning law.

From George E. Gardner, Professor Boston University Law School

In my judgment apprenticeship in a law office while a student is pursuing his studies in the law school is strongly to be deprecated. The three years in the school should be spent in strenuous and unremitting toil over the books. The period is for study and study only. The student ought, with Lord Eldon, to live like a hermit and work like a horse. Even with the most diligent application, this time is all too meagre for the obtaining of that grip upon and mastery over the controlling principles of the law which is the chief qualification of the lawyer, and in the acquisition of which the law school is the student's most efficient aid. If the student is in an office where there is little or nothing for him to do, he had much better be elsewhere. If his apprenticeship is a genuine one, it can only result in a certain mental distraction which must affect unfavorably his work in the school. In a word, the law student should be a student and nothing else. The practice can take care of itself later. If, however, a man has no heart for anything more than a minimum of study, and aims only to pass a bar examination and enter politics or practice law on his wits, the office is a good enough place for him. Otherwise, emphatically not.

From R. M. Bashford, Professor University of Wisconsin College of Law

I think that it is an advantage for a student to enter a law office while pursuing his studies at the law school, in order that he may have access to the library and also to acquire some familiarity with the conduct of business. He cannot, however, properly devote time to office work, which should be given to his studies. The student should first apply himself diligently to the work of the school, and his employment in the office should be considered of secondary importance.

From Edward R. Taylor, Dean of the Hastings College of Law (University of California)

In answer to the question, "Is apprenticeship in a law office desirable while pursuing a course of study in a law school?" I beg to say that in my opinion such an apprenticeship is not desirable, but, on the contrary, is very detrimental. The student in the law school, just the same as when pursuing his academic career, should have nothing on hand during his work in the law school except that work, and to this he should give his undivided time. If he be in an office his duties in the office will be inevitably looked upon by him as primary, and his duties in the law school as secondary. I have never known an instance where this did not occur, nor where absences from class were not frequently excused on account of law office work. It is important that the student, during his whole student life, should breathe the atmosphere of that life. Unless he do so, it is impossible, in the nature of things, for him to derive the benefit from such a life as is his due. A law office life gives to a student, in the absence of a very considerable knowledge of the law, a false sense of the value of things done in the office. He sees so many things, and is himself a part of so many things, done there in matter of mere detail and routine, as to lead him to fancy that the practice of the law (and indeed the law itself) is hardly more than such detail and routine. This will tend to narrow his legal horizon, and to make him little better than a routinist. The ideal law student life, as it seems to me, is constant and assiduous attention to all the duties of the law school, with no outside distractions of any kind; and on the conclusion of that work, and only then, a year or two in an office of general practice.

IV. Students

Chapter 64

Legal Education as Training for Hierarchy

1982

Duncan Kennedy

Duncan Kennedy is professor at Harvard. This article has appeared in 32 *Journal of Legal Education* 591 (1982).

Law schools are intensely political places despite the fact that the modern law school seems intellectually unpretentious, barren of theoretical ambition or practical vision of what social life might be. The trade-school mentality, the endless attention to trees at the expense of forests, the alternating grimness and chumminess of focus on the limited task at hand, all these are only a part of what is going on. The other part is ideological training for willing service in the hierarchies of the corporate welfare state.

To say that law school is ideological is to say that what teachers teach along with basic skills is wrong, is nonsense about what law is and how it works; that the message about the nature of legal competence, and its distribution among students, is wrong, is nonsense; that the ideas about the possibilities of life as a lawyer that students pick up from legal education are wrong, are nonsense. But all this is nonsense with a tilt; it is biased and motivated rather than random error. What it says is that it is natural, efficient, and fair for law firms, the bar as a whole, and the society the bar services to be organized in their actual patterns of hierarchy and domination.

Because students believe what they are told, explicitly and implicitly, about the world they are entering, they behave in ways that fulfill the prophecies the system makes about them and about that world. This is the linkback that completes the system: students do more than accept the way things are, and ideology does more than damp opposition. Students act affirmatively within the channels cut for them, cutting them deeper, giving the whole a patina of consent, and weaving complicity into everyone's life story.

In this chapter, I take up in turn the initial first-year experience, the ideological content of the law school curriculum, and the noncurricular practices of law schools that train students to accept and participate in the hierarchical structure of life in the law.

The First-Year Experience

A surprisingly large number of law students go to law school with the notion that being a lawyer means something more, something more socially constructive than just doing a highly respectable job. There is the idea of playing the role an earlier generation associated with Brandeis: the role of service through law, carried out with superb technical competence and also with a deep belief that in its essence law is a progressive force, however much it may be distorted by the actual arrangements of capitalism. There is a contrasting, more radical notion that law is a tool of established interests, that it is in essence superstructural, but that it is a tool that a coldly effective professional can sometimes turn against the dominators. Whereas in the first notion the student aspires to help the oppressed and transform society by bringing out the latent content of a valid ideal, in the second the student sees herself as part technician, part judo expert, able to turn the tables exactly because she never lets herself be mystified by the rhetoric that is so important to other students.

Then there are the conflicting motives, which are equally real for both types. People think of law school as extremely competitive, as a place where a tough, hardworking, smart style is cultivated and rewarded. Students enter law school with a sense that they will develop that side of themselves. Even if they disapprove, on principle, of that side of themselves, they have had other experiences in which it turned out that they wanted and liked aspects of themselves that on principle they disapproved of. How is one to know that one is not "really" looking to develop oneself in this way as much as one is motivated by the vocation of social transformation?

There is also the issue of social mobility. Almost everyone whose parents were not members of the professional/technical intelligentsia seems to feel that going to law school is an advance in terms of the family history. This is true even for children of high-level business managers, so long as their parents' positions were due to hard work and struggle rather than to birth into the upper echelons. It is rare for parents to actively *disapprove* of their children going to law school, whatever their origins. So taking this particular step has a social meaning, however much the student may reject it, and that social meaning is success. The success is bittersweet if one feels one should have gotten into a better school, but both the bitter and the sweet suggest that one's motives are impure.

The initial classroom experience sustains rather than dissipates ambivalence. The teachers are overwhelmingly white, male, and deadeningly straight and middle class in manner. The classroom is hierarchical with a vengeance, the teacher receiving a degree of deference and arousing fears that remind one of high school rather than college. The sense of autonomy one has in a lecture, with the rule that you must let teacher drone on without interruption balanced by the rule that teacher can't *do* anything to you, is gone. In its place is a demand for a pseudoparticipation in which one struggles desperately, in front of a large audience, to read a mind determined to elude you. It is almost never anything as bad as *The Paper Chase* or *One-L*, but it is still humiliating to be frightened and unsure of oneself, especially when what renders one unsure is a classroom arrangement that suggests at once the patriarchal family and a Kafkalike riddle state. The law school classroom at the beginning of the first year is culturally reactionary.

But it is also engaging. You are learning a new language, and it *is* possible to learn it. Pseudoparticipation makes one intensely aware of how everyone else is doing, providing endless bases for comparison. Information is coming in on all sides, and things that you knew were out there but you didn't understand are becoming intelligible. The teacher offers subtle encouragements as well as not-so-subtle reasons for alarm. Performance is on one's mind, adrenaline flows, success has a nightly and daily meaning in terms of the material assigned. After all, this is the next segment: one is moving from the vaguely sentimental world of college, or the frustrating world of office work or housework, into something that promises a dose of "reality," even if it's cold and scary reality.

It quickly emerges that neither the students nor the faculty are as homogeneous as they at first appeared. Some teachers are more authoritarian than others; some students other than oneself reacted with horror to the infantilization of the first days or weeks. There even seems to be a connection between classroom manner and substantive views, with the "softer" teachers also seeming to be more "liberal," perhaps more sympathetic to plaintiffs in the torts course, more willing to hear what are called policy arguments, as well as less intimidating in class discussion. But there is a disturbing aspect to this process of differentiation: in most law schools, it turns out that the tougher, less policy-oriented teachers are the more popular. The softies seem to get less matter across, they let things wander, and one begins to worry that their niceness is at the expense of a metaphysical quality called rigor, thought to be essential to success on bar exams and in the grown-up world of practice. Ambivalence reasserts itself. As between the conservatives and the mushy centrists, enemies who scare you but subtly reassure you may seem more attractive than allies no better anchored than yourself.

There is an intellectual experience that somewhat corresponds to the emotional one: the gradual revelation that there is no purchase for left or even for committed liberal thinking on any part of the smooth surface of legal education. The issue in the classroom is not left against right, but pedagogical conservatism against moderate, disintegrated liberalism. No teacher is likely to present a model of either left pedagogy or vital left theoretical enterprise, though some *are* likely to be vaguely sympathetic to progressive causes, and some may even be moonlighting as left lawyers. Students are struggling for cognitive mastery and against the sneaking depression of the preprofessional. The actual intellectual content of the law seems to consist of learning rules—what they are and why they have to be the way they are—while rooting for the occasional judge who seems willing to make them marginally more humane. The basic experience is of double surrender to a passivizing classroom experience and to a passive attitude toward the content of the legal system.

The first step toward this sense of the irrelevance of liberal or left thinking is the opposition in the first-year curriculum between the technical, boring, difficult, obscure legal case and the occasional case with outrageous facts and a piggish judicial opinion endorsing or tolerating the outrage. The first kind of case—call it a cold case—is a challenge to interest, understanding, even to wakefulness. It can be on any subject, so long as it is of no political or moral or emotional significance. Just to understand what happened and what's being said about it, you have to learn a lot of new terms, a little potted legal history, and lots of rules, none of which is carefully explained by the casebook or the teacher. It is difficult to figure out why the case is there in the first place, difficult to figure out whether you have grasped it, and difficult to anticipate what the teacher will ask and what one should respond.

The other kind of case—call it a hot case—usually involves a sympathetic plaintiff—say, an Appalachian farm family—and an unsympathetic defendant—say, a coal company. On first reading, it appears that the coal company has screwed the farm family by renting their land for strip mining, with a promise to restore it to its original condition once the coal has been extracted, and then reneging on the promise. And the case should include a judicial opinion that does something like award a meaningless couple of hundred dollars to the farm family rather than making the coal company perform the restoration work. The point of the class discussion will be that your initial reaction of outrage is naive, nonlegal, irrelevant to what you're supposed to be learning, and maybe substantively wrong into the bargain. There are "good reasons" for the awful result, when you take a legal and logical "large" view, as opposed to the knee-jerk passionate view; and if you can't muster those reasons, maybe you aren't cut out to be a lawyer.

Most students can't fight this combination of a cold case and a hot case. The cold case is boring, but you have to do it if you want to become a lawyer. The hot case cries out for response, seems to say that if you can't respond you've already sold out; but the system tells you to put away childish things, and your reaction to the hot case is one of them. Without any intellectual resources, in the way of knowledge of the legal system and of the character of legal reasoning, it will appear that emoting will only isolate and incapacitate you. The choice is to develop some calluses and hit the books, or admit failure almost before you've begun.

The Ideological Content of Legal Education

One can distinguish in a rough way between two aspects of legal education as a reproducer of hierarchy. A lot of what happens is the inculcation through a formal curriculum and the classroom experience of a set of political attitudes toward the economy and society in general, toward law, and toward the possibilities of life in the profession. These have a general ideological significance, and they have an impact on the lives even of law students who never practice law. Then there is a complicated set of institutional practices that orient students to willing participation in the specialized hierarchical roles of lawyers. Students begin to absorb the more general ideological message before they have much in the way of a conception of life after law school, so I will describe this formal aspect of the educational process before describing the ways in which the institutional practice of law schools bear on those realities.

Law students sometimes speak as though they learned *nothing* in school. In fact, they learn skills to do a list of simple but important things. They learn to retain large numbers of rules organized into categorical systems (requisites for a contract, rules about breach, etc.). They learn "issue spotting," which means identifying the ways in which the rules are ambiguous, in conflict, or have a gap when applied to particular fact situations. They learn elementary case analysis, meaning the art of generating broad holdings for cases so they will apply beyond their intuitive scope, and narrow holdings for cases so that they won't apply where it at first seemed they would. And they learn a list of balanced, formulaic, pro/con policy arguments that lawyers use in arguing that a given rule should apply to a situation despite a gap, conflict, or ambiguity, or that a given case should be extended or narrowed. These are arguments like "the need for certainty" and "the need for flexibility," "the need to promote competition" and the "need to encourage production by letting producers keep the rewards of their labor."

One should neither exalt these skills nor denigrate them. By comparison with the first-year students' tendency to flip-flop between formalism and mere equitable intuition, they represent a real intellectual advance. Lawyers actually do use them in practice; and when properly, consciously mastered, they have "critical" bite. They are a help in thinking about politics, public policy, ethical discourse in general, because they show the indeterminacy and manipulability of ideas and institutions that are central to liberalism.

On the other hand, law schools teach these rather rudimentary, essentially instrumental skills in a way that almost completely mystifies them for almost all law students. The mystification has three parts. First, the schools teach skills through class discussions of cases in which it is asserted that law emerges from a rigorous analytical procedure called legal reasoning, which is unintelligible to the layperson but somehow both explains and validates the great majority of the rules in force in our system. At the same time, the class context and the materials present every legal issue as distinct from every other—as a tub on its own bottom, so to speak—with no hope or even any reason to hope that from law study one might derive an integrating vision of what law is, how it works, or how it might be changed (other than in any incremental, case-by-case, reformist way).

Second, the teaching of skills in the mystified context of legal reasoning about utterly unconnected legal problems means that skills are taught badly, unself-consciously, to be absorbed by osmosis as one picks up the knack of "thinking like a lawyer." Bad or only randomly good teaching generates and then accentuates real differences and imagined differences in student capabilities. But it does so in such a way that students don't know when they are learning and when they aren't, and have no way of improving or even understanding their own learning processes. They experience skills training as the gradual emergence of differences among themselves, as a process of ranking that reflects something that is just "there" inside them.

Third, the schools teach skills in isolation from actual lawyering experience. "Legal reasoning" is sharply distinguished from law practice, and one learns nothing about practice. This procedure disables students from any future role but that of apprentice in a law firm organized in the same manner as a law school, with older lawyers controlling the content and pace of depoliticized craft training in a setting of intense competition and no feedback.

The Formal Curriculum: Legal Rules and Legal Reasoning

The intellectual core of the ideology is the distinction between law and policy. Teachers convince students that legal reasoning exists, and is different from policy analysis, by bullying them into accepting as valid in particular cases arguments about legal correctness that are circular, question-begging, incoherent, or so vague as to be meaningless. Sometimes these are just arguments from authority, with the validity of the authoritative premise put outside discussion by professorial fiat. Sometimes they are policy arguments (e.g., security of transaction, business certainty) that are treated in a particular situation as though they were rules that everyone accepts but that will be ignored in the next case when they would suggest that the decision was wrong. Sometimes they are exercises in formal logic that wouldn't stand up for a minute in a discussion between equals (e.g., the small print in a form contract represents the "will of the parties").

32. Austin W. Scott, Lecturing at Harvard. The semiotics of the space and acts are apparent to all who will look for them. (*Courtesy of Art & Visual Materials, Special Collections Department, Harvard Law School Library.*)

Within a given subfield, the teacher is likely to treat cases in three different ways. There are the cases that present and justify the basic rules and basic ideas of the field. These are treated as cursory exercises in legal logic. Then there are cases that are anomalous—"outdated" or "wrongly decided" because they don't follow the supposed inner logic of the area. There won't be many of these, but they are important because their treatment persuades students that the technique of legal reasoning is at least minimally independent of the results reached by particular judges and is therefore capable of criticizing as well as legitimating. Finally, there will be an equally small number of peripheral or "cutting-edge" cases the teacher sees as raising policy issues about growth or change in the law. Whereas in discussing the first two kinds of cases the teacher behaves in an authoritarian way supposedly based on his objective knowledge of the technique of legal reasoning, here everything is different. Because we are dealing with "value judgments" that have "political" overtones, the discussion will be much more freewheeling. Rather than every student comment being right or wrong, all student comments get pluralist acceptance, and the teacher will reveal himself to be either a liberal or a conservative rather than merely a legal technician.

The curriculum as a whole has a rather similar structure. It is not really a random assortment of tubs on their own bottoms, a forest of tubs. First, there are contracts, torts, property, criminal law, and civil procedure. The rules in these courses are the ground rules of late-nineteenth-century laissez-faire capitalism. Teachers teach them as though they had an inner logic, as an exercise in legal reasoning, with policy (e.g., commercial certainty in the contracts course) playing a relatively minor role. Then there are second- and third-year courses that expound the moderate reformist program of the New Deal and the administrative structure of the modern regulatory state (with passing reference to the racial egalitarianism of the Warren Court).These courses are more policy oriented than first-year courses, and also much more ad hoc. Teachers teach students that limited interference with the market makes sense and is as authoritatively grounded in statutes as the ground rules of laissez-faire are grounded in natural law. But each problem is discrete, enormously complicated, and understood in a way that guarantees the practical impotence of the reform program. Finally, there are peripheral subjects, like legal philosophy or legal history, legal process, clinical legal education. These are presented as not truly relevant to the "hard" objective, serious, rigorous analytic core of law; they are a kind of playground or finishing school for learning the social art of self-presentation as a lawyer.

This whole body of implicit messages is nonsense. Teachers teach nonsense when they persuade students that legal reasoning is distinct, *as a method for reaching correct results*, from ethical and political discourse in general (i.e., from policy analysis). It is true that there is a distinctive lawyers' body of knowledge of the rules in force. It is true that there are distinctive lawyers' argumentative techniques for spotting gaps, conflicts, and ambiguities in the rules, for arguing broad and narrow holdings of cases, and for generating pro and con policy arguments. But these are *only* argumentative techniques. There is never a "correct legal solution" that is other than the correct ethical and political solution to that legal problem. Put another way, everything taught, except the formal rules themselves and the argumentative techniques for manipulating them, is policy and nothing more. It follows that the classroom distinction between the unproblematic, legal case and the policy-oriented case is a mere artifact: each could as well be taught in the opposite way. And the curricular distinction between the "nature" of contract law as highly legal and technical by contrast, say, with environmental law is equally a mystification.

These errors have a bias in favor of the center liberal program of limited reform of the market economy and pro forma gestures toward racial and sexual equality. The bias arises because law school teaching makes the choice of hierarchy and domination, which is implicit in the adoption of the rules of property, contract, and tort, look as though it flows from and is required by legal reasoning rather than being a matter of politics and economics. The bias is reinforced when the center liberal reformist program of regulation is presented as equally authoritative but somehow more policy oriented, and therefore less fundamental. The message is that the system is basically OK, since we have patched up the few areas open to abuse, and that it has a limited but important place for value-oriented debate about further change and improvement. If there is to be more fundamental questioning, it is relegated to the periphery of history or philosophy. The real world is kept at bay by treating clinical legal education, which might bring in a lot of information threatening to the cozy liberal consensus, as free legal drudge work for the local bar or as mere skills training.

It would be an extraordinary first-year student who could, on his own, develop a theoretically critical attitude toward this system. Entering students just don't know enough to figure out where the teacher is fudging, misrepresenting, or otherwise distorting legal thinking and legal reality. To make matters worse, the two most common kinds of left thinking the student is likely to bring with her are likely to hinder rather than assist in the struggle to maintain some intellectual autonomy from the experience. Most liberal students believe that the left program can be reduced to guaranteeing people their rights and to bringing about the triumph of human rights over mere property rights. In this picture, the trouble with the legal system is that it fails to put the state behind the rights of the oppressed, or that the system fails to enforce the rights formally recognized. If one thinks about law this way, one is inescapably dependent on the very techniques of legal reasoning that are being marshalled in defense of the status quo.

This wouldn't be so bad if the problem with legal education were that the teachers *misused* rights reasoning to restrict the range of the rights of the oppressed. But the problem is much deeper than that. Rights discourse is internally inconsistent, vacuous, or circular. Legal thought can generate equally plausible rights justifications for almost any result. Moreover, the discourse of rights imposes constraints on those who use it that make it almost impossible for it to function effectively as a tool of radical transformation. Rights are by their nature "formal," meaning that they secure to individuals legal protection for as well as from arbitrariness—to speak of rights is precisely *not* to speak of justice between social classes, races, or sexes. Rights discourse, moreover, simply presupposes or takes for granted that the world is and should be divided between a state sector that enforces rights and a private world of "civil society" in which atomized individuals pursue their diverse goals. This framework is, *in itself*, a part of the problem rather than of the solution. It makes it difficult even to conceptualize radical proposals such as, for example, decentralized democratic worker control of factories.

Because it is logically incoherent and manipulable, traditionally individualist, and willfully blind to the realities of *substantive* inequality, rights discourse is a trap. As long as one stays within it, one can produce good pieces of argument about the occasional case on the periphery where everyone recognizes value judgments have to be made. But one is without guidance in deciding what to do about fundamental questions and fated to the gradual loss of confidence in the convincingness of what one has to say in favor of the very results one believes in most passionately.

The alternative left stance is to undertake the Procrustean task of reinterpreting every judicial action as the expression of class interest. One may adopt a conspiracy theory in which judges deliberately subordinate "justice" (usually just a left liberal rights theory) to the short-run financial interests of the ruling class, or a much more subtle thesis about the "logic" or "needs" or "structural prerequisites" of a particular "stage of monopoly capitalism." But however one sets out to do it, there are two difficulties. The first is that there is just too much dreck, too much raw matter of the legal system, and too little time to give everything you have to study a sinister significance. It would be a full-time job just to give instrumental Marxist accounts of the cases on consideration doctrine in first-year contracts. Just exactly why was it that late-nineteenth-century capitalism needed to render an uncle's promise to pay his nephew a handsome sum if he didn't smoke till age twenty-one, a legal nullity? Or was it the other way around: that capitalism *needed* such promises to be enforceable?

The second difficulty is that there is no "logic" to monopoly capitalism, and law cannot be usefully understood, by someone who has to deal with it in all its complexity, as "superstructural." Legal rules the state enforces and legal concepts that permeate all aspects of social thought constitute capitalism as well as responding to the interests that operate within it. Law is an aspect of the social totality, not just the tail of the dog. The rules in force are a factor in the power or impotence of all social actors (though they certainly do not determine outcomes in the way liberal legalists sometimes suggest they do). Because it is part of the equation of power rather than simply a function of it, people struggle for power through law, constrained by their limited understanding and limited ability to predict the consequences of their maneuvers. To understand law is to understand this struggle as an aspect of class struggle *and* as an aspect of the human struggle to grasp the conditions of social justice. The outcomes of struggle are not preordained by any aspect of the social totality, and the outcomes within law have no "inherent logic" that would allow one to predict outcomes "scientifically" or to reject in advance specific attempts by judges and lawyers to work limited transformations of the system.

Left liberal rights analysis submerges the student in legal rhetoric but, because of its inherent vacuousness, can provide no more than an emotional stance against the legal order. The instrumental Marxist approach is highly critical of law but also dismissive. It is no help in coming to grips with the particularity of rules and rhetoric because it treats them, a priori, as mere window dressing. These theories fail left students because they offer no base for the mastery of ambivalence. What is needed is to think about law in a way that will allow one to enter into it, to criticize it without utterly rejecting it, and to manipulate it without self-abandonment to *their* system of thinking and doing.

Student Evaluation

Law schools teach a small number of useful skills. But they teach them only obliquely. It would threaten the professional ideology and the academic pretensions of teachers to make their students as good as they can be at the relatively simple tasks that they will have to perform in practice. But it would also upset the process by which a hierarchical arrangement analogous to that of law school applicants, law schools, and law firms is established within a given student body.

To teach the repetitive skills of legal analysis effectively, one would have to isolate the general procedures that make them up, and then devise large numbers of factual and doctrinal hypotheticals where students could practice those skills, knowing what they were doing and learning in every single case whether their performance was good or bad. As legal education now works, on the other hand, students do exercises designed to discover what the "correct solution" to a legal problem might be, those exercises are treated as unrelated to one another, and students receive no feedback at all except a grade on a single examination at the end of the course. Students generally experience these grades as almost totally arbitrary—unrelated to how much you worked, how much you liked the subject, how much you thought you understood going into the exam, and what you thought about the class and the teacher.

This is silly, looked at as pedagogy. But it is more than silly when looked at as ideology. The system generates a rank ordering of students based on grades, and students learn that there is little or nothing they can do to change their place in that ordering, or to change the way the school generates it. Grading as practiced teaches the inevitability and also the justice of hierarchy, a hierarchy that is at once false and unnecessary.

It is unnecessary because it is largely irrelevant to what students will do as lawyers. Most of the process of differentiating students into bad, better, and good could simply be dispensed with without the slightest detriment to the quality of legal services. It is false, first, because insomuch as it does involve the measuring of the real and useful skills of potential lawyers, the differences between students could be "leveled up" at minimal cost, whereas the actual practice of legal education systematically accentuates differences in real capacities. If law schools invested some of the time and money they now put into Socratic classes in developing systematic skills training, and committed themselves to giving constant, detailed feedback on student progress in learning those skills, they could graduate the vast majority of all the law students in the country at the level of technical proficiency now achieved by a small minority in each institution.

Law schools convey their factual message to each student about his or her place in the ranking of students along with the implicit corollary that place is individually earned, and therefore deserved. The system tells you that you learned as much as you were capable of learning, and that if you feel incompetent or that you could have become better at what you do, it is your own fault. Opposition is sour grapes. Students internalize this message about themselves and about the world, and so prepare themselves for all the hierarchies to follow.

Incapacitation for Alternative Practice

Law schools channel their students into jobs in the hierarchy of the bar according to their own standing in the hierarchy of schools. Students confronted with the choice of what to do after they graduate experience themselves as largely helpless: they have no "real" alternative to taking a job in one of the conventional firms that hires from their school. Partly, faculties generate this sense of student helplessness by propagating myths about the character of the different kinds of practice. They extol the forms that are accessible to their students; they subtly denigrate or express envy about the jobs that will be beyond their students' reach; they dismiss as ethically and socially suspect the jobs their students won't have to take.

As for any form of work outside the established system—for example, legal services for the poor and neighborhood law practice—they convey to students that, although morally exalted, the work is hopelessly dull and unchallenging, and that the possibilities of reaching a standard of living appropriate to a lawyer are slim or nonexistent. These messages are just nonsense—the rationalizations of law teachers who long upward, fear staus degradation, and above all hate the idea of risk. Legal services practice, for example, is far more intellectually stimulating and demanding, even with a high caseload, than most of what corporate lawyers do. It is also more fun.

Beyond this dimension of professional mythology, law schools act in more concrete ways to guarantee that their students will fit themselves into their appropriate niches in the existing system of practice. First; the actual content of what is taught in a given school will incapacitate students from any other form of practice than that allotted graduates of that institution. This looks superficially like a rational adaptation to the needs of the market, but it is in fact almost entirely unnecessary. Law schools teach so little, and that so incompetently, that they cannot, as now constituted, prepare students for more than one career at the bar. But the reason for this is that they embed skills training in mystificatory nonsense and devote most of their teaching time to transmitting masses of ill-digested rules. A more rational system would emphasize the way to learn law rather than rules, and skills rather than answers. Student capacities would be more equal as a result, but students would also be radically more flexible in what they could do in practice.

A second incapacitating device is the teaching of doctrine in isolation from practice skills. Students who have no practice skills tend to exaggerate how difficult it is to acquire them. There is a distinct lawyers' mystique of the irrelevance of the "theoretical" material learned in school, and of the crucial importance of abilities that cannot be known or developed until one is out in the "real world" and "in the trenches." Students have little alternative to getting training in this dimension of things after law school. It therefore seems hopelessly impractical to think about setting up your own law firm, and only a little less impractical to go to a small or political or unconventional firm rather than to one of those that offer the standard package of postgraduate education. Law schools are wholly responsible for this situation. They could quite easily revamp their curricula so that any student who wanted it would have a meaningful choice between independence and servility.

A third form of incapacitation is more subtle. Law school, as an extension of the educational system as a whole, teaches students that they are weak, lazy, incompetent, and insecure. And it also teaches them that if they are willing to accept dependency, large institutions will take care of them almost no matter what. The terms of the bargain are relatively clear. The institution will set limited, clearly defined tasks and specify minimum requirements in their performance. The student/associate has no other responsibilities than performance of those tasks. The institution takes care of all the contingencies of life, both within the law (supervision and backup from other firm members; firm resources and prestige to bail you out if you make a mistake) and in private life (firms offer money but also long-term job security and delicious benefits packages aimed to reduce risks of disaster). In exchange, you renounce any claim to control your work setting or the actual content of what you do, and agree to show the appropriate form of deference to those above and condescension to those below.

By comparison, the alternatives are risky. Law school does not train you to run a small law business, to realistically assess the outcome of a complex process involving many different actors, or to enjoy the feeling of independence and moral integrity that comes of creating your own job to serve your own goals. It tries to persuade you that you are barely competent to perform the much more limited roles it allows you, and strongly suggests that it is more prudent to kiss the lash than to strike out on your own.

The Modeling of Hierarchical Relationships

Law teachers model for students how they are supposed to think, feel, and act in their future professional roles. Some of this is a matter of teaching by example, some of it a matter of more active learning from interactions that are a kind of clinical education for lawyerlike behavior. This training is a major factor in the hierarchical life of the bar. It encodes the message of the legitimacy of the whole system into the smallest details of personal style, daily routine, gesture, tone of voice, facial expression—a plethora of little p's and q's for everyone to mind. Partly, these will serve as a language—a way for the young lawyer to convey that she knows what the rules of the game are and intends to play by them. What's going on is partly a matter of ritual oaths and affirmations—by adopting the mannerisms, one pledges one's troth to inequality. And partly it is a substantive matter of value. Hierarchical behavior will come to express and realize the hierarchical selves of people who were initially only wearers of masks.

Law teachers enlist on the side of hierarchy all the vulnerabilities students feel as they begin to understand what lies ahead of them. In law school, students have to come to grips with implications of their social class and sex and race in a way that is different from (but not necessarily less important than) the experience of college. People discover that preserving their class status is extremely important to them, so important that no alternative to the best law job they can get seems possible to them. Or they discover that they want to rise, or that they are trapped in a way they hadn't anticipated. People change the way they dress and talk; they change their opinions and even their emotions. None of this is easy for anyone, but progressive and left students have the special set of humiliations involved in discovering the limits of their commitment and often the instability of attitudes they thought were basic to themselves.

Another kind of vulnerability has to do with one's own competence. Law school wields frightening instruments of judgment, including not only the grading system but also the more subtle systems of teacher approval in class, reputation among fellow students, and out-of-class faculty contact and respect. Left students sometimes begin law school with an apparently unshakable confidence in their own competence and with a related confidence in their own left analysis. But even these apparently self-assured students quickly find that adverse judgments—even judgments that are only imagined or projected onto others—count and hurt. They have to decide whether this responsiveness in themselves is something to accept, whether the judgments in question have validity and refer to things they care about, or whether they should reject them. They have to wonder whether they have embarked on a subtle course of accommodating themselves intellectually in order to be in the ball park where people win and lose teacher and peer approval. And they have, in most or at least many cases, to deal with actual failure to live up to their highest hopes of accomplishment within the conventional system of rewards.

A first lesson is that professors are intensely preoccupied with the status rankings of their schools, and show themselves willing to sacrifice to improve their status in the rankings and to prevent downward drift. They approach the appointment of colleagues in the spirit of trying to get people who are as high up as possible in a conventionally defined hierarchy of teaching applicants, and they are notoriously hostile to affirmative action in faculty hiring, even when they are quite willing to practice it for student admissions and in filling administrative posts. Assistant professors begin their careers as the little darlings of their older colleagues. They end up in tense competition for the prize of tenure, trying to accommodate themselves to standards and expectations that are, typically, too vague to master except by a commitment to please at any cost. In these respects, law schools are a good preview of what law firms will be like.

Law professors, like lawyers, have secretaries. Students deal with them off and on through law school, watch how their bosses treat them, how they treat their bosses, and how "a secretary" relates to "a professor" even when one does not work for the other. Students learn that it is acceptable, even if it's not always and everywhere the norm, for faculty to treat their secretaries petulantly, condescendingly, with a perfectionism that is a matter of the bosses' face rather than of the demands of the job itself, as though they were personal body servants, utterly impersonally, or as objects of sexual harassment. They learn that "a secretary" treats "a professor" with elaborate deference, as though her time and her dignity meant nothing and his everything, even when he is not her boss. In general, they learn that humane relations in the workplace are a matter of the superior's grace rather than of human need and social justice.

These lessons are repeated in the relationships of professors and secretaries with administrators and with maintenance and support staff. Teachers convey a sense of their own superiority and practice a social segregation sufficiently extreme so that there are no occasions on which the reality of that superiority might be tested. As a group, they accept and willingly support the division of labor that consigns everyone in the institution but them to boredom and stagnation. Friendly but deferential social relations reinforce everyone's sense that all's for the best, making hierarchy seem to disappear in the midst of cordiality when in fact any serious challenge to the regime would be met with outrage and retaliation.

All of this is teaching by example. In their relations with students, and in the student culture they foster, teachers get the message across more directly and more powerfully. The teacher/student relationship is the model for relations between junior associates and senior partners, and also for the relationship between lawyers and judges. The student/student relationship is the model for relations among lawyers as peers, for the age cohort within a law firm, and for the "fraternity" of the courthouse crowd.

In the classroom and out of it, students learn a particular style of deference. They learn to suffer with positive cheerfulness interruption in midsentence, mockery, ad hominem assault, inconsequent asides, questions that are so vague as to be unanswerable but can somehow be answered wrong all the same, abrupt dismissal, and stinginess of praise (even if these things are not always and everywhere the norm). They learn, if they have talent, that submission is most effective flavored with a pinch of rebellion, to bridle a little before they bend. They learn to savor crumbs, while picking from the air the indications of the master's mood that can mean the difference between a good day and misery. They learn to take it all in good sort, that there is often shyness, good intentions, some real commitment to your learning something behind the authoritarian facade. So it will be with many a robed curmudgeon in years to come.

Then there is affiliation. From among many possibilities, each student gets to choose a mentor, or several, to admire and depend on, to become sort of friends with if the mentor is a liberal, to sit at the feet of if the mentor is more "traditional." You learn how he or she is different from other teachers, and to be supportive of those differences, as the mentor learns something of your particular strengths and weaknesses, both of you trying to prevent the inevitability of letters of recommendation from corrupting the whole experience. This can be fruitful and satisfying, or degrading, or both at once. So it will be a few years later with your "father in the law."

There is a third, more subtle, and less conscious message conveyed in student/teacher relations. Teachers are overwhelmingly white, male, and middle class; and most (by no means all) black and women law teachers give the impression of thorough assimilation to that style, or of insecurity and unhappiness. Students who are women or black or working class find out something important about the professional universe from the first day of class: that it is not even nominally pluralist in cultural terms. The teacher sets the tone—a white, male, middle-class tone. Students adapt. They do so partly out of fear, partly out of hope of gain, partly out of genuine admiration for their role models. But the line between adaptation to the intellectual and skills content of legal education and adaptation to the white, male, middle-class cultural style is a fine one, easily lost sight of.

While students quickly understand that there is diversity among their fellow students and that the faculty is not really homogeneous in terms of character, background, or opinions, the classroom itself becomes more rather than less uniform as legal education progresses. You'll find Fred Astaire and Howard Cosell over and over again, but never Richard Pryor or Betty Friedan. It's not that the teacher punishes you if you use slang or wear clothes or give examples or voice opinions that identify you as different, though that *might* happen. You are likely to be sanctioned, mildly or severely, only if you refuse to adopt the highly cognitive, dominating mode of discourse that everyone identifies as lawyerlike. Nonetheless, the indirect pressure for conformity is intense.

If you, alone in your seat, feel alienated in this atmosphere, it is unlikely that you will do anything about it in the classroom setting itself, however much you gripe about it with friends. It is more than likely that you'll find a way, in class, to respond as the teacher seems to want you to respond—to be a lot like him, as far as one could tell if one knew you only in class, even though your imitation is flawed by the need to suppress anger. And when some teacher, at least once in some class, makes a remark that seems sexist or racist, or seems unwilling to treat black or women students in quite as "challenging" a way as white students, or treats them in a more challenging way, or cuts off discussion when a woman student gets mad at a male student's joke about the tort of "offensive touching," it is unlikely that you'll do anything then either.

It is easy enough to see this situation of enforced cultural uniformity as oppressive, but somewhat more difficult to see it as training, especially if you are aware of it and hate it. But it is training nonetheless. You will pick up mannerisms, ways of speaking, gestures, that would be "neutral" if they were not emblematic of membership in the universe of the bar. You will come to expect that as a lawyer you will live in a world in which essential parts of you are not represented, or are misrepresented, and in which things you don't like will be accepted to the point that it doesn't occur to people that they are even controversial. And you will come to expect that there is nothing you can do about it. One develops ways of coping with these expectations—turning off attention or involvement when the conversation strays in certain directions, participating actively while ignoring the offensive elements of the interchange, even reinterpreting as inoffensive things that would otherwise make you boil. These are skills that incapacitate rather than empower, skills that will help you imprison yourself in practice.

Relations among students get a lot of their color from relations with the faculty. There is the sense of blood brotherhood, with or without sisters, in endless speculation about the Olympians. The speculation is colored with rage, expressed sometimes in student theatricals or the "humor" column of the school paper. ("Put Professor X's talents to the best possible use: Turn him into hamburger." Ha, ha.) There is likely to be a surface norm of noncompetitiveness and cooperation. ("Gee, I thought this would be like *The Paper Chase*, but it isn't at all.") But a basic thing to learn is the limits of that cooperativeness. Very few people can combine rivalry for grades, law review, clerkships, good summer jobs, with helping another member of their study group so effectively that he might actually pose a danger to them. You learn camaraderie and distrust at the same time. So it will be in the law-firm age cohort.

And there is more to it than that. Through the reactions of fellow students—diffuse, disembodied events that just "happen," in class or out of class—women learn how important it is not to appear to be "hysterical females," and that when your moot court partner gets a crush on you, and doesn't know it, and is married, there is a danger he will hate you when he discovers what he has been feeling. Lower-middle-class students learn not to wear an undershirt that shows, and that certain patterns and fabrics in clothes will stigmatize them no matter what their grades. Black students learn without surprise that the bar will have its own peculiar forms of racism, and that their very presence means affirmative action, unless it means "he would have made it even without affirmative action." They worry about forms of bias so diabolical even they can't see them, and wonder whether legal reasoning is intrinsically white. Meanwhile, dozens of small changes through which they become more and more like other middle- or upper-middle-class Americans engender rhetoric about how the black community is not divided along class lines. On one level, all of this is just high school replayed; on another, it's about how to make partner.

The final touch that completes the picture of law school as training for professional hierarchy is the placement process. As each firm, with the tacit or enthusiastically overt participation of the schools, puts on a conspicuous display of its relative status within the bar, the bar as a whole affirms and celebrates its hierarchical values and the rewards they bring. This process is most powerful for students who go through the elaborate procedures of firms in about the top half of the profession. These include, nowadays, first-year summer jobs, dozens of interviews, fly-outs, second-year summer jobs, more interviews, and more fly-outs.

This system allows law firms to get a *social* sense of applicants, a sense of how they will contribute to the nonlegal image of the firm and to the internal system of deference and affiliation. It allows firms to convey to students the extraordinary opulence of the life they offer, adding the allure of free travel, expense-account meals, fancy hotel suites, and parties at country clubs to the simple message of big bucks in a paycheck. And it teaches students at fancy law schools, students who have had continuous experience of academic and careerist success, that they are not as "safe" as they thought they were.

When students at Columbia or Yale paper dorm corridors with rejection letters, or award prizes for the most rejection letters and for the most unpleasant single letter, they show their sense of the meaning of the ritual. There are many ways in which the boss can persuade you to brush his teeth and comb his hair. One of them is to arrange things so that almost all students get good jobs, but most students get their good jobs through twenty interviews yielding only two offers.

By dangling the bait, making clear the rules of the game, and then subjecting almost everyone to intense anxiety about their acceptability, firms structure entry into the profession so as to maximize acceptance of hierarchy. If you feel you've succeeded, you're forever grateful, and you have a vested interest. If you feel you've failed, you blame yourself, when you aren't busy feeling envy. When you get to be the hiring partner, you'll have a visceral understanding of what's at stake, but by then it will be hard even to imagine why someone might want to change it.

Inasmuch as these hierarchies are generational, they are easier to take than those baldly reflective of race, sex, or class. You, too, will one day be a senior partner and, who knows, maybe even a judge; you will have mentees and be the object of the rage and longing of those coming up behind you. Training for subservience is training for domination as well. Nothing could be more natural and, if you've served your time, more fair than that you as a group should do as you have been done to, for better and for worse. But it doesn't *have* to be that way, and remember, you saw it first in law school.

I have been arguing that legal education is one of the causes of legal hierarchy. Legal education supports it by analogy, provides it a general legitimating ideology by justifying the rules that underlie it, and provides it a particular ideology by mystifying legal reasoning. Legal education structures the pool of prospective lawyers so that their hierarchical organization seems inevitable, and trains them in detail to look and think and act just like all the other lawyers in the system. Up to this point I have presented this causal analysis as though legal education were a machine feeding particular inputs into another machine. But machines have no consciousness of one another; inasmuch as they are coordinated, it is by some external intelligence. Law teachers, on the other hand, have a vivid sense of what the profession looks like and of what it expects them to do. Since actors in the two systems consciously adjust to one another and also consciously attempt to influence one another, legal education is as much a product of legal hierarchy as a cause of it. To my mind, this means that law teachers must take personal responsibility for legal hierarchy in general, including hierarchy within legal education. If it is there, it is there because they put it there and reproduce it generation after generation, just as lawyers do.

The Student Response to Hierarchy

Students respond in different ways to their slowly emerging consciousness of the hierarchical realities of life in the law. Looking around me, I see students who enter wholeheartedly into the system—for whom the training "takes" in a quite straightforward way. Others appear, at least, to manage something more complex. They accept the system's presentation of itself as largely neutral, as apolitical, meritocratic, instrumental, a matter of craft. And they also accept the system's promise that if they do their work, "serve their time," and "put in their hours," they are free to think and do and feel anything they want in their "private lives."

This mode of response is complex because the messages, though sincerely proffered, are not truly meant. People who accept the messages at face value often seem to sense that what has actually transpired is different. And since the law is neither apolitical nor meritocratic nor instrumental nor a matter of craft (at least not exclusively these things), and since training for hierarchy cannot be a matter merely of public as opposed to private life, it is inevitable that they do in fact give and take something different than what is suggested by the overt terms of the bargain. Sometimes people enact a kind of parody: they behave in a particularly tough, cognitive, lawyerlike mode in their professional selves, and construct a private self that seems on the surface to deliberately exaggerate opposing qualities of warmth, sensitivity, easygoingness, or cultural radicalism.

Sometimes one senses an opposite version: the person never fully enters into "legal reasoning," remaining always a slightly disoriented, not-quite-in-good-faith role player in professional life, and feels a parallel inability ever to fully "be" their private self. For example, they may talk "shop" and obsess about the day at work, while hating themselves for being unable to "relax," but then find that at work they are unable to make the tasks assigned them fully their own, and that each new task seems at first an unpleasant threat to their fragile feelings of confidence.

For progressive and left students, there is another possibility, which might be called the denunciatory mode. One can take law school work seriously as time serving and do it coldly in that spirit, hate one's fellow students for their surrenders, and focus one's hopes on "not being a lawyer" or on a fantasy of an unproblematically leftist legal job on graduation. This response is hard from the very beginning. If you reject what teachers and the student culture tell you about what the first-year curriculum means and how to enter into learning it, you are adrift as to how to go about becoming minimally competent. You have to develop a theory on your own of what is valid skills training and what is merely indoctrination, and your ambivalent desire to be successful in spite of all is likely to sabotage your independence. As graduation approaches, it becomes clearer that there are precious few unambiguously virtuous law jobs even to apply for, and your situation begins to look more like everyone else's, though perhaps more extreme. Most (by no means all) students who begin with denunciation end by settling for some version of the bargain of public against private life.

I am a good deal more confident about the patterns that I have just described than about the attitudes toward hierarchy that go along with them. My own position in the system of class, sex, and race (as an upper-middle-class white male) and my rank in the professional hierarchy (as a Harvard professor) give me an interest in the perception that hierarchy is both omnipresent and enormously important, even while I am busy condemning it. And there is a problem of imagination that goes beyond that of interest. It is hard for me to know whether I even understand the attitudes toward hierarchy of women and blacks, for example, or of children of working-class parents, or of solo practitioners eking out a living from residential real-estate closings. Members of those groups sometimes suggest that the particularity of their experience of oppression cannot be grasped by outsiders, but sometimes that the failure to grasp it is personal rather than inevitable. Often it seems to me that all people have at least analogous experiences of the oppressive reality of hierarchy, even those who seem most favored by the system—that the collar feels the same when you get to the end of the rope, whether the rope is ten feet long or fifty. On the other hand, it seems clear that hierarchy creates distances that are never bridged.

It is not uncommon for a person to answer a description of the hierarchy of law firms with a flat denial that the bar is really ranked. Lawyers of lower-middle-class background tend to have far more direct political power in the state governments than "elite" lawyers, even under Republican administrations. Furthermore, every lawyer knows of instances of real friendship, seemingly outside and beyond the distinctions that are supposed to be so important, and can cite examples of lower-middle-class lawyers in upper-middle-class law firms, and vice versa. There are many lawyers who seem to defy hierarchical classification, and law firms and law schools that do likewise, so that one can argue that the hierarchy claim that everyone and everything is ranked breaks down the minute you try to give concrete examples. I have been told often enough that I *may* be right about the pervasiveness of ranking, but that the speaker has never noticed it himself, himself treats all lawyers in the same way, regardless of their class or professional standing, and has never, except in an occasional very bizarre case, found lawyers violating the egalitarian norm.

When the person making these claims is a rich corporate lawyer who was my prep school classmate, I tend to interpret them as a willful denial of the way he is treated and treats others. When the person speaking is someone I perceive as less favored by the system (say, a woman of lower-middle-class origin who went to Brooklyn Law School and now works for a small, struggling downtown law firm), it is harder to know how to react. Maybe I'm just wrong about what it's like out there. Maybe my preoccupation with the horrors of hierarchy is just a way to wring the last ironic drop of pleasure from my own hierarchical superiority. But I don't interpret it that way. The denial of hierarchy is false consciousness. The problem is not whether hierarchy is there, but how to understand it, and what its implications are for political action.

Chapter 65

Admission and Exclusion of Law Students

1932

Charles E. Clark

Charles E. Clark (December 9, 1889-December 13, 1963) was Stirling Professor and Dean of Yale from 1929 to 1939, after which he became judge on the United States Court of Appeals for the Second Circuit. This article first appeared in 7 *American Law School Review* 397 (1932).

My function on this program, as I understand it, is to recount some experience in the selective admission of law students. Because of my lack of knowledge, this experience must naturally be that of my own School, Yale, though I do not understand it to be inconsistent with that of other schools. I fully realize that the problem is a much bigger one than merely the success of this system of admission in attaining its immediate objective. That I think it well does; the intellectual calibre of the student body as a whole is materially raised under it. The more indirect implications of a policy of restricted admission on other schools, on the bar and on the community as a whole, I do not feel competent to discuss authoritatively, though I shall venture a few general thoughts upon them at the conclusion of this paper.

So far as I have discovered from the catalogues, the principle of selective admission of law students, that is, that not all candidates with the required preliminary education and character are eligible, is followed only at five schools: Chicago, Columbia, Pennsylvania, Northwestern, and Yale. I might say, if I am in error as to this I shall be glad to be corrected. You will note that I am stating these are the only schools so far as the catalogue shows, so far as I have been able to discover, that do not make a purely educational requirement or an educational and character requirement combined. The first three do not limit to a specific number; at Northwestern the student body may number only 400; while at Yale the entering class is restricted to 100. The number limitation may seem arbitrary, but it does have the advantage of stating a definite standard both to one's self and to the applicants and of serving as a warning that there will be no special cases admitted. Such at least was the advantage we felt after earlier experience with no limitation; though I ought to say that other schools report good results without it.

Our procedure in making selection of students is not particularly involved or occult. A Committee on Admissions of the faculty has before it a complete file for each applicant and it aims to select from among all applicants that particular group of one hundred who seem to it most promising for the study of law. The file of each candidate contains the following: An application blank duly completed containing various formal details; a full transcript of his college record; at least two letters of recommendation from college instructors, giving data about him; the result of his legal aptitude test; and an interview blank containing his answers to questions and the observations of the interviewer in his case.

I will now explain some of these details further.

The importance of the college grades is clear. So far as our methods are subject to statistical check they have been tabulated by the Department of Personnel Study at Yale which is greatly interested in all forms of selective choice of men. From tables of this Department it appears that the correlation between average college grades and success in the law school is substantially high—about +50—with a correlation of even +72 between Yale College and Yale Law School grades. The story told by the college grades is, however, well supplemented by the other material. Thus the personal interview is carefully framed to bring out, among other things, the extra-curricular activities of the student. The interviewer may propound such questions as he sees fit, but the blank before him reminds him that he is to obtain information in detail under the following heads: (1) The applicant's educational background, including all college activities, (2) his economic background, dealing with the question how far he has had to earn money by outside work and what financial assistance he will need in the law school, (3) health, (4) family background, dealing with educational and professional or other attainments of family, (5) vocational background dealing with his reasons for and expectations in the law, and lastly the interviewer's general impressions of the candidate.

As might be expected, many of the letters of recommendation tend to be of a formal nature. We give explicit instructions, however, that details as to the men's intellectual and character qualifications for the study of law are needed and that otherwise the letters will be disregarded. In increasing numbers we are receiving information which seems to be dependable from various college instructors, and each year we become better acquainted with more such men, who understand our purpose and who assume responsibility for their recommendations. It is often thrilling to see the enthusiasm of a teacher who thinks he has uncovered an ugly duckling with possibilities. We have acted upon such hunches at times with the most satisfying results.

The legal aptitude test deserves special mention. It is discussed in a paper by Professor A. B. Crawford of our Department of Personnel Study read before the National Conference of Bar Examiners at Atlantic City last September and to appear, I think, in the next number of the American Law School Review. At first we made use of the Thorndike C.A.V.D. test lasting four hours or longer and also a twenty minute test originated by the late Professor J. Crosby Chapman of Yale. The correlation between the tests and first year law grades was various in different years but the average for the Thorndike test was +45 and for the Chapman test about +40. These were lower, as we see, than the correlation between college and law grades. It was thought that a more effective paper could be prepared and this the Department of Personnel Study undertook to supply with help from various sources. Our law faculty furnished some problems of a legal type. Two one-hour tests were developed and tried out last year. They were given to all the first year class, to editors of and competitors for the Yale Law Journal, and to such members of the faculty as were willing to perform the sacrifice. It had happened by the strangest chance that the faculty had triumphed over the Journal editors at the annual baseball contest of the previous spring. The editors now challenged the faculty to a test of brain power, while admitting that the faculty had shown superior brawn. Much local excitement developed; but the sad details of the score had better be covered by silence.

The results of the new tests seem quite promising. The averages obtained from it correlated with first year law grades to the extent of +64. This is high when it is recalled that tests even of narrower functions seldom correlate higher than +70 with the capacity they are designed to measure, and since the first year class is a selected group with the law grades showing little differentiation numerically between success and failure (25 points between a D and an A). As had been planned, the most discriminating material, as shown by the tabulations, was chosen to make up a single one-hour test. This particular material, which is being tried out further this year, yielded a correlation of +78 with first year law grades. As yet the aptitude grades are most useful as cumulative evidence; we are not now contemplating exclusive reliance upon them to determine our selection of men.

Usually our class of 100 is selected from among 230 to 300 applicants or a little more than one out of three. Since not all applicants finally go through and accept selection the range of final choice is somewhat less, perhaps one out of two. Last spring the number increased, in spite of the financial depression, and our present first year class is unusually satisfactory.

Our experience of about five years convinces us of the success, even the ease of operating, the plan. One must guard against overconfidence, for as indicated by the tabulations referred to above, it seems easy to go farther than we do and indicate the future position in the class of many of the men. Of course we have no interest in going as far as this; we wish merely to select a group which fits our purpose. Our data gives a pretty complete picture of each student. Probably three-fourths of those we would select are obvious choices; the remaining one-fourth naturally causes more difficulty, but an error in choice either way in this group will affect the class average only slightly. True it does affect the individual, but our whole plan is based on our announced purpose of selecting only a group for our School, and our decision means no more than this. It must be so taken by the applicant if he chooses to offer himself. Moreover, we have tried to provide means whereby the late flowering genius may disclose his possibilities and if none are indicated in the data, the presumption seems justified that none exist.

In addition to our conviction that we have secured a student body of greater intellectual power, we have the confirmation shown by fewer exclusions of students during the law course. It is true that Professor Ben D. Wood and others have shown us how subjective all examinations are and perhaps our conviction affects our examination standards. But we are not conscious of any change in our marking system and actually we have eliminated much of the waste to students and school involved in dropping large numbers. We now exclude less than ten per cent of the first year class instead of the previous two and a half to three times that number. Last year the exclusions were nine from the first year class and one other, a second year transfer student. This number, too, is higher than a strict application of our theories would require; since each year it seems desirable to accept a very few candidates about whom we are doubtful but in whom others whose judgments we respect have confidence. This group furnishes a large part of the failures and serves to confirm the effectiveness of our general system.

We have a picture of the working of our system from another angle, for we have some reports from other schools showing that the mortality elsewhere of students whom we have rejected is very high.

We conclude, therefore, that the plan is eminently successful for its immediate objective as applied to our own school. I might add testimonials from our group, for example, as to the ease with which these men accommodate themselves to the newly instituted seminar and individual work of the first year, but that, I expect, is another story. I turn to my final question—should the plan be adopted in many other schools?

Now the limits to which the theory of intellectual aristocracy in admissions to the bar may be carried are not clear. One may venture to believe, however, that we are yet a long way from such limits, wherever they should be established. This Association and the American Bar Association have announced objectives for preliminary education and standards of admission to the bar which are far from being attained and are unlikely to be for many years. Several recent estimates, including one in the December, 1931, number of The Bar Examiner, the new organ of the National Conference of Bar Examiners, concur in believing that more than twice as many lawyers are being admitted yearly than is necessary to maintain the already high percentage of lawyers to total population in this country. If some schools—as many as are now in a position to do so—move for yet higher intellectual qualifications of their students, this would seem for the present at least a highly desirable step.

The problem remains whether such a course may not force the weaker students to schools or communities already overburdened with such men. The difficulty is obvious and in particular cases may cause serious disadvantages. But to suggest as a remedy that schools should refrain from raising their standards as they see them because of the problem is to cast doubt upon the whole program of raising standards in legal education. Furthermore, it is against the teaching of experience. The A.B.A. standards, whether fully complied with or not, have been most effective in stimulating improvement in school and state bar admission requirements. The way to press forward is for those who can to take such steps as to them are possible, and this, if experience is any guide, will ultimately result in a considerable advance along the entire front.

Chapter 66

Migration of Students

1932

Edson R. Sunderland

Edson R. Sunderland (August 29, 1874-March 29, 1959), an expert in procedure and judicial reform, taught at the University of Michigan from 1901 to 1959, becoming an emeritus in 1944. This article first appeared in 7 *American Law School Review* 397 (1932).

There are two types of migration of students from one law school to another. The first is a migration of poor students who have failed in their work, and who move on to other schools, less exacting in their requirements, through which they hope to obtain ultimate admission to the bar. The second is a migration of the abler and more ambitious students, who attend more than one school in order to enlarge their outlook, extend their experience and contacts and get new points of view.

I.

The first type of migration is a by-product of modern methods of law school administration. The weak student is not, of course, directed to try his fortunes in another school, but is merely dropped. It is well known, however, that the effect of such action, in a large number of cases, will not be to turn the student away from the law but only to force him to transfer to some other institution. What appears superficially as merely a matter of internal regulation designed to protect school standards, in reality produces compulsory migration.

This aspect of our educational policy has not received the attention it probably deserves. We have almost no statistical information regarding it. How many students, dropped for unsatisfactory work, are thereby deterred from further effort in the field of the law? How many merely find another school in which they can continue their course? What types of schools admit these students? How many ultimately enter the profession and with what result? None of these questions can be answered.

Involuntary migration of the type here referred to, probably accounts for the majority of current transfers from one school to another. Some of these men, for special reasons or on certain conditions, are able to go into other schools of equal rank, but the movement is almost entirely from schools considered relatively good to schools considered relatively poor.

If the better schools employed a system of instruction adapted only to students of superior ability, while the poorer schools used methods relatively more effective for those of inferior ability, the migrating student might gain by the transfer. It has never been demonstrated, however, that the poorer students require a different method of instruction from that employed for the better students, nor is there any evidence that the good schools and the poor schools have in fact organized their work along different lines with a view to serving students whose minds are on different intellectual levels. All schools compete for the good students and try to satisfy their demands, and any school which should hold itself out as specially equipped to deal with those of mediocre ability would probably have no students at all.

It is quite clear, I think, that involuntary migration is not for the benefit of the student himself, and that its direct result is to lower the quality of the bar by bringing in men with an education inferior to that which they would have received had they not been forced to transfer to other schools.

We justify the process on the score of the benefit resulting to the students who remain in the schools after the weaker men have been eliminated. It is possible, however, that we have overestimated the harm necessarily resulting from the presence of the less capable students, and that we have not made a sufficient study or available ways and means for dealing effectively with the lower levels of the student body. In view of the direct and vital interest which society has in giving every prospective member of the bar the best possible legal training, it ought not to be too readily assumed that the present system of forced migration to poorer schools is the final solution of the problem. Ways might be found, if we sought them diligently, for organizing and operating our law schools so that those weaker students who are determined and destined to enter the profession, might be accorded the benefits of superior instruction without serious injury to the better men. Certainly neither school pride nor traditional prejudice should have controlling influence. The question is one of the balance of advantage, and it seems sufficiently important to warrant a more thorough investigation than it has yet received.

II.

The other type of migration is one which has never been encouraged in American universities, although it has been for generations a characteristic feature of higher education in continental Europe, particularly in German speaking countries.

Professor Conrad, in his classic book on The German Universities, writing of the migration of students during the nineteenth century, states that the average number of semesters spent by students at one university varied from 4.12 in the decade 1831-41, to 3.28 in the decade 1871-81. Almost every student, he says, attends two universities, and spends at each nearly one half of his time. Figures for the early eighties showed that at Munich only 70% of the students were Bavarians, at Strassburg only 23% were from Alsace-Lorraine, and at Heidelberg only 38% were from Baden (the German Universities for the Last Fifty Years).

Matthew Arnold, writing in 1882, was impressed by the "very free circulation of the German students through the universities of the fatherland" (Higher Schools and Universities in Germany, p. 135).

Professor Paulsen, discussing the situation in the first decade of the present century, notes the persistence of the custom which prescribes that a student shall not complete his academic education at one university, but shall attend several in succession (German Universities, p. 301).

As late as the last year before the great war, an American observer, Price Collier, writing upon German Universities, reported that few students resided during their whole course of study at one university, but after remaining for a year or two, moved on in order to hear other professors and to see something of the best work being done elsewhere (53 Scrib. Mag. 46).

While the poverty due to the war has somewhat diminished the amount of student migration in Germany, one gathers the impression from Dr. Flexner's recent book that the system is still as firmly established as ever (Universities: American, English and German, pp. 315-327).

The German system of student migration was a feature of the great expansion of intellectual activity during the past century which centered in the universities. Complete reciprocity between the different institutions of higher learning developed a singleness of educational purpose which exalted the university idea rather than the separate university foundations. All scholars were considered coworkers in the search for truth, and were unaffected by geographical or institutional limitations, jealousies or traditions.

Two results followed.

On the one hand, each professor found himself engaged in a nation-wide competition with every other man in his field. Courses announced at each institution were in effect offered to the entire student body of Germany. Each course was appraised on what appeared to be its own merits, irrespective of the university where the lectures happened to be given. Students came to hear the individual teacher, not to attend the institution. When I was a student of philosophy at Berlin, most of the men whom I met were there because they wanted to hear Professor Harnack. The prestige of the University counted for little; the ability and the attainments of the teacher were everything. Such a system could not fail to be profoundly stimulating to the men who made up the faculties.

On the other hand, the students enjoyed unparalleled opportunities for hearing the most eminent men of their time. In the course of their university career they could come into personal contact with all the more important scholars in a given field, and were able to develop a breadth of view and a soundness of understanding which no single institution could give.

Accordingly, the migration system appears to confer a double benefit. It makes better teachers by enlarging their opportunities and extending their influence; and it gives to the students a vastly broader education. These results are accomplished in the most highly individualized manner, by stimulating the personal initiative and ambitions of the teacher and by encouraging personal enterprise on the part of the student. Organization. with its accompanying mass action, plays no part.

If the migratory system has been so successful and beneficial in Germany, may it not have suggestions of value to us? American educational institutions are suffering from the influence of the machine age. We regiment our student body, we organize our faculties, we standardize our methods. We work and think in groups. All this is inimical to the highest form of intellectual life. Scholarship is the product of individuals, not of organizations. Faculties or committees can assemble, compare and coordinate, but they cannot create. In the world of ideas the pioneer works alone. It is originality, not conformity, which pushes forward the boundaries of knowledge.

If a more liberal interchange of students would help to give the American law teacher a universal instead of an institutional outlook, and thereby inspire him to freer intellectual effort, and if it would open the educational resources of the nation to a larger number of students having the ability and desire to use them, its encouragement would be a matter well worthy of consideration and experiment. There are, of course, administrative obstacles standing in the way. Would the plan require a mutual recognition of credits at face value between all schools which adhered to it? If so it could operate only among a limited group of schools. But a small group would be comparatively easy to organize, and additional schools could be brought in as fast as conditions warranted.

Universal migration would be a much more remote possibility, for it would doubtless involve an abandonment of our credit system and the substitution of a comprehensive test of proficiency in the law, as a basis for the granting of a degree. This is, of course, the German system and there is much to recommend it. But a discussion of that problem is beyond the scope of the present paper.

Chapter 67

Law School Fraternities

1903

Nathan Abbott

Nathan Abbott (July 11, 1854-January 29, 1941) taught at Michigan, Northwestern, Stanford, and Columbia. This article first appeared in 1 *American Law School Review* 33 (1903).

Whatever may be said about the usefulness of college fraternities,—and a great deal has been said and printed both pro and con,—it is safe to say that they are an inevitable element of student life. A recent publication of a small college has the names of over fifty different associations. There were literary, scientific, and athletic societies, societies for speaking French and German, for fencing and for acting, for eating and for walking, for painting and for music, and so on through the list. A recent authority (Sheldon, Student Life and Custom, p. 218) gives the membership in college fraternities as about 150,000. They own club houses. They publish papers, and in some colleges they are a dominant factor in college life. The discussion of college fraternities has divided faculties, has forced the resignation of presidents, and has nearly wrecked one university. It is not a topic that can be disposed of offhand or briefly, and the disposition of it will not be attempted here.

College societies fall, for our purpose, into two classes,—the open and the secret. In spite of the approval of the former and the severe condemnation of the latter, it seems to me that the former are not all good, nor the latter all bad. Any agency that will supplement the college curriculum, or enrich the college life, that will give a home to the homeless student and a welcome to the graduate, is useful, whether it is open or secret in its organization. And any society that impairs the effect of good instruction, or cultivates caddishness and an undemocratic spirit among students, or that, by alliances with others, interferes improperly in elections and college social life, is a detriment, whether it has a Greek name spelled with English letters or with Greek initials only. That it is secret or open has very little to do with its usefulness. What I do regret, and what seems amazing to me, is that, in spite of the work of education in schools and colleges, there can be found a vast number of students who prefer the babyishness of tuppenny "secrets" as a part of their social life, and that thousands of educated men can tolerate the claptrap in secret societies incident to the use of oaths, signs, grips, and passwords that might be expected in the dark ages or among Bushmen.

There are two Greek-letter fraternities whose members are confined to law students and law school graduates,—the Delta Chi, and the Phi Delta Phi. There may be others, but I do not know of them. It seems to me that the most useful way for me to treat this subject is to say something about the Phi Delta Phi association, of which I am a member, and something about its influence, so far as I have seen it here and in other law schools.

Phi Delta Phi was organized in 1869. It is not a secret society, except as to its name, grip, and passwords, and it might well dispense with secrecy even as to those details. The preamble to its constitution reads as follows: "We, the undersigned students of the Law Department of the University of Michigan, in order to promote a higher standard of professional ethics and culture in this and other law schools and in the profession at large, and desiring to unite ourselves in the endearing bonds of affection and brotherly love, for the purpose of compassing these ends do associate ourselves into a fraternity to be known as the Phi Delta Phi." This is not an unworthy object, and, if consummated, is a useful addition to law school work. It also extends beyond the law schools into professional life. During the past thirty-three years more than thirty chapters have been added to the association in a corresponding number of the best law schools. There are not far from three hundred and fifty active members annually, and there are more than six thousand graduate members. Who will say that such a number of students, well chosen, and loyal to the purpose of the society, may not be an important factor in our law schools? And what may be true of this society should be true of similar legal fraternities.

However enthusiastic and well-meaning the founders of a society may be, unless they are particular in their successors they are not likely to have a permanent influence. Nor are their successors likely to carry out the ideas of the founders unless the machinery therefor is suited to the ends. And, if other chapters be organized, there is a considerable danger that the intensity of the influence of the parent chapter will decrease with the distance from it. This is certainly true of the ordinary college fraternity. There is as much variety among the different chapters as there is between different fraternities. One chapter may make scholarship the test for admission, another chapter of the same fraternity in another college may make a record in athletics the standard. I have heard of a fraternity from one chapter of which a member was expelled for getting drunk, whereat a member of the same fraternity in another college said a member would be expelled from his chapter who didn't get drunk.

What method has the Phi Delta Phi taken to perpetuate the declared object of its founders, and how has it safeguarded this in connection with other chapters in other institutions? It has done this, first, by a provision as to the admission of members: "No persons shall be admitted to the fraternity save by a unanimous vote of all the active members of an undergraduate chapter." Certainly this provision cannot be said to err on the side of undue laxness. My own opinion is that it would be better to elect some number, say ten new members, in this way, and then for these unanimously to elect their associates. The law school fraternity cuts horizontally across the other college fraternities as well as the nonfraternity student body, and the unanimity rule will tend to prevent any one society predominating in the law society. Of course, a few members can block the voting, but, as a rule, this rarely happens, and I think the provision has worked well at Michigan and in other institutions. At the University of Michigan, when I was there, the membership was made up of a very even selection from all the fraternities and from the nonfraternity students. Again: "Members may be expelled by a four-fifths vote of the entire chapter." A provision is also made for sending reports of the condition of the society to the central council. This seems to be all in the constitution regarding the matter, and probably it is wise not to overburden the fraternity with regulations. Certainly the chapter at Michigan is a credit to the fraternity and a useful adjunct to the law school.

With regard to the formation of other chapters, the requirements seem likely to result in high standards in new chapters. The fraternity magazine is advocating that petitioners "should show three things: (1) University connection of petitioner's law school; (2) a three-year law course; and (3) a year's lease of club rooms." It is not infrequent for a petition to be rejected, and applications are more stringently regarded than ever.

The internal management of each chapter is a matter of much consequence, and the following chapter program taken from Vol. 3, page 439, of The Brief, the fraternity publication, is quoted as the second influence tending to carry out the objects of the founders: "Chapter effort should in the main be directed along the following lines, and in the following order: (1) Pick out the strongest men of the entering class for the first initiation. Select men for personal worth, rather than for fit of clothes or papa's rating. (2)

Lease chapter rooms, and get them convenient, comfortable, and not too expensive. (4) Weekly meetings should be held for quizzes, reviews of class work, etc. In those schools where practice in moot court work is not given, take up such work at these meetings. (5) Hold a somewhat more pretentious monthly meeting during each month of the college year. The social element may well enter into such meetings. There should be a good dinner. As many of the faculty as possible should be present; and invite to it the alumni, faculty, and prominent members of the local bar. Hops, 'at homes,' and social functions can be given, according to the nature and disposition of the various chapters; but these should be subordinated to the legal work. Use the prescribed form at the initiations. Don't indulge in 'horse play.' * * * Finally run the chapter's finances in such a way that your successors will not be obliged to shoulder a deficit." It is submitted that this is good advice; that it suggests a dignified course of procedure, in which the predominant thought is legal work, with an opportunity for sociability and companionship. It would be difficult to get a fraternity composed of Choates and Websters, but a fraternity made up of the better element in a law school, which element is usually well meaning, and all the better for a fair amount of relaxation, cannot help but be benefited by association with such aims, nor fail to be a salutary influence in the school as a whole. Another feature of the fraternity is the relation of the faculty of the law school to the chapter of the fraternity in the school. The deans of twenty-two law schools are members of the fraternity, and from the last annual letter from the parent chapter it appears that fourteen members of the faculty of the University of Michigan law school are members of the fraternity, and generally throughout the country the faculty are members of the fraternity. This personal relation of the members of the faculty to the association, although they are not allowed an active voice in its management, nor to vote, ought to have a useful influence; and, so far as my experience goes, the students are most cordial in their treatment and considerate of opinions and advice from the faculty members.

The tendency of any fraternity is to be colored by local influences. This can be counteracted by intercourse with other chapters and by the restraining influence of some central authority. The central authority may be permanent in the form of a council, or occasional in the form of a convention. Both are provided for in the constitution of the fraternity, and are the third influence tending to maintain the original purpose of the organizers. The fraternities may be kept in touch with one another best of all by way of some publication. That is provided for in this fraternity by a quarterly publication called "The Brief." It is no more than fitting to say that its editorial work is excellent; that it not only provides admirable leading articles, but by way of reports from all chapters keeps each in touch with the other, and is a distinctly stimulating force in the fraternity. The Brief is a credit to its editor, and should be highly esteemed by every member of the fraternity.

What evidence is there that this fraternity is actually living up to its original purpose?

One department of The Brief is devoted to "Chapter News," and I will quote from the last number: "Mr. Wollman read a carefully prepared paper on the Trust problem." "Judge Mayer outlined the history and work of the New York City criminal court, special sessions." "Judge Delahanty took as his subject the crowded condition of the court calendars." (Feb. Meeting, N.Y. City Phi Delta Phi Club.) "Delay in the administration of law in New York was the topic of the evening's discussion." (March meeting.) The April meeting was occupied with addresses by distinguished lawyers and judges on the administration of criminal law in New York City. "The members of the club sat down to a quiet social dinner, where acquaintances could be made, and where plans for the club's work in the fall were discussed." (May meeting.) The Washington Phi Delta Phi Club reports that it attended the laying the foundation stone of the Marshall Memorial. "Prof. Maynard Daggy read a very interesting paper entitled 'Some Eloquent Lawyers.'" (Harlan Chapter.) "We had the pleasure of listening to a most interesting and instructive address by Professor E. D. Jones on 'Commerical Development, and Its Influence on the Legal Profession.'" (Kent Chapter.) To these could be added reports of dinners and smokers, and of admissions of weakness and efforts to improve. But, generally, the impression from reading the letters is that the fraternity is a living organization, and fulfilling its purpose. It is not claimed that this or any legal fraternity is perfect. But it is probable that their members are average students, with good purposes. Another element of strength of the organization is the character of its members. Many of them are college graduates; and the maturity of their judgment is likely to counteract some of the tendencies of undergraduate life. And, so far as my observation has gone, the members are loyal to the fraternity, and, on the whole, I believe it is a salutary influence in a law school.

I have used the Phi Delta Phi fraternity as a type, and without meaning to disparage any other fraternity, nor to imply that there are not others equally good, if not better, and because a concrete illustration may be of service in meeting the objections that are made to Greek-letter societies.

Chapter 68

Not Only the Judges' Robes Were Black

African-American Lawyers as Social Engineers

1994

Paul Finkelman

Paul Finkelman is John Seiberling Chair in Constitutional Law at the University of Akron School of Law. This review essay of J. Clay Smith, Jr., *Emancipation: The Making of the Black Lawyer, 1844-1944* (Philadelphia: University of Pennsylvania Press, 1993) was first published at 41 *Stanford Law Review* 161 (1994).

Department of History, Virginia Polytechnic Institute and State University. B.A., 1971, Syracuse University; M.A., 1972, Ph.D., 1976, University of Chicago; Fellow in Law and History, 1982-83, Harvard Law School. I thank Richard Aynes, Hayward Farrar, John Hope Franklin, Tom Green, Jeremy Harrison, James and Lois Horton, Beryl Jones, Allison Lindsey, Jenni Parrish, Judith Schafer, and Peter Wallenstein for their conversations and comments about this essay. I also thank the William S. Richardson School of Law at the University of Hawaii for providing office space and research facilities for me while I worked on this article.

When he was in the eighth grade, Malcolm Little thought he might like to be a lawyer. His white teacher had other ideas.

> Malcolm, one of life's first needs is for us to be realistic. Don't misunderstand me, now. We all here like you, you know that. But you've got to be realistic about being a nigger. A lawyer—that's no realistic goal for a nigger. You need to think about something you can be. . . . Why don't you plan on carpentry?[1]

It is too bad that Malcolm Little's teacher did not know what J. Clay Smith, Jr., teaches us in *Emancipation: The Making of the Black Lawyer, 1844-1944*. If he had, he might have given a different answer to his young student, and we can only imagine what kind of lawyer Malcolm X would have made.

Today, of course, no one doubts that there is room at the bar and on the bench for African-Americans.[2] During the past two decades the number of black law students, lawyers, judges, and law professors has grown steadily.[3] While their representation in the legal profession falls far short of their percentage in American society, African-American lawyers are no longer rarities, found only here and there, to the surprise of most observers.

In *Emancipation*, Smith, former dean of the Howard Law School, recalls an earlier era, when black lawyers were unknown in most of the nation. Smith's book represents the first study undertaken to chart the history of blacks in the legal profession from before the Civil War to World War II, just before the beginning of the modern civil rights movement.

Smith has uncovered the first black men and women lawyers in most states, the first black students at Ivy League law schools and on law reviews, the first black judges and prosecutors, and one of the first blacks to write serious legal scholarship.[4] He chronicles the history of the first black admitted to practice before the United States Supreme Court[5] and the first to argue a case before that Court.[6] He shows us black lawyers flourishing in places where few African-Americans lived and black lawyers struggling against segregation in the deep South. This book is an unparalleled treasure trove of information. Smith has painstakingly tracked down, state-by-state, hundreds of black lawyers who practiced between 1844 and 1944. *Emancipation* is a veritable encyclopedia of the accomplishments of African-Americans, most of whom found success in the face of incredible adversity. The sheer amount of information that Smith presents can be numbing, but the cumulative effect of his research is impressive and instructive. This important book will doubtless became an indispensable source for all scholars of race relations, African-American history, and the history of the legal profession.

33. Thurgood Marshall (1908-1993). As a prominent litigator in the twentieth-century campaigns for civil rights and as a justice of the U.S. Supreme Court, Marshall lived the words of his dean at Howard, Charles Hamilton Houston: "A lawyer's either a social engineer or . . . a parasite on society." (*José R. Lopez/New York Times Co./Archive Photos.*)

Given the obstacles that confronted these first lawyers, some of Smith's findings are truly counterintuitive. Smith writes of all-black firms and black solo practitioners representing white clients in the late nineteenth and early twentieth centuries and of black lawyers working in predominantly white firms long before civil rights legislation and affirmative action programs led some firms to open their doors to nonwhites. Many of these black lawyers carved out successful practices in places where virtually no other blacks lived. For example, Thomas McCants Stewart moved in 1898 from New York to Hawaii, where he became active in municipal government and later argued five cases before the United States District Court for the Territory of Hawaii.[7] Similarly, John D. Posten practiced law in Lincoln County, Montana, from 1890 to 1924 while also serving as a census taker and a commissioner of the United States District Court. Throughout this period, according to the census, he was the only black in the county.[8]

Smith has found black lawyers who achieved surprising success in the South during the high tide of racial segregation, the period between 1900 and 1940.[9] Thomas Gillis Nutter, for example, served in the West Virginia state legislature in 1918 and 1919, in an era when there were virtually no black officeholders in the South.[10] Twenty years later, he represented white business interests in a land dispute worth $12 million.[11] In 1929, the American Bar Association admitted Nutter, despite the organization's ban on black members. Smith speculates that "it is not likely that the association was aware that he was black."[12] Similarly, Scipio Africanus Jones, who became a lawyer in Arkansas in 1889, "a time when the Negro lawyer was a strange creature,"[13] served as a special judge in 1915, presiding over the prosecution of a black accused of harming other blacks.[14] A decade later Jones won election as chancellor of the Pulaski County Court and later served on the County's Legal Advisory Board.[15]

Lawyers like McCants, Posten, Nutter, and Jones were unusual men in unlikely places. Although each individual lawyer might have been considered an anomaly, Smith's mammoth study shows how these lawyers helped break down racial barriers. The emergence of black lawyers also undermined several gender barriers. According to Smith, some of the first female law students in the nation were African-Americans,[16] as was the first woman law professor, Lutie A. Lytle.[17] In 1897, Lytle gained admission to the Tennessee and Kansas bars.[18] As a professor at Central Tennessee College of Law, she was the first woman law professor—black or white—in the United States and probably in the Anglo-American world.[19] Howard Law School, which has produced more black attorneys than any other law school in the country,[20] was a pioneer in the battle against gender discrimination in legal education. Between 1872 and 1904, at least eight black women and seven white women graduated from the "black" Howard Law School, which, in 1869, became the first law school in the nation to establish an admissions policy that did not discriminate on the basis of race or gender.[21] In the early twentieth century, a number of white law schools began to admit women, and consequently white women ceased to attend Howard.[22] However, Howard remained the most plausible destination for African-American women seeking a law degree, and at least twenty graduated from the law school between 1900 the end of World War II.[23]

Smith chronicles the history of many previously unknown blacks who struggled to become lawyers. They developed diverse practices, and their careers took them down divergent paths, but for most there was a common thread: They overcame prejudice and discrimination in building their practices and, in so doing, they inevitably aided in the struggle for racial equality.

The stories of these early black attorneys collectively illustrate the complexity of American race relations. The enormous amount of information in Smith's book allows us to see that nearly every black attorney in those early years became a de facto advocate for social change. Throughout the century covered by this book, 1844-1944, the United States Constitution held African-Americans in a subordinated and precarious status. At the beginning of this period, slavery was legal in half the United States, and nearly 90 percent of African-Americans were held in bondage.[24] At the end of the period, 1944, racial discrimination was still constitutionally permitted, and the overwhelming majority of American blacks lived in states that mandated racial segregation in schools, public accommodations, and other areas of life.[25] It is this ongoing context of social and legal oppression that makes the story of pioneering black attorneys so significant to our nation's history and self-definition. But in order to fully appreciate this story we must also understand the history of the many firsts achieved by our nation's earliest black lawyers.

I. The Black Lawyer and Social Change in the 1920s and Beyond

In 1929, Charles Hamilton Houston began rebuilding Howard University School of Law into a powerhouse training ground for black lawyers.[26] At this time, a few blacks were studying at predominantly white law schools in the North.[27] Houston himself had attended Harvard, where he was the first black to serve on the *Harvard Law Review*.[28] Between 1890 and 1934, a smattering of other blacks gained election to the Order of the Coif,[29] graduated with honors,[30] gave class orations,[31] or earned advanced law degrees

(LL.M. and S.J.D.) at such law schools as Harvard University, Yale University, University of Pennsylvania, New York University, University of Michigan, University of Chicago, Boalt Hall, University of Pittsburgh, Iowa University, Ohio State University, University of Cincinnati, Cornell University, University of Colorado, and Boston University.[32] In 1921, three men simultaneously became the first African-Americans to serve on law reviews: Jasper Alston Atkins (Yale), Charles Hamilton Houston (Harvard), and William Edwin Taylor (Iowa).[33] In 1924, Clara Burrill Bruce became the first African-American woman on a law review (Boston University). In 1925, she became the first black editor-in-chief.[34] In 1926, two black students served simultaneously on the *University of Pennsylvania Law Review*, while William Henry Hastie joined the *Harvard Law Review* in 1928, and William Robert Ming, Jr. "became a member of and published in the inaugural issue of the *University of Chicago Law Review* in 1933."[35]

The arrival of blacks on law reviews was more than just a symbolic victory against discrimination. It also led to publication of student notes and articles chosen by students that raised questions about racial inequality. In Volume 1 of the *University of Chicago Law Review*, William Ming published his article *Constitutional Law—Validity of Party Resolution Depriving Negro Rights to Vote in Party Primary.*[36]

Despite the academic success at elite law schools of these, and a few other African-Americans, for most blacks, white schools were too expensive and too difficult to get into. In an age when many private universities maintained official or unofficial quotas on how many blacks, Jews, and other minorities could enter their doors, there simply was not enough space for blacks.[37] Most of the elite Universities allowed only a limited number of blacks in their graduate and professional programs. The great African-American historian John Hope Franklin recalled that when he was studying for his Ph.D. in the 1930s:

> There were few blacks at Harvard in those days. One was completing his work in French history as I entered. As in Noah's Ark, there were two in the law school, two in zoology, and two in the college. There was one in English and one in comparative literature; there were none in the Medical School and none in the Business School.[38]

Like the Harvard medical and business schools in 1939, many law schools set the quota for blacks at zero. Thirty-four of the eighty-eight accredited law schools had policies excluding blacks.[39] Thus, for many blacks, Howard represented their best and often their only hope for receiving a legal education.[40] After becoming Resident Vice-Dean in 1929, Charles Hamilton Houston brought a missionary zeal to his task of turning Howard into a first-rate law school and the major center for the training of black lawyers. His former student Oliver W. Hill, who later became the leading civil rights lawyer in Virginia, recalled that Houston "was a tough disciplinarian,"[41] while his Howard Law School colleague William H. Hastie remembered Houston as an "unremitting task master."[42] Moreover, "[h]e kept hammering at us all those years that, as lawyers, we had to be social engineers or else we were parasites."[43]

Houston succeeded in rebuilding the school and training many effective social engineers. Under his direction, Howard gained full accreditation from the American Bar Association and full membership in the Association of American Law Schools.[44] He lengthened the academic year, reorganized the curriculum, and raised admissions standards.[45] His handpicked faculty included William Henry Hastie, Jr., who later became the first black federal judge.[46] Spottswood William Robinson III, who became a student shortly after Houston left the law school to become special counsel to the NAACP, also became a Howard professor and later a federal judge.[47] William Benson Bryant, who began studying at Howard in 1933, became the first black chief judge of the United States District Court for Washington, D.C.[48] Oliver W. Hill, class of 1933, eventually became the first black member of the Richmond City Council in the twentieth century and the leading civil rights attorney in Virginia.[49] Hill's classmate and lifelong friend, and Howard's most successful graduate was Thurgood Marshall.[50] Long after he had won the *Brown* case[51] and been appointed to the Supreme Court, Justice Marshall claimed that Houston "was the engineer of all of it" and that "if you do it [civil rights] legally, Charlie Houston made it possible."[52]

The importance of these midcentury black lawyers is well known and well documented.[53] Beginning in the 1930s, and taking off in the mid-1940s, black attorneys—many of whom taught or studied at Howard—took the lead in challenging and defeating segregation in the courts.[54] Houston himself pioneered this effort in *Hollins v. Oklahoma*,[55] the first Supreme Court victory by a black attorney representing the NAACP.[56]

Well before Charles Hamilton Houston and his colleagues at Howard began to implement the idea of training black lawyers to become social activists in the 1930s, many black lawyers had already self-consciously played the role of social engineers. Indeed, virtually every black attorney instigated a small social revolution merely by becoming a lawyer or walking into a courtroom. To understand why this was so, we must begin by examining a time when the number of black lawyers in America could be counted on two hands, with fingers left over, and when their own status under the United States Constitution was uncertain.

II. Black Lawyers Practicing Law When They "Had No Rights"[57]

In 1857, in *Dred Scott v. Sandford*,[58] Chief Justice Roger B. Taney explored whether blacks could ever be citizens of the United States and, as such, have the right to sue in a federal court under diversity jurisdiction. Chief Justice Taney wrote:

> The question is simply this: Can a negro, whose ancestors were imported into this country, and sold as slaves, become a member of the political community formed and brought into existence by the Constitution of the United States, and as such become entitled to all the rights, and privileges, and immunities, guarantied by that instrument to the citizen? One of which rights is the privilege of suing in a court of the United States in the cases specified in the Constitution.[59]

Did blacks "compose a portion of" the people of the United States and were they thus "constituent members of this sovereignty"?[60] Chief Justice Taney's answer was blunt:

> We think they are not, and that they are not included, and were not intended to be included, under the word "citizens" in the Constitution, and can therefore claim none of the rights and privileges which that instrument provides for and secures to citizens of the United States. On the contrary, they were at that time considered as a subordinate and inferior class of beings, who had been subjugated by the dominant race, and, whether emancipated or not, yet remained subject to their authority, and had no rights or privileges but such as those who held the power and the Government might choose to grant them.[61]

In language that has become infamous, Chief Justice Taney argued that at the time of the American founding blacks were

> regarded as beings of an inferior order, and altogether unfit to associate with the white race, either in social or political relations; and so far inferior, that they had no rights which the white man was bound to respect; and that the negro might justly and lawfully be reduced to slavery for his benefit.[62]

The Chief Justice carefully couched his "no rights" phrase in historical terms, but the implications were clear. Because blacks "had no rights" in 1787, they could claim no rights in 1857, and presumably never could.

Chief Justice Taney, a profoundly racist proslavery ideologue, hoped that a single decision giving the South a decisive victory in the sectional debate would settle the problem of slavery in the territories and in American politics.[63] Such goals help explain his sweeping and controversial decision. Yet even the Chief Justice's political motivation and overt racism did not require that he completely read blacks out of the American legal system, reducing all free blacks to people with "no rights." Why, then, did he take such an extreme position—extreme even by the standards of 1857? There is strong evidence that the preservation of the racial status quo was an intensely *personal* goal of Chief Justice Taney's. As Don E. Fehrenbacher explained:

> What needs to be emphasized . . . is that [Taney's] *Dred Scott* opinion was written with an emotional commitment so intense that it made . . . logic utterly subservient. . . . [T]he opinion was essentially visceral in origin—that law and history were distorted to serve a passionate purpose. Taney's real commitment . . . was not to slavery itself, for which he had no great affection, but rather to southern life and values, which seemed organically linked to the peculiar institution and unpreservable without it.[64]

But the desire to eliminate all black rights cannot be attributed only to Taney's personal animus, extreme as it was. The Chief Justice's opinion reflected the racism and recalcitrance that pervaded the South. An important aspect of the fears of whites such as Chief Justice Taney arose from the changing status of free blacks in the North. By 1857, the bars of Maine, Massachusetts, New York, and Ohio had been admitting black lawyers for more than a decade.[65] While few in numbers, their participation in the legal system threatened the racial hierarchy Taney and many of his contemporaries held dear and symbolically undermined America's racial status quo. Chief Justice Taney's opinion can be seen as a reaction to the slow yet significant advances of free blacks; advances in which black lawyers formed part of the vanguard.

III. The Emergence of Black Lawyers in the Antebellum North

At the time of the *Dred Scott* decision, some 200,000 blacks lived in the free states of the North,[66] where their rights varied greatly from state to state and within each state.[67] In some places, they could vote,[68] attend public schools with whites,[69] and even intermarry with whites.[70] Even where blacks lacked all of these rights, they possessed most or all of the same fundamental economic rights as whites. They could own property, sign contracts, and generally seek employment in virtually any profession or trade they wished.[71] For example, on the eve of the Civil War, the free black population of Philadelphia owned real property valued at more than $2.5 million.[72] While some of the nearly 250,000 free blacks living in the South also owned substantial property,[73] they were legally barred from many professions, prohibited from getting an education in most places, and always restricted in their movements and other rights.[74] By contrast, in the North, by the mid-1850s, there were black ministers,[75] school teachers,[76] newspaper publishers, journalists, printers,[77] gunsmiths,[78] dentists, doctors,[79] and—perhaps most important for the future of civil rights—lawyers.[80]

Macon Bolling Allen became the first black lawyer in America when the Maine Bar admitted him in 1844.[81] In addition to Allen, who was also admitted in Massachusetts,[82] at least four other blacks were admitted to practice before 1857.[83] Among his many valuable contributions in *Emancipation*, Smith resurrects these early black lawyers.[84] Their history—indeed their very existence—will surprise many lawyers, legal academics, and historians. Chief Justice Taney may not have been surprised, but he was surely appalled and concerned by the existence of black lawyers. He also surely knew it was inevitable that one of these black attorneys would eventually enter a federal court on behalf of a client. Such an occurrence would shake to the core the edifice of white supremacy and proslavery constitutionalism.[85]

Black lawyers threatened in many ways the proslavery establishment that dominated antebellum American politics and law.[86] First, they symbolically threatened the established order of white supremacy. For example, in 1857, the year of *Dred Scott*, Edward Garrison Draper, a free black, applied for admission to the bar of Maryland, Chief Justice Taney's home state. The Maryland bar refused to admit Draper, even though he was found qualified in all respects except for his race.[87] Despite its huge free black population,[88] Maryland, a slave state, could not breach what Judge A. Leon Higginbotham calls the "cultural symbolism" of racial exclusion in the courtroom without undermining both the subordination of blacks and the existence of slavery within the state.[89] Nevertheless, the fact that a black even tried to gain admission to legal practice in a slave state foreshadowed the emerging threat to the ideology of white supremacy and to the southern way of life.

African-American attorneys also undermined slavery because they gave free blacks, fugitive slaves, and perhaps Southern slaves a voice that they never before had. If black attorneys could represent clients in federal courts in the North, they might also seek similar access to southern federal courts, Southern state courts, or even the United States Supreme Court. Eventually, some black lawyer might run for Congress, and some abolitionized district might actually have the votes to elect such a person. After all, by 1857, black lawyers had held office in Ohio and Massachusetts, and run unsuccessfully for office in New York.[90] In *Dred Scott* Chief Justice Taney effectively headed off such a grim and dangerous future for the South and the federal courts.[91] If blacks "had no rights" under the Constitution, then they could not appear in federal courts or in any other federal venue, regardless of their status in some Northern states.[92]

A. Massachusetts: The Emergence of the Black Lawyer Activist

In 1857, it seemed likely that black attorneys would soon disrupt the pristine whiteness of the federal courts. Perhaps it would have been in the United States District Court in Maine where, in 1837, Judge Asher Ware had allowed a black to sue a white and testify against him in an admiralty case.[93] Moreover, Maine was the first state to admit a black lawyer to its bar. In 1844, Macon Bolling Allen, a native of Indiana, moved to Maine where General Samuel Fessenden, the most prominent lawyer in the state and an ardent abolitionist, successfully sponsored him before the Maine bar.[94]

In theory, the people of Maine had the kind of antislavery principles and racial tolerance that might have supported a successful black attorney and even permitted him to litigate in a federal court. However, as the saga of Macon Allen illustrates, it was extremely difficult for black attorneys to find clients outside a strong and supportive black community, notwithstanding the encouragement and occasional financial patronage of principled whites. As a result, Allen, Maine's only black lawyer, moved to Massachusetts, a state with a larger black population and potential client base. Massachusetts provided more than just fertile ground for a young black lawyer looking for a practice. It also provided an atmosphere of equality that allowed black lawyers to challenge prevailing notions of race relations at the local, state, and eventually the federal level. In the decade before *Dred Scott*, Allen and a second black lawyer in Massachusetts, Robert Morris,[95] had already begun the legal assault on the color barrier in the American courtroom. Their uphill fight to enter the courtroom as lawyers surely threatened the world that Chief Justice Taney wanted to preserve: a world in which blacks would have no rights.

In 1847, Governor George N. Briggs, a Massachusetts Whig with antislavery leanings, appointed Allen a justice of the peace.[96] As Smith notes, this made Allen "the first black lawyer in the history of the nation to be appointed to a judicial post."[97] But being first was not Allen's most significant contribution. As with so many of the "firsts" that Smith catalogs, even more significant than the fact of primacy is the context in which a "first" occurred. Allen became a justice of the peace at the very time when the South, the federal courts, and Congress were limiting the legal rights and protections available to free blacks.[98] Allen's new status directly flew in the face of this racist trend.

While Allen was pioneering as a judge and officeholder, Robert Morris was playing a similar role in the state courts. Morris began his legal career as a "copyer" for the Boston abolitionist attorney Ellis Gray Loring.[99] He passed the Massachusetts bar in 1847, shortly after his twenty-first birthday. In his first case he won a judgment for "services rendered" for a black plaintiff, [100] thus laying the groundwork for his involvement in the struggle to integrate Boston's schools.

In 1840, black and white abolitionists in Boston petitioned the school board to integrate the city's schools, but the Board ignored them.[101] Four years later, another group petitioned the school board on this issue, but the Board rejected their petition without written explanation.[102] In 1846 this group again asked the board to end segregation in the schools. This time the board acknowledged the petitioners, only to reject their request,[103] despite the dissents of two anti-slavery members.[104]

In the face of these failures, Benjamin F. Roberts, the father of five-year old Sarah Roberts, retained Morris in a suit over Sarah's right to attend the school nearest her home. According to Smith's account, which offers new information on the case, Roberts filed the initial lawsuit in 1848.[105] In 1849 the case—the nation's first challenging school segregation—went to the Massachusetts Supreme Judicial Court as *Roberts v. City of Boston.*[106] Although he had initiated the case, Morris deferred in oral argument to his co-counsel, the more experienced, better trained, and politically connected Charles Sumner.[107] Taking the case pro bono, Sumner made what turned out to be a prescient argument against segregation. In his brief, which was published and widely circulated as a pamphlet,[108] Sumner outlined an argument against segregation that, with only a few changes and some new social science data, would prevail nearly a century later in *Brown v. Board of Education.*[109] Sumner even discussed the psychological damage of segregation, despite the absence of developed techniques for measuring that harm in 1849.[110]

Notwithstanding his brilliant argument, Sumner lost the case. Chief Justice Lemuel Shaw ruled that separate but equal facilities were not inconsistent with the Massachusetts Constitution.[111] Nearly half a century later, the United States Supreme Court would use Shaw's opinion to help justify its own support for segregation in *Plessy v. Ferguson.*[112] Although the desegregation supporters in Boston lost the battle, they soon won the war. In 1855 the Massachusetts legislature prohibited segregation in the state's public schools.[113]

Despite the negative outcome in *Roberts v. Boston*, Robert Morris had made his mark as the first black attorney to appear before any state's highest court. Although there is no indication that he addressed the court, the official report of the case lists him as an attorney of record. After *Roberts*, it would seem only a matter of time before Morris or another black attorney would attempt to practice before a federal court.

In 1851, Morris almost broke the color line in the federal courts. Ultimately, however, he wound up as a defendant, rather than as an attorney of record. In February of that year, federal marshals seized a black waiter known as Shadrach and brought him before United States Commissioner George T. Curtis under the Fugitive Slave Law of 1850.[114] Several attorneys, including Morris, immediately offered to represent Shadrach. Morris was apparently the first lawyer to formally petition Commissioner Curtis for an extension of time so that Shadrach could mount a defense.[115] When the hearing on this petition began, four white abolitionist attorneys, but not Morris, represented Shadrach.[116] However, spectators observed Morris sitting and talking with the attorneys of record.[117] If the hearing had continued, he probably would have become a formal part of the defense team, thus breaching the wall of segregation in at least one federal courtroom. Although he would have argued before a United States commissioner at a rendition hearing, rather than before a full-fledged United States District Court judge, the symbolic meaning of a black lawyer defending another black in a federal courtroom would have been clear. While Morris never got the chance to defend Shadrach in court, he was instrumental in obtaining Shadrach's freedom. Commissioner Curtis granted the request for a delay, and the marshal ordered the courtroom cleared. At this point, someone—most probably Morris—opened the door to the courtroom, and a mob of blacks stormed in. They grabbed Shadrach and whisked him from the scene before the startled and outnumbered court officers could act. Shadrach quickly fled to Canada.[118]

Federal authorities later sought treason indictments against Morris, alleging that he helped plan the rescue and opened the door to let Shadrach escape. However, the federal grand jury in Boston only indicted him for a misdemeanor.[119] After two trials, a jury acquitted Morris.[120] By the end of the case, Morris had spent a great deal of time in federal court, but not as an attorney. In his own case, two white antislavery lawyers, Richard Henry Dana, Jr., and United States Senator John P. Hale of New Hampshire, represented him.

Morris' early career illustrates the challenge he and other black lawyers posed to the views of Taney and other proponents of a lily-white judicial system. By the time Morris was twenty-five years old, he had appeared before the highest state court in Massachusetts and had filed papers with a United States commissioner. Soon, he would have requested admission to practice in the federal courts, a development which would have severely undermined the premises of *Dred Scott*. If blacks had any rights, then surely the free black members of the bar in Massachusetts, Maine, New York, and Ohio had the right to argue cases in the federal courts and ultimately in the United States Supreme Court. Chief Justice Taney's extreme position in *Dred Scott* helped delay that eventuality until after Taney's death in 1864.

B. Robert Morris as a Prototype Social Engineer

Pioneering black lawyers were, by definition, social engineers. Their very presence in courtrooms altered the way whites and blacks viewed race relations. The experiences of Robert Morris bear this out in several ways. Morris' involvement in the *Roberts* case is an example of the social engineering Charles Hamilton Houston had in mind when he urged his students not to become "parasites."[121] Of course, *Roberts* might well have gone forward without Morris or any other black lawyer in Boston. There were many white abolitionist lawyers in the city who would have proudly taken the case. Moreover, the leader of the school integration movement, a black journalist named William C. Nell, was an ardent integrationist and a close associate of such white abolitionists as William Lloyd Garrison and Wendell Phillips.[122] Nell, a brilliant speaker, organizer, and activist, surely could have found white attorneys willing to initiate this and similar suits.

In fact, the Boston black community honored Nell, not Morris, after the legislature finally prohibited segregated education.[123] However, despite his ultimate status as hero in this enterprise, Nell's "extreme dedication to integration might have caused some ambivalence among the black masses of the city."[124] Thus, at the grass roots level, a black attorney like Morris was probably critical to the case.

Smith's discussion of Morris' role in the *Roberts* case, and indeed, much of the rest of his book, confirms Mark Tushnet's findings that successful civil rights litigation requires a community base and grass roots support.[125] In the *Roberts* case, for example, Benjamin Roberts and his black allies went first to Morris, not to a white attorney, when they were ready to litigate the case.[126] Similarly, in the Shadrach case, Morris' race may have been a critical factor in how the events unfolded. While any of Shadrach's lawyers could have filed a petition seeking a delay in the proceeding, Morris provided the vital link between the attorneys and the black community. It appears that he discussed the case with members of the black community, which led to Shadrach's quick rescue.[127] As the connection between the community and the courtroom, Morris might just as easily have served as part of the defense team if the case had gone to trial. Indeed, it is quite possible that Shadrach would have had greater trust and confidence in his lawyers precisely because one of them was black.[128]

IV. The Complexities of Social Engineering

During the 1930s, some of Charles Hamilton Houston's students, such as Thurgood Marshall, became full-time social engineers, through their affiliation with civil rights groups like the NAACP. But most lawyers—even black abolitionist lawyers in antebellum Boston—did not consistently have high-profile cases with political and civil rights overtones. To fill their plates at home, they needed paying clients in the office, so Robert Morris and most of the other attorneys that Smith writes about took cases that would provide a steady income while serving clients.

Emancipation illustrates that for most black lawyers in practice before 1944, there was no clear distinction between the roles of "social engineer" and a traditional lawyer. While Smith does not stress this theme, the facts speak for themselves. For most of our early history, black lawyers ushered in many types of social change merely by doing their jobs well. First, merely by becoming lawyers, blacks changed the social landscape of America. For the century Smith covers, the number of black lawyers was so small that any black admitted to the bar became living proof of the possibility of black accomplishment and success. Second, by simply opening a practice, black lawyers made legal services available to black clients who otherwise would have had no access to them. Black lawyers serving black clients improved the quality of life for African-Americans, particularly those living in the segregated South of the twentieth century. Third, black lawyers undermined the pervasive psychology of racism. Every time a black lawyer won a case against a white lawyer or represented a white client, he or she exposed the fraud of white supremacy. Even in defeat, a black lawyer could demonstrate the competence of African-Americans to white judges, lawyers, jurors, and spectators who otherwise might have resisted notions of racial equality.[129] The mere presence of black lawyers—especially in the South—chipped away at segregation. Fourth, black lawyers served as leaders within the black community, using their skills and knowledge to move from the legal arena to political forums. Finally, the pioneering black lawyers about whom Smith writes could challenge the racial status quo in small ways, on a case-by-case basis, without necessarily taking on the self-conscious role of social engineer. Even though prisons and jails were segregated, and the jury boxes held only a sea of white faces, and separate bibles were used to swear black witnesses,[130] the black lawyers still sat where white lawyers traditionally sat and stood in the same place as white lawyers when addressing the court.[131] Indeed, by the late nineteenth century and well into the twentieth, the courtroom was one of the very few places in the South where blacks could stand toe-to-toe with whites without breaking written or unwritten laws of racial subordination.[132]

A. The Paucity of Black Lawyers

According to census figures,[133] in 1940 there were 176,475 white lawyers in the United States serving 118,214,870 whites, or one white lawyer for every 670 whites. That same year the census found 1,052 black lawyers serving a population of 12,865,518, or one black lawyer for every 12,230 blacks in the country.[134] This paucity of black lawyers was further exacerbated by their distribution. While about 80 percent of all blacks lived in the South at this time, two-thirds of black lawyers lived in the North.

For most of the period covered by *Emancipation*, Southern blacks were socially, economically, and politically disenfranchised. The one exception was during the Reconstruction, when blacks in parts of the South acquired a degree of political power and influence in the legal system as judges, prosecutors, and police officials.[135] A number of black lawyers practiced in the South during this period, as well. Some remained in the South for the rest of their careers, but after the end of the century the number of southern black lawyers precipitously declined.

Starting in the 1890s, white-dominated southern governments began to disenfranchise and segregate blacks as a backlash against the Civil War and the goals of the Reconstruction.[136] As blacks lost their newly acquired rights, black lawyers disappeared from the scene. For example, in 1900, Mississippi had twenty-four black lawyers, and South Carolina had twenty-nine.[137] A decade later Mississippi was down to twenty-one black lawyers and South Carolina had seventeen.[138] In 1920, both states had only fourteen black lawyers, and by 1930, Mississippi had only six black lawyers, and South Carolina had thirteen.[139] In 1940, there were just three blacks practicing law in Mississippi, and five in South Carolina.[140] It is striking that while black lawyers were disappearing from the South, the black population there was still growing. The black population in Mississippi rose from 908,000 in 1900 to 1,075,000 in 1940, and South Carolina's black population grew from 782,000 to 814,000 during the same period.[141]

This decline in the numbers of black lawyers in the deep South reflected broader trends in the rest of the South.[142] In 1930, for example, the seventeen southern states had a black population of 9,494,000, which was 80 percent of the total black population in the United States.[143] There were a total of 389 black lawyers in the South serving this population.[144] At the same time, there were 868 black lawyers in the rest of the nation, serving the other 20 percent of the black population.[145] By 1940, the number of southern black lawyers had declined to 289, while the number of black lawyers in the rest of the nation had dropped to 763.[146] The number of black lawyers in the South declined by approximately 25 percent, twice the rate of decline in the North.[147] While the overall decline in black lawyers was probably due to the Great Depression, the rate of the decline in the South was nevertheless staggering.

The huge decline in the number of black lawyers in the South was a result of segregation, racism, and violence, which discouraged black lawyers from settling there. In 1935, Charles Hamilton Houston complained that

> it has been extremely difficult to get the most promising law graduates to go South. Even students Southern born and bred are loathe to return. They point out that they have no future in the South in politics; little or no voice in determining the officials who administer the law. They are uniformly excluded from the benefits of membership in bar associations, and have little opportunity for professional improvement through free and equal association with their white members of the bar.[148]

Among the few who did go there, many left after a short time. Houston noted that "[t]he percentage of young graduates who get discouraged and give up the practice within the first five years is much higher in the South than in the North."[149]

In sum, the number of black lawyers in the North rose in the period from 1900 to 1930 and subsequently declined slightly over the next decade due to the Depression. In the South, however, with a vastly higher proportion of the nation's black population, the number of black attorneys steadily declined from 422 in 1900 to 289 by 1940. In the North, where a small fraction of the nation's black population lived, the number of African-American lawyers grew from 296 in 1900 to 763 by 1940.[150]

Because of their small numbers, virtually every black lawyer in the South was a crusader for social change. In offering legal services to African-Americans, black lawyers gave a disenfranchised group a modicum of power and protection. The problem, of course, was that there were far too few black lawyers to either provide adequate legal services to their community or to combat effectively Southern segregation and discrimination.

B. The Role of Legal Services for Southern Blacks

Although always too few, the small number of Southern black attorneys empowered African-Americans to protect some of their rights and property. Some Southern white attorneys were willing to represent blacks, especially if the case did not directly challenge the racial status quo. But, whenever Southern blacks confronted whites in a courtroom, it was an implicit challenge to the dominant racial regime. Even a simple lawsuit not involving segregation or race relations could rock the racial boat if, for example, a black witness, plaintiff, or defendant, contradicted or challenged the testimony of a white. In some instances, such as the 1934 murder trial of George Crawford, no white attorney would represent a black defendant.[151] Without black attorneys, such defendants probably would have gone to trial without the benefit of counsel, or with reluctant or inept counsel appointed by the court. This happened in the Scottsboro cases, when appointed white counsel simply did not provide an adequate defense.[152] A similar situation arose in the trial of three black tenant farmers who were accused in Mississippi of murdering a white planter. One of the appointed white defense attorneys "later admitted" that they "offered only an anemic defense" and "had been largely going through the motions of defending their clients."[153]

Given the history of justice towards blacks in the South, many, if not most, southern blacks felt less comfortable with their fortunes, freedom, or lives in the hands of white attorneys. White lawyers, who depended mostly on white clients, had a greater incentive than black lawyers to settle cases or simply not seriously fight them, since to do so might have undermined accepted racial norms.[154]

Although Robert Morris lived in the North, his career illustrates the political nature of any litigation involving a black client and a black lawyer. Such cases were not only legal arrangements, but powerful political symbols as well. In his first case, Morris represented a black man suing a white for "services rendered."[155] Morris later recalled that when the jury returned the favorable verdict, "My heart bounded up, and my people in the courtroom acted as if they would shout for joy."[156]

Although this case involved an economic victory for only a single black worker, it signaled the beginning of a new era for the black community of Boston—an era in which someone who understood them and looked like them could represent them in court. This case also underscored the strong connection between property rights and civil rights.

The tactics of a group of black attorneys in Tulsa, Oklahoma, demonstrated the importance of property rights in the larger struggle for black equality. After the 1921 Tulsa race riot, in which the black area of town was destroyed by fire and violence, white city officials attempted to replace the devastated black neighborhood with a railroad terminal and other industrial facilities.[157] As part of a 2-pronged attack, the mayor first directed the city commissioners to "'immediately get in touch with all the railroads with a view to establishing a Union station on this ground.'"[58] Second, the City Commission adopted an ordinance requiring all new buildings in the area to be fireproof. "The effect of the ordinance was to prevent some black Tulsans from rebuilding their burned homes where they had been"[159] because they could not afford to rebuild dwellings of two stories or more with the concrete, steel, or brick, required by the new ordinance.[160]

In response to this ordinance, Buck Colbert Franklin, a leading black attorney in Oklahoma, organized massive rebuilding in direct violation of the discriminatory city ordinance. Franklin urged his clients and other black citizens to erect any structures they could in order to stifle the ordinance and frustrate the efforts of the City Commission.[161] Concurrently, Franklin, working out of a makeshift law office in a tent, filed suit to overturn the city fire ordinance. In *Lockett v. City of Tulsa*, Franklin persuaded a three judge panel to strike down the ordinance as an uncompensated taking of private property.[162]

Without this combination of direct action, community organizing, and legal strategy, a large segment of the black community would probably have been forced out of Tulsa. It is unlikely that in the tense days following the riot any white attorney would have been willing to represent the needs and rights of the black community. Most Southern white lawyers readily accepted black clients for routine economic cases—property, tort, contract, debt, insurance—and minor criminal cases that did not threaten the South's system of racial hierarchy. It was virtually impossible, however, to find a Southern white lawyer who would accept a major criminal case involving a white victim or a politically charged case that in any way challenged segregation. In the *Lockett* case, the black community in Tulsa survived largely because Franklin and other black lawyers were able to defend the community's interests.

According to Smith, besides protecting property rights, black attorneys played a critical role in protecting black rights within the criminal justice system.[163] While many black defendants were doubtless guilty of illegal behavior, others were unjustly arrested, charged, and jailed by racist police, prosecutors, and judges. Throughout the South (and in much of the rest of the nation), all-white police forces frequently arrested excessive numbers of blacks, creating persistent conflict between blacks and the police.[164] In a system in which blacks were almost universally excluded from Southern juries, black defendants were more frequently convicted and often received harsher sentences than whites convicted of the same crimes.[165]

Since the colonial period, the criminal justice system has been used as a vehicle for the social control of blacks and to maintain racial subordination.[166] The very appearance of a black defense lawyer in a courtroom was a powerful political act and a direct challenge to the racial status quo.

In some parts of the North black lawyers practiced almost exclusively criminal law, primarily in defense of black male clients.[167] Some black lawyers became so skilled in criminal law that they also began representing white defendants. Smith argues that "[t]he reputation of the black lawyer was most significant in the area of criminal law, because his expertise there had won white clients, mostly immigrants, prior to World War I in both the North and the South."[168] A closer reading of Smith's book indicates that black representation of whites was almost exclusively a Northern phenomenon.[169] These twentieth century black criminal defense lawyers followed in the footsteps of pioneer black lawyers like Robert Morris, who often represented Irish immigrant defendants, and John Mercer Langston, who "speedily made his mark in the backwoods as a criminal lawyer," usually defending white clients.[170] Black representation of white clients was yet another way in which black lawyers challenged the status quo of American race relations.

As it developed a national strategy to attack segregation, the NAACP in the 1930s recognized the value of a black criminal defense bar for African-Americans. As previously noted, Charles Hamilton Houston won his first Supreme Court victory for the NAACP in 1935 in a case involving segregated juries.[171] Perhaps even more important than that victory was the emergence of black attorneys who were able to represent African-Americans at the trial level. After all, most black defendants lost their cases in local courts, received stiff sentences, and were unable to appeal. In 1934, Houston, along with Leon A. Ransom, Edward P. Lovett, and James G. Tyson, represented George Crawford, who was accused of brutally murdering a wealthy white woman in Loudoun County, Virginia. No white lawyer would take Crawford's case. The crowd packed into the courtroom to see the first defense ever mounted by black attorneys in that county. What the crowd saw was quite impressive: four accomplished, courageous, and talented black attorneys standing up for the rights of a black defendant.[172] Houston and his colleagues considered it a great victory when they convinced the jury to recommend a sentence of life imprisonment rather than death. Some of the jurors later said "that Houston's moving appeal for Crawford had saved him from the electric chair."[173]

More common than Houston's defense of Crawford in a high visibility case were the hundreds of routine defenses of black defendants in the North and the South, handled by a handful of black lawyers. For example, in Durham, North Carolina, Robert McCants Andrews, a 1918 graduate of Howard Law School, used his "superb legal skills" to save "the lives of several blacks convicted of murder."[174] In Indiana, Joseph Kent Brown, "a 1906 Howard University law graduate, defended a black man charged with raping a white woman," at a time when most white lawyers were unwilling to take cases of this nature.[175] Although he lost the first trial, Brown won a retrial and ultimately secured an acquittal for his client.[176]

Despite the successes of McCants, Brown, and others, the lack of resources and limited availability of black lawyers undermined due process for most black defendants in a criminal justice system already skewed by racial discrimination in jury selection and the racism of many judges and prosecutors. In 1888, Emanuel D. Molyneaux Hewlett, a prominent black Washington, D.C., lawyer, asserted that "because the Negroes had no means to engage a lawyer," they often "did not have real trial[s]."[177] In other instances, black lawyers often took serious criminal cases without a fee or at a very reduced rate.

In the South and the North, the black community expected the black lawyer to defend any black man charged in a capital case, even if there was no money to pay legal fees. . . . The community expected the black lawyer to defend blacks against the police, because "lawyers [were] luxuries" to the black poor, "to be used when the devil catches them." The black lawyers obliged.[178]

Even when black defendants could afford lawyers, the small number of black attorneys lawyers in the South, and the fact that some southern "county courts . . . barred black lawyers" meant that "[s]ome black defendants appeared without representation."[179]

C. A Living Testimony Against Racism

The mere presence of black attorneys contradicted the prevalent racist notions about black inferiority.[180] Robert Morris recalled that when he argued his first case in Boston, "[t]he courtroom was filled with colored people, and I could see on the faces of every one of them, a wish that I might win the first case that had ever been tried before a jury by a colored attorney in this country."[181] Morris' victory proved to both blacks and whites that blacks could triumph in the white legal system. Similarly, when John Mercer Langston argued his first case, so many people arrived "to witness the novel spectacle" of an African-American lawyer that the justice of the peace had to move "the trial from his home office to a capacious barn."[182] Langston's victory against an experienced white attorney led to an immediate boom in his practice and a subsequent political career in antebellum Ohio.[183]

Long after the end of the Civil War, black attorneys in the South continued to experience much the same reaction that Morris and Langston encountered in the antebellum North. For instance, in 1927, Robert Andrews' presence as an attorney packed the courtroom in Chester, North Carolina. "[B]oth white and colored people . . . were curious to see and hear Andrews plead his case [before a white jury]."[184] Andrews also broke new ground by using blacks as expert witnesses before white jurors. In a successful suit against an insurance company, Andrews used "two Negro surgeons, and three Negro physicians, one white clinician, one white specialist, and one white chiropractor."[185]

After Charles Hamilton Houston's defense of George Crawford, Virginus Dabney, Virginia's leading political commentator, described Houston in these laudatory terms: "The dignity, the poise, and the ability with which this thirty-six-year-old honor graduate of Amherst and Harvard conducted the defense impressed everyone."[186] One of the state's most important newspapers, the *Richmond News-Leader*, further declared that Houston and his colleagues "demonstrated to the Virginia public that there are negro lawyers in the country who can be courageous without being obsequious, lawyers who can make a fight without arousing racial antagonisms."[187] In a 1916 routine civil case, a New York judge publicly praised a black lawyer for "his sound knowledge of legal procedure."[188] This seemingly small compliment was reported in a Florida newspaper,[189] suggesting the importance of the courtroom as a showcase for black ability and success. Throughout the North and South, successful representations by black lawyers and black expert witnesses undermined the racist ideology of black inferiority that perpetuated segregation in America from the post-Reconstruction period until the modern civil rights era.

D. Black Lawyers as Leaders

Although black lawyers have served the black community as role models, providers of legal services, and protectors of property and civil rights, many of the best-known and most influential black leaders have not been lawyers. Smith argues that after Frederick Douglass died, "it was left to the black lawyer to give meaning to his words in all public forums."[190] However, this comment greatly overstates the importance of black lawyers. Indeed, although lawyers worked closely with other leaders to champion the community's causes, there are very few lawyers who can be considered among the greatest leaders in African-American history. A listing of arguably the greatest African-American leaders—Frederick Douglass, Booker T. Washington, W.E.B. DuBois, and the Rev. Dr. Martin Luther King, Jr.—contains no lawyers.[191] Moreover, among a host of other past leaders—Rev. Richard Allen, Mary McLeod Bethune, Blanch Bruce, Father Divine, Medger Evers, James Forten, Thomas T. Fortune, Henry Highland Garnet, Marcus Garvey, John Hope, Rev. Absalom Jones, The Honorable Elijah Muhammad, Carl Murphy, Congressman Rev. Adam Clayton Powell, Jr., Hiram Revels, Mary Church Terrell, William Monroe Trotter, Sojourner Truth, Ida Bell Wells-Barnett, Walter White, and Malcolm X—none were attorneys.[192] Several black leaders who were lawyers, like James Weldon Johnson, John Roy Lynch, and George Washington Williams, are remembered for other achievements.

There may be a number of reasons why black lawyers have not had a more prominent role in African-American leadership.[193] Lily-white law schools and segregated bars (including the American Bar Association),[194] limited the educational and professional opportunities of black lawyers. Hostility toward black lawyers may have driven many talented blacks away from the law and into the ministry, education, journalism, and business, where more leadership and development opportunity was available.

Notwithstanding this trend, many black lawyers have provided important forms of community leadership beyond the courtroom. In Boston, for example, Robert Morris "used his legal talents not only to achieve prominence but to provide effective leadership for his community."[195] Before the Civil War, John Mercer Langston launched a successful political career which included election to local offices. Langston later became the first dean of Howard Law School and the first black Congressman from Virginia. George Lewis Ruffin, the first African-American graduate of Harvard Law School, entered politics almost immediately after his admission to the bar and held a variety of elected and appointed political positions between 1870 and his death in 1886.[196] James Weldon Johnson began his career as a lawyer in Florida and eventually became an ambassador and the Secretary of the NAACP.[197]

Before the Second World War, many southern black lawyer-politicians focused, out of necessity, on improving conditions for their constituents within a segregated society. Thus, Thomas Nutter, a black West Virginia legislator, fought for the establishment of separate hospitals and schools for blacks, rather than seeking to integrate existing "white" facilities.[198] Similarly, Charles W. Anderson, who served in the Kentucky legislature in the 1930s, successfully championed legislation to provide money for blacks to attend universities outside of the state.[199]

Smith profiles many other black lawyers who forged political careers in the period covered by *Emancipation*. He notes that the success of these lawyers was due in part to political patronage and the power of black voters at the local level.[200] From 1866 until Franklin Roosevelt's administration, there were always a few jobs for black lawyers in Republican national administrations.[201] Smith suggests that, from 1901 until 1929, lawyers in the federal government were the de facto national black political leaders because during that time there were no blacks serving in Congress.[202]

While these black lawyer-officeholders were significant, Smith probably overstates their importance. For example, he asserts that Perry W. Howard, a Mississippi lawyer who served as a special assistant to the United States Attorney General, "became the most powerful black man in the nation."[203] As a member of the Republican National Committee, Howard probably was the most powerful black Republican politician in the 1920s and early 1930s, but by that time blacks were losing influence and status within that party.[204] During the same period, however, other blacks, including Marcus Garvey, W.E.B. DuBois, Walter White, James Weldon Johnson, A. Philip Randolph, and the publishers Robert Vann, Robert Abbot, Charles Johnson, and Carl Murphy surely wielded more power than Howard did in the black community.[205]

E. Fighting Segregation

In 1869, John Roy Lynch began his political career as a justice of the peace in Mississippi and led a distinguished career in politics until 1896, at which time he decided to sit for the Mississippi bar exam.

Lynch's decision to study law in part reflected his belief that he could more effectively battle segregation as a lawyer than as a politician. He passed the bar on his second try.[206]

In 1938, Pauli Murray sought to attend graduate school in her former home state of North Carolina. However, school officials at Chapel Hill rejected her before she could formally apply, informing her: "Members of your race are not admitted to the University."[207] Murray considered fighting the issue in court, but the NAACP lawyers with whom she consulted decided that because of her change of residence to New York, hers was not the right case with which to challenge segregated graduate education in the South.[208] In 1941, she enrolled at Howard Law School "with the single-minded intention of destroying Jim Crow."[209] Likewise, Oliver W. Hill remembered, "I went to law school so I could go out and fight segregation."[210]

The motivations driving Lynch, Murray, and Hill recall Charles Houston's hope that his students and all other black lawyers would use the law to fight segregation. Of course, the less politically motivated black lawyers studied law because it could lead to an interesting career that provided opportunities for personal advancement and perhaps, if they were fortunate, a middle-class lifestyle and income.[211] Nevertheless, as Smith demonstrates, regardless of their original intentions, sooner or later most black lawyers fought segregation in one way or another. Every black client who walked into their law offices, brought a potential civil rights case. Every black defendant in the South faced all-white juries, white judges who often called him "nigger" or otherwise treated him with disrespect, and a system of justice skewed against him.[212] The black lawyers representing these clients were forced to challenge the racial status quo whether they intended to or not.

The very availability of black lawyers encouraged many blacks to seek legal help for civil rights violations. In 1898, for example, John Robert Clifford represented a black teacher in West Virginia who successfully challenged that state's unequal salary structure.[213] In *Williams v. Board of Education*,[214] one of the few civil rights victories in a southern state's highest court before the turn of the century,[215] the West Virginia Supreme Court declared that "[d]iscrimination against the colored people, because of color alone, as to privileges, immunities, and equal legal protection, is contrary to public policy and the law of the land."'[216] Without an African-American attorney like Clifford, it is doubtful that a black teacher would have been able to bring such a suit.

Although black lawyer-politicians were unable to directly challenge segregation through legislation, they occasionally were able to do so in the courts. In their roles as politicians, Thomas Nutter of West Virginia and Charles Anderson of Kentucky were forced to accept the reality of segregation and work within existing structures to improve conditions for blacks in separate facilities.[217] As lawyers, however, they were more willing and able to challenge the status quo.

In 1929, stepping out of his legislative role, Nutter unsuccessfully challenged a racially restrictive covenant in a deed, taking on the legal norms of property ownership he could not have challenged as a politician.[218] Similarly, Charles Anderson "mounted the first major challenges to desegregate public education in Kentucky" through the courts, even as he acquiesced to separate schools as a legislator.[219] As in the *Williams* case,[220] it is unlikely that the clients who proposed these civil rights challenges could have found local white lawyers who would have taken their cases.

Some black lawyers had an important role in working as local counsel for the NAACP and other national organizations that were fighting segregation in the state courts. In Louisiana, Alexander Pierre Tureaud, an expert in the civil law, usually represented blacks in cases that did not directly concern race. However, in addition to his legal practice, Tureaud "published many articles concerning United States Supreme Court decisions that affected the rights of black people"[221] and "handled many civil rights cases as local counsel for the NAACP in the 1940s."[222] He successfully argued a case to equalize salaries in the Orleans Parish school district in 1941.[223] Working with Thurgood Marshall and fellow New Orleans attorney Joseph A. Thorton, Tureaud won his biggest civil rights victory in *Hall v. Nagel*,[224] a voting rights case. "The decision meant that at least one federal court in [the New Orleans] region would not rubber stamp a state law that restricted the voting rights of blacks."[225]

In Texas, James Madison Nabrit, Jr., led a team of black Houston attorneys who sued the Texas Democratic Party for barring blacks from primary elections.[226] This early litigation laid the groundwork for the NAACP's final victory against the Texas white primary in *Smith v. Allwright*.[227] Similarly, Zephaniah

Alexander Looby, a Tennessee lawyer, "often assisted Thurgood Marshall in handling NAACP cases in his state."[228]

The careers of Nabrit, Looby, and other black lawyers in the period illustrate the strong connection between the practice of law and social activism. At the local level, most black lawyers became leaders and social activists simply by opening their offices. The role came with the job; the mere existence of black attorneys contradicted racist norms. For blacks, simply applying to the bar was a challenge to the status quo and made the applicant a social engineer.

V. Challenging Racism in the Legal Profession

The white legal establishment erected many barriers to black entry. Thus, the very process by which blacks became lawyers often constituted a direct challenge to segregation within the legal profession. Once admitted to the bar, black attorneys faced racism and discrimination at every turn. In the South, black attorneys were sometimes assaulted, run out of town, or even killed for practicing their profession.[229] In addition to these social pressures, black attorneys felt the effects of racism from within their own profession. Prior to World War II, many law schools would not accept black applicants,[230] and most local bar associations refused to admit black lawyers.

Acceptance of black lawyers by members of the legal profession was very slow in coming. Black attorneys often had to stand up for their own rights in order to effectively practice law. When Frederick Charles Carter tried to use the library of the Virginia Court of Appeals in 1941, a librarian ordered him, under threat of arrest, to sit out of sight of the white library patrons. Carter stood his ground, and the policeman whom the librarian had summoned refused to arrest him.[231] This confrontation eventually came to the attention of Virginia's Chief Justice, who declared that the court had not authorized Jim Crow rules regarding the library and that Carter could sit where he chose.[232] This incident represented a small but significant victory for African-Americans in a profession that generally sought to exclude and demean blacks who entered its ranks.

Such intraprofession discrimination against blacks was not limited to the South. In 1936, a black lawyer in Pennsylvania forced a state judge to publicly apologize for his racist comments.[233] Lawyers working in the federal government were not immune from racism. Smith recounts the story of Robert Vann, who gained one of the few patronage positions available for a black lawyer in Franklin Roosevelt's Department of Justice. When Vann arrived, he had "no office, no desk, and no stenographer assigned to him for at least six weeks."[234] The stenographers ultimately assigned often refused to work with him because of his race, and Attorney General Cummings never met with Vann. Dissatisfied with his restricted role, Vann left the Department in 1936.[235]

Vann was not the only black attorney to experience the New Deal as a "Raw Deal."[236] In 1933, an administration official told one black lawyer seeking a position in the National Recovery Administration that "the position was reserved for whites only."[237] The disappointed and disgruntled applicant complained to Charles Hamilton Houston that "one is driven to hate either his color or his country."[238]

Indeed, except in a few large Northern cities, marginalization seemed to be the rule for black lawyers across the country from the end of Reconstruction until the beginning of World War II. However, the greatest challenge facing blacks was not their status within the profession, but gaining entry to the profession in the first place.

A. The Challenge of Legal Education

As a learned profession—and usually a regulated one—law required some training followed by some type of entrance examination. Before the 1890s, most lawyers "read" law under the tutelage of an experienced practitioner.[239] By the turn of the century, however, the profession had begun moving toward requiring formal training in a law school as a prerequisite for admission to the bar.[240] Both systems presented obstacles for blacks. To read law, a black student had to find a lawyer who was willing to bring the student into his or her office, a rare occurrence. To enter law school, a black applicant needed money and, by the early twentieth century, an undergraduate degree as well. Equally important, the applicant would need to find a school that accepted black students and was located in a place where he or she could afford to live.[241]

1. Reading Law

At the beginning of the period covered by Emancipation, the few existing law schools trained only a small fraction of the nation's lawyers. In 1840—just four years before Macon Bolling Allen earned admission to the Maine bar—there were only nine university-affiliated law schools in the United States.[242] By 1860 the number had grown to twenty-one.[243] Most lawyers, however, especially those of humble origins, "read" law. Black students needed to find established lawyers to serve as mentors and sponsors. Before the Civil War—and indeed for most of the nineteenth and early twentieth century—this meant finding a white lawyer to train a black. It was an unusual white attorney who was willing to take a black into his office.

Although Smith hints at the importance of legal sponsors, both before and after the Civil War, he never discusses the issue of sponsorship at length, and thus deprives his reader of important context for his vast research. Smith writes that some blacks read law with white Southern lawyers during and after Reconstruction, but he never delves into the political meaning of these relations. For example, in the late 1870s, George H. White studied law under the direction of North Carolina Judge William J. Clarke.[244] Likewise, Joseph W. Morris received "financial and substantive" support for his legal education from Chief Justice Franklin J. Moses, Sr. Morris graduated from law school and passed the South Carolina Bar in 1876.[245] Around 1880, John E. Patterson was admitted to the Arkansas bar after "studying law under Judge R.F. Crittinden and S.P. Swepton of Marion, Arkansas, both of whom were white."[246] Similarly, Smith reports that as late as 1939, two white lawyers in Austin, Texas, tutored Kenneth R. Lampkin, who "later assisted Thurgood Marshall in the early development of *Sweatt v. Painter*."[247] Surely the relationships between these black law students and these Southern judges and lawyers deserves some analysis. Unfortunately, Smith offers us no information on these Southern white lawyers and why they spent their own money and perhaps risked their careers to help train black lawyers.

Antebellum Northern white attorneys who sponsored blacks were usually motivated by abolitionist and egalitarian sentiments.[248] A good example of this kind of attorney is General Samuel Fessenden. Fessenden tutored Marcus Bolling Allen and sponsored him for the Maine bar.[249] At the time, Fessenden had the largest law practice in Maine and was a leader of the state bar. He had been a Federalist member of the Massachusetts legislature and a member of the Maine legislature after 1821, when Maine entered the Union as a separate state. Yet despite these conventional affiliations, in the 1830s he joined the Maine Anti-Slavery Society, abandoned traditional party politics because of his opposition to slavery, and later ran as the Liberty Party candidate for Congress and for the governorship.[250] After being admitted to the Maine bar, Allen moved to Boston, where he found another abolitionist patron, Samuel E. Sewell.[251]

Similarly, John Mercer Langston benefitted from sponsorship from sympathetic whites and abolitionists. Langston first worked with Sherlock J. Andrews, an abolitionist lawyer from Cleveland, former Congressman, and Ohio superior court judge. Like Fessenden, Andrews was "a man sympathetic to the idea of full citizenship rights for blacks."[252] However, his heavy load of political and legal business prevented Andrews from giving Langston a proper education. When Langston applied to the proprietary law school at Ballston Spa in Saratoga, New York, to continue his education, the faculty rejected him solely on racial grounds. Fearing that his admission would drive away tuition-paying Southern students, the school suggested that Langston pass himself off as "a Spaniard or Frenchman from some part of the Americas." Langston, however, declared that he would rather die than "consent to the humiliation and degradation implied" by the proposition.[253]

After several other law schools denied Langston admission, including Timothy Walker's Cincinnati Law School, Langston abandoned the idea of entering the profession until 1853, when he became an apprentice to Philemon Bliss, a former judge and active Ohio politician. Bliss openly supported his new student while attacking those, including Timothy Walker, who had refused to educate Langston.[254] Bliss' support proved crucial to Langston's success. Langston reportedly "'staggered' the examiners with his proficiency."[255] Nevertheless, two of the three examiners protested admitting a "colored" man to the bar.[256] The presiding officer, however, reminded the panel that "Judge Bliss is taking care of [Langston's] case,"[257] and that Bliss was the coalition party's congressional candidate. This was sufficient for the examiners to declare that the light-skinned Langston was "white enough" to become a lawyer.[258] A month later, Bliss won election to Congress,[259] proving that his support for Langston had not been politically unacceptable to his constituency in northern Ohio.

Like Macon Allen, Robert Morris[260] also had a leading abolitionist attorney as a mentor and patron. Morris studied under Ellis Gray Loring, who, along with Samuel E. Sewell, was the most important abolitionist attorney in Boston at the time.[261] John Swett Rock initially studied law with Robert Morris, although an obscure white attorney named T.K. Lothrop later sponsored him for the bar.[262] On February 1, 1865, Senator Charles Sumner sponsored John Rock as the first black admitted to practice before the United States Supreme Court.[263] Smith describes Rock's admission as paving the way for other African-Americans to appear before lower courts by delegitimizing race as a qualification for admission to the bar.[264]

Well-placed sponsors could not always overcome institutionalized racism, even within the legal world. George Vashon had the support of a prominent Pennsylvania politician, Walter S. Forward, but this powerful patron could not get the Allegheny County bar to overcome its racism in twice rejecting Vashon.[265]

2. Studying Law at a Law School

In the last third of the nineteenth century, there was a dramatic rise in professionalism in the United States. In medicine, for example, the American Medical Association and state medical societies set standards of practice, which limited entrance into the field to doctors with proper educational credentials.[266] Between 1875 and 1900, the number of pharmacy schools rose from eight to thirty-eight, nearly a 400 percent increase. While there were no schools of veterinary medicine in 1850, the nation had fifteen by 1900.[267] In higher education, this trend was reflected in the rise of graduate programs and the holders of Ph.D.s teaching at colleges and universities, as well as the creation of professional academic organizations, such as the American Historical Association.[268]

Lawyers also participated in this sea change of regulation and institutionalization. For example, in 1842, "New Hampshire provided that any citizen over twenty-one was entitled to be admitted to practice," but in 1872 the legislature empowered the state bar to regulate admission to practice.[269] At this time, most lawyers read law under the tutelage of an experienced practitioner. But this was changing. After its creation in 1878, the American Bar Association agitated for increasingly higher standards— including written exams for admission to the bar.[270] By the turn of the century, advocates of higher professional standards focused on requiring an undergraduate degree and a law school education for admission to the bar. In this period, "[t]he ABA's urge to upgrade the legal profession, a revived intellectual interest in law and related disciplines, and the emergence of the modern university closely paralleled one another."[271] By the 1920s, this trend had led to numerous university-affiliated law schools and a proliferation of free standing and proprietary schools. In addition, by 1920, the YMCA was operating law schools in ten cities. These were designed to accommodate the needs of the "worthy poor."[272]

In the years after Reconstruction, blacks continued to follow the traditional apprenticeship path, but some also began to attend law schools. As more black law schools opened their doors, black students began to find formal legal education a viable option. After its founding in 1869, Howard provided the most spaces for black law students of all law schools in the country. Other black law schools, such as Lincoln University Law School (1870-1873), Shaw University Law School (1878-1916), and Central Tennessee (1879-1921), opened and closed during this period.[273] These schools lacked resources, funding, and sometimes even students. But perhaps the biggest challenge the schools faced was the hostility of the whole legal establishment. The American Bar

Association, for example, under the guise of improving the standard of the profession, revamped its accreditation criteria in such a way that black law schools were unable to meet them and were pressured to close.[274]

Occasionally, blacks obtained a law school education with the help of white philanthropists. Mark Twain financed the legal education of Warner T. McGuinn at Yale, and a dean at the University of Pennsylvania helped Raymond P. Alexander go to Harvard Law School.[275] Silas N. Strawn, a former president of the American Bar Association, paid the expenses of Euclid Taylor, who attended law school in Chicago.[276] But while wealthy white sponsorship may have benefitted the rare black student, for most blacks, as Smith details, obtaining a legal education proved difficult and expensive.

B. Passing the Bar

In an age before impersonal, standardized bar exams, applicants gained admission to the bar by oral examination and interview. Many blacks "took the bar examination . . . faced with the possibility that racism rather than [a] knowledge of the law would govern its outcome."[277]

In 1847, the bar in Allegheny County, Pennsylvania, refused to admit George B. Vashon because he was black.[278] Vashon later became a lawyer in New York. Jonathan Jasper Wright failed in his first attempt to be admitted to the Pennsylvania bar, "presumably because of racism."[279] Yet less than a decade later, Wright served with "considerable ability" on the South Carolina Supreme Court.[280] This suggests that had it not been for his race, Wright would have easily been admitted in Pennsylvania, but not until several months after the Civil War ended was Wright admitted there.[281]

While there is ample evidence of racism in the North, it appears that blacks had less trouble joining the bar in Northern states after 1865 than in the South, where racism continued to be an enormous barrier to bar admission. Racism could sour an otherwise successful examination. When James Weldon Johnson finished his oral examination in Duval County, Florida, one examiner declared, "He's passed a good examination." But Johnson recalled that another examiner was still unprepared to witness the first black admitted to the Duval bar, and "blurted out in my face . . . 'Well, I can't forget he's a nigger and I'll be damned if I'll stay here to see him admitted.'"[282]

VI. The Changing Role of the Black Lawyer

Emancipation details the involvement of black lawyers in civil rights cases from the time blacks first became lawyers until the middle of World War II. Smith's expansive research reveals that their role in civil rights litigation changed dramatically during the century covered by his book. In the middle of the nineteenth century, black lawyers usually facilitated litigation, or litigated, solely at the local level. But starting in the mid-1930s, the nation watched as black lawyers became key players at all levels of civil rights litigation.

As I discussed earlier, Robert Morris' career, including the *Roberts* case and his involvement in the Shadrach affair, illustrates the relationship between the black lawyer's dual roles of legal technician and social engineer. In both cases, Morris took an active role at the beginning of the litigation, but white lawyers took the lead when these cases reached the Massachusetts Supreme Judicial Court and the United States Circuit Court.

This should not, however, come as a surprise, for when *Roberts* went to the Massachusetts Supreme Judicial Court, Morris was an inexperienced, twenty-three-year-old lawyer. The goal of the litigation was to win a decision against segregation and not to showcase a black attorney. Thus, it seems natural that the lead counsel would be the experienced, Harvard-trained, and brilliant Charles Sumner.

Smith shows that this pattern of white lawyers arguing cases prepared by blacks remained fairly constant until the 1930s. When a group of New Orleans blacks in the 1890s organized the Citizens' Committee to Test the Constitutionality of the Separate Car Law, they sought white attorneys to represent them, acknowledging the political wisdom and necessity of this choice.[283] Louis Andre Martinet, a black lawyer in Louisiana and prime mover in this organization, initiated the test case of railroad segregation that led to *Plessy v. Ferguson.*[284] But from the start of the case, Martinet sought white counsel because he did not think the black lawyers in the state had the experience necessary to handle such a case.[285] "Excluding himself, Martinet described black members of the bar as 'practic[ing] almost exclusively in the police courts.'"[286] Almost none had the appellate experience "needed to take the case to the United States Supreme Court."[287] Thus, Martinet turned to two white lawyers—Albion Winegar Tourgee, then living in

New York, and James C. Walker—to represent Homer Plessy at the state level.[288] When the case went to the United States Supreme Court, Tourgee arranged for Samuel F. Phillips, a former Solicitor General of the United States, to join the case.[289] Like Sumner in *Roberts*, Tourgee argued Plessy without a fee.[290]

This pattern continued well into the twentieth century. A recent black graduate of Harvard Law School, Benjamin J. Davis, Jr., initially defended the black communist organizer Angelo Herndon when he was arrested for sedition and treason against the State of Georgia.[291] Davis' presence in the courtroom "infuriated Georgia authorities."[292] The presiding judge read a newspaper when Davis addressed the Court, while the prosecutor referred to Davis, Herndon, and Davis' African-American co-counsel, John H. Geer, as "niggers" and "darkeys."[293] Davis' participation in the case was important to the politics surrounding the defense. However, when the case went to the Supreme Court, Herndon relied on high-powered white lawyers Whitney North Seymour, Sr., Herbert Wechsler, and Walter Gellhorn. Eventually, they won a reversal of Herndon's conviction in 1937, after two trips to the nation's highest court.[294]

In its early years, the NAACP relied heavily on white attorneys, much to the chagrin of some black lawyers.[295] Smith concedes that "[t]his may have been a strategic move, given the hostility of the courts to civil rights litigation," yet he also argues that "the use of white lawyers to fight for black rights made the black lawyer seem incompetent in the eyes of an already doubting black community."[296] Whether this was true or not—Smith's evidence for the proposition is slim—the NAACP clearly had few resources of its own and made good use of these pro bono services. As long as "the foremost lawyers" of the nation—such as Louis Marshall or Moorfield Storey, a former president of the American Bar Association—were willing to donate their services to the NAACP, the organization could ill afford to reject their offers.[297] In the 1930s, however, a growing group of black lawyers—led by Charles Hamilton Houston, his colleagues, friends, and students—began to assume greater leadership and control over the direction of civil rights litigation. Through their struggle for a legal education, they had acquired the training and experience to become "the foremost lawyers" in America.

VII. Research in Search of a Theme

Smith offers pathbreaking information about black lawyers in *Emancipation*, and from this wealth of data a number of themes emerge. The major theme, discussed at some length above, is that as African-Americans sought entry to the legal profession, they thrust themselves into the fight against racism and segregation, regardless of their original intentions. A second theme concerns the importance of how black lawyers worked with sympathetic whites and other minorities to achieve equality in and under the legal system. Unfortunately, Smith's organizational structure submerges these themes and forces the reader to tease them out of what turns out to be an important, but sometimes structurally confusing, book.

For example, Smith's evidence demonstrates the importance of political participation in securing employment for black attorneys. Many of the early black lawyers gained admission to the bar through the political and professional clout of their white sponsors, many of whom held public office. In addition, a surprising number of black lawyers had careers that included election to local, state, or federal offices. Even if Smith does not emphasize it, this evidence demonstrates that social mobility for blacks, like other minorities, has been tied to political activity. Moreover, the combined political power of black lawyers, white sponsors, and abolitionists created avenues for social change. But, given the structure of Smith's book, it is extremely difficult to tie this important information to Smith's overall topic.

Smith's decision to limit this book "to the first one hundred years of the sojourn of the black lawyer in America"[298] undermines the book's usefulness. While this limited temporal scope produces a degree of symmetry, it does little to advance the book's theme. All scholars agree that World War II brought dramatic changes in American civil rights. Black veterans returned from the war against racism abroad to begin a renewed effort to challenge racism at home. Thus, a logical place to end this book would have been 1940, the eve of the war, or 1945, the end of the war, or perhaps in 1950, so that Smith's analysis could have used the census materials to understand the previous decade. Extending the book's coverage to 1950 might have been a daunting task, because Smith would have had to investigate the impact of the G.I. Bill on black and legal education. The difficulty of that task, however, does not explain why this book abruptly ends part way though the war. There is nothing talismanic about a "century" or a "hundred years," and unfortunately, this book suffers somewhat from Smith's belief to the contrary.[299]

A. BLACK AND JEWISH LAWYERS: THE FRUITFUL COALITION

In an age when some African-American and some Jewish leaders seem to be at each other's throats, Smith offers us a timely reminder that the alliance between Jews and blacks began long ago and produced many victories against discrimination in the legal profession and in the law. Smith's work permits us to piece together a story of mutual interest, cooperation, and respect in which blacks and Jews have worked together since the late nineteenth century to reform the legal profession and American law itself.

Smith chronicles instances where, together, black and Jewish students successfully protested and overcame the discrimination experienced by both groups.[300] He notes that when law clubs at Harvard discriminated against both groups, "blacks and Northern Jewish students formed their own club."[301] When the dean at the University of Pennsylvania Law School tried to prevent a black woman, Sadie Mossell Alexander, from serving on the school's law review, Philip Werner Amram, a Jewish student and son of a faculty member, "publicly objected to the dean's actions, and he prevailed."[302]

Allied blacks and Jews also challenged discrimination within the profession. The career of Ellis Rivers, a black graduate of Columbia Law School, illustrates this coalition. Most white firms were uninterested in the young black lawyer, despite his recent Columbia law degree. However, Jonah J. Goldstein hired him for his small firm, Goldstein and Goldstein. Rivers later moved to another "Jewish" firm, Finkelstein and Welling. Meanwhile, the New York State Bar Association rejected Rivers' application for membership on grounds of race. In 1923, Louis Marshall, who at the time was President of the American Jewish Committee and a member of the board of the NAACP,[303] led a group of prominent lawyers that forced the New York State Bar Association to admit Rivers,[304] and in 1929 Rivers became the first black admitted to the Association of the Bar of the City of New York.[305] By 1942, Rivers, who had become a Manhattan prosecutor, attempted to break the color barrier of the American Bar Association. When the ABA refused to admit him—solely on the basis of race—Jonah Goldstein, by this time a judge in New York City, resigned in protest. This led to other resignations, and in 1943 the ABA changed its policy declaring that membership was "not dependent upon race, creed or color."[306] The story of Rivers is similar to that of Hugh Ellwood Macbeth, Sr. In 1927, Macbeth, a black graduate of Harvard Law School, led a group of black and Jewish lawyers in successfully challenging the exclusion of both groups from the California Bar Association.[307]

In an era when most "white" firms refused to hire blacks, Smith has uncovered evidence of blacks working at Jewish firms, and many Jewish lawyers working with blacks to fight discrimination.[308] The first black attorney appointed to defend a white in New York was appointed by a Jewish judge.[309]

Blacks and Jews also worked closely together on civil rights litigation in the NAACP. For many years, Louis Marshall, a prominent Jewish lawyer, argued cases on a pro bono basis for the NAACP. Felix Frankfurter was a leader of the Jewish community, an active Zionist, and a close adviser at the NAACP. As the only Jew on the Harvard Law School faculty, he too faced a great deal of discrimination,[310] which may have made him the logical choice as an advisor for black law students. Justice Frankfurter was a mentor to Charles Hamilton Houston and other black Harvard Law students.[311] Frankfurter was also the mentor of Nathan Margold, a Jewish law student, who preceded Charles Hamilton Houston at the NAACP, where he won the second Texas white primary case.[312] After World War II, another young Jewish lawyer, Jack Greenberg, began working at the NAACP and quickly became Thurgood Marshall's chief lieutenant. Meanwhile, organizations like the American Jewish Committee, the Commission on Law and Social Action of the American Jewish Congress, and the Anti-Defamation League of B'nai B'rith often filed amicus briefs in NAACP-sponsored litigation.[313]

Smith also describes how a number of Jews participated in the development of black law schools. Justice Frankfurter recommended Charles Hamilton Houston for his position at Howard and gave him advice once he was there.[314] Louis Brandeis also indirectly influenced Houston's appointment at Howard. When Mordecai Johnson became president of Howard, he embarked on the process of revamping the entire university. For advice on how to reform the law school, he turned to America's most prominent Jewish attorney, Supreme Court Justice Louis Brandeis. Johnson wanted the cold truth, and Brandeis gave it. The aging justice, who had been on the forefront of social reform throughout his life, bluntly told Johnson to "get yourself a real faculty."[315] As Justice Brandeis' most recent biographer notes: "The implication of his letter to President Johnson of Howard was that he thought that a black law school *could* be first-rate."[316] Johnson was able to use the arguments of Justice Brandeis to convince any doubters that his course of revamping the law school was the correct one. Johnson then turned to Justice Frankfurter, a protege of Brandeis, who in turn urged Johnson to hire his protege, Charles Hamilton Houston.

The relationship between black and Jewish lawyers was not one-sided. Jewish leaders and lawyers fully understood that discrimination was indivisible—that segregation against blacks legitimated segregation against Jews. No better example of the union of the black and Jewish causes exists than the struggle to eliminate restrictive covenants and housing discrimination. Smith explains how in Chicago, for example, five black lawyers challenged the constitutionality of restrictive covenants that excluded both blacks and Jews from certain neighborhoods.[317] In 1926, Louis Marshall had lost a case in the Supreme Court challenging restrictive covenants,[318] so it must have been with great satisfaction that Justice Frankfurter heard the arguments of his former student, Charles Hamilton Houston, against restrictive covenants. Justice Frankfurter's opinion for a unanimous court in *Shelley v. Kraemer*[319] vindicated Houston's position and was a fitting conclusion to the relationship between the two lawyers.

B. Blacks Lawyers in Geographic and Historical Contexts

Smith claims to have organized the book according to "geographical regions (and the states within) established by the American legal system."[320] But the geographical groupings place states together in an illogical way. Smith attempts to assuage our confusion by describing these arrangements as the "established historic and legal geographic lines."[321] In fact, the "system" he uses, which he never explicitly states, is the West reporter system. Developed by a private corporation, this layout can hardly be considered "the American legal system," and Smith fails to justify or explain his use of it.

Using this system results in a truly bizarre organizational structure for the book. Smith reasons that New England warrants a separate chapter because he found records of the first black lawyer in this region. But Smith's "New England" consists solely of Massachusetts and Maine. He discusses Connecticut and Rhode Island in the chapter on the Atlantic States while Vermont and New Hampshire seem to have disappeared altogether from the history of New England, although they offered African-Americans complete equality in the antebellum period, including access to the public schools and the voting booth.

Smith also curiously places New York, which had a black lawyer some years before Massachusetts, in the same region as Ohio, Illinois, and Indiana, which he labels the "Northeast." The West reporter system may call these states "Northeastern," but no one else does. The history of each of these states is quite unique, and Smith's decision to group them together weakens the book's usefulness in describing the social and legal trends relating to black lawyers. In the antebellum period, for example, blacks with property could vote in New York, which never restricted black migration into the state.[322] During the same period, Ohio, Indiana, and Illinois were in the Northwest, or the "Old Northwest," as it was called in the 1850s. Today, they are generally known as Midwestern states. These states were notorious for their racism and discrimination against blacks both before and after the Civil War.[323] While Ohio repealed most of its notorious black code in 1849,[324] the other two states did not repeal their discriminatory laws.[325] Indeed, on the eve of the Civil War, Indiana and Illinois had the dubious distinction of being the most racist states in the North.[326] Furthermore, after the Civil War, de jure segregation existed in all three states for many years.[327] By contrast, New York was one of the most liberal states on race relations before the war, and passed civil rights legislation after the war as well.[328]

Smith also discusses Maryland and Delaware in the same chapter as Pennsylvania, New Jersey, Connecticut, and Rhode Island. By lumping them together, Smith fails to examine the contrasts among these states on racial issues. Maryland and Delaware, for example, maintained slavery until 1865 and racial segregation through the 1960s, while the other states had substantial racial equality in the antebellum period, as well as after the Civil War. For example, New Jersey and Pennsylvania passed civil rights laws in the 1880s,[329] while Maryland and Delaware consistently tried to reduce their black residents to second-class citizens.

Smith's organizational scheme prevents him from comparing the development of the black legal profession in the Northeast with the Midwest, or the South with the North.[330] It is not even possible to compare experiences within regions. For example, Smith discusses Georgia and South Carolina together with Virginia, and not with the rest of the deep South, yet he analyzes Maryland and Delaware, which historically belong with Virginia and North Carolina, in the same chapter with Pennsylvania. Similarly, Smith places Oklahoma in the same chapter with California, as a "Pacific" state, even though Oklahoma should be compared with its neighbors Texas and Arkansas.

This peculiar geographic organization jeopardizes the ability of author and reader alike to draw conclusions about change over time. In the book's current form, the reader must constantly flip back and forth, from chapter to chapter, to get a sense of the ebb and flow of the historical trends in the participation of black lawyers in the American legal system.

Smith does not even exploit his regional organization. For example, it seems peculiar to lump New York together with three states in the Midwest, Ohio, Indiana, and Illinois. But, having done that, Smith fails to compare developments in these states. Three of them—New York, Ohio, and Illinois—were industrial, urban, and had large immigrant populations as well as growing black populations in the twentieth century. How did these conditions affect the development of a black bar in these states? Did Cleveland and Chicago, with their large Eastern European Catholic populations, differ from New York, with its huge Jewish and Italian populations? Were black lawyers better off in the machine politics of Chicago or the "good government" politics of Cleveland? These kinds of questions would have placed the development of the black bar in a broader and more useful social context.

Perhaps *Emancipation* would have been coherent had it followed a scheme that grouped states in geographic regions based on their shared history and culture. Alternatively, Smith could have placed more emphasis on chronology to show how the practice of law changed over time for blacks in the profession. A combination of the two approaches would have been ideal. Instead, we have an impressive amount of important research presented in a confused manner.

VIII. Conclusions

Emancipation offers a new and deeper perspective on the critical importance of black attorneys in shaping American civil rights law. While Smith concentrates on individual lawyers and their personal stories, his book will prove invaluable to other scholars who want to explain why things happened as they did. Smith reminds us that the integration of the legal profession was glacially slow, but that the emergence of a small but effective cadre of African-American attorneys had a transformative effect on the civil rights agenda. Smith also demonstrates that civil rights progress historically arose from biracial alliances and cooperation, particularly in the early years when white attorneys argued the most important cases before all-white judges and juries.

In 1928, Howard University President Mordecai Johnson told the National Bar Association:

> We need in the next 25 years great legal minds to carry out every legal decision handed down by the Supreme Court of the United States, protecting the humblest citizens in the smallest communities. We need men who know and interpret the law, and they must have means to carry on the cases to fight the representative battles of the poor in a peaceful way before the courts of the country in a continuous cycle of test cases.[331]

To a great extent, Johnson's wish was granted. Charles Hamilton Houston, William Hastie, Spottswood Robinson, Pauli Murray, and Thurgood Marshall became this very leadership of the civil rights bar. Thanks to J. Clay Smith, we now know better where they came from and who their role models were.

Notes

1. The Autobiography Of Malcolm X 36-37 (1965).
2. This review essay uses the terms "African-American" and "black" alternatively for stylistic purposes.

3. In the 1977-1978 academic year, there were 5304 black law students in 160 American Bar Association (ABA)-approved law schools, and in 1992-1993 there were 8698 black students in 173 ABA-approved schools. AMERICAN BAR ASSOCIATION, A REVIEW OF LEGAL EDUCATION IN THE UNITED STATES 68 (1993). The total number of black judges (federal, state, and municipal) has grown from only 58 in 1961, to 214 in 1970, to 819 in 1986, to 895 in 1991. JOINT CENTER FOR POLITICAL AND ECONOMIC STUDIES & JUDICIAL COUNCIL OF THE NATIONAL BAR ASSOCIATION, ELECTED AND APPOINTED BLACK JUDGES IN THE UNITED STATES 1991, at 5-6 (1991). For a discussion of black law students before the 1970s, see Ernest Gellhorn, *The Law School and the Negro*, 1968 DUKE L.J. 1069.

4. In 1914, Alfredo Bonito Cosey, a graduate of Howard Law School practicing in New Jersey, published AMERICAN AND ENGLISH LAW OF TITLE AND RECORD, 1535-1911 (1914). More recently, Smith has written about black legal scholarship in the late 19th century. J. Clay Smith, Justice and Jurisprudence *and the Black Lawyer*, 69 NOTRE DAME L. REV. 1077 (1994). This article contains a long discussion of an organization called the Brotherhood of Liberty, which arranged for the publication of JUSTICE AND JURISPRUDENCE: AN INQUIRY CONCERNING THE CONSTITUTIONAL LIMITATIONS OF THE THIRTEENTH, FOURTEENTH, AND FIFTEENTH AMENDMENTS (1889, reprinted 1969) [hereinafter JUSTICE AND JURISPRUDENCE]. This was a "philosophic account of the jurisprudence of race-prejudice, and of the history of its lineal descent from the ancestral jurisprudence of slavery." *Id.* at 42, *quoted in* Smith, *supra*, at 1087. A group of blacks, including a number of lawyers and at least three women, formed the Brotherhood of Liberty in June 1885 in Baltimore. Smith argues that blacks participated substantially in the writing of this huge book, but also notes the participation of a white lawyer hired by the Brotherhood of Liberty. Smith, *supra*, at 1079-80. It seems to me that the authorship of this treatise is far less important than the institutional support from a group of blacks that led to the writing and publication of the book. It is in fact likely that no single person wrote the book, although the white lawyer may have been the primary author. Smith notes that the Brotherhood of Liberty sought to eliminate "restrictions . . . prohibiting blacks from becoming members of the Maryland bar," p. 143, and claims that "as a direct result of the agitation of the Brotherhood of Liberty, this purpose was realized when Everett J. Waring was admitted to the Maryland bar after his graduation from Howard University's law school in June, 1885," Smith, *supra*, at 1083.

5. John S. Rock was admitted in 1865. P. 113.

6. Everett J. Waring argued Jones v. United States, 137 U.S. 224 (1890). P. 178 n.176.

7. P. 492. He later became a justice on the Supreme Court of Liberia. Pp. 492-93.

8. P. 502.

9. "Today most historians understand that *de jure* segregation began before the Civil War, increased massively during Reconstruction, and continued to expand in the 1880s right through the Progressive Era." Paul Finkelman, *Introduction* to THE AGE OF JIM CROW: SEGREGATION FROM THE END OF RECONSTRUCTION TO THE GREAT DEPRESSION vii, viii (Paul Finkelman ed., 1992) [hereinafter AGE OF JIM CROW].

10. During this period, Kanawha County, where Nutter lived, had the largest population of any county in the state. According to the 1920 census, of the 119,650 people in the County, only 8929 were black. 3 FOURTEENTH CENSUS (1920): POPULATION 1106 tbl. 9. The 1910 census found 6476 blacks out of a total county population of 81,457. We cannot be certain, but it seems reasonable to assume that most of the black population of the county lived in Nutter's district.

11. P. 239.

12. P. 544.

13. P. 325 (quoting NATIONAL BAR ASSOCIATION: PROCEEDINGS OF THE SIXTH ANNUAL CONVENTION 30, 31 (1930) (statement of Scipio A. Jones)).

14. "Special judges were elected by attorneys present in court, a procedure commonly followed when a judge was disqualified from hearing a case." P. 326.

15. P. 327. Smith asserts that this last appointment, in 1929, was "influenced by President Woodrow Wilson," although he does not explain how, since Wilson had been dead for five years. *Id.*

16. P. 55. Smith notes:

> Mary Ann Shadd Carey, a black woman, claimed that she was admitted to Howard University's first law class in 1869; if her contention is true, this makes her and Lemma Barkaloo, who entered Washington University's law school in Missouri in the same year, the first women admitted to an American law school.

P. 55. This claim seems very tentative. Apparently Smith, who is a former Dean of Howard Law School, was unable to find any record of Carey, or else, I assume, he would have cited such evidence. Smith is less tentative in asserting that Charlotte E. Ray was the first black woman to graduate from a law school (Howard) and that she was admitted to the bar in 1872. P. 55. The most important work on the history of law schools in the United States asserts that Lemma Bankaloo was admitted to the Missouri Bar in 1870 and that Ada Kepley received her law degree from Chicago's Union College of Law (now Northwestern University Law School) in 1870. ROBERT STEVENS, LAW SCHOOL: LEGAL EDUCATION IN AMERICA FROM THE 1850S TO THE 1980S 82 (1983).

17. P. 344.

18. P. 344. Smith offers an important correction to Peter Wallenstein's pathbreaking work on female lawyers in Virginia. Peter Wallenstein, *"These New and Strange Beings": Women in the Legal Profession in Virginia, 1890-1990*, 101 VA. MAG. HIST. & BIOG. 193 (1993). Wallenstein claimed that Marian Poe was the first black female lawyer in the South, *id.* at 210, but Smith discovered two women who came earlier: Estelle A. Henderson, who was admitted in Alabama in 1919, p. 301, and Lutie Lytle, who was admitted in both Tennessee and Kansas in 1897. P. 344. Findings like these illustrate the exhaustive and groundbreaking nature of Smith's research.

19. P. 344.

20. Although no direct evidence exists for this assertion, the fact that Howard is the oldest law school in the country devoted to educating blacks suggests that it has produced the most black lawyers. Most other predominantly black law schools disappeared, while those that remain—North Carolina Central, Texas Southern, and Southern University—are much newer. Few predominantly white law schools ever enrolled more than a token number of blacks before the late 1960s, and many law schools would not even admit blacks until the 1960s. In 1939, 34 of the 88 accredited law schools had a policy of excluding blacks. P. 50. In 1967, only about 200 blacks graduated from predominantly white law schools, while that year Howard had just under 400 black students enrolled. Although enrollment figures are not the same as graduation figures, it is implausible that any other single law school ever had more black graduates than Howard; and the cumulative effect of more than a century of black law graduates makes Howard the most consistent educator of black lawyers. See p. 64.

21. P. 54.

22. Between 1869 and 1878, women graduated from Iowa Law School, Michigan Law School, and Hastings College of Law. There were five women lawyers in the United States in 1870, 75 in 1880, and 1010 by 1900. STEVENS, *supra* note 16, at 83. In 1918, 177 women were studying law in D.C., but only three were at Howard. The others (presumably all white) were at Washington College of Law (later absorbed into American University), George Washington University School of Law, and National Law School (later absorbed into George Washington University). 9 WOMEN LAW. J. 6 (1919).

23. Pp. 54-55, 83 n.215.

24. U.S. CENSUS BUREAU, NEGRO POPULATION IN THE U.S., 1790-1915, at 57 tbl. 6 (1918) [hereinafter NEGRO POPULATION IN THE U.S.].

25. U.S. BUREAU OF THE CENSUS, THE STATISTICAL HISTORY OF THE UNITED STATES FROM COLONIAL TIMES TO THE PRESENT 43 (rev. ed. 1965). In 1940, there were 13,190,395 native born "non-whites" in the United States. Of these, some 11,460,000 lived in the South, and the vast majority were probably black.

26. See generally GENNA RAE MCNEIL, GROUNDWORK: CHARLES HAMILTON HOUSTON AND THE STRUGGLE FOR CIVIL RIGHTS 63-105 (1983).

27. P. 64. During Reconstruction, a small number of blacks attended the public University of South Carolina law school, and three blacks attended the Maryland University Law School between 1887 and 1890. However, only two of the three students were allowed to stay long enough to graduate. Pp. 37-38. Otherwise, no blacks attended historically white law schools in the South until the 1940s.

28. P. 39. Houston remained at Harvard and became the first black to earn an S.J.D. at that school. *Houston, Charles Hamilton, in* DICTIONARY OF AMERICAN NEGRO BIOGRAPHY 328, 328 (Rayford W. Logan & Michael R. Winston eds., 1982) [hereinafter DANB].

29. Jasper Alston Atkins (Yale, 1922), William Edward Taylor (Iowa, 1923), Richard F. Jones (Pittsburgh, 1923), Leon A. Ransome (Ohio State, 1927), Iven McLeod (Cincinnati, 1929), and Robert Ming, Jr. (University of Chicago, 1933). P. 39.

30. Harry Pace graduated with honors from the University of Chicago in 1933; Clara Bruce had the highest grades in her class at Boston University in the mid-1920s. Although Smith does not say so, presumably she graduated with honors. P. 39.

31. Rufus Lewis Milford Hope Perry was the class orator at New York University Law School in 1891. Smith notes that Perry also wrote his bar examination answers in Latin. P. 38. Unfortunately, Smith relegates to a footnote the fact that neither Perry nor his only black classmate, James Henry Hilton, had legal careers. Perry became a linguist and translator; Hilton was a postal worker when he died. P. 68 n.56. The failure of these men to find a career in law is surely as significant as their success in law school.

32. Pp. 35-40. Mason Nelson, who received an LL.M. from Michigan in 1892, was the first black to earn this degree. P. 40.

33. P. 39.

34. P. 39.

35. Pp. 39-40.

36. 1 U. CHI. L. REV. 110 (1933). This article appeared in the wake of a temporary victory in Nixon v. Condon, 286 U.S. 73 (1932), against the whites-only Texas Democratic Party primary.

37. P. 50. For a discussion of college admissions quotas imposed on Jews, see HENRY L. FEINGOLD, ZION IN AMERICA: THE JEWISH EXPERIENCE FROM COLONIAL TIMES TO THE PRESENT 266-70 (1974).

38. JOHN HOPE FRANKLIN, RACE AND HISTORY: SELECTED ESSAYS, 1938-1988, at 284 (1989). Franklin went on to be the first black chair of a history department at a predominantly white school (Brooklyn College), the first black chair at an elite school (University of Chicago), and the first black president of the American Historical Association, the Organization of American Historians, and the Southern Historical Association. He ended his teaching career at Duke Law School, where he taught Constitutional History. *Id.* dust jacket; see also AUGUST MEIER, BLACK HISTORY AND THE HISTORICAL PROFESSION, 1915-1980 (1988).

39. P. 50.

40. Throughout this period, there were a few other law schools which primarily served black students. Between 1870 and 1880, four black law schools opened and closed. A fifth, Central Tennessee College of Law opened in 1879 and remained in operation until 1921. Five other black law schools opened and closed between 1881 and 1916. Freylinghuysen University, founded for "colored working men and women" in 1907, "produced a trickle of lawyers at its John M. Langston Law School, until 1927." Pp. 56-59. STEVENS, *supra* note 16, at 195. Virginia Union's law school graduated 23 students between 1922 and 1931, but only six passed the bar. Simmons University in Kentucky had only a few law graduates in the 1920s. *Id.* at 201 n.34.

41. RICHARD KLUGER, SIMPLE JUSTICE 128 (1975) (quoting Hill).

42. MCNEIL, *supra* note 26, at 83 (quoting William H. Hastie, Jr.).

43. KLUGER, *supra* note 41, at 128 (quoting Oliver W. Hill).
44. P. 49.
45. Pp. 49-50.
46. P. 51.
47. Houston went to the NAACP in 1935. MCNEIL, *supra* note 26, at 131. Spottswood Robinson entered Howard Law School in 1936, graduated in 1939, and immediately began teaching at the law school. P. 52; KLUGER, *supra* note 41, at 197.
48. MCNEIL, *supra* note 26, at 83.
49. KLUGER, *supra* note 41, at 128. Richard Kluger incorrectly asserts that Hill was "the first Negro ever to serve on the city council of Richmond, capital of the old Confederacy." *Id.* In fact, between 1871 and 1898 "thirty-three blacks served on the city council" of Richmond. Michael B. Chesson, *Richmond's Black Councilmen, 1871-96, in* SOUTHERN BLACK LEADERS OF THE RECONSTRUCTION ERA 191, 191 (Howard N. Rabinowitz ed., 1982) [hereinafter SOUTHERN BLACK LEADERS].
50. KLUGER, *supra* note 41, at 179. Other civil rights lawyers who studied under Houston include Leslie S. Perry, Coyness L. Ennix, Edward P. Lovett, and James G. Tyson. MCNEIL, *supra* note 26, at 82-83.
51. Brown v. Board of Educ. of Topeka, 347 U.S. 483 (1954).
52. MCNEIL, *supra* note 26, at 3 (quoting *College Honors Charles Houston '15*, AMHERST MAG., Spring 1978, at 14 (quoting an address by Justice Marshall)).
53. See KLUGER, *supra* note 41; MCNEIL, *supra* note 26; MARK V. TUSHNET, THE NAACP'S LEGAL STRATEGY AGAINST SEGREGATED EDUCATION, 1925-1950 (1987). For further background, see the collected essays in AFRICAN AMERICANS AND THE LEGAL PROFESSION IN HISTORICAL PERSPECTIVE (Paul Finkelman ed., 1992).
54. See KLUGER, *supra* note 41; MCNEIL., *supra* note 26, at 131-175; TUSHNET, *supra* note 53, at 21-137. A number of white attorneys, especially Jack Greenberg, Thurgood Marshall's second-in-command at the NAACP Legal Defense Fund, were also involved in this desegregation struggle. Justice Marshall later recalled that of "some two dozen lawyers" involved in the school desegregation cases, "only two hadn't been touched by Charlie Houston." MCNEIL, *supra* note 26, at 3 (quoting Justice Marshall).
55. 295 U.S. 394 (1935) (per curiam) (reversing the murder conviction of a black because blacks had been excluded from jury service); see also Roger W. Cummins, *"Lily-White" Juries on Trial: The Civil Rights Defense of Jess Hollins*, 63 CHRON. OKLA. 166 (1985), *reprinted in* RACE AND CRIMINAL JUSTICE 158 (Paul Finkelman ed., 1992).
56. KLUGER, *supra* note 41, at 161. Before this period, the NAACP victories in the Supreme Court had been by such white attorneys as Louis Marshall and Moorfield Storey who "argued all five of the NAACP's Supreme Court cases between 1913 and 1927." TUSHNET, *supra* note 53, at 16.
57. Dred Scott v. Sandford, 60 U.S. (19 How.) 393, 405 (1857).
58. *Id.*
59. *Id.* at 403.
60. *Id.* at 404.
61. *Id.* at 404-05.
62. *Id.* at 407.
63. DON E. FEHRENBACHER, THE DRED SCOTT CASE 559-61 (1978).
64. *Id.* at 559.
65. See notes 81-83 *infra* and accompanying text.
66. In 1850, the U.S. Census recorded 197,711 free blacks living in the North; by 1860 the figure had risen to 225,227. In the South, the numbers were 235,569 and 258,346, respectively. NEGRO POPULATION IN THE U.S., *supra* note 24, at 55 tbl. 2. Quite likely another 10,000-20,000 fugitive slaves lived in the North but avoided the census takers. For a discussion of the problem of relying on census figures, especially for blacks, see note 133 *infra*.
67. Paul Finkelman, *Prelude to the Fourteenth Amendment: Black Legal Rights in the Antebellum North*, 17 RUTGERS L.J. 415, 421-30 (1986).
68. "Blacks in the North could legally vote in every New England state except Connecticut and, if they met the property qualifications, in New York." *Id.* at 477. Blacks also voted in school board elections in Michigan and Ohio. *Id.* at 425, 478. Ohio's highest court ruled that mulattoes were not black and therefore could vote under that state's constitution. Jeffries v. Ankeny, 11 Ohio 372, 376 (1842); Thacker v. Hawk, 11 Ohio 377, 380 (1842); Anderson v. Millikin, 9 Ohio 568, 580 (1859). In 1844, blacks voted in Michigan in large numbers despite the prohibition against such voting. DAVID M. KATZMAN, BEFORE THE GHETTO: BLACK DETROIT IN THE NINETEENTH CENTURY 33-40 (1973).
69. Finkelman, *supra* note 67, at 463-71. In Boston, for example, only 7.6% of adult blacks were illiterate. Two-thirds of these illiterate blacks were born in the South or outside the United States. Of those born in Massachusetts, only 2.5% were illiterate. JAMES OLIVER HORTON & LOIS E. HORTON, BLACK BOSTONIANS 13 (1979). Smith gives literacy figures for all free blacks in the country, asserting that in 1850 "nearly 60 percent [were] in the illiterate class." P. 10. This 60% figure is misleading because it does not distinguish between Northern free blacks, who had relatively high literacy rates, and Southern free blacks, who had dramatically lower rates. Throughout the South it was illegal to teach slaves (and in some places free blacks) to read and write, and there were no public schools for free blacks. In the North school attendance was on the rise for blacks, as was literacy. Smith also asserts that the high level of illiteracy among blacks after the Civil War limited their job prospects to primarily service occupations. P. 10. Smith's observation that some blacks entered such occupations as bookkeepers, stenographers, and electricians is questionable since these professions required literacy. For figures on black school attendance, see Finkelman, *supra* note 67, at 472-75.

70. In 1843, Massachusetts repealed its laws restricting interracial marriage. Act of Feb. 25, 1843, ch. 5, 1843 Mass. Acts 4. For a history of this law, see Louis Ruchames, *Race, Marriage, and Abolition in Massachusetts*, 40 J. NEGRO HIST. 250 (1955), *reprinted in* RACE AND LAW BEFORE EMANCIPATION 448 (Paul Finkelman ed., 1992).

71. Finkelman, *supra* note 67, at 476-77.

72. RICHARD R. WRIGHT, JR., THE NEGRO IN PENNSYLVANIA: A STUDY IN ECONOMIC HISTORY 44 (1912).

73. IRA BERLIN, SLAVES WITHOUT MASTERS: THE FREE NEGRO IN THE ANTEBELLUM SOUTH 217-49 (1974) (stating that a number of free blacks "prospered [and] accumulated property"); JOHN HOPE FRANKLIN, THE FREE NEGRO IN NORTH CAROLINA, 1790-1860, at 150-62 (1943) (noting that several free blacks "amassed a considerable amount of property during their lifetime"); LUTHER PORTER JACKSON, FREE NEGRO LABOR AND PROPERTY HOLDING IN VIRGINIA, 1830-1860 (photo. reprint 1969) (1942) (arguing that despite the legal and political restrictions imposed on free blacks, property holding was widespread among them); MICHAEL P. JOHNSON & JAMES L. ROARK, BLACK MASTERS: A FREE FAMILY OF COLOR IN THE OLD SOUTH xi-xii (1984) (pointing out that while most free blacks were poor, William Ellison, a free person of color, was wealthier than 90% of the whites in South Carolina); CARTER G. WOODSON, FREE NEGRO OWNERS OF SLAVES IN THE UNITED STATES IN 1830, at v (1924) (pointing out that "a considerable number of Negroes were slave owners themselves, and in some cases controlled large plantations); John H. Russell, *Colored Freemen as Slave Owners in Virginia*, 1 J. NEGRO HIST. 233, 234 (1916) (noting that some black Virginians held other blacks as slaves).

74. See generally BERLIN, *supra* note 73.

75. There were many slave "preachers" throughout the South who led services either with the acquiescence of their owners or without their knowledge. However, most of the slave states strictly regulated (or at least tried to regulate) black religious services because slaveowners understood the revolutionary potential of slaves and free blacks preaching to each other. Nat Turner, who led the bloodiest slave rebellion in the antebellum period, planned his revolt at religious services where he was the preacher. On the other hand, most Northern black communities of any size had one or more black churches and ministers. In 1791, Richard Allen founded the A.M.E. Zion church in Philadelphia. Allen's colleague, Absalom Jones, remained in the Episcopal Church, where he became its first black priest and in 1794 organized the African Church in Philadelphia. Many black abolitionists, such as Samuel E. Cornish, Alexander Crummell, Jermain Loguen, and J.W.C. Pennington were also clergymen. For information on these individuals, and the others cited in the rest of the notes for this sentence, see DANB, *supra* note 28.

76. All of the Southern states prohibited teaching slaves to read, and at various times some of these states also prevented any free blacks from gaining an education. Many Northern blacks taught school. For example, George B. Vashon, an early black lawyer, taught in Chillicothe, Ohio while in college. One of his students was the future attorney and dean of Howard Law School, John Mercer Langston. Lewis Hayden, a runaway slave and an abolitionist, founded a school in Detroit.

77. The slave states generally prohibited slaves and free blacks from working in the field of journalism. BERLIN, *supra* note 73, at 229. The most famous antebellum, Northern black newspaper publisher was Frederick Douglass. Others involved in this profession were Martin Delany, William C. Nell, David Ruggles, and the New York lawyer George B. Vashon. P. 392. In 1827, Samuel E. Cornish and John Russwurm began publishing *Freedom's Journal*, the first black owned and operated newspaper in the country.

78. James M. Cheeves, a mulatto gunsmith in Providence, Rhode Island, owned almost $4000 worth of real property. ROBERT J. COTTROL, THE AFRO-YANKEES: PROVIDENCE'S BLACK COMMUNITY IN THE ANTEBELLUM ERA 99, 124-125 (1982). On the importance of blacks being able to own weapons, see Robert J. Cottrol & Raymond T. Diamond, *The Second Amendment: Toward an Afro-Americanist Reconsideration*, 80 GEO. L.J. 309 (1991).

79. Among the antebellum black physicians were the abolitionist publisher Martin Delany and the abolitionist writer William Wells Brown. In 1854, John DeGrasse became the first black admitted to the Massachusetts Medical Society. John Rock was a dentist and a physician before becoming a lawyer. George A. Levesque, *Boston's Black Brahmin: Dr. John S. Rock*, 26 CIV. WAR HIST. 326, *reprinted in* AFRICAN AMERICANS AND THE LEGAL PROFESSION IN HISTORICAL PERSPECTIVE, *supra* note 53, at 166.

80. Finkelman, *supra* note 67, at 476. Not all northern states allowed blacks to become lawyers. In 1847 the Allegheny (Pennsylvania) County Bar rejected the admission of George Boyer Vashon because he was not white. P. 152.

81. P. 8.

82. P. 94.

83. These four were Robert Morris, Sr. (Massachusetts, 1847), p. 96, Aaron Alpeoria Bradley (Massachusetts, 1856), p. 100, George Boyer Vashon (New York, 1848), p. 152, and John Mercer Langston (Ohio, 1854). P. 34. In 1861, John Rock and Edward Garrison Walker gained admission to the Massachusetts bar. P. 100. Rock eventually became the first black admitted to the bar of the Supreme Court of the United States. See text accompanying notes 262-264 *infra*. Walker immediately joined a white lawyer already in practice and later became the first black elected to a state legislature in the United States. P. 100.

84. Smith asserts that in 1860, a black named C. Clay Morgan, "about whom little more is known," was admitted to the bar in Louisiana. P. 282. The source that Smith cites also lists a mulatto named Norbert Villère as practicing law in New Orleans in 1860-61. David C. Rankin, *The Origins of Negro Leadership in New Orleans During Reconstruction*, *in* SOUTHERN BLACK LEADERS, *supra* note 49, at 186, 189. This information is most likely incorrect. While free blacks in antebellum Louisiana had more rights than they did in any other southern state, they could not become notaries, much less practice law. According to Marie Windell, archivist for the Supreme Court of Louisiana, there is no record that either Morgan or Villère was admitted to the Louisiana bar before or after the Civil War. Furthermore, neither is listed as a lawyer in any city directory between 1856 and 1868, nor in *Gardner's New Orleans Directory* for that period. It is possible that Morgan and Villère gave legal advice to blacks in New Orleans, holding themselves out as lawyers within the black community. They may have told the census takers that they were

lawyers even though were not actually admitted to the bar or allowed to represent parties in court. Letter from Judith Schafer, Associate Director, Murphy Institute, Tulane University, to Paul Finkelman (Mar. 29, 1994) (on file with author).

This raises the problem, never addressed by Smith, of how to define a lawyer. If Morgan and Villère held themselves out as lawyers and told census takers the same, were they in fact lawyers? Peter Wallenstein notes that, according the 1880 census, a black woman named Providence Crute claimed that she was a lawyer practicing in Richmond, Virginia. She shared an abode with Nelson Crute, who was either her husband or a blood relative, who also reported to the census takers that he was a lawyer. Wallenstein, *supra* note 18, at 193. Wallenstein concludes: "The Crutes may indeed have been doing legal work, but the Richmond city directories do not list them as lawyers, and neither appears ever to have been admitted to practice in any court." *Id.* at 194 n.2.

85. For examples of proslavery constitutionalism, see PAUL FINKELMAN, AN IMPERFECT UNION: SLAVERY, FEDERALISM, AND COMITY 236 (1981) (examining the development of federal case law on slave transit); Paul Finkelman, *Slavery and the Constitutional Convention: Making a Covenant With Death, in* BEYOND CONFEDERATION: ORIGINS OF THE CONSTITUTION AND AMERICAN NATIONAL IDENTITY 188 (Richard Beeman, Stephen Botein & Edward C. Carter eds., 1987) (discussing the evolution of the Constitution into a national compact that favored slavery); Sanford Levinson, *Slavery in the Canon of Constitutional Law,* 68 CHI.-KENT L. REV. 1078 (1993) (discussing the way proslavery jurisprudence shaped constitutional development); William M. Wiecek, *Slavery and Abolition Before the United States Supreme Court, 1820-1860,* 65 J. AM. HIST. 34 (1978), *reprinted in* LAW, THE CONSTITUTION, AND SLAVERY 544 (Paul Finkelman ed., 1989) (discussing the historical context of Chief Justice Taney's proslavery constitutionalism).

86. The same was true of black attorneys in South Africa. It is perhaps not surprising that the most influential antiapartheid leader, Nelson Mandela, began his career as an attorney. See A. Leon Higginbotham, *Racism in American and South African Courts: Similarities and Differences,* 65 N.Y.U. L. REV. 479, 503-13 (1990).

87. Pp. 163-64. Draper left the United States to pursue a legal career in Liberia.

88. In 1860, Maryland had 83,942 free blacks—the most of any state—and 87,189 slaves. NEGRO POPULATION IN THE U.S., *supra* note 24, at 57 tbl. 6.

89. See Higginbotham, *supra* note 86, at 550. Higginbotham discusses segregation mainly in the South African courts, but also draws the parallel to the outright exclusion of blacks from American courts. *Id.*

90. In 1855, John Mercer Langston won the office of township clerk in Brownhelm, Ohio, to become the first black elected to public office by popular vote in the United States. WILLIAM CHEEK & AIMEE LEE CHEEK, JOHN MERCER LANGSTON AND THE FIGHT FOR BLACK FREEDOM, 1829-65, at 260 (1989). In 1847, Macon Bolling Allen was appointed a justice of the peace in Massachusetts. P. 96. In 1855, George B. Vashon became the first black to run for public office in New York State when he ran for attorney general on the Liberty Party ticket. CHEEK & CHEEK, *supra,* at 122 n.28. Although the product of a weak third party, the nomination nevertheless signaled the movement of blacks into statewide electoral politics. In 1857, Thomas Howland was elected as election warden in Providence, Rhode Island. COTTROL, *supra* note 78, at 93. At least one black held federal office before the Civil War. In 1845, Thomas C. Larkin, the United States Consul in Monterey, California, Mexico appointed William Alexander Leidesdorff as his vice-consul. Leidesdorff was the son of a Danish planter and a mulatto mother. Despite his mixed racial background, he was able to emigrate to the United States, gain citizenship, and briefly hold a federal position. He was active in California politics and a member of the school board before his untimely death in 1848. *Leidesdorff, William Alexander,* in DANB, *supra* note 28, at 394, 394. It is likely that some blacks served on school boards in Ohio and Michigan during this period because blacks were allowed to vote for those officers where there were separate schools and school boards.

91. Some jurisdictions responded to Chief Justice Taney with open defiance. A month after the decision, voters in Oberlin, Ohio, elected John Mercer Langston as township clerk. He won reelection in 1858. CHEEK & CHEEK, *supra* note 90, at 296.

92. Relying on *Dred Scott,* the Mississippi court asserted that it did not have to recognize the free status of a black living in the North. Mitchell v. Wells, 37 Miss. 235 (1859).

93. See Polydore v. Prince, 19 F. Cas. 950 (D.C.D. Me. 1837) (No. 11,257). For a discussion of that case, see FINKELMAN, *supra* note 85, at 243-45.

94. P. 2. For a discussion of Fessenden, see text accompanying note 250 *infra.*

95. Pp. 96-99.

96. P. 96.

97. P. 96.

98. See FINKELMAN, *supra* note 85, at 181-284. The federal assault on black rights began with Justice Joseph Story's opinion in Prigg v. Pennsylvania, 41 U.S. (16 Pet.) 539 (1842). For a discussion of that case, see Paul Finkelman, *Sorting out* Prigg v. Pennsylvania, 24 RUTGERS L.J. 605 (1993); Wiecek, *supra* note 85. The most sweeping limitation on the rights of free blacks was the Fugitive Slave Law of 1850, ch. 60, 9 Stat. 462 (1850).

99. HORTON & HORTON, *supra* note 69, at 56.

100. *Id.*

101. See JIM CROW IN BOSTON: THE ORIGIN OF THE SEPARATE BUT EQUAL DOCTRINE X (Leonard W. Levy & Douglas L. Jones eds., 1974) [hereinafter JIM CROW IN BOSTON].

102. *Id.* at x-xi.

103. See REPORT TO THE PRIMARY SCHOOL COMMITTEE, JUNE 15, 1846, ON THE PETITION OF SUNDRY COLORED PERSONS FOR THE ABOLITION OF THE SCHOOLS FOR COLORED CHILDREN 3-4 (Boston, J.H. Eastburn 1846), *reprinted in* JIM CROW IN BOSTON, *supra* note 101, at 3.

104. See REPORT OF THE MINORITY OF THE COMMITTEE OF THE PRIMARY SCHOOL BOARD, ON THE CASTE SCHOOLS OF THE CITY OF BOSTON 29-30 (Boston, A.J. Wright's Steam Press 1846), *reprinted in* JIM CROW IN BOSTON, *supra* note 101, at 43.
105. P. 97.
106. 59 Mass (5 Cush.) 198 (1849).
107. In the 1850s and 1860s, Sumner became the most vocal opponent of racial discrimination in the United States Senate. See generally DAVID DONALD, CHARLES SUMNER AND THE COMING OF THE CIVIL WAR (1960).
108. CHARLES SUMNER, ARGUMENT OF CHARLES SUMNER, ESQ. AGAINST THE CONSTITUTIONALITY OF SEPARATE COLORED SCHOOLS, IN THE CASE OF *SARAH C. ROBERTS VS. THE CITY OF BOSTON* (Boston, B.F. Roberts 1849), *reprinted in* ABOLITIONISTS IN NORTHERN COURTS: THE PAMPHLET LITERATURE 493 (Paul Finkelman ed., 1988).
109. 347 U.S. 483 (1954).
110. See DONALD, *supra* note 107, at 180-81. Historians Leonard Levy and Harlan Phillips observed that "Sumner's argument before Shaw deserves to be included in a volume of great documents on American democracy, for its nobility of sentiment, literary excellence, and grasp of principles which have been validated by modern sociology." Leonard W. Levy & Harlan B. Phillips, *The* Roberts *Case: Source of the "Separate But Equal" Doctrine*, 56 AM. HIST. REV. 510, 512-13 (1951), *reprinted in* AFRICAN AMERICANS AND THE LAW 282, 284-85 (Paul Finkelman ed., 1992).
111. Roberts v. City of Boston, 59 Mass (5 Cush.) 198, 206-09 (1849).
112. 163 U.S. 537 (1896). The use of *Roberts* in *Plessy* seems particularly inappropriate because in *Roberts* Chief Justice Shaw interpreted the Massachusetts Constitution of 1780, which lacked an equal protection clause. In *Plessy*, however, the Court interpreted the 14th Amendment, which had been adopted explicitly to give blacks equality and which included a guarantee of "equal protection of the laws." U.S. CONST. amend. XIV, § 1. For a discussion of this historical note, see Roderick T. Baltimore & Robert F. Williams, *The State Constitutional Roots of the "Separate But Equal" Doctrine: Roberts v. City of Boston*, 17 RUTGERS L.J. 537 (1986); see also Levy & Phillips, *supra* note 110.
113. Act of March 25, 1855 in Amendment of "An Act concerning Public Schools," Mass. Acts 256.
114. See Fugitive Slave Law of 1850, ch. 60, 9 Stat. 462 (1850); JANE H. PEASE & WILLIAM H. PEASE, THEY WHO WOULD BE FREE: BLACKS' SEARCH FOR FREEDOM, 1830-1861, at 219-21 (1974).
115. See REPORT OF THE PROCEEDINGS AT THE EXAMINATION: CHARLES G. DAVIS, ESQ., ON A CHARGE OF AIDING AND ABETTING IN THE RESCUE OF A FUGITIVE SLAVE (Boston 1851) [hereinafter REPORT OF THE RESCUE], *reprinted in* 1 FUGITIVE SLAVES AND AMERICAN COURTS: THE PAMPHLET LITERATURE 573, 589 (Paul Finkelman ed., 1988) [hereinafter FUGITIVE SLAVES]; see also HORTON & HORTON, *supra* note 69, at 105 (further details on Morris' representation of Shadrach).
116. The attorneys were Samuel E. Sewall, Ellis G. Loring, Charles List, and Charles G. Davis. REPORT OF THE RESCUE, *supra* note 115, at 576.
117. See REPORT OF THE RESCUE, *supra* note 115, at 583.
118. HORTON & HORTON, *supra* note 69, at 105.
119. See United States v. Morris, 26 F. Cas. 1323 (C.C.D.Mass. 1851) (No. 15,815); BENJAMIN QUARLES, BLACK ABOLITIONISTS 206 (1969). Smith erroneously asserts that Morris was tried for treason. P. 98.
120. See PEASE & PEASE, *supra* note 114, at 220-21; QUARLES, *supra* note 119, at 205-06.
121. See KLUGER, *supra* note 41, at 128 (quoting Houston).
122. HORTON & HORTON, *supra* note 69, at 58-59.
123. See TRIUMPH OF EQUAL SCHOOL RIGHTS IN BOSTON: PROCEEDINGS OF THE PRESENTATION MEETING HELD IN BOSTON, DEC. 17, 1855 (Boston, R.F. Wallcut 1856), *reprinted in* JIM CROW IN BOSTON, *supra* note 101, at 267. This pamphlet details the testimonial given "to Mr. William C. Nell, for his disinterested and untiring exertions in procuring the opening of the public schools of the city to all the children and youth within its limits, irrespective of complexional differences." *Id.* at 267.
124. HORTON & HORTON, *supra* note 69, at 59.
125. See generally TUSHNET, *supra* note 53, at 138-66 (drawing conclusions about the NAACP's attempts at social reform).
126. P. 97. As far as I know, no historian has ever pointed this out or commented on it.
127. Other black activists performed a similar role as liaisons in their communities. In the 1851 "Jerry Rescue" in Syracuse, the black minister Rev. Jermain Loguen coordinated the efforts of both white abolitionists and the black community to carry out the mission. PEASE & PEASE, *supra* note 114, at 223-25; QUARLES, *supra* note 83, at 209-11.
128. For example, in 1854, the fugitive slave Anthony Burns initially rejected an offer of legal help from the white attorney Richard Henry Dana, Jr. 3 THE JOURNAL OF RICHARD HENRY DANA, JR. 625-26 (Robert F. Lucid ed., 1968). It is possible that Burns would have been more receptive if Robert Morris or Macon Allen had approached him.
129. See text accompanying notes 171-173 *infra* (discussing the defense of George Crawford by Charles Hamilton Houston and other black lawyers).
130. See C. VANN WOODWARD, THE STRANGE CAREER OF JIM CROW 69 (3d ed. 1974).
131. Judge Higginbotham describes the threat to the apartheid system in South Africa when a black lawyer, Godfrey Pitje, who was "serving the obligatory post-law school apprenticeship with the law firm of [Nelson] Mandela & Tambo," refused to sit or stand in a place designated for nonwhites in the courtroom, but demanded to address the court from the same place as a white lawyer. Higginbotham, *supra* note 86, at 503-11. Curiously, even at the height of racial segregation Southern judges in the United States never attempted to segregate lawyers or defendants into separate sections of a courtroom. This situation may have arisen from the historical fact that black lawyers first practiced in the South during Reconstruction, which was before segregation became fully institutionalized. During this period, some blacks served on the bench in the South, while others served as prosecutors and jurors. Even after Reconstruction, blacks remained part of the legal system in some places. In 1886,

George H. White won election as the solicitor of Edgecomb County, North Carolina, and held that post until 1894. ERIC ANDERSON, RACE AND POLITICS IN NORTH CAROLINA, 1872-1901, at 317. In parts of Texas, blacks served on juries into the 1880s. Donald G. Nieman, *Black Political Power and Criminal Justice: Washington County, Texas, 1868-1884*, 55 J. S. HIST. 391, 399 (1989), *reprinted in* RACE AND CRIMINAL JUSTICE 281, 289 (Paul Finkelman ed., 1992).

132. Not all Southern whites could tolerate the idea of blacks facing whites on a level of equality. In 1871, three white men in Arkansas murdered attorney Wathal G. Wynn after a political argument. It seems likely that Wynn's role as a lawyer made him particularly vulnerable to lethal white hatred. A county judge, who was also black, ordered the arrest of the three whites. Shortly thereafter a mob of blacks sized the three white men and lynched them. Pp. 322-23.

133. The use of census figures for African-Americans has always been problematic. Smith uses them, as I do in this essay, because there is no alternative. But it is important to understand that virtually every census has undercounted blacks, including black lawyers. Recent attempts by big-city mayors to overturn the findings of the 1990 census based on persistent undercounting of blacks and other minorities illustrate the historical tendency of census takers to ignore nonwhites. In City of New York v. United States Dep't of Commerce, 822 F.Supp. 906 (E.D.N.Y. 1993), the District Court acknowledged that every census has resulted in an undercount and that "[m]ore troubling than the undercount itself . . . is that racial and ethnic minorities are undercounted to a greater degree than the population as a whole. This problem, known antiseptically as the 'differential undercount,' has skewed every census since the Bureau started measuring it in 1940." *Id.* at 911; see also City of Detroit v. Franklin, 4 F.3d 1367 (6th Cir.1993). In fact, this problem skewed the counting of blacks, and black lawyers, well before 1940. Fugitive slaves in the North always avoided being counted. For details on the misrepresentations of blacks in the 1840 census, see Albert Deutsch, *The First U.S. Census of the Insane (1840) and Its Use as Pro-Slavery Propaganda*, 15 BULL. HIST. MED. 469 (1944) *reprinted in* MEDICINE, NUTRITION, DEMOGRAPHY, AND SLAVERY 15 (Paul Finkelman ed., 1989).

The counting of black women lawyers in Virginia illustrates the problem of inaccurate census figures. Three black women, Marian Poe, Bertha Douglass, and Inez Fields, all practiced law in Virginia from the late 1920s through 1960. However, the 1930 census recorded only one black woman practicing law in the state. The 1940 census found three black women lawyers in the Commonwealth, as did the 1950 census. However, the 1960 census reported none at all. In fact, by 1950, other black women lawyers had begun to practice in Virginia. Thus, from 1930 to 1960, only the 1940 census had the correct number of black women lawyers in the state. See Wallenstein, *supra* note 18, at 195, 211, 213. For a discussion of the 1880 census and the problem of Providence Crute, see note 84 *supra.*

134. ERIK W. AUSTIN, POLITICAL FACTS OF THE UNITED STATES SINCE 1789, at 466-69 (1986) (census figures on blacks). For census figures for lawyers, see pp. 634-37 tbl. 13. The best source for statistics on blacks before 1915 is NEGRO POPULATION IN THE U.S., *supra* note 24.

135. JOHN HOPE FRANKLIN, RECONSTRUCTION AFTER THE CIVIL WAR 85-103, 127-51 (1961).

136. The best history of this period is RAYFORD W. LOGAN, THE BETRAYAL OF THE NEGRO (1965). For a debate on the development of segregation, see Howard N. Rabinowitz, *More than the Woodward Thesis: Assessing the Strange Career of Jim Crow*, 75 J. AM. HIST. 842 (1988), *reprinted in* AFRICAN AMERICANS AND THE LAW, *supra* note 110, at 470; WOODWARD, *supra* note 130; see also AGE OF JIM CROW, *supra* note 9 (collected essays on segregation).

137. Pp. 624-25.

138. Pp. 626-27.

139. Pp. 628-32.

140. Pp. 634-35.

141. See AUSTIN, *supra* note 134, at 466-69.

142. The only exceptions seem to be Maryland and Missouri, where there were substantially more black attorneys in 1940 than in 1900. Pp. 624-25, 634-35. This may be attributable to the fact that both states were in the upper South and had very large cities—Baltimore and St. Louis—with large black communities able to support black attorneys while also providing them with some security and safety.

143. AUSTIN, *supra* note 134, at 463-69. The 17 include the 15 states that maintained slavery in 1860 Plus West Virginia and Oklahoma. For a discussion of how to define the South, see Paul Finkelman, *Exploring Southern Legal History*, 64 N.C. L. REV. 77, 85 (1985).

144. In 1930 the 17 Southern states had the following number of black male lawyers: Alabama, 4; Arkansas, 16; Delaware, 2; Florida, 10; Georgia, 14; Kentucky, 25; Louisiana 8; Maryland, 33; Mississippi, 6; Missouri, 55: North Carolina, 27; Oklahoma, 53; South Carolina, 13; Tennessee, 26; Texas, 20; Virginia, 57; West Virginia, 20. Pp. 631-32. According to Smith, there were only 24 black women lawyers in the nation in 1930, but he does not indicate where they lived. Pp. 631-33.

145. Pp. 631-33.

146. Pp. 634-37.

147. Pp. 634-37

148. Charles H. Houston, *The Need for Negro Lawyers*, 4 J. NEGRO EDUC. 49, 51 (1935), *reprinted in* AFRICAN AMERICANS AND THE LEGAL PROFESSION IN HISTORICAL PERSPECTIVE, *supra* note 53, at 149, 151.

149. *Id.* at 52, *reprinted in* AFRICAN AMERICANS AND THE LEGAL PROFESSION IN HISTORICAL PERSPECTIVE, *supra* note 53, at 152.

150. Pp. 624-37.

151. See notes 172-173 *infra* and accompanying text.

152. P. 303. The convictions were overturned in Powell v. Alabama, 287 U.S. 45, 71 (1932) (overturning the rape conviction of a black on the grounds that he did not have adequate counsel).

153. Richard C. Cortner, A "Scottsboro" Case in Mississippi: The Supreme Court and Brown v. Mississippi 29 (1986). This led to the Supreme Court decision in Brown v. Mississippi, 297 U.S. 278, 287 (1936) (reversing the murder convictions of three black tenant farmers because the convictions were based on testimony coerced by brutal physical torture including whippings and a mock hanging).

154. However, many black lawyers in the South avoided controversial cases because they did not want to undermine their own financial security or their safety. In 1935 Charles Hamilton Houston complained that generally the "older Negro lawyers in the South . . . have tended to avoid highly inflammable issues and stay in the less controversial fields of strictly civil work and office practice." Houston, *supra* note 148, at 52.

155. Horton & Horton, *supra* note 69, at 56.

156. *Id.*

157. Scott Ellsworth, Death in a Promised Land: The Tulsa Race Riot of 1921, at 84 (1982).

158. *Id.* at 85 (quoting testimony of Mayor T.D. Evans before the City Commission of Tulsa).

159. *Id.*

160. *Id.*

161. Telephone interview with John Hope Franklin (Mar. 29, 1994) (based on Buck C. Franklin's unpublished autobiography).

162. Ellsworth, *supra* note 157, at 86-88. The *Lockett* case seems to be unreported, but was noted in a Tulsa newspaper. *Id.*

163. In the North, many white lawyers were willing to take civil rights cases. Depending on the era, some of these lawyers were associated with antislavery organizations, the Republican Party, the NAACP, the American Civil Liberties Union, or even the Communist Party. Some were politicians, law professors, or civic minded attorneys who believed that racial discrimination was unjust. Some other white organizations—particularly Jewish organizations— made common cause with blacks in fighting restrictive covenants and other forms of housing discrimination as well as discrimination in employment and university admissions. In contrast to the North, it was almost impossible to find Southern white lawyers willing to take cases that challenged the racial status quo, except during Reconstruction. Thus, in the South, blacks had to rely on African-American lawyers or white Northerners to represent them in controversial cases. Since Northerners could not participate in cases at the trial level, blacks in the South could generally rely only on black lawyers. As a result, particularly in cases were a black defendant was charged with raping or killing a white or violating segregation laws, and in cases where blacks sued to enforce the "equal" aspect of "separate but equal," effective counsel was difficult to find.

The Scottsboro cases illustrate this phenomenon. The Scottsboro boys were charged with raping two white girls. Because no white lawyers would take their case and because the appointed counsel refused to provide an effective defense, the boys were denied effective representation. Indeed, the Supreme Court overturned one conviction on this ground in Powell v. Alabama, 247 U.S. 45 (1932), which was argued by Northern white attorneys. This case later led to Brown v. Mississippi, 297 U.S. 278 (1936). See text accompanying note 153 *supra.*

164. See, e.g., Howard N. Rabinowitz, *The Conflict Between Blacks and the Police in the Urban South, 1865-1900,* 39 The Historian 62 (1972), *reprinted in* Race and Criminal Justice 318 (Paul Finkelman ed., 1992). Post-Reconstruction Atlanta did not have black police officers until the late 1940s. Michael J. Klarman, Brown, *Racial Change, and the Civil Rights Movement,* 80 Va. L. Rev. 7, 63 (1994). Similar changes in police hiring policy in Raleigh, North Carolina, and Macon County, Alabama, did not take place until that same period. *Id.* at 63-64.

165. See generally Benno C. Schmidt, Jr., *Juries, Jurisdiction, and Race Discrimination: The Lost Promise of* Strauder v. West Virginia, 61 Tex. L. Rev. 1401 (1983). The current debate over Batson v. Kentucky, 476 U.S. 79 (1986) (holding that prosecutor cannot use peremptory challenges to exclude jurors solely because of their race), illustrates how the problem of jury exclusion continues. See, e.g., Susan N. Herman, *Why the Court Loves* Batson: *Representation-Reinforcement, Colorblindness and the Jury,* 67 Tul. L. Rev. 1807 (1993). For a discussion of blacks on juries in one Southern jurisdiction during and after Reconstruction, see Nieman, *supra* note 131.

166. Paul Finkelman, *The Crime of Color,* 67 Tul. L. Rev. 2063 (1993).

167. Pp. 162, 303.

168. P. 13 (footnote omitted).

169. P. 28. This makes sense for two reasons. First, by World War I there were so few black lawyers in the South that most Southern whites could not have found a local black lawyer even if they had wanted one. See notes 133-150 *supra* and accompanying text. Second, any advantage a Southern white defendant might have gained from the experience of a black attorney would have been undermined by the hostility directed at the black lawyer and the white client, who, by choosing a black attorney, challenged traditional notions of Southern racial etiquette. Charles Hamilton Houston noted that black lawyers in the South suffered from "subtle propaganda spread by the lower-class white lawyer to the effect that a Negro throws away his case in getting a Negro lawyer because a Negro lawyer has no influence with the Court." Houston, *supra* note 148, at 51.

170. Cheek & Cheek, *supra* note 90, at 246.

171. Jess Hollins was convicted of raping a white woman and sentenced to death. The Supreme Court subsequently overturned the conviction because of racial discrimination in the jury selection. On retrial, an all-white jury again convicted Hollins, but recommended a life sentence rather than the death penalty. Cummins, *supra* note 55.

172. P. 234.

173. Kluger, *supra* note 41, at 153. Houston could have appealed the case on the grounds that the jury pool had contained no blacks. Even if such an appeal might have resulted in a victory before the United States Supreme Court, it would have only led to a new trial. It seems improbable that Houston or any of the other lawyers believed that George Crawford was innocent,

id. at 154, so a new trial would probably have only led to another conviction, with the possibility of a death sentence. In this case, Houston fully understood that a life sentence for a black man found guilty of brutally murdering a white woman in Virginia was in fact a huge victory.

174. P. 208.

175. P. 389.

176. P. 389

177. P. 132.

178. P. 12.

179. P. 303.

180. In the antebellum period, scholars seriously debated whether blacks were even the same species as whites and engaged in extensive "research" to prove that blacks were intellectually inferior to all other races. See generally WILLIAM R. STANTON, THE LEOPARD'S SPOTS: SCIENTIFIC ATTITUDES TOWARD RACE IN AMERICA, 1815-1859 (1960). By 1900, this had changed only slightly.

> [M]ost of the social scientists of the Progressive era believed that Negroes were inferior to whites but capable of improvement. . . . Accepting the concept of higher and lower races as determined by differences in historical achievement, [scholars] rated the blacks above the Tasmanians and Red Indians, who had shown no adaptability or capability of improvement.

GEORGE FREDERICKSON, THE BLACK IMAGE IN THE WHITE MIND: THE DEBATE ON AFRO-AMERICAN CHARACTER AND DESTINY, 1817-1914, at 313-14 (1971). In 1896, Franklin Henry Giddings asserted that

> The Negro . . . yields easily to environing influences. Deprived of the support of the stronger races, he still relapses into savagery, but kept in contact with the whites, he readily takes the external impress of civilization, and there is reason to hope that he will yet acquire a measure of its spirit.

FRANKLIN HENRY GIDDINGS, THE PRINCIPLES OF SOCIOLOGY (1896), *quoted in* FREDERICKSON, *supra*, at 314.

181. P. 96.

182. CHEEK & CHEEK, *supra* note 90, at 245.

183. *Id.*

184. Pp. 207, 254 n.132 (quoting a story in the *Chester News* with the headline "Probably First Colored Attorney to Appear Here").

185. P. 208.

186. KLUGER, *supra* note 41, at 153.

187. *Id.*

188. P. 13.

189. P. 13.

190. P. 4.

191. My analysis should not be misunderstood as denying that some black lawyers, such as Thurgood Marshall, deserve a place in the pantheon of heroes of American liberty. But there is a clear difference between lawyers involved in social change and leaders of movements. What makes the African American community different from the white community is the paucity of lawyers in positions of political and social leadership. Even today it is difficult to name any African-American lawyers whose influence in the black community reaches the same level as Rev. Jesse Jackson or Rev. Louis Farrakhan.

192. DANB, *supra* note 28, contains biographical sketches of these African-American leaders.

193. DANB, *supra* note 28, lists 77 African-Americans as "Civil Rights Leaders." Only 17 of these are also listed as lawyers. Out of 88 politicians, only 25 are also listed as lawyers. The book lists 139 educators, 88 politicians, 85 members of the clergy, 80 editors, and 77 civil rights leaders, but only 55 lawyers. *Id.* at xi, xiii-xiv, xvi-xix. This rather crude estimate is surely imperfect, but it does suggest that black lawyers, especially in the period under consideration, were not nearly as important to the black community as Smith thinks.

194. Smith discusses the segregation of the American Bar Association at pp. 541-610.

195. HORTON & HORTON, *supra* note 69, at 57.

196. P. 103.

197. *Johnson, James Weldon*, in DANB, *supra* note 28, at 353, 354.

198. P. 239. As an attorney, when not in the legislature, however, Nutter battled segregation. See note 218 *infra* and accompanying text.

199. P. 352. As an attorney, when not in the legislature, however, Anderson battled segregation. See note 219 *infra* and accompanying text.

200. See, e.g., pp. 135-49, 396, 402-03.

201. For example, William H. Lewis was an assistant United States attorney in Boston under Theodore Roosevelt and later an assistant Attorney General in the Taft administration. Pp. 106-07. James Adlai Cobb had served as a special assistant to the Attorney General under Roosevelt and Taft and actually continued on for the first two years of the Wilson administration. Cobb later served two terms on the municipal court of the District of Columbia, appointed by Coolidge and reappointed by Hoover. P. 139. Perry Howard was a Special Assistant Attorney General under Harding and Coolidge. Pp. 136-37. Similarly, Louis Rothschild Mehlinger, "whose father was Jewish and mother black," served in the Department of Justice under Coolidge and Hoover. P. 137. However, as John Hope Franklin notes, "What patronage [blacks] enjoyed under the Republican presidents during the late nineteenth and early twentieth centuries had diminished perceptibly under Wilson." JOHN HOPE FRANKLIN,

FROM SLAVERY TO FREEDOM: A HISTORY OF NEGRO AMERICANS 383, 384 (5th ed. 1980). Moreover, by the 1920s, blacks saw their few patronage appointments as "political crumbs." *Id.* For further details on Howard and Lewis, see DANB, *supra* note 28.

202. In 1928, Oscar De Priest won a seat in Congress from a black district in Chicago. "De Priest's position was peculiar. He represented not only his own district, but all the Negroes of the United States." JOHN HOPE FRANKLIN & ALFRED A. MOSS, JR., FROM SLAVERY TO FREEDOM 343-44 (6th ed. 1988).

203. P. 303.

204. John Hope Franklin relates that, by 1928,

> Prominent black Republican leaders, such as Benjamin Davis of Georgia, Perry Howard of Mississippi, and William McDonald of Texas, lost influence in their states as the Republican high command began to recognize white leaders in those states to seat white delegates at the national convention instead of the Negro delegates who presented themselves.

FRANKLIN, *supra* note 201, at 384. The DANB entry on Howard concludes that "[m]any Negroes believed that he, like the other Negro Republican state committeeman, Benjamin J. Davis, Sr., did little to advance their cause." Howard, Perry Wilson, in DANB, *supra* note 28, at 331, 331.

205. Compare the discussion of these individuals with that of Howard in DANB, *supra* note 28. Smith makes the mistake of assuming that appointed political positions reflected power within political parties or the national government, and that this power was more significant than the power and influence of black leaders within their own communities. Moreover, it is clear that many blacks who held no formal offices—like editors Carl Murphy and Robert Vann or organizational leaders like Walter White—had a far greater influence over national politics than did the token black officeholders like Perry Howard. Black Republicans, for example, dutifully supported Herbert Hoover's nomination of John J. Parker to the Supreme Court, while Walter White and other leaders helped lead the successful fight against his confirmation. See FRANKLIN, *supra* note 201, at 383-85; KLUGER, *supra* note 41, at 141-43. The Christian Science Monitor called the defeat of the Parker nomination "[t]he first national demonstration of the Negro's power since Reconstruction days." *Id.* at 144 (quoting the newspaper report).

206. P. 289; see REMINISCENCES OF AN ACTIVE LIFE: THE AUTOBIOGRAPHY OF JOHN ROY LYNCH 365-69 (John Hope Franklin ed., 1970).

207. PAULI MURRAY, THE AUTOBIOGRAPHY OF A BLACK ACTIVIST, FEMINIST LAWYER, PRIEST, AND POET 115 (1987).

208. *Id.* at 115-16.

209. *Id.* at 182.

210. KLUGER, *supra* note 41, at 471.

211. In 1932-1934, Howard Law School graduates who returned to the South averaged less than $500 in their first year of practice. Thus, Charles Hamilton Houston concluded that "[T]he average Negro law graduate who goes South expecting to make a lot of money is doomed to disappointment." Houston, *supra* note 148, at 51-52.

212. Pp. 207-08; see text accompanying note 293 *infra*.

213. Pp. 237-38.

214. 31 S.E. 985 (1898).

215. For a discussion of the general state of civil rights in this period, see DONALD G. NIEMAN, PROMISES TO KEEP: AFRICAN-AMERICANS AND THE CONSTITUTIONAL ORDER, 1776 TO THE PRESENT 78-113 (1991).

216. *Williams*, 31 S.E. at 986.

217. During his tenure in the West Virginia legislature, Nutter "fought for the establishment of a mental hospital for blacks and for an industrial school for boys and girls." P. 239. As a member of the Kentucky legislature, Anderson worked to pass the Anderson-Mayer State Aid Act, which authorized "the annual appropriation of $17,000 to assist Negro boys and girls to pursue courses of higher educaton [sic] outside of Kentucky." P. 330 (footnote omitted).

218. P. 239.

219. P. 330.

220. See text accompanying notes 214-216 *supra.*

221. P. 287.

222. Pp. 287-88.

223. P. 288.

224. 154 F.2d 931 (5th Cir.1946).

225. P. 288.

226. P. 349. At this time Texas was essentially a one-party state. The winner of the Democratic primary invariably won the general election. Thus, by banning blacks from the primary, the Democratic party, which claimed to be a private organization, was able to effectively disenfranchise black voters without any state action that would have violated the 14th or 15th Amendments.

227. 321 U.S. 649 (1944).

228. P. 343.

229. In North Carolina some

> lawyer s faced violence when they attempted to represent their clients, especially when the victim was white. Armond W. Scott, a graduate of Shaw [University's] law school, was run out of Wilmington in the early part of the twentieth century for defending a black man accused of raping a white woman. He fled to Washington, D.C.

P. 206.

In 1895, a mob of whites in Tuskegee, Alabama, attacked Thomas A. Harris because they "did not want any Negro lawyer" in their community. Pp. 272, 304 n.20. Harris survived a gunshot wound in the leg, but he "never practiced law in Tuskegee" after the attack. P. 273. Smith also reports that "assaults against black lawyers were prevalent in Alabama before 1895." P. 273. In 1871, three white men in Arkansas murdered Wyathal G. Wynn, a graduate of Howard University Law School, but Smith does not indicate if the murder was racially motivated. Pp. 322-23.

In Missouri and Tennessee, attacks on black attorneys were common. Smith notes that "[b]lack lawyers arguing civil rights cases in some parts of Missouri were physically assaulted by white mobs," p. 352, while "lawyers defending black men charged with rape in Tennessee were, on occasion, forced to flee the state after their clients were lynched." P. 353.

230. Most Southern law schools did not accept blacks. See notes 20 & 39 *supra* and accompanying text. The first case on this issue was Missouri *ex rel.* Gaines v. Canada, 305 U.S. 337 (1938). While Lloyd L. Gaines won the case, he disappeared after the Supreme Court ordered the University of Missouri School of Law to accept him. He may have been murdered by opponents of integration. In Sipuel v. Oklahoma State Bd. of Regents, 332 U.S. 631 (1948), the Court ordered the integration of the University of Oklahoma School of Law. The integration of the University of Texas School of Law was ordered in Sweatt v. Painter, 339 U.S. 639 (1950). However, the law schools of the deep South remained segregated until the end of the next decade.

231. P. 235.

232. P. 235.

233. The judge in this instance "had stated that blacks accused of raping white women should be lynched." P. 159. While not directed at black attorneys per se, statements like this clearly undermined their credibility within the profession.

234. P. 156.

235. P. 156.

236. KLUGER, *supra* note 41, at 155, uses this term for a chapter title. It was also used during the 1930s by leftist critics of Roosevelt.

237. JEROLD S. AUERBACH, UNEQUAL JUSTICE: LAWYERS AND SOCIAL CHANGE IN MODERN AMERICA 188 (1976).

238. Letter from Nelson H. Nichols, Jr., to Charles Houston (Feb. 24, 1934), quoted in AUERBACH, *supra* note 237, at 188, 342 n.52. Even with such instances of discrimination and overt racism, Roosevelt broke new ground for black lawyers, when he appointed William Henry Hastie to be the nation's first black United States district judge and later a civilian aide to the Secretary of War. Pp. 51-52.

239. LAWRENCE M. FRIEDMAN, A HISTORY OF AMERICAN LAW 606 (2d ed. 1985).

240. *Id.* at 606-20 (describing the development of legal education from before the Civil War to the turn of the century).

241. In the early 20th century, a number of law schools opened in conjunction with the night education programs at various YMCAs. Many blacks might have been able to afford these inexpensive schools, but most of them were in Northern cities, while most blacks—more than 80%—lived in the South.

242. STEVENS, *supra* note 16, at 8.

243. *Id.* at 21.

244. P. 204. White later served in Congress and was the last Southern black in Congress until the modern period. On White, see generally ANDERSON, *supra* note 131.

245. P. 223.

246. P. 324.

247. P. 350. Sweatt v. Painter, 210 S.W.2d 442 (1948), *rev'd*, 339 U.S. 629 (1950), led to the desegregation of Texas Law School and effectively eliminated the "separate but equal" doctrine as a defense of segregated graduate and professional schools.

248. The willingness of abolitionists to train black lawyers undermines the arguments by scholars such as Jane and William Pease that abolitionists were racists. See William H. Pease & Jane H. Pease, *Antislavery, Ambivalence: Immediatism, Expediency, Race*, 17 AM. Q. 682, 685-86 (1965), *reprinted in* 14 ARTICLES ON AMERICAN SLAVERY: ANTISLAVERY 356, 359-60 (Paul Finkelman ed., 1989).

249. P. 93.

250. William A. Robinson, *Fessenden, Samuel*, in 6 DICTIONARY OF AMERICAN BIOGRAPHY 346 (Allen Johnson & Dumas Malone eds., 1931). Smith describes Fessenden as a "white liberal." P. 93. This anachronistic description makes no sense, since "liberal" in the antebellum period had no political meaning. Nor was Fessenden a "liberal" in the modern sense. His membership in the Maine Anti-Slavery society and his affiliation with the Liberty Party put him on the fringe of white society. He was, in modern language, quite "radical."

251. P. 95. Smith inexplicably says that Sewell, one of the two most prominent abolitionist lawyers in Boston, was from Maine.

252. CHEEK & CHEEK, *supra* note 90, at 132.

253. *Id.*

254. *Id.* at 226-29.

255. *Id.* at 233.

256. *Id.* at 233-34.

257. *Id.* at 234.

258. *Id.*

259. *Id.*

260. For a discussion of Morris' career, see text accompanying notes 99-128 *supra.*

261. Smith's description of Loring, as "a white man connected with the anti-slavery movement," p. 96, is curious. Historians generally use "antislavery" as generic term covering the whole spectrum of opposition to slavery. Abolitionists—which Loring was—were more radical, more uncompromising, and more likely to support racial equality. Loring was a key advisor to William

Lloyd Garrison and was deeply involved in a number of cases involving slaves in transit or fugitive slave and other abolitionist activities. See PAUL FINKELMAN, SLAVERY IN THE COURTROOM 10, 25, 28-29, 86-87, 225, 234 (1985).

262. Levesque, *supra* note 79, at 166.

263. Pp. 100-102. Smith has also located "the first time in the history of the Supreme Court [that] a Negro introduced a white man as qualified to practice before that court." P. 415 (footnote omitted). In 1914, William R. Stewart, a black lawyer from Youngstown, Ohio, moved to admit Emil J. Anderson, also of Youngstown, to the Supreme Court bar. P. 415.

264. Even admission to the bar of the Supreme Court of the United States did not eliminate the stigma of race. Upon Rock's return trip to Baltimore, the ticket agent refused him passage for lack of a valid travel pass. Rock offered his certificate of admission to the Court as proof of his right to travel to Washington, D.C., but the agent rejected it as fraudulent. P. 102. This incident may reflect either the racism of the particular agent in charge or the scarcity of black lawyers in the United States, or it may indicate that until the previous day none had ever been admitted to practice before the Supreme Court. It may simply be that the cautious agent overseeing rail travel out of wartime Washington did not believe the certificate was real because it may not have conformed to any acceptable proof of Rock's status.

265. P. 152.

266. See MAGAILI LARSON, THE RISE OF PROFESSIONALISM 21-23 (1977) (discussing the medical profession's efforts at monopolization). One result of this professionalism was a restriction in the availability of abortion rights as the AMA used its growing power to prevent midwives and other professionals from performing abortions. See JAMES C. MOHR, ABORTION IN AMERICA: THE ORIGINS AND EVOLUTION OF NATIONAL POLICY, 1800-1900, at 160-70 (1978).

267. BURTON T. BLEDSTEIN, THE CULTURE OF PROFESSIONALISM: THE MIDDLE CLASS AND THE RISE OF HIGHER EDUCATION IN AMERICA 84 (1976).

268. See *id.* at 86.

269. STEVENS, *supra* note 16, at 9.

270. See *id.* at 25, 27; see also FRIEDMAN, *supra* note 239, at 606-20.

271. STEVENS, *supra* note 16, at 73.

272. *Id.* at 80.

273. Pp. 41-65.

274. P. 42; see also FRIEDMAN, *supra* note 239, at 648-54 (describing the development of the ABA, its exclusionary practices and motivations, and the development of formal bar admission requirements); STEVENS, *supra* note 16, at 92-111 (same). These changes were directed at a wide variety of groups, including Jews, Italian immigrants, and other non-Protestants, as well as blacks. In defending the requirement that all law students first complete an undergraduate degree, one New York lawyer declared it was "absolutely necessary" that lawyers be "able to read, write and talk the English language— not Bohemian, not Gaelic, not Yiddish, but English." *Id.* at 101.

275. Pp. 35-40.

276. P. 601 n.218.

277. P. 152.

278. P. 152

279. P. 153.

280. Robert H. Woody, *Jonathan Jasper Wright, Associate Justice of the Supreme Court of South Carolina, 1870-77*, 18 J. NEGRO HIST. 114, 120-22 (1933), *reprinted in* AFRICAN AMERICANS AND THE LEGAL PROFESSION IN HISTORICAL PERSPECTIVE, *supra* note 53, at 508, 514-16.

281. *Id.*

282. P. 279 (quoting JAMES WELDON JOHNSON, ALONG THIS WAY 141 (1933)). Despite the racism of one of the examining judges, Johnson did pass the examination and became a member of the Florida bar.

283. CHARLES A. LOFGREN, THE PLESSY CASE: A LEGAL-HISTORICAL INTERPRETATION 29-31 (1987).

284. 163 U.S. 537 (1896).

285. LOFGREN, *supra* note 283, at 31.

286. *Id.*

287. P. 284.

288. P. 284

289. LOFGREN, *supra* note 283, at 148.

290. *Id.* at 30. Walker, who served as local counsel for the case in Louisiana received a fee of $1000. *Id.* at 31. This is a rare example of a white willing to file suit in a racial discrimination case in the post-Reconstruction South.

291. CHARLES M. MARTIN, THE ANGELO HERNDON CASE AND SOUTHERN JUSTICE (1976).

292. P. 200.

293. P. 200.

294. Herndon v. Lowry, 301 U.S. 242 (1937). Herndon's conviction was not reversed in Herndon v. Georgia, 295 U.S. 441 (1935), as Smith incorrectly asserts. P. 251 n.70.

295. P. 16.

296. P. 16.

297. TUSHNET, *supra* note 53, at 1-2, 16.

298. P. xiii.

299. For a discussion of civil rights litigation following World War II, see JACK GREENBERG, CRUSADERS IN THE COURTS (1994).
300. Pp. 36, 158, 486.
301. P. 36.
302. Pp. 158-59. Smith suspects that the dean's action may have been based on gender discrimination rather than race, because a black man also served on the law review that year. However, the dean may also have opposed the selection of a second black on the law review. For a perceptive analysis of the phenomenon of limiting the number of blacks in any institutional setting, see DERRICK BELL, AND WE ARE NOT SAVED: THE ELUSIVE QUEST FOR RACIAL JUSTICE 140-161 (1987).
303. P. 402; FEINGOLD, *supra* note 37, at 213-15; see also David G. Dalin, *Marshall, Louis, in* JEWISH-AMERICAN HISTORY AND CULTURE: AN ENCYCLOPEDIA 379 (Jack Fischel & Sanford Pinsker eds., 1992).
304. P. 402.
305. P. 402.
306. P. 545.
307. Pp. 486-87.
308. Pp. 401-02.
309. P. 403.
310. KLUGER, *supra* note 41, at 115.
311. PHILIPPA STRUM, LOUIS D. BRANDEIS: JUSTICE FOR THE PEOPLE 332 (1984).
312. *Id.*; see Nixon v. Condon, 286 U.S. 73 (1932).
313. FEINGOLD, *supra* note 37; Will Maslow, *American Jewish Congress, in* JEWISH-AMERICAN HISTORY AND CULTURE: AN ENCYCLOPEDIA, *supra* note 303, at 28. For example, in Shelley v. Kraemer, 334 U.S. 1 (1948), the successful assault on restrictive covenants, there were separate amicus briefs from the American Jewish Congress, American Jewish Committee, and a group of private Jewish citizens of Beverly Hills, California.
314. MCNEIL, *supra* note 26, at 64, 67.
315. KLUGER, *supra* note 41, at 125 (quoting Justice Brandeis).
316. STRUM, *supra* note 311, at 333.
317. Pp. 383, 401-02.
318. Corrigan v. Buckley, 271 U.S. 323 (1926).
319. 334 U.S. 1 (1948).
320. Pp. 19-20.
321. P. 20.
322. See Finkelman, *supra* note 67, at 422-24.
323. See note 327 *infra*; see also LEON LITWACK, NORTH OF SLAVERY: THE NEGRO IN THE FREE STATES (1961).
324. Act of Feb. 10, 1849, 47 Ohio Laws 17 (1849).
325. See note 327 *infra*.
326. See note 327 *infra*; FINKELMAN, *supra* note 85.
327. For the antebellum period, see EUGENE BERWANGER, THE FRONTIER AGAINST SLAVERY: WESTERN ANTI-NEGRO PREJUDICE AND THE SLAVERY EXTENSION CONTROVERSY (1967); N. DWIGHT HARRIS, THE HISTORY OF NEGRO SERVITUDE IN ILLINOIS AND THE SLAVERY AGITATION IN THAT STATE, 1719-1864 (1904); Paul Finkelman, *Evading the Ordinance: The Persistence of Bondage in Indiana and Illinois*, 9 J. EARLY REPUBLIC 21 (1989); Mason Fishback, *Illinois Legislation on Slavery and Free Negroes*, 1818-1865, *in* TRANSACTIONS OF THE ILLINOIS STATE HISTORICAL SOCIETY 414 (1904). For the later periods, see DAVID GERBER, BLACK OHIO AND THE COLOR LINE, 1860-1915 (1976); EMMA LOU THORNBROUGH, THE NEGRO IN INDIANA: A STUDY OF A MINORITY (1957). For a book which illustrates the racial fairness in some parts of the Midwest, see kenneth l. Kusmer, A GHETTO TAKES SHAPE (1978). For a discussion of the complexity of race relations in the Midwest, see Finkelman, *supra* note 67.
328. Paul Finkelman, *The Protection of Black Rights in Seward's New York*, 34 CIV. WAR HIST. 211, 211-34 (1988); David McBride, *Mid-Atlantic State Courts and the Struggle With the "Separate But Equal" Doctrine*, 17 RUTGERS L.J. 569, 570 (1986).
329. McBride, *supra* note 328.
330. Unfortunately, Smith also perpetuates the old Bluebook style of not giving first names of authors in footnotes and in his bibliography. This antiquated style, which even the Bluebook finally abandoned, undermines the utility of his otherwise superbly useful bibliography. I am mystified as to why Smith did this, or why the University of Pennsylvania Press—which as a serious academic press ought to know better—allowed it to occur. Other aspects of the book, including less than adequate proofreading suggest that the publisher did not serve the author well.
331. P. 558 (quoting Johnson).

Chapter 69

First Women

The Contribution of American Women to the Law

1994

Sandra Day O'Connor

The author is an associate justice of the United States Supreme Court. This foreword first appeared in 28 *Valparaiso University Law Review* XIII (1994).

This issue of the *Valparaiso University Law Review* is devoted to the contributions of some "firsts" among women in the law. Each of these women was the first to engage in a wide variety of activities previously thought to be impossible or improper for women to do. All of us owe a great debt of gratitude to our determined predecessors who, despite daunting obstacles, made possible the professional and other opportunities women lawyers enjoy today. As another woman who was the first to serve in a position formerly held only by men, I can appreciate with particular sensitivity the strength of character and the determination these adventurous women demonstrated in pursuing their career goals against far more formidable barriers.

These earlier legal pioneers faced a profession and a society that espoused what has been called "the cult of domesticity," a view that women were by nature different from men, suited only for motherhood and homelife—compassionate, selfless, gentle, moral, and pure. Their minds were attuned to art and religion, not logic. Men, on the other hand, were thought to be fitted by nature for competition and intellectual discovery in the world—battle-hardened, shrewd, authoritative, and tough-minded. A male attorney of the period commented, "[A] woman can't keep a secret, and for that reason if no other, I doubt if anybody will ever consult a woman lawyer."[1]

The four women honored in this volume had more spunk, spirit, and wit than they were given credit for by their male contemporaries. One of the first American women to seek admission to the bar, Myra Bradwell of Chicago, studied law under her husband and applied to the Illinois bar in 1869. Despite the fact that she had passed the necessary examination with credit, she was refused admission. The Illinois

34. Chancellor MacCracken Addressing the Class. Under the auspices of the Dr. Henry Mitchell MacCracken, Chancellor from 1891 to 1910, New York University offered law classes, taught by several lecturers, to women in the 1890s, although the law school was then open only to men. In this chapter, Justice O'Connor depicts the admission and education of four nineteenth-century women. (*Engraving courtesy of New York University Archives.*)

Supreme Court reasoned that, as a married woman, her contracts were not binding, and that contracts were the essence of an attorney-client relationship. The court also proclaimed that "God designed the sexes to occupy different spheres of action, and that it belonged to men to make, apply and execute the laws."[2] The Supreme Court of the United States agreed. Justice Bradley, concurring in the Court's opinion, cited the natural differences between men and women as the reason Bradwell could not be admitted: "Man is, or should be, woman's protector and defender. The natural and proper timidity and delicacy which belongs to the female sex evidently unfits it for many of the occupations of civil life."[3] Bradwell did not again apply for admission, instead devoting herself to women's suffrage and legislative reforms to remove other legal disabilities imposed upon women, including the prohibition on women retaining their own earnings. In 1890, when Bradwell was fifty-nine, the Illinois Supreme Court, acting on her original motion filed twenty-one years earlier, admitted her to practice law in the state; two years later, she was admitted to the bar of the United States Supreme Court.

A few years after Myra Bradwell finally succeeded in her campaign for admission to the bar of Illinois, Antoinette Dakin Leach petitioned for admission to the bar of Indiana. Thirty-four years old in 1893, Leach had received a law degree in Tennessee. The Supreme Court of Indiana granted her petition, despite a provision of the Indiana Constitution which limited bar membership to persons with the power to vote. After her admission, there was some hostility from the male members of the profession, one of whom commented that "'no one seriously thought that a woman could be admitted. . . . There was not prejudice against her admission, but simply an understanding that it was impossible.'"[4] Despite this negative sentiment among her colleagues, Leach practiced law in Indiana for the remainder of her life, and she was one of the first to use a typewriter for preparing legal filings. After her death in 1922, a memorial at the Indiana State Bar Association remarked on her fine personality and described the breadth of her law library, noting that she "'knew how to find therein the decisions which supported her theory of a case.'"[5]

Clara Shortridge Foltz was truly a "first" among women: the first woman to study law at the Hastings College of Law; among the first women admitted to the bar of California; the first woman lawyer in San Diego; the first woman in California to serve as a deputy district attorney; and the founder of the *San Diego Bee.* She was thwarted early in her professional ambitions when she asked a prominent local attorney whether she could study law in his office. He responded:

> My high regard for your parents, and for you . . . forbid encouraging you in so foolish a pursuit,—wherein you would invite nothing but ridicule if not contempt. A woman's place is at home, unless it is as a teacher. If you would like a position in our public schools I will be glad to recommend you, for I think you are well-qualified.[6]

Foltz could give as good as she got, however. When an opposing attorney once suggested in open court that she had better be at home raising children, Foltz retorted: "'A woman had better be in almost any business than raising such men as you.'"[7]

Crystal Eastman of New York, pacifist, feminist, and ardent reformer, used her law degree and master's degree in sociology as a lifelong fight against a broad range of social ills, which she saw as suppressing human freedom. One of her early endeavors was a comprehensive study of the effect of industrialization on urban workers, *Work Accidents and the Law,* published in 1910. She was appointed by Governor Charles Evans Hughes to be the only woman member of the New York State Employer's Liability Commission, and she helped obtain the passage of one of the first worker's compensation laws. Always true to her convictions, when she divorced her first husband she refused to accept any alimony, asserting that "'[n]o self-respecting feminist would accept alimony. It would be her own confession that she could not take care of herself.'"[8] She spent much of her life working for women's suffrage, and she lived to see the passage of the Nineteenth Amendment in 1920.

It is through the courageous and determined efforts of these woman and the many like them that aspiring young women of today can more easily attend law school, join the bar, and participate in our legal system. Women today represent nearly thirty percent of attorneys in this country and over forty percent of law school graduates. They also represent over seven percent of judges, eighteen percent of

35. Sandra Day O'Connor was nominated by President Ronald Reagan and became the first woman to serve as a justice of the Supreme Court, taking the oath of office on September 26, 1981. (*AP/Wide World Photos.*)

state legislators, seventeen percent of state executives, six percent of Members of Congress, and just over twenty-two percent of United States Supreme Court Justices. Until the percentages approach fifty percent, perhaps we cannot say we have succeeded. Nonetheless, the progress of the last century has been astounding. And it is due in large part to the explosion of the myth of the "true" woman through the efforts of real women such as those described in this volume.

NOTES

1. Virginia Elwood-Akers, *Clara Shortridge Foltz, California's First Woman Lawyer*, 28 PAC. HISTORIAN 23, 25 (1984).
2. *In re* Bradwell, 55 Ill. 535, 539 (1869).
3. Bradwell v. Illinois, 83 U.S. (16 Wall.) 442, 446 (1873).
4. James E. Farmer, *Women in the Law: A Centennial Legacy of Antoinette Dakin Leach*, 37 RES GESTAE 106, 108 (Sept. 1993).
5. *Id.* at 110.
6. Mortimer Schwartz et al., *The Battles of Clara Shortridge Foltz*, 1 CAL. DEFENDER 7 (Spring 1985).
7. Nicholas C. Polos, *San Diego's "Portia of the Pacific": California's First Woman Lawyer*, 2 J. SAN DIEGO HIST. 185, 189 (1980) (quoting Clara Shortridge Foltz).
8. NOTABLE AMERICAN WOMAN 1607-1950, at 544 (Edward T. James et al. eds., 1971) (quoting Crystal Eastman).

V. Faculty

Chapter 70

Between the Harvard Founders and the American Legal Realists

The Professionalization of the American Law Professor

1985

John Henry Schlegel

John Henry Schlegel is Associate Dean and Professor of Law, State University of New York at Buffalo. This article first appeared in 35 *Journal of Legal Education* 311 (1985).

An earlier version of this article was presented at the annual meeting of the American Society for Legal History, Williamsburg, Virginia, on October 27, 1979. I am grateful to Marjorie, Bob, Al, and Fred. each of whom took the time to read and comment on one or another draft of this piece and to Kevin Fay who resuscitated the long dormant footnotes.

Few people other than Robert Stevens[1] and Jerold Auerbach[2] seem to have spent much time thinking about the generation and a half of law teachers between the founders of modern legal education—Langdell, Ames, Thayer, and Gray at Harvard—and the reconstructors of legal education—the Realists at Columbia, Yale, and Johns Hopkins. True, everyone has heard of Wigmore[3] and Williston,[4] some perhaps of Joseph Beale,[5] maybe William Keener,[6] conceivably Austin Wakeman Scott[7] and Wesley N. Hohfeld,[8] but who other than a compulsive reader of old law reviews would know about the likes of Ernest W. Huffcutt,[9] Harry Richards,[10] William Reynolds Vance,[11] or Eugene Wambaugh.[12] There is no good reason why anyone should have heard of these men. They are a rather standard-issue group of humans with the usual percentage of fools and knaves, wise and dumb, exceptionable only for a surplus of what might be called "hot dogs." This slight surplus in the direction of a characteristic eagerness for their work, however, defines these law professors in a useful way.

36. George W. Kirchwey (1885-1942) served as professor and dean at Albany and then Columbia before becoming the Warden of Sing Sing Prison. (*Photograph courtesy of Columbia University School of Law.*)

When Stevens looked at this in-between generation, he noted what he called the triumph of the Harvard Structure—the spread of the full-time, three-year, day, university law school enrolling mostly college graduates and teaching a largely prescribed, generally identical curriculum of private law subjects.[13] He ascribed this triumph of rising standards to the nativism of an upper middle class that sought to limit the access to the legal profession of the poor generally and the immigrant poor in particular. Auerbach agreed, though in somewhat stronger words.[14] Quite obviously both men are correct in their assessment. Stevens also commented on what he called the triumph of the Harvard Approach—casebooks, large classes, Socratic dialogue, and single written examinations—but he had a harder time giving any reason, other than a financial one, why this package of nostrums was easily sold.[15] He suggested vaguely that the importance of the development of large corporate practice, the "intellectual value" of the case method and the magic of science in the late nineteenth-century world together eased the sale. Auerbach, on the other hand, saw a tension between the law professors and the organized bar, which he ascribed to a professorial interest in "law reform."[16]

While neither man was seeing ghosts, the observations of each raise problems. The triumph of the case method may well have been more verbal—a triumph of casebooks—than real;[17] and any careful look at law professors as reformers finds them substantially to the right of even the now much maligned progressives.[18] But, these criticisms aside,[19] there are similiarities in the questions these men sought to answer and in their failure to deal with them adequately.

Both scholars attempted to explain how and why law schools—particularly university connected law schools, staffed not with practitioners but with full-time academics—sprang up like mushrooms after a rain during the years around 1890. They answered these related questions by looking largely within the "law box."[20] In doing so they came up with one solid observation—that it was in the class-based interest of legal professionals to raise standards—plus a few other observations that did not quite fit. Had they looked outside the law box they might have noticed something curious. Though the key date would have to be shifted, the questions they asked could have been posed about a half a dozen modern disciplines—anthropology, economics, history, political science, psychology, and sociology—the social sciences as we know them. Now, as Dorothy Ross has shown, histories of these other disciplines disclose a largely coherent pattern to the "how" and begin to suggest, a reasonable plausible "why."[21] In each field a small group of scholars created an academic discipline where none had been before. Each group began by staking out part of the intellectual world as its "turf," adopting a particular way of looking at that turf, a method as it were, and moving to cut out the "amateurs" who formerly had a claim to that turf. Finally they justified those activities by pointing to the "mission" of the discipline. Such is the process of academic professionalization, a common objective for the middle class of the late nineteenth and early twentieth century. This "how" and "why" fits for law schools too and so explains Stevens's and Auerbach's observations. It also illuminates such intriguing questions as whether anyone ever took Langdell seriously when he suggested that law was a science and as a science it was best studied by studying appellate cases, a proposition that for twenty years was treated as daft by most everyone outside of Austin Hall.

The rough outlines of the Langdellian conquest, really creation, of the modern law school are well known.[22] In 1870 Christopher Columbus Langdell came to Harvard and announced that henceforth law was to be taught from cases, largely old English cases assembled in chronological order, and by means of class discussion. Simultaneously he uttered some generalities about law being a science, proceeded to toss out of the law course almost everything except private law, and set to the task of lengthening the curriculum to three years. while restricting admittance to college graduates. Within the span of fifty years, his method and curriculum had taken over legal education.

The standard version of this tale stresses the roles of Langdell and Ames; William Keener, who brought the revolution to Columbia; and the regulatory efforts of the ABA and the new Association of American Law Schools. Generally overlooked are the "missionaries,"[23] the individuals who pressed the Langdellian revolution throughout the provinces, including such men as Nathan Abbott, who helped Wigmore bring the case method to Northwestern, thereafter became dean at Stanford and finally a professor at Columbia;[24] or James Parker Hall, who helped Abbott at Stanford and then became the first regular dean at Chicago;[25] or Ernest W. Huffcutt, who started teaching at Indiana, then moved to Northwestern, and finally to Cornell where he became that school's first academic, rather than practitioner, dean;[26] or Harry S. Richards, who kept the Harvard tradition alive first at Iowa and then at Wisconsin;[27] or William Reynolds Vance, who worked harder at moving up than most men, starting at Washington and Lee and then hitting George Washington and Minnesota before sticking at Yale;[28] or Eugene Wambaugh, the first graduate from a major law school at both Iowa and Western Reserve.[29]

When these men entered law teaching there was no profession. There were effectively two kinds of law schools, one staffed largely or exclusively by practicing lawyers or judges;[30] the other with a very small faculty of "retired"—that is, either aged or unsuccessful—practitioners or judges, assisted by a few active practitioners.[31] Neither of these types of law schools died out in the next thirty years. Indeed, in a real sense they thrived. But alongside developed a third and ultimately dominant type of law school, the law school staffed largely, preferably exclusively, by such academics as Huffcutt and Richards. These academics created this niche for themselves largely through hard work and effective propaganda. Wherever they went they pushed their own distinctiveness—their distinctive way of teaching,[32] their distinctive conception of the subject matter to be studied,[33] and their distinctive status in the profession.[34] They pushed themselves too. Quite obviously, they set to the task of converting the heathen and to stocking the missions thus established, largely through an effective old boy network.[35] And they were a combative lot. They would fight about anything: the elective system,[36] the honor system,[37] the use of practice courts,[38] participation in intercollegiate athletics[39] (a real problem in schools that were, as most were, primarily undergraduate),[40] law school fraternities,[41] and the diploma privilege.[42] They were organizers as well. They jumped into the ABA's Section on Legal Education once it was formed[43] and then they jumped into the AALS when it became clear that the Section would not be their distinctive preserve.[44] Throughout it all, they managed to produce a vaguely respectable body of scholarship to fill the pages of the law reviews they created.

While these academics were taking over and, on occasion, founding law schools, they were also busy talking about what they were doing. The earliest significant explanation came from Thayer who emphasized the importance of great works of scholarship designed to present the Harvard doctrinal universe in a scientific fashion—that is, orderly and carefully researched, especially in its historical aspects.[45] Five years later Ames, while pushing the importance of "full-time" law teachers at a major law school that still relied heavily on practitioner-teachers, presented a more ambiguous "vocation" for his brethren by emphasizing the teaching of law somewhat at the expense of scholarship.[46] Subsequent to Ames's attempt, presidents of the AALS and others felt obliged to help along this matter of professional definition. One suggested that working to raise the educational standards for admission to the practice of law was a sufficient role;[47] another that working to develop "American law into a single harmonious system" through establishing "national law schools" was enough.[48] A third found that "the ultimate function" of the law teacher was to work to "adapt the law . . . to the needs of society under existing industrial and sociological conditions,"[49] being careful to point out the "ever-present necessity of maintaining the continuity of the great current of the law that has come down to us through the centuries."[50]

The common academic enterprise that resulted from all this effort did not appear fully formed all at once. How long the effort took can be judged in several ways. The outside parameters are 1870 and 1921, the year of Langdell's arrival at Harvard and the year that the ABA formally recognized the academic's claim to primacy in teaching law. Within those dates there are several potential measures. An indirect one, appropriate for a capitalist economy, is the interest of the capitalists in the law school market. In the years after the Civil War, major treatises were easily published. Indeed, by 1890 there were four or five major book publishers.[51] Yet during these same years authors of casebooks had a more difficult time. Langdell had his first two books—on contracts and sales—published by Little, Brown, but six years later he ended up publishing his work on equity pleading himself. Although Gray and Thayer shared a publisher, the prolific Ames could not find a regular outlet for his work. Starting in the late 1880s other scholars began to publish casebooks here, there, and everywhere, sometimes with major law book publishers, sometimes with relative unknowns. Quite plainly, however, no publisher was willing to risk publishing more than a few isolated volumes. In the nineties the West Publishing Company tried to start a series of casebooks, and Little, Brown offered half a dozen volumes. Both subsequently gave up the effort. Then the Harvard Law Review Association emerged as a major casebook publisher, though with a rather narrow range of authors. The market was simply too thin; and the Harvard monopoly of Harvard authors, begun no doubt in response to commercial publisher hesitancy, made matters worse. Ten years later the market had improved sufficiently that West began publication of its American Casebook Series, "treating all the important subjects ordinarily covered in a law school curriculum."[52] Even then it hedged its bets by starting a Hornbook Case Series, shorter casebooks for use with West's Hornbooks in those schools that still used text and cases.[53] The publishers were far from sure of the law school's direction.

Another view of this hesitant growth of the profession is furnished by West's "Intercollegiate Law Journal," distributed free to "students in law schools"—*The American Law School Review.* From its beginning in 1902 the editor saw that law professors were a major market for his wares. But initially there were other markets as well, for the journal reported news of the ABA Section on Legal Education and material on legal ethics and bar admission.[54] Quite soon ABA affairs began to lose their prominence, and reports of the annual meeting of the AALS increased in length and comprehensiveness.[55] By 1908 ill-tempered criticisms of case-method instruction,[56] while plainly publishable, drew disclaimers from the editor and a reminder that his journal "is not published for the benefit of any particular class of law schools, nor for the advancement of any special method of legal instruction."[57] Within a few years, however, such criticisms had disappeared, and the journal had begun publishing transcripts of AALS meetings.[58] More revealing still are changes at the micro level, in the *Review's* gossip column, "Notes and Personals." This column, dependent on self-reporting, contained obituaries of deans and biographies of successors, together with notices of appointments, excerpts from speeches, bits of what might pass for legal humor, and announcements of courses and enrollments. At this level the content of the column did not change, but its details show quite a shift. In 1902 deanships were routinely passed from ancient judges, learned in the law, to well-known lawyers, deeply interested in legal education.[59] Ten to fifteen years later the retiring dean was lucky to rate more than passing mention in an article that introduced an academic, inevitably an authority on something or other, and emphasized that the faculty now had three or four full-time teachers and had adopted modern methods of instruction.[60] In 1902 most announcements of faculty appointments could list little more than degrees and a period in practice, often in some places so unexpected that one wondered how the school and the individual got together.[61] Fifteen years later the typical announcement included an extensive list of teaching credits.[62] The pattern of these credits even reveal a nascent pecking order among law schools—Montana and North Dakota were the pits; Kansas and Missouri, a step up; then Illinois, Wisconsin, and Minnesota, with Iowa and perhaps Nebraska after Pound, a half-step in between; and finally the big time, Chicago, Michigan, Columbia, and Harvard.

During these same twenty-five or thirty years, similar patterns of activity were evident in other parts of the university, notably in the emergence of a whole new cluster of scholarly disciplines—the social sciences

37. Dane Hall. Nathan Dane's money led to the construction of this then-opulent building, which is now dwarfed by the complex of buildings that has grown up behind and around it. So do institutions grow. (*Courtesy of Art & Visual Materials, Special Collections Department, Harvard Law School Library.*)

as we know them. These new disciplines followed parallel patterns of development. Hours in public meetings and pages in the journals were devoted to delimiting each discipline's field of inquiry, methods of teaching and of research.[63] From time to time, leaders, actual or hopeful, suggested various "missions" that the group could undertake or had undertaken.

The parallel between the activities of the lawyers and the social scientists is striking. During the last years of the nineteenth century each group created a professional discipline. To identify this broad phenomenon is not, however, to explain it. When it comes to explanation Magali Larson's analysis of professionalization fits the data very well.[64] She argues that professionalization is an attempt by a part of the middle class to improve its social and economic position through a strategy of market control. In order to make this strategy work each group of individuals has to create an identifiable product in a recognizable market. Because the product is an intangible, the traditional tasks of product standardization and differentiation—so important to toothpaste, detergent, or margarine manufacturers—are especially difficult. Standardizing and identifying the product must be accomplished indirectly by gaining control over the providers of service. This control is acquired in two ways: through state sanctioned exclusion of potential competitors and through control of the production of producers. Together, these methods perform the usual function of limiting supply in order to raise price. At the same time, in the proper setting, in the modern university, exclusion of others and control of production permits another kind of control—that over the production of knowledge in the profession. Obtaining control over the production of knowledge is important to a professional group because by doing so the group can supplement state established exclusions of potential competitors. Standardization of knowledge also aids product differentiation, for members of the group thus come to share a common cognitive base, a distinctive kind of knowledge leading to an exclusive possession of tools and techniques of the defined trade. In short, to establish a modern profession one needs state sanction for exclusive possession of distinct knowledge based on university production of certified professionals. The key social institutions for professional advance are the state and the university. These two institutions are only necessary, they are not sufficient. To them must be added the standardized, differentiated product—the cognitively delimited and unified field of knowledge possessed by all members of the profession.

Larson's analysis illuminates the Langdellian revolution. The academic lawyers who established the twentieth-century law school faced problems similar to those confronted by other nascent professionals: creation of an identifiable product, exclusion of others from the market for that product, and justification of the resulting market control. These problems are most easily taken up in reverse order.

Academic lawyers attempted to justify their claim to a privileged market position in three ways. First, they sought to define a role, vocation, or mission for themselves which was of "service" to society: improving the law, elevating standards of the profession, advancing knowledge. More important than the content of the role is that the role was always yoked to a program of product standardization and competition exclusion by means of higher standards. A second justification, aimed more directly at the profession, worked at the intraprofessional distinction between teachers and practitioners. Here the dominant note was of division of labor between equals, advanced, of course, by the less equal party. This justification of the academic's market position stressed the difficult work of systematic scholarship and teaching, recurring themes from Thayer and Ames. The third and last justification is less obvious, but no less crucial. It is no accident that these law teachers saw and presented themselves as university law professors, for it was their connection with the university that provided a separable justification for the privilege they sought. The university with its panoply of middle-class attributes—rank, order, meritocratic advancement through graded work, the creation of knowledge for use—was a powerful symbol and an increasingly powerful institution around the turn of the century. Law professors stuck to it like glue. Thayer emphasized the university connection as did everyone thereafter, at times only to lament its absence. One finds great concern among these law professors with all the trappings of the academy—the nomenclature of degrees,[65] the necessity for examinations,[66] the honor system (said to be impracticable unless the student body be "drawn from those classes in the community which understand each other's conditions and points of view"),[67] and scholarship in the German historical mode.[68] So much for justification.

The matter of market exclusion is the aspect of this equation that has heretofore been more emphasized. By their campaign for higher standards, law professors assisted the bar's attempt to keep lower-class and immigrant populations from entering practice.[69] But in so doing these men[70] were not simply swinging with the ABA nativist moguls. In seeking state sanction for exclusionist admissions policies they were seeking to establish their monopoly of law teaching, for by definition the full-time, day law school, enrolling only college graduates would be the preserve of the academic law professors. State support for the one was tantamount to state support for the other, especially since the call for higher standards for lawyers and thus students was far easier to justify than a call for higher standards for law professors, particularly when teaching practitioners were around. At the same time, state support for physical exclusion was only part of the task. Intellectual poachers had to be excluded from the law professor's territory too. This job, however, carries over into the territory of product definition and standardization. The two are best considered together.

Great effort went into developing the law school's equivalent of the Model T. Enormous amounts of thought and pages of print were devoted to such matters as standardization of credits,[71] standardization of degrees,[72] and standardization of examinations.[73] The entire discussion about prelegal education was in fact a question of product standardization.[74] But the standardized unit of output is possible only if the head of the standardized law student is filled with a standardized but unique unit of knowledge. And here we must return to that most improbable of accidents—Christopher Columbus Langdell.[75]

The bearded prophet of Austin Hall was mad, as Holmes said in print[76] and as Gray did in private.[77] His ideas about law were ultimately incoherent. The suggestion that law was a science—a body of systematic principles resting on evidence—made perfect mid-nineteenth century sense (indeed law had been a science for Blackstone, too). His accompanying observation, however, that the data for this science were to be a small fraction of the reported cases, mostly old English ones, studied inductively in a library, suggests that Langdell really did not understand the difference between Blackstone's science, Newton's science, Lyell's science, and Darwin's science. His curricular emphasis on litigation was, by 1890, hopelessly unrepresentative of the work of the practicing bar he served, and his Socratic method offered nothing distinctive in thought. Indeed, his dialogue was something of a throwback to old catecistic recitations of the New England college and ignored that important educational "innovation" from Germany—the lecture.[78] Ultimately, the soundness of Langdell's ideas about science, content of curriculum, and teaching method mattered little, however. What he offered the law schools was an intellectual Model T, a wholly complete, conceptually unified universe to put in the mind of the standard student.

Much ink has been used over Langdell's "system," relatively little, over his curriculum. But the choice to cast public law out of the lawyer's world and to justify private law doctrine internally, as a matter of logic, not as a matter of ends, may have been a stroke of genius. The resulting curriculum of "pure law" was utterly without competing claimants in the late nineteenth century. Stripped of the political and economic theory, once part of the study of law, and thus intellectually impoverished, Langdell's curriculum allowed its champions to avoid such messes as Theodore Dwight's fight with Burgess's School of Political Science at Columbia over the place of public law.[79] All that was left was for Ames to suggest that thinking like a lawyer was a teachable method[80] and the job was done.

Of course, not just any hermetically sealed intellectual universe would have done. It is surely important that Langdell's world was not debilitating to the needs of elite practitioners. Instead, it was familiar to them and may even have created an employee who, through his research skills, could actually earn his keep while learning to practice, just as the old copyist apprentices did. Nor did it hurt that his notion of historical development was, if not inherently, at least easily, a conservative brake on doctrine and his emphasis on appellate cases support for judicial, and thus relatively elite, control of the law-making machinery. And his internal, logical justification of existing rules put to one side questions of the instrumental character of those rules, just as the fathers of his students would have wished. But despite these matters, it still would be hard to find yourself at a better place at a better time than did C. C. Langdell.

The importance of conceptual unification of law for the nascent professionalization of academic lawyers can, of course, be overemphasized. While it can, in part, explain the success of Langdell's method over that of John Norton Pomeroy's equally grand scheme put into practice at Hastings in 1878,[81] it deals less successfully with the demise of Dwight's comprehensive method at Columbia.[82] Nonetheless, many otherwise curious events become more comprehensible if the social role of the law professor's conceptual universe is remembered.

For example, all the palaver about the necessity for uniform law even at the cost of losing control of law making to the legislature,[83] the attempts to portray *the* system of *the* law as a coherent whole in casebook after casebook, the several tries in the 1910s to shore up that notion culminating in the Restatement project,[84] and even Hohfeld's analytic craziness[85] make better sense when understood as having both potential political and intellectual significance. By struggling to keep the doctrinal universe pure, the pre-World War I law professors worked not only to push along the academic peanut but to secure their special place in the division of labor. This is reflected in the line that separated friendly criticism by insiders from threatening ideas.

When Albert Kales, a fine future interests scholar from Northwestern, suggested that the next logical development of the casebook was to create casebooks for scientifically teaching the particular law of a single state, everyone looked up.[86] Law professors from state law schools, sensing an attack on the eastern establishment, offered praise;[87] but that establishment, less than amused, brought out the big guns. First came William Draper Lewis, dean at Pennsylvania, who thought the idea disposed of with the observation that "the average law school teacher, or at least, the teacher in the best schools, knows something beyond the casebook" and then lamented how narrowing it would be not to know the opinions of Lord Eldon.[88] When that did not end the dispute, George W. Kirchwey, dean of Columbia, ranged all over the field—from the impetus for local law reform coming from exposure to the law of other jurisdictions, to the lack of time to do everything, to a patriotic appeal for "an American law."[89] Finally came Dean Ames's turn to chastise one of his own strayed sheep:

> The writer of the paper and I seem to differ radically as to the object of the three years at the law school. I should infer from the paper that to the author the main object is knowledge. The object arrived at by us at Cambridge is the power of legal reasoning, and we think we can best get that by putting before the students the best models to be found in the history of English and American law, because we believe that men who are trained by examining the opinions of the greatest judges that the English Common Law System has produced are in a better position to know what legal reasoning is and are more likely to possess the power of solving legal problems than they would be by taking up the study of the law of any particular state.[90]

Ames chose to ignore Langdell's science, law reform, and even his own scholarship, as he struck a note more reminiscent of a nineteenth century justification of the study of Greek and Latin as "mental discipline" than of the modern university. Conceptual unity was important indeed.

NOTES

1. See Robert Stevens. Law School: Legal Education in America from the 1850's to the 1980's (Chapell Hill, 1983) [hereinafter cited as Stevens. Law School]; Robert Stevens. Two Cheers for 1870: The American Law School. 5 Persp. Am. Hist. 405 (1971) [hereinafter cited as Stevens. Two Cheers].

2. See Jerold Auerbach, Unequal Justice: Lawyers and Social Change in Modern America (New York, 1976).

3. (1863-1943). A.B. 1883. LL.B. 1887, Harvard. Private practice, 1887. Boston. Prof. 1889, Keito University, Tokyo, Japan. Prof. 1893, dean 1901, Northwestern University. His most famous work is John Wigmore, A Treatise on the Law of Evidence (Boston, 1904-1905). See generally William Roalfe, John Henry Wigmore: Teacher, Scholar, Reformer (Evanston, 1977).

4. (1861-1943). A.B. 1882, A.M. 1888, LL.B. 1888, Harvard. Private practice, 1889, Boston. Asst. Prof. 1890, Prof. 1895, Harvard. Williston drafted the Uniform Sales Act (1906), and was later the chief reporter of the American Law Institute's Restatement of Contracts. His most famous works are Samuel Williston, The Law of Contracts (Boston, 1920-1922), and Samuel Williston, The Law Governing Sales of Goods at Common Law and under the Uniform Sales Act (New York, 1909).

5. (1861-1943). A.B. 1882, A.M. 1887, LL.B. 1887, Harvard. Private practice, 1887, Boston. Lecturer 1890, Inst. 1891, Asst. Prof. 1892. Prof. 1897, Harvard. His most famous work is Joseph Beale, A Treatise on the Conflict of Laws (New York, 1935).

6. (1856-1913). A.B. 1874, Emory College; LL.B. 1887, Harvard. Private practice. 1878. New York City. Asst. Prof. 1883, Prof. 1888. Harvard; Prof. 1890, Dean 1891. Prof. 1901. Columbia. Judge, New York Supreme Court 1902. Private practice, 1903. New York City. His most famous work is William Keener, A Treatise on the Law of Quasi-Contracts (New York, 1893).

7. (1884-1981). A.B. 1903. Rutgers; LL.B. 1909. Harvard. Inst. (mathematics) 1903, Rutgers; Inst. (law) 1910, Asst. Prof. 1910, Prof. 1914, Harvard. His most famous work is Austin Scott, The Law of Trusts (Boston, 1939).

8. (1879-1918). B.A. 1901, U. Cal.; LL.B. 1904, Harvard. Lecturer 1905, Hastings; Inst. 1905, Asst. Prof. 1907, Assoc. Prof. 1908, Prof. 1909. Stanford; Prof. 1914, Yale. Wesley Hohfeld, Some Fundamental Legal Conceptions as Applied in Judicial Reasoning, 23 Yale L.J. 16 (1913), is his most famous work.

9. (1860-1907). B.S. 1884, LL.B. 1887, Cornell. Private practice, Minnesota, 1888. Prof. 1890, Indiana; Prof. 1892, Northwestern; Prof. 1893, Dean 1905, Cornell. Chairman, ABA Section on Legal Education, 1901; Sec.-Treas., 1901-1903, Pres. 1903, AALS. Ernest Huffcut, A Treatise on the Law of Agency (Cambridge, 1895), is his only famous work.

10. (1868-1929). Ph.D. 1892, Iowa; LL.B. 1895, Harvard. Private practice, Missouri, Iowa. 1895. Prof. 1899, Iowa; Dean 1903, Wisconsin. Pres. 1912, AALS. Harry Richards, Cases on Private Corporations (St. Paul, Minn., 1912), is his only significant scholarship.

11. (1870-1940). A.B. 1892, A.M. 1893, Ph.D. 1895, LL.B. 1897, Washington and Lee. Asst. Prof. 1897, Prof. 1898, Dean 1900, Washington and Lee; Prof. 1903, Dean 1905, George Washington; Prof. 1910, Yale; Dean 1912, Minnesota; Prof. 1920, Yale. Pres. 1914, AALS. William Vance, A Treatise on the Law of Insurance (St. Paul, Minn., 1904), and William Vance, Cases and Other Materials on the Law of Insurance (St. Paul, Minn., 1914), are his major publications.

12. (1856-1940). A.B. 1876, A.M. 1877, LL.B. 1880, Harvard. Private practice, Cincinnati 1880. Prof. 1889, Iowa; Prof. 1892, Harvard. Eugene Wambaugh, The Study of Cases (Boston, 1894), is his most famous work.

13. Stevens, Law School, *supra* note 1, at xv.

14. Auerbach, *supra* note 2, at 106-09.

15. Stevens, Two Cheers, *supra* note 1, at 63-64.

16. Auerbach, *supra* note 2, at 76-85.

17. It is extremely difficult to obtain accurate information about the teaching of one's colleagues. It is disproportionally more difficult to obtain accurate information about teaching seventy-five years ago. Nevertheless scraps and pieces suggest that beyond establishing a norm of some *in class* dialogue, reports of the rigor of case-method teaching before World War I are, like reports of Mark Twain's death, an exaggeration. Ignoring Harvard, for which no thoroughly reliable, comprehensive history exists for the years after 1908, the frequency of comments in law school histories that a faculty member did not pursue the Socratic method "in all its rigor" and the much lower frequency of comments that a faculty member was a "master" of it or a "terror" in the classroom should make one pause before suggesting that the use of casebooks brought an end to lecturing.

18. See e.g., William Vance, The Ultimate Function of the Law Professor, 3 Am. L. Sch. Rev. 2 (1911) one of Auerbach's more important examples of law professors and reform, Gerald Fetner, The Law Teacher as Legal Reformer: 1900-1945, 20 J. Legal Educ. 508 (1977), is largely concerned with activities after World War I.

19. These criticisms should not obscure the fact that without the work of Stevens and Auerbach, saying anything about late nineteenth and early twentieth century law professors would be impossible.

20. Robert Gordon, J. Willard Hurst and the Common Law Tradition in American Historiography, 10 Law & Soc'y Rev. 9, 10 (1975).

21. Dorothy Ross, The Development of the Social Sciences, in The Organization of Knowledge in Modern America, 1860-1920, 104 (A. Oleson & J. Voss ed.; Baltimore, 1979).

22. My version is a caricature, of course. The most sensible rendition of this story is found in Stevens, Law School, *supra*, note 1, at 35-64.

23. See John Henry Wigmore to James B. Thayer, May 6, 1984, Box 18. Thayer Mss. Harvard Law Library ("I feel like a 'legal missionary'" in bringing the case method to Northwestern).

24. (1854-1941). B.A. Yale, 1877. Private practice, Massachusetts, 1881. Prof. 1891, Michigan; Prof. 1892, Northwestern; Dean 1895, Stanford; Prof. 1906, Columbia, Pres. 1904, AALS.

25. (1871-1923). A.B. 1894, Cornell; LL.B. 1897, Harvard. Private Practice, 1897, Buffalo. Assoc. Prof. 1900, Prof. 1902, Dean 1904, Chicago. Pres. 1922, AALS.

26. *supra* note 9.

27. *supra*, note 10.

28. *supra*. note 11.

29. *supra*, note 12. Wambaugh was hired at Western Reserve in 1892 but resigned before teaching there in order to accept an appointment at Harvard. See Charles Cramer, The Law School at Case Western Reserve University 29 (Cleveland. 1977).

30. See, e.g., Irving Browne. The Albany Law School. 2 Green Bag 153 (1890); Charles Norton, The Buffalo Law School, I Green Bag 421 (1889); C. Stuart Patterson, The Law School of the University of Pennsylvania. I Green Bag 99 (1889); George Swasey, Boston University Law School, I Green Bag 54 (1889).

31. See e.g., Charles Clafin Allen, The St. Louis Law School, I Green Bag 283 (1889); Chancellor Green. The Law School of Cumberland University, 2 Green Bag 63 (1890); Emlin McClain, Law Department of the State University of Iowa, 1 Green Bag 374 (1889); Charles Slack, Hastings College of the Law, I Green Bag 518(1889). One can discern these two patterns and intuit variations by examining the courses of study in various law schools as listed in 1891 in 1 Report of the Commissioner of Education for the Year 1890-91, 414 (1894).

32. The literature between 1890 and 1915 on teaching methods is voluminous. Robert Stevens, Law Schools and Legal Education 1879-1979: Lectures in Honor of 100 Years of the Valparaiso Law School, 14 Val. U. L. Rev. 179, 214-15 (1980), samples some of the more obscure literature as a debate between advocates and opponents of the case method. On a substantive level, this is true, but equally important, in general the proponents of the case method are full-time academics associated with "university" law schools and the opponents are practitioners, part-time teachers, or "owners" of proprietary law schools.

33. Here the argument is generally one of theory—law as a "science" versus practice—and again the participants turn up on predictable sides. The distinctive (Socratic/case) method held dear by the academics, however, was criticized almost immediately as "undermin[ing] the scientific treatment of law for which Langdell and his associates had called." Stevens, Law School, *supra* note I, at 118. See Josef Redlich, The Common Law and the Case Method in American University Law Schools 50 (New York, 1914). The relationship between case method and late-nineteenth-century "legal science" is at best poorly understood. For an examination of this relationship, see Thomas C. Grey, Langdell's Orthodoxy, 45 Pitt. L. Rev. 1 (1983).

34. Auerbach, *supra* note 2. at 75-85.

35. See John Henry Schlegel. American Legal Realism and Empirical Social Science: The Singular Case of Underhill Moore, 29 Buff. L. Rev. 195 (1980); David McKown. The Dean: The Life of Julian C. Monnet 117-130 (Norman. 1972) suggests the existence and effectiveness of the old boy network. I infer intentionality from the pattern of provincial employment of young law teachers, examples of which are to be found in notes 3, 9-12 *supra*. Roalfe, *supra* note 3, provides some support for these notions.

36. See Ernest Huffcut, The Elective System in Law Schools, 1 Am. L.Sch. Rev. 248 (1904); Discussion, 1 Am. L. Sch. Rev. 262-63 (1904).

37. Survey, The Honor System, 2 Am. L. Sch. Rev. 400 (1910); William Draper Lewis, The Honor System of Conducting Examinations in Law Schools, 2 Am. L. Sch. Rev. 454 (1910); John Lile, The Honor System, 2 Am. L. Sch. Rev. 456 (1910); Discussion, 2 Am. L. Sch. Rev. 464-70 (1910).

38. See e.g., Gavin Craig, Moot Courts as a Part of the Law School Curriculum, 3 Am. L. Sch. Rev. (1913); William Hastings, Practice Courts, 3 Am. L. Sch. Rev. (1912); McClain, *supra* note 31. at 384.

39. See Andrew Bruce, Law School and Intercollegiate Athletics, 1 Am. L. Sch. Rev. 37 (1903).
40. *Id.* at 39-41.
41. See Nathan Abbott, Law School Fraternities, 2 Am. L. Sch. Rev. 33 (1903) [reprinted as chapter 67 in this book].
42. See Stevens, Law School, *supra* note 1, at 95, 98; Robert Henry, Admission to the Bar on Diploma, 3 Am. L. Sch. Rev. 522 (1914).
43. See Stevens, Law School *supra* note 1, at 95, 114-16.
44. Indeed, the Section "was open to any ABA member" from its formation, Id. at 105 n. 26. See Alfred Z. Reed, Present-Day Law Schools in the United States and Canada 23 (New York, 1928). Stevens credits the creation of the AALS by the ABA to pressure from the new breed of academic lawyer . . . for the establishment of an organization of "reputable law schools." Id. at 96.
45. See James B. Thayer, The Teaching of English Law at Universities, 9 Harv. L. Rev. 169, 179-81 (1895).
46. "Of this vocation the paramount duty is, of course, that of teaching. Having mastered his subject, the professor must consider how best he can help the student learn it also." James Barr Ames, The Vocation of the Law Professor, in Lectures on Legal History and Miscellaneous Legal Essays 351, 362 (Cambridge. 1913) (address delivered on February 21, 1901, at the dedication of the new building of the Department of Law of the University of Pennsylvania).
47. Harry Richards, Progress in Legal Education, in Handbook of the Association of American Law Schools and Proceedings of the Fifteenth Annual Meeting, 60 (1915), repr. 4 Am. L. Sch. Rev. 83 (1916).
48. George Kirchwey, American Law and the American Law School, in Proceedings of the Eighth Annual Meeting of the Association of American Law Schools, 11, 15, 17 (1908), repr. 2 Am. L. Sch. Rev. 194 (1909).
49. William Vance, The Ultimate Function of the Teacher of Law, in Proceeding of the Eleventh Annual Meeting of the Association of American Law Schools, 137 (1911), repr. 3. Am. L. Sch. Rev. 2(1911).
50. *Id.* at 38.
51. Support for the assertions of this paragraph, unless otherwise noted, is to be found in Lester Mazor, Bibliography of American Casebooks (1981) (unpublished manuscript).
52. The American Casebook Series, 2 Am. L. Sch. Rev. 276 (1909).
53. See e.g., Am. L. Sch. Rev. back cover (Spring 1913) (advertisement). The debate between those who would use texts and those fond of casebooks was carried into the pages of the Review—itself published by West. See, e.g., George Chase, A Comparison of the Use of Treatises and the Use of Case-Books in the Study of Law, 3 Am. L. Sch. Rev. 81(1912) ("side-by-side" comparison of the issue of "Presumption of the Continuous of Life" as treated in *Greenleaf on Evidence* (and) *Thayer's Cases on Evidence*). The author of this piece, noting the comparative brevity of the textbook's treatment, declared that "a law school using treatises as the fundamental basis of instruction can cover the same field of legal knowledge in a shorter time than schools which confine themselves to casebooks." *Id.* at 82.
54. See, e.g., The Meeting of the Section of Legal Education of the American Bar Association, 1 Am. L. Sch. Rev. 150 (1904); American Bar Association Canons of Ethics, 2 Am. L. Sch. Rev. 223; Hoffman's Fifty Resolutions in Regard to Professional Deportment, 2 Am. L. Sch. Rev. 230; Teaching Legal Ethics in Law Schools, 2 Am. L. Sch. Rev. 377 (1910); A Special Request from the Committee on Standard Rules for Admission to the Bar, 2 Am. L. Sch. Rev. 191, (1908); Recent State Bar Examination Questions, 2 Am. L. Sch. Rev. 559 (1911): A. W. Richter, Reform in the Requirements for Admission to the Bar in Wisconsin, 3 Am. L. Sch. Rev. 432 (1914).
55. Indeed, from 1915 to 1922 the *Review* dedicated an entire issue to the meetings of the AALS. See e.g. Meeting of the Association of American Law Schools—1915, 4. Am. L. Sch. Rev. 65 (1916).
56. See Charles Carusi, A Criticism of the Case System, 2 Am. L. Sch. Rev. 213 (1908).
57. See Notes and Personals, 2 Am. L. Sch. Rev. 237 (1908).
58. See *supra* note 55.
59. See e.g., Law School Personals, 1 Am. L. Sch. Rev. 24 (1902).
60. See e.g., Notes and Personals, 3 Am. L. Sch. Rev. 582 (1914).
61. See e.g., Law School Personals, 1 Am. L. Sch. Rev. 24 (1902).
62. See e.g., Notes and Personals, 3 Am. L. Sch. Rev. 582 (1914).
63. *supra* note 21.
64. Magali Larson, The Rise of Professionalism (Berkeley, 1977). A colleague, among others, has criticized the argument that follows for its failure to isolate any social "push" for such a development. The source of the push however seems relatively obvious. As Andrew Barlow has shown is the case for Harvard, professionalization is a plausible response on the part of an upper class that feels it is losing its previously informal control over social relations, that is, undergoing an informal "crisis of authority." See A. Barlow, Coordination and Control: The Rise of Harvard University (unpublished Ph.D. thesis 1979). At the same time a further push comes from a middle class that by the 1880s or 1890s was wealthy enough and numerous enough to be able to invest marginal dollars in education as a mark of class distinction. Similarly, the failure of the English legal profession to bring forth an academic wing as it became a modern profession is easily explained by the differing social context in the two countries. In America by 1880 academic law training had become recognized as a way of supplementing an apprenticeship. William Johnson, Schooled Lawyers (New York, 1978). No such development had taken place in England, indeed the reverse had occurred. Lacking the necessary social institutions English development took a different course, one that built on the available form—the practitioner's treatise.

A far more significant problem for the argument would be the apparent failure of any of the developing social science professions to seek state sanction for its exclusionist program. Here the subsequent history of psychology and the recent calls for the licensing of public opinion pollsters suggests that one may need a certain minimum number of nonacademic practitioners before state sanction becomes a serious problem. With less than that number less formal social control is adequate.

65. See e.g., Nathan Abbott, Address, 1 Am. L. Sch. Rev. 323, 325 (1905).

66. See e.g., John C. Townes. Organization and Operation of a Law School, 2 Am. L. Sch. Rev. 440, 445-47 (1909).

67. William Draper Lewis, The Honor System of Conducting Examinations in Law Schools, 2 Am. L. Sch. Rev. 4543, 455 (1910). The *Review* was in fact a forum for the debate; *supra* note 37.

68. See generally Jurgen Herbst, German Historical School in American Scholarship (Cambridge, 1965).

69. See Auerbach, *supra* note 2, at 95-129; Stevens, Law School, *supra* note 1, at 99-103.

70. There were, as best as can be seen, no women except for the venerable Ellen S. Mussey of the Woman's Law Class, later the Washington College of Law. See Stevens, Law School, *supra* note 1, at 82-84.

71. See, e.g., Martin P. Burks. Law School Credits. 2 Am. L. Sch. Rev. 174 (1908).

72. See, e.g., Abbott, *supra* note 65.

73. See, e.g., Final Examinations Questions in Prominent Law Schools, 3 Am. L. Sch. Rev. 640 (1915); John Grant, The Single Standard in Grading, 29 Colum. L. Rev. 920 (1929), repr. 6 Am. L. Sch. Rev. 781 (1930); Lawriz Vold, Impersonal Law Examinations, 6 Am. L. Sch. Rev. 214 (1923).

74. See, e.g., Arthur Hadley, Is the B.A. Degree Essential for Professional Study. 1 Am. L. Sch. Rev. 379 (1906). Although certain to raise the level of students' abilities and qualifications, such a requirement was also "an introduction of a sort of caste system in the worst form." *Id.* at 380.

75. For a different view of the significance of Langdell than the one that follows see Anthony Chase, The Birth of the Modern Law School, 23 Am. J. Legal Hist. 329 (1979); Anthony Chase, Origins of Modern Professional Education: The Harvard Case Method Conceived as Clinical Instruction in Law, 5 Nova L. J. 326 (1981).

76. See Book Notice. 14 Am. L. Rev. 233 (1880) (unsigned review of Christopher Langdell, Selection of Cases on the Law of Contracts. Boston, 1879). In the review, Holmes refers to Langdell as "the greatest living legal theologian" with some veiled distaste; seeing Langdell as divorced from reality, he remarks that "we might call him a Hegelian in disguise, so entirely is he interested in the formal connection of things, in logic, as distinguished from the feelings which make the content of logic, and which have actually shaped the substance of the law." *Id.* at 234. For a good history of the interaction of Holmes's and Langdell's philosophies, see Mark DeWolfe Howe, Justice Oliver Wendell Holmes: The Proving Years 155-59 (Cambridge. 1963).

77. See Letter from John C. Gray to Charles W. Eliot, Jan. 8, 1883 (Harvard Archives), repr. in Howe, *supra* note 76, at 158 ("Langdell's intellectual arrogance and contempt is astounding . . . a school where the majority of the professors shuns and despises the contact with actual facts, has got the seeds of ruin in it and will and ought to go to the devil.")

78. See, Lawrence Veysey, The Emergence of the American University 37-38 (Chicago. 1965).

79. Columbia Univ. Found. for Research in Legal History, A History of the School of Law, Columbia University 85-89 (New York, 1955) [hereinafter cited as Columbia].

80. Stevens, Law School *supra* note 1, at 41, 56.

81. See Thomas Garden Barnes, Hastings College of the Law: The First Century 88-118 (San Francisco, 1978).

82. Columbia, *supra* note 79, at 119-32. See Jospeh Beale, A Treatise on the Conflict of Laws 150, 2d ed. (Boston, 1935).

83. See, e.g., William Schofield, Uniformity of Law in the Several States as an American Ideal, 21 Harv. L. Rev, 510, 519-26 (1908).

84. See, e.g., Joseph Beale, The Necessity for the Study of Legal System, Proceedings of the Fourteenth Annual Meeting of the Association of American Law Schools 31, 42-43 (1914), Alexander, Memorandum in re Corpus Juris, 22 Green Bag 59(1910). Schlegel, *supra* note 35, at 195, 234, n. 241.

There is a deep connection between the American Law Institute project and the professionalization of law teachers. Money for the restatements was secured from the Carnegie Foundation through the intervention of Elihu Root. Root was asked to approach the foundation by William Draper Lewis, dean at Pennsylvania, and general AALS Poobah. The two men met when they both served on the ABA Committee on Legal Education which forged the compromise that finally legitimated the position of the academic law professor by suggesting that apprenticeship was no longer an acceptable route to the bar but that a degree from a part-time night school was, so long as that the school required four, not three years to complete its degree. See Philip C. Jessup, Elihu Root (Hamden, 1938); Stevens *supra* note 1, at 115.

85. Hohfeld, *supra* note 8.

86. Albert Kales, The Next Step in the Evolution of the Casebook, in Proceedings of the Seventh Annual Meeting of the Association of American Law Schools 82, repr. in 21 Harv. L. Rev. 92 (1907); Albert Kales, A Further Word on the Next Step in the Evolution of the Casebook, 4 Ill. L. Rev. 11(1909).

87. See, e.g., John Lawson, Discussion in Proceedings of the Seventh Annual Meeting of the Association of American Law Schools, 5 repr. 2 Am. L. Sch. Rev. 116 (1907).

88. William Draper Lewis, Discussion in Proceedings of the Seventh Annual Meeting of the Association of American Law Schools, 3, repr. 2 Am. L. Sch. Rev. 116 (1907).

89. George Kirchwey, Discussion in Proceedings of the Seventh Annual Meeting of the Association of American Law Schools 8, repr. 2 Am. L. Sch. Rev. 117 (1907). See also Kirchwey, *supra* note 48.

90. James Barr Ames, Discussion in Proceedings of the Seventh Annual Meeting of the Association of American Law Schools 16. repr. 2 Am. L. Sch. Rev. 119 (1907).

Chapter 71

The Historical Origins, Founding, and Early Development of Student-Edited Law Reviews

1985

Michael I. Swygert and Jon W. Bruce

© Copyright 1985 by Michael I. Swygert and Jon W. Bruce. All rights reserved. Michael I. Swygert is Professor of Law, Stetson University; B.A., 1965, J.D., 1967, Valparaiso University; LL.M., 1968, Yale University. Jon W. Bruce is Professor of Law, Vanderbilt University; B.A., 1966, Hanover College; J.D., 1969, College of William and Mary.

If we fail, we shall at least have the satisfaction of believing that our work has been honestly done in the interest of the law school and of its alumni.[1]

The American law review properly has been called the most remarkable institution of the law school world. To a lawyer, its articles and comments may be indispensable professional tools. To a judge, . . . the review may be both a severe critic and a helpful guide. But perhaps most important, the review affords invaluable training to the students. . . .[2]

Most accredited law schools in the United States publish a student-edited law review containing scholarly writing about recent court decisions, unresolved issues of law, and other topics of interest to the legal community.[3] Begun a century ago by law students as an academic experiment,[4] law reviews have achieved a prominent and influential position in the legal profession.[5] Much has been written both praising[6] and criticizing[7] these periodicals, particularly with respect to the unique phenomenon of law students managing and editing journals to which academic and practicing professionals submit articles for evaluation, revision, and publication.[8] This process stands in stark contrast to that employed in most other disciplines, in which scholarly journals are edited by recognized authorities in the field and works are selected for publication by a panel of expert referees.

The authors of this Article, however, do not wish to enter the debate regarding the value or appropriateness of law reviews as they presently exist. Nor do we quibble with the frequent assertion that these periodicals have an enormous impact on our courts and law schools, and thus on the legal profession in general.[9] Rather, it is our purpose to explore a long neglected subject—the historical origins, founding, and early development of student-edited law reviews—and by so doing, to shed light on the reasons for the existence of this significant legal institution.

This Article begins with an analysis of the evolution of early forms of legal writing, a process that led to the founding of the first law reviews in the late nineteenth century. Next, the Article focuses on the initial attempts to establish student-edited law reviews, with particular attention to the birth of the *Harvard Law Review* in 1887. Although by all accounts the *Harvard Law Review* is this country's most prestigious and imitated legal periodical,[10] it was not, contrary to popular belief, the first student-edited law journal.[11] Finally, the Article traces the early development of student-edited law reviews into the beginning of the twentieth century, by which time the foundation for their present stature had been laid, and examines the expanding role of law reviews in legal education and their subsequent influence on the legal profession.

Historical Origins

All the earlier forms of legal writing—treatises, law reports, and periodicals—influenced the founders of law reviews, but the growth of legal journalism in America during the nineteenth century provided the groundwork upon which law reviews were built.[12] The "concise and casual" legal writing found in legal periodicals introduced during this period contrasted sharply with the tedious and encyclopedic treatises of Blackstone, Kent, and Story.[13] The newer research and writing, which was somewhat less historic and academic in its orientation, was aimed at the practitioner.[14] These early journals typically highlighted recent court decisions, local news, and editorial comments. During the middle to late 1800's, new legal periodicals appeared with great frequency.[15] Thus, by the time the *Harvard Law Review* commenced publication in 1887, a total of 158 different legal periodicals had been published in the United States.[16]

The reasons why these professional and academic periodicals came into existence are complex and properly addressed only by examining earlier forms of legal writing. This section first examines the early treatises and law reports, and then analyzes the commercial law journals that served as models for the initial student-edited law reviews.

Early Legal Writing: Treatises and Law Reports

Before the advent of legal periodicals, two principal forms of legal writing existed: doctrinal writing in the form of treatises, and case reporting in the form of law reports. The treatise was a lengthy academic exposition of a body of legal doctrine.[17] The law report, on the other hand, contained court decisions, summaries of court opinions, and reporter's comments about the opinions.

Treatises

The only major law-related work produced in England during medieval times[18] was Littleton's *Tenures.*[19] The *Tenures,* written in law French,[20] had enormous significance because Littleton, rather than merely summarizing or abridging court decisions, construed and explicated a "coherent body of legal doctrine" in an expository style.[21] His work demonstrated that court pronouncements were not necessarily a hodge-podge of ad hoc resolutions unrelated to human experience.[22] The *Tenures* showed that the common law "possessed principles and doctrines . . . founded upon the actual problems of daily life."[23] Littleton took one important subject—land law—and treated it extensively and comprehensively in a distinctive literary form.[24] Thus, the *Tenures* came to serve as an important model for monographic writing centuries later.[25]

The next significant English legal work was Coke's *First Institute,* published in 1628.[26] Coke, after serving as chief justice of the King's Bench,[27] authored various law reports[28] and a series of doctrinal expositions called *Institutes.*[29] His *First Institute*—also referred to as *Coke upon Littleton*—was intended to modernize the *Tenures.*[30] The result was a legal encyclopedia of various branches of the law.[31] Eventually, the text of Coke's *Institute* "came to be treated as though it were itself the law; it was regarded with a reverence approaching that accorded an actual statute."[32] Consequently, Coke exerted enormous personal influence in shaping the common law.

Coke's various *Institutes*[33] were followed by the publication of Hale's *Analysis of the Law of England* in 1713, reportedly the first effort to systematize the law by a rational scheme other than that of alphabetical abridgment.[34] Hale's *Analysis* in turn served as the organizational model for the immeasurably influential Blackstone's *Commentaries*,[35] which appeared from 1765-1769.[36]

The Commentaries, which have been aptly described as the "great legal publishing event" of the eighteenth century,[37] constituted the most complete and the most literary book of English law that had yet appeared.[38] Blackstone combined a lucid style with superb literary judgment and a faithful accuracy in recounting the legal principles of the case authorities upon which the *Commentaries* relied.[39]

The *Commentaries* were based on a series of lectures Blackstone delivered at Oxford University beginning in 1753.[40] The academic roots of the *Commentaries* foreshadowed a revived emphasis on the teaching of law, first in England and later in America.[41] To teach law, one must make legal doctrine understandable, and to Blackstone's credit his *Commentaries* combined "the language of the scholar and the gentleman"[42] into one "great readable, reasonable book about English law."[43]

In addition to the institutional books of Coke, Hale, and Blackstone, various monographic works appeared in England in the eighteenth century.[44] The most prolific monograph writer of the century was Sir Geoffrey Gilbert, who authored fifteen treatises in a span of thirty-three years.[45]

Few important legal works were produced in the United States during the 1700's,[46] but certain English treatises were republished,[47] especially the editions of Blackstone's *Commentaries*.[48] The first "significant

38. The Editors and Staff of the *Harvard Law Review*, 1937. Both a laboratory for student writing and editing and a forum for legal scholarship, as well as a way of signaling to employers which students received high first-year grades, the law reviews have been an integral component of the twentieth-century school. (*Courtesy of Art & Visual Materials, Special Collections Department, Harvard Law School Library.*)

expository work" by an American author was Zephaniah Swift's *System of the Law of Connecticut,* published in 1795-1796.[49]

In the early 1800's, the pace of publication of treatises quickened in England and the United States.[50] The popularity of such works thrived, and the treatise became the predominant form of legal writing in the nineteenth century.[51] A significant feature of this period was the extent to which law students studied these doctrinal writings.[52] Roscoe Pound, legal historian and educator, has written that the legal monographs, commentaries, and treatises "became and remained the basis of law teaching down to the present century."[53] It is unsurprising that foremost among the nineteenth-century American treatise writers were two university law professors—James Kent of Columbia and Joseph Story of Harvard.

Chancellor James Kent was appointed the first professor of law at Columbia in 1793. Although Kent left academia to serve in various judicial capacities, he was reappointed professor of law at Columbia in 1823.[54] Shortly after his second appointment, he meticulously drafted an extensive set of lectures.[55] The result was Kent's four-volume, "hugely successful" *Commentaries,* published between 1826 and 1830.[56] In the preface, Kent wrote that he produced those volumes "for the benefit of American students,"[57] and benefit they did. Early editions were in great demand. Upon arriving at Harvard in 1829, one new professor noted that at least a half-dozen copies of Kent's *Commentaries* were needed for student use.[58] Edition after edition appeared. The twelfth, published in 1873, was edited by Oliver Wendell Holmes, Jr.[59] Holmes added extensively to an earlier version, including over twenty-five years of English and American case authority that had been decided since the eleventh edition.[60] This laborious task took three years,[61] but the Holmes edition of Kent's *Commentaries* quickly became a "classic."[62]

The other American giant among nineteenth-century treatise writers was Joseph Story, first holder of the Dane chair at Harvard Law School where he served from 1829 until his death in 1845.[63] Story was prolific even though his career as a treatise writer did not commence until 1832, when he was fifty-two years of age.[64] Over the next thirteen years, he authored nine *Commentaries,* various monographic volumes on the topics of bailments,[65] constitutional law,[66] conflict of laws,[67] equity,[68] pleadings,[69] agency,[70] partnerships,[71] bills of exchange,[72] and promissory notes.[73] Unlike Blackstone's and Kent's books, Story's treatises were not prepared from lecture notes.[74] Story's *Commentaries on the Conflict of Laws,* published in 1834, is generally considered his best work. It was "for its time, so far ahead that it was a new creation rather than a development of the existing state of literature."[75] Story was, in short, a prototype of the academic scholar of the late nineteenth century.

Although Kent and Story were the most significant American treatise writers during the mid-1800's, several others became known by the topic of their labors.[76] For example, even today scholars refer to these nineteenth-century authors and their respective treatises as: "Greenleaf on Evidence,"[77] "Wharton on Criminal Law,"[78] "Sedgwick on Damages,"[79] "Parsons on Contracts,"[80] and "Washburn on Real Property."[81] These texts were largely the product of legal education.[82] They served as the basis of most classroom legal instruction until Langdell's revolutionary case method of teaching diminished, but did not eliminate, their influence.[83]

More significant than their pedagogic value for legal education was the extent to which practitioners and courts turned to these treatises as "authoritative statements" of the "received common law during the formative era" of American jurisprudence.[84] Doctrinal writing played a "much greater part in the growth of the common law . . . than our juristic theory admits."[85] The treatises often influenced judges as to what the law was or ought to be, so in time a particular author's view might actually become the law.[86] Without these treatises, American law would not have developed the consistency, uniformity, and sophistication that it has.[87]

Some commentators have suggested that the quality of the American law treatises declined following the Civil War,[88] in part because the widespread publication of reported American cases provided newer sources of authoritative statements of the law.[89] Nevertheless, the authorship of great treatises rebounded in the twentieth century. "Ultimate treatises"[90] were written between 1904 and 1951 by John Wigmore, Samuel Williston, Joseph Beale, Jr., Austin Wakeman Scott, William Prosser, and Arthur Corbin.[91] Three of these scholars, Wigmore, Beale, and Williston, had been students at Harvard Law School during 1887 and members of the first editorial board of the *Harvard Law Review.* They studied the nineteenth-century treatises; then they authored the twentieth-century treatises. In between, near the turn of the century, they helped to produce a new form of legal writing—the student-edited law review.

Law Reports

Although nineteenth-century treatise writers typically cited and commented on numerous cases, they often wrote in a discursive style, expounding their own theories as well as rules developed by the courts. Moreover, the treatise writers frequently analyzed older cases, often focusing on English cases in which the factual situations did not parallel those arising in a younger nation at a later time.[92]

American courts meanwhile were rendering numerous decisions, and lawyers needed to know their latest pronouncements. Thus, it was inevitable that this need would be filled by publishing American court decisions or "reports." This happened first at Litchfield, Connecticut, in 1789[93] in a publication called *Kirby's Report,* which contained decisions of the Connecticut Superior Court from 1785-1788.[94]

Law reports were not new; they had been printed in England for centuries. These case summaries were essential to the development of the common law because they were considered to contain "the highest and most authentic evidence of the principles and rules of the common law."[95] As W. S. Holdsworth, the highly respected legal historian, noted, "[S]ince the principles and rules of the common law could only be learned by attending to the decisions of the courts, reports of cases made by lawyers for lawyers became absolutely essential."[96] The oldest of these reports was the *Year Books* written in law French from the reign of Edward I through the reign of Henry VIII, a period of nearly 200 years.[97] Originally, reports in the *Year Books* were written by lawyers in longhand from notes taken in court[98] primarily to instruct pleaders.[99] The *Year Books,* therefore, were essentially summaries of "arguments used by the bar and the bench,"[100] rather than reports of case resolutions. The last of the *Year Books* was published in 1537.[101]

Thereafter, various members of the bar, including Coke, privately published the first English collections of cases.[102] These early English reports usually contained "histories of the several cases, with a short summary of the proceedings, . . . the arguments on both sides and the reasons the court gave for its judgment,"[103] rather than the written decisions of the judges.

Case reports were a natural by-product of the English judicial system.[104] A common-law judge occupied a permanent position and "so tended to follow his decisions."[105] If the judge was considered a learned jurist, his decisions were important to other jurists and lawyers as well.[106] The importance of stare decisis had its roots in such notions.

The publication of case reports in this country apparently was delayed by the American Revolution, which among other things produced a "strong dislike for everything English, including the English common law."[107] As noted above, the *Kirby Reports* of 1789 were the first general American law reports. Next came the *Dallas Reports in* 1790, containing Pennsylvania and United States cases.[108] After the turn of the century, an explosion of published American case reports occurred. By 1836, 473 volumes of reports had been published,[109] plus a dozen or more works on specific cases such as *Trial of Selfridge for Killing Austin*[110] and *Robertson's Report of Burr's Trial.*[111]

The late scholar Anton-Hermann Chroust wrote that one of the most remarkable phenomena of the post-Revolutionary period in American law "was the publication of American law reports."[112] Chroust pointed out that the appearance of the first printed reports had "lasting effects" upon later generations of lawyers.[113] Two factors contributed to the significant impact of the American law report. First, the legal treatise was becoming less important to the practitioner. Natural law thinking, incorporated into many legal treatises, was beginning to give way to a more positivist attitude about the nature of law.[114] Second, "fresh intelligence of court proceedings became almost as much of a necessity as that of the general current news of the day."[115] This need continued, and case reporters gained popularity throughout the nineteenth century. In the 1870's and 1880's, West Publishing Company established the national reporter system that is used extensively today.[116]

Early American Legal Periodicals

In the early 1800's, the current news of the day in America was provided mainly by general circulation newspapers, which frequently reported recent court decisions. These journalistic accounts, however, often contained inaccuracies and inevitably were incomplete.[117] Hence, members of the legal profession "demanded a medium of their own."[118] The publication and growth of case reports was one response to this demand. Yet the case reports failed to meet all the needs of the bar. Practitioners desired a publication devoted specifically to bar-related matters.

By the early 1800's, American lawyers had settled throughout the nation. Unlike England, in America the practice of law was largely decentralized. The decentralization resulted in a disjointed body of common law. The development of the American common law along different paths was due not only to the vast geographic distances involved, but also to differences among the court systems in each state. Consequently, the treatises, which tended to be national or universal in scope, did not fully meet the needs of practitioners,[119] whose law practice was primarily local or state oriented.

Furthermore, the treatises and commentaries discussed law developed decades in the past, but the states were rendering new decisions daily. Although the newly published case reports contained accounts of recent decisions, there were so many cases being decided in so many jurisdictions that one could hardly keep up. Moreover, the reporters rarely analyzed or commented upon these cases.

Finally, although the competent practice of law required knowledge of numerous and specific legal principles, rules, and procedures, it also involved dealing with judges, lawyers, and clients—people about whom it was expedient to be informed. Lawyers needed publications that would set out "the literature of the bar, especially its biographical and statistical material, questions of legal reform, chit-chat, and gossip, and [even] an enlivening anecdote."[120] Thus, "concise and casual" legal publications devoted to the American practitioner became inevitable.

First American Legal Periodicals

The first legal periodical in America was the *American Law Journal and Miscellaneous Repertory,* published in 1808 at Philadelphia.[121] In the preface to the first issue, editor John E. Hall declared: "The feeble exertions of a youthful individual, unaided by the impressive sanction of experience, can effect but little without the cordial cooperation of those from whom he has some right to claim assistance."[122] Not only was Hall unaided by the sanction of experience, he was unguided by the example of an American precedent.

The *American Law Journal and Miscellaneous Repertory,* like many journals to follow, was in essence a transitional publication between the earlier case reporters and the later legal magazines that developed in the mid-nineteenth century. As the first of these transition periodicals, the *American Law Journal and Miscellaneous Repertory* deserves special study. It primarily contained long excerpts of judicial opinions. Hence, to a degree it was another "reporter." But unlike the reporters, it also contained a short biography, some notices and brief descriptions of recent law books, and a commentary or editorial section titled "The Adversaria." It was issued irregularly in six volumes through 1817.

The *American Law Journal and Miscellaneous Repertory* had no lasting reference value, but as the original American antecedent of today's legal periodicals, the work is historically significant.[123] It is not known why it was not published after 1817. Whatever the reason for the demise of the *Repertory,* after a four-year publishing hiatus Hall tried again in 1821 to found an American legal periodical. The *Journal of Jurisprudence* was described as a "New Series" of the *American Law Journal and Miscellaneous Repertory.*[124] This venture died after only one volume was issued.[125]

Hall was not the only American attempting to edit and produce a legal periodical during the period of 1800-1825. Three other short-lived journals were published during these years. First, Joseph Gales of North Carolina founded *The Carolina Law Repository* at Raleigh in 1813.[126] It survived until 1816; the entire series consisted of only two volumes.[127] The issues are said to have contained reports of North Carolina decisions, digests of other American and English cases, biographical sketches, and various comments and addresses.[128] The inclusion of speeches and commentary by nonlawyers led one reviewer to conclude that *The Carolina Law Repository* was "only partially a law magazine."[129]

In 1818 another legal periodical appeared: *The New York Judicial Repository,* published in New York City.[130] This monthly magazine consisted almost exclusively of reports of trials, especially criminal trials and those thought to have a mass appeal. The published reports included cases dealing with assault and battery on a wife, assassination, conspiracy, a duel challenge, grand larceny, libel of a son-in-law, swindling, and rape. This journalistic venture into legal sensationalism lasted only six months; the last issue of the *New York Judicial Repository* appeared in February 1819.[131]

The final effort at publishing a legal periodical during this period was also short-lived. The *United States Law Journal and Civilian's Magazine* was produced by members of the Connecticut and New York bars from 1822-1826, during which time only two volumes were published.[132] Like the earlier *New York Judicial Repository, the United States Law Journal* apparently tried to be a magazine for the general populace.[133] And like the *Repository,* it failed.[134]

Each of these early legal periodicals was unable either to define or to carry out its mission. By featuring case reports, these publications were similar to the numerous established reporters. And, by attempting to attract a wide audience, at least two of these periodicals were too general for practicing attorneys yet overly technical for the general readership.

Although none of the legal periodicals published in the first quarter of the nineteenth century attained a position of literary distinction or lasting influence, they represent the first step toward a new form of legal publication. The next move in that direction was taken in 1829 when Joseph Angell, an official reporter for the courts of Rhode Island,[135] began editing *The United States Law Intelligencer and Review,* a legal journal that has been properly described as the "first publication displaying the distinctive features of the law magazine" as it exists today.[136] The *Law Intelligencer and Review* was distinctive because it included what came to be called "lead articles," a writing format which eventually produced some of the most significant legal scholarship of the times and foreshadowed the mainstay of modem law reviews.[137] In particular instances, these articles approached the treatise in stature, respect, and influence.

The *United States Law Intelligencer and Review* also contained case reports and general news, but the lead article, "well considered, upon live subjects,"[138] was its hallmark. Unfortunately, this periodical ceased publication in 1831 after only three volumes.[139] Its demise may have been due to financial difficulties rather than deficiencies in its content.[140]

Many early journals failed because publishers were either unable or unwilling to extend the necessary financial support.[141] Of course, as discussed above, several journals could not carve out a niche in the marketplace because they were too similar to law reports, too local in flavor, too broadly focused, or too technical. Thus, the failure rate of legal periodicals during this period was very high. By 1850, approximately thirty law journals had been attempted in America, but only about ten survived.[142] Nonetheless, the phenomenon of legal journalism was spreading across the United States,[143] and a more sophisticated, nationally oriented law journal evolved. Two journals founded during the mid-1800's—the *American Law Register* in 1852[144] and the *American Law Review in* 1866[145]—qualitatively advanced legal journalism in this country.

American Law Register and American Law Review

In 1852, two members of the Philadelphia bar, Asa Fish and Henry Wharton, compiled and edited the first issue of the *American Law Register.*[146] The monthly issues of the *Register* were distinctive because they contained more scholarly articles than the other journals. Roscoe Pound described the *Register* as the prototype of the "academic-professional type of periodical" which became the "characteristic American type."[147] In the *Register,* "along with popular articles and addresses there were more scientific articles from a general, even . . . a comparative law standpoint."[148] This scholarly emphasis no doubt contributed to the *Register's* most significant achievement—its survival. Indeed, it exists today under the title of the *University of Pennsylvania Law Review.*[149]versity of;; College of Philadelphia;<I>University of Pennsylvania Law Review<D>[University of Pennsylvania Law Review]

Although it was more scholarly than the other journals, the contents of the *Register*'s early issues were not unique. Lead articles were followed by a section entitled "Legal Miscellany," which included digests of and notes about recent decisions, as well as professional news items. Each issue concluded with "Notices of New Books," a section that included reviews of recently published volumes of case reports.[150]

The Register's original editors, Fish and Wharton, compiled and edited the first nine volumes for the Philadelphia publishing house of D.B. Canfield & Co. The *Register,* like all previous American law journals, began as a commercial venture not associated with a university. Beginning with Volume Ten, however, various boards of editors consisting of practicing attorneys, jurists, and law professors operated the *Register.*[151] The first noteworthy legal academic to serve on the *Register's* editorial board was Thomas Cooley of the University of Michigan.[152] The addition of Cooley, a former Chief Justice of the Michigan Supreme Court and one of the leading American treatise writers of the mid-1800's,[153] enhanced the *Register's* professional and academic credibility.

Another editorial board member, William Draper Lewis of Philadelphia, had an even greater impact on the *Register.* Following his appointment as dean of the University of Pennsylvania Law School in 1895, Lewis arranged for the *American Law Register* to be published by the law school he headed,[154] apparently because he believed "that an important attribute of a good law school was a law journal."[155] This conclusion reflected developments in legal education at the time; by 1895 Harvard and Yale already had established successful law school periodicals.

In 1896, law students at Pennsylvania began to edit the *Register.*[156] The name of the publication was changed in 1900 to the *University of Pennsylvania Law Review and American Law Register* and modified in 1945 by deleting the "American Law Register" portion.[157] The *University of Pennsylvania Law Review* goes on, now into its 132nd year, making it the oldest continuously published legal periodical in America.[158]

Another prominent legal periodical that emerged during the mid 1800's was the *American Law Review,* which was first published in Boston in 1866 by Little, Brown & Co. Unlike the monthly schedule of the *Register,* the *Review* was issued quarterly. This schedule may have allowed for more careful writing, selection, and editing of its contents. Certainly, that was the result; the first issue of the *American Law Review* was a breed apart. There were five substantial lead articles dealing with conceptual and institutional issues of national interest.[159] The editors, John Chipman Gray and John Codman Ropes,[160] successfully appealed to the intelligentsia of the nation's legal profession. In Volume One under the heading "Summary of Events," they declared that it was not their "desire or intention to give the *American Law Review* a local tone or circulation" and added that they would "spare no pains in the future to bring together matters of general interest from all quarters."[161] They called on their "professional brethren throughout the Union" to provide the editors with any information as to "judicial appointments, deaths of leading lawyers, important decisions, legislative changes, interesting trials, or other legal news."[162]

The *American Law Review's* aims "were evidently higher than those of most of its competitors, in that it was hospitable to theoretical essays and was as much concerned about the developments in the law of England as with the current American scene."[163] The editors' efforts produced an immediate success. Even the *Review's* competitors wrote of it in glowing terms, one declaring that it was a publication of which the "profession may well feel proud."[164] The *Review,* containing "dignified and elaborately prepared articles upon legal topics," possessed a "vigorous tone" which "earned for it a large measure of influence."[165] Its value to lawyers, the editorialist continued, "can hardly be overestimated," adding that Gray and Ropes established for themselves "an enviable reputation for their ability and discriminating taste."[166]

By including scholarly lead articles, honestly critical book reviews,[167] news of legal events having regional and national interest, and contributions from the best available legal minds, the *American Law Review* quickly became and arguably remained the most important American legal periodical of the nineteenth century. Its role as a model for the later student-edited law reviews[168] made the *American Law Review an* important link in the evolutionary chain of American legal periodicals, which began in 1808 with publication of Hall's *American Law Journal and Miscellaneous Repertory.*[169]

At this stage, however, in the latter half of the nineteenth century, many developmental paths were still open in the field of legal journalism.[170] If the *American Law Review's* birth in 1866 heralded a more "academic" future for the American legal periodical,[171] the emergence of other law journals suggested the continuation of a more "professional" orientation.[172]

Professional Journals

Lead articles in the *American Law Review* usually had an academic orientation. They were written primarily to educate—to enhance the reader's knowledge and awareness of legal principles. Most legal periodicals published in the 1870's, however, were designed primarily to inform—to discuss recent decisions, developments in the law and in legal education, efforts at codification, and news in a journalistic rather than in a scholarly style. These practitioner-oriented journals typically began with comments or editorials, followed by brief articles, case reports, digests, and concluded with book notices. The few "articles" typically did not "lead" the issue, but were buried in the middle. Yet, as mediums of information about legal matters of interest to lawyers and judges, a few of these publications performed superbly.[173]

One journal in particular understood its informational function and successfully performed it for nearly forty years. This publication, The *Albany Law Journal,* commenced on January 8, 1870, in Albany, New York.[174] Although an academic review might publish only quarterly, an informational magazine must appear more frequently to be of value. The *Albany Law Journal* commenced as a weekly, a schedule that placed a burden on its editor, Isaac Grant Thompson.[175] Its publisher hailed the *Journal* as a "medium of conveying to the profession of the country the latest intelligence of interest on all subjects pertaining to the law" and solicited "[b]rief contributions on legal topics, notes of decisions, and items of general legal news."[176]

The first issue of the *Albany Law Journal* began with two pages of advertisements, including those of practicing lawyers,[177] followed by a lengthy editorial comment, "On the Study of Forensic Eloquence."[178] This unsigned exhortation, which probably was written by Editor Thompson, was directed primarily at students. It concluded:

> These examples [of Cicero, Lord Chatham, Pitt, Erskine, and Daniel Webster] will teach [the student] that God has set a price on every real and noble achievement; that success in oratory, as in everything else worth succeeding in, can be purchased only by pain and labor; . . . that those who would follow in their steps must give their days and nights to study. . . .[179]

These lines reveal two characteristic thrusts of the *Albany Law Journal*: the topic of legal education and the espousal of the work ethic. These themes recurred in the ensuing issues.[180]

The *Albany Law Journal* often raised its voice in behalf of better education of lawyers and for higher standards for entry into the profession.[181] The *Journal*'s continuing concern for improving the public image of lawyers was typified by its reaction in its initial issue to a letter in the New York *Independent* newspaper that criticized the legal profession for producing "so few saints, so few martyrs, so few moral heroes."[182] *The Journal* responded that "[nearly] every trace of social and religious liberty on earth is due to lawyers," adding that it was "high time that the vulgar notions about lawyers were done away with."[183]

In certain ways, the *Albany Law Journal* of the late nineteenth century resembles the *American Bar Association Journal* of the mid-twentieth century. For example, each reportedly had the largest circulation of any legal periodical of its time.[184] In addition, both journals sought the support of the entire legal profession. One important distinction is that the American Bar Association, a professional organization, publishes the *American Bar Association Journal,* but the *Albany Law Journal* was not affiliated with any bar organization.[185] As might be expected, these publications did not coexist; the American Bar Association began publishing its *Journal in* 1915,[186] seven years after the demise of the *Albany Law Journal.*[187]

The significance of the *Albany Law Journal* has been misconstrued. Although one writer has asserted that the *Albany Law Journal* established a general pattern of articles which was followed by student-edited law reviews,[188] this view is incorrect. The general pattern of scholarly lead articles was established principally by the *American Law Review* and, to a lesser extent, by the *American Law Register.*[189] The most significant aspect of the *Albany Law Journal* was its spectacular success. The great majority of nineteenth-century legal periodicals failed within a few years for a lack of readers.[190] The *Albany Law Journal,* however, had broad appeal due to the wide variety of topics covered, the general quality of its writing, and its willingness—even eagerness—to take a public stand on controversial legal topics of the day.

The success of the *Albany Law Journal* spawned a score of other professional journals during the early 1870's. One of its better "imitators" was the *Central Law Journal,* located in St. Louis, Missouri, and published weekly to achieve "the highest degree of usefulness."[191] The format of the *Central Law Journal* was substantially the same as that of *the Albany Law Journal.* Like the *Albany Law Journal,* the *Central Law Journal* desired submissions to be brief, stating that "few persons can afford the time or find the patience to peruse long articles; nor can a weekly journal, dealing with a great variety of topics, afford space to print them."[192] The *Albany Law Journal,* however, published a great variety of topics of general and national appeal, while the *Central Law Journal* focused on court decisions and items of interest to the Mississippi Valley region of the United States.[193]

Other similar regional periodicals soon sprang up throughout the country; no longer was the publication of legal periodicals centered in the northeast. By 1875, law magazines such as the *Western Jurist* (Des Moines), the *Chicago Legal News, the Louisiana Law Journal* (New Orleans), the *Pittsburgh Legal Journal, the American Law Record* (Cincinnati), the *Forum* (Baltimore), the *Southern Law Review* (St. Louis), the *Washington Law Reporter* (District of Columbia), and the *Monthly Western Jurist* (Bloomington, Illinois) were being published.[194] Several specialized periodicals also appeared by 1875. They included the *Insurance Law Journal,*[195] the *Medico-Legal Journal,*[196] *The Bankrupt Register,*[197] the *Internal Revenue Record and Custom Journal,*[198] and the *American Civil Law Journal.*[199] More would soon follow. The number of legal periodicals published in this country leaped from seventeen in 1870 to forty-two in 1886.[200]

Several factors contributed to this explosion of commerical ventures in legal periodical publishing. The success of the *Albany Law Journal* was one. Another was the deprofessionalization of the bar. As notions of Jacksonian egalitarianism spread throughout the country[201] and barriers to entry into the profession were lowered, more persons began to practice law.[202] Many of these new, often unschooled lawyers probably were concerned less with the universal principles of law found in the treatises than with cases and news of their particular region or state.[203] The new legal periodicals fulfilled their need.

In summary, the "concise and casual" style, which combined scholarly insight and historical perception with a professional and practical focus, was the creation of nineteenth-century American legal journalism. In time, the treatises lost some of their appeal, not only to practitioners, but also to many authors. The more modern style of legal writing and the medium in which it was published, the legal periodical, eventually became the predominant mode of written discussion about the law. In an 1872 editorial comment on "legal journalism," the editors of the *Albany Law Journal* wrote:

> [T]he province of legal journalism is enlarged and made to be an almost indispensable auxiliary to the profession by . . . well-written, able and elaborate articles on new or doubtful legal subjects. Law journals are also the means of the dissemination of the views of distinguished men upon topics of vital interest. . . . [T]here is abundant reason to believe and to hope that we are in the beginning of an era of legal journalism which shall be brilliant in success, powerful in the accomplishment of law reform, indispensable in the . . . improvement . . . of the profession, and distinguished for the literary . . . lustre which it shall reveal in the law. . . .[204]

Thus, American legal periodicals paved the way for the student-edited law reviews by developing formats for legal writing, by demonstrating that legal periodicals could be useful to the profession, and by creating a widespread audience for articles combining scholarly insights with a professional focus. Although English authors originally dominated doctrinal writing (treatises and institutional works), the Americans blazed the new path of legal journalism that eventually led to student-edited law reviews.[205]

The Founding of Student-Edited Law Reviews

Student-edited law reviews emerged in the late nineteenth century. Contrary to popular belief, the *Harvard Law Review* was not the first student-edited law review.[206] Law students at two other institutions, Albany and Columbia, produced short-lived law journals prior to the publication of the first volume of the *Harvard Law Review* in 1887. Before discussing the founding of the *Harvard Law Review,* we must first examine these earlier efforts.

Initial Ventures at Albany and Columbia

With publication of the *Albany Law School Journal* in 1875, the American law periodical was no longer exclusively in the hands of "professionals. " This journal, whose name bore a close resemblance to that of the successful *Albany Law Journal*,[207] did not last long. Apparently, it survived only one academic year.[208] Yet this publication is significant because it was started and edited by students of Albany Law School. Thus, that institution was the first to produce a student-edited legal periodical.[209]

The efforts of the Albany law students did not go unnoticed by the commercial legal periodicals of the day. "The boys at the Albany Law School have had the enterprise to start a law journal," wrote the *Central Law Journal* on February 25, 1876, adding, "Altogether it is quite creditable. Of course it is not a man's law journal."[210] The *Central Law Journal* review of this new student enterprise continued:

> The editorial contributions are evidently for the most part in the storm-and-stress period. Each one of these boys is an immense aggregation of force which must needs [sic] work itself off in some direction; and it is much better that such electric batteries should be turned upon a novel experiment like this, than that they should expend their energies in stopping chimneys and robbing suburban hen-roosts.[211]

This "novel experiment" consisted of a few short articles, reports of moot court dispositions, news items, and information about the law school's clubs.[212] The *Albany Law School Journal* attempted to be a chronicle of law school events and a magazine of general interest to graduates and members of the profession. This concept was unique in the history of English and American legal periodicals.

The Central Law Journal tempered its relatively cool reception of this new student-edited venture by noting that the initial issue of the *Albany Law School Journal* did contain some "good contributions," "interesting items of news," and even "one question of practical interest."[213] This practical question concerned whether, at the conclusion of a lecture, it was better for a law student to go to the library and read the authorities cited or to go to the textbooks and read about the subject discussed.[214] The student editors answered their own question by arguing for the textbook option.[215] The *Central Law Journal* editors felt otherwise:

> It seems to us that reading from a text book would simply be reading another lecture on the subject. We believe that nothing can take the place of an exploration of the original sources from which text writers and lecturers generalize the knowledge which they present. The law is an applied science; and nothing short of a wide and attentive examination of adjudged cases will give the student a practical idea of how the various questions arose. . . .[216]

It is noteworthy that the *Albany Law School Journal* produced a mini-debate on the pedagogy of legal education.[217] By 1875, the methodology of legal education had undergone dramatic transformation at one law school,[218] and the debate over whether casebooks or textbooks constituted better educational study material was about to begin in earnest.[219] The "boys" of the *Albany Law School Journal* and the "men" at *the Central Law Journal* fought an early skirmish.

The editors of the commercially published *Albany Law Journal also* noticed the student experiment in legal journalism taking place in their city.[220] An editorial in that periodical stated that the new student venture was "the outgrowth of a very commendable spirit—that of furnishing a medium of expression for the legal mind of the school and a chronicle of the events of the school year."[221] The editorialist also opined that even though the student editors "cannot hope to rival in usefulness to the profession their legal contemporaries of a more sober and practical character, they can at least be the instruments of encouraging an endeavor among law students toward a higher legal education."[222]

As mentioned above, the *Albany Law School Journal* ceased publication after one year.[223] It is unlikely that the journal had much of an impact even at Albany Law School. In a lengthy address to the graduating class of the school delivered on May 17, 1876, Judge Lyman Tremain made no mention of the new venture although the students who had produced the volume were surely present.[224] Moreover, a detailed description of the Albany Law School in an 1877 issue of the *Albany Law Journal* does not mention the student journal,[225] nor does a history of the school written by Irving Browne and printed in an 1890 issue of *The Green Bag*.[226]

Despite the failure of the first student-edited legal periodical, other efforts were made. In February 1885, almost ten years after the demise of the *Albany Law School Journal,* six young men at Columbia Law School started the second student-edited legal periodical—the *Columbia Jurist.* They apparently did so without knowledge of the earlier student effort at Albany.[227] The Columbia law students modeled their effort after other periodicals being published by some academic departments in Columbia College.[228] The editors of the *Jurist* explained their intentions in the initial issue: "We think that the *Columbia Jurist* will supply a want long felt. The other departments of this College are each supplied with a paper or publication. Why are not we? Let each member of the Law School contribute heartily with pen and purse."[229]

The editors declared that the weekly *Jurist's* greatest value would be as a reference work for students and that it would include notes from class lectures, moot court decisions, plus "all news that can interest Law Men."[230] Upholding at least half of its motto "Quality before Quantity," the first issue consisted of four pages.[231] In that issue the editors noted that the faculty at Columbia Law School had given them encouragement[232] to proceed, several even promising to contribute articles.

Like the editors of the earlier *Albany Law School Journal,* the student editors of the *Jurist* did not focus solely on internal matters of the law school. They also took note of developments in the law and, in imitation of the successful commercial law journals, published casenotes of recent decisions and lead articles by "persons of acknowledged merit."[233] By calling on contributors from both inside and outside the college, the student editors of the *Columbia Jurist* "made their magazine the forerunner of the modem university law review."[234]

The second volume of the *Jurist* was of a higher quality than the first and, in some respects, more controversial. It contained numerous signed and unsigned articles and several reprints of works from commercial law journals.[235] Interspersed among these diverse and useful writings were editorials, news items, and notes of class lectures.

The *Columbia Jurist* was not received with open arms by its commercial brethren. The second volume of the *Jurist* contained five separate articles concerning "Mr. Dudley Field's Civil Code,"[236] and the student editors became embroiled in a journalistic controversy with the *Albany Law Journal* and the *American Law Review* over the proposed Field Code. The commercial publications had endorsed the codification effort and asserted that the *Columbia Jurist* editors, who espoused the opposing view, had "indulged themselves largely in an intemperate" reaction.[237] In 1886, the *American Law Review* editors decried the "amateur legal journalism" of the *Jurist*'s editorials.[238] Conceding that the *Jurist*'s content had "been enriched by several essays of [Columbia law professor] Theodore Dwight and other eminent men," the *American Law Review* nonetheless claimed to examine each table of contents "to prepare ourselves for whatever assault or criticism the learned and exacting editor of the *Columbia Jurist* may have launched at us."[239]

Weekly issues of the *Jurist* continued to appear for only another year. After Volume Three, Number Eighteen had been published in 1887, the *Jurist* died. The *Albany Law Journal* commented that the *Jurist*:

> ha[d] succumbed after a long disorder, manifested by an inveterate hatred to codification. The disease lately took a bad form, and with a gasp the *Jurist* expired on January 29th last. . . . *The Jurist* died penitent, and by a singular fact made a public confession of its wicked life and its unholy antipathy to codification. With its last breath it feebly murmured, the need of codification is confessed on all sides, and then it died. May so die all enemies to codification! We don't want them to die, but when they die, we want them to die penitent.[240]

The real reason for the demise of the *Columbia Jurist,* notwithstanding *the Albany Law Journal's* romantic belief to the contrary, was the inability of the new student editors to meet the grinding task of putting out a weekly publication.[241]

Despite its short duration the *Columbia Jurist,* unlike the earlier *Albany Law School Journal,* had a significant impact on the development of student-edited law reviews in this country. A copy of the *Jurist* attracted the attention of Harvard law student John Jay McKelvey in the fall of 1886.[242] The Columbia venture motivated McKelvey and other Harvard students to start a student-edited law review of their own.[243] Indeed,the initial issue of the *Harvard Law Review* appeared in the spring of 1887[244] with McKelvey as editor-in-chief.[245]

Although there is no evidence that McKelvey or his fellow Harvard editors were aware of the earliest student-edited periodical, the *Albany Law School Journal,* they certainly were familiar with the *Columbia Jurist.* For example, the *Jurist's* publication of lecture notes is mirrored by the publication of summaries of class lectures in early issues of the *Harvard Law Review.* Moreover, knowledge of the Columbia students' venture in legal journalism surely contributed to the overall concept of the Harvard publication.[246] Thus, the *Jurist* influenced the founding and early content of the *Harvard Law Review.*[247] The origin of the *Harvard Law Review,* however, cannot be attributed solely to the influence of the *Jurist.* The development of a student-edited legal periodical at Harvard resulted from the interaction of numerous influences, persons, and events, a complex topic which the next section explores.

Harvard Law Review

To do something daring and to do it well requires talent and inspiration.[248] Support from others is also helpful. In the matter of the birth of the *Harvard Law Review,* talent, inspiration, and support combined to produce a legal publication that has had an enormous impact on the legal profession.

The talent emanated from a small group of Harvard students who formed a club for the writing of legal essays;[249] a group Samuel Williston[250] later described as including "several brilliant men who afterwards attained distinction."[251] The inspiration came from speeches delivered at the 250th celebration of the founding of Harvard University[252] and from the tone and content of certain earlier legal journals.[253] The support consisted of encouragement offered by faculty members[254] and financial contributions made by alumni.[255]

During the 1880's, student clubs were common at Harvard Law School.[256] Their principal function was to organize "Moot Courts," which were an important part of the curriculum.[257] In the fall of 1886, eight third-year students formed a new club, the Langdell Society, "for the serious discussion of legal topics and for other serious work on law."[258] In addition to conducting mock trials, the members planned to write legal essays to be read at meetings.[259] The intention of writing essays only for their own use soon gave way, however, because "it was felt that the . . . writers deserved a wider circulation than was originally proposed and the founding of the *Harvard Law Review* was the result."[260]

Of course, it was not quite that simple. The prospective editors presented the plan to the faculty, who displayed "differing degrees of warmth in support offered."[261] In particular, the students consulted Professor James Barr Ames.[262] As one student founder, Julian Mack[263] explained: "The suggestion that the *Harvard Law Review* be established met at once with the response: 'Let's consult Mr. Ames. If he approves, we'll do it.' The project received his cordial support; the editors his encouragement and advice."[264] Ames was a likely consultant because his general availability for counseling made him the students' "best friend" during this period.[265] As Joseph Beale,[266] a student founder and later a Harvard law professor, recounted: "Ames approved [the idea for the review] without reserve, wrote the first leading article, and became the chief advisor and helper of the editors throughout his life."[267] Clearly, Professor Ames, more than any other person, influenced the talented group of law students that comprised the original editorial board of the *Harvard Law Review.*[268]

The faculty played no role in managing the review, although apparently the students had invited them to do so.[269] With the exception of Ames, they may not have had high hopes for the new venture because faculty minutes initially referred to the periodical as a "paper" rather than as a "journal" or "review."[270]

John Chipman Gray, who had been co-editor of the prestigious *American Law Review* when it commenced publication in 1866, was a prominent member of the Harvard Law School faculty at this time.[271] Although Gray could have provided the students with a wealth of practical advice,[272] there is no indication that he, or Dean Langdell, for that matter, supported the establishment of the *Harvard Law Review.* Despite the apparent lack of involvement of an experienced editor like Gray, the enthusiastic assistance and encouragement of Ames must have helped to keep the embryonic project alive. Moreover, the entire faculty encouraged the student editors, if not directly by their assistance, then indirectly by their enthusiasm for scholarly activities.[273]

The students were also inspired by the heady times at Harvard in November 1886. The occasion was the 250th anniversary celebration of the founding of the university.[274] Lasting three days,[275] the celebration included speakers James Russell Lowell and Oliver Wendell Holmes, Jr.[276] Even President Grover Cleveland attended.[277]

During this event, the Harvard Law School Association,[278] a recently-formed group of alumni, held a general meeting in the law building.[279] Holmes delivered an inspirational address to the gathering.[280] He recounted the influential history of the Harvard Law School and ended with an exhortation for the school and its future graduates:

> [T]he business of a law school is not sufficiently described when you merely say that it is to teach law, or to make lawyers. It is to teach law in the grand manner, and to make great lawyers. . . .
>
> Yes, this School has been, is, and I hope will be, a centre where great lawyers perfect their achievements, and from which young men, ever more inspired by their example than instructed by their teaching, go forth in their turn. . . .[281]

The students who founded the *Harvard Law Review* were certainly impressed by Holmes and the other speakers. Wigmore, later discussing the birth of the journal, bluntly stated that the celebration of the 250th anniversary "put pride into our hearts, and the conviction that the Harvard Law School had a message for the professional world."[282]

This conviction became the key to the eventual success of the daring, perhaps even rash, student experiment in legal journalism.[283] The mission of the publication was to be a vehicle for the "faculty's scholarship, . . . not so much as an organ for ourselves."[284]

Indeed, the founding of the *Harvard Law Review* gave the faculty, and Ames in particular, a new outlet for their scholarship.[285] Prior to the *Review*'s birth, Ames and Professor James Bradley Thayer[286] had begun research on legal history topics, but did not publish the results until the *Review* was in existence.[287] The *Review*'s editors unabashedly relied on such faculty articles to justify the new venture in legal publishing.[288] "We *knew* that our faculty comprised scholars of the highest standards and accomplishments in their fields. . . . We *knew* that their pioneer work in legal education was not yet but ought to be appreciated by the profession. We yearned to see the fruits of their scholarship in print."[289]

A problem of funding remained. The project was not an official part of the law school program, and it needed outside support. At the suggestion of Ames, the student editors sought assistance from alumnus Louis Brandeis,[290] secretary of the newly created Harvard Law School Association.[291] Brandeis gave the editors money and placed them in touch with other members of the Boston bar who were likely to support the project.[292] Student editor McKelvey also solicited alumni in the New York City area for subscriptions, which reportedly numbered around 300 by the first issue.[293]

The stage was set. It was time for the student editors to produce an enduring, first-rate academic journal. Although the result was not radically different from leading legal periodicals of the time, the review clearly reflected a law school orientation.

The initial issue of the *Harvard Law Review*, published in the spring of 1887, consisted of two lead articles, notes about happenings at the school, reports of moot court arguments, summaries of class lectures, case digests and comments, book reviews, and a list of books received. The editors declared that their goal was to be a vehicle for the publication of research centered at Harvard Law School, to furnish news about the school to alumni, and to spread the word of the new method of instruction introduced at Harvard.[294]

The reference to the "Harvard system of instruction,"[295] of course, concerned the "case method:" the use of casebooks, rather than textbooks, and Socratic, rather than lecture, pedagogy. The person most responsible for instituting this system at Harvard was Christopher Columbus Langdell, who became dean of Harvard Law School in 1870[296] and transformed the institution into a model of the modern law school.[297]

The case method of instruction sought, through the use of casebooks and Socratic questioning, to engage students in classroom discussion.[298] This method stood in stark contrast to the prevailing method of law teaching, which employed textbooks and classroom lectures.[299] The *Harvard Law Review* editors were apparently won over to this new teaching method used not only by Langdell and Ames, but also by an able young professor, William Keener, who later became Dean at Columbia Law School.[300] These innovative teachers were role models for the new editors who were about to embark on a bold venture of their own.

Certainly the intellectual excitement produced by the effective use of casebooks and Socratic dialogue played a critical role in the founding of the *Harvard Law Review*.[301] The student editors thus were not mere purveyors of Harvard's "message for the professional world,"[302] they were a part of it because they were the products of the new casebook method. They had been taught to analyze, not merely to recite from rote memory like schoolboys.[303] And they wanted the legal profession to take notice.

Although the student editors of Volume One of the *Harvard Law Review* were imbued with great enthusiasm for disseminating the Harvard message, they did not lose sight of the competition: the numerous commercial law journals of the day.[304] These periodicals, together with the defunct *Columbia Jurist,* served as organizational models for the Harvard publication.[305] Early issues of the *Harvard Law Review* included two features which were imitations of the *Columbia Jurist*:[306] one section entitled "In the Moot Court," which described cases in the moot court clubs,[307] and another feature, "From the Lecture Room," which contained summaries of class lectures.[308]

Joseph Beale was the student editor responsible for lecture notes in Volume One. At one point, he went to Dean Langdell seeking permission for the *Review* to print notes from one of Langdell's lectures.[309] Langdell instead decided to write an article on the topic covered in the lecture.[310] The result was a seventeen-year project in numerous installments—"A Brief Survey of Equity Jurisdiction"—the original segment of which was the lead article in the second issue of Volume One.[311]

Student editor Wigmore was in charge of the recent cases department.[312] Although established commercial journals all had similar departments run by well-respected editors,[313] Wigmore and his fellow students did not hesitate to become "criticasters of judicial decisions."[314] The primary object was to select cases "which bore directly upon topics discussed" in the classroom.[315] Wigmore also was involved in writing notes about law school news.[316] On occasion these notes were "calculated to induce in . . . [the students] a complacent feeling that . . . Harvard Law School . . . was achieving things."[317]

In sum, the new editors included critical comments on recent cases while promoting good feelings about their school. They also were willing to take chances. For example, student editor Beale wrote a lead article for the initial issue.[318] Publishing a student work as a lead article was adventurous; also out of the ordinary was the chosen topic—"Tickets"—a subject not covered in any law school course.[319]

Another provocative characteristic of the early *Harvard Law Review* is typified by an experience Williston related in his autobiography:[320]

> I had ventured to disagree with . . . Professor Ames . . . and I now undertook to argue the question in print. It illustrates the spirit that has made the Harvard Law School what it is . . . that Professor Ames encouraged me in my plan and discussed in an unbiased way . . . the reason for deciding the problem in one way or another. My essay was published in the second volume of the *Review*.[321]

A final feature of the publication deserves mention. United States Supreme Court Justice Felix Frankfurter wrote that the *Harvard Law Review* was a democratic institution "permeated by ethical presuppositions and assumptions and standards."[322] Students became members of the *Review* if they excelled academically; there were no other considerations.[323]

One of the principal purposes for establishing the *Harvard Law Review* was to convey to the professional world the message and the scholarship of the Law School's faculty.[324] To this end it performed ably. A review of the index to the *Harvard Law Review* discloses that Professor Ames contributed twenty-eight signed articles, Dean Langdell authored twenty-seven, Professor Thayer produced nineteen, and Professor Gray wrote twelve.[325] Student editor, and later Harvard Professor, Joseph Beale, Jr., contributed an astonishing fifty-one articles.[326] Another early student editor who became a Harvard law faculty member, Samuel Williston, was almost as productive; he contributed thirty-four articles.[327] Law professors who arrived at Harvard shortly after the publication's founding also contributed numerous works to the *Review*.[328] Thus, the growth in the prestige of the Harvard Law School may have resulted in part from the dissemination of the scholarship of its faculty through the pages of the early volumes of the student-edited *Harvard Law Review.*

Early Development of Student-Edited Law Reviews

The *Harvard Law Review* rapidly developed influence in academic and professional circles.[329] The impact on the academic world of the first successful student-edited law review is reflected in the creation of similiar periodicals at other institutions. In the legal world at large, its articles soon began to affect judicial decisions and legislative deliberations.

Expanding Role in Legal Education

In a twenty year period following the founding of the *Harvard Law Review*, five of the nation's then most prestigious law schools—Yale (1891), Pennsylvania (1896), Columbia (1901), Michigan (1902), and Northwestern (1906)—modeled legal periodicals after the Harvard prototype.[330] During the next two decades, the law review tide swept the country as many other law schools started and nurtured student-edited periodicals.[331]

The phenomenon of the early growth of law reviews did not occur solely because other institutions modeled one aspect of their programs after the country's leading law school. To be sure, an element of "keeping up with Harvard" motivated the establishment of law reviews at other law schools. Other factors, however, contributed significantly to the increase in the number of law reviews. Most important, the law schools recognized the educational benefits of such student-run operations.[332] In addition, the existence of a law review was, and still is, considered to be the mark of a mature educational institution, one whose reputation is partially based upon the students' academic product.[333] Moreover, law schools made a positive statement about their commitment to legal scholarship by including a law review in their curricula.[334]

The validity of these assertions about the early development of law reviews is best tested by examining the creation of the five reviews noted above. The first wave of *Harvard Law Review* imitators were located at excellent law schools. Thus, once these institutions adopted the Harvard model, the die was cast for legal education. Thereafter, a law school without a law review was considered a lesser institution.

Yale was the first law school to successfully emulate Harvard in this area.[335] Yet the student editors of Volume One of the *Yale Law Journal*, published in 1891, failed to mention their well-established counterpart at Harvard. Unlike the lofty mission of the *Harvard Law Review*, the initial goals of the *Yale Law Journal* were to unite those connected with the institution and to serve as "a mark of the vitality of the school."[336]

> As stated in its first volume, the purpose of the *Journal* was conceived to be threefold: to provide a means of communication between graduates and students, to serve them both as a common arena for discussion of legal matters, and to aid in the education of student editors and contributors.[337]

The *Yale Law Journal*, unlike many of its commercial brethren, had little or no financial trouble in its infancy.[338] Only much later did the *Journal* require outside financial support, and in 1920, after several years of operating in the red, the *Journal* was assured of continued funding from the Yale Law Alumni Association.[339]

Frederick C. Hicks, writing the history of Yale Law School, asserted that one aspect of the *Yale Law Journal* set it apart from law reviews at other institutions: "For many years, the *Journal* was somewhat more receptive than its rivals in other law schools to articles not intended for practitioners."[340] Although early issues of the *Yale Law Journal* did contain articles on legal education and legal history,[341] it is not clear that these volumes were broader-gauged than the efforts of other early reviews.

During the 1890's, several more law schools began publishing legal periodicals.[342] Except for the journals begun at the University of Pennsylvania Law School in 1896 and the Dickinson School of Law in 1897, however, all these publications died around the turn of the century.[343] Each of the surviving periodicals followed an unusual pattern of development. As discussed previously, the Pennsylvania effort did not originate at the school. Instead, University of Pennsylvania law students assumed the editorial chores for the already thriving *American Law Register* in 1896.[344] The publication was brought into the law school by Dean William Draper Lewis, former *Register* co-editor,[345] who sought to enhance the prestige of the institution by becoming associated with "a legal publication of established reputation and national interest and circulation."[346] Renamed the *University of Pennsylvania Law Review*,[347] the publication is the oldest continuously published legal periodical in America.[348]

The Dickinson periodical also underwent a name change during its early development. Christened *The Forum* at its birth in 1897,[349] it was renamed the *Dickinson Law Review* in 1908.[350] The new title reflected modifications in the nature of the publication. Initially, "it was published monthly and its content was principally social; the pages . . . were devoted to comments concerning . . . students and . . . alumni, reports of . . . moot court cases, . . . and the like."[351] Such a publication cannot properly be considered a law review as that concept is generally understood.[352] Much later, the Dickinson publication began to include the "discussion of legal questions and contributions by well-known writers" promised by the student editors of its first issue.[353] Thus, before 1900 only three institutions—Harvard, Yale, and Pennsylvania—produced law reviews that would endure to the present.

During the first decade of the twentieth century, three other prominent law schools—Columbia, Michigan, and Northwestern—established law reviews,[354] thereby virtually assuring a permanent position in legal education for such publications. The establishment of an enduring law review at Columbia University was accomplished only after a series of fitful starts. As noted above, the earliest effort, the *Columbia Jurist*, lasted only three years, from 1885 through 1887.[355] The second attempt to establish a law review at Columbia took the form of a monthly periodical known as the *Columbia Law Times*.[356] This student publication was born in the fall of 1887 and died in 1893, reportedly from lack of revenue.[357]

In 1901, Columbia law students made their third attempt to publish a law review, this time with happier results. In the late 1890's, the law school at Columbia moved to more spacious quarters and acquired the services of a professional law librarian.[358] "As a result, no doubt, of the improved library facilities after the removal, there was a revival of interest in legal scholarship among the students, and a new student publication [the *Columbia Law Review*] was founded to publish its results."[359] Dean William Keener, however, was concerned that the publication have a longer life than its predecessors at Columbia.[360] He therefore required that the student editors solicit professionals to write the lead articles and book reviews and that commitments be obtained from authors for the entire year before publication of the first issue.[361] Dean Keener also demanded that "the new periodical follow closely the pattern of the *Harvard Law Review*."[362]

The student editors of the *Columbia Law Review* adhered to Dean Keener's wishes and sought advice from their counterparts at Harvard.[363] The first issue of the *Columbia Law Review*, published in 1901, carried an editorial that contained the following statement: "In particular, we wish to thank the editors, past and present, of the *Harvard Law Review*, not only for setting before us a standard to which we some day hope to attain, but also for their kindly suggestions."[364] This third attempt to establish a permanent student-edited law review at Columbia obviously succeeded. Today the *Columbia Law Review* is one of the most frequently cited law periodicals in the country.[365]

The efforts of the next two universities to publish enduring law reviews, Michigan and Northwestern, are noteworthy for reasons other than their early entry into the field of law school publication. First, the creation of law reviews at these institutions marked an emergence in the midwest of what previously had been largely a northeastern phenomenon.[366] Second, and more important, the journals at Michigan and Northwestern were initially operated by the faculty.

In 1902, the editors of the first issue of Volume One of the *Michigan Law Review* proclaimed that their purpose was "to give expression to the legal scholarship of the University" and to meet the needs of the legal profession, particularly in the northwest.[367] The publication took substantially the same form as its predecessors at Harvard, Yale, and Columbia, but the makeup of its editorial board was distinctly different. While the three earlier reviews relied on student editors, the *Michigan Law Review* was edited and managed by the faculty.[368]

It is unclear why the Michigan law faculty chose to operate the publication themselves. Possibly they believed that such control was necessary for the success of the venture in view of their experience with an earlier legal publication at the school. In the 1890's, a pamphlet entitled the *Michigan Law Journal* was published for a short time at the law school and then elsewhere.[369] The *Journal*, which displayed a curious mixture of law school, bar, and commercial interests, lasted only seven years.[370] The Michigan law faculty certainly desired a better fate for the new *Michigan Law Review.* Thus, their experience with the *Journal* may have been the determining factor in the decision to place the *Michigan Law Review* "under the editorial management of a member of the faculty, assisted by [a Faculty] Advisory Board."[371] The students, of course, were involved, but only as "editorial assistants." As the *Michigan Law Review* became firmly entrenched in the school's program of legal education, however, the situation changed. "Over the years, the Law Faculty tended to turn over more and more of the editorial work of the *Review* to the student editors. . . ."[372] By the late 1930's, the students had "taken over a much larger share of the total responsibility, with the faculty serving primarily in an advisory capacity."[373]

Northwestern was the next law school to produce an enduring law review. The publication at Northwestern, founded in 1906, followed the format of the *Harvard Law Review,*[374] but was more closely aligned to the *Michigan Law Review* in two respects. First, it was designed to fill a need of the legal community in a particular area of the country—Illinois.[375] Second, it was initially edited by the faculty with some student assistance.[376] The relatively narrow focus of the Northwestern publication is explained in its first issue. There the editors commented:

> Undoubtedly, the field for law reviews of a general character is already overcrowded. Moreover, it must be conceded that such reviews, however excellent, enlist the interest of but a small minority of the practicing lawyers of Illinois. It is believed, however, that there is genuine and widespread need of a live periodical primarily devoted to the discussion and exposition of Illinois law, and of matters of special practical value to the Illinois bar. In that belief, and with the purpose of supplying that need, this *Review* is launched.[377]

Given this perspective, it is easy to understand why the Northwestern faculty chose to call its journal the *Illinois Law Review.*[378] The local orientation of the review also was the reason[379] that the University of Chicago and the University of Illinois law schools united with Northwestern for several years in the late 1920's and early 1930's to produce this publication.[380] Although the cooperative editorship apparently was successful, Northwestern resumed sole control of the *Illinois Law Review* in 1932.[381] Two decades later the review's name was changed to the *Northwestern University Law Review* to reflect the identity of its publisher and the expanded scope of its content.[382]

As in the case of Michigan, it is difficult to determine why the Northwestern law faculty assumed control of the review and initially permitted only limited student involvement. The dean of the school at the time was John Wigmore, who had been one of the student founders of the *Harvard Law Review.*[383] Nevertheless, Wigmore apparently did not advocate an entirely student-edited journal, but supported the concept of a faculty managed publication involving only a few student associate editors.[384]

Perhaps the limited use of student talent in the early days of the review was due in part to the involvement of a Chicago attorney in the establishment of the *Illinois Law Review.*[385] The attorney, Nathan MacChesney, had attended the University of Michigan and was aware of the *Michigan Law Review.*[386] He proposed to Dean Wigmore that Northwestern start a similar journal, and he made a financial contribution toward that end.[387] MacChesney's admiration of the *Michigan Law Review* may have influenced Northwestern's decision to follow the Michigan model of faculty editors, rather than the Harvard model of student editors.[388] His involvement may also explain the inclusion of alumni on the review as associate editors.[389]

Restricted student participation in the early issues of the *Illinois Law Review* also has been attributed to the Northwestern faculty's commitment to scholarship, rather than to doubts about the adequacy of student talent at Northwestern.[390] Indeed, over time the law students at Northwestern played an expanding role in the publication of the *Illinois Law Review.*[391] Following a quarter of a century of faculty control, "complete responsibility for the *Review* was turned over to the students of the law school and in 1932 the first student editor-in-chief was chosen."[392]

Although six years intervened between events at Northwestern and the development of the next enduring law review,[393] the trend was established. Once law reviews emerged at the leading law schools described above, it was a foregone conclusion that the remaining institutions would join the movement.

This proved to be the case.[394] By 1930, forty-three law schools featured law reviews,[395] although "the division of work and responsibility between the faculty and the students of the law-review-publishing schools varie[d] considerably."[396] Whatever their editorial makeup, law reviews already had assumed significance in addition to their educational value to the students. Almost from the beginning, election to an editorial position proved to be a ticket to attractive placement opportunities.[397] For example, "[b]y 1914, at least, the value of *[Columbia] Law Review* training was so generally recognized . . . that the School was unable to supply the demand for graduates who had been editors."[398] In the broader perspective, Justice Cardozo noted: "More and more, the law reviews are becoming the organs of university life in the field of law and jurisprudence. The advance in the prestige of the universities has been accompanied, as might be expected, with a corresponding advance in the prestige of their organs."[399]

Influence on the Legal Profession

It is difficult to assess precisely how the early reviews influenced the legal profession.[400] Certainly some commercial law journals did not think very highly of these competitive journalistic efforts by law students.[401] Nonetheless, there is substantial evidence that law reviews had an almost immediate impact on the development of the law in the courts and the legislatures.[402]

The best-known example of an influential early law review article is *The Right to Privacy*, written by Samuel Warren and Louis Brandeis, which appeared in the *Harvard Law Review in* 1890.[403] Shortly after its publication, the article was cited by a judge, who apparently based his opinion on its contents.[404] Eventually the article produced a broadbased change in the law.[405]

> We have here, obviously, an example of how the attention of the world of common law jurisprudence was brought to focus on an area of human life which the common law up to that time had left unprotected. Originating in the minds of lawyers . . . the columns of a law review afforded a forum for its dissemination and suggestion as to its recognition. . . . [O]ther legal scholars took it up in other reviews until the courts recognized its rightful place in our common law.[406]

The impact of *The Right to Privacy* on the development of the law was not a singular occurrence. Other works published in early law reviews were cited in the briefs of counsel and in court decisions.[407] The stature of student-edited law reviews was particularly enhanced when the Supreme Court of the United States began to cite their articles.[408] This first happened in 1897 when Justice Edward White referred in his dissenting opinion in *United States v. Trans-Missouri Freight Administration*[409] to an article entitled *On Contracts in Restraint of Trade,* written by Amasa Eaton for the *Harvard Law Review.*[410] Three years later, a Supreme Court majority opinion for the first time cited a law review article. In *Chicago, Milwaukee and St. Paul Railway Co. V. Clark,*[411] Chief Justice Fuller cited an article by Harvard Professor James Ames on contract consideration.[412]

Although neither of these articles played a pivotal role in the Court's deliberations, their mere mention gave law reviews additional credibility. The members of the Supreme Court, as well as other judges, gradually increased their reliance on law review articles over the years until by the mid-1920's the impact of law reviews on judicial decision-making was well recognized.[413] In this regard, one commentator noted: "When a Supreme Court Justice was first told by some friend that the *Harvard Law Review* declared his latest decision *wrong,* he may have pretended to scorn the disapproval as the theoretical conclusion of an immature student, but it hurt just the same."[414]

Justice Benjamin Cardozo was particularly complimentary of law reviews. He "found law review articles of conspicuous utility in the performance of [his] judicial duties"[415] and concluded that "[i]n the engulfing flood of precedents the courts are turning more and more to the great scholars of the law schools to canalize the stream and redeem the inundated field."[416] "Judges have at last awakened . . . to the treasures buried in law reviews."[417]

Early law review articles also influenced the thinking of legislators. Many articles contained the recommendation that a certain legal problem could best be solved legislatively.[418] Consequently, the law reviews served "as a mine for legislative drafting bureaus;"[419] numerous statutes resulted from the suggestions of authors of law review articles.[420] One authority has even suggested that the National Conference of Commissioners on Uniform State Laws was created in response to law review criticism of existing law.[421] The Commissioners, of course, have prepared numerous uniform statutes over the years for the consideration and enactment by state legislatures.[422]

Attorneys practicing in the late 1800's and early 1900's felt the impact of law reviews in still other, more subtle ways. Practitioners who subscribed to these periodicals became more aware of current legal thinking and recent developments in other jurisdictions than those who did not.[423] Lawyers of the era also soon discovered that law reviews often were "a more reliable source of information . . . than the ideas and conclusions of . . . law clerks."[424] The usefulness of the publications led many firms to look favorably on job applicants with law review experience.[425]

Over the years, student-edited law reviews became more influential in each of the various spheres of the legal profession discussed above.[426] Although the powerful status of law reviews today is subject to criticism on several counts,[427] it is unlikely that the pervasive influence of this institution will wane appreciably in the foreseeable future.

Conclusion

Student-edited law reviews were founded for a variety of reasons. Many failed, while others exceeded their founders' expectations. Yet all were representative of the nineteenth-century development of a more casual, informative, and topical approach to writing about law. This "legal journalism" in part reflected changing jurisprudential notions taking place in America away from natural law and toward a positivist attitude.

Practitioners found the formal doctrinal works less useful because authors usually adhered to natural law theories. Instead, attorneys wanted information about the latest decisions of America's geographically diverse and politically sensitive courts. They desired news of the profession. New periodicals, calling themselves repositories, journals, registers, and reviews, responded to these needs. They offered case digests, then case comments, and in time, lead articles.

These publications were intended not only to serve the legal profession, but also to turn a profit. As commercial ventures, many succeeded, at least for a time. Certain periodicals even achieved a position of prestige in the legal community.

The early law school reviews imitated the format, style, and content of the more influential commercial publications. Even so, the student-edited law periodicals that appeared near the end of the nineteenth century and in the early years of the twentieth century were unique in three respects. First, "not one iota of commercialism" inspired the commencement of any of the student-edited law reviews.[428] They were designed instead to facilitate academic scholarship. Second, the student-edited reviews began as a "medium of extracurricular training."[429] The editors were not paid,[430] nor did they receive academic credit for their law review work.[431] And third, the student-edited reviews were managed, edited, and at least partially written by nonprofessionals.[432]

The idea that individuals who have not yet graduated from law school select, edit, and publish critical writings for the legal profession still causes concern among critics.[433] Yet few voices are raised scorning the efforts of students who edit law school reviews today. This situation stands in sharp contrast to the published outcry of a century ago deriding the attempts of law students at Albany and Columbia to establish unprecedented law school-related legal periodicals.[434] For the most part, the derision and skepticism of the early years soon subsided as America's law school reviews came of age.

Notes

1. 1 Harv. L. Rev. 35 (1887).

2. *Messages of Greeting To The U.C.L.A. Law Review*, 1 U.C.L.A. L. Rev. 1 (1953) (offered by Earl Warren, Chief Justice of the United States).

3. The term "law review" is used in this article to refer to student-edited scholarly reviews, journals, quarterlies, or similiar periodicals published by law schools. The typical law review is divided into two major sections. The first section contains articles composed by experienced professionals and edited by law students. The second is comprised of works written and edited by law students. *See generally* Fidler, *Law Review Operations and Management*, 33 J. LEGAL EDUC. 48 (1983); Lee, *Administration of the Law Review*, 9 J. LEGAL EDUC. 223 (1956).

4. See *infra* notes 208-328 & accompanying text.

5. See E. GRISWOLD, LAW AND LAWYERS IN THE UNITED STATES 53-55 (1965); M. MAYER, THE LAWYERS 110-13 (1966). See generally Bard, *Legal Scholarship and the Professional Responsibility of Law Professors*, 16 CONN. L. REV. 731, 739-41 (1984); Bernstein, *The Supreme Court and Secondary Source Material: 1965 Term*, 57 GEO. L.J. 55 (1968); Burgess, *Law Reviews and the Practicing Lawyer*, 51 NW. U.L. REV. 10 (1956); Cane, *The Role of Law Review in Legal Education*, 31 J. LEGAL EDUC. 215 (1981); *Douglas, Law Reviews and Full Disclosure*, 40 WASH. L. REV. 227 (1965); Fuld, *A Judge Looks at the Law Review*, 28 N.Y.U. L. REV. 915 (1953); Havighurst, *Law Reviews and Legal Education*, 51 NW. U.L. REV. 22 (1956); Hoffman, *Law Reviews and the Bench*, 51 NW. U.L. REV. 17 (1956); Maggs, *Concerning the Extent to Which the Law Review Contributes to the Development of the Law*, 3 S. CAL. L. REV. 181 (1930); Marke, *Legal Research: Growth, Value of Law Reviews*, N.Y.L.J., Nov. 18, 1980, at 4; Marsh, *The Law Review and the Law School: Some Reflections About Legal Education*, 42 ILL. L. REV. 424 (1947); Newland, *Legal Periodicals and the United States Supreme Court*, 7 U. KAN. L. REV. 477 (1959) [hereinafter cited as Newland, *Legal Periodicals*]; Newland, *The Supreme Court and Legal Writing: Learned Journals as Vehicles of an Anti-Antitrust Lobby*, 48 GEO. L.J. 105 (1959); Thompson, *The Law Review Meets the Marketplace*, STUD. LAW., Dec. 1984, at 14; Wilson, *The Law Schools, the Law Reviews and the Courts*, 30 CORNELL L. Q. 488 (1945); Comment, *Legal Periodicals: Their Use in Kansas*, 7 KAN. L. REV. 490 (1959); Preface, *The Northwestern University Law Review*, 1906-1956, 51 NW. U.L. REV. 2 (1956); Survey, *The Law Review—Is It Meeting the Needs of the Legal Community?*, 44 Den. L.J. 426 (1967); *Why Law School Reviews?*, 4 FORDHAM L. REV. 1 (1935).

6. See, *e.g.*, Cribbet, *Experimentation in the Law Reviews*, 5 J. LEGAL EDUC. 72 (1952); Edmunds, *Hail to Law Reviews*, 1 J. MARSHALL J. PRAC. & PROC. 1 (1967); McKelvey, *The Law School Review 1887-1937*, 50 HARV. L. REV. 868 (1937); Richardson, *Law Reviews and the Courts*, 5 WHITTIER L. REV. 385 (1983); Traynor, *To the Right Honorable Law Reviews*, 10 U.C.L.A. L. REV. 3 (1962); Westwood, *The Law Review Should Become the Law School*, 31 VA. L. REV. 913 (1945); *The University of Detroit Law Journal's 40th Anniversary*, 34 U. DET. L.J. 247 (1957).

7. See, *e.g.*, Cane, *supra* note 5; Kelly, *Faculty Ponders Alternative Journal*, HARV. L. REC., Feb. 10, 1984, at 6; Mewett, *Reviewing the Law Reviews*, 8 J. LEGAL EDUC. 188 (1955); Murray, *Publish and Perish-By Suffocation*, 27 J. LEGAL EDUC. 566 (1975); Rodell, *Goodbye to Law Reviews*, 23 VA. L. REV. 38 (1936); Rodell, *Goodbye to Law Reviews—Revisited*, 48 VA. L. REV. 279 (1962).

8. Compare K. LLEWELLYN, THE BRAMBLE BUSH 107 (1930):

[The] law review is a scientific publication on which in good part the reputation of the school depends. . . . Here is a thing Americans may well be proud of. There is not, as far as I know, in the world an academic faculty which pins its reputation before the public upon the work of undergraduate students—there is none, that is, except in the American law reviews. . . . Such an institution it is an honor to belong to.

with Mewett, *supra* note 7, at 190: "The student, as such, has no place on a law review at all. . . . I am unable to understand this insistence upon publishing the attempts of students at all. I am not convinced that they write any better merely because their names may appear in print. . . ."

9. See *supra* notes 5-6.

10. See Bernstein, *supra* note 5, at 67; Maru, *Measuring the Impact of Legal Periodicals*, 1 AM. B. FOUND. RESEARCH J. 227 (1976); Newland, *Legal Periodicals*, *supra* note 5, at 478.

11. See *infra* text accompanying notes 206-41. The misconception that the *Harvard Law Review* was the first student-edited law school periodical apparently stems from the assertion in an early history of the Harvard Law School that "the *Harvard Law Review* [was] the first legal journal issued in a Law School." 2 C. WARREN, HISTORY OF THE HARVARD LAW SCHOOL 440 (1908). But see F. HICKS. MATERIALS AND METHODS OF LEGAL RESEARCH 207 (3d ed. 1942).

12. See *infra* text accompanying notes 117-204.

13. See *infra* text accompanying notes 17-92, In the early nineteenth century, Professor David Hoffman used the phrase, "concise and casual essays," to refer to writing in legal periodicals. D. HOFFMAN, A COURSE OF LEGAL STUDY 666 (2d ed. 1836).

14. See *infra* text accompanying notes 117-70.

15. See *infra* text accompanying notes 142-200.

16. E. WOODRUFF, INTRODUCTION TO THE STUDY OF LAW 25 (1898) (citing L. JONES, INDEX TO LEGAL PERIODICAL LITERATURE (1888)).

17. See Simpson, *The Rise and Fall of the Legal Treatise: Legal Principles and the Forms of Legal Literature*, 48 U. CHI. L. REV. 632, 633-34 (1981).

18. *Id.* at 634.

19. T. LITTLETON, TENURES NOVELLI (London ca. 1491). Harvard law professor Eugene Wambaugh described the *Tenures* as one of the "most famous books ever written," adding that it was the "first important law book that is thoroughly English." LITTLETON'S TENURES at xi-xii (E. Wambaugh ed. 1903). Historian W. S. Holdsworth declared the *Tenures* to be "the first great book upon English law not written in Latin and wholly uninfluenced by Roman Law." W. HOLDSWORTH, SOURCES AND LITERATURE OF ENGLISH LAW 137 (1925).

20. Law French, a Norman-French language which was substituted for the ancient Saxon language after the Norman Conquest, was used in all law proceedings and was the language of writs, records, and pleadings until the time of Edward III.

Writers continued to use law French in books about the law even after English became the official language of the courts. 2 BOUVIER'S LAW DICTIONARY 1859 (1914).

21. W. HOLDSWORTH, *supra* note 19, at 138.

22. *Id.*

23. *Id.*

24. The *Tenures* was "the first exposition of English land law as a system based on principles instead of as a number of disconnected formulae concerning the procedure of real actions." P. STEIN, REGULAE IURIS 159 (1966); see also W. HOLDSWORTH, *supra* note 19, at 139-40.

25. Before the next great English law book, Coke's FIRST INSTITUTE, was produced in 1628, over 70 editions of the *Tenures* had been published. W. HOLDSWORTH, *supra* note 19, at 139.

26. See Simpson, *supra* note 17, at 635-41.

27. W. HOLDSWORTH, *supra* note 19, at 140.

28. *Id.* at 141.

29. *Id.* at 141-43.

30. *Id.* at 141.

31. *Id.*

32. Simpson, *supra* note 17, at 635.

33. Coke wrote four *Institutes* in all: the SECOND INSTITUTE (1642) commented on English statutes, the THIRD INSTITUTE (1644) concerned criminal law; and the FOURTH INSTITUTE (1644) discussed the history and jurisdiction of the courts. W. HOLDSWORTH, *supra* note 19, at 142. See generally T. PLUCKNETT, A CONCISE HISTORY OF THE COMMON LAW 281-84 (5th ed. 1956).

34. Simpson, *supra* note 17, at 640. Abridgments were condensations of case reports. They appeared only in the 13th and 14th centuries. See generally J. COWLEY, A BIBLIOGRAPHY OF ABRIDGMENTS ETC. (1932). These condensations at times were prepared and used by law students in much the way . . . "briefing" of cases occurs today. See T. PLUCKNETT, *supra* note 33, at 273-76.

35. Simpson, *supra* note 17, at 640.

36. *Id.* at 652.

37. *Id.*

38. W. HOLDSWORTH, *supra* note 19, at 155-56.

39. *Id.*

40. Simpson, *supra* note 17, at 652. A few years after commencing these lectures, Blackstone was appointed Vinerian Professor of English Law at Oxford in 1758. The endowment of this chair had derived in part from the other major legal publication of the century, Charles Viner's twenty-three volume abridgement (1741-57)." *Id.* (citing C. VINER, A GENERAL ABRIDGEMENT OF LAW AND EQUITY (Aldershot 1742-1753)).

41. W. HOLDSWORTH, *supra* note 19, at 155, 160-61.

42. *Id.* at 156.

43. *Id.* (quotation ascribed to Maitland).

44. See Simpson, *supra* note 17, at 652-62.

45. *Id.* at 654. Gilbert's works included: TREATISES OF TENURES (1730), LAW OF EVIDENCE (1734), and TREATISE ON RENTS (1758). See Simpson, *supra* note 17, at 654 nn.138, 142 & 147.

46. See Simpson, *supra* note 17, at 668.

47. *Id.*

48. *Id.*

49. *Id.* at 669.

50. *Id.* at 669-74.

51. See *Id.*; see also R. POUND, THE FORMATIVE ERA OF AMERICAN LAW 138-67 (1938).

52. See R. POUND, *supra* note 51, at 144, 163-64.

53. *Id.* at 144.

54. 1 J. KENT, COMMENTARIES ON AMERICAN LAW at ix (14th ed. 1896).

55. *Id.*

56. Simpson, *supra* note 17, at 670.

57. J. KENT, *supra* note 54, at iii.

58. A. SUTHERLAND, THE LAW AT HARVARD: A HISTORY OF IDEAS AND MEN, 1817-1967, at 100 (1967).

59. S. BENT, JUSTICE OLIVER WENDELL HOLMES 13 (1932).

60. *Id.*

61. See C. BOWEN, YANKEE FROM OLYMPUS 251-53 (1944).

62. S. BENT, *supra* note 59, at 139. "For America, it [the Kent-Holmes edition] was a pioneer work. Nothing so searching and critical had been done before." C. BOWEN, *supra* note 61, at 252.

63. Simpson, *supra* note 17, at 670.

64. *Id.*

65. J. STORY, COMMENTARIES ON THE LAW OF BAILMENTS (Cambridge 1832).

66. J. STORY, COMMENTARIES ON THE CONSTITUTION OF THE UNITED STATES (Boston 1833).

67. J. STORY, COMMENTARIES ON CONFLICT OF LAWS (Boston 1834),
68. J. STORY, COMMENTARIES ON EQUITY JURISDICTION (Boston 1836).
69. J. STORY, COMMENTARIES ON EQUITY PLEADINGS (Boston 1838).
70. J. STORY, COMMENTARIES ON THE LAW OF AGENCY (Boston 1839).
71. J. STORY, COMMENTARIES ON THE LAW OF PARTNERSHIP (Boston 1841).
72. J. STORY, COMMENTARIES ON THE LAW OF BILLS OF EXCHANGE (Boston 1843).
73. J. STORY, COMMENTARIES ON THE LAW OF PROMISSORY NOTES (Boston 1845).
74. A. SUTHERLAND, *supra* note 58, at 107. Story's treatises, however, were intended "as suitable texts for students." *Id.*
75. *Id.* at 115.
76. For a list, see R. POUND, *supra* note 51, at 140-41.
77. *Id.* at 141.
78. *Id.*
79. *Id.*
80. *Id.*
81. *Id.*
82. *Id.* at 144.
83. See *infra* text accompanying notes 297-300.
84. R. POUND, *supra* note 51, at 151.
85. *Id.* at 138.
86. *Id.* at 138-39, 151-53. Most early treatise writers subscribed to the "natural law" theory of jurisprudence. *See* Simpson, *supra* note 17, at 665-67. This view, having roots in Greek philosophy, holds that law embodies and should reflect universal principles—principles of right reason—which courts and other entities have the duty to discern and reveal. *See* R. POUND, *supra* note 51, at 13-16, 144-45, 147-48.

Natural law theory in part explains why various legal writers chose to write treatises, especially from 1750 onward. They felt obliged to unravel the confusion of countless court decisions and to explain how and where these courts had on occasion gone astray from universal principles. Thus, with the belief that decided cases are only of transitory interest vis-a-vis their underlying principles, many legal authors in the 18th and 19th centuries approached their writing with missionary zeal. For example, the American treatise writer Joel Bishop declared that his task was "to unfold the rules, the principles, the reasons, . . . which not only governed former decisions, but are to govern subsequent ones." J. BISHOP, THE FIRST BOOK OF THE LAW 126 (1868). The obligation of the legal writer, in short, was "to discover the true rule" and to reveal it in his writings for the enlightenment of all. Simpson, *supra* note 17, at 674.

The prevalence of natural law thinking, especially in America, was not limited to legal writers. Many judges believed that their juristic role was to discover and unfold the "true rule" and, if no voice came to their aid in the middle of the night, then readable books by the likes of Blackstone, Kent, and Story would have to do. *See generally* R. POUND, *supra* note 5 1, at 3-30.

87. R. POUND, *supra* note 51, at 145-52.
88. *Id.* at 157.
89. See *infra* text accompanying notes 107-16.
90. Simpson, *supra* note 17, at 674.
91. *Id.* The full titles of these treatises are: J. BEALE, TREATISE ON THE CONFLICT OF LAWS (1935); A. CORBIN, CORBIN ON CONTRACTS (1950); W. PROSSER, HANDBOOK OF THE LAW OF TORTS (1941); A. SCOTT, THE LAW OF TRUSTS (1939); J. WIGMORE, A TREATISE ON THE ANGLO-AMERICAN SYSTEM OF EVIDENCE (1904-1905); S. WILLISTON, THE LAW OF CONTRACTS (1920-1922).
92. See generally D. HOFFMAN, A COURSE OF LEGAL STUDY 656-57 (2d ed. 1836).
93. *American Legal Periodicals*, 2 ALB. L.J. 445, 445 (1870).
94. D. HOFFMAN, *supra* note 92, at 659. One authority contends that Francis Hopkinson's work, *Judgments in Admiralty in Pennsylvania* (1789), was the first volume of law reports published in this country. J. WALLACE, THE REPORTERS ARRANGED AND CHARACTERIZED WITH INCIDENTAL REMARKS 571 n.2 (4th ed. 1882). But see Briceland, *Ephraim Kirby, Pioneer of American Law Reporting*, 16 AM. J. LEGAL HIST. 297, 315 n.68 (1972) (discussing why Kirby should be listed first). Kirby's work was a general, "fully developed" reporter not, like Hopkinson's, limited to a specialty area. *Id.* at 315. Kirby's volume, therefore, is the more significant one for the purpose of this Article.
95. READINGS ON THE HISTORY AND SYSTEM OF THE COMMON LAW 295 (R. Pound & T. Plucknett 3d ed. 1927).
96. W. HOLDSWORTH, *supra* note 19, at 75
97. *Id.* at 78.
98. *Id.* at 80-81.
99. *Id.* at 82-83.
100. *Id.* at 87.
101. Note, *Abridgements of the Year Books*, 37 HARV. L. REV. 214, 214 (1923).
102. W. HOLDSWORTH, *supra* note 19, at 89-91.
103. 1 W. BLACKSTONE, COMMENTARIES ON THE LAWS OF ENGLAND *71.
104. Pound, *Types of Legal Periodical*, 14 IOWA L. REV. 257, 259 (1929).
105. *Id.*
106. *Id.*

107. Chroust, *The Dilemma of the American Lawyer in the Post-Revolutionary Era*, 35 NOTRE DAME LAW. 48, 48 (1959); see also Surrency, Law Reports in the United States. 25 Am. J. LEGAL HIST. 48, 54-55 (1981).

108. D. HOFFMAN, *supra* note 92, at 285, 659. Dallas became the first reporter for the Supreme Court of the United States. See Joyce, *The Rise of the Supreme Court Reporter: An Institutional Perspective on Marshall Court Ascendancy*, 83 MICH. L. REV. 401 (1985).

109. D. HOFFMAN, *supra* note 92, at 657.

110. *Id.* at 660.

111. *Id.* at 664.

112. Chroust, *supra* note 107, at 75. See generally Joyce, *supra* note 108.

113. Chroust, *supra* note 107, at 75.

114. This jurisprudential shift was gradual. For a discussion of the influence of natural law theories on treatise writers, see *supra* note 86.

115. *American Legal Periodicals*, supra note 93, at 445.

116. Surrency, *supra* note 107, at 62.

117. *American Legal Periodicals, supra* note 93, at 445.

118. *Id.* "After 1800, . . . [l]awyers looked to legal magazines as well as to other activities to maintain professional cohesion and power." R. STEVENS, LAW SCHOOL: LEGAL EDUCATION IN AMERICA FROM THE 1850'S TO THE 1980'S, at 8 (1983).

119. "The idea that periodicals were especially needed in the United States because of the diversity of law between [sic] the states was emphasized in the forewards to many of our early journalistic attempts." F. HICKS, supra note 11, at 215.

120. *American Legal Periodicals, supra* note 93, at 445.

121. F. HICKS, *supra* note 11, at 202-04; Glasier, *Early American Periodicals*, 28 A.B.A. J. 615 (1942); *American Legal Periodicals, supra* note 93, at 445. Sometimes the last word in this periodical's title is incorrectly listed as "Repository." *See* Pound, *supra* note 10.4, at 262 n.4.; *American Legal Periodicals, supra* note 93, at 445-46. In any case, beginning with the fourth volume published in 1813, the last part of the correct title—"and Miscellaneous Repertory"—was dropped, leaving the journal with *American Law Journal* as its official name.

122. 1 AM. L. J. at v, vii (1808).

123. See Glasier, *supra* note 121, at 615; *American Legal Periodicals, supra* note 93, at 446.

124. D. HOFFMAN, *supra* note 92, at 670.

125. *Id.*

126. *American Legal Periodicals, supra* note 93, at 446.

127. D. HOFFMAN, *supra* note 92, at 670.

128. *American Legal Periodicals, supra* note 93, at 446.

129. *Id.*

130. See 1 N.Y. JUD. REPOSITORY (1818).

131. Letter from Marlene D. McGuirl, Chief, Law Library, American-British Law Division, Library of Congress, to Craig Laporte, research assistant (July 1982) (copy on file with *The Hastings Law Journal*).

132. D. HOFFMAN, *supra* note 92, at 670.

133. See *American Legal Periodicals, supra* note 93, at 446.

134. *Id.*

135. *Id.*

136. *Id.*

137. *Id.* The lead article concept was described by the editor of the *Albany Law Journal* in 1874 as follows:

> A newspaper or journal that only contained news that was a mere record of passing events, would be a short-lived anomaly. The reader requires something more than news. When he has read the telegrams and summary, he turns with unabated interest, and generally with increased interest, to the other parts of the newspaper or journal. He sees in the summary that a new play was brought out last night, and he wants to know whether it was good, bad or indifferent. A telegram tells him that there has been another revolution at Madrid; he wants to know what the newspaper thinks about the affair, and turns to the leader. There has been a ministerial defeat, and the first thing he reads is the leader on the political crisis. . . . The criticisms and the articles are not merely expressions of opinion, but are chiefly instructive essays. The writer of the leading article gives life and interest to the curt telegram.

Editorial, *Legal Journalism*, 9 ALB. L. J. 106 (1874).

The editor pointed out that life and interest can also be put into legal matters by the use of lead articles in law periodicals. *Id.* at 107. Indeed, in 1888 the editors of the *American Law Review*, quoting from an earlier source, opined that "a greater benefit from the study of lead articles may be derived than can usually be gained from the study of the textbooks" because the authors in the law periodicals are "specialists discussing subjects with a well defined object in view." Note, *Leading Articles in Law Periodicals*, 22 AM. L. REV. 786, 786 (1888).

138. *American Legal Periodicals, supra* note 93, at 445.

139. F. HICKS, *supra* note 11, at 20-4.

140. See 11 ALB. L. J. 1 (1875).

141. *Id.*

142. *Id.* But see Glasier, *supra* note 121, at 615 ("Approximately fifty publications with some claim to be classed as legal periodicals were started between 1808 and 1850.").

The most important periodicals that had ceased publication during the mid-1800's were the *American Jurist and Law Magazine* (1829-1842), the *Pennsylvania Law Journal* (1842-1848), and the *Law Reporter* (1838-1866). The quarterly *American Jurist and Law Magazine* has been described as the "first compact, methodical and comprehensive law periodical" published in America. *American Legal Periodicals, supra* note 93, at 447. David Hoffman, while Professor of Law at the University of Maryland in 1836, advised his students to improve their leisure hours by the perusal of the legal periodicals, especially the "admirable works" in the *American Jurist.* D. HOFFMAN, *supra* note 92, at 669. Commenting on the *Jurist* and the earlier *American Law Journal,* Hoffman noted that America had taken a decided lead over England in the area of "repositories of legal essays." *Id.* at 83. *The American Jurist* survived until 1842. A reviewer later described the *Jurist's* volumes as characterized by "good taste and scholarship." *American Legal Periodicals, supra* note 93, at 447.

The *Pennsylvania Law Journal* was started in 1842 at Philadelphia. *Id.* Later to become the *American Law Journal,* the publication stressed Pennsylvania court decisions, but included articles and legal news items. *Id.* This journal is important because it partly served as a model for another Philadelphia based legal periodical, the *American Law Register,* which in turn was one of the most important legal reviews extant in 1886 when students at Harvard Law School sought examples to emulate.

The third significant but ill-fated publication of this era was the *Law Reporter,* a monthly published at Boston under the editorship of Peleg W. Chandler. *Id.* at 448. Twenty-seven volumes were issued before it too was discontinued in 1866. *Id.* Although the *Law Reporter* contained lead articles, news, and comments in addition to reports of cases, its demise was in part due to keen competition. *Id.*

143. The *Western Law Journal,* published in Cincinnati, was the first legal periodical in the United States published outside of the east or southeast. *American Legal Periodicals, supra* note 93, at 447. According to one listing of twenty-one periodicals commenced from 1808 through 1850, six were based in Philadelphia, six in New York City, three in Boston, and one in each of the following cities: Providence, Rhode Island; Burlington, New Jersey; Charleston, South Carolina; Raleigh, North Carolina; Nashville, Tennessee; and Cincinnati, Ohio. *Id.* at 445-48. Within the next 25 years, by 1875, at least one legal periodical was published in each of the following locales: Minneapolis; Chicago; St. Louis; Cleveland; Albany, New York; Bloomington, Illinois; Rochester, New York; Austin, Texas; Topeka, Kansas; Louisville, Kentucky; Baltimore, Maryland; St.Paul, Minnesota; Newark, New Jersey; Pittsburgh, Pennsylvania; Richmond, Virginia; Columbus, Ohio; Scranton, Pennsylvania; and Washington, D.C. See *Digest of Cases in the Law Periodicals,* 21 AM. L. REV. 329 (1887)

144. 1 AM. L. REG. 55 (1852).

145. 1 AM. L. REV. 1 (1866).

146. 100 U. PA. L. REV. 69 (1951). *The American Law Register* was an outgrowth of a local periodical, the *Pennsylvania Law Journal* (1842-1848) and its successor, the *American Law Journal* (1849-1852). Pound, *supra* note 104, at 264.

147. Pound, *supra* note 104, at 264; see also *infra* note 172 (further discussion of the Pound article).

148. Pound, *supra* note 104, at 264.

149. See 100 U. PA. L. REV. 69 (1951).

150. See, *e.g., Review of Swan's Tennessee Reports,* 1 AM. L. REG. 382 (1853).

151. 100 U. PA. L. REV. 69 (1951).

152. *Id.*

153. *Id.*

154. *Id.* see *infra* notes 344-48 & accompanying text.

155. 100 U. PA. L. REV. 69 (1951).

156. *Id.*

157. *Id.* From 1892 through 1897, the periodical's full title was *American Law Register and Review.* In 1898, it again was called *American Law Register.*

158. Douglas, *supra* note 5, at 228.

159. *See* 1 AM. L. REV. 1-83 (1866).

160. Both Gray and Ropes received law degrees from Harvard Law School in 1861. SUTHERLAND, *supra* note 58, at 140. These same men founded the Boston law firm bearing their names shortly after their graduation from Harvard. *Id.* at 185. Gray later was appointed to fill the first Story Professorship at Harvard Law School in 1875. *Id.* Roscoe Pound discussing his days as a student at Harvard Law School, commented that Gray was "master," a "great scholar," and "an outstanding influence with me." Sutherland, *One Man in His Time,* 78 HARV. L. REV. 7, 11-12 (1964).

161. Comment, *Summary Of Events,* 1 AM. L. REV. 206, 206 (1866). 162. *Id.*

163. M. HOWE, JUSTICE OLIVER WENDELL HOLMES: THE SHAPING YEARS: 1841-1 at 264 (1957).

164. *American Legal Periodicals, supra* note 93, at 449.

165. *Id.*

166. *Id.*

167. The *American Law Review* became well known for its candid and often critical book reviews. Although the *Albany Law Review* described the *American Law Review's* book notices as "fearless and impartial," *Id.,* the *Central Law Journal* contended that they sometimes were . . . "conceived . . . in a spirit of faultfinding." 1 CENT. L.J. 24 (1874). The *Central Law Journal* also commented that a recent issue of the *American Law Review* contained "the usual amount of 'heavy' editorial matter, 'grated down and filed away with thought,'" adding that the first article of that particular issue "is a fifty-page discussion." *Id.*

168. See *infra* notes 205, 304 & accompanying text.

169. See *supra* notes 121-25 & accompanying text.

170. See Pound, *supra* note 104, at 265.

171. *Id.* at 259.

172. *Id.* By the early twentieth century, a mixed academic-professional journal emerged as the predominant form of American legal periodical. In a 1928 paper read at the annual meeting of the Association of American Law Schools, Roscoe Pound placed legal periodicals into three categories: academic, professional, and mixed. He generalized that the purely academic journal primarily had been published in Continental Europe, while the purely professional was produced in England. This paper was subsequently published in the *Iowa Law Review*. *Id.* at 260-65.

173. See, e.g., *infra* notes 174-90 & accompanying text.

174. This publication should not be confused with the later *Albany Law Review* or the shortlived *Albany Law School Journal*. See *infra* notes 208-26 & accompanying text.

175. The *Albany Law Journal* published two volumes each year.

176. 1 ALB. L. J. 2 (1870) (advertisement).

177. The advertisements for lawyers merely stated the firm name and location, such as "Hilton & Whitney, Counsellors at Law, St. Louis, Mo." Other advertisers were publishers, stenographers, and court reporters. *Id.* at 1-2.

178. 1 ALB. L. J. 3 (1870).

179. *Id.* at 5-6.

180. See, e.g., *Method and objections of Law Reading, with Reference to Apprehension-Memory-Judgment*, 1 ALB. L. J. 226 (1870).

181. Such efforts certainly helped unify the national movement in American law which began in the 1850's and gathered momentum after the Civil War. See Pound, *supra* note 10-4, at 263. "By 1870, professional journals were vying with one another in appeals for improving the legal profession." R. STEVENS, *supra* note 118, at 24.

182. Comment, *The Moral Standing of the Legal Profession*, 1 ALB. L.J. 10, 10-11 (1870).

183. *Id.*

184. *Our Second Volume*, 2 ALB. L.J. 1 (1870).

185. No national bar organization existed in 1870. The American Bar Association was not formed until 1878. R. POUND, THE LAWYER FROM ANTIQUITY TO MODERN TIMES 270 (1953).

186. See 1 A.B.A. J. 1 (1915).

187. The last issue of the *Albany Law Journal* apparently was published in 1908.

188. Edmunds, supra note 6, at 9-10.

189. See *supra* notes 144-62 & accompanying text.

190. Why had the majority failed? One answer is suggested in an 1875 issue of the *Albany Law Journal*, which states that the majority of American legal journals have "mistaken the true province of legal journalism." 1 ALB. L.J. 261, 262 (1875). The editorial continues:

> A journal which is simply a series of reports, or a compilation of reported cases, can hardly claim the name of "legal journal." . . . The true function of legal journalism is principally to present the various phases of the legal profession, disquisitions on legal topics, a condensed record of legal events, and a summary of the most recent legal decisions. A journal which does this will not fail. . . .
>
> *Id.*

Attempts to "out report" the reporters and not provide "disquisitions" or lead articles on law-related topics typically resulted in a periodical that failed to win sufficient support to survive. Thus, it was reported in 1887 that the *Texas Law Review*, "lately of Austin, Texas, has already succumbed to the rivalry of two sets of '*Reporters*' which are taking the whole land for their province, and making hopeless the future of those local journals which find a pretext for existence in case reporting." *Changes in Legal Journalism*, 21 AM. L. REV. 140 (1887).

191. 1 CENT. L.J. 1 (1874).

192. *Id.*

193. *Id.* The provincial nature of the *Central Law Journal* is also revealed by its repeated inclusions of excerpts from other midwest area law periodicals such as the *Chicago Legal News*. See, *e.g.*, Comment, *The Purpose of a Law Review*, 1 CENT. L.J. 463 (1874).

194. See *supra* text accompanying notes 174-93. The *Chicago Legal News* was edited by Mrs. Myra Bradwell, who may have been the first woman editor or an American law periodical. Comment, *Female Lawyers*, 1 CENT. L.J. 487 (1874). Another woman, Mrs. Catherine Waite, was the editor of the later *Chicago Law Times* which began publication in 1887. 35 ALB. L. J. 21, 22 (1887).

195. The *Insurance Law Journal* was first published in September 1871. Book Notices, 4 ALB. L.J. 195 (1871).

196. 27 ALB. L.J. 481, 483 (1883).

197. *American Law Periodicals*, *supra* note 93, at 449.

198. See *Id.*

199. This periodical first appeared in 1873. Book Notices, 7 ALB. L.J. 94 (1873).

200. See Bloomfield, *Law v. Politics: The Self-Image of the American Bar* (1830-1860), 12 AM. J. LEGAL HIST. 306, 309 (1968) (listing the number of legal periodicals in existence in 1870); *Digest of Cases in the Law Periodicals*, 20 AM. L. REV. 281 (1886) (listing legal periodicals being published in 1886).

201. Kommers, *Reflections on Professor Chroust's* The Rise of the Legal Profession in America, 10 AM. J. LEGAL HIST. 201, 209 (1966); see also Bloomfield, *supra* note 200, at 306-08; Pound, *supra* note 104, at 262.

202. See Bloomfield, *supra* note 200, at 306-08; Pound, *supra* note 104, at 262.

203. See Pound, *supra* note 10.4, at 262. "[In] the late nineteenth century . . . American law became associated with precedents rather than principles and with ad hoc rationalizations, as the judges moved from case to case. Instead of attempting

to discover 'the underlying theory of law' the American lawyer looked 'for cases "on all fours"'. . . ." R. STEVENS, *supra* note 118, at 132-33. See generally Bloomfield, *supra* note 200.

204. Editorial, *Legal Journalism*, 6 ALB. L.J. 201 (1872).

205. There were few outstanding English legal periodicals prior to the 1885 publication of the *Law Quarterly Review* in London. See 50 HARV. L. REV. 862 (1937). Yet by that year, America could boast of scores of legal journals, several of which were being edited with a high degree of professionalism. The *Law Quarterly Review*, moreover, imitated the approach of the earlier *American Law Register* and *American Law Review*. The *Quarterly Review* was distinguished by the intellectual superiority of many of its lead articles and the leadership of its esteemed editor, Sir Frederick Pollock. Even the *Albany Law Journal* commented that the articles in *Quarterly Review*'s initial issue were "excellent," adding that its contents were . . . "much less soporific" than that of other English law periodicals. 31 ALB, L.J. 81 (1885). See Goodhart, *The Jubilee of the Iowa Law Review*, 50 IOWA L. REV. 1 (1964) (discussing the impact of the *Law Quarterly Review* on American student-edited law reviews).

206. See *supra* note 11 & accompanying text; *infra* notes 207-47 & accompanying text.

207. See *supra* note 174.

208. See F. HICKS, *supra* note 11, at 207.

209. *Id.*

The old University of Albany had joined Union College, located in Schenectady, New York, in 1873 to form Union University. Browne, *The Albany Law School*, 2 THE GREEN BAG 153 (1890). The Albany Law School remained in Albany, but became a department of the new University. *Id.* The oldest law school in the state, it occupied only one room in the south wing of the Medical Building in 1875. *Id.* at 155. The school required that students complete at least one academic year of study even before such a requirement was prescribed by the New York bar authorities. *Id.* Isaac Edwards headed the Albany Law School in 1875, and he reportedly "endeared himself to the students by his gentle and winning manners and his kind and sincere nature." *Id.* at 159. Given such a description, it is easy to imagine that Edwards was receptive to the revolutionary idea that students compile and publish a law periodical.

The first law school publication of any kind was the 1822 journal ("minutes of proceedings") of the law school at Needham, Virginia. F. HICKS, *supra* note 11, at 206-07. See generally W. BRYSON, LEGAL EDUCATION IN VIRGINIA 1779-1979, at 592-93 (1982) (discussing the Needham Law School). Only one volume was produced. F. HICKS, *supra* note 11, at 206-07. For a chronological listing of all law school periodicals appearing from 1822-1941, see id, at 207-09.

210. *The Albany Law School Journal*, 3 CENT. L.J. 136 (1876).

211. *Id.*

212. *Id.*

213. *Id.*

214. *Id.*

215. *Id.*

216. *Id.*

217. The earlier *Albany Law Journal*, *supra* note 174, had addressed itself to professional standards rather than to classroom methods.

218. See *infra* notes 297-99 & accompanying text.

219. See McKelvey, *supra* note 6, at 878 (discussion of the quality of legal education and its effect on "the welfare of the human race").

220. Notes, 13 ALB. L.J. 31, 31 (1876); see *supra* notes 174-90 & accompanying text.

221. Notes, *supra* note 220, at 31.

222. *Id.*

223. Unfortunately, the authors have been unable to locate the volume produced in 1875.

That the *Albany Law School Journal* failed after only one volume is not surprising, particularly in view of its several attempts at humor. Consider this sample: "A man rushed excitedly into a lawyer's office last week and said: 'A man has tied a loop in my horse's tail; can I do anything about it?' 'Yes; go and untie it—fee $5.'" *Id.*

224. Tremain, *Address to Law Students*, 13 ALB. L.J. 376 supp. 1 (1876).

225. *The Albany Law School*, 16 ALB. L.J. 115 (1877).

226. Browne, *supra* note 208. *The Green Bag* was an excellent monthly periodical which was first published in 1899. Its title refers to the practice of mid-nineteenth century lawyers of carrying a "green bag of common professional shape and using the same in his practice in a professional manner." R. POUND, THE LAWYER FROM ANTIQUITY TO MODERN TIMES 217-18 (1953) (quoting from the bylaws of the Wilkes-Barre Law Association).

227. A HISTORY OF THE SCHOOL OF LAW, COLUMBIA UNIVERSITY 103 (J. Goebel, Jr. ed. 1955) [hereinafter cited as A HISTORY OF COLUMBIA LAW SCHOOL].

228. *Id.*

229. 1 COLUM. JURIST 2 (1885).

230. *Id.*

231. *Id.*

232. *Id.*

233. *Id.*

234. A HISTORY OF COLUMBIA LAW SCHOOL, *supra* note 227, at 102.

235. At this time it was commonplace for periodicals to borrow liberally from each other and then to cite back to the source. *See* Note, *Stolen from Thieves*, 20 AM. L. REV. 573 (1886).

236. See 2 COLUM. JURIST 325, 327, 337, 340, 373 (1886).

237. Note, *Amateur Legal Journalism*, 20 AM. L. REV. 421, 422 (1886). The *Jurist* editors were also critical of the New York bar examination, claiming that the questions were often irrelevant. *See The Learned Fifth*, 1 COLUM. JURIST 89 (1885) (noted in R. STEVENS, *supra* note 118, at 32 n.39).

238. Note, *supra* note 237, at 422.

239. *Id.*

240. *The Columbia Jurist*, 35 ALB. L.J. 242 (1887).

241. A HISTORY OF COLUMBIA LAW SCHOOL, *supra* note 227, at 103. The new editors were selected from the student body on the basis of "competitive essays" submitted to a committee. *Id.* at 103. Grades were of no use for selection purposes because they were only given when a student took examinations at the conclusion of his course of studies. *Id.* at 430 n. 100.

242. CENTENNIAL HISTORY OF THE HARVARD LAW SCHOOL 1817-1917, at 139 (1918) [hereinafter cited as CENTENNIAL HISTORY].

243. *Id.* at 140.

244. The initial issue was dated April 15, 1887, and numbered 54 pages. 1 HARV. L. REV. 1 (1887).

245. *Id.* at 35. Other members of the editorial board listed on the initial masthead were Joseph H. Beale, Jr.; Bertrum Ellis, treasurer; Wm. A. Hayes, Jr.; Julian W. Mack; John Wells Morss; John H. Wigmore; Alexander Winkler; Bancroft G. Davis; Marland C. Hobbs; Blewett H. Lee; Henry M. Williams; John M. Merriam; Geo. R. Nutter; and Paul C. Ransom. *Id.*

246. See *infra* text accompanying notes 306-08.

247. Other journals arguably had a greater influence on the format and content. See *infra* notes 304, 313 & accompanying text.

248. "It was rather daring, even rash, was it not, for students still in law school to believe that they could start and edit a worthwhile law review?" wrote John Wigmore, one of the student founders of the *Harvard Law Review*, fifty years later. He went on: "Why should we suppose that we should and could do this novel thing?" Wigmore, *The Recent Cases Department*, 50 HARV. L. REV. 862 (1937).

249. See *infra* text accompanying notes 256-60.

250. Williston, later a distinguished member of the Harvard Law School faculty and treatise author, was not one of the original *Harvard Law Review* editors, but joined the editorial board in the fall of 1887. His name first appeared on the masthead of the issue dated October 15 of that year. See 1 HARV. L. REV. 144 (1887).

251. S. WILLISTON, LIFE AND LAW, AN AUTOBIOGRAPHY 82 (1940).

252. See *infra* text accompanying notes 274-82.

253. See *infra* notes 304, 313 & accompanying text.

254. See *infra* text accompanying notes 261-73.

255. See *infra* text accompanying notes 290-93.

256. M. HOWE, *supra* note 163, at 189. The more famous of these clubs included the Pow-Wow Club and the Thayer Club. *See* W. ROALFE, JOHN HENRY WIGMORE, SCHOLAR AND REFORMER 11 (1977); Williston, *Joseph Henry Beale, A Biographical Sketch*, 56 HARV. L. REV. 685, 686 (1943).

257. M. HOWE, *supra* note 163, at 189.

258. CENTENNIAL HISTORY, *supra* note 242, at 139.

259. *Id.*

260. Williston, *supra* note 256, at 686.

261. Beale, *James Barr Ames His Life and Character*, 23 HARV. L. REV. 325, 328 (1910); see also W. ROALFE, *supra* note 256, at 11.

262. Having graduated first in his class from Harvard Law School in 1868, Ames was Langdell's first appointment to the law faculty after Langdell became Dean in 1870. Beale, *supra* note 260, at 328. Roscoe Pound, among many others, described Ames as a "great teacher." Sutherland, *One Man in His Time*, 78 HARV. L. REV. 7, 11 (1964).

263. The first Harvard Law School graduate to be awarded the Parker Fellowship, Mack subsequently taught at Northwestern University Law School, then became a state judge in Illinois. He was appointed a United States Circuit judge at large in 1913, a post from which he retired in 1941. Hand, *Julian W. Mack*, 57 HARV. L. REV. 96-97 (1943).

264. J. Ames, *Memoir of James Barr Ames*, in LECTURES ON LEGAL HISTORY AND MISCELLANEOUS LEGAL ESSAYS 21 (1913) [hereinafter cited as *Memoir*].

265. Beale, *supra* note 261, at 328.

266. After graduating from Harvard Law School in 1887, Beale was appointed to its faculty in 1891. He was a prodigious author of books, treatises, and law review articles throughout his career. See Williston, *supra* note 256, at 685-89. Harvard Law School Dean Ervin Griswold later said about Beale that: "It is one of the finest experiences of life that young men can feel the influence of older men upon them. It was Beale's privilege to influence greatly the lives of many men." Griswold, *Mr. Beale and the Conflicts of Law*, 56 HARV. L. REV. 690, 694 (1943).

267. Beale, *supra* note 261, at 328.

268. *Id.* This group also included John Wigmore, who later became a distinguished treatise writer and law school dean at Northwestern Law School. See *infra* text accompanying notes 383-84. He wrote several works on evidence and other topics. See generally W. ROALFE, *supra* note 256.

269. CENTENNIAL HISTORY, *supra* note 242, at 140. "The Faculty were invited to take an active part in the management, but thought 'that the interests of the paper would be more advanced by their remaining in the background.'" *Id.*

270. *Id.*

271. See *supra* text accompanying notes 159-67.

272. See R. GRAY, JOHN CHIPMAN GRAY 21 (1917); Thayer, *John Chipman Gray*, 28 HARV. L. REV. 539 (1915).

273. One of the student founders, Judge Julian Mack, would later write:

> Trained as I was in the school of Langdell, Ames, and Thayer, I came to attach great value to their penetrating historical researches. . . . I find myself today pleading in defense of my teachers, the legal giants of their day, that they were truly progressive and not wholly unaware of the relation between the law and the other sciences, in an age when sociology was virtually unknown and economics was far remote from the actual working world. . . ."

Mack, *Introduction* to J. FRANK, LAW AND THE MODERN MIND at x (1930).

274. 2 C. WARREN, *supra* note 11, at 439-40.

275. A. PIER, THE STORY OF HARVARD 204-07 (1913).

276. *Id.* Williston would later recall "the thrill that ran through the audience in Sanders Theatre" at Lowell's oration. S. WILLISTON, *supra* note 251, at 82. Lowell was renowned in both the realms of literature and the law. He held the Longfellow's Smith Professorship at Harvard and later was the United States Ambassador to the Court of St. James. A. SUTHERLAND, *supra* note 58, at 118-19. Holmes. of course, later became one of the most prominent jurists to serve on the Supreme Court of the United States. See generally M. HOWE, JUSTICE OLIVER WENDELL HOLMES (1957).

277. S. WILLISTON, *supra* note 251, at 82.

278. The Harvard Law Association was organized on September 23, 1886, and then solicited former students and alumni to meet at Harvard during the 250th celebration in November 1886. 2 C. WARREN, *supra* note 11, at 439.

279. *Id.*

280. Wigmore, *supra* note 248, at 862.

281. O. HOLMES, *The Use of Law Schools*, in COLLECTED LEGAL PAPERS 37, 46-47 (1920).

282. Wigmore, *supra* note 248, at 862.

283. *Id.*

284. *Id.*; see also W. ROALFE, *supra* note 256, at 16.

285. Beale, *supra* note 261, at 328.

286. Thayer was Weld Professor of Law at Harvard at the time of his death in 1902. During his 27 years on the faculty he often gave advice and assistance to editors of the *Review*. 15 HARV. L. REV. 568 (1902).

287. M. HOWE, *supra* note 163, at 140.

288. Wigmore, *supra* note 248, at 862.

289. *Id.*

290. Landis, *Mr. Justice Brandeis and the Harvard Law School*, 55 HARV. L. REV. 184, 188 (1941).

291. Wigmore, *supra* note 248, at 862-63.

292. Landis, *supra* note 290, at 188.

293. Wigmare, *supra* note 248, at 863. In 1890 Brandeis persuaded the Harvard Law Association to purchase sufficient copies of the *Review* to distribute to all Association members. Landis, *supra* note 290, at 188.

294. 1 HARV. L. REV. 35 (1887).

295. *Id.*

296. CENTENNIAL HISTORY, *supra* note 242, at 27. Langdell succeeded Professor Theophilus Parsons as Dane Professor of Law in December, 1869. He was selected Dean the following year. J. GARDINER, HARVARD 75 (1914).

297. A. SUTHERLAND, *supra* note 58, at 162.

When Langdell arrived at Harvard as a faculty member in late 1869, he encountered a law school patterned after a poorly run lawyer's office. J. GARDINER, *supra* note 296, at 75. The students read from textbooks and listened to lectures from a faculty consisting of three instructors. No examinations were required either at the end of a course or for a degree. *Id.* The library was in a shambles, *Id.*, and the school did not have a dean. A. SUTHERLAND, *supra* note 58, at 162. The conditions prompted two recent graduates, Oliver Wendell Holmes, Jr. and Arthur Sedgwick, to publish a comment in the *American Law Review* decrying the Harvard Law School as "a disgrace to the commonwealth of Massachusetts" which injured the profession and discouraged "real students." Summary of Events, *Harvard Law School*, 5 AM. L. REV. 177 (1870) (discussed in A. SUTHERLAND, *supra* note 58, at 164). Holmes and Sedgwick contended that a degree from Harvard Law School during this period was nearly valueless. But their comment ended on an upbeat note, pointing to one recent change for the good—the adoption of a requirement that examinations be passed for the LL.B. degree. *Id.* As a consequence of the adverse publicity, pressure was put on Harvard President Charles Eliot to create a committee to review the condition and prospects of the law school. J. SELIGMAN, THE HIGH CITADEL, THE INFLUENCE OF HARVARD LAW SCHOOL 29 (1978).

Amidst these generally gloomy conditions, the Langdell era at Harvard Law School began. Almost immediately the fortunes of the institution took a dramatic upturn. Not only were the examination requirements continued, A. SUTHERLAND, *supra* note 58, at 171-74, but admission standards were raised significantly. *Id.* at 167-68; see also J. GARDINER, *supra* note 296, at 78. The library became a top priority, J. GARDINER, *supra* note 296, at 76; the course of study was extended from eighteen months to three years, S. WILLISTON, *supra* note 251, at 83; a new building for the school was constructed, S. MORISON, THREE CENTURIES OF HARVARD 338 (1965); see also 2 C. WARREN, *supra* note 11, at 434-37, and the faculty was increased by the addition of such first-rate scholars as Ames, Gray, and Thayer. S. MORISON, *supra*, at 337; see also J. GARDINER, *supra* note 296, at 76-77. The

Ames appointment in 1873 was especially noteworthy. "[Ames] was a new sort of law teacher, a man comparatively young, whose professional accomplishments all were to be in writing, teaching, and in educational administration, with no preliminary experience in practice or on the bench." A. SUTHERLAND, *supra* note 58, at 164; see also S. WILLISTON, *supra* note 251, at 73. In short, Ames was the prototype for law teachers of the future. The most dramatic change, however, was the introduction of a new method of instruction. L. FRIEDMAN, A HISTORY OF AMERICAN LAW 531 (1973).

298. Much has been written about the Langdell case method. For a generally favorable description, see A. SUTHERLAND, *supra* note 58, at 174-80. For a less charitable view, see J. SELIGMAN, *supra* note 297, at 33-38; see also A. REED, TRAINING FOR THE PUBLIC PROFESSION OF THE LAW 369-88 (1921); R. STEVENS, *supra* note 118, at 117-23; J. Frank, *Both Ends Against the Middle*, 100 U. PA. L. REV. 20, 21-22 (1951).

299. L. FRIEDMAN, *supra* note 297, at 531.

The textbook-lecture mode of instruction had been used almost exclusively in American law schools from the time Litchfield Law School, the nation's first law school, opened its doors in 1784. A. SUTHERLAND, *supra* note 58, at 27-28. The College of William and Mary established the first professorship of law in this country in 1779. George Wythe, teacher of John Marshall, was its initial occupant. *Id.* at 26-27. See generally A. DILL, GEORGE WYTHE: TEACHER OF LIBERTY (1979).

Early law teachers utilized treatises as the basic instructional tool. See R. POUND, *supra* note 5 1, at 161. Later they wrote their own texts which, like the traditional treatises, covered only one subject. *Id.* In the classroom, law teachers lectured and law students took copious notes. L. FRIEDMAN, *supra* note 297, at 529-30. There was little, if any, dialogue, but some law teachers quizzed students about their rote memory of the assignment. *Id.* at 529; Ames, *The Vocation of the Law Professor*, 48 AM. L. REGIS. 129, 138-39 (1900). "In every law school, the method used to teach law was dogmatic, and uncritical. . . . L. FRIEDMAN, *supra* note 297, at 529.

At this low point in the history of legal education, Langdell introduced his innovative system of casebook instruction. *Id.* at 530. Langdell explained:

> Law, considered as a science, consists of certain principles or doctrines. To have such a mastery of these as to be able to apply them with constant facility and certainty to the ever-tangled skein of human affairs, is what constitutes a true lawyer; and hence to acquire that mastery should be the business of every earnest student of law. . . . [T]he shortest and best, if not the only way of mastering the doctrine effectually is by studying the cases in which it is embodied. . . . It . . . [is] possible to take . . . a branch of the law [such] as Contracts, for example, and . . . to select, classify, and arrange all the cases which had contributed in any important degree to the growth, development, or establishment of . . . its essential doctrines. . . .

C. LANGDELL, A SELECTION OF CASES ON THE LAW OF CONTRACTS at v-vii (1871), *quoted in* S. KIMBALL, HISTORICAL INTRODUCTION TO THE LEGAL SYSTEM 575 (1966).

Much was left to the student to discover because casebooks usually contained only cases and no commentary. L. FRIEDMAN, *supra* note 297, at 548. These volumes of raw material thereby accentuated the "most striking characteristic of the teaching style they reflected . . . the Socratic masquerade: the act of saying everything while appearing to say nothing at all." *Id.*

By the time the editor-to-be of Volume One of the *Harvard Law Review* matriculated at Harvard Law School in 1884, not only had Langdell authored a casebook, so had Ames. *Id.* Moreover, the controversy between proponents of casebooks and advocates of textbooks was in full bloom. McKelvey, *supra*, note 6, at 878; see also Note, *The Columbia and New York Law Schools*, 5 HARV. L. REV. 146-47 (1891).

The new casebooks were used by several Harvard law professors. Ames was considered the master, clearly better than Langdell, at employing the casebook method of instruction. Beale, *supra* note 26 1, at 328; see also S. WILLISTON, *supra* note 25 1, at 73-74. Ames used the assigned case or cases as a basis for Socratic discussion during which he drew out the key legal principle from the students. *Memoir, supra* note 264, at 8. By virtue of his adeptness with the Socratic method, Ames has been credited with making the casebook teaching system successful. *Id.* It was said that he "baptized men in brain fire" and that his students were "interested, stimulated, tantalized." *Id.* at 9.

300. S. WILLISTON, *supra* note 251, at 74. "William A. Keener [was] a man of acute mind and an excellent teacher." *Id.*; see also *infra* text accompanying notes 360-63.

Langdell, Ames, and Keener apparently were not the first to break away from the lecture method at Harvard Law School. Joseph Story, the great treatise writer, served on the Harvard Law faculty from 1829 until his death in 1845. He used in the classroom "the dialectic which we have come to ascribe to [these later teachers]." A. SUTHERLAND, *supra* note 58, at 105.

301. Brandeis, *The Harvard Law School*, 1 THE GREEN BAG 10 (1889). "The intellectual self-reliance and the spirit of investigation which this new method of instruction engenders, have produced the 'Harvard Law Review'. . . ." *Id.* at 23.

302. Wigmore, *supra* note 248, at 862. See generally R. STEVENS, *supra* note 118, at 35-72 (discussing the impact the early Harvard Law School had on legal education).

303. Ames, *supra* note 299, at 139.

304. Wigmore, *supra* note 248, at 862. Wigmore considered the *American Law Review* the best of the lot. He also thought that good articles appeared from time to time in the *Central Law Journal*, the *Albany Law Journal*, the *American Law Register*, and Frederick Pollock's *Law Quarterly Review*. *Id.* "Probably the *Harvard Law Review* could and would have been born without our example, but it is a reasonable supposition that we did something to prepare the way for it." Pollock, *Editor's Note*, 51 L.Q. REV. 10 (1935).

305. Wigmore, *supra* note 248, at 862.

306. CENTENNIAL HISTORY, *supra* note 242, at 140.

307. See, *e.g.*, *In the Moot Court*, 1 HARV. L. REV. 38, 38-41 (1887).

308. See, *e.g.*, *From the Lecture Room*, 1 HARV. L. REV. 41, 41-42 (1887).
309. Beale, *Professor Langdell—His Later Teaching Days*, 20 HARV. L. REV. 9, 11 (1906).
310. *Id.*
311. 1 HARV. L. REV. 55 (1887).
312. CENTENNIAL HISTORY, *supra* note 242, at 140.
313. Wigmore, *supra* note 248, at 863.
314. *Id.* at 864. "[M]ost of the cases were merely abstracted without any critical or expanded comment." *Id.* at 865.
315. *Id.* at 865.
316. *Id.* at 866-67.
317. *Id.* at 866.
318. 1 HARV. L. REV. 17 (1887). The practice of publishing lead articles by students was in time discontinued. A separate section for student works was developed.
319. Williston, *Joseph Henry Beale, A Biographical Sketch*, 56 HARV. L. REV. 685, 686 (1943). "The choice of an unusual topic, wholly outside the somewhat restricted curriculum of the School at the time, and the keen and thorough treatment of the subject were characteristic of [Beale]." *Id.*
320. See S. WILLISTON, *supra* note 251.
321. *Id.* at 255.
322. FELIX FRANKFURTER REMINISCES 19 (H. Phillips ed. 1960).
323. *Id.* at 27. The meritocracy, however, operated only with respect to individuals who were already Harvard law students. There were no female Review members in the first years of the publication because Harvard, as well as Columbia and Yale, did not admit women students during this period. Robinson, *Women Lawyers in the United States*, 2 THE GREEN BAG 10, 12 (1890).
324. HARVARD LAW REVIEW, CUMULATIVE INDEX AND TABLE OF CASES, VOLUMES ONE TO FIFTY 1887-1937 (1938) [hereinafter cited as INDEX].
325. *Id.*
326. *Id.*
327. *Id.*
328. For example, Jeremiah Smith was appointed to a professorship at Harvard in 1890. 2 C. WARREN, *supra* note 11, at 444. He contributed twenty articles to the *Review*. See INDEX, *supra* note 324.
329. One of first tangible signs of success of the *Harvard Law Review* was the heavy demand for early volumes of the *Review* that developed around the turn of the century. 15 HARV. L. REV. 219 (1901).
330. Maggs, *supra* note 5, at 181-83.
331. *Id.*; see F. HICKS, *supra* note 11, at 207-08.
332. See generally Maggs, *supra* note 5, at 184-86 (discussing the positive impact of law reviews on law teachers, law students, and law schools).
333. *Id.*
334. *Id.*
335. Three other law school periodicals—the *Counsellor* (New York Law School), the *Intercollegiate Journal*, and *The Law Bulletin of the State University of Iowa*—also first appeared in 1891, but none survived for long. F. HICKS, *supra* note 11, at 207; see also *infra* notes 342-43 & accompanying text.
336. 1 YALE L.J. 30 (1891); see also *The First Half-Century*, 50 YALE L.J. 740 (1941).
337. F. HICKS, YALE LAW SCHOOL: 1869-1894 INCLUDING THE COURT HOUSE PERIOD 68 (1937).
338. *Id.* at 66-68.
339. *Id.* at 68.
340. *Id.* at 69.
341. *Id.*
342. See F. HICKS, *supra* note 11, at 207 (listing law school periodicals published during this period). These publications took various forms, but most can be characterized as law reviews. See *supra* note 3.
343. F. HICKS, *supra* note 11, at 207. Two of these journals survived for at least a decade. One was *The Law Bulletin of the State University of Iowa*, which first appeared in 1891. The *Bulletin*, published by the Iowa law faculty, ceased publication in 1901. It was revived in 1915 as the *Iowa Law Bulletin* and became the *Iowa Law Review* in 1925. See 1 IOWA L. BULL. 29 (1915); Notes, The *Iowa Law Review*, 11 IOWA L. REV. 66 (1925). The other journal was the *Kansas University Lawyer* (1895-1911). F. HICKS, *supra* note 11, at 207.

Most of the other law school publications begun in the 1890's survived for only a short time. For example, an attempt to create a monthly *Cornell Law Journal* ended after the publication of one issue in 1894. The law students at Cornell tried again in 1895. This time six monthly installments of a periodical entitled the *New York Law Review* were produced before publication ended. Forrester, *Introduction to Volume 50, Cornell Law Quarterly*, 50 CORNELL L.Q. 1 (1964); see also *infra* text accompanying notes 369-70.

One other entry on Professor Hick's list requires explanation. The *West Virginia Law Quarterly* is listed as a law school periodical first published in 1894. F. HICKS, *supra*, note 11, at 207. This is not entirely accurate. A periodical entitled the *West Virginia Law Quarterly and the Bar* was published by the West Virginia University law faculty beginning in 1917 as the successor to a monthly publication of the West Virginia Bar called *The Bar* that originated in 1894. Foreward, 25 W. VA. L.Q. at i, 56

(1917); see 1 THE WEST VIRGINIA BAR 1 (1894). The *West Virginia Law Quarterly* remained the "official publication of the West Virginia Bar Association." In 1949, its name was changed to the *West Virginia Law Review*. 52 W. VA. L. REV. 56 (1949).

According to Professor Hicks, the other law school periodicals which were commenced during the 1890's were the *University Law Review* (University of City of New York) (1893-1897), *Western Reserve Law Journal* (1895-1901), and *Boston Law School Magazine* (1896-1897). F. HICKS, *supra* note 11, at 207.

344. See *supra* text accompanying notes 146-58.

345. 44 AM. L. REG. 63 (1896); 100 U. PA. L. REV. 69 (1961).

346. 44 AM. L. REG. 63 (1896).

347. The publication was renamed the *University of Pennsylvania Law Review and American Law Register* in 1908 and in 1945 the title was shortened to its current form—*University of Pennsylvania Law Review*. 100 U. PA. L. REV. 69 (1951); see *supra* notes 149, 154-58 & accompanying text.

348. See Douglas, *supra* note 5, at 228.

349. 1 THE FORUM 1 (1897).

350. Editor's Note, 13 DICK. L. REV. 32 (1908).

351. 50 DICK. L. REV. 195 (1946).

352. See *supra* note 3.

353. 1 THE FORUM 1 (1897). It was not until 1904 that *The Forum* published its first article, Trickett, *Character-Evidence in Criminal Cases*, 8 THE FORUM 121 (1904), a work written by the Dean of Dickinson Law School. 50 DICK. L. REV. 195 (1946). Gradually, the Dickinson publication developed into the law review that it officially became in name in 1908. See Editor's Note, 13 DICK. L. REV. 32 (1908). Even after the name change, twenty years passed before the *Dickinson Law Review* switched from a monthly to a quarterly production schedule and discontinued its heavy emphasis on moot court reports. 50 DICK. L. REV. 195 (1946).

354. A few other law schools established law reviews during this period, but none of these journals endured. See F. HICKS, *supra* note 11, at 207; see also *infra* note 393.

355. See *supra* text accompanying notes 227-41.

356. A HISTORY OF THE COLUMBIA LAW SCHOOL, *supra* note 227, at 103, 182; see also Book Review, 1 HARV. L. REV. 209 (887) (noting that the *Law Times* "is evidently modeled on our *Review*").

357. A HISTORY OF THE COLUMBIA LAW SCHOOL, *supra* note 227, at 182. A financial crisis resulted when the *Law Times* discontinued its practice of publishing class notes and thus became less attractive to student purchasers. *Id.*

358. *Id.* at 181-82.

359. *Id.* at 182.

360. *Id.* at 183,

361. *Id.*

362. *Id.*

363. See *Id.* at 184.

364. 1 COLUM. L. REV. 50 (1891).

365. See generally Maru, *supra* note 10, at 227.

366. By 1902 a few short-lived law reviews had been attempted at schools outside the northeast. See F. HICKS, *supra* note 11, at 207; see also *supra* note 343; *infra* note 376. In addition to those law reviews previously mentioned, Professor Hicks lists the *Maryland Law Review* (Baltimore Law School) (1901-1903) and the *Oregon Law School Journal* (1902-1917). F. HICKS, *supra* note 11, at 207.

367. 1 MICH. L. REV. 58 (1902).

368. *Id.* at 59.

369. E. BROWN, LEGAL EDUCATION AT MICHIGAN 1859-1959, at 328-29 (1959).

370. See *Id.* The last issue of the *Michigan Law Journal* appeared in June, 1898. See 7 MICH. L.J. 157 (1898). In September 1898, "ex-editor" R. T. Speed wrote a faithful subscriber that: "The *Michigan Law Journal* would be alive today if all our patrons had acted as fairly as yourself: our inability to collect subscriptions has left us several hundred dollars in debt." Letter from R. T. Speed to A.H.R. Fraser (Sept. 23, 1898), reprinted in 7 MICH. L.J. (1898).

371. 1 MICH. L. REV. 58, 59 (1902).

372. E. BROWN, *supra* note 369, at 331.

373. *Id.* at 332 (quoting Dean Stason's 1951-1952 report to the President of the University of Michigan).

374. Edmunds, *supra* note 6, at 13.

375. MacChesney, *An Old Tradition—The Same Review But a New Name*, 47 NW. U.L. REV. at iii, vi (1952); 1 ILL. L. REV. 39 (1906).

376. See *Law Reviews and Legal Progress: Herein of Past Services and Future Responsibilities*, 51 NW. U.L. REV. 2, 7 (1956) [hereinafter cited as *Law Reviews and Legal Progress*.] An earlier student-edited law review at Northwestern had failed. For four years (1893-1896), *The Northwestern Law Review* was "published monthly during the school year by students of the Northwestern University Law School." 1 NW. L. REV. 17 (1893); see F. HICKS, *supra* note 11, at 207.

377. 1 ILL. L. REV. 39 (1906).

378. See *Law Reviews and Legal Progress*, *supra* note 376, at 13.

379. See *The New Management of the Review*, 19 ILL. L. REV. 161 (1924).

380. MacChesney, *supra* note 375, at iv; *Law Reviews and Legal Progress*, *supra* note 376, at 3.

381. MacChesney, *supra* note 375, at iv; *Law Reviews and Legal Progress, supra* note 376, at 3.
382. MacChesney, *supra* note 375, at vii-viii.
383. See *supra* text accompanying notes 312-17.
384. Dean Wigmore served as one of the associate editors from the Northwestern faculty. ILL. L. REV. 39 (1906).
385. MacChesney, *supra* note 375, at iii.
386. *Id.*
387. *Id.*
388. For a discussion of the wisdom of the decision, see Maggs, *supra* note 5, at 189-90. The failure of an earlier student-edited law review at Northwestern may also have contributed to the decision to utilize faculty editors. See *supra* note 376.
389. MacChesney naturally was one of those chosen to fill a slot as an "Associate Editor of the Alumni." 1 ILL. L. REV. 39 (1906).
390. *Law Reviews and Legal Progress, supra* note 376, at 7. Dean Wigmore also used the *Illinois Law Review* to editorialize on a wide range of newsworthy legal issues. *Id.* at 5-7.
391. See *Id.* at 7-9.
392. *Id.* at 3.
393. See F. HICKS, *supra* note 11, at 207. In 1912, Georgetown University and the University of California each began publishing a student-edited law review. There was, however, some new activity on the law review front during the 1906-1912 gap between the founding of the journal at Northwestern and the birth of similar periodicals at Georgetown and California. First, *The Forum* took steps toward law review status by regularly publishing short articles and assuming the name *Dickinson Law Review.* See *supra* notes 349-54 & accompanying text. Second, the University of Maine School of Law established the *Maine Law Review* in 1908. See 1 ME. L. REV. 30 (1908). The review at Maine lasted as long as the school-until 1920. 14 ME. L. REV. at vii (1962). See generally *The Law Review,* 12 ME. L. REV . 32 (1918). The law review was resurrected in 1962, shortly after the University of Maine School of Law re-opened. 14 ME. L. REV. at vii (1962).
394. Nearly all law reviews followed the Harvard, Yale, Columbia, Michigan, and Northwestern format. See, *e.g., Beginning the Second Fifty Years: A Glance at the First Fifty,* 51 U. COLO. L. REV. 5 (1979). The author comments: "The *Review*'s format was patterned after the established formats of the *Harvard Law Review, Michigan Law Review,* and *Yale Law [Journal].*" *Id.* at 7.
395. Maggs, *supra* note 5, at 181-82.
396. *Id.* at 183.
397. HISTORY OF COLUMBIA LAW SCHOOL, *supra* note 227, at 185.
398. *Id.*
399. B. CARDOZO, SELECTED READINGS ON THE LAW OF CONTRACTS at vii, ix (1931).
400. See generally Maggs, *supra* note 5, at 186-89 (discussing the positive impact of early law reviews on various facets of the legal profession).
401. See *supra* text accompanying notes 210-22; see also McKelvey, *supra* note 6, at 880.
402. See L. FRIEDMAN, *supra* note 297, at 547-48; McKelvey, *supra* note 6, at 880.
403. 4 HARV. L. REV. 193 (1890). See generally A. MASON, BRANDEIS 70-71 (1946) (discussing reasons why Brandeis and Warren wrote *The Right to Privacy*); C. PEARE, THE LOUIS D. BRANDEIS STORY 99-100 (1970) (same). Other significant works appeared in early law reviews. For example, Harvard's Dean Langdell wrote a series of influential articles under the umbrella title, *A Brief Survey of Equity Jurisdiction.* See *supra* notes 309-11 & accompanying text.
404. Note, *The Right to Privacy,* 5 HARV. L. REV. 148 (1891).
405. Edmunds, *supra* note 6, at 3-4.
406. *Id.* at 3.
407. See Maggs, *supra* note 5, at 186-88.
408. The authors wish to express their gratitude to research assistants Craig A. Laporte of Stetson University College of Law and Stephen L. Anderson of Vanderbilt University School of Law for their work in locating citations to law review articles in early Supreme Court cases.
409. 166 U.S. 290, 350 n.1 (1896).
410. 4 HARV. L. REV. 128 (1890).
411. 178 U.S. 353, 365 (1899).
412. Ames, *Two Theories of Consideration,* 12 HARV. L. REV. 515 (1899).
413. See generally Maggs, *supra* note 5, for an excellent empirical study and analysis of this subject.
414. McKelvey, *supra* note 6, at 880 (emphasis in original).
415. Maggs, *supra* note 5, at 186 n.11a.
416. B. CARDOZO, *supra* note 399, at vii, ix.
417. B. CARDOZO, THE GROWTH OF THE LAW 14 (1927). Recent studies indicate that today judges rely heavily on law review articles for insights into various legal issues. See *supra* note 5.
418. Maggs, *supra* note 5, at 188.
419. *Id.*
420. *Id.* For example, the Warren and Brandeis work, *The Right to Privacy, supra* note 404, precipitated New York legislation on the subject. Jones, *The Problem of the Law School,* 1 CAL. L. REV. 1, 6-7 (1912).
421. Maggs, *supra* note 5, at 188-89. "[T]he creation of the Commissions on Uniform State Laws and the numerous statutes

prepared by them . . . are probably due to the criticisms of the Negotiable Instruments Law made by Dean Ames in his articles in the Harvard Law Review." *Id.* at 188.

422. *Id.*
423. *Id.* at 186.
424. McKelvey, *supra* note 6, at 880.
425. A HISTORY OF COLUMBIA LAW SCHOOL, *supra* not, 227, at 185; Maggs, *supra* note 5, at 186.
426. See *supra* note 36.
427. See *supra* note 7.
428. See McKelvey, *supra* note 6, at 871.
429. *Id.*
430. CENTENNIAL HISTORY, *supra* note 242, at 143.
431. *Id.*
432. K. LLEWELLYN, *supra* note 8, at 107.
433. See *supra* note 7.
434. See *supra* text accompanying notes 210-41.

Chapter 72

The Vocation of the Law Professor

1901

James Barr Ames

James Barr Ames (June 22, 1846-January 8, 1916) was the first assistant professor at Harvard Law School (see chapter 70), an architect of the casebook (see chapter 1), and dean from 1895 to 1910. This address was reprinted in Ames's *Lectures on Legal History and Miscellaneous Legal Essays* (Cambridge: Harvard University Press, 1913).

On a broad shaded street in one of the most beautiful of New England villages, stands an attractive old Colonial house, the residence, at the close of the American Revolution, of a Connecticut lawyer. Hard by the house was the owner's law office, a small one-story wooden building much resembling the familiar district schoolhouse. There was nothing about it to catch the eye, but it has a peculiar interest for the lawyer, as the birthplace of the American Law School. For it was to this building that young men came from all parts of the country to listen to the lectures of Judge Reeve, the founder of the celebrated Litchfield Law School.

It is indeed a far cry from the small lecture room of Judge Reeve to this noble structure destined to be for centuries the spacious and well-appointed home of a great university law school. From her humbler home in Cambridge, I gladly bring the greetings and congratulations of the elder to the younger sister, and I am deeply sensible of the privilege of saying here a few words upon a topic that is near to the hearts of both.

On this red-letter day in the history of law schools, we may look back for a moment upon the path of legal education, if only to take courage for further achievement, as we watch the steadily growing conviction, in this country at least, that law is a science and as such can best be taught by the law faculty of a university.

With the revival of interest in the Roman Law, students flocked to the medieval universities, notably to Bologna and Paris; and in countries where the system of law is essentially Roman, the tradition of obtaining one's legal education at a university has continued unbroken. Indeed, upon the continent of Europe a university law school is the only avenue to the legal profession. But the English law was not Romanized. For this, any one who thinks of trial by jury, of the beneficence of English equity, and of the unrivaled English judiciary, may well be thankful. But as a consequence of the non-acceptance of Roman Law, early English lawyers were not bred at Oxford or Cambridge. For the universities were in the hands of the ecclesiastics, who naturally confined their attention to the canon and civil law. Another reason may be found in the well-known dialogue between Lord Chancellor Fortescue and the young Prince of Wales in praise of the laws of England. The Prince having asked why the laws of England were not taught at the universities, the Chancellor replied: "In the universities of England sciences are not taught but in the Latin tongue, and the laws of the land are to be learned in the three several tongues, to witte, in the English tongue, the French tongue, and the Latin tongue."

39. James Barr Ames (1846-1910) was a student in Langdell's first case-method lecture and became not only his successor as dean but also the keeper of the flame of case-method instruction. (*Courtesy of Art & Visual Materials, Special Collections Department, Harvard Law School Library.*)

English lawyers, therefore, obtained their legal training in London, and, in early times, at the Inns of Court, which, with the dependent Chancery Inns, were called by Fortescue and Coke a legal university. In the days of these writers the term was not inapt. The membership of the inns was made up of students, resident graduates, called barristers, readers, or professors, and benchers, or ex-professors, all living together in their dormitories and dining-halls, in that spirit of comradeship which has added so much to the attractiveness and influence of the legal profession. They lived, too, in an atmosphere of legal thought. Every day after dinner, and every night after supper, there were discussions of legal questions after the manner of a moot-court. There were also lectures by the old barristers, which were followed by discussions of the chief points of the lectures. But the lectures and discussions came in time to be regarded as too great a burden upon the lawyers. They were at first shortened, and finally, in the latter half of the seventeenth century, given up altogether.

A legal education being no longer obtainable in the Inns of Court, students of law trusted to private reading, supplemented at first by experience in attorneys' offices, but after Lord Mansfield's day, in the chambers of special pleaders, conveyancers, or equity draughtsmen.

The decay of the Inns of Court seems not to have excited, for two hundred and fifty years, any adverse comment. But towards the middle of this reforming century many influential lawyers were impressed with the need of a better preparation for admission to the Bar. In 1846 a Parliamentary Commission, after hearing the testimony of a large number of witnesses, reported that the state of legal education in England was "extremely unsatisfactory and incomplete," and "strikingly inferior to such education in all the more civilized states of Europe and America," and recommended that the Inns of Court should resume their ancient function of a legal university. Five annual courses of lectures in law were the meagre result of this report.

In 1855 a second Parliamentary Commission, including Vice-Chancellor Wood, Sir Richard Bethell (Lord Westbury) and Sir Alexander Cockburn, recommended that a university be constituted with a power of conferring degrees in law. This recommendation had no effect. Some twenty years later, under the leadership of Lord Selborne, an attempt was made to bring about the establishment of a general school of law in London by the action of Parliament. But the attempt was unsuccessful. Finally, six years ago, a third Parliamentary Commission reported in favor of a Faculty of Law in the proposed teaching University of London. And there the matter rests, although Lord Russell has recently expressed the hope "that the effort may once more be made, and this time successfully made, to establish what Westbury and Selborne hoped and worked for, a great school of law."

As a result of the agitation of the last sixty years, six readers and four assistant readers give some thirty hours of legal instruction per week throughout the year, and only those may be called to the Bar who have passed successfully certain examinations. These examinations represent about one third of the work covered by those of the Law School of the University of Pennsylvania, and, in the opinion of competent judges, do not afford any trustworthy test of adequate knowledge of the law. No attendance is required at the readers' lectures or classes, and the actual attendance is small. There is no permanent teaching staff. The teachers are appointed for a term of three years. They may or may not be reappointed. Incredible as it may appear, at the end of their term, in 1898, the ten readers and assistant readers were all dropped and replaced by a wholly new decemvirate. The reason for this clean sweep is almost more surprising than the change itself. The Council of Legal Education, as one of the members informed Lord Russell, "thought if they did not effect frequent changes, and thus permitted the idea to grow up that the teachers should be continued in office so long as they did their work well, it would be interfering with them in the pursuit of their profession, and it would be unfair to remove them later." Lord Russell, in criticising this novel conception of a professorial staff, says truly that "such a policy renders it impossible to look to the creation of an experienced professional class of teachers." There is obviously a wide gap between this school of the Inns of Court and the leading law schools in this country with a three years' course, compulsory attendance, searching annual examinations, and a faculty of permanent professors.

One naturally asks, Why did not the universities assume the work of legal education which the Inns of Court abandoned? The answer is simple. The traditions of centuries were against such an innovation. It is true that the Vinerian professorship of the Common Law, to which we owe the world-renowned Commentaries of Blackstone, was established at Oxford in the middle of the last century, and this was followed some forty years later by the similar Downing professorship at Cambridge. But only within the last thirty years has really valuable work been accomplished at the universities by a body of competent and permanent teachers. Even now the department of law at Oxford and Cambridge is not and does not claim to be a professional school. A large part of the curriculum devoted to Roman Law, Jurisprudence, and International Law, and a large majority of those who take the law course are undergraduates who propose to take their B.A. degree in law. Mr. Raleigh, one time Vinerian Reader in English Law, tells us that the best men at Oxford seldom begin the study of law until they go to London, and he thinks, in common with many others, that the ancient universities committed a grave mistake when they placed law among the subjects that qualify for the degree of B.A.

I regret to find that Sir Frederick Pollock considers this mistake irrevocable. American law professors would generally agree that a college student had better let law alone until he has completed his undergraduate course. Until the law course is made exclusively a post-graduate course, and Roman Law, Jurisprudence, and Intertional Law are made electives in the third year of the curriculum, instead of required subjects of the first year, and the staff of permanent professors materially enlarged, those of us who would like to see a strong professional school of law at the English universities, are not likely to have our dreams realized.

There must be, of course, some sufficient reason why, notwithstanding the recommendations of successive Parliamentary Commissions, and the earnest efforts of men like Lord Westbury, Lord Selborne, and Lord Russell, so little progress has been made, either in London or at Oxford or Cambridge, towards the establishment of a law school comparable to the best schools in other countries. A distinguished lawyer of this city suggested, many years ago, the quaint explanation that in a country in which the law consists of the decisions of the judges, "it might be politic not to encourage academic schools of the national jurisprudence lest ambitious professors and bold commentators should obtrude their private opinions, and instil doubts into the minds of the youth." The true explanation, it is believed, is that which was suggested by another eminent Philadelphia lawyer. Mr. Samuel Dickson, to whom we have had the pleasure of listening to-day, in his interesting address at the opening session of this school eight years ago, pointed out that no public inconvenience was felt from the calling to the Bar of gentlemen who were incompetent or unwilling to practise. For the barristers being engaged, under the English custom, not by the clients, but by the attorneys or solicitors, who were themselves experienced in law, the ignorant or incompetent barristers had no chance of obtaining any business, and dropped out of sight. Furthermore, the concentration of the entire body of barristers in London, and the unrivaled honors and emoluments that reward the successful lawyer so developed competition and so stimulated the ambition of the ablest men, as inevitably to produce a Bench and Bar of the highest merit and distinction.

If we turn now to this country, we find a marked contrast with the English experience in legal education. To the College of William and Mary, in Virginia, belongs the distinction of having the earliest law professorship in the United States, a distinction due to the fertile genius of Jefferson, who, being appointed visitor to the college in 1779, wrote to a friend, in a tone of great satisfaction, that he had succeeded in abolishing the two professorships of divinity and substituting two others, one of medicine and one of law and police. Judge George Wythe, commonly known as Chancellor Wythe, was appointed professor, doubtless through the influence of Jefferson, who had been a pupil in his office. It is an interesting fact that John Marshall, as a student of the college, attended the first course of lectures given by the first American law professor.

Three similar professorships were established in the last century, at Philadelphia, New York, and Lexington, Ky. It seems probable that these professorships were created with the hope that they would soon expand into university schools of law. Such an inference derives support from the high character of the first incumbents. Professor Wythe was a distinguished judge of the high Court of Chancery of Virginia, Professor Wilson, at Philadelphia, was an Associate Justice of the Supreme Court of the United States, and both were signers of the Declaration of Independence. Professor Kent, though a young man when first appointed, already ranked as a lawyer of exceptional ability and legal learning. To these honored names should be added that of Henry Clay, who, although the fact seems to have escaped his biographers, was for two years professor of law at Transylvania University, being the youngest full law professor, as well as the youngest senator, in our country's history. But the hopes that may have been entertained of developing schools of law out of these professorships were in the main doomed to dispointment. The private law school at Litchfield had for nearly twenty-five years no competitor, and throughout the fifty years of its existence was the only school that could claim a national character.

The oldest of the now existing law schools in this country is the school at Cambridge, which was organized in 1817. But for the first dozen years of its existence, the Harvard School was a languishing-local institution. I cannot better present to you the gloomy outlook for this school at that time than by quoting from Provost Duponceau. In an address before the Philadelphia Law Academy 1821, he advocated earnestly the establishment in Philadelphia of a National School of Law, and after alluding to the law lectures at the University of Cambridge, added: "If that justly celebrated University were situated elsewhere than in one of the remote parts our Union, there would be no need, perhaps, of looking to this city for the completion of the object which we have in view. Their own sagacity would suggest to them the necessity of appointing additional professors, and thus under their hands would gradually rise a noble temple dedicated to the study of our national jurisprudence. But their local situation precludes every such hope." Nor are the law schools of the University of Maryland, Yale, and the University of Virginia, which were established between 1824 and 1826, in any sense rivals of the Litchfield School. At the termination of that famous private school in 1833, there were only about 150 students at seven university law schools. In the dozen years following, new schools were organized, and the school at Cambridge under the leadership of Story, in spite of its unfortunate situation, became a national institution. In 1850, when the Law School of the University of Pennsylvania was established by the auspicious election of Judge Sharswood as Professor of Law, our schools numbered fourteen, and in 1860 the number had risen to twenty-three, with a total attendance of about 1000 students, all but one of these schools forming a department of some university. In the thirty-five years since the Civil War more than eighty new schools have been organized, so that we have to-day 105 law schools, with an attendance of about 13,000 students. Twenty-five years ago in none of the schools did the course exceed two years. To-day, fifty of the schools have a three years' course. Nearly ninety of these schools are departments of a university.

Valuable as the lawyer's office is and must always be for learning the art of practice, these figures show how completely it has been superseded by the law school as a place for acquiring familiarity with the principles of law.

It is an interesting illustration of the law of evolution that we Americans, starting from radically different traditions of legal education, by a wholly independent process, without any imitation of continental ideas, have adopted in substance the continental practice of university legal training.

What is the significance for the future of this remarkable growth of law schools? It means, first of all, the opening of a new career in the legal profession, the career of the law professor. This is a very ancient career in countries in which the Civil Law prevails. In Germany, for instance, a young man upon completing his law studies at the university, determines whether he will be a practising lawyer, a judge, or professor, and shapes his subsequent course accordingly. The law faculties are, therefore, rarely recruited from either practising lawyers or judges. This custom will never, I trust, prevail in this country. Several of my colleagues at Cambridge think that a law faculty made up in about equal proportions of men appointed soon after receiving their law degree and of men appointed after an experience of from ten to twenty years in practice or upon the Bench would give the best obtainable results. I should be willing to take the chances of a somewhat larger proportion of the younger men, if I believe them to have the making of eminent counselors or strong judges; and surely, men lacking these qualifications ought never to be thought of as permanent teachers in a first-class law school. The experience of the new law school at Leland Stanford University may fairly be expected to throw light on this problem. Next year, four of the five law professors in that school will be men who received their appointment within two years after taking their degree in law. They all graduated with distinction, and might look forward with confidence to a successful career at the Bar or on the Bench. I venture the prediction that this California school will erelong be in the front rank of American law schools. One of their faculty told me that their ambition was to make the Stanford Law School better than the best Eastern law schools, and added, with commendable enthusiasm, that he believed they would succeed within twenty-five years. May God speed them to their goal!

But whatever question there may be as to the just proportion in a law faculty of professors from the forum and from the university, there ought to be no doubt that the faculty should be made up almost wholly of men who devote the whole of their time to the university. The work of a law professor is strenuous enough to tax the energies of the most vigorous and demands an undivided allegiance.

At the present time about one fourth of the law professors of his country give themselves wholly to the duties of their professorships, while three fourths of them are active in practice or upon the Bench. These proportions ought to be, and are likely to be, reversed in the next generation. At the law schools of Harvard, Columbia, University of Virginia, Washington and Lee, Cornell, Stanford and as many more, nearly all the professors give themselves exclusively to the academic life. The University of Pennsylvania, I am confident, will not be long in joining this group. There are, of course, occasional instances of men of exceptional ability, facility, and capacity for work, and of such abundant loyalty—I need not go beyond the walls of this building for illustrations—from whom it is better to accept the half loaf that they are ready to give, than the whole loaf of the next best obtainable persons. There is always the hope, too, that such men may, sooner or later, cast in their lot for good and all with the university. But it is a sound general rule that a law professorship should be regarded as a vocation and not as an avocation.

Of this vocation the paramount duty is, of course, that of teaching. Having mastered his subject, the professor must consider how best he can help the students to master it also. Different methods have prevailed at different times and places. At the Litchfield School, Judge Reeve and Judge Gould divided the law into forty-eight titles and prepared written lectures on these titles which they delivered, or rather dictated to the students, who took as accurate notes as possible, which they afterwards filled out and copied for preservation. A set of these notes, filling three quarto volumes of about five hundred pages each, was presented to the Harvard Law Library. The donor in his letter accompanying the gift wrote that these notes were so highly prized when he was a student at Litchfield that $100 and upwards were frequently paid for a set. At a time when there were very few legal treatises, this plan of supplying the students with manuscript text-books served a useful purpose. But with the multiplication of printed treatises, instruction by the written lecture, which Judge Story, as far back as 1843, characterized as inadequate, has been rightly superseded. The recitation or text-book method was for many years the prevailing method, and is still much used. A certain number of pages in a given text-book are assigned to the students, which they are expected to read before coming to the lecture-room. The professor catechises them upon these pages, and comments upon them, criticising, amplifying and illustrating the text according to his judgment. In the hands of a master of exposition, who has also the gift of provoking discussion by putting hypothetical cases, this method will accomplish valuable results. But the fundamental criticism to be made upon the recitation method of instruction, as generally handled, is that it is not a virile system. It treats the student not as a man, but as a schoolboy reciting his lesson. Any young man who is old enough and clever enough to study law at all, is old enough to study it in the same spirit and the same manner in which a lawyer or judge seeks to arrive at the legal principle involved in an actual litigation. The notion that there is one law for the student and another law for the mature lawyer is pure fallacy. When thirty years ago Professor Langdell introduced the inductive method of studying law, it was my good fortune to be in his first class at the Harvard Law School, so that we had an opportunity to compare his method with the recitation system. We were plunged into his collection of cases on Contracts, and were made to feel from the outset that we were his fellow students, all seeking to work out by discussion the true principle at the bottom of the cases. We very soon came to have definite convictions, which we were prepared to maintain stoutly on legal grounds, and we were possessed with a spirit of enthusiasm for our work in Contracts, which was sadly lacking in the other courses conducted on the recitation plan.

There are some very suggestive sentences in Lord Chief Baron Kelly's testimony before the Parliamentary Commission of 1855. He was giving his reasons, derived from his own experience, for setting a much higher value upon the experience in the chamber of barrister or special pleader than upon courses of lectures. "Perhaps," he says, "there was too much copying. But there was also this—there were constant debatings, there were constant investigations of every case that came into the barrister's or pleader's chambers for his opinion and looking up of cases; and then the students, each giving his own opinion upon the case, and saying why he formed that opinion, by referring to authorities; and then the barrister saying, my opinion is so and so, upon such and such grounds, correcting the errors of the one student, and approving of the course resorted to by the other. That was the way in which I learned the law, together with reading; and if I am to compel anybody to go through any course at all, it would be just that course." The Lord Chief Baron was exceptionally fortunate in his student experience. He was in truth at a private law school conducted on the sound principle of developing the student's powers of legal reasoning by continual discussion of the principles involved in actual cases. With the extinction of the special pleader there are few such schools left, even in London, and none at all in this country. One of my colleagues has said that if a lawyer's office were conducted purely in the interest of the student, and if, by some magician's power, the lawyer could command an unfailing supply of clients with all sorts of cases, and could so order the coming of these clients as one would arrange the topics of a scientific law-book, we should have the law-student's paradise. This fanciful suggestion was made with a view of showing how close an approximation to this dream of perfection we may actually make. If we cannot summon at will the living clients, we can put at the service of the students, and in a place created and carried on especially for their benefit, the adjudicated cases of the multitude of clients who have had their day in court. We have only to turn to the reported instances of past litigation, and we may so arrange these cases by subjects and in the order of time as to enable us to trace the genesis and the development of legal doctrines. If it be the professor's object that his students shall be able to discriminate between the relevant and the irrelevant facts of a case, to draw just distinctions between things apparently similar, and to discover true analogies between things apparently dissimilar, in a word, that they shall be sound legal thinkers, competent to grapple with new problems because of their experience in mastering old ones, I know of no better course for him to pursue than to travel with his class through a wisely chosen collection of cases. These "constant debatings" in the class have a further advantage. They make easy and natural the growth of the custom of private talks and discussions between professor and students outside of the lecture rooms. Any one who has watched the working of this custom knows how much it increases the usefulness of the professor and the effectiveness of the school.

But the field of the law-professor's activity is not limited to his relations with the students, either in or out of the classroom. His position gives him an exceptional opportunity to exert a wholesome influence upon the development of the law by his writings. If we turn to the countries in which the vocation of the law-professor has long been recognized, to Germany, for instance, we find a large body of legal literature, of a high quality, the best and the greater part of which is the work of professors. The names of Savigny, Windscheid, Ihering, and Brunner at once suggest themselves. These and many others are the lights of the legal profession in Germany. The influence of their opinions in the courts is as great or even greater than that of judicial precedents. Indeed, to our way of thinking, too much regard is paid to the opinion of' writers and too little to judicial precedents, with the unfortunate result that the distinction of the continental judges is far less than that of the English judiciary. The members of the court do not deliver their opinions *seriatim*, nor does one judge deliver his written opinion as that of the court. The opinions are all what we call *per curiam* opinions. Furthermore, one may search the reports from cover to cover, and not be able to find the number or the names of the judges who constitute the highest court in the German Empire.

But, while the Germans might well ponder upon the splendid record and position of the judges in England and in the best courts in this country, we, on the other hand, have much to learn from them in the matter of legal literature. Some of our law-books would rank with the best in any country, but as a class our treatises are distinctly poor. The explanation for this is to be found, I think, in the absence of a large professorial class. We now at last have such a class, and the opportunity for great achievements in legal authorship is most propitious. Doubtless no single book will ever win the success of the Commentaries of Blackstone or Kent. And no single professor will ever repeat the marvelous fecundity of Story, who, in the sixteen years of his professorship, being also all those years on the bench of the Supreme Court, wrote ten treatises of fourteen volumes, and thirteen revisions of these treatises. We live in the era of specialization, and the time has now come for the intensive cultivation of the field of law. The enormous increase in the variety and complexity of human relations, the multiplication of law reports, and the modern spirit of historical research, demand for the making of a first-class book on a single branch of the law an amount of time and thought that a judge or lawyer in active practice can almost never give. The professor, on the other hand, while dealing with his subject in the lecture-room, is working in the direct line of his intended book, and if he teaches by the method of discussion of reported cases, he has the best possible safeguard against unsound generalizations; for no ill-considered theory, no doctrinaire tendency can successfully run the gauntlet of keen questions from a body of alert able young men encouraged and eager to get at the root of the matter. He has also in his successive classes the gratuitous services of a large number of unwitting collaborators. For every one who has ever written on a subject, which has been threshed out by such classroom discussion, will cordially agree with these words of the Master of Balliol: "Such students are the wings of their teacher, they seem to know more than they ever learn; they clothe the bare and fragmentary thought in the brightness of their own mind. Their questions suggest new thoughts to him, and he appears to derive from them as much or more than he imparts to them."

Under these favoring conditions the next twenty-five years ought to give us a high order of treatises on all the important branches of the law, exhibiting the historical development of the subject and containing sound conclusions based upon scientific analysis. We may then expect an adequate history of our law supplementing the admirable beginning made by the monumental work of Pollock and Maitland.

But the chief value of this new order of legal literature will be found in its power to correct what I conceive to be the principal defect in the generally admirable work of the judges. It is the function of the law to work out in terms of legal principle the rules which will give the utmost possible effect to the legitimate needs and purposes of men in their various activities. Too often the just expectations of men are thwarted by the action of the courts, a result largely due to taking a partial view of the subject, or to a failure to grasp the original development and true significance of the rule which is made the basis of the decision. Lord Holt's unfortunate controversy with the merchants of Lombard Street is a conspicuous instance of this sort of judicial error. When, again, the Exchequer Chamber denied the quality of negotiability to a note made payable to the treasurer for the time being of an unincorporated company they defeated an admirable mercantile contrivance for avoiding the inconvenience of notes payable to an unchartered company or to a particular person as trustee. Both mistakes were due to a misconception of the true principle of negotiability and both were remedied by legislation. It would be difficult to find an established rule of law more repugnant to the views of business men or more vigorously condemned by the courts that apply it, than the rule that a creditor who accepts part of his debt in satisfaction of the whole, may safely disregard his agreement and collect the rest of the debt from his debtor. This unfortunate rule is the result of misunderstanding a *dictum* of Coke. In truth, Coke, in an overlooked case, declared in unmistakable terms the legal validity of the creditor's agreement. In suggesting these illustrations of occasional conflict between judicial decisions and the legitimate interests of merchants I would not be understood as reflecting upon the work of the judges. Far from it. The marvel is that in dealing with the many and varied problems that come before them, very often without any adequate help from the books, so few mistakes are made. From the nature of the case the judge cannot be expected to engage in original historical investigations, nor can he approach the case before him from the point of view of one who has made a minute and comprehensive examination of the branch of the law of which the question to be decided forms a part. The judge is not and ought not to be a specialist. But it is his right, of which he has too long been deprived, to have the benefit of the conclusions of specialists or professors, whose writings represent years of study and reflection, and are illuminated by the light of history, analysis, and the comparison of the laws of different countries. The judge may or may not accept the conclusions of the professor, as he may accept or reject the arguments of counsel. But that the treatises of the professors will be of a quality to render invaluable service to the judge and that they are destined to exercise a great influence in the further development of our law, must be clear to every thoughtful lawyer.

It is the part of a professor, as well as of a judge, to enlarge his jurisdiction. Mention should, therefore, be made of the wholesome influence which the professor may exert as an expert counselor in legislation, either by staying or guiding the hand of the legislator.

The necessity of some legislation to supplement the work of the judges, and the wisdom of many statutory changes will be admitted by all. But the power of legislation is a dangerous weapon. Every lawyer can recall many instances of unintelligent, mischievous tampering with established rules of law. One of the worst of such instances is the provision in the New York Revised Statutes of 1828, which changed radically the rule against perpetuities, and which called forth Professor Gray's criticism "that in no civilized country is the making of a will so delicate an operation and so likely to fail of success as in New York." Equally severe criticism may be fairly made upon the revolutionary legislation in the same State, in 1830, in regard to the law of trust. This new legislation has produced several thousand reported cases and has given to New York a system of trusts of so provincial a character, that in the opinion of Mr. Chaplin, the author of a valuable work on trusts, the ordinary treatises on that subject are deprived of much of their value for local use. A part of this provincial system worked so disastrously, and caused, as Chief Justice Parker has said in a recent opinion, so many "wrecks of original charities—charities that were dear to the hearts of their would-be founders, and the execution of which would have been of inestimable value to the public," that it was at last abolished and the English system of charitable trusts restored. No one will be so rash as to regard the law professor as a panacea against the evils of unwise legislation. But I know of no better safeguard against such evils than the existence of a permanent body of teachers devoting themselves year after year to the mastery of their respective subjects. Then again the spirit of codification is abroad. It is devoutly to be wished that this spirit may be held in check, until we have a body of legal literature resting upon sound generalizations. If, however, codification must come prematurely, it is the part of wisdom to bring to the work the best expert knowledge in the country. The commission to draft the code should be composed of competent judges, lawyers, and professors, and, in the case of commercial subjects, business men of wide experience. The draft of the proposed code should be published in a form easily accessible to any one, and the freest criticism through legal periodicals or otherwise should be invited during several years. In the light of this criticism the draft should then be amended and revised. In Germany, where by far the best of modern codification is to be found, these cardinal principles are followed as a matter of course. They were almost completely ignored, and with very unfortunate results, in the preparation of the Negotiable

Instruments Act, adopted by several of our States. We should surely mend our ways in future codifications. In Germany much of the best work in the drafting of the code and of the criticism of the draft is done by the professors. There is no reason why under similar methods the same might not be true in this country.

This, then, is the threefold vocation of the law professor—teacher, writer, expert counselor in legislation. Surely, a career offering a wide scope for the most strenuous mental activity, a stimulus to the highest intellectual ambition, and gratifying in abundant measure the desire to render high service to one's fellowmen. If the professor renounces the joy of the arena, and the intellectual and moral glow of triumphant vindication of the right in the actual drama of life, he has the zest of the hunter in the pursuit of legal doctrines to their source, he has that delight, the highest of purely intellectual delights, which comes when, after many vigils, some original generalization, illuminating and simplifying the law, first flashes through his brain, and, better than all, he has the constant inspiration of the belief that through the students that go forth from his teaching and by his writings, he may leave his impress for good upon that system of law which, as Lord Russell has well said, "is, take it for all in all, the noblest system of law the world has ever seen."

To those of us who believe that upon the maintenance and wise administration of this system of law rests more than upon any other support the stability of our government, it is a happy omen that so many centers of legal learning are developing at the universities all over our land. May the lawyers and the university authorities see to it that these law faculties are filled with picked men. Until the rural legislator has enlightened views of the value of intellectual service, we cannot hope to have on the bench so many of the ablest lawyers as ought to be there. But the universities, many of them at least, are not hampered by this difficulty. They have it in their power to add to the inherent attractiveness of the professor's chair such emoluments as will draw to the law faculty the best legal talent of the country. I have the faith to believe that at no distant day there will be at each of the leading university law schools a body of law professors of distinguished ability, of national and international influence. That the Law School of this University will have its place among the leaders is assured, beyond peradventure, by the dedication of this building. The lawyers of future generations, as they walk through these spacious halls, and see this rich library, and the reading-rooms thronged with young men working in the spirit of enthusiastic comradeship, will say: "Truly it was a noble nursery of justice and liberty that the lawyers and citizens of Philadelphia erected in 1900"—but as they call to mind the distinguished lawyers and judges among the alumni, and they read over the names of the jurist-consults on the professorial staff, men teaching in the grand manner, and adding luster by their writings to the University and to the legal profession they shall add: "But those men of Philadelphia builded even better than they knew."

Chapter 73

The Metamorphosis of Legal Education

1985

Peter L. Strauss

Peter L. Strauss is Betts Professor at Columbia Law School. This article first appeared at 30 *New York Law School* 637 (1985).

Professor Brook's remarks this morning provide a context for my own. I mean to say a word or two for the classical era. One of the characteristics of legal education over the past half century or so, one that we ought not give up, has been its passion for order in a chaotic world. Striking as it is to say that "a passion for order ill suits a chaotic world,"[1] the world has ever been chaotic—and that passion, our principal defense. The question is, with what principles of order do we exercise that passion, to subdue unruly fact. Do we look to doctrine, to the characteristic tools of the legal profession, to understandings economic or semiological? Recent years have seen a shift in focus concerning what constitutes order, at least from a pedagogic perspective. We have turned our attention to the instrumental or vocational side of the legal profession, as distinct from concern for the content of law and the public order aspirations to which law may relate. That shift seems to me reflected in Professor Gorman's comments.[2]

Professor Gorman's concerns about legal education are concerns that I share, and that are widely shared. The problem is always how to respond. What strikes me is that the three reforms he chose to discuss in his paper sound rather more on what might be described as the vocational or instrumental side of one's approach to the problem of finding order in a chaotic world than on the intellectual or disciplinary side. One can hear them as moving towards the bar and, at least in the hearing, towards a view of the lawyer as rhetorician rather than as person of learning. These reforms include: more instruction about the legal profession, greater use of the practicing bar to sharpen professional skills, a third-year program of concentration intended to develop progression—an end on which all of us might agree, but which is illus-trated largely by its prospect for developing a wide range of lawyerly skills. Evidently this last reform has room for law and economics, interdisciplinary perspectives, planning, counseling, drafting, and other matters of that character. What I want to do, if only by way of creating a contrast that may sharpen later discussion, is to call attention to the risk that the knowledge to be sought will be defined vocationally and instrumentally rather than in the context of a search for critical understanding. While I doubt that it could be said of Columbia, as it recently was of Yale, that appreciation of the legal profession is a scarce commodity, our discussions do tend to look more often in the latter direction.

None of us doubt that changes are coming—whatever our view of their speed and direction. One could start with Professor Chase's reminder to us that even dramatic change may come gradually to those involved in it.[3] The case method did not sweep Harvard, much less the rest of us, overnight. Indeed, as Dean Simon reminded us,[4] New York Law School owes its very existence to resistance to the case method, and its initial success to the soundness and attractiveness of Professor Dwight's alternative teaching techniques. That the case method ultimately did prevail owes a bit to Harvard's special position, but mostly to its effectiveness in producing engagement among students and, as important, professional success among alumni, at an acceptable cost. As what we have heard today will confirm, those three measures—student engagement, professional success, and acceptable cost—remain common reference points in thinking about curricular change.

Note how different we are from other graduate faculties in talking about these subjects and measuring our impact in these terms—indeed, in planning for curricular and pedagogic reform at all. Our professional association's journal is the *Journal of Legal Education*, in contrast to the substantive orientation of professional journals in such fields as economics or comparative literature. Columbia and other schools offer seminars on legal education. That our faculties concern themselves as deeply as this conference suggests with issues of effective pedagogy equally distinguishes us from other university faculties, who rarely convene on these subjects or rank teaching with scholarship in considering advancement. The very fact of that professional orientation is a symptom of what Thomas Bergin once characterized as our peculiar schizophrenia—our indecision between the profession and the academy.[5]

Let me begin with the subject of "student engagement." Save perhaps for the first few months of legal education, or for the advanced elective in which professor and student share the search for knowledge, "student engagement" today generally signals the clinic or its close relatives rather than the Socratic class. None of us really doubt that; we have given up on Socrates. Twenty or thirty years hence, Northeastern's cooperative program or the extraordinary and innovative program at CUNY-Queens may well prove to have been this generation's Langdellian case method. The effectiveness of such programs—of clinical teaching generally—in engaging student effort across a broad range of professional skills appears to be enormous. They need only prove competitive in cost (which is going to be difficult) and succeed in the placement wars to shift all of us in that direction.

I hope to be forgiven the thought that for all of this, disciplined attention to the law's intellectual structures had best not disappear. In this respect I suppose I am guilty of preferring Andrew Wyeth to Jackson Pollack. That we have become disillusioned with law, that the impossibility of encompassing doctrine has spurred our instrumentalism, that our present curricula are too given to private law and judicial action; I suppose all of this is commonplace.[6] Consider, if you will, the recent flood of pabulum produced by reasonably accomplished members of our profession in the form of outlines, nutshells, and black letter student trots written for no other purpose than fostering a superficial grasp of doctrine for examination-takers. What are their implications? For our students, these may be welcome shortcuts through the thickets of cases and literature; for us, surely, they constitute an admission that this stuff no longer has importance, that sophistication in the management of doctrine or development of lawyers' critical sense is not to be demanded. Yet it is hard to imagine a more enthusiastic embrace of the demeaning view of lawyer as mere rhetorician, than a curriculum that abandons law for the techniques of using it. For students to achieve the capacity to learn how to learn law, alone, is not enough. Even from a professional point of view, one wants to know what the law is, as well as how to relate and work within it. I imagine few of us would be interested in being operated on by a surgeon whose education had been limited to the instrumental aspect of modern medicine. What those structures are, and how one achieves coherence, remain important questions indeed; acknowledging their importance is the crucial step.

Professor Gorman has referred to the real-world problems that necessarily influence and constrain the direction of change.[7] We ought not to think about the coming years as if all else will be held equal. The search for engagement among students and success among alumni is going to occur in a declining market and in a changing environment. It bears importantly on the possibilities for reform if the coming years will not be ones of abundant resources, or if the teaching context will be changing in ways that require response.

The resource problems are probably the best known. Paul Samuelson once remarked to my faculty that the number of lawyers is not written in heaven and that the hog/corn cycle has its lessons for those who run law schools. We have been through a period of abundance and we are going to have to adjust to less. Law school applications are dropping sharply and applications from the students law schools would most like to have are dropping the most sharply of all.[8] Bruce Zimmer, the head of the Law School Admissions Council, remarked recently that he would not be surprised to find fifty schools using open admissions standards within three years. Does that mean a return to planned attrition in first year classes? What implications would that have for us? Even without the student risks that would revive, the economic attractiveness of a legal education is also open to question. Today's graduates will all spend their professional careers under the bulge created by the baby boom and the past ten years of law school growth. At the current median entry salary for law graduates, Mr. Zimmer said, a cost/benefit analysis of legal education will suggest doing something else. The increasing vocationalism of American college students—the number of business majors has doubled in a period that saw literature, English, and classics majors halved—suggests that many students will be making that calculation. It may speak as well to the intellectual equipment and expectations with which our students reach us. It certainly promises significant competitive and cost pressures. And we ought not forget how much Langdell's success owed to its competitive and cost advantages. We may also have reason for concern that the heavy debt with which so many students leave us will not only constrain their choice of professional paths today but also, in the repaying, make it less likely we will have their support in the successful years of tomorrow.

We also face changes in the teaching context important to consider in figuring the next decade. We do a lot of talking about pedagogy but, as I think Professor Feinman may also be saying,[9] not enough about considering how learning occurs. Today's students, and especially tomorrow's, come to us from a different learning environment than characterized early schooling even to the middle of this century. Has there *never* been a time when vicarious participation in socratic education was a fact, as Professor Shreve asserts?[10] I can recall little speculation about the impact of television on what we do and how well we succeed, yet I wonder what Marshall McLuhan would have to say about the impact of growing up with television on the possibilities of vicarious participation on which the Socratic method is premised. What are the implications of the day, not far distant, when our students will have lived through their intellectual growth with a computer, not just as a tool for learning (for which it offers some promise in the area of acquiring knowledge of law), but as a teacher of logic or structured thinking? At the same time as others stress the techniques of policy analysis and literary criticism, we may find ourselves with students trained in forms of logic to an extent we have not previously experienced and do not know.

We confront changes in ourselves as well as in our students and in the prior educations from which they come to us. Where previously we have been individuals divided against ourselves, in Bergin's characterization,[11] increasingly we seem to be divided faculties. Clinical faculties are rapidly gaining a status equivalent to traditional law academics, and yet a distinct one, with questions about cost and what constitutes an appropriate contribution to the academic enterprise not fully answered. Whether, for example, a faculty teaching with the commitments entailed by the CUNY approach will find the time or have the inclination for scholarship remains to be seen; that has been for many of us a large issue on the clinical side. Tony Chase suggested that the answer to the problem was that faculty members could put in twice the hours for the same pay. That puts extraordinary weight on faculty altruism, unless one believes the market for teachers will become so crowded as to permit such a lowering of compensation. What can be said with more confidence is that the focus of clinical teachers' attention is almost entirely instrumental, and on the vocational side. One need not deny that problem solving has intellectual rigor and variety—it plainly does—to observe that it is quite a different activity from the study of legal norms.

Those of us on the academic side sometimes seem to be looking away from the profession and towards the academy. I have made no survey, but the impression is strong that we academicians are writing for each other and our colleagues in other disciplines more often; for lawyers and judges, less. We do not so much expect to be read there, and we are not. In class, and in our writings, we build theoretical models and investigate the languages and analytical techniques of other disciplines, where once we sought to understand law on its own terms and to convey its own terms of analysis. Within our faculties we seem to wish to reconstruct the great diversity of discipline and perspective that surrounds us in the university as a whole. For academicians, as for clinicians, law appears to be becoming the subject of our attention, more than it is the center of our being.

In observing this, I do not mean to convey that it is wrong—only that it is happening and that, in its way, it constitutes as radical a movement within our tension between profession and academy as does the move to embrace the profession suggested by Professor Gorman and others we have heard today. From the perspective that the university is a place to seek out knowledge and understanding, indeed, this movement is ideal; as is the other movement from the warring perspective, now ascendant among students, that the university is where you go to prepare for a job.

Do I owe a proposal from all this? There is no reason all of us must take the same path, perhaps every reason not to. The coming competition for this shrinking, changing student body will be eclectic. It would be good to see some schools respond by seeking out the fading liberal arts core. One of the unique aspects of American legal education in the world view is that we so radically separate undergraduate from professional education. Do we need to do so? The time may be upon us for at least some law schools to go back to the model suggested by Professor Kirchwey in the remarks that Professor Brook read earlier this morning,[12] the model in which the law student not only wanders by the rooms where political science and philosophy are taught, but actually goes in.

Would there be a place for a program thoroughly integrating legal with undergraduate education? Imagine a course of education from high school to legal degree that is still seven years long, yet begins to incorporate law in its third year. Imagine a student who nonetheless also pursues an undergraduate major and writes an honors thesis. The university might find cost and learning advantages in using a full economics department, rather than having its law school duplicate existing resources by employing its own economist—a teacher who, to some degree, must always feel herself out of her element. Genuine cross-fertilization may occur if students learning law and learning sociology at the same time produce for themselves, and for their more compartmentalized professors, continuing insights denied when learning occurs in serial fashion. A thesis written in the final years of legal as well as undergraduate education would provide the intensive learning Bob Gorman seeks, and also foster integration of liberal arts and legal perspectives. It may be that, by mixing the two, one could achieve a richness of education at the same time as one maintains a parsimony of resources.

In a world increasingly oriented to vocation, a few backfires might be lit. The *New York Times* recently reported the announcement by the heads of several multi-national corporations of a new program to support the liberal arts; middle management may come from business training, they remarked, but at the top a broader vision is required.[13] In law, as well, the turn to vocationalism warrants some resistance.

NOTES

1. Meltsner, *Whither Legal Education*, 30 N.Y.L. SCH. L. REV. 579, 589 (1985). Professor Meltsner's article appears in this issue.

2. Gorman, *Assessing and Reforming the Current Law School Curriculum*, 30 N.Y.L. SCH. L. REV. 609 (1985). Professor Gorman's article appears in this issue.

3. Chase, *American Legal Education Since 1885: The Case of the Missing Modern*, 30 N.Y.L. SCH. L. REV. 519, 519 (1985). Professor Chase's article appears in this issue.

4. Simon, *Introduction*, 30 N.Y.L. SCH. L. REV. 517, 518 (1985). Dean Simon's introduction appears in this issue.

5. Bergin, *The Law Teacher: A Man Divided* Against *Himself*, 54 VA. L. REV. 637, 638 (1968).

The hard center of this insight is that the modern law teacher has been suffering from a kind of intellectual schizophrenia for the past twenty-five years—a schizophrenia which has him devoutly believing that he can be, at one and the same time, an authentic academic and a trainer of Hessians.

Id.

6. Woodard, *The Limits of Legal Realism*, 54 VA. L. REV. 689 (1968) is an early assessment that still rewards reading.

7. Gorman, *supra* note 2, at 613-15.

8. For a general discussion on student demographics and the effect of declining enrollments on law schools, see Vernon & Zimmer, *The Demand for Legal Education: 1984 and the Future*, 35 J. LEGAL EDUC. 261 (1985).

9. See Feinman, *Reforming and Transforming*, 30 N.Y.L. Sch. L. Rev. 629, 634-35 (1985). Professor Feinman's article appears in this issue.

10. Shreve, *Two Cheers for the Case Method*, 30 N.Y.L. Sch. L. Rev. 601, 602 (1985). Professor Shreve's article appears in this issue.

11. Bergin, *supra* note 5, at 638.

12. Brook, *A Comment on Style: The Elevator as Metaphor*, 30 N.Y.L. Sch. L. Rev. 547, 553 (1985). Professor Brook's article appears in this issue.

13. Gutis, *Executive Education's Unconventional Side*, N.Y. Times, Mar. 24, 1985, § 3, at 17, col. 1.

Chapter 74

Striving to Make Great Lawyers—Citizenship and Moral Responsibility

A Jurisprudence for Law Teaching

1989

Michael I. Swygert

Copyright © 1989 Michael I. Swygert. The author is Professor of Law at Stetson University. Work on this thesis began while Professor Swygert was a Visiting Member of the Faculty of Law at Cambridge University during 1986-87, and continued while he was a Visiting Professor at Emory University during the fall semester, 1988. This article first appeared in 30 *Boston College Law Review* 803 (1989).

I. Introduction

Over one-hundred years ago, Oliver Wendell Holmes challenged a Harvard Law School gathering[1] by declaring that the business of legal education is not merely to teach law, or to make lawyers, it is "to teach law in the grand manner, and to make great lawyers. . . ."[2] Whether Holmes' timeless exhortation may be considered a moral precept for the law teaching community,[3] it surely intimates that law teachers share pedagogic responsibilities that go beyond instilling doctrinal sophistication and nurturing lawyering skills.[4]

This article sets out one view of what these additional responsibilities entail. This view suggests that, to teach law in the "grand manner," law teachers should continually teach law, lawyering, and citizenship, and also persistently consider claims of moral obligation as well as the nexus between moral and legal obligations.[5] The argument concludes that law teachers have normative responsibilities in part because their power, positions, and promises engender trust in their students. The trust takes the form of expectations and reliance—expectations that law teachers know best what issues ought to be raised to prepare students for law practice, and reliance by students coming to law school and affording teachers the opportunity to instruct them. Because expectations and reliance serve as cornerstones of moral responsibility, law teachers share moral obligations in law teaching that extend beyond teaching law.

In substance, this article describes a jurisprudence of law teaching. It begins by comparing three related yet distinct teaching pedagogies. Next, it analyzes the derivation of moral obligation. This analysis is followed by a discussion of how moral and legal obligations relate. The discussion responds to the question of why the moral pedagogy of law teaching requires law teachers to address moral issues. This in turn is followed by a discussion of the difficulties, real and apparent, of raising moral considerations in the law school context. The article ends with an affirmation of the benefits to society, to the student, and to the individual teacher of bringing moral scrutiny into the law school classroom.

II. Teaching Law, Lawyering, and Citizenship

A. The Doctrinal Pedagogy

The thesis of this discourse is that law teachers ought to teach law, lawyering, and citizenship. By "teaching law" is meant primarily an examination of the body of legal doctrine consisting largely of prescriptive and proscriptive rules. Teaching law also includes analyses of the policies underlying the doctrine. These changing doctrinal formulations primarily derive from court adjudications, legislative enactments, and administrative agency activities. Throughout this examination the law teacher and his or her students jointly consider the origin, evolution, application, interpretation, and manipulation of these evolved and evolving doctrinal rules. The predominant pedagogic focus is on facilitating the student's understanding of, and an adeptness in making *arguments* about, how the doctrines apply in terms of a person's or other legal entity's legal rights and obligations. This traditional and analytic approach might be called the doctrinal teaching pedagogy.[6] The doctrinal and analytic emphasis often includes a sprinkling of legal history, jurisprudence, and comparative law, but generally only a sprinkling.[7] To be sure, at certain law schools where law may be taught more as a liberal arts curriculum than a vocational one, perspective or normative courses and content will be emphasized to a greater degree. Nonetheless, doctrinal coverage is still the principal focus.

B. The Practice Pedagogy

Teaching law also has come to include, especially in recent years[8] and especially in America,[9] a deliberate effort to create in the law school environment opportunities for students to be introduced to the skills of lawyering. This might be called "teaching lawyering." The goal is to assist students in developing a minimal proficiency in legal research and writing, appellate advocacy, legal drafting, client counseling, conciliation, negotiation, fact marshalling, and pretrial and trial practice. The pedagogic focus in lawyer training is on the techniques of competent lawyering. Consequently, skills training might be labeled the *practice pedagogy*.

Due in part to the high cost of effective skills training, law schools still have a long way to go in developing skills programs that benefit the entire student population. But there is more to the slowness in the development of skills' programs than their cost. The recognition and implementation of this practice pedagogy tends to cause law school faculties to become de facto divided into two camps: the substance (or academic) camp, and the skills (or lawyering) camp. This division reflects a nearly two-century-old tension in America between those that view teaching law as an academic mission and those that see it as primarily vocational training.[10] Still, the resulting divisiveness is unfortunate, as it taps energy more productively expended in pursuing the shared educational objective of striving to make "great lawyers." Moreover, the occasional sparring between the academics and the skills segments of a law faculty obscures the fact that the law faculty has a shared obligation to teach both the skills as well as the substance of lawyering.

Why an obligation, one might ask. Because entering law students, and the public they will soon serve, expect lawyers to have acquired in their formal training both the knowledge and the skills appropriate to lawyering.[11]

C. The Moral Pedagogy

The public also expects that their lawyers "will go to town for them" (to borrow a phrase often used by Professor Thomas L. Shaffer),[12] and will do right by them. To do right means to act as a responsible citizen, which in turn means to act not only competently, but also to act morally—to do what is proper, not only what is legal. To be sure, what is right is not always clear. But the question must be raised in the law school classroom because law teachers, as explained below, have a continuing obligation to address the morality of good citizenship as well as the substance and skills of lawyering. Fulfilling this obligation requires persistently raising claims regarding what is right, what is proper, and what is ethical.[13]

Teaching the morality of citizenship also involves the persistent consideration of the normative bases for individual, corporate, and governmental responsibilities. These responsibilities extend beyond the mandates of the positive law. They can be framed best as claims of moral obligation. Throughout this consideration, claims and arguments about the requirements of citizenship are routinely raised by the teacher and by his or her students. The pedagogic focus is on notions of individual, institutional, corporate, and governmental morality.

When considering the moral dimension of a problem, the inquiry should never end with the question of what the appropriate legal doctrine does (or might) require. Rather, a further question—what ought the person or corporation do, or have done, under the circumstances—is always relevant.[14] This morally-required dimension to law teaching might be called the *moral pedagogy*. The moral pedagogy foremost involves discussions centering around claims of moral obligation. The sources of these moral obligations are next considered.

III. The Derivation of Moral Obligations

Notions of moral obligation are often attacked as involving largely an individual's subjective opinions.[15] But these arguments are not well-founded. For one thing, beliefs as to specific moral obligations are widely, although not universally, held. This shared belief is evidenced by various legislative enactments prohibiting discrimination on the bases of gender, race, age, and physical handicap.[16] Moreover, convincing arguments have been put forth that normative principles are distinct from positive law and from an individual's subjective opinions.[17] These principles have force and effect in society independent of positive law. Professor Ronald Dworkin has argued that these normative principles become the bases for courts' resolutions of "hard" cases.[18] In addition, these principles, when particularized to concrete situations, become the foundations for claims of specific moral obligations. Lawyers should have ample opportunities to make these claims provided they have become aware of their importance.

A normative morality of higher principles includes reasoned beliefs held by most law-trained persons relating to human dignity, human aspiration, procedural fairness, due process, equal treatment, fundamental human rights, and so on. These beliefs, it is submitted, give rise to expectations that take the form of normatively-based moral obligation.

Normatively-based obligations arise primarily in response to the community's expectations in reference to the positions we hold (our positional or role responsibilities); the language we use, particularly the promise (our promissory responsibilities);[19] and the activities we engage in (our participatory responsibilities).[20] And although we may disagree over whether moral obligations derive from community-based expectations, universal and immutable principles, an unfolding of reason, utilitarian self-interest, or from divine revelation, there can be little disagreement that at least the perception of moral obligations clearly influences our private, professional, and public lives. Presidential candidates, vice-presidential candidates, lawyers, and yes, law teachers sooner or later learn this truth.

My own view of the derivation of moral obligation relates in part to a person's engendering of trust and in part to religious beliefs and an obligatory responsiveness to the miracle and gift of life. The response is my obligation to be caring toward my fellow human beings.[21]

As to the engendering of trust, moral obligations derive from normative expectations about personal, professional, and civic responsibilities that go beyond the mandates or legal duties imposed by positive laws. These responsibilities become obligatory because our positions, language, activities, and group memberships all cause others to depend upon and to place trust in our positions, words, and actions.[22] Because dependencies and trust often reach a level of community expectations, each of us in the web of society is relied upon and trusted in countless, specific ways. This trust is a natural, logical, and predictable response to our promises, positions, activities, and associations. The web of trust goes to the heart of our socialization, the result of which is that we are not autonomous human beings, free to do whatever we desire. Rather, we are persons morally responsible to all other persons in our community. We live in a community of relationships with others.[23] These relationships result in reciprocal expectations.

Others may expect me to do or refrain from doing specific things: to participate in games, activities, to go about my business in predictable and definite ways; or, naturally to assume responsibility for a particular state of affairs.[24] In turn, I have expectations of those around me. My expectations take the form of beliefs that others with whom I interact will do right by me by fulfilling my expectations of trust, a trust generated by their words, positions, and associations.

As noted earlier, these normative expectations in turn serve as bases for claims about moral obligations. These claims may be general and abstract, or specific and concrete. Examples of general claims include all promises, even gratuitous ones, ought to be kept;[25] law teachers ought to deal fairly with their students;[26] employers ought to treat their employees with respect;[27] and, good sportsmanship ought to be observed while participating in or coaching games.[28]

These claims of general and abstract moral obligations should not be ignored or slighted in teaching. This is so because they reflect expectations that not only help shape our conduct, but also serve as a predicate for tomorrow's positive laws. Indeed, a significant segment of our positive law largely incorporates our society's normative expectations and beliefs.[29]

Nor should normative claims be ignored; it is from general claims or statements about moral responsibilities that specific claims are deduced or interpreted. The general claim, for example, that law teachers ought to treat law students fairly is the basis for the more specific claim that law teachers should use identical evaluative criteria in grading a set of examinations—that it is *right* to evaluate students on the same objective basis and wrong not to do so.[30] Being treated the same in reference to objective grading criteria is a law school, community-wide normative expectation, one that law students expect law teachers to follow.

Consider for a moment important equal protection and due process decisions of American constitutional law. These cases not only reflect the doctrine of precedent, or *stare decisis*, itself a normative principle, but they also and more significantly are the United States Supreme Court's pronouncements of our nation's highest moral aspirations. The Court's decisions often reflect previously existing normative beliefs and claims of what the positive law ought to be.[31] As these beliefs and claims change over time, so do the Supreme Court's responses and interpretations. Thus, we have *Plessy v. Ferguson*,[32] a half-century or so after it was decided, becoming *Brown v. Board of Education*.[33]

It is essential to recognize, moreover, that both the general and the particularized claims and expectations about what the law ought to be exist in lawyers' minds prior to a court's (including the Supreme Court's) pronouncements.[34] Consequently, tomorrow's judicial rulings may be anticipated by identifying and focusing upon society's, especially the legal profession's, normative beliefs. Future interpretations of existing laws will to a significant degree reflect the community's—certainly the lawyering community's—evolving expectations of the normative responsibilities pertaining to its individuals and to its business and governmental institutions.

If only to shed light on the legal process perspectives of how new legal requirements come into being and why interpretations of existing rules change over time, law teachers should persistently consider claims of normative obligations. But other arguments support the proposition that law teachers ought to routinely consider claims of moral obligations. One argument concerns the nexus between moral and legal obligations.

IV. The Relationship Between Moral and Legal Obligations

Philosophical explanations of morality, as well as speculations about law, posit the central notion of obligation.[35] In a reductionist sense, an obligation may be said to be any source of compulsion that, when disregarded, causes the disobeying party to be put at risk of losing something that society (not necessarily the party at risk) prefers or values. In this sense, obligations may be thought of as externally compelled. They are imposed upon individuals without regard to their consent.

In our Judeo-Christian society, normative preferences typically include the perceived values of freedom, trust, wealth, love, friendship, divine approval, integrity, power, rectitude, and respect.[36] Given these preferences or values, it becomes apparent how moral and legal obligations are related because each represents a societal compulsion one disobeys at one's peril. To act at peril is to risk losing a preferred value. Consequently, moral as well as legal obligations shape conduct. Thus, from a behavioralist perspective, positive law and notions of morality are not separate spheres, but are intertwined.

Limiting our discussion of obligation to legal duties (as many theorists and law teachers do) causes us to emphasize in our teaching the remedial or "rights" side of the law and morality milieu. In turn, lawyers may tend to emphasize their clients' legal rights while neglecting a mutual exploration of their own and their clients' moral responsibilities. This pedagogical imbalance in teaching, which may be later reflected in lawyering, contributes to the notion that a legal cure must exist for every illness, frustration, disgrace, and disappointment. This is a corrupting notion because it teaches the falsehood that we do not have responsibility for our own well-being, let alone our neighbor's.[37]

The linkage between moral and legal obligations becomes evident when considering the good citizenship responsibilities of lawyers as well as those of law teachers. As suggested above, to be a responsible citizen, one must acknowledge and respond to both moral and legal obligations. This is so because the community expects and trusts that each of us as a citizen of the community will try to fulfill both kinds of obligations. When we do so, we do right by our community. We fulfill its trusts and legitimate expectations not only in reference to our membership in the community, but also and more importantly in reference to our position or role within the community.

The community's trust and expectations are especially acute when it comes to the roles lawyers play.[38] In times of trouble, clients come to lawyers for help in response to the special powers, skills, and influence lawyers are presumed to have. Clients expect (or ought to expect) their lawyers to do right by them by giving them the best advice, legal skills, and moral counsel the lawyers are capable of giving. To give moral counsel does not mean preaching morality. Rather, it involves raising and discussing with the client moral issues and the moral ramifications of alternatives. This moral dialogue, according to Shaffer, is the essence of the law office conversation.[39]

And even if clients do not expect moral guidance, they still get it from their attorneys in positive or negative fashion. For the influence of lawyers extends to their serving as good or bad role models of citizen responsibility. Thus, if clients are to understand fully and respond to their legal and moral obligations, lawyers must give good moral counsel and set good examples in their lawyering and in interactions with clients and other persons and institutions.

Likewise, teachers, all teachers, set examples for their students, tomorrow's citizens. Law teachers in their roles as legal educators have special responsibilities to their law students.[40] Because law teachers, like lawyers, occupy positions of power and influence,[41] they serve as role models to their students of what it means to be good lawyers and good citizens. Because law teachers control the agenda of what is perceived that law students *need to know* (a moral determination), law teachers, like lawyers, are specially trusted, trusted to do right by their students in deciding what ought to be covered both in the curriculum and in the classroom. In short, whether or not we stop to think about it, what law teachers choose to teach, how we teach, and how we choose to act toward our students are moral decisions having far reaching ramifications. The fact is that law teachers are enormously trusted to make the right decisions. And that, of course, raises some nagging and potentially troublesome questions, questions about what law teachers are doing and not doing.

For one, are we, the nation's nearly five thousand law teachers, even cognizant of (let alone fulfilling) the enormous trust conferred upon us? Are we meeting our moral obligations to our students who depend on us and to the public who will in turn depend upon them?

To do right, to fulfill our trust, we must teach not only substantive doctrinal analysis and rudimentary lawyering skills, but we must also address a lawyer's obligation to be a good citizen.[42] We can do this in part by persistently raising claims and arguments concerning a lawyer's moral as well as legal obligations. We can also do it by being cognizant of and responsive to our own moral obligations.

To respond to our own moral obligations as law teachers means that we must routinely reexamine matters we take for granted, such as the curriculum and the case books we use. To do right means that we must care, sincerely care,[43] about our students' education and preparedness to serve the public competently and morally. We are, as Professor David Vernon has reported it, the "intellectual and moral gate keepers" of the legal profession.[44]

To do right does not require that law teachers teach morality, but it minimally demands that we morally teach. While teaching morality suggests taking a stand for particular claim *of* morality, to teach morally requires taking a stand *for* morality by acknowledging and responding to our own and to others' normative responsibilities.

Moreover, as role models of citizen responsibility for our students, we are morally obligated to live our lives as morally sensitive and responsive individuals, professionals, and legal educators. Moral teaching cannot be separated from moral living. We cannot extol virtue in our professional roles and tolerate immorality in our private affairs. Our acknowledgment, response, and example-setting, I submit, are all required in striving to teach law in the grand manner. In our striving to do right by our students, we will be responding to our own profession's moral obligation to assist law students in their striving to become great lawyers for the benefit of their clients, the courts, the legal profession, and society.

V. The Challenge of Teaching Both Law and Citizenship

Given the above argument that law teaching ought to include the persistent consideration of claims about moral obligation and citizen responsibility, it is appropriate to raise the question of whether law teachers are, by and large, doing so. Although the evidence is not easily discernible, and even though claims of morality are undoubtedly being raised by law teachers, a few clues intimate that moral discussions are not being persistently emphasized either in our law school classrooms or in our teaching materials.[45]

For one thing, it may be easy, too easy, to restrict one's teaching and writing about law to a positivist view of obligation.[46] Certainly, the announced doctrinal rules are easier to set out and discuss than are the more confusing, speculative, and at times opposing claims in reference to moral obligations.[47] (Bar examiners do not ask what the law ought to be. Nor do most law school examinations.) Analytic jurisprudence, or asking what the law "is" and stressing reasoning by precedent—or economic analysis, asking, for example, economically how to best lower the cost of accidents—seem far safer and easier to deal with than discussing the amorphous world of "oughts." Legal and economic "rules" tend to be "hard." Moral "oughts" tend at times to be "soft."[48] While rules can be coached, oughts tend to be slippery. And law teachers do not like to fumble the ball.[49]

But to shirk our moral responsibilities is dangerous pedagogy. For if we escape or deny responsibility for what is right, best, or good for society in this fashion, in time so will our students likely emulate our isolationism in their roles as lawyers.

Another challenge to teaching a moral pedagogy is the current popularity of the law and economics emphasis, on the one hand,[50] and the critical legal studies perspective, on the other.[51] The problem is that both of these perspectives, for different reasons, minimize the relevancy of moral obligation and, as a result, do not place moral claims high on their respective agendas. Morality, normative principles, natural law, even social utilitarianism seem to have been pushed aside by many modern legal theorists and academicians in favor of largely economic or political explanations of human conduct and aspiration.

Now these newer perspectives are not necessarily negative developments. These largely American views have widened the intellectual parameters of legal education and have given teachers and students deeper insights into our legal system and its functioning. The problem is that each view attempts to explain too much, and thereby minimizes the role of moral obligations and the nexus between law and morality. Law involves far more than wealth maximization and political manipulations.

Another difficulty of teaching a moral pedagogy is the typical, doctrinally-weighted law school curriculum. The curriculum contains few normative offerings. Many law teachers apparently believe that discussions of moral obligation can be either omitted or left to elective jurisprudence courses and seminars. This approach, however, as others have said, amounts to too little, too late, for too few.[52]

Given these and other impediments to raising routinely law and morality claims in the law school context, I am left after two decades of teaching law with the uneasy feeling that many law teachers, perhaps by accident more than through intellectual scrutiny, come to believe that legal and moral obligations are distinct worlds and that the claims of morality are best kept outside the law school classroom. But this moral isolationism[53] ignores the intertwining of moral and legal obligations, which together establish the responsibilities of citizenship.

As this article has pointed out, moral as well as legal obligations extend to law teachers' professional responsibilities. In response to these obligations, we law teachers have a responsibility to examine routinely the claims of moral obligations in our classrooms, in our writings, and in our roles as citizens and as legal educators. The public's and our students' trust require it.

VI. Benefits of the Moral Pedagogy

Students exposed to the moral pedagogy in their law school experience will benefit. Most importantly, they will be able to hold on to the normative beliefs that they typically bring to law school. These normative beliefs may include the notion that law is related to, and a means to attain, justice. One who is concerned about justice is concerned about "right" outcomes. In addition, students will see how legal rules often incorporate principles of morality. Indeed, students' normative beliefs in justice, fairness, honesty, and human dignity will not be discarded, but rather will become more fully developed as a result of persistent exposure to discussions centering on normative obligations and responsibilities. Students will perceive how legal and moral obligations are intertwined when it comes to defining one's responsibilities.

Consider a parent's responsibilities to his or her child, responsibilities that include the legal obligations of furnishing care and support.[54] Various general and abstract normative claims about parental obligations are routinely made in and out of legal contexts. The legal criteria espoused by courts involving decisions mandating consideration of the best interests of a child are predicated upon notions of moral obligations involving trust, love, and care. At what point do the legal obligations end and the moral responsibilities continue? Can they be separated at all? Family law teachers have to deal constantly with the overlays of legal and moral obligation. The intertwining of law and morality pervades many other segments of the law school curriculum as well—labor, torts, constitutional law, contracts, and so on. Do we as law teachers sufficiently recognize and respond to this social fact? If we do, our students surely benefit.[55] If we do, those of us who teach will reap personal benefits as well.

In emphasizing normative obligations, the law teacher may come away from his or her teaching and scholarship with a generally positive attitude regarding the potential for people, law, and institutions to operate in mutual harmony. The uplifting aspect of acknowledging that citizens have moral obligations concerning their harmonious well-being and that moral obligations are coterminous only to a point with their legal duties is the resulting affirmation of the existence and importance of human dignity, altruism, love, care, and charity. These acknowledgments also remind us that a society's positive laws can never serve as the all-purpose glue to keep society together. In addition, acknowledging moral obligations in teaching may also reflect a teacher's personal religious beliefs. This can be a personally harmonious, even a joyous, experience as the exercise of religious beliefs through one's thoughts and behavior need not be taboo in the law school classroom.[56]

Law teachers focusing on claims of moral obligation as an ingredient of teaching in the grand manner may or may not perceive law as essentially a tool of class oppression exercised by a nefarious power elite to protect their power, position, and wealth. Although admitting of social and economic injustices, one holding a view of law teaching and law study as including consideration of moral obligations probably will not dwell on the paradox of the claims of law vis-a-vis the realities to the point of personal or professional cynicism. A moral perspective looks with hope to the future without being overly judgmental about the past.

Nor does a moral view of obligation isolate one value—maximization of wealth—as underpinning or explaining the entire legal and social system. To the contrary, a view of moral obligation relating to citizen responsibility acknowledges many invisible hands at work in addition to those of Adam Smith's and the proletariat's. The hands at work within society include those normative, moral, and religious forces taking the form of expectations, trusts, and religious beliefs. These beliefs and trusts, along with resulting reliances and expectations, over time help shape a society's normative ethos—an ethos that relates to such values as human life, aspiration, and dignity, and incorporates principles of freedom, justice, and procedural fairness.[57]

VII. Conclusion

A law teacher's persistent consideration of normative principles along with more particularized claims of moral obligations is itself a morally obligatory responsibility. It is a necessary ingredient in striving to teach law "in the grand manner" in an effort to "make great lawyers."[58] A moral pedagogy that explores the responsibilities of citizenship and the moral obligations of the community's members is, in the end, the appropriate jurisprudence for law teaching.

Notes

1. The occasion was in connection with the 250th anniversary celebration of the founding of Harvard University. See 2 Warren, *History of the Harvard Law School* 439-40 (1908). Holmes addressed a gathering sponsored by the recently formed Harvard Law School Association. The principal orator for the celebration was James Russell Lowell. See Samuel Williston, Life and Law: An Autobiography 82 (1940).

2. O.W. Holmes, *The Use of Law Schools*, in Collected Legal Papers 37, 47-48 (1920).

3. Holmes felt that law and morality should be separated when discussing legal concepts. Nonetheless, he acknowledged the pervasive force of morals, even in the development of the positive law. See Holmes, *The Path of the Law*, 10 Harv.L.Rev. 457, 459-62 (1897). "The law is the witness and external deposit of our moral life. Its history is the history of the moral development of the race." *Id.* at 459. "The practice of [morality] . . . tends to make good citizens. . . ." *Id.*

4. Having been a full-time law teacher for the past twenty years, I have become convinced that collectively we fail in legal education to address sufficiently the important issues of moral and ethical citizenship. We tend to be satisfied with teaching legal doctrine, rule manipulation, and the techniques of lawyering. Simply having a required course in professional responsibility and a jurisprudence elective seem to me to be insufficient to the challenge. On the other hand, pervasive teaching of legal ethics is one positive development where that occurs. Still, the concept of the pervasive teaching of legal ethics may not be in harmony with the realities at most law schools. For a description of the difficulties of a pervasive ethical or moral pedagogy, see *infra* notes 44-53 and accompanying text. For an interesting analysis of the normative dimensions of the law and their implications to law teaching, see Terrell, *Flatlaw: An Essay on the Dimensions of Legal Reasoning and the Development of Fundamental Normative Principles*, 72 Calif.L.Rev. 288 (1984).

5. Teaching the claims of morality is not the same thing as teaching virtue. Indeed, educators have long been aware of the problems of whether virtue can be taught at all. *Cf.* Eisele, *Must Virtue Be Taught?*, 37 J. Legal Educ. 495 (1987) (Eisele sets out a normative argument that virtue can and must be taught). For an amusing yet sobering portrayal of how religious and ethical values are generally absent in the context of the modern American law school, see Shaffer, *Moral Implications and Effects of Legal Education: Or: Brother Justinian Goes to Law School*, 34 J. Legal Educ. 190 (1984); see also Neuhaus, *Law and the Rightness of Things*, 1 Christian Legal Soc'y No. 3, 7 (1980).

6. As Luban has elaborated:

> Doctrinal analysis assumes two main forms. First is the articulation of the meaning of a line of cases: a theoretical description of the development of law as it emerges. I call this "rational reconstruction." Second is the analysis of law in terms of the rational considerations that inform it. I call this "policy analysis." Luban, *Against Autarky*, 34 J. Legal Educ. 176, 177 (1984).

7. "An honest look at the law school world today requires the confession that we rarely fulfill this larger [normative] obligation." Cramton, *Beyond the Ordinary Religion*, 37 J. Legal Educ. 509, 510 (1987).

8. The growth in the teaching of lawyering skills in American law schools has in part resulted from the influence of the 1979 report of the American Bar Association Section of Legal Education and Admissions to the Bar, commonly referred to as the *Cramton Report.* This report recommended that law schools provide instruction in the "fundamental skills of lawyer competence." A.B.A. Sec. Legal Educ. & Admissions to Bar, Task Force on Lawyer Competency: The Role of Law Schools (1979).

9. In Britain the academic and skills training of lawyers, including solicitors and barristers, are separated. The academic segment is normally taught as an undergraduate curriculum at either university or polytechnic institutions. Very little in the way of skills training other than doctrinal analysis is addressed. More specialized lawyering skills are presented in either the Inns of Court School of Law (the barristers' professional school), or at one of the Law Society's various Colleges of Law (the solicitors' professional schools). Even so, the skills of lawyering continue to be learned for the most part in England and Wales through apprenticeships, known as "pupillages" in the case of barristers and "articled clerks" in the case of solicitors. See THE BAR ON TRIAL 68-82 (R. Hazell ed. 1978); M. BERLINS & C. DYER, THE LAW MACHINE 33-54 (2d ed. 1986).

10. "[T]he law school, as a professional school, performs the twin tasks of teaching substantive knowledge and also of training practitioners. As law professors, we have become accustomed to . . . academic tensions that these roles generate." Redlich, *Law Schools as Institutional Teachers of Professional Responsibility*, 34 J. LEGAL EDUC. 215, 216 (1984); see also R. STEVENS, LAW SCHOOL: LEGAL EDUCATION IN AMERICA FROM THE 1850'S TO THE 1980'S 5 (1983). From the time of Litchfield Law School in Connecticut, "the dichotomy between the teaching of law as a liberal and liberating study and the teaching of law as a technical and professional study was already established." STEVENS, *supra*, at 5.

11. Although I am unaware of empirical evidence to substantiate these expectations, it is difficult for me to believe that clients, when initially engaging lawyers, do not expect them to be both knowledgeable and skillful. Similarly, I strongly suspect that entering law students expect to acquire the requisite knowledge and skills appropriate for lawyering during their law school tenure. *Cf.* Eron & Redmount, *The Effect of Legal Education on Attitudes*, 9 J. LEGAL EDUC. 431 (1957).

12. See Shaffer, *Preface* to M. SWYGERT & R. BATEY, MAXIMIZING THE LAW SCHOOL EXPERIENCE: A COLLECTION OF ESSAYS iii, v (1983) ("'Attorney' means someone who goes to town for you," quoting Miss Maude, speaking about her attorney, Atticus Finch, in TO KILL A MOCKINGBIRD).

13. "My defense for putting larger normative questions on our teaching agenda rests on a notion that a university law school has a broader function than a cooking institute, a barber college, or some other trade-oriented technical school." Cramton, *supra* note 7, at 510. Judges decide "who has met the responsibilities of citizenship. . . ." R. DWORKIN, LAW'S EMPIRE 1 (1986).

14. "Today, even ardent defenders of positivism concede that it is a legitimate function . . . of the law student and law professor . . . to ask of a legal rule, once it is determined analytically what it says and what it means, 'Is it just?'" Berman, *Toward an Integrative Jurisprudence: Politics, Morality, History*, 76 CALIF.L.REV. 779, 784 (1988). In teaching contracts, I often ask whether a litigated dispute could have been avoided if one or other of the disputants had done what was morally right under the circumstances. For representative cases that I discuss in my contracts course, see, e.g., Mills v. Wyman, 20 Mass. (3 Pick.) 207 (1825), or Feinberg v. Pfeiffer Co., 322 S.W.2d 163 (Mo. 1959). See also Holcomb v. Zinke, 365 N.W.2d 507 (N.D. 1985) ("[T]he ancient rule [caveat emptor] is no longer an expression of American mores.").

Moral claims as they relate to the legal issues raised by abortion, privacy, preferential hiring, self defense, and euthanasia, among others, are the focus of a provocative book by Judith Jarvis Thomson titled RIGHTS, RESTITUTION, AND RISK: ESSAYS IN MORAL THEORY (1986).

15. Ronald Dworkin has described a community's popular morality as its set of opinions about justice and other political and personal virtues that are commonly held by most members of the community or by a "moral elite" within it. See R. Dworkin, *supra* note 13, at 97.

16. Under the common law, putative fathers were held only to have a "moral obligation" to support their illegitimate children. Bastardy statutes providing for support payments upon conviction represent one example of the codification of moral obligations. For a discussion of the incorporation process, see Fiege v. Boehm, 210 Md. 352, 123 A.2d 316 (1956); see also Holcomb v. Zinke, 365 N.W.2d 507 (N.D. 1985).

17. See, e.g., R. DWORKIN, TAKING RIGHTS SERIOUSLY 26, 97-101 (1978).

18. R. DWORKIN, *supra* note 13, at 87-89; see also Forer, *Autonomy and Responsibility: A Search for New Bases of Legal Rights and Responsibilities*, 1986 UTAH L.REV. 665, 686-88.

19. For one argument supporting the moral basis of promissory obligation, see C. FRIED, CONTRACT AS PROMISE: A THEORY OF CONTRACT OBLIGATION 7-22, 40-43 (1981); see also Swygert & Smucker, *Promissory Estoppel in Florida: Growing Recognition of Promissory Obligation*, 16 STETSON L.REV. 1, 15-19 (1986); Locke, *The Object of Morality, and the Obligation to Keep a Promise*, 2 CAN. J. PHIL. 135 (1972).

20. These activities include such daily routines as driving our cars, going shopping, and socializing with friends and neighbors.

21. Mark 12:31: "'Thou shall love thy neighbor as thyself.'"

22. See Locke, *supra* note 19; MacCormick, *Voluntary Obligations and Normative Powers*, 46 ARISTOTELIAN SOC'Y PROC. 50-59 (Supp.1972).

23. "[A] deeper understanding of one's individuality involves an affirmation of the relatedness between the self and the other person." Alexander, *Beyond Positivism: A Theological Perspective*, 20 GA.L.REV. 1089, 1130 (1986).

24. Certain obligations "involve not a duty to act, but instead a responsibility that a state of affairs exists, or will exist." A.M. TETTENBORN, AN INTRODUCTION TO THE LAW OF OBLIGATIONS 1 (1984).

25. Locke, *supra* note 19, at 135-39; see also Swygert & Smucker, *supra* note 19, at 15-19.

26. For a discussion on how to deal fairly with students in the areas of sexual relations, use of student work in research, and in grading and reviewing examinations, see the timely article by Freedman, *The Professional Responsibility of the Law Professor: Three Neglected Questions*, 39 VAND.L.REV. 275 (1986); see also L. PATTERSON, LEGAL ETHICS: THE LAW OF PROFESSIONAL RESPONSIBILITY 1-5 (1982).

27. In the marketplace, workers may value respect as much or more than compensation levels. My fourteen years as a part-time mediator and arbitrator have made this clear to me.

28. The fact that certain basketball coaches or tennis pros are not universally admired attests to the validity of this claim.

29. John Rawls in his highly influential discourse, A THEORY OF JUSTICE (1971), sets out a contractarian theory of law whereby the persons in the community consent to the law maker's pronouncements because the pronouncements reflect the community's shared principles of justice. See also J.W. HARRIS, LEGAL PHILOSOPHIES 11 (1980).

30. See O'Connell, *The Wages of Virtue: Better Symbols for Law School Grades*, 24 J. LEGAL EDUC. 362 (1972); see also Swygert, *Putting Law School Grades in Perspective*, 12 STETSON L.REV. 701 (1983).

31. For a description of the United States Supreme Court's normative interpretation of the Constitution, see R. DWORKIN, *supra* note 13, at 355-99.

32. 163 U.S. 537 (1896).

33. 347 U.S. 483 (1954); 349 U.S. 294 (1955) (*Brown* II).

34. The now somewhat quaint expression, "Brandeis brief," which brings to the Court's attention social data as relevant factors to be taken into consideration in its decision making, underscores this point. Moreover, judges as well as legislators "usually make laws which they believe to be morally right. . . ." P.S. ATIYAH, LAW AND MODERN SOCIETY 76 (1983).

35. See generally P. DEVLIN, THE ENFORCEMENT OF MORALS 12-17 (1965). See also J. HARRIS, *supra* note 29, at 83-85. To achieve results, law "must persuade or compel people to behave in the desired fashion. . . . [C]ompulsion is the more important of these two." P.S. ATIYAH, *supra* note 34, at 53.

36. See, *e.g.*, the list of eight values consisting of power, respect, enlightenment, wealth, well-being, rectitude, skill, and affection, set out by Lasswell and McDougal in *Legal Education and Public Policy: Professional Training in the Public Interest*, 52 YALE L.J. 203 (1943).

37. Swygert, *The Moral Basis of Obligation: A Critique of "Obligation-Duty" Contemporary Analyses*, 16 STETSON L.REV. 557, 560-61 (1987); see also R. NOZICK, ANARCHY, STATE AND UTOPIA (1982) (especially Chapter Three, "Moral Constraints and the State"). Instead of incorporating rights into the end state to be achieved, one might place them as side constraints upon the actions to be done. R. NOZICK, *supra*, at 29.

38. "[T]he public needs lawyers who acclaim the hope and expectation that [their] rights will be enforced." Carrington, *Of Law and the River*, 34 J. LEGAL EDUC. 222, 228 (1984).

39. Shaffer, *The Practice of Law as Moral Discourse*, 55 NOTRE DAME LAW. 231, 232 (1979). "The beginning and end of a lawyer's professional life is talking with a client about what is to be done. . . . [T]his is a moral conversation." *Id.* at 231; see also G. HAZARD, ETHICS IN THE PRACTICE OF LAW 1-14 (1978). It should not be forgotten that "many laws are designed to serve ethical purposes." P.S. ATIYAH, *supra* note 34, at 76.

40. "American law faculties are to the American legal profession what the Old Testament prophets were to Israel." T. SHAFFER, ON BEING A CHRISTIAN AND A LAWYER 177 (1981).

41. "Law teachers have the power to influence the process by which law students can numb themselves to many of their more desirable human impulses." Carrington, *supra* note 38, at 224.

42. "Is there not also a commitment, both for the law teacher and student, to search for the good?" Cramton, *supra* note 7, at 511.

43. See Sandalow, *The Moral Responsibility of Law Schools*, 34 J. LEGAL EDUC. 163 (1984). "Students ought not to be regarded merely as instruments, . . . not even in the setting of a professional school. They are . . . sources of value in their own right." *Id.* at 167.

44. Vernon, *Ethics in Academe—Afton Dekanal*, 34 J. LEGAL EDUC. 205, 211 (1984).

45. "[M]ost casebooks and courses, in design and effect, are doctrinally rather than normatively driven." Wasserstrom, *Legal Education and the Good Lawyer*, 34 J. LEGAL EDUC. 155, 159 (1984). Indeed, the absence of any pervasive coverage of morality as related to law is gleaned from perusing published works for law students authored by both American and British law teachers. These casebooks, texts, and legal guides for the most part reveal few references to notions or theories of normative responsibility or moral obligation. There are exceptions, of course, including the extensive writings of American law professor Thomas L. Shaffer. See, e.g., T. SHAFFER, *supra* note 40; T. SHAFFER, AMERICAN LEGAL ETHICS: TEXT, READINGS, AND DISCUSSION TOPICS (1985); Shaffer, *supra* note 39, at 231; Shaffer, *The Legal Ethics of the Two Kingdoms*, 17 VAL.U.L.REV. 3 (1983).

46. "The prevailing model of law study and law teaching in the United States probably is one of legal positivism (law treated as a system of rules). . . ." Van Doren, *Implications of Jurisprudence to Law Teaching and Student Learning*, in SWYGERT & BATEY, *supra* note 12, at 55.

47. "Many teachers find it difficult or inappropriate to raise the fundamental questions in class or in their writing. It is difficult, because they are often hard and controversial questions." Cramton, *supra* note 7, at 512 (citing Shaffer, *Moral Theology in Legal Ethics*, 12 CAPITAL U.L.REV. 179, 184-90 (1982)). "[There are] very real difficulties of discussing fundamental moral issues in the law school classroom. . . ." *Id.* at 512 n.11; see also Bartlett, *Teaching Values: A Dilemma*, 37 J. LEGAL EDUC. 519 (1987) ("The dilemma is that we cannot be value-neutral in our teaching . . . , but neither can we teach values. . . .").

48. Student concerns about justice or fairness are often dismissed in the classroom as founded on "mushy and naive appeals to sentiments, sympathies, or [moral] commitments that [are thought to] have no place in the harder . . . life and mind of the lawyer." Wasserstrom, *supra* note 45, at 159.

49. "[O]ne of the characteristics of the role of the professor is that it provides a position from which one can be aggressive. . . . [T]he professor may carry on an essentially one-sided battle. . . . I believe this to be highly important as a motivating factor to

those who become law professors." Watson, *The Quest for Professional Competence: Psychological Aspects of Legal Education*, 37 U.Cin.L.Rev. 91, 114 (1968).

50. See generally R. Posner, The Economic Analysis of Law 1 (1972) (economic reasoning is based on the assumption that "man is a rational maximizer . . . of his self interest"); see also Coase, *The Problem of Social Cost*, 3 J.L. & Econ. 1 (1960); Epstein, *A Theory of Strict Liability*, 2 J. Legal Stud. 151 (1973).

51. See Tushnet, *Following the Rules Laid Down: A Critique of Interpretivism and Neutral Principles*, 96 Harv.L.Rev. 781 (1983). For a bibliography of literature of the critical legal studies movement, see Kennedy & Klarem, *A Bibliography of Critical Legal Studies*, 94 Yale L.J. 461 (1984).

52. Wasserstrom, *supra* note 45, at 159.

53. Shaffer, *supra* note 39, at 239-40.

54. Professor Frank Alexander has noted that insights of religious traditions central to our Judaic-Christian heritage can "provide significant perspectives" on legal relationships including those of the family. Alexander, *supra* note 23, at 1126. The covenant tradition of authority between God and people can be focused on family members, the tradition "stand[ing] as a call for the greatest degree of . . . responsibility." *Id.* at 1128, 1131.

55. "If we can engage one another on the level of our convictions, . . . our views of law will be enriched." *Id.* at 1134.

56. "Virtually all of the conceptual pillars of liberal democracy—impartial adjudication, judicial review, . . . the presumption of innocence, habeas corpus, equal protection of the laws, good faith—have an origin or justification in the Judeo-Christian tradition. . . ." Gedicks & Hendrix, *Democracy, Autonomy and Values: Some Thoughts on Religion and Law in Modern America*, 60 S.Cal.L.Rev. 1579, 1618-19 (1987).

57. R. Dworkin, *supra* note 13, at 404. "Citizens . . . aim to be governed justly and fairly and with due process. . . ." *Id.* at 406.

58. See Linowitz, *Point of View: Law Schools Must Help Make the Practice of Law the Learned and Humane Profession It Once Was*, The Chronicle of Higher Education A52 (Sept. 14, 1988) ("The test of a system of justice is whether it serves people whose need is great—by their measurement, not ours. . . .").

VI. Scholarship

Chapter 75

Law And and the Methodology of Law

1997

Edward L. Rubin

Ed Rubin moved from the University of California, Berkeley, to be Professor at the University of Pennsylvania Law School. This article first appeared at 1997 *Wisconsin Law Review* 521.

For the last few dark and stormy decades, ever since it irreversibly dismantled its formalist home, legal scholarship has been traipsing from door to door, looking for a methodological refuge.[1] The doors at which it has knocked have included literature, philosophy, economics, political science, and sociology. Most of the residents have turned legal scholarship away with a meager handout and an explanation that they had problems enough of their own. Economics, which suffers few such doubts, invited it in and tried to gobble it up. For the most part, legal scholarship has kept knocking and tried to make the best of what it was given. A few of its members have abandoned the whole process and, out there in the darkness, tried to reconstruct the law's autonomous home.

This article briefly canvasses the various efforts to link law to other disciplines, a process that has acquired the appropriately indeterminate name of "law and." It argues that legal scholarship adopts a unique stance toward its subject matter that precludes the direct application of another field's methodology. But because of its internal features, legal scholarship needs to rely on other methodologies, particularly social science, to provide an understanding of the forces that act upon the legal system and of the impact of legal decisions. The article then considers two interesting arguments that have been recently advanced to restore the autonomy of law—the autopoietic theory of Niklas Luhmann[2] and Gunther Teubner,[3] and the theory of discursive modalities developed by Philip Bobbitt[4] and extended by Dennis Patterson.[5] While these approaches have much to recommend them, they ultimately do not alter the fact that legal scholarship needs social science to prosper, if not to survive.

Part I considers law and—the relationship of law to other academic disciplines. In the process, it identifies the salient features of legal scholarship. Part II then defines the methodology of legal scholarship with greater precision, discusses its particular relationship to social science, and explains why it cannot function as an autonomous discourse.

I. Law And

The primary concern of this discussion will be standard legal scholarship. This may be defined as work which frames recommendations, or prescriptions, to legal decision-makers.[6] In some cases the work critiques an existing judicial decision, statute, regulation, or constitution, and the recommendation is simply that the decision-maker should act differently. Less commonly, it merely offers a recommendation, with no comment about an existing decision. Most often, the work combines a critique of an existing decision with a prescription, whether general or specific, for a different approach. And sometimes it even suggests that the decision-makers are doing exactly the right thing. All this work, however, is characterized by its normative quality and the direct engagement of its recommendations with identifiable legal decision-makers.[7]

To be sure, many other types of work are recognized as legal scholarship—legal history, legal sociology and jurisprudence, for example. The present discussion is thus properly regarded as an analysis of the most common, characteristic mode of legal scholarship, rather than of every work that can be included in that category. There are, however, some conceptual as well as statistical reasons for defining standard legal scholarship in the manner proposed. To the extent that legal history or legal sociology are history or sociology about legal topics, their methodology is simply the methodology of those scholarly disciplines. As for jurisprudence, some of it can be treated as a special brand of moral or political philosophy. A good deal of the remainder, including this Symposium, involves an analysis of standard legal scholarship, and thus depends upon an understanding of that category.

There is also a substantial body of work that simply describes the law, without offering prescriptions or relying on a recognized academic methodology. This is distinctively legal, but it is generally not regarded as scholarship. It consists of practitioner manuals, summaries of current developments, and nonanalytic treatises. The sociological fact that this work is not regarded as true scholarship within the legal academy suggests the centrality of prescription as a distinguishing feature of the field, since the subject matter of the two categories is obviously indistinguishable Treatises, moreover, tend to cross the boundary into scholarship to the precise extent that they criticize the decisions they describe, and thus propose or imply prescriptions for alternative approaches. Some purely descriptive work does qualify as scholarship, however; typically, it is either comparative, or it is so general that it is recognized as jurisprudence. Such work is relatively uncommon, however. Joseph Raz's work is descriptive jurisprudence[8] but Ronald Dworkin's is standard legal scholarship;[9] although it is written at a fairly high level of abstraction, its central focus is a prescription to judges about the way to decide legal cases.

This definition of standard legal scholarship provides the basis for the claim that other academic methodologies are only indirectly relevant to law, and cannot aid legal scholarship in its search for a methodological home. The fields that will be discussed are natural science, literary criticism, moral philosophy, and social science. In each case, the standard methodology of the field will be described. One caveat is necessary, however: all of these standard methodologies have recently come under assault from postmodernism, an assault which has been sufficiently effective to make any statement of such standard methodologies appear naive. Nonetheless, they are the methodologies that the vast majority of scholars actually employ, and the ones that legal scholarship has sought to borrow. There is no point in borrowing a deconstructed methodology.

As for postmodernism itself, it offers many valuable insights, but it is a kind of intellectual blunderbuss. It is easy to trigger, and it hits a few targets now and then, but the difficult task is to identify the precise shape of the various targets and the way they relate to one another—in other words, the standard modalities of academic discourse. The analysis in this article is based on a sociology, not an epistemology, of academic disciplines—the working methodologies that these disciplines employ to generate their content, not the epistemological claims by which they establish the validity of the entire field.

A. Legal Scholarship and Natural Science

Natural science was the ideal to which legal scholarship aspired in its formative and formalist period,[10] and it exercises a continued fascination because it can produce definite results that are generally regarded as persuasive.[11] In all likelihood, the claim that law could be made into a science was always to be understood in a metaphorical sense, but close examination undercuts even the metaphor. The crucial problem is that the discourse of natural science is essentially descriptive rather than prescriptive. It begins from the premise that there is a real world "out there," separate from conscious human control. Prescriptive statements about this world would be meaningless, but descriptions can yield a model of its behavior that possesses a publicly accessible level of coherence. That, at least, is the working premise of academic natural scientists.[12] It can be challenged on philosophic grounds, but, as a sociological observation about scientists' beliefs, it remains as true today as it was before our epistemological doubts took hold.

Legal scholarship differs from natural science in the prescriptive purpose it adopts. This difference follows, as an almost necessary consequence, from our present vision of the law itself. The scientific aspirations of the formalists were based on the idea that legal principles were "out there," beyond the reach of conscious decision-makers in the same sense as the principles of natural science. As a result, the formalists believed that the task of legal scholarship was to describe those principles, and then construct prescriptions that would be fully dependent on them. But no one really believes this to be true at present, no matter what one's theory of law. Modern legal scholars regard law as the product of conscious decision by public decision-makers, and possibly others. There is thus no fixed reality, but rather an ongoing process by which people in certain positions make decisions; in bald terms, law is created, not discovered. This sentiment has led to prescriptive efforts to improve the quality of those decisions according to the scholar's own views about law or public policy.

Another major contrast between legal and scientific scholarship is that the external information on which natural scientists rely consists of data, whereas the external information for legal scholars consists of events. The distinguishing characteristics of data, as opposed to events, is that they are generated, defined, and given significance by the academic discipline that studies them.[13] To begin with, data are a passive subject of research that must be generated by the discipline itself. This is true even of scientific fields that rely heavily on observation, like geology, and it is apparent in more experimental areas. The biologist who investigates the chemical composition of a mackerel's heart by grinding it up and separating its components in a centrifuge is manipulating the external world in a way that implies its passive and dependent quality. The discovery of a new subatomic particle, a new chemical reaction, or a new dinosaur bone may be an occurrence of great importance, but it is the product of scholarly effort, and thus consistent with the vision of external reality as a passive subject for research. Judicial decisions, legislative enactments, and administrative regulations, on the other hand, are neither discovered in law libraries nor unearthed in the field, but generated by nonacademic actors. In dealing with this external information, legal scholarship necessarily adopts a reactive approach.[14]

Secondly, the nature of the discovered phe-

40. William Draper Lewis (1867-1949). Trained as both a lawyer and an economist, Lewis served as dean of Penn during a period of great expansion in that program and had influence as director of the American Law Institute. (*Courtesy of the Biddle Library Department of Special Collections, University of Pennsylvania Law School.*)

nomenon in science is defined by the discipline, whether this definition consists of determining the discovery itself, like the subatomic particle; the boundaries of the discovery, like the chemical reaction; or the mere fact that it is new, like the dinosaur bone. Events, as opposed to data, come to a scholarly discipline prepackaged, either by their human originator or by a pattern of human observations that is much broader than the one that the discipline establishes.

The third feature that distinguishes data from events is that the significance of the former is determined by scholars. It is the scientist who tells us if the newly-discovered dinosaur bone is just a piece of Cretaceous garbage that some local museum can display to visiting Boy Scout troops, or whether it changes our basic understanding of what dinosaurs were like. The explosion of a volcano may seem like an event, being independently generated and defined by broadly-based, nonscientific opinion, but is only an historic event; whether it has scientific importance will be determined by Professor Magma and his graduate students who go clambering up its sides, There is some element of this process in legal scholarship; an obscure state court decision can be hailed as a triumph of judicial reasoning, or a Supreme Court opinion can be identified as a jurisprudential Armageddon whose implications had escaped the justices at the time when it was handed down. More typically, however, the decision will correctly identify its own importance, and very often it will establish its importance by means of that identification.

A final difference between the law and natural science lies in the noncumulative quality of legal scholarship. It has always been a source of envy to other academic disciplines that science actually progresses, that existing controversies are resolved, and that new insights can be based on those resolutions.[15] To be sure, Thomas Kuhn's theory of successive scientific revolutions, engendered by changes in the underlying paradigm of scientific understanding, has challenged this vision of cumulation.[16] Kuhn adds a needed note of nontriumphant realism to the process of discovery, but he does not refute the basic fact that over long periods of time, the area of scientific agreement increases, and the new problems addressed are increasingly sophisticated and complex.

What underlies the cumulation of scientific knowledge is a unified theory of causality. Scientists are not only involved in a descriptive enterprise, but they are in agreement that their enterprise involves an effort to explain the causes of observed phenomena. They further agree about the sorts of statements that will count as explanations.[17] Viewed from this perspective, natural science is not a group of disciplines, but a single discipline with a broad range of topics. The astronomer and the geologist share the same basic methodology, their fields being distinguished primarily by a difference in altitude. They are prevented from switching from one field to another by the amount of information to be learned, but they can readily accept each other's results and often utilize these results, in a methodologically effortless manner, when their fields overlap.

It is precisely such a theory that legal scholars lack. They lack it because they are not trying to describe the causes of observed phenomena, but to evaluate a series of events, to express values, and to prescribe alternatives. This does not lend itself to the notions of causality that lie at the base of natural science and its cumulative method. It does not, moreover, involve the sort of statements about external reality that can be verified or falsified by data, the process through which the cumulation of scientific knowledge is effected.

B. Legal Scholarship and Literary Criticism

Another source of methodological assistance for legal scholarship is literary criticism, in many ways the diametric opposite of natural science. "Law and literature" once referred to compilations of literary works depicting lawyers—an enterprise that any law-trained person would need to be a masochist to undertake—but now constitutes an important theme in modern jurisprudence.[18] At first, the comparison between legal scholarship and literary criticism appears to be a rather close one. Both literary critics and legal scholars can be properly regarded as engaged in a process of interpretation, an effort to discover the meaning of a preexisting text. This interpretive process may attempt to discern the intent of the author, but that is only one approach to legal or literary meaning; there are numerous others, such as assessing the text's effect upon the reader, or its range of possible meanings, or its interaction with a broader set of social attitudes. All these approaches seem common to both legal scholarship and literary criticism, and have produced a body of writing that can be described, in both cases, as largely reactive and largely noncumulative. Their starting points are works that are generated outside the discipline, and whose character and boundaries are defined by their human originators. Their products are noncumulative, although they rely upon a general background of knowledge and sensibility. The task that both groups of scholars set themselves is to evaluate, rather than to explain; they possess no theory of causality and generate no statements that can be verified or falsified by empirical means.

Despite the similarities between literary criticism and legal scholarship, many scholars maintain that the two fields are ineluctably separated by the fact that law involves the deployment of political power, that it exercises direct consequences in our lives that literature lacks.[19] Passing over, for the moment, this difficult argument, which depends upon some theory about the real nature of both law and literature themselves,[20] there remains a basic difference in the purpose of these academic fields, a difference in the scholar's stance toward her subject matter. Literary criticism adopts an essentially nonprescriptive stance. The critic does not address the author with instructions on how to create more realistic characters or construct a better plot, the way the legal scholar instructs judges how to interpret precedent, use social policy, and reason through to their conclusions. This difference in purpose stems from the opposing attitude of legal scholars and literary critics toward their subject matter, an opposition that can be captured by the qualities of involvement and respect.

Involvement is a relationship in which the scholar's efforts potentially affect the subject matter. Literary critics are not involved, in this sense of the term, with the texts that they interpret. Many authors of great interest to contemporary critics are well beyond the reach of earthly instruction, and the creation of literary works in general is not regarded as a rational process that can be improved by academic argument. As a result, there is no felt need to address prescriptive arguments to the creators of literary texts, and no strong sense that anything would be achieved by doing so.

For legal scholars, the situation is largely the reverse; they are inevitably and intensely involved with the subject matter of their research. They regard the law as the deliberate action of state decision-makers that can conceivably be affected by the sorts of academic arguments that they articulate. In such circumstances, prescription is a natural, and rather appealing, mode of discourse.[21]

In place of the legal scholar's sense of involvement, the relationship of literary critics toward their subject matter can be characterized as one of respect. Literary critics regard a work as worthy of scholarly attention because they respect it, because they find in it a source of meaning or of inspiration.[22] One need only imagine a scholarly work about a novel that the scholar did not respect—a Gothic romance, for example, whose cover shows a winsome woman in a filmy dress embracing a dark-haired man amid a bed of flowers—to recognize that it would not be a work of literary criticism at all, but something quite different, such as a sociological study of the "Gothic romance phenomenon." Critics, in other words, assume what Martin Buber would call an I-Thou relationship with the work under consideration.[23] In essence, they regard the author as a person of genius perhaps, or talent at least, whose work they are in a position to interpret and evaluate, but not improve.

This is generally not true of legal scholars, who adopt very much of an I-It relationship with the decision or statute they are analyzing. Deep down inside, legal scholars tend to think that they could do a better job than the judge. Thus, their interpretive efforts to determine the meaning of a particular opinion are often preliminary to prescriptive statements that evaluate the desirability of the determined meaning. As Charles Collier suggests, this is fatal to the enterprise of law and literature, which can only be advanced by treating judges as poets, and according them an artificially created intellectual status that the actuality of their work product confounds. For most scholars, the judge is someone whose work should be improved, not plumbed for the deeper meaning that its obscurities or implausibilities reveal. To be sure, there are interpretive elements in most works of standard legal scholarship, but the addition of a prescriptive element, and the effect of this element on the character of the description, distinguishes legal scholarship from literary criticism.

The relationship between the scholar's interpretive and prescriptive efforts will be determined by the level of the decision-maker to whom the article is addressed. If it addresses its prescriptions to the author of one particular decision, treating the rest of the world as a fixed background, it will tend to take a purely interpretive stance toward prior decisions or a controlling statute. The prescriptive question will be how these decisions should be interpreted, and whether the author of the decision in question interpreted prior decisions or statutes correctly. Alternatively, an article may address itself to the entire judiciary. In that case, it will tend to speak prescriptively about all the relevant decisions, but it may treat the statutory provision on which they depend in a purely interpretive way. Not only does legal scholarship contain these additional prescriptive elements, but their inclusion produces a particular kind of engaged, argumentative interpretation which is qualitatively different from most literary criticism. In addition, modern legal articles often rely on underlying social policy considerations. In that case, there will be no purely interpretive discussion, and interpretation will be used only as the basis for prescription.

A somewhat different claim, advanced by James Boyd White,[24] Ronald Dworkin,[25] and Stanley Fish,[26] is that legal scholars and judges comprise a single interpretive community which collectively defines the law. Whatever merits this view has, it does not bring the scholar any closer to the literary critic. Literary critics may well constitute an interpretive community, but that community does not include the author, the creator of the subject matter that the literary critic studies. In fact, the whole point of the modern "interpretive community" approach to literature is that the author's intentions and internal thought processes are opaque, so that critics—and readers—must construct that meaning for themselves. But the idea that judges and legal scholars define the law as an interpretive community necessarily depends upon a close cultural link between them, and on their ability to understand each other. It is precisely this linkage that generates legal scholars' sense of involvement and the corresponding prescriptiveness of their approach.

It might be argued that literary criticism is also prescriptive, if not to the author of the work, then at least to its reader. This is certainly the import of modern hermeneutic theory, which views criticism as a way to aid readers in the construction of meaning, rather than a way of revealing to them real, preexisting meanings.[27] But this sort of prescriptiveness would only be analogous to the legal practitioner literature; it addresses the users, however creative their role, not the originators. In fact, the prescriptiveness of legal scholarship distinguishes it rather sharply from literary criticism. The analogy between the two fields is useful for purposes of clarification, but any effort to give it more substantive effect would founder on this prescriptive quality in legal scholarship, and the underlying lack of respect that it implies. There appears to be no reason why legal scholars would grant judges or legislators a donné, why they would presume that apparent mistakes were intended originalities, or why they would treat ambiguity as a virtue that opens up new vistas of meaning or imagination.

The nonprescriptive character of literary criticism tends to dampen its reactivity and noncumulation, thus further distinguishing it from legal scholarship. This decreased reactivity stems from literary criticism's internally-generated standards of significance. It is the critic who decides which works merit attention, not the authors themselves, and not general opinion as embodied in the *New York Times* bestsellers list. These judgments of significance have a cumulative quality: the proper way to interpret a particular work never really becomes settled, but the fact that the work is worth interpreting does become a matter of consensus. To be sure, authors come into favor or fall out of it, and assiduous critics are occasionally able to persuade their colleagues that some acknowledged classic merits the perdition of oblivion, or that some previously unknown novel is a "minor *War and Peace*." But over the course of time, literary judgments seem to stabilize, and the familiar canon of great literature takes shape.

The adoption of this attitude implies a standard, an aesthetic of some sort, by which the literary work is judged as admirable or great. Judgments of significance are cumulative because this standard functions for critics the way a theory of causality does for scientists; it provides a basis for agreement about the criteria by which scholarly work is to be judged. Of course, the critics have no way of verifying or falsifying their conclusions. The cumulative process they are left with, therefore, depends entirely on consensus of the critics, a democratic principle much weaker than the authoritarianism of empirical results. As stated, this Article's discussion is an effort to characterize the basic practices of various academic disciplines, and thus avoids engaging with postmodernist critiques. The concept of a canon has absorbed so much deconstructive punishment in recent years, however, that the entire concept has contracted a certain air of illegitimacy. But most of this controversy acknowledges the idea that judgments of significance are possible, and only disputes the criteria by which the standard judgments have been formulated.[28]

It is, once again, the factor of respect that makes literary criticism more cumulative than legal scholarship. Legal scholars write about cases and statutes because external forces, whether the originators of those products or the general opinion of society, have identified them as significant. In fact, they employ no internally-generated standard, and thus have no basis for agreement, or a cumulation based on judgment. To the extent that legal scholars do make independent assessments of significance, it might be suggested—not altogether facetiously—that their standard is more often based upon contempt than admiration. Generally speaking, articles that seize with glee on obscure errors and drag them into the spotlight of analysis seem more common than those which celebrate some inglorious, if not entirely mute, Milton of the judicial or the legislative art.[29]

C. Legal Scholarship and Moral Philosophy

Philosophy, and more specifically moral philosophy, serves as another potential source of methodology for legal scholarship. It is a current subject of debate among philosophers whether morality is descriptive. Moral realists assert that a system of morality can be derived from some state of the world external to morality itself, most typically human reason.[30] Most moral philosophers, on the other hand, take the position that morality is a matter of judgment or choice, so that its statements are normative rather than descriptive.[31] To the extent that moral philosophy is descriptive, it again differs from law, since realist arguments are even rarer in modern jurisprudence[32] and are almost absent from any more specific discussions of legal principles. Ronald Dworkin's analysis bears a resemblance to such arguments, but his principles exist within law, as a matter of cultural experience, not in the external, transcendental realm of reason. Moreover—and this is indicative of the stance which legal scholars adopt—he rarely attempts to catalogue the principles that guide the law; most of his writing recommends that judges use those principles, or find those principles, in their own decision-making process.[33]

Most moral philosophers, however, see themselves as engaged in a normative enterprise, as legal scholars do. As such, they are necessarily involved with their subject matter; they assert, and indeed insist, that ethical systems affect human life, and their own efforts are intended to affect the formulation of those systems. Sometimes, their writings are addressed to individuals, and sometimes specifically to public decision-makers, suggesting to them how to think, how to live, and how to act. Philosophers evince no particular respect toward their subject matter, whether that subject matter is the world, the soul, or other philosophers. Their general attitude, instead, is one of critical inquiry, a refusal to take things on faith or to defer to the genius of one's predecessors.

Many philosophical ideas are quite useful in the normative debates that constitute the essence of standard legal scholarship;[34] this phenomenon is hardly surprising, since these ideas are general ones, intended to apply to all forms of knowledge and argument. But the particular methodology of moral philosophy cannot be readily assimilated by legal scholarship; while both fields are normative, the type of normativity involved is rather different. To follow Kant's distinction, most moral philosophy is phrased categorically, rather than contingently[35]—the question is how one should behave, not how one should behave if one wants to achieve a particular objective. Legal scholarship generally has some contingent objective at its source, some set of accepted purposes on which its prescriptions are based. Standard legal scholarship is hardly concerned with exploring the underlying function or significance of law. The question it addresses usually involves the proper decision to be made within an existing legal framework.[36]

Apart from the different quality of its normative stance, philosophy is distinguished from law by its nonreactive quality, its ability to set its own agenda. Philosophy certainly responds to broad-based changes in the intellectual climate of society, but so does everything else; its focus on the underlying nature and significance of events precludes more direct influence. To an even greater extent than natural science, philosophy generates, defines, and gives significance to any phenomena to which its practitioners respond; in fact, the very subject of philosophy is the process by which ideas are created, defined, and deemed important, in other fields as well as its own. Philosophers are not entirely immune to events, but it is hard to imagine any occurrence that they would regard as rivaling the significance of a newly-published work by another philosopher.

The one trait that moral philosophy does share with legal scholarship is its lack of cumulation. Philosophic problems rarely become settled to the general satisfaction of those active in the field; for every philosopher who sees increasing levels of conceptual sophistication, there is another who thinks things have run pretty much downhill since Aristotle. There are, however, two elements of philosophic discourse that seem to possess cumulative properties. First, important philosophers generate new categories, distinctions, or perspectives which become part of a vocabulary that expands with time. One need not accept Hume's distinction between "is" and "ought," or Kant's definition of the categorical and hypothetical imperatives, but one cannot ignore them in discussing issues to which they apply. Moreover, one need not struggle to articulate those concepts; although they required extensive and inspired argument to establish, they can now be readily invoked, and used as elements in further argument.

Second, there are certain philosophic issues that in fact are settled over time, not because they can be resolved by philosophic argument, but because they pass out of its ambit into other disciplines. This process is more common in other branches of philosophy, an obvious example being Aristotle's *Physics*, but it appears in moral philosophy as well. Thus social hierarchy, a dominant moral idea in pre-Enlightenment society, was justified by reference to the hierarchical ordering of nature, and divine purpose was deduced from nature's ordered design.[37] Evolutionary theories pretty much eliminated the first argument, and natural selection got rid of the second, to the continued irritation of the faithful.[38] It is considered impolite to treat philosophy as a precursor of science,[39] but the fact remains that certain philosophic inquiries have been resolved this way. The sense of cumulation, therefore, lies in the ability to eliminate certain questions from an otherwise noncumulative field.

Both these limited means of philosophic cumulation have their parallels in law, but to an even more limited extent. Law certainly develops a specialized vocabulary; the difficulty is that its categories, being set within a reactive discipline, are often generated by events, not by scholars, and can always be abolished by those same events, even if scholars remain attached to them. As for cumulation through exclusion rom the field, the law's reactivity means that this process, although it does occur, is not in the control of legal scholars. External social forces decree that certain subjects, such as theology or the alienation of affections, are to be banished from the law, but these same forces introduce new subjects just as readily. Not only does this fail to reduce the aggregate, but it means that the exclusion process is simply not the product of the scholarship. Any exclusions, therefore, merge into the general pattern of events to which the scholarship reacts, and lose their quality as a cumulative tradition. In short, it may be useful to philosophize about the law, but the method of moral philosophy, whether applied to law or something else, is quite different from the methodology of standard legal scholarship.

D. Legal Scholarship and Social Science

A final source of methodology for legal scholarship, and by far the most commonly invoked, is social science. This particular affinity is not primarily motivated by a sense of envy, as is true of natural science. The present state of social science as an academic discipline is not an enviable one; in fact, the field has itself been prey to considerable academic envy, as its very name suggests. Rather, the instinctive tendency to make comparisons between law and social science stems from the enormous substantive overlap between these disciplines. Anthropologists, in analyzing a different culture, often focus on that culture's law as a major object of attention; sociologists frequently concern themselves with criminal behavior, the police, law-related business practices, or even lawyers themselves; political scientists study law-making, law implementation, and judicial dispute resolution; economists are concerned with the transactions that law governs, and the effects of the laws that govern them.

These substantive overlaps are of great importance, but they can obscure the basic comparison at issue here, which is between the methodologies of social science and legal scholarship. The extent to which legal scholars incorporate social science concepts will certainly go far toward determining the nature of the discipline. But nothing can be incorporated, in any coherent fashion, until the methodology for incorporation, and for research in general, is determined.

With respect to prescriptiveness, social science exhibits a considerable range. Sometimes social scientists, consistent with their aspiration to be scientists, take an entirely descriptive stance, treating their subject matter as a fixed phenomenon, "out there" beyond the control of rational decision-makers. Thus, they will write about the psychological condition of various people without taking a position on their relative depravity, or about political behavior of large groups without decrying its disastrous effects.[40] At other times, social scientists assume an interpretive position toward their subject matter, trying to reconstruct its meaning the way literary critics reconstruct a text. This is generally thought to involve participation in the conceptual and normative framework of their subjects—an active understanding of the way the people who are being studied create meaning for themselves.[41] At still other times, however, social scientists frame contingent prescriptions, addressed to particular decision-makers;[42] they recommend monetarist policies to the Federal Reserve because they increase wealth, or design some form of oversight for Congress that can control administrative misbehavior. Such prescriptions are contingent because they rely on an underlying objective—that wealth should be increased, or administrative behavior should be subject to control.

Although the complexity of the social science enterprise precludes easy characterization, its dominant approach appears to be descriptive, thus distinguishing it from legal scholarship. Ever since its inception, social science has aspired to describe social phenomena and explain their causes. We have become increasingly dubious about the sanguine expectations of the field's progenitors, but the basic discourse they established continues to the present day. Contemporary doubts about its truth value or its objectivity are often well-founded, but the effectiveness of the critique should not obscure the nature of basic social science methodology. As in natural science, the critique is often expressed at the level of grand theory, while the day-to-day research within the discipline continues largely undisturbed.

The interpretive and contingently prescriptive modes of social science tend to function as modifications of the field's basically descriptive stance, rather than as truly alternative visions. These modifications are partially determined by varying degrees of involvement and respect. Interpretation begins from a position of respect, a belief that human beings should be treated as creators of meaning rather than as agglomerations of measurable characteristics or observable behaviors. From this, it follows that social scientists, who are themselves creators of meaning, must participate in the beliefs of their subjects, and must actively understand how the people they are studying perceive the world, The analogy between understanding social phenomena and interpreting texts is a natural outgrowth of this approach. Interpretivism is certainly a useful counterweight to the reductionist tendencies of microeconomics, behavioral psychology, and statistical sociology, but it could not function without the elaborate, well-established descriptive techniques that typify social science. A literary text that is being interpreted can be located by an assistant librarian, but a social phenomenon or distant culture must be extensively researched. It is essentially a descriptive task to determine how a people construct meaning, and the fact that the social scientists must understand, empathize or even participate in that process in order to describe it does not change the basic purpose of the enterprise.

The prescriptive mode of scholarship in social science, as in law, emerges from a sense of involvement. When the actions of a particular decision-maker affect the scholar's life, and might be affected by the scholar's work, the desire of the scholar to address prescriptions to that decision-maker will be strong. But in social science, these prescriptions are also built upon a descriptive base; it is the ability to describe and explain social phenomena that gives social scientists their authority. As a result, their prescriptions are often stated as analyses of past events, or as predictions about the future based on extrapolations from a descriptively-understood reality. Thus, the prescriptive mode, like the interpretive one, is a modification of a basically descriptive discipline. Of course, prescriptions inevitably involve normative choices, but what makes such a prescription a work of social science—what places it within the scholarly discourse—is its descriptive basis. Moreover, the field covers many subjects with which scholars are not involved; it is just as concerned with decisions made by long-dead kings affecting long-dead subjects, or the social customs of minute bands of subsistence farmers with no GNP whatsoever, as it is with the political and economic phenomena that affect our lives today. This reflects the basically descriptive style of social science, and in turn supports and validates that style. If legal scholarship resembles social science in its basic tone, it resembles only the prescriptive aspect of that field, rather than its descriptive core.

The reactivity of social science displays a range that is similar to its range of prescriptive attitudes. At one limit, social science can be as nonreactive, or independent, as natural science, treating external phenomena as a body of data to be discovered, defined, and evaluated. This is typical of fields that deal with individual behavior, such as psychology, sociology and microeconomics. As the focus of a discipline moves toward collective behavior, it is likely to become more reactive, allowing external phenomena to assume the character of events. Thus, historians react to social upheavals, political scientists react to elections, and macroeconomists react to depressions. In all these cases, however, the reaction is tempered by an independent research program that can be brought to bear on the event in question. A running commentary on day-to-day, or even year-to-year events, is regarded as the province of journalism, not social science scholarship.

Such reactivity as social science does display, moreover, generally does not affect the entire field. While all these upheavals, elections and depressions are taking place, the exploration of long-past occurrences by historians, the research into ongoing governmental behavior by political scientists, and the model-building by macroeconomists continue to take place. In many cases, moreover, an event that is seemingly external is in fact the product of a process internal to the discipline. The historian's sensational new document is likely to be some moldy set of records that everyone in the office knew was stuffed behind the water heater, but whose significance had gone unrecognized; the archeologist's great find is often some prominent topographic feature, filled with apparent trash, on which the local populace had spent centuries breaking its plows and cutting its feet. In short, although social science varies greatly in its quality of reactivity, it does not seem to be as reactive as legal scholarship.

The pattern of cumulative knowledge in social science is also complex. The field seems to proceed along parallel paths; one can identify a number of different schools in anthropology, psychology, political science, and virtually any other field, that seem to cumulate knowledge among their own advocates, but not with other members of the discipline.[43] The probable explanation is that each discipline contains several different theories of causality. In other words, while all the natural sciences comprise a single discipline, divided into categories only on the basis of their subject matter, every social science field actually consists of multiple disciplines, which share the same subject matter but employ different modes of explanation. Cumulation does occur, but only within each separate school of thought.

In reality, the situation is not as chaotic as it might seem, because theories of causality that proceed for a while in a single field, only to collide with a rival theory or vanish in the thicket, often reappear somewhere else with new-found energy. Thus, the utilitarian, rational-actor view of human beings not only governs much of economics, but also represents a growing trend in political science and anthropology. Marxist dialectical materialism has similarly expanded beyond its economic origins, appearing in virtually every social science field. Less definitive approaches to human behavior also exhibit the same ubiquity; thus, the analysis of cognitive devices for integrating deeply felt emotional experiences crosses such fields as psychology, political science, sociology, anthropology, and history.

Social science is also cumulative in that it has developed a variety of means for the verification or falsification of its hypotheses: structured observation, statistical survey data, laboratory experiments, simulations, and mathematical models are all employed to garner general acceptance for social science propositions. To be sure, the results obtained have not achieved such acceptance, but the really trenchant criticisms are generally directed toward the underlying theory of causality, rather than the method of verification. While some aspects of history, anthropology, or psychology seem closer to the interpretive mode of literary criticism, most social science traditions have demonstrated an ability to cumulate knowledge that is accepted within that tradition, and that serves as a basis for further research.

For the most part, legal scholarship does not display even the fractured cumulativity of the social sciences. It does not divide into subdisciplines whose participants are able to agree upon a theory of causality and a method of verification. Rather, it tends to divide among a variety of normative positions that do not bear any obvious relationship to one another. A feature of recent decades—that is, of the "law and" era—is that many of these positions tend to become linked, or hard-wired, into a particular methodology, for no apparent epistemological reason. Thus, political conservatives have become linked to economics;[44] political progressives to deconstruction,[45] or what Pauline Rosenau calls skeptical post-modernism;[46] race or gender-oriented progressives to constructive postmodernism;[47] political moderates to interpretivism or law and literature.[48] With the exception of law and economics, where one can rely on a rather crisply articulated social science methodology, these separate positions generally do not develop cumulative traditions. They have, however, made normative debate among those with differing affiliations more difficult to sustain.

II. The Methodology of Law

Having thus surveyed legal scholarship's relationship to other disciplines, it is now possible to offer a general characterization of the field. This characterization begins by considering the epistemological status of legal scholarship's distinctively prescriptive stance. The argument, in essence, is that the field is epistemologically coherent because it is a prescriptive practice, not a theoretically-derived category of knowledge. Its distinctiveness as a practice explains why the methodologies of other disciplines cannot be applied in any direct fashion. Additional aspects of the practice, however, specifically its reactivity and involvement, establish a need to seek the aid of other disciplines in characterizing various interactions between law and external phenomena. Not surprisingly, the discipline that holds most promise, given its subject matter, is social science, and current developments in social science seem particularly promising as means of characterizing legally-relevant phenomena. Thus, law is a distinct academic discipline, but it is not an autonomous one.

A. The Nature of Legal Discourse

The defining feature of standard legal scholarship is its prescriptive voice; as shown in the preceding section, it is this feature that distinguishes it from other academic fields. The most important distinction is between this prescriptive voice and the descriptive voice that characterizes natural and social science. As Max Weber perceived, both are modes of discourse that possess their own intrinsic form of rationality,[49] and can thus support an academic discourse.[50] Prescription and description do not appear to be conceptually coherent categories, however. According to most modern theories of knowledge, there is no such thing as pure description.[51] We cannot achieve unmediated contact with reality, or indeed, even conceive of what such contact would consist of. Rather, all our descriptions are theory-laden; they emerge from a vision of the world in which our norms and our beliefs are deeply embedded.

Applied to legal scholarship, this approach suggests that the prescriptions of legal scholarship could not be articulated without a well-developed vision of the entities to which the prescriptions are addressed. This vision presents the legal scholar with the information that renders her prescriptions meaningful. Thus, the scholar's recommendations, albeit normative, are derived from her vision of reality itself, not from some normative theory that exists apart from that reality. We possess a set of beliefs, beliefs that are a product of our culture and our historical position in that culture. Description and prescription are both based on those beliefs; they derive from a basic world view, a "fore-understanding," that cannot be placed in either category. The point is not that there is no reality—that is itself an unprovable metaphysical position and one we obviously do not live by—but that the reality that we perceive is a product of interpretation.

But this does not end the matter, nor does it require us to abandon the perception that the distinction between social science and legal scholarship lies in their use of descriptive or prescriptive discourses. To argue that the distinction cannot be maintained because it cannot be justified in theory assumes that epistemological theory is the only possible source of distinctions among academic disciplines. This seems to deny the very insight that leads to the rejection of the epistemological distinction in the first place—that reality is socially constructed. After all, this insight means only that there is no unmediated access to reality, not that social constructions constitute a single, undifferentiated mass. If a society constructs its image of reality, then it is perfectly capable of constructing a distinction between descriptive and prescriptive academic disciplines as one part of that image. Social science is a separate discipline from law because it perceives itself as separate, and that perception is based on its further perception that it is describing reality. Legal scholarship, by its own account, makes no such claim. To the extent that it describes anything, it describes a human artifact, and its main claim is that it can prescribe alternative approaches.

Social science and legal scholarship, therefore, are not epistemologically-derived positions; rather, they are social practices, ways of speaking about things that are important to us. The fact that they emerge from our system of pre-empirical beliefs makes them meaningful, not invalid.[52] In this context, it becomes possible to reconstruct the distinction that epistemology erases. We know, as a matter of our academic discourse, the difference between description and prescription. We can recognize a statement that purports to tell us how judges actually behave, and we can distinguish it from a statement telling judges how they ought to behave. The distinction is entirely meaningful to us, and because of that, it establishes and maintains the boundaries between two disciplines whose subject matter overlaps. That boundary belongs to the realm of attitude, or belief; rather than separating two theoretically distinguishable disciplines, it separates two disciplines that represent different practices of scholarly endeavor.

The socially constructed distinction between social science and law raises a further question, however. Why have we constructed this distinction, and why do we maintain it? One could, following the methodology of social science itself, provide an institutional explanation and speak of scholars' desire to maintain their cushy jobs, or of the legal profession's need to provide cannon fodder for the capitalist artillery. J.M. Balkin offers precisely such an explanation for law's continued resistance to other disciplines and its continuation as an independent field.[53] Alternatively, one could follow the methodology of law, and ask whether the distinction ought to be maintained as a matter of public policy. Pierre Schiag adopts this approach, arguing that prescriptive scholarship should be abandoned because it contributes to the maintenance of an oppressive political and social regime.[54] The question being asked here, however, is epistemological. Without denying the significance of other explanations, it asks whether there is some additional reason, grounded in the discourse of the disciplines themselves, for the continued distinction between a descriptive and prescriptive approach to government.

In fact, there is such a reason, and it resides in the general structure of an academic discipline. A discipline, as a body of mutually understood intellectual discourse, must involve certain structuring assumptions that define an approach to the world. We think of disciplines in terms of their topics—biologists study living organisms, art historians study paintings, sculpture, and architecture—but reflection indicates that these topics, by themselves, cannot possibly define a field. Every field needs a methodology, and with that methodology comes a basic stance toward its subject matter. The choice between description and prescription is part of that stance.

But this stance does not come unencumbered; in the case of both law and social science, it carries with it major implications about the attitude of these two disciplines toward their common subject matter. Social scientists treat the people they are studying as objects, while legal scholarship treats them as participants, or as a potential audience for their recommendations. Of course, social scientists exhibit a range of attitudes toward their subject matter, and the proper stance is a highly contested issue at the present time. As Weber argued, real understanding of human behavior requires some degree of participation in that behavior by the social scientist.[55] Nonetheless, the point of this participation is to understand the behavior, not to change it, and the aspiration of the social sciences, whatever the level of participation, remains the objective, generalized description of human behavior.[56]

Legal scholarship is distinguished from political science because legal scholarship treats the people it studies as equals, and thus as a proper audience for its prescriptions. The legal scholar is involved with her subject; she speaks directly to that subject, with recommendations about the proper way to make decisions. Of course, she may assert superior knowledge or analytic ability, but she assumes that she is speaking to a person like herself, who can understand and respond to her argument. The aspiration, therefore, is not to be objective, but to be significant and persuasive.[57]

This stance is the source of legal scholarship's particular methodology. While the distinction between "is" and "ought" may have been dissolved at the epistemological level, it is vitally and frustratingly alive in all our theoretical and practical discourses. We have no methodology to move directly from the discourses we perceive as descriptive, such as natural or social science, to decisions about the way to organize our society and the kinds of laws we should establish to effect that organization. Nor does it seem likely that we will be able to develop one. There is no scientific fact about human gestation that is likely to resolve the abortion debate one way or another; there is no analysis of human preferences and macroeconomic structure that is likely to determine how redistributive our economic policies should be. For decisions such as these, we will continue to need methodologies, of which legal scholarship forms one part, that channel normative debate. We need to decide what features of external events are relevant, how consistent with each other our responses to them should be, how these responses should be implemented and which of these responses and means of implementation conform to other norms of public governance.

But the stance of legal scholarship as an academic discourse should not be oversimplified. Participation through recommendation is not only an effort to persuade legal decision-makers, but also an effort to achieve understanding, in the precise sense that Weber used this term. By engaging in an ongoing normative debate about particular decisions, legal scholars achieve an understanding of the issues and the decision-making process of a sort that is simply not available to someone who adopts the stance of social science. Political science analysis of judicial decision-making, for example, tends to treat these decisions as a reflection of the judge's ideological attitude, and to test its conclusions by trying to predict future decisions.[58] But no matter how accurate this analysis may be, it cannot achieve an understanding of the way that judges create, interpret, and deploy legal doctrine. Doctrine is an inherently normative activity, and there are aspects of it that can only be understood by direct involvement in this process. In short, the prescriptive stance of law is not only an effort to influence public decision-makers, but also a mode of understanding, and it should be judged by its insights as well as its influence.

B. The Limits of Legal Discourse

The discursive distinction between description and prescription thus divides law from other disciplines, and establishes it as a distinctive academic methodology. It appears, however, to leave legal scholarship in a worse state than before; no one seems very certain what its separate methodology should be, and it appears as if there is even less reason to hope that other fields might be of assistance in this quandary. By casting doubt on the entire "law and" enterprise, moreover, this conclusion seems to run counter to the most powerful and seemingly promising trend in current legal scholarship.

A partial answer to this question is that there is no reason why the prescriptive discourse of legal scholarship cannot draw on other prescriptive fields, particularly political theory and epistemology. The idea that law is an autonomous discourse, a position associated with formalism, and partially revived by legal process, [59] was never so comprehensive that it would preclude arguments based on political theories such as utilitarianism, egalitarianism, or philosophic liberalism. To these can be added the epistemological theories that have become current in recent years, such as pragmatism, hermeneutics, and discourse ethics. These various approaches, which are general enough to be applied in any field, provide the debates in legal scholarship with a depth and breadth that they would otherwise lack. The epistemological theories represent a particular advance because they add prescriptions based on the possibilities for human understanding to those based on desirable results. In other words, they are process theories, and thus provide the basis for arguments that particular decisions will instantiate values such as human emancipation or the unfolding of our culturally embedded legal principles.

The answer is only partial, however, because these theories, however broadly or abstractly phrased, serve only as particular positions in the ongoing debate, not as a general methodology. More seriously still, the other features of legal scholarship, apart from its prescriptiveness, that emerge from the survey of its relationship to other disciplines suggest that these prescriptive theories leave many questions unaddressed. Legal scholarship, to a much greater extent than natural science, literary criticism, moral philosophy, or social science, is reactive and involved. It is reactive because it responds to external events that are not generated, defined, or given significance by the field itself but by other actors, and it is involved because its prescriptions are addressed to identifiable, external decision-makers.

These intense relationships to external forces suggest that legal scholars need to obtain an understanding of the external events to which they react, and of the effects on such events that their recommendations to legal decision-makers will produce. There is no fully developed theory that addresses this issue, but the traditional answer has been that these understandings can be generated within legal discourse itself. This answer rests on the premise that the events are already characterized in legal terms, and the recommendations will affect decisions that are conceived in those same terms. Thus law is an autonomous discipline; the legal system is closed and self-contained so that it can be fully described by its internally generated discourse. The idea is linked to the further idea that there is a unity of discourse between judges and legal scholars.[60] Because of this shared discourse, legal scholars do not need the methodology to characterize external events or to measure the effects of their predictions; all they need to do is to use the discourse of law that they share with judges.

This traditional position is certainly a familiar one, but it has two extremely serious defects. The first is that it cannot possibly apply to any legal decision-maker other than a judge. Legislators and administrators do not speak or think in the closed discourse of legal doctrine. Typically, theirs is a public policy discourse; they are trying to reach decisions that have desirable social consequences, not ones that fit with, or build upon, existing legal doctrine.[61] If one were to examine the materials that appear before a judge when making his decision, one would typically see a set of oral arguments and briefs asserting that "every legal precedent supports my client's position; there is not a shred of support for the opponent's argument; to accept this argument would involve a radical alteration of the law." These briefs, again typically, would cite positive law and previous decisions of, in order of preference, the court, other courts in the jurisdiction, and other courts in other jurisdictions. But if one were to examine the materials that appear before a legislator, one would find oral arguments and briefs arguing that "my position will produce the following good results, whereas my opponent's would be a disaster for the nation." One might also see at least some survey data, economic projections, or other social science sources. An examination of the materials that administrators use would reveal oral arguments, briefs, and written comments of a similar nature, and a somewhat larger number of surveys and projections. Clearly, legislators and administrators cannot be treated as participating in a self-contained or autonomous legal discourse.

The solution for many legal scholars—one which is not astonishing only because it has become so familiar—is to limit their audience to judges, and thus preserve their ability to remain within the boundaries of legal discourse.[62] This enables legal scholarship to continue without a means of understanding external events or effects, but it does so at a great and ever-increasing price. Modern law is largely created, interpreted, and applied by legislators and administrators; judges are important, but their relative importance has been steadily declining for at least a century.[63] Of course, legal scholars should study judges, and of course there will be some scholars, given the levels of specialization of modern academics, who will focus exclusively on judicial decision-making. Biologists should study one-celled organisms, and some will devote all their efforts to this topic. But for the entire field of legal scholarship to concern itself exclusively with judges, and ignore all the multi-cellular organisms of our governmental system, is to condemn itself to a severely limited perspective, and ultimately to paleozoic irrelevance.

The second serious defect with the traditional approach of treating law as an autonomous discourse is that it is not even a particularly accurate or useful means of relating to judges. Ever since the Brandeis brief, the judiciary's need for information that lies outside the boundaries of legal discourse has been well-recognized. The more administrative our legal system becomes, the more relevant such information will be, because an increasing amount of the judge's efforts will involve interpreting legislative and administrative provisions that were drafted on public policy grounds. One hundred years ago, judges were still the primary creators of the law, and other judges could understand this law within the framework of legal discourse. While judges still create law, legislators and administrators are its primary originators, and a purely legal interpretation will often be an impoverished one. It is possible to construct a theory of interpretation that relies solely on the text of these enactments, as Justice Scalia has,[64] but the result is a profoundly, if intentionally, uncomprehending approach to the material being interpreted. Justice Scalia may assert that he is using a neutral, constitutionally legitimated approach that provides the best interpretation of the text, but he has fooled virtually no one.

C. The Use of Social Science in Legal Discourse

Combining the separate discourse of legal scholarship, the reactive and involved nature of that discourse, and the recognition that the discourse cannot function autonomously, leads to a fairly obvious conclusion: legal scholarship must rely on other disciplines to characterize external events and effects, although it must continue to develop its own methodology for framing its characteristic prescriptions to legal decision-makers. The separate methodology of law is essential, but it is a relatively thin one because of its reactivity and involvement. Thus the "law and" question is crucial, and the recent efforts of legal scholars in shopping among other disciplines has not been misplaced. What is being sought, however, cannot be a methodology for legal scholarship itself, for no other discipline addresses the same issues and adopts the same stance toward them. Rather, the real promise of the "law and" enterprise is that it can provide the characterization of events and effects that legal scholarship is lacking and can no longer aspire to develop.

The crucial question for interdisciplinary legal scholarship, therefore, becomes the simplest one. Other disciplines should not be canvassed for their methodology, but for their subject matter. The most useful discipline will be the one that addresses the same events to which legal scholars react, and the same effects that their recommendations are intended to achieve. Of course, any explanatory force that such a discipline possesses necessarily depends upon its methodology. But the simple, uninteresting conclusion is that legal scholars are not shopping for a methodology, but for a correspondence in subject matter.

Having said this, it is apparent that the discipline to which legal scholars should turn is social science. While some of the internal discourse in the legal field, particularly the creation and development of legal doctrine, lies beyond the reach of social science, virtually all the external events and effects for legal scholarship are well within its ambit. In particular, political science, economics, and sociology are all directly concerned with the events to which legal scholars react, or the effects which their recommendations produce. The value of social science is that it enables legal scholarship to develop realistic models of the law's relationship to society in general; it provides a means of understanding an array of forces and effects that are not explicable within the confines of a prescriptive discourse.[65]

Consider, for example, a typical work of legal scholarship. The Supreme Court has just decided a case interpreting some federal regulatory statute in an unexpected way, and the usual spate of law review articles appears critiquing the decision and recommending an alternative approach. The decision could be analyzed as nothing other than an interpretation of the statutory text, but this would be regarded as a rather retrograde approach these days. Instead, there would be at least some effort to understand the purpose of the statute and the political forces that produced it. This could involve a traditional interest group analysis, or it could employ public choice or positive political theory. In addition, the effects of the Court's decision would need to be considered, and this could involve both political science and economic analysis. All this information would be of great value to the legal scholar in framing a recommendation, although none of it could determine what the recommendation should be. In framing this recommendation, moreover, the effects of the proposal would be a matter of considerable interest, one where political and economic analysis are likely to provide substantial insights. Again, however, the analysis of the results can only provide information; it cannot resolve the underlying question.

This model of law's relationship to social science tracks Weber's model of society in general. Weber distinguished between value rationality (the debate about desirable social norms) and instrumental rationality (the search for the optimal means, as empirically determined) to achieve a predefined end.[66] He believed that instrumental rationality should serve the purposes determined by value rationality. Indeed, being instrumental, it must serve some purpose that is defined by another mode of discourse, and we would be irrational to take it as an end in itself. Weber was concerned that instrumental rationality—the discourse of technology and bureaucracy—would become so dominant a mode of thought that it would preclude or obscure normative inquiry and thus engender this irrationality.[67] In legal scholarship—not surprisingly, for the subject matter of law and social science overlaps—the relationships are the same. The essence of the field is the structured debate about social norms, or value rationality in Weber's terms. Social science is an instrument that enables law to achieve those purposes that this normative debate defines in the most instrumental or empirically valid manner. As such, it has an extremely valid role to play, but should not—it cannot rationally—be taken to resolve the debate about the proper choice of purpose. Thus, social science plays an essential but subordinate role in legal scholarship.

A considerable body of scholarship linking law and social science now exists, and it has begun to display the cumulative quality to which most academic disciplines aspire. There appear, at this point, to be three principal impediments to further progress. First, a lack of clarity about the methodology of legal scholarship itself sometimes generates the claim that a social science discipline, most commonly economics, can definitely resolve legal issues.[68] This is distracting, as distracting as claims from within the discourse of legal scholarship that interpretation of a text can produce such a result. The whole point of legal scholarship is to organize and maintain a normative debate. The distinction between descriptive and prescriptive discourse, socially constructed though it may be, is central to the way we think about these matters. Claims that social science can resolve this debate, rather than merely informing it, serve only to induce hostility to the entire law and social science enterprise among those who do not practice it, while leading its practitioners off the path of further insight with beguiling mirages of normative certainty.

The second impediment to further progress is essentially the converse of the first, and results from the fractured cumulativity of social science. Within any given social science field, different theories of causality contend with one another; this produces lines of cumulative research that proceed on parallel paths, or occasionally run headlong into each other, generating a considerable amount of confusion and debris. Confronted with this chaotic prospect, legal scholars have often been tempted to select social science methodologies that seem to support their own normative position, rather than using social science to clarify the nondoctrinal premises and consequences of that position. Thus, political conservatives have linked themselves to economics, although economics itself can support virtually any position that is currently under discussion by legal scholars. Similarly, political progressives have often embraced post-modernist approaches, although the lessons of postmodernism do not really align with any particular political position either.[69]

The final impediment to the effective use of social science in legal scholarship is more specific, but, until recently, has probably been the most severe. Social science does not seem to provide direct answers to many of the things that legal scholars want to know. Even if one is clear that social science will not resolve a normative debate, and even if one avoids using social science methodologies as an argument in that debate, the relationship of social science to law often seems uncertain. A large part of the reason for this uncertainty lies in what James Coleman calls the macro-micro problem;[70] that is, the problem of developing explanatory accounts that link individual and collective behavior. This is a problem that social science, thus far, has failed to solve, but it is central to the enterprise of legal scholarship. The prescriptive stance of legal scholarship means that it will tend to be addressed to individual decision-makers, or at least structured around the kinds of decisions that individuals make. But virtually all the decisions of legally significant actors occur in an institutional setting—legislatures, government agencies, business firms, or non-commercial private organizations. Individuals acting on their own commit torts and crimes, display deviant behavior, vote, select consumer products, and relate to family members. Social science often studies these behaviors, but these are generally the areas of social science that are most remote from law. Rather, law deals with institutional responses to these behaviors; the individuals whose behavior it addresses are those who frame these responses as part of an organization.

It might appear that there is one vast exception to the principle that legal actors inhabit institutions, that being judges. But, of course, the judiciary is an institution. It possesses collective norms, a hierarchy, an internal structure regulating workload, a boundary controlling information flow, and all the other institutional attributes. It is, however, an institution where many individuals have substantial, and often relatively equal, amounts of discretion, like a law firm or a research laboratory. This, combined with the formalist image of an individual judge deriving his decision from an immediate contemplation of legal texts, has tended to obscure the institutional character of the judiciary.[71] As a result, legal scholars have been less assiduous in seeking social science models for judicial behavior. Social science, in its turn, has not offered much help as a result of the macro-micro problem. It can model the behavior of individuals or the behavior of institutions, but when an institution is primarily composed of semi-independent, discretionary decision-makers, only an account which links both levels will provide a satisfactory image of the totality.

One of the more interesting trends in modern social science has been the development of several separate efforts to address Coleman's macro-micro problem. The first is called "new institutionalism" and emerges from the sociological study of institutions. In essence, it steers a middle path between the personalistic approach of human relations theory, where the institution itself tends to disappear, and the impersonal, mechanistic approach of general systems theory, where the people tend to disappear. In doing so, it builds on Herbert Simon's decision theory,[72] which focuses on the institutional position of the decision-maker—her position in the hierarchy, the information she receives, and the tasks she is expected to accomplish. This approach has been extended and deepened through the analysis of institutional norms and systems of meaning carried out by John Meyer, James March, Johan Olsen, Paul DiMaggio and Walter Powell.[73] It has explored the process by which the belief systems of individuals combine and react to create institutional behaviors.

A second development, called new institutional economics, has emerged at roughly the same time through the work of Douglass North and Oliver Williamson.[74] It is, as its name suggests, an economic analysis, but it breaks with the neoclassic approach that generated standard law and economics by following Simon's idea that people are only boundedly rational;[75] that is, their rationality is limited by the information they receive and their own capacity to process that information. This has been combined with an analysis of norm formation within institutions, and of the transaction costs involved in various institutional arrangements. The goal is to develop a way to explain the behavior of institutions on the basis of the individual's motivational structure.

These efforts promise to provide a social science account of institutional behavior that is particularly useful for legal scholars.[76] In addressing prescriptions to individuals, the most crucial information involves the constraints on that individual's decision-making powers, and the effects that the individual's decision is likely to produce. Of greatest concern, of course, are legal decision-makers—those who create, interpret, and apply legal rules. Since law is both a set of norms and a system of meaning, an account of the decision-maker's relationship to the organization that is phrased in these terms is likely to be particularly useful. None of this will resolve the normative debates that animate legal scholarship. What it might do, however, is to provide a rich empirical context to channel those debates, indicating the range of realistic options and the consequences that will flow from them.

D. The Non-Autonomy of Law

In recent years, two sets of rather interesting, sophisticated arguments have been advanced that, in effect, revive the rather unsophisticated claim that law is an autonomous discourse. The first of these, which may be called the theory of discursive modalities, was developed by Philip Bobbitt in two books about constitutional law,[77] and extended into a general analysis of legal reasoning by Dennis Patterson.[78] As Patterson interprets it, this theory is based upon the epistemology of the later Wittgenstein.[79] The second approach is autopoietic theory, developed by Nicholas Luhmann and Gunther Teubner.[80] It is drawn from continental social theory, specifically the systems theory that Luhmann has developed.[81] Both approaches suggest that legal scholarship possesses its own discourse and cannot profitably borrow empirical insights from social science. Considering them will serve to clarify the contrary assertion that this Article advances.

According to Bobbitt, judicial review in constitutional law is a practice, not a theory. It consists of six forms, or modalities, of argument: historical argument, which relies on the intent of the framers; textual argument, which relies on the language of the Constitution itself; structural argument, which relies on the relationships among constitutional provisions; doctrinal argument, which relies on judicial precedent; ethical argument, which relies on those moral commitments of the American ethos that are reflected in the Constitution; and prudential argument, which "seeks to balance the costs and benefits of a particular rule."[82] A proper, or legitimate legal argument is one that uses these modalities. Thus, searching for a theory that would justify judicial review is meaningless because it depends, in Bobbitt's terminology, on a Langdellian belief that legal propositions are statements "about the world," verifiable in the same way as the propositions of natural science.[83] Instead, law is a normative discourse, part of our social construction of reality. Legal arguments are legitimate to the extent that they are properly articulated within this normative discourse; there is no theory behind these arguments that provides their justification. "If we want to understand the ideological and political commitments in law," Bobbitt writes, "we have to study the grammar of law, that system of logical constraints that the practices of legal activities have developed in our particular culture."[84]

Patterson expands this account into a general theory of legal justification, that is, what makes a statement of law true. His answer is that truth in law is determined by the forms of legal argument, not the correspondence between a legal statement and some external justification. Thus, a proposition of constitutional law, such as "anti-abortion laws violate the Bill of Rights," is validated by arguments that employ one of Bobbitt's six modalities. It is not validated by reference to some external justification, not even the positivist justification of enacted law backed by a rule of recognition.[85] As Patterson states, "the positivist conceives of law as a matter of certain (social or institutional) facts, which can then be used in the same manner as scientific propositions (e.g., confirmation). But law is not as the positivist supposes (i.e., akin to science). The truth of a proposition of law is the product of an activity (justification) and is not a matter of correspondence between a proposition and a social fact."[86]

This theory of discursive modalities addresses law in general, not legal scholarship, and neither Bobbitt nor Patterson focuses on the use of social science in law. Nonetheless, there is at least a mood, and perhaps an implication, in their work that legal discourse can function autonomously, that is, using arguments that are internal to the legal system. As a corollary, arguments that are not part of that system only become relevant if translated into legal terms.

To a considerable extent, the theory of legal scholarship presented in this Article is in agreement with Bobbitt's and Patterson's approach. Because legal scholarship is prescriptive, because it belongs within the general realm of the normative, it is indeed the case that other methodologies, specifically those designed to describe the physical or social world, cannot resolve the issues that are at stake in legal scholarship. On the other hand, legal scholarship affirmatively needs to use these methodologies to characterize events and measure effects that are external to the legal system. It is in this area that the theory of discursive modalities requires clarification.

Although Bobbitt relies on the social construction of reality to distinguish between legal propositions and empirical statements, his own approach to legal discourse is somewhat positivistic, in the epistemological sense.[87] He approaches legal discourse as an observer, rather than a participant, and asks about its form or structure rather than its meaning. But if one focuses on meaning—that is, what the actors think that they themselves are doing—a discontinuity appears in his list of modalities. Five of the six, namely, the historical, textual, structural, doctrinal, and ethical, are methods of interpreting legal texts, in Bobbitt's case the Constitution. The sixth, prudential, does not involve interpretation of a text, but the consideration of nontextual matters, such as the social costs and benefits of particular decisions.[88] Traditionally, we think of legislators and administrators as making these kinds of arguments, while we think of judges as interpreting texts. That is wrong, however; legislators and administrators regularly interpret texts, and judges regularly make public policy, that is, reach conclusions on a prudential basis, and not on the basis of a text.[89] There has, however, been a good deal of discomfort with this judicial function, and a tendency to exclude it from the range of legitimate judicial discourse.

Bobbitt's first five modalities, which are all recognizably ways of interpreting a text, can be accurately described as internal to the legal system; all of them, even the historical modality, are methods that lawyers and law professors have developed and that comprise part of the recognized methodology of legal argument. The sixth modality, however, depends heavily on methodologies external to the law, specifically those of social science. By melding this essentially non-legal mode of discourse into his list of modalities, Bobbitt creates the impression that legal discourse is much more comprehensive than our ordinary understanding would suggest. In fact, this discourse is essentially limited to a particular kind of normative debate linked to a particular kind of textual analysis. It stops short at precisely the point where empirical, or prudential, considerations are perceived as relevant. To incorporate these considerations, traditional legal methodology is not sufficient, and both legal actors and legal scholars must have recourse to social science. This is the source of the discomfort we experience when judges, who are not traditionally regarded as policymakers, use prudential arguments like cost-benefit analysis.

Bobbitt and Patterson also convey the sense that legal discourse is more comprehensive, and more autonomous, than it is generally perceived to be by describing it as a practice. While the characterization itself is a persuasive one, it is important to avoid attributing excessive content or significance to the concept. To say that law or legal scholarship is a practice is to anchor it in intersubjective or cultural conditions, rather than in strong epistemological claims of validity. But this does not determine the content of the discourse or its relationship to other discourses. Such determinations require a separate theory about the way that discourses relate to one another.

As a first approximation, we can distinguish among discourses that are closed to unmediated inputs and outputs, discourses that are open to unmediated inputs, discourses that are open to unmediated outputs, and discourses that are open to both unmediated inputs and outputs. To be open to an unmediated input or output means that the validity of some proposition within the discourse is determined by a proposition that lies outside it. If the proposition outside the discourse generates the proposition within it, the proposition outside the discourse is an input; if the proposition outside the discourse is determined by a proposition within the discourse, the proposition outside the discourse is an output.

Mathematics is an example of a truly closed or autonomous discourse. External events do not serve as inputs that determine its developments; information must be mediated or restated in mathematic terms in order to be relevant. Similarly, the application of a mathematical proposition to other fields, though obviously of interest, does not affect the truth of that proposition; the mathematical validity of imaginary numbers, for example, is not affected by their subsequently-discovered use in modeling electro-magnetic fields. Literary criticism, in contrast, is open to inputs, but not outputs; for most branches of criticism non-literary facts about the author's biography or culture serve as inputs that are relevant to the validity of various propositions.[90] But the usefulness of a literary critic's argument outside the realm of literature is generally not regarded as affecting its validity. Consequentialist ethics may be thought of as a field open only to outputs.[91]

Legal scholarship, however, has a dual openness, at least with respect to policy issues; social science insights about external events help determine the validity of many propositions, so it is open to inputs, while social science insights about the effects of legal propositions help determine their validity, and represent the field's openness to outputs. This suggests that Bobbitt's and Patterson's categorical statements that legal propositions are only arguments, and not statements about the world, need to be modified, or at least clarified. Because of its dual openness in the policy area, some legal propositions really are statements about the world, even if they also function as legal arguments. Many legal scholars, for example, believe that a legal rule is not valid if it produces certain nonlegal consequences;[92] for example, general rules about the enforceability of contracts are invalid if they increase inequalities in wealth.

The tendency to treat practices as autonomous, that is, closed to both inputs and outputs, may stem from a mischaracterization of the basic concept. Alasdair MacIntyre, in one of the seminal modern works about the concept of a practice, uses the game of chess as an example of a practice.[93] But chess is an example of one particular type of practice, namely games. While the concept of play in general may be broader,[94] the term "game" generally refers to a type of practice that involves play and that is closed to both inputs and outputs. That is what makes it a game. No external event affects professional baseball in an unmediated way, and more significantly, the results of any baseball game do not have any direct consequences outside the game. But this is not true of other, non-game practices, like law or politics. It is cute to describe national elections as a game, but the election process, like law, possesses a dual openness; it is directly affected by many non-electoral events, and, of course, it has many direct external consequences. In other words, there are different kinds of social practices; the mere fact that something is a practice does not, contrary to MacIntyre, tell us anything about the practice's relationship to other practices. The language of Bobbitt's and Patterson's work seems to imply that social practices are necessarily closed, but their work need not be read this way, and it is preferable not to do so.

A second analysis that suggests the autonomy of law, in this case quite explicitly, is the autopoietic theory of Luhmann and Teubner. While the theory is far too sophisticated to allow for rapid summary, the basic idea is that society in general is a self-regulating system of communication. Certain fields within society can become, in their turn, specialized, self-regulating sub-systems. As Teubner says, these sub-systems "have constituted autonomous units of communication which are self-reproductive. They produce their own elements, structures, processes, and boundaries. They construct their own environment and define their own identity."[95] Such sub-systems are "operationally closed, but cognitively open to the environment."[96] This means that the legal system responds to that external phenomena, but not directly; rather it constructs an internal model of these phenomena. External phenomena function as disturbances to the legal system that induce it to develop, or alter, this internal model.

Teubner points out that it is relatively easy to describe conflict resolution, which is closely allied to the judicial interpretation of texts, as an autopoietic system.[97] Legislation presents a more difficult case, but his analysis suggests that economic legislation does not control "the economy"; rather, it controls legal actors whose effect on economic systems is uncertain. Thus, the legal system does not affect the economy directly but "observes itself" making certain changes in response to a disturbance.[98] The effect is an indirect one because law and external phenomena exist on different ontological levels. There is thus a clear connection between this theory and the Bobbitt-Patterson theory of discursive modalities.

Although Luhmann and Teubner sometimes suggest that law is necessarily autopoietic, most of their argument is empirical, not theoretical. They demonstrate convincingly that law, even regulatory law, can be autopoietic, but not that it must be. In fact, law often possesses this quality; legislators rely on testimony, lobbyists' arguments, and various alternative views, rather than social science data, in drafting a statute, and they look to judicial decisions, rather than systematic evaluations, to gauge the statute's effects. But this is a defect in the legislative process; it produces bad law. It is also possible for legislators to rely on real data, to evaluate the performance of their enactments, and thus to link the legal system with other modes of social discourse.

Legal scholars, being less constrained than legal actors, can facilitate this process. While they can be part of an autopoietic legal system, they need not be. Instead, they can make direct use of social science to understand the events that affect the legal system and to measure the effects of the legal system on external phenomena. By doing so, they can frame prescriptions that reflect a deeper understanding of the system, and that may be particularly useful to legal actors. Legal scholars would indeed be playing an influential and valuable role if they could penetrate the system's dysfunctional and somewhat old-fashioned autopoieticism.

The apparent link between autopoieticism and closure comes from attributing too much content or significance to the idea of self-regulating social sub systems. In a complex, sophisticated society such as ours, these sub-systems can take many forms. If the participants in a system can create a boundary, they can also penetrate that boundary; if they can establish an autonomous discourse, they can also reestablish a discourse that incorporates relevant findings from other fields. The new institutionalism suggests the complexity of social institutions, and the multiplicity of levels on which they operate; new institutional economics suggests that individuals can strategize against constraints, as well as be limited by them. Legal scholars are capable of penetrating the boundaries of legal discourse, and using social science where it offers direct and useful insights for the study of law. They may even be capable of teaching other legal actors how to carry out this process.

III. Conclusion

The purpose of this article is both cautionary and hortatory. It suggests that the "law and" enterprise should be approached with caution. While other fields may produce many beguiling insights, they cannot supply standard legal scholarship with a methodology. The contingently prescriptive stance this scholarship adopts is simply different from the descriptive stance of natural or social science, the interpretive stance of literary criticism, or the categorically prescriptive stance of moral philosophy. Given the methodological quandaries of contemporary legal scholarship, this appears to be bad news.

However, some of legal scholarship's most serious quandaries do not stem from its prescriptive character, but from its engagement with events and effects that lie outside the field. Here, "law and" can be particularly valuable because other fields provide a way of understanding these events and effects. The most useful fields are the ones whose subject matter overlaps with that of law and legal scholarship—most obviously social sciences such as economics, political science, and sociology. Of course, these fields suffer from their own discontents, and they cannot offer definite solutions to the debates which animate existing legal scholarship. Nonetheless, they have already generated a range of interesting results, and the current directions of these fields offer further possibilities.

NOTES

1. See, e.g., Charles W. Collier, *Interdisciplinary Legal Scholarship in Search of a Paradigm*, 42 DUKE L.J. 840 (1993); Robert Post, *Legal Scholarship and the Practice of Law*, 63 U. COLO. L. REV. 615 (1992); Geoffrey Miller, *A Rhetoric of Law*, 52 U. CHI. L. REV. 247 (1985) (reviewing JAMES BOYD WHITE, WHEN WORDS LOSE THEIR MEANING: CONSTITUTIONS AND RECONSTITUTIONS OF LANGUAGE, CHARACTER, AND COMMUNITY (1984)).

2. NIKLAS LUHMANN, SOCIAL SYSTEMS 437-88 (John Bednarz, Jr. trans., 1995); Nikias Luhmann, *The Unity of the Legal System*, *in* AUTOPOIETIC LAW: A NEW APPROACH TO LAW AND SOCIETY 12 (Gunther Teubner ed., 1987).

3. GUNTHER TEUBNER, LAW AS AN AUTOPOIETIC SYSTEM (Zenon Bankowski ed. Anne Bankowski & Ruth Adler trans., 1993); Gunther Teubner, *Evolution of Autopoietic Law in* AUTOPOIETIC LAW, *supra* note 2, at 217.

4. PHILIP BOBBITT, CONSTITUTIONAL INTERPRETATION (1991).

5. DENNIS PATTERSON, LAW AND TRUTH (1996).

6. See Paul Brest, *The Fundamental Rights Controversy. The Essential Contradictions of Normative Constitutional Scholarship*, 90 YALE L.J. 1063, 1067-89 (1981); William Eskridge & Gary Peller, *The New Public Law Movement: Moderation as a Postmodern Cultural Form*, 89 MICH. L. REV. 707, 746-58 (1991); George Fletcher, *Two Modes of Legal Thought*, 90 YALE L.J. 970, 995 (1981); Edward L. Rubin, *The Practice and Discourse of Legal Scholarship*, 86 MICH. L. REV. 1835, 1847-53 (1988); Pierre Schlag, *Normativity and the Politics of Form*, 139 U. PA. L. REV. 801 (1991); Mark Tushnet, *Legal Scholarship: Its Causes and Cure*, 90 YALE L.J. 1205, 1208-15 (1981).

7. In this article, the term "prescription" is used as a sub-category of "normative"; a prescriptive statement is a normative statement addressed to a specific person or group of persons, like judges, or Americans, or women, as opposed to human beings in general. This terminology is adopted for convenience only, and no part of the argument turns on it.

8. *E.g.*, JOSEPH RAZ, THE AUTHORITY OF LAW: ESSAYS ON LAW AND MORALITY (1979); JOSEPH RAZ, THE CONCEPT OF A LEGAL SYSTEM: AN INTRODUCTION TO THE THEORY OF A LEGAL SYSTEM (1970).

9. *E.g.*, RONALD DWORKIN, FREEDOM'S LAW: THE MORAL READING OF THE AMERICAN CONSTITUTION (1996) [hereinafter DWORKIN, FREEDOM'S LAW]; RONALD DWORKIN, LAW'S EMPIRE (1986) [hereinafter DWORKIN, LAW'S EMPIRE].

10. See Thomas Grey, *Langdell's Orthodoxy*, 45 U. PITT. L. REV. 1 (1983); Dennis Patterson, *Langdell's Legacy*, 90 NW. U. L. REV. 196 (1995). As Patterson points out, Langdell did not really use the methodology of natural science. He certainly claimed he did, however.

11. Frances J. Mootz III, *Desperately Seeking Science*, 73 WASH. U.L.Q. 1009 (1995).

12. See ERNEST NAGEL, THE STRUCTURE OF SCIENCE: PROBLEMS IN THE LOGIC OF SCIENTIFIC EXPLANATION (1961); KARL POPPER, THE LOGIC OF SCIENTIFIC DISCOVERY (1959). This view of the working premises of science is shared by its critics. See MARTIN HEIDEGGER, *The Question Concerning Technology*, *in* BASIC WRITINGS FROM BEING AND TIME TO THE TASK OF THINKING 319 (David Krell ed., 1976); EDMUND HUSSERL, THE CRISIS OF THE EUROPEAN SCIENCES AND TRANSCENDENTAL PHENOMENOLOGY: AN INTRODUCTION TO PHENOMENOLOGICAL PHILOSOPHY 3-84 (David Car trans., 1970). Recent developments in particle physics seem to challenge this view of reality, see NIELS BOHR, ATOMIC PHYSICS AND HUMAN KNOWLEDGE (1958), but do not alter either the methodology of science or, for present purposes, the more important principle that the observations, though they may be affected by the observer, are not determined by conscious human effort.

13. See generally IMRE LAKATOS, THE METHODOLOGY OF SCIENTIFIC RESEARCH PROGRAMMES (1978).

14. Ronald Collins & David Skover, *The Future of Liberal Legal Scholarship*, 87 MICH. L. REV. 189 (1988). See BRUCE ACKERMAN, RECONSTRUCTING AMERICAN LAW 24-28 (1984). These uses of the term "reactive" are related, although not identical, to its use here.

15. It was this model of cumulative knowledge, for example, that served as the basis of Comte's effort to create a science of society. See AUGUSTE COMTE, A SYSTEM OF POSITIVE PHILOSOPHY (1875-77).

16. THOMAS KUHN, THE STRUCTURE OF SCIENTIFIC REVOLUTIONS (2d ed. 1970). There is much to be said for his theory, particularly because the view of science it attacks is so appealing that it cannot possibly be right. But, as critics have pointed out, Kuhn ultimately overstates his ease; the scientific revolutions he observes may represent important shifts in scientists' perception of the world, but the nature of the scholarly discourse allows these changes to be rather quickly assimilated by the discipline, without any major discontinuities in either its ongoing program or its sociological structure. See JAMES HARRIS, AGAINST RELATIVISM (1992); LAKATOS, *supra* note 13, at 8-101; HARVEY SIEGEL, RELATIVISM REFUTED: A CRITIQUE OF CONTEMPORARY EPISTEMOLOGICAL RELATIVISM (1987); Margaret Masterman, *The Nature of a Paradigm*, in CRITICISM AND THE GROWTH OF KNOWLEDGE 59 (Imre Lakatos & Alan Musgrave eds., 1970) [hereinafter CRITICISM]; Stephen Toulmin, *Does the Distinction Between Normal and Revolutionary Science Hold Water?* in CRITICISM, *supra*, at 39. Paradigm shifts seem to represent major revisions, rather than wholesale transformations. Their existence indicates that the cumulation of scientific knowledge is not a smooth progression, but an irregular succession of advances, retrenchments, wrong turns, and frustrating impasses.

17. Whether this is because scientists are in the process of determining the true nature of the real world, or because they have managed to project a self-persuasive pattern on the aleatory phenomena that their experiments produce, remains a matter of debate. See PAUL FEYERABEND, AGAINST METHOD (1974); KUHN, *supra* note 16; LAKATOS, *supra* note 13; BRUNO LATOUR, THE PASTEURIZATION OF FRANCE (Alan Sherdan & John Law trans., 1988); NAGEL, *supra* note 12; POPPER, *supra* note 12; HILARY PUTNAM, REASON, TRUTH AND HISTORY (1981).

18. See e.g., RONALD DWORKIN, *How Law Is Like Literature*, *in* A MATTER OF PRINCIPLE 146 (1982); JAMES BOYD WHITE, WHEN WORDS LOSE THEIR MEANING (1984); Ronald Dworkin, *Law as Interpretation*, 60 TEX. L. REV. 527 (1982); Sanford Levinson,

Law as Literature, 60 TEX. L. REV. 373 (1982); Richard Weisberg, *Theory into Text: A Literary Approach to the Constitution*, 20 GA. L. REV. 939 (1986).

19. See RICHARD A. POSNER, LAW AND LITERATURE: A MISUNDERSTOOD RELATION (1988); Robert Weisberg, *The Law-Literature Enterprise*, 1 YALE J.L. & HUMAN. 1 (1988); Robin West, *Adjudication Is Not Interpretation: Some Reservations About the Law and Literature Movement*, 54 TENN. L. REV. 203 (1987).

20. For a contrasting view, see Sanford Levinson & J.M. Balkin, *Law, Music and Other Performing Arts*, 139 U. PA. L. REV. 1597 (1991). The authors make a persuasive case for the lessons that other disciplines can teach, but these lessons operate at a very general level; in essence, they convey a postmodern mood. It is not clear that these other disciplines can provide law with a methodology.

21. There are, of course, subjects of legal scholarship where the sense of involvement is lacking, such as the law of Ancient Rome or of modern Saudi Arabia. It is in these situations that legal scholarship loses the prescriptive quality that characterizes its standard version, and becomes more similar to a literary interpretation of texts.

22. See, e.g., TERRY EAGLETON, LITERARY THEORY: AN INTRODUCTION 1-16 (1983); STANLEY FISH, IS THERE A TEXT IN THIS CLASS? 147-73 (1980); FRANK KERMODE, THE CLASSIC LITERARY IMAGES OF PERMANENCE AND CHANGE (1975).

23. MARTIN BUBER, I AND THOU (2d ed. 1958).

24. WHITE, *supra* note 18.

25. Dworkin, *supra* note 18.

26. STANLEY FISH, DOING WHAT COMES NATURALLY: CHANGE, RHETORIC, AND THE PRACTICE OF THEORY IN LITERARY AND LEGAL STUDIES (1989); Stanley Fish, *Anti-Professionalism*, 7 CARDOZO L. REV. 645 (1986).

27. *E.g.*, DAVID COUZENS HOY, THE CRITICAL CIRCLE: LITERATURE, HISTORY, AND PHILOSOPHICAL HERMENEUTICS (1978); RICHARD PALMER, HERMENEUTICS 194-253(1969).

28. *E.g.*, HENRY LOUIS GATES, BLACK LITERATURE AND LITERARY THEORY(1984); ARNOLD KRUPAT, ETHNOCENTRISM: ETHNOLOGY, HISTORY, LITERATURE (1992); ELAINE SHOWALTER, A LITERATURE OF THEIR OWN: BRITISH WOMEN NOVELISTS FROM BRONTE TO LESSING (1977); ERLENE STETSON, BLACK SISTER: POETRY BY BLACK AMERICAN WOMEN, 1746-1980 (1981).

29. But *cf.* Francis J. Mootz 111, *Legal Classics: After Deconstructing the Legal Canon*, 72 N.C. L. REV. 977 (1994). Mootz points to decisions such as Hadley v. Baxendale, 156 Eng. Rep. 145 (Ex. Ch. 1854), as constituting a canon of texts that possess "the progenitive force behind a public discourse and continues as the focal point for a shared effort to define social identity." *Id.* at 1035. While certain common law cases that play this role gained their prominence from legal scholarship, most such cases, and usually all constitutional cases, statutory cases, statutes, and regulations have been forced down the canon's throat by their own self-declared significance.

30. *E.g.*, ALAN DONAGAN, THE THEORY OF MORALITY (1977); ALAN GEWIRTH, REASON AND MORALITY (1978); R.M. HARE, FREEDOM AND REASON (1963).

31. *E.g.*, MARK JOHNSON, MORAL IMAGINATION: IMPLICATIONS OF COGNITIVE SCIENCE FOR ETHICS (1993); ALASDAIR MACINTYRE, AFTER VIRTUE: A STUDY IN MORAL THEORY (2d ed. 1985) [MACINTYRE, AFTER VIRTUE]; ALASDAIR MACINTYRE, WHOSE JUSTICE? WHICH RATIONALITY? (1988); J.L. MACKIE, ETHICS: INVENTING RIGHT AND WRONG (1977); HILARY PUTNAM, REALISM WITH A HUMAN FACE 135-213(1990); MARTHA C. NUSSBAUM, THE FRAGILITY OF GOODNESS: LUCK AND ETHICS IN GREEK TRAGEDY AND PHILOSOPHY (1986); MICHAEL J. SANDEL, LIBERALISM AND THE LIMITS OF JUSTICE (1982); SAMUEL SCHEFFLER, HUMAN MORALITY (1992); BERNARD WILLIAMS, ETHICS AND THE LIMITS OF PHILOSOPHY (1985).

32. *E.g.*, JOHN FINNIS, NATURAL LAW AND NATURAL RIGHTS (1980); Michael Moore, *Moral Reality*, 1982 WIS. L. REV. 1061; Michael S. Moore, *Moral Reality Revisited*, 90 MICH. L. REV. 2424 (1992).

33. See DWORKIN, FREEDOM'S LAW, *supra* note 9; DWORKIN, LAW'S EMPIRE, *supra* note 9; RONALD DWORKIN, TAKING RIGHTS SERIOUSLY (1977).

34. Francis J. Mootz III, *Law and Philosophy, Philosophy and Law*, 26 U. TOL.L. REV. 127 (1994).

35. IMMANUEL KANT, GROUNDING FOR THE METAPHYSICS OF MORALS (James W. Ellington trans., 3d ed. 1993). Kant, of course, took the position that morality was descriptive of human reason, but see RICHARD ELDRIDGE, ON MORAL PERSONHOOD: PHILOSOPHY, LITERATURE, CRITICISM, AND SELF-UNDERSTANDING (1989), but his distinction is equally applicable to moral theories based on judgment.

36. One possible exception is legal ethics, where scholars actively debate whether moral philosophy applies, see e.g., DAVID LUBAN, LAWYERS AND JUSTICE (1988); Susan G. Kupfer, *Authentic Legal Practices*, 10 GEO. J. LEGAL ETHICS 33 (1996); Deborah Rhode, *Ethical Perspectives on Legal Practice*, 37 STAN. L. REV. 589 (1985); Richard Wasserstrom, *Lawyers as Professionals: Some Moral Issues*, 5 HUM. RTS. 1 (1975), or whether the only significant issues involve specialized professional norms, see, e.g., MONROE FREEDMAN, UNDERSTANDING LAWYER'S ETHICS (1990); Stephen Ellman, *Lawyers and Clients*, 34 UCLA L. REV. 717 (1987); Stephen L. Pepper, *The Lawyer's Amoral Ethical Role: A Defense, A Problem and Some Possibilities*, 1986 AM. B. FOUND.RIIS. J. 613; William Simon, *Ethical Discretion in Lawyering*, 101 HARV. L. REV. 1083(1988); David Wilkins, *Two Paths to the Mountaintop? The Role of Legal Education in Shaping the Values of Black Corporate Lawyers*, 45 STAN. L. REV. (1993). This debate, however, highlights the distinction between moral philosophy and legal scholarship, since it is restricted to one set of issues, and is quite distinct from the majority of standard legal scholarship.

37. See ARTHUR O. LOVEJOY, THE GREAT CHAIN OF BEING: A STUDY OF THE HISTORY OF AN IDEA (1936); BERTRAND RUSSELL; RELIGION AND SCIENCE (1935); NINIAN SMART, PHILOSOPHERS AND RELIGIOUS TRUTH (1964).

38. For efforts to reconstruct these notions, to a limited extent, see TEILHARD CHARDIN, THE PHENOMENON OF MAN (Berdard Wall trans., 1959); LECOMTE DU NOUY, HUMAN DESTINY (1947).

39. See PETER WINCH, THE IDEA OF A SOCIAL SCIENCE 1-14 (2d ed. 1990).

40. *E.g.*, PETER M. BLAU, INEQUALITY AND HETEROGENEITY: A PRIMITIVE THEORY OF SOCIAL STRUCTURE (1977); GEORGE CASPAR HOMANS, SOCIAL BEHAVIOR: ITS ELEMENTARY FORMS (rev. ed. 1974); ROBERT K. MERTON, SOCIAL THEORY AND SOCIAL STRUCTURE (3d ed. 1968); PETER C. ORDESHOOK, A POLITICAL THEORY PRIMER(1992); TALCOTT PARSONS, THE STRUCTURE OF SOCIAL ACTION (1968); TALCOTT PARSONS & NEIL J. SMELSER, ECONOMY AND SOCIETY (1956); OLIVER E. WILLIAMSON, THE MECHANISMS OF GOVERNANCE (1996).

41. *E.g.*, ZYGMUNT BAUMAN, INTIMATIONS OF POSTMODERNITY (1992); CLIFFORD GEERTZ, THE INTERPRETATION OF CULTURES (1973); MAX HORKHEIMER, CRITICAL THEORY (Matthew J. O'Connell et. al. trans., 1972); MICHAEL POLANYI, PERSONAL KNOWLEDGE (1962); ALFRED SCHUTZ, COLLECTED PAPERS; WINCH, *supra* note 39.

42. See generally AARON WILDAVSKY, SPEAKING TRUTH TO POWER: THE ART AND CRAFT OF POLICY ANALYSIS (1979); Austin Sarat & Susan Silbey, *The Pull of the Policy Audience*, 10 LAW & POL'Y 97 (1988).

43. For a description, see SOCIAL THEORY TODAY (Anthony Giddens & Jonathan Turner eds., 1987) (describing ten different approaches).

44. See ALAN S. BLINDER, HARD HEADS, SOFT HEARTS: TOUGH-MINDED ECONOMICS FOR A JUST SOCIETY (1987).

45. See J.M. Balkin, Deconstructive Practice and Legal Theory, 96 YALE L.J. 743 (1987); John Stick, *Can Nihilism Be Pragmatic?*, 100 HARV. L. REV. 332 (1986).

46. PAULINE M. ROSENAU, POST-MODERNISM AND THE SOCIAL SCIENCES 14-17,138-66 (1992).

47. Edward L. Rubin, *The New Legal Process, the Synthesis of Discourse, and the Microanalysis of Institutions*, 109 HARV. L. REV. 1393 (1996).

48. See Eskridge & Peller, *supra* note 6; Anthony T. Kronman, *Alexander Bickel's Philosophy of Prudence*, 94 YALE L.J. 1567 (1985).

49. MAX WEBER, ECONOMY AND SOCIETY 3-26 (Gunther Roth & Claus Wittich eds., 1978).

50. If one also includes the distinction between prescriptive discourse and the interpretive discourse of literary criticism, the resulting categorization then resembles Habermas' tripartite division of the forms of communicative action. 1 JÜRGEN HABERMAS, THE THEORY OF COMMUNICATIVE ACTION, 273-337 (Thomas McCarthy trans., 1983). Habermas attaches considerable significance to these distinctions, but his argument depends upon some complex claims about the nature of speech that are debatable and, for many people, counterintuitive.

51. See PETER L. BERGER & THOMAS LUCKMANN, THE SOCIAL CONSTRUCTION OF REALITY: A TREATISE IN THE SOCIOLOGY OF KNOWLEDGE (1966); HANS-GEORG GADAMER, TRUTH AND METHOD 235-341, 397-447 (Garrett Barden & John Cumming eds., 1975); NELSON GOODMAN, WAYS OF WORLDMAKING (1978); MARTIN HEIDEGGER, BEING AND TIME 188-210 (John Macquarrie & Edward Robinson trans., 1962); PUTNAM, *supra* note 17; W.V. QUINE, FROM A LOGICAL POINT OF VIEW (1953); RICHARD RORTY, PHILOSOPHY AND THE MIRROR OF NATURE (1979); WINCH, *supra* note 39.

52. Stephen Feldman makes this same point in response to J.M. Balkin regarding substantive values such as justice. Stephen M. Feldman, *The Politics of Postmodern Jurisprudence*, 95 MICH. L. REV. 166 (1996).

53. J.M. Balkin, *Interdisciplinarity as Colonization*, 53 WASH. & LEE L. REV. 949 (1996).

54. Schlag, *supra* note 6. Schlag's analysis is discussed below, at text accompanying notes 60-65.

55. WEBER, *supra* note 49, at 4-13. See also CLIFFORD GEERTZ, THE INTERPRETATION OF CULTURES (1973).

56. Given the preceding point about our theory-laden vision of reality, it might seem that the notion of an objective description must be meaningless, but that is not the case. Objectivity, like pure description, can be a characteristic of a scholarly practice, even if it is not possible as an epistemological position. The mere fact that one must make some assumptions to create a discipline, or to think at all, does not mean that there is no difference in making additional assumptions. Assuming that causality operates and asserting that the Democrats are right about employment policy represent two different levels of analysis. The existence of causality is an assumption we all share, and that only becomes an issue in the academic discourse of philosophy. The correctness of the Democrats is very much a matter of current debate within our society. It is meaningful to be objective, or neutral, about such contested issues, even if one must rely on general but contestable assumptions or beliefs to do so.

57. Jules Coleman and Brian Leiter argue that judges are capable of achieving "modest objectivity" and should be evaluated on that basis. Jules L. Coleman & Brian Leiter, *Determinacy, Objectivity and Authority*, 142 U. PA. L. REV. 549, 620-25 (1993). Modest objectivity is defined as a judgment that the entire community would reach under ideal epistemic conditions. This is somewhat related to Habermas' position in his recent analysis of law and democracy. JÜRGEN HABERMAS, BETWEEN FACTS AND NORMS (William Rehg trans., 1996). However, the concept describes the methodology of judicial decision-making, not the methodology of scholarship. Scholars often argue that judicial decisions, although "objective" in the sense described, are wrong according to some other standard. But even if they do not invoke another standard, and instead use the one Coleman and Leiter propose, they are not striving for the kind of objectivity that the judge is striving for. Rather, they are evaluating the judge's effort to be objective, using criteria that lie outside the judge's decision-making framework (e.g., is there really a consensus, were the conditions ideal, did the judge get it right?).

58. See, e.g., GLENDON SCHUBERT, THE JUDICIAL MIND: THE ATTITUDES AND IDEOLOGIES OF SUPREME COURT JUSTICES, 1946-1963 (1965); GLENDON SCHUBERT, QUANTITATIVE ANALYSIS OF JUDICIAL BEHAVIOR (1959); JEFFREY SEGAL & HAROLD SPAETH, THE SUPREME COURT AND THE ATTITUDINAL MODEL (1993); HAROLD SPAETH, SUPREME COURT POLICY MAKING (1979).

59. For discussion of this phenomenon, see ACKERMAN, *supra* note 14, at 6-22; ROBERTO M. UNGER, THE CRITICAL LEGAL STUDIES MOVEMENT 5-14 (1983); Richard A. Posner, *The Decline of Law as an Autonomous Discipline*, 100 HARV. L. REV. 76 1-66 (1987).

60. Rubin, *supra* note 6, at 1881-86.

61. For a fuller discussion of this mode of judicial decision-making, see MALCOLM FEELEY & EDWARD RUBIN, JUDICIAL POLICYMAKING AND THE MODERN STATE: HOW THE COURTS REFORMED AMERICA'S PRISONS (forthcoming 1998).

62. See Collier, *supra* note 1; Donald H. Gjerdingen, *The Future of Our Past: The Legal Mind and the Legacy of Classical Common-Law Thought*, 68 IND. L.J. 743 (1993); Edward L. Rubin, *The Concept of Law and the New Public Law Scholarship*, 89 MICH. L. REV. 792 (1991).

63. See GUIDO CALABRESI, A COMMON LAW FOR THE AGE OF STATUTES (1982); JAMES M. LANDIS, THE ADMINISTRATIVE PROCESS (1938).

64. *E.g.*, Kaiser Aluminum & Chem. Corp. v. Bonjorno, 494 U.S. 827, 857 (1990) (Scalia, J., concurring); K Mart Corp. v. Cartier, Inc., 486 U.S. 281, 324-25 (1988) (Scalia, J., concurring in part, dissenting in part); INS v. Cardoza-Fonseca, 480 U.S. 421, 452-53 (1987) (Scalia, J., concurring in the judgment). See William N. Eskridge, Jr., *The New Textualism*, 37 UCLA L. REV, 621 (1990); Michael J. Gerhardt, *A Tale of Two Textualists: A Critical Comparison of Justices Black and Scalia*, 74 B.U. L. REV. 25 (1994); William D. Popkin, *An "Internal" Critique of Justice Scalia 's Theory of Statutory Interpretation*, 76 MINN. L. REV. 1133 (1992).

65. This account can be contrasted with Jack Balkin's lively discussion of interdisciplinary studies as colonization. Balkin, *supra* note 53, adopts the positivist, external stance toward legal scholarship that is typical of traditional social science. This point of view is revealed in the metaphors he employs, such as interdisciplinary studies as colonization, academic methodologies as cultural software, the survival of different methodologies as Darwinian evolution and interdisciplinary scholars as "turncoats and invaders." *Id.* at 955-56, 960-62. The present article, in contrast, adopts an internal, phenomenological perspective toward legal scholarship, and tries to understand the meaning of the field, and its interdisciplinary efforts, for those scholars who are involved in it. Balkin's account represents an illuminating, if somewhat traditional, perspective; to the extent that he implies that it is the exclusive account—that legal scholarship has no meaning for its participants—it is highly implausible.

66. WEBER, *supra* note 49, at 3-26.

67. See MAX WEBER, THE PROTESTANT ETHIC AND THE SPIRIT OF CAPITALISM (Talcott Parsons trans., 1976).

68. See, e.g., RICHARD A. POSNER, THE ECONOMIC ANALYSIS OF LAW (4th ed.1992).

69. See J . M. Balkin, *Transcendental Deconstruction, Transcendent Justice*, 92 MICH. L. REV. 1131 (1994). Feldman does not take issue with Balkin on this point, *see* Feldman, *supra* note 52; his critique is that Balkin tries to derive our sense of justice from transcendent values, rather than recognizing it as a socially constructed value, as postmodernism suggests. As Feldman points out, postmodernism treats all our views about justice in this manner, and thus does not necessarily favor one or the other.

70. JAMES COLEMAN, FOUNDATIONS OF SOCIAL THEORY 19-23 (1990).

71. See Collier, *supra* note 1, at 842 48; Edward Rubin, *Legal Reasoning, Legal Process and the Judiciary as an Institution*, 85 CAL. L. REV. 265 (1997).

72. HERBERT SIMON, ADMINISTRATIVE BEHAVIOR (2d ed. 1961).

73. THE NEW INSTITUTIONALISM IN ORGANIZATIONAL ANALYSIS (Walter Powell & Paul DiMaggio eds., 1991); James March & Johan Olsen, Rediscovering Institutions (1989); ORGANIZATIONAL ENVIRONMENTS: RITUAL AND RATIONALITY (John Meyer & W. Richard Scott eds., 1983); John Meyer & Brian Rowan, *Institutionalized Organizations: Formal Structure As Myth and Ceremony*, 83 AM. J. SOC. 340 (1977); Mark C. Suchman & Lauren B. Edelman, *Legal Rational Myths: The New Institutionalism and the Law and Society Tradition*, 21 LAW & SOC. INQUIRY 903 (1996).

74. DOUGLAS NORTH, INSTITUTIONS, INSTITUTIONAL CHANGE AND ECONOMIC PERFORMANCE (1990); OLIVER WILLIAMSON, THE ECONOMIC INSTITUTIONS OF CAPITALISM (1985); OLIVER WILLIAMSON, THE MECHANISMS OF GOVERNANCE (1996).

75. SIMON, *supra* note 81, at xxiv.

76. See Rubin, *supra* note 47, at 1411-24.

77. PHILIP BOBBITT, CONSTITUTIONAL FATE (1982); BOBBITT, *supra* note 4.

78. PATTERSON, *supra* note 5.

79. WITTGENSTEIN, *supra* note 62; see also PATTERSON, *supra* note 5, at 163-79.

80. See LUHMANN, *supra* note 2; TEUBNER, *supra* note 3.

81. For the most recent statement of this theory, see LUHMANN, *supra* note 2.

82. BOBBITT, *supra* note 4, at 12-13.

83. *Id.* at 45-57.

84. *Id.* at 24.

85. See PATTERSON, *supra* note 5, at 146-79.

86. *Id.* at 64.

87. It also seems quite positivistic in the legal sense. Bobbitt argues that justice is external to the law; the six modalities leave room for considerations of justice because they do not always agree, but they do not necessarily generate just results. BOBBITT, *supra* note 4, at 141-79. This could suggest that these modalities are just a big, fuzzy rule of recognition. See H.L.A: HART, THE CONCEPT OF LAW (1961). Patterson argues quite convincingly that this is not the case, that the theory of discursive modalities reflects embedded cultural practices that are more meaningful, and less mechanical, than Hart's formulation. PATTERSON, *supra* note 5, at 59-70.

88. Thus, Bobbitt is a bit unfair to Robert Bork in criticizing him for inconsistency during the hearings on his nomination. Bork claimed to be a strict textualist, thus deploying only one of the modalities, but then said that prudential considerations, such as the stability of law, would prevent him from overruling established precedents on textual grounds. Bobbitt believes that this is inconsistent, in that Bork invoked a second modality, and that Bork's textualism was self-deceptive. BOBBITT, *supra* note 4, at 83-108. But if Bobbitt's first five modalities are all methods of interpreting a text, while his prudential modality is

qualitatively different, then Bork is not being inconsistent. He is choosing a textualist mode of interpretation, but modifying it with non-interpretive, policy-based considerations.

89. See note 58, *supra*, citing sources; FEELEY & RUBIN, *supra* note 68.

90. This is not true for New Criticism, see, e.g., CLEANTH BROOKS, THE WELL-WROUGHT URN (1947); CLEANTH BROOKS & ROBERT PENN WARREN, UNDERSTANDING POETRY (1938); AUSTIN WARREN, THEORY OF LITERATURE (1949); WILLIAM K. WIMSTATT, THE VERBAL ICON (1954), but it is just this closure that makes New Criticism controversial.

91. Kantian ethics is a closed field, and situational ethics is open to inputs and perhaps outputs. It follows that, if one takes ethics as a whole, it is dually open.

92. See CASS R. SUNSTEIN, LEGAL REASONING AND POLITICAL CONFLICT 33-61 (1996).

93. MACINTYRE, AFTER VIRTUE, *supra* note 31.

94. See, e.g., GADAMER, *supra* note 51, at 91-119, 445-47; JOHAN HUIZINGA, HOMO LUDENS: A STUDY OF THE PLAY ELEMENT IN CULTURE (1970).

95. TEUBNER, *supra* note 3, at 69.

96. *Id.*

97. *Id.* at 70.

98. *Id.* at 77-97.

Chapter 76

Victorian from Beacon Hill

Oliver Wendell Holmes's Early Legal Scholarship

1990

William P. LaPiana

William P. LaPiana is Professor of Law, New York Law School, and the author of *Logic and Experience: The Origin of Modern Legal Education* (Oxford Univeristy Press, 1994). This article first appeared in 90 *Columbia Law Review* 809 (1990).

In the years leading up to the publication of *The Common Law*[1] Oliver Wendell Holmes wrote extensively, publishing numerous articles and many book reviews in the *American Law Review*. After taking his seat on the Massachusetts Supreme Judicial Court in 1883 he wrote far less frequently for publication and the vast majority of his work, of course, is his opinions. In his article on Holmes's Supreme Judicial Court opinions Professor Tushnet rightly emphasizes the difficulties of using those opinions as gauges of Holmes's thought.[2] The content of the opinions is constrained by the nature of the questions before the court, and Holmes's addressing of those questions is further constrained by the need to carry his colleagues with him, at least in majority opinions. These constraints of collegiality often removed Holmes himself from the work he produced.[3] Occasionally, however, Holmes himself shines through and he is able to apply his ideas about law to the case at hand.[4]

Still, on the whole, it is in those early writings, culminating with *The Common Law*, that Holmes's ideas were formed. Those ideas remained with Holmes for all of his long life, although as Professor Tushnet observes, they underwent a change in emphasis, certain themes moving into greater prominence and others receding deeper into the background.[5]

Investigating Holmes's thought is not a straightforward undertaking. Neglect of his early writings and concentration on his judicial opinions has led to distortions, especially exaggerated assertions of his originality and pivotal place in American legal thought.[6]

The themes were present from the beginning, however, and a careful teasing out of the various strands of thought present in the early work provides the indispensable framework for evaluating Holmes both as a thinker and as a judge. This Essay examines Holmes's early writings through the publication of *The Common Law* from the perspective of their relationship to Anglo-American legal thought of the time. The salient characteristics of Holmes's thought—the empirical nature of legal science and the importance of studying law as it is rather than as it should be—are a fundamental part of the legal culture in which Holmes came to intellectual maturity. Much of what we associate with Holmes as his unique contribution to legal thought, especially his "bad man" theory of the law and his refusal to equate law with morality, are elaborations of a rich stream of legal thought in which he was a participant. Even the antidemocratic aspects of his thought that have caused much discomfort to some commentators were shared among Victorian legal thinkers.[7] By putting Holmes into context, this Essay hopes to illuminate one aspect of the legal culture of the past.[8]

I. Holmes and Victorian Legal Thought

Oliver Wendell Holmes, Jr., came of age at an exciting time in the intellectual history of Anglo-American law and of thought about society in general. One of the most important developments was the emergence of the new idea of legal science. Turning away from the moralism of the preceeding generations, the new legal scientists sought to study law as it was without considering what it should be. Their goal was to develop a jurisprudence that would properly classify and arrange the principles of the law. Holmes played an important role in American attempts to refine and apply the new legal science. Along with his companions in the Metaphysical Club, especially Nicholas St. John Green, he labored to break the hold of an antiquated moralism on the study of the law. He eventually came to place the greatest importance on facts—in certain factual situations, the power of the state forces individuals to conform to standards of behavior.

Holmes came to this empirical approach to law through the study of history, which confirmed for him the basic truth of John Austin's assertions about the nature of law. Holmes blended historical and analytical jurisprudence, concluding that the former confirmed the latter. His final position was shared by the law teachers who were transforming the Harvard Law School. The case method itself is a reflection of the new scientific approach to law, and Holmes himself is in some ways an intellectual comrade of Christopher Columbus Langdell. Scholarly treatment of Holmes's ideas has suffered from the lack of appreciation of his deep immersion in the new legal thought.

A. A New Legal Science

About the time of the American Civil War thinkers on both sides of the Atlantic had begun to examine critically and to refashion the general approach to society that had held sway over earlier generations.[9] In the field of law this change was symbolized by the writings of John Austin and Henry Maine. These two men became the exemplars of two "modern" approaches to law, the analytical and the historical.

For Austin, understanding could be reached only by separating what he called positive law from positive morality. Granted, Austin's thought is subtle and is often expressed in convoluted prose.[10] In addition, he never finished his great project to restate definitively the science of the law. The posthumous publication of Austin's work in the early 1860s, however, set loose upon the common law world two important ideas. First, law could and should be separated from morality, at least for purposes of study. Second, all law is directly or indirectly the command of the sovereign. Both of these ideas have long reverberated in Anglo-American legal thought.

Austin was not an amoral monster, nor did he share in the atheism of most utilitarians. Much of his first published work, *The Province of Jurisprudence Determined*,[11] is taken up with an elaborate discussion of ethics. The precise role of this discussion in his thought is a matter of dispute, but it is clear that for Austin the study of the science of law meant the study of law as it is, without consideration of what it should be. The study of what law ought to be is the province of the science of legislation.[12]

If Austin sought scientific accuracy through the separation of the is and the ought, Maine sought it through the investigation of the origin of legal rules in the past, especially the Roman past, and through explanation of the mechanisms by which the law had changed in response to changes in society. Maine clearly emphasized his work's scientific character:

> If by any means we can determine the early forms of jural conceptions, they will be invaluable to us. These rudimentary ideas are to the jurist what the primary crusts of the earth are to the geologist. They contain, potentially, all the forms in which law has subsequently exhibited itself.[13]

Ignorance of these early forms is responsible for the "unsatisfactory condition in which we find the science of jurisprudence."[14] By ignoring the facts of legal history jurists place assumption over observation. The result is that:

> [t]heories, plausible and comprehensive, but absolutely unverified, . . . enjoy a universal preference over sober research into the primitive history of society and law; and they obscure the truth not only by diverting attention from the only quarter in which it can be found, but by that most real and most important influence which, when once entertained and believed in, they are enabled to exercise on the later stages of jurisprudence.[15]

The philosophic aspect of *Ancient Law* was overshadowed by what was assumed to be the historical message of the work.[16] It seems that for many readers only one phrase in the entire book was important: "[W]e may say that the movement of the progressive societies has hitherto been a movement *from Status to Contract*."[17] Although as Frederick Pollock noted "it is not clear how far Maine regarded the movement of which he spoke as a phase of the larger political individualism which prevailed in the eighteenth century and a great part of the nineteenth, or what he would have thought of the reaction against this doctrine which we are now [in 1906] witnessing," many of Maine's readers found in his assertion support for their faith in laissez-faire.[18] They also found a convenient weapon with which to fend off Austin's analytical jurisprudence. Commentators often stated that Maine's historical jurisprudence proved that the law was not a command of the state but an organic growth. Holmes, however, never shared that opinion.

B. Holmes and the New Jurisprudence

The ferment in legal thought did not go unremarked in Boston. As Christopher Columbus Langdell was settling into his new job as Dean of the Harvard Law School, a "distinguished group of young intellectuals" in the Boston area had been investigating legal science for some years, discussing their findings in a group that would be known to history as the Metaphysical Club and publishing some of their work in the *American Law Review*.[19] Among the Club's members were Nicholas St. John Green and Holmes.

1. The Collapse of the Old Order. The goal of the advocates of a new legal science was familiar: they sought to order the principles of the common law. They also recognized, however, that the traditional ordering schemes were no longer viable. Holmes quite explicitly pointed out the obsolescence of the old science of procedure. "We cannot help saying that useful as books often are which gather under a remedy or class of remedies, such as injunction or action, the rights which it protects," he wrote in 1871, "the day for such an arrangement is passed."[20] Such arrangements were useful "earlier in the history of jurisprudence," when procedure was more highly developed than were rules, "but now we want principles as they are related to each other, not according to the accidental differences in the way of enforcing them."[21] The science of ordered principles fared no better.

The goal of earlier legal scientists like Joseph Story had been the creation of a proper understanding of the system of law through the intelligent application of inductive methods. Because the system that was to be revealed had an independent existence in the very nature of things, and because the forms of action provided a practical ordering of legal knowledge, before the Civil War there was little explicit discussion of how the much talked-of legal principles were to be arranged. In a sense, the proper arrangement merely awaited revelation; legal scientists did not need to construct it. There were, however, some explicit attempts at ordering—Blackstone's broad arrangement of his lectures around the law of persons and the law of things, itself a reflection of Roman law ideas, was something of a paradigm, which could at least be pointed to as an example of science. The most prevalent theme of American descriptions of orderly science was the superiority of the classificatory scheme of the Roman law.[22] Appeals to Rome meant little, however, to Holmes and Green.

In 1871 Holmes contributed an article to the *American Law Review* on "Misunderstandings of the Civil Law."[23] He gave several examples of the misuse of civil law concepts in the common law, including Lord Holt's opinion in *Coggs v. Bernard*,[24] famous for its attempt to explain common law rules of liability in bailment in terms of Roman law principles and often regarded as a paragon of legal science. Holmes's principal point, however, was that study of the civil law had no place in the training of American lawyers because "it tends to encourage a dangerous reliance on what Mr. Choate would have called glittering generalities" at the expense of "the exhaustive analysis of a particular case, with which the common law begins and ends."[25]

As early as 1869, in a review of Benjamin's treatise on the law of sales, Holmes set forth his own vision of a proper philosophical arrangement of the law. "A book of reference on any subdivision of the law," he wrote, "must set forth at length, not only the principles constituting the specific difference of the subject-matter, but also those common to it and to many other classes of the same genus."[26] Fraud, for instance, should be treated as an aspect of contract "or possibly under some still wider head, rather than repeated in every text-book dealing with every one of the different sorts of contract known to modern commerce."[27]

2. *The Turn to Facts.* Holmes's analysis of the shortcomings of traditional legal thought led him to the conclusion that a truly scientific system would have to be built from the bottom up, from the cases that give examples of the legally significant facts on which recovery is based. The system thus created may be based on "rights," or "obligations," or "duties," but the foundation must be factual. Holmes made this point quite clearly in a letter to John Chipman Gray written in July of 1877. The two friends had spent an evening discussing an article Holmes had recently written.[28] In a letter written a few days later, Holmes described to Gray "my ultimate object":

> viz: to point out a distinction which is of the first importance to a philosophical classification—which has two distinct things to do (1) to enumerate the groups of facts which generate a right or obligation—(2) to enumerate the facts which do not generate either, and yet give a man the right or obligation *as if* the generative fact were true.[29]

The facts, of course, are to be sought in the cases. As Nicholas St. John Green wrote, dismissing John Townsend's theorizing about slander and libel in terms of malice, "[t]he latest decided cases upon this subject *make the law.*"[30]

Holmes seems to have first formulated his belief about the primacy of facts in the series of lectures on jurisprudence that he gave at Harvard College in the spring of 1872. These lectures seem, at least at first glance, to have grown out of a rejection of Austin's ideas. The substance of what Holmes said is preserved only in the form of a "Book Notice" in the *American Law Review*, nominally a review of an article on Austin by Frederick Pollock.[31] According to Holmes, law, at least "in the more limited meaning which lawyers give to the word," consists of the rules enforced by the courts; such rules are not necessarily the commands of the sovereign.[32] Such a statement is, of course, a rejection of one of Austin's basic premises and is, in turn, the result of a rejection of Austin's concept of sovereignty. Holmes pointed out that the identity of the sovereign is defined by power. "That is to say," Holmes wrote, "the will of the sovereign is law, because he has power to compel obedience or to punish disobedience, and for no other reason."[33] There are, Holmes maintained, real limits on the power of the political sovereign, a statement he supported by showing in his lectures "that there might be law without sovereignty, and that where there is a sovereign, properly so called, other bodies not sovereign, and even opinion, might generate law in a philosophical sense against the will of the sovereign."[34] He pointed out that in the end, no command of the sovereign could prevail against the "physical power" of that "large number" which in most states has even been a "numerical majority of males, who have had no share in the political power."[35]

Once the Austinian conception of sovereignty was disposed of, it was easy for Holmes to show that judges decide cases on many motives "outside their own arbitrary will, beside the commands of their sovereign."[36] All the lawyer is concerned with, as he pointed out, is what the judges will do in the future because "in a civilized state" what "makes lawyers' law" is not the will of the sovereign "but what a body of subjects, namely, the judges, by whom it is enforced, *say* is his will."[37] The true subject of jurisprudence, the true source of law, therefore, is any motive for judicial decision which lawyers can reasonably rely on to be used by other judges in the future, which they can use to predict a future outcome. This first appearance of Holmes's "prediction theory of law" grew out of a belief that what judges do is the law.[38] Holmes's early work on the factual basis of law laid a solid foundation for that belief.

II. The Contours of Holmes's Thought

When Holmes set out to formulate his own views on the issues that agitated legal thinkers of his day, he drew first on history. Keeping in mind Austin's admonitions on the source of law and Maine's use of history to illustrate existing legal rules, Holmes searched the past for the origins of current legal doctrine. Those origins were to be found in the reality of the past rather than in transcendent principles that somehow simply existed. Not surprisingly, he took an increasingly empirical view of law, grounding legal science in the facts of human life, among which were judicial decisions. His view was shared by the first generation of modern law teachers and in this respect, contrary to what many have assumed, Holmes and Langdell were more intellectual allies than enemies.

A. The Role of History

By the spring of 1872, then, Holmes seems to have made a public repudiation of total faith in Austin. He continued for the next year or so in the Austinian task of classification, albeit on the basis of duties. After the publication of "The Theory of Torts" in 1873,[39] however, the charts showing the arrangements of the duties disappeared. His next article, "Primitive Notions in Modern Law" published in 1876, marks an important transition.[40] In that essay Holmes carried forward the aim of "The Theory of Torts" to show that liability for tortious acts does not depend on culpability, as Austin maintained, but rather on the failure to come up to the standard of behavior established by the community. His methodology was historical. He pointed out that at least in some cases "which Austin, following the jurists of the mature period of Roman law, had interpreted on grounds of culpability," the root of liability was in fact "the much more primitive notion, that liability attached directly to the thing doing the damage."[41] He attempted to "explain that primitive notion more at length, to show its influence on the body of modern law, and to trace the development from it of a large number of doctrines which in their actual form seem most remote from each other or from any common source."[42]

Holmes's next article, "Primitive Notions in Modern Law. No. II," appeared in July of 1877.[43] Its purpose was "to prove the historical truth of a general result, arrived at analytically" in "The Arrangement of the Law."[44] Holmes's earlier article rested on his belief, which had formed for some time an important part of his view of law, that "all special rights are legal consequences of a special group of facts."[45] Supporting that belief required Holmes to explain why some "continuing rights [which] are incidents to a situation of fact, [and] which can only be filled by the first person entitled to the rights in question," can "be succeeded to by another who cannot fill the situation."[46] The conventional description of this situation uses the notion of "privity" to explain the relationship between the first holder of the right and his successor. In "The Arrangement of the Law" he analyzed the concept of privity in terms of an abstract *persona* that is the thing to which the fact situation attaches, an idea that in turn is traced to the treatment of heirship in the Roman law.[47] He came to the conclusion, as he put it in "Primitive Notions in Modern Law. No. II" "that in such cases there is a fictitious identification of distinct persons for the purpose of transferring or completing the right."[48] That article found the origin of that fictitious identification in an analogy to inheritance. Thus Holmes could explain the seemingly anomalous situation he described at the beginning of the essay. If a person uses a way over his neighbor's property in order to reach his own, the person who buys the land

and continues to use the way "can add the seller's time of adverse user to his own, for the purpose of making out an enjoyment long enough to give him a right by prescription."[49] Someone not a buyer (one who has unlawfully dispossessed (disseised) the original adverse user), however, cannot add (tack) his period of use to that of his predecessor. The idea of tacking arose from analogizing the purchaser to the heir who succeeds to all the rights of the deceased by assuming his *persona*; he is not in the eyes of the law a different person. Since heirship is always lawful or right, the analogy cannot be applicable to a disseisor. Holmes traces the use of this analogy through Roman, Germanic and English law.[50]

Holmes still faced a legal puzzle, however. The lack of privity between disseisee and disseisor arose from the apparent unwillingness to conceive of a "wrongful" succession by inheritance, or as Holmes put it, "without the element of consent, there was no likeness to be laid hold of."[51] In spite of this limit to the analogy, it seems that at common law, although the matter is not without doubt, a disseisor does have an action against anyone who obstructs a right of way over another's land (an easement) obtained by the disseisee through adverse use. The puzzle is compounded by the undoubted legal fact that an easement is incapable of possession, being "an ideal creation of the law."[52] The answer is found, Holmes believed, in the tendency, common in one period of the development of the human mind, to endow inanimate things with a personality, a concept he had already discussed in his earlier article on "Primitive Notions in Modern Law."[53] Rights obtained by prescription were "built up out of similes drawn from legal persons" at the time when personification was still common in criminal law, "and then, as often happens, language reacted on thought, so that conclusions were drawn as to the rights themselves from the terms in which they happened to be expressed."[54] Again Holmes traces this idea through Roman and English writers and uses it to explain one of the knotty concepts of the land law, the rule that privity of estate is necessary in order for a covenant to run with the land.[55]

It is important that the difference between the historical method of these later articles and the analytical method of the earlier be understood. In the earlier article on arrangement of the law, Holmes attempted to explain the problem of succession by showing that the notion of privity logically arose from the fictitious identification of decedent and heir. In the later articles he shows through the examination of legal thought of treatise writers how the fictitious identification was extended to other areas by analogy. This process was governed by ideas like the personification of inanimate objects, which his age did not accept and which are emphatically not logical. In these later works, Holmes is writing a sort of intellectual history that attempts to ground legal ideas in the more general ideas of a specific historical era as well as in the operation of the human mind. Thus the difference between the treatment of easements and covenants cannot be explained by classifying them as rights *in rem* or obligations, or by differentiating between rights obtained by grant and those obtained by prescription. An accurate explanation requires an understanding of the intellectual (but not necessarily rational) processes that clothed an estate with something akin to personality.[56]

Holmes is not concerned, however, with testing his hypothesis against evidence other than that provided in commentaries and treatises. Regarding his conclusion that easements and like concepts were seen as part of the land itself, he wrote:

> If evidence of a general tendency, in the early communities and manors, to impress a permanent character on particular parcels of land, or that services were due from or to their respective occupants simply by reason of their occupation, were necessary for the present argument, it would probably not be hard to find. But there is no need of going into further details.[57]

He did, however, add to this passage a footnote citing the work of the French scholar M.E. de Laveleye and his own lengthy footnote to Kent's discussion of the history of alienation in his edition of Kent's *Commentaries on American Law*.[58] The footnote is an elaborate discussion of what historical evidence Holmes could find, much of it in secondary sources, about the origins of property and the nature of village communities. He was not disdainful of the facts of social history, but the focus of his inquiry was ideas.

Holmes's thought continued in the empirical channel, as evidenced by his increasing concern with history. He published his next article, "Possession," in July of 1878.[59] It is most important for its expression

41. Oliver Wendell Holmes, Jr. (1841-1935) was twice a professor at Harvard. His book *The Common Law* is a classic, as are many of his opinions as a justice at the U.S. Supreme Court. This photograph was taken in 1880. (*Courtesy of Art & Visual Materials, Special Collections Department, Harvard Law School Library.*)

of Holmes's notion about the relationship between facts and law and its rejection of a priori approaches to the law. In the second division of the article Holmes deals explicitly with the question, which, he points out, has been the focus of German scholarship on this subject, "whether possession is a fact or a right?"[60] The question, in Holmes's view, should never have been asked, at least by lawyers who are not concerned with what philosophers or moralists mean by the question. Every right "is a consequence attached by the law to a group of facts which the law defines."[61] If the facts exist with regard to a certain person, that person has the right in question. Possession, therefore, "is such a group of facts; and, when we say of a man that he has possession, we mean to affirm directly that all the facts of that group are true of him, and we convey, indirectly or by implication, that the law will give him the advantages of the situation."[62]

The importance of this definition, which Holmes believed is true for every substantive area of the law, becomes evident when he contrasts it to German ideas about possession. According to Holmes, all the best known German jurists are both scholars of the Roman law and disciples of some version of Kantian or post-Kantian philosophy.[63] Roman possession was "that of an owner or of one on his way to become owner."[64] Savigny took this fact of Roman law to the conclusion that "intent to deal with the thing as owner, is in general necessary to turn a mere physical detention into juridical possession."[65] This view in turn harmonizes with Kant's view of law. For him, possession was part of the ego, a manifestation of the will which can only be restrained when it interferes with the freedom of others. The intent necessary for possession, therefore, must be an intent to make oneself owner.[66] This intent should be protected because the entire legal system must respect the manifestations of the human will.[67] Holmes had already shown in the first part of the essay, however, that the common law gives possessory remedies to persons who are not owners.[68]

Holmes's entire view of the law becomes clear in his explanation of the inadequacies of the German position and the rightness of the common law approach. First, he reiterates the idea that legal duties come before legal rights. He makes explicit his view that "the direct operation of the law is to limit freedom of action or choice on the part of a greater or less number of persons in certain specified ways; while the fact that the power of removing or enforcing this limitation is generally confided to certain other private persons is not a necessary or universal correlative."[69] In other words, the law prevents people from interfering with other people. In fact, the law does this directly in the case of the protection of possession. The intent which must be found in order to protect possession is the intent not to make oneself owner, but to exclude others.[70]

Holmes then demonstrates through the analysis of cases that the common law protects as possessors those who have the intent to exclude others. He admits that his proposed general test of intent does not fit the case of servants who are considered not to have possession of property entrusted to them although it is true that a servant clearly intends to exclude the world at large. The reconciliation is found in history. "A servant is denied possession," Holmes asserted, "not from any peculiarity of intent with regard to the things in his custody either towards his master or other people by which he is distinguished from a depositary, but simply as one of the incidents of his status."[71] The status still bears many of the marks of its origin in slavery and the possession of a slave was the possession of the owner. Here again history gives an answer which logic cannot. As Holmes put it, "there is no adequate and complete explanation of the modern law, except by the survival in practice of rules which lost their true meaning when the objects of them ceased to be slaves."[72] Just as the rules regarding easements and covenants are explained not by the concept of privity but by the operation of analogy and the survival of the idea of personification of objects, so the inability of servants to have possession is understandable only by understanding history.

Holmes was not quite done. He maintained not only that the common law actually required that the possessor have the intent to exclude but that "no more should be required on principle."[73] Possession is protected not for the philosophical reasons of the Germans regarding the will and personality, but because "man, by an instinct which he shares with the domestic dog, and of which the seal gives a most striking example, will not allow himself to be dispossessed, either by force or fraud, of what he holds, without trying to get it back again."[74] The grounds of this part of the common law are, therefore, empirical. "Indeed, those who see in the history of law the formal expression of the development of society will be apt to think that the proximate ground of law must be empirical, even when that ground is the fact that a certain ideal or theory of government is generally entertained."[75]

In "Possession," for the first time, all of the themes of Holmes's thought are brought together into one argument. First, the definition of law as the application of force on individuals is expressed as the source of the primacy given to duties. Second, the object of the study of law is the facts which must be true in order for the law to act. Third, no matter what sort of conclusions about general rules and principles can be drawn from the exploration of the facts that invoke the public power (an investigation which is itself historical, based on the records of the law), perfect symmetry can never be expected because the workings of the human mind in history are not perfectly logical. Reasons for rules have disappeared, yet the effects of the rules persist. Finally, the study of the law is not concerned with philosophical systems, but rather with the realities of life in the world, which realities are not particularly lofty. Possession is protected because man—like other animals—defends what he has acquired.

B. Empirical Law

The state of Holmes's thought at the time of the publication of "Possession" seems settled enough to attempt to assess the influence of the two major groups of ideas that dominated American legal thought in the period: the analytical and historical approaches to jurisprudence. In the first place, Holmes was critical of Austin. The definition of law as the command of a sovereign simply did not convince Holmes. He saw too many instances of the sovereign being powerless to make law in the face of power held by others, that "numerical majority of males"[76] who in the extreme could undo the sovereign's law by taking to the streets. What should not be overlooked, however, is that for all his criticism of Austin, Holmes still finds the source of law in the facts of power.[77] The complaint of some anti-Austinians was that the command theory promoted the unacceptable notion that the legislature could make any law it wanted, even if that law interfered with property rights in an effort to effect the redistribution of wealth, an aim which was totally contrary to the true nature of law, the rights of property being above and beyond human meddling. Holmes shared no such belief. What the public power enforces is the law. Given Holmes's belief about the instinct to preserve one's property, he might find something short of naked confiscation unwise, but it seems unlikely that he would say that something inherent in the nature of law deprived the legislature of such power. He came close to saying that might makes, if not right, at least law of the kind lawyers must study. Rejection of Austin's conception of the absolute nature of the sovereign's power does not entail, at least for Holmes, a rejection of the basic idea of the nature of law which Austin expressed.[78]

Nor did Holmes's abandonment of the attempt to classify the law on the basis of duties signify a complete rejection of Austin. In "Possession" he wrote: "The business of the jurist is to make known the content of the law; that is, to work upon it from within, or logically, arranging and distributing it in order from its *summum genus* to its *infima species*."[79] Holmes repeated this passage almost verbatim in *The Common Law*, adding the words "so far as practicable" at the end.[80] This qualification of the need to classify symbolizes exactly to what extent Holmes rejected Austin's thought. His abandonment of the attempt to classify or arrange the law according to a schedule of duties marked the end of his engagement with "Austin's classificatory mania."[81] The passage from "Possession" reproduced in *The Common Law* is the only discussion of legal duties in the book. By 1883 Holmes had come to doubt whether there was any use in the concepts of rights and duties. "The primary duty," he wrote Pollock, "is little more than a convenient index to, or mode of predicting the point of incidence of the public force."[82] More than thirty years later Holmes wrote to John Chipman Gray in answer to Gray's inquiry about "an article of yours, I think in the Am. [sic] Law Review to the effect that the best classification of the Law was on duties."[83] Holmes replied:

> The duty basis was the theme of my first article in the law Rev. Oct. 1870-Vol. 5 p. 1. "A long time ago, gentlemen," as old Parsons used to say in a melancholy voice, "a very long time ago." Later I became convinced that the machinery of rights and duties was a fifth wheel—and partially expressed it in an address to the Boston Law School Jan 8/97 ["The Path of the Law"] that was printed in the Harv. Law Rev. My theme and present view is expressed in American Banana Co. v. United Fruit Co. 213 U.S. 347, 356 [1908] "Law is a statement of the circumstance in which the public force will be brought to bear upon men through the Courts."[84]

Five years earlier, Holmes had been even more blunt in a letter to Gray on the same topic: "Personally I don't care a damn for the rights and duties business preferring to regard only the prophecy as to the incidence of the public force" as he discussed in "The Path of the Law."[85]

The evolution of Holmes's ideas about torts further illustrates his growing disillusionment with the concept of duties as well as with his prior adherence to Austinian ideas. In "The Theory of Torts,"[86] Holmes had put forward the idea that negligence is a question of fact, asking whether or not an actor has lived up to what the average member of the community would do in the circumstances. This view rests all negligence law on facts which are to be investigated through the means of decided cases. As Holmes put it, "an enumeration of the actions which have been successful, and of those which have failed, defines the extent of the primary duties imposed by the law. . . ."[87] He then proceeded to classify the law of torts according to duties by relating subjects of the substantive law to duties depending on the facts involved.[88] To remove the duties from the scheme leaves legal categories and facts, the only subjects he has discussed based on evidence of what courts really do. Duties truly are a "fifth wheel."

Holmes's modifications of Austin's ideas are, therefore, an extension of the empirical side of Austin's thought. If Austin's conception of law was based on the reality of power, his scheme for the classification and arrangement of legal ideas nevertheless partook of more abstraction than Holmes was willing to accept. One of the strains of thought which led Holmes to his position was his appreciation of history. Holmes's view of the sovereign was based on what history showed to be the limits of the political sovereign's power.[89] His conception of the non-logical side of the law was grounded on an understanding of the extent to which ideas and, in some cases, institutions long without any real life in contemporary thought still exercised influence through the existence of rules based on them.

The realization that Holmes was a historian of ideas sheds light on his treatment of the role of morality in law. Like Austin, Holmes believed that for purposes of study, law and morals must be separated. Holmes had made the point in print quite early. In 1867 he reviewed the ninth edition of Story's *Equity* Jurisprudence by Issac Redfield,[90] former chief justice of Vermont, whose eulogist had praised him as an ideal lawyer always concerned with sound principles and the morality of the law.[91] The young Holmes saw matters differently. Although Redfield was "an eminent and able man,"[92] his editing of Story exhibited the same flaws all of his works did. "One of them," Holmes wrote, "is a habit of moralizing, which is notably out of place among the rules and precedents of courts."[93] He then quoted Redfield's criticism of an English judge for doing justice rather than adhering to principle, something always to be deprecated by those who believe in principle and trust "'consequences to Him with whom are all the issues of life.'"[94] Holmes's comment on that statement clearly ruled morality out of court: "When the learned editor calls in the authority of religion to make weight against the authority of the Master of the Rolls, by doing so he only renders the want of legal authority more conspicuous."[95] In "Possession" he was more explicit:

> We may leave on one side the question of their [legal rights'] relation to moral rights, and whether moral rights are not in like manner logically the offspring of moral duties; these are for the philosopher who approaches the law from without, as part of a larger series of human manifestations. The business of the jurist is to make known the content of the law. . . .[96]

Morality did not decide cases. It did, however, have a role to play in the growth of the law. Holmes explained that role in a passage near the end of the chapter in *The Common Law* on "The Theory of Torts":

> But in the main the law started from those intentional wrongs which are the simplest and most pronounced cases, as well as the nearest to the feeling of revenge which leads to self-redress. It thus naturally adopted the vocabulary, and in some degree the tests, of morals. But as the law has grown, even when its standards have continued to model themselves upon those of morality, they have necessarily become external, because they have considered, not the actual condition of the particular defendant, but whether his conduct would have been wrong in the fair average member of the community, whom he is expected to equal at his peril.[97]

Ideas of morality are one more component in the intellectual history of the law. It must be taken into account in describing law's growth and even its current state. The notion of the average member of the community is at least in part shaped by community ideas of right and wrong. The tests of the law, however, do not address the moral state of the actor and moral standards have no inherent authority apart from their use to help set the objective legal test.[98]

C. Holmes and Legal Education

Since the ultimate basis of the sort of systematic legal science sought by Green and Holmes was the decided case, they might be assumed to be advocates and allies of the transformation that was occurring at Harvard Law School at the very time they were formulating the ideas examined above. Indeed, Green, Holmes and Gray occupied lectureships in Cambridge during this period. Green, however, left the reforming Harvard to help found the new law school at Boston University in protest against the new methods. Holmes wrote critical reviews of Langdell's work in the years before publication of *The Common Law*, and the intellectual relationship between Holmes and the dean has become a controverted point.[99] Saul Touster has maintained that Holmes moved from criticism of Langdell's reliance on cases to acceptance of the case method, a transformation which led Holmes in *The Common Law* to ignore "moral ideas" and "philosophy" in favor of a narrow, formalistic approach to law.[100] Like most assertions of a basic transformation in Holmes's thought, Langdell's assumed influence, exerted through his teaching technique, is misconstrued. Holmes quarreled with the dean, but their differences have obscured important areas of agreement.

Holmes was the author of the highly critical notice of the Harvard Law School which appeared in the *American Law Review* in 1870.[101] He found the school inadequate in almost every particular. He seems to have been soured on law schools by his experience at the unreformed Harvard. The next year, in reviewing Bryce's urgings that common lawyers study the civil law, Holmes observed that "[t]he common law begins and ends with the solution of a particular case," and that "the best training," therefore, "is found in our moot courts and the offices of older lawyers."[102] The implication is that the best learning comes by doing, a belief perfectly compatible with the ideas about education that accompanied the introduction of the case method to the law school.[103]

In the first years of the new regime at Harvard, the case method was used exclusively by Langdell and was known to the outside world through his casebooks. Holmes's review of the first part of Langdell's contracts casebook was full of praise for its historical arrangement. "Tracing the growth of a doctrine in this way," Holmes wrote, "not only fixes it in the mind, but shows its meaning, extent, and limits as nothing else can."[104] Holmes went on, however, to criticize Langdell's treatment of the cases on forbearance as "collected with an overscrupulous minuteness." Langdell, it seems, had paid too much attention "to the other side of what is now settled."[105] This failing did not, however, detract from the usefulness of the work.[106] The publication of the complete work later in 1871 was greeted by another anonymous Holmes review that praised the dean for using a philosophical rather than a manual method of arrangement and that also pointed out the importance of the principles to be deduced from the cases, at least for the instruction of students.[107] While Langdell's innovation was still new, Holmes had some reservations about Langdell's scholarship. Holmes approved the study of cases as the source of the law—as a place where the principles are found—but found Langdell's practice of the study defective.

Holmes expressed these same attitudes much more fully in his review of the second edition of the contracts casebook published in 1879. In this review Holmes characterized the dean as "perhaps, the greatest living legal theologian," concerned only with "the formal connection of things, or logic, as distinguished from the feelings which make the content of logic, and which have actually shaped the substance of the law."[108] What those "feelings" are is most simply said to be the lessons of history of the sort Holmes dealt with in his contemporaneous writings. The core of Holmes's criticism, however, is the same point he made in his first review of Langdell's work. The tendency to "overscrupulous minuteness" seen in 1871 had blossomed into the dogmatism—"the effort to reduce the concrete details of an existing system to the merely logical consequence of simple postulates"—seen in the extensive summary of the law of contracts which Langdell added to the second edition of the casebook.[109] Having published his idea of a complete system for the first time, clearly Langdell was determined to prove his point even if that meant reconciling decisions "which those who gave them meant to be opposed" by drawing them together "by subtle lines which never were dreamed of before Mr. Langdell wrote."[110]

Holmes specifically disagreed with Langdell on the notion of equivalency, a concept involved in understanding the role of consideration in bilateral contracts. Broadly put, Langdell's observation was that in the case of a contract made by giving a promise for a promise, the performance of one is payment for the performance of the other and therefore, as Holmes put it, neither party "can call on the other to perform without being ready at the same time himself."[111] This becomes in turn an important principle for understanding the role of conditions in contract law. Holmes, however, did not believe that the proper judicial treatment of conditions depended on the working out of a principle of equivalence.

> Suppose A promises B to do a day's work for two dollars, and B promises A to pay two dollars for a day's work. There the two promises cannot be performed at the same time. The work will take all day, the payment half a minute. How are you to decide which is to be done first, that is to say, which promise is dependent upon performance on the other side? It is only by reference to the habits of the community and to convenience.[112]

Theory, the idea that "on the principle of equivalency a man is not presumed to intend to pay for a thing until he has it,"[113] is not sufficient to answer the question. The work is payment for the money and the money for the work. There is no reason in logic to say one person "intends" to pay before he has what he has bought and the other intends to give before he has been paid. What does give the answer, what explains the cases, is that amalgam of practice and belief which is summed up in history and which is the law.

> The fact that employers, as a class, can be trusted for wages more safely than the employed for their labor, that the employers have had the power and have been the law-makers, or other considerations, it matters not what, have determined that the work is to be done first. But the grounds of decision are purely practical, and can never be elicited from grammar or from logic.[114]

Holmes's fourth sentence of *The Common Law* was the same sentence he had used in the review which described Langdell as a "legal theologian": "The life of the law has not been logic: it has been experience."[115]

Langdell's system was too logical, too devoted to drawing distinctions and reconciling cases on grounds that had life only in his own mind. Holmes felt himself to be firmly grounded in the reality of history, human nature and the practicalities of life in the world. The heart of Holmes's criticism is an objection to Langdell's intellectual rigidity and a priori approach, to his creation of what Pollock called "the Langdellian ether of a super-terrestrial Common Law where authority does not count at all," not to the study of the law through the study of cases.[116]

Perhaps the most dramatic example of the basic agreement between the two men can be seen in a letter Langdell wrote to Theodore Dwight Woolsey of Yale soon after assuming the deanship discussing the study of jurisprudence. The new dean had been appointed secretary of a "Committee on Jurisprudence" which appears to have been the relevant committee of the American Social Science Association. He does not appear to have been particularly honored by the appointment and wrote Woolsey to profess his bewilderment at exactly what he was expected to do as well as "to offer for your consideration the following suggestions in regard to the study of jurisprudence":

> [I]t [the study of jurisprudence] does not specially concern lawyers or those intending to become lawyers, but other portions of the community as well; some perhaps more, e.g., those aiming at public life or a high order of journalism. The chief business of a lawyer is and must be to learn and administer the law *as it is*; while I suppose the great object in studying jurisprudence should be to ascertain what the law *ought to be*; and although these two pursuits may seem to be of a very kindred nature, I think experience shews that devotion to one is apt to give more or less distaste for the other.[117]

In fact, the study of jurisprudence does not even belong in the law schools, but rather should be part of the postgraduate studies available in the university and should be carried on by "University men who devote themselves to the higher education, and not lawyers, whether on or off the Bench, not even professors in Law Schools."[118] Like Holmes, Langdell shared the Austinian belief in the separation of the is and the ought. All that there is of law is in the cases. Anything else is the province of another field of study.

D. Holmes and the Scholarly Tradition

If this explication of Holmes's thought through the period ending with the publication of *The Common Law* is correct, it is necessary to reassess claims that Holmes was startlingly original in his thought and that his ideas underwent a far reaching transformation during his long career. Indeed, it seems that Holmes shared in widely held beliefs about the nature of law and about the way to go about studying it. Commentators have identified as his most notable contributions ideas—such as the prediction theory, the "bad man" view of law, and the separation of law and morality—which were firmly rooted in the advanced legal culture of his younger years and which he himself held from the 1870s.[119] In particular, "The Path of the Law" represents not a new start or even a turning point, but the making explicit of his empirical approach to law and the emphasis on law as a coercive mechanism which he first described in his earliest articles. Even the aspects of his thought that have caused revulsion in the present day were a part of the legal culture in which he came to intellectual maturity.

Holmes's scorn for the mob, his almost cynical treatment of the democratic process has been much noted in recent scholarship. Grant Gilmore in particular found Holmes "savage, harsh, and cruel, a bitter and lifelong pessimist."[120] Most commentators seem to explain this aspect of Holmes by pointing to the influence of "social Darwinism," which was heightened by Holmes's experiences as a soldier.[121] Distrust of democracy, however, was a common theme in Anglo-American legal thought throughout the mid- and late-nineteenth century. Austin himself was appalled by the progressive extension of Parliamentary suffrage.[122] Maine was no happier with political developments that extended the power of the "people" in politics.[123] Holmes's friend, James Fitzjames Stephen, was perhaps the most prominent antidemocrat of the Victorian age. His *Liberty, Equality, Fraternity*[124] was a withering attack on the premises of democracy. Stephen's basic assertion was that the vast majority of people were ignorant and vicious and dedicated to levelling society through the destruction of private property.[125]

The ignorance of which these thinkers complained was ignorance of the "truths" of classical political economy. In a sense, Adam Smith and Malthus were their guiding lights.[126] Holmes was one of the true believers. He found socialism stupid because it ignored economic truth. Indeed, he wrote to Pollock that rereading Malthus pleased him "immensely" but left him "sad." "A hundred years ago he busted fallacies that politicians and labor leaders still live on. One thinks that an error exposed is dead, but exposure amounts to nothing when people want to believe."[127] Holmes's belief in life as struggle, therefore, had at least some of its roots in an adherence to the tenets of classical liberal economics widely shared by his contemporaries. Unlike some of those contemporaries, however, he also believed that Austin's basic insight into law as power meant that he could not enforce those tenets on an unwilling polity. Holmes's early adherence to Austinian positivism is thus the direct ancestor of his judicial dismissal of freedom of contract as "an economic theory which a large part of the country does not entertain" in his dissent in *Lochner v. New York* in 1905.[128]

Conclusion

Holmes began his legal career as a student of the two dominant strains of the legal culture of the time. Drawing from both the analytical and the historical schools, he attempted to create a science of law that would supersede the previous generation's belief in an ordered system of a priori principles. By separating law and morality, as Austin counselled, Holmes believed he could free the study of law from irrelevant considerations of what should or must be in favor of an empirical study of what the law really is. By studying history, Holmes believed he could demonstrate that legal doctrine did not develop according to logical rules, but rather reflected a society's social structure as well as its conscious judgments about policy.

Holmes had definite beliefs about how those policy decisions should be made. His policy preferences were based on classical liberal economics. When it came to judging, however, Holmes's beliefs about the nature of law proved stronger than his economic views. Having located the source of law in power, he refrained as a judge from opposing what he saw as expressions of society's will, even when those expressions were, in his eyes, stupid. As it happened, his restraint led to a reluctance to invalidate progressive legislation. Thus, with some careful editing of the record, he could be lionized as a "liberal" even though he was "liberal" only in the nineteenth century sense of that term. His disregard for individual rights,[129] except perhaps in the area of political speech, offends contemporary liberal ideas, but was at its base simply a reflection of his deference to the power of the majority. His scorn of the mob, and perhaps of the very idea of democracy, was a common posture among nineteenth century Anglo-American legal thinkers.

The connections between Holmes and other students of the common law have been neglected, in part because the Justice outlived them all.[130] Towards the end of his life, admirers half his age transformed him into a paragon of liberal virtue. The rediscovery of his true views has led to studies which concentrate on the man himself rather than on the legal culture in which he came to intellectual maturity. When those connections are reexamined, Holmes can be seen as a part of his times, as one of several Victorian legal thinkers, most of whom simply did not manage to hold an important judicial post well into the twentieth century.

This reexamination also reveals a final irony, one that Holmes might have appreciated. He once wrote that his epitaph should read "Here lies the supple tool of power."[131] Perhaps he should have said, "Here lies the supple tool of law professors." The legal realists seized him as their patron saint, the one true mature judge who had overcome formalism. Yet in his thought he did adhere to a formalism of a sort; he believed that the laws of the dismal science were true and inescapable. If he is the ancestor of any branch of current American legal thought, those who should erect his shrine are the advocates of law and economics. In Holmes they can find a thinker who knew that society and its law should be organized along the lines dictated by the "science" of economics. All they must do is ignore his appreciation for the role the irrational plays in the life of the law.

NOTES

1. O.W. Holmes, The Common Law (1881).

2. Tushnet, The Logic of Experience: Oliver Wendell Holmes on the Supreme Judicial Court, 63 Va.L.Rev. 975, 978 (1977).

3. *Id.* at 978-79.

4. See, e.g., Vegelahn v. Guntner, 167 Mass. 92, 104-09, 44 N.E. 1077, 1079-82 (1896) (Holmes, J., dissenting) (discussion of policy issues involved in labor dispute picketing); Norcross v. James, 140 Mass. 188, 192, 2 N.E. 946, 949 (1885) (historical discussion of covenants running with the land).

5. Tushnet, *supra* note 2, at 978.

6. See G. Aichele, Oliver Wendell Holmes, Jr.: Soldier, Scholar, Judge 123-24 (1989); Tushnet, *supra* note 2, at 1005-12. One exception is The Formative Essays of Justice Holmes: The Making of an American Legal Philosophy (F. Kellogg ed. 1984), which reprints the early essays and finds them important clues to Holmes's legal thought.

7. See, e.g., G. Aichele, *supra* note 6, at 162-64; G. Gilmore, The Ages of American Law 48-49 (1977).

8. Holmes's personality seems to have fascinated those who have studied him even more than have his ideas. See, e.g., G. Aichele, *supra* note 6, at 3, 20, 69; White, The Rise and Fall of Justice Holmes, 39 U.Chi.L.Rev. 1, 51-52 (1971). The net effect of this personalized approach to Holmes is to find the source of his ideas in his personality. Holmes's family life, his difficult relationship with his father and his experiences in war all undoubtedly contributed to his outlook on life in general and his views of law in particular. To focus so intensively on these aspects of the man, however, obscures the extent to which he consciously thought about the matters that engaged his interest and the extent to which he consulted, accepted and rejected the views of others. This approach also puts us in danger of losing sight of the extent to which Holmes was a person of his times, participating in the general culture of his world.

The great attention paid to Holmes as judge says much about the state of legal history in America. On the whole, American legal history lives in America's law schools rather than in graduate faculties of arts and sciences. Its practitioners often are lawyers first and historians second, even when they have done graduate study in history. As lawyers, they are wedded to the text in which the law is found, and this focus on the specific document sometimes tends to limit historical inquiry. At the extreme, such an attitude has probably contributed to the strength in current legal thought of a congeries of ideas and attitudes loosely grouped under the term "deconstructionism." Perhaps it is not surprising that many of the law school adherents of these new ideas have been drawn to the study of history. See P. Novick, That Noble Dream: The "Objectivity Question" and the American Historical Profession 555- 57 (1988).

9. For concise explanations of traditional common law thinking, see D. Lieberman, The Province of Legislation Determined: Legal Theory in Eighteenth-Century Britain 1-176 (1989); G. Postema, Bentham and the Common Law Tradition 3-38 (1986).

10. The fullest treatment of Austin's thought is W. Rumble, The Thought of John Austin: Jurisprudence, Colonial Reform, and the British Constitution (1985).

11. J. Austin, The Province of Jurisprudence Determined (1861).

12. *Id.* at 71-87.

13. H. Maine, Ancient Law: Its Connection with the Early History of Society and Its Relation to Modern Ideas 2-3 (F. Pollock ed. 10th ed. 1906) (London 1861). See generally R. Cocks, Sir Henry Maine: A Study in Victorian Jurisprudence 33-34 (1988) (discussing Maine's historical approach to law); G. Feaver, From Status to Contract: A Biography of Sir Henry Maine, 1822-1888, at 45-64 (1969) (Maine hoped to demonstrate that a greater appreciation of the social basis of all legal institutions would be achieved by using historians' techniques). Cocks emphasizes Maine's use of comparative method, which was widely regarded at the time as the highest form of scientific inquiry. See R. Cocks, *supra*, at 34-38.

14. H. Maine, *supra* note 13, at 3.

15. *Id.* at 3. Maine hoped to break the hold of such a priori concepts on legal thought and substitute for them a scientific understanding of the growth of law. His chapter on the early history of property is a model of his method. See *id.* at 237-94. He criticizes the belief, given classic form by Blackstone, that occupancy is the foundation of private property. The whole law of private property, according to Blackstone, is "a natural development from the physical appropriation of unowned things." Utz, Maine's *Ancient Law* and Legal Theory, 16 Conn.L.Rev. 821, 833 (1984) (footnote omitted); see also H. Maine, *supra* note 13, at 245-46. The gradual development of permanent ownership thus appears to be the natural accompaniment of progress towards modernity. Maine, however, denigrated this sort of reasoning:

> These sketches of the plight of human beings in the first ages of the world are effected by first supposing mankind to be divested of a great part of the circumstances by which they are now surrounded, and by then assuming that, in the condition thus imagined, they would preserve the same sentiments and prejudices by which they are now actuated,—although, in fact, these sentiments may have been created and engendered by those very circumstances of which, by the hypothesis, they are to be stripped.

H. Maine, *supra* note 13, at 246-47. In this case, the sentiment or prejudice which is assumed to be always in existence is "an instinctive bias towards the institution of Property." *Id.* at 249. In Maine's view, however, occupancy, or "mere possession," as a means of gaining ownership can arise only after the institution of property has been well established. Only after society accepts "a presumption, arising out of the long continuance of that institution, that *everything ought to have an owner*" can the person who merely asserts ownership acquire permanent, inviolable rights. *Id.* In short, talk of the almost mystical primacy of private property is misplaced. See Utz, *supra*, at 824-38. Once the jurist had untangled the developments leading to law as it was today he would have a collection of principles which could be properly ordered into a code of law. R. Cocks, *supra* note 13, at 5.

16. See Utz, *supra* note 15, at 823-24.

17. H. Maine, *supra* note 13, at 165.
18. F. Pollock, Introduction and Notes to Sir Henry Maine's Ancient Law 424 (1906). Maine's biographer emphasizes his "Whiggish flexibility and lack of dogmatism" on contemporary economic questions. G. Feaver, *supra* note 13, at 293 n. 45.
19. G. Aichele, *supra* note 6, at 95.
20. Holmes, Book Notices, 5 Am.L.Rev. 534, 534-35 (1871) (reviewing A. Dicey, A Treatise on the Rules for the Selection of the Parties to an Action (1870)).
21. *Id.* at 535.
22. See generally Hoeflich, Law and Geometry: Legal Science from Leibniz to Langdell, 30 Am.J.Legal Hist. 95, 108-18 (1986) (the geometric paradigm in Anglo-American law).
23. Holmes, Misunderstandings of the Civil Law, 6 Am.L.Rev. 37 (1871).
24. 92 Eng.Rep. 622 (1703).
25. Holmes, *supra* note 23, at 41. He made the same point several times during the next two years, denying "that fundamental principles are more clearly brought out in the Roman than in the English law" and emphasizing the importance of "the solution of a particular case" to the common law. Holmes, Book Notices, 7 Am.L.Rev. 320, 320 (1873) (reviewing T.W. Greene, Outlines of Roman Law (1872)). In fact, the much vaunted principles of the civil law are meaningless to the modern world, since they "are obscured by traditions which prevented their consistent application, by historical difficulties which have to be overcome before the law can be understood, by principles of classification that have lost their significance, and by a philosophy which is no longer vital." *Id.*
26. Holmes, Book Notices, 3 Am.L.Rev. 541, 541 (1869) (reviewing J. Benjamin, A Treatise on the Law of Sales of Personal Property (London 1868)) [hereinafter Holmes, Review of Benjamin]. For similar expressions, see Holmes, Book Notice, 1 Am.L.Rev. 375-76 (1867) (reviewing D. Power, Roscoe's Digest of the Law of Evidence in Criminal Cases (6th ed. Philadelphia 1866)); Holmes, Book Notice, 5 Am.L.Rev. 113, 113 (1870) (reviewing J. Schouler, A Treatise on the Law of the Domestic Relations (1870)); Holmes, Codes, and the Arrangement of the Law, 5 Am.L.Rev. 1, 12-13 (1870) (Holmes's first major article).
27. Holmes, Review of Benjamin, *supra* note 26, at 542.
28. Letter from Oliver Wendell Holmes to John Chipman Gray (July 13, 1877), Oliver Wendell Holmes, Jr. Papers, box 33, folder 26, Harvard Law School Library Manuscript Division [hereinafter Holmes Papers], reprinted in Microfilm Edition of the Holmes Papers, reel 53, frames 256-59 (original) (1985); *id.* reel 24, frames 544-45 (typed transcript). The article referred to is evidently Holmes, Primitive Notions in Modern Law. No. II, 11 Am.L.Rev. 641 (1877) [hereinafter Holmes, Primitive Notions in Modern Law. No. II].
29. Letter from Oliver Wendell Holmes to John Chipman Gray (July 18, 1877), Microfilm Edition of the Holmes Papers, *supra* note 28, reel 53, frames 260-61 (original); *id.* reel 24, frame 546 (typed transcript).
30. Green, Slander and Libel, 6 Am.L.Rev. 593, 612 (1872) (reviewing J. Townsend, A Treatise on the Wrongs Called Slander and Libel, and on the Remedy by Civil Action for those Wrongs (2d ed. 1872)).
31. Holmes, Book Notices, 6 Am.L.Rev. 723 (1872) (reviewing The Law Magazine and Review New Series No. 3 (April 1, 1872)) [hereinafter Holmes, Review of Pollock].
32. *Id.* at 723.
33. *Id.*
34. *Id.*
35. *Id.*
36. *Id.* at 724.
37. *Id.*
38. *Id.*
39. Holmes, Theory of Torts, 7 Am.L.Rev. 652 (1873).
40. Holmes, Primitive Notions in Modern Law, 10 Am.L.Rev. 422 (1876).
41. *Id.* at 423. Holmes first criticized Austin's conception of culpability in Holmes, Review of Pollock, *supra* note 31, at 725.
42. Holmes, *supra* note 40, at 423.
43. Holmes, Primitive Notions in Modern Law. No. II, *supra* note 28.
44. *Id.* at 641. The article referred to was Holmes, The Arrangement of the Law: Privity, 7 Am.L.Rev. 46 (1873) [hereinafter Holmes, Arrangement of the Law].
45. Holmes, Primitive Notions in Modern Law. No. II, *supra* note 28, at 641 (summarizing his earlier article on Arrangement of the Law).
46. Holmes, Arrangement of the Law, *supra* note 44, at 49.
47. *Id.* passim.
48. Holmes, Primitive Notions in Modern Law. No. II, *supra* note 28, at 641.
49. *Id.* at 641-42.
50. *Id.* at 643-53.
51. *Id.* at 647.
52. *Id.* at 654.
53. Holmes, *supra* note 40, at 423.
54. Holmes, Primitive Notions in Modern Law. No. II, *supra* note 28, at 654-55.
55. *Id.* at 656-60.
56. *Id.* at 657-58.

57. *Id.* at 657 (footnote omitted).
58. 4 J. Kent, Commentaries on American Law 441-42 n. 1 (O.W. Holmes 12th ed. Boston 1873). Several articles by Laveleye are referred to in footnote one, as is Holmes's "Arrangement of the Law." *Id.*
59. Holmes, Possession, 12 Am.L.Rev. 688 (1878).
60. *Id.* at 698.
61. *Id.*
62. *Id.*
63. *Id.* at 700.
64. *Id.* at 701.
65. *Id.*
66. *Id.* at 700-01.
67. *Id.* at 717.
68. *Id.* at 696-98.
69. *Id.* at 702.
70. *Id.*
71. *Id.* at 707.
72. *Id.* at 710.
73. *Id.* at 702.
74. *Id.* at 719.
75. *Id.*
76. Holmes, Review of Pollock, *supra* note 31, at 723.
77. See R. Cosgrove, Our Lady the Common Law: An Anglo-American Legal Community, 1870-1930, at 113-14 (1987).
78. See H. Pohlman, Justice Oliver Wendell Holmes and Utilitarian Jurisprudence 48-75 (1984).
79. Holmes, *supra* note 59, at 702.
80. O.W. Holmes, *supra* note 1, at 219.
81. R. Cosgrove, *supra* note 77, at 113.
82. Letter from Oliver Wendell Holmes to Frederick Pollock (Mar. 25, 1883), reprinted in 1 Holmes-Pollock Letters: The Correspondence of Mr. Justice Holmes and Sir Frederick Pollock, 1874-1932, at 20-21 (M. Howe ed. 2d ed. 1961) [hereinafter Holmes-Pollock Letters].
83. Letter from John Chipman Gray to Oliver Wendell Holmes (undated), Holmes Papers, *supra* note 28, box 33, folder 23.
84. Letter from Oliver Wendell Holmes to John Chipman Gray (Oct. 27, 1914), Holmes Papers, *supra* note 28, box 33, folder 26.
85. Letter from Oliver Wendell Holmes to John Chipman Gray (Nov. 3, 1909), Holmes Papers, *supra* note 28, box 33, folder 26. The article referred to is Holmes, The Path of the Law, 10 Harv.L.Rev. 457 (1897).
86. Holmes, *supra* note 39.
87. *Id.* at 659-60 (footnote omitted).
88. *Id.* at 660-63.
89. For a discussion of the relationship between Austin's, Maine's and Holmes's ideas of sovereignty, see H. Pohlman, *supra* note 78, at 54-66.
90. Holmes, Book Notices, 1 Am.L.Rev. 554 (1867) (reviewing Story, Commentaries on Equity Jurisprudence (I. Redfield 9th ed. (1866)).
91. Phelps, Issac F. Redfield, in Orations & Essays of Edward John Phelps, Diplomat and Statesman 222-23 (J.G. McCullough ed. 1901).
92. Holmes, *supra* note 90, at 554.
93. *Id.*
94. *Id.*
95. *Id.*
96. Holmes, *supra* note 59, at 702.
97. O.W. Holmes, *supra* note 1, at 161-62. See also Holmes's discussion of fraud, in which he states that "the moral starting-point of liability in general should never be forgotten." *Id.* at 137.
98. On Holmes's rejection of the authority of morals apart from their acceptance by a majority, see R. Cosgrove, *supra* note 77, at 117-18.
99. See, e.g., Book Notice, 14 Am.L.Rev. 233, 234 (1880) (reviewing C. Langdell, A Selection of Cases on the Law of Contracts, with a Summary of the Topics Covered by the Cases (2d ed. 1879)) [hereinafter Holmes, 1880 Review of Langdell]. The involved story of the attribution of the review to Holmes is told in Touster, Holmes a Hundred Years Ago. The Common Law and Legal Theory, 10 Hofstra L.Rev. 673, 695 n. 91 (1982). The link between Holmes and Langdell was most clearly made by Grant Gilmore. See G. Gilmore, *supra* note 7, at 48-56; G. Gilmore, The Death of Contract 14-22, 35-43 (1974). For a critical assessment of recent Holmes scholarship, including observations on the connection between Holmes and Langdell, see H. Pohlman, *supra* note 78, at 144-64.
100. See Touster, *supra* note 99, at 694-704.
101. Holmes, Harvard University, Law School, 5 Am.L.Rev. 177 (1870).
102. Holmes, Book Notice, 5 Am.L.Rev. 715, 716 (1871) (reviewing J. Bryce, The Academical Study of the Civil Law (1871)).

103. See Chase, The Birth of the Modern Law School, 23 Am.J.Legal Hist. 329, 329-48 (1979); Chase, Origins of Modern Professional Education: The Harvard Case Method Conceived as Clinical Instruction in Law, 5 Nova L.J. 323, 323-40 (1981).
104. Holmes, Book Notice, 5 Am.L.Rev. 539, 540 (1871) (reviewing C. Langdell, A Selection of Cases on the Law of Contracts (1870)) [hereinafter Holmes, 1871 Review of Langdell].
105. *Id.*
106. *Id.*
107. See Holmes, Book Notice, 6 Am.L.Rev. 353, 353-54 (1872) (reviewing C. Langdell, A Selection of Cases on the Law of Contracts (1871)).
108. Holmes, 1880 Review of Langdell, *supra* note 99, at 233.
109. *Id.* at 234.
110. *Id.* at 233.
111. O.W. Holmes, *supra* note 1, at 335.
112. *Id.* at 337.
113. *Id.*
114. *Id.* at 338.
115. *Id.* at 1; Holmes, 1880 Review of Langdell, *supra* note 99, at 234.
116. Letter from Frederick Pollock to Oliver Wendell Holmes (Sept. 17, 1897), in 1 Holmes-Pollock Letters, *supra* note 82, at 80.
117. Letter from Christopher C. Langdell to Theodore D. Woolsey (Feb. 6, 1871) Woolsey Family Papers, Series I, box 23, folder 433, Yale University Library Manuscript Division.
118. *Id.*
119. See, e.g., G. Aichele, *supra* note 6, at 124-62.
120. G. Gilmore, *supra* note 7, at 48-49.
121. See Aichele, *supra* note 6, at 61, 144.
122. See W. Rumble, *supra* note 10, at 196-205.
123. See R. Cocks, *supra* note 13, at 131-40.
124. J. Stephen, Liberty, Equality, Fraternity (1873).
125. See B. Mylchreest, The Anglo-American Dialogue on Constitutionalism, 1860-1920, at 215-19 (1988) (unpublished dissertation available at Cornell University).
126. See B. Mylchreest, *supra* note 125, at 115, 216-19; W. Rumble, *supra* note 10, at 201.
127. 1 Holmes-Pollock Letters, *supra* note 82, at 219; see also G. Aichele, *supra* note 6, at 149; B. Mylchreest, *supra* note 125, at 218.
128. 198 U.S. 45, 75 (1905) (Holmes, J., dissenting).
129. See G. Aichele, *supra* note 6, at 148-49.
130. Three exceptions to this neglect are R. Cosgrove, *supra* note 77; B. Mylchreest, *supra* note 125; H. Pohlman, *supra* note 78.
131. G. Aichele, *supra* note 6, at 145.

Chapter 77

The Place of Research in the American Law School

1926

Orrin K. McMurray

Orrin K. McMurray (born November 25, 1869) taught at Columbia, Michigan, and Stanford, and served as professor and dean of the school of jursiprudence in the University of California, Berkeley, from 1907 to 1926. This article first appeared at 5 *American Law School Review* 631 (1926).

Address of the President of the Association of American Law Schools, delivered at the Twenty-Third Annual Meeting in Chicago, December 29, 1925. The discussion following the President's address will be found on page 672 et seq. of this magazine.

The Association of American Law Schools this year completes a quarter century of life. It was organized at Saratoga, August 28, 1900; it has met annually since that date, except in 1917 and 1918, when the meetings were omitted because of the war. During this period, it has had a part in the initiation of practices and movements fraught, in all probability, with considerable importance for our national welfare. It is not my purpose to rehearse in detail these achievements nor to claim for the Association the sole merit for things that must be shared with other agencies. But briefly, and without multiplying details, it may be of interest to mention a few constructive activities in which the Association may claim some share.

In 1902, a former president of this Association, Mr. Ernest W. Huffcut, in an address before the American Bar Association, pointed out that more than one-half the law schools of the country required not even a high school training for entrance, while only seven out of ninety-eight schools studied required any preliminary college training. A fundamental principle of our organization is the necessity of some degree of general education on the part of those preparing for the bar. The original articles required that members should demand of candidates for a degree the completion of a high school course of study or its equivalent. Even this modest requirement was not deemed possible of strict enforcement in the early years of the century. A construction placed upon the article in 1903, under a resolution of the Association, allowed "occasional exceptions in special cases." Standards of preparation have been steadily increased in the case of our members, until now the requirement of preliminary education is in effect two years of work in a college of liberal arts. Meanwhile, the number of law schools demanding at least two years of preliminary college study has increased from seven in 1902 to sixty-five in 1925, and the number demanding at least three years of such study is now twelve.

The three-year law course was another standard by which the Association has firmly stood since its organization. For the first five years of its existence, however, the requirement was, under the terms of the Article establishing it, suspended in its operation. To-day, as we are informed by the latest bulletin of the Carnegie foundation for the Advancement of Teaching, one hundred forty-two schools demand the three-year course in law of all candidates for degrees, while thirty-five per cent of the law students of the country are enrolled in schools demanding a program of work that occupies their full time for at least three academic years. The powerful influence of the American Bar Association supports the position of this Association with respect to preliminary and law school training, and intelligent public opinion rather generally recognizes the desirability of better educational standards for the bar.

From the very beginning we favored the requirement of an examination of all applicants for admission to practice law by boards appointed by the Supreme Courts of the various states, and the abandonment of the privilege of admission to the bar upon the presentation of the diploma of a law school. Almost universally, such boards have been created, examinations now required, and the former privileges withdrawn. It is believed that there has been a general improvement in the character of the examinations.

Unfortunately, many of our people are spending time and money pursuing law courses that demand no test of fitness or standard of preparation, and that fail utterly to equip them for the practice of law under modern conditions. In some cases, these so-called law courses are little more than devices for enriching their promoters.

Too much emphasis may easily be placed upon such external indications of improvement in the standards of the legal profession as are afforded by evidence of an increase in the average time for preparation demanded of lawyers. Other causes have contributed to the possibility of requiring higher demands from candidates for the bar. The diminution during the last quarter of a century in the gross number of working hours annually required by our people to earn a living wage has enabled a greater number to prolong the period of preparation for active life, has increased the annual supply of leisure, and has forced the expansion in numbers and programs of high schools, colleges, and universities, as it has of hotels, motion picture palaces, and other institutions even more definitely pledged to amusement than our colleges.

A recent research bulletin of the National Educational Association has given some statistics in respect to the expense of primary and secondary education in the period from 1890 to 1924, which indicate as well as any other facts that might be adduced the extent to which youth has been released from bondage to physical labor during this time. In 1890, the country expended in this part of its educational program $140,000,000; in 1924, the annual budget had mounted to $1,580,000,000. The sums devoted to higher education have increased correspondingly. More of our people's time and money can be spent on school and college than has ever been the case in our history.

Legal education, without particular merit or fault on the part of teachers, has been forced to share in the forward movement, both for good and evil. The current of events has swept us onward whilst all the time we have imagined that our efforts were shaping progress.

However, there is some merit in moving forward with events. Without the stimulus of this Association and the efforts of the American Bar Association and of state and local bar association, standards of legal education and of admission to the bar might generally have remained until the present day where they were in 1900. The easiest course for the members of this Association to have followed would have been to open their doors to all who might apply, to reap the material profits and reputation that inevitably flow from numbers.

So far as our program has been based on renunciation our position is impregnable to criticism. But must we not admit that we have yielded to compromise in the matter of educational standards? Have we really appropriated to the improvement of legal education so much of the leisure, so much of the economic power of our nation, as we are fairly entitled to, having regard to the great social importance of our profession? At most periods in the history of the English and American bar, I think it is safe to assert that the lawyer, in addition to his technical training, has had a degree of general culture equal at least to that of his clients. Do our requirements preserve this relation between the special culture of the bar and the general culture of the community? Can a university law school justify its position in admitting students with only two years of work in the college of letters, when the business world has adopted a standard demanding a college degree for its higher grades of stenographers, bookkeepers, and clerks? The only excuse is a stultifying admission that time spent in the college of arts is time wasted; that the arts degree signifies nothing. There is no very important reason why one should wear trousers, or bathe frequently—one might call dressing and washing a waste of time. The due proportions of our social life, however, require these conventions. If there is no better basis for requiring the A.B. degree from the lawyer—though I am unwilling to concede that there is none—one can rest the demand upon the fact that it is the prevailing fashion, the need of preserving a degree of harmony among the various elements of our life.

But there is a better reason. With all its faults, the college of letters opens to sentient beings with the intelligence to receive it some vision of science and civilization. As Sir Walter Scott says: "A lawyer without history and literature is a mechanic, a mere working mason; if he possesses some knowledge of these, he may venture to call himself an architect." If the law of the more or less static society in which Scott lived demanded for its true comprehension studies beyond the technique of practice, what of a legal system in a dynamic state of society like ours? The lawyer of a former era might with fidelity to his client confine his learn-ing to procedure, criminal law, the law of real property, a modicum of commercial law. The modern lawyer must have an adequate knowledge of the fundamentals of private law, it is true, but increasingly the activities of the state cut across those of the individual—constitutional law, conflict of laws, administrative law, a body of scientific, historical, and economic knowledge, are some of the weapons he must possess. And back of all is required the critical intelligence demanded to understand the complex conditions of commercial and industrial life, the intricate adjustments of conflicting social interests. A period of preparation that allows the lawyer to embark upon his profession at the age of twenty-five is not too long to equip him for his life work.

Some of our university law schools have recognized both the need and the opportunity, and have insisted on the bachelor's degree in arts as a prerequisite to entrance into the law school. Yet less than a dozen years before Yale University had adopted this requirement, President Hadley, in his report delivered at Yale Commencement in 1902, publicly declared the policy of that University to be against increasing the standards of preliminary education for the law. One of the great benefits from the study of the past is that we may acquire courage in meeting the problems of our own day, by considering the fears and doubts of honest and intelligent men regarding innovations that now have become commonplaces. Archbishop Lee, who in 1525 wrote to Henry VIII from Bordeaux, informing him that an Englishman had just translated the New Testament and intended to import it into the King's realm, "whiche cannot long endure if thies bookes maye come in," the Lord Chancellor in the mid-Victorian period who had rather know that a French army was invading his country than that a deceased wife's sister's marriage bill should become law, the prophets of evil who predicted Jeremiads of woe if workmen's compensation, railroad commissions, blue sky commissions, were established—all such and legions of others testify against that "repose on a formula which prolonged means death."

The conversion of Yale University so soon after her President's carefully deliberated utterance is a particularly striking evidence of the power of truth to get itself established. Mr. Hadley said: "We have our choice concerning the question whether we shall increase this difficulty (the difficulties of the early days of practice) by requiring a long course of secondary education prior to the beginning of professional study, or shall try to minimize it by putting the opportunity for such study within reach of the graduates of our high schools as soon as they are qualified to enter thereon. If we adopt the former system, as so many of our universities are now tending to do, we enhance the artificial difficulties, which are already great enough at best, and tend to make the professions of law and medicine places for the sons of rich men only. The bad effect of such a policy seems to me to be obvious. It is an introduction of a sort of caste system in the worst form. During the past generation we have gradually gotten rid of the traditional distinction between learned and unlearned professions. We have come to the full appreciation of the fact that the work of the manufacturer and the financier, the engineer and the journalist, involves the same sort of ability and character, and carries with it the same sort of social privileges and responsibilities that are involved in that of the lawyer, the physician, or the minister. The gain from this source has been so great that it has been sufficient to offset some of the dangers by which democracy has been menaced. It would be a serious mistake for society if our best universities by their action should attempt to undo any of this work or impose any artificial restrictions which should single out one group of professions as the peculiar property of those who have enjoyed inherited wealth and collegiate education." The answer to the argument is that, ten years after it was made, Yale Law School, under Mr. Hadley's presidency, rejected it in toto.

Besides standing in the vanguard as a defender of standards in legal education, this Association has to its credit such accomplishments as the publication of the Select Essays in Anglo-American Legal History, the Continental Legal History Series, and the Legal Philosophy Series. The outlook both of the bar and of the law school teacher has been materially broadened by the opportunity afforded by these publications to become acquainted with some of the best juristic thought of the world. Also closely interwoven with the history of the Association are the establishment of the Council of Legal Education of the American Bar Association and the creation of the American Law Institute. If not the efficient cause in an Aristotelian sense, it may lay some claim to be a contributing cause of the existence of these important agencies.

In the latest attempt by the bar to solve some of the problems of our jurisprudence, through the efforts of the American Law Institute, not the least interesting feature has been the recruiting of law teachers for aid in the task. The law teacher, thanks in some slight measure to this organization, has become conscious that he belongs to a distinct profession, and the bar and the community have also become aware of him as a contributor to the evolution of our legal system. At the same time he has been recognized by his university confreres as possessing value in the life of the university and to a certain extent engaged like them in the hunt for facts and their possible relations. The broadening of his interests has been reflected in the annual programs of the Association. The great controversy, Case Method of Teaching versus all Persons, has long since been laid on the upper shelf where the classics repose. Even the problems of the curriculum—precisely where shall Agency or Equity be taught, and for how many hours, or shall they be taught at all—by no means awaken the enthusiasm they evoked a dozen years ago.

An increasing number of the law teachers of the present have shifted their interest to that portion of the field of jurisprudence that deals with the relations of the law to actual life. They want to know how the law works, rather than how this rule or that doctrine harmonizes with other rules or doctrines laid down by judges and text-writers, or how the rule or doctrine came to be what it is. Indeed, a tendency may even be noted to peep over the juristic fence into territory belonging to their neighbors. In other words, a curiosity for discovery is awake. The universities must provide in some manner that the enthusiasm may be turned to the service of discovery.

In general, the law school has been oblivious to the value of investigations carried on for their own sake, and has afforded little encouragement or opportu-nity to teacher or student to embark upon such tasks. Both are held to rather strict rules with reference to hours of teaching and units of credit. Neither lei-sure nor physical means are provided for the inquisitive searcher after new relations or new methods. Existing curricula condition the productive activities of our teachers. To be sure, there have been some exceptions, and a few printed volumes attest the value of the modest experiments that have been attempted. Our law reviews also occasionally contain articles transcending current controversies over recent decisions and dealing in the spirit of truth-finding, with the broader and more fundamental aspects of juristic science. But, in the main, research in the law has received little encouragement.

One must not overlook the great treatises on special branches of the law that have been produced by our legal scholars, chiefly within the law schools. They have contributed much to our legal development. But in the main their production involved a utilitarian end—to make available the results of judicial decisions for use by the bar in the work of litigation and in counseling clients. In the main, they have not attempted to study the interrelation of law and the social structure, nor to develop critical methods of approach and investigation. Moreover, the law schools have not in general recognized that the production of such works is one of the purposes for which law schools exist.

In a sense, of course, the lawyer, and even more the law teacher, is constantly engaged in research; he deals with original sources, and he is immensely diligent in their analysis and study. But his investigations are nearly always directed toward an immediately practical purpose—the lawyer's toward winning his case; the teacher's toward organizing and simplifying his material. The free play of intelligence upon the materials of jurisprudence, this is the sort of thing for which our law schools with their rigid teaching programs have allowed little scope. And the co-operative spirit, which has furthered the advancement of science to such a high degree, has been almost wholly absent from such investigations as have been made independently by legal scholars.

It is easy to suggest reasons for the lack of development of the law school on this side. First and foremost, the naïve philosophy of the layman, maintained, indeed, by many intelligent lawyers, regards the law as a field in which discovery is impossible, since it is something given or revealed, complete and finished. "Poor will be the judge," says James C. Carter, "who does not acknowledge that he is a seeker among divine sources for pre-existing truth." If that be so, there is no need for the encouragement of the sort of research that has made possible the physical and biological sciences. Second, and closely related with the former reason, an instinctive conservatism, natural to every profession and reflected in public opinion, has engendered the fear that free research in law, as indeed in any of the social sciences, may ultimately have consequences detrimental to the existing social status. But the reason that has chiefly prevailed in preventing the university school of law from developing a program of research comparable with those developed in history, economics, psychology, or natural science, may best be found in the nature of the law school and its problems during the last half century—the period of the birth in our country of the scientific spirit.

It is not necessary before a group of law teachers to dwell upon the history of the American law school. The medieval cleft in legal education that existed between Universities and Inns of Court produced a tradition that was received by our people with the common law of England. That law had been in the main the work of a self-governing co-optative group, which bore the burden of preparing its own prospective members. Corporately it had sadly neglected this obligation but its duty of educating future barristers was still carried in England by individual members of the profession, who received pupils. Though the self-governing bar disappeared in our states, the idea persisted that the training of lawyers might reasonably be left to the bar. Indeed, the necessities of pioneer communities could scarcely provide other means for a legal education. The pupils of the English barrister became the students of the American attorney. In general, the latter felt no obligation toward the young men in his office, between whom and himself there was usually lacking the cash nexus that was found in England. Occasionally, however, an American lawyer would receive students who paid fees; with such, it became a natural matter to transform a group of such students into a school. The law schools, such as they were, of fifty years past, were incurably affected with the professional point of view implicit in their origin.

When our country became conscious of the claims of scientific study in the '70's of last century, and girded itself for the task, it found the law schools almost exclusively in the hands of the legal profession. The notion of sweeping the law school into the orbit of the University, or organizing graduate work in legal science as it was organized in history, or philosophy, or natural or political science, very naturally fell outside the plan of the University builders of that era. They took the popular appraisal of the lawyer and of his work, and organized the scientific activities of the University, omitting law from the circle. Frequently, indeed, the law school was loosely connected with the University—sometimes even controlled by an independent body of trustees.

It is obvious that the progress of the law schools of the country during the last generation has been closely bound up with the development of the Universities. The school buildings are now usually found on the University campus. A differentiation has occurred between the legal practitioner and the teaching profession. To use an old expression, the law faculty has become a learned faculty. That the complete domestication of the law school in the University may lead to results fraught with consequence to the development of our legal system I should be the last to deny. Fortunately, it is not necessary to predict the future. It may be that we shall have one law of the University and another law of the forum, as in old Germany; it may be that our law will lose the toughness of the law taught in the Inns of Court before the English renaissance. One's views as to the desirability of this or that detail in organization or curriculum may be consciously dependent upon his historical enthusiasms, but the final result will be determined by forces which we can but moderately control or direct.

The great improvements in legal education during the last quarter of a century seem to indicate that the time is auspicious for the University Law School to begin a broadening of its field, by welcoming independent research on the part of its faculty and advanced students. This means, of course, the provision of physical opportunities (libraries, rooms, materials) and of proper clerical and other assistance; it means, also, the release of the investigator from too rigid a curricular program. Above all, it involves the eagerness and enthusiasm of the workers. It is not a vain hope that at the bar, as well as in the teaching profession, will be found men willing and able to carry on the work.

That a great task lies ahead in the patient study of legal rules, doctrines, and institutions from every possible angle of approach is apparent to every man who thinks. Take such questions (by no means among the most important awaiting solution) as those involved in the treatment by society of negligent injuries. The increasing volume of such injuries is becoming a matter of significance in our social economy. Has the law met the problem? Plainly an investigation on such a topic carries one out of his library, though that must be ransacked for material to discover the experience of others. The actual results of negligence litigation must be studied, not only from the statistics of lawsuits, but from the testimony of those who have participated in them. The expenses of public service companies and others must be analyzed. Safety devices, police control, a hundred matters, must be investigated. One can conceive the application of the mathematics of probability and the results of psychological experiments to aid in formulation of rules of behavior. And what is true on such a subject is equally the case with every problem of adjustment of law to a changing society.

What an advantage it would be to such an organization as the National Crime Commission, or the American Law Institute, if our country had possessed for many years such an institution as Von Liszt's Seminary in Criminal Law, with its hosts of experts, versed in this or that phase of the general problem. Permit me to quote from Professor Lorenzen's description of that seminar, given some twenty years since, for the reason that it affords a model of what might well be undertaken in our own country:

> It occupies about half a dozen rooms at Charlottenburg, and has a library on criminal law containing over fifteen thousand volumes. The Seminary meets every two weeks, at which time a member gives an address, or report upon a subject upon which he is working. A discussion follows, which is sometimes continued in an extra session. The special object here is to give to the student a chance to profit by the criticism of the instructor or fellow members before he gives final form to his paper. In this way, his attention is often directed to a point overlooked. He is led to re-examine more carefully the positions taken, and perchance to change them upon more mature reflection. Since the winter semester of 1903 to 1904, the increase in the number of students desiring to do seminary work has caused Professor Von Liszt to divide his Seminary into sections, seven in number—the dogmatic; the criminal psychological; the criminal statistical; the criminal political; the philosophical; the historical; and the one on criminal procedure. These hold sessions for discussion and study. Several of them have undertaken larger pieces of work. One of them, for example, has collected all the material, legislative and other, concerning diminished responsibility for crime; another has collected, arranged, and published everything written in recent years on the general principles of criminal law in connection with the movement for the revision of the present German Criminal Code. A great many of the articles, prepared in the Seminary, appear in the Review of Criminal Law, of which Von Liszt is one of the editors; others appear elsewhere in reviews or as independent publications. In 1903 the productivity of the Seminary had reached such a degree as to justify the publication of an independent review by the Seminary, called 'Transactions of the Judicial Seminary in Criminal Law,' in which the more able papers are printed. Traveling fellowships have been awarded by the Seminary from time to time for the study of problems in criminal law or criminal procedure abroad. In this and other ways the members of the Seminary are encouraged and stimulated to do their best.

If the necessary development of our law is to proceed with order, we must have many working in the field, each contributing his bit. Possibly ninetenths of the theses produced in our Universities purporting to be pieces of original research are worthless; possibly the encouragement of so-called research has resulted in attracting mediocre men, entering the field of scholarship and teaching. But even mediocre men may contribute something to the development of knowledge, and if one-tenth or even one-hundredth of the annual crop of theses contain some germinating seed for scientific progress, the waste involved is amply paid for.

It may be urged that the work of research in law may be left to Foundations and Institutes. They have their place, and an important place, in the intellectual and social structure. But the divorce between teaching and research must not be permitted, if the most fruitful results are to ensue. We must preserve the reproductive capacity in learning, and that can find its protection only in an association of scholars teaching as well as learning.

The means for putting into effect a modest program are at hand. All that is needed in many of our schools is the release from a part of their teaching obligation of a few members of the faculty, who indicate a desire and a capacity for research work, and a corresponding release of some of the ablest students, who may desire to undertake such work, from a part of their program. In our rigid and formalistic educational system, it may be that this cannot always be accomplished, but I believe that in many places in our country it is possible, and, where it is possible, can there be a question as to its desirability?

Suppose, as an experiment, that one-half of the regular curriculum of the last year of the law school work were given up by ten per cent of the students, and one member of the faculty were relieved from all save one course, that he might conduct a seminar in industrial law, or in procedural reform, or in problems in corporate reorganization, or in the organization and financing of community apartment houses, or in the legal history of a state, or in any other topic that might be selected, would or would not the morale of that school be improved? Suppose that these able students were thus forced to omit evidence and trusts and corporations from their law school course in exchange for the efforts put forth in their seminar, would the sacrifice be too great for the benefits derived? I admit that the ideal seminar would be constituted of men who have finished their professional courses, and who, after some experience in the world as lawyers or teachers, desire to pursue some special studies.

In time—and possibly within a very short time, if we can judge by the manner in which students of law, without compulsion, have flocked to schools demanding the highest standards of admission—graduates would enroll themselves in the seminars, not necessarily for credits in units or degrees, but because of the opportunity to study thoroughly, and in association with other men of ability, some outstanding problems of law. I believe there is a body of such men in nearly every large center of population, and that many of them could find time for advanced studies leading to deeper insight into the problems of the law. Indeed, even more than the medical profession, the legal profession seems to have a unique potentiality for such sort of development. The admission of members to the seminar must lie in the hands of the teacher advised by the other members. Freedom, indeed, must be its very life.

I do not advocate a particular program. Indeed, it is of the essence of the idea that each investigator possess freedom to develop his program independently. The central notion is the creation of groups of investigators, guided by legal scholars, or by teachers who may evolve into legal scholars. In some cases, it may be desirable to relieve the investigator wholly from the conduct of professional courses. Generally, however, it would be more feasible to gather together a small group, consisting of advanced students, and, if possible, of practicing lawyers and faculty members, under the guidance of a member of the faculty best prepared or best disposed to undertake the conduct of the studies—in short, a permanent round table.

During the last generation, because the opportunity and the will were present, we have been able to develop professional schools with high standards of learning and with high ideals. Is it not possible that we can establish foci of creative activity, which, within the next generation, will serve a great purpose in the process of aiding in the reshaping of our law to the conditions of our national life? To me it seems that the evolution of the law school into a true place of research is inevitable, if only we address ourselves to the task.

Chapter 78

Why Law Professors Should Not Be Hessian-Trainers

1988

Robert M. Jarvis

Robert Jarvis is Professor at Nova Southeastern University Center for the Study of Law. This article first appeared at 13 *Nova Law Review* 69 (1988).

I. Introduction

In his thoughtful remarks on the current state of legal scholarship, Professor Clark Byse touches on many of the questions which today surround legal education.[1] Among the issues discussed by Professor Byse, and the one to which I wish to speak, is the conflict between the law professor's duty to teach and the law professor's obligation to engage in scholarship.

As Professor Byse notes, the seminal work on whether law professors should pursue excellence in the classroom or in the library is Professor Thomas F. Bergin's classic work in which he described the law professor as a man (and now also a woman) divided against himself.[2] In Professor Bergin's opinion, almost all law professors belong to one of two camps, which Professor Bergin has classified as "authentic academics" and "Hessian-trainers."[3] According to Professor Bergin's thesis, those who belong to the former camp possess unique scholarly abilities, while those in the latter camp excel at preparing law students for careers at the private bar.[4]

In Professor Bergin's view, the existence of these two camps has caused law professors to suffer from intellectual schizophrenia by making them (as well as others) believe that law professors should be both authentic academics and Hessian-trainers at the same time.[5] The result, according to Professor Bergin, is highly counterproductive: authentic academics attempt to teach, with miserable results, while Hessian-trainers struggle to engage in scholarship, with equally miserable results.[6] To cure this schizophrenia, Professor Bergin urges that both camps be liberated so that the authentic academics and the Hessian-trainers can be "fully one or the other."[7] Thus, Professor Bergin would allow authentic academics to devote all of their time to scholarship and would permit Hessian-trainers to spend all of their time teaching.[8]

In revisiting Professor Bergin's article twenty years later, Professor Byse has come to the conclusion that Professor Bergin is wrong, and argues forcefully that law professors have an obligation both to teach and to engage in scholarship. Although he believes that law professors can choose which task to emphasize,[9] Professor Byse is firm in his view that all law professors must contribute to "both roles to the full extent of our abilities."[10]

Is Professor Bergin right? Should both the authentic academics and the Hessian-trainers be allowed to follow their own callings? Or is Professor Byse correct when he states that except in a few elite institutions, law professors are "morally bound" to be authentic academics and Hessian-trainers? As the title of my response indicates, I believe that both Professor Bergin and Professor Byse are wrong with respect to how the schizophrenia of law professors should be cured. In my opinion, authentic academics should not co-exist with Hessian-trainers in law schools and law professors should not strive to be both authentic academics and Hessian-trainers. Rather, law professors should be—indeed, must be—authentic academics, and should leave Hessian-training to other members of the legal profession.

II. The Law Professor's Agenda

As Professor Byse notes, law professors have remarkable control over the setting of their professional agendas.[11] The right (for it is always described as a right rather than a privilege) to set one's own agenda as a law professor is variously defended as a necessary part of academic freedom and an important counterweight against the lure of the greater financial rewards offered by private practice.[12] Moreover, as Professor Byse points out, the right is not a completely unfettered one, for all law professors must devote "an irreducible minimum of time and effort" to "nondelegable" obligations, such as preparing for and teaching classes, drafting and grading examinations, judging moot court competitions, serving on law school and university committees, and supervising student papers.[13]

Thus, it may strike some as heretical for me to suggest that both tenured and untenured law professors have an agenda which requires as its primary order of business the continuing production of scholarship.[14] Although Professor Byse agrees that law professors should be producing more scholarship than they do at the present time,[15] and argues that stricter tenure standards combined with decanal and peer pressure may be useful in achieving this goal,[16] he stops short of saying that law professors have an actual duty to either engage in scholarship (if they are not already engaged in scholarship) or engage in more scholarship (if they are already engaged in some scholarship). Rather, Professor Byse opts for an individualistic standard in which "the decision to or not to engage in scholarship" is seen as a highly personal one which "must be made by each of us in a conscientious and responsible manner."[17] Although Professor Byse ends his remarks by saying that all law professors have an (undefined) moral duty to engage in scholarship to the extent that our abilities (as well as our non-teaching obligations, professional and otherwise) permit, he answers Charles Frankel's important question[18] by writing that mastering the art of teaching is as important as mastering the art of scholarship.[19]

III. Why Law Professors Must Make Scholarship Their Single Most Important Task

Why must law teachers make scholarship the single most important item on their professional agendas? Why can't members of law school faculties live in a world composed of authentic academics and Hessian-trainers, as Professor Bergin suggests? Why isn't it enough for law professors to strive, within their own limits, to be both authentic academics and Hessian-trainers, as Professor Byse believes? There are two reasons, which are really two sides of the same coin.

First, law professors are not equipped to be Hessian-trainers, although other members of the legal profession are very well equipped to be Hessian-trainers. Second, law professors are very well equipped to be authentic academics, while no other members of the legal profession are equipped to be authentic academics. Since I take as a given that society needs both authentic academics and Hessian-trainers,[20] the question becomes one of resource allocation: in what activity can the efforts of the law professor make the greatest contribution?

Turning to my first proposition, which states that law professors are bad Hessian-trainers while other members of the legal profession are good Hessian-trainers, Professor Byse's comments are accurate but incomplete. As Professor Byse states, "Our students come to us, for the most part, to be educated to become practicing lawyers. . . ."[21] As a result, law students and law professors differ in a way which is much more fundamental than what Professor Byse describes as the absence of a "community of scholarly purpose."[22] Not only do law students not seek to do what their professors do, as Professor Byse points out,[23] law students seek to engage in the very activity that their professors are prohibited from engaging in.[24] While law students enter law school to join the practicing bar, law professors join law school faculties by leaving (some might say by escaping) the practicing bar.[25]

Given the disparity of goals between law students and law professors, it is clear that law professors are not suited to being Hessian-trainers, regardless of whether they themselves ever were proficient Hessians. If the law professor once was a successful Hessian, he cannot remain one over time. At some point in his career as a law professor he will become too far removed from the actual practice of law to remain a modern Hessian-trainer, living as he must on worn-out war stories and telling students about how law used to be practiced.[26] On the other hand, if the law professor was a bad Hessian, then he will be a bad Hessian-trainer from the very beginning, and will remain so.[27]

Even if a law professor could somehow be or become skilled at Hessian-training, one must ask whether there is any reason for him to do so. The answer is clearly no. The legal profession, which has witnessed explosive growth in the past fifteen years, already has more than a sufficient number of Hessian-trainers. These Hessian-trainers can be found in the associate training programs of both small and large firms, in the growing number of continuing (and in some jurisdictions now mandatory) legal education programs conducted across the country, in the seemingly endless number of practical articles and treatises which are produced each year, and in the myriad of other self-improvement efforts in which the organized bar participates regularly. Thus, even if law professors could become Hessian-trainers of the highest caliber, there is no reason for them to undertake such an effort.

This fact leads to my second proposition, which is that only law professors have the possibility of becoming and remaining authentic academics. To understand fully this proposition, one must keep clearly in mind how few law professor positions exist in this country. As anyone who in recent times has tried to become a law professor knows, obtaining a tenure-track position in a law school is nearly impossible.[28]

Those who are lucky enough to become law professors[29] have a social responsibility to choose carefully what they do with their professional time. Since law professors can structure their professional lives with a freedom unknown to other members of the legal community,[30] and since there are so few law professor positions in the country, law professors must not conduct projects which could be done as well (or done well enough) by non-law professors.

As an example of my second proposition, consider the following. Although any member of the legal profession may write an article geared to the practitioner or produce a text on some practical aspect of lawyering, only law professors have the time, not to mention the library and research assistant resources, necessary to produce a *scholarly* article or a *scholarly* book. Similarly, law professors make poor use of their time when they act as Hessian-trainers. Since we have more than enough Hessian-trainers, law professors should be seeking out and engaging in activities which only they can do, namely, the production of scholarly works which are marked not only by thorough research (whether such research is doctrinal or empirical in nature) and ample citation (whether such citation is to legal or non-legal sources), but by the sort of informed and thoughtful analysis which can come only through long periods of unhurried consideration, reflection, study and discussion with others, the sort of periods which no practitioner could ever record on his timesheet.[31]

IV. Conclusion

Should I be understood as saying that law professors should be bad teachers? That they should come to their classes either unprepared or not at all? That they should have little or no passing familiarity with the content of the textbooks they assign? Of course not. After all, the mere size of our students' tuition notices prohibit any such thing. What I am saying is that law professors should realize that their *highest* obligation is to scholarship, and that this obligation does not begin in the year before they come up for tenure and end in the year after tenure is obtained. It is lifelong, it is constant, it is the justification for our collective existences.[32] Hessian-training, on the other hand, should be primarily left to the Hessians, of whom there are plenty and who are much better at it anyway.[33]

In short then, Professor Bergin is wrong in his belief that law schools have a place for both authentic academics and Hessian-trainers alike. They do not, because there simply are not enough law faculty places to go around. Likewise, Professor Byse is wrong that law professors should strive to be successful authentic academics and successful Hessian-trainers. Whether a law professor is successful or fails totally at becoming a Hessian-trainer will be irrelevant in the lives of his students, since they will be surrounded by Hessian-trainers forever as soon as they leave law school and join the practicing bar. What law students will have only for a brief time, however, is the chance to be surrounded by authentic academics.[34] Moreover, if law professors fail to become and remain authentic academics, they will be robbing society and the profession of the unique scholarly contributions which only a person leading the life of a law professor will ever be able to make.'[35]

NOTES

1. Byse, *Legal Scholarship, Legal Realism and the Law Teacher's Intellectual Schizophrenia*, 13 NOVA L. REV. 9 (1988).

2. Bergin, *The Law Teacher: A Man Divided Against Himself*, 54 VA. L. REV. 637 (1968).

3. *Id.* at 638. Although Professor Bergin admits that some individual law professors represent distillates of both personalities, and pronounces such persons "healthy," he contends that their numbers are few. *Id.*

4. *Id.* at 656-57.

5. *Id.* at 638.

6. *Id.* at 656-57.

7. *Id.* at 657.

8. Professor Bergin also suggests that the law school curriculum be redesigned to offer students a choice between earning a practical degree (which would be called an LL.B.) or an academic degree (which would be called a Ph.D. in law). *Id.*

9. Byse, *supra* note 1, at 30.

10. *Id.* at 31.

11. *Id.* at 29.

12. See further Christie, *The Recruitment of Law Faculty*, 1987 DUKE L.J. 306.

13. Byse, *supra* note 1, at 29. See also Stubbs, *Only Nine Hours a Week!*, 21 J. LEGAL EDUC. 566, 566-67 (1969).

14. To a certain extent, of course, non-tenured law professors have such an agenda forced upon them due to the relatively short period of time (normally five to seven years) between appointment and tenure review and the requirement that they have published prior to receiving tenure. See further Abrams, *Sing Muse: Legal Scholarship for New Law Teachers*, 37 J. LEGAL EDUC. 1(1987); Kane, *Some Thoughts on Scholarship for Beginning Teachers*, 37 J. LEGAL EDUC. 14 (1987); Richmond, *Advice to the Untenured*, 13 Nova L. Rev. 79 (1988).

15. Byse, *supra* note 1, at 30 (*citing* Swygert & Gozansky, *Senior Law Faculty Publication Study: Comparisons of Law School Productivity*, 35 J. LEGAL EDUC. 373 (1985)). See also Ellman, *A Comparison of Law Faculty Production in Leading Law Reviews*, 33 J. LEGAL EDUC. 681 (1983). But see Kaye & Ellman, *The Pitfalls of Empirical Research: Studying Faculty Publication Studies*, 36 J. LEGAL EDUC. 24 (1986).

16. Byse, *supra* note 1, at 30.

17. *Id.*

18. Frankel, *Reflections on a Worn-Out Model*, DAEDALUS, Fall 1974, at 25, 29-30.

19. Byse, *supra* note 1 at 31.

20. As Professor Bergin observes, society needs authentic academics to improve the social performance of law and requires Hessian-trainers to assure an adequate supply of practicing lawyers. Bergin, *supra* note 2, at 638-39.

21. Byse, *supra* note 1, at 19.

22. *Id.* at 20.

23. *Id.* at 19.

24. The rules of the American Bar Association state that a law school shall have no fewer than six full-time faculty members, and defines a full-time faculty member as:

> one who during the academic year devotes substantially all working time to teaching and legal scholarship, and has no outside office or business activities and whose outside professional activities, if any, are limited to those which relate to major academic interests or enrich the faculty member's capacity as a scholar or teacher, or are of service to the public generally, and do not unduly interfere with one's responsibility as a faculty member.

American Bar Association Standards for Approval of Law Schools Standard 402(b) 1987. Nevertheless, it would be the exceptional law professor who could honestly say that he does not believe that at least one of his colleagues (whether at his own law school or at another law school) is not ignoring the proscriptions of Standard 402(b).

25. While many law professors have practiced before joining a faculty (although a sizeable minority have not), the reality is that those who have practiced usually have done so for three years or less. Indeed, it generally is agreed that a person who has practiced for more than five years is a less-than-ideal law professor candidate. See further Glickstein, *Law School Where the Elite Meet to Teach*, 10 NOVA L.J. 541 (1986). But see Jacobs, *Law Schools Find Niche for New Breed of Professor*, MANHATTAN LAW., Apr. 12-18, 1988, at 3, col. 1 (profiling several young law professors who came to teaching only after long periods of service outside academia and reporting that Professor John Coffee, chairman of the Appointments Committee at Columbia University, believes that increasing emphasis is being placed on experience when looking for new law faculty members).

26. Even if he chooses to ignore standard 402(b) and serves as an active consultant to private law firms, *see supra* note 24, such consulting cannot serve as a complete substitute for actual practice.

27. Dean Prosser long ago concluded, however, that those who fail in the practice of law only rarely are hired to serve as law professors. See Prosser, *Lighthouse No Good*, 1 J. LEGAL EDUC. 257, 260 (1948) ("With due allowance for the inevitable exceptions, the venerable gentlemen who compose our faculties were once, whatever they may be now, the most promising young men in the practice of law.").

28. See further Zenoff & Barron, *So You Want to be a Law Professor?*, 12 J. L. & EDUC. 379 (1983). Although no one knows how many persons seek to become law professors, see Bruce & Swygert, *The Law Faculty Hiring Process*, 18 HOUS. L. REV. 215, 221 (1981), it is clear that there always have been many more applicants than positions. See Prosser, *Advice to the Lovelorn*, 3 J. LEGAL EDUC. 505, 507 (1951). That there is intense competition for the few available law professor positions is not surprising, especially when one considers the demographics of the legal profession. As Professor Byse points out, there are currently 4,500 law professor positions in the United States. Byse, *supra* note 1, at 14. By the same token, there are now 700,000 attorneys in the United States, a number which is expected to grow to 1 million by the year 2000. T. Morgan & R. Rotunda, *Professional Responsibility—Problems and Materials* 2 (4th ed. 1987). Thus, at current levels, only 1 out of every 156 lawyers can be a law professor at any given time. Moreover, it has been predicted that the need for new law professors in the future will be considerably less than in previous times, when the entrance of women and minorities into the legal profession, the opening of new law schools, and the growth in the scope and breadth of course offerings (due to the addition of such new courses as environmental law), created an unparalleled demand for new teachers. See Pye, *Legal Education in an Era of Change: The Challenge*, 1987 DUKE L.J. 191, 195. It is true, however, that if one does manage to find a position as a law professor, the likelihood of receiving tenure is quite high. Although in recent times there have been a few highly publicized cases of persons affiliated with certain scholarship movements being denied tenure, such as Clare Dalton at Harvard University and Drucilla L. Cornell at the University of Pennsylvania, see Moss, *Would This Happen to a Man?*, 74 ABA J. 50 (June 1, 1988), the reality is that most law professors do receive tenure. See Christie, *supra* note 12, at 310. In comparison, a recent study found that the chances of making partner in a New York City law firm ranged from ten to twenty percent. Wise, *Psst! Wanna Make Partner?*, NAT'L L.J., Oct.26, 1987, at 1, col. 2. See also Christie, *supra* note 12, at 308.

29. In using the word "luck," I do not mean to imply that those who receive positions as law professors in any way are not qualified for their jobs. Rather, I simply mean to say that in addition to possessing the proper academic and past employment qualifications, see Glickstein, *supra* note 25, one must also be in the right place at the right time, since most law school faculty recruiting committees seek to hire not the best available candidate but the best available candidate who can fill the law school's curriculum needs. See further Zenoff & Barron, *supra* note 28, at 401. See also Prosser, *supra* note 28, at 507-08.

30. Zenoff & Barron, *supra* note 28, at 391. As Dean Prosser once wrote: "The professor works when he feels like it; and if, on any given afternoon, he decides to go to a ball game, he merely closes his office and walks away, whistling cheerily as he goes." Prosser, *supra* note 27. The disparity between the freedom enjoyed by law professors and other members of the legal profession in general, but particularly with respect to being able to pursue scholarship, has become very pronounced as law firms have increased associate salaries to astronomical levels. In some New York City law firms, the starting salary for new law school graduates now has reached $76,000-per-year. See Lyne, *Weil, Gotshal Sets $76,000 Going Rate*, MANHATTAN LAW., July 5-11, 1988, at 1, col. 2. In exchange for such large salaries, firms insist that associates concentrate on nothing but the firm. As Professor Roger C. Cramton of Cornell University has noted: "Law firms not only expect a lawyer to be zealous on behalf of the client, but they expect the young lawyer to make the law firm his or her principal commitment—ahead of family, friends, and outside interests." Behof, *For Love or Money?*, STUDENT LAW., Nov.1987, at 16, 19. In an attempt to make themselves more attractive to graduating students, some law firms are now allowing associates to "buy back" some of their time by accepting reduced salaries in return for having the opportunity to pursue non-firm matters. See, e.g., Kilbourne, *The 77% Solution: Kronish, Lieb Offers Yale Grads More Freedom at Lower Pay Scale*, MANHATTAN LAW., Nov. 17-23, 1987, at 3, col. 3 (reporting that the Manhattan law firm of Kronish, Lieb, Weiner & Hellman is offering Yale Law School students the opportunity to join the firm at 77 percent of its usual starting salary in return for being allowed to spend up to one-third of their time on such pursuits as "public interest law, scholarship or even politics.").

31. In some circumstances, however, it can be very helpful for a law professor to engage in writing projects which are practical rather than scholarly in nature. As Professor Robert H. Abrams of Wayne State University has demonstrated ably, the production of what he terms "busy work" (including bar journal articles, survey pieces, and previews of U.S. Supreme Court cases) and "lower order" work (typified by glorified casenotes, state-of-the-law articles, and treatise sections) can be a useful first step towards the production of such "higher order" work as affirmative thesis articles, law reform articles, and frontal attacks on citadels of major legal doctrine. Abrams, *supra* note 14, at 2-3.

32. Of course, many believe that the primary (or only) justification for the existence of law professors is that they train future

lawyers, and that the requirement that law professors publish is one imposed not by the bar (which is indifferent to whether law professors engage in scholarship) but by the universities with which law schools have chosen to affiliate. See further Chase, *The Legal Scholar as Producer*, 13 NOVA L. REV. 57 (1988), and Hurst, *Research Responsibilities of University Law Schools*, 10 J. LEGAL EDUC. 147 (1957). While I have no doubt that the bar does see law professors in this way, and that this fact accounts for the constant law professor-bashing which is carried out by the bar, see, e.g., Hazard, *Competing Aims of Legal Education*, 59 N.D.L. REV. 533, 544 (1983), I reject as improper a vision of law professors as mere robots relentlessly turning out the massive number of associates needed to keep law firms stocked with new lawyers.

33. If law students come to law school to learn how to be Hessians, and if law professors were to follow my view that Hessian-training should take place after law school, one may legitimately wonder what I believe law students should do while in law school. Although I wish I had an original answer to this seemingly provocative question, the answer has already been given by Professor Bergin: law schools, led by law professors, should be focusing on policy training. Bergin, *supra* note 2, at 650. See also Cramton, *Demystifying Legal Scholarship*, 75 GEO. L.J. 1, 11 (1986) ("The professional orientation of American law schools, while contributing to their success as professional training grounds, does interfere with the contribution that they have made and can make to better understanding of law and justice."). I differ from Professor Bergin only in approach. Whereas he suggests that law schools establish a uniform first year curriculum and then require students to choose after the first year whether they wish to follow a practitioner or academic program, see *supra* note 8, I would require all law students to follow an academic program, leaving all Hessian-training to post-law school programs (formal or otherwise) run by non-law professors. This position also places me at odds with Professor Byse, who would have law professors combine academic training and Hessian-training. I recognize that my position is "old-fashioned," and that I am swimming against a tide of sentiment which favors practical legal education. See, e.g., Wald, *Teaching the Trade: An Appellate Judge's View of Practice-Oriented Legal Education*, 36 J. LEGAL EDUC. 35 (1986); Goldstein, *No Straight A's for the Law Schools*, N.Y. TIMES, Jan.15, 1988, at 10, col. 3 (nat'l ed.). The basis for my position, however, is twofold. First, I believe strongly that one only can make the best possible Hessian by giving him the ideas of the academic and then the tools of the practitioner, rather than trying to give him only the tools (as Professor Bergin would do), or attempting to give him both the ideas and the tools at once (as Professor Byse favors). Second, for the reasons stated earlier in this response, I am certain that law professors, removed from the experience of day-to-day practice, can never become or remain proficient Hessian-trainers. Of course, it could be argued that law schools could be very proficient at Hessian-training if they hired only Hessians and then required such Hessians to continue to spend a large portion of their time as Hessians. The recent unhappy experience at CUNY Law School leads me to believe that such a model is inherently unworkable. See generally Kleinberg & Barnes, *CUNY Law School: Outside Perspectives and Reflections*, 12 NOVA L. REV. 1, 34 (1987). See also Shipp, *As Its Students Fail the Bar, A Law School Faces Changes*, N.Y. TIMES, Dec. 26, 1987, at 1, col. 3 (nat'l ed.). I do, however, favor CUNY's emphasis on teaching law students humanistic professionalism. See further Burns, *The Law School as a Model for Community*, 10 NOVA L.J. 329, 371 (1986); Merton, *The City University of New York Law School: An Insider's Report*, 12 NOVA L. REV. 45, 49 (1987).

34. Although today's law student comes to law school possessing, at a minimum, a bachelor's degree, and in a number of cases a master's degree or even a doctoral degree, I do not believe that the experience of having been surrounded by non-legal authentic academics is an adequate, or even partial, substitute for being surrounded by authentic legal academics.

This is not to say, however, that law students want to be surrounded by authentic academics while in law school, nor is it to say that they will enjoy being in such an atmosphere. In fact, quite the opposite is and will be true. As has been noted elsewhere, law students want their law professors to be Hessian-trainers, as do their future employers. See McFarland, *Students and Practicing Lawyers Identify the Ideal Law Professor*, 36 J. LEGAL EDUC. 93 (1986) (reporting that both law students and practicing lawyers believe that the ideal law professor is one who prepares law students for the active practice of law). Moreover, law professors are giving in to this demand, for a variety of reasons. See D'Amato, *The Decline and Fall of Law Teaching in the Age of Student Consumerism*, 37 J. LEGAL EDUC. 461 (1987). Of course, some legal educators believe that far from "acquiescing" to student pressure, this is how law school ought to be. See Rohr, *The Law School for the Consumer*, 13 NOVA L. REV. 101 (1988).

35. One point on which Professor Byse and I do agree is that valid legal scholarship can take many different forms, including policy science, legal process, economic analysis, rights thesis, critical legal studies, feminist legal theory, and literary theory. Byse, *supra* note 1, at 11-13. See also Brown, *A Cure for Scholarship Schizophrenia: A Manifesto for Sane Productivity and Productive Sanity*, 13 NOVA L. REV. 39 (1988), and Kissam, *The Evaluation of Legal Scholarship*, 63 WASH. L. REV. 221 (1988).

Chapter 79

The Most-Cited Law Review Articles Revisited

1996

Fred R. Shapiro

Fred Shapiro is a librarian of Yale Law School and the co-editor of *The Oxford Anthologoy of Legal Stories* (Oxford University Press, 1998) and editor of *The Oxford Dictionary of American Legal Quotations* (Oxford University Press, 1995). This article first appeared at 71 *Chicago-Kent Law Review* 751 (1996).

Associate Librarian for Public Services and Lecturer in Legal Research, Yale Law School; Editor, OXFORD DICTIONARY OF AMERICAN LEGAL QUOTATIONS (1993); S.B., Massachusetts Institute of Technology; J.D., Harvard University; M.S.L.S., Catholic University of America. I would like to thank my research assistant, Tracy L. Thompson, for her outstanding work and Ann C. Davidson for excellent research help. I am deeply indebted to David Pendlebury of the Institute for Scientific Information for supplying me with crucial data. Akhil Amar, James Lindgren, Richard Delgado, and Jean Stefancic were each in their own way godparents of this project, and I owe much to each of them. Thanks also to Blair Kauffman for his encouragement and support, to Yale Law School Associate Dean Stephen Yandle for generously approving funds for research assistance, and to Ian Ayres for helpful comments.

This Article presents two lists updating my previous study of *The Most-Cited Law Review Articles*, published in the *California Law Review* in 1985.[1] The first list sets forth the one hundred most-cited legal articles of all time, that is, most often cited within other articles. This list is more comprehensive than the original study because it has no chronological restrictions and because it includes interdisciplinary journals that were formerly excluded. Since eleven years have transpired, the new roster also encompasses a new generation of legal scholarship.

The second list presented here enumerates one hundred most-cited articles of recent years, consisting of the top-ten most-cited articles published each year for the ten most recent years for which meaningful data are available. This contemporary list reveals a striking phenomenon. A very high percentage of the articles included are written by women, feminists, minority scholars, critical race theorists, critical legal studies scholars, and other "outsiders." The percentage of such participation is so high as to raise the question of whether, at least in the world of the law reviews, the outsiders have become insiders.

I

In the preface to my book, *The Oxford Dictionary of American Legal Quotations*, I wrote: "Law is the intersection of language and power."[2] The body of that book, however, is devoted to another kind of intersection: *legal documents are the intersections of other legal documents.* The links between the documents (I am avoiding the term texts because it is freighted with trendy baggage) are called "quotations" or, more broadly, "citations."

Citations are strings of names and numbers incorporating the language and power of one source in another source. Judges' opinions usually have citation links with other judges' opinions and with statutes and regulations. Law review articles usually have citation links with other law review articles, with judges' opinions, and with statutes and regulations.

Links between documents (I am avoiding the terms *intertextuality* and *hypertext*) are more important in law than in any other discipline, even the literary and computer-science fields that have given rise to the concepts of intertextuality and hypertext. In judges' opinions in the common-law system, citation links, which carry the weight of precedent and legislative mandate, are more significant than the words that surround the citations.

In law review articles, readers often peruse the citation links (footnotes) with an occasional glance at the "top of the page" text, rather than the other way around, because the really interesting scholarly conversation is taking place at the bottom. The great legal iconoclast and footnote-hater, Fred Rodell, missed the point.[3] Yes, footnotes are abominations destroying the readability of legal writing, but they proliferate and become discursive because they are where the action is. If I am right that citations are the crux of legal documents, then it is inevitable that legal writers will be drawn to insert text in the footnotes where the citations live.[4]

The centrality of citations is reflected in a variety of legal institutions. The *Shepard's Citations* system of indexes dutifully records every citation link and thus creates a powerful tool for verifying the authority of case precedents and finding cases and other sources relating to a given subject. The citation networks are so pervasive that it is said that a researcher can find the entire universe of cases relevant to his or her issue by starting with a single case and tracing citation links forward and backward. *LEXIS* and *Westlaw*, the two full-text online legal databases, also spotlight citation links and facilitate citation-based research.

The Bluebook,[5] a manual of citation form for law students and lawyers, exerts a despotic influence over legal writing. Citation form even has economic and public policy ramifications, as was proven recently when a major legal publishing company, a public-interest group, the Department of Justice, and other players engaged in an epic lobbying battle over a proposed change in the method of citing court decisions.[6]

I have contributed to citation obsession in the legal community with two studies ranking the most frequently cited law review articles. In 1985 I published *The Most-Cited Law Review Articles*,[7] enumerating the fifty most-cited law review articles since 1947 (the upper crust of these pieces were then collected in full text in an anthology with the same title[8]). Six years later I published *The Most-Cited Articles from* The Yale Law Journal,[9] that journal's thirty most frequently cited articles on the occasion of its centennial.

The *Yale Law Journal* study summarized the rationale of citation analysis as follows:

> Citation analysis is now extensively used by information scientists and sociologists to study the history and structure of the natural sciences and other disciplines. . . . Authors too have been evaluated through tabulation of citations to their writings. Citation counts have been utilized in assessing scholars' work for purposes of grant awards, tenure, or promotion decisions.
>
> Those using citation data for evaluative purposes have justified such use by pointing to research demonstrating a high correlation between the total of citations to a scientist's or

> scholar's writings and judgments by peers of the " 'productivity,' 'significance,' 'quality,' 'utility,' 'influence,' 'effectiveness,' or 'impact' of scientists and their scholarly products." One investigator has gone so far as to say that "citations and peer ratings appear to be virtually the same measurement."
>
> Almost all citation analysts, however, are careful to note that citation counts measure a "quality" which is socially defined, reflecting the utility of the writing in question to other scholars, rather than gauging its intrinsic merit. Furthermore, the value of the counts may be lessened by limitations in the accuracy, coverage, or time-frame of the source data. For these reasons and others, evaluative use of citation analysis has remained controversial.
>
> Even with their acknowledged limitations, citation counts are attractive as relatively objective tools for assessing scholarly impact. They can be used not only to gauge the impact of a given author or writing, but also to identify which writings are the most frequently cited, taken to be a rough measure of the writings which have had the most extensive impact.[10]

Reactions to my previous studies have ranged from denunciation:

> [R]anking by citation counts could become an invidious virus in the world of scholarship. It bears no relationship to scholarly merit. It is nondiscriminating in its discrimination. It is not even a reliable indicator that the work cited was read, let alone understood by the citer.[11]

to adulation:

> Footnotes nowadays are not phony excrescences; they are the raw data used by the hottest new school of legal scholarship, the citation analysts. These bibliotechs have shown once and for all that nobody reads the text of other people's articles anyway. Anybody who is anybody in any field you care to name has already said the same thing in different words a dozen times before. There is nothing new under the sun. The only thing that is important is who cites whom. If you're cited, that means you're identified as a player in the game: a scholar of significance.[12]

Well, tongue-in-cheek adulation.

I have tried to stake out a middle ground in which I present lists of most-cited articles as rosters of high-impact contributions worthy of recognition, but I do not claim too much significance for the compilations. Most of the supercited articles are probably articles of great merit, but the connection is by no means assured, there being a variety of reasons why an article might be very frequently cited, of which merit is only one. For example, an article might summarize a particular idea or issue effectively so that it becomes a convenient or reflexive cite long after it has ceased to influence scholars or even to be read. On the other hand, a brilliant or influential article might fail to make a most-cited list for a number of reasons.

In any case, here I go again.

II

This updated study is really a substantial expansion of the original "most-cited law review articles" concept. I have compiled two lists, one historical in nature and the other focusing on contemporary scholarship. Table I is a compilation of the one hundred most-cited legal articles. Table II is a listing of the ten most-cited legal articles published each year for the years 1982 through 1991, the most recent years for which there is meaningful data available.

These lists are comprehensive, in a way that my original study was not, in two respects. First, the tables now are based on data from the *Social Sciences Citation Index*, a marvelous tool that lists, for any publication, articles from over one hundred legal journals and over one thousand social science journals citing that publication. Where *The Most-Cited Law Review Articles* was a ranking of the most-cited articles published in traditional law reviews, such as *Harvard Law Review* or *Yale Law Journal*, measured by citations in other traditional law review articles, the new study is broader.

"Law and" journals such as *Journal of Law and Economics*, *Journal of Legal Studies*, *Harvard Civil Rights-Civil Liberties Law Review*, *Law and Society Review*, and *Supreme Court Review*, some of which are very important outlets for law-related scholarship, are covered here both as sources of articles included among the most-cited and as part of the "citing" universe from which the citation counts are drawn. As a result, *The Most-Cited Law Review Articles Revisited* takes a genuinely interdisciplinary view, embracing the law and economics movement and the law and society movement and, for all articles, counting impact on social science as well as impact on legal scholarship narrowly defined.

I went even one step further and also included some articles published in economics journals, sociology journals, and the like, if the majority of citations to the article occur in legal or "law and" journals. My theory in doing so was that I wanted to represent law-related scholarship as comprehensively as possible, and that a predominance of citations in law-related journals seems to identify an article as being law-related. Under this rule, an article by Stewart Macaulay,[13] an article by Henry G. Manne,[14] and two articles by Catharine A. MacKinnon[15] qualified for my lists even though they were all published in "nonlegal" journals.

Conversely, I excluded some highly cited articles appearing in "law and" journals because the majority of their citations occur in nonlegal journals. For example, Sam Peltzman, *Toward a More General Theory of Regulation*,[16] has received over seven hundred citations, but the great majority have been in economics and political science journals. A number of other articles have citation totals high enough to make the "top 100" list but have been similarly excluded because of this criterion. They are as follows: Benjamin Klein, Robert G. Crawford, and Armen A. Alchian, *Vertical Integration, Appropriable Rents, and the Competitive Contracting Process*;[17] Oliver E. Williamson, *Transaction-Cost Economics: The Governance of Contractual Relations*;[18] Eugene F. Fama and Michael C. Jensen, *Separation of Ownership and Control*;[19] Harold Demsetz, *Why Regulate Utilities?*;[20] and Gary S. Becker and George J. Stigler, *Law Enforcement, Malfeasance, and Compensation of Enforcers*.[21]

The second respect in which this study is more comprehensive than the original one is chronological coverage. Before, only articles published in 1947 or later were included, and articles published after 1977 had not had enough time to amass sufficient citations to qualify. The present lists expand the coverage in both directions.

Because the source data from the *Social Sciences Citation Index* have no beginning date for cited publications, older articles can be encompassed. Thus, articles going as far back as the infancy of law review publishing in the 1890s appear here. However, the *SSCI*'s citing coverage does have a commencement date of 1956, i.e., citations in pre-1956 journals are not counted, so pre-1956 articles are disfavored in this respect. Samuel Warren and Louis D. Brandeis's article, *The Right to Privacy*,[22] was published in 1890 but gets no credit for any citations to it between 1890 and 1956. Because of this factor, only a few early articles make the "top 100" list based on their post-1956 citations. Therefore I have appended a special roster, arranged chronologically, of a dozen "Additional Older Articles." These did not qualify for the all-time listing but would, I believe, have qualified had the data included pre-1956 citations.

In addition to classic older articles, these lists reflect a generation of scholarship uncounted by the previous study. The data, prepared eleven years later, are consequently eleven years more up-to-date, but I have ensured that contemporary trends are measured in another way as well. An overall list of the one hundred most frequently cited articles of all time will not fully represent recent articles because even a very high-impact article will take a half-dozen or more years to reach the threshold level of citations. Therefore I have separately enumerated the ten most-cited articles published in each of the years from 1982 to 1991. This way recent articles fairly compete only with their own cohort. I believe that it is too early for data for years subsequent to 1991 to be meaningful.

For those interested in further details of how I compiled this study, a Methodological Appendix is included after the most-cited lists.

III

The Most-Cited Law Review Articles Revisited charts a dramatically different scholarly landscape than *The Most-Cited Law Review Articles.* The two lists in the new study, one a long-term historical view and the other a snapshot of contemporary activity, make it plain that there has been a striking change in recent years in the composition and perspective of legal scholars.

One dimension of the change is demographic. On the all-time list of the 100 most-cited articles (actually 102 articles because of a four-way tie at the bottom), only three of the articles are written by women, with those being recent publications near the end of the ranking.[23] Only one is by a minority author.[24] The list of 100 recent most-cited articles, however, yields quite different statistics.

Of the 100 articles on the recent listing (actually 103 because of ties), 29 are by women. The representation of women grows stronger as more recent years are examined. Over the most recent five years (1987-91), the numbers are 20 out of 51. Focusing on the top five of each of those years rather than the top ten, an actual parity emerges: 13 of 26 top-ranking articles from 1987-91 are written by women.

Racial composition shows a similar trend. The 103 recent articles include 19 written by African Americans, Latinos, or Asian-Americans. Again, the representation is greater in recent years. Seventeen of the 51 articles in the 1987-91 period are by minority scholars.

If we combine women and minority scholars into one demographic "outsider" category, we find that 39 of 103 articles in the latest ten-year period and 28 of 51—a majority—in the latest five years are "outsiders" in this sense. The minority majority reaches an astonishing level if only the top five of each year from 1987 to 1991 are tabulated. Seventeen of 26 top-ranking articles from these five years are outsider-authored. The number goes to 19 of 26 if openly gay scholars are added in to the demographic outsider definition. Clearly, outsiders in this period have achieved some kind of insider status in the law reviews, if not outright dominance.

There are other ways of defining outsiderhood than demographics. The list of most-cited recent articles can also be analyzed from a political perspective. A trio of movements in the legal academy—feminism, critical race theory, and critical legal studies—loom very large in this compilation. Precise categorization is difficult, but I would estimate that about 45 of the 103 included articles fall within these tendencies. The numbers grow as the decade progresses: for the latest five years (1987-91) most of the articles are "outsider" in their politics, and for 1990 and 1991 the fraction is two-thirds.[25]

I do not want to portray this political trend, or the demographic trend, as an inevitable historical march to the left or toward diversity—it may be that I merely happened to end my study at a time when a short-term wave was cresting—but the numbers are hard to dismiss. No one could maintain that leftist politics or feminism or racial minorities are reigning triumphant in American society in the 1990s (quite the contrary appears to be the case), but in the realm of legal scholarship, or at least in the realm of the law reviews, the outsiders may have achieved something resembling a dominant position.

Legal scholarship's other celebrated movement of recent decades is law and economics. This school also figures very prominently in the most-cited rankings. Of the 102 articles on the "all-time" list, at least 12 belong to law and economics. They include the overwhelmingly number-one ranked article and three others in the top twenty-five. In comparison with its towering citation landmarks of the 1960s, 1970s, and early 1980s, law and economics's representation for recent years appears to be a bit less strong, although the top-ten articles of each year may be too small a slice to permit generalizations of this sort. If there has been a decline, the explanation could lie in the tendency of a scholarly movement in a mature phase to focus on narrower issues, resulting in fewer citations per paper, than was true in a formative phase characterized by articles of wide application.[26]

Another school, the "law and society" movement, places only three articles on the all-time list, but two of them are blockbusters ranking in the top fifteen.[27] Law and economics, law and society, feminism, critical race theory, and critical legal studies can all be characterized as rebellions against traditional doctrinal scholarship and interdisciplinary departures from the notion of law as an autonomous field. Lumped together, their performance in this study is a formidable one. By the 1980s, traditional doctrinal articles are few and far between among the citation elite.

Turning to individual articles, the runaway citation champion is R. H. Coase, *The Problem of Social Cost.*[28] This renowned paper has been recognized, along with Coase's other work, with a Nobel Memorial Prize in Economics. It is frequently said to be the most-cited article both in law and in economics. I have not verified this assertion as to economics, but its citation preeminence in law is dramatic, as it has amassed almost twice as many citations as any other law-related article. The methodology of my original study necessitated the omission of *The Problem of Social Cost,* but its inclusion is one of the principal benefits of the more comprehensive data used in this update.

The original study anointed Gerald Gunther's 1972 equal protection piece[29] as number one. Gunther still ranks near the top (third), but Herbert Wechsler, *Toward Neutral Principles of Constitutional Law,*[30] has now pulled ahead into the second position. Charles A. Reich, *The New Property,*[31] one of the genuinely original breakthroughs in legal thought, is number four. Fifth, despite a passage of time that would have ended most articles' citation careers and despite being denied the benefit of decades of pre-1956 cites, is Oliver Wendell Holmes, Jr., *The Path of the Law*[32] (probably first among law review articles in jurisprudential importance and surely first from the standpoint of literary merit). Another venerable classic overcoming similar obstacles is Samuel D. Warren and Louis D. Brandeis, *The Right to Privacy,*[33] whose scholarly influence was accompanied by a profound influence on the courts.

One function of such a study is to spotlight the work of certain scholars whose impact is evidenced by multiple appearances on the lists. Only one author has four articles on the all-time list: Henry M. Hart, Jr. Three of Hart's articles rank in the top forty. Scholars with three articles each on the all-time list are: Alexander M. Bickel, Guido Calabresi, John Hart Ely, Lon L. Fuller (all three in the top fifty), Frank I. Michelman (also all three in the top fifty), and William L. Prosser. Those with two articles each are: Robert H. Bork, William J. Brennan, Jr., Paul Brest, Owen M. Fiss, Henry J. Friendly, Marc Galanter, Kenneth L. Karst, Duncan Kennedy, Richard A. Posner, Joseph L. Sax, Cass R. Sunstein, Herbert Wechsler, and Harry H. Wellington. If the Additional Older Articles are added in, then Karl N. Llewellyn has four articles listed, Fuller picks up a fourth article, and Harry Kalven, Jr. gets a second.

The list of most-cited recent articles features, for the most part, a different group of authors with more than one contribution. Towering over this group is the impressive record of Cass R. Sunstein. Sunstein has eight articles listed, including a 1985 article that has in a short time already climbed to 38th on the all-time list[34] and a 1988 one that is the youngest item in that top 100.[35] After Sunstein, the most prolific participant is Frank H. Easterbrook. Easterbrook, in addition to coauthoring the most-cited article of the 1980s, a 1981 article which is already 24th all-time,[36] produced five articles among the yearly leaders for the early 1980s before entering upon a judicial career.

Next among recent-article authors is Richard Delgado with four publications. Those with three each include: Akhil Reed Amar, John C. Coffee, Jr., William N. Eskridge, Jr., Catharine A. MacKinnon, Mari J. Matsuda, and Margaret Jane Radin. The two-timers are: Bruce A. Ackerman, Robert M. Cover, Kimberlé Williams Crenshaw, Daniel R. Fischel (for a total of three between the all-time and recent lists), Owen M. Fiss (for a total of three between the all-time and recent lists), Philip P. Frickey, Ronald J. Gilson, Reinier Kraakman, Charles R. Lawrence III, Frank I. Michelman (for a total of four between the all-time and recent lists), Gary Peller, Frederick Schauer, and Joseph William Singer. Duncan Kennedy and Richard A. Posner each have one for a total of three between the all-time and recent lists. Abram Chayes, Gerald E. Frug, and Richard B. Stewart each have one to go with another one they have on the all-time list.

This is an appropriate point to insert some caveats about the incompleteness of this study as a pantheon of the highest-impact legal scholars. The principal incompleteness relates to the fact that scholarship in book form is not reflected. Although most scholarly legal writing does occur in articles, there is a substantial literature in books. Much significant work is therefore unnoted on my lists, and some major scholars' oeuvres are slighted or omitted altogether.

Hart's and Wechsler's positions would be further enhanced if their federal courts casebook[37] were encompassed, and Hart's still more so if the Hart and Sacks legal process materials[38] were covered. Holmes's *The Common Law,*[39] Prosser's torts treatises, and the books of Bruce Ackerman, Alexander M. Bickel, Charles L. Black, Jr., Guido Calabresi, John Hart Ely, Lon L. Fuller, Felix Frankfurter, Harry Kalven, Jr., Karl N. Llewellyn, Catharine A. MacKinnon, Richard A. Posner, Roscoe Pound, Laurence H. Tribe, and

Charles Warren would add to their respective authors' citation record were this an articles-and-books compilation. Some other major scholars are not mentioned at all on my lists because their contributions have predominantly appeared in books. Ronald Dworkin, Jerome Frank, Grant Gilmore, J. Willard Hurst, John Henry Wigmore, and Samuel Williston are examples.

Some articles' citation totals might be curtailed because they are turned into books, which then may be cited instead of the articles. Alexander M. Bickel, *The Supreme Court, 1960 Term—Foreword: The Passive Virtues,*[40] which became a chapter in Bickel's book, *The Least Dangerous Branch,*[41] illustrates this category. Conversely, the articles near the top of the all-time list might have had more modest totals if they had been made into books.[42]

There is another bias tilting the playing field against certain articles. As I have pointed out before, "Some topics have a far larger scholarly literature than others, resulting in much greater citation potential for an article in a popular subject area than for one in an area less frequented by law reviews."[43] A constitutional law article will have countless opportunities to pick up law review citations, but the most brilliant article on wills would have so few opportunities that it could never qualify for a most-cited list. John H. Langbein, *The German Advantage in Civil Procedure,*[44] has received a remarkable number of citations for an article on comparative law, but this is a field with a modest-sized literature, so Langbein's paper falls just short of the most-cited list for 1985.

Returning to the data, it may be of interest to analyze the listed articles by law reviews and author affiliations. The following are the numbers of articles from particular law reviews.

ALL-TIME LIST (LAW REVIEWS)

Harvard Law Review	42
Yale Law Journal	18
Columbia Law Review	5
Journal of Legal Studies	5
Stanford Law Review	5
University of Pennsylvania Law Review	4
California Law Review	3
Minnesota Law Review	3
University of Chicago Law Review	3
Journal of Law and Economics	2
Supreme Court Review	2
American Sociological Review	1
Boston University Law Review	1
Buffalo Law Review	1
Indiana Law Journal	1
Journal of Political Economy	1
Law and Contemporary Problems	1
Law and Society Review	1
New York University Law Review	1
Signs	1
UCLA Law Review	1

RECENT-ARTICLES LIST (LAW REVIEWS)

Harvard Law Review	30
Yale Law Journal	16
Stanford Law Review	9
Columbia Law Review	7

Michigan Law Review	6
University of Chicago Law Review	6
California Law Review	3
Harvard Civil Rights-Civil Liberties Law Review	3
Southern California Law Review	3
University of Pennsylvania Law Review	3
Virginia Law Review	3
Duke Law Journal	2
Journal of Legal Studies	2
Signs	2
UCLA Law Review	2
Boston University Law Review	1
Journal of Law and Economics	1
Maryland Law Review	1
New York University Law Review	1
Northwestern University Law Review	1
Texas Law Review	1

It is clear that *Harvard Law Review* and *Yale Law Journal* continue to dominate the production of the most frequently cited articles. *Harvard Law Review*'s preeminent position seems even stronger than Harvard Law School's historical preeminent position in general law school prestige. Nine of the top 12 articles, and 18 of the top 29, are from this review.[45] *Stanford Law Review*, *Michigan Law Review*, and *University of Chicago Law Review* may be ascending in importance, although the sample is too small for firm conclusions. Particularly noteworthy is the presence of two nontraditional and young journals, *Journal of Legal Studies* (founded in 1972) and *Harvard Civil Rights-Civil Liberties Law Review* (founded in 1966), alongside the hoary traditional reviews. Their showing reflects the strength of law and economics and critical race theory in the rankings.

The academic affiliations of the authors on the lists at the time of publication, counting authors more than once if they have multiple articles included, are as follows:[46]

All-Time List (Authors' Academic Affiliations)

Harvard	22
Yale	18
University of Chicago	10
Stanford	7
Columbia	5
University of California, Berkeley	4
UCLA	4
University of Wisconsin	3
Duke	2
George Washington	2
University of Minnesota	2
(schools with 1 are omitted)	

Recent-Articles List (Authors' Academic Affiliations)

University of Chicago	15
Harvard	15

Yale	11
Columbia	6
Stanford	6
University of Michigan	5
University of Minnesota	5
Boston University	4
Georgetown	4
University of Southern California	4
UCLA	4
University of Wisconsin	4
University of Colorado	3
University of Hawaii	3
Northwestern University	3
American University	2
University of California, Berkeley	2
University of Virginia	2
(schools with 1 are omitted)	

Here we see, on the all-time list, Yale a closer second to Harvard in author affiliations than it is in law reviews. The University of Chicago is third all-time, and on the recent-articles list it ties Harvard for first. One cannot help but speculate that Chicago would have run away with first place on the latter list had Easterbrook and Posner not become judges.

Finally, I have tabulated the authors' law degrees by schools (see Table III). Again, authors are counted more than once if they have multiple articles.[47]

All-Time List (Authors' Law Degrees)

Harvard	41
Yale	23
University of Chicago	13
Columbia	7
Stanford	5
University of Minnesota	3
University of California, Berkeley	2
New York University	2
(schools with 1 are omitted)	

Recent-Articles List (Authors' Law Degrees)

Harvard	33
Yale	29
University of Chicago	11
University of California, Berkeley	6
Columbia	3
University of Hawaii	3
New York University	3
University of Southern California	3
University of Michigan	2
UCLA	2
(schools with 1 are omitted)	

Harvard's historical flagship role as a producer of leading scholars is apparent from these figures. For the recent time-period, Yale runs a close second to Harvard. It should be noted, however, that Yale and University of Chicago both have much smaller alumni populations than Harvard's; on a per-capita basis, Yale would probably rank first. Together, Harvard, Yale, and Chicago train over 70% of the authors of the most highly cited legal articles. All in all, looking at the numbers for law reviews, authors' affiliations, and authors' law degrees, Harvard, Yale, and Chicago clearly form a triumvirate dominating legal scholarship, or at least that portion of it published in article form.[48] Stanford, Columbia, and University of Michigan are probably comparable to Chicago in overall prestige, but do not appear to be its equals in scholarly importance.

Conclusion

I have previously written that "the historical and structural insights of citation analysis could provide grist for a sociology of legal scholarship."[49] I have not belabored the rationale and prospects of legal citation analysis here, but interested readers will find in my first two essays on the subject the sketch of a methodological roadmap.[50] The present study is a modest example of sociology of legal scholarship. I believe the results will be of interest to the legal and scholarly communities, particularly the finding that outsider groups may have become insiders in the legal academy.

Citation analysis can also provide grist for the intellectual history of law. On one level, "the historical development of areas of legal thought could be charted by means of network diagrams showing citation connections between recent and older writings, or time series of co-citation maps."[51] Such charts could be converted into narrative accounts of specific landmark scholarship, of specific patterns of influence, or of the development of specific scholarly movements.

On another level, citation maps and the sort of citation-classic list presented here can form the basis for generalizations about the nature of innovation in legal thought. I do not by any means think that all of the articles on my lists are pathbreaking, but some of them certainly are, and such lists can help to identify the truly seminal legal writings. What are the conditions under which breakthroughs are made? What are the characteristics of landmark scholarship and scholars? How does influence exert itself in law? What social, political, and economic factors facilitate or work against legal change? If, as I have suggested, citation links are the crux of legal discourse, then the analysis of those links can be crucial to answering these and other questions leading to an understanding of the history of legal ideas.

Table I: Most-Cited Law Review Articles of All Time Compiled by Fred R. Shapiro[52]

1.	1741	R. H. Coase, *The Problem of Social Cost*, 3 J.L. & Econ. 1 (1960).
2.	968	Herbert Wechsler, *Toward Neutral Principles of Constitutional Law*, 73 Harv. L. Rev. 1 (1959).
3.	913	Gerald Gunther, *The Supreme Court, 1971 Term—Foreword: In Search of Evolving Doctrine on a Changing Court: A Model for a Newer Equal Protection*, 86 Harv. L. Rev. 1 (1972).
4.	728	Charles A. Reich, *The New Property*, 73 Yale L.J. 733 (1964).
5.	719	Oliver Wendell Holmes, Jr., *The Path of the Law*, 10 Harv. L. Rev. 457 (1897).
6.	645	Abram Chayes, *The Role of the Judge in Public Law Litigation*, 89 Harv. L. Rev. 1281 (1976).
7.	609	Robert H. Bork, *Neutral Principles and Some First Amendment Problems*, 47 Ind. L.J. 1 (1971).
8.	582	Richard B. Stewart, *The Reformation of American Administrative Law*, 88 Harv. L. Rev. 1667 (1975).

continued on next page

TABLE I - *continued*

9.	578	Samuel D. Warren & Louis D. Brandeis, *The Right to Privacy*, 4 HARV. L. REV. 193 (1890).
10.	550	Duncan Kennedy, *Form and Substance in Private Law Adjudication*, 89 HARV. L. REV. 1685 (1976).
11.	542	Guido Calabresi & A. Douglas Melamed, *Property Rules, Liability Rules, and Inalienability: One View of the Cathedral*, 85 HARV. L. REV. 1089 (1972).
12.	523	Frank I. Michelman, *Property, Utility, and Fairness: Comments on the Ethical Foundations of "Just Compensation" Law*, 80 Harv. L. Rev. 1165 (1967).
13.	489	Marc Galanter, *Why the "Haves" Come Out Ahead: Speculations on the Limits of Legal Change*, 9 LAW & SOC'Y REV. 95 (1974).
14.	460	Joseph Tussman & Jacobus tenBroek, *The Equal Protection of the Laws*, 37 CAL. L. REV. 341 (1949).
15.	454	Stewart Macaulay, *Non-Contractual Relations in Business: A Preliminary Study*, 28 AM. SOC. REV. 55 (1963).
16.	446	John Hart Ely, *The Wages of Crying Wolf: A Comment on* Roe v. Wade, 82 YALE L.J. 920 (1973).
17.	436	William W. Van Alstyne, *The Demise of the Right-Privilege Distinction in Constitutional Law*, 81 HARV. L. REV. 1439 (1968).
18.	402	Owen M. Fiss, *The Supreme Court, 1978 Term—Foreword: The Forms of Justice*, 93 HARV. L. REV. 1 (1979).
19.	384	Henry G. Manne, *Mergers and the Market for Corporate Control*, 73 J. POL. ECON. 110 (1965).
19.	384	Frank I. Michelman, *The Supreme Court, 1968 Term—Foreword: On Protecting the Poor Through the Fourteenth Amendment*, 83 HARV. L. REV. 7 (1969).
21.	370	William L. Prosser, *The Assault Upon the Citadel (Strict Liability to the Consumer)*, 69 YALE L.J. 1099 (1960).
22.	360	Anthony G. Amsterdam, *Perspectives on the Fourth Amendment*, 58 MINN. L. REV. 349 (1974).
23.	357	Robert H. Mnookin & Lewis Kornhauser, *Bargaining in the Shadow of the Law: The Case of Divorce*, 88 YALE L.J. 950 (1979).
24.	356	Frank H. Easterbrook & Daniel R. Fischel, *The Proper Role of a Target's Management in Responding to a Tender Offer*, 94 HARV. L. REV. 1161 (1981).
25.	355	Henry M. Hart, Jr., *The Supreme Court, 1958 Term—Foreword: The Time Chart of the Justices*, 73 HARV. L. REV. 84 (1959).
26.	346	William J. Brennan, Jr., *State Constitutions and the Protection of Individual Rights*, 90 HARV. L. REV. 489 (1977).
27.	341	Henry M. Hart, Jr., *The Power of Congress to Limit the Jurisdiction of Federal Courts: An Exercise in Dialectic*, 66 HARV. L. REV. 1362 (1953).
28.	340	H.L.A. Hart, *Positivism and the Separation of Law and Morals*, 71 HARV. L. REV. 593 (1958).
29.	338	Laurence H. Tribe, *Trial by Mathematics: Precision and Ritual in the Legal Process*, 84 HARV. L. REV. 1329 (1971).
30.	337	Paul Brest, *The Misconceived Quest for the Original Understanding*, 60 B.U. L. REV. 204 (1980).

TABLE I - *continued*

31.	336	John Hart Ely, *Legislative and Administrative Motivation in Constitutional Law*, 79 YALE L.J. 1205 (1970).
32.	327	Roberto Mangabeira Unger, *The Critical Legal Studies Movement*, 96 HARV. L. REV. 561 (1983).
33.	323	Thomas I. Emerson, *Toward a General Theory of the First Amendment*, 72 YALE L.J. 877 (1963).
34.	319	Alexander Meiklejohn, *The First Amendment Is an Absolute*, 1961 SUP. CT. REV. 245.
35.	317	Bruce J. Ennis & Thomas R. Litwack, *Psychiatry and the Presumption of Expertise: Flipping Coins in the Courtroom*, 62 CAL. L. REV. 693 (1974).
36.	306	Lon L. Fuller, *Positivism and Fidelity to Law—A Reply to Professor Hart*, 71 HARV. L. REV. 630 (1958).
37.	303	Henry M. Hart, Jr., *The Relations Between State and Federal Law*, 54 COLUM. L. REV. 489 (1954).
38.	301	Cass R. Sunstein, *Interest Groups in American Public Law*, 38 STAN. L. REV. 29 (1985).
39.	299	Richard A. Posner, *A Theory of Negligence*, 1 J. LEGAL STUD. 29 (1972).
40.	292	Joseph L. Sax, *Takings and the Police Power*, 74 YALE L.J. 36 (1964).
41.	291	Robert M. Cover, *The Supreme Court, 1982 Term, Foreword: Nomos and Narrative*, 97 HARV. L. REV. 4 (1983).
42.	290	Duncan Kennedy, *The Structure of Blackstone's Commentaries*, 28 BUFF. L. REV. 205 (1979).
43.	288	Lon L. Fuller & William R. Perdue, Jr., *The Reliance Interest in Contract Damages* (pts. 1 & 2), 46 YALE L.J. 52, 373 (1936-37).
44.	287	Friedrich Kessler, *Contracts of Adhesion—Some Thoughts About Freedom of Contract*, 43 COLUM. L. REV. 629 (1943).
44.	287	Harry Kalven, Jr., *The New York Times Case: A Note on "The Central Meaning of the First Amendment,"* 1964 SUP. CT. REV. 191.
46.	284	Lon L. Fuller, *The Forms and Limits of Adjudication*, 92 HARV. L. REV. 353 (1978).
47.	282	Thomas C. Grey, *Do We Have an Unwritten Constitution?*, 27 STAN. L. REV. 703 (1975).
47.	282	Frank I. Michelman, *The Supreme Court, 1985 Term—Foreword: Traces of Self-Government*, 100 HARV. L. REV. 4 (1986).
49.	278	Richard A. Epstein, *A Theory of Strict Liability*, 2 J. LEGAL STUD. 151 (1973).
49.	278	William L. Cary, *Federalism and Corporate Law: Reflection Upon Delaware*, 83 YALE L.J. 663 (1974).
51.	271	Guido Calabresi, *Some Thoughts on Risk Distribution and the Law of Torts*, 70 YALE L.J. 499 (1961).
52.	268	Mark V. Tushnet, *Following the Rules Laid Down: A Critique of Interpretivism and Neutral Principles*, 96 HARV. L. REV. 781 (1983).
53.	267	Alexander M. Bickel, *The Original Understanding and the Segregation Decision*, 69 HARV. L. REV. 1 (1955).
54.	266	Dallin H. Oaks, *Studying the Exclusionary Rule in Search and Seizure*, 37 U. CHI. L. REV. 665 (1970).
55.	264	Henry J. Friendly, *Some Kind of Hearing*, 123 U. PA. L. REV. 1267 (1975).

continued on next page

TABLE I - *continued*

56.	256	Paul Brest, *The Supreme Court, 1975 Term—Foreword: In Defense of the Antidiscrimination Principle*, 90 HARV. L. REV. 1 (1976).
57.	255	Felix Frankfurter, *Some Reflections on the Reading of Statutes*, 47 COLUM. L. REV. 527 (1947).
57.	255	George P. Fletcher, *Fairness and Utility in Tort Theory*, 85 HARV. L. REV. 537 (1972).
59.	254	Henry J. Friendly, *In Praise of Erie—and of the New Federal Common Law*, 39 N.Y.U. L. REV. 383 (1964).
60.	253	Owen M. Fiss, *Objectivity and Interpretation*, 34 STAN. L. REV. 739 (1982).
61.	253	Charles R. Lawrence III, *The Id, the Ego, and Equal Protection: Reckoning with Unconscious Racism*, 39 STAND. L. REV. 317 (1987).
62.	252	William L. Prosser, *Privacy*, 48 CAL. L. REV. 383 (1960).
63.	251	Henry P. Monaghan, *The Supreme Court, 1974 Term—Foreword: Constitutional Common Law*, 89 HARV. L. REV. 1 (1975).
64.	250	William L. Prosser, *The Fall of the Citadel (Strict Liability to the Consumer)*, 50 MINN. L. REV. 791 (1966).
65.	249	Marc Galanter, *Reading the Landscape of Disputes: What We Know and Don't Know (And Think We Know) About Our Allegedly Contentious and Litigious Society*, 31 UCLA L. REV. 4 (1983).
66.	245	Henry M. Hart, Jr., *The Aims of the Criminal Law*, 23 LAW & CONTEMP. PROBS. 401 (1958).
67.	244	John Hart Ely, *Flag Desecration: A Case Study in the Roles of Categorization and Balancing in First Amendment Analysis*, 88 HARV. L. REV. 1482 (1975).
68.	243	Bruce A. Ackerman, *The Storrs Lectures: Discovering the Constitution*, 93 YALE L.J. 1013 (1984).
69.	242	Herbert Wechsler, *The Political Safeguards of Federalism: The Role of the States in the Composition and Selection of the National Government*, 54 COLUM. L. REV. 543 (1954).
69.	242	Paul M. Bator, *Finality in Criminal Law and Federal Habeas Corpus for State Prisoners*, 76 HARV. L. REV. 441 (1963).
71.	241	Joseph Goldstein, *Police Discretion Not to Invoke the Criminal Process: Low-Visibility Decisions in the Administration of Justice*, 69 YALE L.J. 543 (1960).
72.	240	Felix S. Cohen, *Transcendental Nonsense and the Functional Approach*, 35 COLUM. L. REV. 809 (1935).
73.	238	Alexander M. Bickel, *The Supreme Court, 1960 Term—Foreword: The Passive Virtues*, 75 HARV. L. REV. 40 (1961).
73.	238	Martha Minow, *The Supreme Court, 1986 Term—Foreword: Justice Engendered*, 101 HARV. L. REV. 10 (1987).
75.	232	Jerome A. Barron, *Access to the Press—A New First Amendment Right*, 80 HARV. L. REV. 1641 (1967).
76.	231	Marvin E. Frankel, *The Search for Truth: An Umpireal View*, 123 U. PA. L. REV. 1031 (1975).
77.	230	Richard A. Posner, *An Economic Approach to Legal Procedure and Judicial Administration*, 2 J. LEG. STUD. 399 (1973).
77.	230	Harry H. Wellington, *Common Law Rules and Constitutional Double Standards: Some Notes on Adjudication*, 83 YALE L.J. 221 (1973).

Table I - *continued*

79.	229	Archibald Cox, *The Supreme Court, 1965 Term—Foreword: Constitutional Adjudication and the Promotion of Human Rights*, 80 Harv. L. Rev. 91 (1966).
80.	228	Gerald E. Frug, *The City as a Legal Concept*, 93 Harv. L. Rev. 1057 (1980).
81.	226	Alexander M. Bickel & Harry H. Wellington, *Legislative Purpose and the Judicial Process: The Lincoln Mills Case*, 71 Harv. L. Rev. 1 (1957).
82.	225	Alan David Freeman, *Legitimizing Racial Discrimination Through Antidiscrimination Law: A Critical Review Of Supreme Court Doctrine*, 62 Minn. L. Rev. 1049 (1978).
83.	224	James B. Thayer, *The Origin and Scope of the American Doctrine of Constitutional Law*, 7 Harv. L. Rev. 129 (1893).
83.	224	Frances E. Olsen, *The Family and the Market: A Study of Ideology and Legal Reform*, 96 Harv. L. Rev. 1497 (1983).
85.	222	Robert H. Bork, *The Rule of Reason and the Per Se Concept: Price Fixing and Market Division* (pts. 1 & 2), 74 Yale L.J. 775 (1965), 75 Yale L.J. 373 (1966).
86.	221	Arthur Allen Leff, Unconscionability and the Code—The Emperor's New Clause, 115 U. Pa. L. Rev. 485 (1967).
87.	220	Guido Calabresi & Jon T. Hirschoff, *Toward a Test for Strict Liability in Torts*, 81 Yale L.J. 1055 (1972).
88.	218	Charles Fairman, *Does the Fourteenth Amendment Incorporate the Bill of Rights?—The Original Understanding*, 2 Stan. L. Rev. 5 (1949).
89.	217	Philip Areeda & Donald F. Turner, *Predatory Pricing and Related Practices Under Section 2 of the Sherman Act*, 88 Harv. L. Rev. 697 (1975).
90.	216	Charles L. Black, Jr., *The Supreme Court, 1966 Term—Foreword: "State Action," Equal Protection, and California's Proposition 14*, 81 Harv. L. Rev. 69 (1967).
91.	212	John P. Brown, *Toward an Economic Theory of Liability*, 2 J. Legal Stud. 323 (1973).
92.	211	Joseph L. Sax, *Takings, Private Property and Public Rights*, 81 Yale L.J. 149 (1971).
93.	208	Cass R. Sunstein, *Beyond the Republican Revival*, 97 Yale L.J. 1539 (1988).
94.	207	Albert W. Alschuler, *The Prosecutor's Role in Plea Bargaining*, 36 U. Chi. L. Rev. 50 (1968).
95.	206	Kenneth L. Karst, *Equality as a Central Principle in the First Amendment*, 43 U. Chi. L. Rev. 20 (1975).
96.	205	Sanford H. Kadish, *Methodology and Criteria in Due Process Adjudication—A Survey and Criticism*, 66 Yale L.J. 319 (1957).
96.	205	Harold Leventhal, *Environmental Decisionmaking and the Role of the Courts*, 122 U. Pa. L. Rev. 509 (1974).
96.	205	Catharine A. MacKinnon, *Feminism, Marxism, Method, and the State: Toward Feminist Jurisprudence*, 8 Signs 635 (1983).
99.	204	William J. Brennan, Jr., *The Supreme Court and the Meiklejohn Interpretation of the First Amendment*, 79 Harv. L. Rev. 1 (1965).
99.	204	William M. Landes, *An Economic Analysis of the Courts*, 14 J.L. & Econ. 61 (1971).
99.	204	Kenneth L. Karst, *The Supreme Court 1976 Term—Foreword: Equal Citizenship Under the Fourteenth Amendment*, 91 Harv. L. Rev. 1 (1977).
99.	204	George L. Priest & Benjamin Klein, *The Selection of Disputes for Litigation*, 13 J. Legal Stud. 1 (1984).

Additional Older Articles[53]

Roscoe Pound, *Mechanical Jurisprudence*, 8 COLUM. L. REV. 605 (1908).

Julian W. Mack, *The Juvenile Court*, 23 HARV. L. REV. 104 (1909).

Wesley N. Hohfeld, *Some Fundamental Legal Conceptions as Applied in Judicial Reasoning*, 23 YALE L.J. 16 (1913).

Charles Warren, *New Light on the History of the Federal Judiciary Act of 1789*, 37 HARV. L. REV. 49 (1923).

Karl N. Llewellyn, *A Realistic Jurisprudence—The Next Step*, 30 COLUM. L. REV. 431 (1930).

Max Radin, *Statutory Interpretation*, 43 HARV. L. REV. 863 (1930).

Karl N. Llewellyn, SOME REALISM ABOUT REALISM—RESPONDING TO DEAN POUND, 44 HARV. L. REV. 1222 (1931).

Karl N. Llewellyn, *What Price Contract?—An Essay in Perspective*, 40 YALE L.J. 704 (1931).

Lon L. Fuller, *Consideration and Form*, 41 COLUM. L. REV. 799 (1941).

Harry Kalven, Jr. & Maurice Rosenfield, *The Contemporary Function of the Class Suit*, 8 U. CHI. L. REV. 684 (1941).

Harold D. Lasswell & Myres S. McDougal, *Legal Education and Public Policy: Professional Training in the Public Interest*, 52 YALE L.J. 203 (1943).

Karl N. Llewellyn, *Remarks on the Theory of Appellate Decision and the Rules or Canons About How Statutes Are to Be Construed*, 3 VAND. L. REV. 395 (1950).

TABLE II: MOST-CITED LAW REVIEW ARTICLES OF RECENT YEARS COMPILED BY FRED R. SHAPIRO[54]

1982

253	Owen M. Fiss, *Objectivity and Interpretation*, 34 STAN. L. REV. 739.
193	Frank H. Easterbrook & Daniel R. Fischel, *Corporate Control Transactions*, 91 YALE L.J. 698.
186	Catharine A. MacKinnon, Feminism, Marxism, *Method, and the State: An Agenda for Theory*, 7 SIGNS 515.
178	Peter Westen, *The Empty Idea of Equality*, 95 HARV. L. REV. 537.
170	Duncan Kennedy, *Distributive and Paternalist Motives in Contract and Tort Law, with Special Reference to Compulsory Terms and Unequal Bargaining Power*, 41 MD. L. REV. 563.
165	Richard B. Stewart & Cass R. Sunstein, *Public Programs and Private Rights*, 95 HARV. L. REV. 1193.
158	Steven Shavell, *Suit, Settlement, and Trial: A Theoretical Analysis Under Alternative Methods for the Allocation of Legal Costs*, 11 J. LEGAL STUD. 55.
156	Judith Resnik, *Managerial Judges*, 96 HARV. L. REV. 374.
152	Abram Chayes, *The Supreme Court, 1981 Term—Foreword: Public Law Litigation and the Burger Court*, 96 HARV. L. REV. 4.
134	Richard Delgado, *Words That Wound: A Tort Action for Racial Insults, Epithets, and Name-Calling*, 17 HARV. C.R.-C.L. L. REV. 133.
134	Frank H. Easterbrook, *Ways of Criticizing the Court*, 95 HARV. L. REV. 802.
134	Margaret Jane Radin, *Property and Personhood*, 34 STAN. L. REV. 957

1983

327	Roberto M. Unger, *The Critical Legal Studies Movement*, 96 HARV. L. REV. 561.
291	Robert M. Cover, *The Supreme Court, 1982 Term, Foreword:* Nomos *and Narrative*, 97 HARV. L. REV. 4.
268	Mark V. Tushnet, *Following the Rules Laid Down: A Critique of Interpretivism and Neutral Principles*, 96 HARV. L. REV. 781.

TABLE II - *continued*

249	Marc Galanter, *Reading the Landscape of Disputes: What We Know and Don't Know (And Think We Know) About Our Allegedly Contentious and Litigious Society*, 31 UCLA L. REV. 4.
224	Frances E. Olsen, *The Family and the Market: A Study of Ideology and Legal Reform*, 96 HARV. L. REV. 1497.
205	Catharine A. MacKinnon, *Feminism, Marxism, Method, and the State: Toward Feminist Jurisprudence*, 8 SIGNS 635.
189	Paul C. Weiler, *Promises to Keep: Securing Workers' Rights to Self-Organization Under the NLRA*, 96 HARV. L. REV. 1769.
177	Frank H. Easterbrook, *Statutes' Domains*, 50 U. CHI. L. REV. 533.
139	Frank H. Easterbrook & Daniel R. Fischel, *Voting in Corporate Law*, 26 J.L. & ECON. 395.
122	Richard A. Posner, *Statutory Interpretation—in the Classroom and in the Courtroom*, 50 U. CHI. L. REV. 800.

1984

243	Bruce A. Ackerman, *The Storrs Lectures: Discovering the Constitution*, 93 YALE L.J. 1013.
204	George L. Priest & Benjamin Klein, *The Selection of Disputes for Litigation*, 13 J. LEGAL STUD. 1.
203	Joseph William Singer, *The Player and the Cards: Nihilism and Legal Theory*, 94 YALE L.J. 1.
198	Owen M. Fiss, *Against Settlement*, 93 YALE L.J. 1073.
191	Frank H. Easterbrook, *The Supreme Court, 1983 Term—Foreword: The Court and the Economic System*, 98 HARV. L. REV. 4.
179	Robert W. Gordon, *Critical Legal Histories*, 36 Stan. L. Rev. 57.
163	David Rosenberg, *The Causal Connection in Mass Exposure Cases: A 'Public Law' Vision of the Tort System*, 97 HARV. L. REV. 849.
163	Cass R. Sunstein, *Naked Preferences and the Constitution*, 84 COLUM. L. REV. 1689.
162	Gerald E. Frug, *The Ideology of Bureaucracy in American Law*, 97 HARV. L. REV. 1276.
161	Ronald J. Gilson & Reinier H. Kraakman, *The Mechanisms of Market Efficiency*, 70 VA. L. REV. 549.

1985

301	Cass R. Sunstein, *Interest Groups in American Public Law*, 38 STAN. L. REV. 29.
168	Gary Peller, *The Metaphysics of American Law*, 73 CAL. L. REV. 1151.
162	H. Jefferson Powell, *The Original Understanding of Original Intent*, 98 HARV. L. REV. 885.
152	Bruce A. Ackerman, *Beyond Carolene Products*, 98 HARV. L. REV. 713.
137	Clare Dalton, *An Essay in the Deconstruction of Contract Doctrine*, 94 YALE L.J. 997.
112	James Boyle, *The Politics of Reason: Critical Legal Theory and Local Social Thought*, 133 U. PA. L. REV. 685.
101	Akhil Reed Amar, *A Neo-Federalist View of Article III: Separating the Two Tiers of Federal Jurisdiction*, 65 B.U. L. REV. 205.
92	Michael S. Moore, *A Natural Law Theory of Interpretation*, 58 S. CAL. L. REV. 277.
89	Frederick Schauer, *Easy Cases*, 58 S. CAL. L. REV. 399.
89	Stephen D. Sugarman, *Doing Away With Tort Law*, 73 CAL. L. REV. 555.

1986

282	Frank I. Michelman, *The Supreme Court, 1985 Term—Foreword: Traces of Self-Government*, 100 HARV. L. REV. 4.

continued on next page

Table II - *continued*

192 Jonathan R. Macey, *Promoting Public-Regarding Legislation through Statutory Interpretation: An Interest Group Model*, 86 Colum. L. Rev. 223.
162 Suzanna Sherry, *Civic Virtue and the Feminine Voice in Constitutional Adjudication*, 72 Va. L. Rev. 543.
125 Robert M. Cover, *Violence and the Word*, 95 Yale L.J. 1601.
124 Cass R. Sunstein, *Legal Interference with Private Preferences*, 53 U. Chi. L. Rev. 1129.
119 Elizabeth M. Schneider, *The Dialectic of Rights and Politics: Perspectives From the Women's Movement*, 61 N.Y.U. L. Rev. 589.
111 John Stick, *Can Nihilism Be Pragmatic?*, 100 Harv. L. Rev. 332.
106 Lucinda M. Finley, *Transcending Equality Theory: A Way Out of the Maternity and the Workplace Debate*, 86 Colum. L. Rev. 1118.
102 John C. Coffee, Jr., *Shareholders Versus Managers: The Strain in the Corporate Web*, 85 Mich. L. Rev. 1.
86 John C. Coffee, Jr., *Understanding the Plaintiff's Attorney: The Implications of Economic Theory Through Class and Derivative Actions*, 86 Colum. L. Rev. 669.

1987

253 Charles R. Lawrence III, *The Id, the Ego, and Equal Protection: Reckoning with Unconscious Racism*, 39 Stan. L. Rev. 317.
238 Martha Minow, *The Supreme Court, 1986 Term—Foreword: Justice Engendered*, 101 Harv. L. Rev. 10.
179 Margaret Jane Radin, *Market-Inalienability*, 100 Harv. L. Rev. 1849.
151 Cass R. Sunstein, *Lochner's Legacy*, 87 Colum. L. Rev. 873.
143 Mari J. Matsuda, *Looking to the Bottom: Critical Legal Studies and Reparations*, 22 Harv. C.R.-C.L. L. Rev. 323.
143 Patricia J. Williams, *Alchemical Notes: Reconstructing Ideals from Deconstructed Rights*, 22 Harv. C.R.-C.L. L. Rev. 401.
141 William N. Eskridge, Jr., *Dynamic Statutory Interpretation*, 135 U. Pa. L. Rev. 1479.
130 Akhil Reed Amar, *Of Sovereignty and Federalism*, 96 Yale L.J. 1425.
129 Cass R. Sunstein, *Constitutionalism After the New Deal*, 101 Harv. L. Rev. 421.
127 Daniel A. Farber & Philip P. Frickey, *The Jurisprudence of Public Choice*, 65 Tex. L. Rev. 873.

1988

208 Cass R. Sunstein, *Beyond the Republican Revival*, 97 Yale L.J. 1539.
200 Frank I. Michelman, *Law's Republic*, 97 Yale L.J. 1493.
195 Kimberlé Williams Crenshaw, *Race, Reform and Retrenchment: Transformation and Legitimation in Antidiscrimination Law*, 101 Harv. L. Rev. 1331.
166 Robin West, *Jurisprudence and Gender*, 55 U. Chi. L. Rev. 1.
97 Frederick Schauer, *Formalism*, 97 Yale L.J. 509.
82 T. Alexander Aleinikoff, *Updating Statutory Interpretation*, 87 Mich. L. Rev. 20.
79 Ernest J. Weinrib, *Legal Formalism: On the Immanent Rationality of Law*, 97 Yale L.J. 949.
78 Martha Fineman, *Dominant Discourse, Professional Language, and Legal Change in Child Custody Decisionmaking*, 101 Harv. L. Rev. 727.
73 Alan Schwartz, *Proposals for Products Liability Reform: A Theoretical Synthesis*, 97 Yale L.J. 353.
66 Joseph William Singer, *The Reliance Interest in Property*, 40 Stan. L. Rev. 611.

TABLE II - *continued*

1989

193	Mari J. Matsuda, *Public Response to Racist Speech: Considering the Victim's Story*, 87 MICH. L. REV. 2320.
145	Cass R. Sunstein, *Interpreting Statutes in the Regulatory State*, 103 HARV. L. REV. 405.
123	Richard Delgado, *Storytelling for Oppositionists and Others: A Plea for Narrative*, 87 MICH. L. REV. 2411.
117	Antonin Scalia, *The Rule of Law as a Law of Rules*, 56 U. CHI. L. REV. 1175.
98	Joan C. Williams, *Deconstructing Gender*, 87 MICH. L. REV. 797.
95	Ian Ayres & Robert Gertner, *Filling Gaps in Incomplete Contracts: An Economic Theory of Default Rules*, 99 YALE L.J. 87.
93	Kimberlé Williams Crenshaw, *Demarginalizing the Intersection of Race and Sex: A Black Feminist Critique of Antidiscrimination Doctrine, Feminist Theory and Antiracist Politics*, 1989 U. CHI. LEGAL F. 139.
93	Randall L. Kennedy, *Racial Critiques of Legal Academia*, 102 HARV. L. REV. 1745.
84	Jed Rubenfeld, *The Right of Privacy*, 102 HARV. L. REV. 737.
82	Kathleen M. Sullivan, *Unconstitutional Conditions*, 102 HARV. L. REV. 1415.

1990

142	Angela P. Harris, *Race and Essentialism in Feminist Legal Theory*, 42 STAN. L. REV. 581.
129	Katharine T. Bartlett, *Feminist Legal Methods*, 103 HARV. L. REV. 829.
107	William N. Eskridge, Jr., *The New Textualism*, 37 UCLA L. REV. 621.
105	Charles R. Lawrence III, *If He Hollers Let Him Go: Regulating Racist Speech on Campus*, 1990 DUKE L.J. 431.
94	William N. Eskridge, Jr. & Philip P. Frickey, *Statutory Interpretation as Practical Reasoning*, 42 STAN. L. REV. 321.
67	Richard Delgado, *When a Story Is Just a Story: Does Voice Really Matter?*, 76 VA. L. REV. 95.
66	Michael W. McConnell, *The Origins and Historical Understanding of Free Exercise of Religion*, 103 HARV. L. REV. 1409.
65	Vicky Schultz, *Telling Stories About Women and Work: Judicial Interpretatons of Sex Segregation in the Workplace in Title VII Cases Raising the Lack of Interest Argument*, 103 HARV. L. REV. 1749.
64	Margaret Jane Radin, *The Pragmatist and the Feminist*, 63 S. CAL. L. REV. 1699.
61	Gary Peller, *Race Consciousness*, 1990 DUKE L.J. 758.

1991

106	Akhil Reed Amar, *The Bill of Rights as a Constitution*, 100 YALE L.J. 1131.
56	Mari J. Matsuda, *Voices of America: Accent, Antidiscrimination Law, and a Jurisprudence for the Last Reconstruction*, 100 YALE L.J. 1329.
56	Dorothy E. Roberts, *Punishing Drug Addicts Who Have Babies: Women of Color, Equality, and the Right of Privacy*, 104 HARV. L. REV. 1419.
55	Catharine A. MacKinnon, *Reflections on Sex Equality Under Law*, 100 YALE L.J. 1281.
55	Mark J. Roe, *A Political Theory of American Corporate Finance*, 91 COLUM. L. REV. 10.
51	Kathryn Abrams, *Hearing the Call of Stories*, 79 CAL. L. REV. 971.
51	John C. Coffee, Jr., *Liquidity Versus Control: The Institutional Investor as Corporate Monitor*, 91 COLUM. L. REV. 1277.

continued on next page

TABLE II - *continued*

49	Richard Delgado, *Campus Antiracism Rules: Constitutional Narratives in Collision*, 85 NW. U. L. REV. 343.
49	Ronald J. Gilson & Reinier Kraakman, *Reinventing the Outside Director: An Agenda for Institutional Investors*, 43 STAN. L. REV. 863.
45	Lani Guinier, *The Triumph of Tokenism: The Voting Rights Act and the Theory of Black Electoral Success*, 89 MICH. L. REV. 1077.
45	Pierre Schlag, *Normativity and the Politics of Form*, 139 U. PA. L. REV. 801.

METHODOLOGICAL APPENDIX

I obtained citation totals for articles in the following manner. For each article checked, I searched for citations to that article using the Socscisrch database on *Westlaw*, corresponding to the printed *Social Sciences Citation Index* from 1972 to the present. The searches took this form (the article in this example is Akhil Reed Amar, *The Bill of Rights as a Constitution*, 100 Yale L.J. 1131 [1991]):

cr("amar ar, 1991, v100!") cr("amar a, 1991, v100!") cr("amar, 1991, v100!")

I chose this form to catch the variants under which the author's name might be entered in the database, and to catch variations based only on page number. It was not possible to search for the few misspelled authors' names or other typographical errors in the database. Each article was checked at source to make sure that there was no ambiguity in the search based on two articles by the same author or different authors with the same surname appearing in the same volume and year of the journal.

For articles published before 1972, I also counted totals of citations from the printed 1956-65 cumulation of the *Social Sciences Citation Index*, the printed 1966-70 cumulation of the *SSCI*, and the printed 1971 volumes. These totals were added to the citation totals obtained from *Westlaw*.

I determined which articles to check by a combination of methods. First, I scanned *Shepard's Law Review Citations* and checked those articles with longer lists of citations in that source. Second, I used printouts, very generously given to me by the Institute for Scientific Information (publishers of the *SSCI*) some years ago, which list, for twenty-one key law reviews and interdisciplinary journals,[55] all articles with over twenty citations. Third, I used printouts given to me, again generously, by ISI very recently which list, for twelve key interdisciplinary journals,[56] all articles with over twenty-five citations. Fourth, I asked several knowledgeable scholars in law and economics to check off articles, published since 1979 in the *Journal of Law and Economics* and *Journal of Legal Studies*, they thought likely to have been highly cited. Fifth, I pursued a variety of research methods, by necessity unsystematic, to catch articles from journals not covered by the four methods above.

Because of the nature of these methods, which are the only methods available for such a task but which have limitations, I cannot assert with certainty that I have caught all of the most-cited articles from interdisciplinary journals. There is also a slight possibility that I have missed some older articles from journals not included in the list of twenty-one key journals for which I obtained printouts from ISI.

The final data were assembled in May 1995, and therefore represent citation totals as of that date.

NOTES

1. Fred R. Shapiro, *The Most-Cited Law Review Articles*, 73 CAL. L. REV. 1540 (1985).
2. The OXFORD DICTIONARY OF AMERICAN LEGAL QUOTATIONS ix (Fred R. Shapiro ed., 1993).
3. Rodell's classic attack on footnotes occurs in his *Goodbye to Law* Reviews, 23 VA. L. REV. 38, 40-41 (1936).
4. J. M. Balkin, *The Footnote*, 83 NW. U. L. REV. 275 (1989), states the case for the footnote possibly being more important than the text far more eloquently than I can.
5. THE BLUEBOOK: A UNIFORM SYSTEM OF CITATION (15th ed. 1991).

6. For a survey of this controversy, see Kelly Browne, *The Ins and Outs of a Uniform Citation System*, NAT'L L.J., July 17, 1995, at C5.
7. Shapiro, *supra* note 1.
8. Fred R. Shapiro, THE MOST-CITED LAW REVIEW ARTICLES (1987). This anthology is published by William S. Hein and Company.
9. Fred R. Shapiro, *The Most-Cited Articles from* The Yale Law Journal, 100 YALE L.J. 1449 (1991).
10. *Id.* at 1453-54 (footnotes omitted). For more extensive discussion of citation analysis, see Shapiro, *supra* note 1, at 1540-44; Shapiro, *supra* note 9, at 1453-58, and sources referred to in those articles.
11. Joseph Goldstein, *Commentary*, 100 YALE L.J. 1485, 1485 (1991).
12. Herma H. Kay, *In Defense of Footnotes*, 32 ARIZ. L. REV. 419, 426 (1990) (footnote omitted).
13. Stewart Macaulay, *Non-Contractual Relations in Business: A Preliminary Study*, 28 AM. SOC. REV. 55 (1963).
14. Henry G. Manne, *Mergers and the Market for Corporate Control*, 73 J. POL. ECON. 110 (1965).
15. Catharine A. MacKinnon, *Feminism, Marxism, Method, and the State: An Agenda for Theory*, 7 SIGNS 515 (1982); Catharine A. MacKinnon, *Feminism, Marxism, Method, and the State: Toward Feminist Jurisprudence*, 8 SIGNS 635 (1983) [hereinafter MacKinnon, *Feminist Jurisprudence*].
16. Sam Peltzman, *Toward a More General Theory of Regulation*, 19 J.L. & ECON. 211 (1976).
17. Benjamin Klein, et al., *Vertical Integration, Appropriable Rents, and the Competitive Contracting Process*, 21 J.L. & ECON. 297 (1978).
18. Oliver E. Williamson, *Transaction-Cost Economics: The Governance of Contractual Relations*, 22 J.L. & ECON. 233 (1979).
19. Eugene F. Fama & Michael C. Jensen, *Separation of Ownership and Control*, 26 J.L. & ECON. 301 (1983).
20. Harold Demsetz, *Why Regulate Utilities?*, 11 J.L. & ECON. 55 (1968).
21. Gary S. Becker & George J. Stigler, *Law Enforcement, Malfeasance, and Compensation of Enforcers*, 3 J. LEGAL STUD. 1 (1974).
22. Samuel D. Warren & Louis D. Brandeis, *The Right to Privacy*, 4 HARV. L. REV. 193 (1890).
23. Martha Minow, *The Supreme Court, 1986 Term—Foreword: Justice Engendered*, 101 HARV. L. REV. 10 (1987); Frances E. Olsen, *The Family and the Market: A Study of Ideology and Legal Reform*, 96 HARV. L. REV. 1497 (1983); MacKinnon, *Feminist Jurisprudence*, *supra* note 15.
24. Charles Lawrence III, *The Id, the Ego, and Equal Protection: Reckoning with Unconcious Racism*, 39 STAN. L. REV. 317 (1987).
25. Although the outsider political movements taken together increase their presence as this decade progresses, one component, critical legal studies, fades in the later years.
26. See William M. Landes & Richard A. Posner, *The Influence of Economics on Law: A Quantitative Study*, 36 J.L. & ECON. 385, 407 (1993), for essentially the same point.
27. Marc Galanter, *Why the "Haves" Come Out Ahead: Speculations on the Limits of Legal Change*, 9 LAW & SOC'Y REV. 95 (1974); Macaulay, *supra* note 13.
28. R. H. Coase, *The Problem of Social Cost*, 3 J.L. & ECON. 1 (1960).
29. *Gerald Gunther, The Supreme Court, 1971 Term—Foreword: In Search of Evolving Doctrine on a Changing Court: A Model for a Newer Equal Protection*, 86 HARV. L. REV. 1 (1972).
30. Herbert Wechsler, *Toward Neutral Principles of Constitutional Law*, 73 HARV. L. REV. 1 (1959).
31. Charles A. Reich, *The New Property*, 73 YALE L.J. 733 (1964).
32. Oliver Wendell Holmes, Jr., *The Path of the Law*, 10 HARV. L. REV. 457 (1897).
33. Warren & Brandeis, *supra* note 22.
34. Cass R. Sunstein, *Interest Groups in American Public Law*, 38 STAN. L. REV. 29 (1985).
35. Cass R. Sunstein, *Beyond the Republican Revival*, 97 YALE L.J. 1539 (1988).
36. Frank H. Easterbrook & Daniel R. Fischel, *The Proper Role of a Target's Management in Responding to a Tender Offer*, 94 HARV. L. REV. 1161 (1981).
37. HENRY M. HART, JR. & HERBERT WECHSLER, THE FEDERAL COURTS AND THE FEDERAL SYSTEM (1953).
38. HENRY M. HART, JR. & ALBERT M. SACKS, THE LEGAL PROCESS: BASIC PROBLEMS IN THE MAKING AND APPLICATION OF LAW (tent. ed. 1958).
39. OLIVER WENDELL HOLMES, JR., THE COMMON LAW (1881).
40. Alexander M. Bickel, *The Supreme Court, 1960 Term—Foreword: The Passive Virtues*, 75 HARV. L. REV. 40 (1961).
41. ALEXANDER M. BICKEL, THE LEAST DANGEROUS BRANCH (1962).
42. The opposite argument can also be made, however: a book could enhance the visibility of the author's articles, increasing the articles' citations.
43. Shapiro, *supra* note 9, at 1459-60.
44. John H. Langbein, *The German Advantage in Civil Procedure*, 52 U. CHI. L. REV. 823 (1985).
45. The annual series of Forewords to the Supreme Court issue of the *Harvard Law Review* accounts for a remarkable 13 articles on the most-cited all-time list. An additional two articles appear among the most-cited recent articles. See Mark V. Tushnet & Timothy Lynch, *The Project of the Harvard 'Forewords': A Social and Intellectual Inquiry*, 11 CONST. COMMENT. 463 (1994), for a fascinating intellectual history of these Forewords. My original study, Shapiro, *supra* note 1, gave only crude approximations of the citation totals of the Forewords, because *Shepard's* does not fully cover them, but the present data accord them equal treatment with other articles.
46. If two coauthors of an article were affiliated with the same school, I counted this as one affiliation for that school. If coauthors were affiliated with two different schools, I counted this as one affiliation for each school.

47. See *supra* note 46 for treatment of coauthors.

48. I do not believe the inclusion of books would alter the dominance of these three schools.

The only tabulations above in which the three are not obviously 1-2-3 in some order are those of law reviews, where *University of Chicago Law Review* is a bit further down on both all-time and recent-articles rankings. If, however, *Journal of Legal Studies, Journal of Law and Economics,* and *Supreme Court Review,* all of which are produced at the University of Chicago Law School, are added in, Chicago rises to third on both rankings.

One other school is competitive with the "Big Three" if we compile "where are they now" data on the *current* academic affiliations of the authors on the most-cited recent articles list (authors with multiple articles counted more than once). Georgetown has 12 in this analysis, tied with Chicago for third behind Harvard's 17 and Yale's 13. For the last five years covered (1987-91), Georgetown easily ranks first in current affiliations of the authors.

49. Shapiro, *supra* note 9, at 1457.

50. See *supra* note 10.

51. Shapiro, *supra* note 9, at 1457.

52. The column of numbers on the left is the ranking. The second column is the total number of citations in the *Social Sciences Citation Index* from 1956 through May 1995. See Methodological Appendix after Table II for more detailed explanation.

53. These articles, ordered chronologically, did not qualify for the all-time listing but would, I believe, have qualified had the data included pre-1956 citations.

54. The column of numbers on the left is the total number of citations in the *Social Sciences Citation Index* through May 1995. See Methodological Appendix after Table II for more detailed explanation.

55. *American Bar Association Journal, California Law Review, Columbia Law Review, Cornell Law Review, Georgetown Law Journal, Harvard Law Review, Journal of Criminal Law and Criminology, Journal of Law and Economics, Journal of Legal Studies, Law and Contemporary Problems, Michigan Law Review, Minnesota Law Review, New York University Law Review, Northwestern University Law Review, Stanford Law Review, Supreme Court Review, Texas Law Review, University of Chicago Law Review, University of Pennsylvania Law Review, Virginia Law Review, Yale Law Journal.*

56. *Administrative Law Review, American Bar Foundation Research Journal, Harvard Civil Rights-Civil Liberties Law Review, Journal of Criminal Law and Criminology, Journal of Law, Economics and Organization, Journal of Law and Economics, Journal of Legal Education, Journal of Legal Studies, Law and Human Behavior, Law and Social Inquiry, Law and Society Review, Supreme Court Review.*

VII. Deans and Administration

Chapter 80

The History of Law School Administration

1997

James M. Peden

James M. Peden is Associate Dean and Professor at the Thomas M. Cooley Law School.

Preface

When one is writing a historical treatment of any subject, one looks for evolution in the subject matter. Especially, one looks for milestones; events which are of such magnitude that they make a dramatic impact and a lasting difference in the way in which future events unfold. Sometimes these changes are brought about through the efforts of individuals, or groups of individuals, acting with intent and by plan. Other times the changes are more fortuitous. This chapter will explore the milestones that have occurred in American legal education over the last two centuries from the perspective of the administrators, the individuals who are charged with the duty of ensuring that the law school survives through the years and operates smoothly on a daily basis.

Former Dean of Harvard Law School and President of Harvard University Derek Bok, in analyzing the performance and success of higher education in America, posits that there exists a high degree of competition among our institutions of higher learning.[1] It is not difficult to apply this premise to legal education. Individual law schools, whether through the success and notoriety of their alumni and faculty, library size, or sheer survival for an extended number of years, contend for status, because increased status enhances the viability of the institution. This correlation between status and continued existence directly affects the administration of a law school.

There is a discernible cycle in legal education: Superior law schools enjoy excellent reputations among laypeople and professionals, locally or nationally. The reputation of the institution is necessarily linked to the reputation of its graduates and its faculty. Enhanced institutional reputation attracts a large consumer pool of candidates for admission with high scholastic aptitude, allowing the law school the freedom to choose both the size and the quality of the student body. A law school with a student body made up of the best and brightest college graduates will attract faculty of high ability. The result of having the best faculty teaching the best students is the production of higher-quality professionals, which then magnifies the reputation of the institution.

As President Bok further points out, this cycle is driven by the needs and demands of four differing interest groups: the professors or "academy," the students, the profession, and society.[2] Throughout the history of legal education, and to the present, these interest groups continue to affect the way law schools operate. Key to the adaptability of law schools in meeting the demands placed upon them by the various interest groups have been the individuals concerned with the administration of the institutions. Law school administration, as will be seen, did not develop according to any preconceived plan. The early years were marked by the efforts of individuals who copied some management structures from other academic institutions, invented new ones, and in the process created a unique organization for a professional school. Eventually, this organization became standardized in a process that has come to diminish the role of individuals and emphasize adherence both to a detailed plan as described by the professional organizations most intimately connected with legal education—the American Bar Association (ABA) and the Association of American Law Schools (AALS)—and to the increasingly specific parameters of federal regulation.

Any discussion of law school administration must, initially, center upon the deanship, originally an academic office utilized in undergraduate institutions. No two law school deanships are exactly alike. The nature of each deanship and the parameters of decanal authority vary with the age of the institution, its organizational structure, the size and quality of its faculty and student body, and the individual occupying the office. Even so, within these parameters certain obligations remain constant to each deanship, particularly in the current milieu.

The dean in a modern law school must function in a variety of roles responding to President Bok's four main interest groups. Thus, the decanal role in a modern law school includes responsibilities as "administrator, advocate, ambassador, arbitrator, budget officer, counselor, diplomat, director, envoy, fund raiser, intellectual intercessor, judge, liaison, mediator, mentor, negotiator, ombudsperson, planner, public relations officer, public servant, representative, university official, and visionary leader."[3] Most critically, the modern law school dean is the leader of a management team of assistants and staff, dedicated to maintaining the operational capability of the school.

The office of the dean has grown in responsibility, power, and size from humble beginnings, influenced by many things. Once, the most significant influence was surely the individuals who served in that office. Yet, in the twentieth century, with the advent of accreditation and federal regulations, more administration time and energy are devoted to compliance with external standards than to creative development within the institutions. A history of the administration of law schools is therefore, at least initially, a history of the deanship, the individuals who helped define it, and their responses to external forces that affected the institutions over which they had authority.

THE FIRST CENTURY: APPRENTICES AND PROFESSORS

Around the time of the Revolutionary War, the colonies were beginning to experience a shortage of lawyers. This shortage was attributable to a steady increase in population and an increase in commerce with other nations, two trends that would accelerate once independence from Great Britain had been achieved. The initial response of the established legal profession to this need was increased utilization of the existing apprenticeship system, which had been imported from England.[4]

In the colonies there were two types of apprenticeship. An individual could work in the offices of a court clerk performing clerical duties, learning how the court system worked and gaining an appreciation of the court's reasoning in rendering its decisions through observation. This very practical knowledge stood these apprentices in good stead when they later became practitioners, as long as the problems that they encountered were explicable within the parameters of the scant information they had encountered as understudies. Cases and situations that presented issues outside of their somewhat limited experience presented "grave difficulties."[5]

The second option available to individuals wishing to enter the legal profession was to enter the office of a willing practitioner to, again, perform scriveners' duties and to receive such instruction as the master lawyer was inclined to give. Students paid for this sort of educational opportunity "a fee of perhaps $100 or $200. If the lawyer were a man of distinction, the amount was sometimes as high as $500."[6]

As the legal profession grew in numbers and influence, its leading members became concerned both with the intellectual quality of its novitiates and with the quality of instruction they were receiving at the hands of practitioners who were willing to undertake the "instruction" of those able to pay the fee. Whether through the desire to maintain exclusivity or a desire to insure competence, the leading members of the bar sought to impose formal educational prerequisites for admission to the practice of law.[7]

At first, bar associations eased entry requirements for those who had college educations. In 1756, in New York, college graduates were required to apprentice with a practitioner for three years, while individuals without the benefit of a college education were required to apprentice for seven years.[8] The Suffolk, Massachusetts, bar gave a clear indication of its concern in 1771 by decreeing, "consent of the bar . . . shall not be given to any young gentleman who has not had an education at college, or a liberal education equivalent in the judgment of the bar."[9] There was thus a clear incentive for aspiring lawyers to secure a university or college education.

University instruction in law had recently begun at Oxford University. There, William Blackstone had lectured on the common law in 1752 and was subsequently appointed to the Vinerian chair in 1758.[10] The American colleges followed a similar pattern, at first teaching law-related subjects as part of the undergraduate curriculum.[11] It was not until the late 1700's that the first professorship in law was proposed by the president of Yale College, Ezra Stiles. Upon his election to the office of president in 1777, he proposed endowing professorships in law, oratory and medicine.[12] President Stiles proposed a professorship in law because

> The Professorship of Law is equally important with that of Medicine; not indeed towards educating Lawyers or Barristers, but for forming *Civilians*. Fewer than a quarter, perhaps of the young gentlemen educated at College, enter into either of the learned professions of Divinity, Law or Physic. . . . And yet perhaps the most of them in the Course of their Lifes are called forth by their Country into some or other of the various Branches of civil Improvement & the public offices in the State. Most certainly it is worthy of great attention, the Discipline and Education of these in that knowledge which shall qualify them to become useful Members of Society, as Selectmen, Justices of the Peace, Members of the Legislature, Judges of Courts, delegates in Congress. . . . It is in this view chiefly, & principally for this end, that the several States may see the Expediency of endowing Professorships of law in the Colleges.[13]

But disagreement between the Assembly of Connecticut and the Yale Corporation over how much influence each would have in filling the appointments prevented the creation of the professorships.

Thomas Jefferson, upon being appointed governor of the Commonwealth of Virginia and visitor of the College of William and Mary, revised the organization of that college to include a professorship of law, the first in the nation.[14] In 1779, Jefferson's friend and teacher, Judge George Wythe, was appointed as the first professor of law at William and Mary. The trustees and boards of regents of several colleges passed similar resolutions in the next three decades. Columbia, then King's College, voted to establish three professorships in law in 1784, one of which was filled by James Kent in 1793.[15] The College of Philadelphia, later to be the University of Pennsylvania, created a professorship of law in 1790.[16] Princeton established its law department in 1795 with undergraduate instruction in law.[17] The University of Transylvania created a law department in 1799.[18] The Dartmouth College Trustees approved a law professorship in 1808.[19] In 1816, the University of Maryland established a law chair, as did Middlebury College in Vermont.[20] Although the study of law had found its way into the regular college curriculum and perhaps gained a limited degree of academic legitimacy, these early efforts did not provide a whole legal education, replete with practical applications.

The Litchfield Law School provided what was, by most accounts, the most complete legal education of its time. Founded in 1784 by Judge Tapping Reeve of the Connecticut Superior Court, later Chief Justice of the Connecticut Supreme Court, it existed until 1833. The curriculum at Litchfield under Reeve's successor, James Gould, is described thus:

> According to the plan pursued by Judge Gould, the Law is divided into forty-eight Titles which . . . he treats in systematic detail. . . . The Lectures, which are delivered every day, and which usually occupy an hour and a half, embrace every principle and rule falling under the several divisions of the different Titles. . . . The examinations, which are held every Saturday, upon the lectures of the preceding week, consist of a thorough investigation of the principles of each rule, and not merely of such questions as can be answered from memory without any exercise of the judgment. . . . There is also connected with this institution, a Moot Court for the argument of law questions, at which Judge Gould presides. . . . The whole course is completed in fourteen months, including two vacations of four weeks each. . . . No student can enter for a period shorter than three months. The terms of instruction are $100 for the first year, and $50 for the second. . . .[21]

Although other private law schools operated contemporaneously with Litchfield, it was the most renowned. By the time Judge Reeve's school closed its doors in 1833, over a thousand students had attended and many had gone on to serve the growing nation in politics and government.[22]

Harvard College first established a law professorship in 1815. Its first Professor of Law, Chief Justice Isaac Parker, recommended that a separate professional school be established for the sole purpose of educating future lawyers, because he felt that law students needed a specialized educational environment in which to carry on their studies, separate and apart from what they were accustomed to as undergraduates.[23] The Harvard College Law School that resulted in 1817 would be the predominant model for law schools until the present day.

For the first century of its existence, formal admission to the practicing bar in each individual state, or sometimes county, was in the hands of the various courts, which usually required that the prospective practitioners pass an examination by the court or more commonly a committee appointed by the court. In most cases this procedure involved an oral examination.[24] If the applicant's responses proved to be adequate in the estimation of the examiners, admission to the practicing bar was granted. Often, the influence of family and position played as important a role in the process as did legal acumen. The examinations were more casual than rigorous, and the study of law was not required for application for oral examination.[25] There was, therefore, no incentive to spend the time and resources to secure a legal education at any of the educational institutions if one could become a practitioner by simply passing the examination. One solution to this problem was as controversial as it was significant from a historical perspective.

Theodore William Dwight, a professor of law at Hamilton College in Clinton, New York, hit upon a solution that would enrich law school enrollment and provide an influx of competent individuals for the profession. Through his persuasion, in 1855, the New York state legislature passed an act that allowed graduates of the law department of Hamilton College to be admitted to the practice of law upon examination by lawyers who were members of the law faculty at the school.[26] This sort of arrangement, termed the "diplomate privilege," had been utilized briefly in Virginia and Louisiana, but with Dwight it became a cause.[27] He was a staunch believer in formal training at a law school for those aspiring to be lawyers. He therefore concluded that the best way to ensure that only competent individuals be allowed entry into the practice of law was by requiring that the young aspirants demonstrate to members of the academy that they possessed sufficient knowledge.

The obvious attraction of the privilege approach quickly spread to other institutions because of its potential to attract students. Four years later, law graduates of the University of Albany were granted admission to the practice "upon the mere presentation of a diploma, provided the candidate had been in attendance at least three terms of twelve weeks each."[28] When Dwight later went to Columbia, he secured the same privilege for its graduates in 1860.[29]

The members of the profession became concerned that this procedure gave control of entry into the practice to the members of the academic community rather than active members of the profession. Under the new system, apprenticeship was not required or even desirable to the applicants, some of whom had read about but never seen an actual pleading or interviewed a client. Furthermore, law schools unable to secure the privilege for their graduates were concerned by the obvious threat to their admissions. Lewis Delafield, president of the American Social Science Association, was definitely opposed to the privilege, stating that, "lawyers are public officers and upon principle no private body should appoint to public office."[30] By 1890, the privilege would extend to twenty-six law schools in sixteen states. However, it gradually came under attack and was finally eliminated in New York in 1882.[31] It would persist elsewhere, in some form, until the present day.[32]

The fact that the diplomate privilege was adopted on such a broad scale suggests that a dramatic shift had occurred in American legal education in the years between the Revolutionary War and the Civil War. The apprenticeship system had trained lawyers in much the same way that craftsmen had been trained, by hands-on experience. The proprietary schools that came next, of which Litchfield was probably the best, demonstrated that law could be taught in a formal way, quite apart from any apprenticeship experience, "as a science, and not merely nor principally as a mechanical business, nor as a collection of loose independent fragments."[33] Law had become a proper subject for university instruction first as part of the general undergraduate curriculum and later in separate schools within the university.

Gradually, the profession's control over the education and training of those entering its ranks had diminished. While it is true that some form of apprenticeship would continue to be a requirement for entry into practice in various jurisdictions past the Civil War, the profession's influence had been significantly reduced. True, Dwight's introduction of the diplomate privilege into the mainstream of legal education at Columbia meant a final concession to the academy that the practicing bar would not willingly make. Nevertheless, by 1860 it was clear that acceptance of the formal instruction in law had become a rapidly expanding movement that would gradually replace the dominant apprenticeship model.[34]

The Reconstruction Era: Decanal Appointments and Professional Organizations

American society emerged from the social upheaval surrounding the Civil War determined to restructure itself. As a result, Americans developed a concern for progress, professionalism, and occupational stratification. Educational institutions, including law schools, were affected by these social, economic, and educational reformations.[35] In the years after the Civil War, law school deanships became the dominant force in law school administration. Theodore William Dwight became Columbia's first dean, although the office was termed "warden," in 1864.[36] The deanship at Yale was first assumed by William C. Robinson, by agreement among the faculty consisting of Robinson and two others, in 1873.[37] Hastings College of the Law appointed its first dean, Serranus C. Hastings, in 1878.[38]

The office of the dean was an established component of undergraduate institutional administration. Typically, the dean was an academician who would step forward from the ranks of his colleagues to assume administrative responsibility for the institution in addition to teaching duties for a period of time. At the expiration of his term as dean he would return to teaching as his sole professional responsibility, while one of his colleagues undertook the duties of dean. These deans were individuals whose main interest was in teaching and research and who assumed additional, administrative duties for a period of time. Early law school deanships were of this nature, the dean considered to be *primus inter pares*, first among equals. Gradually, however, law school deanships in the United States assumed a new structure and character. Individuals who would be dean of a law school still had to be acceptable to the academicians, as members of the faculty. In addition, they had to possess skills of administration equal to the task of ensuring the smooth operation of a large institution. The office of dean slowly took on so many administrative functions that the individual occupying the office became primarily an administrator who could perform as a faculty member rather than a faculty member who could also administer.

Michigan Creates a Dean

An excellent example of the evolution of a deanship can be traced through the record of the University of Michigan Law School. The "Record of the Department of Law" at the University of Michigan of October 3, 1859, reflects that the three newly appointed professors of law, James Valentine Campbell, Charles Irish Walker, and Thomas McIntyre Cooley, were present at the first meeting of the board and elected as their dean Professor Campbell; Cooley was named as secretary. None of the three professors lived in Ann Arbor, site of the university. Soon, Cooley moved to Ann Arbor, became "resident professor," and assumed the many administrative tasks necessary to ensure the smooth running of the Law School.[39] Historical evidence is scant about the early deanship of Professor Campbell, and available sources indicate that he made only one recorded appearance as dean, when he delivered an address that formally opened the Law Department.[40]

However, there is, in the records of the proceedings of the Board of Regents, a series of resolutions in which the resident law professor (Cooley) was given extra compensation for lectures to be delivered to the Academical Department, the medical graduating class, and the senior class, covering such subjects as constitutional history, medical jurisprudence, and constitutional law.[41]

There is also no record of formal proceedings in which Dean Cooley was elected as a successor to Dean Campbell. The extant evidence shows that, although the university catalogue of 1871-1872 and the 1873 proceedings of the Board of Regents refer to Cooley as Dean, he did not sign his communications as dean until 1875.[42] "Thus between 1872 and 1875, the duties which Cooley had performed as 'Secretary of the Law Faculty' and as the 'Resident Professor of Law,' had been recognized as the duties of the chief administrative officer of a university department, and Cooley was accorded the title of Dean."[43]

Columbia Opts for Expertise

It was with some trepidation that the trustees at Columbia College in New York resolved to start a law school in 1858. Previous attempts to institute a program of legal education at Columbia had not been terribly successful. The first attempt had been in 1793, when Professor of Law James Kent offered a series of lectures on constitutional law and government.[44] These were canceled in 1798 because of underenrollment.[45] His second effort, in 1823, received a better response, but because he was heavily involved in other pursuits, the program died in 1826.[46] It did not escape the Columbia trustees that there had also been an attempt to start a law school, planned by Benjamin Butler at the University of the City of New York in 1838.That school, however, quickly failed because of financial problems.[47]

Nevertheless, the Columbia trustees decided to solicit Theodore Dwight from Hamilton College to be the head of this new endeavor as professor of municipal law.[48] Dwight was an energetic man who had studied law at Yale in 1841 but had withdrawn from the program to return to his *alma mater*, Hamilton College, as a tutor in 1842.[49] There, in 1846, he was appointed professor of law, history, civil rights, and political economy. He secured establishment of a regular Department of Law in 1853 and, as mentioned before, the diplomate privilege for Hamilton law graduates in 1855.[50]

His belief in formal instruction in the law led him to the conclusion that the apprenticeship method was too haphazard to provide a comprehensive legal education. His teaching methodology was based on the learning of a set of legal principles from a textbook and Socratic interchange with the students.[51] He was a practitioner, and a participant in nearly all the professional organizations of the time in New York. In addition to being one of the founders of the New York City Bar Association, he was associate editor of the *American Law Register* and legal editor of the *Cyclopedia of Literature and Science*.[52]

At Columbia, he successfully inaugurated the diplomate privilege as he had done at Hamilton, established "prizes" for qualified students, and instituted a series of interdisciplinary lectures.[53] His appointment was an unqualified success, for in 1864, when the college adopted a series of regulations for the law school, "[it] was obvious that the continued existence of the school was entirely dependent upon Theodore Dwight's continued connection with it. If, in the sixties, Dwight had withdrawn to establish an independent law school of his own . . . the Columbia College Law School would shortly have died of inanition."[54] When Columbia College adopted statutes for the governance of its various programs in 1864, Dwight's importance to the law school was quite clear, for they provided:

1. There shall be a Warden of the Law-School; and the Profesor of Municipal Law shall be the Warden.

2. It shall be the duty of the Warden to take charge, and have a general care of the Buildings used for the purposes of the Law School, and of the movable property therein.

3. He shall report to the Trustees as occasion shall require concerning the State of the Law School, and the measures which shall be necessary for its future prosperity, first submitting such reports to the Committee of the Law School.

4. It shall be his duty to see that the Course of Instruction and the discipline of the School be faithfully executed, and to rectify all deviations from the same.

5. He shall have the power to grant leave of absence from the school for a reasonable cause, and for such length of time as he may judge the occasion may require.

6. He shall preside, in the absence of the President of the College at Commencements of the Law School, and at all meetings of the Faculty, and shall sign all diplomas for degrees duly conferred.[55]

Dwight would be the dominant influence in the growth and development of the Columbia Law School for thirty-three years. He had urged the use of the term "warden" rather than "dean" to describe his position. Had he allowed the Trustees to use the term "dean," he would have been the nation's first. As it was, that distinction would fall to Christopher Columbus Langdell at Harvard.

Harvard Gambles on an Unknown

In 1869, the Harvard Corporation elected Charles W. Eliot as president of Harvard College.[56] He was then thirty-five years old. He was a graduate of the class of 1853, assistant professor of mathematics and chemistry at the Lawrence Scientific School from 1858 to 1866, and assistant professor of chemistry at Harvard from 1861 to 1863.[57] He was concerned that among those holding LL.B.'s and M.D.'s there were too few who also held a bachelor of arts degree. "The term 'learned profession' is getting to have a sarcastic flavor," he wrote.[58] That he was bent on producing change became quickly evident as reflected in a letter written by Oliver Wendell Holmes to John Lathrop Motley in 1870.

> "How is it, I should like to ask," said one of our number the other day, "that this Faculty has gone on for eighty years managing its own affairs and doing it well,—for the Medical School is the most flourishing department connected with the College,—how is it that we have been going on so well in the same orderly path for eighty years, and now, within *three or four months* it is proposed to change all our modes of carrying on the School? It seems very extraordinary and I should like to know how it happens."
>
> "I can answer Dr.——'s question very easily," said the bland, grave young man: "There is a new President."[59]

Eliot believed that the study of law should be approached as a science, one of his biographers noting that "[r]eforms during Eliot's administration moved the professional faculties away from practical preparation for a craft and toward theory and research."[60] In January of 1870, President Eliot brought Christopher Columbus Langdell to Harvard as Dane professor.[61] Langdell had attended Harvard College without earning a degree. However, he later attended Harvard Law School and received an LL.B. in 1853. He was then admitted to practice in New York, although Langdell was never very interested in active court work. As a young lawyer, he preferred the library of the New York Law Institute to the courtroom and "attracted the attention of many of the leaders of the Bar and . . . was frequently employed by them on the preparation of briefs, opinions, and pleadings. . . ."[62] By 1864 he was a partner in the firm of Stanley, Langdell and Brown but still preferred the study of law to the courtroom, establishing his bedroom in connection with his law office which, presumably allowed him to devote more time to his studies.[63]

In September of 1870, at a meeting in Eliot's office, Langdell was elected dean of Harvard Law School, an office he would hold until 1895.[64] As Eliot said in a dinner speech of the Harvard Law School Association in 1886:

> "He [Langdell] then told me, in 1870, a great many of the things he has told you this afternoon: I have heard most of his speech before. He told me that law was a science: I was quite prepared to believe it. He told me that the way to study a science was to go to the original sources. I knew that was true, for I had been brought up in the science of chemistry myself; and one of the first rules of a conscientious student of science is never to take a fact or a priciple out of second-hand treatises."[65]

Langdell, speaking to the same group, defined what he believed to be the qualifications of one who would teach law: "What qualifies a person, therefore, to teach law is not experience in the work of a lawyer's office, not experience in dealing with men, not experience in trial or argument of causes—not experience, in short, in using law, but experience in learning law. . . ."[66]

Before Langdell, law schools did not have rigid admission criteria for incoming students. Under his leadership a minimum age of nineteen was required for admission to the Harvard Law School, and "all who did not have a baccalaureate degree should be required to pass an entrance examination."[67] Later, the Harvard faculty would require that admissions be limited to graduates of approved colleges or those qualified to enter the senior year at Harvard College.[68]

The length of the course of study at most schools was usually one year, with two notable exceptions: Harvard, which required a year and a half, and Yale, which required two years.[69] Then in 1876, Harvard's faculty decreed that the course of study be lengthened to three years. Students were also required to complete their first-year classes successfully before being allowed to take second and third- year courses.[70]

Langdell required that only full-time law professors, not active practitioners or sitting judges, teach at Harvard Law.[71] One of the most notable examples of this philosophy was his appointment of James Barr Ames as an assistant professor in 1873. Ames had practically no experience as a practicing lawyer, but Langdell had appointed him because of his "scholarly and teaching potential."[72] So successful was Ames that when he attempted to resign in 1877, the Harvard Corporation voted to create a new professorship in order to retain him.[73]

Finally, as any modern law professor can relate, (and many modern law students lament), it was Dean Langdell who instituted the case method of teaching.

All of these innovations were unique at the time, and any one would have afforded Langdell prominence in the annals of legal education. For them all to occur under his and Eliot's leadership was as extraordinary as the fact that they are, in one form or another, accepted, even required, features of legal education to this day.[74]

These first deanships at Michigan, Columbia, and Harvard are instructive because they illustrate some basic differences in the way the office of the dean was perceived in its earliest form and because they created a model for future deanships. Cooley's deanship had arisen out of circumstance. He was the member of the three-member faculty who was willing and available to undertake the administrative duties necessary for running the school. In this sense he was an example of the classic English dean, truly *primus ex pares*.

Dwight was brought to Columbia because he had a proven record of success in developing the law department at Hamilton. He had very definite ideas about the formal instruction of law and how it should be implemented. He was also a practitioner recognized by the influential members of the bar and government in New York. In short, he was appointed because of his proven administrative ability, his vision, and also because his choice was politic at a time when the trustees were concerned about the viability of their newly conceived law school. It is difficult to discern whether he was chosen because any one of these qualities outweighed the others in the deliberations of the trustee. What is important to note is that he was an individual, external to Columbia, retained by the trustees to perform the specific function of organizing and running the law school. This is much more suggestive of the modern deanships that we have come to know.

Similarly, Eliot secured the services of Langdell at Harvard. The differences between Langdell's situation and Dwight's are subtle, more than either compared to Cooley's. Eliot promoted Langdell at Harvard because he had been impressed with Langdell's scientific approach to legal education. Langdell did not have extensive practical experience, and in his opinion such experience was not required or desirable in a law professor, as evidenced in his hiring of Ames. Between the two, Eliot and Langdell defined and detailed an institution that became the paradigm of the American law school, with Langdell as the example of the new, proactive law school administrator.

The Harvard example did not go unnoticed at the University of Michigan. There, the deanship would be defined differently after the departure of Thomas M. Cooley. As the student enrollment grew larger, so did the faculty. As the faculty grew larger, so did the administrative duties of running the law school. "The precise relationship between the dean of the Law School and the faculty remained dependent upon the personal character of the Dean, but the generalization may be made that the period between 1859 and 1959 was marked by the development of the office from a purely titular designation to that of an executive with broad powers and the prime responsibility for the internal functioning of the Law School."[75]

Such a transition is clearly seen during the deanship of Harry Burns Hutchins at Michigan, in 1894, about which some interesting observations can be made with regard to the administration of the law school. Hutchins was appointed by the Board of Regents as dean. He was the first to initiate regular faculty meetings and keep departmental student records.[76] As a result of increased faculty interaction, the faculty became involved in student issues such as misconduct and cheating or special admissions.[77] It is evident that dealing with such matters became onerous to the faculty, because there is an indication that they soon gave up at least some of their authority to act in certain cases. For instance, they placed authority to act on determining the status of students who asked for advanced status in the dean and the secretary. They also reasoned that the dean and the secretary could pass on all matters that "they deemed formal and record their action as that of the faculty."[78]

Cooley had become dean largely because circumstances required that a single individual be responsible for overseeing the operation of the newly created department of law. Hutchins was appointed dean and assumed a much more proactive role, involving faculty in the issues that confronted the school and maintaining institutional records. The faculty responded by recognizing that there were instances in which the office of the dean should be able to act on behalf of the academy without consultation. In twenty years a change had occurred in the nature of the deanship at Michigan, the emphasis had shifted from the dean's office as one of a faculty member with extra responsibilities to that of an individual whose primary function was to administer the school.

The years between the Civil War and the turn of the century were important to legal education because of the emergence and development of formalized institutional instruction in law, and the creation of the first deanships. These changes within the legal cloister turned largely on the influence and leadership of the individuals who were deans. Even as the personal influence of these individuals grew, pressure from without the cloister was growing also. Actions taken by the legal profession, and by a newly conceived national academy, as well as the federal government, would dramatically and permanently alter law school administration.

Two Professions Get Organized

Although law schools were beginning to graduate more entrants to join the ranks of the legal practitioners, there was still no reliable mechanism for ensuring that these new lawyers were competent. Bar examinations were by no means standardized, or even, in many locales, written.

In 1877, American Social Science Association president Lewis Delafield advocated the formation of a national association of lawyers.[79] Delafield believed that the practice of law should be a public calling, self-regulating and limited to those who were "worthy" contrary to the current practice of "easy admission allowed to all applicants."[80] He also believed that "[t]he best system would be . . . to require that all applicants should learn the principles of law in a school, then apply them for at least a year in an office, and finally pass a public examination by impartial examiners appointed by the courts."[81] In his opinion, a national organization of lawyers could exert considerable influence over the manner in which individuals were admitted to the practice of law. If such an organization could establish qualifications for entry into the practicing bar, it might then logically create educational requirements for those wanting to enter practice.

The American Bar Association was established in 1878 because of this perceived need for quality in the profession and excellence in educational instruction. Simeon Baldwin, a Yale professor, authored its constitution, defining its mission, which remains the same to this day:

> to advance the science of jurisprudence, promote the administration of justice and the uniformity of legislation throughout the Union, uphold the honor of the profession of law, and encourage cordial intercourse among members of the American Bar.[82]

In a more practical vein, the new association established standing committees, one of which was the Committee on Legal Education and Admissions to the Bar. A resolution was adopted:

> That the Committee on Legal Education and Admissions to the Bar be instructed to report, at the ensuing annual meeting, some plan for assimilating throughout the Union, the requirements of candidates for admission to the bar, and for regulating, on the principles of comity, the standing throughout the Union, of gentlemen already admitted to the practice in their own States.[83]

The committee ambitiously gathered data and, during the next several years, issued several recommendations relating to the length of course of study, appropriate subject matter for instruction, and bar admission procedures. By 1892, the committee was able to present a distillation of these recommendations to the association as resolutions, which were then adopted. First, it was resolved,

> "That the American Bar Association strongly recommend that the power of admitting members to the Bar, and the supervision of their professional conduct, be in each State lodged in the highest court of the State." Second, "That at least two years of study should be required of every student before he presents himself for examination. . . ." Third, "That, in the opinion of this Association, it is a part of the highest duty and interest of every civilized State to make provisions when necessary for the maintenance of law schools, and thorough professional education of all those admitted to practice law."[84]

In 1897 it would recommend three years of study at a law school. In 1909, 1911, and again in 1912, the section recommended that one should have four years, training in a law office, or three years in a law school followed by a year of either graduate work or practical experience in a law office, before being admitted to the practice.[85]

In 1900 ABA membership was not large, with only about 1.3 percent of all lawyers enrolled as members.[86] However this number included the highly influential members of the commercial bar and a growing number of academic lawyers, whose main concern was legal education. Legal educators had been active in the association from the beginning. Simeon Baldwin, who had submitted the draft of the first ABA constitution, was a professor at Yale, later chairman of the Section of Legal Education and Admissions to the Bar and president of the ABA.[87] Carleton Hunt, the first chairman of the Standing Committee on Legal Education and Admissions to the Bar, taught law at the University of Louisiana.[88] Henry Wade Rogers served as the first chairman of the section while he was president of Northwestern University (he was later dean at Yale). In 1894, when the section considered the use of the case method, both Dean William Keener of Columbia and Dean Emlin McClain of Iowa joined the debate.[89] Professors Blewett Lee from Northwestern University and Thayer from Harvard, among others, joined discussions in the section over what should be taught at the law schools at the 1896 meeting of the section.[90] It became evident that this new constituency, whose primary concern was legal education, required an organization of its own. Consequently, the ABA recommended the formation of an association of law schools.[91]

In 1900, the Association of American Law Schools (AALS) was formed, initially consisting of twenty-five member schools.[92] The first order of business was the adoption of minimum requirements for membership.

It was decided that member schools needed to own or have access to a library with a minimum collection of state and Supreme Court reports, must require two years of acceptable study, and must admit only those with a high school education or its equivalent.[93] In the ensuing twenty years, the AALS would, through its membership requirements, place increasing demands on the law schools. In 1905 it required that members offer a three-year course of study; in 1912, schools with day and night programs of equal length were denied membership; by 1916 member schools were required to have what the association considered full-time faculty.[94]

In the first two decades of the twentieth century, the ABA and the AALS, each proclaiming its pursuit of excellence for the profession, at times seemed to be in competition to decide which could author a set of standards more demanding than the other. The result was fairly predictable. Many schools could not or would not join the AALS although they had perfectly viable programs, because they did not measure up to the high standards required for membership. "In 1901, 52 percent of law students were in AALS schools, leaving 48 percent in non-AALS schools. By 1910, the balance had changed; the figures, respectively, were 46 percent and 54 percent. By 1926, the contrast was even more noticeable, standing at 35 percent in AALS schools and 65 percent in non-AALS schools."[95] The same principle applied to the standards promulgated by the ABA. Other than being able to proclaim that the school utilized the current set of ABA recommendations, there was no incentive to respond, institutionally, to the requirements.

However, all this was about to change. In 1921 the ABA issued recommended minimum standards for all law schools:

1. The American Bar Association is of the opinion that every candidate for admission to the bar should give evidence of graduation from a law school complying with the following standards:

   a. It shall require as a condition of admission at least two years of study in a college.

   b. It shall require its students to pursue a course of three years' duration if they devote substantially all of their working time to their studies, and a longer course, equivalent in the number of working hours, if they devote only a part of their working time to their studies.

   c. It shall provide an adequate library available for the use of the students.

   d. It shall have among its teachers a sufficient number giving their entire time to the school to ensure actual personal acquaintance and influence with the whole student body.

   e. It shall not be operated as a commercial enterprise and the compensation of any officer or member of its teaching staff shall not depend on the number of students or on the fees received.

2. The American Bar Association is of the opinion that graduation from a law school should not confer the right of admission to the bar, and that every candidate should be subjected to an examination by public authority to determine his fitness.

3. The Council on Legal Education and Admissions to the Bar is directed to publish from time to time the names of those law schools which comply with the above standards and of those which do not and to make such publications available so far as possible to intending law students.[96]

Pursuant to these standards, the first list of ABA- approved law schools appeared in 1923.[97] However, investigating schools' compliance with the standards proved problematic. It was not until 1927 that the section appropriated sufficient funds to hire H. Claude Horack to oversee the approval procedure as the first adviser to the section.[98] Although the two organizations, at times, created confusion over their constantly changing recommendations and standards, they were apparently successful in persuading law schools to adopt them. In 1927, "166 of 176 law schools had a course lasting three years or more, and 100 had at least a nominal requirement of two college years for admission"[99] Still, these recommendations did not have real effect in the law schools until the states amended their bar admissions laws to give preference to individuals graduating from ABA approved schools.

By the end of the 1930's, increased student enrollment had created a need in most institutions for larger facilities, libraries, and faculty.[100] The ABA requirements affected the competitive environment of the law schools, placing limits on various phases of their operation, where as before they had been free to be much more creative in their approach to legal education. As chief administrators, deans became increasingly involved with issues of regulatory compliance rather than innovation. It also became clear that a single individual could no longer administer the larger schools without assistance.

The Second Wave: Adding Administrators

When Roscoe Pound was appointed dean of Harvard Law School in 1916, he took over his predecessor's administrative staff of two, the dean's secretary May McCarthy, and Richard Ames, secretary of the school. The dean was required to

> provide and administer an expensive complex physical plant. He must maintain and increase a library adequate to scholarship in any field of man's law and government. He must house all of this activity, not only conveniently, but with sufficient grace to show that in his school men study the law, as Holmes put it, "in the grand manner." All this Pound, with an astonishingly small staff of administrators, did well at Harvard.[101]

Even so, by 1928, Dean Pound needed assistance. After all, fifteen hundred students were enrolled in the law school and the faculty had grown to thirty-two. Professor Joseph Warren was appointed to the newly created position of vice dean.[102] Additional administrative staff was forthcoming; "The faculty created an Administrative Board on which sat the vice dean, the chairman of graduate courses, and a chairman of the courses of each of the three LL.B. years, together with the secretary of that board."[103]

In 1923, the trustees at Columbia voted to create the position of assistant to the dean to help in the performance of mounting administrative duties.[104] Robert Goldsby was appointed to the position in July of 1923, although his name is not mentioned in the minutes of the Faculty of Law meetings until October 12, 1923.[105] Mr. Goldsby was apparently not a law graduate, nor was he a lawyer, being referred to as simply Robert E. Goldsby, B.S.[106] His tenure was short, for the minutes of the April 11, 1924, Faculty of Law meeting indicate that he resigned on February 15, 1924.[107]

At the October 10, 1924, meeting of the Faculty of Laws, Dean Jervey announced that William T. Taylor was the new assistant to the dean, as well as secretary of the faculty.[108] Taylor was a product of Columbia's undergraduate program (A.B. 1921) and Law School (LL.B. 1923).[109] When he resigned in 1927, he was replaced by John Grant, who was a graduate of West Point and received his LL.B. from Columbia in 1927.[110] Mr. Grant, however, was apparently not satisfied with the title of assistant to the dean. The minutes of a special Faculty of Law meeting held on April 11, 1930, are of interest:

> The Dean reported to the Faculty that Mr. John L. Grant, Assistant to the Dean and Associate in Law, had indicated his unwillingness to continue his relations with the school after June 30, 1930, unless he were given faculty rank.
> On motion duly seconded and carried it was
> Resolved: That Mr. Grant should not be given Faculty rank.[111]

His successor, James P. Gifford, was appointed assistant to the dean and assistant professor of law, the next day, April 12, 1930.[112] However, he fared better than his predecessor:

> On motion duly seconded and carried it was
> Resolved: That Mr. James P. Gifford be recommended for appointment as Assistant Professor of Law and as Assistant to the Dean for a period of two years beginning July 1, 1930 and ending June 30, 1932 and that he be assigned a seat on the Faculty of Law.[113]

At the University of Michigan, although the faculty had given broad discretion to a special committee made up of the dean and the secretary to act in many matters, it went further in 1905 and voted to allow the creation of a standing executive committee of three.[114] The dean was to be chairman and the committee was to pass "all petitions to the faculty asking special examinations, elections of work not according to the regular schedule, changes from a special to a regular student, and other matters of a formal nature and not involving the status of the student in the Department."[115] In addition, the faculty created an

Administrative Committee in 1906, consisting of four members with the dean as chair, which primarily dealt with students in academic trouble.

To this Committee the semester reports shall be referred, and the committee shall make inquiry, personal if possible, as to the cause of failure by any student who has failed in two or more subjects. Recommendations for faculty action shall then be made by the Committee to the Faculty, accompanied, if any reasonable excuses are offered by the students, by explanations of the failures. The Committee has authority to warn students, or put them on probation, and its action in these regards shall be final unless special faculty action is taken.[116]

This committee, with the dean's office, apparently provided adequate service to the school for many years. Although the regents, in 1939, had agreed that an assistant dean should be selected, the matter had been deferred for inclusion in budgetary considerations.[117] It was not until 1956 that Michigan had both an associate and an assistant deanship, created pursuant to a planning committee's recommendation, as the dean reported to the university's president,

> The faculty Planning Committee, in collaboration with the Dean, has given careful consideration to this problem and has recommended to the faculty the creation of the office of Assistant Dean to be responsible for a considerable number of administrative duties, including those previously performed by the Secretary of the faculty as well as certain duties that in recent years have been performed by other faculty members. It was further recommended that the office of Associate Dean be created to be directly responsible for research in legal education and for alumni relations development, and to have advisory functions in regard to recruitment of faculty personnel and budget problems.[118]

The creation of additional administrative mechanisms, whether through the office of an assistant dean or associate dean or a committee, gives an indication that the number and complexity of the administrators' duties had steadily increased. Interesting too are the titles used in referring to these new administrators. The terms "vice dean," "assistant dean," "associate dean," "assistant to the dean," and "secretary" were not generally interchangeable. As the case of the unfortunate Mr. Grant makes clear there were real distinctions in these titles that affected the administration of the school.

Certainly some of the dean's responsibilities had to be delegated if the schools were to operate smoothly. Along with that responsibility came the grant of authority to act. Where the individual administrators were required, in the execution of their duties, to make decisions affecting the faculty or fundamental parts of the educational program, faculty status was necessary to convey authority and secure consensus and support. The more basic administrative chores could be performed just as easily by someone not of faculty status. Faculty committees could, as at Michigan, still have some administrative or advisory functions, especially with regard to students, curriculum, and faculty recruitment. Yet the dean was still the recognized head of the school, in most cases, with ultimate responsibility for its operation.

This "second wave" of administrators also signaled a trend toward specialized administrative functions. Functions that faculty committees had handled previously were turned over to offices created to perform specific functions, such as the director of admissions, the registrar, and the office of student affairs.

In the years between World War I and World War II, the administrators of the various schools had to comply with an increasing number of ABA regulations as well as with the AALS membership rules. It became apparent that the administration of the schools had become a full-time proposition. By publishing its annual list of "approved" law schools, the ABA had become, in effect, an accrediting body, lending its seal of approval to some programs and not to others. Schools sought the approval because it meant that their programs subscribed to the high ideals of the profession, but beyond that there was no imperative that schools be approved. The situation would change as states began to incorporate graduation from an ABA- approved law school as one of the requirements for taking their bar exam. In 1939, "101 of a total 180 law schools in the United States had been approved. . . . Five new jurisdictions adopted the ABA's minimum standards, bringing the total to 41."[119]

Graduation from an ABA-approved law school meant status within the profession; Consequently

ABA-approved schools attracted students because of the effect that graduation from such a school would have on their future. Indeed, because most states required attendance at an approved school for admission to their bars, students graduating from an approved school could take the bar examination and be admitted to practice in any number of states. Those who graduated from unapproved schools would eventually be limited to practice in the state in which the school was located. Hence professional status and mobility were conferred upon graduates of schools successfully completing the approval and accreditation process.

When the Department of Health, Education and Welfare gave the ABA its accrediting authority in 1952, students attending accredited schools could qualify for government loans. This added financial incentive made attendance at an ABA approved school even more desirable than attendance at a nonapproved school.

Although the AALS has never been an accrediting organization for law schools, attending a member school had advantages. A law school's AALS membership did not benefit its students as directly as did ABA accreditation. The primary benefit of membership in the AALS was the status it gave to the faculty and the school in the academic community. A secondary effect was that member schools could, as a result of this status, attract faculty which nonmember schools could not. The clear implication was that the quality of education was better at AALS membership schools. Although the AALS has never been an accrediting body, in 1941, when the ABA decided that it would be desirable to "inspect" the schools it had approved periodically to guarantee continued compliance, it relied on information gathered by the AALS because it could not fund such inspections itself.[120]

By 1940, the simple list of recommended standards published in 1921 had been greatly enlarged in scope and detail. The list of ABA standards had grown to fifteen "Factors Bearing on the Approval of Law Schools."[121] The "factors" having most to do with the schools' administrations were:

1. Autonomy of the school and its relationship to the university or parent body.
2. Relationship of the law school to a separate board of trustees as in the case of an independent law school.
3. Extent of the authority of the dean over such matters as admissions, dismissals, readmissions, employment of the faculty and determination of the curriculum.
4. Function of the faculty with reference to action taken on account of poor scholarship, applications for admission, for advanced standing, etc.
5. Frequency of regular faculty meetings, agenda of such meetings and record of proceedings.
6. Policy of the school as to tenure of teaching staff.
7. Preparation and approval of annual budget.
8. Secretarial aid to the dean and faculty.
9. Policy as to sabbatical leaves.
10. Scholarship and fellowship.[122]

The list of AALS requirements for membership had grown in a similar fashion. Faculty and decanal authority in the administration of law school programs became the subjects of an increasing number of regulations.

World War II and the Veterans

The ABA, as the voice of the profession, and the AALS, as the voice of the academy, had certainly established their roles as the guarantors of quality legal education by the 1940's. Until that time, there was little doubt that their ever-increasing rules and regulations served a valid purpose: quality control of the legal profession. High-quality legal education benefitted the students, better equipping them with the knowledge they needed to practice law. More knowledgeable lawyers benefitted society at large. World War II would have a drastic effect on how the law schools interpreted this syllogism. Just as the ABA and the AALS seemed to have everything well in hand, events over which they had no control were about to cast doubt on this perception.

The war took its toll in student enrollment and faculty availability; as a result, changes were necessary in the course of study at many law schools. Semesters were shortened; exams were waived in some cases, or administered in other states, at military bases.[123] There was also the problem of faculty and administrators leaving the schools for government service.

Chairman of the National Conference of Bar Examiners John K. Clark remarked, "The various departments are so filled with deans and professors, it must be a very large proportion that Uncle Sam has taken to his breast, not for fighting, but for intellectual pursuits."[124] Student enrollment was even more drastically affected. Section Chairman Albert Harno, dean of University of Illinois law school reported:

COMBINED ENROLLMENTS OF THE 110 LAW SCHOOLS

1938	28,184
1941	18,449
1942 (fall)	7,887
1943 (March)	5,686

Dean Harno predicted that "By next fall [1943] . . . this company will have dwindled yet further. . . ."[125] In that same year NCBE chairman Clark indicated that, if the war continued for another year, "perhaps 20 to 40 of the nation's law schools would close due to lack of enrollment."[126]

Students were, in some cases, allowed to take the bar exam before graduation, if they were in their last term of law school.[127] In some jurisdictions, students were admitted to the practice without taking a bar exam if they had a degree from an approved school (even where no formal diplomate privilege existed)[128] before completing the entire course of study. The situation caused Herbert W. Clark, who would later serve as chairman of the section to lament that,

> in the name of war emergency, there may be foisted upon the public, the courts, and the profession successive crops of poorly equipped, poorly taught lawyers to aid [in] solving problems whose importance, complexity and difficulty cannot be equalled in history.[129]

The dire predictions proved to be correct, for in the fall of 1944, the section reported, "law school enrollment had decreased by 83 percent since 1936."[130] Through the war years, there was increasing pressure from the law schools to change the ABA standards that had been adopted in the prewar era and that were becoming increasingly difficult to comply with. Although the ABA resisted a formal retreat from the standards that had been adopted, Dean Harno, as chairman of the section, declared in 1943 that "there has been no lowering of the substance and the spirit of the standards. The council has approved adjustments in the school programs that were essential because of decreases in enrollments, and on account of the loss of faculty members to the armed forces and to governmental service."[131]

If the war years had proved lean for law schools, the postwar years were a time of plenty. Not only were the returning veterans eager to pursue professional careers; they were financially enabled to do so by the provisions of the G.I. Bill, which funded their education. Many who would have been financially precluded from attending law school could now enroll in ABA-AALS schools. With an increase in enrollment fueled by veterans who could afford a legal education through the G.I. Bill, law schools grew in size and number again. Enrollment numbers were significant: "In 1947, there were 51,015 law students, far more than any earlier year."[132] With an ample supply of students, both the ABA and the AALS resumed their pursuit of excellence through ever "higher" standards.

POSTWAR REGULATION FROM WITHIN AND WITHOUT

After World War II, both the ABA and the AALS resumed efforts to ensure professional competence and quality legal education. There were two areas of immediate concern. First, there was the problem of attorneys returning from military service, trying to resume private practice after a four-, five-, or six-year hiatus. Second, there were schools whose programs, because of the problems associated with the war, had been granted variances from the prewar standards required by both the ABA and the AALS.

To address the first problem, the ABA made refresher courses available to the lawyers returning from service through the Practicing Law Institute. The AALS had experts in various legal fields write articles surveying the changes that had occurred in their areas of expertise during the war years.[133] Correcting the second problem was only a matter of time. Inspections conducted by the AALS of schools that had fallen out of compliance during the war revealed that those programs quickly recovered and once again came up to the prewar standards.[134]

In 1930, the AALS had required candidates for admission to member schools to have completed "one-half of the work acceptable for a bachelor's degree granted on the basis of a four year period of study by the state university or the principal college in the state where the law school is located."[135] By 1950, the AALS standard was three years or three-quarters of the proposed work acceptable for a bachelor's degree.[136]

In 1930 four full-time faculty were required by the AALS.[137] By 1950 the bylaws had been amended to require four full-time faculty and a full-time dean.[138] This last requirement, that of a full-time dean, was at least an indirect acknowledgment that law school administration had become a full-time proposition, at least by one of the organizations responsible for the ever-increasing standards.

Not only were there more standards; they were more pervasive, affecting every aspect of the typical law school's operation, its "washrooms, floor space, and record keeping."[139] As the standards and recommendations proliferated, with no end in sight, even members of the issuing associations wondered about their efficacy. Karl Llewellyn, president of the ABA in 1950, remarked in 1961 that such concern was "the damndest waste of time that any intelligent organization ever indulged in."[140]

Yet the standards, for all their detail, took into account some very important elements of law school administration. While it is true that the central figure in law school administration is the dean, it is equally true that other agencies, the board of trustees or directors, the regents, university presidents, and, of course, the faculty all play a role in the administration of a school. The ABA and AALS standards set parameters for the necessary interaction of these factions in such a way as to minimize conflict and define each one's responsibilities to the institution.

With few notable exceptions, early deans of law were chosen on the British model, first among equals, a member of the faculty who undertook the administrative tasks necessary to keep the institution running, not unlike a steward. Deans chosen or elected by the faculty and respected by their colleagues fostered cooperation and collegiality. Where the president, regents, or trustees of the larger University were charged with the responsibility of appointing the dean, the process was more complex. A particular individual might be sought from outside the law school because of his or her political influence or educational philosophy. Of course, the imposition of this sort of governance from without could be problematic with the faculty.

Both the ABA and the AALS have, in the course of time, recognized a balance of authority that has to be maintained between the faculty of a law school and the administration. The standards and regulations of both organizations have been modified through the years so as to require that law schools have such a balance in power.

The ABA describes the flow of authority for its accredited law schools: "The law school shall be governed by a board whose members are dedicated to the maintenance of a sound educational institution, possess the capability of participating in the formulation and development of such an institution, and have no financial interest in the operation of the school."[141] When a law school is not university-affiliated, the board "should empower the dean to serve as the chief executive or chief academic officer of the law school and should define the scope of the dean's authority. . . ."[142]

However, both the ABA and the AALS recognize the importance of faculty involvement in choosing or retaining deans:

> The law faculty shall have a substantial degree of involvement in the process by which a law dean is selected, appointed, or . . . reappointed. . . . Except in rare cases and for compelling reasons, a law dean shall not be appointed or reappointed over the objections of a majority of the law faculty.[143]

The AALS has a similar requirement in decanal appointments:

> The faculty shall exercise substantial control over decanal and faculty appointments or changes in faculty status, such as promotions, tenure designations and renewal or termination of term appointments.[144]

In recognition of the complexities of the deanship, both the ABA and the AALS state that the job of being dean is full-time.[145] In a like manner, however, both organizations stress faculty involvement and control of the educational program. "A member school shall vest in the faculty primary responsibility for determining institutional policy."[146] Similarly, the dean and the faculty of the law school shall have the responsibility for formulating and administering the program of the school, including such matters as faculty selection, retention, promotion and tenure; curriculum; methods of instruction; admission policies; and academic standards for retention, advancement, and graduation of students.[147]

Both organizations had as their genesis the desire to ensure quality, and that is reflected in their regulations:

> A faculty's competence shall be judged primarily with reference to its full-time members. Competence shall be determined in the aggregate, with emphasis upon the following criteria: 1. Quality of teaching and attention given to law students both as individuals and as a group; 2. Breadth, depth, and variety of the faculty's training and experience; 3. Scholarly interests and performance; and 4. Responsible participation in the group deliberative processes of the law faculty.[148]

The ABA requires that,

> The members of the faculty shall possess a high degree of competence, as demonstrated by education, classroom teaching ability, experience in teaching or practice, and scholarly research and writing.[149]

There is very little doubt among lawyers, legal educators, members of the public, and law students that these standards promote the sort of educational environment that is best for the production of graduates who will, in short order, be competent professionals. But the standards, increasing in number and detail each year, seem to allow less and less variance in the institutional model they describe. Whether or not their prescription for excellence also makes allowance for sufficient programmatic variety to ensure progress and reform other than that contemplated by the standards has become a persistent question.

The Modern Era

In the years following World War II, American society entered a period of dramatic change. The Cold War, the Civil Rights movement, the Vietnam War and later the Watergate scandal contributed to changes in the way the citizens of the United States looked upon themselves and their government.

Beginning in the early 1960's, Congress enacted a series of laws designed to correct long-standing problems in public and private institutions. The main thrust of the legislation, from the Civil Rights Act of 1964 to the Americans with Disabilities Act of 1990, has been to guarantee freedom from discrimination and the protection of individual rights. These laws have affected all institutions of higher education and, although simple in concept, have added significantly to the administrative responsibility of operating a law school.

Civil Rights Legislation

Passed into law in 1964, the Civil Rights Act did not become applicable to law schools until 1972. Title

VII of the act prohibits discrimination based on sex, race, color, religion, or natural origin in employment decisions including hiring, firing, pay, status, working conditions, and privileges.[150] It also provides remedies for individuals who have been the victims of discrimination in the workplace. Title VI of the act prohibits such discrimination in any activity that is federally funded.[151] Executive Order 11,246, which was issued in 1965, requires that employers and recipients of federal contract funds take affirmative action to ensure that there is no discrimination in the recruitment of, or the promotion or retention of, or termination of individuals in any employment situation.[152]

The passage of these laws, in the mid-1960's, heralded wide societal changes. Higher education, it appeared, was going to be made available to everyone equally, and law school was no exception. Affirmative action plans were adopted at colleges and universities across the nation with the goal of attracting and retaining more members of minorities, particularly African American students. Schools changed their policies with regard to recruitment and admissions of minority group members. New sources of financial aid were sought to help those who were capable, but could not afford the cost of a legal education. Indeed, increased African American enrollment in the nation's law schools was noted through the sixties and into the seventies.[153]

Then, a leveling off occurred in the number of minority students applying to law school, either because the Civil Rights movement was no longer central to the public's interest or because, even with the racial consciousness of the law schools being raised, the total number of applicants worked an indirect discrimination on minority members who were disadvantaged financially or because of inadequate undergraduate preparation.[154]

Slowly, the number of minority law students is increasing. This trend is partly due to an increase in the number of African American lawyers who established themselves in the 1960s and early 1970s and who today find themselves able to encourage young individuals in the pursuit of a legal education. It is also partly the result of ABA requirement 212, which requires law schools to attract more minorities:

> [accredited law schools must] demonstrate, or have carried out and maintained, by concrete action, a commitment to providing full opportunities for the study of law and entry into the profession by qualified members of groups (notably racial and ethnic minorities) which have been victims of discrimination in its various forms.[155]

Further, the Civil Rights Act of 1991 places a burden on law schools as employers to refrain from employment practices that create a "disparate impact" on individuals because of their race, sex, color, or national origin.[156]

These laws made law school administrators more sensitive to possible discriminatory practices in every phase of a school's operation. It is not enough to comply with regulations such as Section 212; The real challenge to present-day administrators is to foster an atmosphere within their institutions that minimizes the likelihood that discrimination will occur at all. The administration must see to it that the school has an antidiscrimination policy which is clear and applicable to all faculty, staff, and students.

For instance, faculty discrimination claims most frequently arise in connection with the promotion and tenure process. Institutional policies for scheduling of teaching loads, awarding of sabbaticals, and evaluation for promotion must be written and enforced by the administration without regard to sex or race. A teacher who has taught an approved elective class in women's rights or African American employment issues must be given academic credit equal to that accorded the teaching of any other approved elective.

Faculty recruitment committees must affirmatively advertise and seek out minority candidates for faculty and decanal positions. Many schools have adopted affirmative action policies to ensure minority student recruitment and retention. Administrators must closely monitor hiring of support staff and their subsequent conduct. Registrars and admissions officers must carefully adhere to the school's policies in the execution of their offices.[157]

Sexual harassment is a form of gender discrimination which can occur in a variety of settings within the law school whenever there are unwelcome sexual comments or contact between individuals. The result is often liability for the institution and a public relations nightmare for the administration. Allegations of faculty harassing students or other faculty members, students harassing students or faculty, or either harassing staff can occur in any number of contexts.[158]

It is important that each school have a written policy concerning sexual harassment that contains investigation and disciplinary procedures. Students, faculty, and staff should be apprised of the policy and assured that claims of this nature will be pursued in a thorough and timely fashion.

FERPA

Enacted in 1974, the Family Educational Rights and Privacy Act applies to all public and private institutions that receive federal educational funding. Its purpose is to allow students full access to their school records while limiting such access by other individuals. In this way the students can control access to their files and be sure that only accurate information is disclosed.

Practically every educational institution that keeps student records must comply with the act. Students, regularly request that information in the form of transcripts or letters of commendation be forwarded to prospective employers, the government, or other educational institutions. It is therefore very important that all individuals within the institution be advised of the circumstances under which student information can be accessed, by whom, and for what purposes.

THE ADA

The Americans with Disabilities Act became law in 1990.[159] The purpose of the act was to provide equal opportunity for individuals with disabilities by making it unlawful to discriminate against them because of their disabilities. The broad provisions of the act apply to employment and education. The effect on postsecondary education is and will prove to be most significant. The act, when taken in conjunction with Section 504 of the Rehabilitation Act of 1973, applies to legal education in many ways.[160]

These provisions prohibit law schools from discriminating in any way, at any time, on the basis of an individual's "handicap" status. Schools cannot require information concerning an individual's possible disability during the admissions process.[161] While attending law school, individuals who have a disability must receive accommodation for their disability at their request.[162] In practical terms, this means that the physical plant of the law school as well as the academic and auxiliary programs of the school must accommodate those individuals who have disabilities. New construction at law schools must be disability friendly. Libraries must make accommodations to assist individuals who cannot physically use the facilities as can nondisabled individuals. Classroom activities must be altered to accommodate individuals with disabilities. All of these affect the administration of the institution.

For instance, a hearing-impaired individual may require that a signer be present in the classroom. A visually impaired individual may require that written information be translated into Braille. Individuals with learning disabilities that affect the comprehension of the spoken word may require note-takers in class or the tape recording of lectures. Disabled individuals may require extra time to complete examinations. There are issues of expense in alteration of the physical plant of the school, which must conserve its financial resources. There are issues of evaluating student disabilities, which requires the services of trained individuals to review technical psychological and medical data. There are faculty academic freedom issues that the administration must be prepared to address. A professor may not want his or her lecture tape-recorded or may not want to reformat the final examination from essay to multiple choice. Yet all these scenarios are distinct possibilities, in some cases realities, which arise under the Rehabilitation Act and the ADA. Each school must provide a grievance procedure to address the petitions of students who feel that the administration has not dealt with their disabilities in a proper fashion under the terms of these laws.

The number of students for whom the ADA and the Rehabilitation Act applies is sizeable. Some estimates run as high as nine percent of the entire law student population.[163] These numbers are likely to increase when students who throughout their lives have been accommodated under ADA, the Rehabilitation Act and the Education for All Handicapped Children Act begin entering post-secondary education.[164]

THE PROFESSION RESPONDS

The ABA has adopted regulations which embody the intent of these federal laws and are binding upon schools wishing to be accredited. Presently, Standard 211 provides that a law school wishing to attain or maintain accreditation,

> . . . shall maintain equality of opportunity in legal education including employment of faculty and staff, without discrimination or segregation on ground of race, color, religion, national origin, or sex.[165]

Affirmative action is the thrust of ABA Standard 212 which states:

> Consistent with sound educational policy and the Standards, the law school shall demonstrate, or have carried out and maintained, by concrete action, a commitment to providing full opportunities for the study of law and entry into the profession by qualified members of groups (notably racial and ethnic minorities) which have been victims of discrimination in various forms.[166]

The Americans with Disabilities Act and Section 504 have been incorporated in Standard 213:

> The law school shall not discriminate against persons with disabilities in its program of legal education . . . [and] shall not discriminate on the basis of disability in the hiring, promotion and retention of otherwise qualified faculty and staff.[167]

Law schools that do not abide by the standards run the risk of not being accredited or reaccredited, as the case may be. There is also the possibility of civil liability for violation of the federal statutes from which the Standards have been drawn. It is therefore necessary that policies be drafted and compliance with the policies be enforced by the administration at each law school. In practical terms, this creates a need for enlarged administrative staffs. Presently Harvard has two deans, one administrative dean, one vice dean, two associate deans, and four assistant deans. Columbia Law School has a dean, a vice dean, four associate deans, and two assistant deans. The University of Michigan Law School has one dean, two associate deans, and four assistant deans.[168]

AN OLD DEBATE

The true mission of formalized legal education has been debated from its earliest days. One faction would have law taught and studied as a science, the end goal being the production of legal scholars. Another would insist on what it considers a much more practical goal of producing individuals who are ready and able to practice law. A third faction would assert that the difference between the first two is one of teaching methodology only, and that either approach, done well, produces a high-quality candidate for the bar. Still, the differences between practitioners and the academic lawyers that originally led to the formation of the AALS have persisted and have recently been addressed by the ABA.

The MacCrate Report was generated at a conference sponsored by the ABA, the University of Minnesota Law School, and West Publishing Company, held in September 1993 to discuss issues now confronting the profession and the law schools. It had its genesis in a 1992 report of the ABA Section of Legal Education and Admissions to the bar, "Legal Education and Professional Development: An Educational Continuum," edited by Task Force chair Robert MacCrate, past president of the ABA.[169] In attendance were twenty-four law school deans, seven state supreme court justices, six past ABA presidents, twelve past Section Chairs and forty-nine law professors.[170] The participants convened over concern for a perceived crisis in the profession. Public perception of the profession and the justice system, it was felt, had never been lower. The legal profession was concerned that the practice of law had become but a business.[171]

Chairman Robert MacCrate, in his closing remarks of the conference, quoted from the report of the Task Force:

> If a single public profession of shared learning, lawyering skills and professional values is to survive into the 21st century, the law schools together with the bar and the judiciary must all work for the perpetuation of core of knowledge together with the fundamental lawyering skills and professional values that identify a distinct profession of law throughout the United States.[172]

The report addresses a multitude of problems in education and practice. Curious because it reiterates some themes that are eminently historical, the Summary of Group One contains the following recommendations:

1. increased and better supervised law school externship programs;
2. pedagogical innovations within the law school;
3. broadening the scope of tenurable research and scholarship in law schools;
4. an improvement of the relationship between law teachers and law practitioners; . . .
6. a reconfiguration, or perhaps abandonment of the bar exam and;
7. further studies of apprenticeship-internship programs, such as those used in medical schools.

The guidestar of any of these solutions must be "to improve the general quality of legal practice."[173]

Thus it seems that, in one sense, the same debates still plague the legal community. "There has been a historical mutual disdain between these two groups, academics and practitioners, a disdain which has exacerbated the problem of 'bridging the gap.'"[174]

Many schools, in general, have successfully incorporated skills-oriented classes into their curricula without much problem, although many in the academic community who remain convinced that actual training in the practice of law is a task that should remain the burden of the profession, not the law schools. However, establishing and maintaining live client clinics or providing quality externships has proved much more problematic for law schools.

Because law students require close supervision when representing individuals, most in-house clinical programs can be made available to only a limited number of students each year. This means that when the budget of the law school is examined, fewer students are being educated through this sort of clinic than are being taught in the larger lectures. The problem is made somewhat worse when one considers that one or more members of the full-time faculty are usually assigned to the clinic operation.

Externships are subject to all the criticisms of the old apprenticeship system. It is difficult for a law school to monitor the quality of an externship program, where students are working under the supervision of private practitioners. In a similar way, student experiences may vary widely from term to term depending on what cases the firm can provide for the students to work on. Finally, the ABA's authority to prescribe the essentials of an educational program through the process of accreditation has been called into question.

ABA Authority Questioned

There is growing belief in the law school community that the ABA accreditation process has become too cumbersome, the requirements too stringent. In a larger sense, the extensive requirements placed upon law schools have the result of demanding that institutions of all sizes adapt to a plan that ensures uniformity. Attention to some requirements necessarily means that other areas of the educational programs cannot receive resources and, as a result, remain undeveloped. In trying to ensure the same high quality from every law school, the ABA has created a climate in which creativity and innovation are increasingly difficult for some institutions and impossible for others.

The recent controversy surrounding the denial of ABA accreditation to the Massachusetts School of Law highlights these issues. In 1993 Lawrence Velvel, dean of the Massachusetts School of Law, brought suit to have the ABA's accrediting authority revoked, after his school was denied accreditation. Both the Department of Education and the Department of Justice began investigations of the ABA accreditation process in 1994, based upon antitrust allegations arising out of the ABA's monopoly of the accreditation process.[175] The Massachusetts school is anything but orthodox when compared to other schools, and therein lies the problem, at least from the perspective of the ABA:

While the ABA frowns on a school's having too many adjunct professors, or having professors who are also administrators, MSL's administrators teach, its teachers administer and its teachers practice law or do research in varying combinations, with few of the restrictions the ABA favors.[176]

The question that the MSL situation poses is whether the ABA should strive to ensure quality education by requiring uniformity in all programs throughout the nation or require that law schools be held to comply with a core of basic standards while allowing them to diversify thereby broadening educational offerings generally. The frustration that many administrators feel was voiced by Dean Velvel:

> The ABA standards say to us you cannot do it, because if you do not meet their faculty student ratios . . . and if you do not have the number of professors they say you should have, or do not use the LSAT as they say you should, or if your teachers teach more than eight credit hours a semester, you are not a quality school. . . .[177]

It was not long before other members of the legal education community voiced their concerns over the process as well. In May of 1994, a group of fourteen law school deans signed a letter seeking assistance from other deans around the country in trying to modify the accreditation process. Their chief complaint is:

> We find the current process overly intrusive, inflexible, concerned with details not relevant to school quality (perhaps even at odds with maintaining quality), and terribly costly in administrative time as well as actual dollar costs to schools.[178]

The letter also points out that, today, the student pool of college graduates is declining. The members of the profession are finding that the practice of law is not as financially rewarding as it once was (and, presumably, with growing numbers of lawyers, less exclusive in terms of status). The profession has become more diverse in terms of the types of practice in which its members engage. Yet the requirements placed upon the law schools do not recognize the needs of the profession.

The letter recognizes that some schools educate their students by exposing them to the broader concepts of law, studying law as a science. Others educate their students in the skills necessary to practice. Some have faculty devoted primarily to the exploration of new horizons of law. However,

> [a]ll schools are interested in providing preparation for a variety of careers our graduates may undertake. . . . Our differences provide choices to prospective students and enrich the profession and the community. . . . Different responses to the changes in the profession are to be expected and applauded. . . . It is perhaps peculiarly the academic lawyers' responsibility to preserve and protect these differences and this diversity.[179]

The ABA Section created the Wahl Commission in April 1994 to study the accreditation procedures as part of a programmatic review which is conducted "every five years."[180]

Conclusion

The administrative structure in a law school, or in any other school for that matter, exists for two reasons, preservation of the institution and promotion of its mission. To accomplish this goal, the administration must monitor and exercise control over a wide variety of daily occurrences in the institution. Most of what the administration does on a daily, weekly, or even yearly basis seems terribly mundane to the strictly academic mind yet is essential to the academic mission of the school. Class size must be determined, rooms need to be assigned to lectures and seminars, a teaching schedule must be drafted in accordance with the curriculum, and sufficient faculty must be retained to teach the subject matter. Having resolved long-range planning problems, an administration must also quickly respond to inevitable short-term, rapidly occurring problems. Faculty can become ill and unable to teach, requiring the location and procurement of replacements; there are occurrences of student misconduct that require attention; the ceremonies that are part of every institution, such as orientation, honors convocations, and graduation, must be planned and executed. It becomes quickly apparent that the modern law school requires a sizable administrative force to carry out its mission.

Yet, the dean remains the central figure in law school administration, representing the law school to the university and to the public while maintaining control of internal faculty and student concerns. But increasing external constraints and bureaucratization have both enlarged the number of things that a dean must do and defined how those duties are to be carried out. As a result, there has been a dramatic change in the nature of law school deanships which is easily discerned when one compares the duties of the modern law school dean with the accomplishments of the early deans.

The model deans of the nineteenth century, Cooley, Langdell and Dwight, achieved notoriety by innovation. While each shared the same goal—the training of sound lawyers—each found success through personal innovation.

Columbia acquired Dwight because of his record of administrative success at Hamilton. Once at Columbia, he instituted the diplomate privilege, which he had first developed at Albany, and offered cash rewards for high academic performance. As a result of actions such as these, acceptance at Columbia became very competitive among prospective law students. The school was also accorded prestige within the legal and academic community.

Christopher Langdell was an educational innovator. Others had lectured at law as a science, but Langdell taught it in a laboratory. He eschewed hiring practitioners as teachers at Harvard, preferring scholars whose philosophy of legal education was similar to his. Thus was born the case law system of legal instruction, the dominant teaching methodology to this day.

Although technically not the first dean at Michigan's Law School (the often absent Dean Campbell preceded him), Thomas Cooley was a scholar of the law, producing not only opinions but significant treatises. Yet his duties at the nascent law school ranged from overseeing the physical plant to teaching classes in the law and medical schools.

Each of these men defined their deanship according to their own creative strengths, Dwight as a manager, Langdell as an innovator, and Cooley as a caretaker and scholar.

Unfortunately, the survival of the modern law school as an institution no longer depends so much on the individual creativity of the dean as it does on the adroitness of the dean at abiding by regulations and compliance with statutes. A major turning point in law school administration was the imposition of these external standards and the somewhat coercive effect of state licensure laws which gave preferential treatment to graduates from accredited schools. Because the standards took on a life of their own, increasing in number and applying to more and more facets of a school's program, particularly in the years after World War II, administration of the schools became decidedly more complex. It is fair to say that no dean since World War II has achieved notoriety in any way approaching that of the early deans.

Dean search committees in modern law schools seek candidates who are accomplished academicians, skilled problem-solvers and individuals with vision. A dean must be acceptable to the academic community at large so that his authority is recognized by both the faculty of the school and the academic community at large. Moreover, it is obvious that in any institution the size of the modern law school, the ability to solve problems is a necessary attribute of its leaders. When the dean assumes responsibility for the resolution of the recognized problems that confront the modern law school, the faculty are able to concentrate more on academic pursuits. Last, most law schools want a dean who can plan for the future in ways that will advance the school's mission. This may involve such things as enlarging the skills component of the school's curriculum or enhancing the school's technological capabilities. Although most decanal candidates are capable of performing in these respects, few are adept in all three. The result is fairly predictable: "If a choice must be made [for a dean], faculty members opt for the financially or politically skilled caretaker in preference to the accomplished scholar, the intellectual maverick or the educational innovator."[181]

In recognition of the complexity as well as the bureaucratic regularity of the modern deanship, both the ABA and AALS have developed aids for those who would be dean. In 1993, the AALS finally published a Law Deanship Manual. This work describes, in general terms, the roles and duties of the modern law school dean and is evidence of how radically the office has changed with the passage of time. Dwight's correspondence file at Columbia contains numerous letters written to the parents of students dunning them for late payments of tuition.[182] By contrast, the Law Deanship Manual advises that "The amount of time that the dean must spend on fund-raising can vary from ten or twenty percent to sixty or seventy percent."[183] The need for decanal involvement in the financial well-being of the school is further emphasized, "It [fund-raising] cannot be the bottom item on the list but likely must be among the top item on the list every week."[184]

In 1993, the ABA Section on Legal Education inaugurated a yearly, two day informational conference especially for new law school deans. The format of the conference varies, but in general, topics such as faculty relations, law school finances, long range planning and fund-raising are addressed in a series of lectures and discussions. Some sessions address issues that are more personal to the dean, such as how to maintain a personal life while in the limelight of the deanship, the proper time and manner in which to socialize with faculty, and how to adapt to a new school following an appointment as dean.[185]

It seems then that we have reached a point in law school administration where there is general consensus among legal educators of what the duties and responsibilities of the law school dean are. A logical next step would be to consider an administrative model that can be taught in a formalized way. As it is presently, it is not unusual for a decanal candidate to take graduate level courses in management, accounting, business, or higher education to enhance his or her qualifications. There is no question that the law dean of the twenty-first century will still be the central administrative figure of the school. However, when one considers the current trend toward institutional specialization, whether or not these individuals will be possessed of a specialized degree such as a Doctor of Decanal Science is an interesting question to contemplate.

NOTES

1. DEREK BOK, HIGHER LEARNING 14 (1986).

2. *Id.* At 75.

3. ASSOCIATION OF AMERICAN LAW SCHOOLS, LAW DEANSHIP MANUAL 4 (November 1993).

4. ESTHER LUCILE BROWN, LAWYERS AND THE PROMOTION OF JUSTICE 22 (1936).

5. *Id.* At 22.

6. *Id.* At 23.

7. *Id.* At 23 n.2. See the "Record Book of the Suffolk Bar." reproduced in 19 Proceedings of the Massachusettes Historical Society, First Series 150 (December, 1881).

8. ROBERT STEVENS, LAW SCHOOL: LEGAL EDUCATION IN AMERICA FROM THE 1980S (1983) 11 n.12.

9. BROWN, *supra* note 2, at 23. As an oracle of things to come that same body, in 1780, limited the amount that practitioners could charge appentices to "'one hundred Pounds sterling[]' [and two years later decreed that] 'no gentleman in the future shall have in his office more than three students at the time'" *Id.* 23 n.3.

10. ARTHUR E. SUTHERLAND, THE LAW AT HARVARD, 20 (1967).

11. ESTHER LUCILE BROWN, *supra*, at 24.

12. 1 CHARLES WARREN, HISTORY OF THE HARVARD LAW SCHOOL AND OF EARLY LEGAL CONDITIONS IN AMERICA 165 (1970).

13. *Id.* at 166.

14. *Id.* at 169.

15. *Id.* at 174.

16. *Id.* at 172.

17. *Id.* at 178.

18. *Id.* at 177.

19. *Id.* at 178.

20. *Id.* at 170-180.

21. *Id.* at 184-185.

22. *Id.* at 181-182

23. Isaac Parker, Harvard's first law professor wrote "It is believed that a school at Cambridge, under the immediate care of a learned lawyer, whose attention would be principally directed to the instruction of his pupils, would afford opportunities for laying a solid foundation of professional knowledge, which would be cheerfully embraced, and would be found highly

beneficial. The undersigned proposes that there should be a vote of the Government, establishing such a school, and constituting a department connected with the University." *Id.* at 305.

24. Stevens, *supra*, at 25.
25. *Id.* at 25.
26. N.Y. Laws 1855, c.310 (enacted April 12, 1855). See Foundation for Research in Legal History, A History of the School of Law Columbia University (Julius Goebel, Jr., Dir.) 34 n.5(1955).
27. Stevens, *supra* note 49, at 26.
28. N.Y. Laws 1859, c. 267 (enacted April 12, 1859). See Goebel, ed., *supra* note 52, at 402.
29. N.Y. Laws 1860, c. 202 (enacted April 7, 1860). *Id.* at 403 n.55.
30. Stevens, *supra* note 51, at 26.
31. *Id.* at 27.
32. *Id.* at 99 n.52.
33. *Id.* at 4 n.10.
34. The apprenticeship system is not completely gone. In California, Vermont, Virginia, and Washington individuals can still sit for the bar examination without having attended law school but by "reading law" for a designated period of time under the direction of a practioner. ABA Journal, February 1995, pg 28-29.
35. Stevens, *supra* at 20. As part of this "rebirth," American society was marked by a "thirst for eighteenth-century 'rationalism' often dressed up in 'scientific forms.'" Occupational groups felt an urge "to professionalize and to stratify. . . ." The effects of this renaissance were felt in all realms of American life and were crucial to the "development of universities and the legal profession." *Id.*
36. Goebel, ed, *supra* note 110, at 59.
37. Frederick C. Hicks, Yale Law School Journal 4 (1937).
38. Thomas Garden Barnes, Hastings College of the Law, The First Century 44. (1978).
39. "Cooley was on hand. He could appear before the Regents and represent the Department. He could order blank books and control the amount of gas used to light the Law Library. Elizabeth Gaspar Brown, Legal Education at Michigan, at 32. (1959).
40. *Id.* at 32.
41. *Id.* at 34-35.
42. *Id.* at 36-37 nn.25-26.
43. *Id.* at 37.
44. Goebel, ed, *supra*, at 15.
45. *Id.* at 17.
46. *Id.* at 21.
47. *Id.* at 22.
48. *Id.* at. 29.
49. *Id.*
50. *Id.* at 34.
51. *Id.* at 37.
52. *Id.* at 41.
53. *Id.* at 45.
54. *Id.* at 57.
55. *Id.* at. 58-59.
56. 2 Charles Warren, History of the Harvard Law School and of Early Legal Conditions in America 355 (1970).
57. *Id.* at 354.
58. William P. LaPiana, Logic & Experience 7 (1994).
59. 2 Warren, *supra*, note 4, at 356-357.
60. LaPiana, *supra* note 4, at 8.
61. 2 Warren, *supra*, at 359.
62. *Id.* at 359.
63. *Id.* at 360.
64. Sutherland, *supra*, at 167.
65. 2 Warren, *supra*, at 361 [reprinted as Chapter 52 of this book].
66. *Id.* at 361.
67. Esther Lucile Brown, *supra* at 30.
68. *Id.* at 30.
69. *Id.* at 29.
70. *Id.* at 30.
71. *Id.* at 30.
72. Stevens, *supra*, at 38.
73. 2 Warren, *supra*, at 404.
74. American Bar Association, Standard for Approval of Law Schools and Interpretations (1993) (hereinafter ABA stndrd.)
75. Elizabeth Gaspar Brown, *supra*, at 32.

76. *Id.* at 43.
77. *Id.* at 45-46.
78. *Id.* at 46 n.75.
79. Stevens, *supra*, at 27.
80. *Id.* at 27.
81. *Id.* at 27 n.62.
82. Susan K. Boyd, The ABA's First Section, Assuring a Qualified Bar 5 (1993).
83. *Id.* at 4.
84. *Id.* at 7.
85. Stevens, *supra* note 34, at 96.
86. *Id.* at 97.
87. Boyd, *supra*, at 5.
88. *Id.* at 5.
89. *Id.* at 7-12.
90. *Id.* at 12-13.
91. Stevens, *supra*, at 96.
92. *Id.* at 96.
93. boyd, *supra*, at 15.
94. Stevens, *supra*, at 97.
95. *Id.* at 108 n.44.
96. Esther Lucile Brown at 45-46.
97. *Id.* at 46.
98. Boyd, *supra*, at 28.
99. *Id.* at 29.
100. "By 1938, there were 101 ABA-approved with 63.7 percent (23,827) of the national law school student body.," Stevens, *supra*, at 180.
101. Sutherland, *supra*, at 243.
102. *Id.* at 287.
103. *Id.* at 287.
104. Goebel, ed, *supra* note 12, at. 180.
105. Minutes of the meeting of the Faculty of Law, Columbia Law School 1 (April 12,. 1923).
106. 1923 Columbia Reports. 244.
107. Minutes of the meeting of the Faculty of Law, Columbia Law School 180 (April 11,. 1924).
108. Minutes of the meeting of the Faculty of Law, Columbia Law School 187 (October 10, 1924).
109. *Id.*
110. 1927 Columbia Reports. 389.
111. Minutes of the meeting of the Faculty of Law, Columbia Law School 359 (April 11, 1930).
112. *Id.* at 360.
113. *Id.*
114. Elizabeth Gaspar Brown, *supra*, at 46.
115. *Id.* at 47 n.77.
116. *Id.* at 47.
117. *Id.* at 58.
118. *Id.* at 65.
119. boyd, *supra*, at 40.
120. *Id.* at 40-41.
121. American Bar Association, Standards for Legal Education (1940) 3.
122. *Id.* at 15.
123. *Id.* at 46.
124. *Id.* at 44-45.
125. *Id.*
126. *Id.* at 45.
127. *Id.* at 46.
128. *Id.* at 45.
129. *Id.* at 46.
130. *Id.* at 48.
131. *Id.* at 47.
132. Stevens, *supra*, at 205.
133. 4 Journal of Legal Education 425.
134. *Id.*
135. Association of American Law Schools, Handbook and Proceedings of the Annual Meeting, 173 (1930).
136. Association of American Law Schools, Proceedings of the Annual Meeting, 156 (1950).

137. Association of American Law Schools, Handbook and Proceedings of the Annual Meeting, 173 (1930).
138. Association of American Law Schools, Proceedings of the Annual Meeting, 155 (1950).
139. Stevens, *supra*, at 208.
140. *Id.* at 208 n.29, cited in first, "Competition in the Legal Education Industry," 393.
141. ABA stndrd, *supra*, sec. 203.
142. *Id.* Interpretation 203.
143. *Id.* Interpretation 5 of sec. 205.
144. Association of American Law Schools, Proceedings of the Annual Meeting, By-Law 6.6(c) (1993) (hereinafter AALS By-Law).
145. ABA stndrd, 402(a); AALS By-Law 6.5(b).
146. AALS By-Law 6.6(a).
147. ABA stndrd 205.
148. AALS By-Law 6.4(c).
149. ABA stndrd 401.
150. 42 u.s.c.a. § 2000e, et seq. (West Supp. 1974).
151. 42 u.s.c.a. § 2000d, et seq. (West Supp. 1974).
152. Exec. Order No. 11,246, 30 Fed. Reg. 12,319 (1965).
153. 12 T. Marshall L. Rev. 436-437.
154. *Id.* at 444-445.
155. ABA stndrd 212.
156. Civil Rights Act of 1991, Pub. L. No. 102-166, 105 Stat. 26 (codified as amended in scattered sections of 42 U.S.C. and 29 U.S.C. 626(e)).
157. Kent M. Weeks, complying with Federal Law, A Manual for College Decision Makers 3-5(1995).
158. *Id.* at 7 et. seq.
159. 42 u.s.c.a. § 12101-12213 (1990).
160. 29 u.s.c. § 794 (1988).
161. 34 c.f.r. § 104.42(b)(4)(1981).
162. 42 u.s.c.s. § 12182(A)(i-iii) (1994).
163. Association of American Law Schools, Proceedings of the Annual Meeting, 293 (1992).
164. 20 u.s.c.a. § 1401-1461 (1988).
165. ABA stndrd 211.
166. *Id.* at Standard 212.
167. *Id.* at Standard 213.
168. Association of American Law Schools, The AALS Directory of Law Teachers 1993-1004 42-43, 59-60, 77-78 (1993).
169. The McCrate Report, Building the Educational Continuum, Editor's Note (1994).
170. *Id.* at 3 (Welcoming Remarks by Dean Robert A. Stein).
171. *Id.* at Editor's Note.
172. *Id.* at 146.
173. *Id.* at 131.
174. *Id.*
175. Do Law School Graders Measure Up?, The National Law Journal, Feb. 20, 1995., at 1.
176. *Id.*
177. *Id.* at A27.
178. Letter from Law School Deans to Michael P. Cox, Dean, Thomas M. Cooley Law School, 1 (April 28, 1994).
179. *Id.* at 2.
180. Do Law School Graders Measure Up?, The National Law Journal, Feb. 20, 1995., at. A27.
181. Clara M. Lovett, College Leadership and the Dangers of "Magical Thinking," The Chronicle of Higher Education, April 27, 1994, at A44.
182. Theodore Dwight Correspondence, Theodore Dwight Papers, Columbia University Law School Treasure Room.
183. Association of American Law Schools, AALS Law Deanship Manual 59 (1993).
184. Telephone Conversation between the author and Dean Frank T. Read, December 6, 1995.
185. ABA Section on Legal Education, Conference Materials: Seminar for New Law School Deans (June 16-18, 1994).

Chapter 81

Letters to Students

1890-1891

Theodore W. Dwight

Theodore Dwight (July 18, 1822-June 29, 1892) was founder and Professor in the law school of Hamilton College and was Professor and Warden of Columbia Law School from 1858 to 1891. His lectures and influence are described in chapter 1 and his deanship in chapter 80. See also his lecture and notes in chapters 23 and 24 and student notes of his lectures in chapter 26.

March 18 [1890?]

W. Gates Lawrence, Esq.

Dear Sir:

In reply to your favor of the 17th inst. I beg to say, that a regular attendance of three years is prerequisite to the conferring of the degree of LL.B.

I do not think there will be any difficulty of your coming here in having your time at Cornell counted in your favor, provided that you pass an examination upon the studies of our first and second years course. Still, I cannot say by authority, as the details have not been settled yet, but will be pretty soon. I will send you a copy of our "Circular of Information" for 1890-91 as soon as published.

Yours very truly,
Robert Senfiner

March 19 [1890]

John M.L. Nash, Esq., Treasurer etc.

Dear Sir:

Mr. Robert W. Toppan a few days ago sent his check to us as he is in the habit of doing to the amount of $150, directing, that it should be used for the prize in Political Science for the current year.

On referring the subject of prizes for this year to the Law Committee a few days ago, it was their unanimous opinion that the prizes should only be awarded to the Senior class, and as there is now no Senior class, but only a Middle class, they could not be awarded for the present year. I mentioned this fact to Mr. Toppan who replies to me in a letter under date of March 15th, that if the Treasurer of the College will simply make a memorandum on his books, that he has received the $150 for the prize in Political Science for the year 1891, there is no reason why the check should not be endorsed to his order at the present time.

I write this note for the purpose of ascertaining whether you will adopt Mr. Toppan's suggestion or whether I shall return the check to him. The check being payable to my order, I have no authority to endorse it, except on the terms prescribed in his letter.

Yours very truly,
Theodore W. Dwight
Warden etc.

March 21st [1891?]

John M.L. Nash Esq., Treasurer etc.

My Dear Sir:

Referring to yours, dated March 21st, relative to the money for the Toppan prize in Political Science, I enclose Mr. Toppan's check for $150 payable to my order and endorsed to you as Treasurer, which I request you in his behalf to note on the Treasurer's books to be used for the prize in the year 1891. Please acknowledge the receipt to me.

Yours very truly
Theodore W. Dwight
Warden etc.

42. Theodore W. Dwight (1822-1892) as Warden (or dean) of Columbia, ran an essentially entrepreneurial school, which became more merged with university administration throughout his tenure. (*Courtesy of Art & Visual Materials, Special Collections Department, Harvard Law School Library.*)

November 24 [1890?]

Thos. F. Gilroy, Jr. Esq.

Dear Sir:

Prof. Dwight directs me to inform you that unless you see him without delay and explain your continued absence from the lectures, your name will be stricken from our roll.

Yours very truly
Robert Senftner
Sec'y

November 24 [1890?]

Richard C. Bunzl, Esq.

Dear Sir:

Prof. Dwight directs me to inform you that unless you see him without delay, and explain your continued absence from the lectures, your name will be stricken from our roll.

Yours very truly
Robert Senftner
Sec'y

Dec. 9th [1890?]

John H.V. Arnold Esq.

Dear Sir:

I am directed to inform you that your son's name has been dropped from the class roll for continued absence from the lectures.

Yours very truly
Robert Senftner
Sec'y

Mch 25th [1891]

John M.L. Nash, Esq.
Treasurer etc

Dear Sir,

Please find enclosed my check for $5.00 in payment for extra examination fee from W.H. Moller.

Respectfully yours,
Robert Senftner
Sec'y
Warden etc.

March 25

John M.L. Nash Esq.
Treasurer etc.

Dear Sir:

I beg to acknowledge the receipt of yours of the 22 inst. And in reply to say, that Mr.Landes is credited in our Law School register with the payment of $55 for the first term of 1888-89. He withdrew Feby 4, 1889 and did not take a degree.

Yours respectfully,
Robert Senftner
Sec'y

March 27th

John M.L. Nash Esq.
Treasurer etc.
Dear Sir:
I mailed you on the 21st inst. Mr. Robert M. Toppan's check for $150.00
Please let me know whether the check has been received.

Yours very truly,
Theo. W. Dwight
By Sec'y.

April 2

Gerard Beekman Esq.
My dear Sir:

I find in examining my files of the resolutions of the Trustees of Columbia College, that there are missing or wanting certain minutes. It may be that in some of the months none were printed, but I give them numbers as I find them.

It has occurred to me that you might have copies in hand in your office which you could supply to me, so as to make my files complete. If so, I would like two copies, one for the Secretary's office, and one for my own.

The following are the missing numbers:

1885 all before December
1886 Jan'y, June and October
1887 Jan'y, Febr'y and December
1888 May
1889 Jan'y, March and October

making it in all 19 numbers.

I have a bound volume running to 1888, but it is often a convenience to consult the separate numbers.

The Secretary will find it a great convenience in his office to have one of the bound volumes, no copy of that has been sent to him.

Yours very truly,
Theodore W. Dwight
Warden &c

Chapter 82

Afterword

Why Deans Quit

1987

Paul D. Carrington

Paul D. Carrington is former president of the AALS and dean of Duke, where he is professor.
This article first appeared at 1987 *Duke Law Journal* 342.

Author's note: The time between preparation of the submitted manuscript and publication of this article was very brief. In that time, the author did receive a number of very helpful insights of readers of the draft, many of which are not reflected in the article only because the author was too late to change it. It is clear from these responses that more is to be said on this subject, and an enlarged treatment should be prepared and presented at another time. Meanwhile, the author is especially grateful for the comments of Francis Allen, John Cribbet, Tom Ehrlich, John Ely, Charles Galvin, Dave McCarthy, Dick Merrill, Jeff O'Connell, and Frank Strong. Dick Maxwell and Ken Pye made helpful comments on a previous draft, and I have drawn on experiences of many others, some of whom may well prefer to remain unnamed.

In 1980, Jeffrey and Thomas O'Connell published their thoughtful reflections in The Five Roles of the Law School Dean.[1] Their aim in part was to explain why the average deanship tenure is less than four years. While Jeffrey O'Connell is a well-traveled law professor and Tom an experienced administrator, neither had served as a law school dean. It is a wisdom attributed to Mark Twain that people who write about places they have never been tend to be boring. Yet the O'Connells' work has survived scrutiny by those who have been there, perhaps demonstrating that there is not much to this deaning business that does not meet the eye of the careful outside observer. Their identification of a dean's five roles, as leader, manager, envoy, energizer, and intellectual, remains a helpful taxonomy to those contemplating service as a dean or bearing the responsibility of selecting a dean.

Nevertheless, it seems fair to say that the O'Connells stopped short of tendering a full explanation of the short tenure of law deans. Perhaps it would be useful for a wizened veteran such as myself to put their observations in a slightly different light by trying to count the costs and the benefits of service in the office. It is after all true, as one might suppose, that the reason for the high turnover is that the rewards of the job are for many too meager in relation to the burdens. Understanding why this is so may be helpful not only to those who are considering employment as a dean, and for those seeking to hire one, but also perhaps to those who advise or supervise one, not only as university officers, but also as members of boards of visitors or other advisory groups. In this vein, I add my thoughts to those of the O'Connells.

I. The Dean's Rewards

On the one hand, consider the rewards. There are few deans who do not make some financial sacrifice to the job; sometimes rather substantial sacrifices. It is true that most deans are paid more than they received as professors, and many are paid significantly more than their senior colleagues. But there are unavoidable personal costs associated with the role, and there are sometimes substantial opportunity costs for a dean who makes a full investment of self in the job.

There is of course the gratifying noneconomic effect of being regarded by one's friends, colleagues, and family as a 'leader' or a decision maker. That benefit will carry some deans for a few weeks, and others for some months, but will carry very few for a period of years. Colleagues do learn rather quickly to regard the dean most of the time as a mere support player; indeed, one of the occasional decanal roles not enumerated by the O'Connells is that of community fireplug. The status of the professor is already very high; the dean is scarcely elevated in relation to the professor; and the former dean enjoys the effect without paying the cost of being a dean.

Then there is the fame, the imagined public recognition. Some persons may nourish the illusion that what deans say is more important, or at least more widely perceived, than what professors say; but experience teaches the falsity of that perception.

Finally, there is the reality of a bit of power over an institution, surely an attraction to those of us who study the exercise of power for years without engaging in it. Little enough power, to be sure. Just enough perhaps to force the question, power to do what? Power will not feed and clothe the children; it is useful only if one can imagine a consequence of its exercise. What might a dean expect or be expected to accomplish with the crumbs of power conferred on the office?

When one thinks of the narrow institutional goals to be served, these are likely to be conceived by the dean's constituencies and supervisors in the shallow terms of peer impressions: can this school be moved from eightieth to sixtieth, or from eighth to sixth, on the fraternal pecking order in the period of a deanship? A mature person contemplating success measured in that way is likely soon to find, if he or she did not perceive it in advance, that the gratification associated with the effective exercise of power to achieve the goal is inadequate compensation for the pain associated with its attainment, to say nothing of the painful risk of failure and negative results.

One who seeks rewards in the results of performance had therefore best come to it with a reasonably firm sense of the values to be served by performance in the office; for such persons, there is a possibility at least that they can draw their pay at the window of internal gratification derived from having advanced those values even through occasions of defeat and rejection. Alas, it is probably true that many of the persons who find themselves to be deans lack any such sense of mission, and hence are doomed to be undercompensated.

Having values, it should be emphasized, is very different from having objectives. A wise dean will, I think, avoid having plans specifying objectives to be achieved. Such plans are an impediment to the exploitation of opportunity. If they are not the product of widely shared institutional deliberation, they invite opposition because they are manipulative. If they are the product of such deliberation, they will be made at the cost of institutional energy invested in questions that need never arise, and will likely lack ambition because of the institutional tendency to avoid hard questions that have not yet arisen. There are times when academic institutions are justified in undertaking elaborate planning, but they are fewer than is supposed by persons infected by the dictates of management science. Law school deans, and other academic leaders as well, do better to concetrate understanding on why decisions are to be made than on matters of how, what, and when.

II. The Dean's Constituents

At the same time that the pay is limited, the job is hard. The difficulty derives because there are so many constituencies to be served, many of them capable of insistence on service. Even more so than the work of most practicing lawyers, the job of dean is freighted with contradictions and conflicts of interest that preordain a measure of failure. As the O'Connells describe,[2] the traits required for the job include in good measure those that enable the officeholder to endure frustration and rejection.

The first constituency of a dean is, of course, the faculty. Almost all success in the job, however success may be reasonably defined, must be derived from the success of the faculty. A dean lacking satisfactory collegial relations with the faculty needs to address that problem first and last; if relations cannot be redeemed, there is little use in continuing as a dean. It is almost inevitable that the relation will in time become frayed, and this fact alone is usually sufficient justification for terminating a deanship that is in its second decade.

There are in fact two faculty constituencies, one comprised of invidual members, and one of the faculty entity. There is conflict of interest with respect to each. In the relationship with individuals, the dean, like the shipboard Laundry and Morale Officer, has a duty to help resolve personal as well as professional problems of the faculty, to do whatever can be done to keep each individual member of the group in the most productive mode attainable. This may involve concern with support service, or pay, or fringe benefits, or spouse employment, or medical care, or, perhaps most of all, encouragement or moral support. Most, maybe all of us, have weeks, months, or years when we need community support such as a sound and effective institution can provide. While wise senior colleagues and others can be a big help, it is generally the dean alone who has the motive and opportunity to detect and provide the help that is needed by individual colleagues. In general, this requires above all that the dean be ready to approve and encourage the efforts of colleagues, to be an appreciative and sympathetic audience. Yet, at the same time, like the Laundry and Morale Officer, the dean must, because no one else will, hold colleagues to account when they neglect duties and fail to achieve. If there is a case of faculty harassment of a student, or an involuntary medical leave that must be imposed, or a reappointment to be denied, it is the dean who wears the mantle of adversary to the unfortunate colleague. Moreover, the dean should also provide intellectual criticism of colleagues whose work is not up to attainable standards. There is a manifest inconsistency in these roles. As with the military, no one should be required to serve with the same officer for too long.

Similarly, in relation to the faculty as a group, the dean is cast as advocate for group decisions, as the champion of faculty governance. Faculty governance is important for several reasons, but not least is the relation to faculty morale; those who are devoting their lives to the institution require substantial control over it if they are to retain enthusiasm for it, if they are not to become passive drones. While being the champion of faculty governance, the dean should, however, inhibit some of the political impulses of the faculty, partly to prevent the waste of emotional energy that can result in an environment in which competition for control is too keen and too pervasive. A good faculty can render itself almost useless by too large an investment in internal politics; when that occurs, the dean has failed. The contradiction is again apparent.

In regard to faculty relations, there is also a related conflict between the roles of the dean as leader and as energizer of the faculty. As the O'Connells recognize, a faculty of self-regarding lawyers can be led, if at all, only by the gentlest and least-constraining of means. But law faculty committees are rarely energetic risk-takers; from the perspective of individual professors, institutional committee work is not professionally rewarding, and almost any program change is a threat to some personal relationship rightly valued by some member of a committee. So, as the O'Connells observe,[3] it is the dean who has a primary interest in the advancement of the institution, and who may have the energy and the willingness to take risks needed to accomplish most of the possible improvements that it might occur to anyone to make. But the performance of this function of energizer risks personal conflicts with colleagues and raises the visibility of the dean, thus impairing the ability of the dean to lead by effectively gentle means.

These opportunities for conflict are increased and magnified by their divergence from the many other constituencies with which the dean maintains a relationship as envoy. The most important envoy role of the dean is with those who provide support for the school.

One major constituency is the one that appointed the dean, the President and Trustees, who usually act through a subordinate academic officer, a Vice President or a Provost. The dean can survive a moderate amount of friction with the university hierarchy, but, depending on the character of the officers involved, there is a limit to the support a law school will receive from university leadership that is a bit down on the dean. Law schools that are blessed with reasonable financial formulae have deans who are a bit less dependent, but most universities do place the law school dean in the role of annual mendicant. The weight of this burden depends in part on whether the university is genuinely supporting the law school, as only a few private schools do, or whether the law school is made to bear its own full financial weight.

In some public schools, it may be desirable, even important for the dean to maintain a good relationship with the chair of the state senate finance committee, or other political officials who exercise control over the state fisc. Or, to maintain the institutional political base, it may be important to maintain close relations with the organized bar of the state.

Especially if the institution is a private one, the dean as envoy must also maintain relations with past and prospective benefactors, at least those who are in the major gift category. It appears that most law deans have seriously neglected this set of relationships; a decade of such neglect inflicts permanent harm on the institution. A momentary lapse in manners, or even a forgotten appointment, can undo the benefits of a decade of earnest labor at the other tasks of the dean. Major gifts are rarely received out of the blue or from supporters of a school whose dean is regarded with disfavor by the benefactor.

A complication with this set of constituent relationships lies in the conflict of interest of the university administration. Law school deans are often charged by the university with a duty to raise funds, sometimes in large amounts. At the same time, the university is also raising funds for other purposes and other programs, often in competition with the law dean. It is an experience common among law school deans to have major prospects cultivated over a period of years diverted by the university to other programs. Indeed, a dean is sometimes given a list of 'prospects' on whom the university development officers have given up, and it is not rare for the dean to find that any progress in kindling the interest of a person on such a list is rewarded by a re-direction of the resulting gift to some other program.

Before most persons become eligible for the role of benefactor, they are of course alumni. The dean is the chief envoy to that group. General alumni relations and an effective annual giving program require attention, and for some schools much travel. While much of this can be delegated to administrative staff or to colleagues, the ultimate responsibility remains with the dean, and the dean does need a positive relationship with at least those alumni who are helpful in organizing such activities. For some alumni, the appropriate means of communication is through the activities of the organized bar, and few deans can afford to ignore those activities even if their schools are private and have no use for a political base from which to influence the public fisc. For other alumni, the avenue of communication is continuing education; it is not a bad idea for a dean to be visible in that activity.

While the foregoing constituencies are important for the needed support they give the law school, there are a number of others who are important because of their claim to regulate the school. First on this list will normally be the Provost or academic Vice President who, in addition to exercising some power of the purse, will also impose constraints on the law school usually justified by reference to a presumed need to fit the practices of the school to those of the larger institution of which it is a part. Although first on the list, this source of regulation is rarely a problem. The Vice President, like the dean, has a strong interest in the welfare of the law school, and, if experienced, has learned that the law school and its faculty is a potentially powerful ally of the central administration, if for no other reason than that law professors are not by definition hostile to the making of decisions by officers, and are often more balanced in their political and institutional judgments than their less worldly colleagues in some other disciplines. As long as the dean is not asking for too much of the university's money, most problems of regulation by the central administration can be managed even by a dean of modest administrative skill.

This may be less so if the Vice President or Provost is subject to the dominion of the university faculty or its committees. Prospective deans should be quite wary of being responsible for a law faculty whose appointments or other important recommendations are subject to the approval of an 'advisory committee' of the university faculty. When new powers are suggested for university faculty bodies or committees, it is the unfortunate dean who must place his or her body across the tracks.

In regard to tenure appointments, of course, such committees can perform a useful role by preventing bad appointments to weak schools or departments. Even in regard to these recommendations, however, such a committee can be a very troublesome adversary of the law faculty. Being proponents of values of the academic rather than the legal profession, they elevate research to transcendent importance. Such committees are often death to clinical appointments, and are a formidable threat to the careers of academic lawyers drawn from the ranks of practitioners, who are sometimes a bit slow to produce scholarly writing in the bulk expected. More subtly, and perhaps more importantly, such committees threaten the collegial responsibility of the law faculty and transfer the authority of the collegium over its junior members to a faceless group of references at other universities, diminishing the incentives of the young law teacher to maintain constructive relations with law colleagues, law students, and the legal profession. If the law faculty's recommendations on tenure are to be subject to close scrutiny by an outside group, the law school dean is well advised to insist that the reviewing group be at least largely composed of law professors from other law schools rather than other kinds of academicians closer at hand.

Certainly, in any case, tenure decisions are important and it must be expected that the law school will have to justify them to higher authority within the university. The dean will be the person to make the justification. The duty of the dean to be candid with the university on these matters can bring the dean into serious conflict with the faculty. The dean is obliged to disclose weaknesses in the recommendation, and if the dean is himself opposed to the recommendation, this too must be disclosed. Such disclosures are very likely to result in a disapproval of the faculty's recommendation, leading to much recrimination by the majority making the recommendation. Few deanships could withstand such an event.

Review procedures can be an unqualified nuisance to the law school and to the dean with respect to matters of rank. Given the traditions of law schools, tenured faculty members must have full rank if they are not despised. This reality can be denied by a university faculty committee. Indeed, this is likely to be the case because of the tradition in other fields of reserving full rank as a recognition of additional achievement. My own judgment is that this is a perverse tradition representing poor personnel management; it demeans and alienates an underclass in order to give a useless satisfaction to a favored group. But despite the unwisdom of fine-tuned class distinctions among the members of a tenured faculty, it is the tradition and a university rank committee can be expected sooner or later to seek to impose it upon a professional school.

Similarly, many law schools have a number of endowed chairs, which serve as an additional emblem of rank. In a few universities, there is an 'advisory' committee to counsel against the dilution of standards by promiscuous appointments to chairs. If such a committee is taken too seriously by the university, the regulatory scheme can confer on a group outside the law school, and having no particular interest in its welfare, a very sizable destructive power over it.

A dean unable to secure an appropriate rank for a colleague deemed within the law school to be deserving of that rank is likely soon to lose not only any positive ties to the faculty, but some of the most ornamental and promising members of that faculty as well, resulting in a total failure of the deanship. Thus, all of these advisory committees pose a serious threat to a law school dean, one that can be reduced but not controlled by the dean's ability to maintain a positive relation with university faculty.

The risk is magnified if a rank committee is appointed to perform a representative, political function. It is also magnified if members are inexperienced in the exercise of small power, underemployed, insecure in their own professional status, or self-important; alas, all of these traits can be found among esteemed university faculty, and are likely to recur among those serving on rank committees. When these traits manifest themselves, the rank committee is very likely to be tougher than it is good, gratified by an opportunity to elevate its members by denying rank to a professional school colleague, and quite immune to the pleading and cajolery of a dean.

Occasionally, a university faculty committee may claim other powers over a professional school, such as the power to disapprove a new program, or even to control salaries. Once entrenched, such prerogatives are difficult to remove. Yet the presence of such powers makes the law school deanship a hazardous venture which places the best and most creative work at uncontrollable risk.

Other officers of a university may also propose to regulate aspects of a law school program. For a private school especially, the most noisome of these regulators is likely to be the university development office, which will try to restrict the law school's access to possible benefactors. University development is a tough, competitive game, and many of the players have limited job security. Few if any university development officers perceive the law school as a major source of political support, and they are accordingly driven to take what they can away from law schools for the benefit of programs nearer and dearer to the central administrators who supervise them. Raising funds from foundations and corporations is at many universities an especially competitive game played by rules that are unstated, changed for the occasion, and administered unevenly. More than a little guile, tact, and aggression is required if a law school is to hold its own in this universe of activity.

Also important may be the employment or human relations officer who has the task of administering federal and state employment laws and of protecting the university from ruinous internal competition for the best employees. Such officers can obstruct sound administration when they deny a raise or promotion in rank to a secretary or administrator. These matters often can be as important to the school as they are difficult.

Then there are the regulators outside the university. For local institutions, it is often crucial for the dean to maintain a positive relation with the state supreme court, the bar examiners, and other organized bar leaders who exercise some power to regulate law schools. More important to a larger number of schools is the Section on Legal Education and Admissions to the Bar. For about twenty years or so, that Section, through its accreditation committee, has become increasingly aggressive in regulating law schools. The Section has a legitimate, indeed important, function in ensuring that approved law schools, whose graduates are allowed to sit for bar examinations in most states, adhere to appropriate minimum standards regarding the size and qualifications of the law faculty and its dedication to the teaching mission of the school, the qualifications of the students, the adequacy of library facilities to sustain effective study, and the sufficiency of the curriculum to train students for the performance of legal services. In the last two decades, however, the Section has used its accreditation power to coerce improvements by universities in an effort to conform each law school, as near as may be, to the vision held by the Section for that school. Thus, in 1980, one officer of the Section explained to over a hundred assembled deans that the turnover rate in their offices required that the Section assume some decanal responsibilities for planning and developing the 170 or so approved schools. This activity of the Section has been encouraged by some deans, some of whom may indeed have secured at least momentary advantages from their universities as a result of this kind of leverage. This well-intentioned program to improve law schools is a serious threat to the governance responsibility of the faculty, and to the general quality of many law schools. A dean whose school falls into the receivership of the Section has failed, even if some short-term monetary support is won thereby, because the benefit will accrue at the cost of the law school's control over its own destiny.

One hopes that the Section will return soon, as it has been advised, to its appropriate function of maintaining minimum standards of preparation for law practice, leaving to deans and faculties of most law schools full responsibility for their own fates. But meanwhile, the Section must be yet another significant constituency for many deans, one which has the power to undo a decade's achievement.

Not a regulator of the law school, but certainly a threat is the communications industry. While, as I have said, few reporters or readers of the press or viewers of the media are interested in the words of a dean with respect to issues on which a dean might wish to be heard, there are other matters on which a dean must speak even if there is no benefit to the school to be gained by the utterance. Preeminent on the list of issues on which deans must speak to the press is the bar examination result, a clear no-winner for any dean. There are other less routine questions regarding the profession or students of the university on which the press will smoke out a dean. And a dean is often included on the list of persons to whom a petition is circulated for signature prior to publication. The press relations dimension of the job has been magnified by the advent of the journalism of the legal profession. Lurid reportage of innocent events can and does cause substantial harm to a dean or to a school. It is often the business of these journalists to make stories even where there are none. Doubtless some positive results can be achieved by working with this branch of the press, although such results must be very rare, and are alien to my own experience. In any case, an effective dean serving as a public information officer for the law school must strive to maintain a suitably positive relation with the media, even while knowing that most journalists have interests that are adverse to those of the school.

There are two constituencies among the general public to which the dean has an envoy relationship. These are the law firms and other employers who do, or might do, business through the law school's placement office and prospective admissions applicants. Individuals in either of these groups can make reasonable demands on the time of a dean. Because neither of these groups is organized, it is not generally the case that a dean's mistake in dealing with an individual will be a deadly one. Yet because they are not organized to insist on their views, someone must champion their interests in deliberations on school policy. Often that someone is the dean.

Additionally, the dean is envoy to a number of smaller groups of individuals who are significant to the school. One group consists of those members of the university faculty who have interests extending to law or some aspects of law; some of these persons may or should teach law students from time to time, and others ought to participate in other ways in the intellectual community of the school. A second group consists of international visitors, some of whom may teach, but many of whom may serve usefully as friends of the school on the basis of a single day's positive impressions. A third group is the adjunct faculty, which, especially for a school ambitious to maintain a substantial clinical program of quality, can be an important group that can be often and easily slighted by the regular faculty. A fourth group, of critical importance, are prospective recruits to the faculty; indeed, this group may be, over the longer term, the single most important constituency of the dean, for a failure of positive relations with this group has dreadful consequences that are obvious.

Yet another set of groups to which the dean is envoy is comprised of student organizations. Each school has at least one organ that is representative of the entire body of law students. Sometimes, this group can be energetic and constructive; more often, it is passive and sociable; sometimes it can become confrontational and a real difficulty for the dean. Not always will such a group be wrong when it is confrontational; law students are a critical and perceptive audience and are not unwilling to take public note of a dean's shortcomings. On other occasions, the group will pit itself against the faculty, perhaps putting the dean in the crossfire. Sometimes, such a group will simply make unjustifiable demands that must be rejected. If possible, a wise dean will engage the support of the full faculty on such an occasion, but this may not always be possible.

Sometimes incendiary is the relation to other student organizations. Organizations responsible for a publication can pose serious problems; more than a few function far below the par of quality that the students are capable of achieving. Such organizations can also manage their affairs in such matters as membership selection in ways that adversely affect other school activities. An effective dean can try to elevate standards and inhibit activities that are harmful to others, but traditions of institutional autonomy are an impediment. Similarly, moot court programs run by students can develop negative traditions, habits and standards; a dean can hope for help from a faculty adviser, but ultimate responsibility does rest in the dean's office. Additionally, there are the special interest student groups, each of which may have special expectations to which a dean may have to respond.

A common characteristic among student organizations is a short time perspective. Unwise 'traditions' can be invented and entrenched by a single three-year generation of students. The ability of group members to distinguish such traditions from the longer term and broader interest of the law school is limited not only by short memory, but also by short foresight. It is a function of the dean to try to correct the consequences of such defects of vision.

Much of the work with student organizations can be delegated to an assistant dean, but not the part giving rise to serious conflict. When there is an odium to be borne in such matters, it is likely to be the dean's, and it is likely to have some effect on other relationships as well.

In addition to student organizations, there is another student constituency—the unorganized mass of students. This group exercises the real power of socialization over its members. What most think and do will influence the thinking and action of many. The dean's and faculty's relation with the mass will be influenced by the relationship with student organizations, or with student members of faculty committees, but the mass should not be mistaken for its representatives. A dean not having a satisfactory relation with the mass of students exposes to risk not only the deanship, but also faculty and staff who may need the support of a dean, and the longer-term goodwill of younger alumni.

Owing in part to the high teacher-student ratios prevalent in law schools, the power of the student constituencies is greater than an outsider might imagine. Law teachers are, in part, performing artists, and are strongly influenced by audience reaction; this pressure on the faculty is subtle and sometimes unperceived, but more than a few bad decisions have been made by professors and faculties to avoid the lash of audience rejection. Indeed, the timidity of otherwise courageous professors in the face of even limited and temporary student odium can sometimes be remarkable. It is then the role of the dean to deflect, and if necessary, to absorb such an odium that would otherwise befall one or more colleagues, or to urge the faculty to resist an improvident impulse of student opinion.

I have now identified a couple of dozen constituencies of the dean to whom that officer bears the relation of envoy. Others arise from the role to which the O'Connells refer as managerial. The dean as manager has yet another full set of constituencies to whom relationships should be maintained.

First, of course, there is the administrative infrastructure of the law school, the people who do the work of making the institution run, the associate and assistant deans and the director of the library. These persons are almost universally underappreciated by the students and by the faculty. Often there are serious questions of job title and status or even tenure; many of these are matters for the faculty to decide even if they are not directly dependent on the individual for help. A dean who fails to get and retain the right kind of help in these positions is in serious difficulty, to say the least.

In addition, there is the staff supervised by the deputy administrators. The dean must be careful not to tread on the roles of delegates, and to leave them ample room to make their own mistakes and maintain their own relations with subordinates. At the same time, it is desirable to maintain a possibility of direct communication with the cataloguers in the library, the admissions secretary, and dozens of other individuals who are on the institutional front lines. Without some communication with these sources, it is impossible to judge the administrative skill of delegates or to form a satisfactory opinion on relative budget needs, or to be effective in doing battle with university personnel officers with regard to raises and promotions. Moreover, staff members are sometimes drawn into heated issues which the dean cannot avoid, such as complaints by the faculty about secretarial services, or by students about library or placement services. On such occasions, the dean needs knowledge of the office and a relationship with the people in it.

Of course the largest constituency within the school is made up of students in their individual capacities. Except in a very small school, it is impossible for the dean to have a personal relationship with each student. But the management role does require involvement in crises. Student suicide is only the most serious of a range of matters requiring the dean's attention. Some of these matters can place the dean in an adverse relation with a faculty member or with a deputy. They also bring the dean into contact with other significant constituencies who may be concerned with student conduct, including especially parents, but also the police or the fitness committee of the bar examiners. The latter pose an especially noisome conflict between the dean's role as teacher- counselor and his role as an officer of the profession obliged to disclose pertinent information to a licensing authority. Even in a small school, one can expect several individual student crises each year.

In a more positive vein, the dean may have opportunities to help individual students with their careers. This is most likely to be the case with judicial clerkships. Even this role is not free of conflict, because alumni do ask, and some expect, a preferment in the advice given by the dean to students considering offers of employment.

As manager, the dean may also have a relationship with admissions applicants and with employers. These will again involve the crisis situations in which there are opportunities to make institutional friends and enemies. Most deans must at some marginal level become involved with admissions decisions involving candidates favored by supportive alumni; usually the dean's interest in such matters is rightly resisted by the faculty. On occasion, also, problems arise with employers using the placement service. Sexual harassment of a student by an interviewer or summer employer presents the dean with an especially onerous obligation for confrontation, sometimes with alumni.

There is another large constituency outside the law school for whom the dean is accountable to those within it. These are the university support offices, which may include the campus police, food service, the parking office, the bursar's office, housekeeping, and a half dozen other bureaucracies. Often these offices have acquired a self-centered view of the university and have lost the sense, if they ever had it, that their mission is to support the efforts of those who teach and learn. In order to secure satisfactory services, the dean may be required to spend valuable good will with higher university officials. If the services are unsatisfactory, it is often the dean who bears the odium of the dissatisfaction. Again, much of the routine contact with these offices can be delegated, but not when the heat is up.

Finally, perhaps most urgent of all obligations, the dean has duties to an immediate office staff with whom satisfactory relations are indispensable. Like the dean, persons working in the office of the dean must deal with many constituencies, hopefully without adding to the complexity by interjecting yet more conflict into these relations. Like the family cat, it is they who are closest at hand when something needs to be kicked. A dean supported by a competent and even-tempered staff is very fortunate; a wise dean will make the appropriate care of such a staff a very high priority.

As the number of constituencies approaches a third dozen, I should note that intersecting almost all these relationships is the responsibility of the dean as budget officer of the law school. For those who have shared the experience of spending millions of institutional dollars, it is no surprise to learn that there seems to be very little discretion to be exercised, so fixed are the expectations reflected in the way things have been done recently. Yet there is endemic dissatisfaction with whatever the budget allows, and every dollar that a dean spends on one purpose is in fact taken from twenty-five others.

Much of this is obvious, but it is possible that the reader has not before attempted to count these diverse groups to whom a law school dean must account. When one also considers that most of these very numerous and conflicting constituencies are articulate and aggressive, it seems fair to say that the job is as complex as any other job within the university. The accomplishment of any specific objective by a dean must be regarded as improbable. These features are, of course, for some of us the charm of the job.

III. Lifestyle

Thus far, I have dealt with the substantive complexities of the job. These complexities are not what generally causes deanships to end in the third or fourth year. The cost-benefit analysis of deaning tilts still more to the cost side when consideration is given to the lifestyle of the dean. It is at all times clear that the lifestyle of a professor is to be preferred by almost any taste to the lifestyle of the dean.

Some deans find their in-boxes to be unbearable companions.[4] I have never minded mine so much, but I learned early to be ruthless in dealing with it. Over half of my mail each day is disposed of in a round file in less than three minutes, and I will have disposed of much of what remains within seven minutes by penning the initials of another person in the upper right-hand corner. This is not to say, of course, that my own in-box, or that of every dean so far as I know, is not sometimes an appalling sight, especially the second in-box, where I hold those few daily items that require fuller attention. It is a special discipline not to be governed by the mail; failure to master the technique of handling most paper only once and usually as briefly as possible can make the job an intolerable burden.

There is likewise the telephone. It rings too much, too often with messages one would prefer not to receive and much too often with calls placed by persons other than the callers, for whom one is asked to wait, a practice that I revile. An attraction of being a former dean is the freedom it allows to greet with a dead line those persons whose secretaries announce their call. (I do not know how many others share my own reaction, which is to measure the maturity and integrity of a person by his or her willingness to dial a telephone. I know federal judges, senators, and university presidents who do, and assistant bureaucrats who do not. It may be useful parenthetical advice to rookie deans to do their own dialing.) Of course, one can ask that incoming calls be controlled, but this is the counterpart of having a secretary place your calls: it risks offense to callers; and it always turns out that the calls one most wanted to receive are the ones that are held.

Then there is the calendar of appointments and committee meetings, which are sometimes seemingly incessant. Most troubling is that the appointments one often should have kept are the ones that are never made, because the occasion for them was not known. It is not bad practice for a dean to cruise the building, daily if possible, especially to remain in contact with the faculty, but also to see and be seen by the secretaries, the librarians, and of course the students. A dean without time for a visit to the faculty coffee pot or lunch table invites serious trouble and disappointment. It also seems necessary to see most assistant and associate deans frequently, some daily and some weekly, maybe the library director monthly. In general, for most deans, because the usual work week is already chopped to pieces by calls and mail and appointments, it makes sense to leave the office door open and receive most callers on demand; this is good for relations with faculty and students and costs less than one might suppose.

Then there is ceremony. Some ceremonies, such as commencement or meeting an incoming class, can be especially gratifying. But the number of events in between can wear a fellow down. And for some deans there is the travel. For national law schools, alumni and benefactors are everywhere. An effective dean may need to spend thirty to sixty nights a year away from home, usually in a lonely hotel room, and often after too much food, too much drink, and not enough exercise.

If the dean is to perform at all as an intellectual leader, it is essential to maintain at least a passing acquaintance with contemporary news events and with recent legal developments. It is necessary to read at least most of what the faculty writes, in draft and with comments if possible. It is also desirable to participate in the intellectual life of the faculty by attending lectures and workshops, and contributing useful comments on papers presented whenever possible. And it is perhaps most important for a dean to retain some personal life of the mind by reading novels, history, science, or other writings that carry the mind some distance from the institutional routine so that its owner can return to work from a different place, at least from time to time.

If the dean is not planning to leave academic life at the end of the deanship, it is essential that the dean also teach. Perhaps for the wrong reasons, students will, fortunately for a dean, minimize their claims on outside time of a dean-teacher. It is, however, inevitable that the dean's teaching will be less careful, and less effective, than it would be without the distractions of other decanal duties. For this reason, teaching is not without risk. Pity the dean who must deal with student unrest about the quality of his or her own teaching!

Moreover, a dean who contemplates a possible return to academic life must also write. Writing is also important if one is to keep one's status as a member of the intellectual community of the school. As with teaching, this activity must be limited, and is seriously impeded by the incessant demands of the in-box, the telephone, and the appointments calendar.

Adding these activities together, it is clear that they occupy more hours and days than there are. Over-commitment of time is thus an independent additional reason why a dean is doomed to experience substantial failure and frustration. This is also a reason why, in the end, a dean's neglected spouse is likely to blow the whistle if no one else does.

Indeed, it should be noted that the family bearing that burden of neglect can be an enormous, even an essential, help in keeping the stresses of the dean's job in perspective; the dean's family is always his or her most important, if not only, 'support group.' It is perhaps for this reason that few unmarried persons have served long terms as deans. But this means that the office is in a sense filled by two persons (or more), not one. Even a spouse who limits his or her ceremonial and social activities is making a substantial, if involuntary, contribution to the institution. Rarely is this recognized by an institution. I am, however, told that there are now a few enlightened institutions that provide salaries for spouses of executive officers. If commencing anew, I would perhaps insist on such an arrangement.

IV. Conclusion

Would I undertake such a job again? Yes, on conditions. Would I recommend it to a friend? Yes, on the same conditions, I would recommend the job for a friend who has a strong marriage (or a suitable surrogate for that), a substantial willingness to take flak as well as give it, and a sense that law and legal education are worthy enterprises. But I would not recommend the job to one who takes himself or herself very seriously, and who expects his or her efforts to be widely and fully appreciated. Appreciation can come to some, but it would be a folly to count on it, and one who performs the job for gratitude will not perform it well.

The conditions I would require and recommend to a friend are several. First, one should not undertake to be a dean to a faculty of which one would not wish to be a member. The previous discussion suggests many reasons why this won't work. This factor often counsels against becoming an 'outside' dean, and there are additional reasons for caution about that, not least of which is the awesome difficulty of establishing positive relations with literally hundreds of people at once; an outsider cannot with any accuracy assess so many unknowns among the many constituencies, and is not likely for many years to be effective in relations with alumni and benefactors. On the other hand, I would for myself again elect to be an outsider once (but never again), given just the right time and place.

Second, one should be assured of enough control of events within the law school that one's failures will result from one's own shortcomings and not the intransigency of an officer or committee that will not share in the responsibility for the failure. Thus, I would never recommend to a friend a deanship of a law school whose important decisions (such as rank) could be reversed by a university faculty committee, or the accreditation committee of the Bar, even if the faculty were the one to which the friend belonged. Better to keep one's options open to leave than to invest the effort and heartache in a losing cause.

Third, in the same vein, one should have a clear understanding about the role of the dean in fund-raising and the nature and extent of any limitations imposed by university development officers. This should probably be reduced to writing. A minimal demand would be that the law school dean be free to ask for support from any alumna or alumnus of the law school at any time, or from corporations or foundations in which they have major offices; a dean without that freedom is in an unacceptably vulnerable position.

Fourth, one ought to be prepared to remain on the job for about a decade, perhaps a bit less for an insider who knows the institution well enough to shorten the learning curve. It takes, at least for most, about half that time to learn the role and the other players. Turnover every three or four years destabilizes too many relationships, and results in the neglect of too many constituencies. It also invests too much institutional energy and emotion in deanship selection. From the school's point of view, it is important that there be periodic reviews, especially of the relationship between dean and faculty. Yet there is a problem with a departure date fixed in advance in that the deanship weakens as the date approaches; for this reason, it will generally be desirable for the dean to quit substantially in advance of any fixed date, and on moderately short notice.

Finally, one should accept employment as a dean only if one is prepared to leave the job early without regret. The job is a prison if the dean does not keep the door open for himself as well as for those seeking his attention. The authenticity of the risk that the dean might quit can give strength in dealing with unruly constituencies, most of whom will prefer the known to the unknown in the job. A dean who cannot quit will be victimized by a constituency whose claim he is unable to resist. Thus, here again there is contradiction inherent in the deanship. One should want the job for its own sake, yet not want it too much. The adversities in the lifestyle of the dean are likely to make this ambivalence easy enough to achieve.

Adaptability to such conditions is a special form of madness. Yet it is said that a key to a happy career is to make one's special insanity useful or even valuable to others. My hope in penning these words is to help a few individuals and institutions make just this kind of match.

NOTES

1. O'Connell & O'Connell, The Five Roles of the Law School Dean: Leader, Manager, Energizer, Envoy, Intellectual, 29 EMORY L.J. 605 (1980).

2. *Id.* at 620-24.

3. *Id.* at 612-17.

4. St. Antoine, On Reasons for Decanal Disenchantment and Their Wider Implications, 20 LAW QUADRANGLE NOTES 8, 9 (1976).

VIII. Accreditation and Association

A. The American Bar Association

Chapter 83

The American Bar Association Law School Approval Process

A Century Plus of Public Service

1995

James P. White

James P. White is the Consultant on Legal Education to the American Bar Association and Professor at Indiana University School of Law. This article was first published at 30 *Wake Forest Law Review* 283 (1995).

In this article, Dean White defends the law school accreditation process as having improved the quality of legal education and legal services provided to the public over the past century. White traces the historical development of the present accreditation process and the fundamental principles upon which the process is based. Although acknowledging that healthy criticism of the accreditation process is to be encouraged, White insists that the process serves a vital public purpose that cannot be overlooked.

The American Bar Association (ABA), through its law school accreditation function, seeks to ensure the quality of American legal education. Recently, the process by which the ABA accredits law schools has become the subject of significant debate.[1] In addition, the ABA currently is reviewing this process to reflect recent educational developments.[2] To understand fully the current examination and debate concerning the law school accreditation process, a review of the history and purposes of this process is necessary. For more than one hundred years, law school accreditation has improved the quality of American legal education and, in turn, the quality of legal services provided to the public.

Legal education and bar admissions requirements were a subject for action at the organizational meeting of the ABA in 1878. It was at that meeting that the assembly took two important steps towards the creation of today's approval process. First, it created the Committee on Legal Education and Admissions to the Bar. Second, it adopted the following resolution:

> That the Committee on Legal Education and Admissions to the Bar be instructed to report at the ensuing annual meeting, some plan for assimilating throughout the Union, the requirements of candidates for admission to the bar, and for regulating, on principles of comity, the standing, throughout the Union, of gentlemen already admitted to practice in their own states.[3]

At this time, most American lawyers still were educated through law office study. The number of law schools was increasing, however, as they often were among the first colleges established at new universities.[4] Given this increase, it is not surprising that in 1879, at the second meeting of the ABA, the Chair of the Committee on Legal Education and Admissions to the Bar reported:

> There is little if any dispute now as to the relative merit of education by means of law schools, and that to be got by mere practical training or apprenticeship as an attorney's clerk. Without disparagement of mere practical advantages, the verdict of the best informed is in favor of the schools.[5]

The Committee then presented four resolutions to the assembly. The first resolution restated the 1878 resolution regarding the establishment of the principles of comity to govern admissions to the bar in the various states.[6] The second resolution recommended that the state and local bar associations of each state be urged to further "the maintenance of public authority of schools of law, provided with faculties of at least four well paid and efficient teachers."[7] The third resolution stated the following:

> *Resolved,* That the said state and other local bar associations be respectfully requested to recommend and further in such law schools a general course of instruction, to be duly divided, for ordinary purposes into studies and exercises of the first year, of the second year, and of the third year. . . .[8]

This resolution also requested that law schools provide at least the following studies: moral and political philosophy; the elementary and constitutional principles of the law of England including the feudal law, the institutes of the municipal law, and the origin and progress of the common law; the law of real rights and remedies; the law of personal rights and remedies; the law of equity; the *lex mercatoria*; the law of crimes and their punishments; the law of nations; the maritime and admiralty law; the civil or roman law; the constitution and law of the United States; the jurisdiction and practice of United States courts; comparative jurisprudence and the constitutions and laws of the several states; and political economy.[9]

The fourth resolution provided the following:

> *Resolved,* That the said state and other local bar associations be respectfully requested to recommend and further in such law schools the requirement of attendance on at least the studies and exercises appointed for said course of three years, as a qualification for examination to be admitted to the bar.[10]

Despite the growing number of law schools, however, law school graduates still were a minority among the practitioners and judges attending the meeting. Consequently, the recommendations of the Committee were not adopted by the ABA assembly.[11]

Thirteen years later, the Committee on Legal Education and Admissions to the Bar presented the following resolutions to the annual meeting of the ABA:

> *Resolved,* That as the American Bar Association strongly recommends that the power of admitting members to the Bar, and the supervision of their professional conduct, be in each State lodged in the highest court of the State. . . .
>
> *Resolved,* That at least two years of study should be required of every student before he presents himself for examination.

> *Resolved,* That, in the opinion of this Association, it is a part of the highest duty and interest of every civilized State to make provisions when necessary for the maintenance of law-schools, and the thorough professional education of all who are admitted to practice law.[12]

The Committee also submitted a resolution to the effect that, if possible, all law schools should maintain programs of postgraduate instruction for lawyers, and particularly for young lawyers.[13] These four resolutions adopted by the ABA in 1892[14] form the basis for today's law school approval process.

This impetus continued into 1893, when the Association recommended and adopted a resolution which created the First Section of the ABA, the Section of Legal Education (Section).[15] The ABA delegated a substantial measure of autonomy to the Section, and continues to do so today. In 1894, this newly created ABA Section held its first meeting. The Chairman of the Section, Henry Wade Rogers, reported that seventy-two law schools existed in the United States, and that of this number, all but seven were associated with universities.[16] He reported that enrollment in these schools for the academic year 1893-94 was 7,600.[17] Rogers stated that "[t]he law schools have grown immensely in the favor of the profession and the best informed and ablest members of the profession are arrayed on their side."[18] In his address, Rogers articulated substantial advances which had been made in law school admission requirements. In 1875, there were no general qualifications for admission to law school; but by 1894, Harvard had announced that no person would be admitted as a candidate for a law degree who had not acquired an academic degree from a list of selected colleges.[19] Rogers further commented favorably on the growing number of law reviews that were being published by law schools.[20] He also reported that, while most law schools provided two years of instruction, a small but increasing number of schools had established a new three-year requirement.[21]

The Section continued in its support of law schools, and in 1921 it adopted resolutions which represent a major evolutionary step in the history of today's approval process. These resolutions, adopted by the Section and moved by chairman Elihu Root[22] to the House of Delegates for adoption, were as follows:

> (1) The American Bar Association is of the opinion that every candidate for admission to the bar should give evidence of graduation from a law school complying with the following standards:
> (a) It shall require as a condition of admission at least two years of study in a college.
> (b) It shall require its students to pursue a course of three years duration if they devote substantially all of their working time to their studies, and a longer course, equivalent in the number of working hours, if they devote only part of their working time to their studies.
> (c) It shall provide an adequate library available for the use of the students.
> (d) It shall have among its teachers a sufficient number giving their entire time to the school to insure actual personal acquaintance and influence with the whole student body.
> (2) The American Bar Association is of the opinion that graduation from a law school should not confer the right of admission to the bar, and that every candidate should be subjected to an examination by public authority to determine his fitness.
> (3) The Council on Legal Education and Admissions to the Bar is directed to publish from time to time the names of those law schools which comply with the above standards and of those which do not, and to make such publications available, so far as possible, to intending law students.
> (4) The president of the Association and the Council on Legal Education and Admissions to the Bar are directed to cooperate with the state and local bar associations to urge upon the duly constituted authorities of the several states the adoption of the above requirements for admission to the bar.
> (5) The Council on Legal Education and Admissions to the Bar is directed to call a Conference on Legal Education, in the name of the American Bar Association, to which the state and local bar associations shall be invited to send delegates, for the purpose of uniting the bodies

> represented in an effort to create conditions favorable to the adoption of the principles above set forth.[23]

In the same year these resolutions were adopted, Alfred Z. Reed published an important study of legal education that suggested that more than one kind of law school could be permitted.[24] The Root Committee disagreed with the Reed premise, believing instead that the intellectual and ethical qualifications are, and should be, the same for all lawyers.[25]

In 1922, in accordance with the 1921 resolution, the ABA convened a conference in Washington, D.C.[26] Chief Justice William Howard Taft, in his keynote address to members of that conference, stated that "[t]he best general education is to be had at our colleges and universities. . . . For no learned profession . . . is a thorough and general college education more necessary than for that of the law."[27] The conference adopted resolutions endorsing the Standards of Legal Education which had been drafted by the ABA.[28]

In 1923, the Council of the Section and Admissions to the Bar, for the first time, published a list of approved law schools.[29] Thirty-nine law schools were listed as complying with the Standards of the ABA[30] and were placed in a so called class "A." Nine schools which had reported to the ABA their intention of complying with the Standards in the immediate future were listed as class "B."[31]

Thus, the years from 1878 to 1923 saw the enactment of many resolutions concerning legal education. Throughout all of these years and resolutions, there remain strong constants. First, a commitment of the leaders of the profession to the development of quality legal education in the United States. Second, a commitment to the law school as a post-baccalaureate professional institution providing this education. A law school that can provide this education is one with adequate resources, one with university affiliation, and one which performs its obligation of service to the practicing bar and the judiciary in such areas as continuing legal education.

Regulation of legal education in the United States is unique among all nations. Under the doctrine of separation of power, authority for bar admissions principally resides in the highest court of each state or admitting jurisdiction.[32] The role the ABA plays as a central accrediting body has allowed accreditation to become national in scope, rather than fragmented among the fifty states, the District of Columbia, the Commonwealth of Puerto Rico, the Virgin Islands, and Guam. The interest of the states and the various admitting jurisdictions in a competent bar obviously is great. Without a nationally recognized accrediting agency, such as that provided by the ABA, ensuring a competent bar would place upon each state or admitting jurisdiction the annual burden of assessing the merits of each applicant's educational qualifications and the merits of his or her law school. Since the 1920s, the vast majority of jurisdictions has obviated this burden by relying upon the ABA's admission process.[33]

I believe that the ABA accreditation process is an example of the profession responding to public need. While there may be criticism voiced of the process, and healthy criticism is to be encouraged, the accreditation process has developed under certain fundamental principles. First, the profession itself is best equipped to form the ultimate judgment of quality. Second, participation by different components of the profession, including the bench, the bar, and the professorate, is the best way to form that professional judgment. Third, a thorough understanding of the operation and legitimacy of the accreditation process is required for the process to be effective. Professional review of law schools engenders confidence in individual state admitting authorities that the public is served by lawyers who have received a legal education meeting standards of the profession. Today, as it has for many years, graduation from an ABA-approved law school qualifies an applicant to sit in any American admitting jurisdiction.[34] The ABA approval process is recognized by the highest courts of the admitting jurisdictions as assuring that the graduate possesses the requisite qualifications to permit his or her entry into the practice of law.[35] This result—instilling states and admitting jurisdictions with confidence in the requisite qualifications of law school graduates and providing them a standard upon which to rely—is the goal of the ABA accreditation process.

The current Standards for the Approval of Law Schools were adopted in 1973 after a review and redrafting process which began in 1969.[36] While the Standards, Interpretations, and Rules of Procedure have been amended periodically, it was apparent in 1990 that there should be a thorough and complete review of the Standards and Interpretations, to assure their validity and reliability and to reflect current and future developments in American legal education.[37] Accordingly, the Section Council directed its Standards Review Committee to undertake a thorough and comprehensive review of the Standards and Interpretations.[38] This review currently is in the final stages of completion and the Committee will present a revised set of the Standards and Interpretations to the Section Council at the August 1995 meeting. Thereafter, in accordance with established procedure, the revised set of standards and interpretations will be circulated widely for comment, public hearings will be conducted, and only after thorough review will they be presented for adoption to the House of Delegates of the ABA.[39]

43. Simeon Baldwin (1840-1927), a case reporter and author, was chief justice and later governor of Connecticut and active in the adoption of accreditation standards by the Section of Legal Education of the ABA. (*Courtesy of Art & Visual Materials, Special Collections Department, Harvard Law School Library.*)

There also should be a periodic review of the accreditation process such as the review that took place in 1988-89 with the Ramsey Committee[40] or the review that is occurring in the current Section Commission to Review the Substance and Process of the American Bar Association's Accreditation of American Law Schools.[41] Indeed, the law school approval process must be reviewed constantly to ensure diversity and freedom of experimentation by American law schools, to prevent stultification of the approval process, to ensure compliance with the United States Department of Education requirements for recognition of accrediting agencies, to assure the acceptance and confidence of the highest courts of the fifty states, and to determine the validity and reliability of the Standards. This vigorous review must be undertaken for the public good.

In his 1959 presidential address to the ABA, then ABA President Ross L. Malone discussed the significance of the adoption of the ABA accreditation process:

> It is doubtful if this Association has ever taken action which had a more far reaching effect upon the legal profession or its relationship with the public. Had the Association never accomplished anything more than the adoption of the resolutions in 1921, implemented by the National Conference in 1922 and the system of inspection and approval of law schools which has followed, the existence of the American Bar Association would have been fully justified.[42]

Thus, the ABA's accreditation process has been viewed for a long time as a core element of the ABA's dedication to public service. The past twenty years have been years of great development in American legal education, witnessing the greatest and fastest changes in the history of American legal education. The demand for legal education has increased dramatically, and the brightest and the best have sought admission to American law schools. The number and quality of American law faculty has also improved dramatically over these years. Student/teacher ratios have permitted smaller classes with various modes of instruction and have exposed students to rapidly developing areas of law. The explosion in law library holdings continues, including use of microform materials and readily accessible on-line data bases. In addition, the following examples demonstrate but a few of the changes in legal education over the past twenty years: rigorous writing experiences; new methods of instruction; new courses reflecting developments in the law and its reliance upon other disciplines; the integration, sometimes reluctant, of courses involving lawyering skills into the law school curriculum; the development by many schools of new post-J.D. programs of instruction; the growth of summer and semester programs conducted by American law schools in foreign countries; and opportunities for American law students to study at foreign institutions through cooperative programs and programs of individual study.[43] Further, higher standards of admission; increased recognition of the obligation of professional service; goals of affirmative action; and increased student support services, including financial counseling, student counseling, and placement, all have been part of the growth and development of American legal education.[44]

During the past twenty years, the ABA, through its accreditation function, has worked to improve the quality of American legal education. By focusing on the quality of legal education, the ABA seeks to insure that graduates of approved law schools provide legal services of high professional quality to the public. Thus, at its essence, the process serves a vital public purpose, a point which we cannot afford to overlook in the current examinations of, and debates concerning, the ABA's accreditation process.

NOTES

1. For a discussion of the current debate surrounding the law school accreditation process, see Ken Myers, *Do Law School Graders Measure Up?*, Nat'l L.J., Feb. 20, 1995, at A1, A27.

2. *Id.* at A27.

3. 1 REPORTS OF THE AMERICAN BAR ASSOCIATION 26 (1878). Please note the term "gentle*men*." Law was not yet a profession to which women were freely admitted and accepted.

4. *Id.*

5. 2 REPORTS OF THE AMERICAN BAR ASSOCIATION 209 (1879).

6. *Id.* at 235.

7. *Id.*

8. *Id.*

9. *Id.* at 235-36.

10. *Id.* at 236.

11. 3 REPORTS OF THE AMERICAN BAR ASSOCIATION 13-24 (1880).

12. 15 REPORTS OF THE AMERICAN BAR ASSOCIATION 9 (1892).

13. *Id.* at 10. This resolution is particularly interesting in light of the *Report of the Section Task Force on Law Schools and the Profession: Narrowing the Gap* (commonly referred to as the *MacCrate Report*). The Task Force makes the following statement:

> The Task Force's collective effort has resulted in the recognition that the task of educating students to assume the full responsibilities of a lawyer is a continuing process that neither begins nor ends with three years of law school study. Having reached this conclusion, the Task Force, in Part III of the Report, has identified the roles of law schools and the practicing bar in assisting prospective lawyers as they move along the continuum from applicant to student to qualified lawyer.
>
> Thus, we have concluded that there is no "gap." There is only an arduous road of professional development along which all prospective lawyers should travel. It is the responsibility of law schools and the practicing bar to assist students and lawyers to develop the skills and values required to complete the journey. To identify those skills and values, to describe what law schools and the practicing bar are now doing to advance the professional development of lawyers, and to recommend how the legal education community and the practicing bar can join together to fulfill their respective responsibilities to the profession and the consuming public has been the central mission of this Task Force.

SECTION OF LEGAL EDUC. & ADMISSIONS TO THE BAR, AMERICAN BAR ASS'N, LEGAL EDUCATION AND PROFESSIONAL DEVELOPMENT—AN EDUCATIONAL CONTINUUM: REPORT OF THE TASK FORCE ON LAW SCHOOLS AND THE PROFESSION: NARROWING THE GAP 8 (1992).

14. 15 REPORTS OF THE AMERICAN BAR ASSOCIATION 20 (1892). For the complete transcript of the amendment process and eventual adoption of these resolutions, see *id.* at 11-20.

15. 16 REPORTS OF THE AMERICAN BAR ASSOCIATION 89 (1893). See also SUSAN K. BOYD, THE ABA'S FIRST SECTION: ASSURING A QUALIFIED BAR 11-14 (1993).

16. BOYD, *supra* note 15, at 12.

17. 17 REPORTS OF THE AMERICAN BAR ASSOCIATION 394 (1894).

18. *Id.*

19. *Id.* at 396-98.

20. *Id.* at 404.

21. *Id.* at 400-04.

22. Elihu Root was a former United States Secretary of State, a former president of the ABA, and a recipient of a Nobel Peace Prize.

23. 46 REPORTS OF THE AMERICAN BAR ASSOCIATION 687-88 (1921).

24. ALFRED Z. REED, TRAINING FOR THE PUBLIC PROFESSION OF LAW 416-18 (1921).
25. 46 REPORTS OF THE AMERICAN BAR ASSOCIATION 681 (1921).
26. 47 REPORTS OF THE AMERICAN BAR ASSOCIATION 482 (1922).
27. *Id.* at 497-98.
28. *Id.* at 495-96.
29. *Id.*
30. *Id.*
31. *Id.*
32. See James P. White, *Legal Education in the Era of Change: Law School Autonomy*, 1987 DUKE L.J. 292, 295 (1987).
33. *Id.*
34. See SECTION OF LEGAL EDUC. & ADMISSIONS TO THE BAR, AMERICAN BAR ASS'N, COMPREHENSIVE GUIDE TO BAR ADMISSION REQUIREMENTS 10-11 (1994).
35. See, e.g., Appeal of Murphy, 393 A.2d 369, 371-72 (Pa. 1978) (holding that Pennsylvania, in premising admission to bar examination upon applicant possessing a law degree from a law school accredited by the ABA, had not unconstitutionally delegated its judicial function to the ABA, since the Pennsylvania Supreme Court's adoption of the results of the ABA accreditation process carried with it an endorsement of standards which the ABA had promulgated for guidance of itself, institutions, and students involved), *cert. denied*, 440 U.S. 901 (1979).
36. AMERICAN BAR ASS'N, STANDARDS FOR APPROVAL OF LAW SCHOOLS AND INTERPRETATIONS II (1994).
37. See *Section of Legal Educ. & Admission to the Bar, American Bar Ass'n, Report of the Special Committee to Study the Law School Approval Process* (1990) [hereinafter *Report of the Special Committee*]. The Standards dealing with law school libraries are in the process of total revision to reflect current and foreseeable developments in the delivery of information. See Memorandum D9495-32, Proposed Revision of ABA Library Standards and Interpretations, from James P. White, Consultant on Legal Education to the American Bar Association, to Deans of ABA Approved Law Schools (Dec. 9, 1994) (on file with author).
38. *Report of the Special Committee*, *supra* note 37, at 69.
39. James P. White, *Adoption of Standards Is a Deliberative Process*, SYLLABUS, Winter 1993, at 2, 2.
40. See REPORT OF THE SPECIAL COMMITTEE, *supra* note 37.
41. A letter sent by Commission Chairperson Rosalie E. Wahl to approximately 1500 legal educators, practitioners and judges identified the following areas for review:

A. An examination of the validity and justification for law school accreditation as designated in the Council of the Section by the United States Department of Education and as delegated by the fifty highest state courts, including the relationship of the Council to the House of Delegates, and to the state courts as the ultimate legal profession regulators.

B. A perspective on the Standards for the Approval of Law Schools, the body of governing principles adopted by the House of Delegates, including the ongoing activities of the Standards Review Committee of the Section currently conducting a complete review and proposed revision of the Standards.

C. An evaluation of the structure and processes by which law school accreditation is administered.

D. A review of the work and findings of the joint commission currently examining the issue of the financing of legal education, including an appraisal of the cost of the accreditation process.

E. A policy perspective on the effects of the recently adopted Department of Education regulations relating to accreditation agencies, especially its regulations relating to agency independence, financing, consumer notification, and protection.

Letter from Rosalie E. Wahl, Chairperson of the Commission to Review the Substance and Process of the American Bar Association's Accreditation of American Law Schools (Dec. 5, 1994) (on file with author).
42. 84 REPORTS OF THE AMERICAN BAR ASSOCIATION 493 (1959).
43. See generally Robert MacCrate, *Preparing Lawyers to Participate Effectively in the Legal Profession*, 44 J. LEGAL EDUC. 89 (1994) (discussing the skills and lessons essential to the creation of qualified attorneys).
44. See generally *id.* (discussing the skills and lessons essential to the creation of qualified attorneys).

Chapter 84

History of the Activity of the American Bar Association in Relation to Legal Education and Admission to the Bar

1930

George Harris Smith

George Harris Smith (November 29, 1873-February 24, 1947) was an attorney in Salt Lake City, mainly representing railways. Annual address of the Chairman of the Section of Legal Education delivered at Chicago, Illinois, August 19, 1930. This article was first published at 7 *American Law School Review* 1 (1930).

Gentlemen—under the mandate of the by-laws of the Section it is the duty of your chairman to at this time make an annual address to the Section. That duty is performed with the consciousness that your present chairman is quite incapable of gracing the occasion either with the legal scholarship or the outstanding personal position and prominence in the Association that his predecessors have brought to the office. It is a matter in which the Section can justly take pride that, during its long existence, its chairmen have heretofore uniformly been outstanding lawyers of distinction and such prominent members of the Association that they brought to the Section a prestige that in itself gave it force and vitality aside from organized effort and effective administration. The present administration of the Section can appeal to you only through its organized and collective efforts to faithfully and with such efficiency as it possesses perform its duty as an administrative agency of the Association. The account of its stewardship will appear in the report of the council of the Section, to be presented at this session.

The work of this Section has of recent years been of such definite nature that the impression has at times been created that questions respecting legal education and standards of admission to the Bar are new subjects of recent consideration. To correct these views and briefly set forth the history and background of the activity of the Bar Association with reference to these items is the purpose of these remarks at this meeting.

The first meeting of the American Bar Association was held at Saratoga Springs, New York, in 1878. A constitution was then adopted which provided in article III for the appointment of a Committee on Legal Education and Admissions to the Bar, consisting of five members to be appointed by the President.[1] At the same meeting it was moved that the Committee on Legal Education and Admissions to the Bar be instructed to report at the next annual meeting some plan of assimilating throughout the Union the requirements for candidates for admission to the Bar and for regulating on principles of comity the standing throughout the nation of gentlemen already admitted to practice in their own states.[2] The first chairman of this Committee was Mr. Carleton Hunt of Louisiana. Mr. Hunt was a distinguished scholar and lawyer and the principal figure on the subject of legal education and the work of the committee on that subject of the Bar Association until 1886.

The year following its inception the Committee presented resolutions that the state and local bar associations be requested to recommend the maintenance by public authority of law schools with at least four "well paid and efficient teachers" and that their diploma should be an essential qualification for admission to the bar, and that such bar associations further be requested to recommend a course of three years in such law schools as qualification for the bar examination.[3] The consideration of these resolutions was postponed until the following year when, after considerable debate, they were rejected and in place thereof a resolution was passed requesting the states to recommend and further the maintenance of law schools.[4] The following year a resolution was passed in which a three-year course in law schools was recommended.[5]

For the next ten years the Committee was apparently inactive. In 1890 it seemed to have taken a new lease on life and a long report was submitted, followed by a further and even more extensive report the next year containing information as to admission requirements in the various states. In 1892 a resolution was passed by the Bar Association recommending that the power of admission to the bar in each state be lodged in the highest courts of the state and that examination of candidates be referred to a permanent commission appointed by the Court. It was also resolved that at least two years of law study should be required before admission to practice.[6] At the same meeting an informal conference was held by a number of gentlemen interested in legal education, at which it was decided to call together at the annual meeting the following year a number of men particularly interested in legal education to a special meeting. In 1893 this special meeting was organized as the Sec-

44. William A. Keener (1856-1913) was brought from Langdell's case-method incubator by President Seth Lowe to "revive" Columbia's law school, although it was the largest in the United States. Replacing Theodore Dwight in a move that split Columbia's faculty, Keener served as dean from 1891 to 1901. (*Courtesy of Art & Visual Materials, Special Collections Department, Harvard Law School Library.*)

tion of Legal Education and Admissions to the Bar under the following by-laws passed at the regular meeting of the Association:[7]

1. "A section of the Association to be known as the Section of Legal Education is hereby established which shall meet annually in connection with the meeting of the Association, but not during such hours as the Association is in session."

2. "Its object shall be the discussion of methods of legal education and it may make recommendations to the Association which shall be referred by the Association to the Committee on Legal Education."

3. "The proceedings of the Section may be published from time to time at the discretion of the Executive Committee and on the recommendation of the Committee on Publications."

4. "All members of the Association who desire may enroll themselves as members of the Section and persons not eligible for membership in the Association but who are engaged in teaching law may be admitted to the privileges of the floor at any meeting of the Section by a vote of the Section."

5. "The Section shall be organized by the annual appointment of a Chairman and Secretary by the Section at its first session."

Twenty-seven men were enrolled in the Section at its first meeting, and Henry Wade Rogers of Illinois was elected the first chairman. Meetings of the Section have been held every year since that time. At the meeting held in 1894, the year following the organization of the Section, Woodrow Wilson appeared and spoke on "Legal Education of Undergraduates." In 1895 a notable address was delivered before the Section by Mr. Justice Brewer of the Supreme Court, which was followed by the introduction of the following resolution:

> "Resolved that the Section recommends to the American Bar Association the passage of the following resolution:
>
> "'Resolved That the American Bar Association approve the lengthening of the course of instruction in law schools to a period of three years and that it expresses the hope that as soon as practicable a rule will be adopted in each state which will require candidates for admission to the bar to study law for three years before applying for examination.'"[8]

This resolution was referred to the Committee on Legal Education in 1896 and was adopted in 1897,[9] together with the following resolution:

> "Resolved that the American Bar Association is of the opinion that before a student commences the study of law it is desirable that he should have received a general education approximately at least equivalent to a high school course and that persons who have not completed the equivalent of such a course should not be admitted into law schools as candidates for degrees."[10]

This declaration may properly be regarded as the beginning of the present standards of the American Bar Association, and it was introduced in response to a resolution adopted in 1896 requesting the Committee on Legal Education in its next report to consider the practicability of establishing a minimum standard for requirements for admission to law schools and to a degree.

In 1905 the Section expressly by resolution disapproved of the diploma privilege, that is admission to the bar without examination on diploma from certain schools.[11] In 1906 a committee was appointed by the Section "for the purpose of drafting a set of rules for admission which if adopted and approved by this Section may be regarded as standard rules."[12]

In 1908 a number of resolutions recommended by the Committee were adopted by the Bar Association. These included resolutions urging the appointment of Boards of Bar Examiners where they were not established; recommending the adoption by the states of a requirement for admission of a high school education or its equivalent; and further stating it to be the opinion of the Association that the interests of the profession and the state would be promoted if two years of college were required. Another resolution approved three years' study of law for candidates who were graduates of law schools and four years for others. Other resolutions disapproved the diploma privilege and expressed the approval of the Association to those night schools that had extended their course to four years.[13] Nothing further of particular importance was accomplished until finally in 1916 the results of this committee's work called "The Standard Rules for Admission to the Bar" were adopted by the Section.[14] These covered the subjects of bar examinations, the diploma privilege which was disapproved, character examinations, comity as to admissions, registrations, etc. Among the other recommendations the two following were of vital importance:

> "No candidate shall be registered as a student at law until he shall have satisfied the Board that he passed the necessary requirements for entrance to the collegiate department of state university of the candidate's state, or of such college or colleges as may be approved by the State Board of Law Examiners, or an examination equivalent thereto, conducted by authority of the state."
>
> "All applicants (after being educationally qualified) should be compelled to study law for four years, the first three of which must be spent in compulsory attendance upon, and the successful completion of and passing the prescribed course of instruction at an approved law school which requires not less than three years of resident attendance for the completion of its course and for graduation therefrom, and then the service of a continuous year of registered clerkship as prescribed, exclusive of all other occupations; provided, however, that (if such clerkship cannot be obtained) the fourth year may be passed in an approved law school in post-graduate work, and that the applicant's law course shall have included (adequate courses) in procedure and practice."

These resolutions were presented by the Section to the Association and referred to the Committee on Legal Education. In the meantime, in 1913, a request was made by the Committee on Legal Education of the American Bar Association and the Executive Committee of the Association of American Law Schools to the Carnegie Foundation for the Advancement of Teaching, to conduct an investigation of legal education along the same lines as it had recently completed for medical education. This report and subsequent supplements have furnished much valuable information on the subject of legal education and the requirements of admission to the bar.

In 1918 the standard rules for admission were presented to the Bar Association by the Council on Legal Education and at that time the following resolution was adopted:

> "Resolved that the American Bar Association approves the action taken by many of the law schools in requiring two years of a college course as a condition of admission to their courses of study, and the Association expresses the conviction that this should be the minimum requirement recognized by law schools of the first class."[15]
>
> The requirement adopted in regard to preliminary education was as follows:
>
> "Every candidate should satisfy the Board that he has passed the necessary requirements for entrance into the collegiate department of the state university of the candidate's state or of such college or colleges as may be approved by the State Board of Law Examiners, or an examination equivalent thereto, conducted by the authority of the state."[16]

In 1920 by-laws of the Section were adopted which charged the council of this Section with the duty of considering measures for the improvement of legal and pre-legal education, including admission to the bar, and requiring an inspection of law schools of the country with power to classify them with regard to standards approved by the Section. A special committee was appointed to report on what action should be taken "to create conditions which will tend to strengthen the character and improve the efficiency of persons to be admitted to the practice of law."[17] The following year, under the chairmanship of Mr. Elihu Root, standards of admission to the bar were presented and approved by the Section and by the American Bar Association in the following form:

"Resolved: (1) The American Bar Association is of the opinion that every candidate for admission to the Bar shall give evidence of graduation from a law school complying with the following standards:

(a) "It shall require as a condition of admission at least two years of study in a college.

(b) "It shall require its students to pursue a course of three years duration if they devote substantially all of their time to their studies and a longer course if they devote it to other studies.

(c) "It shall supply an adequate library for the use of the students.

(d) "It shall have among its teachers a sufficient number giving their entire time to the school to ensure absolute personal acquaintance and influence upon the whole student body."

(2) "The American Bar Association is of the opinion that graduation from a law school should not confer the right of admission to the Bar and that every candidate should be subject to an examination by public authority to determine his fitness.

(3) "The Council on Legal Education and Admissions to the Bar is directed to publish from time to time the names of those law schools which comply with the above standards and of those which do not, and make such publications available, so far as possible, to intending law students.

(4) "The President of the Association and the Council on Legal Education and Admissions to the Bar, are directed to cooperate with the state and local bar associations to urge upon the duly constituted authorities of the several states the adoption of the above requirements for admission to the Bar.

(5) "The Council on Legal Education and Admissions to the Bar is directed to call a conference on legal education in the name of the American Bar Association, and the state and local associations shall be invited to send delegates for the purpose of uniting the bodies represented in an effort to create conditions favorable to the adoption of the principles above set forth."[18]

In 1922 at a conference of delegates from state and local bar associations of the entire country these standards were endorsed, and since that time the work of the Section has been largely directed towards administering the commission thus given it and bring about a fulfillment of the requirements of those standards. In 1927 the resolution was passed recommending the establishment in each state of opportunity for collegiate training where none now exists and urging the states to hold pre-legal examinations to test the qualifications of those candidates claiming the equivalent of two years of college education.[19]

The Section itself still remains as it was created in 1893, although of course changes in the by-laws have from time to time been made. In 1916 the Executive Committee of the Section was enlarged and made into a body of seven called the Council of Legal Education,[20] which was in effect a program-making Committee for the Section.

In 1917 this was changed by another by-law which created a Council on Legal Education and Admissions to the Bar to be appointed by the President of the American Bar Association, consisting of five members with an overlapping tenure of five years.[21] This was followed by formal action doing away with the old Committee on Legal Education and Admissions to the Bar.[22] Under the new constitution adopted in 1919 the Section was empowered to adopt its own by-laws subject to the approval of the Executive Committee of the American Bar Association.[23] The constitution definitely provided for what is the present organization of the Section, namely a chairman, vice-chairman, secretary-treasurer, and a council of eight members. Under the by-laws adopted at the 1920 meeting officers of the Section became ex-officio members of the council and the council members served terms of four years. Also not only members of the Bar Association who might choose to enroll themselves prior to any meeting became members of the Section, but in addition such teachers of law and allied subjects and those interested in the subject of legal education who should be elected by the Section itself.[24]

In 1927 the Bar Association authorized its Executive Committee to take such action as would enable the council to organize an executive force adequate to carry out its duties, which resulted in the creation of the position of adviser.[25] Following that direction an administrative staff was organized that permits of systematic, regular and continuous methods of performing the duties placed upon the Section by its principal, the American Bar Association itself.

Thus it becomes demonstrably clear that from the very beginning to the present moment the American Bar Association has had at heart the promotion of standards of legal education as conditions for entering the public calling of the law. It has from the very first had in mind, as its expressions evidence, the clear recognition that those standards of necessity, and as a matter of natural development in keeping abreast with the march of events, would from time to time be improved and raised to higher levels. The demands of the times are such that all who serve must constantly advance to higher standards of performance. Today not only the lawyer and the doctor but the merchant, the banker, the butcher, the baker, the farmer and the artisan, the maid servant and the butler to say nothing of the traditional candlestick-maker, must all have and possess preparation, knowledge, learning and experience in their calling far above the requirements of a generation ago in order to properly fit into the demands of modern exactions. But the Association is doing much more than meeting material needs. In promoting the standards of legal education and admission to the Bar it is pursuing its primary objective, a noble ideal that looks far beyond the confines of personal status and operates directly upon the preservation of our Government itself. The declared purpose of the American Bar Association, reduced to a single sentence, is to promote and maintain the administration of justice throughout the nation. That is the equivalent of saying that the object of the Association is to support and preserve the Government under which we so proudly live and enjoy liberty under law, because the ultimate aim and object of all governments is and must be in the final analysis the administration of justice. What other purpose can there be for organized society. So in the work of promoting the science of jurisprudence and the administration of justice this organization is striving as best it can to aid in fulfilling the destiny of the nation. And because our profession is, more than any other group of its citizens, part of the machinery set up by the nature of our Federal Union for administering justice, it is in a very real sense performing a function of government in constantly advancing legal learning to higher grounds of individual and collective effectiveness.

We are then, by promoting higher standards of all the essential elements that the public calling of the law must possess, carrying out the objects of the Association and by doing that giving aid and assistance to the preservation of our Governmental institutions. All else aside, support of Government is the first duty of citizenship. This duty is even greater in a lawyer because of his calling. Perhaps never in the history of our Republic was there greater need for undivided devotion to and support of our Government and the preservation of its institutions than at this very time. True, no nation threatens us with violence. No international complications disturb our tranquillity. But our national traditions, our national ideals and our constitutional structure are all being subjected to insidious attack at home and from abroad, from within and from without. There are those in places high and low who would tear down and destroy, if not by violence, by intrigue.

Never before did greater need exist for the lawyer of our nation to quietly survey his country's condition and his own relations, to its institutions, to take stock of his own qualities and his services to the community, to correctly estimate whether his support of established order and authority is running high or low and whether his devotion to the ideals of his noble profession is hot or cold. His group and its correct standards on all these items means more to the nation and its success in the administration of justice than that of any other organization that exists. If the work of this group can add its mite to these ends, if from this and other proceedings of this Association we can in some small measure take away a renewed appreciation of our duties and obligations to the profession that has honored us with its call, if we in turn can bring honor to it and increased fidelity to the ultimate objects and purposes of our glorious Republic and sense within us some renewed loyalty to our system of jurisprudence and government and what they stand for; then the work and profit of this occasion will be of enduring good.

And let it ever be remembered that it is easy to find fault. To criticize requires less ability and effort than any other enterprise that men pursue. To tear down and destroy requires no conscience and often but little effort. But to build, to create, to construct, to continually improve requires infinite labor and skill and a patience that passeth understanding. If the agitator and fault-finder, the dreamer and the demagogue, the internal or foreign enemy of our institutions should ever succeed in destroying this magnificent and stately edifice of constitutional government, conceived and builded by our fathers with a master mind and a skillfulness beyond their own consciousness who among the wise men of all the land can foresee what miserable, what dangerous, what perverted makeshift of government might be set up in its place.

NOTES

1. Vol. 1, Reports of the Am. Bar Ass'n (1878) 16.
2. Vol. 1, Reports of the Am. Bar Ass'n (1878) 26.
3. Vol. 2, Reports of the Am. Bar Ass'n (1879) 14.
4. Vol. 3, Reports of the Am. Bar Ass'n (1880) 40, 44.
5. Vol. 4, Reports of the Am. Bar Ass'n (1881) 28.
6. Vol. 15, Reports of the Am. Bar Ass'n (1892) 9, 20.
7. Vol. 16, Reports of the Am. Bar Ass'n (1893) 7, 10.
8. Vol. 18, Reports of the Am. Bar Ass'n (1895) 406-408.
9. Vol. 20, Reports of the Am. Bar Ass'n (1897) 31, 33.
10. 10 Vol. 20, Reports of the Am. Bar Ass'n (1897) 33, 34.
11. Vol. 28, Reports of the Am. Bar Ass'n (1905) 560, 580.
12. Vol. 30, Reports of the Am. Bar Ass'n (1906) 32.
13. Vol. 31, Reports of the Am. Bar Ass'n (1908) 17-23.
14. Vol. 41, Reports of the Am. Bar Ass'n (1916) 652ff.
15. Vol. 43, Reports of the Am. Bar Ass'n (1918) 72.
16. Vol. 43, Reports of the Am. Bar Ass'n (1918) 75; Vol. 42, Reports of the Am. Bar Ass'n (1917) 464, paragraph 8.
17. Vol. 45, Reports of the Am. Bar Ass'n (1920) 465, 466.
18. Vol. 46, Reports of the Am. Bar Ass'n (1921) 38-47.
19. Vol. 52, Reports of the Am. Bar Ass'n (1927) 111.
20. Vol. 41, Reports of the Am. Bar Ass'n (1916) 9, 28.
21. Vol. 42, Reports of the Am. Bar Ass'n (1917) 90.
22. Vol. 44, Reports of the Am. Bar Ass'n (1919) 192, 193.
23. Vol. 44, Reports of the Am. Bar Ass'n (1919) 89, 124.
24. Vol. 44, Reports of the Am. Bar Ass'n (1920) 465.
25. Vol. 52, Reports of the Am. Bar Ass'n (1927) 112.

B. The Association of American Law Schools

Chapter 85

A Bit of History

Report of the AALS Long Range Planning Committee

1989

This report first appeared in the *Proceedings* of the AALS 1990 Annual Meeting, at page 317.

No one now involved in law teaching remembers a time when there was no AALS. When that day comes in the life of any organization, its institutions and functions are often taken as inevitable. The early history of legal education has been the subject of several books and articles, but a brief look back may be useful to develop perspective on today's AALS.[1]

A. The Early ABA—1878 to 1900

Both the organized bar and the community of law schools are a relatively recent historical development. Indeed, it was just over a century ago, in 1878, that a few prominent lawyers assembled in Saratoga, New York to create the American Bar Association. The new organization's aim was to bring "quality" to what its founders saw as a diverse and disorganized legal profession.

Among the greatest concerns of the ABA organizers was the manner in which lawyers were then being trained. In the late 19th century, less than 20% of the lawyers admitted to practice each year had received formal legal education; most had read law in a lawyer's office. Thus, one of the first acts of the ABA was to create the Committee on Legal Education, which was followed in 1894 by the Section

In 1894, there were 7600 students enrolled in 72 U.S. law schools. The principal early effort of the Section on Legal Education was to have bar admission limited to persons with law school training. Although its ultimate goal was three years of law school, its practical goal was two years.

The Section on Legal Education deliberately chose to include full-time professors among its leadership, although only a minority of law schools had full-time staff. The list of professors active in the ABA was impressive—Ames, Thayer, Williston, Mechem and Wigmore, to name only a few. Many professors, however, were either not members of the bar or were not part of the one percent of lawyers who comprised the American Bar Association.

B. The New AALS—1900 to 1920

In 1900, in order to promote greater participation in discussions about legal education by professors at "respectable" schools, an ad hoc ABA committee invited thirty-five such schools to join an organization that came to be known as the Association of American Law Schools. Thirty-two schools accepted and became charter members. James Bradley Thayer of Harvard became the first president. At the time, the thirty-two AALS member schools were training fifty percent of all U.S. law students.

The AALS was quickly seen to meet a real need among the country's full-time law teachers. Law reviews were only in their infancy, so the AALS became a place for professional and scholarly exchange as well as personal contact. Roundtable discussions of both substantive law and developments in law teaching were a central part of its early annual meetings.

The AALS began law school inspections in this period and imposed continuing reviews to determine whether member schools had maintained membership standards. Several did not, especially when the AALS increased its standards to require that member schools have at least three full-time faculty.

But the impact of the fledgling AALS was not limited to the law schools. The AALS supported creation of the American Association of Law Libraries in 1906, and began publication of essays on Anglo-American Legal History in 1907. Even the founding of the American Law Institute in 1923 can be traced directly to Professor Hohfeld's call at the 1914 AALS Annual Meeting for a "Vital School of Jurisprudence and Law."

In the early years, AALS meetings were routinely held in conjunction with the ABA Annual Meeting. Tension soon arose, however, between academics and practicing lawyers over how legal education should develop. While some practitioners continued to favor a classical education, more advocated a greater emphasis on practice-oriented skills. In 1914, in a move some attributed to a desire to reduce professorial influence, the American Bar Association moved its Annual Meeting from August to October, thus making it almost impossible for law professors to attend.

As a result, the AALS moved its meeting to a more convenient time between Christmas and New Year's, and picked a more central location, Chicago. Professors liked the new freedom, and the practice of holding AALS meetings during Christmas week, most often in Chicago, continued until 1974.

C. Cooperation in Accreditation—1920 to 1945

While ABA and AALS members continued to have differences throughout the 1920s, in an important sense, each knew that the support of the other organization was important to achieving its own agenda for law and legal education. During that period, for example, the ABA (which by then represented 10% of the nation's lawyers) worked to establish the principle that "reading law" was insufficient for admission to a learned profession. After establishing the principle of law school accreditation in 1923, the ABA worked to have the states require graduation from an ABA—accredited law school as a prerequisite for admission to the bar.

The AALS cooperated in this effort and indeed led the way by establishing membership requirements higher than those of the ABA. AALS members had to require three years work for the first degree in law, for example, and more than that if the degree was earned in the evening. In fact, the AALS was so successful at staying ahead of the ABA that, by the early 1920s, AALS member schools were educating only 35% of the country's law students (down from 50% in 1900).

One concern of AALS member institutions was that the ABA might be willing to create a class of accredited law schools with lower standards than those required of AALS members. Indeed, there are suggestions that in both 1920 and 1929, AALS members packed the meetings of the ABA Section on Legal Education to assure election of council members sympathetic to higher accreditation standards.

The ABA, in turn, wanted the example and support of the best schools as it sought to establish a better-educated, more prestigious profession. Thus, it was natural that the two organizations would work together in establishing and applying accreditation standards to law schools.

Indeed, the pursuit of higher standards went beyond concerns about the classroom. In 1930, the ABA and AALS cooperated in supporting the creation of the National Conference of Bar Examiners to oversee production of bar examinations which used essay questions on examinations that resembled those used in the "better" law schools.

The structure of legal education that we know today was largely formed in the period from 1930 through the end of World War II. Among other developments, the process of accreditation became institutionalized, and in 1938 the AALS proposed discussing creation of a standardized law school admission test. Most important, several states were persuaded to impose requirements for at least two years' pre-legal education on top of the requirement of attending law school.

But the Depression did even more to strengthen the position of AALS member schools. Students wanted to attend the best school that would accept them. During the Depression and war years, admission to good schools was relatively easy and operation of weaker schools tended to be unprofitable. Returning veterans might have restored the market for less sophisticated law schools, but the veterans made ABA accredited and AALS member schools their first choice.

D. The Informal Organization Matures—1945 to 1963

The period from 1945 to 1963 was a transition time for legal education and for the AALS. The informality of the AALS was, by present standards, almost beyond belief. AALS activities were managed by a three-member executive committee, plus the president, president-elect and secretary-treasurer, all working from their respective schools.

A faculty appointments register was created in 1948, for example, to "keep a file of persons who desired positions in the teaching profession." The term "file" was meant literally; the program started with 30 names and received 12 inquiries from deans. Over six placements were credited to the fledgling system, however, and the program was considered a success.

Nor did its informal style prevent the AALS from addressing public questions facing legal education and the nation. The 1950 Annual Meeting, for example, resolved that "the Association of American Law Schools opposes the continued maintenance of segregation or discrimination in legal education on racial grounds and asserts its belief that it is the professional duty of all member schools to abolish any such practices at the earliest practicable time." A special committee then was created to consider making compliance with this policy a condition of AALS membership.[2]

In addition, volumes of "Selected Readings" were assembled and published by AALS committees in support of the scholarly and teaching functions of the law schools. In this and other ways, the Association grew in importance both as a link among law schools and as a means of providing services that no one institution could effectively create on its own. Concrete work on an admission test for law schools was begun in 1947, for example, as a way to provide information to member schools about applicants from diverse undergraduate institutions. Later, the Law School Admission Test Council (LSATC) was formally created in 1961.

Concern was expressed as early as 1961 that creation of the LSATC might foreshadow a proliferation of legal education organizations. The new National Association for Law Placement Officers (NALPO) raised a matter of similar concern. The Executive Committee considered whether the work of both new organizations might better be the responsibility of the AALS, but an organization run by part-time officers was in no position to undertake more activities and the idea went no further.

E. Full-Time Leadership Begins—1963 to 1973

AALS activities ultimately became too extensive to be managed by a half-dozen professors in their spare time. The modern AALS can be dated from 1963 when the national office was opened in Washington with Professor Michael H. Cardozo of Cornell as the first AALS Executive Director.

During the first decade of full-time leadership, AALS activities grew dramatically. The Committee on

Academic Freedom and Tenure considered important cases, and production of the Directory of Law Teachers was substantially improved. The "Law Books Recommended" project, begun in 1963 and completed in 1967, became a landmark in the developing sophistication of law libraries. Major studies of public questions were produced, most financed by outside grants solicited by President Walter Gellhorn. In 1967, for example, a report on protection of civil rights lawyers was published, and in 1972, a study on part-time legal education.

The role of the AALS in supporting good teaching was also expanded in the 1960s. In the area of clinical education, the AALS was actively involved in the creation of the Council on Legal Education for Professional Responsibility (CLEPR) in 1966. Further, an ambitious AALS summer teaching clinic, first held in 1969 at the University of North Carolina, was the forerunner of our present professional development programs for new and experienced teachers.

The leadership role of the AALS in opening the legal profession to minorities and women was especially significant during this decade. The AALS preceded the ABA by seven years when it began collecting statistics on minority enrollment in law school in 1964. In 1966, substantial efforts were made to prevent states from closing several historically black colleges and universities which had played a large role in educating the nation's black lawyers. The Association also played central roles in the 1967 creation of the Council of Legal Education Opportunity (CLEO) and the AALS Section on Minority Groups. Moreover, 1971 saw an AALS conference on assimilating minority students in law schools and the Association's active work on an amicus brief defending the constitutionality of affirmative action programs in the *DeFunis* case.

The AALS also became a leader in dealing with issues facing women. A Committee on Women in Legal Education was established in February 1970 and a membership requirement prohibiting sex discrimination at member schools followed in December. The Committee became the Section on Women in Legal Education in 1973. In 1974, Soia Mentschikoff became the first woman president of the AALS.

Finally, during this period, a start was also made at systematizing government relations and relations with other legal education organizations. The AALS produced the first Pre-Law Handbook for college students in 1967, for example, and published it cooperatively with the Law School Admission Council (LSAC) in 1971. Links were established outside the law school community as well, to associations such as the American Council on Learned Societies (ACLS).

F. The Present AALS Develops—1973 to 1989

In 1974, Professor Cardozo was succeeded as Executive Director by Professor Millard H. Ruud, who until then had been serving as ABA Consultant on Legal Education. Except for the period 1980-83, when Professor John A. Bauman served as Executive Director, Millard Ruud held the position until 1987. Under Professor Ruud the AALS successfully dealt with the challenges of the 1970s, a time of several dramatic changes in the nature and scope of legal education.

First, the 1970s were a time of extremely rapid growth in the number of students in law school. Overall enrollment went from about 40,000 in 1968 to about 110,000 in 1975. The opening of new law schools taxed the Association's accreditation function to an extent that had not been known for many years.

Second, the number of new law teachers required to staff the new institutions and to teach the increased numbers of students grew significantly. The need to hire so many new teachers tested the capacity of the Association to facilitate traditional hiring activity at the Annual Meeting. Then, once hired, the newcomers needed assimilation into law teaching, a transition that many schools found difficult to handle entirely on their own.

Third, due in part to the dramatic increase in both the academic quality of law school applicants and the interest of able law school graduates in a teaching career, the proportion of law schools that shared the objectives of AALS member schools increased sharply during this period. Largely gone were the days of a sharp division between "national" and "local" law schools, or between those with a "scholarly" and those with a "practice" orientation. Law schools did—and continue to—differ in their strengths and orientation, but AALS membership became an objective of most accredited law schools. Today, 156 of the 174 ABA-accredited law schools (90%) are AALS members.

One important Association response to these developments was the decision made in 1975 to separate the function of faculty recruiting from the Annual Meeting. This allowed the Annual Meeting to be devoted to the scholarly exchanges that have in fact developed. A second response has been to expand greatly the AALS professional development activities for law teachers. These now consist, for the most part, of events outside the time of the Annual Meeting. They tend to extend over more than one day and bring together faculty with similar interests to talk about substantive issues in teaching and research.

In addition, while Professor Ruud was Executive Director, AALS involvement with other organizations and in government relations continued and expanded. The AALS/ABA Committee on Guidelines for Clinical Legal Education worked for three years to produce an important report issued in 1980. The Joint AALS/ABA/LSAC Student Financial Aid Task Force undertook advocacy before federal agencies and Congress. The Task Force was particularly active in 1982 in resisting cutbacks then proposed in government financial aid programs.

Finally, in 1986, the AALS created a Joint Task Force on Placement in conjunction with the National Association for Law Placement. The Task Force sought effective means to minimize the ways in which the placement function disrupts academic programs at the nation's law schools. Currently, the AALS and NALP are working together on a computer-assisted placement program designed both to assist in that effort and to improve placement opportunities for all students.

Within the space of a single professional lifetime, then, the AALS has moved from a position as an adjunct of the ABA and an informal coordinator of meetings to a major national organization with an annual budget exceeding $1.5 million. The rate of change has been particularly dramatic over the last ten years. There are 50% more AALS sections now than there were in 1978, for example. The number of candidates at the Faculty Recruitment Conference has increased 75% over the same period. Twice as many law teachers registered for the 1989 Annual Meeting as registered in 1980. For the most part, the growth has been managed very well. When Dean Betsy Levin became Executive Director in 1987, however, it was clear to all that the growth in staff prior to her arrival had not matched the increase in duties of the office. Neither was the Association's physical space adequate to accommodate the present size of the program.

Important decisions now must be made about the directions in which the AALS should go. This report seeks to lay the groundwork for those decisions. Its governing premise is that the AALS properly plays a central role in legal education. Nevertheless, it should not try to do either what other organizations can do better, or what the individual law schools can do better for themselves. Thus, Part II of this report turns to a discussion of the Association's proper roles.

Notes

1. This history is based on several sources: M.H. Cardozo, The Association Process 1963-1973 (1975); A.J. Harno, Legal Education in the United States (1953); R.B. Stevens, Law School: Legal Education in America from the 1850's to the 1980's (1983); Seavey, The Association of American Law Schools in Retrospect, 3 J. Legal Ed. 153 (1950); Sullivan, The Professional Associations and Legal Education, 4 J. Legal Ed. 401 (1952); Augustyn, A Historical Survey of Membership Requirements (1986) (memorandum prepared for internal use by the Special Committee on AALS Membership Requirements).

2. Lest Association members take excessive pride in their sensitivity, it should be noted that at the next year's meeting a resolution was adopted making it only an AALS "objective" that member schools maintain "equality of opportunity in legal education without discrimination or segregation on the ground of race or color." A special committee was appointed to "confer and cooperate" with member schools in trying to accomplish this objective. The accompanying report also noted: "Discrimination against women is now not a serious enough problem in fact to be worth Association action. Where it exists, it carries no invidious implications."

Chapter 86

Minutes of the First Annual Meeting

1901

Association of American Law Schools

The first annual meeting of the Association of American Law Schools convened in the Tabor Opera House, Denver, on Wednesday, August 21, 1901, at 3 o'clock P. M.

In the absence of James B. Thayer, of Harvard University, President of the Association, William P. Rogers, of Indiana University, was elected Chairman.

The following schools were represented through the delegates named:

Buffalo Law School: James Parker Hall.
Cincinnati Law School: Charles M. Hepburn.
Cornell University, College of Law: E. W. Huffcut, Frank Irvine.
Harvard University Law School: Joseph H. Beale, Jr.
University of Illinois, College of Law: Wm. L. Drew.
Indiana University, School of Law: William P. Rogers, G. L. Reinhard.
University of Iowa, College of Law: Emlin McClain, Charles Noble Gregory, Harry Sanger Richards.
Iowa College of Law: C. C. Cole.
University of Michigan, Department of Law: V. H. Lane.
University of Minnesota, College of Law: A. C. Hickman, James Paige, H. S. Abbott, Frederick V. Brown.
University of Missouri.: H. B. Babb.
New York University School of Law: Clarence D. Ashley, F. H. Sommer, L. J. Tompkins.
Northwestern University Law School: Edwin Burritt Smith, Edward Avery Harriman.

Your Committee would further report that under the special proviso of subsection 1 of Article 6 of the Articles of Association, it had no discretion in the matter of determining whether schools represented at the Saratoga meeting last year comply with the requirements of said subsection. Some examination of the printed announcements of these schools leads your Committee to believe that not all of them complied with the requirements of this subsection at the time such annoucements were issued. It is to be presumed, however, that they will comply with such requirements by September, 1901. Under the provisions of Article 10 of the Articles of Association it will become the duty of the succeeding executive committee to examine more closely into this matter and determine whether the requirements of Articles 6 and 7 are complied with by all members of the Association. In the judgment of your Committee the usefulness and success of the Association will depend very largely upon the strict adherence to the moderate requirements fixed in the Articles of Association as a condition to membership.

Respectfully submitted.
James B. Thayer,
Chairman.

The recommendations of the Executive Committee were taken up for consideration.

On motion, the following schools, recommended for membership by the Committee, were duly elected:

The Hastings School of Law of the University of California.
University of Colorado, School of Law.
Denver Law School.
University of Kansas, School of Law.
Leland Stanford, Jr., University, Department of Law.

On motion, the delegates present from the above schools were given full standing. These were:

University of Colorado, School of Law: C. M. Campbell, Moses Hallett.
Denver Law School: Tyson S. Dines, G. C. Manley, Lucius W. Hoyt.
University of Kansas, School of Law: W. E. Higgins, J.W. Green.
Leland Stanford, Jr., University; James Parker Hall.

A motion to waive the provisions of the Articles of Association and admit schools which had not filed their application and submitted their proofs to the Executive Committee, was ruled by the Chair to be out of order, as contrary to the constitutional provisions.

The recommendation of the Executive Committee concerning the application of the Chicago Law School was adopted.

It was voted that the Secretary should notify the Chicago-Kent School that on account of its certificate of membership being filed after the 15th of July the same could not be accepted, but that, as an application for membership, it would be referred to the incoming Executive Committee.

On motion, the courtesy of the floor was extended to representatives present from law schools which were not members of the Association.

The report of the Executive Committee upon the application of the Georgetown University Law School was adopted.

It was voted to recommit to the Executive Committee the original resolutions (1 and 2 above) and the substitute resolution recommended by the Committee, and that the Executive Committee be instructed to print next year its report in advance of the annual meeting and send a copy to every law school that may then be a member of the Association.

It was moved that the Committee's substitute for the third resolution referred to it be adopted. It was moved as an amendment that the resolution and the substitute recommended be recommitted.

Upon a vote taken the motion to recommit was lost and the recommendation of the Executive Committee was adopted.

The recommendation of the Executive Committee that the fourth resolution referred to it be referred to a special committee was adopted. On motion, it was voted that the special committee consist of three members and be appointed by the incoming President.

The recommendation of the Executive Committee that members of the Association be requested to print in their annual announcements the fact of their membership in the Association was adopted.

It was voted that the Association recommend that the expenses of delegates to the annual meeting of the Association be paid by the schools appointing them.

On motion, it was voted that the Executive Committee be requested to print its report and mail it to the members of the Association at least twenty days before the annual meetings of the Association.

On motion, it was voted that the incoming Executive Committee consider and report whether it is feasible to amend the Articles of Association so as to require schools to send representatives to each annual meeting, and whether schools in default for two consecutive years should retain their membership.

The committee appointed to audit the Treasurer's accounts reported that it had examined the report and vouchers and found the same entirely correct. On motion, the report was accepted, and the Treasurer's report accepted and approved.

On motion, it was voted that the Executive Committee be requested to confer with the Executive Committee of the Section on Legal Education of the American Bar Association and consider whether it is desirable to prepare a joint programme for the discussion of topics connected with legal education.

The Secretary read a communication from James B. Thayer, President of the Association, concerning a possible defect in the Articles of Association, in that they do not specify any examination test for the passing of students from one year to the next.

On motion, it was voted that the Association express its regret that ill-health prevented the attendance of the President and it was further ordered that his communication be referred to the Executive Committee with the request that the Committee report at the next annual meeting as to the matters concerning which action is suggested.

The Committee on Nominations reported as follows:

For President: Emlin McClain, of the Iowa State University.

For Secretary-Treasurer, Ernest W. Huffcut, of Cornell University.

For members of the Executive Committee: Simeon E. Baldwin, of Yale University; William P. Rogers, of Indiana University; and William S. Curtis, of the St. Louis Law School.

On motion, the report was adopted; the Secretary was instructed to cast the ballot of the Association for the candidates named, and they were declared duly elected.

On motion, the Association adjourned *sine die.*

E. W. Huffcut,
Secretary.

Chapter 87

Report of the Committee on Legal Education and Admissions to the Bar

1906

To the American Bar Association:

The Committee on Legal Education and Admissions to the Bar have the honor to submit the following report:

At the last meeting of the Association, the following resolution was passed:

Resolved, That the Committee on Legal Education and Admissions to the Bar be instructed to ascertain what degree

Pursuant to the resolution, the committee have investigated the subject referred to. The committee find that the forms of degrees at present conferred for legal study, in this country and abroad, are as follows:

Bachelor's Degree

The principal degree of the American law schools is the degree of LL. B. This is the regular degree in ninety-six schools. Of these schools forty-eight require a high school education at least as requisite for admission, and a three years' course of study; sixteen require a three years' course of study, but admit persons with less preliminary education; thirty-two have a two years' course or less. Two schools offer the degree of L. B. or B. L. for a two years' course; two offer B.C.L. and one J. B. for a special three years' course.

In England the bachelor's degree is offered in the universities for three years' of university work.

In Scotland the degree of LL. B. is offered for a three years' course after receiving the A.B., and the degree of L.B. (bachelor of law) for a two years' course following a secondary school education.

In Ireland the degree of LL. B. is given for a two years' course after attaining the degree A. B.

Master's Degree

The master's degree in law is offered in nineteen schools; in all of them it is in the form L.L. M. In all the schools it is given for one additional year of legal study. Eleven of the schools have three year courses, and require a high school graduation for admission; three of them have three year courses without requirements for admission; four have two year courses; one has a one year course. Two give the degree *in absentia*. There are two alternative master's degrees granted for special courses, each by a single school; M. P. L. (master of patent law) and M. C. L. (master of civil law).

No master's degree seems to be given abroad.

Doctor's Degree

Nine schools offer a doctor's degree in course. Six of these offer the degree J. D. In two schools it is the regular degree, given after a three year course; both schools require the completion of an academic course in college before admission to the school. In one school it is offered as a regular first degree to college graduates. In one school it is a regular higher degree, for three additional years' work after the bachelor's degree in law to college graduates only. In two schools it is given as a higher degree to any student who has gained the bachelor's degree in law.

Four schools offer the degree D. C. L.; one of them as an alternative to the J. D. This is given for two years' work after the LL. B. to any holder of that degree. One school offers the L.L. D. for three years' work after the LL. B. to persons not college graduates, the corresponding degree for college graduates being J. D.

In England and Ireland the doctor's degree (LL. D. or D. C. L.) is offered for additional work after the bachelor's degree. In Germany and on the continent of Europe some form of doctor's degree is the regular degree, given for three years of university work after graduation from the college (gymnasium).

The committee deem it advisable that degrees should be used so far as possible to indicate the nature of the training given by the school or required by it for admission; and that the higher degrees should be given only for exceptional training, and such as would be approved by the American Bar Association and the Association of American Law Schools. To attain that end they recommend the following rules, to be recommended by this Association for adoption by the law schools and other educational institutions of the United States:

Bachelor's Degree. The degree of LL. B. or that of B. C. L. or J. B. shall be granted only by day schools having a three years' course and requiring for admission graduation from a high school. Other schools shall grant the degree of L.B.

Master's Degree. The master's degree shall be granted only by schools which are entitled to grant the degree LL. B., and for not less than one full year of additional work done in residence at the school granting the degree after the student has received the LL. B.

Doctor's Degree. The degree LL. D. shall not be granted as a regular degree, but only *causa honoris*.

The degree of J. D. shall only be conferred by schools which have the right to confer the degree of LL. B., and the degree shall not be conferred except upon those who have previously obtained a degree in arts or science.

The degree of D. C. L. shall only be conferred by schools which have the right to confer the degree of LL. B., and the requirement for this degree shall be at least two full years of additional work done in residence at the school granting the degree and after the student has received the bachelor's degree.

The doctor's degree shall be granted only to college graduates. If granted as a first degree in law, it shall be in the form J. D. (standing for *juris doctor*, or in English, doctor of law); if as a second degree in law, in the form D. C. L.

Our reasons for these recommendations are as follows:

As to the bachelor's degrees, the recommendations conform exactly to the practice of the Scotch universities; and the degree L. B. is already used in the South in several two year schools. The two year schools and those having no requirements for admission will not be prevented from granting a proper degree, and one already known in the section in which most schools of the sort are found; on the other hand, the schools whose requirements are higher will be given a proper mark of difference by the form of the degree. A very large majority of those now receiving the degree LL. B. would continue to receive it if the proposed rule were in force.

As to the master's degree, it seems improper to grant this or any higher degree for a course of study which should entitle the student to a bachelor's degree only. The higher degrees should be reserved for serious study of a higher sort than that required of ordinary graduates in law.

The doctor's degrees are given, generally speaking, in two ways; sometimes as a first degree in law following a bachelor's degree in arts and sometimes as a higher degree in law. A distinction in form is desirable; and the prepondering practice already marks out the distinction proposed. It seems undesirable in any event to confer the LL. D. upon a young man for regular work in course. The almost universal use of the degree in this country to signify the highest honor which a university can confer makes it extremely fitting that the degree should be reserved for that purpose; and this it is quite possible to do since the form D. C. L. remains available and is already not uncommonly used as a higher legal degree in course both in England and in this country.

The committee submit herewith as an appendix to this report a table showing the degrees conferred by the law schools of the United States and the conditions on which they are granted so far as the length of the course of study, the entrance requirements and the character of the school, whether day or night, are concerned. Any other information sufficiently definite to be of any value is difficult to obtain.

It would be interesting and no doubt valuable to be able to ascertain definitely the course of study and the entire method of training in the various schools, but it does not appear practical to obtain such information.

There is a similarity in the catalogues in connection with this subject. The various branches of public and private law are taught. In some cases the number of hours devoted to the various subjects is stated in the catalogues, but so much is left to the judgment of the instructors teaching the subjects that any detailed statement is impracticable.

The committee have observed in the proceedings of the Association of American Law Schools at its last meeting that this subject was under consideration and the desirability of a uniform standard referred to. This is a subject worthy the careful consideration of this Association as well as the body referred to. A degree is an academic distinction and it is desirable that the attainments of those holding the same degree should be substantially the same, otherwise the degree in itself means nothing. Fake degrees ought by all means to be discouraged and if possible prevented.

It is the traditional duty of the Bar to train its new members and to protect the profession and the public from incompetent or vicious attorneys.

The committee have observed that the extension of the course of study to three years and in some schools the addition of a post-graduate course has led to the development of the course of study in the direction of historical jurisprudence, political science and public law. This is to be commended.

It is a fact frequently referred to and a matter of common knowledge that the government of this country is largely in the hands of lawyers. Notwithstanding the fact that they constitute but a small portion of the population, their influence is very great, not only in the actual work of legislation and in the administration of justice and in the executive branch of the government, but in guiding public opinion. Any scheme of education which neglects to provide for a training in history, public law, economics and other branches of political science is inadequate and faulty, and your committee are gratified to observe the development of the course of study in the direction which has taken place in late years.

In connection with the subject of degrees, the committee may report that the practice which formerly prevailed throughout the United States of admission to the Bar on the diploma of the law schools without any examination by the courts or other public authority has been generally abandoned. It may be that in the early days of the law schools such laws were helpful to the schools and not injurious to the profession or to the public. But with the increase in the number of schools and the inferior character of some and the practical difficulty in legislation making any distinction between schools, the practice had become a vicious one. In few states does the degree of a law school now admit to the Bar. The privilege is one which the leading schools have formally disapproved of. The American Bar Association at its meeting in 1901 adopted a resolution disapproving of this practice. (See A. B. A. report of 1901, page 580.)

The most powerful influence in elevating the standard of admission to the Bar has been the creation of State Boards of Law Examiners.

The American Bar Association has gone on record on a number of occasions in favor of the creation of State Boards of Law Examiners for every state.[1]

In the following states such boards have been created.[2]

Colorado	Michigan	Pennsylvania
Connecticut	Minnesota	Rhode Island
Georgia	Missouri	Tennessee
Illinois	Nebraska	Texas
Iowa	New Hampshire	Vermont
Kansas	New Jersey	Washington
Louisiana	New York	West Virginia
Maine	North Dakota	Wisconsin
Maryland	Ohio	Wyoming
Massachusetts	Oklahoma	

The laws creating such boards are all very simple. While there are differences in details, such as the number of examiners and the terms for which they are appointed, the length of time a student is required to study, etc., the character of preliminary education, etc., the most important features are the same. The main point is to take away from the lower courts the power to admit to the Bar, and put the matter entirely in the hands of the Court of Appeals or highest appellate court and to create a permanent board to examine the students.

Under the old practice, when members of the Bar of one county were admitted to the Bar of every other county in the state on motion the standard for the state was the county having the lowest standard.

These laws lead to a uniformity of standards for the entire state, prevent evasion of the rules of a particular place, get rid of local or political influences and have a decided tendency under present conditions to raise the standards of admission. Such has been the effect whenever they have been adopted.

The creation of a permanent board leads to a fixed standard and to a policy likely to be progressive.

The same reasons which lead to the adoption of a uniform standard for a state apply to some extent to the country at large. Today the lawyer who has no business in other states has little in his own. It is not difficult to evade a standard so long as lawyers from other states are admitted on motion. The committee have known a number of cases where law students left their own states and went to another to study law because they could get a license in a year, while in their own state they would be required to study three years. As members of the Bar, they could be admitted on motion in their own state and thus save two years of work in the law school. The committee are informed that some law schools have used this argument successfully to induce young men to enter their schools.

The influence of the members of the Bar as a body on public affairs is enormous. The conduct of a few of the very best or worst men need not be considered in connection with admission to the Bar. A man with a superior mind will come to the front no matter whether the standards are high or low. No standard of admission will abolish entirely the shyster. This must be accomplished in another way. It is the mass which is most potent. It is the public sentiment of the Bar which is the powerful influence. There is an average of character and efficiency. It is this average which should be considered. An attorney is not bad, negligent or incompetent whose conduct is that of a man of ordinary capacity and character in his profession. The admission to the Bar of large numbers of men of inferior character and training lowers the average, and is a bad influence. The qualifications of a class so influential in public affairs is a matter of public and general interest.

It is true that a uniform standard of admission to the Bar for the whole country is not practical. What is possible in one place would be far in advance of public sentiment in another. The committee have never proposed such a thing, but we have advocated as one step toward better conditions the creation of State Boards of Law Examiners in every state.

If the power to admit is taken away from all inferior courts and given entirely to the Court of Appeals, uniformity in each state will be attained at once. In some places it would be necessary to begin with an easy examination. A three years' course of study and a preliminary requirement of a high school education would not be difficult to procure in some states. In others, perhaps, only one year without any preliminary education would be all that is practical. But a state board is practical everywhere. Any considerable increase in requirements for admission made suddenly would be unjust and lead to stout resistance. Progress must be gradual. This a matter which is better in the hands of the courts. The standard can be changed from time to time as conditions are favorable. No fixed standard should be established by the legislature. Its activity should be limited to putting the power to admit in the hands of a single body. It is easier to get a court to make changes than the legislature. A reasonable progress may be expected from a court. The plan now is to get state boards in every state. After this is done the next step can be determined on.

This is a subject which has already been considered by this Association. Any further comment at this time is, therefore, considered unnecessary.

So far as your committee have been able to ascertain, such boards have been universally satisfactory. In no state in which such boards have been created have they been abolished. The committee recommend that this Association again exert its influence in favor of the creation of boards in states in which they have not yet been created. In conclusion the committee recommend the adoption of the following resolutions:

Resolved, First, that this Association recommend to the State and Local Bar Associations of the various states and territories and the Bar Association of the District of Columbia the consideration of the subject of admission to the Bar, and such action by such association, as will lead in every state and territory and the District of Columbia the creation of State Boards of Law Examiners and the maintenance of a standard of preliminary educaton equivalent, at least, to graduation from a high school.

Resolved, Second, that the Secretary of this Association be and he is hereby instructed to send a copy of these resolutions to each State and Local Bar Association and the Bar Association of the District of Columbia and the territories.

In connection with the subject of degrees, the committee submit for the consideration of the Association the following resolutions, which have been already mentioned, and recommend their adoption:

Resolved, First, That the degree of LL. B. or that of B. C. L. or J. B. shall be granted only by day schools having a three years' course and requiring for admission graduation from a high school. Other schools shall grant the degree of L. B.

Resolved, Second, that the master's degree shall be granted only by schools which are entitled to grant the degree LL. B., and for not less than one full year of additional work done in residence at the school granting the degree after the student has received the LL. B.

Resolved, Third, that the degree LL. D. shall not be granted as a regular degree, but only *causa honoris.*

Resolved, Fourth, that the degree of J. D. shall only be conferred by schools which have the right to confer the degree of LL. B., and the degree shall not be conferred except upon those who have previously obtained a degree in arts or science.

Resolved, Fifth, that the degree of D. C. L. shall only be conferred by schools which have the right to confer the degree of LL. B., and the requirement for this degree shall be at least two full years of additional work done in residence at the school granting the degree and after the student has received the bachelor's degree.

Resolved, Sixth, that the doctor's degree shall be granted only to college graduates. If granted as a first degree in law, it shall be in the form J. D. (standing for *juris doctor,* or in English, doctor of law); if as a second degree in law, in the form D. C. L.

George M. Sharp,
Henry Wade Rogers,
Joseph Henry Beale, Jr.,
Lucius H. Perkins,
J. Crawford Biggs.

NOTES

1. Proceedings A.B.A.:
1895, p. 380, etc.
1896, p. 543, etc.
1897, p. 367, etc.
1898, p. 503, etc.
1899, p. 518, etc.
1900, pp. 574, 576, etc.
1901, p. 409, etc.
1904, p. 786.

2. Proceedings, 1900, p. 577; 1901, p. 409; 1904, p. 791.

IX. Technology and the Future

Chapter 88

Alternate Futures

The Future of Legal Education

1998

John Mayer

John Mayer is Director of the Consortium, Computer Assisted Legal Instruction, in Chicago, Illinois. Copyright © 1998 John Mayer.

All the notions we thought solid, all the values of civilised life, all that made for stability in international relations, all that made regularity in the economy . . . in a word, all that tended happily to limit the uncertainty of the morrow, all that gave nations and individuals some confidence in the morrow . . . all this seems badly compromised. I have consulted all the augurs I could find, of over species, and I have heard only vague words, contradictory prophecies, curiously feeble assurances. Never has humanity combined so much power with so much disorder, so much anxiety with so many playthings, so much knowledge with so much uncertainty.[1]

Introduction

A somewhat obscure sub-genre of science fiction deals with alternate histories. What if Kennedy wasn't shot? What if the South won the Civil War? What if Napoleon won at Waterloo? I have found these stories fascinating because they always had basis in historical fact with one, small, though quite significant change in what actually did happen. The idea of conceiving of multiple, possible histories gives interesting perspective to the exercise of what possible histories are ahead of us.

I will use this essay to spin some alternate futures for legal education. All of them are plausible to varying degrees and all of them will come true, I believe, to a certain extent. I hope to highlight ideas and experiments that are incubating in legal education today that may mature into these possible futures and also comment on the motivations and barriers that will prevent or encourage these futures to come to pass.

The goal of this essay is not to offer strategic advice to those of us involved in legal education. The limits of this forum and the complexity and broadness of the task would render most advice to mere platitudes. Rather, I hope to stimulate some thinking about the future of legal education that will motivate an ongoing dialogue.

As the Executive Director of the Center for Computer-Assisted Legal Instruction[2], I am keenly interested in the future of legal education. CALI's non-profit mission is to serve legal education with focus on the intelligent use of computer technology as an agent of change. My training, degrees and profession are in Information Technology. I am neither a lawyer nor a professional teacher. However, for more than seven years, I designed, built and managed the computer systems and services at a mid-western law school, and during that time, felt that I joined the community of legal educators as I listened, learned and endeavored to create systems that supported the needs of law school faculty.

In 1991, I organized the first conference to professionalize the area of computers in legal education.[3] In 1998, this conference will celebrate its 8th year and there are strong indicators that computer staffing in law schools has attained viability as an integral partner in legal education in the incredibly short time of less than a decade. At the very first conference, John Hankins, Network Manager at CICnet,[4] boldly told a roomful of librarians, faculty and law school computing staff that in less than two years, we would all be "on" the Internet, (whatever that was) and that we should start planning for it right now. While planning the 1998 Conference, it was difficult to conceive of a session or presentation that did not, in some way, involve the Internet or the World-Wide-Web. The CALI Conference has portended many new advancements in the use of computer technology in legal education. The first Microsoft Windows graphical web-browser, Cello, was demonstrated in beta version by its author Tom Bruce of Cornell law school in 1992. The first electronic casebook, developed by Professor Ronald Staudt while President of CALI was unveiled at a CALI Conference. The first Electronic Library was exhibited at a CALI Conference[5] and the first windows-based word processor was displayed by a vendor at a CALI Conference.[6]

All of these foretold future directions of technology and their eventual application to legal education, but very few of these products exist today in the same form as they were first introduced. Technology, alone, does not create change. It can only make things possible. Change occurs because people use the technology to improve efficiency or educational impact on their students. The acceptance of new technologies is most powerful, however, when it changes the culture of the law school. Rapid change occurs only when a critical mass accepts and uses a new technology. E-mail is an excellent example. If only 20% of a community used e-mail, it would quickly die out as a passing fad. When everyone is connected, the value and potential for communication is exponentially greater and as more and more members of the community log on, the value becomes more and more apparent to everyone.

The number of computer technologies that have achieved critical mass in legal education today can be counted on one hand. Word processing, on-line legal research such as LEXIS or Westlaw, and electronic mail. Almost every law school has a web-page and hundreds of law faculty are creating and using web-pages to support their courses, so it looks like this may achieve critical mass as well. The list of technologies that have not yet reached critical mass is quite a bit longer. Computer-based instruction,[7] electronic casebooks,[8] interactive video lessons, expert systems/artificial intelligence, computers in the classroom (either used by the faculty member to teach from or by the students to type, rather than write, their notes), natural language searching and computer-based exams are all present, but not yet integral to legal education like word processing, e-mail and online research are.

Other technologies are still in the experimental stage and may soon come crashing out of the gates heading for the critical mass finishing line. These include distance learning, video-conferencing and web-based legal research to rival that of LEXIS and Westlaw. The Internet has been transporting text since its inception in the early 1970's. The Web has brought us easy delivery of pictures and sound and crude animations and video. The logical conclusion of this advancement is real-time, effortless video delivery to and from any personal computer, television and cellular phone. It *will* happen. We are only biding our time, waiting for the fiber to be pulled, the satellites to be launched[9] and the technology to stabilize and standardize so that critical mass on a global scale may occur.

Legal education may or may not change, but it is in for quite an interesting ride as these experiments lead to new experiments and as the existing players and new players jockey for position. These new technologies will force us to re-examine the ways that we create, deliver and verify educational goals of our students. Technology will not cure all that ails us. In the short term, it will create many more problems than it solves while we grapple with the possibilities. This essay will examine some of those possibilities in the form of potential future directions for legal education.

Alternate Future: The Monolithic Law School

In the past several years, many colleges and universities around the globe have begun to offer for-credit courses that are taught almost entirely across the Internet. These courses use web pages for the syllabus and course readings, email for submission of assignments and student questions, chat rooms for real-time discussions, downloadable tutorials for self-study and on occasion, sound (and less frequently video) recordings of lectures available anytime, anywhere via the World-Wide-Web. Hundreds of faculty have supplemented their courses using these same technologies. The growth of these has been nothing short of explosive and LEXIS and West have contributed with products and services to support web-based course pages.[10] In early 1998, Harvard Law School and Arthur Miller began offering a non-credit course on Privacy in Cyberspace delivered entirely over the Internet which included a web site, email discussion and pre-recorded lectures delivered via the web. Harvard does not mince words regarding their goals: "We are inaugurating a global cyber school, eventually to serve all languages and all ages."[11]

Distance learning is not new. Correspondence courses, delivered by U.S. Mail have been around for over a century. What is new is the richness of interaction and the ease of delivery that can be achieved by faculty and schools. In anticipation of the unregulated growth of this phenomenon, the American Bar Association's Section on Legal Education issued a set of Temporary Distance Education Guidelines on May 6, 1997. Normally not known for its rapid response, the ABA's warp speed issuance of these guidelines legitimizes and even encourages experimentation in this new educational delivery medium. Not surprisingly, these same guidelines also reiterated the ABA's refusal to grant permission to law schools to grant credit for courses taken by correspondence study.[12]

Despite this impediment, the logical extreme of this phenomenon was obvious to many as evidenced by articles and on-line discussions that have recently occurred in legal academia circles. Could not all classes in [fill in the blank] subject be taught by one faculty member over the Internet? Won't this reduce all other faculty who teach [fill in the blank] to teaching assistants? The short answer is "yes." In the recent past, cross-institution, experimental courses with a large digital component have been taught in areas such as Intellectual Property, Indian Law and Law of the Internet. Online courses covering the core law school materials such as Civil Procedure, Contracts and Torts are sure to follow. In this future, one law school will offer all of its classes and faculty to law students around the world via the Information Superhighway. Real-time or digitized for later download, full motion video lectures will be delivered wherever the student connects. The technology exists to accomplish this today and it is not that expensive either. The largest costs are storage of the digitized video for later access and staff to operate the video cameras while the professor roams the classroom. A full television studio production facility would be a more expensive, but not entirely unlikely, scenario. In this future, every classroom becomes a channel on the Harvard Law Interactive Cyberschool Network.

The quality of the online educational experience is still in question. Proponents of entirely electronic education still have to prove that the same educational goals are being met or exceeded. The groundwork is being laid in the experiments and pilot projects of today for future, for-credit, entirely online, legal education.

Law schools and CLE providers are already using audio, and sometimes video, to augment their web pages to deliver legal education. The economies of scale make this future quite viable. One teacher, teaching to thousands of students. There are very few law schools that could sustain dominance in a global marketplace. It could only work from a top-tier institution with international prestige, plenty of resources and a lot of moxie. Harvard and perhaps a few other institutions might fit that description.

Localized monolithic law schools are possible on the state level. State legislatures, seeking to save money may become attracted to the idea of consolidating the resources of several schools into a single, online school. Salaries and infrastructure costs are reduced, every student is taught by the top instructor, and the marginal cost of adding students to the class are minimal since the student is paying the freight on the delivery to their personal computer.

In 1996, a consortium of western states was formed to deliver online undergraduate curriculum from state universities.[13] California decided to opt out of this consortium.

> With pre-eminent high-tech and entertainment industries as well as prestigious universities . . . California is in a unique position to set up its own world-class online network.[14]

Given California's size, the state is arguably in a position to do this, but the competition for students won't stay within state boundaries. Similar, for-profit ventures have also been launched to compete for the tuition dollars of cyber-savvy students working through high school today.[15]

The biggest barrier to for-credit, online, law school is accreditation from the ABA, but if it can be demonstrated that the quality of education is the same or even better, then things may change. Online education may also meet other needs that will support its growth and accreditation. The Americans with Disabilities Act requires schools to make reasonable accommodations to disabled students. Making changes to infrastructure such as classrooms, staircases and laboratories is quite expensive, but with cyber education, the classroom is the student's home, so few accommodations may be necessary. Online school can provide equal access to minorities and probably for less money. In this future, *University of California Board of Regents v. American Bar Association* is inevitable.

Consolidating all of the law schools in a state means you need less faculty, less infrastructure and less staff. Downsized faculty and clerical workers unions will fight this. The tenure system will have to be re-evaluated, weakened or dismantled. Since its inception, tenure has come up for critical scrutiny many times. The coincidence of the current rumblings about the tenure system and the rise of online education may provide the flashpoint for its final downfall. There will be monolithic law schools in the future—either state-sponsored mega-schools or prestige extensions of existing market leaders. What will the rest of us do in response to remain competitive?

Alternate Future: Law School Mini-Consortia

When the going gets tough, the tough join forces. If a single law school or a group of state-run law schools can go online to attract students from the global applicant pool, then it is possible, even necessary, for small groups of law schools to form mini-consortia that leverage strengths of each member of the consortium. This is a route for private schools seeking competitive advantage in the future.

A small collection of law schools of equivalent stature could join forces to deliver the best of what each has to offer. Students would not attend a single school, but a consortium, taking classes from . . . well, it wouldn't matter from the student's viewpoint. The law schools would have resource-sharing agreements and would normalize their curriculums, tuition and schedules to accommodate the students. Teaching in specialized areas would be stronger overall as faculty from each law school would combine to form virtual centers of excellence in such areas as Environmental Law, Intellectual Property and Labor/Employment. One person departments would be a thing of the past. Some attrition among faculty would naturally occur, but more among non-teaching staff. Why have multiple Admissions, Registrars, Career Services and Libraries? Local infrastructures would be reduced or converted to on-site training sessions in the practice of law. Libraries and librarians are especially vulnerable as more primary and secondary materials become available online.

Despite all the excitement over online education, there are compelling reasons for not delivering all legal education online. Practical skills training, such as that offered by clinics, are becoming increasingly important. Many states are experimenting with a practical component to the bar exam to bridge the gap between academia and practice. The Canadians and Europeans require law school graduates to "apprentice" for a year before being allowed entry to the Bar.[16] The increasing importance of legal writing and analysis skills may not translate well into the cyber-realm.

A geographically dispersed mini-consortia could leverage its under-utilized buildings and classrooms to provide office space and training to students for the practical portion of their education. Clinics would flourish as every student is required to spend several weeks a year working real cases with real clients fulfilling the practical component of their education and preparing for the practice portion of the bar exam. "Boot camps" for legal writing, moot court and skills training that resemble today's intensive trial advocacy courses would increase to meet these needs. A consortium of the top private law schools in the major legal market areas like New York, Chicago, Los Angeles and Houston could present a formidable front to the state-consortiums or the monolithic law school described in the first future above. Given the globalization of law practice, you might add London, Tokyo, and Hamburg to that mix.

Local law schools have always had the advantage of handling the variations in state laws that exist. It might be difficult for a student in Nebraska to take courses from a consortia that doesn't offer any focus on the student's home state. Law schools may learn some things from the for-profit bar preparation companies that are expert at teaching this material- at least as far as passing the bar is concerned.

Again, economies of scale make this future possible, but competitive pressures for a dwindling, quality applicant pool are more compelling reasons. The 1990's has been a period of merger-mania as markets and companies consolidate and globalize. In the legal education arena alone, the number of legal publishers has been tremendously reduced as Reed-Elsivere and Thomson have gobbled up Lexis-Nexis, Matthew Bender, Shepards, West and others in just the past several years. Education will become more commercialized and commodity-like. Private law schools have the further advantage of initiating these coalitions themselves in contrast to state schools where the pressure may come from above in response to cost-cutting. Where is this economic and competitive pressure coming from? Aren't there enough law schools already?

ALTERNATE FUTURE: INVASION OF THE BARBARIANS

The answer in this future is "no, there are not enough law schools." Many pundits decry the glut of lawyers in the United States today and the National Association for Law Placement's recent statistics show that since 1990 law school graduates have increased while those finding jobs in private practice has decreased.[17]

If they are not practicing law, what are all these lawyers going to do? Some will start businesses in the lucrative field of legal education. Legal education is a profitable business. The cost of infrastructure, compared with other areas of study such as chemistry and physics, is quite low. The materials for the study of law are largely in the public domain and almost all primary and many secondary sources are available online or on CD-ROM. No other area of study can boast such thorough digitization. Law schools are often described as the cash cows of private universities.

The faculty of these virtual, private, for-profit law schools would be made up of lawyers tired of practice or better yet, partners taking early retirement from their practice. They have made their money and may see this as a way to contribute to the greater good of society. Lawyers with extensive experience and excellent speaking skills from many trials and litigations could be courted by for-profit firms seeking quality faculty who are not steeped in scholarship. Their reputation and experience in practice would be a selling point to students looking for law degree that gives them a solid, practical understanding of the law. Many business schools advertise that their faculty work for the Fortune 1000 offering "real world" experience in the classroom. Medical students are taught by practicing physicians in teaching hospitals, why should law be different? Perhaps experienced faculty and librarians who have been down-sized in the previously discussed futures will find employment with a for-profit firm offering better benefits, better working conditions and no scholarship requirement or tenure pressure.

For-profit law schools will have less compunction and more flexibility to offer their educational services to other markets such as CLE, foreign businesses and white-collar workers who need to understand some area of law that impacts their jobs. As legal matters pervade our everyday lives, from crime to child care, from taxes to traffic tickets and from sexual harassment to small business, everyday people are intensely curious about the law and many are realizing that they will be more valuable in the job market or better able to perform their current jobs if they have a better understanding of the legal system. A law degree is not their goal. Today, there are few products aimed at this market. Other factors motivate a broader marketplace for legal education in the future. More people will seek legal education to start businesses, defend themselves against lawsuits, create social change or advocate a political issue. Legal literacy may become another fundamentally required skill to be an engaged citizen in a democratic society of the future. For-profit law schools will meet this demand. Extremely low overhead, practical education, flexible hours and a money-back guarantee will overcome the lack of history, tradition and prestige offered by today's law schools.

The ABA has recently accredited a for-profit law school and there are others in the process of obtaining accreditation.[18] Alternatively, there are few examples of for-profit law schools offering correspondence study today over the Internet, and no one seems to be taking them seriously for now. Accreditation with the ABA will be a serious barrier, but if that gets cracked by establishment law schools to allow them to deliver legal education online, then the door will be opened for the barbarians as well.

It's hard to get seriously worried about a group of unemployed lawyers forming up to compete with our venerable institutions of legal education, but what if these lawyers are well-funded, backed by a name-brand steeped in tradition and already possessing vast online experience and resources?

Alternate Future: Law School, Inc.

Welcome to Law School, Incorporated. Instead of small, entrepreneurial start-ups entering the legal education market, large, well-funded and established, corporate entities will. These could include Reed-Elsivere, Thomson or established continuing legal education publishers like the Practising Law Institute. Other possible candidates are BarBri, large accounting firms like Peat Marwick, Ernst & Young or Arthur Andersen that employ more lawyers than even the largest law firms or large law firms seeking to diversify their portfolios.

Many law schools employ adjunct faculty that are already employees at large law firms. A large enough law firm could leverage these teachers to offer courses to potential clients or as a recruiting angle for new associates. Many states require lawyers to take continuing legal educational courses and allow teachers of these seminars to receive credit for their presentations. Law firm teachers can offer the firm's in-house expertise as a selling point as well. They would not only teach the theory of law, but could provide intimate access to the practice of law as well. Practical skills could be gained on real cases. The school *is* a law firm, so no need to add a clinic. The cases would not all be pro-bono and the best students would be offered jobs upon graduation.

These entities have sufficient resources to fund for-profit legal education ventures and many are invested heavily in educational delivery systems already, both traditional and online. The legal publishers have larger libraries of source materials than any single law school and they understand the legal education market better than any commercial entity. Given that it would be a bold move to directly compete with established legal education academia, partnerships are likely. Many professional sports teams now play in stadiums that have been renamed to reflect their corporate sponsorships.[19] These ideas may stick in the craw of venerable educational institutions that will not compromise their values for the bottom line, but if the right combination of competitive pressures, global opportunity and economic incentive can be found, is the Lexis-Nexis-Harvard Cyberschool or the Baker & McKenzie's Yale Online Law School so inconceivable? In the past, such partnerships have been kept at arm's length, but the future is all about new collaborations that leverage the reputations and strengths of the partners. Law faculty would never allow advertising in their classrooms by a vendor, but they are more complacent about vendor presence in their virtual classrooms when they use online services to deliver course materials to their students. For-profit, online law schools would be seeking students that could also become clients, customers and employees.

Accreditation would be an important issue, but these commercial entities have proven their willingness to litigate as part of their business development. Technologically and developmentally, this future is the most probable of all. Culturally and politically, it is also the most problematic. Legal education is at least a billion dollar industry and profits from books and online databases is being assaulted by all the free access to information that can be had for $19.95 per month on the World-Wide-Web. Is it accidental where www.lawschool.com takes you?

Legal Education: 2003

Now that I've thoroughly frightened you, let me say that I doubt that any of these futures will come to pass in any significant degree for at least five years. Changes in education move at glacial speed and the long history of tradition and prestige that law schools enjoy today gives them a powerful momentum that will be difficult to overcome.

There are other reasons why none of these futures may be realized at all. The chaos brought about by rapid change may cause people to cling to known entities and locally trusted institutions. Law schools may hunker-down and weather out the vast changes occurring all around them. A "back-to-basics" movement in education could re-energize law schools to return to smaller student bodies and more personalized attention paid to students. Schools may pick and choose more delicately which technologies they choose to integrate into legal education. Lawyers, law schools and state bar organizations may circle the wagons and effectively repulse the assaults on their right to be the gatekeepers to the practice of law. Lawyering is more than a job or a profession. Lawyers are supposed to have public duties and ethics that transcend personal wishes or money. Lawyers are servants of society-at-large and the rule of law. Can these ideas be effectively passed on to law students from schools whose motives are less than pure? The training of students to think like lawyers occurs through immersion in the study of law. The transformation of legal education to more student-centered learning may run counter to this notion. It may be harder to mold minds via cyberspace.

The next five years will find legal education and all of its participants doing business as usual. There is a lot of infrastructure building happening and a lot of experimentation in computer-integrated legal education. Hundreds of faculty have supplemented their courses with web pages. More and more law schools have someone with "Director" in their title managing computing services and you would be hard pressed to find a law school that didn't have a web page and didn't have e-mail for each and every one of its students, faculty and staff.

Law schools will spend the next five years consolidating their understanding of new, web-based technologies to support existing classes, distance learning experiments, local and overseas partnerships and administrative efficiencies. Publishers such as Thomson and Reed-Elsivere, non-profits such as CALI and institutional initiatives such as Cornell's Legal Information Institute, Harvard's Berkman Center and others will not be idle either. I suspect these will be extremely busy times for all players as we struggle to understand how best to use technology to serve legal education, as the faculty culture becomes more sophisticated in its use of computers and the Internet and the tools leverage more power into the hands of everyone.

Closing Remarks

If you read the last section and were relieved to learn that you can duck your head for five more years, then you have read me wrong. The successful schools are already on the path to the future. Experiments may lead to failures, but each mistake teaches us more about how the system can work when it is scaled up to include an entire faculty and student body in a global marketplace. Experience will be a stern teacher, but will reward the tenacious student. The technologies, programs and services that will seem to burst upon the scene in 2003 are in incubation today being refined, reworked and re-engineered. The successful institutions will have spent the intervening time educating themselves by re-examining every facet of the educational delivery process. Schools with scarce resources should realize that computer-integrated learning is a growth area and should not be underfunded or cordoned off from the "real" education that goes on day after day. The time for gurus, entrepreneurs and change-agents is drawing to a close as we will *all* have responsibilities in creating and managing change. You can sit by the side of the road and wait to learn from others' mistakes, but then you will not be building the habits and tolerance into your institution's culture that the rapid degree of technology change requires. Peter Schwartz, in his seminal book, *The Art of the Long View*,[20] advises us that

> . . . the point is not to "pick one preferred future," . . . Nor is the point to find the most probable future and adapt to it or "bet the company" on it. Rather, the point is to make strategic decisions that will be sound for all plausible futures.[21]

This would be difficult to do if we are not actively engaged in exploring the possibilities of new technologies today in legal education. The future will be decided by our actions today and the actions we take today will determine which future we get.

NOTES

1. Philosopher Paul Valery, "Historical Fact," 1932.
2. CALI is a non-profit consortium of 175 U.S. law schools incorporated in 1982 to support research and development into computer-integrated legal education.
3. Conference for Law School Computing Professionals, more generally known as the CALI Conference.
4. CICnet is the Committee for Institutional Cooperation-net. CICnet operated the wide area IP network that connected the universities of the Big Ten to the Internet.
5. Library of International Relations, LOIS.
6. Wang's UpWord. Copies of the software were provided to all attendees. Unfortunately, the software was never commercially released.
7. Though CALI has been slugging it out for more than 15 years.
8. The recent decision by LEXIS to stop distributing Folio Views for free to law schools does not bode well for this technology in the Folio format. HTML-based publishing is a likely successor, however.
9. "Surfing by Satellite," Angela Hickman, *PC Magazine*, May 5, 1998.
10. The West Education Network (TWEN) from WestGroup and the LEXIS Virtual Classroom from Lexis-Nexis.
11. From http://cyber.law.harvard.edu/metaschool.html, the web site for the Berkman Center for Internet & Society.
12. Temporary Distance Learning Guidelines, American Bar Association Section on Legal Education, www.abanet.org.
13. Western Governors University at www.westgov.org.
14. California Governor Pete Wilson quoted in the *San Francisco Chronicle*, Oct. 3, 1996.
15. *Cyber-Schools May Pose Challenge to Ordinary Colleges*, Daniel Kruger, The Bond Buyer, Inc. 1998.
16. However, legal education is primarily an undergraduate curriculum in Canada and Europe.
17. *ABA Approved Law Schools*, 1998 edition, Macmillan/Simon & Schuster, page 36.
18. Thomas Jefferson School of Law in California received ABA accreditation in August of 1996.
19. Chicago Bulls-United Center, San Francisco Giants-3Com Stadium, etc.
20. *The Art of the Long View*, Currency/Doubleday Publishers, 1991, Peter Schwartz.
21. From the introduction to the paperback edition, p. xiii-xiv.

Chapter 89

In Search of the Origins of the Electronic Casebook

1998

Ronald Staudt

Ronald Staudt is Professor of Law at the Chicago-Kent College of Law of the Illinois Institute of Technology and Vice President for Technology Development, LEXIS-NEXIS. Copyright © 1998 Ronald W. Staudt.

In April 1998, I served as the moderator of a working conference to explore opportunities to improve the US court system using Internet technology. The convening organization had invited judges, court administrators, court clerks, and librarians, who were technology leaders. The group was small enough to develop a sense of camaraderie during the two-day meeting. At one point in a heated discussion about computer based expert systems for pro se divorces, one of the judges made a Potter Stewart-like statement that " We all knew where we want to go. We just need to work out the details." I was struck by the obvious error in the statement. There was no agreement on whether facilitating more pro se divorces was a good idea. There were significant disputes about the means and even the wisdom of almost every proposed change in the court processes. But the camaraderie had been rapidly built and deeply felt. I think the sense of common purpose and fellowship grew from a core of optimism—typical American optimism—irrepressible belief in a better future from hard work and technology.

I offer this essay as a participant observer's trace of some of the pedagogical insights that powered the activities of the Chicago-Kent Center for Law and Computers during its first 10 years. The insights arose out of my own optimism that technology, in the form of digital computing, would make law schools and law practice better.

Clinical Antecedents

From 1983 to 1994 I served as the Director of the Chicago-Kent Center for Law and Computers. In this role I became an evangelist for the benefits of the use of computer technology to improve the teaching and practice of law. Earlier, in 1978-80, I had worked with James Sprowl, then head of the American Bar Foundation's Computer Project and later a colleague at Chicago-Kent, to investigate the use of automated practice systems and other computer tools to assist clinical legal education. The 1978 Chicago-Kent "Law Office of the Future Project" was aimed at using computers to improve the delivery mechanisms of routine legal services to those who were unable to afford lawyers. Optimism about the ability of computers to automate legal analysis and drafting was the fuel for the experiments. Using software engineered on a mainframe computer by Jim Sprowl, the clinical faculty at Chicago-Kent built five automated practice systems to draft documents for simple wills, uncontested divorces, guardianships, etc. Clinical students used these practice systems to prepare first drafts of client documents. The most frequently used system was the simple will system that served up 500 draft wills for senior citizens at Chicago's Old Age Centers.

The Law Office of the Future Project predated the invention of personal computers. Terminals and printers wired to phone lines with acoustical couplers were the tools of information capture and output. My optimism was focused on the promise of automating the dull, repetitive and tedious tasks that lawyers must often perform to obtain a rather ministerial yet important result for a client. Computers were perfectly capable of handling these complex but not creative tasks if proper instructions could be written for the computers and if those instructions were properly and continually maintained to reflect changes in the law. I envisioned computers as able to leverage the research and judgment of good lawyers.

The pedagogical value was also based on this optimism. Clinical courses create special learning tension because students perform professional tasks for clients. This learning tension often motivates students and offers deep and driven learning experiences. Student work on practice systems might draw on this same source of student motivation and add analytical breadth. Student participation in the creation of practice systems would have the real world relevancy of clinical client work and also require extensive and thorough substantive analysis of all the answers that a client might offer in an interview. Mistakes would have real world impact. The intellectual endeavor would also be of challenging breadth.

Today, I am less convinced that practice systems can make a significant inroad into the law school curriculum. During the Law Office of the Future Project, students worked with clinical experts to help refine the practice systems. The work for a student of creating even a small practice system is difficult and narrow enough to tax the educational cost benefit analysis that surrounds the fight for a place in the law school curriculum. This type of project is likely to survive only as an advanced "independent study" or supervised deep research project.

My optimism in those days extended to a vision of a radically changed law profession. Greater productivity seemed within reach, lower legal fees and fewer lawyers. It appears that in the following 20 years, none of these changes have occurred. The number of lawyers grew, fees increased, ministerial work continued to be considered professional and essential to lawyer livelihood. Very few commercially viable practice systems have been built, even to this day.

I remain convinced, despite this evidence to the contrary, that optimism about practice system productivity in the legal profession is justified. Like many technology-driven changes discussed here, the insight may be good and the execution poor and the timing wrong. Practice system tools may need improvement. Professional disinterest driven by financial disincentives to adopt this time saving technology may be to blame. It may be almost impossible for most law firms to invest uncompensated time to build a practice system that will reduce the time it now takes to perform work for which the firm is paid an hourly fee. At the conference described in the opening paragraphs, the judges and court administrators were very enthusiastic about pro se practice systems that could eliminate the need for lawyers but improve the quality of court papers submitted by litigants themselves. Now that most litigants can use computers without fear, there is renewed optimism for this technology.

Legal Writing Antecedents

Personal computers emerged in the early 1980's. By the middle of the decade the IBM PC was on the cover of Time magazine. Chicago-Kent, with IBM's assistance, launched a set of projects to probe all the optimistic possibilities created by the IBM PC. Chicago-Kent's proposal to IBM to fund its Center for Law and Computers described a wide range of innovations and deliverables. The law school agreed to build an IBM PC Classroom with 35 computers arrayed in the first teaching environment designed to teach law with computers. The centerpiece for IBM, however, was a Lawyer's Microcomputer Toolkit and its companion Law Student Microcomputer Toolkit. IBM was fascinated by the PC software industry. New software companies like Ashton Tate, Inc. had made millions with d-Base and Lotus 123 spreadsheet program was the emerging software darling. IBM believed that in the engineering departments of IIT were youthful geniuses who would craft the next WordStar or the next VisiCalc.

Conceptually, the Law Student Microcomputer Toolkit is the predecessor of the electronic casebook. The Toolkit was designed to pull together on one machine as many different professional functions as were then available in a computer. Again, with guidance and some programming from Jim Sprowl, the Chicago-Kent Computer Center built a menu program that could call up LEXIS, word processing, utilities from DOS to manage disks and files, and the computer lessons from CCALI.

Optimism was rampant in the personal computer marketplace and we were attracted to descriptions of a new set of software products that were called "thought processors." Inspired by software guru Neil Larson and others who claimed that Houdini or Thinktank could improve drafting and thinking, we evaluated a series of these programs and eventually crafted an experimental legal writing curriculum that was designed to explore the limits of the power of computing to improve legal writing.

The experimental writing sections used a bundle of software organized by the Toolkit menu system. Its first iteration offered WordStar for word processing, Thinktank for thought capture and outlining, Crosstalk for telecommunications, RoseKey to enable keyboard shortcuts and some homegrown macros to call and interact with the LEXIS desktop software. Later versions of this Toolkit substituted Framework for the word processor and outline processor because Framework offered macro and telecommunications as part of its integrated package. Even later we were delighted to learn that a company called Flexpractice had built an automated document processor on top of Framework. This allowed the program to bring the early insights of the clinical program into the Legal Drafting classes.

Two pedagogical processes were at the core of the early uses of PCs in the first-year Chicago-Kent Legal Writing curriculum: top-down and bottom-up outlining.

1. We taught students to organize writing assignments by building a top-down computer outline that could be expanded conceptually and filled with the detail of exposition. The computer offered easy restructuring of the outline as conceptual understanding emerged. Research notes and pieces of the writing assignment were organized easily in this structure. Later, students could grab pieces of electronic text from LEXIS to capture error free quotes for their writing papers.

2. Bottom-up outlining was an effort to map the available software tools to a rough model of casebook learning. In an ideal Langdellian course students would read the full text of cases in chronological order and would work toward conceptual synthesis. We offered outlining to help students understand and capture the parts of a case, brief the case, and also to cluster cases under long descriptive categories that defined the common law emerging from the line of decisions. As students worked through the assigned readings for the semester, some developed organic outlines of their class notes using these tools. Students prepared maps of the course by using the outline feature to contain electronic case briefs prepared in advance of class and a recap of class notes typed into the emerging outline after class. We stressed that the computer program required explicit assignments of each piece of text, reading notes or class notes, into the outline of concepts. We were convinced that forcing students to think about the relative position of texts in the map of the course would improve their focus on larger synthesis issues and nudge them into more productive studying habits.

As I look back on the guidebooks that we wrote to help students implement these tools as they started law school, I am struck by the complexity of the material that we needed to teach before students could begin to be productive. Most students arrived in law school in 1987 unfamiliar with computers and totally ignorant of the software tools that we used to create these new improved learning opportunities. We taught them everything they needed to know to try these new technologies, from how to format a floppy disk to DOS file naming conventions. It is amazing that some of them learned all of this technology for the first time as they entered graduate school and used these new techniques to help navigate the tasks of the first year of law school.

An Early Experiment: An Electronic Casebook Companion

New hardware and software needed to launch the first electronic casebooks became available in the early 1990's. For electronic casebooks to be convenient, the computer had to be as accessible as a book. First, notebook computers increased in power and reduced in price and weight to a point that made it possible for students to carry them everywhere. On the software side, hypertext tools, like HyperCard, HyperPad and FolioViews, emerged in more and more convenient and inexpensive packages. Hypertext software made it possible for an electronic author or teacher or student to create links between any two points in the texts of the law. Hypertext made it possible to build, in the computer, an image of the fabric of the primary sources, an image that could be navigated, annotated, and cross-referenced.

In my first attempt to harness this set of insights, we built a hypertext companion to a paper casebook. The companion was a repository of my teaching notes, the teaching notes of one of the authors of the casebook and a statutory supplement. The structure of the book was also represented in a series of electronic note cards that mapped to the table of contents of the book. Each note page had links to pages higher and lower in the hierarchy and to LEXIS. We offered a link to the definitions of legal terms on each page. The assigned texts were available only in the print casebook except for a few late breaking cases that the students were told to download from LEXIS and store in the computer for class discussion.

This "study tool" was not received with enthusiasm. Most students tried the tool to humor the professor and then continued their former study and note-taking behavior. My contemporaneous evaluation pointed to student unfamiliarity with graphical interfaces and mice as significant barriers. Looking back, it is obvious that this computer outline of the casebook did not offer enough power to make its use valuable to students. It built on the outlining insights from the legal writing classes by adapting a note-taking machine for a particular course. At best, it helped to organize notes taken in class if those notes neatly fit into the book's table of contents. The students found the statutory supplement, definitions and the convenient links to LEXIS interesting, but there was no compelling functionality offered.

The First Electronic Casebook: Computer Law on Disk

Casebooks are the predominant tools used by faculty to help them teach skills and impart information. Casebooks are conceptually simple. They offer to faculty adopters and their students:

1. a structure for assigned readings,
2. editing of published texts to focus attention on the parts of those texts deemed most relevant by the teacher and
3. authored instructional texts in the form of explanation, analysis, questions, problems or citations to suggestions for additional reading.

The electronic casebooks developed at Chicago-Kent and emulated by the commercial publishers offer some new techniques for reaching these pedagogical goals. The rules, the texts from which they are derived and the texts used to explore legal analysis are all available in digital form. By virtue of the online systems, LEXIS and Westlaw, most of the internal references can be instantly available in full text if the student is connected to a network or phone line. Using software like FolioViews the computer can offer endless editing, easy linking of any text segment to any other, and easy restructuring of the conceptual structures through outline management.

My optimism drove a belief that these tools permitted the author, teacher and student to be interactive with an electronic artifact. I also believe that the artifact itself can be expected to have verisimilitude. The electronic representation of the law delivered in electronic form can be conceptually more true to the nature law itself than flat text in paper form. This more natural artifact, it seemed to me, would offer pedagogical benefits to those who were learning the law for the first time. It would support a more Langdellian pedagogy by allowing a student to wander through the linked texts in the exact relationships defined by the authors of the texts. A more detailed description of the insights about the parallels between law, hypertext and artificial intelligence that fired my imagination can be found in "Legal Mindstorms: Lawyers, Computers and Powerful Ideas." (31 Jurimetrics J. 171, 1991)

Electronic teaching materials in law could offer two other new capabilities: First, the electronic casebook could become a tool for group learning projects. Teachers could modify and reorganize an electronic casebook with ease, make it their own and adapt it to their own style of pedagogy. Students could be given assignments to do deep research and analysis of pieces of the course and offer electronic notes to the class to enhance the texts presented in the course. Second, ubiquitous connectivity delivered by local area networking and the introduction of the Internet added interactive communications power that paper could never offer. Asynchronous communication with the professor or the study group with precise reference to the texts in question could make the electronic casebook itself a repository for electronic discussion.

In 1992, I prepared a completely electronic casebook, using the same HyperPad technology described above, for a course called Law and Computers. The major change from the "companion" approach was that all of the assigned readings were available in the notebook computer in electronic form and nowhere else. In the following year, we rebuilt the same electronic course materials in FolioViews, a software platform used by many publishers in law and accounting to distribute material on CD-ROM. This FolioViews version of the Computer Law on Disk course became the prototype for many of the electronic casebooks now in "circulation." Chicago-Kent used these new course materials to launch a small experimental section of its first year class starting in 1994-5. In 1995-6, a full section of 100 students entering Chicago-Kent was furnished electronic versions of as many of their casebooks as possible.

There are some detailed accounts of Chicago-Kent's early efforts to build electronic teaching materials and the first electronic casebooks. My own account in "Does the Grandmother Come with It? Teaching and Practicing Law in the 21st Century" (44 Case Western Reserve L. Rev 499, 1994) is my best effort to present the issues. Richard Warner's piece "Teaching Electronically: The Chicago-Kent Experiment" (20 Puget Sound L. Rev. 383, 1997) is more objective and a superb presentation of the current state of the art. Peter Martin studied the Chicago-Kent "E-Learn" section and wrote a detailed evaluation and analysis of that most thorough experiment in the pervasive use of electronic casebooks. His account is available in 1998 on the Internet at http://www.law.cornell.edu/papers/kentrprf.htm.

Postscript

It is too early to write a recapitulation of the success or failure of electronic casebooks. We are living the early history of these emerging tools for pedagogy. From 1994 through 1998, I left academic life and managed the product development activities of LEXIS-NEXIS. During that time I helped LEXIS-NEXIS launch electronic products, including a series of electronic casebooks modeled on the Chicago-Kent prototypes. With the perspective of those four years out of the classroom in a business environment, I am more convinced than ever that optimism about the power of technology to make things better is a powerful force. Inside LEXIS-NEXIS, as well as in the Center for Law and Computers at Chicago-Kent, the sustaining drive to try new tools, new products, new courses, new approaches to pedagogy bubbled up from this simple optimism. Often, that optimism was misplaced. Frequently, the new thing went badly. In retrospect, it may have been better to wait a bit before pushing this or that new invention into the classroom or library. But, thankfully, I believe that this optimism in the benefits of new technology is irrepressible. It certainly is in me.

Chapter 90

A Vision of Law Schools of the Future

1998

James Hoover

James Hoover is Professor and Associate Dean for Libraries, Columbia Law School in New York. Copyright © 1998 James L. Hoover.

Presuming to predict the future is dangerous. It seems especially foolish at the ends of centuries. The results do make for often humorous reading decades later. The best we can really do is describe what is possible now and evaluate the implications if new ideas or opportunities become widespread. As technology is now a major driving force in institutional change, our inability to describe possibilities even two years out makes these efforts even more suspect. This looks to be true even of that most resistant of institutions, higher education, and to one of its most traditional of disciplines, legal education.

Over the past twenty-five years my professional life has focused on legal education. For much of this time I have been a law librarian providing traditional research services to faculty and students, primarily at Columbia Law School. Over time the lines between research support and more active involvement in the larger educational role have blurred. Similarly, the ability of a law library to provide services to today's faculty and students became dependent on the most robust computer network and information services staff . Somewhere along the line I accepted responsibility for both the library and computer services. The last major piece was the emergence of a support group for faculty using technology in the classroom and as an adjunct to the classroom; this development was extremely important as we planned the renovation of existing classrooms and the construction of new ones integrating technology which currently seems potentially effective. The web is now where we look to deliver library, computer and instructional services.

Thus what is attempted here is not prediction but description of change and resistance to change. The technology generally works. What often does not keep up with it is focus on how to use it as a tool for education and how to support instructors properly so that they may experiment with it. Of course, some of this failure is financial but even more is vision and leadership. Fundamentally the issue ahead is how to deal with change; the technology is only the symbol of the change. Change happens constantly and all around us. What we need to do is make change part of what we are about as law schools. In that way we also take control of the change rather than just be subjected to it as a result of actions of others. We need to study the experiences and expectations of the students now working their way through high schools and colleges on their way to law school; we need to both support and study new teaching techniques being tried by our colleagues, often our younger colleagues.

What Is Possible Now

Assume all law schools have some if not most classrooms wired for multimedia presentation, network and Internet access by instructor; some classrooms will have network connections to the student desktop either wired or wireless. At least one classroom in each school, and likely more, will have distance learning capabilities for either high speed line or Internet connectivity to other educational institutions or remote speakers or remote attendees. This will allow linked classrooms with other schools for jointly taught courses and courses from one location "broadcast" to multiple locations as Peter Martin is now doing from Cornell.

Students and faculty have access to networked services from offices, classrooms, library, lounges, and residences especially if on campus; these services are supported by the institution. Off campus connectivity to the law school's network is provided either through ISP or supported by institution by dial access.

Schools are now seeing increased use of electronic communication beyond email to class discussion extending the classroom through such means as the web. There is facilitated support for real time and asynchronous discussions.

Research Material Online

We are seeing aggregation and de-aggregation of legal publishing at the same time. The past 10 years has been one of major consolidation of commercial legal publishing. Small niche publishers have emerged with new electronic services though none have yet become key providers. The probable loss or weakening of some aggregators may result as sources decide to publish electronically on their own given the web's ease of distribution. Legal publishing is increasingly dominated by global publishers; this will result in the internationalization of legal tools as the profession itself internationalizes.

Primary Resources

U.S. federal and state coverage is greatly expanding as court decisions, statutes, regulations and other government information is made directly available by agencies through the Internet as a regular part of the work of the agencies. These will often be the most up-to-date source but may not have the organizational or search sophistication of commercial services plus they will necessarily be limited to jurisdictional coverage. However, they will put great pressure on commercial providers for enhanced service

There will be continued gradual expansion in the online availability of primary materials for many countries. The emergence of major international legal publishers will speed this process for major industrial countries. Given the regional differences in the organization of the legal profession and, thus, the economics of using expensive online services, the growth of coverage will be spotty for some time. In many areas the major supplier of online legal information will be the government which can use the web. As with foreign legal coverage, there will be greatly expanded current international resources built over time from organizations, governmental and non-governmental. The globalization of the legal publishing industry will result in much more comprehensive and comparative resources such as multi-jurisdictional digests for the EU based on both regional and national law.

Scholarly Material

Journals will have wide web availability, necessitated to attract quality articles as the web can speed up the publication process. There will be a test of the value of the selection and editorial processes of journals as authors have other alternatives such as self-publishing via the web; similarly, there will be a testing of the importance of formal publication for tenure and scholarly acceptance. Journals may need to go beyond mere publication and begin supporting a wider range of scholarly communication, such as discussion of publications amongst scholars, or enterprises offering such enhancements will get articles rather than the journals that do not.

The development of electronic treatises will continue to be slow as the value of new types of information resources such as audio, video and integrated modeling or database manipulation develop. The need for constant update of these resources will be felt more strongly. These developments will change who authors treatises as traditional main-line scholars abandon them because they will take much more time as they become permanent projects. Treatises may require even broader authoring and may require a significantly different support structure either from the publisher or the supporting educational institutions.

For the individual there will be much expanded opportunity for self-publishing through new channels such as the web. Works in progress will be releaseable to gradually expanding circles of readers; works may remain works in progress for longer periods of time as discussion within the scholarly community takes place even as the piece evolves. The lack of a peer or student journal review process may necessitate new measures of quality but these should be possible either through scholarly organizations or through electronic evaluation of use of the scholarship.

New Resources

Significant increase in the use and availability of non-textual material including images, still and moving, and sound. Use of modeling based on datasets will support new ways of evaluating alternative solutions to issues. Ownership of legal publishing by broadly based international publishers will challenge what is considered legal and non-legal. Lines will blur as the legal profession continues its current heavy use of materials well beyond traditional legal sources. This use will filter down more noticeably into the academic community.

Historical material will continue to have large gaps in the online environment. For U.S. law there will be a slow but continuous growth in electronically available secondary material. Full runs of journals will be available. Material in fields important in the practice of law will be converted as will important historical materials in those fields. Material in the public domain will be a ground much explored by scholars and libraries for resources of continuing significant value. Material still under copyright but out of print will continue to be the most vexing as publishers who will control the material will not necessarily see the financial return on converting but will be reluctant to give up an asset. Authors will have mixed feelings wanting broad scholarly access but with some concern for possible loss of revenue for those small number of publications which earn authors significant royalties.

For many other countries, however, much recent material will be available online but only slightly older material will not. Countries holding copyright in government publications will be pressed to convert them or allow others to do so. Some countries may even lack the historical collections from which to work; cooperative programs will be needed with major research libraries.

Retrieval/Searching

New, more powerful search engines will assist in managing access to the explosion of resources. Added features will include automatic summarization, automatic translation of some degree of usefulness and value indication based on use made of the resource by others making similar inquiries. At the same time there will be a probable loss of some existing aggregators of legal material due to self publishing. The next five years will be quite tumultuous as new tools are developed to help researchers cope with the expansion of online resources. New research techniques will be needed on a continuing basis. New search interfaces such as avatars will become common and ease the use of multiple and increasingly complex databases. It will be interesting to watch their development and evaluate their effectiveness at assisting end users in yet another area where librarians are commonly called upon.

Geography

Law faculty have already become highly mobile with increasingly sophisticated access to a base of services delivered electronically for his/her home institution. Remote access to email, the web, centrally stored files and major legal databases are already assumed. Increasingly there will be access to enhanced services both direct to the end user and facilitated for research support. Students will have very similar remote access to resources and services and potentially even classes.

Impacts

Will law faculty become freelancers with few institutional ties? Already the number of faculty holding appointments at multiple institutions make them look increasingly like symphony conductors flitting from podium to podium. This mobility will decrease the base of faculty committed to the institution for the long term and providing the time and energy necessary to maintain a quality program in legal education. A star system may be evolving out of this phenomenon, which will pull at the fabric that holds faculty together as a community within an institution. At the same time the mobility and communication offered will allow the creation of communities spanning institutions. Scholars of similar interest will find it easier to collaborate both on scholarship and teaching beyond their own schools. The power provided by technology will pull faculty increasingly into non-educational activities while maintaining teaching and scholarly commitments. Efforts to control outside activities will become more difficult.

Students will have similar mobility and it will create issues of importance. It will be more difficult than it already is to hold their interest in the second and third years. Residential requirements will be under great pressure. What part of the law learning process really requires residence. First year for Socratic and similar analysis development seems to require residence and probably second year as well as the next level of analytical process and detailed learning are laid. Third year could continue to benefit from residence but will be under significant pressure. If the third year includes greater amounts of professional/clinical work, variations on how that is conducted could include such models as externships. Teaching methodologies in this environment will be under significant pressure to change to hold student interest and keep them in the classroom. New techniques will also be needed when they are not in the classroom either because part of the class is elsewhere but together or when the students are dispersed. Even greater importance may be attached the first year as it may be the only time the students are totally residential or taking non-specialized courses and are taking courses only with classmates from their school. Institutional loyalty amongst future alumni/ae could be affected if many of the courses are either taken remotely or taught by someone from another school; is this an appropriate factor to consider in determining residence requirements?

Fewer distinctions will exist between schools as curricular offerings are enriched via distance learning. Smaller schools may be able to purchase courses from larger schools or even other types of organizations to enrich their own curricula. The globalization of legal education is already following that of economies and the practice of law. There will continue to be more international and comparative courses including the use of faculty or special lecturers from abroad bringing expertise in other systems in person and via distance learning. Joint classes between schools will become common and also exist across borders. Real time distance learning will play a major role but asynchronous education may become a major tool initially to enhance real time classroom experience and later on its own.

New generations of students may require new teaching methodologies such as those described above. To hold the focus of students more challenging case studies and more practice-type activity in regular (non-clinic) classes may result. Distinctions between clinical and other classes especially after the first year may reduce considerably. Modeling and other visualization tools will be used in courses in and outside the classroom to take legal analysis to new levels. Group learning, acknowledging both what happens already and how attorneys work in practice, will become part of the formal educational process but cannot be at the cost of analytical skill building and intellectual challenge. Classroom time will continue to be very valuable; auxiliary teaching methods to cover "survey" material outside the classroom will be developed to allow use of classroom time for more in-depth analysis.

LIBRARIES/RESEARCH

With ever greater resources to the desk/laptop of student and faculty- empowered end users, they already need to come to a library less and less often to access material. This will be especially true as research services, commercial or local, are available via the web and access becomes ubiquitous throughout all law school spaces. The new, more geographically open educational environment assumes equally open access to research material.

An important role for librarians will continue to exist and grow. They are the primary teachers of research techniques. This includes not only the ever-changing array of sources, but the actual organization of the research process. Librarians must develop new skills for assisting faculty with personal knowledge management through which a faculty member can keep track of the sources automatically set up to bring relevant information to her desktop and to then organize it in useable forms for current use and in the development of a personal resource for ongoing research. As the sources of legal information constantly change, as the research tools for identifying and managing those sources change, librarians must become leaders of change management with the school. It will be their challenge to develop the programs to assist faculty with the constant retraining that most are not now aware they need.

Library collections will continue to be important. They are the training ground for new law students; they are selective resources of important material for faculty, alumni/ae and those within the university community who do not have access to commercial online legal resources. There will be growing importance of archival and special collection materials as distinctions among libraries and schools and to support specialized programs within schools. New types of resources including video, audio, and data will require new forms of indexing and retrieval. The development of search services for both textual and non-textual material will be an important challenge. While the discipline of law will not lead this effort, the time before it will need these materials will be surprisingly short. Critical issues of preservation including electronic materials will continue to haunt us. The scale of preservation projects in a conventional setting like microfilm is daunting; converting materials to electronic form with real search capabilities will be especially daunting, usually beyond the abilities of individual schools and requiring new levels of cooperation between institutions.

INFORMATION TECHNOLOGY

Many of the newest challenges to law schools relate to information technology (IT), both determining its appropriate role and how to support it. There are no rules or guidelines for schools to use in evaluating requests for information technology or in providing the organization and resources needed to support users in academic environments. There are, however, developing measures in the commercial sector to which we should look even if the lessons are painful. Perhaps no other part of a school's operation must recognize forces outside the school.

Central among the primary information technology issues is providing and maintaining the infrastructure. The availability and quality of central university services varies so greatly that many schools have had to provide networking services internally. Schools need to use their institutional clout to ensure that adequate networking services are provided by the parent institution so that the school can focus on value-added functions important to it. Business models are again important in amortizing the cost of both networking and end-user equipment so that the resources will be provided for regular upgrade and replacement. Universities often have no existing procedures for such planning; they must develop them.

IT staffing levels, compensation and retention are again issues where the school cannot ignore what is happening elsewhere. It takes both adequate technology and qualified staff to meet user needs. Unfortunately, law schools now find themselves both paying much lower salaries than the commercial market and having such small, overworked staffs that they are increasingly unable to attract or retain qualified people. Computer folks may very much enjoy what they are doing but that does not mean they do not want to have lives beyond work. IT operations should be recognized as mission critical services needed 24 hours a day, seven days a week and staffed accordingly. There must be depth in staffing so that one departure or illness does not bring down an important function upon which the entire school relies. Schools are now operating utilities and must recognize what it takes for them to serve.

Because IT services within schools are so new, there are no boundaries on user expectations. The school must work to provide those boundaries as it will never have the staff to meet all requests. One function which needs to be within those boundaries is training. Many schools provide advanced and expensive computers to faculty and staff with no serious support on their use. While there are always early adopters who figure things out for themselves, most faculty need support from the school to use technology in teaching and research. It takes a great deal of time and energy to create useful classroom computer applications. Time and expertise beyond that of individual faculty will be needed in most cases to develop those applications. New incentives will be needed to encourage faculty to experiment.

Even students who each year bring greater experience with computer technology and greater expectations need training and support. While students use computers heavily, they do not generally understand the technical issues involved in computing and turn to the school's IT staff for assistance. Increased use of laptops in networked environments only increases that need. In the current competitive environment for the best students support for their computing needs may be important in attracting them. As technology is used more frequently in the classroom and as an adjunct to it, students will need IT support to do their work.

Law School Administration

The administration of law schools has already changed greatly from twenty years ago when there would be a dean and an assistant dean. The library was the largest administrative unit and was the only one that cost much. Now there are many assistant and associate deans and many administrative units in most law schools; the library is just one of them and perhaps no longer even the largest. This trend is a complicated one that cannot be evaluated in detail here but has resulted from factors including increased faculty resistance to non-teaching and research responsibilities such as reviewing admissions files and career counseling as well as inadequate central university services.

As law schools look administratively more like other organizations, there may be efforts to try alternatives to save money or reduce administrative involvement of the Dean. One likely vehicle is outsourcing. Any number of areas might be candidates, with information technology and library services being outsourced in the for-profit community already. Even career services and development might be candidates although somewhat less likely due to the desire to maintain close alumni/ae contact. Admissions is the one area that probably would not be a candidate.

The growing competitive environment among schools for students and faculty is already resulting in major resources being spent to create or maintain distinctions among schools. Marketing and public relations will continue to receive attention for recruitment and fund-raising. They are just the latest administrative areas to divert time and resources from more traditional functions.

Conclusion

Technology will offer legal education intriguing new opportunities. However, it will also offer even greater challenges. Higher education is resistant to change; legal education may be especially resistant. There are few incentives to faculty currently to try new styles of teaching or scholarship. It seems essential for law schools to formalize their goals and relate the use of technology to those goals. Technology alone without the connection will fail. Legal education in the next decade that does not understand and make appropriate use of technology may also fail.

This will be a time when strong leadership and vision will be important to achieve the goals of law schools. This will not be an easy time to be a dean but it could also be wonderfully adventurous, not an adjective often used to describe law school faculty including deans.

Chapter 91

The Role of the Professor in the High-Tech Law School

1998

Steve Sheppard

In a high-tech law school, "Could not all classes in [fill in the blank] subject be taught by one faculty member over the Internet? Won't this reduce all other faculty who teach [fill in the blank] to teaching assistants? The short answer is 'yes.'"[1]

In the future predicted by technology experts, technology will give legal educators the capability to fundamentally change law schools, and economic pressures will make such change practically unavoidable. In the face of the cost savings possible with electronic teaching materials of the kind pioneered by Ron Staudt[2] and John Mayer, and research methods developed and described by Jim Hoover,[3] tomorrow's law school dean will be under pressure from legislators, members of boards of trustees and, increasingly, shareholders to outsource or replace the most expensive components of legal education. The most expensive components of the typical law school budget being library acquisitions costs and faculty salaries, it will not be hard to guess where the first axe blows will be aimed.

I am a law professor who has taught both traditional lecture-hall classes using the case method and feedback-intensive legal writing courses, and I am an avid consumer of the contents of law libraries (a point for which this book must stand as mute testament.) My students have used CALI exercises to good effect, and they will use distance learning courses for their bar examination review courses. On the other hand, my students are *my* students, and I am keenly aware of many of their needs and obstacles as they struggle to reach their goals, a pursuit that I have shared with them.

In that pursuit, I firmly believe that some part of legal education can effectively be automated with an increase in the degree to which the statistically typical student will comprehend and retain considerable portions of the law-school syllabus. On the other hand, I also believe that certain functions of a legal education must be the province of personal experience and cooperation between the teacher and the student and that these functions can never be automated, even by unthinkably powerful computers, without a fundamental loss to the profession and to the student.

In some regard, the division between the teaching functions that can be automated and those that cannot can be represented in the differences of emphasis between the teaching philosophies of Joseph Story and Simon Greenleaf, both Harvard professors in the 1830's.[4] Greenleaf, while talking sometimes about the duty of the lawyer or the lawyer's role in society, was the careful expositor of the lecture drilling his students on the finest points of the black-letter law, and ensuring that they had a comprehensive grasp of the details of each topic set for his syllabus. Story, while lecturing sometimes from his careful and detailed commentaries, was the embodiment of The Law, teling stories about lawyers and judges that emphasized character and the proper virtues of the lawyer. While both emphases can be explored in films and lectures, there is a greater loss of chemistry in attempting to translate Story's pedagogy from the personal to the impersonal frame, just as the diminution of interplay of actor with audience in a film and a stage-play is greater in the soliloquy than it is in the crowd scenes.

Even so, to suggest that there are reasons not to engage in cost efficiency is not, without more, to prove that an inefficiency should continue. It is reasonable to assume that technology can allow distance learning for some types of small seminar, then some types of large lecture, and, eventually, even for skills courses such as advocacy and writing. Why should these courses continue to be delivered by local professors in local schools?

One reason will, for a time, be a technical requirement of state bar licensure, that law faculty representatives certify the character and fitness of their students to practice law. While this requirement today means little more than that an administration certify the student has a record of few arrests or incidents of formal discipline, the requirement at least trades on the notion that students are known to their teachers, which requires there to be a live teacher. This requirement alone, however, cannot justify either the corps of faculty for a school or the monopoly of schools for the requirement. Thus, the character and fitness rule is unlikely to long impede significant changes.

One reason might have been that the courses are much harder to automate than they seem. This would be true if the course really followed a model of Langdell/Ames case method dialogue, in which questions and answers may be too hard to predict to adequately program. However, this century has seen a steady erosion to the easier use of the casebook to support the class quiz, which is especially easy to automate.

One reason may be that the professor has an important role as scholar and public servant, and the law schools serve as unique resources for neutral expertise in the advancement of the law. This argument, already unappealing to anti-intellectuals and radical libertarians, depends upon the empirical truth of the statement, which is not always without doubt.

A more constant reason will be the student's desire for a focus of interest and a source for guidance in any given course. Computer software companies that provide on-line and computer-driven help programs, telephone help lines, and detailed manuals still support live training programs for software users. The student likes having a local trainer, who can be questioned personally, even if the trainer has less information than an on-line source. For law schools to give vent to such a demand by students, would insure that there is an instructor, but it would not insure that the instructor will have the breadth of knowledge or experience within narrow specialties expected currently. A live instructor facilitating distance and on-line learning may support many more courses than the twentieth century stand-up lecturer. Thus, a single teacher may be able, particularly with the aid of non-lawyer guidance and career-counseling specialists, to teach four or five times the current number of students.

In this way, the career of the law teacher may well follow the career of the small-town merchant. Where once each town supported a shoe store, men's clothing store, women's clothing store, and the like, the modern mass market has given the successors to the merchants running these stores a choice, if they wish to stay in the trade. Some few have become specialty producers selling in a niche or producing mass-market goods; the bulk have become part-time employees of national retailers serving a multi-town market. The result has been a higher volume of available goods and variations in style of these goods, albeit of sometimes lower quality and always lesser service, but available at such lower cost that local merchants cannot compete.

So, too, may law professors find themselves faced with a choice, either to join the few national producers of instructional computer-based casebooks or to compete for local positions, of increasing insignificance, as providers of the national media. In some regard such a change would be similar to the local lecturer who builds a syllabus from a national printed casebook, but in other regards, it may more profoundly alter the role of the local teacher, whose students look and listen to other voices as those of authority.

What friction may resist such change, or at least alter its course? First, the needs to teach local law in local schools. State-owned law schools will be especially unlikely to abandon their classes to multi-state and other national approaches exclusively. Second, the need to teach particular skills that are hard, although not impossible, to automate, such as analysis, research, and oratorical skills. Third, and a likely compelling reason for a time, will be the resistance of accrediting authorities.

Still, none of these reasons for internally resisting the changes that are likely to be driven from without have the suasive potential of the reason represented in Joseph Story. While the work done by Greenleaf is replicable and potentially mechanical, the work done by Story is not. Students from whom the law demands character and fitness, drawn from a society that increasingly does not provide such examples, must be given these examples in a compelling, personal way.

The irony is that the professoriate in recent decades has nearly surrendered this role, allowing larger classes and greater distance between itself and the student polity, as well as considering it either an unnecessary or unenforceable job requirement. Even so, it is precisely this role that is the most powerful available reason for professors to continue in their tasks without risk of obsolescence. So long as character, virtue, lawyerly style, and example remain little or no part of the professor's teaching regime, the teacher may as well be replaced by a machine.

NOTES

1. John Mayer, "Alternate Futures: The Future of Legal Education," Chapter 89 in the present work.
2. See Ronald Staudt, "In Search of the Origins of the Electronic Casebook," Chapter 90 in the present work.
3. See James Hoover, "a vision of law schools of the future," Chapter 91 of the present work.
4. See Steve Sheppard, "Casebooks, Commentaries and Curmudgeons," p. X

45. George Wythe (1726-1806) used moot courts and mock legislatures, and supervised reading, lectures, and quiet conversations, to instill in his students a reverence for the ethics and character demanded of a lawyer. How might he have approached a class taught with computer software over a modem? (*Courtesy of The R. W. Norton Gallery, Shreveport, Louisiana.*)

The History of Legal Education in the United States

Commentaries and Primary Sources

Index